HUMBLE OIL & REFINING CO.

FIRST BOARD OF DIRECTORS

R. S. STERLING
President

W. S. FARISH
Vice-President

H. C. WIESS
Vice-President

R. L. BLAFFER
Vice-President

W. W. FONDREN
Vice-President

F. P. STERLING
Vice-President

C. B. GODDARD
Director

JESSE H. JONES
Director

L. A. CARLTON
Director

History of Humble Oil & Refining Company

A STUDY IN INDUSTRIAL GROWTH

by Henrietta M. Larson
and Kenneth Wiggins Porter

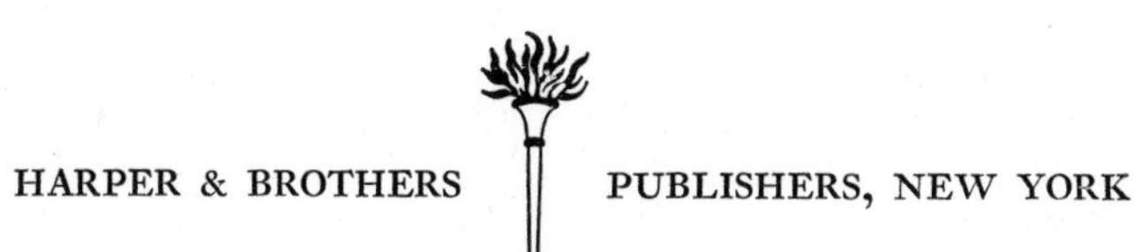

HARPER & BROTHERS PUBLISHERS, NEW YORK

HISTORY OF HUMBLE OIL & REFINING COMPANY

Printed in the United States of America

FIRST EDITION

K-I

Library of Congress catalog card number: 58-8875

Contents

Appendices

Illustrations

The following photographs will be found in a group after page 486:

The above photographs were selected from the collection of Humble Oil & Refining Company and prepared for publication under the supervision of Walter G. Beach. Permission to reproduce certain photographs was granted as follows:

Gittings Studio, Houston: photographs of Hines H. Baker, Rex G. Baker, Morgan J. Davis, Harry W. Ferguson, J. A. Neath, and Carl E. Reistle, Jr.

Moffett Studio, Chicago (for Blank & Stoller): L. T. Barrow, R. V. Hanrahan, and John R. Suman

Maps, Geologic Drawings, and Charts

Tables

Foreword

The *History of Humble Oil & Refining Company* traces the development of a pioneer industrial corporation that expanded from a modest beginning in oil production to an important integrated company during the life of its principal organizers. It is a fascinating and significant record of business achievement, co-operative effort, and corporate maturity. In addition it illustrates the relationship between this operating affiliate and its principal shareholder, Standard Oil Company (New Jersey), a holding company which has owned 50 per cent or more of Humble's stock since 1919.

Although this volume is the result of an independent study undertaken by the Business History Foundation under an arrangement with Humble, it also serves to supplement in many ways the *History of Standard Oil Company (New Jersey)*, which has been one of the major projects of the Foundation since 1947. The first two volumes of the Jersey Standard history—*Pioneering in Big Business* and *The Resurgent Years*—have already led to the re-examination of many popular assumptions. A third volume covering the history since 1927 will soon appear. These volumes, together with the *History of Humble Oil & Refining Company*, will provide an enlightening account of the development of operations within one of the largest concerns in the petroleum industry.

The Board of Trustees of the Business History Foundation consists of the following members: Ray Palmer Baker, Vice-President Emeritus, Rensselaer Polytechnic Institute, President and Chairman of the Board; Alfred D. Chandler, Jr., Associate Professor of History, Massachusetts Institute of Technology; W. Thomas Easterbrook, Professor of Political Economy, University of Toronto; Herbert Heaton, Professor of Economic History Emeritus, University of Minnesota; Ralph W. Hidy, Isidor Straus Professor of Business History, Harvard Graduate School of Business Administration; Ralph M. Hower, Professor of Business Administration, Harvard Graduate School of Business Administration, Secretary; John G. B. Hutchins, Professor of Business History and Transportation, Cornell University; Henrietta M. Larson, Associate Professor of Business History, Harvard Graduate School of Business Administration, Editorial

Director; Ross M. Robertson, Director of Business History Studies and Associate Professor of Business Economics and Public Policy, University of Indiana; and Harold F. Williamson, Professor of Economics, Northwestern University.

RAY PALMER BAKER
President and Chairman of the Board

Hickory Hollow
Averill Park, New York
May 25, 1959

Authors' Preface

The writing of a history of Humble Oil & Refining Company was undertaken by the Business History Foundation, Inc., pursuant to an understanding arrived at in 1947 between the late Professor N. S. B. Gras, president of the Foundation, and the late President Harry C. Wiess, of Humble. The company agreed to make all its records available for research, to arrange interviews with its employees and annuitants and visits to its operations, and to have the manuscript read by present and past executives of the company for criticism and suggestions, but to allow the Foundation full freedom to determine what should ultimately be published. The company also made a substantial gift to the Foundation, one of the first received.

When Mr. Porter was engaged to take charge of the project, the plan was that a draft of the history should be completed approximately three years after his entry upon the work in 1948. This was believed to be a practicable schedule for writing the history, which was originally envisaged as a study primarily of the company's administration, with emphasis on top administrators, policy, and control of operations. In consequence of this planned emphasis, the research in company records was at first confined principally to an enormous collection of administrative correspondence, reports, and memoranda, supplemented by numerous interviews with Humble executives, key employees, and annuitants. Considerable research was also done in published materials, particularly in trade journals; and business executives and others outside Humble were interviewed, including several men associated with other oil companies. By late in 1951 Mr. Porter had completed a draft of the history and had revised chapters on the basis of the criticisms and suggestions of Professor Gras and company readers.

Even before the completion of this draft, however, it had become evident that a history of the company based principally on top administrative records would be inadequate. It had become clear that research in operating records was also required; only those records would yield the necessary insight into the operation of an integrated concern undergoing rapid growth and technological development and into the process of change from a minimum of state regulation of oil production to a highly complex system of control. Although Mr. Porter, who by then was filling a one-year appointment as a visiting professor at the University of Oregon, was eager to continue his academic career, he undertook to add materials obtained by Miss Larson from several months of research in Humble's operating records. This attempt led to the conclusion that a major additional effort was required.

When Mr. Porter was awarded a Fulbright lectureship in Australia, it was arranged that Miss Larson would assume principal responsibility for the necessary additional research and revision of the manuscript as soon as she could be released from other work. Beginning early in 1954, she did research mostly in the records of Humble's staff and operating departments and also in published legal records; her emphasis was on scientific research and engineering, management organization and practices, conservation, and legal aspects of oil production. Utilizing the new materials in connection with Mr. Porter's manuscript and research files, she prepared a revised and expanded draft of the history, every chapter of which was read by Mr. Porter in at least two drafts and modified in the light of his comments and suggestions. In view of the extent of Miss Larson's contribution, it was agreed that she should be recognized as joint author.

The officers and Board of Directors of Humble Oil & Refining Company continued to support the project despite its extension over many more years than originally planned, and despite the fact that before the manuscript was completed all the officers and directors at the time the project was undertaken in 1947 were gone from the board. On all levels within the company, from the President and Chairman of the Board to the worker in refinery or field, help was forthcoming whenever requested. The time given to the project by scores of individuals, active or retired, many in high administrative or operating posts, is literally incalculable.

It is impossible to acknowledge adequately the help received from within the company. Special recognition must go to the late Harry C. Wiess, former President and later Chairman of the Board, for his contribution to the initiation of the project. We are also particularly indebted to Humble's later presidents, Mr. Hines H. Baker and Mr. Morgan J. Davis, for their continued support, and to Mr. L. T. Barrow, former director and Chairman of the Board, and Mr. Rex G. Baker, former director, Vice-President, and General Counsel, for many constructive suggestions. We owe a special debt of gratitude to Dr. Richard J. Gonzalez, who, at first as head of the Department of Economics and Statistics and later with added responsibilities as a director and treasurer of the company, was our liaison and guide within Humble. Our warm thanks also go to the others, active or retired, who contributed generously in various ways.

Many individuals outside the company also gave of their time and knowledge. A number of former employees of Humble who were active or retired executives of Standard Oil Company (New Jersey) were very helpful, as were several independent oil operators and men associated with other major companies. Consulting geologists, engineers and lawyers, newspaper editors and university professors, and our friends and acquaintances in Houston contributed from their knowledge of the company and the industry. Contract drillers, service-station attendants, taxi drivers, businessmen, clerks, and others in Texas and Louisiana, who in the course of their day's work were willing to chat about the oil industry as they had observed it, likewise—generally without knowing our particular interest—contributed to our understanding of the company and its place in the industry and community.

Credit is due the late N. S. B. Gras for envisaging the value of a history of Humble and for making arrangements for the project; and to the late Charles W. Moore and to Dr. Ray Palmer Baker, successive presidents of the Foundation, for their support over the years. Mr. Robert Ferris, Mr. Porter's research assistant, merits special recognition for devoted work. Our warm thanks also go to Miss Ruth Collard and Miss May Q. Garther, Mr. Porter's general assistants, and to Miss Florence K. Glynn, who typed the later drafts, and to Mrs. Elsie H. Bishop, who has had the responsibility for the final editorial checking of the manuscript and for reading proof.

Although countless individuals have contributed to this volume, the authors must bear full responsibility for it—for its sins both of omission and of commission. It has been a matter of particular concern to company executives, as indeed to us as authors, that many employees whose names are not included have contributed as much to the company's success as some who are mentioned. There was neither time nor space for a broad coverage of employees below the higher executive posts, but mention of a few implies recognition of the contribution of the many in the lower ranks.

Our hope is that this study may contribute to a better understanding of modern business. Any institution, to survive, must in the long run not only serve the society within which it operates and do so in ways consistent with that society's values; it must also be sufficiently well understood so that the necessary social controls, whether through education and public opinion or through government regulation, will be constructive rather than arbitrary or punitive. In our complex modern life, neither a company nor business in general is "an Iland, intire of itselfe"; nor can any society remain strong without a vigorous and effective system of production and distribution. One sees in the history of Humble Oil & Refining Company, as in that of many other companies, the emergence of responsible and professional management. One might question whether public understanding of the problems that confront business has made similar progress. This history documents the one and may help to provide a factual basis for the other.

HENRIETTA M. LARSON
December, 1958 *Associate Professor of Business History Graduate School of Business Administration, Harvard University*

KENNETH WIGGINS PORTER
Professor of History, University of Oregon

History of Humble Oil & Refining Company

Chapter 1

AN INTRODUCTION

HUMBLE OIL & REFINING COMPANY has operated within a period of time that can rightly be called the Petroleum Age. For thousands of years from the dawn of civilization even the most advanced peoples depended primarily on the muscles of human beings and animals for energy; only slowly they harnessed the force of the wind and the flow of the river. Not until the eighteenth century did man's use of the water wheel for industrial purposes become so important as to introduce the Water Power Age. After the middle of the nineteenth century man vastly increased the energy at his command by burning coal to produce steam, and thus created the Coal Age. In the twentieth, by the use of petroleum products, he has multiplied, manifold, his stationary and mobile power. In some countries, including the United States, oil and gas at mid-century supply far more energy than water power and coal combined, while throughout the entire world petroleum provides most of the driving power for the vast and complex system of transportation.

Petroleum is not merely an indispensable and versatile source of energy on land and sea and in the air. It also lubricates the wheels that it turns, helps to pave roads, and furnishes synthetic rubber for tires. It heats buildings and also roofs and paints them, waxes their floors, and cleans their windows. It supplies the basic ingredients for the manufacture of synthetics, plastics, and chemical products—literally numberless—for the uses of peace and war. The extent to which petroleum products are used is one measure of the height of a people's material culture today. Of transcendent importance is the strategic place that petroleum has come to hold in these days of international tension and undeclared war.

Although the petroleum industry has developed in many parts of the world and has become of vital significance to East and West alike, the United States is still in the 1950s a leader in both the production and processing of petroleum and the consumption of its products. Oil was produced commercially in Russia earlier than in America, but our country soon after its entry upon commercial production in 1859 attained a primacy which, except for a few years near the turn of the century, it has ever since maintained. According to the best available statistics, the United States has been responsible for nearly half of the world's total production of crude oil and it has consumed an even larger share of world production. It is now using about ten times as much nonanimal energy as all the rest of the world together, but twenty times as much oil energy.

The growth of the oil industry is one of the most significant developments in the industrial history of our country. Other countries have even greater oil resources than our own, and some have deposits that are more easily developed; but possession of these resources has not necessarily meant the development of oil production. No natural resource, however potentially useful and valuable, has economic value until the demand for it has become effective and it can be produced at costs that will make its utilization economically feasible. The American industry has been able to produce, process, and distribute oil at costs that have stimulated the growth of a tremendous market both at home and abroad. Why has this development been possible? And by what means has it been accomplished?

Any consideration of the dynamic growth of the American oil industry must, first of all, recognize the many favorable factors that have affected that industry and, indeed, American economic development in general. Basic to the oil industry, of course, has been the existence of the resource, but other factors have also been vital. This American industry has served the great and growing demand for oil products of a nation of high industrialization, high literacy, and relatively high average income. It has operated under laws governing oil property and the oil business and under conditions of political stability and security that have encouraged the small investor and operator to enter the industry and have enabled companies to grow in size and efficiency. It has drawn on a supply of workers of relatively high ambition, skill, and capacity for improvement. It has had available the resources of schools for advanced education in science, engineering, and other disciplines of significance to business in general and to the oil industry in particular. By no means the least important factor has been the dynamic nature of American society itself, the willingness of its members to move, to assume risks, and to work hard in order to take advantage of the opportunities to rise in the economic and social structure.

Within this favorable situation as to resources, culture, and institutions, the shaping of the oil industry has been the work of men—men who, individually or in partnerships, in small companies or in large integrated corporations, have devoted their capital, knowledge, experience, and efforts to finding, producing, storing, transporting, buying, selling, and processing crude oil, and distributing its products to consumers. Whether as promoters, policy-makers, or managers, or all of these combined, they have had central responsibility for the formation and administration of companies, for their success or failure, for the strength and weakness the industry has manifested, and for its growth.

In few industries has success been less certain, and the rewards potentially greater. Although the oil industry has enjoyed a phenomenal development and is proverbial for the private fortunes to which it has given rise, survival and growth were long relatively rare and success has never been easy to achieve or maintain. The rewards for those who succeeded, however, were sometimes spectacular; for many companies they have been substantial over a considerable period of time. As the industry has matured, however, the spectacular rewards have tended to disappear and the more moderate returns to become characteristic.

A principal reason for the large number of failures and for the relatively substantial rewards to a few has been the extreme riskiness of the industry's primary operation, the discovery and production of oil. A constant and continuing threat even to the well-established producing concern has been, and still is, the possibility of exhausting its basic asset by failing to acquire new reserves as fast as proved reserves are consumed. A second source of difficulty has been the rapidly changing character of nearly all operations, which has meant that operators insufficiently flexible to adapt their methods to change have fallen by the wayside and raised the industry's high percentage of failures.

Extreme riskiness and the concomitant possibility of great rewards long gave the oil industry unusual characteristics. They brought into that business a vast amount of capital for development and also a strong strain of individualism, as well as emphasis on short-run objectives. These characteristics aggravated the industry's inherent propensity toward waste of the natural resource, of men, and of capital. However, the very speculative quality of the oil industry, which so long attracted men interested in making a fortune in a hurry, also contributed to its rapid development.

In this situation the process of natural selection went relentlessly on, certain circumstances and actions making for survival. Obviously, luck has been a substantial element in success, particularly in the discovery of individual oil pools. It is a question, however, whether luck has not been of short-term rather than long duration; its importance, moreover, has diminished with the development of oil-finding technology. An obvious answer, though one that need not be elaborated here, is that long-time success in the oil industry has been determined largely by the administration of companies, by basic policies and management of operations.

But what is meant by success? The fact of survival and growth is one manifestation of success; a broader concept includes other ends and also the means by which those ends are attained. Although any definition of success is necessarily highly personal and subjective, certain general criteria can be applied. To the owners, large or small, the primary test is whether or not a company earns a profit; owners may differ as to what constitutes a satisfactory profit, but clearly in order to command adequate capital for continuing operations a company must be profitable to some degree. Employees have their own tests of what constitutes a successful company—that is, a good company to work for. So, also, have consumers, those who administer public regulation of the industry, and the general public.

The general conception of business success has broadened in recent years. In our society business has become a way of life, and it is judged by its means as well as by its products. But, as an institution whose function is primarily economic, the principal tests of its performance are economic. An increasing consciousness of the importance of a dynamic economy and also changing criteria as to the distribution of income have led to a more and more careful examination of the economic performance of our business system and its individual units. Accordingly, it is asked: Are oil companies and the oil industry making the best possible use of capital, labor, and natural resources? Are they employing them in such ways as to bring the fullest returns, within the limits of what is feasible, to all interests, individually, and to society as a whole?

One consideration has particular significance in relation to the oil industry: the irreplaceability of the natural resource. Do oil companies produce, process, and handle crude oil and its products in such ways as to derive from a natural reservoir or from a barrel of crude oil the greatest volume of useful products technologically and economically feasible? Moreover, are they making every effort within their means to find new resources in order to assure a supply for the future?

The last two questions have for nearly three decades been of great concern to the oil industry and to those responsible for the formulation and administration of public policy. The principle has been established and made widely effective that, as far as is feasible, such production practices must be employed as will result in a minimum of waste in the processing and handling of oil and gas and in the greatest ultimate recovery from a reservoir. Public policy has on the whole been such as to foster an aggressive search for new reserves. This close involvement of industry and public in issues that affect the interests of both is a challenge to the intelligence and sense of responsibility of business firm and citizen alike.

The history of Humble Oil & Refining Company affords much insight into the development and nature of this important American industry. It deals with the policies, practices, problems, and accomplishments of a company that has for many years been the largest oil-producing concern in the United States and that has in general played an important role in the American oil industry. Humble's and its predecessors' history spans two eras in the growth of this industry: the era of pioneering individualism by relatively small business units employing empirical methods; and the later era of more highly technical operations by large companies and small ones and of more stable conditions under a system of public regulation.

Humble is not a typical American oil company, but its experience is representative of a large segment of the industry. It is typically American in origin. Its principal founders—a lawyer, railroad employee, merchant and banker, print-shop operator, farm hand, and so on—first learned the art and the business of oil finding and production through operating in small groups and coping constantly with difficulties in finance, transportation, and marketing. They eventually combined to form Humble Oil & Refining Company. Later, having affiliated with one of the major oil companies, they developed a large system of integrated operations. They constructed pipelines and refineries and increased their production and reserves to supply a rapidly growing market. They were among the leaders in adopting new scientific concepts concerning the behavior of oil in its natural habitat and in using new methods of locating promising geologic structures and bringing such oil as might be found to the surface in the most economical fashion and with a minimum of physical waste. They were among the pioneers in applying new scientific principles in the field of petroleum chemistry to the problem of more effectively transmuting the raw materials into useful products. Meanwhile, they managed the work of an ever-growing body of men engaged in a bewildering variety of complicated operations in a rapidly changing industry.

The history of Humble is, however, more than an account of industrial processes carried on by a large and successful oil company. It is also the history of a group of executives meeting administrative problems and pressures that change and increase with growth in the size and complexity of operations, with changing concepts concerning the responsibilities and functions of managers of business, and with the stresses of depression and war. It is a human story, of managers and men at work, of wealth for more than a few and a good living for many. It is a story of hard, grueling, often discouraging, and yet challenging and eventually rewarding work for men in the administration of the company; and also of workers by the hour or day, some of whom rose to positions of high responsibility while many others found pride and satisfaction in the dexterous performance of their duties and in their sense of being indispensable parts of a respected and thriving organization.

This volume attempts to sketch the efforts of administrators and rank-and-file employees, function by function and decade by decade. From the account emerges a general view of an exceedingly complicated organization and of operations in a highly competitive, flexible, and changing industry, an industry that in the long run is the product and the synthesis of many companies, large and small.

The history of Humble Oil & Refining Company begins in Texas and is largely concerned with operations in that state. However far afield the company has ranged in its search for oil—east into the Everglades of Florida, and west to the California tidelands; north into the Choctaw country of Oklahoma, the Pacific Northwest, and even Alaska, and south of the Rio Grande into Mexico's Tamaulipas—it has always remained essentially a Texas company, administered by native or naturalized Texans.

But this is not only a Texas story, nor should it be of interest to Texans alone or to those many individuals who have been fascinated by the dynamic spirit and growth and the romantic past of the Lone Star State. Though Texas is its home, Humble is the product of many elements drawn from far and wide. Many states have contributed managers, geologists, engineers, and other employees, as well as capital for expansion. The Old World has helped to provide the basis for its scientific and engineering advance. This company, in reality, illustrates the creativity of a dynamic and mobile culture when channeled by effective administrators into the work of transforming the resources of nature into useful products.

The primary concern of Humble Oil & Refining Company and its predecessors has always been the quest for petroleum, liquid or gaseous. This has meant pitting man's skill against nature's obduracy and applying human intelligence to solving the riddle of where oil and gas are stored in the recesses of the earth.

The solution of that riddle has not been easy, as is amply demonstrated by Humble's search for oil and gas. There has, indeed, been no general solution—the riddle is solved only by finding one reservoir after another. Even today, the only way to prove whether or not oil exists in a given place is by drilling. Much has been learned, nevertheless, about the kinds of subterranean structures in which petroleum may be found, and ingenious ways have been devised for locating them.

The earth's crust is made up of countless layers of rock of varying composition and of irregular shape and thickness. Oil and gas have been found predominantly in sedimentary rocks—sandstones, limestones, and dolomites. These rocks, in the process of the building up of the earth's crust, were laid down under seas or lakes or by winds or rivers; they have been in process of formation, layer upon layer, for hundreds of millions of years, since the earliest aeons of the earth's history. They were deposited in strata, some of which have lateral continuity over great areas but may in places have a vertical thickness of only a few feet. Geologists have studied such strata from outcrops on the surface, from subsurface samples of rock, and from data obtained by means of geophysical instruments.

Within many sedimentary strata, in the process of their formation, was deposited organic matter, animal and plant, particularly under marine conditions and in lakes or deltas of rivers. Scientists now generally believe that this organic material, presumably under moderate temperatures but great pressure, was transformed into oil and gas in their natural state.

These materials have not necessarily—perhaps even rarely—remained where they were formed. Because of their own relatively low specific gravity or from the pressure of heavier fluids, they have moved upward in the earth's crust until prevented from further movement by rocks that they could not penetrate. There they were trapped. Some traps were formed by the way strata in the process of their formation were laid down on top of each other; others, by changes after strata had been formed. The earth's crust has not been, and is not, static or rigid. As that crust has been disturbed over the aeons by movements within the earth, strata have been bent, folded, or cracked—where cracked they have sometimes slipped so that the edge of a porous, or permeable, stratum abuts upon a different one that is impermeable to oil and gas. In traps formed in these various ways, oil and gas may remain until some other movement in the earth's crust sets them free to rise to the surface or to move underground again until stopped by some other impermeable rock—or until the bit of a drilling rig penetrates to the formation in which they are held entrapped.

The problem of the producer has been to find where oil has been trapped. When the Humble founders entered the oil industry, very little was known of the petroleum geology of Texas. Practical oilmen in that state for many years looked for such surface manifestations as oil seeps or paraffin dirt. Even when Humble Oil & Refining Company was organized in 1917, knowledge of the petroleum geology of the state was very spotty, merely an accumulation of scattered observations of surface manifestations and of what had been found by examining cuttings brought up in the drilling of wells.

The two accompanying drawings illustrate what has been learned about the structure and composition of the earth's crust and the occurrence of oil under the hills and plains of Texas. One is a drawing of a geologic cross section between two points in eastern and western Texas about a thousand miles apart, and the other is of a cross section between points in northern and southern Texas about four hundred miles apart. The occasional small, black, irregular dots in both these cross sections are of special interest: they indicate some of the reservoirs where oil and gas have been found by drilling.

EAST–WEST GEOLOGIC CROSS SECTION OF TEXAS

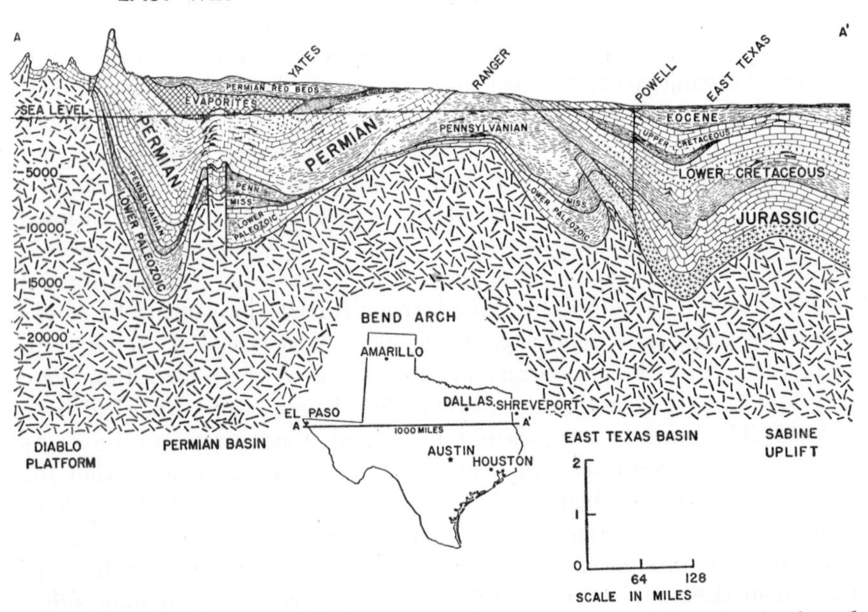

This drawing shows the folding and faulting and the variations in depth and thickness of the strata that constitute different geologic periods. It does not show the different strata within a period. The names of several important fields are shown above the drawing, and names of geologic provinces are shown below.

Finding oil, the interest on which the efforts of Humble and of the oil industry have always primarily been focused, is but the beginning. The oil must be brought to the surface, carried to refineries, processed, and supplied to the market at whatever time and place demanded, in whatever product, quality, or volume required, and at prices that buyers will pay. That is the oil business, the work of Humble Oil & Refining Company from 1917 and of its founders from the time oil in commercial quantities was first discovered in Texas near the end of the nineteenth century.

Humble Oil & Refining Company at the end of 1957 was the largest domestic producer and purchaser of crude oil in the United States. It then had about 9,000 miles of pipeline and a refinery that ranked among a few leaders in range of equipment, processes, and products. It led all other companies in the possession of domestic oil reserves, which it estimated in billions of barrels. It had 19,600 employees and net fixed assets of over one and a quarter billion dollars. During the year it spent $9,287,100 on research, $167,382,000 on payroll and other employee compensations, $121,121,400 on exploring for new oil, and $146,147,800

NORTH–SOUTH GEOLOGIC CROSS SECTION OF TEXAS

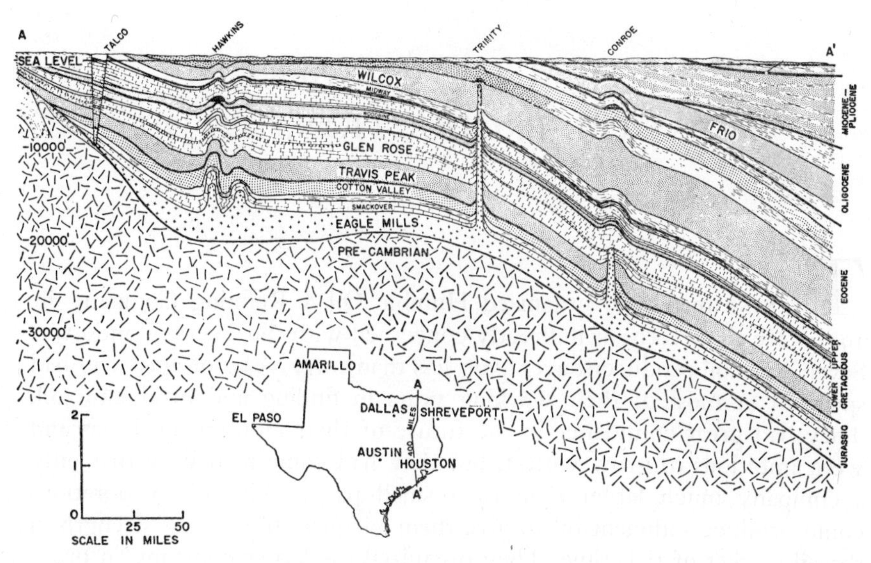

Geologic periods are indicated along the right-hand edge and important strata are named within the drawing. The names of several important fields are given above the drawing.

on drilling 867 new wells (including $61,792,100 for 219 dry holes). Its net income for the year was $175,910,400, of which $96,902,200 was paid to shareholders in dividends and the remainder applied to capital expenditures totaling $235,395,400. During 1957 Humble daily produced an average of 360,600 barrels of crude oil, purchased 418,100, delivered from its trunk pipelines 675,200, and ran to its refinery 234,500 barrels; it also sold daily an average of 1,119,000,000 cubic feet of natural gas. In 1957 Humble acquired more new reserves than it produced and advanced both its gas and oil reserves to record levels.

Chapter 2

THE HUMBLE FOUNDERS IN TEXAS OIL PRODUCTION, 1897-1917

THE NINE men who organized Humble Oil & Refining Company in 1917 were all directly or indirectly concerned with the Texas oil industry. Seven were oil producers, averaging less than forty years of age, who had spent all or most of their working years in finding and producing oil. They had great confidence in the future of their industry in Texas and were ambitious to grow with it, but they had come to believe that only a company much larger than their small partnerships or corporations could produce sufficient oil to give them adequate bargaining strength in the oil market of that time. They organized the larger company in order to develop more effectively and profitably their business of producing oil.

The origins of this larger company and of the Texas oil industry itself are similar to the beginnings of that industry elsewhere in the United States and indeed of much of American business. As in Pennsylvania a generation earlier, so in Texas some men and companies, beginning in a small way in a risky, rough, and ruthlessly competitive industry, were able to acquire operating skills, capital, and administrative capacity with which to develop a large and profitable business for themselves and to help build the industry in their region. The founders of Humble created during two pioneering decades the essential elements of the new Humble company and participated with a host of others in laying the foundations of the Texas oil industry. In 1917 both the company and the industry stood on the threshold of a period of surging growth.[1]

CORSICANA: THE BEGINNING OF THE OIL INDUSTRY IN TEXAS, 1894–1900

The beginning of commercial oil production in Texas in the 1890s coincided with the dawn of the fuel oil age. Kerosene had previously been the principal petroleum product; kerosene lamps were used in all quarters of the globe. During the next twenty years, however, fuel oil was to surpass kerosene as the leading oil product, and the principal use of oil shifted from furnishing light to producing energy—energy to power industrial machines and, particularly, to drive ships and locomotives. The Texas oil industry in its first two decades was concerned principally with producing oil for power.

Corsicana, in east central Texas, was the scene of the discovery in 1894 of the state's first commercial oil field.[2] As so often in the American oil industry, the discovery was accidental—oil was found in the drilling of a water well. The drillers were using a method they had developed in searching for water in South Dakota, a rotary-type mechanism to bore the hole, together with a stream of water to flush the cuttings to the surface. So far as is known, this was the first use of the rotary rig in drilling oil wells.[3]

The development of the Corsicana field followed a pattern familiar in the rise of new oil regions in the United States, one that provides an illuminating background against which to view the Texas oil industry of later times. After the accidental discovery of oil, several local businessmen took steps to develop production. They had neither adequate capital nor experience, but they organized a company and obtained some leases. Then they turned to the original home state of the oil industry and succeeded in inducing the well-known Pennsylvania wildcatters, James M. Guffey and John H. Galey, to drill five wells for a half-interest in their company. A cable-tool rig, the standard drilling rig of that time, was soon at work. The first well was completed in 1895 at a depth of about a thousand feet.

The completion of this well attracted investors and operators from near and far and brought the first oil boom to Texas. By the end of 1897 Corsicana was producing a daily average of 500 barrels of oil from 50 wells and in the following year an average of 2,300 barrels from 287 wells. The production per well was not large, but by the end of 1900 the field had yielded a total of over two million barrels of crude oil.

As in older oil regions, production at Corsicana early outstripped its market. Again the local men sought outside help; the mayor of the town appealed to J. S. Cullinan, a Pennsylvania oilman. After examining the situation, the Pennsylvanian agreed to construct a pipeline, storage tanks, and a refinery and to develop a market, in return for a regular supply of crude oil at a given price. For financial aid Cullinan went to certain Standard Oil officials whom he had known when he had been an employee of a Standard Oil affiliate. The J. S. Cullinan Company, a partnership, was formed with capital supplied indirectly by the National Transit Company, the large pipeline affiliate of the Standard Oil group. This partnership was superseded in 1898 by the Corsicana Refining Company, which also held a majority of the stock of the Corsicana Petroleum Company organized to carry on production.

J. S. Cullinan, thus, with the assistance of Standard Oil capital, established at Corsicana a fully integrated operation, the first in Texas. The Corsicana Petroleum Company was soon second in production among the many small local concerns operating in the Corsicana field. Cullinan's particular contribution was to provide an outlet for the field's production. After he and one of his brothers had demonstrated that Corsicana crude oil could be used for locomotive fuel, he was able to market large quantities of crude for fuel oil. The stills of the Cullinan refinery, the second fully fledged refinery between the Mississippi and the Rockies, were fired on Christmas day in 1898. The first shipment of refined oil left Corsicana in February, 1899.

Corsicana not only started commercial oil production in Texas. It brought to the state the experience, capital, and markets of the highly developed American oil industry. It set the pattern of organization that was to become common in Texas: production became largely the province of local operators, whereas integrated operations—particularly transportation, refining, and marketing—were carried on by or with the help of outsiders. Corsicana's operations helped to establish the use of fuel oil as a source of power for locomotives and ships and to usher in the fuel oil age. This field was the testing ground for a new type of drilling rig, the rotary, which was to play an indispensable part in the subsequent development of oil production in Texas and, indeed, nearly everywhere that oil wells were drilled. Moreover, Corsicana brought about the first legislative enactment in Texas for regulating oil production, a law having to do chiefly with the abandonment of wells.

Corsicana also gave a considerable number of men training in the oil industry, especially in production. Among them were Walter W. Fondren, a subsequent founder and original director of Humble Oil & Refining Company, and the Hamill brothers, who in 1901 drilled the discovery well at historic Spindletop on the Gulf Coast of eastern Texas.

SPINDLETOP AND EARLY GULF COAST DEVELOPMENT

The commercial oil industry in Texas came into being at Corsicana, but Spindletop made the state an important factor in the national oil industry and started the development of oil production on the Gulf Coast.[4] In 1901 the Spindletop field was brought in by a gusher with an initial daily flow of from 75,000 to 100,000 barrels. In the following year it produced over 18,000,000 barrels of crude oil, which amounted to 20 per cent of the production of the United States and 93 per cent of the year's national increase.

Great as was this production, the contribution of Spindletop to the development of the oil industry in Texas has a significance far beyond its spectacular early performance. This field started a lively search for oil that was to bring a considerable development to the Gulf Coast. Important in that development were the geologic observations made at Spindletop, the drilling methods used, and the men who participated in the industry there.

Four unsuccessful attempts to find oil at Spindletop lend emphasis to the success of the fifth effort and to the methods used to achieve it. In 1892 a local company had been organized to test the conviction of Patillo Higgins of Beaumont that oil could be found by drilling on a slight rise in the flat country close to his home town on the Neches River near the eastern boundary of Texas. The company made three efforts to drill and ran out of capital, but found no oil. It then entered into a lease contract with Anthony F. Lucas, a mining engineer of Washington, D.C., who was something of an authority on salt domes. Lucas exhausted his resources in one unsuccessful effort. He, in turn, sought the help of Guffey and Galey, the Pittsburgh wildcatters who had completed the first well in the Corsicana field.[5]

The Pittsburghers promised financial aid and contracted with the three Hamill brothers of Corsicana—Jim, Al, and Curt—to make a further attempt. The Hamills spudded-in the test well in October, 1900. On January 10, 1901, they struck oil at a depth slightly over a thousand feet. The drilling was incredibly difficult, through quicksand and tough and rubbery gumbo, which "heaved" into the hole, and against heavy gas pressure.[6]

The Hamills' success, which has become a Texas legend, was the result of adequate equipment, brawn, and brain. The brothers had plenty of drill pipe and a sturdy rotary rig with sufficient power. They had the prodigious strength and endurance required to drive the pipe down through the loose sands that tended to cave into the hole. And they had the ingenuity necessary to overcome unfamiliar drilling problems. For example, out of a piece of board and an old boot they fashioned a back-pressure valve to keep the heaving quicksand out of the pipe. Their prime innovation was, instead of merely circulating water down the hole to cool the drilling bit and flush out the cuttings as at Corsicana, to use a mixture of water and a claylike mud for performing the cooling and flushing functions and also for supporting the loose wall of the hole and holding the gas pressure in check. Any sort of drilling fluid thereafter was known as "mud." The Hamills climaxed their success by bringing the well, which came in as a gusher, under control by means of a valve rushed to Spindletop from St. Louis.

The Hamills used at Spindletop two new techniques that made drilling possible on the Gulf Coast, with its unconsolidated formations, quicksand, and high gas pressure. The cable-tool rig, which had hitherto been the standard drilling equipment in the American oil industry and which operated on the percussion principle, had served well in hard formations. But in the sands of the Gulf Coast the grinding by the rotating bit of the rotary rig was necessary, as was the use of "mud" instead of water as a drilling fluid. "At Corsicana," Curt Hamill explained, "the formations were hard enough so that a hole would stand up like the neck of a jug, but at Spindletop they were soft, and without 'mud' to plaster the hole and make it stand up it was like taking a brace and bit and trying to drill a hole in a heap of wheat."

The Spindletop boom was possibly more spectacular than anything of its kind in American experience with the exception of the California Gold Rush of 1849.[7] The population of Beaumont, a modest town of rice farmers and lumbermen, in a short time increased from 9,000 to 50,000, as oilmen, land speculators, adventurers, and sight-seers swarmed in from all over the country and even from abroad. Land prices rose to sensational heights. Leases were commonly small and wells were spaced so closely that the legs of neighboring derricks in some places touched each other. The craze for quick and easy wealth attracted countless promoters and investors and stimulated the formation of hundreds of companies, all of them speculative and many, if not most, pure "sucker-traps." Spindletop became known as Swindletop. Here was born the legend of the get-rich-quick Texas oil operator.

The discovery at Spindletop soon led to other discoveries on the coastal plains of eastern Texas and western Louisiana. The low topographic mound under which oil was found at Spindletop was, as was soon realized, the surface expression of a buried salt dome—a type of structure that had been formed by a pillar of salt pushed upward under heat and pressure. In the process, strata had been fractured and sands tilted upward against the salt plug, with the result that traps were formed which might hold oil and gas; a trap might also be formed by a porous rock capping the dome. The early discovery at Spindletop was in such a cap rock. Though many salt domes are buried without trace at the surface of the coastal plains, the Spindletop dome manifested itself in a slight surface elevation on an otherwise featureless plain; that the presence of these domes was sometimes indicated by topographic mounds caused practical oilmen to regard such mounds as possible indications of oil.

Within a few years several salt-dome fields were discovered east and west of Beaumont. The first after Spindletop was discovered at Jennings, Louisiana, in 1901. In Texas the early discoveries of salt-dome fields included Sour Lake and Saratoga discovered in 1902, Batson in 1903, Humble and North Dayton in 1905, and Goose Creek in 1908, all situated between Beaumont and Houston.

Those fields established the Gulf Coast as an oil region of permanent importance. In 1905 Texas produced 28,000,000 barrels of oil, chiefly on the eastern coastal plain. Only the simultaneous growth of oil production in California kept the Lone Star State in second place.

GEOLOGIC CROSS SECTION OF THE SPINDLETOP SALT DOME

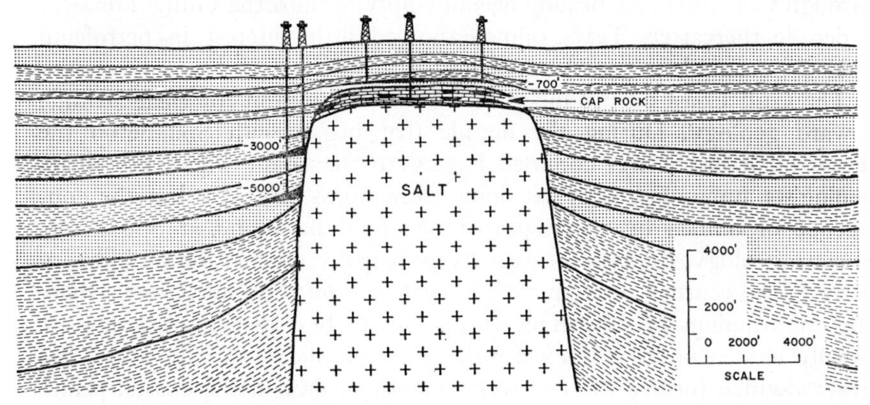

This drawing shows the location of oil reservoirs that have been discovered above and alongside the salt dome. The first discovery was in an anticline above the dome. In later years oil was found in porous zones within the cap rock, just above the salt, and in two strata at different depths on one side. These were trapped by the salt, which oil cannot permeate.

THE EARLY TEXAS OIL INDUSTRY

The basic pattern that was to characterize the Texas oil industry for three decades was set in the early years of oil production and reached its full development within ten to fifteen years. The pattern was not new in the industry, but its manifestation in Texas is of special significance to our interest in Humble, for it was within that pattern that the founders of Humble Oil & Refining Company operated, before and for some time after 1917, as the oil industry spread to other sections of Texas and to neighboring states.

Strikingly characteristic of the Texas oil industry in the early years were the ingenuity of its practical drillers and the nearly complete absence of formal science and engineering. The use of the rotary drilling rig at Corsicana and the brilliant improvisations of the Hamills at Spindletop have already been observed. A particularly important later invention was the Hughes rock bit. These innovations were the work of practical men, not of professionally trained engineers. Practical men also found whatever oil was discovered during nearly two decades of development in Texas.

Petroleum geology was little known or understood in the early years of the Texas oil industry. An illustrated article, which appeared in a Houston newspaper a few days after the discovery at Spindletop in 1901, informed its readers in all seriousness that the well was the result of tapping a great underground "oil stream" flowing from North Texas through Corsicana and Beaumont and emptying into the Gulf.[8] For over a decade thereafter, Texas oilmen showed little interest in petroleum geology as a guide to petroleum deposits.

The Gulf Coast oil producers had some justification for their attitude toward geology. During the decade that began with Spindletop the Texas oil industry was confined largely to the coast, where petroleum geologists, unfamiliar with salt-dome formations, had early lost the confidence of oilmen by denying that oil could be found at Spindletop. Surface geology, the type of geology principally used in the oil industry early in the century, was, indeed, of little use on the Gulf Coast, where the outcroppings of subsurface formations to be found elsewhere were usually hidden under a thick mantle of unconsolidated sands, clays, and gravels which formed the relatively smooth surface of the coastal plains. This initial failure of surface geology on the coast, unfortunately, caused most oilmen to disregard it, even when the search for oil moved into areas of well-bedded sedimentary rocks, where geology could have been of great value.

In Texas, as elsewhere at the time, oil fields were developed rapidly and intensively, with attendant confusion and waste. Such development had accompanied every uncontrolled rush to exploit valuable and irreplaceable natural resources in the United States; but in the exploitation of oil resources rapid and wasteful development was accelerated by the fugitive nature of oil underground and by the prevailing law of property in gas and oil.

Under the laws of the states, minerals underground belong to the owners of the land. Oil, which migrates with change in underground pressure, brought special problems in applying the laws of ownership. In 1889 the Pennsylvania Supreme Court in *Westmoreland Natural Gas Co. v. DeWitt* applied to oil in the earth the old English common law by which wild animals—fugitive creatures of no fixed place—belonged to him who captured them; oil thus belonged to anyone who could gain possession of it through wells drilled on land he owned or had leased. This decision established a precedent that was universally followed in the United States.

The "rule of capture," as the legal principle came to be called, determined the character of the development of oil fields in Texas. Under that rule each operator—landowner or lessee—had to hasten to drill and produce oil before it was drained from under his land by others, experience having shown that rich production, even in the best of fields, was of short duration. Antitrust laws prevented producers from combining to control and restrict production. The result was rapid development, which in turn brought a characteristic production cycle. Field after field experienced a short period of high production from flowing wells, followed by an early decline to a relatively low plateau when production became dependent on pumping. High production at Spindletop lasted less than three years. Again and again as new fields were discovered Texas oilmen experienced the same cycle of production. Not until the late 1920s and 1930s, when new production practices and conservation laws were applied to the Texas oil industry, was the familiar cycle broken.

The rapid development and decline of fields determined other characteristics of the oil industry in Texas; one of these was an erratic price situation. In the period of flush production in a field, prices frequently fell to low levels. Local demand could take only a fraction of the production, and hastily thrown-up earthen levees generally for a time provided the principal storage for the oil. Pipelines soon supplied transportation to refineries or to shipping points, but even pipelines and refineries might not be adequate to cushion the impact on local prices of a greatly increased production. Spindletop illustrates the situation: its first production brought 25 cents a barrel—the earlier price in Texas was $1.00; in the boom that followed, companies with pipeline facilities bought oil at Spindletop for 2 or 3 cents a barrel; after the drop in production in 1903 Spindletop crude again sold for as high as 83 cents a barrel.[9]

Drastic price declines, instead of leading to decreased production, forced operators to increase their volume in order to recoup at lower prices the investments already made in leases and equipment. The operators in a field, therefore, allowed their wells to flow to their full capacity; if one operator failed to do so, his neighbors would drain the oil from under his land.

Producers without storage, pipelines, or refineries generally sold their oil under either the credit-balance or the contract system. Under the first of these a producer would deliver his oil to a company that agreed to run it into storage for a certain period of time; the owner received a storage certificate, which he generally sold for whatever it would bring. This system gave the producer some opportunity to seek competitive buyers or to hold for price changes; at the same time, he was bearing the risks of not finding a buyer, of suffering from a fall in prices while he was paying for storage, and of losing oil by the evaporation allowance to the owners of the storage. Under the contract system a purchasing or refining company would agree to buy all or a specified amount of a producer's production at a fixed price for a period of time, from six months to a year or even longer. When contracts were made during flush production, as is said usually to have been the case, they prevented the producer from benefiting from the subsequent price rise after production declined.

Low prices were especially hard on small producers, who were often near bankruptcy because of costly competitive drilling. A well-informed observer of the early Texas oil industry estimates that ninety-eight out of a hundred failed. Yet the comparatively low cost of producing operations, together with the prospect of a well gushing oil in quantities that would more than compensate for low prices, kept the ranks of the small producers from being depleted.

A serious effect of rapid development was the waste of the resource itself. Little if anything was understood of the tremendous underground waste that resulted from the dissipation of a reservoir's natural energy by the prevailing rapid and unrestricted development of oil fields, but aboveground waste was quite obvious. A great source of loss was the use of earthen storage; evaporation and deterioration, caused by rain, dust, and other foreign matter, were inevitable results of open storage. Loss by fire was a frequent occurrence. So common, however, was the aboveground waste of oil that it came to be regarded as a necessary accompaniment to production. Ignorance of underground waste and the generally tolerant attitude toward all waste were long to stand in the way of adequate conservation of oil resources. A beginning was made when in 1917 an amendment to the Texas constitution declared that "the conservation and development of all of the natural resources of this State . . . are . . . public rights and duties, and the Legislature shall pass all such laws as may be appropriate thereto," and when the Railroad Commission was empowered to administer oil and gas conservation laws.[10] The application of the rule of capture was unaffected, however, and the regulation of the rate of production in order to prevent waste lay in the future.

Boom development and rapid decline were accompanied by poor living and working conditions and an unstable supply of oil-field workers. The general industrial standards were low, to be sure, but the rule of capture would have prevented operators from improving them even had they wished to do so. That rule encouraged, and indeed even necessitated, rapid, competitive, and wasteful production. Rapid exploitation of a field made it difficult, if not impossible, to provide adequate housing; and early decline made it financially impractical. Oil-field workers, consequently, generally lived in tents, shanties, or crowded flophouses. Sanitation was usually bad, and sickness sometimes attained epidemic proportions. Although fires and explosions were common evils, safety measures, camp doctors, and compensation for injuries were almost unknown. Lawlessness was common, violent death not infrequent, and, as generally the case where large numbers of men without families sought work and wealth, gambling and other vices flourished. The *Oil & Gas Journal* as late as 1918 pointed out that Sodom and Gomorrah were oil-field towns.[11]

Low morals and lawlessness manifested themselves not only among migratory workers but also among the operators. Oil-field booms attracted many men in search of wealth at any price, and threat of failure weakened the ethics of others. Sharp dealing, regardless of the industry, has never been uncommon in a rapidly growing business group made up principally of men with little experience and capital and operating with few controls, either of law or of well-formulated opinion. In the early Texas oil industry sharp practices were nearly endemic.

The forces of law and order, honesty and decency, were not, however, entirely idle. The Texas Rangers, a state police force, assisted the local officers in the more flagrant breaches of the peace. Dishonest business practices were dealt with largely by the growing opinion of the industry. The "shrewd customer," though sometimes temporarily prosperous, probably seldom attained great permanent success, whereas individuals whose honesty went even beyond their strict legal obligations might find that their reputation ultimately proved, figuratively, a letter of credit. Honesty and decency, even in the early oil-field booms, proved to have a distinct survival value.

As producing fields were developed in Texas, refineries and pipelines were built. Corsicana, Beaumont on the Neches, and Port Arthur on Lake Sabine were the earliest refining centers. Pipelines were laid from the fields to the refineries and also to river loading points for the shipment of crude oil by tanker. Small refineries were numerous, but even in early Gulf Coast days three were large for their time: the refineries of predecessors of The Texas Company and the Gulf Production Company at Port Arthur and of the Magnolia Petroleum Company at Beaumont. Extensive storage facilities were also built.[12]

As in the oil industry in its earlier decades in Pennsylvania, the participants in the early Texas industry came to be divided roughly into two groups: operators specializing in production; and those with extensive pipeline, storage, and refinery facilities and operations, who also generally had some production. Of the $36,000,000 invested in the Texas Gulf Coast industry between January 1, 1901, and August 15, 1904, only about one-third went into production, the remainder being invested in transportation, storage, and refineries.[13]

This cleavage into two groups was to play an important part in the oil industry in Texas, as it had done elsewhere. The relatively small capitalists of Texas could organize and finance the early operations of producing firms; the management and capital for the development of production were in consequence largely local. To supply the funds for building pipelines, tank farms, and refineries was, however, beyond their resources. Eastern capital, therefore, went into providing those facilities, and to a lesser extent into production. Capital initially supplied by Mellon, Standard Oil, and Sun Oil interests was largely responsible for the extensive early transportation, storage, and refinery facilities in Texas.[14] The companies with roots in the older oil interests—Gulf, Sun, Texas, and Magnolia—became the early majors of the Texas industry.

Out of the cleavage between the small producers, on the one hand, and large transportation, storage, and refining interests, on the other, arose conflict in Texas, as in Pennsylvania a generation earlier. In 1905 the local Texas producers helped to prevent the passing of legislation that would have permitted one corporation to carry on all oil-industry functions.[15] They attacked the big corporations strongly in 1907. The immediate reason was low prices, but another was the decline of flush production in the Gulf Coast fields, which put the small producers in a difficult situation. These developments paralleled the national movement of trust-busting and hostility to Big Business which was a characteristic feature of the years before World War I, but in Texas the movement was reinforced by a strong regional chauvinism. The small native producers blamed the large eastern interests for low prices and financial difficulties.

In 1907 the Texans resorted to the usual instruments of regulation, the legislature and the courts. Texas antitrust laws were already severe; the year 1907 brought stiff amendments. Violation of the law was made a felony, and a corporation convicted of violation was subject to heavy fines and to banishment from Texas, a ban that also applied to any corporation acting in concert with the guilty party and to which the latter might transfer its obligations or its properties. Other provisions of the law put further restrictions on foreign corporations. Texas corporation law was also unfavorable to integration. The statutes treated the conduct of an oil business and the operation of oil pipelines as separate specific purposes for which private corporations could be created, and the courts construed the general corporation statute as forbidding incorporation for more than one statutory purpose.[16]

The Texas courts in the first decade of the century were particularly severe against Standard Oil interests. Contributing factors were undoubtedly the current widespread attack on Standard Oil Company (New Jersey) and its affiliates and the excesses of the Waters-Pierce Oil Company, its marketing affiliate in Texas. The United States Supreme Court in 1909 upheld for the second time the decisions of the Texas courts that the Waters-Pierce Oil Company had violated Texas antitrust laws; the company was fined and its permit to operate in Texas was revoked. The Texas District Court of Travis County, in *State* v. *Security Oil Co., Navarro Refining Co. and Union Tank Line Company*, also decreed the ouster from the state of several companies directly or indirectly associated with Standard Oil: the Security Oil Company, which owned the Burt Refinery at Beaumont; the Navarro Refining Company, which owned the refinery built by Cullinan at Corsicana; and the Union Tank Line Company.

The effect on the Texas oil industry of this drastic action against Standard Oil and of the threat of action against other companies can only be surmised. Whether a more tolerant attitude toward these experienced companies would have enabled them to operate as a stabilizing and progressive influence it is impossible to say, although the rapid and more orderly development of the oil industry in certain other states indicates that such might have been the effect.[17] Most of the larger companies with eastern support continued to operate in Texas, however, and were able, by resorting to one device or another, to carry on several functions. They incorporated holding companies outside Texas to control companies operating in Texas; they purchased producing properties in the name of the stockholders, operated through unincorporated joint-stock companies, and even defiantly engaged in more than one function through a single company. By such means The Texas Company, Gulf, and Magnolia carried on in Texas the various functions of the oil industry. Possibly it was because The Texas Company was so conspicuously integrated that it strove in 1915 to have integration legitimatized by act of the Texas legislature, as will be observed in another connection.

The legal climate of Texas was favorable to the growth of local companies and of small independent producers. Also, the newness of the industry and the many small, shallow fields gave opportunities to a rising class of small capitalists. A young man with little capital could enter the industry as a dealer in leases or oil-storage certificates or as investor in a drilling rig. A number of small operators could pool their resources in a partnership or corporation to buy and develop leases that one of them, alone, could not handle. In 1908 it was estimated that two hundred business units were engaged in production in fourteen fields. The mortality was of course heavy, but in Texas for a considerable span of years production continued to be the game for the man with small capital.[18]

Among the smaller operators who succeeded were the principal founders and original directors of Humble Oil & Refining Company. It was in the risky, individualistic, wasteful, but productive early Texas oil industry that they reaped the harvest of experience and oil properties which they merged in 1917 to form the corporation that developed into the Humble Oil & Refining Company of today.

THE FOUNDERS OF HUMBLE OIL & REFINING COMPANY IN EARLY GULF COAST PRODUCTION

The nine founders and original directors of Humble Oil & Refining Company all participated in some way in the early Texas Gulf Coast oil industry. Seven either were at Beaumont in 1901 when Spindletop was discovered or became involved in the Spindletop boom within a year or two. One began an indirect association with the industry in 1903 as a supplier of feed for draft animals in oil fields; he entered oil production at the Humble field in 1909. The last of the original directors to enter the oil industry became a director of a predecessor company in 1914.

Observations about these men and their early activities yield several generalizations. They represented a wide diversity of family interests and circumstances, education, experience, and capital, thus constituting somewhat of a cross section of the society of the region. Over the years they individually acquired a broad experience in the producing business and added to their capital in the process, most of them having begun with literally nothing. By the formation of small firms and business relations between individuals and groups, they participated in a gradual process of nucleation that in 1917 led to the combination of their interests and operations in one company.

Two of these Humble founders—Walter W. Fondren and Charles B. Goddard—entered the industry by way of the drilling rig and built their careers on success as drillers and producers. They were men without family backing, with little formal education, and with no capital, whose original resources were good health, native intelligence, and strength of character.

Fondren was the first of the group to enter the oil industry.[19] He was born in Tennessee in 1877, the son of a farmer who in 1883 moved his family to Arkansas in a covered wagon. Orphaned at the age of nine or ten, he worked on farms and in sawmills in Arkansas from about the age of twelve until, at seventeen, he set out for Texas "with nothing but a pair of overalls and thirty cents." In 1897 he left his job as a farm hand, at fifty dollars a year and board, to roughneck—to serve as a helper on a drilling rig—at Corsicana. When oil was discovered at Spindletop in 1901 he was prepared to enter the boom as a skilled rotary driller at a high wage. He worked hard and became an independent driller. His first business venture, with an old rig bought partly on credit, was to drill on a tract only twenty feet square. He had trouble and lost his well, but his reputation for dependability enabled him to borrow enough money to finance reworking it. This time he got production, paid his debts, made a small profit, and was on his way as an oil producer.

Fondren moved from field to field as new pools were discovered. He drilled some wells at Sour Lake for a Beaumont group; when those wells stopped flowing, he agreed to pump them on shares, a venture that proved profitable. In 1904 he entered a contract-drilling partnership at Batson with G. Clint Wood, who at the time of the Spindletop boom was with a local lumber company which supplied drillers with fuel and derrick timbers. During and after 1905 Fondren concentrated on the Humble field, operating both under his own name and through about a dozen companies and partnerships. He soon acquired large production.

Prosperous though he was, Fondren was merely a drilling contractor and producer and was dependent on others for transportation and a market. He early tried to escape from that dependence. In 1905 he became vice-president of the Coleman Oil Company, organized to engage in the business of marketing crude oil; in 1908, with Wood and other men, he was "working on a scheme to take over the lines of the Commercial Oil Company at Humble" in order to sell directly to railroads and others.[20] Apparently nothing came of these projects. The efforts illustrate the small producers' lack of success in their attempts to enter marketing.

Charles B. Goddard was another early Spindletop driller who was to play an important part in Humble history. He came from Ohio, where he had been a tool dresser on a cable-tool rig at a time when, as he said, he was so young that he should have been in school. He came of age at Spindletop, where he roughnecked for a year to learn rotary drilling. He subsequently worked as a driller, gauger (measuring oil in tanks), and engineer, and finally began drilling on his own account in the Humble field.

Similar was the background of another Ohioan, Bert Broday, who was long to be associated with Humble Oil & Refining Company although not as a director. Broday had started as a tool dresser in the Lima field in Ohio at the age of sixteen. He learned rotary drilling at the Sour Lake and Humble fields and became a contract driller.

Among the hundreds of young men whom the Spindletop boom brought to Beaumont were William Stamps Farish and Robert Lee Blaffer, founders, original directors, and future presidents of Humble Oil & Refining Company. They met in an oilmen's rooming house in 1902, where they formed an acquaintance that later led them to join their efforts in the oil business. From their partnership developed one of the three major groups that in 1917 were to form the new Humble.[21]

Farish came to Beaumont in 1901 to report on developments at Spindletop for an uncle, a promoter then in England. Born in Mississippi in 1881, of English and Irish ancestry, young Farish was the son of a lawyer and a grandnephew of Jefferson Davis, the President of the Confederate States. He was graduated in law at the University of Mississippi the year he came to Beaumont. Reserved in manner, tall and sturdy of build, and with a prematurely bald brow, young Farish had an appearance of maturity beyond his years.

Petroleum soon entered Farish's bloodstream. After about a year as supervisor of wells for the Texas Oil Fields, Limited, an English syndicate, he organized the Brown-Farish Oil Company. This firm did contract drilling and traded in oil by buying and selling pipeline certificates (documents representing ownership of oil in storage). Brown died, leaving the firm bankrupt; but Farish succeeded in borrowing money and paying all the creditors, thus greatly strengthening his own credit among local oilmen and bankers.[22]

Blaffer came to Beaumont in 1902 to purchase oil for the Southern Pacific Railroad, but within a few months he decided to become an independent operator. Born in the mid-1870s, of South German, Alsatian, and Austrian ancestry, he came from a New Orleans family known for its educational and humanitarian interests. He had left Tulane High School at the age of fifteen to work in a bank, after his father, a brick and lumber merchant, had lost heavily through overinvestment in timberlands. Blaffer was a tall, nattily dressed young man with fair, curly hair.

By 1904 Blaffer and Farish had formed a partnership and from then on they usually operated jointly, though each one also joined others in drilling partnerships. Blaffer & Farish engaged in contract drilling, sometimes taking payment in oil or in an interest in a lease; they also traded in leases, buying blocks for the Gulf and Texas companies and for themselves. For several years they were associated with Ed F. Simms, one of the shrewdest of the early Gulf Coast operators.

In 1905 Blaffer & Farish moved to Houston in order to concentrate on the nearby Humble field. At times they were "broke" and lived in a shack in the field with barely enough money to buy food; Blaffer is said at one time to have offered his gold watch as security for a drilling crew's wages. Their troubles came not only from dry wells and other normal hazards, but also from inadequate equipment and techniques for handling the high gas pressure and from salt-water encroachment in the coastal fields. By 1908, however, they had, in the vernacular, got "such a bundle out of Humble" that, according to the gossipy *Oil Investors' Journal*, Farish was the best catch in Houston and Blaffer a close second.

They made a good team. Their temperaments were complementary, Farish being described as a man of strong feelings, which were normally well under control, and of reserved disposition; and Blaffer as warmhearted, impulsive, and sociable. Both are remembered in oil-field

Shows the location of fields in which the founders had interests and of early Texas refineries.

tradition for acts of unusual generosity, such as arranging and paying for the burial of an oil-field derelict. In business matters, however, Farish was regarded as a "plunger" and Blaffer as conservative. Blaffer was the financial man of the team; Farish's chief interest was in field operations.

The spectacular success of Blaffer & Farish at Humble occurred near the beginning of a period of declining Gulf Coast production and was the firm's last successful venture for several years. After the decline struck them, their ten-dollar-a-week clerk sometimes was able to meet their payroll only by collecting in advance for oil which they were selling to Gulf or Texas on a year's contract at 27½ cents per barrel. Not until 1914 did their condition begin to improve, and then in a region far from the Gulf Coast.

Harry Carothers Wiess of Beaumont,[23] youngest of Humble founders and original directors, entered the oil industry by a route very different from that of these self-made oilmen. A lad of thirteen when oil was discovered at Spindletop, he frequently rode out to the field to see what was happening; in later years he recalled seeing on the grass bodies of men, dead from the hydrogen sulphide gas from the wells. At an age when many local boys began to work in the oil fields, young Wiess was sent to the Lawrenceville School in New Jersey. From Lawrenceville he went to Princeton University, from which he received a degree in civil engineering in 1909. After returning home he engaged in various enterprises, including the management of a print shop, but his father's ill health soon made it necessary for him to assume responsibility for the family's oil interests. Harry Wiess thus entered the oil industry as a second-generation oilman.

William Wiess, the father, a Confederate veteran and in his younger years a steamboat captain, was a substantial Beaumont lumberman, real-estate owner, and banker, nearly sixty years of age when the Spindletop boom rocked his home city. His father, Simon Wiess, a native of Poland, had settled in Beaumont in 1839 after years of experience in mercantile work and shipping in Turkey, New England, the West Indies, and Louisiana.[24]

Although William Wiess entered the oil business as an investor in companies operating in the Spindletop field, his principal activity in the early Gulf Coast oil industry was his part in the organization of the Paraffine Oil Company.[25] The origin of Paraffine was typical of the early Texas oil industry. On a hunting trip in the "Big Thicket" near Beaumont in 1903, Judge W. L. Douglas, walking barefoot around the campfire, detected between his toes a peculiar dirt which he thought contained paraffin. He told of his find to his friends, William Wiess and S. W. Pipkin of Beaumont, and $10,000 was forthwith subscribed, the Paraffine Oil Company was organized, and land was bought at Batson Prairie.

In October, 1903, Paraffine discovered the Batson field, from which it produced 1,250,000 barrels of crude oil in 1904. Batson's was the usual story—flush production with the price falling from 60 to 8 cents a barrel, waste, salt-water flooding, and rapid depletion. The field produced nearly 10,000,000 barrels in 1904 and less than 4,000,000 in 1905. Profits are said to have accrued principally to land speculators, but the Paraffine Company dug earthen reservoirs, which enabled it to hold the oil for higher prices, and obtained an outlet for its oil by laying, in association with the Higgins Oil & Fuel Company, a pipeline to Sour Lake, where it made connections with other lines. Paraffine's board of directors—as a foreshadowing of later developments in Texas—evinced an early interest in conservation by providing that pipeline privileges should not be granted to operators drilling more than one well to an acre. Although the pipeline was unprofitable, Paraffine in 1904 paid dividends of a quarter of a million dollars.

Paraffine also pioneered in two other fields. In 1904, at first in association with the Higgins Company, it purchased a number of leases near the village of Humble, including the subsequently famous "Paraffine forty-acres." Although not the discoverer of the great Humble field, Paraffine was one of its early and large producers. In 1905, again in conjunction with the Higgins Company, it established commercial production in the North Dayton field.

Although in this stage of the industry success can in some measure be ascribed to good fortune, men and management cannot be overlooked. The stockholders and directors of Paraffine, with the exception of Director Robert A. Greer, who was, or had been, a director of the J. M. Guffey Petroleum Company,[26] were not experienced oilmen and, excepting Wiess, had little capital; but neither were they fly-by-night speculators. They were a close group of relatives and friends—respectable, conservative Beaumont citizens—who were eager to take advantage of the opportunities for investment in a rapidly developing industry and region. The directors met frequently and kept in close touch with operations. S. W. Pipkin, general manager and president from 1903 to 1912, was obviously important to the company's success. Under his management a total of $462,000 was distributed in dividends. Paraffine became one of the most successful small companies in the early years of the Texas oil industry.

By 1905, however, the Paraffine Company's production was falling. It shared in the steady decline of the Texas oil industry during the next five years. Well established in three Gulf Coast fields, the company continued to be profitable, but it displayed little further energy and participated in no spectacular discoveries.

In 1907 William Wiess organized the Reliance Oil Company, which issued shares to the value of $67,000 based on properties in the Batson and Humble fields.[27] Wiess had retired from the Paraffine board in 1904, when accused, probably unjustly, of endeavoring to get control of the company for The Texas Company, of which he was a stockholder.[28] Later he did gain control of the Paraffine. In 1909 he bought out the principal stockholders of the Reliance, became its president, and put Barney Flynn, an experienced oilman from Bradford, Pennsylvania, in charge of operations. The Reliance, organized during a period of declining Gulf Coast production, was to find success in another oil region.

Young Harry Wiess began to take an active part in the management of the Reliance and the Paraffine in the period of decline on the Gulf Coast. He was a director and secretary of the former by 1910, devoting his full time to the company's interests and learning the oil business from his father's associates, Barney and his brother Bill Flynn. In 1912 he became president of Reliance. About the same time he was elected director, vice-president, and treasurer of Paraffine. When the father died in 1914, the son also became president of Paraffine. By that time the two companies had established themselves in another region, as will be seen later.

Two other Humble founders and original directors who were interested in the industry in early Gulf Coast days were not, however, active in promoting or managing Humble Oil & Refining Company. One was Lobel A. Carlton, an attorney who had taken up residence in Beaumont in 1897. Carlton and his young law partner, Edgar E. Townes, who was to become the tenth director of Humble Oil & Refining Company, were for many years engaged in private practice in the field of petroleum law and as lawyers represented most of the men who organized Humble Oil & Refining Company. They occasionally yielded to the temptation to invest in some of their clients' oil companies. The other founder-director was Jesse H. Jones, a Houston lumber dealer and real-estate operator, who was probably the least of an oilman of Humble's original directors. Jones some years ago remarked that, although people called him a gambler, the oil business had always been too much of a gamble for him. Nevertheless, he, too, had his fling at Spindletop, in a fashion prophetic of his later career, by buying a lease block some miles from the field, subdividing it, and selling the subdivisions at a nice profit.

The two Sterling brothers, Ross S. and Frank P., were the last of the founders and original directors of Humble Oil & Refining Company to enter the oil industry. In 1911 R. S. Sterling organized Humble Oil Company, which furnished the later company its name, more than half its capital, and a majority of its most active original directors and officers. His brother became a director of the company in 1914.

R. S. Sterling was the chief promoter and unquestioned leader of Humble Oil Company.[29] He was born in 1875 near Anahuac, Texas, of Scottish and Irish ancestry, the son of a carpenter, farmer, storekeeper, and self-educated country doctor, who had been a captain in the Confederate Army. Ross left school when he was twelve and for several years assisted in operating his father's market boat, which carried farm produce to Galveston and returned with supplies. At the age of twenty-one he bought a small store from his father. In 1900 he went into the produce commission business in Galveston, but his place of business was wrecked by the great Galveston storm and flood.

He then turned to the booming oil industry in the vicinity of Beaumont. In 1903 he opened a feed store at Sour Lake to supply grain and hay for the mules used in hauling casing and other supplies and in digging earthen reservoirs for storing the oil of the newly discovered Sour Lake field. He subsequently established branches of R. S. Sterling & Company in the oil-field towns of Saratoga, Dayton, and Humble, operating them in association with some of his half-dozen brothers. Described as "the hardest-working white man you ever saw in your life," Sterling could carry a five-bushel sack of oats from store to wagon.

After the panic of 1907 Sterling—following the time-honored precedent of the small-town merchant—entered banking. He bought a string of banks in small towns where he had feed stores and also organized other banks. He employed his feed stores and banks to help finance his various other business interests. Although his methods sometimes troubled bank commissioners, cashiers, and grain dealers, his creditors were always paid sooner or later, and none of his banks failed.

Late in 1909 Sterling began to invest in oil properties. G. Clint Wood persuaded him to buy, at a bargain, two producing wells in the Humble field [30] and agreed to manage them for a half-interest. Once launched in oil, Sterling continued to acquire oil properties.

Soon Sterling was taking the lead in promoting the organization of a company. He and other individual operators in the Humble field, recognizing that under the current competitive conditions they were drilling themselves to death, decided to conserve effort and capital by pooling their interests in one company. In co-operation with Wood, Sterling, a youthful-appearing man in his mid-thirties, tall and robust, with strong, handsome features and a carriage expressing self-confidence, won the interest of several oilmen: S. K. Warrener, a West Virginian, who had been a gauger for the Sun Oil Company; Charles B. Goddard, Warrener's brother-in-law, who was a successful drilling contractor [31] and producer; M. C. Hale, a rig-building contractor and stockholder in Sterling's Humble State Bank; and J. W. Fincher, cashier of the same bank.

In January, 1911, these men agreed to incorporate with a capital of $150,000, consisting primarily of producing properties valued at $350 for each barrel produced daily. The portion of the 1,500 shares subscribed by the organizers ranged from Warrener's 495 to Fincher's 100; 20 unassigned shares were to be sold for working capital. The six organizers constituted themselves the board of directors, with Sterling as president and Goddard as field superintendent.

The company was named Humble Oil Company after the field in which its organizers were operating. The Humble field, a salt-dome field, as described in the *Oil & Gas Journal* in 1913, was large compared with most Gulf Coast fields, being about two and a quarter miles wide and four long. A distinctive feature was the fact that it was producing from five different pay sands, ranging from a depth of 600 to 3,200 feet. Discovery of deep production in 1917 was to lead to large additional production. The field had been given the name of a small nearby town—with a population of about 700 people, located seventeen miles northeast of Houston—which had been named for Pleasant Humble, a former justice of the peace.[32] Thus, fortuitously, was a large oil company of the future to acquire its deceptively modest name.

The company encountered some difficulty in its incorporation. Its attorney finally learned that the secretary of state of Texas suspected that "Standard Oil" might somehow be involved; if so, he would not grant the charter. Sterling and his associates enjoyed a good laugh over the thought that the great Standard Oil Company could be interested in their little organization. Humble Oil Company apparently proved itself above suspicion, for on February 16, 1911, it was duly incorporated.

During 1911 and most of 1912 Humble Oil Company operated almost exclusively in the Humble field. In 1912 its headquarters were moved to Houston. Its profits were paid out largely in dividends at the monthly rate of 3 per cent on capitalization. Pressure for such large dividends, not uncommon among men who looked upon corporations as little different from partnerships, came from stockholders who were heavily indebted to banks on account of past operations and who by the merger of their properties had given up a personal income. Humble would soon, however, have to decide whether it was a liquidating company or one with ambitions toward permanence, which in the oil industry required constant expansion. The decision to expand was strongly influenced by the promise of Oklahoma.

SEEKING NEW FIELDS IN OKLAHOMA

In the years 1906 to 1910 oil production in Texas fell off sharply and steadily until, in the latter year, it was less than 9,000,000 barrels, which ranked it only sixth among oil-producing states. From ranking next to California in 1902, Texas thus dropped well behind even West Virginia and was only just a little ahead of the original oil state, Pennsylvania. The fall in Texas' production was the result of two conditions. One was the short cycle of flush production and rapid decline of fields owing to wasteful producing methods. The other was the failure to discover important new fields. Surface indications were playing out as guides to new Gulf Coast oil fields because the more obvious evidences of the existence of oil had already been tested by drilling.

The decline of the Texas oil industry turned the attention of some of its oilmen to Oklahoma, which over a score of years beginning with 1907 was to be either the leading oil-producing state or the contender with California for that honor. Shippers and refiners along the Neches and Sabine laid pipelines to the rich pools of their northern neighbor in order to obtain oil, and Texas producers shifted their exploring and producing activities from the Texas Gulf Coast to the hills of Oklahoma.

The Humble founders and constituent companies, however, stuck pertinaciously to the Gulf Coast fields, particularly to the Humble field, for several years after the decline had begun. Not until 1910, 1911, and 1912, when Texas was beginning to regain its lost ground, did they begin to move into Oklahoma, and even then they maintained a strong interest on the Gulf Coast.

The first of the predecessors of Humble Oil & Refining Company to move north were the companies representing the Wiess interests, which were then coming under the management of Harry C. Wiess. In 1910 the Reliance entered Oklahoma, and it was shortly followed by Paraffine. Under the management of the young second-generation oilman these two companies, particularly the Reliance, succeeded in developing production at Wann, Mounds, Healdton, and other important pools in Oklahoma. Sometimes they operated in association with the Gypsy Oil Company, and they had close relations with the Humble and Ardmore companies.

The Ardmore Oil Company [33] was a joint creation of Wiess and Sterling interests, its organization carrying forward that process of nucleation which gradually brought together the founders of Humble Oil & Refining Company. The Ardmore, named after the town of Ardmore in southern Oklahoma, was incorporated in September, 1911, with a capitalization of $20,000, by S. W. Pipkin (Paraffine president), R. S. Sterling (president of Humble Oil Company), and W. M. Babcock (subsequently Humble's lease man in Oklahoma). The secretary of the company was E. E. Townes, the young Beaumont attorney. Ardmore's stockholders were mostly residents of Beaumont who were connected with its American National Bank.

Ardmore's experiences during 1912 to 1916 were discouraging. The tests drilled on its leases in 1912 were failures. In the following year the company purchased an interest in some promising leases from the Paraffine Oil Company, but after production had been proved, the owners of the land sued for and obtained cancellation by resorting to the unscrupulous use of the confusion in Indian titles that gave rise in Texas to the scornful term, "an Oklahoma guarantee." During the first eight months of 1916 Ardmore's profits were less than $400—Townes traded his five or six shares for twenty young pigs. Then came that sudden shift in fortune for which discouraged oilmen have always hoped.

In September, 1916, and January, 1917, Ardmore acquired an interest, with Humble, Paraffine, and Reliance, in three Tubbee leases in the Healdton district and the Martha Potter lease. Ardmore's cash resources had long since been exhausted, but its prospects were strengthened by the fact that Sterling and the Wiess interests had by this time acquired nearly all its shares. Accordingly, Mrs. William Wiess loaned the company $25,000, secured by a mortgage on company property valued at $22,330, and the American National Bank of Beaumont advanced an additional $15,000, on a note endorsed by Harry C. Wiess and R. S. Sterling. The Tubbee and Potter leases proved quite productive.

Humble Oil Company had moved into Oklahoma in 1912, shortly after the Paraffine and Reliance companies. In connection with its decision to try its fortunes in Oklahoma, Humble adopted a more conservative dividend policy and increased its capitalization. Sterling convinced the stockholders that their main objective should be to build up and expand the company and that dividends must therefore be reduced from 3 per cent to a maximum of 1 per cent a month. The capitalization was increased to $300,000; a thousand shares went to Sterling, Warrener, Fincher, Goddard, and others for leases in Oklahoma, while 500 shares at $100 each were prorated among the stockholders in order to provide working capital. Goddard was put in charge of operations in Oklahoma.

Humble's move to Oklahoma immediately proved fortunate. In 1913 its total production increased 70 per cent, despite a 45 per cent decrease in its Texas production; dollar sales more than doubled. Humble seems to have achieved excellent realization on its outlays. The Fox lease in Okmulgee County, Oklahoma, in which it had purchased a half-interest for $125,000, is said to have "paid out" in thirteen months. Humble leased eighty acres in the Healdton field for $8,500, completed two wells on it, and, the acreage being in the heart of the pool, sold a half-interest for $50,000, which was characterized by the *Oil & Gas Journal* as one of the best deals made in that development. The 160-acre Anderson lease, also in Oklahoma, which Humble purchased for $421.50 and developed, in 1914 produced oil selling for over $50,000. While the net earnings on those leases do not appear in the records, these holdings were apparently both productive and profitable.[34]

Humble's experience thus immediately and dramatically justified Sterling's policy of conservative dividends and expansion into Oklahoma. It also testified to the sagacity of its lease purchasers and to the skill of its operators.

Blaffer and Farish were the only founders and original directors of Humble Oil & Refining Company who did not participate in the rush to the Oklahoma oil fields. That, however, was the result of an accident. Farish and Wood once started for Oklahoma to look for leases, but on the way Wood wrecked his car and injured himself so badly that the trip was not completed. Perhaps because Farish did not reach Oklahoma, he and Blaffer participated instead in the development of North Texas production.

REVIVAL OF TEXAS PRODUCTION

Although in 1910 Texas had fallen to sixth place as an oil-producing state, in 1911 its production began to increase steadily and its rank as an oil-producing state to improve. In 1915 and 1916 it was in third place, though still far behind Oklahoma and California. In 1917 the forward surge of Kansas left Texas in fourth place.

The revival of the Texas oil industry was the result of two developments. One was the discovery of new fields in northern Texas. The other was deeper drilling on the Gulf Coast, to horizons from 2,000 to nearly 4,000 feet below the surface.[35] The discoveries were largely accidental. In 1902 a water well being drilled on the Red River Uplift in Clay County gave evidence of oil at 150 feet; oilmen moved in and developed a shallow field. A few years later a rancher in Wichita County struck oil in drilling a series of water wells for his cattle; an oil company leased the ranch and in 1909 brought in the Electra field. This discovery was the forerunner of such Wichita County fields as Burkburnett and Iowa Park, which were discovered in 1913.[36]

The next great oil development in north central Texas was in Eastland and adjacent counties. In 1912 the Texas Pacific Coal Company, in sinking a test hole for coal near Thurber, had found indications of oil; in 1915 it struck an oil sand a few miles from the first hole. Drilling for oil was soon begun, resulting during 1916 in a few small or moderate-sized wells. In March, 1917, the Producers Oil Company, the producing subsidiary of The Texas Company, completed a well in the "Ranger Lime," seven miles southeast of Breckenridge. Although this was the discovery well, the Ranger boom began with a well drilled at Ranger late in 1917 by the Texas Pacific.[37]

Although those new discoveries owed little if anything to geology, the development of production in North Texas was facilitated by improvements in drilling. The rock formations in North Texas were harder even than those at Corsicana. As a consequence, still more powerful engines, higher and stronger derricks, and heavier drilling equipment were needed. The Hughes rock bit, first tested in 1909, made it possible to introduce into North Texas the more modern rotary rig instead of the cable-tool rig, which had previously had a monopoly in that region of hard formations. On the Gulf Coast the rotary rig had proved more efficient than the old cable-tool outfit, but when rotary drilling was first attempted in the hard-rock northern country the fishtail bits then in use simply bounced up and down until they were worn out. The Hughes bit, consisting of two revolving cones which ground and crushed the rock instead of merely shoving and gouging in the fashion of the old fishtail, gave the new producing region the benefit of the rotary system's greater general efficiency.

G. Clint Wood was responsible for bringing Blaffer and Farish into North Texas. Returning to Wichita County after the accident that had prevented Farish and himself from going to Oklahoma, Wood leased 500 acres on the A. J. Schulz farm and also the adjacent Serrien tract in the Burkburnett area. He then formed a partnership with the Spindletopper Ed Prather and with Blaffer and Farish. Wood himself took charge of the drilling. His first well flowed 100 barrels a day.

Fearful of Wood's "gambling" proclivities, Blaffer insisted on incorporation. The Schulz Oil Company was, therefore, organized in June, 1915, with a capitalization of $60,000.[38] Wood (president) and Prather (vice-president) each took 200 shares, whereas Blaffer (secretary-treasurer) and Farish subscribed for 100 each. Blaffer and Farish also took 133 new shares issued the next year, and 5 were allotted to L. A. Carlton, the Beaumont lawyer. Wood was to do the drilling at $6,000 per well. Bert Broday was to serve half-time as field superintendent of the Schulz Company, giving the other half of his time to his drilling partnership with Wood.

By 1916 the Schulz was one of the leading companies in the Burkburnett area; with the unusual record of not a single dry hole, it still was not profitable. The wells, although their high-gravity crude brought a premium price, were only modest producers. Moreover, production was also declining, while expenses were high. The company soon owed more than $40,000, of which $15,000 was in debts to oil-well supply houses for which Blaffer and Farish had given their personal guarantees. Blaffer failed in his attempt to get a $60,000 advance on oil from the Pierce Fordyce Association, but he managed to borrow $75,000 from a Houston bank on the personal endorsement of Schulz stockholders—a testimony to their credit rating. In the summer of 1916, however, he ordered the suspension of drilling.

Certain changes in company ownership and management made possible the resumption of drilling in the autumn. Bert Broday was given full charge of field operations; his drilling partnership with Wood had been dissolved and Wood's shares in the company bought by Broday and by others who already owned Schulz stock. Broday thereafter operated a company-owned rig at a considerable saving in drilling expense. More important still was a rise in prices, from a low of $1.20 a barrel in 1916 to $2.00 in 1917. The company's profits for the first half of 1917 were $35,000.

Though the Humble founders had thus extended their operations to Oklahoma and North Texas, they also continued to operate on the Gulf Coast. Their success in obtaining production in Oklahoma and in Wichita County coincided, indeed, with an increase in their Gulf Coast production which was achieved largely by drilling to deeper horizons in old fields.

In 1914 and 1915 Blaffer and Farish strengthened their ties with other future founders of Humble Oil & Refining Company. In the former year Farish joined three men, including Jesse H. Jones and L. A. Carlton, in purchasing a two-acre tract with eleven producing wells at Sour Lake; increased production and war prices made the investment profitable.[39] Early in 1915 Blaffer & Farish bought from the Paraffine Oil Company a third-interest in a forty-acre tract at Humble; the other two-thirds was owned equally by Paraffine and the J. M. Guffey Petroleum Company, later the Gulf Production Company. Blaffer & Farish took charge of development and, by drilling below 2,900 feet, brought in a 2,000-barrel well.[40] In 1916 and 1917 Blaffer & Farish also brought in some large flowing wells on properties at Goose Creek owned jointly with the Wiess interests.

During the years 1915 to 1917 the Paraffine Oil Company also participated in and benefited from deeper drilling on the Gulf Coast in association with Humble Oil Company. In this way it strengthened on the coast a connection that was already firm in Oklahoma.

Walter W. Fondren as an individual operator also engaged in deep-drilling activities at Humble and Goose Creek. Oil-field gossip held that he had "more cash than anyone else in Houston." The orphan farm boy, through hard work, thrift, honesty, and uncanny drilling skill—and probably some luck—had spun his original 30 cents into not far from half a million dollars.

Humble Oil Company's development of Gulf Coast production was particularly spectacular, and the achievement of remarkable realizations from small initial outlays was as characteristic of its Gulf Coast as of its Oklahoma operations.[41] One of its most successful operations was on the F. B. West lease at Sour Lake; another, on the Armstrong-Wheeler-Pickens tract at Humble. Deeper drilling on the already highly profitable

F. B. West lease at Sour Lake brought in six gushers with a total initial production of 29,600 barrels daily. Near the end of December, 1916, Humble brought in a well at Goose Creek flowing 10,000 barrels daily. This high production influenced the company to purchase over 900 acres of leases, some already in production, for $720,000 ($320,000 in cash) plus one-eighth of the net profits.

Sterling's remark at the first meeting of Humble's stockholders had more than come true: "You boys sit steady in the boat and in five years we will have a million-dollar company." Six years after its incorporation the company's properties were variously valued at from one to four million dollars. During 1916 Humble produced and sold crude for nearly $500,000. The market price of its shares in that year ranged from 24 to 58½ per cent above par.

Humble's success, after an appropriate obeisance to Lady Luck, can be attributed chiefly to management. To recognize potentially productive acreage, to lease it ahead of competitors and without paying too much for it, to raise the funds necessary for leasing and development, and to drill the property and produce the oil efficiently according to the standards of the time, all indicated abilities that not every oilman or oil company possessed.

Humble Oil Company was controlled largely by R. S. Sterling. For voting control, Sterling needed only a few proxies in addition to the voting of the shares owned by himself and his eight brothers and sisters. Frank P. Sterling, an elder brother, became a director in 1914.[42] In 1915 their sister, Florence M. Sterling, became treasurer and in 1916 secretary of the company. The Sterlings' strength in the company, however, depended in large measure on President Sterling's business capacity. He is said to have possessed an intuitive ability to evaluate oil property and to act quickly in obtaining promising acreage. Sterling himself quoted approvingly the maxim of an official of The Texas Company: "The oil game is fast. Shoot, and then see what you've killed."

Sterling, moreover, was responsible to a considerable extent for the well-stocked cartridge belt essential to a rapid-fire policy. His was the insistence of plowing back four-fifths of the profits. He also controlled half a dozen small banks and employed them and his feed stores as sources of funds. Humble's notes outstanding increased from $8,000 in 1912 to $285,000 in 1917; at first these loans were from Sterling's own little banks, but eventually they came from Houston banks, strong evidence of the company's growing financial stature and stability.

Sterling was ingenious both in getting cash and in getting the most out of what the company already had. Humble obtained comparatively little cash from the sale of stock, but it used stock to pay for leases. It also acquired leases and equipment on credit, some of its leases to be paid out of production. A distinctive minor feature was a policy of strict economy. Both administrative and operating expenses were held down. The officers at first received very low salaries, the president none; in 1912, however, both the president and the vice-president were voted $5,000 annually, and in 1916 the president's salary was raised to $10,000. "The old Humble Company was really a poor-boy outfit," one of its employees recently reminisced, indicating that by "poor-boy" he meant excessively economical.

Other men besides its president contributed to Humble Oil Company's success. Three deserve special credit: G. Clint Wood, Charles B. Goddard, and Walter W. Fondren.

Although Wood was connected with Humble only until he sold his stock and retired as director in 1912, the advice and assistance of that shrewd lease buyer and expert production man probably contributed considerably to the company's early success. In fact, without Wood's close association with many of the founders of Humble Oil & Refining Company, and particularly his indispensable part in the organization of Humble Oil Company, the new company of 1917 might never have been organized.

Goddard's contribution was more specific. An original director of the old company, he managed its Oklahoma operations. He was thoroughly able, conscientious and dependable, and Humble's early success in Oklahoma must in large measure have been owing to his experience and ability.

Fondren's strength was particularly in field operations — he was frequently called the *real* oilman of the group. Elected a director early in 1912, he succeeded Wood in charge of Gulf Coast operations on the latter's retirement in the same year. Fondren was generally recognized as probably the leading driller on the Gulf Coast in a day when the driller also served as production superintendent, petroleum engineer, and even geologist. His assumption of control over operations on the coast inaugurated a series of triumphs. His strength was, however, not confined to drilling ability. In a rough and frequently unscrupulous environment, he was distinguished for strict morality, absolute integrity, and personal generosity and was universally popular with men in the field.

Sterling and Fondren, like the Blaffer and Farish combination, constituted an effective team. The two men complemented each other: Sterling, the executive, financier, and trader, the busy, hustling promoter; Fondren, the quiet, modest oilman, the driller extraordinary, interested primarily in field operations. Without Sterling, Humble Oil Company probably would not have existed; without Fondren, it could hardly have achieved its outstanding success on the Gulf Coast.

By 1915, and still more by 1916 and 1917, the Humble founders and predecessor companies were established as successful producers. The sterile period, from the decline of Gulf Coast production to the acquisition of production in Oklahoma and revival on the coast, was at last over. The primary and immediate question in the minds of these oil producers was no longer, "Can we find oil and, if so, where?" It was, "To whom and on what terms can we sell our crude?" Attempts to find a satisfactory answer to this question were to lead to the organization of Humble Oil & Refining Company.

Chapter 3

THE ORGANIZATION OF HUMBLE OIL & REFINING COMPANY

CONCERN over marketing was neither a transient nor an unusual phenomenon in the American oil industry. From the early days of the industry specialized producers had tended to believe that they did not realize from the sale of their crude a fair share of its ultimate market value. This attitude had similarly been characteristic of farmers and ranchers and other producers of basic commodities, who felt that they had inadequate safeguards and strength in the marketing of their products. Indeed, the belief of small, specialized producers of commodities that other functional divisions in the economic process were absorbing more than their just share of the goods' ultimate value probably reaches back to the very beginnings of production for the market in ancient times.

Historically, the producers of commodities sought by various means to strengthen themselves in the market. Political action was a common means. Some form of associative endeavor was frequently employed to achieve greater bargaining strength. Often the problem was quite beyond solution by such means. In American experience the producers' problem not uncommonly came from an inefficient marketing mechanism resulting from a volume too small to support a developed, competitive system. Frequently, what was regarded as the result of exploitation by other functional groups between the producers of commodities and the ultimate consumers was basically the result of low prices in the consumer market. There was no one solution for the problems in marketing, and success in solving them generally depended largely on how well what was done was suited to underlying conditions.

The means finally employed by the founders and early directors of Humble Oil & Refining Company to increase their realization from the oil they produced was the result of years of experience and of a growing understanding of the nature and functioning of the oil industry. The precipitating factor which led to their first significant step, as so often in the history of business, was low prices, but the desire to benefit from rising prices provided a more enduring motivation. Success came from a combination of circumstances, but primarily from decisions that were especially suited to the existing world-wide conditions of the oil industry of the time. This chapter deals with the experience and growing understanding that culminated in the organization of Humble Oil & Refining Company.[1]

MARKETING SYSTEMS AND PROBLEMS

The main market outlets for the independent producers in Texas from the early days of the industry had been the pipeline companies, which took the oil in the fields where it was produced. In the earlier years the pipelines used one or the other of two arrangements: to store the oil for the producer, giving him as evidence of ownership a certificate which he could sell to whomever he wished; or to purchase on contract, for the pipeline or an affiliated company, for a specified term and price. As the years passed, the contract-sales method came to prevail in Texas. When prices were reasonably good and there was no serious difficulty in disposing of the oil, the producers accepted their dependence on the pipelines as purchasers without too much complaint; when the reverse situation arose, they tended to blame the large buyers.

Attempts had been made in early Gulf Coast years to strengthen the marketing of the independent producers. Some of the Humble predecessor companies and founders had tried to acquire storage, build a short pipeline, and market oil directly to local buyers; but, as far as is known, none of these efforts, except Paraffine's construction of earthen storage at Batson, had been successful. Producers had likewise failed in their attempts to establish marketing associations.[2] They had succeeded in preventing the enactment of laws that would have permitted a single corporation to produce, transport, refine, and market oil and oil products under one charter and thus achieve greater strength as against the small producer. The general corporation law, forbidding corporations from engaging in any business except that specifically authorized, had, however, proved ineffectual in preventing integrated operations in the Texas oil industry.[3]

Several strong groups in Texas were carrying on virtually an integrated business. Standard Oil, even before the dissolution of the group by the United States Supreme Court in 1911, had been eliminated by action of the Texas courts except through indirect holdings in what became the Magnolia Petroleum Company. The Texas Company, Gulf, Magnolia, and Sun groups, or their predecessors, were the strongest in Texas, all but Sun having producing, pipeline and storage, and refining facilities. All four had the support of capital from the East and, most important, had marketing connections through their eastern affiliations. The structure of the marketing system in Texas was thus similar to that which generally prevailed in the oil industry throughout the United States; that is, the small independent producer sold his crude oil to the large, integrated concern.[4]

But whereas the structure of the oil market was essentially the same in Texas as elsewhere in the country, its functioning was somewhat different. In Texas the contract system for the sale of crude oil had gradually come to predominate, but elsewhere the posted-price system, under which the producer was paid the price being offered on the day of sale, was in more general use.[5] There was, moreover, a less tangible but very significant element in the situation: in older oil regions the large companies had learned, though they failed on occasion to remember, that long-time good relations with small producers were essential to a continuing supply of oil in adequate quantities and that the only sound basis for such relations was recognition of a mutuality of interest. This attitude had apparently not yet progressed far in Texas, a fact which perhaps was evidence of the immaturity of the oil industry in that state.

Everywhere, however, the working of the system, whatever its structure and practices, was affected by the erratic nature of the oil supply. Local flush production, beyond the capacity of even a large purchaser to store and transport, generally brought about price decline and severe criticism of the purchaser by the small producer. A rise in national or foreign production resulting from the discovery of tremendous fields sometimes similarly affected prices and small producers throughout the whole American oil industry.

Such was the situation that developed during 1915. Excessive production from newly discovered fields in Mexico, Oklahoma, and California, at a time when the demand was temporarily weakened by the war-caused disruption of shipments to Europe, increased the supply much faster than the market could have absorbed it even normally and brought about a crisis in the oil market. Prices fell sharply.[6] The attitude of the independent Texas producers was drastically affected. They were not prepared to recognize the national and international character and the infinite complexity of the problem but instead tended to assign exclusive responsibility for the instability of crude prices to the control of purchasing, transportation, and refining by the big companies.

The price decline affected the independent producers in two ways. The large purchasers passed on to the small producers the lower prices resulting from the rapidly mounting oversupply of oil as promptly as their purchase contracts permitted, a practice to which the producers had become accustomed. But with the price decline of 1915 came a situation new in degree if not entirely new in essence: uncertainty as to whether or not their oil would be taken even at contract prices.

Under the contract system the purchasers wrote into their contracts limitations on the amount of crude they could be required to buy, while generally stipulating that they should have an option on all or part of any remainder at the contract price. The producers had been willing to accept these stipulations so long as the escape clause was not invoked and all their crude was purchased, but they strongly resented a contract purchaser's taking advantage of these provisions to limit the amount he would be required to take even at prices that seemed to the seller excessively low. To the producer it hardly seemed equitable that the purchaser should refuse to buy more than a stipulated minimum when prices were falling, while insisting on his right to take all of a producer's oil when prices were rising.

When this adverse purchase situation hit them in 1915, the Texas independent producers were already disturbed by a major oil company's attempt to obtain legal sanction for a position that to the average small producer already appeared excessively and unwarrantably privileged. Early in January, 1915, it had become known that The Texas Company was sponsoring a bill in the Texas legislature that would give companies the legal right to carry on under a single charter the principal functions of producing, transporting (including buying, storing, and selling), and refining. Such a law would validate The Texas Company's integrated operations in connection with the Producers Oil Company. Other concerns, it was generally known, also owned separate units performing individual functions operated as a single united interest. To legitimatize this situation seemed to the small producers to make inevitable even a further weakening of their own position.

Primarily in order to oppose the so-called Texas Company bill, a group of independent producers organized the Texas Oil Producers and Landowners Association. R. S. Sterling was elected president, and Fondren and Wiess were among its directors. The bill was defeated, but a compromise was passed in the same year that permitted a single company to perform all the functions except producing, thus making explicit an authorization assumed to exist under the Act of 1899. The Texas Company, however, continued to work for its original bill. In the same year a bill was introduced, and supported by the independents, to make pipelines common carriers.[7]

Farish was not a member of the association opposing The Texas Company's bill—according to Sterling he was on the other side—but within a few months he also joined the opposition. A particularly unhappy experience with the contract-sales system was primarily responsible for his change.

In July, 1915, Blaffer & Farish and the Paraffine Oil Company had entered into an eight-months' contract with the Gulf Pipe Line Company for the sale of their oil from a certain lease in the Humble field. The sellers had wanted the pipeline company to agree to take their entire production, up to 3,000 or 4,000 barrels daily, even at the low price of 60 cents per barrel. Gulf, however, had refused to contract for more than a thousand barrels from each, but it had still insisted on an option on any remaining production at the contract price. Before the end of the year crude prices rose suddenly because of a rapid increase in the manufacture of motorcars and a rising demand in Europe for oil for war.[8] The Gulf Coast market price shot up to about a dollar. Gulf now insisted on its right under the sales contract to purchase the entire production of Blaffer & Farish and Paraffine. Blaffer, Farish, and Wiess, seeing their oil running to the Gulf pipeline at 40 cents below the market price, entered suit against Gulf. The decision, which came several years later, was of course in favor of Gulf.[9]

What the producers could have hoped to achieve by entering suit in this circumstance is not clear. Possibly Farish was attempting to appeal to a principle of equity transcending the actual letter of the contract. That the principle of mutuality of benefit in contracts was not altogether foreign to the thinking of the oil industry at the time is evidenced by the fact that, in this very year 1915, Vice-President Bedford of Standard Oil Company (New Jersey) urged the head of his company's Canadian affiliate not to make oil-purchase contracts that would give the company an advantage over the small Canadian producers; the only good contract, he held, was one that was mutually beneficial.[10] Possibly, on the other hand, Farish and his associates merely intended to advertise the deficiencies of the contract-sales system.

Farish at about the same time had another unfortunate experience with a major company. He had succeeded in getting an advantageous offer for the crude from his firm's Thompson lease at Sour Lake delivered at shipside. He asked the Sun Pipe Line Company to give him a rate for carrying the oil in its pipeline. Sun, however, had not built a pipeline for the use of the general public; it was interested in buying and transporting oil for itself. Farish was informed that the line from the tank farm to the dock was a part of the private plant facilities, not of the Sun Pipe Line Company but of the Sun Oil Company.

Gulf, Sun, and other companies were not behaving in this way out of sheer malice. The world petroleum industry was in a state of flux; a few large companies were struggling desperately for larger shares of the expanding world market. The major companies in Texas, operating in a highly competitive environment, were simply utilizing to the full the advantages of large capital and an integrated organization to defend and strengthen themselves. As long as the contract-sales system prevailed in Texas, Gulf could hardly afford to volunteer to pay $1.00 for crude when competitors were getting a large part of their supplies under contract for only 60 cents.

Gulf's policy of refusing to contract to purchase more than a certain amount is, indeed, said to have resulted from an early contract that did not specify a maximum-purchase requirement. When the producer brought in a well flowing several times as much oil per day as Gulf had pipeline and storage capacity to handle and Gulf, accordingly, requested the producer to cut back his production, the latter called attention to the fact that the company had contracted for the entire production. The company's purchase contracts, thereafter, provided for a limit on what the company could be required to take.

Sun's refusal to permit Farish to use its pipeline facilities was also from its viewpoint entirely justifiable. It had constructed a pipeline system in order to supply its own refineries. Why, then, should it permit a producer to use its pipelines in order to supply crude to a rival refinery? In the opinion of Sun, Farish could as logically have expected to receive permission to use one of its still batteries to refine his crude, selling the product in competition with Sun.[11]

The hostility of Farish to the major companies and to legislation that might increase their power had risen to such a point by the end of 1915 that he was prepared to take a strong public stand against the large oil interests. At a meeting of the Texas Oil Producers and Landowners Association to discuss contract prices for the next year, which R. S. Sterling had asked him to address, Farish scathingly denounced the big companies.[12] His exposition of the producers' marketing problem —which was later to be used in an attempt to embarrass him—is doubly significant; it expressed the viewpoint both of a recognized leader of the independent producers and of an ambitious and forward-looking oilman who was to become a principal promoter of Humble Oil & Refining Company: [13]

The producer has never in the history of the industry been paid a fair price continuously. The refining industry has always bought up its flush production at a large discount. . . . I know that supply and demand determine prices, but it is manifestly unfair for the refineries to say to us that they are paying to us the market price. They make the market. Commerce in our product, except through them, has been destroyed. Perhaps I might say that they had destroyed it. Whether it be right or wrong, lawful or unlawful, they have, through allied companies, come almost wholly in control of the production, handling, piping, and refining of oil in the State of Texas. What the little fellow gets for his product is through their grace. What they offer, be it large or small, he must take or go broke. . . . I, for one, feel that if I have to rely on the humanitarian impulses of those who now dominate the whole of the oil business, including its production, I will get but scant rations.

Farish proposed several courses of action. One was to oppose the Texas Company bill, which, he said, would give the refineries "one more cinch in the knot" with which they had tied the producers. Instead of being given greater powers, the companies "should be circumscribed, or at least put under such governmental supervision as would insure to the producers and the public, generally, fair and equitable treatment." He could see no reason why the pipeline companies, which under their charters were public agencies, should not be under governmental control "if the public good so requires." That Farish was not thinking solely of appeal to governmental regulation is, however, shown by two additional suggestions. Asserting that 60-cent coastal crudes would realize $4.00 if refined, he urged the members of the association to endeavor to enlarge their market by making better known to eastern manufacturers the refining value of Texas crude. He also advocated that the old credit-balance, or storage-certificate, system be revived and substituted for the contract method.[14]

As a consequence of Farish's exhortation, the Gulf Coast Oil Producers Association was formed in January, 1916.[15] The new organization was intended to have a broader base than its predecessor and to attract producers who, like Farish, had held aloof from the earlier organization. Among its objectives were closer relations among independent oil producers and "the creation of more stable markets for both crude and refined oils, and better and more permanent relations with producing, pipe-line, refining, and marketing companies." Farish was elected president, R. S. Sterling vice-president, and Wiess a director.

In June, 1916, Farish as president of the association went to the East to confer with refinery managers, presumably of companies without affiliated operations in Texas. He had two objectives: to convince the eastern refiners of the high value of Gulf Coast crudes for manufacturing lubricants and to establish direct sales contacts with them. He found the refiners interested, but he made another important though discouraging discovery. One executive—reportedly an executive of Standard Oil Company (New Jersey)—expressed definite interest and asked how much crude oil he and his associates could supply. When Farish answered that they could supply from 15,000 to 20,000 barrels daily, the executive replied that such an amount would not begin to meet his company's needs, and that, if purchases were made from Farish's independents, the major producing company from which his company was currently purchasing crude oil might refuse to sell to it. In view of the increasing demand for petroleum products, such a danger to a large refining company's crude supply could not be disregarded.

Farish had thus run head on into one of the important realities of the contemporary oil industry. The oil business was Big Business, made so by the tremendous demand for oil products. An adequate and assured supply of crude oil was a primary necessity for the large companies with heavy investments in refineries and other facilities and large commitments as marketers. This was a fact of life in the oil industry that was behind the movement, at home and abroad, to form larger and larger companies and to integrate functionally.

On his return to Texas Farish proposed that the producers pool their production in order to ensure an adequate and steady supply and thus to strengthen themselves in the marketing of their oil. He also urged them to hold out for higher prices. Because of the large capital required and the excessive risk involved, he disapproved, however, of the proposal that the small producers should join in building and operating a large and complete refinery.[16] This attempt to pool the production of independent producers failed, as similar efforts had failed in earlier times and other places. Co-operative action by a large number of producers on a voluntary basis was clearly not the solution to save the small producers.

Various developments in 1916 and early 1917 converged to influence the founders of Humble Oil & Refining Company to take other and more positive action to strengthen their marketing position. With their larger investment in producing properties they had more at stake than earlier. Rising prices were making them even more dissatisfied with the contract system. The majors were growing stronger and might strengthen themselves even further through the enactment of the Texas Company bill. Most important of all, perhaps, the producers had acquired a better understanding of the nature of the oil industry as a whole and of current trends within it, particularly the increasing size and functional integration of individual companies or groups. One of the most important factors in this development was the "education" of Farish and his rise to leadership among the independent producers.

BYPASSING THE MAJORS

The first attempts of the founders of Humble Oil & Refining Company to strengthen themselves, as producers, in the marketing of crude oil took the form of undertaking in small ways several functions ordinarily performed by the majors. Though few and far from spectacular, their efforts showed that they were intent on doing everything possible to increase their realization from the sale of their crude oil. Some entered refining and marketing, while one group acquired a pipeline and purchasing contracts.[17]

Refining was then principally a function of the larger companies. By the end of 1917 there were twenty-six refineries in Texas, valued at $48,950,000 and with an estimated daily capacity of 225,000 barrels. Gulf, Texas, and Magnolia owned about 70 per cent of the Texas refinery capacity, located mostly in the Port Arthur–Beaumont area.[18]

The larger companies occupied this overwhelmingly strong position in refining for a number of reasons. They had the capital for building and equipping refineries and for maintaining an adequate supply of crude oil, and their large refineries supplied a volume output that gave them an advantage in marketing. Fuel oil, which was in strong demand early in the century, characteristically went to railroads, shipping companies, and industrial plants. Such concerns needed large and assured supplies, which the smaller refineries could not provide.

With the coming of the gasoline age in the second decade of the century, however, the demand for petroleum products changed favorably for the small refinery. The demand for gasoline in the United States rose rapidly with the phenomenal increase in automobile registrations from 500,000 in 1910, to 2,500,000 in 1915, and 10,000,000 in 1920.[19] By 1919 one-fourth of the crude oil produced in this country was used in the manufacture of gasoline; moreover, a barrel of crude refined with gasoline as the chief product was worth two or three times as much as a barrel processed primarily to produce fuel oil. Within Texas the increase in the consumption of gasoline meant that the small refinery could find a larger local outlet for its products.

Gasoline of the quality then required could be produced profitably with simple equipment. Innovations in refining that required costly equipment, such as continuous distillation and the Burton process for cracking the oil molecules to produce such lighter products as gasoline, had already come into use. As late as 1917, however, even a good-sized refinery commonly consisted of shell stills, each with a capacity of about 600 barrels, set upon solid walls of masonry, constructed in rows but operated individually. For years to come many refineries were to continue to use the simple batch still, individually or in batteries.

The use of these shell stills to supply the growing local market for gasoline provided an opportunity for the small producer. Three of the Humble founders seized the opportunity to use this type of still to supply the growing local market for gasoline and obtain a larger realization from their crude. A casual experiment at the Humble field by Farish's younger brother was a first uncertain step in this direction.

Stephen Power Farish was, as far as is known, the first person to "cook" a barrel of oil for one of the firms that pooled their properties to form Humble Oil & Refining Company. In March, 1916, when he was in charge of producing operations on the Paraffine forty-acres at the Humble field, a "freak" well came in that flowed 400 barrels daily of high-gravity crude. Partly for amusement and partly as an experiment, young Farish constructed a little "teakettle" refinery consisting of an old boiler with a steam coil inserted, a wooden condenser-box set on pine logs, and a few small bolted tanks. The chemicals for treating the gasoline were mixed in a barrel and poured into the treating tanks from a bucket, and the mixture was stirred with a paddle. The neighbors were then invited to fill the tanks of their Fords with the product.

The "teakettle," though short-lived, convinced Blaffer, W. S. Farish, and Wiess that a small refinery processing a superior grade of crude could compete with the larger refineries in the local gasoline market. They decided to invest $10,000 in a small "topping" plant and incorporated the Globe Refining Company.[20] The firm of Blaffer & Farish furnished one-half the capital, and S. P. Farish and Wiess one-fourth each. The Globe refinery at the Humble field, a single steam still with a capacity of 300 barrels daily, began operations in October, 1916. S. P. Farish supervised both producing and refining operations; Blaffer was sales manager.

Nearby Houston provided a market. A Ford tank truck plied the short distance between Humble and Houston, delivering about 500 gallons of gasoline daily to four principal customers at 17 cents per gallon, a price which the large companies could not meet and apparently did not like. The residue was shipped to Houston by tank car to be sold as fuel at 2 or 3 cents per gallon.

Besides creating conversation and amusement in the South Texas refining industry, the Globe was a source of profits to its owners. Early in 1917 its capacity was doubled in order to process, in addition, the 150 barrels of high-grade crude produced daily from the Schulz-Serrien leases and small quantities purchased from outsiders. The number of the refinery's personnel was increased, a still added, the efficiency of the refining equipment raised, and the tank-truck equipment tripled. Gasoline production then averaged 1,200 gallons daily, while the proportion of gasoline produced from a barrel of crude was raised from 14 to 22 per cent. In the meantime prices also rose. Gasoline sales in dollars increased from a little more than fuel oil sales to nearly twice their amount. During the first nine months the Globe Refining Company netted a profit of $21,000, or 26.5 per cent of sales. Thus the Globe group was able, as Wiess expressed it, to obtain a realization of about $3.00 per barrel of crude instead of 60 cents. The lesson was obvious.

Blaffer and Farish at about the same time were engaged in organizing a "natural gasoline" company in Wichita County, the second in Texas. The Schulz Gasoline Company was an outgrowth of the Schulz Oil Company, of which Blaffer and Farish were the principal owners. By late summer of 1916 they were aware that the gas produced with the high-gravity Schulz-Serrien crude, separated from the oil at the top of the casing and released to the atmosphere, was rich in gasoline. By October they had come to an agreement, with their former associate G. Clint Wood, to build and operate a casinghead gasoline plant to extract the "natural," or "casinghead," gasoline from the gas. They incorporated the Schulz Gasoline Company, owned three-fourths by Blaffer & Farish and one-fourth by Wood. The plant, one of the earliest gasoline compression plants in Texas, went into operation in July, 1917. After blending with a equal amount of purchased naphtha, the product was sold at 17 cents a gallon.

Early in 1917 Humble Oil Company assumed the functions of pipeline transportation, for which it had hitherto depended exclusively on the major companies, and also of purchasing. The pipeline affiliates of the Gulf, Texas, Sun, and Magnolia groups owned most of the state's pipeline network; all but Magnolia purchased crude in the fields and carried it to their affiliated refineries in Texas or to shipping points on tidewater.

R. S. Sterling purchased the Southern Pipe Line Company for Humble Oil Company on January 23, 1917.[21] The Southern provided an outlet from the Goose Creek field to the Houston Ship Channel. Its equipment consisted of 1,000 feet of gathering lines, two 7,000-foot lines of four-inch pipe across Black Duck Bay to Hogg Island, cypress storage tanks with a capacity of 20,000 barrels, a wharf on the Ship Channel, and 500 feet of six-inch line from the tanks to the wharf. The price paid by Sterling was $130,000, half in cash and the remainder contingent upon the fulfillment of Southern's purchase contracts, which represented $103,480 of the company's valuation.

The company had been organized in 1913 with a capital of $20,000. It had rarely paid dividends, probably because of the decline in Goose Creek production until the drilling of wells into deeper sands in 1916. For a time Southern apparently served as the outlet for most of Goose Creek's production, but it was not long before the majors extended their lines to purchase oil from the productive deep sands.

Humble would perhaps have purchased the line in any case to get an assured outlet for its large production, which was about to be increased by the acquisition of an additional large leasehold at Goose Creek, but it undoubtedly also expected to profit from the fact that, through contracts negotiated between August, 1916, and January, 1917, Southern had placed the greater part of Goose Creek production up to July 1, 1917, under contract at 65 cents a barrel. The Southern, moreover, had a contract to sell to Magnolia 600,000 barrels at from 90 to 95 cents. Since prices were rising—the price of Goose Creek crude in March, 1917, was $1.25—there was a chance of even higher returns on whatever Magnolia did not take.

Those contracts placed Humble Oil Company on an unfamiliar side of the crude oil market, and its new role immediately involved it in difficulties. Its attempt to enforce the purchase contracts eventually caused it to resort to the courts; a settlement was finally arrived at in September, 1918.[22] The founders of Humble Oil & Refining Company were thus early confronted with serious problems in their purchase relationships with producers, and they proved as reluctant as the larger companies to relinquish the price advantage that the difference between the contractual and the market price gave them.

By the time of Sterling's purchase of the Southern Pipe Line Company, negotiations were well under way for a merger of the interests of the men and groups whose careers over nearly two decades we have been following. At the same time that they were engaged in small but significant steps toward vertical integration, they were also preparing to effect a general pooling of properties and interests that was to complete the union that had been developing among them for several years.

PRELIMINARIES TO UNION

Some time in 1916 W. S. Farish began to explore the possibility of uniting several independent companies in a single corporation. He envisaged a corporation of sufficient size to bargain advantageously with the larger companies and, particularly, to deal directly with eastern refineries.

Farish confined his discussions to those men with whom he and Blaffer had enjoyed increasingly close ties for many years, that is, the Wiess and Sterling groups. Personal friendships, business relations, and co-operative action in producers' associations had welded the three groups into such a close relationship that for them to unite into one concern was a logical step (see Table 1). Their common problems and opportunities in 1916 provided the motivation, and Farish the initiating leadership.

Discussions went on among representatives of the various interests in those groups throughout 1916, and toward the end of the year, according to Wiess, they were discussing the relative values of the properties involved and were taking a poll to see who were willing to join the new enterprise.[23] The Blaffer & Farish partnership, with a production of 1,200 barrels daily, was committed to the plan. R. S. Sterling favored the combination, and his influence assured Humble's adherence. Sterling's interest was crucial, for Humble Oil Company, with its large assets and average production of 6,000 barrels daily, was of central importance

TABLE 1

PRINCIPAL BUSINESS TIES BEFORE 1917 OF THE ORIGINAL DIRECTORS OF HUMBLE OIL & REFINING COMPANY

A. OWNERSHIP IN PARTNERSHIPS AND CORPORATIONS

Owners	*Blaffer & Farish*	*Paraffine*	*Reliance*	*Ardmore*	*Humble Oil*	*Globe Refining*	*Schulz Oil*	*Schulz Gasoline*	*Farish & Ireland*
Blaffer	x				x		x		
Farish	x				x		x		x
Blaffer & Farish						x		x	
Jones		x							x
Carlton							x		x
Fondren					x				
Goddard					x				
Wiess		x	x	x		x			
R. S. Sterling				x	x				
F. P. Sterling					x				

B. JOINT LEASE INTERESTS OF COMPANIES AND MEN

In Texas

Humble Field
Blaffer & Farish and Humble Oil
Blaffer & Farish and Paraffine
Humble Oil and Paraffine

Goose Creek Field
Blaffer & Farish and Humble Oil
Blaffer & Farish and Paraffine
Humble Oil and Paraffine

Sour Lake Field
Farish, Jones, and Carlton[a]

In Oklahoma

Tubbee Leases
Humble Oil, Paraffine, Reliance, and Ardmore

Martha Potter Leases
Humble Oil, Paraffine, Reliance, and Ardmore

[a] There were probably more such common lease interests of men, but no record has been found of them.

and, indeed, indispensable. The Wiess interests agreed to contribute those properties—representing a total daily production of 1,750 barrels—of the Paraffine and Reliance companies that were shared with the firms cooperating in the Humble and Goose Creek fields in Texas and in Carter County, Oklahoma; their other properties were too widely scattered to be readily integrated into the new project. The Ardmore Oil Company, controlled by R. S. Sterling and Wiess, would contribute all its properties, which produced 2,000 barrels daily. Blaffer, Farish, and Wiess would add the Globe Refining Company to the combination. There was no question about the Southern Pipe Line Company, which was purchased by Sterling after plans for the new organization were well advanced.

Some opposition to the merger manifested itself. Ed Prather, a ruggedly individualistic oilman and a major stockholder in the Schulz Oil Company, with its high-quality production of 150 barrels daily, did not want to lose control of his interest in the Schulz by merger. Prather finally agreed, however, to go along with the other owners of the Schulz when Bert Broday told him that he considered himself "fortunate to have the chance" to join Fondren, Blaffer, Farish, and Sterling. Farish's associates in the Farish & Ireland partnership at Sour Lake were unwilling to contribute such a profitable property, but Farish pledged his share.

Others agreed to join the group as individuals. Among them were W. W. Fondren, Humble Oil Company's vice-president, who would contribute privately owned drilling equipment and a lease interest. J. Cooke Wilson, a former Wiess associate, would also contribute a lease interest.

The general nature of the consolidation seems to have been agreed upon some time in January, 1917. A couple of months were to pass, however, before the principals decided what sort of company they wished to organize and before they could take action to effect the merger.

Several alternatives were considered. A possibility was to incorporate under the liberal corporation statutes of Delaware or New Jersey, as the majors operating in Texas had done. Despite the stringency of Texas corporation laws, the founders decided that they preferred to incorporate in the state where they planned principally to operate and which was their home by birth or adoption. Merging the properties in Humble Oil Company, which would have been a relatively simple procedure, was considered, but the company's charter did not empower it to engage in all oil-industry operations. Early in 1917 the increasing possibility of another alternative delayed the final decision.

That alternative depended on the fate of the Texas Company bill in the legislature. The Texas Company was still endeavoring to persuade the legislature to vote favorably on a bill that would permit a company to engage under a single charter in all the functions of the oil industry. The independent producers, as observed earlier, had particularly objected to the joining of pipelines and production. Early in 1917, however, the situation changed. The Gulf Coast Oil Producers Association, through a committee including Farish, Sterling, Wiess, Wilson, and Wood, won support for a bill constituting pipelines as common carriers, forbidding them to discriminate for or against any individuals or corporations in the transportation of oil, and assigning their regulation to the Texas Railroad Commission. The assurance that a common-carrier bill would be passed reconciled some of the opponents to the union of several functions under one charter.

Early in February the Texas legislature passed a bill that authorized a company organized for the operation of oil pipelines to engage in the oil and gas producing business, but conditioned its right to do so upon separately incorporating and operating oil pipelines. The oil company, however, was permitted to own all the stock of the pipeline company. This modified Texas Company bill was presented to the governor of Texas for his signature on February 12; the common-carrier bill was passed the next day. Both bills were signed on the twentieth day of the month.[24]

The promoters of the merger decided to incorporate under the new law. "They decided," as Edgar E. Townes later remarked, "to start clean and fresh." They wanted a company authorized not only to produce but also to refine, buy and sell oil and oil products, and own a pipeline company. Although Farish seems to have been concerned principally with establishing direct connections with eastern refineries, no one could object to a charter that would permit refining operations or to a name that, as Sterling said, would "give the refining atmosphere."

The fact that the new act was not to go into effect until June 20 created a serious problem for the group. They were eager, for a specific reason, to consolidate their interests as soon as possible: it was expected that the next Congress would pass an excess-profits tax for corporations, with a provision against reducing the rate of profit by increasing capitalization through reorganization. Since many of the organizing groups' properties had appreciated in value since purchase, such a provision might affect the owners and the new company adversely and even dangerously. As will be seen later, an informal union was agreed upon to take effect before the convening of Congress in March.

In the meantime certain preliminaries were carried forward, a most important one being to determine the value of the individual properties to be assigned to the consolidation. Apparently no specific formula was used in arriving at the relative value of the individual properties. Indeed, in the prevailing lack of knowledge of the depth of oil sands and of other indications of oil in a reservoir, no very exact standards could have been applied. Nor was the practice of valuing producing properties by the rough measure of average daily production employed, except perhaps as something of a basis for bargaining. Even identical shares in a single lease were not given the same valuation.

The relative values assigned to each group of properties, according to Townes, were "bargained across the table." Such discussion obviously resulted in the assignment of a lump sum, payable in stock, to each group of properties. The Sterling interests seem to have come off most favorably, the Wiess interests somewhat less so, and the Blaffer and Farish interests least favorably of all. The Sterling group was essential to the organization of the new company. The Wiess interests had over the years played an important role in helping to bring the Blaffer and Farish and the Sterling interests into closer association, but the Wiess group was also needed to strengthen the combination.

According to H. C. Wiess, Farish "was ready to reduce the participation of his own properties . . . in furtherance of the main objective." Doubtless he felt that any losses that his personal and partnership interests might suffer in the process of organization would be more than compensated for by the new company's higher realizations from crudes. Wiess recalled in 1945: "I attended meetings prior to the organization of the company when, except for Will Farish's leadership, vision, and determination, the idea of organizing a new company would have been abandoned. He was the man who came to the fore and called the attention of the group to the fact that the larger advantages of such an organization outweighed any differences as to details or personalities."

THE FINAL ORGANIZATION

Between February 15 and 20, 1917, according to later reports,[25] it was agreed that the properties to be merged in the new company should from March 1 be considered as parts of a joint enterprise in which the various owners should as of that date receive interests proportionate to the values agreed upon for the individual properties. This arrangement was apparently a gentlemen's agreement, for no written record of it exists, but the year-end statements in the new company's ledger cover March 1 to December 31, 1917.

The earliest action in the final organization process of which contemporary written record exists was taken on March 20, 1917. On that day the stockholders of Humble Oil Company authorized the directors of that company to purchase the properties of Blaffer and Farish, H. C. Wiess, and W. W. Fondren, "working out the details to best advantage." Humble's capital stock was increased from $300,000 to $4,000,000, and the number of directors was increased from seven to nine. Farish, Blaffer, Wiess, Jones, and Carlton joined the two Sterling brothers, Fondren, and Goddard as members of Humble Oil Company's Board of Directors.

The next day the new Board of Directors resolved that "certain properties offered to this company by sundry owners . . . should be, and they are hereby, accepted at the prices and on the terms that same have been by the owners offered to the company." These properties included certain interests of the Paraffine Oil Company and the Reliance Oil Company, the Blaffer & Farish firm, including its interest in the Schulz Oil Company, certain personal interests of W. S. Farish and W. W. Fondren, and the Ardmore Oil Company. The Southern Pipe Line Company and the Globe Refining Company were not included, since Humble's charter did not authorize the company to engage in refining and transportation. The properties were purchased as of March 1, 1917, with compensation in stock that would be provided for in the affidavit accompanying the new charter, for which application was to be made under the new Texas Company Act.

On May 17, 1917, Sterling, Farish, and Wiess filed with the Secretary of State of Texas a charter for a corporation to be known as Humble Oil & Refining Company. The charter prepared by Carlton and Townes with the collaboration of Frank Andrews provided for the right to perform all the functions allowed under the new law, including owning the stock of a pipeline company. It is significant that the new law authorized companies to produce only oil and gas, whereas the old law had included the broader classification, minerals. The capital stock of the new company was to be $4,000,000, the same as the recently increased capital of the old Humble Oil Company. The charter affidavit listed properties valued at slightly over that amount.

According to company tradition, these properties were listed at half their market value. One contemporary document lends support to this tradition: the record of the purchase resolution adopted by the stockholders' meeting of Humble Oil Company on March 20, 1917, contains the statement that the properties to be purchased were to be taken over "at a price of one-half the appraised value." This conservative valuation of the properties was consistent with the fact that these company organizers were operating men and not company promoters or stock salesmen. A practical reason for it, however, was to protect the owners of the properties from crippling taxes from capital gains on properties originally acquired at low cost but developed over the years. Since the methods of the federal tax authorities for figuring costs and depletion were not yet clearly developed and hence were uncertain, it seemed wise to E. E. Townes, the company's legal counsel, to value the properties conservatively.

On June 21, 1917, incorporation under the charter filed in May was granted, the first under the new Texas Company Act. On that date, then, the existence of Humble Oil & Refining Company as a legal entity began. The company was immediately organized, and the recently elected directors and officers of the old Humble Oil Company were elected to the same positions in the new Humble company. (The old company's charter was canceled after all its properties had been transferred to the new company.[26])

The distribution of the stock of the new company is significant. Of the $4,000,000 at which the company was capitalized, $3,715,000 went to those who had contributed physical assets or stock in predecessor companies, in accordance with the properties and valuations listed in the affidavit accompanying the application for incorporation. The principal owners were the men whose careers have herein been reviewed, but there were also a number of smaller stockholders. Stock to the amount of $191,000 was reserved for offering to the original stockholders for purchase at par in order to supply working capital, each stockholder being entitled to subscribe in proportion to his stock ownership. Of special significance was the reservation of $94,000 in stock that was "subscribed and paid for by R. L. Blaffer, Trustee, to be appropriated by him to employee stock purchase contracts, it being the intent that faithful employees should have the privilege of purchasing limited amounts of stock at par." Humble Oil & Refining Company was not the first company, nor even the first oil company in Texas, to set up an employee stock-purchase plan.[27] That such a plan should have been an element in the original scheme of organization, at such a confused time, does, however, reveal that the founders at this early period recognized the importance to the company of its employees, particularly the men who had long worked with them in their various enterprises but who had not actively participated in the founding of the new company.

Thus, Humble Oil & Refining Company at its inception was an aggregation of successful but relatively small oil producers with ambitions to form a large integrated corporation. On the material side the company's strength lay in its considerable production. On the perhaps even more important personal side, its founders possessed a great deal of experience in production, a willingness to learn, experiment, and expand, a good general reputation for honesty and ability, and an energetic, ambitious, and aggressive leadership that was on the whole capable and forward-looking. Its principals were confident, and qualified observers felt that their confidence was justified. An official of The Texas Company, in bidding Godspeed to a daring young man who was leaving its employ to work for the new company, told him that he could not lose, adding: "It takes both brains and luck to be successful in the oil business and the Humble company has both." [28]

The new company was launched at a time when the demand for oil products was rising. This was a fortunate circumstance in which to start a company with ambitions to expand. Yet the record of history reveals that there are dangers in such a situation, particularly in the temptation to expand at a faster rate than a concern's capital can support and its management effectively handle. The new Humble was to experience its share of difficulties.

Chapter 4

EXPANSION AND INTEGRATION, 1917-1919

THE INCORPORATION of Humble Oil & Refining Company on June 21, 1917, marked the solution of some problems and the beginning of others. The merging of interests hitherto separately administered by independent, spirited, strong-willed men confronted Humble with the problems of reorganization that inevitably arise out of such circumstances. In addition to the managerial needs resulting from the merger, the company experienced difficulties growing out of its own rapid expansion in a period of war and postwar adjustment. At the same time, also, it became involved in a conflict with organized labor which soon after Humble's incorporation struck the entire American oil industry.

Financing expansion turned out to be Humble's most serious and enduring problem. In order to seize attractive opportunities to expand in refining and sales and especially to purchase lease acreage and develop production, Humble within about a year strained its credit to the limit. By late in 1918 its directors were confronted with the necessity of making an important policy decision. Countless companies in American business had faced the same problem but had chosen various means in their search for a solution. The choice made by Humble's directors brought a fundamental turning point in the company's operations and stands as one of the most important decisions in its history.[1]

EARLY ADMINISTRATIVE ORGANIZATION

From an administrative point of view, the union of successful and aggressive men had both advantages and disadvantages. Quite apart from the advantages of size was the gain from the pooling of the experience, knowledge, and judgment of several men. Such a gain, however, depended on the degree to which hitherto independent men would co-operate in forwarding the interests of the whole. Favorable to such co-operation was the mutual confidence and respect which had developed from close acquaintance during many years. Important also was the fact that these men had complementary interests and capacities. Moreover, the merger of their interests had been motivated by the conviction that they could gain more from operating the larger company than by continuing to operate independently.

The directors and officers of the new Humble during its decisive early months were the men who had been in charge the few months when the consolidation was operating under Humble Oil Company's charter. The old Humble group was most strongly represented. Five of the nine directors—four among the most active—were of the old company. Ross S. Sterling as president, Florence M. Sterling as secretary-treasurer, and Walter W. Fondren as vice-president held the same positions in the new company as in the old, as did Director Charles B. Goddard as manager of the Oklahoma properties. The leaders of the other groups, that is, Farish, Blaffer, and Wiess, were also elected vice-presidents. Thus out of nine directors five were vice-presidents.[2]

Not all the original directors devoted their full time to the company's management. At first all except Goddard in distant Oklahoma usually attended the frequent meetings of the Board of Directors, but only six directors gave their full time to the company's affairs. Lobel A. Carlton, the Beaumont lawyer, was rather inactive and remained so until his death in 1925. Wiess, also a Beaumont resident, was at first occupied with extensive family interests; not until 1919 did he become active in management. Jesse H. Jones, Houston businessman and a late investor in Humble Oil Company, was not himself an operating oilman and was reported to have been elected a director at Farish's suggestion "to accomplish some financing plans," but he sold his stock at a profit within the year and resigned his directorship. E. E. Townes, who early in 1918 succeeded Jones as a member of the board, devoted himself entirely to the company's affairs. No director was elected thereafter except on a full-time basis.

For the most part, although some necessary readjustments were made, the managers of Humble continued to carry out about the same duties in operations as those for which they had been responsible as members of the constituent firms. Goddard, who had managed the old Humble's Oklahoma properties, now assumed responsibility for all the holdings of the new company in that state. Blaffer, who had been in charge of the North Texas production of the Schulz Oil Company and of sales from the Globe refinery at Humble, continued to carry these responsibilities.[3] R. S. Sterling retained a special interest in operations at Goose Creek, where Humble Oil Company had achieved extraordinary production. Farish usually supervised operations at the Humble field, which had been the core of Blaffer & Farish's Gulf Coast interest. Fondren, who had been in charge of Humble Oil Company's drilling and production on the Gulf Coast, appears at first to have been given general oversight of drilling both on the coast and in North Texas. He worked closely with Frank P. Sterling, who, although without operational responsibilities as a director of Humble Oil Company, was now vice-president in charge of producing the oil from Gulf Coast wells after they had been brought in. There was, obviously, much overlapping of authority.

Specialized departments were organized only as they were needed. Certain corporate departments had to be set up at once. At the beginning, Townes constituted a one-man legal department, in which he soon established ad valorem tax, land records and rentals, and claims and right-of-way divisions. The Accounting Department was also organized, and separate accounting for the various operations was soon instituted. Because the company at its beginning had only one operation of any importance—production—the single Operating Department seemed to be all that was needed. However, as old operations were expanded and new ones added, greater specialization became necessary. On October 1, 1917, the Land Department, to have charge of leasing, was set up under Robert D. Farish, a younger brother of W. S. Farish. A Sales Department and a Traffic Department were added early in 1918. A geologist, employed in 1918, constituted the nucleus of a geologic department.

Only in one instance do the records reveal that a director was made fully responsible for a function or a department at this time. Townes after his election to the board in 1918 continued to be in charge of the Legal Department, which had broad operating as well as corporate duties. Whether or not any other director had such exclusive responsibility is uncertain. Blaffer, who had managed sales from the little Globe refinery, may similarly have been given oversight of Humble's product sales after refining operations had been increased and the separate Sales Department set up. Vice-President Farish appears to have had some general oversight of production and was perhaps chiefly responsible for the purchase of leases. Even at an early date he was apparently recognized as *primus inter pares*, a sort of executive vice-president without the title.

In spite of the lack of a rational organization, the directors co-operated effectively during these early years. "The organization was not very well designed as to duties," Townes reminisced three decades later;

but, he said, "the company was small and the active men on the board worked together." There was ample opportunity for sharing opinion in directors' meetings, which were held from one to five times a week. The mutual respect that had helped to bring the Humble founders together in the first place created a willingness on their part to make concessions and, apparently, to handle necessary adjustments in a fashion calculated to cause the least injury to anyone's self-respect. The prosperity of the oil industry and the company's expansion gave all the founders adequate opportunities to exercise responsibilities suited to their special capacities and wishes. Further, the advantages of union helped to compensate for such losses of independence or status as circumstances eventually necessitated.

A more clearly defined organization would have to be worked out in time. The organization of a well-rounded set of departments and the assignment of responsibility for each department to a specific director lay in the future but were foreshadowed in early experience. It took nearly a score of years for the organizational problems resulting from the merger to be entirely solved, but in the meantime a gradual adjustment of the system met the current needs of the company.

FORWARD INTEGRATION

One of the means by which Humble expected to obtain a larger realization from its crude oil was to integrate forward into refining and sales. Although the emphasis continued to be on production, in the short span of its first two years Humble diversified its operations. It even in a small way entered the retail distribution of gasoline.[4]

Before the organization of the new company a beginning in refining and marketing had been made in the successful little Globe refinery at Humble, which continued to operate with increased efficiency and capacity through May, 1919.[5] By the end of 1917 Globe was turning out four or five thousand gallons per month of gasoline, kerosene, and solar oil (a gas oil used for Diesel fuel). It had even produced a few hundred gallons of "lubes." A third crude still was added in 1918, and the throughput for the year nearly doubled. Two two-inch pipelines built to loading racks on the railroad at Humble, one for gasoline and kerosene and the other for fuel oil, were Humble's first product lines. These made possible shipping by railroad tank car rather than exclusively by tank truck.

The Schulz Gasoline Company's casinghead gasoline plant near Burkburnett went into operation in July, 1917. With gas supplied from the Schulz-Serrien leases, this plant, which was managed by Bert Broday, averaged 800,000 gallons of natural gasoline per year. This natural, or casinghead, gasoline was trucked—later piped—to a pressure tank near the loading rack at Iowa Park, ten miles from the plant. There it was blended with an equal amount of naphtha purchased from The Texas Company in carload lots at 17 cents per gallon, and the blended gasoline was shipped to Port Arthur and sold to The Texas Company at the same price.[6] That company thus got an improved gasoline at a low cost, and Humble obtained a market for a product that might otherwise have been wasted.

Ownership of the casinghead plant led Humble to construct its first North Texas "refinery." The thrifty Blaffer objected to the plant's buying gasoline for its own automobiles and tank trucks and ordered that casinghead gasoline should be used. Casinghead, however, was a volatile and tricky fuel, ordinarily used only as a blending agent to improve the quality of gasoline topped from crude; when used alone it was highly inflammable. After a truck had been entirely destroyed and Farish on a visit of inspection had had to stifle the flames from an automobile engine with sand carried in his derby, a step was taken in the interest of safety. A topping plant constructed from a drilling-rig boiler was set up to distill a more dependable fuel from the Schulz-Serrien leases' high-gravity crude oil. The plant produced about 15 gallons of gasoline per barrel of crude and averaged about 400 gallons daily. The residue from the still was mixed with the crude oil sold to The Texas Company—sale of crude on a gravity basis in Texas was still several years in the future.

When in August, 1917, Humble brought in the Serrien No. 13 with an initial flow of from 2,000 to 3,000 barrels daily, a larger outlet was needed than that furnished by the Globe refinery. Humble, consequently, purchased from the Dixie Oil & Refining Company, for about $600,000, a plant at San Antonio with a capacity of 2,000 barrels daily. Included in the purchase were fifty-two tank cars and five bulk plants—at Corpus Christi, San Antonio, Seguin, Yoakum, and Austin.[7]

At first the oil was carried by truck to Iowa Park and then shipped in Humble's own tank cars to the refinery at San Antonio. After February, 1918, however, it was pumped to the railroad through a makeshift line of secondhand four-inch drill pipe. This modest line was the first addition to Humble's crude-pipeline "system" after the merger.

For a short period Humble also had an interest in a refining unit and pipeline in another area. In August, 1917, in order to relieve itself from entire dependence on the Magnolia Pipe Line Company as an outlet for its Healdton crude, Humble bought a half-interest in a refinery at Wilson, Oklahoma. It agreed to furnish the necessary crude and to build a casinghead plant to supply blending material. The Wilson

Refining Company undertook to construct a pipeline from Humble's wells and to buy all its casinghead gasoline from Humble. A year later, Humble for an unrecorded reason disposed of this interest.[8]

The expansion of the Globe refinery and the purchase of the Dixie plant at San Antonio necessitated greater attention to the marketing of refined products, and on January 1, 1918, Malcolm J. Monroe became sales manager for Humble. Monroe's principal early task was to arrange for the distribution of Humble's petroleum products in the Houston area, with which he was already familiar because of his former service as head of the Houston division of The Texas Company's sales. To this work was soon added responsibility for the five bulk plants purchased from Dixie.

The company was not yet particularly interested in retail sales, preferring to market through dealers, but with the purchase in March, 1918, of a bulk plant in Houston it also acquired five retail outlets. These were merely small curb pumps in front of what have been described as run-down wooden shacks. Houston then boasted only two real "drive-in" stations. The whole purchase amounted to less than $83,000. Humble next purchased, for $75,000, a site on Main, Travis, and Jefferson streets to be developed for filling-station and garage purposes. The building, completed in March, 1919, at a cost of some $50,000, was at first a show place. It is still in use, but fortunately other Humble stations did not follow its ornate pattern.[9] Operated by salaried employees, this station was probably intended primarily to put the company's name before the public. For nearly a decade thereafter Humble never owned more than three or four filling stations.

The special transportation problems resulting from the expansion of refining and marketing led to the organization of the Traffic Department in March, 1918. At first its principal function was to keep the tank cars moving from the Wichita Falls area to the San Antonio refinery. A minor daily chore was to move two cars carrying wooden tanks filled with fuel oil from the Humble field to Houston for sale to a railroad.[10]

The expansion of sales forced Humble to assume the unfamiliar role of purchasing refined products. In 1918 its sales amounted to 315,000 barrels, but not all came from Humble's two small commercial refineries. The company manufactured almost no lubricating oils or greases and found it difficult to keep up with gasoline sales. The Sales Department was, therefore, forced to buy all its lubes and a considerable volume of gasoline from the major companies and then to sell in competition with them.

Humble's dependence on purchased products reinforced its early desire to own a refinery as an outlet for its Gulf Coast production.

The managers of the company were aware of the suitability of Gulf Coast crudes for the manufacture of lubricants, but for the time being the rich pool of high-gravity crude discovered in Wichita County in August, 1917, had diverted to the purchase of the Dixie plant funds that had been intended for use in building a Gulf Coast refinery. The hope of acquiring a coastal refinery was kept constantly in the minds of the directors by increasing production in the prolific Goose Creek field. A railroad corporation headed by R. S. Sterling connected Goose Creek with the main line of the Southern Pacific in May, 1918, and created an outlet for such shipments as the 35,000 barrels of crude sold to a St. Louis refinery at $2.00 per barrel.[11] However, neither that outlet to inland points nor the facilities to tidewater provided by Humble's Southern Pipe Line Company eliminated the need for a refinery in the area.

Preliminary steps were taken toward obtaining such a refinery. By June, 1918, Humble was purchasing tracts of land for a refinery site on the Houston Ship Channel near Goose Creek, southeast of Houston. The beginning of these purchases coincided with, and may have been stimulated by, the company's discovery at Goose Creek of a well with an initial flow of 20,000 barrels daily—when a roughneck intending to perforate a casing at 3,000 feet accidentally did so at 2,300 and thereby tapped an unsuspected oil horizon. In July the Humble board voted to build on the new site a refinery with an initial capacity of 2,500 barrels daily, to be increased gradually to 20,000. Willard C. Averill of Beaumont, a Cornell graduate in mechanical engineering who was experienced in the building and operation of refineries, was added to Humble's staff and made general manager of the Dixie refinery. He was entrusted with setting up a laboratory for testing Gulf Coast crudes and drawing up plans for the projected coastal refinery.[12] Although the plans were ready by August, the $1,500,000 estimated as the cost of the new refinery was not available, and construction was indefinitely postponed.

In the course of a little over a year Humble had, nevertheless, made considerable progress in the development of refining, transportation, and marketing. The company had expanded one existing refinery, bought another small one, temporarily acquired a half-interest in a third, constructed a small topping plant for its own use, built two casinghead gasoline plants, and drawn up plans and bought the site for a Gulf Coast refinery. It had set up a sales department, acquired half a dozen bulk plants and five retail outlets, and built a model retail station. It had also facilitated the movement of its crude and refined products by the acquisition of tank cars and numerous tank trucks and by the construction of four short pipelines between field and plant and railroad loading racks. By these additions to its operations Humble set its feet firmly on the path of integration.

INCREASING PRODUCTION AND RISING PRICES

Refining and the marketing of refined products were, however, merely the handmaidens of increasing production. Humble's principal investments then as today were in crude oil production. Early in 1917 the corporation ranked fifth in Texas production, but it took third place the following year, ranking after Texas and Gulf and ahead of Magnolia. It was production that was to make Humble an important oil company.[13]

Several developments accounted for the increase in Humble's production from 3,200,000 barrels in 1917—for the whole calendar year for the properties merged in that year—to 4,290,000 the following year. Increased investments in leases and drilling extended its estimated reserves from 36,000,000 barrels at the end of 1917 to 42,000,000 at the end of 1918. The increase in 1918 was stimulated by rising prices; earnings then enabled the company to carry the heavy rise in costs that came after the United States had entered the war in the spring of 1917. Humble bought leases in such North Texas boom fields as Ranger, Burkburnett Townsite, Electra, and Sipe Springs. By the end of 1918 it had some production in the famous Ranger field.[14] At that time it also brought in a phenomenal well at West Columbia. New production on the Schulz-Serrien leases at Burkburnett and at Goose Creek and Sour Lake, however, accounted for most of the increased output.

Another venture was not so successful. The company's entrance into northern Louisiana in August, 1918, with the purchase for $200,000 of a small acreage and a producing well in the Pine Island district, proved an unfortunate investment. The organization used as much fuel oil for drilling and operating as the lease produced.

An event of decisive importance to Humble's future production and reserves was the appointment as of March 1, 1918, of Wallace E. Pratt as first geologist.[15] Pratt, then thirty-three years old, had been interested in petroleum geology ever since his college days. After receiving his Master of Arts degree from Kansas University in 1909, he had for six years served the United States Bureau of Insular Affairs as geologist attached to the Division of Mines, Bureau of Science, of the government of the Philippine Islands. Reconnaissance in the Philippines and in Borneo for the East Asiatic Petroleum Company, an affiliate of Royal Dutch-Shell, had extended Pratt's experience. On his return to the United States he had accepted a two-year contract as a division geologist with The Texas Company, serving the first year in Mexico and

Costa Rica and the second in North Texas with headquarters at Wichita Falls.

Humble approached Pratt late in 1917. At that time North Texas was on fire with the Ranger boom, and the young geologist was preparing to go into a lease-buying enterprise for himself. Frank Cullinan, who was retiring as The Texas Company's vice-president for production, recommended Pratt to Humble, but Pratt was at first unenthusiastic. He later remarked that Humble had impressed him as just another "fly-by-night Burkburnett outfit," a bunch of young and ambitious promoters who were merely following the lead of the major oil companies in wishing to add a geologist to their staff. After a talk with Farish, however, he was immediately reassured as to Humble's character and future and the potentialities of his own connection with it, for Farish, who for some time had been in touch with geologists and studying geological publications, impressed Pratt as knowing why he wanted a geologist. The geologist, consequently, declined an offer of a raise from The Texas Company and went to work for Humble. Before the end of the year Pratt had a staff of three geologists.

Farish was also at this time influential in helping to bring about a rise in the price received for Humble's crude oil. As president of the Gulf Coast Oil Producers Association, Farish had for two years urged its members to hold out for higher prices. Early in 1918 he demonstrated the validity of his advice by negotiating a contract at Franklin, Pennsylvania, by which Humble sold crude to the Galena-Signal Oil Company at $1.80 per barrel. This contract, which indicated the possibilities of direct sales to eastern refineries, was credited with forcing the big Texas purchasers to fall into line and raise their prices accordingly. Moreover, as a member of the Petroleum Committee of the Council of National Defense, Farish was in a position to exert influence and urge that the government raise the price of Gulf Coast crude to $1.80, which increase was made in the summer of 1918.[16]

Farish was also generally recognized as meriting special credit for the successful organized efforts of Texas producers to bring about a change in the method of purchasing crude oil in Texas.[17] Purchase on long-term contracts at a flat price, which worked a real hardship on producers at a time of rising wartime costs and prices, was abandoned in favor of the method of posting prices, by which a purchasing company periodically made public announcement of the price it would pay per barrel. This method, which had first been introduced by a Standard Oil company in a Pennsylvania field in 1895 to help the producers in a period of low prices, had the advantage of treating all producers alike and of making prices more sensitive to changes in the market for crude and products. In September, 1918, Humble was selling about 80 per cent of its crude oil by daily sales to The Texas Company.

Humble's stature as a producing company was growing. Its attainment of third place in Texas production and a considerable increase in its coastal reserves strengthened its already substantial standing in its region. Farish's membership on the Petroleum Committee of the Council of National Defense projected Humble onto the national oil-industry stage.[18] That membership gave Farish an understanding of the nature and trends of the entire oil industry and contacts among its leaders which were to have an importance, for both himself and Humble, far beyond what anyone might have anticipated at the time.

EMPLOYEE RELATIONS, 1917–1918

Only a few months after its incorporation Humble was involved in a general strike of workers in the Gulf Coast oil industry [19], which sprang from general industrial conditions of wartime rather than conditions peculiar to Humble or to the oil industry in general. Although this episode had little effect on the company's operations, it affords a convenient backdrop against which to view Humble's later attitude toward unionism and relations with its employees.

Behind this particular strike were labor conditions in Texas generally and in the oil industry in particular. The Texas background, particularly on the Gulf Coast, was southern and rural. Conditions were influenced by traditional local occupations, such as cotton planting, lumbering, and the cattle industry, in which the hours were "from can see to can't see" or even longer. The employers' attitude toward workers and unions was colored by the mingled arbitrariness and paternalism of the large planter or ranch owner.

In the oil industry hours of labor were still ten, twelve, or even fourteen hours a day in a seven-day week, but wages were considerably higher even for unskilled and semiskilled labor than in other occupations in Texas. The workers for the most part were native-born white Americans, and some had drifted into the Gulf Coast oil fields from regions and occupations in which unionism had gained considerable headway. Although many workers had a keen consciousness of what they considered their rights, they were largely a migratory group; if they felt that they were being treated unfairly on a job they usually expressed their resentment by simply quitting, individually, and finding work elsewhere.

The executives of the Gulf Coast oil companies had had little or no experience in dealing with employees in any formal way. Hiring and firing were generally left to foremen. In an industry which followed a jagged pattern of boom and bust, employers had not devoted much attention to building up a permanent labor force. Although they were often generous in the treatment of veteran workers or those in need, their approach was paternalistic. As in many other industries, the employers had not taken cognizance of the growth of unionism. In fact, there was little precedent for organized action by workers in the oil industry in Texas.[20]

By 1916 the labor situation was changing throughout American industry. Living costs were soaring as a result of the war in Europe, and industries were competing for workers. Labor organizations were taking advantage of the situation in order to gain higher wages, shorter hours, and union recognition.

In the summer of 1916, under the leadership of the Texas State Federation of Labor and the Houston Trades Council, a local union was formed at Goose Creek, one of the fields particularly important to Humble. The many locals chartered in the area held joint meetings in Houston to discuss methods of improving working conditions.

The oil companies responded to the changing economic conditions, but not directly to the demands of the unions. Some oil companies had early recognized the increasing cost of living by a 10 per cent increase in wages. At the beginning of 1917 the Gulf Coast Oil Producers Association, of which Farish was president, had called for an additional adjustment by a cost-of-living bonus or other wage increase.[21] A general 20 per cent rise over the traditional $3.00 per diem came in September, 1917. When the Gulf Coast locals invited representatives of the producers to meet with them in October to discuss terms of employment, the producers refused.

President Sterling of Humble pointed out that wages had been raised and stated his opinion that in the oil-producing business it was impossible to regulate the hours of labor. "We see no reason why we should confer with outsiders or strangers upon matters which solely concern our employees and ourselves," he remarked, adding that, while Humble had no objection to its employees belonging to a union if it did not interfere with their work, the company would not recognize unions. Sterling declared that Humble would "continue to exercise the right to select its own employees and to deal with them directly and not through the medium of a labor union or other organization."[22]

On the refusal of the Gulf Coast employers to meet with union representatives for discussion, the local unions issued a complete set of demands. They asked for a year's contract providing for an increase in wages to a minimum of $4.00 per day, instead of the recently established $3.60, and an eight-hour day with time-and-a-half for overtime. They also demanded a union shop and the arbitration of grievances. The locals threatened to boycott companies without union contracts.

These demands during a period when the United States was at war did not put the union in a good light before either the companies or the public. The developing opinion was no doubt confirmed in the minds of some, when, at its convention in El Paso in 1918, the oil workers' union adopted a resolution calling for the immediate nationalization of railroads, shipping, and communications, and of the oil, coal, and power industries.[23]

After the employers on the Gulf Coast in October, 1917, had shown no disposition to negotiate with them, the oil-field locals went out on strike. An overwhelming vote on October 20–21 led to a walkout on November 1 by 8,000 to 10,000 production workers in Gulf Coast Texas and Louisiana.

The strike immediately brought government action. The day after it went into effect, army regulars and former Illinois national guardsmen were sent from a camp in Texas to the various oil fields to protect property and operations, not from strikers, according to Governor Hobby, but from enemy aliens. On November 15 the *Oil & Gas Journal* reported the presence of two thousand soldiers. On the second day of the strike, two representatives of the United States Department of Labor also appeared. They remained only a few days and left in the belief that the strike would soon end because the men were already going back to work.[24]

The strike's effectiveness varied from field to field, and Humble appears to have suffered comparatively little. After the first few days workers drifted back to work, and in no field was the number of strikers 100 per cent of those employed. Although for a week Humble's Sour Lake leases were completely shut down, the company was soon able to continue drilling wells that had already been started and to keep completed wells pumping. Supervisors served as drillers and clerical employees worked as roughnecks, roustabouts, and pumpers. Youths from the sandy farmlands and lumberjacks from the pine forests of eastern Texas came to fill unskilled positions. At Humble and Goose Creek the men who stayed on the job were protected by barricades and by armed guards until the arrival of troops.[25]

The *Oil & Gas Journal* reported that the strike was orderly and quiet. Despite the reputation of Texas for gunplay, violence was generally confined to random fisticuffs. The Gulf Coast oil-field strike, though reputedly the largest in the history of the petroleum industry up to that time, contrasted favorably with contemporary struggles in western mining communities.[26]

The strike was five weeks old before steps were taken toward its settlement, and by then many men had returned to work. On December 7, officers of The Texas Company, Gulf, and Invincible and Farish of Humble met with a committee of sixteen drillers. These drillers, who were informal representatives of the field workers, demanded $4.00 per day as the minimum wage, but they dropped all other requests, including recognition of the union. The operators expressed a willingness to employ men without discrimination against members of the unions, but they would not agree to discharge new employees in order to rehire strikers. They offered to meet with one or more representatives of their employees to discuss wages and working conditions and to try, in conjunction with the employees, to standardize the wage scale. They indicated that they might grant a general wage increase[27] but they gave the drillers no specific assurance, possibly awaiting the government's decision concerning the producers' request for an increase in the price of crude.

Some days later federal mediators arrived in Houston. Verner Z. Reed, who was serving on the Federal Mediation Commission, headed the group; he had helped to avert a strike in the California oil fields, where the operators had agreed to the eight-hour day and a $4.00 minimum wage. On December 21 this mediatorial group announced its findings in Texas. It censured the unions for striking before giving the federal government a chance to mediate, and the operators for refusal to confer with representatives of the unions. It declared that the strike should end by Christmas Eve without discrimination against union members and that the eight-hour day should be established without reduction of wages—as a penalty for the workers' premature strike the change in hours was not to be effective until March 1, 1918. It stipulated that a committee representing both operators and unions should agree on a minimum wage by February 1, 1918, and that, if agreement was not reached, the federal government should appoint a special commission to decide the issue.[28]

The union representatives accepted the conditions of the mediators, but the Gulf Coast operators, organized in a producers' association of which Farish was president, appealed to the full Mediation Commission in Washington. Reed had obviously gone beyond the functions of a mediator by announcing the findings as if acting with powers of compulsory arbitration. In their official appeal the producers asserted that before November 1, 1917, they had granted bonuses and pay increases of 20 per cent to oil-field men, who, the employers stated, were better paid than others in comparable work. They also asserted that the eight-hour day would be detrimental to the industry and was not desired by the employees, while acceptance of the mediators' findings would lead to additional labor difficulties. Farish urged members of the new producers' association to write to the Secretary of Labor stating that mediation was not needed and also to ask employees to sign a statement that they were satisfied with conditions.

Over a period of three weeks in January, 1918, conferences between representatives of the Gulf Coast producers' association and the striking oil workers were carried on in Washington under the auspices of the Federal Mediation Commission. The terms of their eventual agreement were announced by the Secretary of Labor on January 30. Wages and hours were left for future adjustment by a committee of the employers' association, with the stipulation that the strikers should have preference for employment by their former employers if they qualified satisfactorily and were not "personally objectionable to the foreman or superintendent." Provision was made in the terms of the agreement for appeal from the recommendations of the association's committee.[29]

The immediate reaction of the strikers is said to have been one of disappointment at the apparent lack of any immediate gains from the strike. Although at this late date it is impossible to know how many strikers held opinions expressed by some a generation later, many of the strikers are said to have felt that they had been tricked into surrendering by the award of the mediation board, and some blamed the union leaders. There was also some bitterness toward the companies, particularly the majors.[30]

In the meantime employment conditions in Texas had improved. It was estimated that 25 per cent of the strikers lost their original jobs, but no general black list was instituted and strikers "not needed" by one company could find employment with another. Less than two months after the formal end of the strike and just after oil prices had begun to rise, Humble and the Gulf Production Company in March, 1918, jointly announced a wage scale which equaled or exceeded the one the unions had demanded. Farish held that the higher price of oil entitled the men in the field to a share in the prosperity of the industry. A little later the producers' association's executive committee, headed by Farish, recommended still another increase in wages, which became effective June 1.[31]

During 1918 Humble also took individual action to improve relations with its employees. In October it announced its second employee stock-purchase plan—supplementing the original one of 1917—which gave all employees the opportunity to participate and attempted to make the conditions attractive. Employees could purchase shares at the issuing price of $250 per share by depositing at least 10 per cent of the total and paying the rest in installments over a period of no more than four years. While deferred payments were to bear 6 per cent interest, all dividends were credited on the purchase price.[32]

Humble late in 1918 undertook at Goose Creek—a field that was a prospective long-term producer[33]—a bungalow-building program, its first effort to provide adequate housing for employees. The Texas and Gulf companies introduced a similar housing program at the same time.

Although it is impossible to assess the indirect effects of the strike separately from those that flowed from the underlying conditions, there were clearly other factors than the strike favoring the workers. The rise in the price of crude, because of its immediate effect on earnings and its stimulus to the development of new production, was an important factor. Humble's own enlarged program of expansion, undertaken after the price increase, doubled the number of its employees. The North Texas boom and the general scarcity of labor made the employers keenly aware of the need for instituting policies that would secure for themselves a steady supply of workers.

Humble's executives, especially Farish, had played an important role in defeating the strike and also in influencing the industry to grant the oil-field workers their most pressing demands. Humble's executives had not been behind other industrialists in employee relations before 1917, but the company had had no formal policy governing those relations. The events of 1917 and 1918 and Humble's efforts in the latter year may have helped prepare the company to introduce within the next three years an advanced program of industrial relations.

FINANCIAL PROBLEMS AND AFFILIATION WITH STANDARD OIL COMPANY (NEW JERSEY)

Humble's greatest and most persistent difficulty in its first two years unquestionably stemmed from its lack of capital for expansion.[34] The only cash on hand at the time of incorporation was $18,000 in the treasury of the old Humble Oil Company; the new corporation's assets were almost entirely in the form of leases and equipment. Humble's early program of expansion and integration strained its resources and credit up to and even beyond their limits—in the oil business, as in Alice's Wonderland, it was necessary to run fast in order to stay in the same place. The company had to purchase leases on a large scale whenever potentially productive property came on the market; with reserves being rapidly depleted, it would otherwise soon go out of business. In 1918 it held an extensive lease acreage and had a development program under way which, in Farish's words, "was swamping us from the standpoint of finances."

While a few hundred thousand dollars came in every month from oil runs, the company was spending twice as much. Meeting the payroll was a first claim on available funds, yet as payday approached The Texas Pipe Line Company, to which Humble sold most of its crude, was sometimes called on for advances. Payment of some bills was postponed. Before the Schulz-Serrien leases came in so profusely in August, 1917, Humble, according to report, was unable to pay its officers. The officers gave notes for various purchases and for loans from banks, which amounted to as much as $100,000. As the dates for payment approached, the notes were often either renewed or paid with money borrowed elsewhere. R. S. Sterling was kept busy getting extensions of loans and negotiating additional ones all over the state.

Loans from Texas banks, however, did not prove adequate for Humble's far-from-humble plans, and loans were sought elsewhere. In October, 1917, Farish negotiated a loan of $250,000 from the Liberty National Bank in New York City, on a ninety-day note bearing the personal endorsement of Sterling, Fondren, Blaffer, and Farish. The loan was obtained at the suggestion and through the good offices of Jesse H. Jones, then a director of Humble and a personal friend of the bank's president, Harvey Gibson. This note was twice renewed.

By February, 1918, the company's financial condition presented a mixed picture. At the annual stockholders' meeting on the eleventh of the month Farish reported that the company was "in very fine condition and its outlook very encouraging." Its net income of over $878,000 after taxes in 1917 was high enough to induce the federal income-tax commissioner to endeavor to collect additional taxes. He refused to accept the argument that the company's invested capital was actually twice its capitalization; the difficulties growing out of this controversy were to plague the company during the many years of life of the properties involved. Despite increasing income, ready cash was lacking in 1918. A 6 per cent dividend was paid partly in Liberty Bonds at par and partly in cash borrowed from Jones. The directors, nevertheless, resolved that the company should go on an annual dividend basis of 10 per cent, payable quarterly. The desire to advance the reputation of the stock of a new company must have been important in the decision. Moreover, the company was over three-fourths owned by directors and their relatives, who were more or less dependent on income from dividends. Even so, only 21 per cent of net income after taxes was paid in dividends in 1918, a dividend policy that under ordinary circumstances would be considered conservative.

The fulfillment of Humble's ambition to become a large, integrated company called in 1918 for additional expansion through large-scale participation in the rapid leasing developments in the Ranger district, the construction of a pipeline to that area, and the building of a coastal refinery. The company's current financial condition, however, rendered such expansion and integration impossible and even the maintenance of its position as a producing company doubtful, unless it could obtain larger amounts on longer terms than the loans available from Texas banks or even the quarter-million-dollar loan negotiated in New York.

In an attempt to obtain the needed funds the Board of Directors authorized Sterling and Farish to borrow two or three million dollars for from four to six years. After a diligent canvass of the financial houses of New York which went on for weeks, the only proposition Sterling and Farish could report was an offer to purchase $4,000,000 of Humble bonds, or preferred stock, at 92. Since these bonds were to yield 8 per cent annually and carry an option to convert them into common stock or preferred stock sharing dividends up to 12 per cent, the proposition was rejected as exorbitant and endangering control of the company. For the time being the directors decided to curtail operations. Even at that, they negotiated another short-term loan of $250,000 from the Guaranty Trust Company of New York on the security of $275,000 in Liberty Bonds.[35]

In the meantime, in September, 1918, Farish continued to seek a large long-term loan in the East. Every day he telephoned a no-progress report to Sterling. Then, finally, came an important new development which Farish announced in a telegram reading, "Had lunch today with the father of them all. . . ," meaning Walter C. Teagle, president of Standard Oil Company (New Jersey).[36] During service on the Petroleum Committee of the Council of National Defense, Farish had become well acquainted with A. Cotton Bedford, chairman of the committee and also chairman of the Board of Directors of Standard Oil Company (New Jersey), and with President Teagle of the same company. Farish's acquaintanceship with Teagle had also been forwarded by their common interest in hunting Texas quail. Perhaps uncertain of the attitude of his own associates toward negotiations with Standard Oil, Farish added to his message, "If you have no objection I will talk to him further about it." "It" evidently meant funds for Humble. Sterling replied, "I don't give a continental damn if you get it from the Czar of Russia or the Emperor of Germany, just so we have the money."

Standard Oil Company (New Jersey) had reason to be interested in Humble. It had not recovered the degree of integration that it had lost in the dissolution of 1911. It had been shorn of nearly all its domestic producing affiliates and of much of its domestic marketing business and transportation facilities and had been left principally a refining and foreign-marketing company. Although in the intervening years it had added to its producing properties, in 1918 it had a low ratio of production to its refining facilities and more European marketing outlets than suitable products. Like other oil companies faced by a greatly increased demand for gasoline and lubricating oils, Jersey Standard was eager to obtain a permanently dependable source of crude oil.[37] It had the money to take the necessary steps. The prodigious current Ranger boom in north central Texas attracted Jersey's attention to the possibilities of that state as an important domestic producer of crude.

At least as early as September, 1917, Jersey Standard's attorneys had been considering ways and means of overcoming the obstacles to their company's entry into production in Texas. In 1913 the company had paid a fine to settle a charge of violating the state's antitrust law, and although it had not then actually been barred from doing business in Texas a general impression to that effect prevailed. The principal possibilities considered for entering the state were (1) to obtain a permit for a producing affiliate, The Carter Oil Company, to do business in Texas, (2) to incorporate a Texas company and hold its stock, or (3) to acquire 51 per cent or more of the capital stock of a Texas company already in operation. Another means which was considered was to acquire and hold leases through individuals.

Obtaining a permit for Carter Oil to operate in Texas, at one time considered the most promising solution, was abandoned when in September, 1918, the Texas attorney general expressed his opposition. This and other proposals were superseded by the plan to purchase a majority of the stock of a going Texas concern, although Jersey's Legal Department considered this and the other possibilities to be unsafe. When Teagle, however, inquired of Frank Andrews, Jersey's Houston attorney, what the legal situation would be if the company purchased 60 per cent of the capital stock of Humble Oil & Refining Company, the Texan replied that such a deal would not in his opinion violate Texas antitrust statutes.[38] Jersey's Legal Department continued to be doubtful, but the view of the Houston attorney prevailed.

Teagle, it is said, had previously suggested to Farish, probably while on a hunting trip in Texas, that Jersey purchase a controlling interest in Humble, but Farish had refused, because his company preferred a loan to selling stock and had still not given up hope of that solution to its financial difficulties. Teagle is said to have taken the initiative, after hearing that Farish was in New York, by telephoning the Texan in his New York hotel and inviting him to the luncheon mentioned in the telegram to Sterling. Several conferences between the two men followed, Farish meanwhile receiving encouragement from his associates in Texas to pursue the matter. Farish then returned to Houston to report. The directors of Humble decided that they were willing to make a trade, and Farish returned to New York, this time to inform Teagle that Humble would double its capital stock and sell half to Jersey "at a price to be agreed on." Jersey Standard immediately sent a party headed by Arthur F. Corwin of The Carter Oil Company to inspect and evaluate Humble's properties. Impressed by what he found during a six-weeks' study, Corwin returned a favorable report.[39]

A large Humble delegation went to New York at the beginning of January, 1919. Sterling, Farish, Wiess, and Blaffer were accompanied by Humble's legal counsel, Carlton and Townes, and its chief geologist, Wallace E. Pratt. The first matter to be discussed was the price of the stock; Sterling valued a half-interest in Humble at $20,000,000, but Jersey Standard's valuation failed to meet this figure by four or five million dollars. The final figure came to $17,000,000 in cash, for which the purchaser was to receive half of Humble's stock, which was to be increased to a par value of $8,200,000.

Even before the price had finally been settled upon, the negotiators were debating the question as to the percentage of the stock to be sold to Jersey Standard. Teagle's original idea had been to purchase 60 per cent; Humble had agreed to sell half. George H. Jones, Jersey's treasurer, suggested, and Chairman Bedford agreed, that Jersey should have at least 51 per cent. Sterling was unwilling, however, to return to Houston to tell Humble's stockholders that control had been sold to the unpopular "Standard Oil Company." Jersey Standard settled for 50 per cent; Sterling assured the Jersey group that he would be glad to sell them some of his stock if they should ever feel that Humble was not "doing things right"; he well knew that Jersey could pick up a few shares on the market. For several years the stock was held in the name of Walter C. Teagle, because of a Texas law which forbade a foreign corporation from subscribing to the capital stock of a corporation the capital of which was being increased. C. O. Swain of Jersey Standard's Legal Department, "in order," as he expressed it, "that there should be no question about the control," ordered the purchase of five additional shares of Humble stock, to be held for Jersey Standard.[40]

By January 13, 1919, Humble and Jersey had agreed on a tentative statement concerning the character of the former's operations. It began: "The present policy of the company is, and the future policy will be, to build up a large producing business in the State of Texas, and to accumulate storage reserves of crude oil." The plans contemplated the construction of a trunk pipeline from Ranger to Galveston and a refinery on the Houston Ship Channel with a capacity of about 4,000 barrels daily to run Goose Creek crude for manufacturing lubricating oil. In addition to plans to spend an estimated $8,000,000 on the projected pipeline and refinery, another $2,000,000 would cover outstanding indebtedness, leaving the remaining $7,000,000 for buying additional lease acreage and for drilling. Jersey Standard's payments were to start with $5,000,000 on receipt of the stock, the balance to be held at 6 per cent interest subject to ten days' call. The agreement provided for shares to be held by a trustee for the benefit of the employees under the stock-purchase plan, and hope was expressed that dividends could be continued at the 10 per cent annual rate. The understanding was embodied in a formal agreement signed January 29, 1919.

The directors of Humble, who could now look forward to a period of expansion, probably derived different individual satisfactions from the outcome of the negotiations. The irrepressible Blaffer, it is reported, jokingly remarked to Farish en route homeward: "Well, Bill, our financial troubles are over! With this $17,000,000 we can lease the whole state of Texas and carry out all necessary developments!" Farish may have been gratified by the unexpected and stupendous success of his 1916 plan for establishing a direct connection with eastern refineries. And Sterling may have recalled that the Texas secretary of state, eight years before, had inquired suspiciously of his proposed $150,000 company, "Does Standard Oil have anything to do with this?"

News of the transaction electrified the oil world, particularly that of the Southwest. In presenting the agreement on February 10 to the annual Humble stockholders' meeting, where it was unanimously ratified, Farish described the purchasers merely as "parties in New York." Probably, however, it was then generally understood that Standard Oil Company (New Jersey) had bought into the expanding Humble. Some asked why such "sharp Pennsylvania Yankee businessmen" as the Jersey people should have paid such a high price for a half-interest in a comparatively new company. The old Spindletopper, Ed Prather, in conversation in 1945 with one of the authors of this history, quoted himself as having said at the time, "They aren't paying that much for any property; they're paying it for those boys! They don't have men like that up there. Before you and I die, those boys will be running the Standard Oil Company!" This jesting remark could have been the serious judgment and prediction of a man aware that a farsighted group of men buy on future anticipation and that in the past companies in which Jersey Standard held stock had contributed leadership to the whole.

In the meantime Humble men had to take a certain amount of "ribbing" by the representatives of large oil firms, who saw a leading "independent" becoming connected with the largest of them all. Underwood Nazro of Gulf called out to Sterling, in the presence of a group of oilmen at the Houston Club, "R. S., I hear that Standard is going to take you over." "Take us over, hell!" Sterling shot back. "We're going to take over the Standard!" Sterling lived to see two Humble men become presidents of Jersey Standard, one of them being William S. Farish.

Humble's changed financial situation in 1919, even apart from the possibilities of future developments, undoubtedly helped the Humble leaders to take in stride the jocular jibes of the men of the major oil companies—and the criticism of some of the independents. Beginning with February 15, 1919, the day on which the additional stock authorized by the directors was delivered to Teagle's representatives, installments of the $17,000,000 began to be deposited to Humble's account with the Guaranty Trust Company. The effects were noticeable on the pages of Humble's account books, which listed for February nearly half a million dollars of bills payable. Two notes, due February 4 and 9, were as usual renewed for thirty days, but all the remaining notes, due on or after the fifteenth and totaling $345,000, were paid in full.[41]

Humble's affiliation with Standard Oil Company (New Jersey) came at a strategic time—the beginning of a long-term rise in the demand for oil products. This rise was both cause and effect of the growth of the oil industry, the industry supplying products in volume and quality and at prices which stimulated demand. How this was accomplished is illustrated by Humble's operations in the 1920s.

The next nine chapters deal with Humble's administration and operations from 1919 to the great depression, a period in which the foundations of the Humble of today were laid. Chapter 5 considers general administration; Chapters 6 through 10 deal with operations, function by function; the next three are concerned with the company's shift to the new production technology.

Chapter 5

ADMINISTERING AN EXPANDING COMPANY, 1919-1929

HUMBLE'S sale of stock to Standard Oil Company (New Jersey) in 1919 was unquestionably one of the most important events in the company's entire history. The new affiliation changed Humble from an independent producing company to one having close relations with a leader in the world oil industry. This change followed a significant oil-industry trend of the times, the growing importance of large groups carrying on integrated operations. To Humble this affiliation meant the realization on a large scale of its organizers' objectives: to assure their company of a satisfactory market and to provide funds with which to finance expansion.

The next decade was to bring great transformations within Humble. The company was to develop from a loose aggregation of small producers and producing properties into a large, complex, and well-co-ordinated organization carrying on all the processes of the industry. At the same time it was to shift from reliance on practical methods learned from oil-field experience to the employment of scientists and engineers to develop and apply advanced techniques. Although the full realization of the developments initiated in the years from 1919 through 1929 was to come later, by the end of the 1920s the foundations of the company as it is today had been laid.

The central factor in this growth and change was Humble's top administration. It formulated policies and planned, directed, and controlled operations. It was the originating and driving element that co-ordinated the capital resources and the men employed in diverse operations into a co-operative effort to supply the market with crude oil and products at a profit.

The present chapter deals with general administration.[1] It considers the powers of the top government of the company with particular reference to Jersey Standard, the composition of the Board of Directors, the policies and programs adopted, and the operating organization created. This chapter also deals in a general way with policies and results in two areas of over-all significance: employee relations and financial management.

THE HUMBLE–JERSEY STANDARD RELATIONSHIP

Humble had the good fortune to obtain the advantages of affiliation with a large concern without losing independence. Its Board of Directors has always in practice maintained full control over the company. This has been as true since the sale of stock to Standard Oil Company (New Jersey) in 1919 as it was before. Though Jersey Standard acquired enough shares within that year to elect the Humble board, it has always from the first delivered its proxies without instructions to officers of the company.

Humble's independence of its majority stockholder was not a usual relationship in such circumstances. Texas oil companies not uncommonly had to look to the East for capital; the promoters at Corsicana and Spindletop, as earlier observed, sought help from the business centers of America's older oil regions. The large companies that had developed from beginnings in those early Texas fields with the aid of capital from the Northeast had their headquarters in New York, Philadelphia, or Pittsburgh and were largely controlled by eastern interests. It has been a common experience throughout the history of business that firms in newly developing regions that have sought help from centers of trade or finance have, for a time at least, lost a large measure of their freedom of action.

The independence of Humble was the result of a number of circumstances. First of all, the company's organizers were proud and strong-willed individualists as well as experienced oilmen with considerable producing properties. They were eager for more rapid growth than they could themselves finance, but they were already making profits—$3,000,000 in 1918—and they were not willing to accept help except on terms that they considered reasonable. Their objective was to obtain funds for expansion without losing control of their company.

Several important considerations caused Jersey Standard to favor independence for Humble. Jersey was in a vulnerable position; at a time when competition for the control of oil reserves was increasing, it needed a tremendous supply for its markets and refineries but had little production of its own. Jersey Standard, however, was deterred by legal and political considerations from entering production in Texas. Though it finally decided to purchase Humble stock, it was well aware of the need to be circumspect in its relations with the company.

Jersey Standard, moreover, was short of production experience and production managers. Its Board of Directors at the time of the Humble purchase did not include even one producing man. The company for a number of years had to hire men from other regions and companies, not always with satisfactory results, to provide managers for its new producing operations in the Mid-Continent, Latin America, and the Dutch East Indies. It could hardly, therefore, do otherwise than give free rein in production matters to such able and aggressive oil producers as the Humble directors had proved themselves to be. In fact, in the purchase negotiations Jersey executives expressed the hope that the management of the Texas affiliate would continue as it was then constituted.[2]

This procedure was entirely in keeping with Standard Oil tradition. In buying into an already established company, Jersey Standard and its predecessors had generally followed the policy of leaving authority and responsibility as much as possible in the hands of the company's existing managers. Carrying on a great variety of operations as it did under a multiplicity of circumstances in many different parts of the world, the company had early learned the advantage, even the necessity, of leaving much authority to local managers.[3]

Administrative control of Humble, accordingly, rested in the company's Board of Directors. Potential control remained with Jersey Standard, which as a majority stockholder could exercise the prerogative of nominating and electing new directors. This prerogative it has never exercised. Nor have Jersey men been elected to the Humble board, excepting two who in the first year of the affiliation joined Humble for special work in operations and were soon elected directors; one remained only a few months. Humble directors and officers have with a few exceptions been men whose associations have been exclusively with Humble and who have worked their way up through the ranks.

Yet Jersey Standard did have a vital influence on Humble from the beginning of their affiliation, an influence that lay chiefly in the large company's importance as a customer of its Texas affiliate. Jersey Standard was concerned that Humble's investments in producing properties, pipelines, storage, refinery equipment, and other facilities should be of the character and dimensions necessary to complement its own and its other affiliates' operations in refining and marketing. To that end it advised and counseled with its Texas affiliate. It kept Humble informed of estimated future needs, and Humble used that information in planning its expansion and operations. Humble, likewise, kept the larger company informed in detail concerning its own operations and plans, frequently seeking advice as to methods and practices. This the larger company gave, drawing upon its long experience and broad contacts. Humble thus gave careful consideration to the needs of its large customer and benefited from its experience. But at the same time it also developed operations beyond that customer's needs.

As a source of financial aid Jersey Standard also had something to say about Humble's use of funds. When asked for a loan on open account, or for support of a new bond issue, Jersey would have to assure itself that the funds were to be used wisely. It might, indeed, take the initiative and offer to help finance the construction of some facility that would be necessary or useful in supplying its own needs.

Although Jersey Standard advised and helped to finance, Humble made the final decisions. Since the two companies' needs were complementary, however, serious differences seldom arose. Sometimes, to be sure, Humble deliberately took its own course against Jersey's advice. Examples of Humble conduct, ranging from cheerful co-operation to obstinate independence, appear in the records of the two companies' relationship.

Close examination of their relations reveals that the larger company influenced its affiliate but did not control its administration or its operations. Although its self-restraint may originally and primarily have been inspired by particular circumstances, as the years passed Jersey Standard was increasingly motivated by the practical advantages of independence in an affiliate operated by able and aggressive executives —men who were willing to benefit from the knowledge and experience of the older company and who could see the advisability of adjusting operations to the needs of Humble's largest customer, but who also could be trusted with full administrative responsibility.

A test of the legality of the relationship occurred in 1923. The attorney general of Texas then filed an antitrust suit against Humble, seeking "to perpetually enjoin and restrain it from doing business in Texas, to forfeit its charter and franchise rights, and to recover the statutory penalties." His grounds were that Standard Oil Company (New Jersey)—which, referring to a Texas court decision of 1913, he alleged had been prohibited from doing business in Texas—had acquired over 60 per cent of the stock of Humble Oil & Refining Company, a Texas corporation, and through its ownership "exercised full and complete control and management" to the extent that Humble had become the means or agency by which Standard Oil Company (New

Jersey) was doing business in Texas in violation of the state's antitrust laws.

The decision of the Civil Court of Appeals in Austin was that Standard Oil Company (New Jersey) had not been ousted from Texas and that it did not control Humble. The court held that the voting of 60 per cent of the stock did not necessarily involve control and that the testimony did "not disclose any effort on the part of the Standard Oil Company of New Jersey to exercise control [of] or manage" Humble. Therefore, Jersey was not doing business within Texas in the meaning of the state's antitrust laws, and Humble "was not in the facts of the case the alter ego, or the means or agency by and through which the Standard Oil Company of New Jersey was doing business." The Supreme Court denied an application for a writ of error.[4]

A new law passed by the legislature of Texas in the following year clarified the legal side of the Humble-Jersey relationship. This act, the passage of which was suggested by Humble to give assurance to investors—who were generally fearful of companies incorporated in Texas—legalized the holding and voting of stock in a Texas corporation by a "foreign" corporation.[5] As a result, Jersey Standard could hold stock in Humble directly, not only through an agent as hitherto, and could vote its stock. Jersey continued, nevertheless, to leave its votes in the hands of the Humble board.

In its relationship with Jersey Standard, Humble was, therefore, in the enviable position of enjoying virtual autonomy while also benefiting from a connection with the stronger and more experienced company as adviser, as a source of funds, and as an assured customer. Humble was thus able to concentrate its efforts on the operations for which it was best qualified, the search for and production of crude oil, but also to undertake and carry forward the development of other operations.

Humble's independence was important in several respects. There were times when quick decisions were necessary, particularly in the purchase of leases. In a rapid lease play, when a few hours or even less time might make the difference between obtaining a valuable lease and failing to do so, the independence of the Humble organization was a distinct advantage.[6] Independence was of continuing importance in that it placed full responsibility on the men who were in a position to have the best understanding of Humble's operations and of the local conditions affecting them.

Ultimate authority and responsibility for the company's administration thus rested with the Board of Directors of Humble Oil & Refining Company. In the final analysis success or failure depended on their ability to administer the changes and to carry on the operations that were implicit in Humble's new relationship.

DIRECTORS AND OFFICERS, 1919–1929

No change in the top government of Humble Oil & Refining Company accompanied the Jersey stock purchase of 1919. The membership of the board remained the same as before, consisting of eight of the original directors and a ninth who had participated in the organization of the company. Seven were production men—field men or managers—who had learned the business and skills of oil production in the oil fields of the region. Two were lawyers. Eight of the nine served the company full time as officers or managers.[7]

The Humble board at the beginning of the period was both a policy-making body and a board of managers. The directors met every morning either as a board or as an operating committee. All except the two lawyers were assigned specific responsibilities in operations, but the influence of the individual members varied considerably. Several were principally departmental in their activities and in their influence on the board; they were Fondren, Frank P. Sterling, and Goddard—all, as will be observed later, production managers rather than central administrators—and Carlton, who was a rather inactive legal counsel. The others—R. S. Sterling, Farish, Blaffer, Wiess, and Townes—also had special responsibilities, but they were all of central importance, either because of their position as corporate officers or by virtue of their particular interest and knowledge and their personal influence.

R. S. Sterling's responsibilities were principally of a general nature, as president until 1922 and chairman of the board from 1922 to 1925. He had nominal charge of pipeline construction, but actual management was left to others. Being primarily a promoter and financier, he found less scope for his talents under the new situation than he had found as president of the old Humble Oil Company and of the new Humble before the Jersey affiliation. Sterling's success as the principal creator of Humble Oil Company, however, no doubt made his leadership a source of assurance to minority stockholders and of confidence in the new Humble on the part of the general public.

R. L. Blaffer was a natural choice for the treasurership. He was also officially in charge of crude oil operations. His undefined general contributions were, however, probably of even greater importance than his immediate official services. His conservatism sometimes caused him to be compared to a balance wheel checking his more impetuous associates, while his genial disposition suggests that he also served as a lubricant to the company organization. He became particularly effective as a one-man employee relations department. Although the workers in field and office might christen a particularly "tight" formation "the Blaffer sand" and swap anecdotes about his lecturing department heads on the excessive use of rubber bands, they nevertheless felt from him a warm current of sympathy which convinced them that he was really interested in them as human beings and not merely as employees. Paradoxically, the thrifty Humble treasurer also won a place in Humble tradition as a "one-man Credit Union" for personally lending money to needy employees.

E. E. Townes, head of the Legal Department and general counsel, soon came to occupy an important and influential policy position.[8] His natural conservatism and his legal knowledge were factors in keeping the expanding company from disastrous involvement in antitrust proceedings. He was particularly fearful of the political effect on Humble of its association with Standard Oil Company (New Jersey) and zealously guarded Humble's independence in its relations with its large stockholder. Townes's influence was not, however, exerted exclusively through the Legal Department. A former instructor in English at the Texas Agricultural & Mechanical College, he was the earliest literary man of the organization and was called upon to compose speeches and articles to inform employees and others concerning Humble's history and purposes. A devout Baptist, the teacher of the largest Sunday-school class in Houston, he was given to emphasizing Humble's moral character and to deriving ethical teachings from its experience. Probably no other member of the Humble board in those early years did so much as Townes to give expression to and help crystallize the company's idea of its own high principles. And more than anyone else on the board he was attuned to Texas public opinion.

Harry C. Wiess, a stocky, boyish-looking man in his early thirties, was a director and vice-president whose primary responsibility was departmental but who early came to be regarded as one of the leading policy men on the board. For several years he was the youngest director and when, in 1919, he assumed his broad responsibilities as head of refining and sales his only management experience had been in two small producing companies. While he was to become singularly successful in both fields, his importance to Humble was not limited even in the early years to his management of the two operations. His interest in research, especially, had an influence that soon permeated Humble's total operations and was a strong factor in determining the company's distinctive character.

W. S. Farish, until he became president in 1922, occupied no position that in itself gave him general oversight of company policies and operations, but he is said to have been the most important man in the company. Officially he was the vice-president in charge of a geographical subdivision of Humble's producing operations and a member of the Crude Oil Committee. Unofficially he was the liaison between Humble and Jersey Standard and the director whose advice was sought most widely within the company. These responsibilities came to Farish because of his recognized position as the best-informed and most farseeing executive in the Humble company and, indeed, in the Gulf Coast oil industry.[9]

Three new members were soon added to the board, bringing the number to twelve. They were specialists, and only one participated in general matters of policy. William S. Smullin, the first director from outside the group, served only a few months in 1920 before he left to join a Jersey affiliate in Colombia.[10] The election as director in February, 1921, of James Anderson, an engineering graduate of the University of Maryland, marked the first addition to the board of a professional engineer. Anderson was a man of much experience in pipeline work with Jersey affiliates, mostly with the Standard Oil Company of Louisiana.[11] A tall, spare, scholarly man of forty-two years, Anderson served as liaison with Humble's pipeline subsidiary, as a member of the Crude Oil Committee, and as manager of crude purchasing. The third addition in those early years was John S. Bonner, who was elected director early in 1922.[12] Forty-six years of age at the time, Bonner was a large, stout man with a genial disposition—a sort of lay Friar Tuck of the oil business. Although officially in charge of the Sales Department under Wiess, Bonner was also a one-man public relations department. He was effective not only with sawmill operators to whom he sold lubricants but also with members of the Texas legislature—the latter role, however, not entirely with Farish's approval.

All these new members of the board were made vice-presidents. Thus all the directors excepting Townes and Carlton of the Legal Department and Goddard in distant Oklahoma were also Humble officers. The vice-presidents who were company founders were, however, tacitly regarded as superior in status to the new vice-presidents.

Late in 1922 was initiated a series of changes in the membership of the board and in the officers of the company that marked the beginning of a significant shift in the administration of the company. The shift came about gradually, a result largely of the developing interests and influence of Farish and Wiess, but it was strengthened and made explicit by changes in officers and board members from late in 1922 to early 1927.

The first step was the election of Farish to the presidency in October, 1922, when R. S. Sterling became chairman of the board. The many-sidedness of Sterling's personality and the diversity of his interests brought this change sooner than might otherwise have been the case. According to some of his earliest and closest associates, the oil business was merely one of the many outlets for Sterling's boundless enthusiasm, energy, ambition, and daring, whereas Farish had deliberately chosen it as his lifetime career and principal means of self-expression.

Although for a decade Sterling had concentrated upon the petroleum industry the fervent heat of his major interest and attention, this had from the first been merely one of his many irons in the fire. Other interests, such as real estate, public life, and charities, were moving into central position in his mind and emotions. This dispersion of his interests and energy came at the very time when the creation of the new Humble required full attention to its affairs.

A few years later Sterling's increasing interest in public affairs brought his resignation from the Humble board. Although he had planned to retire from the company in order to give his whole attention to his private business affairs and his public interests, his resignation was precipitated by his involvement in the Texas gubernatorial campaign of 1924. Sterling had joined Ex-Governor W. P. Hobby in the consolidation of two newspapers to form the Houston *Post-Dispatch,* which supported the Republican candidate for the governorship. Newspapers and campaign speakers supporting Mrs. James Ferguson, the Democratic candidate, alleged that Sterling and the *Post-Dispatch* were supporters not only of the Republican party but also of the Ku-Klux Klan (a secret order devoted to the maintenance of white, Protestant, and native-born supremacy). James Ferguson himself charged that there was a coalition between the Republican party and the Klan to get control of Texas, that "Standard Oil" and other "giant" concerns were backing them, and that Sterling, "the head of Standard Oil in Texas," was financial sponsor of the *Post-Dispatch* and backer of the Klan. This created a difficult situation for Humble, particularly since its charter had in 1923 and early 1924 been threatened by suit under Texas antitrust law. Sterling resigned in February, 1925, at which time he sold a considerable block of his stock to Jersey Standard. His resignation terminated his official association with Humble, to the organization and success of which he had made strategic contributions. He subsequently had an active career in public life, rising to the governorship of Texas.[13]

From at least as early as his election to the presidency of the company in 1922 until his resignation in 1933 to become chairman of the Board of Directors of Jersey Standard—of which board he had been a member since 1927—Farish was the towering figure in Humble Oil & Refining Company. A review of his personal characteristics and a preview of the qualities that he demonstrated as the chief executive of the company afford some indication of the contribution he was to make as its head.

Farish was distinguished in physique and personality. He was large and powerful and had the manner of a southern gentleman. He was self-restrained to a degree that caused some to regard him as cold and distant, but his scrupulous courtesy and consideration,[14] his fairness, and his unquestioned ability rendered him generally popular among his associates. By those close enough to him to perceive the underlying warmth of his nature he was almost idolized.

A student of the oil industry, Farish was an omnivorous reader and sought information from men on all levels. He had a photographic memory and could quote voluminous data with fluency and accuracy, but he was never obsessed with detail or satisfied with a partial view. He wanted to see every situation as a whole. "What do these figures *mean?*" he would ask. "*That's* what I'm interested in."

While Farish followed closely the various operations and problems of his company, he focused his interest on matters of broad significance within the company and in its external relations. A golf enthusiast, a lover of horses and hunting dogs, and a murderous quail shot, he found in field sports relief from the pressures of his office and freedom to face larger issues of company policy and industry problems.

Farish was particularly effective in winning the co-operation of his associates. He picked his executive assistants carefully and then trusted and backed them. He encouraged aggressiveness and a willingness to take a chance. When one of his men "shot and missed," he was quick to defend him. He was never a respecter of rigid organization lines; he believed in letting the best-qualified man do a job, regardless of whether or not it lay in his official province. He kept an open mind, was tolerant of diverse opinions, and never closed the door to further consideration of a matter at issue. He could assimilate views that he had originally questioned, and make them his own. The technologists felt that he understood their special problems and was sympathetic with their difficulties. If he had confidence in a man, he would accept his judgment without following him through all his reasoning. The confidence that he reposed in his associates of lower rank and his willingness to give them credit even beyond what they felt themselves entitled to, made them ready, as one said, "to work their toenails off" for him. "He wasn't a driver," another said, "but he could lead a man almost to death, trying to keep up with him." [15]

It was frequently said that Farish operated by intuition. Actually, the apparently uncanny speed of his decisions was rendered possible by his willingness to depend on the advice and judgment of men in whom he had confidence and by his ability to draw on his own well-stocked store of knowledge and experience. He probably, at that, made more mistakes than if he had been of more deliberate judgment. But he also made more decisions, and in the oil industry the race was often to the swift.

As presiding officer of the Humble company, Farish was dominating but not domineering. Important problems were settled in the board, not by his arbitrary decision or by a majority vote but according to the

Quaker principle of the sense of the meeting—discussion went on until general agreement had been reached. Farish, however, had the knack of speeding up agreement, inside or outside board meetings. He was noted for his power of analysis, his ability to go directly to the heart of a matter; he had the art of synopsizing a report, briefly and forcefully, and of summarizing the thinking of a group. After long discussion, with a single question he could put an issue into proper focus.

Farish's relations with the public were more variable than with his associates. If he was convinced, for example, that the economic situation required a cut in crude prices or the abandoning of certain pipeline connections, he would carry out his plans with inflexibility and with what appeared to some as ruthlessness, regardless of protests or the possible effect on Humble's standing with a particular and important segment of the community. He did not believe in buying good will by being unrealistic in economic matters. In dealing with press and politicians, his knowledge of the oil industry and his willingness to answer questions fully and frankly generally produced a favorable impression. At times, however, irritation at what he considered unfair probings and interpretations—for example, in hearings of legislative committees or administrative agencies—caused him to lose control of his usually well-contained temper; on such occasions he might become undiplomatically plain-spoken.

When R. S. Sterling resigned as Humble chairman in 1925, the vacancy on the board was filled by the election of Chief Geologist Pratt. Here was a notable change in the membership. Sterling's trading capacity, promoting skill, and sheer daring had been indispensable; without these qualities and without Humble Oil Company to build upon, probably no organization comparable to Humble Oil & Refining Company would ever have been incorporated. But Sterling was of the old school of oil producers, whereas Pratt was of the new technological group. Humble would not have existed without Sterling; without Pratt and the group of which he was representative, it could not have become the largest producer of crude in the United States. Sterling's retirement symbolized the passing of one era; Pratt's election, the beginning of another.

John R. Suman, who became a member of the Humble board in January, 1927, further strengthened the high-level emphasis on the new technology. The compactly built, dynamic Suman, a thirty-six-year-old Indianan with a degree in mining engineering from the University of California, had since 1912 been active in Texas oil fields as geologist, engineer, and executive. He had recently been appointed vice-president and general manager of the Rio Bravo Oil Company, a subsidiary of the Southern Pacific Railroad. He was also author of *Petroleum Production Meth-*

ods, a standard handbook. On the recommendation of Pratt, Suman was elected director of production in the Northern division. Suman's election is also an organizational landmark: he took the place of the last director (Carlton, recently deceased) to devote only part time to the company; and he is the only director since Humble's organization to have been elected without a preliminary apprenticeship in the company.

The interests and contributions of Pratt and Suman were by no means exclusively or narrowly technological. Pratt became the philosopher and teacher of the company, who could put the scientific aspects of oil finding and production into clearly understandable form, to the educational advancement not merely of Humble employees and executives and the oil fraternity in general but also of the public at large. Suman was interested in human as well as petroleum engineering and was largely responsible for the extension of the company's industrial relations program. To other operators in production he was also what Bonner was to lumbermen and politicians, a one-man public relations department; he has been described as so diplomatic and persuasive that he could cause agreement to emerge out of a meeting originally composed of twenty-six men with the same number of different opinions.[16]

By the end of the decade the character of the eleven-man Humble board had changed significantly. Farish, Blaffer, and Wiess, of the founders, together with Townes, Anderson, Pratt, and Suman, were the most active directors. The balance of administrative authority had tipped decisively in the direction of professionally trained men; and the hired administrator was beginning to carry heavy weight.

INITIAL POLICIES AND PROGRAM

The basic policy of the Humble board in 1919 was to develop a large, integrated operation with emphasis on production. When stock was sold to Jersey Standard, it was understood that Humble would greatly expand its production, undertake the purchasing and storage of crude oil on a large scale, and build a refinery to supply the larger company with certain products. The Humble board, however, planned to go farther by developing refining beyond Jersey's needs and expanding its own sales. Its object was to create what Farish in 1920 called a "perfect petroleum unit."

The task before the Humble board at the beginning of the Jersey affiliation, therefore, was as rapidly as possible to change a moderately small and essentially specialized producing operation into a large and diversified one. Important decisions concerning the extent and timing of expansion, horizontally and vertically, had to be made, as well as decisions and arrangements to provide the necessary organization and physical facilities.

The heart of the program was the development of production. Change of scale was here the chief requirement, but there was one essentially new requisite—wildcatting. Although some of Humble's organizers had engaged in wildcatting, they had not been successful wildcatters in the sense of discovering new fields; they had, however, been adept at picking up and successfully drilling acreage near producing wells and they had succeeded in locating new producing sands in proved fields. In order to expand production fast enough, it now became necessary to search for new fields. Humble's new geologic group under Pratt was ready to undertake a comprehensive search for oil.

To develop an extensive program of crude oil purchasing was a different matter. This was essentially a new operation for the members of the Humble board. Their nearly two decades of experience as sellers of crude had given them an appreciation of the problems and attitudes of the small independent producers that was to stand them in good stead; their experience on the buyers' side of the crude market, however, in 1919 consisted only of relatively small purchases over about two years.

Since the objective was an adequate supply of crude oil at all times, Humble had to build up reserves in storage against the future scarcity which its large refining customer had been anticipating ever since World War I. This meant that it would have to bear the risk of change in the value of the oil in storage, for there was no way of hedging against changes in oil prices—the oil market, unlike some commodity markets, did not have specialized risk-takers. The Humble board realized that, in order to maintain an adequate future supply, good relations would also have to be established with the independent producers. In other words, in entering upon a program of heavy purchasing Humble faced problems of policy and management that were of first importance and that proved to be difficult of solution.

From the decision to become large producers and purchasers followed as a matter of course the decision to enter upon pipeline construction and operation on a large scale. It was neither efficient nor profitable to depend on others for transportation. Tank-car transportation was out of the question as relatively too expensive;[17] pipeline transportation was both more convenient and more economical. It would be cheaper to supply Jersey's eastern refineries by pipeline to the Gulf and by its own tankers from Gulf ports than by shipment all the way overland through other companies' pipelines.[18] Humble and Jersey would both benefit from Humble's having its own pipeline system, inasmuch as Humble's pipeline profits would be shared by Jersey as a stockholder. Humble, however, had neither the experience nor the organization necessary for building pipelines and had very little familiarity with pipeline operation. Entering this field, therefore, involved a relatively new type of effort, but one which depended for its success less on shrewd policy than on effective management.

The construction of a Gulf Coast refinery was also a part of the program decided upon early in 1919. Although Jersey was in especial need of crude to stock its stills at Bayonne and Bayway, it also required certain refined products which could be more advantageously manufactured by a Gulf Coast than a North Atlantic refinery. Ranger crude could be substituted for the scarce Pennsylvania oil as a cylinder stock, and coastal crudes were a suitable base for the manufacture of the low cold-test lubricants in demand in Europe. To ship these products to Europe directly from the Gulf Coast was more economical than to send crude to the eastern refineries and to ship products from there to Europe.

It was especially in its plans for refining and for the related field of sales, however, that Humble set out on its own course independently of the large stockholder's needs. The directors had decided before affiliation with Jersey to expand the company's refining facilities by building a lubricating-oil plant on the Gulf Coast and had already built up something of a sales organization. The Jersey connection eliminated the immediate necessity for developing sales in Texas, but for reasons of profit and prestige, as well as for developing the independent operations which they had originally planned, the members of the Humble board decided to strengthen their company's sales organization. Building a refinery with a capacity beyond what was necessary for supplying Jersey Standard was an essential part of this program.

The broad program adopted in 1919 called for the continued development of integrated operations. After Humble had decided upon and planned their character and extent, it was necessary to finance and build the appropriate plants and other facilities, to recruit and organize the managerial and working personnel, and to co-ordinate the various operations. The development of individual departmental functions will be considered in separate chapters. The remainder of the present chapter will deal with matters of general importance, that is, building up an adequate managerial organization, developing employee relations policies and programs, and financing growth in all departments.

THE MANAGERIAL ORGANIZATION

The new program required a radical reconstruction of Humble's internal organization. The old Operating Department and Sales Department were obviously insufficient; a more specialized structure was required to meet the needs of greater size and diversity of operations. Because Humble management consisted almost exclusively of production men, it was necessary to find managers for the new operations and to fit the old directors into a reconstructed organization.

In April, 1919, the Humble board agreed on an important organizational policy. Farish had obtained from Jersey a detailed account of how its board operated, with each member in charge of, and responsible to the board for, one or more departments. On President Sterling's recommendation the Humble directors unanimously resolved that each director be given managerial responsibilities in one or more departments, and that an operating committee consisting of the president and the five vice-presidents be set up to exercise general supervision of operations. Thus the directors continued, in effect, to constitute a board of managers. The Board of Directors also adopted recommendations for establishing new departments.

Several administrative and auxiliary departments were organized in the spring of 1919.[19] Two new departments were established to take care of central administrative, or corporate, matters. One was the Treasury Department, headed by Blaffer as treasurer; the other was the Comptroller's Department, the manager of which was responsible to the treasurer. The comptroller, C. B. Deming, in addition to the usual duties also had charge of office personnel. The Legal Department, headed by Townes, was continued as earlier but with an increased staff. The Traffic Department, to direct transportation by other means than pipelines, had been established earlier but was now put under Wiess. A new Purchasing Department, also headed by Wiess, served as a general purchasing agency for the various departments, though purchasing was only gradually centralized. The Warehouse Department, under the treasurer, was given charge of storing and distributing materials and equipment, maintaining inventory control and, in co-operation with the Comptroller's Department, keeping the accounting records necessary under a system of departmental accounting and of joint-account operations in production with other companies.

Separate departments, each under one or more directors, were set up for the various operations. A department was a separate entity, deriving its authority from the Board of Directors and having its own accounting office. The structure of each individual organization varied, being determined not only by the particular function it was to perform but also by available managerial personnel and, in the case of the pipelines, by law.

The Production Department was not a unified operating organization. Inasmuch as most of the Humble directors were producing men with years of successful experience, the organization as a matter of course recognized the contributions and protected the prestige of the four who were to be active in production. Fondren and F. P. Sterling continued to be in charge, respectively, of drilling and production on the Gulf Coast. Farish was placed "in charge of production and leases in North and West Texas, Oklahoma, and Louisiana, and generally speaking, in all territory outside the coastal belt." Goddard continued to occupy a semi-independent status in Oklahoma. The old Land Department for scouting and leasing was retained as an auxiliary group.[20] Another was the geologic staff, whose function was to furnish geologic information and advice with particular reference to leasing.

Crude oil operations were not at first committed to a separate department. Crude purchasing was for a short time handled by Humble Pipe Line Company but in July, 1919, was transferred to the parent company's Production Department. Since crude operations involved heavy financial commitments, it was logical that Treasurer Blaffer should be put in charge of the purchasing of crude, the handling and disposition of the oil, and the advancing of loans on oil in storage. Questions of policy and price were, however, so important as to require the attention of more than one director, and for this reason the Crude Oil Committee was set up. It at first consisted of Blaffer, Farish, and an informal representative of the pipeline company.

Pipeline construction and operations, as required by law, were assigned to a new corporation, Humble Pipe Line Company, organized and owned by Humble Oil & Refining Company. President Sterling of the parent company also served as the first president of the pipeline company, and Blaffer as its treasurer. Since the Humble board had little familiarity with pipelines, however, a full staff of experienced pipeline men from Standard Oil Company of Louisiana joined the Humble organization under the leadership of James A. Anderson as vice-president and general manager of the pipeline company.

The Refining Department was established in April, 1919. Refining presented somewhat the same problem as crude purchasing and pipelines in that no Humble director was familiar with anything but simple and small-scale refining. Because of his engineering degree and his reputation as an able executive, Harry C. Wiess was assigned responsibility for refineries and refinery operations.

The Sales Department rounded out the functional division of operations. Wiess was also the director and vice-president in general charge of sales, an operation ancillary to refining. Although in the summer of 1919 John S. Bonner became manager of sales under Wiess, with special responsibility for the sale of industrial lubricants in Texas and Louisiana, Wiess himself retained chief responsibility for gasoline sales.

These early arrangements for the top administration and the division of the operating organization were modified as time passed in response to changing needs and opportunities, particularly as new men succeeded the old heads of the company. In general the tendency over the decade was for the original board members to delegate managerial duties to others, partly because of the need for specialists in areas in which the old members had insufficient knowledge and experience and partly because of the growth of the company and the increasing need for attention to long-range planning and policy-making.

Further developments occurred in the Humble organization as the decade passed. Formal departmental standing committees were slow to develop; there was a special reason for the establishment in 1919 of the Crude Oil Committee, but other committees appeared late in the decade. Staff organizations became of considerable importance to operations. They were chiefly in three areas: law, the general field of employee relations, and research. One of the interesting developments in this decade was the close integration of the legal staff with operations. Another was Humble's emphasis on men and functions rather than on strict departmental or vertical lines, as can especially be illustrated by the refinery research staff, which for a time carried on research for production and pipelines.

The co-ordination of operations—that is, below the board's responsibilities for planning expansion, allocating funds, selecting management personnel, and in general deciding on policy—was formally performed by the Operating Committee, made up of the president and vice-presidents. An unofficial and informal, but important, body for bringing about both vertical and horizontal co-operation was the regular gathering of board members, departmental managers, and superintendents in the Houston offices on Sunday and holiday mornings. Board members and managers at various levels were also constantly visiting and consulting in headquarters and field. By such means was continued on a larger scale the personal relationship that had characterized the small companies that had combined to form Humble Oil & Refining Company.

A TRANSITION IN EMPLOYEE MANAGEMENT

The growth of Humble necessitated a larger and more varied working force. The "man question," as James Anderson called it in 1920, required attention as never before in Humble's operations. A company with a high fixed investment and heavy commitments as a supplier of crude oil and refined products needed a large and stable working force; moreover, a company carrying on a great variety of operations must have adequately skilled men. More than men and skills was needed, however, to combine a large number of employees into an efficient and smoothly operating organization.[21]

Humble's administrators had certain basic attitudes and objectives that proved to be as suitable to the larger as to the smaller company. They were still thinking in individual human terms about "being fair" and "doing what's right," and they recognized an obligation toward their employees and wanted to behave justly and humanely. While they wished to make relations with employees as agreeable as possible, they were also determined to make the decisions as to the character of those relations. Their motives were not primarily or consciously utilitarian. When R. S. Sterling slapped a driller on the back and addressed him as "Red" or "Slim" or Blaffer gave a greenback to a roughneck with a sick child, they were moved by a warmhearted gregariousness and a desire that people with whom they were associated should be happy. Such actions and attitudes, whatever their motivation, worked for a community of spirit between employer and employee that was conducive to loyal co-operation.

Humble continued for some time to follow its former employee policies. In 1919 it was paying going wages or better, leaving hiring and firing to operating managers and supervisors, working employees the usual long hours, paying accident compensations required by law with occasional additions, laying men off when no longer needed for certain work in a particular location, trying to prevent outsiders from influencing their workers in favor of joining a union, and taking little responsibility for living accommodations for men in the fields. On the whole, employee relations were personal and direct and were left to managers, superintendents, and foremen.

Certain circumstances, however, were at the time bringing to Humble's directors a conscious recognition of the need for more formally organized employee management. Among these were the local revival of the movement for organizing oil workers, a shortage of workers, and Humble's rapidly increasing labor force—as is shown by Table 2. Important also was the fact that change was in the air; some advanced companies were abandoning the more obvious and negative aspects of an old-fashioned labor policy for a positive and, in the long run, more effective system. A leader in this transition was Standard Oil Company (New Jersey), which was to have a strong influence on the development of Humble's employee policies and relations.

Following the example and recommendations of Jersey Standard, Humble in 1920 decided to adopt a benefits program and on a limited scale Jersey's industrial representation plan. J. Perry Moore, a young Texan chosen by Sterling for the job and sent to New York for training under Clarence J. Hicks, head of Jersey's Department of Personnel and Training, was employed to introduce these innovations in Humble.[22] The representation plan was at first confined to the Baytown refinery, but the benefits program was applicable to employees in all branches of Humble's operations.

Humble had previously had some acquaintance with one form of employee benefits—accident compensation—and had in certain cases granted compensation beyond the legal requirement, although purely on a personal and voluntary basis. By 1920, however, it was so enthusiastic in its attitude toward a formal system of annuities and benefits that it considered providing for higher death benefits than Jersey itself. On April 15, 1920, Humble adopted the annuities and benefits plan in

TABLE 2

NUMBER OF EMPLOYEES AND AMOUNT OF PAYROLL
HUMBLE OIL & REFINING COMPANY
1917–1929

	Number of Employees as of December 31					
	Exploration and Production	*Refining*	*Sales*	*Pipelines*	*Total*	*Year's Total Payroll*[a]
1917	....[b]	....	....	....	541	$ 524,000
1918	....	....	....	....	1,078	1,198,000
1919	....	....	....	2,590	7,285	5,055,000
1920	....	....	....	1,573	5,935	8,801,000
1921	1,971	1,349	162	2,277	6,100	8,317,000
1922	1,688	1,280	113	702	4,073	8,640,000
1923	2,285	1,637	173	1,388	5,748	9,277,000
1924	2,696	1,688	192	3,281	8,169	10,889,000
1925	2,572	2,727	214	2,767	8,579	14,694,000
1926	3,011	3,010	225	5,648	12,256	16,626,000
1927	2,497	3,242	330	5,764	12,266	19,556,000
1928	2,656	3,999	412	2,980	10,442	18,757,000
1929	3,044	6,087	658	2,323	12,548	21,874,000

[a] Includes vacations, sickness, accidents, and holidays but not company benefits. The total for 1917 is for six months.
[b] Data not available.
Source: Records of Humble Oil & Refining Company.

effect in the Jersey group for employees with at least a year's service. The principal features of the plan were pensions at sixty-five for employees with twenty or more years of service, death benefits, total and permanent disability benefits, and sickness and accident benefits allowing compensation equal to half-pay.[23]

Another new departure was taken in 1920 with the establishment of the *Humble Magazine*, a publication chiefly for employees. This organ, under Moore's editorship, was designed to improve communication within a company growing too large for any considerable personal contact and to help keep employees informed of developments within the company.

Jersey Standard furnished precedents for the above program, but in

1920 Humble on its own initiative adopted the policy of granting a vacation of two weeks with pay to "all regular men" of a year's service, "including all classes of labor." The lower grades of Humble workers were soon reduced to a week's vacation after two years' service, but elsewhere any sort of vacation for common labor was nearly unheard of at the time.[24]

The new pension and insurance plan, the *Humble Magazine*, vacations with pay, and Humble's already existing employee stock-purchase system were for the benefit of all Humble's employees, but the Baytown refinery served as the nursery for certain practices in employee relations that were not immediately or effectively introduced elsewhere. Activities at Baytown will be considered in connection with the construction and operation of the refinery in those years. Medical and safety work inaugurated at Baytown, however, soon spread to other departments and is, therefore, of general interest.

Dr. Charles M. Aves, the first company physician, joined Humble in August, 1919, to take care of construction workers at Baytown but was shortly brought to Houston to organize a medical department for the whole company. Besides the general objective of raising the employees' health standards and reducing absences from work, there were special considerations growing out of the new annuities and benefits plan. The adoption of the plan necessitated physical examinations for all employees. And, since insurance premiums varied with sickness and accident rates, it was important to keep those rates low.[25]

Accident prevention, however, lagged behind preparation to repair damages. Humble's industrial relations specialist, J. Perry Moore, in 1920 urged the appointment of a full-time man to promote safety; he pointed out that during the first half of the year accidents had totaled 1,553, of which 61 were serious and 6 fatal. Over half these accidents, numbering 884, had occurred among 1,100 refinery employees, as compared with 483 accidents among 2,540 production employees and 154 among 1,190 pipeliners. It was not until 1922, however, that Humble appointed D. J. Wallace as "Safety Man or Safety Engineer." [26]

To mention merely concrete developments in Humble's employee relations is to spell out the letter and omit the spirit. Humble employees even today frequently emphasize the company's "democracy" above such material considerations as wages, insurance, and annuities. Early Humble employees particularly prized the outings, barbecues, and picnics on Labor Day, San Jacinto Day, and Humble Day, at which shirt-sleeved company officials mingled with the employees and their families, calling them familiarly by their nicknames, exchanging friendly talk, banter, and reminiscences, and recapturing something of the intimacy of earlier days. Here the Sterlings, Blaffer, and Bonner in particular, with their warm, outgoing dispositions, scored heavily with the employees of the young company.

The early period of innovation in employee policy and management ended in 1922. In that year Humble's employee relations head resigned, and the *Humble Magazine* ceased publication soon after his departure. The young and enthusiastic Moore was neither experienced nor wholly effective in working with employees and may also have been overzealous and tactless in urging such proposals as the eight-hour day, which the directors considered premature and impractical. Jack Dies, head of Humble's tax division, was appointed to succeed Moore. Dies was not equipped for developing an employee program, and his other duties, which included service as Humble's principal representative at the state capital, left him little time for employee relations. He was, however, expected to do little more than manage a program that had already been set up.

There were no general organized innovations in the next few years, but the effectiveness of Humble's employee stock-purchase plan was increased. The reduction of the par value of the stock to $25.00 in 1922 was something of a stimulus to employee participation. The adoption in 1924 of the Jersey plan, whereby the company contributed 50 cents for every dollar invested by the employee, was what really set the purchase of stock by employees on the way to general acceptance. Under the plan in effect from 1926 to 1929 a total of 22,083 shares were delivered to 3,180 employees, more than a fourth of the company's total personnel.[27]

The weakest point in Humble's employee situation in the 1920s was the continued high accident rate. After his appointment as Safety Engineer in 1922, Wallace organized committees, held meetings, and prepared handbooks; but management was still only moderately concerned with safety, the employees were not yet much interested, and the program was understaffed. The accident rate continued to be high. In the month of October, 1923, fewer than 2,000 Humble production employees experienced 141 accidents. When in 1924 Wallace and most of his staff were moved to Baytown, the care of the widely scattered employees in production and on the pipelines was left to the already overburdened Jack Dies and two assistants. Accident rates and costs continued high: in February, 1925, accidents cost the company an average of $6.14 per employee.

The high accident rate was one of the problems that brought about a revival of activity in Humble's employee management in the years 1926–1929. Other matters that urgently required attention were the length of the work week and the growing need for a stable working force of high quality.

The problem of the long work week was the first to be solved. In

1927 Humble's work week ranged from the five and a half days and forty-four hours of office workers and the six days and forty-eight hours of refinery mechanical forces up through the seven-day week with fifty-six hours of process men in the refinery and "tower" (tour, that is, shift) employees on pipelines, the sixty-three hours of other pipeline employees, and the eighty-four hours worked by production foremen and pumpers and drilling crews.

Humble had for some time been in a somewhat embarrassing position because of its long work week. Jersey Standard had voted the six-day week and eight-hour day as early as 1915, and by 1925 The Carter Oil Company and the Standard Oil Company of Louisiana, wholly owned Jersey subsidiaries operating in or near Humble's territory, had followed Jersey's example.[28] Jersey's president asserted that he would not work seven days a week for anyone, and he would not expect anyone to work seven days a week for him, and Clarence J. Hicks warned Farish that a resolution of the American Federation of Labor calling for "best endeavors . . . in bringing about an eight-hour day and a six-day week in the petroleum industry" was probably the first gun "in a renewed campaign to unionize oil workers."

The seven-day week, however, had long been standard in the Texas oil industry, and Humble's executives accepted it as part of the natural order. Humble's own directors customarily were in their offices Sunday mornings. When the issue was raised in 1927, Humble's reaction as expressed by its new production director, John R. Suman, was that, when the company was "straining every effort to lower . . . production costs" and "labor was very plentiful and contented," it was "a very poor time to inaugurate radical social programs." David B. Harris, superintendent of the Shreveport division and subsequently director and vice-president for industrial relations, says that he considered the six-day week a "Bolshevik idea." In those days, when oil-field workers in boom towns usually did not have their families with them, managers took a gloomy view of the increase in gambling, drinking, and general vice and disorder that might result should the workers be allowed any time off beyond the absolute minimum necessary for eating and sleeping.

Jersey's president was careful to avoid giving orders, but a certain stockholder in the Jersey company was free to speak more bluntly. The younger Rockefeller in 1922 had declared publicly that the twelve-hour day and the seven-day week were "unnecessary, uneconomic and unjustifiable." Now, in what is said to have been almost the only letter from a John D. Rockefeller to a president of Humble, he expressed his strong distaste for any connection, direct or indirect, with a company that worked any of its employees eighty-four hours a week.

The example of the California oil industry apparently influenced the

Humble executives. Director Suman in June, 1928, spent two weeks in producing fields in California, where employee relations had made significant progress. He reported that "after an intelligent study of the situation" the eight-hour day had been universally adopted and employees in practically every company in the state would soon have the day of rest with full pay.

Humble decided to adopt what Farish called the "expensive change" to the six-day week.[29] The board announced what was apparently an innovation in the oil industry in Humble's operating area, "the granting of one day's rest each week to all regular employees without reduction of present earning," to take effect October 1, 1928. The day of rest in the case of rotary crews was cumulative, to be "taken during cement time . . . or at completion of well." [30]

The change to the eight-hour day soon followed. The establishment on February 1, 1930, of the eight-hour day was preceded by none of the controversy that had gone on over the adoption of the six-day week. Vice-President Wiess, however, suggested that, in view of the shorter week and two weeks of vacation, holidays on Humble Day, Independence Day, and Christmas Day be eliminated; the Christmas holiday was retained. When during the great East Texas boom in 1931 a return to the longer day and week was suggested, Suman was even more strongly opposed to any lengthening of the weekly hours than he had originally been to their reduction.

A dramatic development in 1926 convinced Humble of the necessity of instituting a strong safety program. When the hydrogen sulphide gas from "sour" (high-sulphur-content) West Texas crude began to strike down production and pipeline employees, the application of new safety methods became as obviously necessary in production and on pipelines as in the refinery. In the spring of 1926, at Humble's request Jersey Standard's safety director, R. S. Bonsib, toured the fields and refineries with Humble safety men and advised them. Safety committees were reactivated, and Humble's present-day safety program began to get under way.[31]

Improvement was slow but unmistakable. Even after the inauguration of the new safety program, Humble Pipe Line Company's accident rate was at times notably high; in December, 1926, for example, 232 employees were injured, at an average cost of $45.55 to the company for each of 2,960 employees. Eye injuries, alone, on tank building in the Corsicana division in eight months in 1926 cost nearly $7,500. Tank building, which required much welding, was a particularly hazardous occupation. When large numbers of men were working under high pressure and with the equipment of those days, which from a safety viewpoint was poor, some accidents were inevitable. Systematic observation, however, pointed up certain weaknesses. One source of danger was obviously the equipment, but another was the men themselves. The fact that a high accident rate followed certain foremen from job to job revealed that refusal to take even elementary precautions was a principal factor; in some cases the discharge of a foreman proved necessary. Improvement was made by attacking some of the more obvious difficulties, but it was clear that a more intensive and broader attack had to be made on the accident problem.

The Humble directors in 1926–1929 also came to see the need to give special, company-wide attention to the hiring and holding of desirable workers. Excepting in the boom time of 1919–1920, the company had had no central employment offices. To be sure, general directives were sent out from Houston and there was an emphasis on the desirability of holding good workers, but for some time nothing concrete was done about it.

The old system of hiring and firing by superintendents and supervisors according to current needs still prevailed late in the 1920s, but Humble had developed something of a standard in regard to layoffs when there was a surplus of workers. The general policy was to retain the "best" men, and the "good" men as far as possible. When there were more "good" men than could be kept, other things were considered, such as seniority and dependents and—in Baytown in 1927—the way a man managed his own finances. Seniority seems to have been given a higher rating in production than in refining. The Production Department made an effort to retain its best men even when they were not needed; in the depression of 1920 it gave them a ninety-day leave of absence and in 1924 a year's leave. However, the judge of who were the best and the good men was the local supervisor.

Humble's principal officers in the late 1920s became anxious to find a more accurate method of determining who were the best and the good men than by just leaving it to the judgment of the individual supervisor. Farish is said to have been distressed by the necessity of laying off some of Humble's best men during the industry's periodic depressions and to have been interested in a more careful evaluation of individual ability so that layoff programs could emphasize more realistic factors than, for example, length of service. Wiess commented, early in 1929: [32]

> None of us likes to discharge or demote men and for this reason we often find men holding positions that they are not properly filling, with consequent lowering of efficiency, and frequently it has a general bad effect on the department concerned. Observation of our organization and Jersey's indicates that the man is always given the benefit of the doubt, and I think that sometimes we are too reluctant to change. This illustrates the importance of exercising great care in employing men....

The continuity of employment came to be recognized as a matter to be given serious consideration. It was then common in the Texas oil industry for turnover to be high, but it must have come as something of a shock to Humble's top administration to learn that, outside Baytown refinery and Humble Pipe Line Company which themselves had highly shifting working populations, Humble had an average monthly turnover in 1926 of about 10 per cent.

Although the turnover rate was high, a solid core of continuous employment was maintained. A statistical study of the length of service of male employees of the Humble companies as of January 1, 1952, showed that there were 543 still working for Humble after thirty or more years of employment and 2,066 who had started to work for the company between January 2, 1922, and January 1, 1928. This record does not include the men of long service who had retired before 1952.

Several influences converged in 1927 to convince the men responsible for Humble's employee policies that a basic revision of the approach to employee management was needed. A number of years of experience with a large working force had resulted in a better understanding of employee problems and possibilities. The company was increasingly emphasizing specialization, administrative as well as technological. And certain individuals helped to crystallize thinking by making specific suggestions. L. C. Ingram of the Annuities & Benefits division in 1927 presented plans for the entire reorganization of the industrial relations function and particularly for the formation of a personnel department; Suman, the newly elected director for production, was strongly interested in such a department.

Suman's visit to California oil fields in 1928 was a result of this growing interest. His report on employee relations there was concerned primarily with the establishment of an employee relations department, which he strongly recommended. He had found the principal California companies unanimous as to the value of their personnel departments, particularly in safety work. He emphasized, however, that the success of such a department would depend on the personality of the manager and 100 per cent backing by the Board of Directors.

The Humble board accepted Suman's recommendations and elected a committee to have charge of setting up what was then called the Industrial Relations Department. The Industrial Relations Committee consisted of Suman, Wiess, and Ralph V. Hanrahan, the first two being directors in charge of production and of refining and sales, respectively, and the third being president of Humble Pipe Line Company.

The Board of Directors employed H. E. Bell, a lawyer who was chief supervisor of the Oil & Gas Division of the Texas Railroad Commission, to establish the new department. After a few weeks' study of employee relations in California early in 1929, Bell set about to organize the company-wide Industrial Relations Department, which was to take over the existing Annuities & Benefits, Medical, and Safety divisions, add personnel and training, and make the safety work more effective.

On July 1, 1929, R. B. Roaper, previously safety director at the Baytown refinery, was appointed safety director to head a company-wide safety program. The new Safety Department, consisting of the safety supervisor, a first-aid man, and three field men, was smaller than Roaper had recommended, indeed considerably smaller than the safety organization of California Standard. The earliest efforts of the new department may be illustrated by what was done at Raccoon Bend, the first producing field in which the program was put into effect. Here the two newly established departments, Safety and Petroleum Engineering, met on common ground. Chain guards were placed on the rigs, and extra-heavy mud and blowout preventers were used to combat the high gas pressure. This use of safety devices represented the early phase of the safety effort.

While the new safety work was getting under way, Humble's accident rate remained high in virtually all departments. Indeed, in 1929 the company had the worst accident record of all the companies in which Jersey Standard owned a half-interest or more, a record which ranked Humble sixty-fourth of seventy-nine companies reporting to the National Safety Council. Humble's lost-time accidents in the year numbered 1,562, including 13 deaths and 63 permanent disabilities, and cost the two Humble companies over $230,000. Although there were extenuating circumstances, the record was bad, and Humble's executives considered it serious.

By early 1930, however, improvement had begun in all departments, particularly in refining, Gulf Coast production, and the pipeline company. The program set up in 1929 was to be carried forward with notable accomplishments in the next few years.

In 1929 final preparations were made for the organization of a personnel division. Howard S. Warner, a Mississippian and a civil engineering graduate of Cornell, whose close friend David B. Harris had recommended him for the managership of the industrial relations program, went to work on January 1, 1930, as head of the new personnel division. In preparation for this appointment Warner worked six months in the field as roustabout and roughneck, thus establishing the precedent that members of Humble's industrial relations group should have practical experience in the industry, and had three months of training with the Jersey Industrial Relations Department and at Jersey refineries.

In the meantime Bell transferred to the Legal Department, and the Industrial Relations Department acquired a new manager. Charles E. Shaw accepted the appointment after spending several days in November, 1929, inspecting Humble's employee-relations activities and making extensive recommendations. Then thirty-three years of age, Shaw had formerly been manager of employee relations at Jersey's Bayway refinery. He had been educated at Kansas State Agricultural College and Columbia University. He had majored in economics, played football, and captained the track team.[33]

Shaw's appointment came at what proved to be a crucial time. It was fortunate that on the eve of the great depression Humble's industrial-relations program at last was brought into step with progressive principles and organized under trained and able leadership.

FINANCING EXPANSION

Affiliation with Standard Oil Company (New Jersey) supplied Humble with capital with which to expand. Not all the funds obtained from outside Humble were furnished by Jersey, but the large loans obtained elsewhere were supported by its credit. The effectiveness of the new capital was multiplied by the reinvested earnings which the expanded facilities made possible. Humble increased its fixed assets from $13,100,000 at the end of 1918 to $233,200,000 at the end of 1929.[34] (For financial data, see Appendix II, Tables I–VI.)

In the first drive to expand, in 1919–1922, additions to fixed assets averaged over $25,000,000 per year. In 1919–1920 this growth was financed mostly by Humble's stockholders, principally by Jersey Standard in accordance with its policy of making high advances to its promising affiliates in their early years of growth.[35] In addition to the $17,000,000 from the original sale of stock to Jersey, nearly $26,000,000 was realized from the sale of a new issue in the autumn of 1919. Each stockholder was given the right to purchase for every share he held one and a quarter shares at the rate of $100 per share and three-fourths of a share at $250 per share; Jersey Standard purchased its allowance plus enough of the $250 rights to increase its interest to over 56 per cent of Humble's total outstanding stock.[36] In 1919–1920 it also advanced over $30,000,000 to Humble on open account. Jersey's confidence in Humble is demonstrated by the fact that in the early 1920s its advances to that company were larger than those to any other of its affiliates.[37] In 1921 Humble also sold through J. P. Morgan & Company a $25,000,000 issue of two-year, 7 per cent gold notes, which it refunded in an easier money market the following year by selling an issue of ten-year, 5½ per cent gold debentures. In 1921 Humble reduced its indebtedness to Jersey by $11,000,000, but in 1922 it drew on its large stockholder for $9,000,000.

In the period 1919–1922 Humble's net earnings were less than dividends plus federal income taxes, which left no earnings for reinvestment. Costly leases, expensive development, too many dry holes, and a drop in the price of oil to below cost in 1921 resulted in those four years in a loss for the Production Department despite a great increase in the amount of oil produced. Crude oil purchases and sales also resulted in loss except in 1920, when a spectacularly rapid but short-lived appreciation in the value of crude oil in storage produced a substantial book profit. Refinery operations showed an annual loss or an infinitesimal profit; local sales of products were profitable until 1922 but relatively unimportant. The pipeline company's operations, with an annual return ranging from 20 to 30 per cent on the investment, were the exception to the rule of losses or insignificant profits. Some oilmen in those years referred to Humble as "Teagle's sick baby."[38] Depression in the industry, which was worldwide at the time, had struck Humble in the weakness of early expansion.

The year 1922 marked a low point in Humble's investment in new facilities, but it also marked the beginning of a turn for the better in the company's financial condition. Although the company was still losing money, it "hit the jackpot" in production in the fault-line area, it solved the worst of its refining difficulties, and its pipeline subsidiary continued to make handsome profits.

In 1923 the strong upward trend of Humble's expansion was resumed. The year 1925 brought the heaviest investment until then and also the largest net income. Excepting a small loss in the Sales Department in 1923 and in the Crude Oil Department in 1924, all operations were profitable in those years; production in 1924 and 1925 brought an even larger net income than did pipelines.

Humble in 1923–1929 generally met the acid tests of a business corporation's success under the system of private enterprise: ability to grow with the times and to make a profit. It increased its crude production and reserves, pipeline mileage and capacity, crude oil purchases and sales, refinery capacity and throughput, and product outlets and sales, wholesale and retail. It also increased its profits, thus strengthening its financial position.

The precedent of using profits for expansion established by the old Humble Oil Company in 1912 was followed by the new Humble. The profits earned in and after 1923 were largely plowed back into the business, although the stockholders were not forgotten. In the Jersey-Humble discussions of January, 1919, the hope had been expressed that dividends on Humble stock would be continued at 10 per cent per annum; despite heavy losses in 1919–1922, Humble had paid its stockholders a dividend. The fact that this dividend was only about 3 per cent of the market value of Humble stock shows the confidence that most local investors had in Humble's future.

During the profitable years 1923–1925, the annual dividend was increased only from $2,000,000 to $2,100,000. No attempt was made to base payments to stockholders on the company's net earnings; from nearly 60 per cent to a little over 90 per cent of the profits were used in those years for paying debts and for financing expansion. The directors felt that, inasmuch as Humble had paid dividends in the previous loss years and was still engaged in expansion, the company was justified in temporarily holding its dividends to a relatively small return on investment.

The years 1925–1927 were a period of notable expansion. Humble's gross capital investments were increased from $110,100,000 at the end of 1924 to $202,800,000 three years later—approximately $42,000,000 in pipelines, $30,000,000 in production, $18,000,000 in refining, and slightly under $2,000,000 in sales. This expansion could not be paid for entirely out of profits, which declined after reaching a high peak in 1925, falling to a particularly low point in 1927. Tremendous increases in the production of crude and declining prices, coupled with costly expansion from which the company had not yet had the opportunity to benefit, were chiefly responsible for increased outside financing.

Early in 1926 Humble increased its capital stock nearly $30,000,000 by selling 1,250,000 new shares to its stockholders at $25.00 per share, on the basis of two new shares for each three already held. The receipts from this stock sale were used primarily to reduce and, during April, 1927, to liquidate the company's demand-loan account with Jersey, which at the beginning of 1926 had stood at over $32,000,000. Since Jersey by then owned over 60 per cent of the Humble stock, this increase in capital amounted to its changing over $18,000,000 of liquid assets into fixed capital.

The loan positions of the two companies were then reversed—a proud day for Humble. Jersey at the end of May, 1927, owed Humble $4,000,000 on open account, a situation that continued to prevail until the larger company by the end of 1930 was debited with approximately $31,000,000.

In April, 1927, Humble issued $25,000,000 of ten-year, 5 per cent gold debentures for the purpose of acquiring additional stock of its pipeline company issued to finance expansion. The resulting construction of new lines enabled Humble Pipe Line in the three successive years 1927, 1928, and 1929 to attain higher profits than ever before. This, in fact, marked the peak of pipeline profits; never again was Humble Pipe Line Company to earn such large annual profits as in 1928 and 1929.

Humble would have suffered an actual loss in 1927 and 1928 had it not been for its pipeline company's earnings. In 1929, however, when the profits of Humble Oil & Refining Company reached the new peak of over $32,500,000, the pipelines were not entirely responsible. Refining, crude oil marketing, and even local sales of refined products also contributed; production suffered a small loss.

Humble utilized a goodly share of these profits for expansion. During the years 1926 to 1929 it paid out in dividends less than 30 per cent of the profits, which left over $55,000,000 to be plowed back into the business. Whatever the annual profit—whether as low as $7,000,000 or as high as $32,000,000—the dividends were held at a little less than $2.00 per share. Some small stockholders protested, but Farish took the view that the funded debt must be "out of the way, or practically out of the way," before the company increased its dividends.[39] In plowing back most of the company's earnings, Humble's policy was in agreement with that of its largest stockholder, which during 1918–1927 paid out to its owners only 35.7 per cent of its profits.[40]

By the end of 1929 Humble was financially strong. Its net worth was then $171,300,000, as compared with $11,000,000 at the end of 1918. Its financial condition at the end of the period is shown in Table 3.

In 1920 and 1921 Humble built a new home.[41] The million-dollar, nine-story Humble Building occupied half a block in the center of the city. In May, 1921, the company began to move to this building the many offices that had hitherto been housed in various places in downtown Houston.[42]

The Humble Building became the headquarters for all of the company's widely scattered operations—in northern Mexico, in southern Oklahoma and Arkansas, in western Louisiana, and in the various oil regions of Texas. In this building the geologists studied surface and subsurface data gathered from far and wide and thus added to the company's knowledge of the geology of Texas and its neighboring oil regions. Here, also, departmental offices and subdivisions collected information—from a constant stream of visitors to and from the fields and from frequent and periodic reports—and planned and guided operations. And the Legal Department helped to draw up contracts, examined titles, prepared for representing Humble in lawsuits, and advised the Board of Directors and executives on all legal matters. To this building on Sunday mornings came directors and officers, managers, and superintendents to hear of the past week's developments and to discuss and argue about what should and what should not be done. Here the Operating Committee or the Board of Directors daily considered matters of policy and set the company's course. Should Humble add to the enormous quantity of crude oil in storage—with possible loss through price decline—or risk a shortage of supply? Should it invest a million or more in leasing and development in an untested area—which might yield several million dollars' worth of oil or only dry holes? Or build a pipeline into a distant region of recent oil development—which might or might not prove productive enough to justify the investment?

In the accounting offices figures were collected on operating expense

Table 3

Consolidated Balance Sheet
Humble Oil & Refining Company
December 31, 1929

Assets			
Current Assets:			
Cash and Demand Loans		$ 34,086,889.62	
Marketable Securities		2,664,995.00	
Acceptances and Notes Receivable		995,380.64	
Accounts Receivable		7,581,750.53	
Inventories:			
Crude Oil and Refined Products (Costs, Less than Market)	$41,232,920.66		
Materials and Supplies	7,672,014.68	48,904,935.34	$ 94,233,951.13
Permanent Investments:			
Investments in Non-Affiliated Companies		145,102.43	
Miscellaneous Securities		21,879.37	166,981.80
Sinking and Special Trust Funds			788,071.64
Fixed (Capital) Assets:			
Properties, Plant and Equipment		233,278,368.37	
Less: Reserve for Depletion and Depreciation		89,574,308.77	143,704,059.60
Prepaid and Deferred Charges			1,552,263.56
Total Assets			$240,445,327.73
Liabilities			
Current Liabilities:			
Accounts Payable		$ 13,518,914.55	
Accrued Liabilities		9,877,009.86	$ 23,395,924.41
Funded and Long Term Debt:			
Ten Year 5½% Debenture Bonds, Due 1932		23,504,000.00	
Ten Year 5% Debenture Bonds, Due 1937		21,114,000.00	44,618,000.00
Deferred Credits			647,191.93
Capital Stock:			
Authorized and Issued		75,000,000.00	
Less: Treasury Stock Available for Sale to Employees		633,875.00	74,366,125.00
Surplus:			
Capital Surplus Paid in		9,935,118.46	
Earned Surplus Unappropriated		87,482,967.93	97,418,086.39
Total Liabilities			$240,445,327.73

Note: As originally published; not adjusted for subsequent changes in accounting classifications.

and income. As these were totaled, month by month and at year's end, and consolidated into over-all company figures, they revealed whether the company was or was not making profits. One year, or two, or even three did not tell the whole story, however, for oil is produced not at once by act of a board of directors but by long and unremitting effort.

What went on in the Humble Building was principally planning, providing means, and measuring results. This was significant only as it made possible adequate and efficient operations in producing, in transporting, in buying and selling crude oil, in refining, and in the sale of products. Those diverse and widely scattered operations were the ends toward which all the central administrative effort was directed.

To those activities attention is now turned. The principal operations were going on simultaneously, meshed together into a related network of activities, but here they can best be presented singly. Such a separation, however artificial, and an order of some sort, however arbitrary, are necessary to fit the complicated reality of the company's operations into the limitations of a historical presentation. The next eight chapters will deal with Humble's different operations—production, pipeline transportation, purchasing, refining, and sales—until the onset of the depression. These chapters record Humble's great expansion of the 1920s and the beginning of the transition to technologically oriented thinking and practice. The story begins with the search for oil-bearing sands and the production of crude oil.

Chapter 6

UPS AND DOWNS IN THE QUEST FOR OIL, 1919–1926

THE PRODUCTION of crude oil continued in the 1920s to be Humble's most important operation. As had been agreed in the discussion with Jersey Standard executives in January, 1919, the Humble executives' major objective was "to build a large producing business."

The decision to expand came at a turning point in the history of the world oil industry. To the tremendous market for fuel oil that had been developing in the past two decades, a development greatly accelerated by World War I, was now added the rapid increase in demand for gasoline resulting from the phenomenal postwar rise in the number of automobiles in the United States. As the Humble founders had entered the oil business in the early years of the fuel oil age, so the expansion of the company's operations after the war coincided with the appearance of the gasoline age. The expanding market for oil products was a major factor in Humble's, as in the entire oil industry's, subsequent history.

The surging demand focused attention and effort on oil production to an extent the oil industry had never before experienced. The result was an unprecedented drive by oil companies, promoters, and governments to get control of potential oil lands and to develop oil reserves. In most foreign countries believed to be promising for oil production, intense competition for large government concessions ensued; but, once obtained, these could generally be explored and developed in an orderly fashion. In the United States, however, the struggle for oil led to the leasing of relatively small tracts from individual owners and, under the prevailing rule of capture, developing them competitively and hence rapidly. Competition in the 1920s accentuated certain basic characteristics of the American oil producing industry and brought serious problems and significant new developments. Humble, operating in a region with a tremendous potential oil production, had to carry out its program of expansion in a very unstable situation.[1]

Because of the importance and the complexity of Humble's producing operations, it is essential to have some understanding of how those opera-

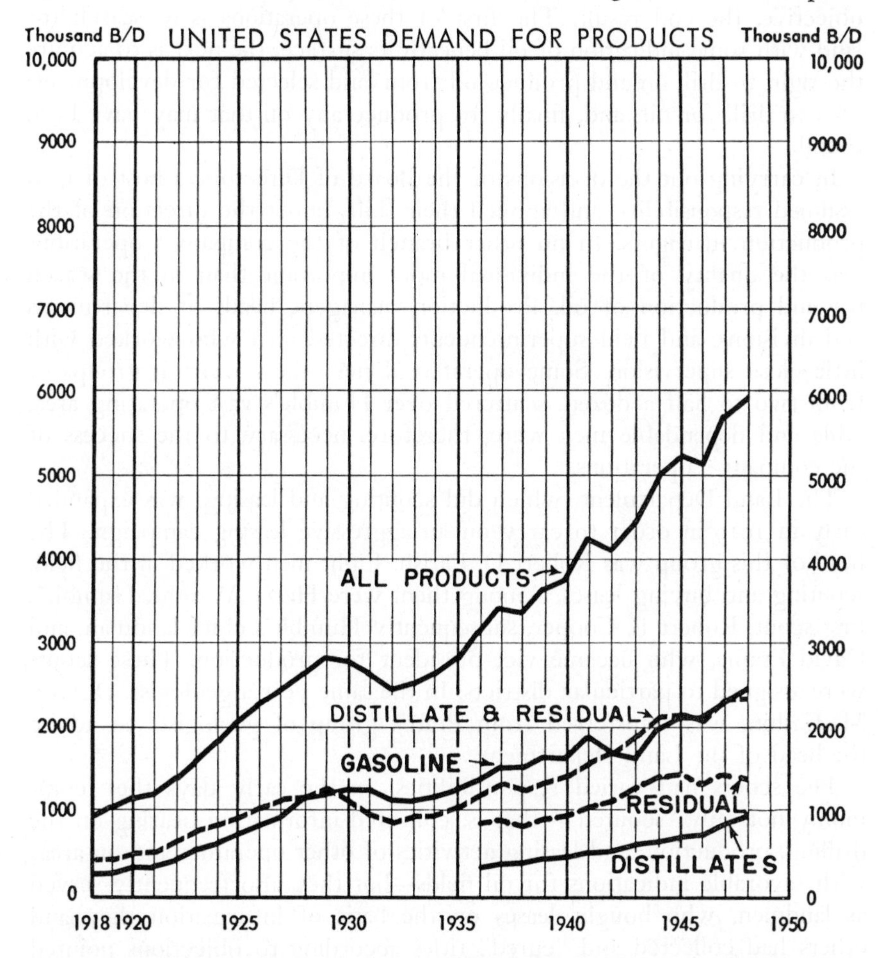

tions were organized and carried on. The following survey of the organization and its work is designed, therefore, to give some insight into production in the 1920s and also to provide background against which to view later developments. The actual production of oil in the decade following affiliation with Jersey Standard is considered in the second section of this chapter.

THE PRODUCTION ORGANIZATION AND ITS WORK

The term "production" as used in the oil industry has both a special and a general meaning. In its special meaning, it refers to a number of activities immediately related to the process of extracting the crude oil from the earth. As a general term, however, production includes a series of related operations of which the actual producing of oil is the objective, the end result. The first of these operations is to search for land with some indication of oil beneath its surface; the next is to acquire the right to drill on and produce oil from land selected for development; then to drill for oil; and, finally, to produce any oil that may have been found.

In carrying out the decisions of the Board of Directors, a host of men assumed responsibility and applied their skills under the direction of the production managers. In no other branch of the company's operations was the quality of the individual more important than in the search for and production of oil. Production managers, heads of departments and divisions, and field superintendents directed men who worked with little close supervision. Some operated alone; others were in groups of from two to half a dozen, scattered over Humble's vast operating area. Able and dependable men were, therefore, necessary to the success of the company's operations.

The Land Department, which did scouting and leasing, was expanded early in 1919 in order to carry on an aggressive leasing campaign. The head of this group was Robert D. Farish. Eight men worked in the field, scouting and buying leases. Among them were Harry Wright, Humble's first scout, Robert B. Cooper, subsequently Humble's chief landman, and David Frame, who became vice-president for production. These scouts were assigned to particular districts. In the same year a geologist, D'Arcy M. Cashin, was transferred from Pratt's group of geologists to advise the head of the Land Department.

The scouts had varied responsibilities. In the early days they commonly not only "scouted"—that is, collected information bearing on the drilling, production, and leasing activities of other operators and on areas with favorable indications for oil fields—but they also frequently served as landmen, who bought leases on the basis of information they and others had collected and "cured" titles according to objections pointed out by the Legal Department. Buying leases and checking titles, as time went on, became increasingly the work of specialists. The scout's primary and enduring function, however, was to collect information.[2]

The scouts looked for all kinds of physical indications of oil, such as gas seeps, sulphur-tasting water, rainbow colors on a pond, and oily soil or sand. A particularly important function of the scouts was to collect cuttings from oil wells being drilled, particularly from wildcats. These and other samples were put into containers with their proper identification and sent to the geologists for analysis.

Another important scouting function was to collect information about the oil operations of other men or companies. In these early years, when Humble's leasing was guided largely by competitors' leasing and wildcatting, it was vital to have correct, speedy, and regular information about these activities. The scouts also reported the location, ownership, and rate of production of producing wells. In collecting such information they worked closely with Humble's field superintendents.

The scout had to be a man of parts. Earlier training in drilling was an asset, but even more important were his physique, temperament, personality, and resourcefulness. In an emergency he had to work twenty-four hours a day, except for a cat nap in his car, and continue on the job seven days a week. He had to be able to listen to, but put no more than the proper value on, local gossip, to win the confidence of, and extract information from, people who were often under orders not to give it. As a last resort he might have to watch drilling operations from a distance with field glasses or even visit a drilling site in disguise—perhaps as a rabbit hunter. But, first and last and most important, the scout had to make friends easily and retain many friends permanently. In return, the company supplied him with a car and paid him as much as $250 a month and expenses—a high salary for that time.

The scout kept a constant stream of reports flowing in to his headquarters. Really "hot" information, for example that some company had discovered a new oil sand, he immediately reported by telephone. During a rapid lease play and important drilling activity, the division scout reported not only to the Land Department but also to the field superintendent and to the division superintendent or geologist. The scout wrote regular weekly reports on the activities of competitors—also including information about Humble's own operations in his area. A monthly report summarized his findings.

One early rule governing Humble scouts established an important precedent. Chief Scout D. E. Woods in September, 1919, instructed the men under him that they "should not acquire directly or indirectly any interest in oil and gas leases, oil and gas production, prospective oil or gas properties or royalties," or "in any way act in capacity of broker in leases or production," or acquire "interest of any kind which might in any way conflict with the interest and business of the Company."[3]

This rule undoubtedly contributed to a high turnover among Humble's exploration employees; although some scouts, geologists, and lease men left the company to cash in on their experience, while in Humble's employ they were expected to devote themselves wholeheartedly to its interest.

The expansion of production changed the scout's work. Co-operative scouting early began to supplement individual scouting. The exchange of information among scouts of various companies at first took place informally and unofficially as the growth of the industry made it impossible for a scout to keep track of all developments in his area. Some of the major companies early recognized the advantage of exchanging information on a more formal basis. In 1920 Humble agreed to exchange drilling and production figures three times a month with some companies, although Farish objected to co-operative scouting with nonparticipants in such an agreement and to the establishment of a central office for the co-ordination of information. The development of the east central Texas boom of 1921–1925 stimulated co-operative scouting.

The work of the scouts was early affected by the growing importance of geology. Although the scouts continued to report on competitors' geologic activities and to collect cuttings for the geologists to analyze, the geologist soon became the key figure in Humble's search for indications of oil. Specialized geologic scouts, indeed, early became a regular part of Humble's scouting organization.

The rise of the geologist to a position of paramount importance in Humble's exploration organization was the most significant new development in the company's producing operations until the late 1920s. This rise was the result of careful and imaginative work by the geologists and of the courage they displayed in backing up their findings with positive recommendations.[4]

Early in 1919 the number of geologists under Pratt was increased from three to ten. Among them were Eugene Holman, who was to advance rapidly in Humble and eventually to become the chief executive officer of Standard Oil Company (New Jersey); David P. Carlton and James E. LaRue, who later became heads of Humble's geophysical work; H. J. McLellan, who rose to become Gulf Coast division geologist; and William E. Hubbard, who in the 1930s became head of the Production Department's Proration division.

The group's headquarters were set up in Fort Worth in the spring of 1919. During the next year most of the geologic work was done in North Texas and the Panhandle. There was some work on the Gulf Coast, with an occasional assignment in Southwest Texas; and there was one assignment in 1919 in Mexico, where Humble incorporated a subsidiary to acquire leases and concessions just south of the Rio Grande.

In the spring of 1920 headquarters were moved to Houston, and the department's staff and activities were expanded. District offices were also established at Ardmore in Oklahoma, Shreveport in Louisiana, and soon thereafter at Cisco and Mexia in Texas. A geologic research laboratory was set up at the Houston headquarters.

Petroleum geology was a relatively new specialty in 1919. The United States Geological Survey and a few individual geologists had early done some work in this field. Geologists had been employed by oil companies in the Mid-Continent for only a few years, but few American universities were giving specialized courses in petroleum geology. And, when geology was used in the search for oil, the emphasis was still on surface geology, particularly on the search for evidences of structural irregularities that might hold oil trapped in porous rocks.

Pratt's first emphasis was therefore logically on surface geology. His staff did important work in exploring and mapping certain areas. Surface geology, however, while indispensable, had serious limitations; for example, indications of higher structures were sometimes misleading in that they did not conform with underlying structures, and on the Gulf Coast surface evidences of underlying structures were hard to find.

The Humble geologists continued to regard surface exploration and mapping as necessary and important and in some areas for several years employed surface geology exclusively, but they gave increasing attention to subsurface work. The geologic research laboratory analyzed samples of cuttings from subsurface formations. Humble's use of micropaleontology as an aid in finding oil was initiated in 1919, at its Fort Worth headquarters, under Alva C. Ellisor. About the same time in 1919 work in micropaleontology was also started by Esther Richards under E. T. Dumble of the scientifically minded Rio Bravo Oil Company, a subsidiary of the Southern Pacific Railroad. Some research in this technique had been done under J. A. Udden of the Bureau of Economic Geology, connected with The University of Texas, but Humble and Rio Bravo were the first oil companies in Texas to employ it in the search for oil. Humble's work in micropaleontology soon became especially important for the Gulf Coast and the fault-line area. The geologists analyzed samples particularly to identify the microscopic fossils they contained, from which were identified successive geologic formations in a given place. By the correlation of findings in different wells and areas, the geologists began to map subsurface structures. Thus they not only helped to discover and outline fields but also to build up a body of information about the geology of Texas.

The samples came from various sources. Some were collected by regular or geologic scouts from wells of Humble and other companies; they were either the regular cuttings, brought up in the process of drilling, or samples taken at the bottom of the hole by a special device called a core barrel. "Dry-hole money"—contributions to the drilling of a wildcat in exchange for underground information and with the agreement that, if the well proved a dry hole, the money need not be repaid—brought many samples to Humble. In 1922 Humble began to do core drilling, that is, the drilling of a hole of small diameter to obtain samples. Light rotary rigs were used; Fondren designed an improved rig which came into use in 1924.

The work of scouts and geologists was focused on helping to answer one crucial question: Where should Humble lease lands to test and develop? When the decision to lease in a given area had been made, the next step was the important and difficult operation of negotiating the desired leases at prices within the limits decided upon.

The Board of Directors determined general leasing policies and plans. It decided how much to spend for leases in a given year, in what regions Humble should expand the search for oil, whether to lease alternate small tracts (checkerboarding) or large blocks, and so on. When leasing was especially competitive, the board had an advantage over some competitors in not having to get authorization from distant superiors.

There was much latitude in leasing in the early days. Although the authority for leasing rested in the Board of Directors, individual directors often assumed that responsibility and lease men in R. D. Farish's Land Department usually carried out the details. A vice-president might consult associates before deciding to purchase leases or he might "make a trade and tell the others after its consummation." Occasionally even a production superintendent would take action without discussing the purchase with an officer. The landman, who generally made the agreement with the landowner, operated under definite but, customarily, rather flexible instructions. Since the Land Department was at first separate from Pratt's geologic group, the latter might make a recommendation that the chief landman would not or could not carry out. The potentialities for disagreement are obvious.

Gradually, however, the chief geologist moved into central position in managing Humble's leasing. W. S. Farish, who had early been given general authority over "all matters pertaining to leases acquiring new land, making of wildcat locations . . . outside the jurisdiction of any particular district," delegated much authority to Pratt. By 1922 the chief geologist was managing the scouting, leasing, and geologic work of the Northern division subject to W. S. Farish, while R. D. Farish remained in charge of scouting and leasing in South Texas and the Gulf Coast division. The finding of oil in a twilight zone in east central Texas, between the Gulf Coast division and the Northern division, caused Pratt, in his zeal to acquire leases, to operate over a larger area. By 1924 the prestige of the geologists was high because of their success at Mexia and Powell, as will be observed later. The management of scouting and leasing was then co-ordinated with geologic study under the chief geologist in the Geologic, Lease and Scouting Department. Humble was one of the first companies to place the responsibility for leasing directly upon a geologist.

After this reorganization, practices in exploration and leasing were gradually formalized. Under Pratt were a chief landman and a chief scout, and in each geographical division a division geologist, landman, and scout. The division geologist reported to both the division superintendent for production and the chief geologist. Interest in a block of leases might begin almost anywhere in the organization and be referred through channels for approval to the chief geologist, to the board, and back to the chief geologist, who would authorize the land-and-lease staff to negotiate the purchases.

Specific decisions concerning leases were arrived at with increasing frequency on the sole authority of the chief geologist. As Pratt said, finding oil is a geologic problem and, when decisions to purchase must be made quickly, one man can act faster than two. The board was supposed to pass on expenditures of $50,000 or more, but in practice President Farish could speak for the board. The chief geologist was responsible for apportioning the amount to be spent. The division geologist, according to Pratt, was authorized to "get all you can up to X dollars per acre within these lines" or to spend "so much money within a local area." The most money was generally spent in divisions where more new fields were being found and operators were most active. As the operating territory grew larger, the division geologist alone had command of adequate local information on which to base a decision, although, unless time was very important, he would seek confirmation from Houston.

Humble's early leasing policy changed with its developing use of geology. In the early years of the decade, the policy was generally to checkerboard lease purchases, that is, to lease a relatively small acreage here and another there, particularly in or near proved fields. As confidence in the geologist increased, the practice developed of estimating the direction in which a newly discovered field was going to "move" and then leasing desirable acreage before the rush began and lease prices shot skyward. To an increasing extent, however, as the geologists' judgments proved valid, Humble leased for wildcatting.

The actual task of negotiating for leases was at first commonly performed by the company's landmen, who often also doubled as scouts, and later more and more frequently through lease brokers. A more or less standard lease form for the industry, known as "Producers 88," had been developed, although each company generally issued its own revised form under this magic number. This lease gave the lessee the exclusive right to explore for oil or gas on the land covered for an agreed number of years and to produce therefrom, after oil was discovered, as long as oil or gas could be produced; the contract provided for an annual stipulated rental until oil was found or the lease expired and a one-eighth royalty on any oil or gas produced. The lease contract usually included a cash bonus to the landowner at the time of execution and also provisions for cancellation.

While Producers 88 had come into general use before Humble's incorporation, lessors were still sometimes able to obtain special provisions. These included, on occasion, a high bonus, an onerously high royalty and, in or near fields of large proved production, the producer's commitment to drill one or more wells within a specific time. Humble's negotiations over the valuable twenty-five acre Gaillard lease at Goose Creek broke down at one time, it is said, because the lessor demanded a clause allowing him to cancel the lease contract if the gates were left open so his cattle could get out. Humble later acquired the property for many times the earlier sum—with the penalty for leaving the gates open still in the lease. Many lease agreements purchased from promoters in the Ranger area obligated Humble to drill within a specific period without provision for substituting a rental payment.

Use of the company's lease form relieved the landmen of many complicated decisions, but the profound question of "How much?" remained. The land to be leased and the bonus, or purchase price, and annual rental to be offered were worked out in advance by the division geologist in consultation with the landmen. For a wildcat lease the bonus ordinarily ranged from $1.00 to $5.00 an acre. Sometimes, however, companies would obtain large blocks in advance of exploration without a bonus and with rentals of from 50 cents to $1.00 an acre.

The landman had to know some law and a good deal about oil. He had to plan carefully and be resourceful in bargaining—a good trader was invaluable. He had to deal with various kinds of individuals, honest and dishonest, ignorant and informed. The experienced landman knew that trying to high-pressure a farmer into a decision would probably only make him stubborn and suspicious. He usually tried to buy the first lease from an influential member of a community and, when possible, avoided paying more to one lessor in a community than to another, thus guarding against a sure way of making enemies. In West Texas, a region of large ranches, trading was relatively easy before much oil had been found there and the landman's title problem was simpler than in East Texas and on the Gulf Coast, where the multiplicity of small holdings and irregularities in titles greatly complicated leasing.

A large company with a good reputation and a long-run view of leasing had an advantage. Scout-landman N. E. Tanner said he was successful because he knew many people and could point to the reputation and skill of his company in finding oil. Humble was well aware that considerate behavior by its various employees was particularly important to its success in lease buying; courtesy and care of fences and other property by pipeliners as well as drillers were essential. "Always treat the farmer so you will be able to come back" was Humble's motto. For example, landman Tanner on one occasion in Winkler County in West Texas shared with a prospective lessor his own information about a new well and offered more than the latter's asking price, thus winning for himself and his company a reputation in that community for fair dealing which over the years was probably worth many times the extra expenditure for the particular lease. While such behavior was not exclusive with Humble, the consistent practice of fair dealing helped to build an enviable reputation for the company. Humble also followed the unwritten law of the major companies of not trying to get a landowner to break an earlier commitment or to gain a "top lease"—a lease to begin when the current one expired.

The problem of clearing title differed from district to district, and the method varied from time to time. At first the company purchased some 90 per cent of its leases without other title examination than checking immediately available official records; it relied for security on the spreading of risk over many leases. In West Texas, where large tracts of land were held under patents granted by the state, most of Humble's leases were bought and paid for after title examination, the lessor being willing to wait for payment during the brief period necessary to clear title. Some landmen, however, regarded it as advantageous in the long run to exhibit complete confidence in ranchers by refraining from holding bonus payments in escrow until clearance of the title. In southern Louisiana and East Texas and Gulf Coast Texas there was more reason for caution. The situation was particularly complex in East Texas, a region of poor, sandy soil covered with piney woods, where holdings were commonly small and farms had frequently been abandoned, sold for taxes, or occupied by heirs without registering change of ownership. If oil was found, claimants were often many.

Humble might specify that the would-be lessor should validate the title within a certain period. One such deal, in about 1926, gave the company an opportunity to demonstrate its capacity for leaning over backward in order to be fair. It had agreed to pay $107,000 for some leases in Southwest Texas, offered by a group of inexperienced would-be oilmen, contingent upon showing a good and merchantable title within thirty days. The lessors did not present the necessary proof until after fifteen additional days, and in the meantime a dry hole had been drilled near the property, which greatly reduced, perhaps wiped out, its potential value. Humble's Legal Department, as a matter of course, held that, since title defects were not cured within the required time, the company was not obligated to purchase the leases. But President Farish, after listening to the lessors' plea for sympathy on the grounds that the group did not understand the oil business very well and simply could not afford to lose all that money, finally agreed to pay the $107,000. This expenditure helped to advertise Humble as a "square-shooting company," but it was expensive publicity.

The Legal Department had top responsibility for examining the abstracts of titles and for passing on the validity of titles, but by the middle 1920s a group of specialized employees known as title men had developed whose function was to cure lease titles, that is, to obtain information or instruments called for by the lawyers who examined the abstracts of titles. Although the work was frequently merely a matter of checking official land records, on occasion a search through widely scattered city directories and family histories was necessary. The tendency throughout the years was increasingly to draw title men from the ranks of recent graduates of law schools.

When titles had been cleared, Humble could proceed to determine the existence or nonexistence of oil by what was, and still is, the only sure method—the penetration of a formation with a drilling bit. Here the drilling organization assumed responsibility for operations.

First the derrick had to be set up. The rig builders worked in crews of six or seven and were highly paid, especially during the booms so characteristic of the early 1920s. The rig builder is, however, rather an offstage figure in the Humble drama, since from the beginning Humble's derricks have usually been built on contract.[5]

Humble generally used its own crews for drilling.[6] At first it used the cable-tool rig in certain hard formations in Oklahoma and North Texas, but with the improvement of the rock bit, which made possible the drilling of even the hardest formations with a rotary, the rotary rig came into general use. The cable-tool drillers, usually Northerners, during the 1920s gave way to the indigenous "round-and-round boys," or "longhorn swivel-neckers," who ran the rotaries.

The rotary crew was headed by the driller, proud veteran of the derrick platform, who was typically an extreme individualist of varied talents. He had to be able to tell from the sound and speed of the drilling machinery what was going on at the bottom of the hole. In addition he had to be something of a steamfitter, plumber, blacksmith, carpenter, and stationary engineer. Responsible for hiring and firing and for the smooth functioning of a crew of individualists, he must also possess organizing and executive abilities of a high order, as well as coolness, vigilance, and resourcefulness in an emergency. Before professionally trained technologists became prominent on Humble's staff, the driller also served as his own geologist and petroleum engineer. On the basis of "returns" from the formations, he had to decide when a producing sand had been reached and it was time to set screen—the perforated pipe for keeping out sand and admitting oil. Lacking in schooling and even illiterate as many of the early drillers were, they were indispensable members of the Humble organization.

The driller's helpers, known by the proud title of roughnecks, usually numbered four. Their most important work came when the drill pipe was "pulled" to change the worn bit and then run back into the hole. Two floormen at the rotary table "broke" the joints of pipe as they came out of the hole, while the derrickman, standing on a platform eighty or ninety feet above the derrick floor, racked the pipes. The fireman, or engineman, assisted the floormen in making a "round trip" of pipe, in addition to seeing to the supply of power for the draw works which raised and lowered the drill pipe and casings and for the turntable which rotated the drill pipe carrying the bit. The driller from his position at the controls of the draw works furnished instructions to a crew, who usually, by necessity and from long working together, were imbued with a strong spirit of teamwork and co-ordination.

The members of the drilling crew, up to and including the driller himself, were trained on the job. If a "boll weevil," as the "greenhorn" roughneck was called, showed willingness, intelligence, and ambition, his fellow workers, headed by the driller, assisted him in learning through observation and experience every task of the crew. Eventually the roughneck might rise to the position of relief driller, in charge for short periods or for an entire tour in the absence of the regular driller. The next step would be to a tour of his own as a full-fledged driller.

The work of the drilling crew was taxing at times, but the opportunities for the ambitious and able were immediate. The crews were on the job twelve hours or more, except on the Gulf Coast, where the working day was traditionally ten—the engineer merely kept the rotary table turning and the mud circulating to prevent the pipe from "freezing" for the two hours between tours—but within the long shift was usually time for a poker game now and then, or for a nap. The roughnecks worked a seven-day week until nearly the end of the decade. There were two exceptions to the long day and week. In April, 1920, the executive committee of the Texas Gulf Coast and Louisiana Oil & Gas Association, headed by Farish, unanimously recommended an increase in pay and the eight-hour day, apparently in recognition of union activity, but depression in 1921 caused Humble and others to revert to the longer hours.[7] Strict enforcement of Oklahoma's Sabbath laws shortened the work week in that state. The roughneck's pay in the 1920s was $4.50 per day, but the ambitious worker had his eye on the driller's job and wage. Although the driller's pay was normally twice as much as that of his helper, during boom periods it rose to $20.00 or $30.00 per day. Many drillers, enjoying their work and lacking the formal preparation for further advancement, were not attracted by positions involving heavier responsibilities. Some, however, rose to the more responsible and higher-paid position of "tool pusher," an experienced driller in charge of as many as four rigs, whose function was to see that rigs had supplies and equipment and that operations were proceeding smoothly. A few rose even higher, an example being Ray H. Horton, who became a director of Humble Oil & Refining Company.

After a well had been brought in, other crews took over the task of producing the oil. Before production could begin, the connection gang installed the combination of pipes and valves—the "Christmas tree"—that controlled the flow of oil from a well and also connected the pipes and valves that conveyed and controlled the flow from well to lease tanks. In the meantime the "bull gang" dug ditches, wrestled with pipe and lumber, and performed the heavier, less skilled jobs.

Once the work of installing and connecting equipment and pipes had been completed, the producing of oil commenced. The crude oil might go through two processes before reaching the lease tank: the first to separate gas from the oil, and the second to break by "treating" an emulsion of oil and water that might have formed. As will be noted in the chapter on refining, some of the gas produced was run through casinghead gasoline plants to separate the natural gasoline from the gas. There was as yet little market for the gas itself. Humble, like other operators in those years, "flared" most of it, that is, burned the gas at the top of pipes high enough to protect the field from the fire. When the oil reached the lease tanks, it was gauged and sampled for the production record.

When wells no longer flowed by natural pressure, the pumps took over. The pumper, frequently a drilling or production man too old for his former arduous responsibilities, for a modest wage accepted twenty-four-hour-a-day responsibility for the efficient pumping of as many as twenty-five wells. The company usually supplied him with a house and a plot for a garden.[8]

The working conditions of the common laborers in production, the "roustabouts" of the "bull gang" and the connection gang, differed somewhat from those of the roughnecks, as did their opportunities for immediate and ultimate advancement. The roustabouts, though paid as much as the driller's helpers and given a shorter day and even Sundays off in slack periods, steadily did heavier work and did not have the immediate and attractive prospect of becoming drillers. The roustabout might, if able and ambitious, become a labor foreman or gang pusher of a crew of roustabouts. The gang pusher did not have such long hours, heavy responsibility, or good pay as the driller. But production men led a more settled life than drillers. Furthermore, there was the opportunity to become a farm boss, the production foreman in charge of producing operations in an entire field who co-ordinated the work of the production gangs, pumpers, and gaugers. A few men rose to even higher supervisory posts.[9] Perhaps it is merely a coincidence that more district superintendents seem to have come up via the production than the drilling ladder. Although there was interchange of men between drilling and producing, the two functions generally appealed to somewhat different temperaments.

Since drilling and producing were different phases of the same function of extracting oil from the earth and often went on simultaneously in the same field, it was logical that they should be co-ordinated by supervisors and executives familiar with both types of operation. On the Gulf Coast, however, as already observed, drilling and production were not so co-ordinated in the 1920s. In other areas tool pushers and farm bosses were responsible to a district superintendent in charge of both drilling and production in a particular field or in closely related fields. The district superintendent, in turn, reported to one of the half-dozen division superintendents in charge of a large geographical area. Above these men were the Production Department managers or the directors for production.

Men for the higher supervisory tasks in the field were at this time occasionally recruited from the ranks, but often they came by other avenues. Goddard, who was in charge of production in Oklahoma, and Broday, superintendent of the Northern division, were indeed practical drillers who had risen from the ranks, but they also had been prominently associated with predecessor companies of Humble Oil & Refining Company and were among its fairly large stockholders. In the early 1920s men of different training and experience began to enter the managerial group. Eugene Holman, who became superintendent of the Arkansas-Louisiana division in 1922 and had served as a geologist and landman, was a 1917 graduate of The University of Texas, where he had specialized in geology; before joining Humble in 1919 he had worked for The Texas Company in Mexico and Central America, and one year with the United States Geological Survey. His assistant and successor, David B. Harris, held a degree in civil engineering from the Texas Agricultural & Mechanical College and had had experience in banking and as an infantry captain in the army. Harris worked for two years as roustabout and farm boss, in 1921 rose to assistant district superintendent, the following year to assistant division superintendent, and four years later to division superintendent. David Frame had attended The University of Texas, had worked in a bank, and had been a captain of artillery before his work as scout and landman from 1919 to 1926 carried him to the post of division superintendent in the Panhandle. Obviously, special training and experience outside the oil industry, added to the necessary native ability and the capacity for tremendous physical and mental exertions, facilitated promotion.

Humble's drilling and producing organizations continued in 1919–1926 to operate basically as they had done earlier and to employ mostly old methods. Changes were made, to be sure, and some of them were important. They were not, however, the result of a systematic and comprehensive examination of existing methods but consisted rather of occasional improvements made here and there.

Some improvements were made in drilling. Fondren was keenly interested in improving machinery and was a nationally recognized authority on drilling equipment.[10] Yet in such obvious developments as the use of steel derricks Humble was a laggard. Although a Gulf Coast hurricane not infrequently leveled every derrick in a field and Humble was considering windproof steel derricks as early as 1919, F. P. Sterling opposed them on the ground that they would rust in the acid soil of the coast, and Bonner of the Sales Department fought them in behalf of the lumbermen, who were Humble's principal customers for lubricants. Humble's superintendent on the Gulf Coast, F. W. Fraley, is given credit for introducing more careful cementing of wells in 1920–1921, when cementing around the lower part of the casing to shut out water and gas was still not a common practice.[11] Farish's Northern division was, perhaps, somewhat readier than the Gulf Coast division to adopt new techniques. The first Mid-Continent well to be drilled with rotary equipment powered by electricity is said to have been a Humble well in Wichita County, in North Texas, completed in April, 1923; Humble did not begin to use electric power for drilling on the Gulf Coast until the following year.[12] The Gulf Production Company with its steel derricks, electric rigs, and weight indicators—dial devices for indicating how long and how heavily a bit bore on the bottom while "making hole" [13]—was probably better equipped for drilling. Humble's frequent blowouts, particularly in the Gulf Coast fields where the gas pressure was high, indicated both the lack of knowledge of gas pressure and inadequate mud and equipment for coping with the gas.[14]

Advances were made in production as well. Frank Bass set up a salt-water disposal plant at Hull in 1920, when it was still customary to allow salt water to run destructively into a creek or on the ground. On the Gulf Coast, also, Humble was one of the first companies to use electricity for pumping and treating, introducing it at Goose Creek in 1919 and at West Columbia in 1921.[15] Harry L. Edwards, general superintendent for production outside the Gulf Coast, designed a treating plant.[16] In 1923 the Northern division acquired a chemical engineer, G. H. L. Kent, formerly of Jersey Standard's Bayway refinery. Kent had been brought to Humble to direct the manufacture and sale of Sealite, a foamy covering to protect storage oil and gasoline from evaporation. When this preparation proved ineffective, he was made assistant to the general superintendent of the Northern division to have charge, particularly, of oil treating.

Humble's greatest weakness at this time was one that it shared with most companies—a disregard of the role of gas in oil recovery. A well would be brought in through open casing and allowed to flow thousands of barrels of oil and sand until it had "blown its head off," that is, until its natural energy was largely exhausted. The well would then be "put on the pump"—to produce less oil at greater expense per barrel than if the oil had been produced more slowly with less waste of its lifting energy. The Rio Bravo Oil Company was one of the few companies that brought in its wells through tubing—a "string" of small pipes run into the well through the much larger casing—instead of through the casing itself; Rio Bravo endeavored by controlling the rate of production through tubing to maintain a proper ratio between gas and oil in production, that is, to produce enough gas to lift the oil but not more.

EXPLORATION AND PRODUCTION IN PARTICULAR REGIONS AND FIELDS

The Humble directors were especially interested in the Ranger area in 1919, and Ranger became the scene of Humble's first vigorous efforts to increase production. The term "Ranger" in its restricted use referred to the field by that name in Eastland County but was also commonly used to designate the entire north central Texas oil-producing area in the belief that such fields as Breckenridge, Desdemona, and Sipe Springs would ultimately connect with one another to form a single vast field. The Ranger area, booming with activity, was considered one of the most promising oil regions in the country, its oil being especially valuable for cylinder stock, which was in short supply.

In the spring of 1919 William S. Smullin joined Humble to direct and co-ordinate operations in the Ranger area as superintendent of drilling and production in North Texas.[17] Smullin was an experienced production man from California, who had been employed by Jersey Standard to examine oil prospects in Texas before its purchase of Humble stock. At the time of his arrival the Ranger boom was at its height. Prices were soaring, competition was feverish, and speculation was rampant. An estimated million dollars a day was being spent in developing the Ranger district, exclusive of the cost of the leases themselves, which ranged to as high as $10,000 per acre—one five-acre lease with a producing well was reported to have been sold for over half a million. Rig builders and drillers received up to $30.00 a day. Contract drillers were charging $12.00 to $15.00 per foot, but even the average cost of $70,000 for drilling a well did not discourage operations. Oil was selling at a premium price of $3.50 per barrel, and the supply was believed to be nearly inexhaustible.

Smullin's background and temperament were suited to such an environment. A man of big ideas, he had become accustomed to large-scale operations in California. He directed the building of an oil-field camp at Cisco to serve as fitting headquarters for an anticipated prodigious field. Humbletown—with its office building, waterworks, ice plant, powerhouse, and employees' cottages, its machine shop, its warehouse full of automobile parts and tires, and its acres of pipe stock—eventually cost more than a million dollars. In order to hold experienced men, who were scarce, Smullin provided housing and food which, compared with usual Texas oil-field standards, were luxurious. Attractive cottages with hardwood floors and built-in copper tubs were matched by a commissary stocked with abundant luxuries and a dining room in which lavish meals were topped off by pint servings of ice cream.[18] Humbletown was established as a veritable Big Rock Candy Mountain of Texas oil-field legend.

Although the great camp at Cisco was the most conspicuous result of Smullin's short stay with Humble, it was probably not the most important. Smullin recommended a number of organizational changes, but some of them were not realistic although theoretically sound. He checked up sharply on tardiness and mistakes, and recommended a better control of expenditures. It was on his recommendation that Humble established an engineering department. He engaged a number of engineers, some of whom were exceptionally well-qualified men from California. And he took an interest in early conservation work.[19]

Meanwhile the scouting and leasing organization and Pratt's geologists, who numbered nearly a dozen, were endeavoring to see that Humble should not be left behind in the rush for promising acreage in the Ranger area. This was a difficult assignment. Favorable structures were determined primarily by surface geology, particularly by "reverse dips" which might indicate a dome or anticline; unfortunately the Ranger limestone did not always conform with the surface rocks. The subsurface formations were studied to a less extent. Although taking cores was not yet possible in northern Texas, where cable tools were still dominant, geologists gathered cuttings, whenever possible, to familiarize themselves with the formations encountered.

Early in 1919 Humble's principal producing assets were believed to be in this Ranger area; and, as arranged in the agreement with Jersey Standard, Humble took over The Carter Oil Company's leases at Ranger. During the first five months of 1919 more than three-fourths of the $4,250,000 that Humble paid out for leases was spent in northern Texas. For a time an average of $50,000 per day was spent on leases in the Ranger area, most of which obligated the company to drill one or more wells per lease. The pace continued into 1920.

Intelligence, money, and energy could not, however, produce oil where oil did not exist. Humble geologists recommended thousands of

AREA OF HUMBLE'S OPERATIONS, 1917–1930

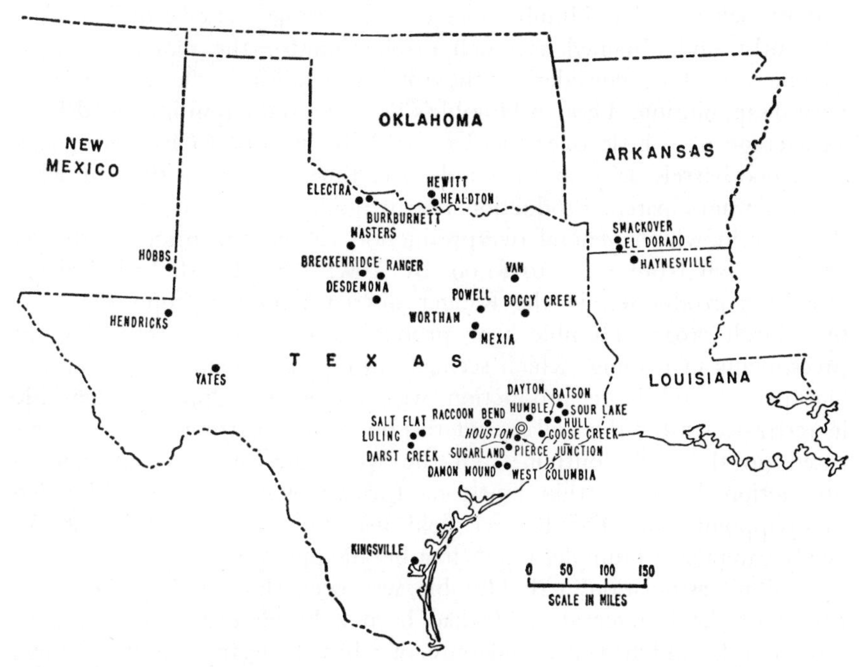

This map shows the location of most of the fields in which Humble had producing operations during this period.

acres, millions of dollars were expended on leases, Division Superintendent Stephen P. Farish had as many as ninety strings of tools operating simultaneously, and Smullin with considerable verve directed the total operations. But the results were small. Unfortunately for Humble, the best territory had already been occupied by Gulf, Texas, and the Texas Pacific Coal & Oil Company. The belief that the early wells in the Ranger area defined a prodigious pool proved erroneous; the "Ranger field" turned out instead to be a number of small pools. Inevitably Humble drilled many dry holes. Even when the initial production from a well was large, production from the Ranger limestone declined rapidly. According to a geologist, "only the first well on each 160-acre tract ever paid," and Humble, even after it had struck a dry hole, was frequently committed by the terms of its leases to drilling several wells on neighboring acreages. Two examples represent the general situation: on the eight-thousand-acre tract near Sipe Springs, where Humble's wildcat well, Moorman No. 1, was proclaimed to be "the forerunner of a real oil pool," the offset well proved a dry hole; in March, 1921, the company bought for a quarter of a million dollars a lease with eight wells producing 800 barrels daily, and within a month the production had fallen to 200 barrels.

Pratt believed that Humble had chosen acreage wisely, drilled wells efficiently, and obtained as much production for the money spent as anyone else, but, considering the total expenditure, the results were very disappointing. Though Humble's Ranger production increased from an average of a little over 200 barrels daily in 1918 to between 3,000 and 4,000 barrels daily in 1919 and 1920, this was only a tithe of what had been anticipated. Production nearly doubled in 1921, but that was the year in which general overproduction caused the price of Ranger crude to fall from $3.50 to $1.00. By May, 1920, Farish had declared Humble's production in the Ranger district a losing proposition, and by March, 1922, Humble was producing only 120 barrels daily.[20] Investments in drilling, which seemed entirely reasonable when oil was high-priced and large production was anticipated, appeared fantastic in retrospect after the collapse of the boom. Furthermore, expectations based on the early output from the wells and the rapid decline in production from the thin limestone formations with a gas drive led to disappointment. The Ranger field was the first big effort of the newly capitalized Humble, and its first big disappointment.

Smullin's association with Humble was even shorter than the boom period of the Ranger area. He had been a Humble director for only four months and had attended only one board meeting when in June, 1920, Jersey Standard "borrowed" him to visit operations in Alberta and Saskatchewan; in September he was made a director of The Tropical Oil Company, which Imperial Oil, Limited, Jersey's Canadian affiliate, had recently purchased, and for a time he had charge of producing operations in Colombia.[21]

Meanwhile the faithful old Gulf Coast helped to compensate for the losses and disappointments in Ranger. From 1919 to 1921 Humble's Gulf Coast production was never less than two-thirds of its total. Even when its North Texas production was at its height, that on the Gulf Coast was three or four times greater, and through 1922 it far exceeded the company's production in any other area. This record was attained in spite of such obstacles as poor roads, heavy rainfall, and terrific coastal storms which frequently leveled scores of derricks.[22]

Organized in a division separate from other Humble producing territories, the administration of the Gulf Coast was itself divided into two departments—drilling and production. The personal qualities of the two officers in charge of the separate functions went far to compensate for organizational deficiencies and the consequent friction. On the lower level, according to a veteran employee, the Gulf Coast division resembled two mules stuck in a mud hole, neither of which would start pulling first. Another old-timer characterized the interdepartmental situation as "just like the World War." However, Fondren, director for drilling, probably had a more thorough practical knowledge of rotary drilling than anyone else on the Gulf Coast. He was open-minded and anxious to keep up with the times, as evidenced by his adoption of a crude though workable method, recommended by a prominent petroleum geologist, for testing possible oil sand.[23] Although F. P. Sterling, production director, was, in the opinion of some, not an easy man with whom to work, the vice-presidents were on friendly terms and both were generally popular with their men.

Among the several Gulf Coast fields that were particularly important to Humble during the years 1919 to 1921, two far outranked the others. Sour Lake, Humble, Batson, Damon Mound, Dayton, and the Hull field all contributed to the company's production from the Gulf Coast, but Goose Creek and West Columbia were the two most important. Goose Creek alone produced nearly as much oil as the entire Ranger district, but the really spectacular field was West Columbia. Humble's property in this area was undeveloped in 1919, but two years later was producing twice as much as the company's total North Texas output. Its first West Columbia well, drilled on three acres bought by R. S. Sterling for $500 on the recommendation of Scout Harry Wright, on the basis of the activities of competitors, was a 10,000-barrel-daily gusher. The highly productive Japhet lease at West Columbia, recently referred to by E. E. Townes as "the most remarkable twenty acres in Humble's history," cost $200,000; this purchase exemplifies Humble's ability to recognize a "strike" when it saw one and to "shell out" for leases.

The Gulf Coast in general and West Columbia in particular offered problems in drilling and production. West Columbia was noted for the tendency of its wells to sand up and for high gas pressure. In the absence of safety devices and with the inadequate drilling mud of the time, blowouts were frequent and in some cases men were seriously injured. In the coastal area generally, bad roads and extremely heavy rainfall necessitated the use of many horses or oxen to haul equipment. Transportation problems, coupled with large production, made it necessary for Humble to use earthen storage tanks, ultimately to a total capacity of 4,500,000 barrels. During one season of heavy rains the Brazos overflowed its banks,[24] and water stood seven feet deep around tanks which, only twelve feet high, were in serious danger of being undermined and of collapsing. Quick and co-operative joint action by drilling and production crews, in the face of almost certain death should the earthen walls give way and release a flood of oil, achieved the siphoning-off of much of the accumulated water and the reinforcement of the walls.

Gulf Coast production continued to rise rapidly and to play a significant part in Humble's output. Older fields were expanded and new ones came into production, including the Hull field, which, with a daily average of 2,250 barrels by August, 1921, ranked next to Goose Creek.[25] Although by 1921 other areas were contributing to Humble's rapidly increasing production, the Gulf Coast remained the most productive (see Table 4). To the smaller output from North Texas in that year were added almost half a million barrels from east central Texas, over a million barrels of production in Oklahoma, and about a third as much in Arkansas and Louisiana. The Gulf Coast production reached nearly 8,000,000 barrels in 1921, its best year until 1930. At that time Humble was responsible for almost a third of the entire crude production of the companies, domestic and foreign, affiliated with Jersey Standard.[26] It was the largest producer of Texas crude, surpassing The Texas Company, its nearest rival.

Though Humble's total production was increasing despite failure in Ranger, the immediate situation at the end of 1921 was not favorable. From 1919 through 1921, because of falling prices, costly leasing, expensive development of new territory, and too many dry holes, Humble's Production Department had not only failed to show a profit but had also suffered a heavy loss. By the middle of 1921 Humble, along with the rest of the nation, was in the depths of a postwar depression. In the oil industry the situation was accentuated by excessive production, particularly in Mexico, which brought a severe drop in oil prices just at the time when the boom and heavy expenditures in Ranger were followed by the bust. The price of lower-gravity Gulf Coast crudes began to drop late in 1920, and that of the high-gravity North Texas and west central Texas crudes early in 1921; in the summer of 1921 prices reached a low point from which there was only a fair recovery in the autumn. The effect on Humble's income from production is shown in Table 5.

The time had come to halt, to reduce costs. Humble cut wages by about 10 per cent, lengthened hours, and laid off a large number of employees, including, according to Farish, many "of the most capable

TABLE 4

ANNUAL NET CRUDE OIL PRODUCTION OF HUMBLE OIL & REFINING COMPANY BY REGIONS, 1917–1930
(Thousands of barrels)

Year	East Texas	Texas Gulf Coast	North Texas	South-west Texas	West Texas	New Mexico	South Louisiana	North Louisiana and Arkansas	Okla-homa	Total
1917	. . .	2,132	371	. . .	. . .	. . .	. . .	. . .	697	3,200
1918	. . .	2,952	908	. . .	. . .	. . .	. . .	4	428	4,292
1919	. . .	4,112	1,683	. . .	. . .	. . .	. . .	8	237	6,039
1920	. . .	5,989	1,222	. . .	. . .	. . .	10	2	603	7,826
1921	448	7,929	2,458	. . .	. . .	. . .	26	367	1,063	12,291
1922	2,167	5,800	1,379	. . .	. . .	. . .	9	749	1,095	11,199
1923	9,207	4,287	1,264	. . .	. . .	. . .	3	1,452	814	17,027
1924	9,816	2,839	949	. . .	. . .	. . .	3	1,504	741	15,851
1925	8,825	3,309	1,537	325	2	. . .	3	3,183	845	18,029
1926	3,887	2,891	2,891	288	46	. . .	3	2,741	960	13,707
1927	2,843	2,089	2,620	195	2,132	. . .	2	1,765	1,602	13,248
1928	1,889	2,106	2,529	199	7,009	. . .	2	1,322	1,171	15,895
1929	2,010	6,592	2,150	5,331	6,161	105	12	543	551	23,457
1930	2,293	9,217	2,529	6,283	4,812	1,016	54	. . .	. . .	26,205

Source: Records of Humble Oil & Refining Company.

type." It also suspended or reduced drilling operations until it was running only 32 rigs, as compared with 146 the previous year.[27] The total production was considerably less in 1922 than in the preceding year.

In the summer of 1921 the self-confidence of Humble's chief geologist was at a similarly low point. Pratt pessimistically felt that his record at Ranger had lowered rather than raised not only his own prestige but that of petroleum geology in general. Fortunately, others had a better opinion both of Pratt and of the possible contributions of his science. Early in the previous year the American Association of Petroleum Geologists had elected him its fourth president. He had received a salary increase, and Farish had said that he believed Pratt could "do some good on the Gulf Coast." The Gulf Coast area, however, offered

TABLE 5

ANNUAL NET CRUDE OIL PRODUCTION, PRICE, AND VALUE
HUMBLE OIL & REFINING COMPANY
1917–1930

Year	*Net Production in Barrels*	*Average Price per Barrel*	*Value*
1917	3,200,086	$1.083	$ 3,467,235
1918	4,292,172	1.826	7,837,567
1919	6,039,188	1.384	8,358,806
1920	7,825,903	2.750	21,521,233
1921	12,291,081	1.319	16,215,012
1922	11,199,269	1.378	15,433,689
1923	17,027,413	1.172	19,956,128
1924	15,851,268	1.555	24,644,126
1925	18,029,298	1.668	30,067,360
1926	13,707,388	1.836	25,167,749
1927	13,250,211	1.226	16,242,191
1928	15,501,996	.938	14,541,897
1929	23,450,569	1.145	26,862,012
1930	26,214,456	1.059	27,760,042

Source: Records of Humble Oil & Refining Company.

serious obstacles to a geologist. Most of the fields that could be located from surface indications had been discovered; the use of subsurface geology and core drilling was just getting under way.[28] The accumulating knowledge of petroleum geology, however, was soon to be tested in other areas.

During the middle years of the 1920s Humble spread out in several new districts, increasingly applied new methods of exploration with success, and continued to be confronted with marked variations in production as well as in prices. Although the company strove vigorously to develop production in other districts, its important new reserve acquisitions during several years following 1921 were chiefly in the fault-line area of east central Texas. It was at this time that geology became an effective part of the production effort, moving into central position in the search for oil-bearing structures.

Late in 1921 the Humble geologists were able to test their knowledge in a new field. Although Texas' first real oil field had been discovered at Corsicana in east central Texas a quarter-century earlier, nothing else had been found in that general area for many years, and it was regarded as the oilmen's graveyard of dead hopes. Early in the 1920s, however, east central Texas began to show increased activity. In 1920 Colonel A. E. Humphreys, with his geologist F. Julius Fohs, leased a block at Mexia in Limestone County, where Alexander Deussen of the United States Geological Survey had noted a fault in 1914 but a later geologist of the Survey had indicated an anticline. By March, 1921, Humphreys and Fohs had a flowing well. As well followed well in the late summer of 1921, acreage began to sell at an average of $1,000, and by early August the boom was on.[29]

For some time Humble remained unimpressed. Pratt knew of the fault but did not recognize its significance at first; neither, apparently, did Deussen, who was now with a company in Texas. Pratt continued for a time to believe that the Humphreys-Fohs pack was "following a cold trail." In April, 1921, he wrote: "We do not consider this well or this District as particularly significant. . . . We are watching it and expect to take care of the situation if we feel any investments are warranted." He brought Dwight J. Edson, a young Dartmouth geologist, from Ranger to study the geology of the area.

For several months Pratt and Edson watched drilling operations, noting well depths and examining the cuttings and returns which E. M. (Gene) Peeples, a geologic scout, collected. Alva C. Ellisor, Humble's micropaleontologist, identified the formations from which the samples came. Production in this area, as it proved, came from the Cretaceous rocks of the Mesozoic age. These were rocks of about the same age as those which constituted the producing formation in the tremendously prolific Mexican fields and have proved to be the most important sources of American petroleum. The producing sand was the Woodbine, from which production had been obtained in southern Arkansas and northern Louisiana. On the basis of the assembled data, Edson used his talent for subsurface work to draw a series of maps showing the depths of the formations in the various wells. From these observations and analyses Pratt and Humble's geologic staff concluded that a fault, not an anticline, had trapped the oil and that the productive Woodbine sand lay principally to the west of the area already proved.

On Pratt's recommendations Humble at the end of August, 1921, began active bidding for leases. Farish scraped together what money he could, and his company got its first leases almost simultaneously with the coming-in of the Desenberg gusher, the best to date, a mile west of the first Mexia well. By September 19 Humble had reputedly spent $400,000 for leases, ranking next to Magnolia among buyers. It paid over $2,000 per acre for some, but it hedged by buying others outside its preferred western area for as little as $100.

Pratt, having taken time to collect evidence and to make up his mind, now had complete confidence in the new field and pushed his company's activity. A leading oil journal stated, "Just what direction the pool will go is only guess-work at this time, as it can go in most any direction, with the north, northeast and south locations said to have the best chance"; Pratt, however, believed in the west, a confidence supported not only by the Desenberg and a later Nussbaum gusher but by the indications of subsurface geology. He spent all the money he had and wanted more. When he appealed to Farish, who was then in New York, for half a million to purchase a hundred acres offsetting the Desenberg, he was not discouraged by an emphatic "No!" He harried Farish by telephone and finally gained permission to take half the lease. Gulf, Humble's keenest competitor, took the other half.

Humble's purchases and activity in Mexia justified the decisions of the geologists. Because of its increased production in this field, Humble for a few days early in 1922 was said to be next to the largest producer of crude oil in the United States, surpassed only by California Standard. Between 1921 and 1931 it produced nearly 5,500,000 barrels at Mexia, over 6 per cent of the field's total production, which was more than half again as much as its percentage of the acreage. At Mexia Humble's geology began to pay off.

Realization of the fact that a fault similar to that at Mexia existed at Powell, Navarro County, north and east of Mexia, led Humble to acquire over a thousand producing acres there even before oil was discovered in a Woodbine sand early in 1923 by another company.[30] Most of this acreage was obtained at low prices, and it included about one-third of the field's productive area. Out of 180 wells drilled at Powell by Humble only five failed to produce, a truly remarkable record. It is significant that at this time a Humble report from the field recognized the economic waste in close spacing: "If each well was given four, five, or six times the area that has been given, everyone would profit by the saving in development costs, and the amount of oil would be produced at less cost per barrel."

Powell became a prodigious commercial producer. According to Pratt, its daily maximum was probably the highest attained up to that time by any field in the United States, and Humble's share was about a third. Humble's production one day exceeded 154,000 barrels; officials attributed this remarkable accomplishment at Powell to the geologists.

Yet the period of flush production was brief. A few excerpts from the company's daily reports from Powell in 1923 illustrate what was happening: June 27, "Our Blumrosen [number] one should be in tonight. . . . We are faced with tremendous flush production"; June 29, "Our Blumrosen number one doing about ten thousand"; July 3, ". . . the eleven wells . . . completed at Powell have a daily production of 56,000 barrels, with 9,000 barrels pinched in"; September 7, "It is my judgment, from the way wells are coming in at Powell yesterday and today, that the gas pressure is pretty well off the pool, and that we will not have a large flowing production for any great length of time . . . . All our previous estimates as to amount of flush production were too high. We have thirty-three completed producing wells today that are pro-

A FAULT TYPE OF TRAP, SIMILAR TO THAT AT THE POWELL FIELD

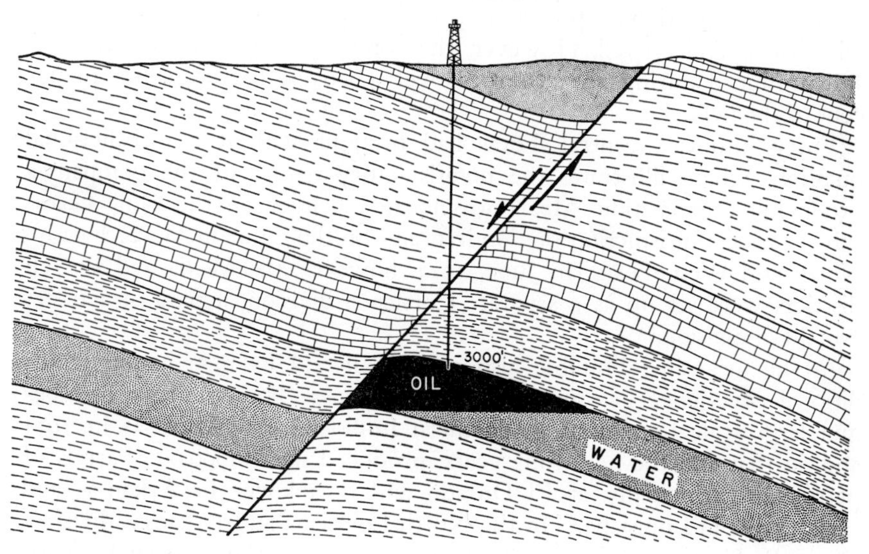

As a result of movement along the fault, a formation permeable to oil abuts one impermeable to oil.

ducing at the rate of about 42,000 barrels. Of this number some are being put to pumping and some are being cleaned out preparatory to pumping"; November 16, "We have thoroughly canvassed situation at Powell and feel that the production has definitely passed peak, rapidly declining. . . . Our production Monday all wells open 120,000 barrels, today 103,000 barrels with four new completions. This is indicative of slump in pool." The course of what was for a short time the most productive oil field in the United States, as of other fields at the time, thus led to early pumping.

In the whole east central Texas area the intense competition, the number of "tight" wells on which it was difficult to get information, and the confused land titles created unusual difficulties for scouts, landmen, and title men, but Wortham, another fault-line field, in Freestone and Limestone counties, added some special problems of its own. The curing of titles on small east central Texas plots was made difficult by the fact that the courthouse at Fairfield, with all the land records, had burned. Humble had to substitute for the lost records such information as that of "Old Man Stubbs," who knew the community intimately, including who had married and who was related to whom. The company had to content itself with limitation titles based on undisputed occupancy. Competitive bidding in this field also forced the scout-landman to jump his bonus offer from $200 per acre to $500.

Humble's managers were disappointed with both their company's total and proportionate production in the Wortham field, as compared with Mexia and Powell. However, the company drilled numerous wells and produced during 1925 to 1930 over 4,000,000 barrels, some 10 per cent of the field.

Entry into east central Texas had brought with it a jurisdictional question, which illustrates the unsatisfactory nature of the company's producing organization. Mexia was located neither on the Gulf Coast, subject to the jurisdiction of Fondren and Sterling, nor in W. S. Farish's North and West Texas. In June, 1923, however, the Mexia and Powell districts were set up as a separate Corsicana division, a part of Farish's Northern division.[31]

In the meantime Humble also gained oil and its men acquired additional experience in a number of other areas. The company had begun large-scale operations in northern Louisiana and Arkansas in 1921 and, in that and the next four years, produced over 7,000,000 barrels of petroleum, principally at El Dorado and Smackover in Arkansas and Haynesville in Louisiana.[32] In the North Louisiana and Arkansas division, David B. Harris and Eugene Holman gained experience in supervisory capacities. However, isolation, lack of adequate transportation facilities, high operating costs, and the viscous character of the crude and its consequent low price made this area a losing proposition.

Humble also became active in Southwest Texas,[33] expanding its geologic knowledge and discovering two new fields and two new oil sands in older fields. The company began in 1922 with a lease on about 800,000 acres of the King Ranch, an early evidence of block-leasing by Humble; but when investigation revealed little of interest Humble dropped the lease. The next year it drilled in the Kingsville field in Kleberg County but failed to get commercial production.[34] Humble in 1923 investigated the possibility of investing in the Luling field, but in Farish's judgment the price asked was too high—the property offered was purchased by Magnolia. During the following year, however, Luling produced over 10,000,000 barrels,[35] and in the spring of 1925 Humble began operations in that field and expanded into others.

Humble's operations in Southwest Texas throughout those years were, however, generally unsatisfactory. Most of the wells drilled were dry holes; those that were productive were either small or short-lived. The greatest disappointment in this area was at Piedras Pintas in Duval County. Though Humble began drilling here late in 1922, it did not strike oil until three years later. The well came in with such high original production that Humble anticipated an output of millions of barrels of high-gravity crude; but after flowing heavily for a short time the discovery well declined, went on the pump, and within a year ceased to produce.[36] Humble acquired no production to speak of during its early years in Southwest Texas; even in 1925 the region contributed to the company's output less than a third of a million barrels and after that its contribution fell off.

In the fields in West Texas and the Panhandle, where after the discoveries in the fault-line area the state's principal oil development took place, Humble played a minor role. In the first years of the decade it had drilled two gas wells and a dry hole in the Panhandle—in Carson and Oldham counties. Pratt believed that this region of magnificent distances would probably be one of gas wells and small oil wells which, with prices as low as in 1923, would not be profitable. The Panhandle's long distance from markets also made it unattractive, and, even when some flowing wells came in and production rose, Humble continued to show little interest. In 1926 Farish was still opposed to engaging in intensive competition for acreage or production in that area.[37] A sudden increase in its output in the early summer, however, led to the appointment of David Frame as superintendent at Amarillo of a new Panhandle division and the undertaking of some development in the area.[38] But Humble never became a large producer in that region, which was later to become important for its oil and, especially, gas reserves and production.

Although Humble started exploring in West Texas in 1922 and had a pipeline to the area by 1926, it did not achieve an appreciable output until 1927. Since the flow from wells in West Texas was often too small to be profitable, Humble's geologists sought structures that would promise adequate production. In the meantime Gulf leased a large portion of four counties. Humble acquired properties in Howard and Coke counties and in the Yates and Hendricks fields of Pecos and Winkler counties, but, having concentrated most of its energies on other areas, it was left behind in the early race for prospective oil lands in West Texas.[39]

Humble was more successful in some of its older divisions. In North Texas it discovered the Masters, or Woodson, field[40] and the small Stover field, which, together with older developments in the area, from 1921 to 1927 produced over 10,000,000 barrels. On the old Gulf Coast during the same years, largely in West Columbia, Goose Creek, and Hull, Humble's production was 27,000,000. Of the newer Gulf Coast fields, the most important was Orange (or Terry), but its best well, owned by Humble, produced 400,000 barrels in twenty-six days and then sanded up. Pierce Junction, near Houston, proved relatively unproductive, as did Blue Ridge in Fort Bend County.[41]

Humble's worst disappointment after Ranger was experienced in east central Texas, the region of its earlier triumphs. Following the fault line northward, the producing organization had decided that a field equal to Powell and worth an estimated $75,000,000 to $80,000,000 probably lay to the northeast in Kaufman County. Humble leased, at a "good stiff price," 11,000 acres in its Mabank block and bought in fee the site for a tank farm. The whole Board of Directors gathered in April, 1925, for the bringing-in of the test well—a million-dollar dry hole. A letter sent at this time to a Humble official by an old-time producer, who had little regard for the new ways, compared a certain young geologist to a pointer, sent to hunt quail, which turned out to have a nose for "chasin butterflies and chippy bur-rds"; the writer asked if the geologist, "or one of his kind," was responsible for Humble's "getting hung" with the "million dollar lemon."[42] This venture pointed up the fact that, while the geologist could find a structure favorable to the accumulation of oil, only the bit could tell for sure whether oil had migrated to and been trapped in that structure. Thirty years later, however, Humble had some production there: four small fields had been discovered, producing partly from the Woodbine formation and lying partly in Humble's Mabank block. During the year following Humble's disappointment at Mabank, its east central Texas production fell off by 5,000,000 barrels.

In the years 1921 to 1925 the fault line had played a dominant part in Humble's development: its output of almost 28,000,000 barrels in the three years, 1923–1925, exceeded that of all Humble's fields in other regions for the same period. By 1925, with a production of over 18,000,000 barrels, Humble was the second largest producer east of the Rockies and the largest producer in Texas,[43] a standing which it owed to the fault-line area. The fields of this region were profitable in themselves, having by 1923 brought the Production Department out of the red; they also laid the foundation for future profits by strengthening the position of the Geologic, Lease and Scouting Department. However, as in other new fields in this period, after rapid development the annual production in the fault-line region soon declined.

Although during the years from 1919 through 1926 Humble's Production Department expanded greatly, in the last of those years the company found itself in a difficult situation. Humble reached the peak of its reserves for the period in 1923, of production in 1925, and of profits also in 1925. At the beginning of 1926 a scarcity of crude oil was threatened. Large though Humble's production had been since 1923, it had never been sufficient to supply the company's regular needs; and in later years there appeared to be no prospect in the near future of supplying any larger share of Humble's own requirements and those of its largest customers. During 1925 east central Texas production had fallen off nearly two-thirds; such production as it achieved elsewhere was not of the proportions or character to promise much for the future. Humble, moreover, was losing position in Texas production; it fell to second place in 1926 and to fourth in the next year.

The company's first reaction to its weakening position in production was to increase its efforts to find oil and to build up reserves and production. The expenditures of the Geologic, Lease and Scouting Department, exclusive of dry hole costs, were increased from $9,400,000 in 1925 to $14,400,000 in 1926; the cost of lease acreage purchased rose from $8,000,000 to $11,500,000. In 1926 the number of wildcats drilled was increased by a third. The result of these increased expenditures could normally, however, not be realized for several years. Humble's production fell from 18,000,000 barrels in 1925 to 13,700,000 in 1926. Despite a slight increase in the average price per barrel in the latter year, the Production Department's profits fell about a third.

FORESHADOWING NEW TECHNIQUES

Yet, there was some reason for optimism. In 1926 a Humble exploration crew discovered a salt dome by using a new geophysical instrument. And in the same year Humble quite experimentally began to attack drilling and production problems in new ways which indicated a developing interest in gas as a factor in oil recovery. These developments mark a turning point in Humble's search for and production of oil.

Geophysics as an aid in finding geologic formations favorable to trapping oil had been introduced experimentally in Texas in 1922. In that year the Rycade Oil Corporation, a subsidiary of Amerada managed by E. L. DeGolyer, began to experiment with a torsion balance brought from Europe. This apparatus was used for measuring the pull of gravity in the hope that it would be useful in locating salt domes and other formations having a density differing from that of surrounding rocks. Late in the same year the Roxana Petroleum Corporation, a Shell subsidiary, also began torsion-balance operations. In March, 1924, the Marland Oil Company, operating through the Alcorn Oil Company, introduced to the Gulf Coast another type of instrument, the refraction seismograph. This instrument was expected to help determine the depth and character of formations by recording the speed and quality of shock waves sent through them and refracted to the surface. Two or three months later the Gulf Production Company began to use both a seismograph and a torsion balance on the Gulf Coast.[44]

Pratt was skeptical at first of the practical utility of those instruments, although he had been impressed as early as 1920 by a discussion by Dr. Udden of seismic methods. In 1922 and 1923 Humble was so successful in acquiring production along the fault line through the use of subsurface geology—it had been more successful in the use of surface and subsurface geology than any other company in Texas—that there was no immediate need to try new geophysical methods of dubious usefulness. Besides, Baron Mintrop of Germany, who held the patents on the one seismograph being used in the oil industry and controlled the only trained crews, signed exclusive contracts with the Gulf and Marland companies. DeGolyer was building a seismograph under an American patent.

After watching developments for a time Pratt became convinced that Humble could not safely neglect geophysics. Possibly he was impressed by the fact that men like DeGolyer, Donald C. Barton, and Sidney Powers of Amerada and L. P. Garrett of Gulf were convinced of the value of geophysics even though at variance as to methods; that Gulf, Humble's principal rival in Texas production, had recently adopted both torsion balance and seismograph may have been decisive. Pratt concluded that Humble should investigate geophysical methods seriously but should proceed experimentally. He recommended that Humble build its own seismograph and develop its own geophysical staff, including field crews; this recommendation was adopted by the Board of Directors.

In June, 1924, work in geophysics was started within the Geologic, Lease and Scouting Department and in July David P. Carlton was put in charge. Some weeks later a Rycade torsion-balance survey furnished the first proof of the practical utility of geophysics by discovering indications of a salt dome in the Nash area.[45] A shop was set up within Humble's new geophysical division to design and construct suitable instruments, and an experienced physicist from the Baytown refinery was put in charge. When he proved a better theoretical than practical scientist and resigned, his assistant, O. H. Truman, was given charge of the shop. Truman, who had degrees in physics and mathematics and had had experience in a bicycle repair shop and in an astronomical observatory, in a short time succeeded in building a seismograph. In April, 1925, Humble sent its first seismograph crew into the field. In the meantime Humble had ordered torsion balances from Hungary and had sent a professor from The University of Texas abroad to study the use and interpretation of torsion-balance data.

A period of research, development, and exploration ensued; the number of instruments was increased and more crews were sent out to the fields. In the first ten months of 1926 Humble spent over half a million dollars on geophysical work. It made its first geophysical discovery on June 1, 1926, when a refraction crew, under Edgar S. (Eddie) Sherar, found the Moss Bluff salt dome in Liberty County, Texas.[46] The preparatory work of the company in this period had thus proved its usefulness, and it was to lead to rich rewards in later years.

In the spring of the same year the Northern division, utilizing the most recent knowledge of the function of gas in oil recovery, began to pump gas under pressure into the oil sand on one of its leases at Powell in an attempt to slow up the decline in production; the results appeared so satisfactory that the method was applied to other fields.[47] Engineer Kent was in charge of this work and was giving special attention by this time to the use of gas in the restoration of reservoir pressure. Another significant new departure was the research on drilling mud undertaken by the research staff of the Refining Department.

Humble was recognized as better equipped than many producing companies in its area, but it was clearly not yet a leader in applying new ideas in petroleum technology. It was not so advanced as John R. Suman's Rio Bravo, E. L. DeGolyer's Amerada, the Pure Oil Company, the Marland Oil Company, and, among the majors, The Texas Company and the Gulf Production Company. Humble had had an engineering department since 1920, but the engineers had been concerned mostly with such activities as surveying, building tanks, and constructing salt-water disposal plants.[48]

The Production Department, in contrast with the Geologic, Lease and Scouting Department, had no one capable of making a systematic and comprehensive effort to improve drilling and production techniques. Able as its managers were, they were limited by their experience. Before the department could make advances comparable to those being made in exploration and refining, a change in both attitudes and personnel was necessary. But the experiments in 1926 were at least a beginning in the right direction.

The year 1926 marks a turning point in Humble's exploration and production methods. A basic factor in bringing about this change was unsatisfactory production in recent years. Serious problems were also met in crude oil purchasing, as Chapter 8 will show. In that year two of the company's most influential executives concerned with production—President Farish and Director Pratt of the Geologic, Lease and Scouting Department—became convinced that, in order to assure Humble of an adequate supply of crude at a cost that gave some certainty of profits, some changes were necessary, not only in the company's own operations but in the entire industry's. Humble's experimenting in 1926 with new techniques in oil finding and production foreshadowed the direction in which the company was to progress.

Fundamental changes in Humble's production policies and operations followed in the next few years. These significant developments will be dealt with after the company's work in transportation, crude oil purchasing, refining, and sales has been considered.

Chapter 7

BUILDING AND OPERATING A PIPELINE SYSTEM, 1919-1930

To ACQUIRE efficient and relatively low-cost transportation became a necessity for Humble when in 1919 it undertook to furnish oil in vast quantities to Standard Oil Company (New Jersey). Accordingly, on March 3, 1919, Humble Oil & Refining Company organized a pipeline subsidiary under the amended charter of the Southern Pipe Line Company. The parent company held all the shares of the new Humble Pipe Line Company and provided eight of its first nine directors, including the president, R. S. Sterling.

Building a pipeline system necessitated planning in what was for the Humble directors a new area of investment and operations. Men could be hired to operate the lines, but the directors had to assume responsibility for determining where and when to make the heavy capital expenditures that the construction of pipelines required. Because of the commonly short period of high production in individual fields under the prevailing system of competitive drilling, the risk involved in building pipelines was considered high. In 1919, however, Humble needed outlets for its oil from two areas where it was developing large operations, areas that the directors believed would prove productive for many years. As for other lines to be built later, the directors would have to consider needs and possibilities as they arose. To guard against loss from the early exhaustion of production in fields or regions to which lines were built, Humble, like other pipeline companies at the time, would seek to minimize the risk by maintaining pipeline rates so high as to recover the capital investment in only a few years. So long as rates could be kept high enough to make possible rapid depreciation—although much lower than railroad charges—lines could be built to furnish transportation even from fields far from refineries or shipping points on tidewater.

In its first six years Humble Pipe Line Company built a network of lines between the Gulf and north central Texas. In 1925–1930 it followed the expanding oil industry into West and Southwest Texas and the Panhandle, virtually completing the system of lines which, with minor changes and additions, was to serve Humble until 1950. While building this system, Humble Pipe Line Company also gathered and stored increasing amounts of crude oil to be carried to refineries and to shipping points on the Gulf.[1]

BUILDING FROM NORTH CENTRAL TEXAS TO THE GULF, 1919–1924

Before Humble Pipe Line Company could begin to build, it had to acquire an operating organization. Humble Oil & Refining Company was not altogether without pipeline experience, but its few miles of lines required no organization capable of constructing and operating pipelines on so large a scale as was planned early in 1919.

For the top operating management of the pipeline company Humble drew principally on Standard Oil Company of Louisiana and, thus, on the long and successful pipeline experience of Standard Oil Company (New Jersey). James A. Anderson was hired as the ninth director and vice-president and general manager, and Ralph V. Hanrahan as general superintendent. Other men also came from Louisiana Standard, several to have long careers with Humble in important executive or supervisory posts and one who was to leave in 1920 to supervise the building of the Andian pipeline of a Jersey Standard affiliate in Colombia. Construction Engineer Fred F. Mellott came from Tide Water in Pennsylvania.

James Anderson, who came of a Scottish family that had settled in Maryland in the seventeenth century, was an engineer with many years of experience on Standard Oil pipelines. Three years after beginning with the old Buckeye Pipe Line Company in Ohio in 1906, he had joined the new Standard Oil Company of Louisiana. There he had worked on pipeline construction and had become superintendent in charge of the purchasing, gathering, and transporting of crude oil.[2]

Ralph Hanrahan, the new Humble superintendent of pipeline construction, was a dark-haired, stocky young man of Irish descent who, though only thirty-three years of age, already had nearly eighteen years of pipeline experience. Born in the old producing and pipeline center of Olean, New York, Hanrahan had begun his career in 1901 with the Indiana Pipe Line Company, an affiliate of Jersey Standard. He had later worked for other Standard Oil pipeline companies in Ohio and Pennsylvania, and in 1909 he had joined the pipeline department of the Standard Oil Company of Louisiana.[3]

Two urgent tasks of construction faced the managers of Humble Pipe Line Company in 1919. The booming Ranger area needed an outlet for its crude to the Gulf, where Jersey Standard tankers would take virtually any amount of oil that could be brought to tidewater. Texas City was chosen as the tanker loading terminal on the Gulf; pipeline right-of-way to Ranger was acquired from an affiliate of the Prairie Oil & Gas Company (a large Mid-Continent corporation which had decided to abandon a project for a pipeline to Galveston);[4] and Comyn was selected as the gathering point for Ranger crude. Construction to the coast over the newly acquired right-of-way began. At the same time, since Humble then anticipated that its projected refinery would depend principally on crude from West Columbia on the Gulf Coast, construction was also started from that field to the refinery site at Baytown. The point of intersection of the two main lines was at Webster, southeast of Houston, which was selected as a tank-farm site convenient to the projected refinery and to tankers at Texas City.

General Superintendent Hanrahan and Dan T. Freel, W. T. Cushing, M. M. Stuckey, and others in charge of construction had to contend with the usual problems of pipeline builders in a hurry. The difficulties normally arising from the lack of sufficient men and materials in the right places were accentuated by an unusually wet season. When the ditching contractor quit out of disgust with the weather, the Humble pipeliners had to assume the entire responsibility for construction. On the West Columbia line the lack of roads and the reddish-brown gumbo of the Brazos River flood plains necessitated the use of yokes of oxen to move pipe and heavy equipment. The Ranger area supplied its own rain and mud,[5] and the long trunk line under construction from Comyn to Webster had to cross the flood waters of four rivers.

Construction in those days called for a great deal of heavy work. Although machinery for digging and pipelaying had been in use for many years, oil companies owned comparatively little such equipment, probably because investment in specialized machines for only occasional use tied up too much capital. Pick-and-shovel work was still predominant in the digging of pipeline ditches, and crews of men with hand tongs screwed and tightened pipe joints.

Although the Humble pipeliners used mostly old and tried techniques, they employed some advanced methods and new equipment. Ditching and pipelaying machines helped to speed the work on the main line. Multicylinder, vertical Diesels burning crude oil, rather than the horizontal type of Diesel then generally used on pipelines, were installed in the six pump stations on the main line from Comyn to Texas City; these 165-horsepower engines seem to have been a Humble "first." They drove plunger pumps, the main-line stations each having two working pumps and a stand-by for periods of repair.

The ability of the construction superintendent and the supervisors to overcome construction problems was no more important than the skill they had to display in dealing with thousands of migratory pipeline laborers. The "typical pipeliner" was a special breed of man, like the lumberjack of the northern forests and the cowboy of the western plains. His employment fluctuated with the rate of pipeline construction and the seasons; to obtain work he must travel far and frequently. In consequence, he was restless and reckless and required particularly expert direction and supervision. But, while the pipeliner was proud of his toughness of speech and behavior, he also took pride in group solidarity. The skilled superintendent or foreman brought out this quality to the full. Most of the workers on Humble's pipeline construction in 1919 and 1920 were Irishmen from the East. Hanrahan, although American-born, had a background that helped him to appreciate and make the best use of their qualities in the tradition of a long line of Irish and Irish-American pipeline superintendents who had worked successfully for Standard Oil—including the pipeline executive, Daniel O'Day, whose sister had married Ralph Hanrahan's uncle. Hanrahan's assistants were also able to win and hold the respect of the men. Among them was "Jap" Neath, a twenty-three-year-old construction foreman of Welsh descent who before joining Humble in 1918 had worked for several years in Oklahoma with an affiliate of The Texas Company and in Texas with Gulf.

The pipeliners usually slept in tents—camp being moved as construction progressed—and frequently had to walk two or three miles to and from a ten-hour day's work wielding pick and shovel, handling heavy joints of pipe, or straining on pipe tongs. The wages varied with the job and the skills required. The ordinary construction laborer received 40 cents an hour for a ten-hour day. The stabber, the pipeline aristocrat who handled the exacting task of steering the pipe for coupling and acted as "straw boss," received $5.50 per day; the tong men of the make-up gang, who screwed the joints in place, $4.50. The men were known as prodigious eaters, but they were well fed in company mess tents at a charge of 75 cents a day. While the lives of most pipeliners consisted of a succession of short, hard, and rough jobs, promotion was a definite possibility for steady men with qualities of leadership.

Despite many difficulties, within a few months oil was flowing through the new lines. By July, 1919, the pipe from West Columbia stretched the 42 miles to Webster Station, and by early November crude was flowing from the Webster tank farm to the new dock and waiting tankers at Texas City. By July of the same year, gathering lines in the Comyn area "made connection" with a number of wells, relieving the congested condition for producers who had previously depended on earthen tanks to receive their oil. Late in January, 1920, crude began to travel through the 290 miles of pipe from Comyn to the coast.[6] Six months later the pipeline men were pumping Ranger oil from Webster to the Baytown refinery.

Within about a year after its organization, Humble Pipe Line had thus established what was to be for five years the essential outline of its system. Before the end of 1920 it was operating nearly 450 miles of eight-inch trunk line, 8 major pumping stations, and 245 miles of gathering lines.

The completion of the two trunk lines early in 1920 was followed by promotions. All the parent company directors withdrew from the pipeline company's board. Anderson was elected president of Humble Pipe Line Company, a position he held only until his election to the board of Humble Oil & Refining Company early the next year, when W. M. Cleaves of Humble's Legal Department succeeded to the presidency of the subsidiary. Hanrahan became director, vice-president, and general manager in 1920, and other men moved up to new positions.

These promotions of 1920 were indeed to be merely the first of many for men who worked on the construction of these early lines. J. A. Neath was to become general superintendent, a member of the board in 1925, vice-president in 1928—and eventually chairman of the board of Humble Oil & Refining Company. A. E. Pecore, who joined the pipeline company as a draftsman in 1919, later became chief engineer, general superintendent, vice-president, and president. On December 31, 1948, the superintendents of four out of five pipeline divisions were men who had worked on early construction; the fifth had joined the company in 1921.

As lines were completed, the pipeline organization began the work of connecting with producing leases and moving the oil produced or purchased by Humble. Both the parent and the pipeline company needed more oil than Humble's own increasing production, the former to supply the requirements of its own refineries and those of Jersey Standard and other customers and the latter to maintain a regular flow sufficient to fill its lines and thus to render operations most economical and profitable.

To obtain enough oil was not easy. The producers, to be sure, were dependent on pipelines as an outlet for their oil, but in the quest for crude the youthful Humble had to pit itself against such seasoned purchasers and pipeline veterans as Prairie, Texas, Gulf, and Magnolia. In the early 1920s, especially, the growing demand for oil products and a widespread fear of a shortage of oil resulted in a rush for connections with new fields and wells like those earlier scrambles for oil as the American petroleum industry had spread across the continent.

The policy of Humble Pipe Line Company was to build rapidly, get to a new field early in order to make connections with as many wells as possible, and achieve and maintain good relations with producers. This policy did not differ from that of other intelligent and successful pipeline concerns except, perhaps, that Humble's newness in the business forced its men to display unusual energy and co-operation with producers. An older pipeline company, for example, could refuse to take oil from a lease several miles from its lines, but Humble pipeliners would build a gathering line to the lease at heavy cost. The problems of the pipeline company were complicated by the fact that most fields flourished only briefly and then rapidly declined. If the lines were to be kept full, customers supplied, and the friendship of producers retained, oil had to be taken both in flush periods, when expensive new lines and storage had to be built, and in decline, when less capacity was required and the proportionate costs of operations were greater.

Throughout the 1920s the primary functions of Humble Pipe Line Company, broadly stated, were two: to build such additions to its lines as were necessary in order to obtain sufficient supplies of crude; and then to move the increasing varieties and grades of crude efficiently and economically through its system. For a few months early in its history Humble Pipe Line was also in charge of crude oil purchasing, but in July, 1919, probably because of the possible complications inherent in the Railroad Commission's jurisdiction over pipeline companies, Humble Oil & Refining Company took over purchasing. The pipeline company thereafter functioned only as a gatherer and transporter.

In the years 1920 through 1924 Humble Pipe Line Company added to its network of gathering lines, expanded storage facilities at existing stations and tank farms, and increased trunk-line capacity by building parallel lines and loops. It also constructed comparatively short branch lines to new fields in which Humble Oil & Refining Company had large production or purchasing, or both.

The location of new trunk lines and principal gathering lines was decided from time to time by directors of the two Humble companies according to current and anticipated needs. Careful planning was necessary in order to guard against overbuilding or underbuilding in any area and also to keep the whole system in balance. A key factor in all such decisions was information about the geology of newly proved fields and of possible producing regions not yet proved. Another decisive consideration was the anticipated demand for crude oil, particularly by Humble's large customer, Jersey Standard, concerning whose needs Farish was in close communication with President Teagle. Farish, Pratt, Anderson, and Hanrahan were the major pipeline planners during the 1920s, subject, in the case of large expenditures, to action by the Board of Directors of Humble Oil & Refining Company.

Gathering lines, tank farms, stations, branch lines, and trunk-line expansion were all of vital importance, but an account of their growth can easily become a wearisome catalogue of lengths, dimensions, and capacities. The statistics of pipeline construction are consequently presented in Appendix II, Table XI. References to a few particularly interesting or significant examples of such construction will, nevertheless, illustrate the general characteristics of the development during the early 1920s.

The growth of production in the coastal Hull and Pierce Junction fields called for the first new extension by Humble. In the summer of 1920, another extremely wet season, the pipeline men built twenty miles of eight-inch pipe from Hull through the swampy bottoms of the Trinity River near Dayton. When this line was added to one extending from Dayton to Goose Creek, purchased from The Texas Company, the crude from Hull could flow to Baytown. Construction of a twenty-mile, eight-inch line the following year linked the Pierce Junction field to Webster.[7]

The development of production in east central Texas along the Mexia-Powell fault line resulted in the building of one of the pipeline's most significant extensions of the decade. Humble was not only a large producer in this area but also a large purchaser, and its pipeline company was the first to build to Mexia, in which oil had been discovered in 1921. By early 1922 the company was operating about seventy miles of eight-inch pipe, in January running its first crude from Mexia via Groesbeck to Hearne, a main-line pump station.[8] Even before Humble drilled its first well in Powell in September, 1923, Humble Pipe had rushed an extension to that field. When Wortham, also a fault-line field, came into production late in 1924, the pipeline men constructed still another gathering system and enlarged their trunk-line facilities.

As production in 1923 and 1924 declined in east central Texas, new discoveries took place in North Texas—in Wichita, Archer, and Wilbarger counties. Humble Pipe Line Company in the summer of 1924 added 110 miles to its Ranger gathering system, extending northward to the Vernon pool in Wilbarger County.

When a gathering line was extended to a field where Humble wanted to become a heavy purchaser but that might turn out to be so large that trunk-line capacity would not be adequate, two alternatives faced the company: to add to the trunk line or to build storage for what would probably be a temporary surplus. In choosing between a large tank-building program or increased pipeline capacity, several considerations had to be weighed. Tanks would provide an outlet for the producer's oil and, when the field declined, furnish oil on which to draw in order to run pipes for a time to near capacity. In some areas Humble chose to build tanks to provide for temporary surpluses, as in 1923 at Powell, where in a short time it built eighty-one tanks with a capacity of 5,500,000 barrels. If oil was needed to meet current demand, pipeline capacity would have to be extended. If, however, the oil was not currently needed, the advantage of gaining immediate revenue from its transportation had to be balanced against the risk of overexpanding the pipeline. The storing of crude oil, furthermore, was expensive and speculative for the Crude Oil Department. The price of crude, its scarcity or abundance, the current demand, and the estimated future of the field and regions beyond were consequently telling factors in the decision to build or not build a pipeline.

Whether the decision was for increased storage or greater pipeline capacity, the pipeline construction men had to move rapidly and use all their ingenuity. When material for regular steel storage was unavailable and time for obtaining it was insufficient, as at West Columbia in 1919, earthen storage could be hastily provided by mules and scrapers.[9] The use of such storage, however, was discontinued as soon as possible because it was wasteful—it was soon forbidden under state regulation. Makeshift machinery, such as old engines, was sometimes used until more satisfactory equipment was available. Pipeliners, if need be, would work all night, as when Superintendent MacMahon's men started work at 7 P.M. on a four-mile pipeline and loading rack and had both ready for use the next day.

Pipeline builders, including Humble men, occasionally took daring direct action. For instance, "borrowing" a competitor's pipe from a railroad siding, although frowned upon by top management, is known to have been resorted to in an emergency, the pipe being replaced as soon as an expected consignment arrived. Superintendents and foremen with reputations to make and schedules to meet got what they needed wherever they could.

Humble pipeline men demonstrated imaginative helpfulness in working closely with producers. Since water was scarce in some of the areas where they built, they were quick to grasp the possibility of carrying that scarce commodity to a lease in return for the privilege of running the oil it produced. The pipeliners also pitched in to help in case of a blowout or other emergency. They would work night and day to connect with a lease so that oil would not be drained underground by more fortunate neighbors with storage tanks or connections with a rival pipeline. Humble Pipe Line Company thus achieved a reputation for bringing transportation and a market to the independent producer, and profited thereby through increasing its share of the coveted crude.[10] The success of the Humble pipelines was, of course, closely connected with Humble Oil & Refining Company's crude oil purchasing (Chapter 8).

By the end of 1924 Humble Pipe Line Company was operating almost 2,000 miles of line. Trunk mileage had not quite doubled since 1920, but gathering lines had increased more than fourfold. The pipeline company's net investment in fixed assets exceeded that of Humble Oil & Refining Company's investment in refining and was not much less than the parent company's investment in production. By 1924 Humble was delivering through its trunk line 79,000 barrels daily, or more than one-fifth of the total crude production of Texas.

EXPANSION THROUGHOUT TEXAS, 1925–1930

Extensive as Humble Pipe Line Company's construction was in the years 1919–1924, it was to be even greater in the next six years. At the end of 1924 the company entered its greatest construction period; it not only built over 4,000 miles of new line but also elaborated the basic pattern of its trunk system by extending its lines to the many new and remote Texas fields. In that period it also made significant changes in construction policies and methods. Hanrahan as president from 1925, Neath as general superintendent, and Stevenson as chief engineer had top responsibility in those years.

The first major extension of the pipeline system was run from Comyn to Kemper, in order to transport a large quantity of purchased crude from West Texas. In December, 1924, at the time of the decision to build, Humble had no production of its own in that area, but it had agreed to buy from the Reagan County Purchasing Company 20,000 barrels daily of Big Lake crude for a period of fifteen years. During 1925 and 1926 the pipeline men built two parallel lines to provide the extension of approximately 200 miles from Comyn to Kemper in West Texas, the first line being put into operation in April, 1925. In order to carry the increased flow, they also had to expand the trunk-line capacity from Comyn to the coast.[11] Until 1927 Humble had the only pipeline serving West Texas and was consequently in a strategic position to purchase oil from new discoveries in the area.

As new fields in West Texas came into production, lines to those fields fanned out from Kemper. In the autumn of 1926 Humble built to the oil fields of McCamey and Crane, a year later to the prolific new Yates field, and in 1928 to Big Springs. Also in that year it built an extension from Crane to Winkler, and in 1930 to the new Hobbs field in New Mexico.[12]

To carry the increasing volume of oil from West Texas soon became a problem. The trunk line from Comyn to Webster City already had a multiplicity of eight-inch, ten-inch, and twelve-inch pipes and loops; a further increase in its capacity of 100,000 barrels a day was impracticable. Moreover, a shorter route from Kemper to the Gulf was obviously desirable.

That shorter route was provided by a line that ran 345 miles from Kemper directly to Ingleside in Southwest Texas and that cut the cost of transportation by eliminating 130 miles of the distance West Texas oil had to travel to reach the Gulf. Ingleside was also the terminus of Humble's Southwest Texas system started in 1925. Although Piedras Pintas, the first field served, proved to be only a one-well field, the 125-mile line to Ingleside from Thompsonville in Jim Hogg County and Bruni in Webb nevertheless proved useful. By summer of 1926 the line was serving a number of fields in Southwest Texas, and as new fields were discovered other branches were built.[13]

New tanker-loading facilities on the Gulf were necessary to accommodate this new West-Southwest Texas system. In order to use tankers with a thirty-two-foot draft, Humble first planned to build sea loading facilities outside Corpus Christi Bay, but the state of Texas, apparently under pressure from certain business interests, obtained an injunction stopping it from carrying out this plan. Humble won the resulting litigation in a decision of the Supreme Court of the state. In the meantime it decided to build the terminal on Harbor Island, just inside the bay, in the expectation that the federal government would deepen the channel through the bar at the bay's entrance.[14] Located one mile from the Gulf, on a passage improved by dredging, the Harbor Island terminal eventually developed into an important oil shipping terminal.

In contrast with the early entrance of its pipelines into West Texas and Southwest Texas, Humble entered the Panhandle only after consideration of various alternatives. In the spring of 1926, when Panhandle production was increasing fast, President Farish opposed taking an active part. The Panhandle was a long distance from tidewater, and its oil possessed the characteristics, unattractive for pipeline transportation and refining, of high viscosity and high content of salt, paraffin, and sulphur. Panhandle oil moved like the proverbial molasses in January, corroded pipes and tanks, and was then little esteemed by refiners. By autumn Humble was planning to set up a 10,000-barrel refinery for the purpose of reducing the crude's viscosity by cracking so that the oil could be pumped through a pipeline. When experiments at the Baytown refinery indicated that about 10 per cent of casinghead gasoline mixed with the crude would similarly reduce its viscosity, the refinery project was abandoned.[15] The Marland Oil Company solved the problem by doubling the number of pump stations and using the exhaust from the station engines to heat the oil and thus render it more fluid.[16]

In December, 1926, the willingness of large producers to contract to sell a large quantity of Panhandle crude at satisfactory prices made Humble favorable to pipeline construction. The difficulty of financing such a large project and the uncertainty of finding a market for such a high-viscosity crude still delayed the decision. Within a few months, however, Jersey Standard, which was chronically fearful of a shortage of crude, encouraged Humble to undertake the project. Humble Pipe Line decided to build. Once the decision had been reached, the pipeline men moved fast. By May, 1927, the Panhandle trunk line was carrying crude the 321 miles from Burnett to the main line at Comyn.[17]

Other extensions of the pipeline system were built in 1929 and 1930. The Salt Flat field in Southwest Texas, discovered in 1928, was provided with an outlet by a 125-mile extension of the original West Columbia line to Luling. A line was also built from Refugio to Ingleside and extended to Pettus.

The increase in production in East Texas brought a new departure in 1930 which provided Humble's crude with an altogether different outlet, although one that had been under consideration since 1924. The occasion was the development of the Van field. Instead of tying this production into the old main line, a ninety-three-mile, ten-inch line was laid to the Louisiana boundary. There at Moore station it joined the pipeline of Standard Oil Company of Louisiana, which carried oil to the large Baton Rouge refinery.

A glance at the accompanying map will reveal certain advantageous features of the Humble pipeline system at the end of 1930. The system by then reached into all the oil-producing regions of Texas, and it had several market outlets. The principal outlets were two tanker-loading terminals on the Gulf, at Texas City and Ingleside, and two major refineries, Humble's at Baytown and Louisiana Standard's at Baton Rouge. Many smaller refineries, several owned by Humble but others by independent refiners, also provided outlets within Texas. This network of pipelines with its several major outlets enabled Humble to move large amounts of crude oil with a high degree of efficiency.

The process of building Humble's pipelines in the years 1925–1930 is of special interest for several reasons. In no similar period of time has Humble Pipe employed so many men on construction or laid so many miles of line. And labor was hard to obtain so far from employment centers. West Texas, especially, presented problems, with its great distances, sparse population, and difficult terrain. To transport equipment, supplies, and personnel from railroad to construction points took much time. Employees were known to have been carried by buses or even trucks on a daily round trip of as much as 180 miles between camp and work. The character of the terrain was sometimes a serious obstacle to construction—West Texas is a semiarid region,

HUMBLE PIPE LINE COMPANY SYSTEM, 1930

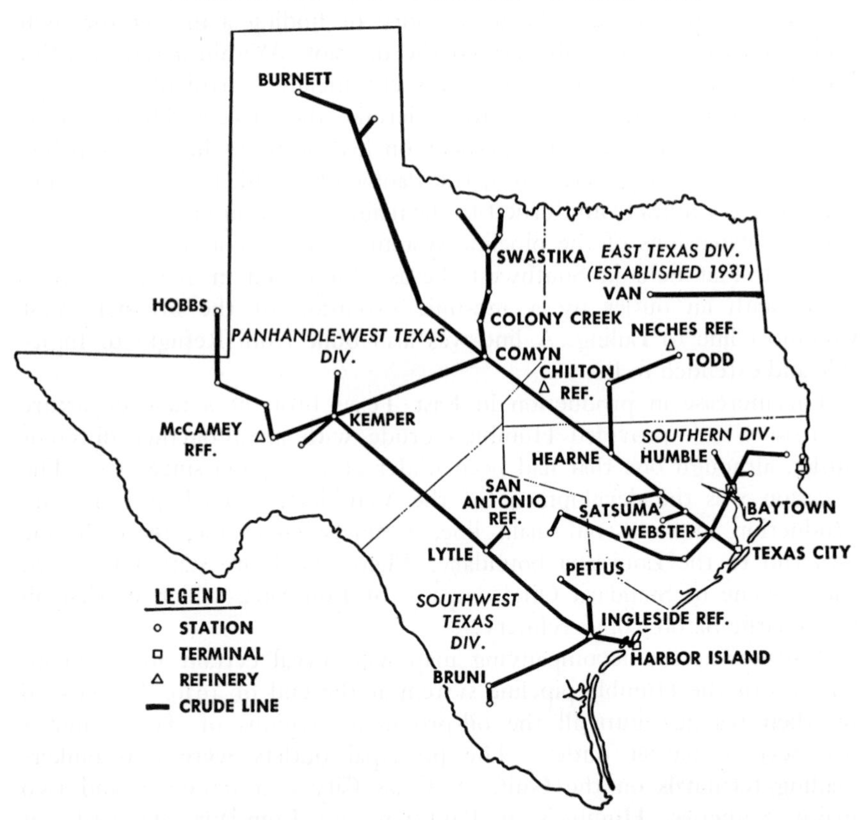

varying from farming land to sand dunes of a desert type and solid rock with little or no vegetation. A survey party, traveling in a stripped-down wagon, took three days to cross twenty miles of shifting sand dunes between Crane and Winkler. A mule team might be required to drag a single section of pipe across long stretches of sand. Trenching in the loose and shifting sand has been compared with ditching in water. It was not uncommon for the winds to uncover and undercut pipes here and there, leaving the exposed sections without support.[18] The Kemper-Ingleside line, on the contrary, had to be cut across the rugged West Texas hills. Here ditching machines at best barely scratched the surface; some men worked with air drills to prepare holes, and others blasted the solid rock with dynamite.[19]

Labor relations on these construction projects were even more difficult than on the construction of Humble's first trunk lines. The homeless, womanless pipeliners lived a rough, monotonous, and isolated life in pipeline camps. In the absence of other types of recreation, they broke the monotony by heavy payday drinking, gambling, and quarreling, by capricious complaints about their meals, and by spasmodic insubordination. Men were fired so frequently for drunkenness or defiance of authority that it was said a pipeline construction project needed three crews—one working, one going, and one coming. However, discharged men could usually obtain work on the next division, if they wished, for each superintendent hired his own crews, and men were scarce. Whatever difficulties occurred were usually the result of individual or spontaneous action.

Success in employee relations still depended on the same qualities as before—the character and skill of the individual foreman and superintendent—and, with the expansion and acceleration of construction, the proportions of the task increased. In 1926 and 1927 Humble employed from 5,000 to 6,000 pipeline men. Work was plentiful and workers were independent. The successful manager was the man who could be fair without weakness and firm without tyranny. These were the years in which, so far as Humble was concerned, the "tough," migratory pipeliners of tradition made their last stand before being superseded in large part by the more stable forces of the pipeline contractor.

The toughness of the workers, especially during the construction of the Burnett-Comyn and Kemper-Ingleside lines, is a favorite theme of Humble pipeline lore. The traditional restlessness of the pipeliner was perhaps accentuated by a final flare-up of IWW activity. Men came and went constantly, at a tempo calculated to exasperate the superintendents and foremen who bore responsibility for the progress of the work. Foreman George Lee, a fabulous figure in Humble pipeline lore, is a symbol of the foremen's ability to outmatch the pipeliner's traditional roughness. Brandishing a two-by-four ripped from the crudely built field office, he once quelled a group of pipeliners who, having quit en masse at a most inconvenient time, insisted on immediate payment of their wages and threatened to enforce their demands by wrecking the office. On another occasion, the same doughty foreman was called one cold night by a frantic hotel clerk, when ingenious pipeliners decided to put out the electric lights with shots from their revolvers; he rushed to the scene and, with swinging fists and fearful objurgations, drove the trigger-happy pipeliners to bed. Not infrequently, employee relations on pipeline construction followed the pattern set by the schoolboys in *The Hoosier Schoolmaster*, who first "tried out" the master and, when he proved capable of dealing with them on their own terms, often gave him their respect and loyalty.

Both history and folklore tend to overemphasize conflict; the less dramatic events and developments have comparatively little place in written records or men's memories. The rapidly growing pipeline mileage, however, demonstrates the presence of general harmony and efficiency in Humble's pipeline construction. Obviously only men of unusual hardihood, determination, and toughness could have achieved Humble's record in pipeline construction in the 1920s; only foremen and superintendents matching those qualities could have inspired their men to such exertion. Respect for and loyalty to such superintendents and foremen as Hanrahan, Neath, and Lee, rather than attachment to Humble Pipe Line Company, were probably responsible for the *esprit de corps* that was a general characteristic of successful pipeline construction—that, for example, made men willing to work long hours to complete a line to a newly discovered field at a time when overtime payment was unheard of.

The application of improved techniques to Humble construction was also characteristic of this period. Humble's large storage program, intended to assure producers of an outlet and customers of an adequate supply of crude in days of ever-anticipated scarcity, gave the company a special interest in improved tank construction. Since about 1922 companies on the West Coast had been experimenting with welding, rather than riveting, the bottoms and roofs of tanks; in 1925 Humble installed welded roofs on six 55,000-barrel tanks at Comyn. Early in 1929 it built an all-welded steel bottom on a 30,000-barrel tank at San Angelo station in West Texas. At about the same time, the use of welding for joining pipes superseded threaded couplings. Humble's first extensive use of this method was on the construction of the Panhandle pipelines in 1926–1927. By the late 1920s, the electric-arc process had begun to take the place of the acetylene-gas method for welding pipe.[20] In 1927 Humble put in service its first floating roof on a tank instead of the traditional rigid roof; the floating roof retarded evaporation and corroded less rapidly than the rigid type.

From 1925 to 1927 Humble Pipe Line Company also changed one of its basic construction policies. Pipeline companies had customarily done their own building, altogether contrary to railroad practice. Humble Pipe Line followed the traditional pattern until the construction of the

Kemper-Comyn line in 1925, but on that project it began a gradual transition to a policy of employing contractors to build new lines.

There seem to have been several reasons for this change. The introduction of heavier, more effective, and consequently more expensive ditching and laying equipment was an important factor. The company managers felt that the extent to which the company itself could use this heavy equipment, because of the interim periods when it would be unused and rusting, would not justify the investment. Also influential was the company's eventual decision to avoid building up a large temporary pipeline personnel during periods of construction. The extent of necessary layoffs after the completion of a line is illustrated by the fact that the 2,600 employees at the end of 1919 had been reduced by about a thousand at the time the main trunk lines were completed. When the pipeline men were pushing into the flush Mexia field in 1921, the total number of workers rose to almost the earlier high but soon declined by about 1,500. In 1926–1927 the total rose to 5,000. The anticipated rapid growth in construction activities in the mid-twenties, which obviously required large crews for a limited time only, may well have influenced the timing of the adoption of the new policy. The subsequent depression was to confirm in the minds of Humble executives the wisdom of contracting pipeline construction and other similar work.

The shift from company to contracted construction was gradual. At the time of Humble Pipe Line's first moves toward the new policy, contracting companies were neither sufficiently numerous nor well financed and equipped to handle all the tremendous tasks of construction confronting Humble. The pipeline company, moreover, still had on hand a large amount of equipment that was not yet obsolete and a good supply of trained men, and it anticipated regularity of employment for a substantial number. On some stretches of line contractors would not only haul and string out pipe, functions that had almost always been contracted even earlier, but would also do ditching. Then the pipeline company would couple, wrap, and lay the pipes—operations requiring greater skill and more care. In time even these operations were turned over to specialists. According to Ralph V. Hanrahan, after 1927 nearly all Humble's major pipelines were laid by contract, though some continued to be built by the company until the mid-1930s.[21]

The construction of Humble Pipe Line Company's vast system of lines enabled the company to become an outstanding transporter of oil. Early in 1928 an important oil-industry journal characterized Humble Pipe Line as "the biggest pipeline company in the world."[22] If pipeline mileage is the criterion, this statement cannot be substantiated, for this or any subsequent year. In 1930, according to the Interstate

Commerce Commission's first report on this subject, Humble was outranked in pipeline mileage by the Prairie, Buckeye, and Stanolind pipeline companies. In that year, however, according to the ICC report, Humble did rank first in the number of barrels of oil transported in the United States, its nearest competitors being Prairie, Shell, and Magnolia. The journal mentioned above was undoubtedly on firm footing when it described President Hanrahan as "one of the best liked, most courteous and able executives in the pipe line industry in the United States," and as a man who had "a great faculty for making friends and holding them" and who had "won the admiration and regard of pipe line men everywhere." [23]

OPERATING THE SYSTEM, 1919–1930

Humble Pipe Line Company was involved in important and sometimes difficult relationships at each end of its operations as a carrier. Jersey Standard had to have adequate supplies of appropriate quality, as also did Humble Oil & Refining Company's other customers and its own refineries. Humble Pipe Line Company, working in close co-operation with Humble's Production Department and Crude Oil Department (the purchasing agency) and with other shippers whom it served, had to be ready to supply storage and transportation whenever either was required. Good relations had to be maintained at all times with those who had oil to sell or to move by pipeline. In achieving and maintaining such relations, quick connections with leases under development and a reputation for fair dealing were of major importance. Humble's crude purchasers and pipeliners co-operated in carrying out Humble's policy of tying independent producers to itself by good service and firm confidence—bonds less easily broken than the pipeline connection itself.

The difficulty of maintaining adequate inventories varied with fluctuations in demand and supply. In the race for oil of the early 1920s pipeline superintendents had to make quick, on-the-spot decisions or lose out to other companies. In subsequent times of shortage or of overabundance of crude oil, the pipeliners had to be ready for any supply situation that might arise in a single field, or in the whole area in which Humble operated, and to meet the demand for moving oil to refinery or tanker.

In the 1920s Humble Pipe Line did not transport much oil for other than its own parent company. Under a Texas law of 1917 it was a common carrier, with published rates applying equally to all shippers, and subject to the authority of the Railroad Commission. But the conditions under which a pipeline company was required to carry for others were such that few of the smaller producers could meet them. In order to ship by pipeline, they had to have at the destination a purchaser or storage or shipping facilities; the pipelines could refuse, moreover, to accept for shipment less oil than the minimum of 10,000 barrels designated by the Commission as the amount considered necessary for efficient operation, a requirement which greatly reduced the number of producers able to take advantage of the pipelines as common carriers.[24] Most important of all, most producers without pipelines preferred to sell their oil at the wells; and the large producers usually had their own pipelines and did not ship by the lines of others, except when mutually satisfactory arrangements could be worked out in special circumstances.

Over the years, Humble's routine relations with producers came to conform to a well-defined pattern. In the early rush days, pipeline superintendents and division gaugers actively solicited connections. Later, producers approached the pipeline division superintendent or went directly to the crude oil purchasing group to "tender" the production of a new well or lease. In any case, the offer had to be passed on to those executives of Humble Oil & Refining Company who were responsible for purchasing. Anderson, after election to the parent company's board in 1921, brought to this group a full knowledge of pipeline needs and problems. Although as a member of the Crude Oil Committee and after 1922 as the manager of the Crude Oil Department he was concerned with purchasing crude for the parent company, in this work he was equipped to consider also the effect of the purchase on pipeline operations. After receiving a geologist's report on the probable reserves of a lease, the manager of the crude oil purchasing would usually recommend a pipeline connection with the lease; the necessary gathering lines would then be constructed.

Pipeline operations began at the tanks on Humble's or other producers' leases with which gathering lines were connected. When a tank was nearly full, the flow of oil into it was temporarily shut off, and the pipeline's gauger measured and tested the oil in the tank before running it into the pipeline company's gathering line. When the tank was nearly empty, the gauger took another measurement in order to determine how much crude the producer had delivered to the pipeline. The "run ticket" was the evidence of the amount delivered.

Possibilities of error in gauging, honest or otherwise, were not lacking. W. S. Farish as an independent producer in earlier years had been convinced that the gaugers of major purchasing companies were deliberately making mistakes in favor of their employers. According to industry lore, the less scrupulous purchasers might instruct their gaugers as to the amount of oil beyond the quantity purchased that they should run per month. Yet, also according to oil-industry tradition, the "error" was not all on one side; some producers tapped the lines of purchasers, ran the crude back into their tanks, and sold it again. Such action, it may be noted, was found not only in the oil industry; in the early days of the wheat industry in a newly settled region it was not uncommon for the purchaser to shade weighing and grading to his own advantage, and farmers were known to have used various means to obtain better grades and higher weights than their grain actually merited. In the oil as in the wheat industry ethical standards improved with the increase in competition, the development of responsible companies, and effective public regulation.

Humble, quite apart from any personal probity of its policy-makers, would probably have followed a policy of strict honesty in crude oil purchasing regardless of the general climate of opinion and practice because it was imperative that no stigma should be permitted to attach itself to Humble Pipe Line Company. Humble was just beginning to engage in the purchase and transportation of crude oil in a period of scarcity and increasing competition and in a region dominated by a number of strong and well-entrenched companies. Under these conditions its success in purchasing crude in the amounts needed to satisfy the requirements of Jersey depended not a little upon a reputation for honesty and fairness.

How Humble accomplished this objective of honest gauging, working through men brought up in an earlier tradition, is not recorded. Reminiscences of some old-timers would seem to indicate that at least occasionally a Humble superintendent—eager to build a reputation for efficiency and economy—may have expected his gaugers to favor the company, rather than the producer, in recording oil measurements. That Humble must have succeeded early in building up a high standard of pipeline ethics may be concluded from the fact that, even when it was most unpopular, it was apparently never accused of dishonesty in measuring crude oil.

The re-education of employees accustomed to an earlier tradition was only a small part of the problem of running a pipeline system. The flow of oil that went on night and day, seven days a week, year in and year out, was complex from the beginning and became increasingly so as oil was handled from more fields and as the quantities and types of crude oil multiplied.

When the oil left the lease tank, it traveled through gathering lines to the nearest main-line station. Oil shipped by independent producers —known as common-carrier oil—was sent on its way at once, except in those rare cases when arrangement had been made for storage; but oil owned by Humble Oil & Refining Company was stored at a trunk-line station until it was needed to feed Humble's stills or to load on a tanker for shipment to Jersey Standard or to other customers.

The pumping stations supplied whatever energy was needed to drive the oil through the lines. Heavy oil in particular required additional force to move it even when gravity was in its favor, and of course all oil had to be pumped up inclines and over hills. The stations themselves ranged from small booster plants to the large trunk-line stations, each with its own tank farms for operating purposes. The most important was the Webster station, of which F. W. Reece, formerly of Louisiana Standard, had charge.

Wherever possible, a pipeline station was located near, and named after, a good-sized town. Such a location reduced the necessity for company-owned housing and also provided shopping, recreational, and educational facilities for pipeline employees and their families. The decisive factor, however, in determining the location of a pumping station was the distance the oil would efficiently flow under certain gravitational conditions and pressures. Some stations in the West Texas region were inevitably remote and lonely.

Three plants on the Kemper-Ingleside line, far from any town, were designated merely as stations A, B, and C. Station C, some thirty-five miles from Kerrville in the Texas hill country, was in a particularly wild and lonely place. The terrain was so rocky that any footgear except the heaviest boots was soon torn to pieces. The company, however, constructed a roadway down a boulder-strewn canyon, hauled in soil for lawns and flower beds, built cottages and a school, and transformed desolation into a friendly oasis.[25]

The men engaged in operating and maintaining the lines were a more stable group than the floating construction workers, though many former construction men transferred to the operating organization—indeed, the core of the operating management had joined Humble Pipe Line in its early years. Operating tank farms and pumping stations, "walking" the lines to look for leaks, and keeping the lines in repair required special skills and the utmost dependability. A relatively large and able supervisory group was necessary; division superintendents remote from headquarters often had to act on their own judgment in matters far from routine. These pipeline operators, both supervisors and rank and file, tended to become permanent employees and thus to participate in the company's program of annuities and benefits.

The dispatcher's office at Houston headquarters, under S. F. Power from Louisiana Standard, was in charge of the complicated work of co-ordinating the movement of the crude oil through the vast pipeline system to refineries and to loading docks on the Gulf. In that office schedules were drawn up and orders prepared and issued to ensure the arrival of sufficient amounts of the right types of crude at the proper times and places to supply refineries or load tankers. The task of co-ordination called for careful planning in advance; transporting oil from Comyn to Baytown, for example, took a week.

Although the dispatcher was informed well ahead of time in regard to the needs of the refineries served and the capacity and time of arrival of tankers loading at Texas City or Harbor Island, he had to be ready for the unexpected. In the era of uncontrolled production the supply might suddenly change. A newly discovered field would pour forth a flood of oil that somehow had to be moved. Late in 1923, as a result of the Powell boom, Humble Pipe Line Company broke all previous records by handling 120,000 barrels in one day from a single field.[26] On the other hand, a field might suddenly go to water, sand up, or otherwise cease to produce, forcing the pipelines to make hasty arrangements for obtaining oil elsewhere. The establishment in Texas of the principle of prorating production according to market demand was to ease the pipeline's supply problems greatly in the 1930s, but in the 1920s adjusting to an oversupply or undersupply of oil was a part of the operational routine.

The work of delivering proper quantities of oil at the right time and place grew with the increasing variety of crudes and the adoption of more exact methods of grading. The varying types and grades, which served different purposes and had different values, had to be kept separate from each other.[27] The gravity and other qualities of crude might vary even in a single field, and in a long trunk line serving a number of fields the oils differed considerably.

When Humble Pipe Line Company began operations in 1919, purchasers, following the practice that had prevailed in most fields in early days, did not demand fine grading. The only grades were the "sweet" North Texas crudes with a high gasoline content, known as Ranger crude, and the Gulf Coast, or Goose Creek, crude, which was well suited for manufacturing lubricants and fuel oil. But when, as soon occurred, crude from the Ranger area proved to be valuable for the production of cylinder oil and refiners were willing to pay a premium price for it, the Ranger crude proper could no longer be run with the other North Texas gasoline crudes, such as the Burkburnett. Gulf Coast crudes were also soon divided into two grades with a price differential. The "A" grade, with little sulphur content, was particularly valuable for the manufacture of lubes and drew a higher price than the "B" grade, which, with a higher sulphur content, was used primarily for fuel oil. New fields added new grades, and in 1922 Texas buyers, following the Mid-Continent practice, began to classify crudes and determine prices in accordance with a gravity scale.[28] By 1929 Humble was handling at least twenty-five grades of crude oil—some say as many as sixty different types.

Humble early devised a plan for avoiding the necessity of keeping common-carrier crudes separate in the pipelines. Whenever possible it would persuade the owner to sell his oil to Humble Oil & Refining Company at the field price and buy an equal amount of the same grade at the destination at the field price plus the transportation cost. The pipeline company was thus not required to keep a particular batch separate from all others, while the original owner was first reimbursed for the crude he delivered and then could buy back a similar quantity and grade at a convenient delivery point. In time, pipeline tariffs provided for common-stream delivery of the same kind and quality of crude rather than the very same crude entrusted to the line.

Various methods, new and old, were used to prevent or minimize the intermixture of different crudes in the lines. Since the movement of oil depended on a continuous flow, some contact and intermixture were inevitable at each end of a particular batch. Running as large a batch as possible was a partial solution, but to keep to a minimum the mixing at each end remained a problem. Water was occasionally used to separate two grades, but it had bad effects on the pipe and also led to emulsification. More successful was the device of running an intermediate grade between a premium grade and one of low quality, but such a "buffer" grade was not always available.

The technique Humble eventually adopted was to follow the movement of the various crudes closely as they moved through the line. The dispatcher's office would notify the operator at a station to put a certain amount of a particular crude into the line behind a crude being pumped. From then on, the dispatcher and pump-station operators along the line would keep in close communication by telephone or telegraph lines paralleling the pipelines, the operators reporting the progress of the crude as gauged and tested from samples, station by station. When a given batch reached its destination, it would be run into appropriate tanks. Succeeding batches would be put through the same process, one following another as scheduled by the chief dispatcher's office in Houston.[29]

Even the most precise methods of testing and checking the stream did not always prove adequate to the complicated task of moving a score or more of different grades of crude oil. Keeping many different crudes separate also called for new equipment. Extra tankage, intricate design and layout of piping, and even the building of duplicate gathering lines were necessary to make possible the handling of the increasing number of types of crude oil.

Auxiliary construction and maintenance crews had responsibility for keeping the lines and stations in order. Maintenance always involved much work, particularly because of the heavy investment—probably well over 85 per cent of the total—in steel tanks and pipes that were subject to corrosion. Besides corrosion, hurricanes and floods and even the winds that uncovered the pipelines in the desert produced sudden emergencies. The pipeliners had to be ready, night and day, to meet these destructive vagaries of the weather.

Corrosion was a constant and continuing problem, one that increased during the 1920s because of the growth of the pipeline industry and its movement into areas with unfamiliar natural conditions. Along with other pipeline companies in the area where it operated, Humble encountered such relatively unfamiliar conditions as briny swamps, soil with great variations in moisture and mineral content, and the moisture-laden atmosphere of the coastal region. Other difficult conditions, such as oil impregnated with salt water and sulphur which corroded the interior of pipes and tanks, although not new had never been solved.

The seriousness of the corrosion problem at the end of the 1920s brought a concerted effort by the oil industry to develop means of prevention. Humble, like other similar companies, had experimented with various types of waterproof coatings to protect the pipes externally; treating the oil in the producing fields had as one of its objectives the removal of such elements, especially salt water and hydrogen sulphide, as would cause internal corrosion of pipes or tanks. The oil industry's widening employment of research and engineering suggested the desirability of a co-ordinated scientific approach to this corrosion problem. Beginning in 1929, committees of the American Petroleum Institute, on which Humble Pipe Line was represented, and of manufacturers of pipe-coating materials jointly sponsored research on the corrosion problem in co-operation with the United States Bureau of Standards. Humble men also began research on tank corrosion, which was directly applicable to Humble Pipe Line's problems.

Until effective preventive measures were developed, Humble and the pipeline industry generally had to keep on repairing heavy damage. Tank corrosion, which was especially rapid at coastal terminals, necessitated much repairing and replacing of parts of tanks. When the faithful linewalker discovered surface evidence of pipeline leaks, repairmen uncovered and dealt with the pipe, which could sometimes be mended by inserting wooden plugs and covering them with gaskets that were in turn covered by a steel patch held in place by bolted clamps. Not until the development early in the 1930s of shielded electric-arc welding did it become common practice to make the repairs permanent by welding the edges of these patches to the pipe. Pipe repair was only one of the routine operations involved in the maintenance of pipeline facilities.

By the end of the period Humble Pipe Line Company was operating over 6,000 miles of trunk and gathering lines. In its peak year, 1929, it gathered a total of about 73,500,000 barrels of crude oil, carried by trunk line nearly 90,500,000, and averaged daily deliveries of nearly 250,000 barrels (see Appendix II, Table XI). It was then carrying about 10 per cent of the total oil production of the United States. Humble, according to the *Oil & Gas Journal*, was recognized as having "pioneered . . . in the design and operating of both gathering and trunk line operations," particularly in developing methods of "batching many grades of crude oil from the fields to refineries and shipping terminals without contamination."[30] In those years was laid the foundation for Humble Pipe Line Company's greatest technical achievement, the expeditious and efficient handling of tremendous quantities of crude oil of many types and grades.

PIPELINE FINANCE, 1919–1930

This first period of Humble Pipe Line Company's history was distinguished by high financial returns. Although final judgment on such financial questions as the profitability of pipelines must rest on an evaluation of a longer term than a decade, to examine a period in the light of the opinion and the conditions of its own time is of some advantage.

Humble Pipe Line Company's financial stature grew over the years with the growth of its facilities. In 1919 its capital stock was $15,000 at par; in 1920 it was increased to $12,000,000, and five years later to $24,000,000; in 1927 the authorized capitalization was increased to $50,000,000, where it has since remained. The pipeline company financed its growth by means of sale of stock to Humble Oil & Refining Company, reinvestment of capital recovered by depreciation, and salvage from abandoned lines. In 1930 its gross investment in fixed assets, not including either storage facilities or oil held to fill the lines for operating purposes, reached approximately $83,000,000. Humble Pipe Line had the advantage of strong financial backing which carried it through its earliest construction, but later its profits provided the necessary funds for expansion—that is, the profits were paid as dividends to the parent company, which bought the increased stock of its pipeline subsidiary.

Despite this spectacular growth, pipeline men in the 1920s, as in earlier years, repeatedly expressed doubts about the continuance of favorable pipeline returns, a concern which, though real enough at the time, is difficult to understand in the light of subsequent developments. The future of new oil fields was then, however, highly uncertain; experience showed that, under the accepted system of uncontrolled production, a field might be virtually depleted in four or five years. The capital investment in pipelines was heavy, and the period of profits might be brief. Pipeline tariffs in consequence were then, as earlier in American pipeline history, generally set high enough to enable a line to get back its investment within a very few years.

The history not only of individual fields but of the Texas oil industry in general lent support to doubts concerning the pipelines' future. Following its boom period of 1901 to 1905, which were its peak years for more than a decade to come, Texas production during the next twelve months dropped 65 per cent and for several years continued to decline. In order to get enough oil, pipeline companies had been forced to push northward into Oklahoma.

Pipeline men in the early 1920s consequently had no assurance that the pleasing early returns on their investment would be continued, especially that the particular fields to which they laid pipe would continue to produce sufficient oil for pipeline operations. No one could know that Texas was on the verge of one of the greatest periods of growth in American oil history and not, as in 1901 to 1905, in a merely temporary and illusive boom. The pipelines reaped the benefits of the large production that their own rapid expansion helped to encourage. Several individual fields followed the pattern of early decline, but numerous newly discovered fields kept the pipelines full.

Several examples illustrate this development. Humble's main line from Comyn to Webster had originally been constructed to run Ranger crude, but by 1922 output from this area was near the vanishing point. Had the line been dependent solely on Ranger, the amount of oil it transported would have fallen off greatly and its profits correspondingly declined. The discovery of oil at Mexia, however, restored the importance of this main line south of Hearne. When the Mexia production fell off, Hanrahan, in January, 1923, envisaged the immediate possibility that the lines from Ranger and Mexia to Webster might run only half their capacity, but his anxiety was lifted when the nearby Powell field came in. Although the production of Powell rapidly declined in its turn, discoveries in north central Texas helped to fill the trunk line. The discovery of oil in West Texas and the Panhandle not only provided a flow for the original line but also called for expansion of its capacity and the building of new lines. Humble Pipe Line benefited from the discovery of new fields comparatively near the original construction and it plowed back profits into branch lines, extensions, gathering lines, loops, and so on, in order to reap further profits. From 1919 to 1930 only about 300 miles of pipeline had to be abandoned and dismantled—a small proportion of the mileage built.

But these developments were not anticipated, and in the 1920s the pipelines followed traditional rate-setting methods. Pipeline rates were determined to some extent by the rates of the competing transportation method, which in a new field was usually a railroad; the rates were always considerably less than tank-car rates because the operating cost of running crude through pipelines was considerably less than that of carriage by tank car. In anticipation of a possible short life for the pipeline, however, rates were determined largely by the amount necessary to amortize the investment within the few years that oil might be available from the flush field or fields that a line was built to serve. This objective of obtaining an early return on a heavy capital investment affected the rates even where pipelines were competing for oil. In proposing Humble's rates in 1919, Farish thought they "should be substantially the same" as those charged by other pipelines, since it would not be advisable to "disturb the rate of transportation of oil within the state." [31]

Humble Pipe Line, in conformity with the rules and regulations of the Railroad Commission, published separate gathering, transportation, and loading charges. The company's original tariff for gathering a barrel of Ranger crude was 20 cents, a charge which for half a century had been almost traditional for this service. The trunk-line rate from Comyn to Texas City in 1920 was 45 cents; the railroad charge for transportation between the same points was $1.00. Two years later, when Humble Pipe Line entered the Mexia field, its tariff from there to Texas City was set at 30 cents; the tank-car rates dropped from 70 to 50 cents.

In comparison with present rates, the pipeline charges of this period appear high, but they must be considered in relation to the earlier situation. Pipeline construction by Humble and other Texas companies actually caused a sharp drop in the cost of transporting crude. Indeed, this reduction in transportation rates made it possible for oil to reach a larger market. The slower, but less expensive, pipeline, wherever available, won out in competition with the tank car.[32]

Despite the reduction in the cost of transportation brought by pipelines, the rates were often under attack. Records of discussion about rates at various times help to indicate the reasons for the differences of opinion. In 1920 Jersey Standard's president expressed the view that Humble's pipeline rates, because of the increase in costs, were not sufficient to yield a fair return on the pipeline value. Humble executives, however, believed that, in view of public opinion and pipeline regulations, it would be a great mistake to raise the question of pipeline rates in Texas. President Sterling wrote: "It is very doubtful in our minds whether we could justify a higher rate than we are now charging." [33] Humble Pipe Line was already making a profit on the gross investment of something over 20 per cent after taxes.

An exchange of letters on rates between Jersey Standard and Humble two years later showed not only that economic conditions had changed but also that other factors were involved. By early 1922 the price of crude oil and other commodities had declined, and Teagle believed that pipeline rates should follow. Jersey Standard was now purchasing a major part of the crude transported by Humble. The Jersey president recommended that the tariffs from Ranger and Mexia should each be cut 5 cents a barrel, a strong argument for the reduction being that other pipelines were charging less than Humble for the same service. Farish replied that the line from Ranger to Texas City had been built at a time of high construction costs and had not been "operated sufficiently long for us to see daylight on our pipe line investment." In his opinion, too, some thought should be given to the fact that the heavy costs of purchasing, holding, and storing oil, although legally the responsibility of Humble Oil & Refining Company, needed to be covered. Nevertheless, after about a month of discussion the rates were reduced.[34]

In 1926 and 1927 Jersey Standard again complained of certain rates, but against a different background from that of either 1920 or 1922.[35] The flood of crude oil that set in late in 1926, together with Humble's desire to dispose of larger quantities to nonaffiliated companies, was largely responsible for a reduction in the Crude Oil Department's charges for buying and selling crude, but pipeline tariffs were little changed. Up to the end of 1930, although some trunk-line rates had been slightly reduced, no general change had taken place; gathering rates, similarly, were reduced in only a few regions.

This period, nevertheless, foreshadowed future changes. A renewal in 1928 of the Jersey-Humble discussion of pipeline rates reveals some of the pertinent factors. Not only Humble's existing competitive position but also the possibility or probability of high profits attracting new competition had to be considered. Increasing attention also had to be given to public opinion. Teagle then expressed his position to Farish in strong terms: "I have felt, and have so expressed myself to you on one or two occasions, that the holding up of pipe line rates in order to exact the fullest possible earnings in the transportation end of the business might not be the wisest policy to pursue." Farish, who was president of a company that was benefiting greatly from pipeline profits and who had firsthand knowledge of pipeline problems, in his reply emphasized the problems and pointed out that high pipeline profits had facilitated the rapid development of the oil industry in Texas and, indirectly, had benefited the public. The pipeline men, he wrote, were finding it difficult and expensive to keep the pipelines running to capacity or near capacity. In order to obtain the oil—and, he might have added as a producer, to take care of new production—they were forced continually to expend a large part of their profits on the extension of lines. These facts, he urged, must be considered before reducing tariffs.[36]

In the meantime, throughout the 1920s the net income of the pipelines steadily rose, and returns on the investment were always excellent. After rising rapidly to 1921, the net income increased slowly but steadily from 1921 to 1923 and then rose rapidly again, with the exception of a slight falling off in 1926. The rate of earnings was always more than 20 per cent, and in 1921, 1924, and 1928 was a fraction over 29 per cent. An unusually high rate of return in 1929 (33.58 per cent) and the sharp drop in 1930 (to 11.08 per cent) were partly—in the latter year, primarily—the result of tax adjustments, although they were also affected by the favorable economic conditions of 1929 and the business decline in the following year. For the years 1919–1930, the pipelines were Humble Oil & Refining Company's biggest earner, dividends from the pipeline company accounting for $124,000,000 out of a total net income of $140,-000,000.

Humble's corporate structure and accounting methods, to be sure, accentuated the pipeline returns. Although the company had once considered a major change aimed at correcting this overemphasis, it actually adopted only a minor one. Late in 1929 Vice-President Anderson suggested that Humble Oil & Refining Company transfer the Crude Oil Department to the pipeline company. The purchase and holding of crude for sale required a large capital and expensive storage and also involved considerable risk, whereas crude sales had normally resulted in only a very small annual profit or even in a net loss. If the Crude Oil Department, with its investment of $27,000,000, could be shifted to the account of the pipeline company, with which its operations were closely associated, the yield on the pipeline investment would be at a lower rate. One can only infer the reasons for not taking a step that was appealing on more than one ground. Humble Pipe Line Company, as already mentioned, had in 1919 ceased to be a purchaser of oil and had since restricted itself to transportation; the same factors that had favored the earlier step, particularly the authority of the Railroad Commission over pipelines, militated against retracing it. Furthermore, while fluctuations in crude prices had on the whole worked against the Crude Oil Department's profits, they could produce inventory profits as well as losses, with the result that the real returns from pipeline operations might be still further distorted. The proposed merger of the Crude Oil Department with the pipeline company was not carried out. Certain duplications in accounting and record-keeping between the Crude Oil Department and the pipeline company were, however, eliminated in 1930.

Humble Pipe Line Company was fully aware that pipeline rates were subject to criticism and realized that the pipelines were yielding larger and steadier returns than had originally been expected. Criticism of its rates came, as already mentioned, from Jersey Standard, from other customers, and from producers; the rates were influenced by declining prices. Action by the Railroad Commission and the legislature was a distinct possibility. High rates and high profits, as always in pipeline history, engendered the beginnings of their own decline as competition was attracted and public opinion aroused. The 1920s, in retrospect, were the golden age of Humble's pipeline operations.

For Humble Pipe Line Company the years 1919–1930 could hardly be regarded from any viewpoint as other than highly successful. Multitudinous problems of construction and operation had been confronted and successfully solved. The system had gathered 368,000,000 barrels of oil in those years and had transported by trunk lines 397,000,000 barrels. Moreover, the pipeline company in this period provided nearly 90 per cent of Humble's consolidated earnings and made available substantial funds for the expansion of other company functions as well as its own growth.

The pipeline company provided an outlet for the oil of countless producers who had no transportation facilities as well as for Humble's own production. In fact, in 1921–1925 Humble's production accounted for slightly more than half of the crude gathered by its pipelines, but in the years 1926–1930 its own production amounted to only about a third of its pipeline gatherings. In serving itself Humble was also serving the rapidly growing production industry of Texas. This was made possible not only by the great pipeline system Humble built in the 1920s but also by the large crude oil requirements of Standard Oil Company (New Jersey).

Chapter 8

CRUDE OIL PURCHASING AND SELLING, 1919–1926

THE same objective that principally motivated the great expansion of Humble's production and pipelines also made the company a heavy purchaser of crude oil: that of supplying Jersey Standard with oil in large volume. So important did Humble's crude purchasing soon become that in some years after 1920, despite greatly increased production, it purchased about four times as much oil as it produced.[1]

No other activity in which the company was engaged involved more complicated problems than did crude oil operations. In this difficult field, moreover, the directors and executives had had little experience, only in a small way as sellers of crude and almost not at all as buyers. Consequently, while plunging into the business in a large way, they had to develop an organization, policies, and methods.

As a seller of crude, Humble dealt with a relatively small number of customers, chiefly with Jersey Standard, which needed tremendous supplies and was for many years haunted by a fear of shortage. Humble had to be able to supply its customers with the kinds and quantities of oil they required at all times and at current prices. The really serious problem was to have adequate crude on hand to meet demands. Indeed, as virtual underwriters of its customers' oil supply, particularly Jersey Standard's, Humble had to perform a variety of costly and risky functions.

Purchasing involved new relationships and unfamiliar operations for Humble's executives. Blaffer and Farish recognized their new position as buyers by resigning from the Gulf Coast Oil Producers Association in March, 1919. They did not wish to appear to be "on both sides of the proposition," although Farish asserted that their interest in a good price for Gulf Coast crude remained as strong as ever,[2] which was a logical result of their own interest as large producers. By the time Humble became a large buyer, the purchasing of crude in Texas on the basis of posted prices had come into general practice.[3] Price remained a crucial question, nevertheless, and producers were seldom satisfied with the prices offered, although a limit was set on what a buyer could pay by what he could get from his customers and by the prices paid by other purchasers. Moreover, if he was to retain the good will of the sellers, the purchaser was not free to buy the amounts he thought best from his own forecasting of prices and of the needs of his customers. If he did not buy what a producer offered, the latter might have to curtail his production, with a resulting loss of oil under his lease from drainage by nearby wells; to avoid such a loss, the producer might seek another buyer. In order to retain the producer's business, the purchaser had to take the oil in flush as well as lean times.

The instability of oil production made the risk heavy with respect to both supply and price. From 1919 to 1927 Humble carried on its crude oil operations in alternating periods of scarcity and overabundance. It was compelled to attempt to develop purchasing policies and practices that would, on the one hand, keep it from being drowned in a superfluity of oil and, on the other, prevent it from being left without crude to fill its pipelines and to supply the stills of its own and its customers' refineries. The processes by which it arrived at its policies and the extent to which these proved successful constitute the major themes of this chapter.

PURCHASING DURING A PERIOD OF SCARCITY, 1919–1920

The importance and difficulty of crude oil operations necessitated the handling of questions of policy and price by the Board of Directors. Sales were negotiated by the company's top administrators. Purchasing required a more complicated organization. Blaffer, Farish, and James Anderson—at first as a representative of the pipeline company—constituted the important Crude Oil Committee, which stood between the board and operations. As has already been observed, Blaffer, as director and treasurer, was officially in charge of purchasing, but W. S. Farish exercised an important influence on policy matters. The actual management of operations in the field was assigned to Humble Pipe Line Company, which at first handled crude purchasing as a part of its own business but from July, 1919, on behalf of the Production Department, to which the crude oil business was then transferred.

The early discussions and agreements with Jersey Standard concerning the terms on which Humble was to supply its large customer with crude established the general pattern of their relationship. The discussions particularly concerned Goose Creek and Ranger crudes for loading on Jersey tankers. Jersey's practice of buying at the posted field price, plus gathering, transportation, and loading charges and a marketing commission, was accepted by Humble. Jersey agreed to pay a commission of 20 cents. These charges—but not the commission—were regulated by the Texas Railroad Commission. Although prices and charges have varied with the times, these general principles have not changed over the years. No written contract has ever covered Humble's sale of crude to Jersey.

The same general pattern also applied to sales to other companies, except that such sales were covered by contracts and that prices were somewhat a matter of negotiation. The marketing commission was 20 cents from early in 1920 to 1926. However, because of the scarcity of oil in the early days of this period, Humble got from outside companies what the trade would pay; the price paid, which might reflect variations in commissions,[4] was a matter of negotiation.

Humble inaugurated and for nearly two years carried on its purchasing in a sellers' market. The years 1919 and 1920 were a period of scarce oil, high prices, and almost frantic efforts by refining companies to keep their stills supplied. The price of crude soared. Jersey Standard was badly in need of cylinder stocks for itself and its customers; Ranger oil, next to Pennsylvania crude, was the best for that purpose. Jersey had first call, but Imperial Oil, Limited (Jersey's Canadian affiliate) and the Vacuum Oil Company (Jersey's traditional supplier of high-grade lubricants, which was in critical need of Ranger crude), reinforced their requests for oil by offers of high commissions or premiums. By the end of July, 1919, Humble had contracts with sixteen companies to deliver nearly half a million barrels of Texas crude and was purchasing nearly three times as much as it was producing.[5]

In order to meet its commitments Humble had to compete successfully with such well-established purchasers and pipeline owners as Prairie, Gulf, Texas, and Sun. The efficiency and tireless efforts of its pipeline company came to be important factors in its success as a purchaser, since the company that got its lines to a lease first usually got the oil. Humble's price policy was a strategic factor in its competition for crude. The company in this period always stood ready to pay the highest market price and refused as a matter of policy to buy oil below posted prices; [6] and in reducing prices it followed others, rather than taking the lead.

In 1919–1920 this price policy was determined largely by the fact that Humble was trying to break into a sellers' market against established buyers. As a producer also, Humble was interested in high prices; it seems to have been particularly ready to take the initiative in raising the price of Gulf Coast crudes, of which it was a large producer. Jersey, as a purchaser, was not always in accord with its affiliate's pricing. However, Humble was expected to meet the current needs of customers and to lay up storage stocks in anticipation of a shortage of supply at the very time that a tremendous demand for Ranger and Burkburnett crudes was forcing prices up. Humble's highest payment for crude was $4.07 a barrel for 300,000 barrels of Ranger in storage purchased from Prairie Oil & Gas Company on June 2, 1920; this was a negotiated price which was 57 cents above the posted price.[7]

Humble's aggressiveness in seeking crude is illustrated by an episode in 1920 which is something of a curiosity in the company's history. Humble bought from Imperial Oil a tanker, capable of carrying 3,100 tons of oil, for bringing to Baytown Mexican oil to be purchased from Jersey. Wrote Farish to Teagle, June 9, 1920: "We believe this boat will prove a valuable investment if for no other purpose than to supply cheaper fuel for our Baytown and Goose Creek consumption." On August 26 the tanker was transferred to American registry and Humble ownership. On August 30 Wiess was informed that the ship would arrive at the Baytown terminal between September 15 and 17 with a cargo of light Mexican crude. The company's records contain no further reference to the *Baytown;* presumably Humble's seagoing effort came to an end because of the overabundance of supply and decline in price that struck the oil industry in the autumn of 1920.

During 1919 and 1920 Humble purchased and produced about 29,000,000 barrels of crude. It sold nearly 21,000,000 barrels, of which three-fourths went to non-Jersey buyers, a far larger proportion than in later years. At the end of 1920 Humble had over 8,000,000 barrels of storage crude, a deliberate accumulation as insurance against scarcity. (See Table 6.)

To provide adequate storage at this time was difficult. Aboveground storage—whether earthen or steel—was costly and wasteful. Earthen storage was made by scooping out, with mule teams and scrapers, large shallow pits in the ground, using the excavated earth for embankments. Wherever possible, those pits were dug down to clay; when packed down hard, the clay would hold water on which the oil would float. Individual pits might be as large as three city blocks and hold oil to a depth of eight feet and to the amount of 400,000 barrels. A particular advantage of this type of storage was that it could be constructed from materials locally available when steel for tanks could not be obtained quickly enough; moreover, it was initially less expensive than steel, an important consideration in the storage of flush production of short duration.[8] But this type of storage would lose by evaporation at least 20 per cent in the course of six months to a year, it seemed to attract lightning, and it was seriously endangered by floods. Humble's executives did not like earthen storage, but they used it to a considerable extent in the early 1920s for storing the heavy Gulf Coast and Smackover crudes.

TABLE 6

SELECTED STATISTICS ON CRUDE OIL OPERATIONS
HUMBLE OIL & REFINING COMPANY
1919–1930

	Crude Oil Purchases (000 B/D[a]*)*	*Total Supply*[b] *(000 B/D)*	*Crude Oil Sales (000 B/D)*	*Crude Oil Stocks at End of Year*[c] *(000 bbls.)*
1919	7.4	23.9	15.5	4,876
1920	33.9	55.3	41.9	8,160
1921	44.7	78.4	58.6	13,152
1922	48.9	79.6	55.3	15,743
1923	51.9	98.6	62.3	20,626
1924	68.2	111.5	69.1	20,515
1925	86.3	135.7	75.3	18,084
1926	100.2	137.8	80.3	15,434
1927	166.0	202.3	110.4	14,699
1928	194.5	236.9	119.8	14,076
1929	216.3	280.5	140.4	15,405
1930	177.7	249.5	114.1	19,632

[a] Barrels per day.
[b] Purchases plus production.
[c] Does not include lease stocks.

Source: Records of Humble Oil & Refining Company.

Steel tanks were necessary for storing the lighter crudes of North Texas, and Humble early adopted the policy of substituting steel storage elsewhere as rapidly as possible, although as late as 1922 it found difficulty in providing sufficient storage of any kind. However, even the steel tanks in use in the early 1920s were not satisfactory. Experiments conducted at Humble's Burkburnett refinery in 1921 revealed that high-gravity Serrien crude stored in a 150-barrel open steel tank in twenty-four hours lost five barrels of oil and two degrees of gravity. Expensive though it was, extensive storage of oil continued to be a necessity for the large purchaser and constituted one of his big problems until proration was established in the 1930s.

Humble's crude purchasing policies during the period of scarcity in 1919 and 1920 consisted, in brief, in trying to get its pipelines to new production ahead of other buyers, generally paying the highest posted price for a given grade of crude, and building up storage stocks against an expected period of scarcity. Near the end of 1920, however, the company was confronted with a situation that necessitated drastic readjustments in its crude oil operations.

PURCHASING DURING A PERIOD OF ABUNDANCE, 1920–1923

Late 1920 inaugurated a period of abundant production of oil in which the problem of the purchaser was not to obtain sufficient oil but to deal with its overabundance. Oil prices began to break on the Texas Gulf Coast in November, 1920. This change in the oil market was brought about by the postwar depression, unusually large domestic production, and the heavy importation of Mexican oil. Such refiners as the Vacuum Oil Company, which in 1920 had frantically begged for more crude, now sought a postponement of deliveries. The average price of Texas oil plunged downward. By summer Ranger crude had fallen from $3.50 to $1.00 a barrel, and Gulf Coast oil from $3.00 to 80 cents.[9] (For the price trend, see table on page 132.)

Humble's first action in dealing with this superabundance of crude was to follow other purchasing companies in cutting prices, its price policy varying with the desirability of the available crudes. At one time Humble refused to purchase the low-gravity coastal crudes—of which it was itself a large producer—excepting royalty oil from its leases and contract oil. Humble's method of dealing with the producers of the particularly desirable North Texas crude illustrates its usual practice, when prices seemed to be on a downward trend, of attempting to strike a balance between the desire to maintain friendly relations and an unwillingness to purchase far beyond current needs or storage capacity. Following the example of The Texas Company, Humble announced that, beginning on December 27, 1920, it would purchase only 50 per cent of the runs to Humble Pipe Line Company but would store the remainder at a charge of 3 cents a barrel per month. About a month later it followed other majors—Gulf, Texas, and Sun—in a series of 50-cent and 25-cent price cuts, with a further cut for oil that had to be run to wasteful earthen storage.[10] These price and purchase cuts inspired a resolution in the Texas legislature, calling upon the attorney general to proceed against those companies as combinations in restraint of trade.

In March, 1921, when crude prices were about half what they had been at the beginning of the year, Humble began an aggressive campaign to accumulate a million barrels of Ranger and the same amount of coastal crudes. By the middle of the month, following Gulf's example, it was ready to buy from the Ranger leases with which it had pipeline connections their total production and also to purchase the oil held in storage for the lease owners. By April, however, its purchases had again reached a saturation point. On April 5 Humble announced that it would prorate runs up to its pipeline capacity of 20,000 barrels and pay $2.00 a barrel for the oil. For whatever it took in addition, which would have to be run to storage, it would pay $1.75. Humble considered increasing pipeline capacity, but the prospective long-run difficulty of keeping such a line full brought, instead, the decision to increase storage. By November, 1921, Humble had added over 2,000,000 barrels of steel tankage.

Prices continued to decline and Humble continued to buy crude.[11] The company was thus following a policy similar to that stated in a Jersey memorandum of June 30, 1921: "We . . . feel that every bit of crude tankage . . . should be full of cheap oil before the . . . market goes up."[12] Buying low-priced oil was one way of bringing down the average cost of crude stocks, in the hope that prices would soon turn upward. Humble's effort to acquire as much lower-priced crude as it could handle was in keeping with the traditional policy of large purchasers, which was a result, primarily, of the large buyers' position as the bearer of the risk of price change.

The headlong descent of crude prices from November, 1920, to June, 1921, threatened to show up very unfavorably in Humble's balance sheet, for by summer the company held nearly 10,000,000 barrels of crude that had been bought at far higher prices than prevailed at that time. The threat to the balance sheet was particularly serious because the company had already floated a loan of $25,000,000 and was expecting to turn to the bankers for another loan within a year. Humble, consequently, tried to get Jersey Standard to bear some of the burden of the loss; Jersey was willing to make further advances, but its executives felt that their affiliate should be responsible for financing its own expansion, including the building up of storage capacity and crude oil stocks.

Despite Humble's strongest effort to reduce the average cost of the storage oil, there was still a prospect of heavy current losses on crude oil operations. Director Wiess, therefore, suggested that Humble's high-cost storage oil be treated as an investment and that only the profit or loss on current purchases and sales be included in making up crude oil operating accounts. Farish's request that Humble's Accounting Department work out some such system was met by the accountants with doubt as to its feasibility; but Gay Carroll and Stuart A. Giraud succeeded in drawing up a plan for two stocks of crude: one, called "permanent stock," to consist of high-cost crude, was intended to be a reserve to be drawn on when current sales exceeded current purchases plus "working stock" inventory; the other, the working stock, to consist of the more recently acquired and less expensive crude, was intended for use in determining the cost of current crude oil sales. The plan was adopted as of January 1, 1922. When current sales exceeded the inventory of working stock, the permanent stock was drawn upon at the per-barrel value of the oldest accumulated stock of the particular grade of crude on which the draft was made. By this method any loss on sales was booked in the month in which the permanent stocks were drawn on.

By adopting virtually what we now know as the Lifo principle (last-in, first-out) of inventory accounting, Humble prepared to meet a serious accounting loss on its storage oil. Twenty years later a plan similar to this suggestion of Farish and Wiess—that the profit or loss on crude sold at a given time should be determined on the basis of the cost of the most recently purchased crudes—was adopted by the Bureau of Internal Revenue for oil inventory accounting.

At the same time that this new system of inventory accounting was put into effect a separate Crude Oil Department was established. The complete segregation of crude oil accounting was apparently the main objective in separating crude operations from the Production Department. The purchase and sale of crude had become so large a business that it was desirable for cost-control and accounting purposes in general, as well as for other considerations of management, to make this separation. This new department was designed to embrace the activities of purchasing, storing, and selling crude oil from the time it left the producers' tanks until it was delivered to the Refining Department or sold to others. The Crude Oil Committee continued to function as before, and James Anderson as director and vice-president, assisted by W. R. Trelford, to have charge of operations. Ralph V. Hanrahan, vice-president and later president of Humble Pipe Line Company, kept in close touch with crude operations and attended important sessions of the Crude Oil Committee. The pipeline company continued to gather oil in the fields and worked closely with the Crude Oil Department in purchasing.

Humble at this time was becoming increasingly conscious of the need to adjust the price of crude more closely to the value of the products. Grading of some kind was an old practice in the American oil industry, one that had varied with different conditions. Humble first distinguished between two grades of Gulf Coast crudes—"A" for manufacturing lubricants and "B" for fuel oil. In October, 1922, however, the company followed the example of the Gypsy Oil Company and The Texas Company in beginning to differentiate among crudes on a gravity basis.[13] The grading and pricing of oil according to gravity was an inevitable result of the need to buy with greater discrimination as to the end product of the crude in a market in which a superfluity of oil was offered and the lighter oils, because of their higher gasoline content, were in relatively greater demand. It was a logical result of this situation that Wiess, the director in charge of manufacturing, was more responsible for the company's grading and pricing by gravity than anyone else in Humble.

There was no basic change in purchasing policies. The company's officials were quite aware of the high cost and risk of aboveground storage. But their choice in flush fields lay between supplying storage for surplus production to the limit of a well's capacity and the operator's ability to get the oil to the surface and risking the loss of a supplier by not supplying sufficient storage and thus forcing him to reduce his production at the risk of drainage by wells on neighboring leases. The general opinion in the oil industry continued to be that storage was the only practical means of taking care of surplus production.[14]

The inequities that could result under the prevailing system of competitive production can be illustrated from Humble's own producing operations. On a tract known as the Japhet twenty-acres in the rich West Columbia field, developed in the years 1918 to 1920, Humble had drilled thirty-one wells and by November 7, 1921, had produced over 8,000,000 barrels. Farish on that date wrote in reference to this production, ". . . we have undoubtedly produced more oil from this property than was originally under the property, as we have unquestionably produced some of our neighbors' oil along with our own." Although this was a somewhat extreme example, and there is no proof that Farish was right in this instance, it illustrates what could happen with unregulated, competitive drilling.

This Japhet experience pointed a moral—and illustrated the advantages of large capital and integrated operations. Once when Teagle of Jersey Standard was in Texas, he and others, while driving from Houston to West Columbia, tried to estimate how much storage would have been required to hold the oil produced from the Japhet twenty-acres. Farish calculated that, if stored, the 8,000,000 barrels produced would have required 148 tanks of a capacity of 54,000 barrels.[15] Humble, because of its assured customer in Jersey, and Jersey, because of its strong position in refining and marketing, had been able to dispose of most of this oil as it was produced; some other producers, unable to market, refine, or store an equal proportion of the oil in place beneath their land, had presumably been forced to submit to drainage. But what if the day should come when Humble would be unable to dispose of most of its oil as produced? Could even such a strong company afford to store such tremendous production? The advantage of producing to supply only current needs was obvious.

Humble in those years of abundance attempted to reduce the actual cost of storage.[16] Although its policy was to discontinue the use of earthen storage, this was not accomplished entirely until near the mid-1920s; however, evaporation was reduced to some extent by building wooden roofs over some of the Gulf Coast earthen pits. Experiments with a patented foam covering, known as Sealite, to reduce evaporation in tanks proved unsuccessful. Evaporation from steel tanks with wooden roofs was, however, reduced by substituting steel roofs or insulated wooden roofs. In 1923–1924 it was found that insulated roofs, which cost only about half as much as steel roofs and did not corrode, were not efficient from an evaporation standpoint and were subject to fire from lightning. Humble was able to effect some saving by following the trend toward tanks of larger capacity, which reduced the per-barrel cost of storage.

Although steel tanks reduced the physical waste of oil, they were themselves wasteful in another way. The cost of constructing a sufficient amount of steel storage to take care of a field's uncontrolled flush production was enormous. Moreover, only a small part of the value of the steel tanks could be salvaged once the field's brief high production was over and tanks were cut up and moved to another field. Also, when steel tanks had been used to store oil with a high sulphur content, the resultant corrosion made the salvage value negligible. Yet the economic waste from excessive construction of steel tankage could not be eliminated so long as unrestricted production prevailed.

During the years 1921–1923, when the development of the fault-line fields in east central Texas brought erratic production and wide fluctuations in prices, Humble continued to pile up inventory. Greatly increased production in this area necessitated a corresponding increase in pipeline and storage facilities and greatly strained Humble's crude oil purchasing and storage policies.

Humble entered Mexia as a purchaser in the autumn of 1921 when the field still had no pipeline outlet. The company decided to build storage, extend a pipeline to the field, and make as many lease connections as possible and buy as much oil as it could provide storage for. Teagle advised that oil be bought instead of stored because experience indicated that independent producers were usually willing to sell their total production at a price that would allow for the expense of storage, whereas they were dissatisfied with the price when the purchaser prorated runs. Humble posted a price of 60 cents, ordered nearly 3,000,000 barrels of steel storage, and soon was handling 50 per cent of the output of the field, nearly half of the runs being its own production. At first about 40 per cent of the oil was shipped by tank car and the rest stored—both costly operations—but by January, 1922, the pipeline that Humble was building from its Comyn-Webster main line reached Mexia and provided an outlet for 20,000 barrels daily.

Humble then negotiated twelve-months' contracts for the purchase of Mexia crude, so pegged to the Mid-Continent price that, at the time the agreements were made, the price was 50 cents above the going price of Mexia oil. As the Mid-Continent price fell because of the large Texas production and the price of east central Texas crude rose because of increased competition for oil in that particular area, the gap between the

Humble contract price and the going Mexia price grew narrower and narrower. In September the posted price for Texas crude exceeded the Mid-Continent's by 25 cents, and before the end of the year by 60 cents, which meant that Humble's contract price was lower than the Mexia posted price. In September, five months before the expiration of the contract, Humble, instead of continuing to take advantage of its favorable contractual price, voluntarily agreed to extend the contract for twelve months at regular posted prices.

By the end of 1922 Humble had crude oil in storage totaling nearly 16,000,000 barrels. Three-quarters was Texas crude and the remainder, in earthen tanks, was from its own production in the newly developed Smackover field in southern Arkansas.

Early in 1923, declining production at Mexia and Smackover, preceded by salt-water encroachment in the prolific southern fields of Mexico, temporarily corrected the situation of overbundance which had prevailed for over two years. Humble and The Texas Company then inaugurated a series of general price increases. These were particularly appreciated in North Texas, where producers were said to have been "forced to move their product at any figure they could get." [17]

An increase in production in the spring of 1923, however, set in motion a new price decline. Then came the great Powell boom.

If Powell—a fault-line field north of Mexia—had been the only flush field at that time, the situation would probably not have been so serious. But its development coincided with unprecedented increases in Oklahoma and in the Los Angeles Basin. Production in the United States increased from 571,000,000 barrels in 1922 to 754,000,000 in 1923; the total end-of-year crude oil stocks rose to over 80,000,000 barrels more in 1923 than in 1922.[18] Prorating pipeline runs was started early in the summer of 1923 in California and the Mid-Continent.[19] The situation was described thus in a report of the Humble "Scouting Department": [20]

> . . . the general economic situation as applied to oil is one that staggers the imagination even of those who are well informed concerning the oil business. The oil industry in America faces an overproduction that is beyond the capabilities of financial resources of the industry to take care of it. Daily production in the United States, if all was being produced, would probably total close to 2,500,000 barrels. The purchasing companies throughout the Mid-Continent area are pro-rating runs on a 70% basis. It is understood, of course, that the Prairie, Sinclair, and some smaller purchasing companies in the Wichita area are pro-rating runs in this area on a 70 per cent basis, and we are just informed today that The Texas Company has inaugurated this policy in the Ranger and North Texas Fields, so, it is readily seen by everyone that the overproduction situation is, to say the least, about to break the back of everyone in the business. . . . To continue to produce oil in Texas by the drilling of new wells in the old

fields, and the overdrilling and overproduction of pools of this character, means nothing less than economic loss and waste to the state.

Humble again built pipeline and storage facilities to take care of a new flood of oil. Jersey, realizing that its Texas affiliate already had as great an investment in crude as it could afford to carry, offered assistance in financing an increase in Humble's pipeline capacity in order to provide an outlet for the company's current production. Humble rushed a pipeline from Mexia to Powell. Instead of increasing the capacity of its trunk line to take care of flush production, it initiated a tremendous tank-building and tank-buying program aimed at an ultimate capacity of over 8,000,000 barrels.

Powell's unprecedented production complicated matters for Humble as for other producers in that field. For a time the company was unable even to take care of its own production, which amounted to approximately a third of the field's total. Tank-car transportation was wasteful and expensive—about 53 cents per barrel to the Coast, compared with trunk-line charges of 25 cents. Many wells, therefore, had to be shut in to await an outlet. Magnolia, principal price-maker in the area, cut its price to 75 cents. Humble kept its posted price at $1.00.[21]

Although Humble had difficulty in taking care of its own large production at Powell, it purchased some oil even during the flush period. These purchases, however, were small compared with its own production, which for over forty days averaged more than 100,000 barrels a day; because Powell was developed largely by the majors, a smaller percentage of the oil it yielded was for sale than was usual in new fields. There are no written records that reveal Humble's purchasing policy at Powell, but J. A. Neath, who was pipeline superintendent in the Mexia-Powell district when Powell was at its height, said in 1955 that Humble took as much oil from wells offsetting its own wells as it did from its own. This prorating, according to Neath, sometimes necessitated the reduction of the flow from Humble's own wells or even the shutting down of the wells when adequate storage was not available.

Humble also at the same time had difficulty in handling the oil offered in the Ranger district. Pipeline outlets from North Texas had been choked and prices there adversely affected by Powell. Humble consequently offered to hold back its own production if those from whom it was purchasing at Ranger similarly curtailed theirs.[22] Beginning August 1, 1923, it followed the example of The Texas Pipe Line Company in reducing its runs in the Ranger district, except those under contract, to 70 per cent of July production. The following significant statement was included in Farish's order to Hanrahan about the prorating of purchases: [23]

For the present, as this pro-rating applies only to purchased oil, instruct your gaugers to run all the production of the Humble Oil & Refining Company. We want it understood, however, that we want your gaugers to know that the policy of the Humble Oil & Refining Company in pro-rating will be not to seek any advantage in producing oil over their neighbors, and that in all areas or districts where production is being pro-rated the Humble Oil & Refining Company will curtail or handle their own production so as to be in line with what is being done on the adjoining properties. It will take several days to thoroughly analyze the situation and to know just what is being done on the adjoining properties; therefore, for the present, I repeat, have them run all the production from the Humble Oil & Refining Company.

Because an insufficient number of operators agreed to prorate, Humble's offer of voluntary reduction of its production was not put into effect. On August 19, following the lead of Gulf and Magnolia, Humble consequently cut its purchases to 50 per cent, but it offered to store the remainder if given an option to purchase.

Humble then adjusted its purchasing to the condition of oil supply. When purchase limitations and price cuts brought a curtailment of North Texas production, it resumed the 100 per cent purchase policy and early in October offered to purchase the storage oil on which it had an option.[24] Late in the month, however, it cut its North Texas prices to between 80 cents and $1.30, depending on gravity, but it did not follow subsequent cuts by Prairie and Magnolia.[25]

In the meantime Powell production had slumped after mid-September, only to increase in October with amazing rapidity. Humble ran to its tanks 90,000 to 100,000 barrels daily, moving 26,000 by pipeline and 20,000 by tank car and storing the remainder. In order to meet this short-lived increase in production, the company revived its tank-building program and bought two tank farms, with the result that by early 1924 it had nearly 11,000,000 barrels of steel storage in the Mexia-Powell area.

A report of a visitor to Powell in November, 1923, conveys a sense of the activities in the field, particularly Humble's: [26]

Today in those cotton fields, 525 derricks are up, of which 450 represent producing wells. There are 113 wells still drilling, of which 32 are being drilled by the Humble Company. As you drive into the field from Corsicana, you are deafened by the pneumatic drills racing to finish the Humble Company's programme of 7,000,000 barrels costing $4,000,000. In a single group the company has forty 80,000-barrel tanks and forty 50,000-barrel tanks. . . . On the farm of R. P. Fleming, the Humble Company brought in five wells, each capable of 10,000 barrels a day, or 50,000 barrels in all, if storage capacity had been available. When storage space had been completed the Fleming wells flowed only 19,000 barrels, an illustration of the reason for the feverish race of production among competitors in an oil field. "The difference between the 50,000 and 19,000 barrel production," said Mr. Farish, "is due to the fact that too many other straws were stuck in the tub." "Straws in a tub" is a perfect illustration of competitive exploitation of an oil field. . . . Out of these 2,400 acres of cotton fields, 25,000,000 barrels of oil have flowed in half a year, selling for $25,000,000. The Humble Oil Co. produced one-third. With what it produced and what it buys, it is today responsible for taking care of fully one-half the total production. There is not a million barrels in storage capacity at Powell outside the Humble's 7,000,000.

Powell's great surge in the autumn of 1923 was its last. In late November and December the field's production fell off rapidly. The period of overproduction brought on by Powell was over, and crude prices began to rise in Texas.[27]

The oversupply of oil resulting principally from flush production in this field brought a threat to Humble's very existence. It spurred a movement in Texas, which had arisen early in 1921 after a severe drop in prices, to attack purchasers of crude oil through the courts. Powell thus helped to bring to Texas one of those crises that had appeared again and again in the history of the American oil industry; one such crisis had sparked the movement which culminated in the dissolution of the Standard Oil group in 1911,[28] and another had set in motion the negotiations that led to the founding of Humble Oil & Refining Company in 1917. In August, 1923, as a direct result of the condition of the crude oil market for which Humble and other majors were blamed, suit was brought against Humble for violating the Texas antitrust laws, on the allegation that Standard Oil Company (New Jersey) was operating in the state through its affiliate.[29]

Although the case was decided in Humble's favor in 1924, the fact that the cancellation of its charter was threatened must have demonstrated vividly how politically vulnerable Humble was. To the purchaser's burden of loss by evaporation, heavy investment in storage facilities and in crude oil in storage, and the risk of loss from the uncertainty of prices was thus added the burden of increased political uncertainty.

Humble's popularity or unpopularity—as traditionally that of all large purchasers of crude oil—was, indeed, to be dependent throughout the years largely on whether or not the company was willing to take all the crude tendered at what the producers regarded as adequate prices. When it was purchasing all the oil from the leases with which it was connected, and particularly when making new connections with wells and raising prices, Humble was in high standing with the independent producers. But price cuts, unwillingness to make new connections, or refusal to purchase all the proffered oil speedily canceled the good will won earlier, despite the fact that, unlike some other companies, Humble was usually willing to store unpurchased oil rather than cast that onerous burden upon the independent producer. As the largest purchaser of crude oil in Texas, Humble more than any other company was generally blamed for falling prices. The problem of keeping the friendship of producers without bankrupting itself was later to become an important factor in the company's developing interest in proration and conservation.

In brief, Powell's flush production severely strained Humble's purchasing and storage policies. It forced the company to build up tremendous storage stocks, which had to be carried at high cost and risk, and challenged the company's policy of treating its suppliers' production as its own. As a result, Humble's executives began to perceive that storage was not the final answer to the problem of maintaining an adequate inventory and that in the future the supplying of current needs would have to be more closely correlated with current production.

RENEWAL OF THE QUEST FOR CRUDE, 1923–1926

Had another flush field followed closely after Powell, the subsequent history of Humble's purchasing and production might have been different. When Powell went into decline, Humble was apparently planning to become more selective in obtaining its crude supply; it was intending, instead of attempting to take all the oil that might be offered, to expand its own production and tie to itself certain suppliers by bonds of self-interest and gratitude. Its sharing of the market during Powell's highest production was evidence of such an intention. But fate again intervened in the form of another interlude of scarcity, a period in which Humble's own production declined sharply, both absolutely and relatively to that of the industry in Texas.

The collapse of the Powell boom late in 1923 ushered in a period of better balance between supply and demand and an upward price trend which was to last nearly three years.[30] Crude prices rose from December, 1923, through May, 1924; then came a sharp downward movement followed by a period of relative stability lasting until early 1925. Texas crude prices then again experienced a rapid rally, after which they remained reasonably high and unusually stable until October, 1926.

Like other companies, Humble early responded to declining production at Powell in the autumn of 1923 by rushing to make contracts and connections.[31] Even with a large supply in storage, it desired to assure itself of a larger share of the rapidly declining production of high-gravity Powell crude, which was then becoming increasingly valuable because of the steeply mounting demand for gasoline. Its eagerness to obtain the crude is indicated by the resumption of its old practice of loaning money to independent operators in return for twelve-months' contracts to purchase their crude at posted prices, the loan to be repaid out of half the proceeds to the sellers.

Humble now found itself in a dilemma as to prices. Higher prices would raise the value of its own production and tremendous storage stocks—over 20,000,000 barrels, some of which had been purchased at high 1919–1920 prices. But Farish warned in a statement of November 27, 1923, that higher prices would stimulate the wildcatters to increased efforts:[32]

> The danger is that somebody, in the interest of improving inventory and presenting a favorable year-end balance sheet, may mark up the price of crude. That would be a grave error. It would set the wildcatters loose again . . . and production would swamp us. . . . The price of crude should, in the interest of the industry, remain low until the next heavy consuming period. . . . If the wildcatters are held in leash by the present unprofitable prices . . . , then by May consumption may have eaten into stocks so that we may be able to dispose of perhaps 125,000,000 barrels at $2.00. The oil industry is sick. An advance in crude at the present time will make it sicker. . . .

In 1924 Humble bought the desirable Powell crude at the comparatively low prices then current. It took the lead, however, in increasing the price of Gulf Coast crudes in the spring on the ground of the importance of those crudes to the Baytown refinery. It canceled a cut in which it had followed Magnolia, explaining that, although the general situation warranted a weak market, most crude was being bought at the earlier prices and the company's connections should not be penalized. It was somewhat slower than other companies in reducing prices in North Texas when production increased.[33]

The company's policy with respect to its crude oil in storage was to attempt to hold the oil for higher prices. The high cost of holding the large stock was becoming a problem—by the middle of 1924 Humble held 22,000,000 of an estimated 471,000,000 barrels in storage in the United States. Some of that oil had been purchased at twice the current prices, and the temptation was strong to hold it, regardless of cost, in the hope that it could eventually be sold without too great loss. Whenever the price of oil declined, moreover, the temptation was strong to buy more oil in order to reduce the average cost of the oil already in storage. The expense of holding the oil was, however, constant and high; it could ultimately become prohibitive.

While Farish was greatly concerned over the "enormous cost and waste" [34] of holding oil in storage, the question was *when* to sell. Over this question a difference arose between the presidents of Humble and Jersey. Late in 1924 Teagle asserted that Humble had actually put 4,000,000 to 5,000,000 barrels into storage. The Jersey president commented: "My view is that the time to take crude out of storage is when you can do so, not when you would like to do so. . . . There may be some wise men . . . who can always reduce stocks at the top of the market and replenish them at the lowest point, but I am not, unfortunately, in this class. . . ." Farish replied that during the preceding seventy-five days Humble had drawn 1,700,000 barrels out of stock, despite a price slump that had brought the average price to $1.25, but it did not wish to dispose of any more Powell-Mexia crude at less than $1.50.[35]

Jersey Standard was not a disinterested party in this controversy. During the last months of 1924, when crude was scarce, Jersey called on Humble for such vast quantities of sweet (nonsulphurous) crude that the latter had to draw 3,000,000 barrels from stock at an average price of about $1.25, which was considerably less than average cost. Jersey also wanted Humble to pledge a regular supply of sweet crude during 1925; although Humble did not refuse to grant this request, Farish pointed out its unprecedented character. He at first thought that a "proper and fair allocation to Jersey would be about half the estimated 90,000 barrels that could be moved daily from Ranger and Powell."[36]

Humble's financial needs soon, however, made advisable the stepping up of sales—the company needed $30,000,000 for expansion and also wished to pay $8,000,000 on its loan account. In January, 1925, it authorized the sale to a pipeline company of 2,400,000 barrels of badly contaminated Smackover crude at $1.05. It also offered in February, 1925, to increase its commitment to Jersey for the months of March through August, 1925, to 56,000 barrels daily, plus a million barrels of Powell-Mexia-Currie crude in storage at Webster, to be moved during the next three months. When Jersey's E. M. Clark, although needing the crude, objected to moving the additional million barrels in the specified time, Humble offered to sell the oil at $2.00—claiming that it could be sold elsewhere at $2.65—and Clark agreed to the purchase.

Humble did not succeed in reducing its crude stocks very much in 1924–1925. In 1924, by curtailing its production and nearly doubling its refinery runs, it was able to achieve a balance between incoming and outgoing oil. In 1925 it reduced crude stocks 2,500,000 barrels, or about 8 per cent. This, although not a large reduction, was the first substantial cut since Humble had begun to build up storage stocks. The total United States stocks were in 1925 reduced only about 2 per cent.

Storage continued to be a problem, but after 1924 Humble's objective was to balance production and purchases with sales and refinery runs, rather than to buy oil to store, however low the price. But this objective was difficult to reach. "There is no happy medium," a leading oil journal observed. "Either the production is far in excess of demand, with a consequent piling up of surplus stocks in steel and earthen tanks, or the output falls off so rapidly that the drill is set to work with a vim." [37] Storage, expensive and wasteful as it was, continued to be the only possibility for some time, as it had been since the beginning of the American oil industry.

From 1924 Humble apparently attempted as a conscious policy to take proportionately as much from its pipeline connections as it ran from its own wells, even at the cost of shutting in a part of its own production. This policy of sharing the market—of ratable purchasing—may be illustrated from the memory of men working in the fault-line area in 1924–1925. A Humble production executive of recent years recalls that in 1923 or 1924, when he was a young superintendent in the Mexia-Powell district, he exclaimed to Farish on one occasion: "Mr. Farish, I sure as hell can't see why we're choking back 75,000 to 100,000 barrels daily of our own production and buying about that much from independents." Farish was silent for a moment, then replied, "Well, Russell, those boys have spent their money just like we have and they're entitled to their share of production." [38] John R. Suman, who in 1927 became a director of Humble, recalls an experience he had in 1924 or 1925. As manager at the time of the Rio Bravo Oil Company he was told that if he wanted to sell his company's oil from the Wortham field he should see "Jap" Neath, then superintendent of Humble Pipe Line Company in that area—so close was the co-operation between pipelines and the Crude Oil Department that it was not unusual for a pipeline superintendent to agree to purchase oil for Humble. According to Suman, Neath turned out to be a burly man, "tough as a boot and hard-boiled as they come," his formidable appearance accentuated by a big cap pulled down over his ears. When asked how much he would take of Rio Bravo's oil, Neath replied that he would take proportionately as much as was taken from Humble's own wells. Suman decided, judging from what was then an unusual practice, that the Humble men were "square-dealing folks." [39]

Humble's practice of sharing the market and its price policy—that is, its unwillingness as a rule to initiate cuts and its frequent refusal to follow others in lowering prices—are given principal credit for its ability to get connections when oil was scarce and to retain them when some refiners were offering a premium price.[40] The company's general willingness to store its connections' oil, rather than to cast the producers adrift, was another source of good will.

As the months passed in 1924 and no new flush fields were discovered, Humble's dependence on the independent producers became more and more obvious. The company became increasingly concerned about its oil supply; as the demand increased, no important new fields were discovered in Texas, and its own production slowed down. Jersey's anxiety concerning a long-time supply of crude also began to revive.

Humble's reaction to this situation was to look for new fields in which to purchase, a search which led into regions more remote than those in which the company had been operating. The principal discoveries in Texas after the Mexia and Powell booms were first in West Texas and later in the Panhandle. Humble did not enter either of those regions as a producer until 1926, and then only on a small scale compared with its production in the older oil regions; but it soon became a large purchaser in both.

Humble entered West Texas as a purchaser in December, 1924. Jersey's need for crude oil then influenced Humble to make a fifteen-year contract with the Reagan County Purchasing Company, Inc., and the Marland Oil Company for the purchase of 20,000 barrels daily from the Big Lake field in West Texas.[41] This deal, which was later to cause Humble much trouble, is said to have been the worst the company ever made. Humble agreed to deliver the crude to Jersey tankers. During 1925 and 1926, as noted in Chapter 7, it built two parallel pipelines from Kemper, near the Big Lake field, to Comyn, and also increased the capacity of the trunk line from Comyn to the Gulf Coast.

During 1925 Humble sold to Jersey nearly 6,000,000 barrels more than in the preceding year. Although a large amount was obtained from West Texas, some was withdrawn from storage. To supply Jersey, Humble also had to cut sales to nonaffiliated companies to 50 per cent of the previous year's sales.

Humble continued to have difficulty in obtaining sufficient oil during most of 1926. The company's own east central Texas production fell off so disastrously that, in order to meet its own and its customers' increasing needs, Humble had to reach out into new areas for more crude. Principally because of this need it built the pipeline from Thompsonville in Southwest Texas to Ingleside on the Gulf. Humble's own production in that region was at the time very small, but on August 30, 1926, it posted its first price for Mirando crude.[42] It also extended the West Texas pipeline to the newly discovered McCamey and Crane and on October 25 began purchasing in those fields.[43]

After much hesitation, owing to uncertainty about the oil future of the region, Humble also moved into the Panhandle. By May, 1926, production had so increased there that Humble decided to begin purchasing; it gathered the oil and brought it to the railroad for shipment by tank car. By December, 1926, the willingness of certain large producers to contract their Panhandle crude to Humble stimulated the latter's interest in building a pipeline to the region. Jersey's concern over an adequate supply of crude was a prime factor in Humble's decision to become a large purchaser in the Panhandle and to extend its pipeline system to that region.

While Humble's fears for the future were influencing it to extend its pipelines and purchasing, oil again became increasingly abundant. Indeed, at the very time that the fear of shortage was making Humble decide to enter the Panhandle as a large purchaser, a crude surplus was beginning to pile up.

In order to obtain contracts for sales to nonaffiliated refiners, such as The Atlantic Refining Company, Humble at this time took a significant step. It reduced its gathering charge at Comyn from 20 to 12½ cents and the commission from 20 to 5 cents. No change was made in trunk-line charges.[44]

In October, 1926, in keeping with a general price reduction, Humble also reduced its prices in the Panhandle.[45] Hostile producers and newspapers consequently accused it of spending $50,000,000 on a pipeline in order to get cheap oil for Jersey Standard, to which Humble replied that, because of the high sulphur and low gasoline content, Panhandle crude was not cheap in the long run. It is true that one of the reasons Jersey's president had advanced for the heavy expenditure for the Panhandle pipeline was that such an outlet might enable Humble to purchase oil at a price less than the cost of producing the oil.[46] Obviously, however, Humble could not afford to construct a 300-mile trunk line, build storage, and then purchase what was regarded as rather low-quality oil at more than the competitive price. As a matter of fact, the "cheap" oil Humble had contracted to buy was becoming a matter of grave concern.

Humble, indeed, was then by no means avid for even low-priced oil inventories. Its stockholders had been advised that henceforth the policy would be "to carry on its business without adding any crude to storage."[47] But Humble had to buy more oil than it wanted in the Panhandle, and Jersey Standard became seriously alarmed over its affiliate's purchases.

Humble and the Jersey group, generally, were caught in the web of their own success. Farish concurred in a statement of Jersey's Coordination Committee in January, 1927, to the effect that Jersey affiliates "could not play fast and loose with the connections with producers and in sound business practice were obliged to take their oil through thick and thin." [48] This statement of policy was not inspired by a greed for low-cost oil but came out of recognition of the necessity for maintaining the good will of the independent producers to whom Humble and the Jersey group looked for much of their crude supply. Regardless of whether or not Humble wanted to increase its oil in storage, dependence on other producers left no alternative to purchasing and storing.

Actually, by the end of 1926 Humble had reduced its crude in storage to 15,500,000 barrels from the high point of 20,500,000 barrels at the end of 1923 (Table 6). This reduction occurred despite the great increase in purchasing resulting from the company's entry into West Texas and the Panhandle. Humble's own refinery runs and its crude oil sales had, of course, increased somewhat. But the reduction came largely from a decline in the company's own production. The crude stock that Humble held at the end of 1926 was still a large and risky investment.

PROFITS: PAST AND PROSPECTIVE

The year 1926 was the most profitable that Humble's crude oil operations had ever experienced. While the book profits were high in 1919 and 1920, the tremendous decline in prices in 1921 produced a substantial loss in that year; a still larger loss would have resulted in 1922 but for the change in inventory accounting. Actually, the department's operating account showed a small profit in 1922 and a more comfortable one in 1923. In 1924 the Crude Oil Department ended the year in the red, as a result of Jersey's large purchases from storage at prices below cost. During 1925, on the contrary, when prices were reasonably high and comparatively steady, Jersey's heavy purchases brought a substantial profit. In 1926 Humble's crude oil sales increased in volume, prices until late in the year were higher than they had been for several years, and Humble reduced its inventory.

Over the eight years, 1919 through 1926, Humble's crude oil operations earned a fair total profit, although the full results could not be measured until the oil in storage at the end of the period had been disposed of and the large investment in storage and gathering equipment had been depreciated. Looking backward from the end of 1926, however, the results were not bad.

A significant point must be noted, nevertheless, in relation to profits in the years 1919–1926. A principal factor was price—both short-term price situations and, especially, long-term trends. Humble was generally able to hold its oil long enough to ride out short-term price declines, the striking exception being 1924; the long-term trend from 1921 until late 1926 was favorable.[49] In such a situation a company with the resources that Humble commanded could normally carry on crude operations successfully under the existing system. But what if the long-time price trend should change?

Late in 1926 Humble executives began to fear such a change. A considerable drop in prices occurred in October, and the tremendous increase in production in that year, both at home and abroad, presaged a long-continuing period of what the oilmen called overproduction—a production so large that prices did not cover costs and yield a fair return on investment. If what they feared became a reality, the strain on Humble's crude oil operations would become dangerously heavy.

In the next few years Humble was to make desperate efforts to reduce the risks and costs of aboveground storage while assuring itself of an adequate supply of oil for its own and its customers' needs. Those efforts were based on such earlier experiences as have been recounted. The particular turn they were to take in the important transition years of 1927–1930 was in large part guided by the changing attitudes of Humble executives toward production and purchasing problems in 1919–1926, particularly as seen in relation to changes in the world oil industry. Those attitudes and changes are the concern of a later chapter.

Chapter 9

TRIALS AND TRIUMPHS IN EARLY REFINING, 1919–1929

In 1919 the stage was set for a dramatic development of Humble's refining. The managers of the company had in 1918 formulated plans for building a refinery to utilize the increasing flow of crude oil from Goose Creek wells in manufacturing low-cold-test lubricating oils. The agreement with Standard Oil Company (New Jersey) of January, 1919, provided both the necessary capital for building such a plant and a market for its products.

The next decade was to bring important developments in the market for petroleum products and radical changes in their manufacture. The driving force was the rising demand for fuel and lubricants for the gasoline engine arising principally from the sharp upward trend in the number of automobiles after the war, an increase which ushered in the gasoline age. The steeply rising demand for gasoline, both absolute and relative to such former leading products as kerosene and fuel oil, stimulated changes in manufacturing methods and in the 1920s gradually brought science and engineering importantly into refining. In 1919, however, experienced practical men and time-tested methods still generally dominated the refining industry.

Humble's directors had to plan and build their company's Baytown refinery at the beginning of this period of change. Consequently, the original construction and early operation of this refinery were influenced by older ideas and methods. It was fortunate for Humble, however, that its directors were not committed to old ways and that the company had no strongly entrenched operating organization to hamper the introduction of the new. Director Wiess, who was given charge of refining, was an engineer by training and was especially receptive to new developments in refining technology. Moreover, he could draw upon the experience and knowledge of a small group of men in Jersey Standard who were introducing new concepts and new processes into their company's manufacturing operations.[1]

Humble's manufacturing in the 1920s was not to be limited to the large Baytown refinery. For many years the directors continued to follow the policy, inaugurated in the early days of the company, of building small manufacturing plants to meet specific needs and to take advantage of particular conditions. At the beginning of 1919 Humble had the Dixie refinery at San Antonio and the small Globe refinery at the Humble field; it also had a casinghead gasoline plant at the Healdton field in Oklahoma and a similar plant, with a related "topping plant," in North Texas. The forces that had brought these plants into existence in 1917 to 1919 continued to be operative for some time thereafter.

SMALL REFINERIES AND CASINGHEAD GASOLINE PLANTS

The small plants were of two kinds and served different purposes. Casinghead plants separated the valuable gasoline from the gas produced with oil, for which there was little if any market at the time; they were consequently built near fields producing particularly gasoline-rich gas. A variety of circumstances influenced the building and location of small refineries or topping plants. Those plants were not necessarily so economical to operate as the larger ones, but they served certain specific purposes well. Most plants of this type met a more or less temporary need; they were generally closed or moved to another location when there was a change in the conditions that had brought them into existence.[2]

The transitory nature of those small plants is illustrated by the fate of Humble's two earliest refineries between 1919 and 1922. The little plant at the Humble field was sold.[3] The Dixie refinery at San Antonio was closed in the summer of 1921 because of depressed business conditions and because other provisions had been made for handling much of the crude of the field from which it had been supplied. Although the discovery of the Mexia field in east central Texas restored the Dixie plant to activity for a short time in the autumn, the next year brought its permanent closing.

Conditions in producing fields in various parts of Texas fostered the building of other small plants. The practice of topping or refining the crude near the oil fields grew principally out of the nature of the raw material and the conditions surrounding its production. The law of property in oil known as the rule of capture encouraged the rapid development of a field, its production having to be stored until transportation was available. Tank cars were scarce and rates high. The high gasoline content of the crudes from the Burkburnett and Ranger areas of North Texas made them particularly susceptible to evaporation. Hence, to avoid the loss of light ends and to reduce the quantity of oil to be shipped, the crude oil was refined or topped near the fields.

Humble's flush production in the Burkburnett and Ranger areas during the years 1919–1921 resulted in several proposals for refinery projects in North Texas. The company abandoned a plan to build a topping plant at Iowa Park in the Burkburnett area because of the expense and its failure to arrange the sale of the distillate to Standard Oil Company of Louisiana. A striking illustration of the transitory conditions governing the use of such plants is the fact that traffic congestion in the busy postwar year 1919 delayed the arrival of equipment at Comyn in the Ranger area until production had declined and the need for a local refinery was over.

By late 1920, however, Humble had decided to build a topping plant at Colony Creek, west of Ranger. The company then had in storage 3,000,000 barrels of high-gasoline-content Ranger crude, which, it was estimated, was suffering a 6 per cent annual loss by evaporation. It consequently undertook to build a plant to top off a portion of the light fractions of the oil. The urgency in building at Colony Creek is indicated by the fact that even such items as window sashes were brought in by railway express and that Humble's newly organized Engineering Department erected more than a score of buildings in two weeks. In about three months, operations at the plant were under way. The "tops" were blended with Ranger crude to improve the latter's quality, and the mixture was transported by pipeline to Texas City for shipment to the Bayonne refinery of Jersey Standard. The "bottoms" were returned to storage. Within a short time the Colony Creek plant had topped the available crude and was no longer needed.

A somewhat different set of circumstances led to the building of a refinery near Burkburnett. Humble had been sending its production from this field to its San Antonio plant, but the high cost of shipping the crude by tank car—almost a dollar a barrel—resulted in the decision to build a refinery near the oil field. Work was commenced in June, 1921, and the Burkburnett plant was operating four months later. This refinery, with a capacity of 1,800 barrels daily, manufactured gasoline, kerosene, and fuel oil. The lighter refined products were delivered to Humble's Sales Department and sold to brokers; the fuel oil was sold to brokers and to railroads. In 1923 the output of this plant was improved by the installation of new equipment. After 1924 the plant was unprofitable, and in 1927 it was abandoned because of decreased crude oil production in the area and unsatisfactory realizations from sales.

Humble's flush production in the Powell field of east central Texas motivated the construction of other facilities in the interior. A refinery with a daily capacity of 7,500 barrels to supply the local market was constructed at Hearne, the junction point of Humble's trunk line and its pipeline to the Mexia-Powell area. This plant went into operation in October, 1923. Although this refinery at Hearne was operated for only two years, it proved both useful and profitable. It provided fuel oil on contract to the International & Great Northern Railroad and delivered kerosene and gasoline to the Sales Department and shipped them to Baytown by tank car. It was closed because of declining production and the termination of the railroad fuel oil contract. Wiess summarized the contribution of the Hearne plant as follows: "[The Hearne refinery] paid for itself handsomely, providing a market for upwards of 4,000,000 barrels of crude, giving perhaps 12½ cents per barrel profit to the pipeline company . . . , plus practically an equivalent in plant operations. . . . We have been further benefited by being able to hold connections in the Powell district . . . and have saved additional pipeline and storage tank investments." [4]

In the later years of the decade Humble added a number of other small refineries for a somewhat special reason. Vigorous competition in the gasoline market led to the company's decision to enter retailing. Since the retail stations which it planned to open at considerable distances from the Gulf could not be supplied profitably from Baytown in competition with rival stations supplied by interior refineries, Humble decided in June, 1927, to build more small refineries. These would distribute their products in the surrounding territories at less cost than if the products were shipped from Baytown, and they would also serve as bulk stations from which tank trucks could transport products directly to retail outlets.

Three such refineries were built in 1927. The Pecos area in West Texas was supplied from McCamey, where a 1,200-barrel refinery, with equipment from the old Hearne plant, went into operation in March. Utilizing crude oil from newly discovered West Texas fields, McCamey supplied Humble's and other marketers in the area and also provided fuel for railroads. North central Texas was served by a new 1,500-barrel skimming plant at Breckenridge, and the Waco area by a plant of the same size and type built at the Chilton pipeline station in east central Texas.

Additional facilities were similarly needed in south central Texas, where Humble was supplying customers partly from purchased gasoline.

Since the company's new pipeline from West Texas ran within twenty miles of San Antonio, plans were made to remodel the inactive Dixie refinery, but the project was abandoned because of the objections of residents of the city. A new 4,000-barrel plant, built outside city limits, went into operation early in 1928, supplying gasoline to Humble's Sales Department and fuel oil to railroads.

The next small refinery began operations at Ingleside, near Corpus Christi, on the Gulf in July, 1928. This plant was constructed at the terminal of one of Humble's pipelines from West Texas in order to take advantage of the increasing flow of crude from West and Southwest Texas. It was originally designed to supply fuel oil to Jersey Standard's tankers and to other ships and railroads and also to furnish gasoline to the markets of Corpus Christi and the lower Rio Grande Valley.

The era of construction of new small refineries terminated with the opening of the Neches refinery near Jacksonville in East Texas in October, 1929. Situated near Humble's Boggy Creek field, this refinery, with a daily capacity of 5,000 barrels and with a connected casinghead gasoline plant, supplied Humble's gasoline market in East Texas. The managers of Humble considered locating refineries in the Panhandle and at Smackover, Arkansas, but rejected both projects.

During the 1920s Humble also added to the number of its casinghead gasoline plants for reasons similar to those leading to the building of small refineries. The gasoline plants helped to provide products for Humble's expanding sales, but they also served a conservation function like that served by topping plants for high-gasoline-content crudes. From the gas produced with crude oil, casinghead plants recovered elements which would otherwise have been wasted and which were valuable for improving the volatility of the gasoline topped or cracked directly from crude oil.

Early in 1920, after surveying various fields, experts from Jersey Standard recommended a location for a new plant near Burkburnett. A gasoline plant with a daily capacity of 2,000 gallons went into operation there the following April. Later in the year, moreover, encouraged by the success of other companies operating casinghead plants on Desdemona gas, Humble built a plant in the Ranger area. In 1923 the company added other facilities in the Powell field, and six years later it built a plant at Jacksonville in East Texas.

Changes in the management of the casinghead plants illustrate adjustment to the problems of a growing company. At first these plants, all near Humble production, were placed under the supervision of the Production Department. With the growth of their importance and the general increase in the attention devoted by Humble to the processing of raw materials, these plants were shifted to the Refining Department.

In August, 1919, Humble's Operating Committee set up a separate Casinghead Gasoline Department, but two years later it was transferred to the Refining Department. Wiess had charge of the operations.

Although the casinghead plants had a fluctuating output, they served their purpose well. Late in 1921 the combined daily capacity of the Humble plants in Texas was 12,500 barrels, which was increased as other plants were built. The product was shipped to Humble refineries to be blended with heavier products or was sold for the same purpose.

The increase in the number of small, scattered refineries and casinghead gasoline plants was a passing although a significant phase in the history of Humble. The small refineries or topping plants saved quantities of the lighter fractions of the high-gasoline-content crudes of Ranger and Burkburnett during the flush production of those areas and helped to supply local markets. But they could not be economically operated in the long run; and for some, because of the fleeting nature of the local oil fields on which they depended, life was indeed short.

CONSTRUCTION AND EARLY OPERATION OF THE BAYTOWN REFINERY, 1919–1921

The construction of a refinery near Houston was a development of permanent significance. And building a large refinery to serve a highly competitive market, at a time when the quality of products was undergoing constant improvement, was quite a different undertaking from building small topping plants or refineries to serve local needs.[5]

Because the products of the projected refinery were to be used largely to supply its markets, Jersey Standard offered to help build and get the plant into operation. Humble accepted the offer, and the men who were added to Wiess's staff in 1919 came mostly from Jersey plants. Among them was Clifford Mackay Husted, who was engaged to become manager of the new refinery—Humble's former refinery manager had resigned, reportedly because of unwillingness to "work for Standard."[6] Husted, a Cornell engineering graduate who had been an assistant superintendent of Jersey Standard's Eagle Works, had had years of experience in a plant that specialized in manufacturing lubricants. The new chief engineer was Thomas Hayden Hamilton, who had recently directed the construction of a section of the BMT subway in New York. Siegfried P. Coblentz came from Jersey Standard to serve as refinery chemist. Additional supervisors were added when work on refinery equipment and operations began. W. A. Eberle, machine-shop foreman from Jersey Standard's Eagle Works, arrived in October, 1919, as superintendent of the refinery. Francis Nicholson Read, who had been ten years with the Galena-Signal Oil Company, a firm with almost a half-century reputation for making superior lubricants, came as assistant superintendent two months later.

Humble's top administrators, who had earlier selected a tract of 2,200 acres thirty miles from Houston on the ship channel just above Galveston Bay,[7] had followed a practice tested by long experience in the American petroleum industry: they chose a location accessible to deepwater shipping. The new refinery, it was decided, should be named Baytown. It could hardly be given so meaningless a name as Goose Creek, after the nearest town, and Baytown was an appropriate name, considering the location. Although the site was favorably located for shipping, the low-lying, boggy rice field surrounded by dense woods presented many obstacles to construction.

On April 16, 1919, a small party of engineers spread out their plans on the porch of an old farmhouse, the only building on the new property. Soon were provided a storehouse, a bunkhouse, and an office building—a wooden shack with chicken wire for partitions. Water wells were drilled by a contractor, the water proving excellent. Surveying, clearing, and draining got under way. Power lines and a railroad began to cut their paths from Goose Creek through the thicket of senna beans covering the refinery site.[8]

Early progress was interrupted when the rains came, the same rains that were then making work difficult for Humble's pipeline builders. Employees remember that it rained "one hundred days straight." Storms, especially in May, harassed workers and wrecked buildings and equipment. At times Baytown was shut off entirely from the outside world.[9] The only way to get around the refinery site was on horseback, the animals sometimes being belly-deep in water.

Rains were not the only obstacle. Tales are told of clouds of flies and malaria-carrying mosquitoes, grasshoppers, office-invading snakes, and bellicose Brahman bulls. The earth, when dry, was as hard as cement and as difficult to break, but, when the rains commenced, it grew slippery and sticky. When the rains ceased, they left a reservoir of heavy mud. It was a common saying a quarter-century later that in the early days the gumbo had claimed enough rubber hip boots to supply the entire working force of the later date. It balled up on the feet and shovels of workers and clogged ditching machines until they racked themselves to pieces. Sometimes four mules were needed to pull an empty wagon.[10] As if these conditions were not enough to try the builders' patience, quicksand added to the difficulties of excavation.

When the summer brought relief from the heavy rains, work proceeded more rapidly. Humble crews could then resume the work of clearing, draining, surveying, and excavating. Transportation facilities to and about the refinery site were improved.[11] By late July the Turner Construction Company, which had contracted to build most of the refinery, could begin pouring concrete. Humble crews started to erect tanks late in August and continued with this and other construction work, such as laying sewer lines and refinery pipelines and building brickwork, except during the torrential October rains.[12]

An inadequate supply of workers handicapped early construction. The workers did not like the terrain, the isolation, or the weather. Skilled labor was particularly scarce because the Ranger boom of 1919 and 1920 drew riggers, tank builders, and other workers away from the Gulf Coast. Negroes and Mexicans, however, who in accordance with Texas tradition were barred from oil-field work, were available for the hard, dirty labor of refinery construction. At the end of 1919 half the construction workers at Baytown were Mexicans or Negroes, principally the former.[13]

Despite all difficulties, by January, 1920, the concrete work on the boilerhouse, crude stills, and filter house was nearly completed, most of the machine shops were operating, and a battery of atmospheric stills was under construction. The first oil was charged to a still on May 11, 1920, an event commemorated for many years by a holiday. The formal completion of the Baytown refinery, however, was not to be celebrated until April 21, 1921—San Jacinto Day, in memory of the final victory of the Texans in 1836 in their struggle for independence from Mexico.

Nearly all the refinery foremen—except in the labor groups—were experienced men from Jersey Standard refineries, known locally as New Jersey Yankees. Many were foreign-born and Roman Catholic, and all were unacquainted with southern conditions. The working force was for the most part inexperienced in refining. It consisted mostly of native white Texans, but included Negroes and Mexicans who could not speak English. Yet the foremen, with hardly an exception, were successful. Their ability to do the work themselves, their willingness to turn their hands to anything that needed doing, and their eagerness to train the inexperienced workers are said to have been important in developing an adequate working force at Baytown.

Optimism prevailed briefly in the spring of 1920,[14] but many months were to pass before the Baytown refinery would be in successful operation. Among the circumstances delaying operations were the enlargement of the original plans, the variety of crudes to be processed, a short boilermakers' strike, and certain managerial and technical difficulties.

According to the original plan the principal units were to have been two batteries of ten atmospheric stills each, primarily for manufacturing lubricating oils, and in addition such necessary units as acid and wash agitators for treating the distillate, filter houses, and filter-wash stills for recovering the naphtha used in washing. By October, 1919, however, because of the rising demand for gasoline, the management had decided to add sixteen Burton stills—a type of still developed some years earlier by Standard Oil Company (Indiana)—to crack gasoline from gas oil after the small quantity of gasoline recoverable from coastal crude by atmospheric distillation had been topped off. Cracking broke the heavy hydrocarbon molecules into lighter fractions by the use of high temperature and pressure. A naphtha treater and steam stills for rerun purposes were part of the enlarged plan.

The various installations were put to use as soon as they were completed. The first battery of atmospheric stills was ready for oil in May, 1920, and the second battery, as well as filter-wash stills, in September.[15] In April, 1921, three of the sixteen Burton pressure stills were fired, and late in the spring the other pressure stills and steam stills for rerunning the distillate from the pressure stills were put into operation. By August, 1921, Baytown was a refinery of twenty atmospheric crude stills, sixteen Burton pressure stills, four steam stills, three filter-wash stills, and a full complement of agitators, treaters, filter houses, boilerhouses, and accompanying equipment. On the ship channel a 600-by-40-foot concrete dock had replaced a timber dock destroyed by fire the previous December.[16] The refinery had cost over $10,000,000, in contrast with the more modest estimate in 1918 of from $1,000,000 to $1,500,000, but the capacity was 10,000 barrels daily compared with the earlier proposal of 4,000 barrels.

A minor complication at Baytown was a strike of the boilermakers in August, 1920, the only strike in the refinery in the 1920s. Those employees were the object of a general organizational drive and struck for 12½ cents more than the current scale of a dollar an hour. Stoppage of work occurred at Humble's refinery and also at neighboring refineries and Louisiana Standard's in Baton Rouge. Wiess explained to the men that Humble was paying higher wages to boilermakers than were several of its competitors. Sterling commented that the company would of course not take back the "agitators," a policy also pursued by Louisiana Standard. The strikers returned to work without winning an increase in wages, but Wiess showed concern over the fact that wages at Baytown were in general lower than at Baton Rouge. Within a few months rates at Baytown were adjusted upward for a number of classifications, although not for the boilermakers.

Another disturbance occurred early in 1921. Drillers and roughnecks who had been laid off because of depressed conditions decided to drive the Mexican workers from Baytown. When, however, the mob appeared at the east gate of the refinery, the superintendent's diplomacy was effective in persuading it to disperse. Humble continued to employ

Mexican and Negro workers and also, as was the custom of the region and the industry, to pay them less than native white laborers, a difference which was eventually eliminated.[17]

Although the original purpose of the Baytown refinery was to process Goose Creek crude, during its first months the plant in fact dealt with a variety of raw materials. Both Humble and its chief customer, Jersey Standard, needed gasoline and cylinder oil early in 1920; Jersey was particularly eager to obtain cylinder stocks from the paraffin-base North Texas crudes. Consequently the oil charged to the first atmospheric-still battery in the Baytown refinery was Burkburnett crude of high gasoline content. After the completion of Humble's pipeline from Comyn to Baytown, Ranger crude was substituted. But the refiners were not successful in manufacturing from Ranger crude a cylinder stock that met specifications.

The coastal crudes also proved difficult to handle and the refinery failed embarrassingly in the filling of orders. Although coastal oil was first run in September, 1920, supplies promised for November were not then ready for delivery, and later orders also could not be filled. Because Baytown's refiners were unable to follow the original plan of cutting the lubricating distillates directly from the crude, they had to rerun the oil. Treating lube distillate made from Gulf Coast crude was then a tricky process, an art rather than a science and one requiring much skill. The refiners lost another six weeks as a result of using what proved to be the wrong grade of acid for treating. The receiving house proved not to have been constructed properly, and several batches of oil were spoiled. The lube distillates went into an emulsion when acid-treated; batches stood around for months, but no one could break the emulsion. Coblentz, the chemist, tried electrical precipitation, even applying for patents on such a process, but his method proved ineffective. In the hundreds of variations of the "treats," as the batches of distillate after acid-treating were called, some were better than others but none was a complete success. Some treats were finished through filtering and some lubes were shipped, but the filter costs were prohibitive and the oil had a poor color. Treater foremen from the East came and went to no avail, and visiting refinery experts from Jersey were of little help. In the meantime the Gulf and Texas companies were putting out merchantable oils directly from their acid agitators without filtering.

Humble for some time failed to emulate the successful methods of its competitors. Several years earlier the refiners of those other companies had succeeded in making lubricating oils from Gulf Coast crudes by running the distillates over caustic soda before acid-treating. Although the Humble managers were not acquainted with the practical workings of the process, they were keenly aware of the associated difficulties and disadvantages. The caustic was notoriously "hell on still-bottoms"; if its use could be avoided, a great deal of wear on equipment would be prevented. Caustic also impaired the value of the fuel-oil residue. Moreover, the men experienced in treating Gulf Coast oils were working for other companies in the area, and the ill feeling aroused by the early hiring of men from among ambitious employees of the major companies, particularly The Texas Company, now made Humble reluctant to approach these expert treaters. Husted and his co-workers sought long, but vainly, for a process that would preclude the use of caustic.

Encountering difficulties in putting a new refinery into operation was certainly not unique in the history of refining. Different types of crude have always demanded special methods for handling, and the men who managed the Baytown plant were not familiar with Gulf Coast oils. Vice-President Wiess, although entirely devoted to his duties, at the beginning of construction and operation at Baytown was not yet a specialist in refining. Husted struggled faithfully with the recalcitrant new raw materials, but shortly before the refinery's formal opening in April, 1921, he took an indefinite leave of absence and soon resigned. No amount of advice, even from such an experienced refining company as Jersey, or work on the part of the men at Baytown could produce an early solution. In the summer of 1921 the Baytown refinery was not yet really in practical commercial operation. Lube oils, the manufacture of which was its original primary objective, were not being made in appreciable quantities.

The men who had faced and accomplished the arduous task of construction had been stopped in their tracks by the Gulf Coast crude oils. They had borne the burden and heat of the day; mostly from the northeastern states, they had labored in a social and psychological environment that was as unfamiliar and baffling to them as the Goose Creek rice field and the coastal crudes. Despite many obstacles, they had built the refinery. But commercial production of lubes proved beyond the capacity of the builders.

BAYTOWN BECOMES A LARGE, UP-TO-DATE REFINERY, 1921–1925

In 1921 several new refinery men were added to Humble's refinery management. John Levi Finley, who was appointed assistant to Wiess, vice-president for refining, had had nearly twenty years of refining experience. Service with Standard Oil Company (Indiana), where the Burton still had originated, had made him familiar with that still's operation. He had also worked with Imperial Oil, Limited, in Canada, where he had handled difficult crude oils. His most recent experience had been in Jersey Standard's asphalt plant at Charleston, South Carolina.[18] Raymond E. Powell was appointed assistant superintendent as of November 1 and superintendent two months later.[19] He had worked with Finley in Charleston, and his experience, dating back to 1907, had been in various Jersey Standard and Imperial Oil refineries. In October, Jesse James Harrington, oil-treater foreman at The Texas Company's refinery at Port Arthur, was on the recommendation of Finley engaged as head treater for Baytown.

Harrington, employing the traditional Gulf Coast method, began to run lube distillates over caustic in the two batteries of atmospheric stills. By December, 1921, Baytown was said to be "producing beautifully finished lubricating oils instead of mere slop."[20] The next task was to cut out an intermediate process in order to meet competitive costs. Humble's rivals were putting out good lubes directly from the acid agitators without the use of filtering. With increased experience Humble's distillers were able to make "heart" cuts which did not require blending, were of better color, and, except in the case of the heaviest distillates, could be finished by the agitators without going through the expensive clay-filtering process. By the spring of 1922 the major portion of Humble's lube oil was prepared for market without filtering. The lubricating plant was at last on a sound operating basis, an auspicious first step in strengthening the Baytown refinery.

Another significant development came at about the same time, the beginning of research at Baytown. Wiess, in a memorandum written in November, 1940, tells of its origin:

> In the fall of 1921 I heard Dr. Lewis [W. K. Lewis of MIT, a Jersey consultant] make a talk to a group of Jersey technical men and executives in New York, in which he pointed out that engineering principles well known in science and in use in other industries were available for immediate application to many problems of the petroleum industry. I was deeply impressed by this talk. We had but one chemical engineer in our employ at that time, Stewart Coleman, a graduate of Rice Institute who also had been a student of Dr. Lewis.
>
> We recognized the necessity of setting up a competent chemical engineering organization at Baytown at the earliest possible time and at once established contact with Dr. Lewis and sought the help of him and Dr. Loomis, [N. E. Loomis, of Jersey Standard's Development Department] in setting up such an organization. We engaged Dr. Lewis as consultant, and early in 1922 had a research program under way in the laboratories of MIT on the development of vacuum stills, heat transfer and other urgent problems.

Thus, under the direct influence of Jersey and its Development Department established in 1919 was inaugurated an interest that was to have a strong effect on the development of the Baytown refinery. For three years Coleman divided his time between Baytown and MIT working on vacuum distillation, which Dr. Lewis believed would solve the treating problem in manufacturing lubricants.

Although the establishment of a research organization at Baytown was to come later, Humble in 1921 thus began to participate in a small way in the movement that was to bring radical change in Humble's and the industry's refining operations. Jersey Standard had in 1919 established its Development Department to keep itself informed of technical progress pertinent to refining, to experiment with new processes and to design equipment for putting them into use, and so far as practicable to carry on basic research. Other major companies were similarly undertaking formal research programs. Indiana Standard, for example, in 1922 appointed Robert E. Wilson, who was Director of the Research Laboratory of Applied Chemistry and Associate Professor of Chemical Engineering at Massachusetts Institute of Technology, to head its refinery research.[21]

In 1922 Baytown undertook an expansion program,[22] one of a series that, except for the depression period of the 1930s, subsequently increased its rated capacity every two or three years. A battery of ten crude stills, specifically intended for rerunning lube distillates over caustic, was added; six steam stills were added to another battery for running pressure distillates, rerunning kerosene, and processing light crudes. These two batteries were equipped with bubble towers and large heat exchangers, then known as Baytown heat exchangers;[23] they were more economically operated than the old equipment, had greater capacity, and gave more uniform results.

Following this expansion, a new program was undertaken that was intended to bring the refinery's equipment into line with the most advanced techniques, particularly for manufacturing a larger percentage of gasoline from crude. The Burton pressure stills installed at Baytown in 1921 were standard for that date, but they were already about to be superseded by other equipment. Cracking the hydrocarbons to produce a larger percentage of gasoline from crude was then an interest of several of the larger companies, which developed or acquired processes of their own. Jersey Standard developed the tube-and-tank process, which it strengthened by acquiring certain Ellis patents. Indiana Standard, Shell, and Texas acquired other processes.[24] The Burton stills were not well adapted to the Gulf Coast crude oils with their asphalt base and highly refractory gas oil. Moreover, the Burton stills at Baytown had deteriorated to such an extent that it had become necessary to reduce the pressure under which they operated.

In 1923 Humble began to construct six tube-and-tank cracking coils, the process referred to above which had been developed by Jersey Stand-

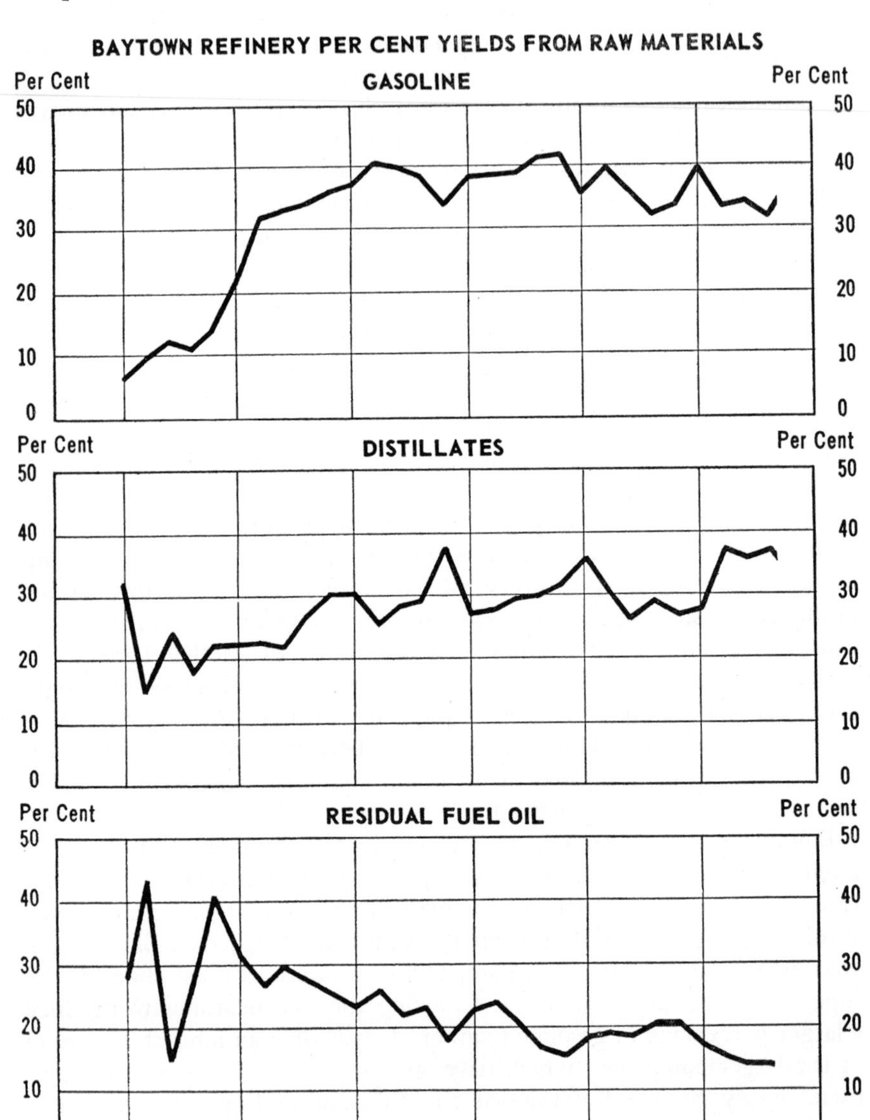

ard. The advantages of this equipment over the Burton stills were that it could be operated continuously, instead of in batches, and could stand a much higher pressure. Humble was at first deterred by Jersey's royalty of 10 cents per barrel of crude stock charged or a flat payment of $100,000 per cracking coil. Because of the experimental character of the process and the low gasoline content of coastal crudes, the charge seemed exorbitant to Humble's directors, but inasmuch as the merits of the method appeared so great they accepted the flat rate. By September, 1923, three of the new units had been installed at Baytown and the Burton stills had been removed from service.

Pleased with the success of the new process and pressed by an increasing demand for gasoline, Humble's managers late in 1924 began to plan the construction of additional tube-and-tank units. They also started what proved a successful campaign to get the royalty reduced, an early example of the company's "standing up to" its large stockholder. Wiess insisted that Humble had built units before the process had been fully developed, that it had contributed considerably to the development of the process, and that it should not be expected to pay the maximum royalty. Since the validity of the patents covering the equipment apparently depended largely on the use of soaking drums, Baytown set to work on an experiment to test whether the cracking coils could be operated profitably without the drums. Humble and Jersey Standard shortly, however, agreed on a contract embodying a paid-up royalty of $50,000 per unit. Baytown immediately started to build ten new tube-and-tank cracking coils; it subsequently added to their number until by August, 1926, a total of twenty units had been put into operation.

The introduction of these cracking coils marked Baytown's definite shift from its original role as a lubricating oil plant to that of a complete refinery, emphasizing gasoline. In terms of percentages figured on the basis of total crude input, the motor gasoline produced from crude at Baytown rose from 11.3 per cent in 1923 to 21.5 in 1925, while the percentage production of lube oil decreased from 21.6 to 13.5.[25]

Humble late in 1923 decided to make another major change at Baytown. This was a result of the research of Coleman and James Harrop on vacuum distillation, followed by the inspection by Wiess and others of California Standard's vacuum-distillation operations—vacuum distillation was then becoming a major interest of large refining companies. Four of Baytown's original battery of atmospheric stills were equipped with bubble towers and heat exchangers, and six were rebuilt so as to operate under vacuum. The first group took off light products from the crude or distillate, and the vacuum stills produced the lubricating cuts. The reconverted battery, completed in 1924, worked well; better distillates could be produced under vacuum straight from the crude than by double runs in atmospheric stills. The second battery of atmospheric stills was reconverted the next year. Its operation, however, was as much an improvement over that of the first battery as the first had been over the older process, an indication of how fast refining was being improved. Coleman's hope that the use of caustic might eventually be eliminated and finished oils obtained directly from the stills was not realized at the time.

Although Humble was not the first company to employ vacuum distillation in the production of lubricants, the scale on which Baytown developed the process and the success with which it operated were noteworthy. A visiting Jersey Standard engineer late in 1925 described the Baytown plant as including "all the improvements ever made in distilling . . . under vacuum."[26]

In 1924 research was formally established at Baytown by the organization of the Development Department. C. R. Johnson, a graduate of MIT and formerly development manager of the Goodyear Rubber Company, was employed to set up and head Humble's new department. Several other MIT men were also hired, including Dr. E. F. Voss, who had had considerable industrial experience and held a doctoral degree in science from the University of Paris. Coleman, who had completed the residence requirements for the doctoral degree at MIT, had returned to Baytown. Harry W. Ferguson, a 1924 graduate in chemical engineering from the University of Michigan, joined the group shortly after graduation. The new department consisted of two divisions, a routine testing laboratory, under W. R. Brison, to carry on "the class of work previously done here," and an experimental division, under Coleman, "to carry on experimental work in connection with plant operation and process. . . ." On Johnson's resignation in 1925, the youthful Coleman was made head of the department.

Dr. Lewis of MIT and Dr. Loomis of Jersey Standard spent two weeks at Baytown immediately after the establishment of the Development Department, and the Baytown research staff had the continuing advantage of communication with the Jersey group and the advice of Dr. Lewis. The latter was an outstandingly creative pioneer in applying chemical engineering to refining. N. E. Loomis and E. M. Clark of Jersey Standard advised particularly on the practical application of new concepts and processes. "Baytown," as Coleman reminisced in later years, "was an experimenter's dream." There the research group did not have to depend upon a laboratory but could have a whole still battery for an experiment.[27]

The work of improvement and expansion at Baytown was continuous. The addition in 1924 of an atmospheric still for topping gasoline fractions from heavy Mexican crude of high viscosity, and in the following year of a battery of twelve stills for running light Mexia-Powell crudes, illustrates the growth of Baytown's capacity and the refinery's ability to handle an increasing variety of crude oils. By the end of

1925 Baytown had a rated capacity of 50,000 barrels daily, and it had become a complete, up-to-date, and efficiently operated refinery. Also in 1925, for the first time, it earned a substantial net profit.

EMPLOYEE RELATIONS AT BAYTOWN, 1919–1929

Because Baytown served as a nursery for several employee relations developments that were later applied to the whole company, the refinery's early employee management merits special consideration. The developments at Baytown were mostly due to particular circumstances, including the necessity at the refinery of managing a large concentrated labor force, the close contact of Baytown with Jersey's refining, and its location some distance from developed communities.

Baytown's experience with a joint management-employee council was especially significant. This was a direct borrowing from Jersey Standard, in whose New Jersey refineries this form of employee representation had been adopted in 1918 under the leadership of Clarence J. Hicks.[28] On December 10, 1920, representatives of Baytown management and employees unanimously adopted an agreement for a Joint Conference similar to that in operation in Jersey Standard's refineries. The stated objective of this new organization was the regular and special meeting of representatives of management and employees to discuss hours, wages, and working conditions, and, if possible, to settle difficulties before they became grievances. The agreement provided for the annual election of employee representatives from the various divisions of the refinery, together with the appointment by management of an equal number.

The agreement included principles and rules concerning employment. Hiring and firing in the petroleum industry were traditionally done by foremen or superintendents. The Baytown employee-management agreement, following Jersey's example, stated specific causes for dismissal and the employee's right of appeal to foremen, employment department, superintendent, division conference, general joint conference, and "the higher officials of the company," all actions being "subject to review by the Board of Directors."[29] The list of offenses for which an employee could be fired without warning was long—sixteen specific ones and the repetition of other offenses after warning; whether or not dismissed employees in the early years availed themselves of the right of appeal does not appear in the records. But at least the agreement recognized in principle that the employee had some protection on his job.

The Joint Conference served as a medium for communication between management and employees, at first particularly to communicate to the employees management's decisions or thoughts on specific matters. For example, in a period of large but intermittent construction, the problem of layoffs called for consideration. In 1922 Superintendent Powell announced to the Joint Conference the principles which should govern layoffs:[30]

> We are getting near the end of this construction program and it means that . . . a large number of our men will have to be laid off. When this layoff comes you are going to keep the best men. . . . So when the layoff comes, impress upon your men that it is the good men that we shall keep. Some good men too will have to go, but first of all should be considered a man's value to the company; then . . . it is a question of seniority; that being equal, it is a question of dependents. . . . Personal feelings, I know, are apt to creep in most every time, but you must disregard that entirely. . . . It is a question of usefulness to the company. . . .

The Joint Conference performed still another function that was important in a new community without municipal government. Typical subjects of discussion were such Baytown community matters as housing and sanitation. For example, an able Negro representative was instrumental in bringing the problem of housing the approximately 300 men of his race to the attention of management and thus achieving some improvement. The conference also served to effect necessary joint action on a number of community problems.

In its early years, however, the Joint Conference at Baytown did not achieve real vigor in discussing major employment issues. The superintendent of the refinery unquestionably dominated the meetings. He was chairman, ex officio, and he had the power to cast the deciding vote, should the conference divide evenly on an issue. Superintendent Powell was of the old school of managers who were familiar only with one-way communication with employees—the communication of orders and management decisions. The conference approach to problems was, indeed, a new technique for the representatives of both employees and management, a technique nowhere mastered in a short time. The gossipy *Humble Bee*[31] complained two years after joint representation had been adopted that only half the employees voted for representatives. Whatever apathy this vote may have represented, there is evidence that working conditions and wages at Baytown were sufficiently satisfactory in these early years, compared with conditions generally in the area, so that the employees may not have had any particular desire to join in urging improvement. The system was to come into broader and more effective use within Humble in the 1930s.

A beginning was also made at Baytown at this time in training ambitious employees. The traditional method was to learn on the job. The refinery went a little beyond this, though the action taken in the 1920s was probably more important as a new departure foreshadowing later development than in its actual accomplishment. In 1922 Coblentz, the chemist, gave a series of lectures to laboratory men. In 1927 Superintendent Powell initiated talks on refining and refinery management; and the next year he gave a course on foremanship, which was open to foremen, members of the Joint Conference, and apparently to other interested employees. These lectures in the 1920s were given on the initiative of refinery men and antedated Humble's formal program for employee training.

Accident prevention was another area of experimentation at Baytown. The high refinery accident rate in 1920—2,266 accidents among a thousand workers, largely on construction—called attention to the need for preventive work. The Baytown Joint Conference in February, 1921, organized safety and health committees, and the refinery employee magazine, the *Humble Bee*, emphasized precautions against accident and illness. A safety director for the company, D. J. Wallace, was appointed in 1922, but in 1924 he was moved with his staff to the refinery, where considerable progress was made in developing safety consciousness and safety methods.[32] From 1927 this work was carried forward under R. B. Roaper, who succeeded Wallace as safety director at Baytown when the latter resigned to accept a similar position with the Mid Continent Oil & Gas Association. Roaper had had no previous experience in either safety work or the oil industry, having been supervisor of the Baytown housing development, but he studied safety problems and ways of preventing accidents. Under his direction at the refinery strict safety rules, safety handbooks, safety shoes and goggles, improved gas masks for workers handling poisonous crudes, and first-aid training contributed to an improved safety record, as also did his emphasis on safety as head of the refinery's welfare program and his editorship of the *Humble Bee*. The refinery's safety record was so much improved that in 1929 Roaper was appointed to head a formal company-wide safety program.[33]

Finally, Baytown provided Humble with experience in furnishing housing and community facilities for its employees which led to a development that marked a departure for the company from company-owned camps, such as the Humble camps in the Goose Creek, West Columbia, and Ranger fields. For several years Humble provided housing for its Baytown employees—a large percentage of whom were temporary construction workers—only in response to pressing needs and without over-all planning. At first employees commuted from private homes in neighboring towns or bunkhouses at Goose Creek, but soon old army tents and barracks were provided near the refinery, with meals at an old farmhouse. By January, 1920, new bunkhouses and mess halls were accommodating a thousand men. Married supervisory employees were early supplied with small houses, as were also some of the skilled workers, but others had to shift for themselves. In 1922 Humble built many one-room and two-room rental houses for the unskilled.[34] Some community facilities were also provided, including schools for native white and Mexican children. Free evening transportation to Goose Creek was furnished for employees who wanted to go shopping or to seek whatever entertainment the village offered.[35]

Plans were made in 1923 for a permanent community to be known as East Baytown. The company by then had a large permanent operating force. At East Baytown Humble adopted the policy of assisting its employees in acquiring homes instead of building homes for them. The management agreed to lay out a tract, build streets and sidewalks, provide utilities, and finance a home-building program. Two years later, when title to the land had been cleared and building could begin, a prospective owner could obtain funds from the company for building a house by making a down payment of 10 per cent of its cost and agreeing to pay the balance in small monthly installments at 6 per cent interest. Within ten months of the first contract, 380 lots had been sold and 145 buildings completed. Following the custom of the region, East Baytown was restricted to native white workers, who also enjoyed the facilities of the fine brick community house with company-sponsored movies established early in 1925. More adequate housing arrangements for the few hundred unskilled Mexican and Negro employees than their small rental houses were not provided.[36]

East Baytown, however, was a village not only for supervisors and skilled employees. That it was possible for unskilled workers to acquire homes there is illustrated by the experience of one employee as recounted by him shortly before his retirement late in the 1940s. An illiterate French-Acadian, he had come to work for Humble in 1919; he had left Louisiana because he was earning only 80 cents a day on a sugar plantation, which was not enough to support his family. Having heard of high wages in the oil industry, he borrowed a few dollars, went to Texas in search of a job, and began to work for Humble as a common laborer for $5.00 a day. He slept in a boiler room until he could buy a tent and for a time subsisted mostly on crackers and cheese. At the end of a year he bought a one-room shack near the refinery, built a one-room addition himself, and then brought his wife and four children to live there. They lived in that shack for several years, adding two rooms to house the family that increased to six children. When land in the East Baytown subdivision was made available, this unskilled worker bought a double lot including betterments for less than $700. On the completion of his seven-room modern house in 1927, he owed only $400, a debt that he paid within a year.[37] Excepting a few hundred dollars from the sale of a small piece of land in Louisiana, this home was paid for by savings from earnings with Humble.

The organization of Humble's Industrial Relations Department in 1929 opened a new chapter in employee relations at Baytown, as in the company generally. Much of the background of experience that went into the creation of the new department had been gained at Baytown in the 1920s, particularly in the Joint Conference, employee training, and safety work.

A GOLDEN AGE IN HUMBLE'S REFINING, 1926–1929

The years 1926–1929 constitute a particularly significant period in Humble's refining history, especially at Baytown. Those years were marked by an increase in capacity, by improved economy of operation and quality of products, and by a generally high level of profits.

Humble continued to expand its refining capacity in the later 1920s. The addition of cracking coils in 1926, observed earlier, had just been accomplished when management recommended adding further equipment. Wiess estimated that another battery of ten cracking coils operating at from 450 to 600 pounds pressure, with ten atmospheric stills to handle sweet crude, would cost $3,250,000 but would pay for itself within a year.

A difference of view concerning the additional cracking units arose between the executives of Humble and Jersey Standard. Speaking for his company, President Teagle commented: "I am reasonably confident that the refinery people at Baytown are no different from . . . refinery people elsewhere . . . they all want to run the maximum quantity of crude. There seems to be an inbred feeling in the refinery fraternity that volume is more important than costs." Teagle thought that Wiess's plan called for running too much sweet crude and that Baytown should instead operate "to the maximum capacity on coastal and other fuel crudes." Farish replied that Humble necessarily produced and purchased certain quantities of light crude and could not operate exclusively on heavy crude oils. "We have not," he declared, "what are called growing pains at Baytown; we have no desire to increase capacity at expense of cost of product. . . ." Although Farish was exasperated, he expressed reluctance to go against Teagle's wishes. Teagle, in the same spirit, observed that the difference of opinion seemed to result from the fact that the Humble managers were "viewing the situation from the standpoint of Humble's entire business, whereas at the outset, at least, we feel the situation should be viewed only from the standpoint of the operations of the Baytown plant."[38]

The difference of opinion, indeed, arose from two diverse ways of looking at the proposed expansion, a diversity inherent in the holding company–affiliate relationship. Managers of Jersey Standard were considering the total costs and volume of products of its own refineries and of the refineries of affiliates; the company's Board of Directors considered gasoline supplies ample for Jersey's market without the installation of new cracking units at Baytown. Humble's administrators, who were as a matter of policy working to achieve a better balance in the various activities of their corporation, desired to expand a successful operation. But they had to face the reality that they were largely dependent on Jersey for a market and, indeed, for funds with which to expand, and that Jersey itself could not honestly encourage refinery expansion for which it could not assure an outlet.

The action finally taken was a modification of the original plan. A conference between representatives of Humble and Jersey Standard in September, 1926, gave opportunity for a frank discussion of all the facts and considerations but left the final decision to Humble. Wiess pointed out that the original six cracking coils were already badly corroded from running high-sulphur-content crudes and that the Baytown refinery needed new equipment to process the increasing quantities of sour crude oils from the Panhandle and West Texas. Because the cracking of heavy distillates was then undergoing rapid changes, he instructed Finley, his assistant, and Coleman, head of the Development Department, to make a careful study of the subject. By December, 1926, Humble's managers had decided to construct at Baytown two high-pressure Cross cracking coils (a process of the Gasoline Products Company), which had been intended originally for Humble's abandoned refinery project in the Panhandle. Hardly had the first one been completed when advances in design led to changes; alloy steel tubes were then becoming available for use in the heating coils in furnaces that eventually made it safe to raise temperatures as high as 1100° Fahrenheit.

These two Cross units, as revamped in 1928 and 1929 and operated at 750 pounds pressure, handled as many barrels of charging stock per day as five tube-and-tank units. These coils also had the advantage of considerably lower construction costs per unit of capacity, and they played an important part in improving the antiknock quality of Baytown's gasoline. Although the new equipment furnished only about half the cracking capacity that the Humble Board of Directors had considered adding, Wiess recommended delaying construction of more such facilities "subject to further consideration and discussion." In the meantime, the refinery group had begun to reconstruct the tube-and-tank units so as to make possible their operation under 750 pounds of pressure and thus to increase their capacity. No new cracking equipment was built at Baytown for nearly a decade thereafter.

Despite an increasing emphasis on gasoline, the Baytown refinery manufactured many other products. During 1926 a battery of ten atmospheric stills, all equipped with bubble towers, was constructed to run the increased production of North and West Texas and the Panhandle and to meet the increased demand for export naphtha and gasoline, kerosene, gas, and Diesel oils. In the same year a vacuum still was added for the manufacture of black oil from light coastal crudes; in 1928 seven additional stills, all but one equipped to operate under vacuum, were constructed to manufacture lubes. This construction released other vacuum stills for running various types of crude and for rerun service. Baytown's rated capacity in 1927 rose to 100,000 barrels daily.

During 1928 and 1929 the emphasis at Baytown was on adding to finishing equipment and improving the quality of products. The large runs of sour crude from West Texas and the Panhandle resulted in trouble with the odor and color of gasoline and other products. In consequence Baytown added a battery of vacuum stills, constructed on the foundations of the old Burton stills, for finishing kerosene and rerunning naphtha. A treater and a second acid agitator were provided to improve the refined oils. In order to upgrade kerosene to the high quality required by the European market, a 6,000-barrel Edeleanu plant was built in which liquid sulphur dioxide was used to reduce the sulphur content and improve the burning quality of refined oils.[39]

Economy received increasing emphasis in Baytown's operations in the later 1920s. During the years 1925–1929, in order to prevent the waste of gas vaporized from the oil at the refinery, an absorption plant and other facilities were constructed for the recovery of naphtha from wet gases. At the end of this period Baytown also added debutanizers to segregate from cracked gasoline the light fractions which caused excessive losses from evaporation of recovered naphtha. By this program Baytown achieved what was then probably the most nearly complete hydrocarbon recovery system in the United States.[40]

Another economy measure was effected early in 1926 by the substitution of natural gas for some of the other fuels used. Baytown had depended on comparatively expensive fuel oil, supplemented after 1925 by gas from the absorption plant. The refinery continued to use cracking-coil coke and low-quality fuel oil, but the managers estimated that the use of natural gas effected an annual saving of $200,000. Baytown was the second major refinery in the coastal region to fire stills with natural gas, the Magnolia refinery at Beaumont having preceded it.[41]

Baytown, it is pertinent to note, had several economic advantages over refineries on the Atlantic Coast, as was indicated by a comparative study made in 1927 by Jersey's Manufacturing Department of manufacturing costs at Jersey refineries in the New York area and in the affiliates' refineries on the Gulf. Baytown, like Baton Rouge, was found to have strong advantages in the cost of fuel and water and in the cost of land and taxes on land. Baytown, particularly, had somewhat lower wage rates for process employees; its rates were set in accordance with those in its own area, which were lower than the rates on the New York seaboard. Baytown also was advantageously located for refining sweet crudes from North and East Texas and for bulk export shipment of products. However, it was less advantageously located for the purchase of certain chemicals, for packaging and shipping products in cans, cases, and barrels, and for refining certain crudes, especially Mexican, Colombian, and Californian oils.

The Development Department played an increasingly important role in strengthening the Baytown refinery, and it experienced a considerable expansion and a multiplication of functions in these later years of the decade. Many new men were added, especially in 1927. Several of Humble's new research men were to have long and important careers with Humble or Jersey Standard. The work of the department continued along two main lines, research and technical service. Although the research activities included work for production and pipelines, the emphasis was on refining. Work continued to be done on such refining problems as oil treating, vacuum distillation, and cracking; a newer interest was hydrocarbon recovery; and late in the decade a hydrogenation research division was added to co-operate with Standard Oil Development Company in a new approach to the problem of providing more and higher-quality gasoline. The major emphasis of the department, however, was on the planning and designing of refinery equipment for utilizing the results of research and on technical service to refining.

A distinctive feature of the Development Department's activities was the excellent relations of research and technical men with those in charge of refinery operations. The technical men worked closely with the operating organization in a staff capacity, and "practical" refinery men were brought into Development Department conferences to contribute from their experience, a practice that was apparently unusual. Dr. W. K. Lewis, who also served as a consultant for other large industrial concerns, expressed the belief that Baytown was particularly distinguished for a lack of jealousy and for a spirit of co-operation among its research workers, technicians, designers, and "practical" refinery men.

The culmination of this process of bridging the gap between the

Development Department and the plant units was the establishment in 1929 of a special Technical Service division. This was an organization of chemical engineers outside the laboratory whose functions were to follow actual operations closely and to be available for advice and consultation in regard to improving the efficiency of operations and manufacturing products of better quality. The establishment of this service at first made operating men fear for their jobs, but the engineers were soon able to convince them that they were there to help and not to replace them.

Baytown's strong technical position received practical recognition in the so-called Mutualization Agreement between Humble and Standard Oil Development Company, an agreement which provided for "exchange of licenses under patents between the two companies" for twenty years beginning January 1, 1928. Wiess had urged such an arrangement ever since the incorporation of Jersey's Standard Development Company late in 1922, although at that early date Humble was a newcomer in the refining world. Within a few years the young company's position in the use of vacuum distillation and the tube-and-tank process had changed, as Frank A. Howard, president of the Development Company, acknowledged. In 1926 Howard said that, relative to its "scale of operations," Humble was "doing at least as much as the Jersey Company in the way of forward-looking work." Wiess did not appreciate the opinion that Jersey Standard, in contrast to Humble, had long since attained "manhood's estate as a manufacturer," but he welcomed an allowance of $100,000 as "compensation . . . for valuable engineering and development work on the Tube-and-Tank Process." This concession was the prelude to discussions that led to the cross-licensing agreement and the consequent cancellation of Humble's unpaid balance on tube-and-tank royalties.[42]

In order to improve the administration of refining and to co-ordinate more closely the various refining activities, Humble's directors in 1929 established a Manufacturing Committee. Heretofore the key figures in refining had reported directly to Wiess, excepting Baytown's superintendent, who reported to Finley. Under this organization, according to Wiess, certain problems, particularly in accounting, record-keeping, engineering, and industrial relations, had not been given as close consideration as was desirable. After consultation with Jersey Standard, which had had a long experience with the committee system, the Humble directors decided to establish the committee in order to broaden responsibilities and authority and provide each man with a better understanding of the entire range of refinery management. Wiess became chairman, Finley vice-chairman, and S. A. Giraud—the accountant who since 1922 had been one of Wiess's assistants—secretary. Each member was responsible to the committee as a whole rather than to an individual. This reorganization was an important step in achieving the co-ordination and integration of the various phases of Baytown operations that were its managers' goals.[43]

At the end of 1929 Baytown was a large, well-equipped, and efficiently operated refinery, with five profitable years behind it. Its rated capacity was then 100,000 barrels daily. According to Bureau of Mines figures it had the same rated capacity as California Standard's refineries at El Segundo and Richmond; its capacity was exceeded by the Gulf refinery at Port Arthur, Texas, and the New Jersey Works of Standard Oil Company of New Jersey, the new operating affiliate of Jersey Standard. The average daily input at Baytown in 1929 was 112,500 barrels (see Appendix II, Table X). The percentage yield of gasoline was 35.8.

Wiess was perhaps not altogether objective in his judgment when, looking back in 1945, he declared that the company at the end of the 1920s had "the best refinery in the United States." But N. E. Loomis, head of Jersey's Development Department, had stated in 1927 that Baytown's cracking-coil operations were setting the pace for Jersey Standard and its affiliates; and Dr. W. K. Lewis, Jersey Standard's principal technical consultant, agreed that throughout the mid-1920s "Baytown set the pace for all the Jersey organization in technical improvements." [44] With their new technical and management organization, Humble's refining executives at the end of 1929 faced the future with confidence, probably as little conscious as other prosperous manufacturers of the problems that the next few years would bring.

Chapter 10

MARKETING PRODUCTS INSIDE AND OUTSIDE TEXAS, 1919–1929

HUMBLE'S entry into large-scale refining necessitated comparable developments in marketing products. Selling products on a large scale was in 1919 a new operation for the company's directors, one that raised many questions as to policy and management. Should Humble depend largely on Jersey Standard to purchase its refinery products or should it seek to develop a considerable market of its own? Should it operate principally as a wholesaler or follow the current trend of producing companies to integrate forward into retailing? How far should the company commit its financial resources and its top administrative talents to marketing and thus divert its efforts from production and related activities aimed at supplying crude oil?

The decisions made by Humble's directors in the years 1919–1929 with reference to these and many other questions relating to marketing will be considered as the story of operations unfolds. Certain decisions, however, were foreshadowed in the agreement to sell stock to Jersey in January, 1919, and in the plans for building the Baytown refinery. The Humble directors then envisaged their company as a wholesaler of products. A large proportion of Baytown's output would be sold to Jersey, but the existing Sales Department would attempt to expand sales to industrial and commercial consumers and to dealers in Humble's home territory.

For carrying on these marketing operations a more formal organization was established at once. Special responsibility on the board level for the management of marketing was assigned to Director Wiess, a logical assignment, inasmuch as he also had been given charge of refining and the other directors who were active in operations were concerned with production. A Marketing Department was established to handle large sales directly from the refinery. Although Wiess was officially head of this department, in practice other directors, especially Farish, participated in negotiations for large sales. The old Sales Department, with a new operating manager, was to continue to sell Humble products in Texas and southwestern Louisiana. No co-ordinating committee of top administrators similar to the Crude Oil Committee was established for marketing at this time.

Humble's entry into the products market came near the beginning of a dynamic and chaotic period in the marketing of refinery products. Demand was to rise rapidly in the next decade, but so also was production. Competition was to increase greatly, prices were to fall, and new competitive practices were to be employed. Forward integration by producing and refining companies, as well as backward integration by distributors and refiners, was already in 1919 changing the organization of the oil industry and, in consequence, of the marketing of products.[1]

WHOLESALING PRODUCTS OUTSIDE TEXAS, 1919–1926

In its early association with Jersey Standard, Humble was equipped neither organizationally nor experientially to negotiate foreign or even large-scale domestic sales. The two companies, therefore, had informally agreed at the time of the sale of Humble stock to Jersey that the latter should negotiate such sales. F. H. Bedford, Jersey vice-president in charge of sales of lubricating oils, was to manage the sale of Humble lubricants for export, Humble naming the price and paying a 5 per cent commission; and F. W. Asche, Jersey vice-president in charge of foreign marketing, was to handle export sales of gasoline, kerosene (refined oil), gas oil, and fuel oil at prices based on the realization but bearing no commission.[2] There were no specific arrangements for domestic bulk sales outside Texas, but Humble also looked to Jersey Standard to handle that business. Jersey itself was recognized as having first call on Humble. The younger company thus became associated with the marketing operations of the world's largest distributor of petroleum products.

The degree of mutual dependence that developed between the two companies is indicated by Humble's products sales to Jersey Standard. In 1920 a total of only 13.4 per cent of the former's refinery products went to the latter, and the next year 17.5 per cent. In 1922, however, with the coming into effective operation of the Baytown refinery, Jersey took 47.1 per cent of Humble's products; in 1923 it bought 79.7 per cent; in

1926, 84.5; and in 1929, 84.7. In other words, Jersey Standard from 1923 took all but a relatively small portion of Humble's products for itself and its affiliates, mostly abroad. (For total refinery sales, see Appendix II, Table X.)

The two companies originally had only general understandings to guide their commercial relations. They had agreed that Humble should from time to time list its supply of refined products and their prices with Jersey "as with other prospective customers." If Jersey wished to buy at the list price, it could do so; if not, it could make an offer below the list price, which Humble in turn could accept or reject. Each deal became a separate negotiation, and each negotiation was dependent on the current market for the given product.

To negotiate deals between the two companies was not so simple a process as it might appear. As its refining expanded, Humble was in the position of having to sell to or through its large customer or being left without an outlet for a large portion of its refinery output. Jersey Standard was similarly dependent on Humble for a large volume of products, but it had to meet strong competition at home and abroad and adjust to a downward trend of prices and severe fluctuations within the trend.

No sooner was the Baytown refinery turning out large quantities of lubricants for Jersey Standard's market than that product ran head on into a difficult situation in Europe. Jersey's European marketing affiliates were selling lubricating oils under contracts that not only protected the purchaser against any rise in the price but also included a "fall clause," which allowed the buyer the benefit of any price decline. Bedford of Jersey Standard urged Humble to agree to a clause providing for a reduction in its price to Jersey corresponding to any decline in the latter's regularly issued price lists. Influenced by the opinion of its legal counsel that, although such a provision would not be positively illegal, it "might as a practical question result in very difficult and possibly embarrassing situations," Humble refused to enter such an agreement.[3] Humble would agree to making adjustments in the case of a break in prices, but then only on an individual basis and on demonstration that Jersey's price to the customer had actually been adjusted.

Humble's dissatisfaction with the export sales of its lubes at this time made it particularly fortunate that Jersey's own Manufacturing Department offered a more favorable outlet. That department was having difficulty meeting the current demand for lubricants, but E. M. Clark, Jersey director with special responsibility for refining, did not wish his company to incur the large expense involved in adding to its own refining equipment. In September, 1922, therefore, he agreed to purchase from Humble regular and large supplies of lubricating distillates to be finished at Jersey's refinery at Bayonne, New Jersey. In providing those distillates Baytown's surplus capacity was utilized and sales averaged $2,000,000 annually over a three-year period. Humble also agreed late in 1922 to ship each month about 15,000 barrels of heavy Polarine at a price subject to such adjustment, in accordance with fluctuations in the price of Gulf Coast crude, as to yield a profit of 50 cents per barrel.

With the aid of Jersey Humble was also able to sell some of its products to large domestic marketing companies. Its sales contracts with such "outside" companies, particularly with concerns operating principally on the Atlantic Coast, were at first negotiated through Jersey executives, who were better acquainted than Humble with current marketing opportunities. James A. Moffett, a Jersey director, negotiated a contract with Standard Oil Company (Indiana) in 1921 that enabled Humble during 1921, 1922, and 1923 to sell annually an average of 150,000 barrels of "red" oil at prices providing for adjustment according to changes in the posted price of Gulf Coast crude. This, according to Wiess, proved "the finest business" on Humble's books; [4] it was a great disappointment to Humble when Indiana Standard began to produce those oils in its own Whiting refinery. Jersey also assisted its Texas affiliate in negotiations for the sale of lubricants to the Vacuum Oil Company and of kerosene to the Union Petroleum Company, a Sinclair affiliate, in the sale of considerable quantities of gas oil to such companies as Standard of New York, and in large fuel oil sales to such concerns as the United Fruit Company and the Bethlehem Steel Company. F. W. Asche was particularly proud of getting a million-barrel sale to the Navy away from the Magnolia Petroleum Company.

Humble, at the same time, was not averse to selling lubes and gasoline directly, and it made some sales to companies in the South and the Midwest. It even sold directly to such a long-standing Jersey Standard customer as The Ohio Oil Company. Most of the gasoline it marketed in the Midwest was probably, however, from the Hearne refinery rather than from Baytown. Humble even considered entering into a contract to sell for shipment to Australia and Africa, but apparently this was not done.

The years 1923–1925 brought sharp disagreements between Humble and Jersey over products sales but also the gradual elimination of most of the circumstances that gave rise to the differences. At this time Jersey's marketers were beginning to meet especially severe competition abroad, and increasing national controls on the oil business were being applied in several countries. Jersey's position in the domestic market was also being challenged as never before by aggressive marketers, including such younger companies as Texas and Gulf and such former affiliates of Jersey as Standard of New York and Atlantic Refining. Prices were falling, and Jersey's own refining was in a bad way. Humble, as a seller of refinery products, was now in the same role as the producer who never thought he was paid enough for his oil; its heavy refinery loss in 1922 gave it a special reason for making the best trades possible.

Humble's top administrators believed that they had legitimate grievances. President Farish was not convinced that his company was receiving as much from foreign lube sales as it should, but he expressed a willingness to go on selling on a cost basis if Jersey believed it necessary in order to hold Humble's place in that business. He pointed out that a part of Baytown's high overhead and consequent loss resulted from an investment of over a million dollars in three practically useless filter houses "put in at New York's request" on the erroneous assumption that Humble oils would have to be filtered to go into the foreign market.[5] In 1924, when the competition of lubes from cheap California crudes further threatened Humble's lubricants, Farish and Wiess urged Jersey executives to establish an efficient sales organization that would push Humble's motor oils as quality products in the domestic market, just as the sales organizations of Texas, Sun, Vacuum, and Standard of California were doing with their products. Farish maintained that the current situation was such that a profit could reasonably be expected. This implied criticism of Jersey Standard's domestic marketing operations was not altogether without foundation, but Jersey was caught in a web of difficult circumstances.[6]

Domestic gasoline sales to Jersey during 1923 and 1924 followed the unprofitable pattern of the sale of lubricants for export. Farish maintained that Humble was selling not only below cost but also below the market, and was doing so only to keep its large refinery running. Baytown, he asserted, had never yet realized an actual profit; it might, he suggested, have been a mistake to build it, although he was convinced its costs were not too high. "We can manufacture as cheaply or cheaper than the best," he stated, "and our sole trouble now is in the matter of realization on our products." Humble, moreover, had turned down offers of a cent to a cent and a half above Jersey's offers. Farish consequently maintained that Jersey was responsible for furnishing Humble an outlet at a profitable price. Teagle in defense of Jersey in 1923 informed Farish that practically all refineries were operating either at a loss or with a very small margin of profit—Jersey's own refinery loss for the year was over $2,000,000.[7]

The gasoline sales controversy centered especially in the determination of the basis of pricing. Farish felt keenly that Jersey, in offering only the Mid-Continent price or very slightly above it for gasoline from Baytown, was depriving that refinery of the advantage of its position on tidewater. Jersey, however, had to consider transportation costs from a product's source to the ultimate buyer, costs which were to some extent a matter of rate differentials beyond its control. In the spring of 1924, although the Baytown tanks were getting full, Farish refused Jersey offers for three cargoes, "because we are not willing to admit as a matter of principle that gasoline at seaboard is worth no more than it is in the interior." [8] Humble did accept subsequent offers, but grudgingly. "Of course," Farish commented, "we are not in a position to refuse to sell as we must look to you for an outlet." By early June, 1924, Humble had shipped only about a tenth of an estimated 2,500,000 barrels of gasoline to be moved that year, and, excepting the promise of some export business, had no prospect of a regular movement of gasoline from Baytown.[9]

Humble's position was weakened by the fact that it was having trouble over the quality of its products. In 1924, apparently for the first time since complaints about lubricants in 1921, Baytown had difficulty with the quality of both gasoline and lubricants. Humble had to call on Jersey for a chemist to test its shipments. And it was spurred by these difficulties to expand its research at Baytown, which was noted in Chapter 9.

In the meantime, Humble had begun to assume a more independent attitude toward marketing outside Texas. Late in 1923 and throughout 1924 it became increasingly willing to bypass Jersey if a favorable opportunity presented itself. For example, late in 1923 it sold a cargo of refined oil (kerosene) to The Atlantic Refining Company—which promptly resold it to Jersey! Farish justified this sale on the ground that Atlantic and other companies had made his company definite offers that indicated a better realization than would have resulted from depending on Jersey's merely tentative offers. Teagle responded with a definite assurance that his company would in the next six months want all the kerosene Humble could deliver. A year later, when Teagle proposed that Humble should quote to outsiders "only on Navy grade" gasoline, Farish informed him that Humble had already sold to the Tide Water Oil Company 200,000 barrels of "Jersey grade gasoline" at a fraction of a cent more than Jersey was paying.[10]

Humble was particularly anxious at this time to sell lubes. "As you know," Farish pointed out to Teagle late in the spring of 1924, "it has been our policy not to look for markets outside of those to whom we are catering." But in October he wrote: "We cannot afford to face another year like this one in which we delivered not over 700,000 barrels of lubricating oil, or around 60 per cent capacity. We feel that we would be justified in taking any steps necessary to book the business which is so essential to the protection of our large investment at Baytown." [11]

The plans and activities of Humble's Marketing Department during October, 1924, indicate what was meant by those justifiable and necessary steps. If there was no possibility of getting back its lubricating business with Indiana Standard, the department was considering aggressive entry into jobbing activities in the Chicago territory. When Vacuum inquired about lubricants for 1925, Farish duly referred the inquiry to Bedford; when the latter did not pursue the matter with the vigor that Humble considered essential, Wiess determined to negotiate directly, despite Bedford's contention that the Vacuum people were his customers and that he should handle the business without Humble's participation. Humble succeeded in making a "satisfactory" sale of 100,000 barrels of lubricants to Vacuum. B. H. Brown of the Marketing Department, in the meantime, was conferring with representatives of the Sinclair Oil & Refining Company and the Tide Water Oil Company in regard to lubricating business that a year or so earlier would have been handled through the Bedford office.

A substantial increase in Jersey's sales—owing to the increase in general demand, on the one hand, and more aggressive marketing and less conservative price policies on the part of Jersey, on the other hand—brought improved relations between Humble and its large customer and better times for Baytown. In October, 1924, Humble was informed that Jersey's "export people" in charge of foreign sales of kerosene and fuel oil would "figure on purchasing" from Humble during 1925 a million barrels of naphtha and 500,000 barrels of kerosene.[12] Bedford wrote that "with luck" his department hoped to be able during 1925 to take from 500,000 to 700,000 barrels of lubricants "for domestic and export business." [13] By the end of the year Bedford's department had definitely booked 335,000 barrels for delivery during the first six months of 1925, including sales to Vacuum and heavy Polarine for Jersey's Manufacturing Department.

Even more gratifying was Jersey's offer "to take 2,200,000 barrels . . . of gasoline . . . in fairly equal monthly quantities over the year 1925 . . . navy grade" at "5½ cents per gallon below the Newark tank wagon market price on the day each cargo is loaded." The price was still the Mid-Continent price, but the large assured outlet and the definite price were satisfactory compensations.[14]

The price of lubricants sold through Bedford's office, however, remained a problem in the improving Humble-Jersey relations. Wiess informed Farish in September, 1925, that sales through Bedford had continued to be at lower prices than the average for other lube sales and that the old difficulty about the "fall clause" had again arisen. Wiess suggested a review of the whole marketing problem. "We have," he wrote, "practically declined all inquiries for all products moving from Baytown over the whole year," except for an occasional sale of lubricating oil in order to get prices to compare with Bedford's. Wiess expressed doubt that Humble should place itself entirely in Jersey's hands.[15] This difficulty was the subject of negotiations between Humble and Jersey throughout the fall of 1925, and it was accentuated by the Jersey Manufacturing Department's dissatisfaction with the quality of lube distillate furnished by Humble.

But, despite such difficulties over sales, Humble's refining operations during 1925 became substantially profitable for the first time since the Baytown refinery had gone into commercial operation. Contributing importantly to this result were a better forecast of the products required, the 2,200,000-barrel gasoline-sales agreement, and the continuance of the profitable sales of lube distillates and heavy Polarine to Jersey's Manufacturing Department. Humble's refining profit in 1925 was, indeed, approximately as much as the year's profits from the domestic refineries operated by both Jersey Standard and its Louisiana affiliate with combined crude runs five times as large as Humble's. Such profits for 1925 left Humble little room for complaint about the sale of its products.

Jersey's large purchases continued to be a major factor in expanding capacity and maintaining capacity operations at Baytown. For example, in March, 1926, Jersey informed Humble that it would take a monthly average of over half a million barrels of naphtha and gasoline, about evenly divided between domestic and export quality. This would add up to nearly twice Humble's total sales for 1924 and approximately a million barrels more than its total sales for 1925. Also, Jersey was figuring on taking from Baytown over the last seven months of the year 190,700 barrels per month of refined oil, which would amount to 400,000 barrels more than Humble had sold during the previous year. Discussions as to price naturally continued, but capacity operations and regular advance orders rendered price of less importance than it had been earlier.

Humble's principal problem for a time thereafter was not to induce Jersey to take more of its refined products or to find outside customers for itself, but rather to turn out products in adequate volume and of a sufficiently high quality to satisfy Jersey's demands. Jersey was planning to put on the market on April 1, 1926, a premium gasoline of improved knock rating, to be known as Esso, and invited Humble to help supply it. Humble apparently had no difficulty in meeting the specifications.

The years ahead were to bring their own problems, but they were also to bring a clearer understanding between Humble and Jersey Standard concerning the pricing of Humble's refinery products. Before those developments are described, however, Humble's efforts to market its products in its home territory will be considered.

SELLING LUBES AND COMPETING IN THE TEXAS GASOLINE MARKET THROUGH BULK-STATION EXPANSION, 1919–1926

In carrying out its decision of 1919 to strengthen sales in its home territory, Humble's first need was to set up an organization to sell lubricants, the primary products of its proposed new refinery. Selling lubes was a field of marketing that required special knowledge of products and their uses. No one in the Humble organization had the necessary knowledge or, indeed, any experience or contacts in the lube market.

Humble met this need by purchasing on July 1, 1919, the assets and operations of the Bonner Oil Company, which held a strong position in the selling of lubricants to sawmills, railroads, utilities, and other types of industrial and commercial concerns on the Gulf Coast of Texas and Louisiana.[16] Bonner's physical assets acquired by Humble included service-station equipment, warehouse stocks, and several bulk distributing plants in eastern Texas and southwestern Louisiana. Humble also took over nearly all the company's personnel, including John S. Bonner (president), B. H. Brown (secretary), and A. L. Dingle (treasurer).

Because of his success and contacts as the managing executive of his company, Bonner was made general manager of Humble's reorganized Sales Department. Malcolm J. Monroe, the department's former manager, was appointed manager, under Wiess, of the division in charge of the distribution of gasoline, kerosene, and motor oils through bulk stations to retail outlets. B. H. Brown was given responsibility for the industrial lubricating oil business; he also was given charge of the purchase of products needed for resale.

The Sales Department was strictly a home-trade organization. It did not attempt to sell outside Texas and that part of Louisiana in which the Bonner Oil Company had been active. In 1928 even the bulk plants in Louisiana from which lubricating oil had been distributed were sold, and thereafter sales to commercial and industrial users in Louisiana, as in other states, were on a limited basis, f.o.b. Texas points.

The Bonner salesmen sold lubricating oils and greases as effectively for the Humble Sales Department as they had for the Bonner Oil Company. Until Humble produced marketable lubes, they continued to sell oils purchased as before and under the old Bonner brands. They were so successful that their sales in more than one year saved the Sales Department from large losses.

To establish Humble in a satisfactory position in the sale of gasoline and products other than lubricants and greases was far more difficult. Humble for some time not only had to buy products from other refining companies but also had to enter a market where those companies were already well established. It had to compete with such able and established marketers as the Texas, Gulf, and Magnolia companies. All three were strong and aggressive marketers; The Texas Company, especially, and Gulf had extensive marketing operations outside Texas. In Texas those three competitors, besides having extensive bulk operations, owned or controlled under lease many filling stations. Humble, on the contrary, owned only three retail outlets and planned to sell primarily as a bulk-plant operator; its directors did not believe that their company should compete with its own customers and hoped that it would not have to engage generally in retailing.[17] The company's newly acquired funds were earmarked for oil leases and wildcat drilling and for the construction of a pipeline system and a large refinery, not for an expensive campaign to acquire filling stations.

One of the areas in which Humble's directors early had to make policy decisions was in pricing. They at first adopted an open, one-price policy. This was contrary to the practices of competitors, who made such price concessions to dealers as rebates for quantity and discounts to match the so-called commercial-car discounts given by the dealers, which enabled preferred customers to drive up to a filling station and get gasoline at the tank-wagon price—sometimes for even less. Humble's policy was explained by Bonner as follows: "We believe that gasoline should be sold to all dealers in the same locality at the same price. We do not believe in . . . cash rebates, over-delivery, so-called commercial car discounts, or two prices at filling stations, or cash discounts on coupon books, etc." Humble particularly objected to the secrecy with which rebates and discounts were granted. For counteracting these special inducements, its bulk-station agents assertedly employed only such competitive devices as the uniformly high quality of all products, hard work day and night, good and prompt service, twenty-four-hour shipments, accurate measurements, and fair dealing in general.

One reason for Humble's price policy is clear. Some ethical considerations may have been involved, for Humble's policy-makers had in earlier years suffered from price discrimination in the sale of crude, but on this subject the records are silent. The directors' unfamiliarity with the products market may also have been a factor; they had not experienced the rough-and-tumble competition and the pricing practices that had come to characterize that market. But they did know that in affiliating with Jersey Standard Humble became a prime target for politicians. Moreover, in the early 1920s gasoline prices were under country-wide attack and investigation; early in 1923 a Congressional committee, of which Senator Robert M. La Follette was chairman, reported its findings, charging collusion among Jersey Standard and its former affiliates with resulting exorbitant prices and waste. The Federal Trade Commission's report in 1927, based on an extensive study, contradicted many of the charges and inferences in this La Follette report of 1923, but in the intervening years many individual companies and the American oil industry in general were under a cloud. Because of its association with Jersey Standard, Humble was especially conscious of the need to be careful. Humble itself, moreover, was under political attack in Texas, as were certain other companies, after the crude price decline of 1920–1921. And in 1923 the attorney general of the state brought suit against Humble under the state's antitrust law, alleging that it was the medium through which Jersey Standard was illegally operating in Texas and threatening the cancellation of Humble's charter. When this suit was decided in Humble's favor early in 1924, the company's legal position was strengthened. Humble's administrators, nevertheless, under the careful direction of its legal counsel, continued to be fearful of adopting practices which certain of its competitors were employing with impunity.

Humble's effort to expand bulk sales without adopting its competitors' practices succeeded only in a very limited and temporary fashion. The Monroe brothers (Malcolm J., the head of the bulk-station division, and his brother, Dan T., of the same division), with the fighting spirit of true Texans, advanced their bulk stations into debatable territory. Although they succeeded in greatly increasing Humble's gasoline sales, the profits from such sales were small or nonexistent. The Sales Department earned a net profit in 1920—by far its best year before 1927—but gasoline showed a very small profit and fuel oil a loss; profits were then derived principally from lubricating oils and refined oils and greases, which were the major products sold. During the next two years both gasoline and fuel oil sales experienced losses which, despite profits on lubes and greases, resulted in a small profit in 1921 and a loss in 1922.

Early in April, 1922, Humble "elected to make a fight," as B. H. Brown said, by adopting its competitors' commercial-car rate as the basis for its own price to dealers; that is, it adopted a differential of 3 cents between the price to dealers and the retail price. This reduction below cost temporarily brought about the discontinuance of commercial-car rates and, according to Malcolm J. Monroe, "made a very wholesome market," though at a high cost to the gasoline sales account. By June, however, the earlier situation had been re-established,[18] and the summer saw Humble's gasoline sales falling off and competition becoming increasingly severe. Pressure from new dealers and local refineries was causing the major distributors to resume or extend the granting of rebates and commercial-car discounts and "furnishing pumps practically free." The Texas Company, the most aggressive of the major distributors, was said to be selling coupon books with discounts to dealers and consumers and to be offering to lease filling-station equipment at 10 per cent per annum on the value.

Humble in 1923 continued to advocate that the major distributors should be "willing to . . . sell gasoline . . . on a clear-cut open policy basis without differential in favor of preferred customers and without rebates to dealers." [19] Wiess, however, recommended that Humble be aggressive at all points where the company had "an even break"; inasmuch as this would "necessarily involve the cutting of prices," Humble's bulk-station agents, most of whom had recently been put on commission, would have to be returned to a salary basis wherever competition was particularly keen.[20] Humble's gasoline war of 1923 was, however, even less successful than that of the previous year.[21] Gasoline sales again fell off slightly and, though the loss on such sales was halved, other losses and expenses were more than the usual large lubricating oil profits could cover.

Humble, obviously, could not indefinitely continue to challenge the policies of its major competitors through bulk-station expansion and expensive, and at best merely temporarily effective, price wars. Eventually it would be forced either to give up a losing business or adopt more effective methods of competition. The major competitors, far from being subdued, were obtaining exclusive outlets for their products by buying filling stations and pumps from independent dealers and leasing them back at a nominal rental [22]—the so-called lease-and-license system [23]—although the attorney general of Texas took the position that such a practice was contrary to the state's antitrust laws.[24]

Humble obviously was at a disadvantage in not being a retailer, but its own background and Jersey's interest and practices were against its entering a retail sales campaign. Jersey was interested in getting supplies from Baytown, not in a diversion of products into Humble's own markets; moreover, Jersey's own policy in the early 1920s was not to go heavily into the retail business—in 1919 it owned only eleven filling stations [25] —and it was skeptical of the wisdom of making the large expenditure for stations essential to an aggressive filling-station program. Nothing in Humble's own experience indicated any interest on its part in becoming a large retailer, and its Legal Department was well aware of the legal risks should Humble adopt the lease-and-license system.

By 1924, however, Humble was sufficiently conscious of the critical situation to consider entering retailing, that is, to expand beyond its three old outlets in Houston. It may have been influenced by the favorable decision in its crucial antitrust suit. It may also have been influenced by the fact that Jersey itself, although it would not adopt the lease-and-license system, had finally instituted in its marketing territory on the Atlantic Coast a "program of owned service station expansion . . . as an

PRESIDENTS OF HUMBLE OIL & REFINING COMPANY ELECTED 1917–1948

R. S. STERLING
1917–1922

W. S. FARISH
1922–1933

R. L. BLAFFER
1933–1937

H. C. WIESS
1937–1948

HINES H. BAKER
1948–1957

DIRECTORS ELECTED TO BOARD 1917–1937

JAMES A. ANDERSON

HINES H. BAKER

L. T. BARROW

JOHN S. BONNER

WALLACE E. PRATT

WILLIAM S. SMULLIN

JOHN R. SUMAN

EDGAR E. TOWNES

This 25,000-barrel-a-day flow from three Humble wells in the West Columbia field gushes into an earthen pit, common practice in pre-conservation days.

In the early days of Spindletop development, wooden derricks stood shoulder to shoulder, often touching at the base.

This 1918 traffic jam in the famous Northwest field, Burkburnett, was typical of the early days. Here the young Humble Oil & Refining Company started on its way to becoming one of the nation's leading producers of crude oil.

First dock, pump station, and tank farm owned by Humble Oil & Re
Company in Goose Creek field. This and a few miles of gatherin
were the beginnings of Humble Pipe Line Company in 1919. (Facing

R. V. Hanrahan, president of Humble Pipe Line Company from 1925 to 1950.

Coating and lowering line were all handwork in the early days of pipeline construction.

Larger numbers of men used hand methods for laying pipelines. Heavy timbers propped up lines; hand-operated tongs joined sections.

This gusher in the Corsicana field in 1923 is typical of how wells in early Texas boom fields were brought in.

fully equipped, motorized geophysical
rew of 1926. Humble began building
eophysics equipment in 1924; made
st seismograph recording in 1925. (Fac-
g page)

Large dynamite shots and long pick-up lines were used in the Gulf Coast area in the search for salt domes in the late 1920s.

Early type of geophysical equipment in field use. Improvements were made rapidly from the middle 1920s.

Team of 10 horses hauls heavy gas engine to location in the Desdemona field in early 1920. Roads were often a morass of mud.

A typical drilling crew on a Humble well in Louisiana, about 1922.

Scene in the Sugarland field, a few miles southwest of Houston, which Humble brought in in 1928. Here Humble first practiced 20-acre spacing in the interest of conservation.

At the height of development in 1922 the West Columbia field looked like this. Storage pit in foreground holds water.

Humble transportation crew moves 28,000-pound boiler to a drilling location at West Columbia by horse team in 1919.

Baytown refinery, growing out of a low, boggy rice field, in 1919 begins to take shape. Construction workers' tents are in background.

In 1922 Baytown refinery looked like this through a panorama camera. Building in left foreground is the laboratory. Unit with two stacks is the high-pressure still. At right are several batteries of crude stills and the filter house.

In the 1920s Humble built a number of small refineries near flush production. This is Burkburnett refinery in 1925.

Big truck trains hauled gasoline and other refined products from small inland refineries to sales centers in the late 1920s, the first era of marketing expansion.

Small bulk stations like this one at Graham served marketing during the 1920s when emphasis was on wholesale sales.

Humble's first service station in Houston, and the type of equipment used for distributing products in 1919.

Inspection party, from Humble offices and operations, which visited Baytown refinery on October 12, 1920, while plant was under construction. Bottom row: Messrs. Hanna, Eberle, Husted, Sterling, Anderson, Buerbaum, Hill, Carroll, Thompson, Meadows. Middle row: Messrs. Maloney, Broday, Vaughan, Attwell, Clark, Hanrahan, Moore, Edwards, Moffett. Top row: Messrs. Harris, Applegate, Freel, Pardee, Farish, Reeger, Armstrong, Styron, Behling, Stanton, Stovall, Downs, Schneider, Bowman, Hamilton, Bates, Sinclair, Read.

Humble's only tanker, at the Baytown docks, acquired in 1920 to bring Mexican oil to the refinery.

Automobiles parked around "Dad" Joiner's well in East Texas. After the crowd had dispersed on the evening of October 3, 1930, the well brought in the largest field in the United States.

Humble president, Ross Sterling (center), speaks to employees at the first Humble Day barbecue, held in May, 1920, at Baytown.

Polk Street view of Humble Building shortly after completion in 1921. Typical tank wagon and driver of the era in foreground.

Steel and wooden derricks stand side by side in the Barbers Hill field during the 1928–1930 development of newly found deep sands. Oil had been found here in shallow sands in 1918.

Hu M. Harris, developer, and the first unitized draw works, perfected in 1932. Unit now stands on The University of Texas campus and bears memorial plaque. Unitization speeded up the moving of drilling equipment.

antidote for the lease-and-license program of competitors."[26] Even so, Humble was reluctant to incur such expense until it had tested the possibilities of other competitive methods.

For example, Humble increased its advertising. Despite the intensely competitive atmosphere, it had hitherto demonstrated little interest in advertising and publicity as a means of stimulating the demand for its Flashlight Gasoline and Velvet Motor Oils. It had in 1922 substituted a new trade-mark, showing a gear wheel and the inscription "Humble Oils," for the old Dixie Products circle devices.[27] As late as 1923, however, it was spending only $5,000 for advertising for the whole year. Early in 1924 it began to display a consciousness of the possibilities of advertising, and in May and June it contracted for work amounting to nearly $40,000. It also distributed a booklet containing road maps, eulogistic descriptions of Humble products (particularly motor oils), and a ringing reaffirmation of the company's sales policy. At the same time it began to assist dealers by running advertisements in their local papers.[28]

More significant still was the way in which, during 1924 and 1925, Humble began to adopt the widely prevailing competitive practices. In the summer of 1924 it issued coupon books to dealers, which provided for a discount of 2 cents per gallon to commercial users of gasoline—the hitherto much-condemned commercial-car discount. In August, 1925, it decided to meet the discounts for quantity granted to dealers by Magnolia, Gulf, and Texas. Wiess further recommended that Humble sell on a very narrow margin, keep the tank-wagon price close to the delivered tank-car price, push tank-car sales, and further extend discounts for quantity. This "comparatively free-handed policy" should be an open one, Wiess advised, so that it would not be confused with secret rebating and similar practices.[29] To determine how closely the price could be shaved, the Sales Department on November 1 adopted an accounting system that separated the selling costs of gasoline from those of lubricating oils and other products.

Another step toward falling into line with its competitors was Humble's adoption late in 1925 of the policy of furnishing dealers with gasoline pumps, which Wiess as early as the spring of 1923 had admitted might prove a necessary alternative to building filling stations. In November, 1925, several dealer-customers stated that they would cease purchasing from Humble unless they could lease pumps from the company on approximately the same terms as from its competitors. Inasmuch as a district court the previous year had upheld the right of the refiner to require a filling-station operator to sell only the refiner's product through equipment leased or rented to the retailer, the Humble Operating Committee yielded and appropriated $250,000 for the purchase of over 500 old pumps owned by Humble's bulk commission agents—who had supplied them to their retail dealers—and 200 new pumps, all to be rented for $1.00 a year.[30]

By the beginning of 1926 Humble had given up at several points its attempt to conduct its local sales on a one-price-to-all basis. It had yielded on rebates for quantity and to some extent on commercial-car discounts, as well as on furnishing its dealers with gasoline pumps at a nominal rental. It still, however, held out against expanding its retailing.

Humble had hardly completed the formulation of this new sales policy when it was confronted by serious competition in quality, particularly from Gulf No-Nox gasoline and what Wiess himself described as a "superior product" sold by The Texas Company "at no advance in price." [31] Customers were then becoming increasingly quality-conscious because of product differentiation in advertising and the better performance of their cars when using certain gasolines. New engine design, which was raising the compression of automobile engines, made detonation a serious problem for refiners. The Humble sales group felt that the improvement of the "knock" rating of gasoline at the refineries would eventually be necessary. In the meantime, a quicker and less expensive method of meeting competition would be to obtain the right to use Ethyl Compound for addition to gasoline to make its "knock" rating equal to that of premium gasoline. Humble put Humble Ethyl gasoline, a premium grade, on sale in September, 1926,[32] but despite large advertising expenditures and reportedly better performance, results proved very discouraging. The public was apparently still alarmed over the dozen or so deaths that the manufacture of the tetraethyl lead mixture had caused; it was not convinced, despite the lesson of experience, that the new gasoline was not harmful to the motorist or to the station operator.[33]

The Sales Department, with all its changes in policy and practice and the increase of its bulk stations in 1925, was still unable to advance Humble toward a sales position in Texas corresponding with its importance in other operations. It achieved a slight increase in gasoline sales in 1924 and a larger one in 1925, but it also took a heavy and increasing loss on those sales. The sale of lubricants and the resulting profits were, however, increased markedly; the advertising program's stress on Humble motor oils doubtless contributed, but the Bonner group's industrial lube business was probably still the principal basis for such success as the Sales Department enjoyed.

The department ended 1924 with a small profit and earned a somewhat larger profit the following year. During 1926, however, although its gasoline sales expanded by about a fifth and for the first time brought Humble's total annual sales in Texas to over a million barrels, the

Sales Department's proportion of the state's gasoline sales, which had never reached 6 per cent, fell off slightly. The total profits that year were cut back to what they had been in 1924, the result of a considerable loss in the gasoline account. The Sales Department was saved from actual loss in 1926, as in the past, by profits on lubricants, particularly on motor oils. The problem of how to derive a profit from Humble's gasoline sales in Texas seemed further from solution than ever before.

RETAILING IN TEXAS, 1927–1930

In April, 1927, a meeting of Humble sales agents was called to take "a broad look" at the whole selling effort.[34] At least one of its conclusions seemed almost inevitable. Although Humble had met competitors' methods in almost every respect except the ownership and leasing of filling stations, its gasoline sales position was still far from what it should be. The logical next step was to undertake aggressive competition through controlled retail outlets.

Wiess had resisted the adoption of a company-owned retail-station policy from the beginning of his connection with the Sales Department. Late in 1925 he had weakened so far as to suggest the possible acquisition or financing of one retail station in each Texas town in which Humble had a bulk station, but a year later he was still opposed to "leasing and taking over the control of filling stations."[35] He later admitted that Humble's marketing methods were responsible for its products not having "the reputation that they deserve." Texas, Gulf, and Magnolia were each doing about 20 per cent of the gasoline business in Texas, and Humble only between 5 and 6 per cent. But Magnolia owned about 500 Texas filling stations, and the Texas and Gulf companies controlled over 1,000 each through lease-and-license arrangements; Humble, with the exception of three stations in Houston, was without either ownership or control of retail stations. Humble's directors had come to believe that their company was too important in other branches of the Texas oil business not to be more strongly represented in retail distribution, but they also knew that such representation would require a substantial filling-station investment.[36]

Nevertheless, out of the sales agents' meeting and subsequent discussion in the Board of Directors came the decision that Humble "must attempt to retail more . . . products and establish a more definite, direct contact with the consumer." Following the board's decision, the Sales Department undertook to expand Humble's sales efforts throughout the state wherever its principal competitors could not supply products more cheaply than Humble.

To enter a market where strong competitors were already established would obviously be expensive at best and could succeed only if both quality and costs were competitive. Humble's Baytown refinery, with its expanding research and improved processes, could by the late 1920s compete in quality on the whole; but it had been built with a view to filling tankers, not supplying the consumer a thousand miles away in West Texas. Poor roads and the scarcity of rail lines, and the high cost of transportation by both, posed serious cost problems.

In June, 1927, Humble decided to meet this cost problem by supplying gasoline from local refineries to dealers in certain areas who could not be economically supplied from Baytown. This arrangement would serve the double purpose of eliminating a high transportation charge and using the refineries as bulk stations from which tank trucks could deliver supplies to the retail stations in the area they served. Local refineries were either built or adapted to serve this program. (See Chapter 9.) They were located in parts of Texas in which crude oil was easily available but which were a considerable distance from Baytown.

These refineries could not economically supply all the outlying localities in which Humble undertook to establish retail outlets, that is, at the end of 1928 in the territory west of Alpine in distant West Texas, the Panhandle, the Fort Worth–Dallas area, and the vicinity of Beaumont, Port Arthur, and Orange. By the purchase or exchange of gasoline Humble could even supply some of those areas almost as cheaply as its competitors. Wiess felt that especially in the Fort Worth–Dallas and the Beaumont–Port Arthur areas, which contained large percentages of the state's population, Humble could not "forego representation." The company's principal effort, however, should be in parts of the state accessible to products from its own plants. The next step was to build up chains of filling stations along the main highways within the company's territory.[37]

Even before this refinery program was well under way in the summer of 1927, Humble acquired some retail stations. Its bulk commission agent in the Rio Grande Valley decided to retire and offered his fourteen retail stations for sale; and the Austin bulk-station agent, who had four retail stations, was offered a higher commission by another company. Humble chose to buy the stations rather than to lose the business in those areas and thus found itself launched on an extensive program of retail expansion.

In anticipation of expansion, Humble's sales territory was split into a northern and western division and a coastal, or southern, division. The first was to be served principally by the new interior refineries; the coastal, by Baytown.

The program of acquiring retail stations, accompanied by the addition of more bulk stations, was carried forward until checked by the full onset of depression in 1930. In 1927 and subsequent years through 1930 the number of Humble's bulk stations was increased from 68 to 143; the company-owned retail stations were increased from 3 to 220, and 56 were obtained on long-term leases. Most of the new filling stations were constructed according to the Sales Department's special design, prepared by the sales engineering staff. The net fixed assets of the department were increased from a little over $1,000,000 to over $7,500,000. Substantial as this increase was, Humble's retail organization was still small compared with that of its principal competitors.

For several years the policy of expanding retail outlets apparently justified itself. McCamey, the West Texas center for production, pipelines, and refining, was responsible for a large part of Humble's increased Texas gallonage, and it provided an example of what could be accomplished even under the most difficult conditions by a combination of interior refineries, tank-truck trains, and company-owned filling stations. Indeed, the McCamey effort illustrates the lengths to which Humble went in increasing the sale of gasoline.

McCamey was an oil-boom town on a belated frontier, in a region where nature was untamed and inhospitable and at a time when prosperity made difficult the hiring of men to work in such a region. Humble's refinery and sales personnel, accordingly, were not without some unusually picturesque and intractable characters; according to Dan T. Monroe, they included a circus strong man and a punch-drunk prize fighter.

From McCamey, gasoline was carried by trucks with four-wheel drives, each of which pulled two trailers carrying from 4,000 to 6,000 gallons. Roads were virtually nonexistent in parts of West Texas of that day. According to the memory of certain Humble men, the drivers—each equipped with a week's provisions, a sleeping bag, and a couple of bales of hay to put under the wheels should the truck get stuck in the seemingly bottomless sand—used to chart their course across country by stars or compass. One driver, it is said, was always accompanied by a large bulldog for companionship and to frighten the coyotes away from his lonely bivouacs. At McCamey, too, the Industrial Workers of the World made one of its last stands by bringing about a "strike" among Humble's drivers—who were replaced within sixteen hours by men brought in from Breckenridge.[38]

The McCamey refinery, which at first was the only one in the West Texas area and as such met little competition, was for a time highly successful. During 1927 it brought the Refining Department a substantial profit, and its trucking operations saved so much on transportation that the same method was introduced in the San Antonio, Corpus Christi, and Waco areas.

The problem of price competition, however, was being progressively intensified everywhere as the growing surplus production pressed upon the market and as lower prices stimulated the distributors' efforts to expand their sales volume. By 1928 the practice of "giving away more than the other fellow to get business," as Farish described it, had gone so far that the industry called on the American Petroleum Institute to establish a code of ethics for marketing.

Such a code was adopted by the API board in December, 1928, subject to approval by the Federal Trade Commission; but it could be put into effect only through general acceptance by the individual refining and marketing companies. The code expressed disapproval of the refiners' and wholesalers' practice of offering retailers concealed inducements to handle their products.[39] Before the code went into effect, some companies increased their efforts to expand their retail business by employing methods that were specifically opposed by the code. These included leasing independent stations and then re-leasing them to the same dealers at a lower rent or no rent at all; leasing to dealers pump and tank equipment, particularly at municipal airports, at a dollar a year; offering commercial-car discounts; and indiscriminately issuing "courtesy cards" which entitled the bearers to gasoline at commercial-car rates.

Humble at this time, because of its large recent investment in retail stations and equipment, decided to follow competition in some respects. It yielded first on commercial-car discounts to dealers, and in October, 1929, it agreed to compensate its dealer-customers for all commercial-car discounts. It at first restricted these discounts to vehicles licensed as commercial, but within a few months it liberalized the regulations until the discount applied to practically all gasoline sold on credit.

In the final analysis, however, the continuing success of Humble's Sales Department depended primarily on the quality of the products sold. Quality alone was not enough but it was necessary for continuing success, especially in the strong buyers' market and amidst the rigorous competition that characterized the market for petroleum products in the late 1920s. Humble's efforts to improve the quality of its refinery products at this time are considered elsewhere (Chapter 9). Gasoline, especially, was under competitive pressure in Texas, and Humble's refining and research departments co-operated with the Sales Department in improving its quality. In 1928 Humble introduced an improved brand of regular gasoline, which was believed to be equal in quality to any rival brand. At Bonner's suggestion, it was named Flashlike, instead of the former Flashlight. In 1929 the premium grade was also changed to Ethyl Flashlike gasoline.

Humble then undertook an extensive advertising campaign to make these new products known. The campaign was explained in a booklet distributed to dealers. According to the booklet: "The Company thoroughly appreciates that well-planned, truthful and consistent advertising is of powerful assistance to the dealer in stabilizing the demand for Humble Products . . . . We are using practically every worth-while newspaper in the entire territory, and in many instances are using two and oftentimes more papers in a single town." The keynote of the entire campaign was to be "Service Insurance for Your Car," and dealers were advised to "capitalize on this by a few explanatory remarks whenever they sell Humble Oils." To acquaint dealers with the more important talking points to be used, copies of sixteen different advertisements were included in the dealers' booklets.

The dealers were also provided with a forty-page booklet for distribution to customers as a means of making known to them the high quality of Flashlike gasolines and Velvet motor oils. The booklet contained sectional road maps of Texas; it described the research, analysis, and testing that went into the manufacture of Flashlike gasolines, and "what it means to your motor"; and it explained the importance of regular lubrication. Besides, it contained aviation and waterways maps of Texas and the state's fish and game laws.

For several years the expansion program that Humble's Sales Department had inaugurated in 1927 seemed to justify itself. In the years 1927 through 1929 total gallonage doubled. Tank-car sales, although unimportant in comparison with sales through bulk and filling stations, contributed to the increased gallonage. But all the major distributing companies were expanding as fast as Humble, or even faster, an expansion made possible by a tremendous increase in demand. The appointment in 1925 of Ross S. Sterling, former Humble president, as Texas highway commissioner had marked the beginning of a highly successful program of "getting Texas out of the mud." As automobile travel became possible over a rapidly expanding area and as prosperity spread, the number of cars owned in Texas in proportion to population substantially increased, and the average annual consumption of gasoline per car in the state rose by 100 gallons.

With all its efforts, Humble's Sales Department succeeded only moderately as compared with the major competitors. Its percentage of gasoline sales in Texas actually fell off slightly in 1927. In 1929, for the first time, it raised its proportion of such sales to over 6 per cent but remained in fifth place—a very bad fifth as compared with the three leading competitors. However, for the first time since 1920, gasoline sales produced a profit, one that even exceeded the profit from the sale of lubricants.

Although relatively unimportant in Humble's total operations, the Sales Department's accomplishments were not without significance. The department had established Humble as a substantial marketer in its home state, even in retailing, despite the strength of such well-established and able marketers as Gulf, Texas, and Magnolia. And Humble's retail stations—which from the range of their services could be classed as service stations—were becoming favorably known for their appearance and service.

SOLVING QUALITY AND PRICE-DETERMINATION PROBLEMS IN REFINERY MARKETING, 1927–1929

While Humble was striving to strengthen its sales position in the home market, its products met an equally strong if not even stronger competition in the domestic market outside Texas and in the foreign market. Within Humble's own operating area its marketers were meeting competitors who, like Humble itself, drew their supplies from Texas and sold to Texans, thus working within one economy and under similar conditions. This was also essentially true elsewhere in domestic markets. In Europe, on the contrary—the export market to which the major portion of Humble's refinery products went—there was no such basic similarity or balancing of supply and of competitive conditions. The products of the Royal Dutch-Shell group, the Anglo-Persian Oil Company, and the Burmah Oil Company, Limited, in many markets had appreciable cost advantages over oil from Texas and indeed from elsewhere in the United States.

Jersey Standard's relative marketing position in the Eastern Hemisphere was in the 1920s being weakened by several developments. One was the competition of cheap oil from expropriated Russian properties. Another was the greatly increased strength after World War I of the Royal Dutch-Shell group and Anglo-Persian, both of which had strong backing by their home governments and relatively low-cost production on large government concessions. Royal Dutch in the 1920s became a large producer in Venezuela, where it had low-cost production as compared with American oil and also a transportation cost to European markets lower than the cost from the Texas Gulf Coast. Furthermore, several of Jersey's competitors at home were aggressively strengthening their position in European markets.

Russian oil was a special problem to Jersey Standard. It came from expropriated properties in which Jersey had a large ownership, and it especially threatened Jersey's position in the United Kingdom as a wholesale supplier to the Anglo-American Oil Company, Limited. From 1922 to 1927 Jersey took a strong position in a movement to boycott Russian oil unless the owners of the expropriated properties were given some remuneration, but by 1927 this movement had definitely failed. Jersey, consequently, in an effort to strengthen its competitive position against Russian oil in Great Britain, initiated negotiations for the purchase of the stock of Anglo-American so that it could assume a more aggressive position in the British market. The negotiation was to lead to the purchase in 1930 of the Anglo stock by the Standard Oil Export Association. This concern, organized under the Webb-Pomerene Act, which enabled American companies, under certain conditions, to associate for the purpose of carrying on business abroad without being subject to attack under federal antitrust law, was owned by four of Jersey's domestic affiliates until it was liquidated in 1936 and the stock of the British company was transferred to Jersey.[40] Humble owned 30 per cent of the stock of Standard Oil Export.

From about 1927 the basic disturbing element abroad, as at home, was world-wide overproduction. Jersey Standard—then the weakest of the three leading international oil marketers in the volume and cost of its own controlled crude supply—was interested in an effort to stabilize markets in the Eastern Hemisphere and Latin America and to reduce marketing costs to a level more nearly commensurate with falling prices. In 1928 it accepted a statement of principles, known as the Achnacarry Memorandum, looking toward those objectives. Whatever activities were carried on in accordance with those principles seem to have had little if any effect, however, in the years with which we are presently concerned.[41]

It was in such a market that Humble's largest customer was operating in the later 1920s. Jersey Standard had to meet fundamental problems of oversupply, greatly reduced prices, and increasingly stiff competition. Could it continue to take a sufficiently large volume of Humble's products to make possible the continuation of capacity operations at Baytown, and could it take the products on such terms as would enable Humble to operate the large refinery profitably? The answers to these questions depended on Humble as well as on Jersey.

The quality of Humble's products was of primary importance. Quality was becoming of increasing competitive significance, and refiners were universally having trouble. A buyers' market is always more selective than a sellers'. By the later 1920s, moreover, the public had become educated to a greater appreciation of quality differences; and improved motors, especially for airplanes but also for automobiles, were requiring better lubricants and gasoline of lower "knock" rating ("octane rating" had not yet come into the vocabulary of the oil trade). The refiners who wanted to maintain their position, or to strengthen it, had to work constantly to improve their products and yet keep costs within economic limits. The needs of the market were thus forcing what came to be virtually a revolution in the manufacture of petroleum products.

Humble's first insistent quality problem at this time involved refined oil, or kerosene. This was no new development in the marketing of that product—late in 1926 and in 1927 Humble's kerosene ran into a quality problem similar to that which Standard Oil kerosene from the Lima field had encountered late in the 1880s.[42] Humble was making kerosene from West Texas crudes, which were relatively low-priced but which, like Lima crude, had a high sulphur content. In order to make a satisfactory product, Humble's refineries could cut only a small fraction from those crudes. To meet quantity commitments it therefore had to distill disproportionately large amounts of kerosene from the more valuable East and North Texas sweet crudes. Even so, Humble was more than once forced to purchase a part of its requirements. Either source of supply—manufacture from sweet crudes or purchase—was relatively expensive. It was with the objective of assuring itself of a high quality of kerosene in adequate volume that Humble in 1929 built the plant at Baytown to treat this oil by the Edeleanu process. This new plant made it possible to meet the requirements of the European market adequately, and with a more economical use of the raw material.

Humble's lubricants at the same time faced serious trouble in the domestic market outside Texas. The quality of the company's lubes, indeed, was not infrequently a source of complaint by Jersey and its customers, complaints that came especially from commercial and industrial buyers, who were progressively demanding a higher quality. It was becoming increasingly difficult for lubricants from Texas naphthenic base crudes to compete with oils made from paraffin crudes produced in the northeastern states.

Wiess had in 1926 become concerned over the lubricants problem. He then expressed to Jersey's Director E. M. Clark the hope that the construction of vacuum stills on the eastern seaboard for the manufacture of lubricants would not go so far as to offer competition with Humble's business. A month or two later he voluntarily suggested a cut in the base price for distillate from which to manufacture the Polarine brand of lubricants—for over a year Jersey's Manufacturing Department had been dissatisfied with Humble's distillate. This reduction, he explained, was possible because deep flush production from Spindletop had made available at a reduced price large quantities of a crude that was better adapted than "the average stream of Heavy Coastal" to the manufacture of lubricants, and also because of "improvement in the operation of vacuum stills."[43]

The sale of Humble lubricants in the domestic market rallied in 1927, perhaps because of this price concession, but thereafter it continued to decline. By the end of 1929 the company had lost a "considerable volume of its lube sales to New York refineries and to increased demand for paraffine oils." [44] Export sales, however, increased sufficiently so that in 1928, despite the decline in the United States, Humble's total lube sales were over 2,000,000 barrels.

Humble responded to this lubricants problem by initiating an extensive research effort to improve its lubes. But several years of research would be required to solve the problems posed by Texas crudes adequately to enable Humble to manufacture a grade competitive with the best products from the paraffin-base Pennsylvania crudes.

Gasoline and naphtha encountered problems of their own. Late in 1926 and early in 1927 Humble had difficulty in meeting specifications for export naphtha, and there were complaints about the color of domestic gasoline. By the end of the 1920s it had become imperative to supply gasoline of high quality in large volume, and of course at competitive costs. The inauguration of Humble's extensive hydrogenation research program and the adoption in 1929 of a plan to build a hydrogenation plant resulted from the need to manufacture gasoline of high quality in large volume.

Farish and Wiess, in the meantime, were making progress in their pricing relations with Humble's large customer. There was still much discussion, and even serious disagreement, but a new spirit was manifested in the discussions. In the earlier years, in the face of what seemed to be temporary difficulties, Farish had been able to hold out stubbornly for better realizations. By these later years of the decade, however, the world oil market had entered upon what appeared to be a downward price trend of considerable duration. Farish especially, among Humble executives, was becoming more cognizant of the serious condition of the oil industry; indeed, as will be seen later, at this time he became one of the leading promoters in this country of new methods for reducing wasteful overproduction and the cost of producing oil.

An important development in the Humble-Jersey marketing relationship during the late 1920s was the working-out of a formula for arriving at what were intended to be mutually satisfactory prices for gasoline, kerosene, and fuel oil sold by Humble to or through the Delaware Company (Standard Oil Company of New Jersey, incorporated in Delaware in 1927 to take over the domestic operating functions of the parent company). Jersey Standard and Humble had originally agreed that the former would handle the export sale of the latter's refined products, except lubricants, at prices based on realization from sales, that is, according to the prices actually received in the export market. Trouble had arisen, however, from the fact that better prices could be obtained in one market than in another. This problem increased with the growth of competition. It became obviously unfair, in these circumstances, to require Humble to supply products to a market in which, for example, a price war was going on, so that the price received for those products would be drastically reduced, while the better markets might be left to the refineries of Jersey's wholly owned affiliates.

In 1928 Humble, because of its large sales for the export trade, was suffering severely from the competitive situation in England. A gasoline price war was going on there between the Russians and Royal Dutch-Shell. Companies were obliged to meet their quotations or suffer a serious decline in sales. During the first five months of 1928 the Delaware Company's sales to Anglo-American Oil Company, Limited, resulted in a loss of about $1,000,000; the loss in June was $1,500,000, and it was estimated that during the rest of the year the monthly loss would average nearly $1,000,000. Delaware, in consideration of Russian competition, had agreed with Anglo to assume the loss in case the realizations were below the current Gulf schedule; and Humble, since its price was based on realizations, was forced to assume about half of such losses. Farish declared that Humble's share of the monthly loss was more than the profit could be "with everything working right" at the Baytown refinery. "A few more contracts like this," he declared, "and we will all be sick or in our graves . . . . We are not in position here to judge the value of the future business with Anglo, but it will have to be extremely valuable to stand this kind of pressure."[45]

Jersey and Humble were already working on the problem. Late in 1927 it was suggested that these market differentials could be equitably adjusted as follows. As soon after the end of each month as possible, the actual realizations for both domestic motor gasoline and export naphtha during that month would be "worked back" to "an average equivalent price in the Gulf." This would mean, in the case of the Atlantic Coast refineries, that from the actual average realization per gallon would be subtracted handling costs and tanker freight from the Gulf for domestic gasoline and "the established selling price differential between New York and the Gulf" for export naphtha. Fixed differentials would be used to determine the price for products of superior or inferior quality. Baytown and Baton Rouge would receive the Gulf price thus determined for deliveries during the previous month, while Bayonne would receive the Gulf price plus the established differential, according to whether domestic gasoline or export naphtha was involved.[46]

A memorandum embodying these principles was informally accepted on February 8, 1928, as a basis for doing business during that year, and discussion over a formal contract continued for several months. One difference of opinion arose from the fact that the plan as originally proposed included only two-thirds of the Delaware Company's gasoline business—its export sales and its domestic sales to other companies—and omitted sales through its own domestic marketing organization. Wiess and Farish believed that the sales through Delaware's and Standard of Louisiana's marketing departments should also be included. They further maintained that gasoline sold through Humble's own Sales Department, supplied principally from interior plants, should not be included, inasmuch as the current effort was primarily to work out a fair price for gasoline from Baytown and the new Ingleside refinery, which was regarded as an extension of Baytown. The final agreement, dated July 1, 1928, included gasoline sold through Delaware's and Louisiana's marketing departments, but on a different basis, namely, the price at which Delaware sold gasoline to Standard of New York and Louisiana to Standard of Kentucky. Otherwise the arrangements were essentially the same as those embodied in the preliminary memorandum.

Gasoline was not the only product with differentials calling for correction. Since cracking now made it possible to turn a much larger percentage of a barrel of crude into gasoline than had formerly been possible, and since gasoline was more valuable than kerosene, kerosene became scarce and large gasoline purchasers adopted the practice of requiring certain amounts of kerosene to be sold to them along with the gasoline, frequently on what was to the manufacturer "a very unsatisfactory price basis." Because of this practice, Jersey's kerosene sales to Anglo during 1928 suffered losses, which were particularly heavy in November. Most of these losses, however, ultimately fell on Humble, which therefore suggested "a kerosene price agreement along the lines of the gasoline price agreement." Such an agreement went into effect as of January 1, 1929, as also did a fuel oil agreement based on similar principles.[47]

Despite heavy competition and quality problems, the volume of sales to or through the Delaware Company zoomed, a result in part of more aggressive marketing by Jersey interests as well as of a rapidly growing demand for petroleum products. The total products sales to or through Jersey—which had been 18,053,000 barrels in 1926 and 27,858,000 in 1927—rose to 40,967,000 barrels in 1929. Inasmuch as a refinery operates up to its capacity at diminishing costs per unit of product, the situation in 1929 was impressively gratifying.

Despite the heavy losses through sales to the Anglo-American Oil Company, Limited, 1928 was a good year for Humble's Marketing Department. In that year the Refining Department, with over 80 per cent of its products going to the Delaware Company, made the largest profits in its entire history until 1950.* This result came principally from an increase of over $15,000,000 in value of its gasoline sales; the value of its lube sales, for the third successive year, was less than in 1925. The coincidence of an increased volume of sales and somewhat more stable prices contributed to this impressive profit record.

During 1929 Humble sold more barrels of every principal product than it had in any previous year. Its refining profit, however, fell off somewhat from the 1928 peak, owing to extensive foreign purchases of lubricating oil for stock during 1928, competition with New York-manufactured paraffin-base lubricants, Rumanian and Russian competition in the foreign markets, and generally lower prices. Humble's refining profit, nevertheless, was still higher than in any year before 1928. With its principal refinery operating with a high degree of efficiency and at capacity and with satisfactory marketing arrangements with the Delaware Company, Humble had reason to be satisfied with the marketing of its refinery products.

From most points of view, Humble's directors and executives could look back with not a little satisfaction on what had been accomplished in selling crude oil and products since 1919. The company had acquired a wholesale market for oil and products of dimensions far beyond initial plans. Moreover, it had succeeded in establishing excellent relations as a purchaser of crude oil and in developing a seller-buyer relationship with Jersey that had satisfactorily reconciled the interests and problems of both companies. Humble had also broken new paths for itself in the market of its own region, even broadening operations by entering firmly into retailing. As a final test of accomplishment, its sales activities had earned a fair profit over the years.

But Humble's administrators had no feeling of assurance about the future. In the later years of the 1920s Farish and other Humble directors, along with many other oil-industry executives at home and abroad, had become convinced that there was something fundamentally wrong with the oil industry. Why and how Humble's directors had come to this realization and what action they had already taken to strengthen their company and industry are considered in the next three chapters.

* Inasmuch as reference is made at various places in this volume to the estimated earnings or rates of return of major operating departments, it is well to point out that these estimates are based on interdepartmental billing prices and practices and are, therefore, subject to the qualification that the results might have been different if each department had been a separate company dealing with outside parties in market transactions. The assumptions on which departmental profit estimates are calculated have changed at various times in accordance with what was deemed reasonable by the company's executives. Consequently, the estimates of departmental profits cannot be regarded as more than approximations used as a management tool in the light of intimate knowledge of all the considerations involved.

Chapter 11

CHANGING ATTITUDES TOWARD SUPPLY PROBLEMS, 1919–1926

THE YEAR 1927 introduced a period of transition in Humble's production and purchasing. By that time several of Humble's directors had concluded that their company must increase its effectiveness in finding oil, cut production and storage costs, and bring supply operations into closer relationship with current market demand. Furthermore, they had become convinced that more than individual company action was required, that some measure of control of production would have to be established. They had come to believe that only production research and engineering could provide the basis for the realization of these objectives.

This changed attitude toward supply problems was the result of a process of experience and education. The actual experience with production and purchasing has already been dealt with. The educational process is the special interest of the present chapter. It is concerned with Humble's top administrators' thought about their company's problems in connection with its supply operations and with methods of solving them. The chapter begins with the expansionist drive of the early years, deals with the company's reaction to oversupply and to proposals for government controls in 1923–1925, and shows the decisive effect on several Humble executives in 1926–1927 of the new petroleum technology. Two developments in their attitude toward supply problems were especially important: the emergence of a new concept of waste; and the realization that, if waste was to be avoided, the adjustment of oil supply to demand could not be left to unrestricted competition.[1]

EXPANSION AND THE BEGINNINGS OF CONSERVATION, 1919–1923

In the first four years following affiliation with Jersey Standard Humble's dominant objective in production and purchasing was to increase oil stocks and reserves in order to supply a tremendously dynamic market. The economic thought of the company's top administrators was cast in the mold of individualism. Their methods were the usual methods of practical oilmen, except that in the search for likely places to drill for oil Pratt led Humble along but slightly known geologic trails.

Humble's drive to expand in those early years, as has already been observed, was a part of the intense world-wide competition for oil production and reserves that had arisen during World War I. The current rapid increase in demand—coupled with recognition by certain countries of the importance of the control of oil supply to national security and a general belief that the consumption of oil might before long press upon the limits of world oil resources—made investors, oil companies, and governments throw their available funds and their influence into a race for the control of oil lands. Private funds went not only into established companies, thus augmenting the earnings plowed back into the business, but also into new, often speculative, concerns promoted to gain control of possible oil-bearing lands. Certain governments backed their nationals in countries where possible oil resources were still undiscovered or undeveloped.

Concomitant with this intensification of the efforts to augment and control oil supply, a movement developed for the conservation of petroleum resources through some form of government regulation or control. This movement, which originated in the same fear of shortage that drove the oil industry to rapid expansion, was stimulated by the waste that resulted from the uncontrolled production and frequent market chaos of the American oil industry. At first in large part resisted by oilmen, the conservation movement eventually was accepted not only as necessary for the more efficient recovery and use of an essential resource but also as a means of solving or easing some of the industry's economic problems.

In Texas the regulation of the oil industry in the interest of conservation had its effective beginning in 1919, although, as in other oil states, some regulations went back a number of years earlier. The laws of 1899, 1905, and 1913, however, had dealt only with such matters as the plugging of abandoned wells, proper casing of wells, and the prevention of waste from gas wells. As the years went by, the state and certain oilmen had manifested greater and greater concern for the future. In 1916 J. S.

Cullinan, who was known as the dean of Texas oilmen, even proposed federal control in the interest of conserving petroleum resources.[2] In 1917 an amendment to the Texas constitution broadened conservation by declaring that to conserve and develop natural resources was a public duty and right, and an act of the legislature assigned responsibility for the administration of the state's conservation laws to an existing agency, the Railroad Commission. Finally, an act of June 18, 1919, gave the Commission broad regulatory and enforcement powers for the conservation of oil and gas, including the prevention of underground waste.[3]

The Commission at once undertook the task of formulating the rules under which it should operate in carrying out these new responsibilities. It proceeded to study oil production in the state and to hold public hearings to guide in the development of specific regulations. The result was a set of rules under which the Railroad Commission in the autumn of 1919 began to issue orders to the oil producers.

Humble executives apparently accepted state regulation in principle and were favorably impressed by the early attitude and procedures of the Railroad Commission. In 1919 Farish wrote in regard to the hearings before the Commission, then in the process of formulating the new rules: "I found the Railroad Commission of Texas in a very satisfactory frame of mind and attitude toward the oil business. I am very well pleased, as all others were, with the hearing on conservation rules and regulations and on pipeline rules and regulations. I think when these rules are finally adopted by the Railroad Commission, they will be in very satisfactory form." [4]

Farish's preference, like that of most oilmen, was for self-regulation by the industry wherever possible. In the summer of 1919 he joined Underwood Nazro of Gulf in recommending voluntary proration of pipeline facilities among the wells in the northwestern extension of the Burkburnett field. When the Commission took over and ordered the prorating of pipeline runs in the field for a limited period, however, Farish held that the Commission's order—its first—was "strictly within their legal rights and duties." [5]

Farish and other Humble executives welcomed the Commission's rule of greatest permanent importance, Rule 37, which was aimed at the uneconomical practice of "crowding half a dozen wells on about five acres." This rule forbade drilling a well nearer than 300 feet to a completed well or to one being drilled, or nearer than 150 feet to any property line—but it contained an exception which enabled the Commission to grant permits to drill wells closer to each other and to property lines than the stated distances. Even before the announcement of this rule Farish and Nazro of Gulf had agreed that a requirement of as much as

500 feet between wells would be acceptable to them, and Humble had ordered its drillers to place wells a minimum distance of 400 feet from a property line.[6]

Humble men were also in agreement with the Commission's attitude toward earthen storage, although Farish was concerned over its announced intention in 1922 of enforcing the prohibition of such storage. He was well aware of the waste in open, particularly earthen, storage; experiments at the Burkburnett refinery had demonstrated the effectiveness of gastight tanks in reducing the loss in volume and gravity from evaporation. The company had instituted a program to eliminate or cover earthen tanks but was delayed by the current steel shortage; there was difficulty in providing sufficient storage of any kind for the large volume of oil it was producing and purchasing. This was an industry problem, a fact which the Commission recognized by granting time for complying with the storage order.

Humble executives were apparently less sympathetic with the Commission's orders to prevent the waste of gas from oil wells under production. In 1920 the company protested an order to shut in a well, flowing 300 barrels a day, because gas was being wasted; Farish commented that if "they can get away with this, they can make us do anything." [7] His company's view was essentially that it was entitled to blow into the air any amount of gas in the course of producing oil. Oilmen then generally believed that gas was not wasted, even when it was blown, if it had served to lift the oil. There was at the time no commercial outlet for gas—even Houston did not begin to use natural gas until 1926.

Humble also objected to the proposed enforcement of the Commission's Rule 40, which prohibited the use of vacuum pumps. Such pumps sometimes stopped the flow from offset wells. One of Humble's production men asked, "If you are going to prohibit vacuum, why not prohibit working barrels, sand pumps, or the many other devices that have been perfected to stimulate production, such as wire lines, air, etc.?" His chief objection was the effect the enforcement of the rule would have on the production of casinghead gas. Bert Broday, one of Humble's veteran production superintendents, was authorized to join other operators in a petition against the order. This move was followed by modifications in the rule, including the insertion of an exemption in favor of using vacuum pumps for casinghead gas.[8]

In general Humble's attitude toward such regulations sprang from a combination of tradition, necessity, and a lack of knowledge of what went on in the reservoirs from which oil was being produced. The company, like the oil industry generally, accepted the older regulations for the prevention of flagrant and obvious aboveground waste. Humble was probably ahead of a considerable part of the industry in its welcome to new spacing regulations. But regulations to prevent underground waste were another matter. The basic reason for Humble's reluctance to take steps to prevent or minimize such waste was, undoubtedly, the fact that no one in the company at that time had much comprehension of the function of gas in oil recovery. It is true that in May, 1920, Chief Geologist Pratt, in referring to certain wells, questioned the efficiency of the recovery methods employed: "I can't get away from the idea that the flow from such wells does not represent the total volume of oil in the reservoir. . . . I doubt if these wells flow as much as 50% of the total volume available." [9] He made no suggestion for improving recovery, which indeed was not within the scope of his responsibilities, but it is significant that he was even thinking about the problem.

Actually, there was then no certainty as to what constituted better production practices or what really was meant by underground waste. The term first appeared in Texas law in 1919; the idea that there was underground waste was old, but there was still little more than empirical evidence to support it. It is significant that the 1917 edition of Van Hise's pioneering work on conservation, although condemning the waste of natural gas, did not mention underground waste or waste in production.[10] John R. Suman's *Petroleum Production Methods*, first published in 1920 and issued in a third revised edition in 1923, had nothing to say about pressure maintenance or repressuring.

Although various theories had developed about the behavior of oil underground, its study was then only in an early stage, where geology had been a generation earlier. In 1917 the United States Bureau of Mines had set up its Petroleum Experimental Station at Bartlesville, Oklahoma, among other objectives "to carry on certain experimental work and to devise new methods for the improvement of present practices." [11] In the same year J. O. Lewis, who for a time headed the station, in a publication of the Bureau of Mines dealing with methods of secondary recovery recognized the function of gas in oil production.[12] In 1919 a member of the station's staff wrote that it had been estimated that not over 20 per cent of the petroleum underground was being recovered and that the "engineers of the bureau strongly feel that it is now time to start investigations on methods for increasing recovery," such as "the control of flowing wells by producing against back pressure." [13]

That many operating oilmen gave consideration to the work of the Bartlesville station is doubtful. The oil industry, particularly in Humble's operational area, as yet lacked an integral group of specialists who could keep the top executives—mostly practical oilmen without technical training—informed concerning the latest developments in the technology of oil production. Petroleum technologists, moreover, were by no means in agreement. Early in 1921 a member of the staff of the Bureau of Mines published a paper demonstrating the value of reasonably slow controlled production and the waste from premature and irregular water encroachment.[14] Later in the same year, however, another publication of the Bureau of Mines stated a position with contrary implications; a paper prepared by W. W. Cutler, Jr., and Walter S. Clute reported that in a certain Oklahoma district production was greater from wells spaced three acres to a well than from those on fifteen-acre spacing.[15] When specialists disagreed diametrically on fundamentals, what should practical oilmen think? Until oil executives had strong evidence of the fact and nature of underground waste, they were likely to go their old ways.

Although Humble executives were not yet greatly concerned over the physical waste of gas and oil, they were troubled in 1920–1922 by the effect of excessive drilling upon prices. Drastic price decline was really serious for Humble with its large inventory of high-cost oil, but the company's executives at this time looked to neither state nor federal government for help. A common plea in the oil industry in this period of overabundance was for a tariff on imports, but there is no evidence that Humble joined in this plea. The recommendation of Humble's most articulate production manager was to reduce excessive drilling by wider spacing—which would also cut costs—and to shut down operations; Farish looked to "the industry to regulate and take care of the distressing situation."[16] This position was consistent with Humble's philosophy, which represented the view of most of the industry at the time, that the oil business was the responsibility of the men running the oil companies.

The supply situation became even more serious in 1923. The development of production on Osage Indian lands in Oklahoma and in the Los Angeles Basin in California and the fault-line fields in Texas accelerated the rate of increase of production over consumption. Although there was some decrease in imports owing to the fall in Mexican production, crude oil stocks in the United States rose from 283,000,000 barrels at the end of 1922 to 364,000,000 at the end of 1923.[17] Pipelines were choked, storage was hard to supply, independent producers were dissatisfied, and there was increasing criticism of the industry for being wasteful.

Humble as a purchaser of crude oil was in a difficult situation. Although scarcely able to take care of its own production at Powell, as was observed earlier, it finally began to buy ratably from other producers. In North Texas it reduced its purchases, urging upon suppliers a voluntary cut in production. An antitrust suit, which threatened Humble's very existence, was brought against the company in the Texas courts.

Yet Humble continued to maintain that the industry should take care of itself, and it met the crisis by increasing its storage capacity. Its faith in storage as a balance to overabundance was, however, shaken severely in the struggle with flush production at Powell. The company executives consequently decided to reduce inventory in the hope that, by increasing Humble's own production and establishing a firm relationship with selected independents, a better ratio between additions to and withdrawals from storage could be maintained.

Humble's answer to serious overproduction in 1923, therefore, was the old answer—reliance on its own management and resources. The company continued to maintain that position in the next two years despite a new movement for regulation.

RESISTANCE TO FEDERAL REGULATION, 1924–1925

To anyone conversant with the history of the oil industry, the movement for government regulation that arose in 1923 could have come as no surprise. Such maladjustment between market demand and supply as occurred in that year had in the past brought falling prices, dissatisfied independent producers, chaos in marketing, and pleas for government interference. To this development was added in 1923 the prevailing fear of a petroleum shortage, which focused attention upon the wastefulness of the oil industry and called for comprehensive regulation by the federal government in the national interest.

This movement had a multiple origin. It was part of a general demand in the early 1920s for government regulation of enterprises dealing with basic commodities. The low prices and the general chaos that characterized the oil business for several years from 1921 made that industry especially susceptible to suggestions for regulation, but certain specific developments and circumstances had a strong influence in making the movement articulate and effective. An investigation of the oil industry, undertaken in 1922 by a committee of the United States Senate headed by Robert M. La Follette and focused on prices, resulted in the very critical report of March, 1923, which alleged that certain companies, including Jersey Standard, had conspired to rob both the small producer and the consumer. The Teapot Dome affair of the same year put the industry in a bad light before the public. George Otis Smith of the United States Geological Survey, who was deeply concerned over the rapid depletion of the nation's oil resources, at the same time urged upon President Coolidge the need for conservation. In 1923 the American Petroleum Institute, on the urging of Henry L. Doherty and Edward W. Marland, assigned to a committee of four men, of which Doherty was a member, the task of surveying the situation and reporting to the Institute's board. The resulting report held that oil production was wasteful and violated important principles of conservation; it recommended action in order to forestall legislation harmful to the industry. But Doherty's proposal for federal regulation was rejected by the board.[18]

Henry L. Doherty had by this time become convinced that drastic action was required, and during the next three years he worked zealously to win acceptance of his conservation views. He had become alarmed by the sensational discoveries and intensive development in the Los Angeles Basin. And he was perhaps better informed than any other oil-company executive concerning the natural conditions affecting the production of oil. He had followed closely the researches at Bartlesville; he had financed one of the Bureau's early reservoir research men, C. E. Beecher, in studying the relations between gas and oil in a reservoir. He was familiar with the research of D. B. Dow and Carl E. Reistle, Jr., of the station's staff, reported in an article published in July, 1924, which demonstrated the great need for utilizing gas for driving oil through a reservoir sand.[19]

Doherty emphasized both economic and physical waste. He asserted that the excessive drilling of California wells was contributing to the dissipation of gas pressure, to water encroachment, and to the decline of production to a point where even pumping was unprofitable. He held that proper conservation of gas would make possible the recovery of virtually every barrel of oil without pumping. He also stressed the effect of the "awful surplus of oil" on the market and the advantages, from the viewpoint of conservation and economy, of storing oil in "natural ground reservoirs." To build up "real ground reserves," however, he recognized as impossible without some regulation of production that would limit competitive drilling.[20]

Few thoughtful men acquainted with the oil industry could have differed with Doherty's analysis of the problems of the industry. Farish held the same view on excessive drilling, for economic rather than physical reasons, but he accepted flush production as normal and inescapable under the rule of capture, as indeed did Doherty. He was certainly impressed with the terrible problem of oversupply with its high costs, waste, and risk, with the advantages of storing oil in its natural reservoirs, and with the impossibility of accumulating "ground" reserves under existing laws.

Farish, and oilmen in general, however, apparently did not at the time comprehend Doherty's position on underground waste. The study of waste in the oil reservoir, as has been observed, was still in the laboratory stage, and only the Bartlesville laboratory was giving serious attention to the problem. This work was probably known to few oil-company executives; if they were familiar with the views of specialists on the subject of oil recovery, they were probably more likely to know of Cutler's theory, which received attention in oil industry journals and was popularly interpreted to mean that the more wells were drilled in an oil pool the more oil was recovered.[21]

While industry leaders, despite their slight understanding of reservoir mechanics, accepted much of Doherty's analysis of industry problems, most of them, including Humble's Farish, strongly opposed his main proposal for solving the problems. This was a plan to require the development of each pool as a unit by the creation of oil districts, similar to drainage and irrigation districts, under federal administration. District trustees, under his plan, would "settle with the individual land holders according to the calculated amount of oil or gas underlying each man's land." Doherty held that under this system reserves could be withheld from production until needed, that the plan would eliminate the virtual necessity under the rule of capture of competitive and wasteful exploitation, and that it would make possible orderly and efficient production gauged to actual needs. In other words, Doherty proposed what later would have been described as compulsory unitization under federal control.[22]

The Doherty plan was denounced among oilmen as unconstitutional, impracticable, and unnecessary. Yet widespread feeling existed among oil industry executives that some plan for coping with overproduction was needed. Some took a positive stand. For example, representatives of the important Texas Company held that the state had wide powers to prohibit waste; the company's general counsel recognized that there was "doubtless an enormous underground waste of oil." [23]

In December, 1924, as a result of the increasing problems of the industry and mounting criticism, the Federal Oil Conservation Board was established. This was to prove a very important step in the development of the conservation movement. In announcing the board's formation, President Coolidge declared that, although there was no immediate danger of a shortage of oil, there was overproduction, resulting in cheapness, which encouraged waste. The President called for extensive study of the industry's problems and invited oilmen to co-operate.[24]

The presidents of Humble and Jersey discussed this request for industry co-operation with particular reference to the position to be taken at the forthcoming meeting of the board of directors of the American

Petroleum Institute, of which they and the chairman of the Jersey board, A. Cotton Bedford, were members. Farish and Teagle agreed upon a statement which they presented to Bedford.[25] They proposed two alternative courses to follow, neither of which, they agreed, would be effective unless backed by about 80 per cent of the members of the Institute's board, a percentage which, they said, would represent a substantial majority of the industry.

One alternative was "direct opposition to the idea that complete conservation could be accomplished" under existing laws. If the board took this position, then would it not be dangerous to offer to co-operate with the Federal Oil Conservation Board? Would not co-operation suggest, the two men queried, that it was considered feasible to work out a plan of conservation, which would lead the public to blame the industry in case of failure, "thus paving the way for making government control of the oil business a very real political issue?"

The other alternative was "wholehearted co-operation with the government." If 80 per cent of the API board would co-operate with the government and with one another in an effort to bring about improvement, "but without any idea that complete conservation of our future supplies can ever be realized," then, Farish and Teagle suggested, this other route should be chosen. They held: "If, as a very appreciable number of those engaged in the industry feel, sooner or later government intervention in some form or another in the management of the oil business is inevitable, then it would seem that the President's present attitude and the appointment of this commission offer an opportunity for effectual co-operation between the government and the industry, to correct certain ills from which the industry is now suffering. . . ."

The nature of the co-operation proposed by the two presidents is significant. First, it should look toward modifying existing laws—they clearly had antitrust laws in mind. This should be followed by "teamwork" within the industry itself, which the modification of existing laws would make legally possible. The basis for industry co-operation would be "a code of business ethics" to be formulated and agreed upon by the API board to "cover all of the various operations from the drilling of a wildcat well to the sale of the finished products to the ultimate consumer." The adoption of such a code "would materially assist in rectifying some of the present unsound conditions and be a real step in the direction of the conservation of the future oil supplies." The two presidents envisaged that the public would be protected by a code that "would have the effect of exercising in behalf of the consuming public an adequate price control."

Such industry co-operation was an expression of Farish's basic political philosophy. He had consistently contended that the oil industry could take care of itself if legal obstacles to co-operation were removed. The suggestion, moreover, was in keeping with a movement in the United States in the 1920s for self-government of business through trade associations, a movement which was to find concrete expression a decade later in the National Industrial Recovery Act. Whether their proposal of industry co-operation was a genuine preference in 1925 on the part of Farish and Teagle, or merely a means of undercutting a drive toward federal regulation, it is impossible to say. Whatever the motivation, in the meeting of the API board on January 12, 1925, Jersey's Chairman Bedford proposed a resolution offering full co-operation with the Federal Oil Conservation Board.

The resolution was adopted, and a committee of eleven members was appointed to study the problems of the industry.[26] Farish was a member of this committee and also the ranking member of its subcommittee on crude supply. Pratt of Humble was the chairman of a special eleven-man committee which prepared a report on supply.[27] This report, dealing with the question of the adequacy of oil resources, provided the major support of the committee's conclusions.

The report of the Committee of Eleven contained the following significant statement on oil supply and waste: [28]

> Waste in the production, transportation, refining and distribution of petroleum and its products is negligible.
>
> There is no imminent danger of the exhaustion of the petroleum reserves of the United States.
>
> It is reasonable to assume that a sufficient supply of oil will be available for national defense and for essential uses in the United States beyond the time when science will limit the demand by developing more efficient use of, or substitutes for, oil, or will displace its use as a source of power by harnessing a natural energy.
>
> The availability of future supplies . . . depends upon adequate incentives . . . . There must be:
>
> (a) Security in the ownership of lands and the right to lease.
>
> (b) Conditions of exploration and development by owners or lessees permitting exercise of initiative, liberty of action, the play of competition and the free operation of the law of Supply and Demand.
>
> (c) Prices that will provide a return to producers, refiners, and distributors commensurate to the risks involved and the capital invested.

The report's great weaknesses were that it included hardly the slightest suggestion for improvement and was resolute in the denial of evils of which individual members of the committee must have been well aware. It dodged entirely Doherty's plan for unit operation. And it went as far in denying any danger of an oil shortage as the zealous conservationists, in their endeavor to frighten the public into exerting pressure on the oil industry, had gone in overemphasizing the danger of imminent exhaustion.

Farish's own position, as spokesman for Humble, was set forth in his reply to a questionnaire of January 10, 1925, sent by the Federal Oil Conservation Board to leading executives and specialists in the industry.[29] Farish denied that there was any significant overproduction or waste, including underground waste, or that there was any danger, immediate or remote, of exhausting the petroleum resources of the United States. He maintained that, in the absence of danger of exhaustion of supplies, "it was not within the function" of the federal or the state governments "to control the manner of production or use of oil." Exploitation of reserves, however, "could be delayed and held in check if the companies who own same were permitted by law to enter into pooling agreements that would tend to delay development."

To draw from this reply definite conclusions about Farish's thinking at the time is impossible. His answers to questions concerning waste followed oilmen's old modes of thinking, which, it is true, had not yet been effectively disproved by scientific research though doubt had been cast upon them. His nearly complete denial of waste was not, however, consistent with his earlier references to enormous waste from overproduction,[30] though at that particular time the menace of overproduction had somewhat subsided. His position that the exploitation of reserves could be delayed and held in check if voluntary pooling was permitted was entirely consistent with his earlier thought.

It is probably fair to conclude that the position of Farish and of other members of the committee was more a measure of their attitude toward government regulation, especially federal, than anything else. Pratt in 1927 virtually repudiated the contention of industry leaders that reserves were ample as only an opinion inspired by fear of burdensome government restrictions.[31] H. C. Wiess wrote in 1930: "The immediate reaction of a considerable part of the petroleum industry was based on the feeling that an admission of the charges [of waste] made would result in some form of federal control which would be unsatisfactory."[32] Farish's attitude unquestionably derived in large part from fear of government control.

In those years of controversy for the oil industry, Humble's top executive had thus taken a definite stand on a number of issues. Most emphatically Farish had opposed the extension of government regulation of the industry. His position on waste was enigmatic, inspired largely, it seems, by fear of government but founded essentially on ignorance of, or a lack of conviction concerning, the natural conditions that affected recovery from a reservoir. In so far as co-operative action was needed to improve the industry, he believed the action should be taken by the industry itself. But he held that before any such action could be taken by oilmen, the restrictive influence of state and federal antitrust laws would have to be removed.

BEGINNINGS OF THE SCIENTIFIC AND ENGINEERING REVOLUTION IN PRODUCTION, 1925–1926

The years 1924–1925 produced the heat of conflict, but they also produced light. Farish and other Humble executives then became aware of an emerging scientific and engineering revolution, a development without which the fundamental problems of oil production could not have been successfully attacked. During 1926 the education of executives of Humble and other oil companies progressed rapidly.

Henry L. Doherty's continuing crusade for reform by unit operation of oil pools under federal administration was influential in furthering interest in the subject.[33] Farish, who in 1925 was a strenuous opponent of Doherty's proposals, in 1928 made the *amende honorable* by writing to him: "I wish you to know that whereas I have differed with you, as to methods, I want to thank you for the part you have played in making the industry realize the need for better producing methods." [34]

The Federal Oil Conservation Board served as an important educational agency.[35] Its public hearings, which began in February, 1926, were obviously aimed at an objective investigation of the industry's ills and possible remedies. Production engineers and company executives found in the hearings the opportunity both to make their own positions known and to learn from others. No less an authority than Charles Evans Hughes discussed the legal issues involved in federal and state regulation.[36] As the hearings progressed, the oilmen's fear of federal intervention diminished.

In the long run, the most important development was that professional men and executives in the oil industry increasingly gave special consideration to production problems and methods. The research men of the Bureau of Mines began to address meetings of petroleum engineers and executives. The American Institute of Mining and Metallurgical Engineers provided in its Petroleum Division an important forum for discussion of the scientific and engineering and even economic and legal aspects of production. Such papers as those presented late in 1925 by Edward L. Estabrook and Clarence M. Rader on the "History of Production of Salt Creek Oil Field, Wyoming," and in 1926 by L. L. Dunn and James O. Lewis on the "Advantages of Unit Operation in New Pools" were significant contributions. Meetings of the Association of American Petroleum Geologists, the American Petroleum Institute, and the American Bar Association similarly began to contribute to the process of education.

At the same time, publications concerned with production problems increased. Professional journals, the published transactions of association meetings, and oil trade periodicals provided articles and addresses dealing with production engineering and research, economics, and law. Notable among the published proceedings of meetings of professional associations are the annual publications for 1925 and 1926 of the AIMME, entitled *Petroleum Development and Technology*. A significant periodical article was Lester C. Uren's "A Comparison of Methods of Oil Field Development," which appeared in January, 1926, in the *Oil Bulletin*. Addresses and articles by engineers emphasized the need for conservation, the extent of waste, and the role of gas in the recovery of oil. Particularly important were demonstrations—such as in Beecher and Parkhurst's important paper of 1926—not only that gas exerted a propulsive force but also that, when dissolved in the oil, it decreased the oil's viscosity and increased the ease of its movement toward the well, thus contributing to maximum recovery.[37] Such articles also emphasized the potential contribution of unit operations to the conservation of gas and oil and to economical production.[38] To the few path-breaking papers on fundamental questions published before 1925,[39] by staff members of the Bureau of Mines and others, was thus added a considerable literature.

On the whole, the years 1925 and 1926 were most important as a period of exploration, of preparation for definitive accomplishment in later years. There was much disagreement over both theory and practice, but disagreement nourished investigation and discussion. There were wide differences even among technologists on such important matters as well-spacing and unit operations and on such basic issues as the behavior and function of gas in the production of oil. The important achievement was not so much positive accomplishment in the solution of industry problems as it was the development of a new attitude. A growing group of trained and experienced scientists and engineers, as well as some industrial leaders, became convinced that traditional theories and techniques were inadequate and that new ones should be sought. The technologists, the men best fitted to guide in such a search, gained increasing influence. Thus the barrier of tradition was broken and the way was opened to change.

Farish and Pratt of Humble followed the new developments closely. Pratt, though previously concerned almost exclusively with the search for possible oil-bearing structures and but slightly with the underground behavior of oil, quickly recognized the significance of the new scientific and engineering developments in production. He became the interpreter of these developments to Humble in general and to Farish in particular.

He was the first to urge that Humble add to its organization a trained petroleum engineer, recommending John R. Suman, who was outstanding as both engineer and executive.

Farish, then the president of Humble and head of its largest producing division, gave increasing support to these new developments as the year 1926 progressed. At the public hearings of the Federal Oil Conservation Board in February, 1926, speaking as president of the American Petroleum Institute, Farish declared that the industry would participate in finding methods to prevent waste and announced a gift of half a million dollars from John D. Rockefeller for carrying on scientific research in this area. If this natural resource was being wasted, he said, the $9,000,000,000 investment in the oil industry was being jeopardized.[40] As president of the American Petroleum Institute in 1926, Farish was a figure of national importance and as such was frequently called upon to speak before bodies ranging from the West Texas Chamber of Commerce in June, 1926, to a conference on education and industry at the University of Chicago in October.

Statements in these addresses bore little resemblance to Farish's position in the previous year. He declared: "Petroleum is a wasting asset. Whenever a barrel of oil is consumed, our total supply is permanently diminished in exactly the amount. . . . . Our Federal Government has properly . . . urged the necessity of conserving the remainder of this essential natural resource." The petroleum industry, he stated, lacked cohesion and intelligent direction, adding, "Competition is intense and totally unreasoning." The rule of capture and state and federal laws precluding agreements between operators rendered "wasteful drilling and overproduction inevitable" and real conservation impossible. He no longer denied the possibility of overproduction, which he said had endured for "a prolonged and trying period." He spoke favorably of unit operation, even employing that very controversial term.

Farish no longer appeared as a thick-and-thin defender of the oil industry, denying the very existence of overproduction and waste, but as a moderate critic. He called for a program of reform, though on a purely voluntary basis. He publicly advocated no legislation, save to make voluntary co-operation legally possible.[41]

The progress of Farish's thinking was actually greater than those public statements indicated, even as his stand of the previous year was probably not adequately representative of his real knowledge and views. An understanding of the function of gas in petroleum recovery had begun to span the gap between the laboratories of the Bureau of Mines and the offices of oil companies. Such perceptive executives as Farish were at last becoming persuaded that underground waste was a reality, but one that might in large measure be overcome.

Humble executives in 1926 began to put new ideas into effect in their company's operations and, indeed, to help provide a broader base for them. Farish and Pratt, like other more progressive leaders of the oil industry, were earlier convinced of the importance of gas conservation than of any other conservation principle. As early as April, 1926, Humble production superintendents were experimenting successfully with maintaining production by pumping the gas back into the sands. But individual action for gas conservation was seen to be of limited utility; by June, 1926, Farish was urging upon H. E. Bell, oil and gas supervisor of the Texas Railroad Commission, that all gas produced in the Panhandle "be returned to the sand . . . whether . . . processed for gasoline or not."

By October Humble directors were discussing with John R. Suman the possibility that he might join Humble to develop its petroleum engineering. Farish, whose presidential duties had become heavy, saw the need of turning his own responsibilities as production manager over to someone who could give close attention to producing problems. Under the urging of Pratt and his own conviction of the importance of a new approach to production, he looked for a man familiar with new producing concepts and techniques.

In the meantime, the preliminary report of the Federal Oil Conservation Board of September, 1926, did much to allay the fears of oil executives and to further the acceptance of emerging conservation principles.[42] Temperate in tone, it placed the burden of protecting petroleum resources "upon the normal commercial initiative of private enterprise," but it firmly insisted upon the necessity for such protection. It emphasized the vast wastage of gas, recommended that doubt as to the legality of co-operative methods should be removed by appropriate legislation, and urged state action, under the police power, to stop the waste of gas and to prevent the draining of oil without compensation from beneath one owner's land to another's well. This report provided evidence that the issue had been taken out of federal politics and had been changed basically into a search for facts and practicable methods. Pratt and Farish, in company with other progressive oil executives, were ready to participate in such a search.

A NEW THREAT OF OVERPRODUCTION

Only a few weeks later a new and menacing threat of overproduction added its weight to Humble's and the industry's interest in new production principles and techniques. Humble had long maintained that the problem of overproduction was an industry problem, and since the time of flush production at Powell, as has been noted, the company had tried to reduce its inventory and put its supply operations on a more nearly current basis. In this, however, it had enjoyed little success.

One factor in the supply situation, the upward tendency of oil prices, had hitherto been favorable but it had a somewhat artificial base. The enormous aboveground storage of crude had evened out the effect of the great fluctuations in supply from flush production in new pools, with the result that prices from time to time did not fall so far as they might otherwise have fallen. Moreover, the continuing fear of an eventual shortage of oil had given crude in storage or underground a speculative value. The result was that the average price apparently declined relatively slowly in periods of flush production as compared with the rate of price increase when the supply declined.[43]

Throughout the history of the oil industry, the market had usually absorbed the oil offered at prices sufficiently above costs so that oil production was on the whole profitable. Before 1911 the Standard Oil group, great storers and aggressive marketers, had a stabilizing effect on crude oil prices. Their willingness to buy oil for storage in periods of flush production, within the limits of their facilities, and their sale of that oil when crude production decreased had tended to make price fluctuations less extreme than they might otherwise have been. Of basic importance was the fact that the demand for oil products was so dynamic that the market until in the later 1920s took the oil that was produced at prices that were generally profitable to producers. Periods of difficulty did occur, such as the one in 1915 which contributed to the organization of Humble Oil & Refining Company, but they were usually regarded as resulting from special circumstances or as more or less temporary.

In the 1920s, however, certain developments complicated the supply situation. One was the unusually strong drive to acquire reserves and develop production. Another was the increase in the ability to discover oil and to produce such discoveries effectively as a result of improvements in petroleum geology and engineering. Still another was improved refining methods, which increased the gasoline gallonage obtained from a barrel of oil. The question was whether crude production and the market for refined products could be so balanced as to keep the price of crude in a reasonable relationship to costs of production.

In 1926 trouble was obviously brewing. Numerous new fields began to add tremendously to the world supply. In the United States notable discoveries were made in the Mid-Continent, Texas, and California. In Humble's own region the discovery of the great Seminole pools in Oklahoma and large new production in West Texas and the Panhandle made the situation increasingly acute. At the same time, new sources of oil abroad were beginning to threaten American oil in foreign markets. The great Maracaibo Basin of Venezuela, with an improved outlet for its oil, began to add heavily to the world's oil stream; in Colombia and Sumatra new discoveries and pipeline outlets also contributed. Especially portentous was the threat of oil from expropriated properties in Russia, which was already being offered by the Soviet government at prices far below the costs of private companies.[44] In October, 1926, prices began to decline steeply.

In his speech delivered in Chicago in October, 1926, Farish predicted that during the next two years there would be low prices and an oversupply of both gasoline and crude oil. Several months later Wiess held that in the next two years or longer the petroleum industry would be on a fundamentally new basis of chronic oversupply, as contrasted with relatively short periods of overabundance in the past, and that, no matter how low prices fell, they would not correct the long-term prospects. The price-cost situation, he held, spelled disaster for the average operator if it continued over a period of two years or more.

By the end of 1926 several of Humble's leaders had thus reached certain definite conclusions concerning what was wrong with the oil industry and with their own crude supply operations, and the company had begun to do something about its problems. Pratt was convinced of the necessity of applying research and engineering to production in order to recover a larger percentage of oil in a given pool and to produce it more efficiently. Farish had publicly recognized that disorganization, waste, and overproduction did exist and did constitute problems.

Privately he was at least upon the brink of deciding that only public authority could adequately deal with the monster that was menacing the stability, prosperity, and perhaps even the very existence of the oil industry by preventing the building-up of large and secure reserves, the employment of efficient and economical production methods, and the sale of crude at prices that would yield a profit. Near the end of the year Farish and Pratt were discussing with J. Edgar Pew of Sun Oil and with members of the Texas Railroad Commission the possibility of enacting a law to enable the regulatory body to prevent the waste of gas from oil wells. Wiess, though fully occupied with his own responsibilities in refining, was lending men from his department for research in production and was giving his support to the new approach to production and supply problems. Strong evidence of the attitude of the members of Humble's Board of Directors was their invitation to John R. Suman to join them in order to introduce and develop in Humble's production new production engineering methods—the only time that an outsider has ever been elected a director of the company.

Although the principal problems of their industry had by the end of 1926 been clarified in the minds of several of Humble's top administrators, how to solve those problems was far from clear. The search for solutions was to be a major concern of the Humble organization in the years 1927–1930, and indeed for several years thereafter. Out of that search were to develop new policies and practices of fundamental importance to Humble's future operations.

Those developments were to be the product not merely of a few top executives but rather of the co-operative efforts of executives, research men, engineers, lawyers, and, indeed, production men on all levels. Their efforts were applied in two separate but closely related areas. On the one hand, Humble men through research and engineering contributed to more efficient operations within the Humble organization itself; on the other, they provided leadership in the conservation movement, which during the 1930s was to work profound changes in the American oil industry. Those efforts constitute the central themes of the next two chapters.

Chapter 12

THE BEGINNING OF A NEW ERA IN HUMBLE'S PRODUCTION, 1927–1930

At the beginning of 1927 Humble's principal problem was to reverse the downward trend in reserves, oil production, and profits that its producing operations had experienced in recent years. It was obviously necessary to acquire large and relatively inexpensive and dependable reserves, to reduce the cost of producing oil to a level commensurate with the lower prices resulting from the competition of low-cost crude in national and world markets, and to sell at prices sufficiently above costs to earn a reasonable return on the investment.

Humble worked along several lines to strengthen its production. The present chapter will focus attention on the company's attempts to increase its reserves and to improve its operations through a greater utilization of science and engineering. The next will deal with its participation in the movement to improve the entire industry's producing methods and its efforts to help develop regulation by the states in the interest of less wasteful and less erratic production.[1]

OVERPRODUCTION: AN OIL-INDUSTRY PROBLEM

Humble's policies and practices in these years can be understood and evaluated only in the light of an increasing overproduction of oil. The situation that Farish foresaw late in 1926 and that Wiess predicted in March, 1927, as a "chronic and continued oversupply, as contrasted with . . . past experience of relatively short periods of acute oversupply alternating with similar periods of either approximate balance or draft on stocks," was more than realized in subsequent years. Late in 1926, indeed, the oil industry entered a condition of overproduction that was to plague it for over a decade.

The term "overproduction" had several connotations at the time. Oilmen generally meant by it a production so large as to drive prices below the level necessary to cover costs plus a normal profit margin. Men who had assumed responsibility for purchasing and storing crude also considered the industry as overproducing when the volume of production exceeded transportation facilities and market demand, so that oil stocks in storage materially increased. Government specialists who were anxious over the waste of natural resources, and some oilmen, particularly those who purchased and stored crude, further regarded the waste of oil and gas as indicative of overproduction. Thus the term came to have three general meanings: a volume of production that drove prices below the profit level, production beyond the effective market demand, and production that was wasteful of the resource.

Even in an industry accustomed to periods of glut, the condition that prevailed for many years, beginning late in 1926, was unprecedented. It was, however, the logical result of the world-wide, decade-long fear of a shortage which had brought a rush of capital into the development of oil production; it was also a result of the development of new techniques for finding and producing crude oil and for manufacturing products. Oil consumption, to be sure, simultaneously increased rapidly, but at a slower rate than reserves and productive capacity.

American oil in the later 1920s was threatened in foreign markets and at home by the growing volume and even greater potential of crude oil production in foreign countries. New fields were discovered in Sumatra, Persia (Iran from 1935), and Iraq; new pipeline outlets were provided for the production of the rich Infantas structure in Colombia; particularly threatening was the rapidly increasing volume of crude that flowed from the Maracaibo Basin in Venezuela. Some of these new oil regions had lower transportation costs to certain markets than did oil from the United States; but the greatest advantages of these new fields were that they were large and not very deep and that, being on large government concessions, they were developed under one management at great savings in costs as compared with competitive development in the United States. A special case was the oil from properties expropriated by the Russians, which was offered at prices far below normal cost of production elsewhere.

While oil from abroad was beginning to menace United States oil from the viewpoint of costs, so far as overproduction was concerned the really critical situation was at home. At this time large production was developing in West Texas, and prolific fields were opened in other regions, notably Oklahoma City in the Mid-Continent and Santa Fe Springs (deep) in California. Despite a considerable holding-back of production, only a small increase in imports, and some increase in consumption, the stocks of crude oil and refined products in the United States rose from

CRUDE OIL PRODUCTION OF PRINCIPAL STATES

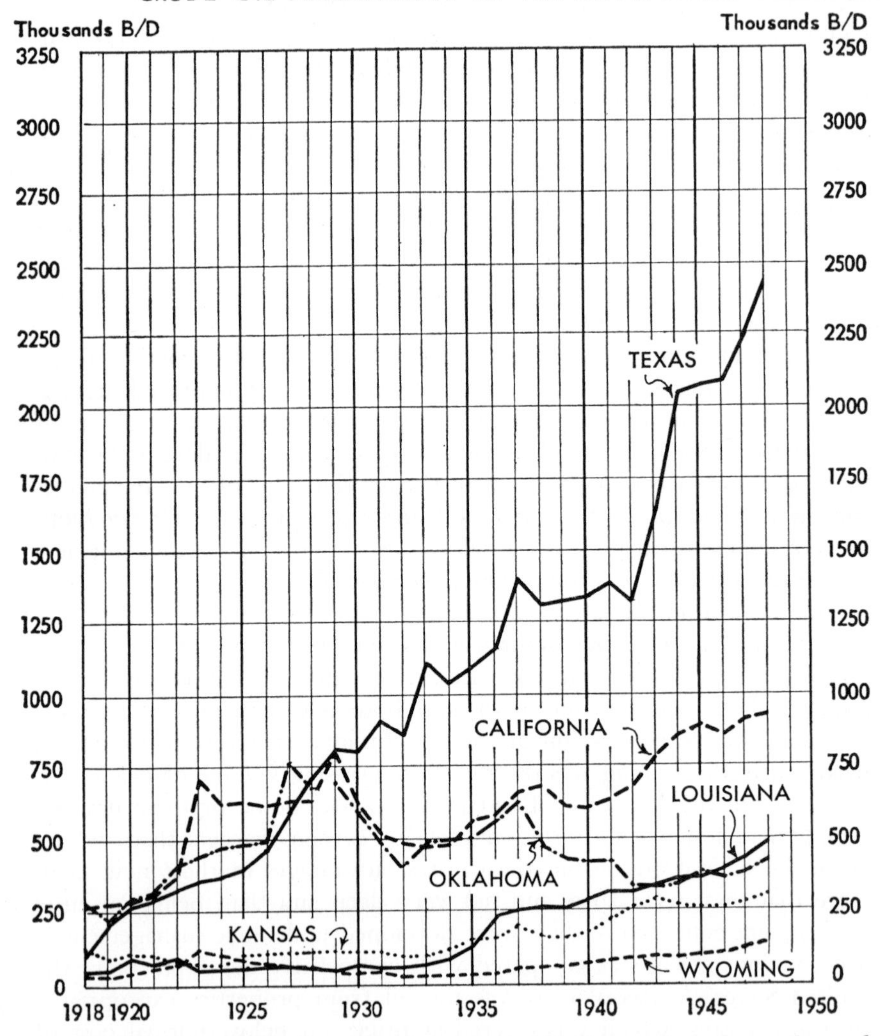

520,000,000 barrels at the end of 1926 to 666,662,000 barrels at the end of 1930.[2] The current success in finding new oil deposits threatened a further deterioration in the inventory situation.

American oilmen and government specialists were soon in agreement that overproduction was serious. The former were especially worried about prices. The effect on prices was, indeed, critical—a decline from a national annual average price at the well of $1.88 a barrel in 1926 to $1.19 in 1930 and in Texas from $1.85 to 99 cents.[3] This drop in oil prices was greater than the fall in the general wholesale commodities price level.

Overproduction and low prices were major factors in determining Humble's policies in the decade after 1926. They were, to be sure, important to the whole American and the world oil industry. Humble, however, with a less balanced integration than many companies and with heavy investments in production and commitments as a purchaser, was in an especially difficult position.

SUCCESS IN THE SEARCH FOR OIL PROSPECTS AND RESERVES

By 1927 Humble had become firmly committed under the leadership of Pratt to a new policy in acquiring acreage to develop, that of leasing large blocks of land. No longer was the company to depend mainly upon checkerboarding its leases, only occasionally obtaining a larger tract. Block-leasing was not practicable or wise in all circumstances, but the new policy set an objective which the company in subsequent years increasingly approached. Humble was particularly careful to avoid scattered acreage in regions where the development of large pools appeared a possibility.

The adoption of this leasing policy was largely a result of the new attitude of several executives toward the company's production problems. By 1927, as has been observed, those executives had become convinced that the only solution to the problem of competitive drilling—with its attendant flush production, high cost, low recovery, and waste—was the development of the oil pool as a unit. The unit plan did not necessarily mean one-company ownership, but that was its simplest and most indubitably legal form. If a company could acquire an entire field, it could operate that field efficiently and economically, drill only the number of wells necessary to develop the field properly under the obligation of the leases, conserve gas and oil, and, when the price of crude was below cost of production, reduce production without danger of drainage by offset wells. Such an operation would have the additional advantage of decreasing transportation difficulties and the number of camps for production employees, both important from the viewpoint of costs. Even though a whole field could not be leased, block-leasing, if also practiced by other companies, might facilitate unit development, which Humble urged.

A field of one's own, to experiment with and to operate according to the best principles, required something more than recognition of its desirability. Besides the problem of finding and obtaining the right to test and develop a structure that was not already partly leased, success depended upon the command of sufficient capital to purchase a block of acreage covering an entire structure, reasonable success in finding oil, and petroleum engineering adequate for developing and producing such a field in the most economical fashion.

Block-leasing was a more difficult way of acquiring oil lands than the old checkerboarding method. First of all, it meant finding prospective fields where leasing a large area was still possible. Where such a prospect was believed to exist, negotiations had to be made for the right to test the land by actual drilling and to develop production if oil was found. In East Texas with its small individual holdings this would require scores or even hundreds of leases, but in Southwest or West Texas a desired block might lie within a single ranch. Brokers commonly purchased blocks of leases for resale; and independent drillers or producers acquired leases in order to drill a wildcat and, if oil was found, to sell the leases.

Whether one or scores of separate acquisitions were required for the purchase of a block of acreage, a crucial question was the cost. This involved not only bonuses, rentals, and royalties, but also such other matters as the time of testing, rate of development, and cash payments and overriding royalties to brokers or others. Large lease purchases, for example a ranch or a block of leases held by an independent operator, usually involved heavy commitments and required special contractual terms.

Such negotiations, consequently, were either carried on by the executives responsible for exploration and leasing or were closely directed and supervised by them. Nearly all the larger trades at this time were negotiated by Wallace E. Pratt, director for geology, leasing, and scouting. Other large purchases were negotiated by Chief Geologist Eugene Holman in 1927 and 1928 and, beginning in 1929, by his successor, L. T. Barrow, or by other geologists or landmen to whom they might delegate the responsibility, but always in close consultation with and under the direction of Pratt. Robert B. Cooper, Humble's chief landman, at this time began to participate in negotiating important trades. However, on Pratt particularly, and on Holman and Barrow successively, devolved the primary responsibilities for carrying out Humble's block-leasing policy.

As the trades became larger and the terms more involved—not the relatively simple "Producers 88" contract used earlier—Humble's legal staff moved into a position of even greater importance than earlier in the acquisition of oil land. The curing of titles had always been and continued to be a vital part of the work; where unit operations were contemplated, however, or even the acquisition of a large portion of a field, it was even more important than under the previous checkerboarding of leases that all titles should be sound and that so far as possible no vacancies or claims to limitation titles should be overlooked. As the contracts in the larger trades became more complicated, especially those involving a second party between the original lessors and Humble, the responsibilities of the lawyers in their formulation became correspondingly heavier.

In those later years of the 1920s, Rex G. Baker of Humble's Legal Department was in charge of the company's title and contract work, a responsibility which he was to continue to carry throughout the next decade. A measure of the quality of the work done by Baker and his associates is the relatively small amount of Humble's litigation involving lease titles and contracts in subsequent years. It was not always possible, of course, to obtain absolutely clear titles, and questions inevitably arose over the application or interpretation of specific contractual terms However, although the oil industry then normally experienced a large percentage of challenges of its land titles and lease contracts, Humble suffered relatively little loss from such claims or from resultant litigation.

While the executives negotiated the purchases of large lease blocks and the lawyers cured titles and drew up contracts, the scouts, geologists and geophysicists, and landmen, under the direction of the chief geologist, looked for prospective oil lands to lease, test, and develop. Block-leasing, because it required going into unproved areas more than did the earlier checkerboarding, made geologic and geophysical exploration on a large scale especially important. Since Mexia-Powell days Humble geologists had not been so successful as those of certain other companies, but the executives were especially encouraged by the accomplishments of the company's geophysicists, who in the latter part of 1926 discovered the Moss Bluff salt dome. Although Moss Bluff did not become an important producing field, its discovery confirmed Pratt and other Humble executives in the belief that geophysical methods were potentially valuable.

By the beginning of 1927 the Geophysics Department of Humble's Geologic, Lease and Scouting Department, after two and a half years of experimentation, was ready to begin its great contribution to Humble's production and reserves. The work was directed by David P. Carlton and James E. LaRue, who co-operated closely; in so far as there was any division of their duties, Carlton devoted somewhat more of his attention to seismic field work and research and LaRue to gravity and interpretation. In 1927 the department consisted of a small research group, a machine shop, and fourteen geophysical parties—fifty-eight men in all. Three crews then operated refraction seismographs; four, torsion balances; and seven, magnetometers. Humble's success in finding much-needed oil reserves depended largely on these geophysicists, with their relatively new instruments for geologic exploration.

The geophysicists worked in the later 1920s along several closely related lines. The research group, with O. H. Truman in direct charge, worked with the machine shop in developing more sensitive, more rapid, and more fieldworthy instruments. In 1927 work was begun on designing and building a gravity meter, an instrument which LaRue urged as potentially very valuable. The geophysicists also studied the analysis and interpretation of data, at first being helped especially by the field men's accumulation of data on known structures. In the field, seismographic exploration was the special charge of Stuart Sherar. The field men were principally concerned with gathering data on undeveloped areas in the hope that such data would reveal structures that might be oil-bearing.

The instruments used in the field by Humble geophysicists, as by other companies, at this time measured various phenomena of significance in studying structures. The magnetometer measured the variation of the earth's magnetic field at a given point; by comparing variations in the earth's magnetic field at different points, men familiar with the interpretation of such data derived clues to differences in the composition of the subsurface geology from place to place. This instrument was used principally on the Gulf Coast, but without much success. The torsion balance measured the pull of gravity, which varied with the density of rocks and thus indicated differences in the rocks at the various points where measurements were taken. This instrument was useful in locating anticlines, but it was especially helpful in finding salt domes; its serious weaknesses were the great care and long time required in its operation. The refraction seismograph, which recorded sound waves sent into the earth by an explosion and refracted to the surface, gave an indication, by the speed and quality of the waves recorded, of the nature of the strata shot. Comparison of results at different points indicated variations in subsurface formations. This instrument was used chiefly to locate shallow salt domes.

The year 1927 proved notably successful for the geophysicists. After a flowing well had been brought in at Boggy Creek in East Texas as a result of surface geologic mapping, seismic work proved the existence of a salt dome and by outlining the dome guided in the purchase of further leases. In a seismic play in East Texas in the spring of the year, salt domes were indicated at other places. The discovery of the East Tyler dome was one of those strokes of luck in which the oil industry has been so prolific: a Humble seismograph operator, hearing on his radio an order given to a competitor's crew to set off the charges, set his own instrument and got a recording that indicated a salt dome. Quick work the following day outlined the dome, and Humble lease men got a large block with no competition. The crew that set off the charge missed the dome altogether. The crowning achievement of the geophysicists in 1927, however, was the discovery of the Sugarland salt dome.

Because of the importance of the acquisition of large blocks, some of which became major fields, it is well to note the procedures by which Humble acquired the rights to test and develop them and also the conditions agreed upon. Both the procedures and the conditions may be illustrated by two blocks of which Humble obtained complete control at this time and on which major fields were developed, the Raccoon Bend and Sugarland fields.

The first of these blocks, acquired in 1926 and 1927, was in an unusual swing in the Brazos River known as Raccoon Bend.[4] The block had been leased in 1925 and early 1926 by Harry Pennington. A Texan with a degree in engineering from the University of Michigan, Pennington had come to believe that efficient recovery could be maintained in a field by holding a proper ratio of gas to oil in the production process, a subject on which he wrote a series of articles published in *The Oil Weekly* beginning in 1923. Since maintaining such a ratio would require control of a whole field, he looked for a likely prospect. He concluded that Raccoon Bend was underlain by a salt dome and accordingly was a prospect for oil, and he leased as much land as he believed would cover the prospective field. He thereby acquired obligations to drill many wells, but he could not himself command the necessary capital for development, which he estimated would cost $7,500,000. He succeeded in interesting H. T. Staiti, a Gulf Coast independent operating in sulphur and oil properties, in the prospect. On behalf of the Valley Oil Corporation of which he was president and principally on the basis of gas flows in shallow wells, Staiti agreed in return for an interest to drill the many wells required by Pennington's leases. Pennington assigned his leases to Staiti's corporation.

After some preliminary work on the land, Staiti turned to Humble. Frith Owen, a geologist working under Raymond Goodrich, then Humble's Gulf Coast division geologist, was sent to check Pennington's report to Staiti on the block. Owen strongly recommended that Humble acquire an interest in the block if it could be obtained on a satisfactory basis.

Pratt conducted the negotiations with Staiti that eventuated in the contracts of June 7, 1926, whereby Humble acquired an undivided one-half interest in the leases then owned by the Valley Oil Corporation and undertook to operate the properties on joint account for itself and Valley Oil. Humble agreed to pay the corporation a cash bonus of $20,000 and to expend an additional $165,000 in examining the titles of the many scores of separate leases in the block, in surveying the tracts, and in drilling a specified number of wells to given depths. If on the completion of the test wells Humble chose not to develop the field, it could reassign its interest to Valley Oil—a "stop-loss" provision that limited its original risk. The terms of these and other contracts were spelled out by Rex G. Baker and the legal representative of Valley Oil, and Baker had charge of the examination of the title of each individual lease and of Humble's rights and obligations thereunder.

Humble's exploratory drilling at Raccoon Bend met with modest success. In the spring of 1927 the discovery well was brought in and the other test wells were drilled. These early wells were not spectacular performers, but the prospect soon took on the aspects of a major field. After the discovery Humble obtained full control of the field by purchasing from the Valley Oil Corporation on May 21, 1927, the remaining one-half interest in the leases concerned. Staiti offered to make this trade in order to be relieved of the obligation to stand half of the cost of developing and operating the properties after Humble's original expenditure of $185,000. Under the new arrangement, Valley Oil received a one-fourth interest in net profits and $150,000 in cash. In 1934 Humble also purchased for nearly $500,000 a quarter of that one-fourth interest, thus reducing Valley Oil's participation in net profits to three-sixteenths.[5]

Raccoon Bend has special historical significance as Humble's first important wholly controlled and operated field. Boggy Creek was the earliest, but its structure was such that there was little advantage in unit operations. Raccoon Bend was, therefore, the company's first opportunity to test its growing conviction of the importance of unit operations.

Humble's next large acquisition, which also led to the development of a field operated as a unit, was a large collection of holdings on which the Sugarland field was developed. A somewhat different procedure was followed in acquiring this block than at Raccoon Bend; some land was purchased in fee, some in individual leases, and a major part as a large block of leases. Most of the early purchases were negotiated by Pratt, with the advice and assistance of Chief Geologist Holman and Landman Cooper; other early trades were directed and supervised by Holman. As in the Raccoon Bend purchase, Rex G. Baker had charge of the legal work for Humble.[6] Sugarland illustrates how complicated the process of acquiring a large block could be.

The search for oil in the Sugarland area had begun many years earlier. In May, 1921, a wildcat well had been drilled about half a mile north of the northern edge of the present field but had been abandoned at 3,810 feet. Later the Gulf Production Company had leased a block on which it made a refraction seismograph survey but found no salt dome and consequently gave up the block. In the summer of 1926 Humble geophysicists examined the area with a seismograph; probably because the dynamite charges used were too light, this refraction shooting failed to yield any indication of a salt dome. In September, 1927, Joe Rostrom, Humble scout, reported that he was sure some leases were being taken in the area by H. C. Cockburn and Smith & Gates, following torsion-balance work by the North American Exploration Company. A Humble refraction crew was moved back into the area immediately; it used the same shot points as in 1926 and set the instruments up at the same locations but used 400 instead of 225 pounds of dynamite for each shot. The records obtained, though not interpreted to indicate definitely the presence of salt, nevertheless encouraged Humble to explore the area again. The company therefore decided to spend $25,000 in acquiring leases on which to explore.

The first acquisition was the outright purchase in fee of an 835-acre farm owned by Mary E. Hamner, a ninety-year-old widow. The negotiations for this purchase were carried on for Humble by its landman at Cisco under the direction of Chief Geologist Holman; Mrs. Hamner was represented by her son, Judge Edward J. Hamner of Sweetwater. Humble proposed to lease the land, having no desire to be encumbered with the management of a farm, but Hamner wanted to sell. The farm had earlier been offered to another party at $25.00 per acre, in cash and notes, but the prospective buyer had been unable to raise the necessary cash. Humble was offered the farm for $25,000, which it agreed to pay. The deed was signed by Mrs. Hamner on October 3, 1927, and was delivered to Humble after the title had been approved.

A suit which subsequently arose over this purchase illustrates in a general way a not uncommon development with respect to oil lands leased or purchased—claims of heirs after oil has been found. In the spring of 1928, after Mrs. Hamner's death and the discovery of oil on a neighboring tract, Judge Hamner's brothers and sisters brought suit, charging that he and Humble had conspired to defraud the mother and seeking the cancellation of the deed. A settlement was agreed upon whereby the plaintiffs withdrew all charges reflecting on Humble and Judge Hamner and recognized the validity of Humble's deed; Humble on its part agreed to pay the heirs $250,000 in cash and to grant them a one-sixteenth royalty on oil and one-half the customary royalty on other minerals, including sulphur. A judgment in accordance with this agreement was rendered by the court in April, 1929. Humble on its own initiative then made a gift to Judge Hamner and to his children, who had refused to participate in the suit although in their grandmother's will they were designated as heirs to one-sixth of the property. The company's gift to the children was the equivalent in cash and royalties of their proportionate share under the will.[7]

The major part of the prospect that was to become the Sugarland field was offered to Humble by H. C. Cockburn, a Houston lease broker, who, in association with Smith & Gates and the North American Exploration Company, had leases and options on leases totaling 3,564 acres. As of October 24, 1927, Pratt on behalf of Humble made a trade with Cockburn and his associates under which the company acquired a thirty-day option to purchase this lease block plus leases which the Cockburn group might acquire under option contracts or otherwise in the Sugarland area. Humble paid $10,000 for this option. The contract stipulated that, if Humble chose to exercise the option, it would pay Cockburn an additional $50,000 for his leases and at its own cost drill a well on the center of the dome to a depth of 3,500 feet. Upon the completion of that well, Humble had the option either to assign the leases to the Cockburn group and to be relieved of further liability or to retain the leases and make an additional cash payment of $200,000. The contract further provided that, if Humble chose to hold the acreage, it would keep at least one rig constantly drilling, with no more than sixty days between wells, until the leases were reasonably developed. After 500,000 barrels of oil had been produced out of Humble's net working interest, the company would pay Cockburn and his associates an additional $260,000 out of one-fourth of five-sixths of the production. The group, furthermore, retained overriding royalties of one-twenty-fourth on oil and gas and of 50 cents per long ton on sulphur. Humble was of course obligated to pay the original lessors the royalties stipulated in their lease contracts.

During the thirty-day option period, Humble moved the refraction crew back into the area. This time the geophysicists used dynamite charges of from 450 to 950 pounds and longer shot-lines. Their findings clearly indicated a salt dome at what they estimated to be below a depth of about 3,300 feet.

Humble chose to exercise its option and on November 19, 1927, obtained an assignment of the nine leases Cockburn then held. The company soon began drilling, and in March, 1928, it brought in the No. 1 Sugarland Industries well, on a 280-acre lease, as the field's discovery well.

During the exploration period and later Humble rounded out its holdings to cover the entire field. It leased two tracts before the Cockburn option was exercised; and in May, 1928, it found six unleased acres just off the productive Sugarland Industries acreage, which it then leased. In March, 1929, Humble obtained the assignment of four leases in the area from the Gulf Production Company, with the obligation to begin drilling within sixty days. Humble assumed all royalty obligations and paid Gulf $275,000; Gulf retained the right to participate, to the extent of one-half of the net profits from the acreage covered by the leases, after Humble had recovered from production its payments to Gulf for the assignment, rentals, and development costs, together with interest on these at 6 per cent. Only one of these four Gulf leases proved productive. In March, 1931, Humble purchased a thousand-acre tract, part of which was covered by a lease assigned to Humble by Cockburn. In 1938 it purchased in fee a 4.17-acre tract within its Hamner purchase, on which the seller had obtained a limitation title. Humble paid $30,000 in cash for this small tract, assumed the obligation to drill two wells on it within eight months, promised a further payment of $20,000 out of one-fourth of six-sevenths of the production from the tract, and obligated itself to pay a royalty of one-seventh of production—these terms illustrate how much might have to be paid for oil land in order to protect a block and also how onerous terms could be from the point of view of both physical and economic waste.

The discovery of the Sugarland field was significant far beyond the importance of the field itself. Sugarland was the first major oil field, of which there is record, discovered on the basis of the findings of the new art of seismic surveying. It was also the first fairly deep salt dome to be discovered through the use of geophysical instruments. Its discovery had immediate significance in the use of such instruments because it demonstrated that larger charges of explosives and longer shot-lines were necessary for locating the deeper salt domes.

The discovery of Sugarland inaugurated the search for more deeply buried domes. Humble gravity crews were moved from West Texas to the coast, and the refraction crews began to use larger charges and longer shot-lines. Late in 1928, as a result of the work of the research division, seismograph crews were outfitted with electronic, in place of mechanical, seismographs and with instruments that could be used in water. An active seismic play developed in coastal Louisiana, where Humble's crews found several promising prospects.

Humble by this time was easily the leader among Jersey affiliates in geophysical exploration. It entered an agreement with Standard Oil Development Company, as of January 1, 1929, to make the results of its geophysical research available at cost. Humble had then already supplied seismographic equipment and personnel to Jersey Standard's Venezuelan operations; in 1929 it sent additional crews to Venezuela and one to Jersey Standard's affiliate in the Far East. For several years Humble continued to co-operate with Jersey affiliates in this way.

The growing demand for geophysical work and the obvious need for better instruments and more effective interpretation of data resulted in an expansion of the company's geophysical research program which got under way in 1929. Several men were added to the group, including Dr. L. W. Blau, who brought with him some partially developed improvements on the torsion balance, particularly for shortening the observation time. M. M. Slotnick, a mathematician who joined the group in 1930, initiated work that contributed to the interpretation of geophysical, particularly seismic, data.

By the end of 1930 the research group had made considerable progress in the improvement of geophysical instruments. Advances had been made in the tropicalization of instruments, which improved them for use in the swampy and humid regions of Louisiana and Texas and in the Tropics. Truman, after about four years, had brought the gravity meter to a point where it gave definite promise of being effective—a very important development, since this instrument was the most likely substitute for the slow and cumbersome torsion balance. Substantial improvements had also been made on a new type of seismograph, the reflection instrument, developed by the Geophysical Research Corporation, under the sponsorship of E. L. DeGolyer, through research directed by J. C. Karcher. This instrument recorded sound waves shot into the earth by an explosion and reflected back to the surface. To a skilled interpreter the record gave indication of the density and thickness of the successive strata. The reflection seismograph had the advantage of yielding information in greater detail on a larger variety of structures than its predecessor, the refraction instrument.

Humble, which had been later than a few other companies in beginning to use geophysics in exploration, was strengthening its competitive position. In January, 1930, of 98 seismographs in Texas and Louisiana, Shell was operating 26, Humble 16, and Gulf 14, while, of 101 torsion balances, Gulf was operating 24, Humble 17, and Shell 14. Humble and Shell had by this time ceased to use the magnetometer. Humble thus, in the number of seismographs and torsion balances in the field, stood between the two large companies which had preceded it in the use of geophysical instruments.

For Humble's geophysical crews, however, the years 1929 and 1930 were discouraging. Seismic and torsion-balance crews continued to search for prospects in the coastal districts of Louisiana and Texas, but they accomplished little; the undiscovered salt domes that their instruments could detect were apparently becoming rare. The year 1930, according to a departmental report, marked the completion of "the first phase of the application of geophysics to the discovery of petroleum on the Coast," practically all the shallow domes having by then been located.[8] It was clear that future success would depend largely on those new and untried instruments, the gravity meter and the reflection seismograph. Humble's gravity meter was not yet fieldworthy, but in the autumn of 1930 reflection instruments began to be used in the fields and early in 1931 the last refraction instruments were withdrawn from use. Time would tell whether the more than doubled expenditures of the Geophysics Department—increased from $577,000 in 1929 to $1,300,000 in 1930—would pay off.

While the company's geophysicists during 1927–1930 operated mostly on the Gulf Coast, where their instruments were most effective, the geologists worked nearly everywhere. Their findings were often used as a basis for geophysical work, but in regions where geophysical instruments were not then sufficiently effective the geologists had full responsibility for exploration.

The geologists ranged widely in West Texas and the Panhandle but they made no important discoveries in either. Probably their work was not intensive enough. Humble, as always, had to decide where expenditures for exploration appeared to promise the best results, and its success elsewhere indicates that it had at this time what seemed to be sufficient reasons for spending more on exploration in other regions than in West Texas.

Humble geologists also worked in Southwest Texas, where late in the 1920s they achieved marked success.[9] From 1920 to 1928 that part of Texas had been for Humble a region of that "hope long deferred which maketh the heart sick." Although its search for oil there was not comparable to its activities in the old Gulf Coast area or East Texas, Humble had explored widely, leased considerable acreage, and drilled many wells in Southwest Texas. Yet in the years 1927 and 1928 its production in the area averaged less than 200,000 barrels. These disappointing years were in the long run not unproductive, however, for each shallow-well test and every dry hole contributed to the company's knowledge of the region's geology.

The results of the efforts of a small field staff of geologists, scouts, and landmen and of Fondren's drillers began to be realized in 1928. During that year subsurface work by L. T. Barrow, who was in charge of geology in the area, and surface work by L. F. McCollum, assistant geologist, together with scouting information contributed by L. S. McGee, led Humble to achieve a strong position at Salt Flat, near the Luling field. Several leases were obtained from brokers and a one-half interest was purchased in a block owned by the Luling Oil & Gas Company. Humble's eagerness to acquire new production at the time is illustrated by the speed with which this purchase was made; R. B. Cooper and L. T. Barrow, on authorization by Holman, negotiated the trade on a Saturday, agreeing to pay the asking price of $100,000, and by Monday the contract had been drawn up and signed. In October, 1928, the

Salt Flat field was discovered by the Sun Oil Company. In 1928 also, after surface work by McCollum had mapped faulting in the area, Humble acquired acreage at Darst Creek. In the next year Humble acquired considerable production in the Darst Creek field, which was discovered by The Texas Company.[10] Through the intelligent use of geologic information accumulated during seven years of patient and persistent effort, Humble had thus finally succeeded in establishing itself in Southwest Texas.

L. T. Barrow, who was in charge of geologic work in Southwest Texas, was as of January 1, 1929, appointed chief geologist of Humble. He had joined the company in 1924, after receiving the Master of Arts degree in geology from The University of Texas. He was to serve as chief geologist until shortly after he became a director of Humble in 1937, that is, through a period of notable additions to the company's reserves.

Statistics give some indication of the success of Humble's efforts to expand its oil reserves during the years 1927 through 1930. Humble then followed a more selective lease program than earlier. The total expenditure for leases was only about half as large in 1927 as in 1926 and even less per year in the next three years. The amount of leased acreage dropped was greatly increased as compared with earlier years. And yet, while lease expenditures declined, Humble drilled more wildcats—a total of 153 in the years 1927–1930 as compared with 86 in the preceding four years. These wildcats, moreover, were comparatively more successful, since in the later period they resulted in the discovery of nine fields —one out of seventeen—and, in the earlier, of only three, or one out of approximately twenty-seven. Humble's proved reserves, according to recently corrected estimates, tripled from the end of 1926 to the end of 1930. Yet the company at the latter date held only a slightly larger percentage of the industry's proved reserves in its region than it had in 1926.

PETROLEUM ENGINEERING AND PRODUCTION RESEARCH

On New Year's Day, 1927, John R. Suman, who was about to join Humble as a director, entered the Humble Building to look around and found the company's directors in their usual Sunday or holiday morning meeting. Farish invited Suman to join them and handed him a report, prepared late in 1926, which estimated the Producing Department's loss for that year to be $3,500,000. "What's this?" asked Suman. "I thought you were supposed to *make* money, not *lose* it. Why have you lost all this money?" "That's what *you're* supposed to find out," was Farish's reply.[11]

Humble's new petroleum engineer and production executive had been hired, of course, not merely to find out why the Production Department was losing money but also to remedy the situation, whatever the causes. Several members of the Humble board had realized that their producing operations, although excellent according to old standards, were inefficient according to the new. No Humble executive, however, had the combination of management experience and knowledge of petroleum engineering necessary for introducing the new methods into the company's producing operations. Pratt, the geologist, was aware of some of the company's weaknesses but had neither sufficient knowledge of production nor time to repair them. Wiess, of the Refining Department, was convinced of the value of scientific methods based on research and experimentation. Farish, who only recently had been converted to the necessity of adopting new methods, had his hands full as chief executive and realized that he should turn producing matters over to a qualified person. Thus, it was Suman's job to change Humble's Production Department from an organization of practical men following customary ways to one employing the latest and most effective methods and over the long term producing the most oil at the lowest cost. In accepting his new Humble appointment, Suman had, indeed, stipulated that he be given the opportunity to develop engineering in the Production Department.

Suman's first step was to make a survey of the various fields in the Northern division, the only region in which he had clearly defined authority. He noted the type and condition of the equipment in each field, the special techniques being employed, and particular field problems and needs. And in conference with the local managers he planned changes and the application of certain new practices.

He was especially interested in experimenting with returning gas under pressure to certain wells and leases. For example, he reported with reference to the Burkburnett district: "The most important matter which we have under consideration in this district is the putting of gas pressure on the Serrien lease. The short study which we have made of the subject indicates very conclusively that the production could be materially increased here by the application of gas pressure from central wells. We intend to send our engineer into this territory in the near future to make a thorough study of this subject." With reference to "the Rock Crossing district in the Waggoner Pasture, Wichita Falls Division," he wrote: "There is no question but that the application of compressed gas to this structure would also be a material aid to greater recovery and we intend to take this matter up in the near future and will see what can be worked out with the Phillips Petroleum Company." [12]

Better control of costs, Suman discovered, was an obvious need. Costs were found to vary greatly from field to field. For example, accounting-department figures for the month of December, 1926, showed the following variations in the cost of treating oil: Fox pool, 25 cents a barrel; Nocona, 12 cents; Haynesville lease, 23 cents; Irma, Arkansas, 11½ cents.

After this survey of the Northern division, Suman began to develop an organization. He recommended that full-time treating, gas, and electrical engineers be employed; and that each division, in addition to the usual geologist and civil engineer, should have a production engineer. By July, 1927, he had placed "production or gas engineers" in the North Texas, Corsicana, and newly organized West Texas divisions, and had established a "specialized petroleum engineering" service, with headquarters at Houston, under the supervision of Chief Engineer Rex G. Hamaker. This engineering service, in addition to mapping, abstracting, and civil and construction engineering work, included electrical engineering, gas and air lift and pressure restoration, oil treating, and the testing of materials and equipment.

Although Humble's producing organization had been far from backward in improving and maintaining its equipment, the new manager found much room for improvement through the application of recent developments in engineering methods and equipment. Suman himself was then a member of the committee of the American Petroleum Institute on the improvement and standardization of equipment, which did important work in developing standard specifications for drilling and producing equipment.[13] During 1927 Humble's Engineering Department, in its own laboratory and with help from Rice Institute, made several thousand tests on belting, belt clamps, sucker rods, wire lines, high-pressure gate valves for flowing wells, rotary drilling draw works, and so on. As a result of these tests, certain types and makes of equipment were adopted, thus improving the quality of and standardizing Humble equipment. Suman estimated in May, 1928, that resultant savings in purchasing equipment might amount to from 20 to 30 per cent.

Other problems were more difficult to solve. One was that of oil-well cementing. Another had to do with drilling mud. The greatest challenge, however, was to find ways of increasing the efficiency of oil recovery from reservoirs, with which Suman's organization was already experimenting by means of air lift and repressuring.

A study of reservoir conditions in the Desdemona field, then already under way, dramatized the need for improved recovery. This study was carried on under Harry W. Ferguson in the field and Stewart Coleman as head of the Development Department of the Refining Department. A preliminary analysis by Coleman of the data collected on the recovery of natural gasoline in that field indicated that the "recovery by flowing and pumping methods in Desdemona has been less than ten per cent." [14] On the basis of this preliminary study, work was continued in the field with the advice of Dr. W. K. Lewis and in co-operation with research for Humble at the Massachusetts Institute of Technology, the objectives being to estimate the amount of oil that remained in the producing sand and to learn how recovery might be increased.

This experiment, which was to go on for a number of years, was the first study undertaken by Humble that combined the recording and analysis of actual producing data with laboratory experiments in order to develop a scientific basis for production. In this study the research men began to correlate basic scientific work with observation and experimentation in the field, a combination that was later to lead to important developments.

Suman early became convinced that petroleum engineering should be organized separately under an experienced petroleum engineer. Consequently, when Chief Engineer Hamaker accepted an offer to head the research department of the Reed Roller Bit Company, the Engineering Department was disbanded and its personnel and work distributed among three new departments: civil engineering, sales engineering, and petroleum engineering.[15]

The Petroleum Engineering Department was organized as of June 1, 1928, under a new manager, W. W. Scott. A graduate of Stanford University in engineering, with a course in petroleum engineering, Scott had been a member of the early group in production research in the United States Bureau of Mines. After leaving the Bureau, he had for a year been with Royal Dutch-Shell in Borneo on work having to do especially with controlling water in the oil fields and also with new methods of producing and cementing wells. On his return to the United States he was employed by the Pure Oil Company as a petroleum engineer for two years before joining Humble in 1928.[16]

Scott's first task was to build an organization. Recruits were sought among Humble's own engineering groups, and many engineering graduates of 1928 were hired, particularly from the University of Oklahoma, which was then the only institution in the general region offering a degree in petroleum engineering. Another group of new engineers was hired in 1929. In that year the department's work was organized in five divisions: electrical, gas, chemical, equipment, and petroleum engineering service, each under a senior engineer. At the end of 1929 the Petroleum Engineering Department had forty-five employees.

As the names of these various divisions indicate, the range of the work carried forward by the department was broad. In 1929 its activities consisted mostly of electrifying oil-field equipment, starting work on the standardization of rigs, setting up equipment service records, and working on oil treating, cementing, and gas repressuring. Attention was also given to straight-hole drilling, and the engineers worked with the new Production Research Department in building a pressure maintenance plant at Sugarland and repressuring equipment at Olney. Work was also started on improving drilling mud. A standard tank battery was developed in the East Texas field. The Equipment Committee was formed, with Suman as chairman, to review equipment studies and tests and establish Production Department equipment specifications; this committee also began to work with the American Petroleum Institute on the further standardization of drilling and production equipment.

At the same time several circumstances made Humble executives consider expanding the production research that since 1926 had been carried on by the Development Department of the Refining Department. A basic reason for this greater interest in research was the necessity of getting more oil out of a given pool at less cost. Professor Uren's challenging of the old belief that more oil was recovered with closer spacing of wells had great significance to oilmen anxious over the high cost of close drilling, as Farish had been since the beginning of the decade. The growing emphasis on unitization—with its promise of recovering a larger percentage of the oil in a pool—highlighted the need for a better understanding of the nature of reservoirs and their behavior under the production process. Such publications as Beecher and Parkhurst's "Effects of Dissolved Gas upon the Viscosity and Surface Tension of Oil" opened up great possibilities for studying and improving recovery.[17] Another important factor was the oil industry's growing interest in investigating the function of gas in oil recovery. Humble's Farish was on a seven-member Gas Conservation Committee established by the American Petroleum Institute early in 1927; Suman was made chairman of its technical subcommittee for Texas and Louisiana. Suman was also chairman of the API's Division of Development and Production Engineering. Humble executives contributed leadership to this study movement and learned from it. Farish, Pratt, Suman, and Wiess, especially, among Humble's directors, early became convinced that Humble should expand its production research.[18]

What form such research should take, however, was then far from clear. In 1927 and 1928 oil companies were doing little production research aside from certain work that was essentially along engineering lines. Amerada was probably the only company in Humble's territory at the time that had what might be called an organized program of production research. One question was whether Humble's projected production research department should do theoretical research or leave that to schools. Humble had already arranged with the Massachusetts Institute of Technology to do the research in connection with the study of the Desdemona field, and the American Petroleum Institute had made similar arrangements for the advancement of production research. There was no question concerning the continuation and expansion of field research. The decision as to fundamental research was left to the new department.

The Production Research Department was established as of March 1, 1929. Its nucleus was furnished by the Baytown Development Department, including H. Dayton Wilde as head of the group. Among the original members, besides Wilde, were Thomas W. Moore, Thomas V. Moore, and George Cannon. By the summer of 1929 this new research department had a staff of eight technical men and their assistants.

The results of Humble's production research, like the research results of the Geophysics Department, were to be made available through Standard Oil Development Company to affiliates of Standard Oil Company (New Jersey). The Development Company had recently established a Department of Petroleum Production Engineering with three divisions: laboratory research, field research, and engineering services. The function of the department was principally to facilitate the exchange of research findings and engineering developments among Jersey affiliates. Humble, according to an arrangement with the Development Company, was to bill the latter for a sum equal to two-thirds of the cost of its research and pay a sum equal to one-third of the cost of the research results that it received. Humble was then the only Jersey affiliate with an organized production research program.

Humble's Production Research Department in its earlier years worked chiefly on the study of gas as a factor in production. That gas was important in oil recovery was then widely accepted, but very little was known about how it performed its function under varying reservoir conditions. Humble's research was based on the assumption that, if production methods were to be improved intelligently, the fundamental laws of nature governing the movement of oil through the reservoir sands and up the wells must be understood. At first it was believed that gas in the reservoir, particularly gas dissolved in the oil, was the most important factor determining the movement of oil. Gas in solution was known by theorists to decrease the viscosity and surface tension of the oil particles so that they could move more easily through the sands. Maintaining the gas in solution was believed to be of primary importance. Within a short time scientists also came to recognize the importance as a propulsive force of gas above the oil zone in a reservoir (a gas cap). Since the effectiveness of gas in a reservoir depended on pressure, the objective was to produce the oil in such a way as to maintain the reservoir pressure to the greatest possible extent. The maintenance of pressure, it was believed, would lengthen the flowing life of a field, make expensive pumping unnecessary, and result in the recovery of a larger percentage of the oil.

The Humble research group investigated the problems of pressure maintenance and efficient recovery by making studies under different conditions. Many scientists were working in the laboratory on these problems, especially under the sponsorship of the American Petroleum Institute, but few added to such studies experiments in the oil fields. Although the Humble production research group from the first carried on laboratory studies of the solubility of gas in oil and of the effect of gas in solution on the movement of oil, its most important work in those early years was its field studies. The most distinctive and valuable feature of Humble's field research in those early years was its emphasis on quantitative studies. This, first of all, required measuring volumes and pressures; next, making mathematical calculations and attempting to construct general formulas.

The early work of this research group was somewhat crude in the light of later knowledge, although it was good within the assumptions on which it was based and was significant in its method of attack on problems. It was later learned that the assumptions tended to oversimplify the complex problems studied. Indeed, although this early research led to certain generalizations that were to stand the test of later studies, it was in essence an exploration of a new field of scientific study and a necessary preparation for the more refined and precise research of later years.

A key problem in the beginning was to devise instruments for taking the measurements required for quantitative studies. The first serious need was for some way of measuring the pressure at the bottom of a well, that is, the pressure in the reservoir. It was a simple matter to obtain the gas-oil ratio at the top of the well by separating the gas from the oil and measuring the volume of each by ordinary meters, but new instruments had to be designed for measuring bottom-hole pressures. Amerada had a bottom-hole pressure gauge, but it was so large that it could be lowered only through the casing, thus necessitating the removal of the tubing through which the oil was being produced before lowering the gauge.

The Humble research men, in order not to interrupt production, for a time ran a flexible quarter-inch tube down through the producing tubing, sealed off gas leakage at the top, forced the liquid out of the small tube, made allowances for hydrostatic pressure, and then measured the gas pressure at the top of the tube. A less cumbersome device was soon designed by T. V. Moore. California Standard's affiliate, Standard Oil Company of Texas, was then using in West Texas a gauge small enough to be lowered through the producing tubing, but it was not considered sufficiently accurate or dependable. Moore devised another gauge, in which the spring was extended under pressure and was subjected to less friction than was the one used in the California gauge. This gauge the Humble men considered adequate for measuring pressure at the bottom of a well. Since it did not, however, come into use until in 1931, the Humble men in their early research had to depend chiefly on "macaroni" tubing for the measurements from which to calculate bottom-hole pressures.

Effective work in the fields also required the co-operation of engineers and field men. Humble's research men were particularly fortunate in receiving such co-operation. They had the advantage of strong and intelligent support from the principal managers concerned with field operations. This favorable situation was in contrast to that in another major company whose scientists did valuable work in the laboratory but who, because of the production manager's opposition to new scientific and engineering methods, did not have the opportunity to test their theories in the fields.

Studies in four fields, two of which Humble controlled completely, were especially important in those early years. Work at Sugarland was started even before the Production Research Department had been formally organized, and the study of the Olney field was begun late in 1929. The work at Desdemona and also at the Yates field was continued.

The Sugarland study was the first attempt to make a quantitative investigation of the factors influencing the decline in the reservoir pressure of a field under production.[19] For all wells careful records were kept of gas-oil ratios (number of cubic feet of gas produced per barrel of oil) and bottom-hole pressures. Wells were carefully spaced and their volume of production was controlled with the objective of reducing gas-oil ratios and maintaining bottom-hole pressures. By the spring of 1930, 5,000,000 barrels of crude had been produced with a gas-oil ratio of about 460 cubic feet of gas per barrel. It was then estimated that, if Sugarland had been produced the usual way without consideration for ratios and pressures, the ratio would have been a thousand per barrel. During the course of the study it was decided to install a pressure maintenance plant, and on April 1, 1930, the return to the oil sands of the gas produced with the oil was begun. The injection of from 80 to 90 per cent of the produced gas lowered the ratio to a net of 35 per barrel. Production was held to 12,000 barrels daily. The Sugarland experience was convincing evidence that in fields with gas drives the cost of conserving and returning the gas to the reservoir was amply repaid by the reduction in lifting costs and increase in recovery.[20]

Olney was a research man's dream, a pool which could be used as a laboratory for experimentation. Humble already held most of Olney, an exhausted field of sixty acres with twenty-five wells, and it acquired the few leases held by others. The research there was intended to test the effect of gas injection on oil recovery. It was impossible to give an exact demonstration at Sugarland, or at any other field where oil was being produced, of the effect of maintaining gas pressure. Olney was small enough to serve as a pilot plant and, it was reasoned, if commercial recovery was restored in this commercially exhausted field, the amount of oil subsequently recovered would give some indication of what the results would have been had the reservoir pressure been maintained. The field was repressured with gas purchased near by; and, after the pressure had been restored, production was again started with one producing well to each 7.5 acres. The experiment was continued several years. Suman reported in 1934 that Olney provided "eloquent and incontrovertible evidence of the increased ultimate recovery obtainable by the control and efficient utilization of reservoir energy. . . ." [21]

At the Yates field, which was being operated under a proration agreement, Humble research men and engineers participated in the collection and study of data to guide in determining the most equitable basis for prorating production among wells. An easy solution was to treat the production of a well under open and uncontrolled flow as a measure of its potential, but Humble's research men held that open-flow production was injurious to well and field. At Yates, then, study was aimed at discovering a better way of measuring a well's potential preparatory to prorating a field's allowable production among its wells.[22] Similar tests without open flow were made in the Hobbs field in New Mexico.[23]

The production research group did not, however, confine itself to reservoir and production studies. It early gave attention to drilling mud. It studied cementing, in both laboratory and field. And it studied the evaporation and contamination of oil in pipelines.[24]

By the fall of 1929 Humble's production research men and petroleum engineers were participating in meetings of professional organizations devoted to producing problems. Coleman, Wilde, and T. W. Moore then presented before the American Institute of Mining and Metallurgical Engineers a paper, the data for which were drawn from Sugarland, entitled "Quantitative Effect of Gas-Oil Ratios on Decline of Average Rock Pressure." [25] This paper, which was representative of the thinking and the methods of the Humble production research group at the time, marked the beginning of quantitative studies of reservoir behavior. In the winter of 1930 Wilde, before the same organization, discussed cementing problems on the Gulf Coast.[26] Papers presented by Wilde and Mercer Parks before the Production Division of the American Petroleum Institute at its fall meeting of the same year dealt with repressuring experiments at Sugarland and Olney. T. W. Moore also gave a paper, based largely on data from the Yates field, on the determination of the potential production of wells without the use of open-flow tests. Humble's Scott saw the maintenance of equitable production among wells as a problem of controlling the relative pressures underground as between wells, thus pointing to the great issue of the 1930s: the regulation of production so as to give to each operator in a field the opportunity to recover the oil originally in place under his land.[27] Scott, who was then associate vice-chairman of the Petroleum Division of the AIMME, was already active in gathering data on well-spacing for presentation at a symposium on this subject.

The Humble Production Research Department thus in those early years was already performing two functions. It was assisting the Humble engineers and field men to devise ways of producing a field more efficiently. And it was helping to develop the basic knowledge of the mechanics of oil reservoirs that was essential to efficient production and was a necessary foundation for laws for the equitable regulation of production.

STRENGTHENING DRILLING AND PRODUCING OPERATIONS

Humble's drilling and producing operations during those years were concerned with both increased recovery and lower costs. Future oil supply was contingent not only upon finding more oil but also upon controlling production so as to keep crude oil reserves in their natural storehouses until needed and to recover ultimately a larger percentage of the oil in a pool. Furthermore, in order to meet the current low prices resulting from increasing domestic and foreign competition, costs had to be reduced. These objectives could not be realized immediately or even within a few years. Here we are especially concerned with changes of long-run significance that were inaugurated in 1927–1930. The principal changes of this character were the geographical shift of producing operations, the unification of the production organization, and the introduction of the new technology into field operations.

A basic and recurrent decision in the oil business is in answer to the question: "Where shall we operate?" No company possesses unlimited resources; capital must be applied where it is believed the largest returns will result. When capital has once been invested in a region, withdrawal is difficult. In the years from 1927 through 1930 Humble's producing operations shifted in a southwesterly direction as new regions were developed and old ones abandoned.

The new regions that showed the most promise by 1927 were Southwest and West Texas, in neither of which Humble had previously manifested much strength. During several discouraging years its geologists had failed to locate any very good prospects in Southwest Texas, and the company had developed only small production there. In West Texas it had first leased in Howard and Coke counties, after which discoveries by other operators had encouraged the purchase of leases in the Yates and Hendricks fields in Pecos and Winkler counties. Humble had showed a greater interest in purchasing crude than in production in Southwest and West Texas, and in 1926 it had built pipelines to both regions.

As Humble geologists began to be successful in Southwest Texas in those later years, the company entered into drilling and producing operations there on a large scale. When the Salt Flat field was discovered in October, 1928, David B. Harris, superintendent of the Arkansas and Northern Louisiana division, was transferred to the new field. By the next spring Humble had fourteen rigs at Salt Flat drilling furiously to bring the company's production up to the proportion justified by its ownership of half the producing acreage. Humble's production in the region rose from 200,000 barrels in 1928 to 5,000,000 in 1929; it was so successful that, late in 1928, operations there were separated from the Gulf Coast division and organized as the Southwest Texas division with headquarters at San Antonio.

Humble for several years had watched and in a small way participated in developments in West Texas, but not until 1927 did it undertake a strong drive to develop production there. Its geologists had failed to find any important oil prospects, but when it became obvious that large fields were developing Humble moved in. Early in 1927 the West Texas division was organized, with headquarters at San Angelo, and David Frame was transferred from the Panhandle to take charge of development. William E. Hubbard, an engineer, succeeded Frame as head of Panhandle operations. The company's production in West Texas increased from 200,000 barrels in 1926 to 2,000,000 the next year and 7,000,000 in 1928, principally from the Hendricks field. Humble's Production Department participated in two important proration developments in 1927 and 1928, which will be discussed in another connection. The operations of the West Texas division extended across the state boundary into New Mexico's Hobbs field, where oil was discovered in 1928. Early in 1930 Humble brought in a well that proved to be the field's first large producer, and in that year Hobbs contributed a million barrels to the West Texas division's production.[28]

Expansion into Southwest and West Texas and New Mexico was followed by the abandonment of operations in Oklahoma, Arkansas, and northern Louisiana. Oklahoma operations had at one time been fairly profitable; the others, however, had never been. By 1927 the production of each was comparatively small and also static or declining. Technologically, the Oklahoma operations were not progressive. Furthermore, those properties were not an integral part of Humble's production, refining, and transportation system; oil from their wells went neither to Humble pipelines nor to Humble refineries. Since the capital and energy that Humble was expending in those regions could obviously be more profitably employed elsewhere, the properties were sold in 1929—those in Oklahoma to The Carter Oil Company and the others to Standard Oil Company of Louisiana, both affiliates of Standard Oil Company (New Jersey).

Humble then also abandoned its interest in developing oil production in Mexico, the only foreign country in which it has ever undertaken operations. It had entered northern Mexico in 1919 through a subsidiary, Compañía Petrolera Tamaulipas, S. A., organized to acquire lands for development; but not until after the Calles-Morrow agreements had led to a clarification of Mexico's regulation of the oil industry did the company test its holdings. However, after a deep well had been drilled in 1929 without a show of oil, Compañía Tamaulipas became inactive. Although there was no recovery of capital in this instance, there were obviously more promising opportunities in other areas for developing production.

The sale of properties released $5,000,000 for use elsewhere, and relatively small additional fixed investments in producing properties in the new divisions brought large increases in volume. By the end of the decade two of the company's three most productive divisions were the Southwest and the West Texas. The third was the Gulf Coast division, which to its faithful old fields added new ones, notably Sugarland and Raccoon Bend. East Texas and North Texas, however, never during those years attained their 1926 production. This regional shift in Humble's producing operations had the additional advantage of a closer relationship of the company's production with its pipeline system, which not only supplied transportation to the company's refineries and Gulf Coast shipping points but also increased Humble's profits.

In 1929, also, a more rational organization was established for the management of drilling and production. Suman's position as director in charge of petroleum engineering had given him authority in that line in all Humble's producing operations. Scott in 1928 had similarly taken over the management of petroleum engineering for the whole department. In the next year three founder-directors, who had occupied semi-independent positions, retired as operating managers. One had been manager of the Oklahoma operations, and the other two had had separate responsibilities in the Gulf Coast division. The appointment of

David B. Harris to the superintendency of that division in 1929 in effect unified its management. Henceforth, each of Humble's producing divisions was under one manager, and those managers were not founders or large owners but men who had risen as company employees. This process of unification was completed on October 1, 1930, when David Frame became general superintendent of production.

While shifts in areas and changes in management were occurring, a transition that was of major significance to all areas and on all levels of Humble's drilling and producing was taking place: the introduction of the new technologist and technology into operations. From the early days of the Industrial Revolution such a transition from old to new ways had been resisted because of its threat of human obsolescence. Humble, like the oil industry generally, experienced more or less resistance.

For several years there was considerable opposition within Humble's producing operations to new men and methods. Many old-timers had difficulty in accepting the new technology. The opposition of a few division superintendents was particularly serious. They were practical men of much experience, who had achieved excellent results in such prolific fields as West Columbia and Powell when oil was in heavy demand and prices were still relatively good. In the petroleum engineers, who endeavored to introduce methods more suitable to a period of intense competition and low prices, these men could at first see only rivals who menaced their authority and even their jobs. Many men in drilling and producing crews similarly saw their security threatened by new skills. Illustrative of a feeling of resentment was the name given to weight indicators installed on drilling rigs to record the pressure of the bit; they were called "stool-pigeons" because they "tattled" if the crew shut the rig down for coffee or an early morning nap.

The managers, then, were confronted by human as well as technological problems. To solve the latter it was necessary first to solve the former, particularly to develop integrated effort between the staff men and the line organization on all levels. This development was so successful that staff-line co-operation became a distinctive feature of Humble's field operations.

The top-level production managers deserve much credit for the development of such close integration of staff and line. Suman from the very first made it clear to operating men that the engineers were there to help them, not to take over their jobs. "It must be distinctly understood," he wrote to division superintendents in regard to the new engineering work in 1927, "that these operations are all under the division superintendents in their respective divisions . . . , there being no desire to interfere with our present organization." Scott, as manager of the Petroleum Engineering Department, assisted the young engineers in their effort to learn how they could best work with the old-time drillers. David Frame, general superintendent of production from 1930, had the major responsibility for the acceptance by the field men of the engineers and research men. Each one of these managers was unusually effective in his relations with the men; each one had their confidence, respect, and loyalty. Most important of all was the example of close co-operation by Scott and Frame as managers of production and petroleum engineering.

Co-operation was something that could not be imposed from above; it had to be learned by the lower ranks of both technologists and practical men, by staff members and linemen. The introduction of many newly graduated engineers after the establishment of the Petroleum Engineering Department in 1928 aroused much opposition among the field workers. Suman and Scott soon saw that the young engineers needed, first of all, to acquire some understanding of work and workers in the field. The next annual crop of new engineers was, therefore, put to work for a year as roughnecks or roustabouts—thus establishing a precedent that Humble long continued to follow. The old field men frequently subjected those "book-educated smart alecks" to more than a normal amount of hazing. If a young engineer demonstrated, however, that in spite of his diploma he was not afraid of hard work, the old-timers would usually soon cease making things difficult for him and help him instead. The engineer was then on the way to acceptance at least as a fellow worker, the first and indispensable step toward success in his eventual role as petroleum engineer. After a year or so of nontechnical work in the field, the young engineer was given a technical assignment as an engineer.

The improvements in operations resulting from the work of the engineers and research men were, so far as the field men were concerned, the ultimate test of the value of the technologist and his new techniques. Any driller who had faced the danger of blowouts could appreciate the value of the new blowout preventers and of more effective drilling mud. To burn automatically controlled gas instead of expensive fuel oil under the boilers that supplied power was an obvious economy and convenience. Obvious also were the savings from producing a field under its own reservoir energy instead of by using pumps, which were costly to purchase and install and to operate.

Gradually, mutual appreciation of engineers and operating men developed. The old field men came to see that the technical men were there to help them, and the engineers and scientists learned to respect the practical skill of the field workers. Eventually, the latter not only began to bring their problems to the former but also to contribute ideas and suggestions from their experience in the field. The drillers and production men also began to take personal pride in what was being accomplished—and to send their sons to engineering schools.

This development took time, and some of the old linemen and of the new engineers were unable to adjust to the new integration of effort. Such engineers apparently did not stay long in the Humble organization. The problem was more difficult to solve when old and loyal operating men failed to co-operate. Those who could not be convinced of the utility of petroleum engineering and research eventually gave place—by retirement or by separation from the company—to men able and willing to accept the new ideas and methods.

While this process of integration was going on, the engineers and researchers were bringing great changes in Humble's drilling and production methods. Those changes were in two broad areas, the improvement and standardization of equipment and the more effective use of nature's own energy in bringing oil to the surface.

The standardization and improvement of equipment, which Suman had started on a large scale in 1927, went forward rapidly under Scott. In the next three years a significant beginning was made in standardizing and improving equipment quality and design. Moreover, steel derricks were substituted for wooden ones, and the use of gas instead of oil as fuel to furnish power for drilling equipment was begun. These changes not only reduced costs; accidents were also reduced by better design of machinery and equipment from a safety viewpoint and by the installation of protective devices.

The more revolutionary developments in those years, however, came from a better understanding of the function of gas in oil recovery and from the development of ways of effectively applying that understanding to production. Producing the oil through tubing—which, according to Suman, Humble first used at Boggy Creek in 1927—gave better control of the rate of production. Gas-oil ratios and bottom-hole pressures provided the basis for determining, well by well, the rate of production most effective in preserving the natural gas energy in a reservoir.

Something was also accomplished in increasing recovery in older fields. Humble, it has been observed, first experimented with repressuring in 1926, and it continued to carry on "rejuvenation" operations—to use the current term—in the later years. Because of incomplete knowledge of reservoirs and their behavior, however, these experiments were not always successful. Nevertheless, a report on Humble's rejuvenation operations in fields in Oklahoma, Panhandle, North Texas, and near Corsicana stated that in 1929 those operations had brought a substantial increase in the production of oil and casinghead gasoline and in the profits therefrom.

The most significant innovation, however, was the establishment of unit operations in several fields. "There existed with us always," said Farish late in 1929, "a dream or desire to control or own an entire structure, and the attempt to fulfill this desire or dream has really been the mark at which we have been shooting the past few years." This dream was first realized by Humble at Boggy Creek and Raccoon Bend in 1927 and first successfully fulfilled in the important Sugarland field in 1928. It was also realized, for experimental purposes, at Olney in 1930.

Those fields were operated in such ways as to utilize their reservoir energy as efficiently as was possible at the time. Wells were spaced with a view to both economy in drilling and efficient production. At first the emphasis was on maintaining gas pressure in the reservoir by controlling the gas-oil ratio. In 1930, as already observed, a pressure maintenance plant was installed at Sugarland, and in the same year production was resumed at Olney, which had been repressured experimentally by the research group. Also, the decision was made to build at Raccoon Bend a plant for returning gas produced with the oil to the producing formation.

Although some mistakes were made, the total result was notably successful. The pressure maintenance project at Raccoon Bend, decided upon in 1930 but not undertaken until 1931, was not successful; the formation there, as was later learned, was too broken up to make repressuring effective. The nature of the propulsive forces in pools was then incompletely understood, particularly the importance of the water drive. Yet those early experiments with the development of a pool as a unit obviously marked a tremendous improvement over the old competitive drilling and producing. Fields that under the old system would have been "put on the pump" in a few months continued to flow under their own power. Pressure maintenance proved relatively inexpensive. Wider spacing brought economy in drilling. Finally, the oil producer could exercise some control over the rate and volume of his production and over his reserves.

A report made in 1929 by a member of the staff of the Texas Railroad Commission contains an interesting statement about one of Humble's unitized fields. Boggy Creek, it states, was being operated better than any other pool in Texas, not excepting those pools where proration was in effect. The report continues: [29]

> The wells are drilled carefully, brought in properly, produced sensibly, and the ultimate recovery should be much greater than . . . under ordinary operating conditions. . . . Some of the wells are flowing with as high as one thousand pounds back pressure . . . practically no waste oil on the ground and nowhere on the Neches River can you find a rainbow of oil.

Sugarland may be pointed to as a symbol of the revolution that was beginning to take place in Humble's producing operations late in the 1920s. Sugarland is Humble's oldest pressure maintenance field, and in retrospect it can be seen to have been both a valuable laboratory and a commercially profitable field. The Humble Board of Directors made the then radical decision not to have pumps installed at Sugarland; through a misunderstanding pumping foundations were installed, but they were never used. The research men's early understanding of the forces exerting pressure in the reservoir was not complete; late in the 1930s it was discovered that the field had a water drive as well as a gas-cap drive. But, when demand increased after gas injection was discontinued during a period of low allowables, it was correctly decided that the water drive was too weak to produce the field efficiently at the higher rates and injection was resumed. So successful has been the combination of drives made possible by reinjecting the gas that during World War II Sugarland was able to produce for a short period a peak of 10,000 barrels a day. Today its maximum efficient rate has declined with its state of depletion to 5,000 barrels; however, with proration the field is producing considerably less. The establishment of pressure maintenance by gas injection and the orderly development of Sugarland nearly three decades ago have thus been effective in increasing recovery from this field. Although it is impossible to calculate the exact financial results, the increased percentage recovery and the savings on drilling, producing, and storage have been significant, while the cost of pressure maintenance has been relatively low.

Humble's executives were soon convinced that unit development and operation of fields was of major importance in solving the industry's problems. Unitization not only reduced underground waste and maintained reserves in the ground until they were needed; it also reduced the cost of production. Farish said late in 1929: "The economic trend is toward lower production costs, and these in turn impel us toward unit operations. . . . We must have low-cost production if we are to survive as producers." He pointed to the fact that three large companies in Venezuela had an average production cost of 25 cents a barrel.[30]

The extent to which one company alone, under the laws of property in oil and gas in the United States, could carry on unit operations was, however, decidedly limited. In order to put unitization into effect, co-operative production was necessary. To such co-operation Humble gave strong support, both through trying to bring it about in the oil fields and through working for legislation that would make it unquestionably legal. The company's own success in the fields where it controlled the total production was strong evidence of what might be accomplished by unitized development and production.

One more Humble producing policy and practice in those years was of significance: the curtailment of production in accordance with the condition of the local or general market. Humble abandoned its earlier practice of producing its wells to their full potential, and, wherever possible, exercised a considerable amount of self-restraint. In keeping with a broad movement developing in the American oil industry at the end of the 1920s, it voluntarily reduced production, sometimes because of a glut in certain fields and sometimes because of general overproduction.

Such curtailment was most practicable where Humble controlled a whole field. The company held production at Sugarland and Raccoon Bend substantially below potential. At Moss Bluff late in 1929 it gave royalty owners nearly half a million dollars in advance payments for the privilege of delaying development work. In competitive fields, such as Salt Flat, Humble asserted in 1929 that it was running rigs only to protect leases, especially from producing or proved drilling offsets. For several weeks in the spring of 1930 it shut down all its operations, including production, on Sundays in response to a suggestion of the Federal Oil Conservation Board that refinery operations be stopped one day a week. In March, 1930, the company was reported to have shut in from 150,000 to 200,000 barrels daily of its own production.[31]

The volume of Humble's production in those later years is, therefore, not a true measure of the success of the company's operations. In 1927 the volume of crude produced was even slightly lower than in the low year, 1926, and in 1928 it was not much higher—about the same as in 1924 and less than in 1923 and 1925. Even with greatly increased production in West and Southwest Texas in 1929 and 1930, Humble's production just barely held its own, percentage-wise, in the total production of the area in which it operated.

If profits were the only measure of the Production Department's operations in 1927–1930, the record would be one of failure. Heavy net losses were incurred in 1927 and 1928; a small net profit was earned in 1929, and a very moderate one in 1930. For the four years there was a total net loss—a loss half as large as the total net profits for the four preceding years. An important factor in this situation was, of course, price—the average price Humble received per barrel of crude oil fell from $1.836 in 1926 to $0.938 in 1928, rose to $1.145 in 1929, and fell to $1.059 in 1930.

Although the Production Department in 1927–1930 was conspicuously unprofitable and did not until the end of 1930 hold a larger percentage of the estimated industry reserves in its region than it had held in the low year of 1926, Humble's executives were nevertheless convinced that those years had been years of progress. The full results of their new science and engineering and of the strengthening of management could obviously be realized only over a longer time. Those results, however, depended not on Humble alone, but on the extent to which new concepts of efficient and controlled production could be generally realized through joint action of producers and wise regulation by government. Side by side with the improvement of their own company's operations, therefore, Humble's executives participated in the development of such co-operation and regulation.

Chapter 13

A CO-OPERATIVE APPROACH TO PRODUCTION PROBLEMS, 1927–1930

By the beginning of 1927 several Humble executives were already urging certain steps toward achieving some form of industry-wide action to reduce waste of oil and gas and to make production and prices less erratic. During the next few years they were to propose and promote various fundamental measures for joint action within the industry and for regulation by the states. In its own state Humble in those years played a leading role in what came to be called the conservation movement.

The history of that movement may be divided into three periods. In the first, about the years 1923 through 1926, a few oil industry executives and government specialists challenged the petroleum industry to face the problems of underground and aboveground waste of a limited natural resource. It was during this early phase that Farish and Pratt of Humble awoke to the necessity of change in their company's and the industry's attitude and operations, particularly in regard to the need for greater regulation by state government. (See Chapter 11.) In the third period, about 1931–1935, effective regulation by a few states was established. The middle period, about 1927–1930, is the one with which we are now concerned.[1]

This period, as Farish phrased it, was a time of growth of knowledge. A mounting crisis of overproduction and waste in the oil industry combined with the pioneering leadership of a few companies and men, in industry and federal and state governments, to produce increasing support for conservation efforts. Of fundamental importance was the reservoir research of the United States Bureau of Mines and a few companies, which also experimented with controlled production in specific fields. Important also was the "organized study"—to quote an authority on the history of the conservation movement[2]—conducted by such institutions as the Federal Oil Conservation Board, the United States Bureau of Mines, the American Institute of Mining and Metallurgical Engineers, the American Petroleum Institute, and the American Bar Association. Through periodic meetings, committees, and publications, these and other institutions considered industry problems and ways of solving them.

In all aspects of this movement Humble executives, engineers, and lawyers participated with energy and conviction. They took part in meetings and committees of industrial and professional organizations to study industry problems and make recommendations for solutions. Most important, Farish and several of his associates were active in a series of campaigns in Texas for the control of production and prevention of waste through gas conservation, unit operation, wide spacing of wells, ratable withdrawals from reservoirs, and proration according to market demand.

Within Humble this was a team operation. Suman, Scott, and Wilde and their associates provided technical information on the reduction of waste and on better operating methods. Hines H. Baker was chiefly responsible for searching out legal principles that would warrant joint action by companies and regulation by states. Farish, as the company's chief and most widely known executive, was the company's spokesman. Pratt and Suman, also, were active in national organizations. Suman was particularly influential in Texas Railroad Commission hearings and in encouraging co-operation on the part of producers in the oil fields.

In view of the traditional attitude of oilmen toward government regulation, the position the company took in regard to legislation and regulation in the interest of conservation was little short of revolutionary. This change can be explained only as the response of a farseeing and responsible management to conditions that made old ways of thinking unrealistic and old operational methods obsolete.

IN QUEST OF OLD LEGAL PRINCIPLES TO MEET NEW NEEDS

A primary problem in bringing about co-operation within industry and between industry and government, state or federal, for the improvement and regulation of production was to devise ways and means acceptable under American law.[3] The conservation movement cannot be understood without some comprehension of the problems involved in adapting established legal principles to such radically new objectives. As a preliminary to a consideration of Humble's early struggle for conservation, therefore, brief attention must be given to the thinking of company executives on the legal problems involved in this process. First of all, they had to arrive at a clear understanding of existing law and precedent.

It is a basic principle of common law in the United States that the landowner, as owner of minerals in the subsoil, owns the oil and gas in place under his land and is entitled to a reasonable opportunity to recover those resources. In the absence of regulation he may drill as many wells as he pleases on his land, wherever he wishes to locate them, and produce them to capacity. When a landowner or his lessee drills a well on a particular tract of land, the law recognizes another basic principle—that all the oil and gas he obtains from the well on his land becomes his property. This rule of capture was first applied to oil production in the United States by the Supreme Court of Pennsylvania in 1889. It is a rule of convenience arising out of the difficulty of determining the underground source of the oil produced at the surface.

This difficulty derives from the fact that oil and gas are fugacious in nature. They migrate from areas of high to areas of low pressure. When a well is completed and begins producing, a low-pressure area is established at the bottom of the well, and oil migrates from the surrounding area to the bottom of the well and through the well bore to the surface. Thus, if one owner drills on his land and his neighbors fail to do so, all of the oil within that area capable of being drained by the well will in time migrate to and be produced through that well. Neighboring owners, therefore, in order to prevent their oil from being drained away, must drill offset wells on their own land. Under unrestrained competitive conditions, once oil is found in a well all offsetting owners must drill as quickly as possible and produce their oil with the utmost speed in order to prevent drainage by wells on adjoining lands. This, in the past, led to mad drilling races, wide-open production, often far in excess of market requirements, and rapid dissipation of reservoir energy. Such practices inevitably resulted in underground waste—that is, leaving in the reservoir vast quantities of oil unrecoverable by ordinary and economically feasible methods. Moreover, the surface storage of large amounts of oil, particularly in earthen pits but also in steel storage, resulted in the waste of oil.

Oilmen had early come to realize that, although such competitive practices brought flush production and market chaos and also speedily reduced the energy of a pool so that wells had to be pumped, there was little they could do about it. The only early legal restraint on a producer was another common-law principle, the obligation not to commit surface nuisances. Agreements of producers to restrict production would have contravened still another legal principle, first of the common law and later recognized by federal and state statutes, that combinations in restraint of trade were illegal. Moreover, the usual form of redress, suit for damages, was not open to the oil producers, because there was no way of determining how much oil, if any, was drained from under a given tract through a well on a neighbor's land and thus no way of obtaining evidence of damage that would stand up in a court of law. So long as an oil pool was *terra incognita*, there was little possibility of recourse by such legal process in private litigation.

Some statutory limitations were early placed upon the production of oil and gas for the purpose of conserving the resource in the public interest. Late in the nineteenth century laws prohibiting certain obviously wasteful practices were enacted by several oil states. Such laws were challenged by operators as unconstitutional, particularly as depriving them of property without due process of law under the Fourteenth Amendment. A landmark in the legal history of oil and gas was one such case, which originated under an Indiana statute to prevent waste and was appealed to the United States Supreme Court as *State* v. *Ohio Oil Company*. The court in 1900 upheld the statute's constitutionality on the ground that the state had the authority to use its police power for the protection of the public interest and the rights of individual owners in a common oil or gas pool. Thus the highest court sanctioned the use of a state's police power both to prevent waste and to protect correlative rights.

The state of Texas in its oil and gas law followed the ordinary precedents. It adopted the prevailing rules of property. However, it applied to the oil industry antitrust laws that were more severe than those in most states. Through conservation legislation under the state's police power, supported by an amendment to its constitution in 1917 and administered by its Railroad Commission, as has already been noted, there developed a considerable regulation of oil production to prevent waste.

The application of the police power in Texas and elsewhere was limited, first, by the narrowness of the prevailing concept of waste and, secondly, by the inability to define correlative rights in an oil pool because of a lack of the necessary knowledge of reservoir conditions. Until that concept and that knowledge were enlarged, little further regulation of production would be possible.

Such, in general, was the law applying to oil production when the conservation movement first got under way. A primary question was:

How could laws to allow co-operation within the industry and to provide extensive state regulation be fitted into this legal framework?

This problem was analyzed by James A. Veasey of The Carter Oil Company in 1927 in an address before the American Bar Association, which is a landmark in the development of the study of conservation law.[4] The speaker explored such fundamental matters as the source of the authority to regulate oil production and the powers under which that authority might be exercised. If conservation could not be effected by action of the industry, he held, compulsory legislation should be enacted, if it could be "upheld under any theory of constitutional law." Measures under the police powers, he suggested, might be upheld by the courts. Veasey called upon the members of the bar to give careful and studious consideration to the problem.

The study of oil law spread rapidly. A Committee on Conservation of Mineral Resources was set up in 1927 by the Section of Mineral Law of the American Bar Association. In the same year the American Petroleum Institute appointed a Committee of Five to study legal questions. Three prominent authorities on oil law were appointed by the American Bar Association to the Committee of Nine, which was established under the Federal Oil Conservation Board to represent the public, the bar, and the oil industry in the study of the industry's problems. In the various professional and oil-industry associations and within oil companies the study of legal methods of solving industry problems went forward.

Within the existing legal framework and with close attention to current developments in the study of the law of oil and gas, Humble's Legal Department worked to guide the company's conservation efforts along correct legal routes. Edgar E. Townes, who had skillfully steered Humble through the shoals of antitrust law and along the early course set by the Texas Railroad Commission, was the senior member of the company's team of lawyers. Hines H. Baker, beginning with proration at Yates in 1927, was assigned special responsibility for studying and giving advice on the legal aspects of conservation. Baker, who had joined Humble in 1919, had served his apprenticeship in title work but had soon been called upon to do consultation work with various operating departments and to write legal opinions on corporate and other problems. These assignments had given him broad familiarity with the operations of both Humble and the industry in the region of the company's principal activity.

Before the Legal Department began to give special attention to conservation, Humble's general position had been expressed by President Farish, who was himself a law graduate and a former member of the Mississippi bar. In his presidential address to the American Petroleum

Institute in December, 1926, referring to the invitation of the Federal Oil Conservation Board to the oil industry to co-operate in the study of oil-production problems, he commented thus on the recommendations which the Institute might make:[5]

> Any action to be recommended must rest upon sound premises, and must give proper protection to the industry and to the public. . . .There is no one, I believe, who would seek either from Congress or from the states any form of legislation which would result in restraint of trade. . . , meaning specifically as to oil, the control of production for the purpose of controlling price. Such legislation would be contrary to the spirit of our institutions. Competition is necessary, not merely as a protection to the consumer, but also to the development of the industry. Co-operation must stop somewhere short of this properly forbidden territory.

Here Farish pointed to an issue that was to be closely interwoven with the oil conservation movement, the effect of regulation on prices. From the very first, Humble executives saw in the regulation of production a means of checking erratic production of individual fields and also general overproduction, but they consistently based their efforts in support of conservation on what they believed to be sound legal principles. (Their position on the relationship of proration and prices is considered in Chapter 18.)

Although Hines H. Baker carried the chief responsibility within the company for the study of conservation law, he had the help of other members of the Legal Department. This help consisted mainly of discussion, which took the form of searching for new interpretations of old legal principles that would make them applicable to the current problems of the oil industry. Townes provided the challenge of old points of view until he himself was converted to the new. Rex G. Baker, whose special responsibility was for title and contract work, contributed by active participation in discussion and in the study of precedent.[6]

Townes, the head of Humble's legal staff, in 1927 followed traditional lines of thought sanctioned by law and usage in Texas. Gas conservation, then believed by many to be the key to the solution of industry problems, should, he held, be provided for by state legislation embodying a general prohibition to be administered under the state's police power by a commission. Townes did not share many of his contemporaries' fear of administrative commissions. His experience with the Texas Railroad Commission had, on the whole, been satisfactory; and he believed that, as knowledge of and public interest in conservation developed, commissions would also grow in knowledge and responsibility.

The pooling of different interests in a field for operations under one management, then currently advocated, involved considerations of antitrust law, which was unusually severe in Texas. Townes advised that the only way to unitize a proved field under Texas antitrust law was for the state by legislation to authorize the Railroad Commission to administer producers' agreements for voluntary unitization. But he could see no "legal basis for the idea that the government can compel adjoining owners to pool their properties for oil and gas purposes." He did not, indeed, see how the state's police power could be used for such purposes. Townes held that, without permissive legislation for voluntary unitization by all producers in a field, unitization could be achieved in only one way, by merging all interests in a potential oil field before oil was discovered. If oil was found, unit development and operation could then be carried on.[7] The Legal Department, apparently at the suggestion of Farish and Pratt, drew up a form for such a pooling agreement for purposes of exploration, which provided for development and operation if oil was discovered.

Humble's design for conservation law did not appear at once full-blown; it was to develop from several years of experience, observation, study, and discussion. The company's legal staff followed closely the work of others in oil law, including such attorneys in private practice as Robert E. Hardwicke and John E. Kilgore and such company counsels as Lewis Foster of Sun Oil, W. O. Crane of The Texas Company, W. P. Z. German of Skelly, and James A. Veasey of Carter Oil. Humble's lawyers also worked closely with operators; Hines H. Baker, in particular, was cognizant of the problems resulting from overproduction and of the growth in the understanding of oil reservoirs and their behavior. The key to a legal solution of industry problems, he believed, lay in the prevention of waste. But what was waste? The answer was being supplied, on the one hand, by the technologists and, on the other, by the increasing overproduction resulting in wasteful and uneconomic storage and use. Baker's close relations with scientists, engineers, and operating men in the Production Department—particularly with W. W. Scott—probably accounted in large measure for his increasing surefootedness in the maze of petroleum law. He acquired an understanding of reservoirs and their behavior that gave him a new comprehension of underground waste and a sense of its vast significance to the law of oil and gas. Drawing both from the technologists and from his own and others' study of the law, he led Humble executives to conclusions that as early as 1929 embodied the essential legal ideas which they were to follow in their work for conservation legislation.

A statement written by Baker in June, 1929, entitled "Some Underlying Principles Controlling the Solution of the Problem of Oil and Gas Conservation," indicates his own and his company's position as it had developed to that time.[8] It was prepared as a summary for company use with special reference to a draft of an interstate compact that Northcutt Ely, Assistant Secretary of the Interior and head of a committee of the Federal Oil Conservation Board, had proposed for consideration at a conference of governors, called by the Secretary of the Interior, which was to meet at Colorado Springs in June, 1929. The statement's main points will, therefore, be mentioned, omitting legal details and engineering technicalities.

The primary objective of the conservation movement, according to Baker, was the prevention of waste:

> . . . first, to lessen or prevent actual physical waste of these products [oil and gas] in the methods by which they are produced and brought to market, involving the prevention of such waste both underground and upon the surface . . . , and, second, to maintain the supply of these limited and irreplaceable resources for present and future needs by the maintenance of adequate underground reserves and the production of the products in response to actual market demand only. . . .

"The problem of oil and gas conservation," the statement continues, "arises largely out of the nature of these products and the rules of property that have evolved controlling their ownership and production." From this it comes that "oil and gas are not produced in response to market demand" but rather, where divergent ownership obtains, from "a mad rush among operators to secure an advantage in production." This in turn results in "loss in the quantity of oil and gas recovered in the aggregate from the particular field," and it "is the primary cause of the cycles of over-production and under-supply that run their course in the industry."

"The nature of oil and gas and the elemental principles controlling their production can not be changed"—so the exposition continues. Nor can legal principles be altered: "It is generally believed that the rules of property now obtaining are the most reasonable rules that may be evolved controlling production and ownership of these products." Moreover, these rules "have given rise to vested rights that under our constitution cannot be taken away."

The exposition then considered how, in view of the existing laws of nature and of property, competitive production within individual pools could be carried on without waste. The answer was to operate the pool as the natural unit that it is. This objective could be accomplished by voluntary co-operation among producers, but such co-operation would involve serious difficulties, including lack of agreement as to the relative value of individual properties and particular production practices and also fear of antitrust laws. In order to achieve co-operation among producers in a pool, it would be necessary to remove the restraints of antitrust laws and to establish "some measure of coercion to compel the respect for the rights of other operators and the public on the part of hard-headed or selfish individuals or units, and to compel the adoption of methods and practices for the prevention of waste."

This suggestion of coercion raised a cardinal point, which Humble had from 1927 steadfastly answered in one way. Whatever control is established, continues Baker's statement, "must be by the exercise of the police power," a power that resides in the states and not in the federal government.

More was required, however, than the action of a single state or of producers in the individual pool. The "co-ordinated efforts of the producers throughout the industry and of the various State agencies exercising the police powers of the States" are required to deal with "general over-production with its attendant evils" that "results from over-production in several pools." Such co-ordination could be accomplished through an interstate compact, a form of interstate co-operation authorized by the Constitution of the United States and "not repugnant to" the constitution of the states.

A compact between the principal oil-producing states could perform several functions, the exposition continued. It could establish an agency to serve as a fact-finding body to determine the nature and extent of overproduction—"that is, production resulting in actual physical waste and beyond current market demands." This agency could "allocate as between the states the proper amount of oil to be produced therein necessary to meet the current market demands." It might also be "given power and authority in the public interest to approve contracts between producers of the various states involved to carry out the allocations so made by such body."

An interstate compact was envisaged as a channel through which to deal with the restraint that antitrust laws placed on co-operative action by oil producers. Under an interstate compact, the states "might agree to remove the restraints of their anti-trust laws so far as may be necessary to enable agreements . . . for unit development and operation" and for "carrying out the allocations made by the fact-finding body. . . ." Similarly, "Congress by its approval might remove the restraints of the Federal anti-trust laws. . . ." Baker defended the removal of such restraints on two grounds: first, an agreement for the co-operative development and operation of a single pool "makes the pool in fact (as it is in nature already) the unit of production and competition and places the oil producing industry on the same footing as are other mining and manufacturing businesses." Secondly, the removal of the restraints applying "to larger areas during periods of over-production . . . results in the conservation of a product of a very limited and irreplaceable character in which the public has a vital and direct interest."

While this summary statement envisaged broad and important functions to be performed under an interstate compact, it held that no agency established by such a compact could have any enforcement powers. It was firm in the position that such an agency could not employ the police power, since that power resides in the states. Moreover, it maintained that to delegate the police power to a joint board containing representatives of several states was neither practicable nor possible under the existing constitution of Texas.

The discussion concluded with an optimistic statement of the belief that, if an interstate compact providing for "the fact finding board and for the removal of the anti-trust restraints" could be "supplemented within the several States by adequate conservation measures vesting in a State agency the authority to prevent waste, . . . proper legislation and proper administrative machinery" would be secured "to enable the industry by co-operative effort within itself and with the conservation agencies to work out an actual, practical operating solution of the oil and gas conservation problem."

Humble's blueprint for a legal solution of the problems of the oil industry was thus complete by the end of the 1920s. Many of its details were similar to recommendations made by various committees and other agencies engaged in the study of oil and gas law. Three features were particularly significant: insistence that only the states through their police power had authority to regulate production; emphasis on holding production to current market demand as a conservation measure; and the acceptance of the idea of an interstate compact for the establishment of an agency to allocate among the states the respective proportion each might produce of the current market's total requirements.

In three years Humble had progressed far in its position on conservation: from urging gas conservation under the Texas Railroad Commission to advocating nationwide restriction of production to current market demand through the police power of states. The company's early efforts to apply these principles in order to advance control of production by means of producers' co-operation and government regulation is the theme of the remainder of this chapter.

GAS CONSERVATION AND UNIT OPERATIONS

The progressive leaders in Humble, as in the industry generally, were converted to gas conservation earlier than to any other conservation principle. The company's initial stand on gas conservation was along traditional lines: it advocated state legislation for conserving gas, under the police power, to be administered by a commission. As early as June, 1926, Farish proposed to the Oil and Gas Supervisor of the Texas Railroad Commission that all the gas produced in the Panhandle "should be returned to the sand . . . whether . . . processed for gasoline or not."[9] By the end of 1926 Farish and Pratt were discussing with their company's lawyers and with members of the Texas Railroad Commission the possibilities of a law that would enable that regulatory body to prevent waste of gas from oil wells, just as it already was empowered to prevent the waste of gas from gas wells.

Humble's interest in gas conservation was based on a broad concept of waste. Pratt wrote a broad definition of the waste of gas:[10] To produce more gas than was necessary for efficient production of oil was wasteful; to permit the gas thus produced to be blown into the air was also wasteful, "provided that there is any possible chance of utilizing it commercially either as a fuel in the ordinary sense, or for the restoration of pressure in oil sands, or for the manufacture of carbon black." Farish regarded the waste of gas as generally uneconomic as well as wasteful of the resource itself. He wrote: "Certainly some day the oil industry is going to have to answer for the uneconomic and wasteful way in which gas and oil are being used . . . 'wasteful' . . . in the actual waste of gas . . . and economic waste as applied to production. . . . If this gas was conserved and put back into the sand, or pressure maintained in the well and less gas used, . . . more oil could be lifted at less cost. . . ."[11] Farish understood from the first that conservation measures, in order to succeed, would have to be sound from the viewpoints of economics, science, and public policy.

Humble and Farish were not alone in the industry in urging gas conservation. E. W. Marland, who shared with Henry L. Doherty the honor of having proposed conservation in the early 1920s, sponsored a gas conservation bill before the Oklahoma legislature in 1927. J. Edgar Pew of the Sun Oil Company displayed all the zeal of a recent convert. Marland, Pew, and Farish worked closely together in providing leadership for the movement, nationally and in their own operating regions—Marland being at the forefront in the Mid-Continent as Farish was in Texas and Pew in both regions.

Their efforts encountered strong opposition within the industry. President Teagle of Standard Oil Company (New Jersey), although sympathetic with Farish's objectives, was fearful that the Texan was trying to go too far too fast. He reminded Farish of their joint statement in 1925 in favor of regulation by the industry itself, urged that a plan be worked out "by practical men," and warned of the current opposition to government regulation among leaders of the industry.[12] F. C. Proctor, special counsel of the Gulf companies, who was then known as the dean of oil lawyers in Texas and who was a member of the API Committee of Five to study oil law, was more emphatic. He described gas conservation laws as a "nostrum worthy of a blather skite politician, but not of the leaders of a great industry."[13] The president of the API was strongly opposed to legislation.[14] Another API officer proposed as a substitute that landowners should enter suit for injunction and damages against neighbors who took more than their share of the gas in a common pool.

Charles Evans Hughes, distinguished legal counsel of the API, saw three possible routes that conservation efforts could take: federal legislation, state legislation, or action within the industry itself. As between the first and second of these, he seemed to prefer federal legislation, perhaps through "prohibiting the shipment in interstate commerce of oil produced under circumstances involving the waste of gas." He held that the difficulties with state legislation "were chiefly practical rather than constitutional or political." The states had "the constitutional power to legislate in furtherance of the conservation of oil and gas"; but he doubted that states would legislate wisely or administer effectively, and he feared that they might be encouraged to go too far in other industrial legislation. He held that the industry could make its greatest contribution through a campaign of education.[15]

Farish was in complete agreement with Hughes on the need for education, but he also saw an immediate necessity for government action: "I still feel that the only solution of the trouble of the oil industry is in government control and help, with overproduction, no profit, excessive competition, and no conservation. . . . The industry is powerless to help itself. . . . We must have government help, permission to do things we cannot do today, and perhaps government prohibition of those things (such as waste of gas) that we are doing today. . . ."[16]

To Teagle's suggestion that some plan for gas conservation should be drawn up by men in the industry, Farish had an answer:

> You seem to assume that it is possible for someone in the industry—you call them "practical men"—to work out an ideal formula for the conservation of gas. . . . There is no one in the industry today who has sense enough or knows enough about it to work out this plan. . . . What will fit today will not fit tomorrow; what will fit one field will not fit another. . . . We can only pass a law prohibiting waste and enforcing conservation, and leave it up to some board to write the rules and apply same. . . .

Humble's solution was to leave the administration of gas conservation laws to a commission. Although neither Farish nor Townes was altogether happy about entrusting this power to a governmental agency, both continued to urge that such a body of specialists would improve with the advance of knowledge and the development of public opinion. Moreover, it was clear to them that a legislature could not possibly draw up a code of rules applicable to all fields and circumstances; legislation could prohibit waste and provide for enforcement, but only a commission could prepare and administer sufficiently flexible rules. To resort to suits for damages would, in Farish's judgment, be leaving highly technical matters to the exceedingly limited technical knowledge of judges and juries.

Farish, however, in spite of his convictions in regard to gas conservation, soon at least temporarily relaxed his efforts to bring about gas conservation legislation in Texas. The failure of Marland's bill in Oklahoma, the uncompromising opposition of F. C. Proctor whose friendship Farish valued and whose standing as an authority on oil law he respected, and the opposition or general apathy within the industry all had their effect. An element of uncertainty and a feeling of disappointment crept into his correspondence. In June, 1927, he wrote to Teagle: "I have come to the conclusion that there are more individual fools in the petroleum industry than in any other business. They do not know the meaning of co-operation and teamwork." [17]

Farish and his associates did not thereafter cease to work for gas conservation legislation, but their energies were directed principally along other lines. Farish had come to realize—as Teagle had urged—that a great deal of "education" was necessary before co-operation within the industry could be established. He apparently decided as a practical matter to emphasize less unpopular measures until operators had become better informed.

One such measure was unit operation by action of the producers, which Farish had already begun to promote and for which he had great hopes. Unitization was then much discussed by engineers as a means of effecting the most efficient recovery; it would give control of production, and it should appeal to those oilmen who believed that the industry must save itself. As early as May, 1927, Farish was ready to believe that the only solution for competitive drilling with its excessive waste was the unit plan. Since one company alone could rarely get control of an entire reservoir, an effective unit plan necessarily meant co-operation among producers.

In May, 1927, Farish and President Teagle of Jersey Standard took action that was probably intended rather to arouse discussion than to bring about immediate practical results. They presented to the chairman of the Federal Oil Conservation Board a plan to curb overproduction and waste under which interested producers would purchase undivided fractional interests in a block of acreage and test and develop it as a unit under the management of a committee, each participant to receive his percentage of oil from every well drilled on the property.[18] The plan, apparently suggested by Townes and drawn up by the Legal Department, was believed to be admissible under antitrust law because it provided for the complete merging of interests before a tract was proved to contain oil.[19] This plan was designed to put a curb on what Pratt called "the carefree wildcatter," who, in testing unproved territory, had little concern for whether or not the market could absorb more oil.

Unit operations by joint agreement, however, were difficult to negotiate. In May, 1927, Humble proposed that the Marland Oil Company join it in such an arrangement in a prospective field in West Texas. The proposal was that the two companies, each owning large blocks of the area, should merge their interests, participating in costs and possible production in proportion to the amount of land held. Marland was to drill the test well and to develop and operate the field if it proved to yield oil. Marland did not accept the proposal.

Humble continued to urge that no wildcat wells be drilled until every effort had been made to pool an entire prospective area, but not until March, 1928, did it succeed in negotiating a joint agreement for unit operations. This was for the testing and development of leases in Coleman County, west central Texas, held by Humble, the Continental Oil Company, and three other operators. Continental, with 36.5 per cent, held the major interest and was in charge of development; but Humble, with the smallest interest, was credited with having fostered the plan. By May Humble had constructed gathering lines connecting the field with its trunk line to Comyn.[20]

Few would join in such a venture. The operators, who were optimists or they would not have been in the oil game, hesitated to enter into agreements prior to development lest their percentages prove too small. A carefully worked-out method of adjusting the percentages during development might have provided an answer to this objection, but confidence was then still widely lacking in the engineers' ability to make such calculations, and the antitrust laws offered a convenient and substantial reason for not co-operating.

Unit operations, like gas conservation, clearly would not progress far until at least a large segment of oil-industry leaders and of government officials concerned with the administration of gas and oil law had become convinced that conservation was necessary and practicable. A wide range of interests, indeed, had to become persuaded that conservation was sound science and technology, sound business, sound law, and sound public policy. But those immediately concerned as industrial leaders and public administrators needed, first of all, to be educated.

The education of industrial leaders and government officials was, however, proceeding rapidly. Humble contributed to this process by making public the findings of its researchers and engineers and by having its executives and specialists serve on committees to study new developments and recommend policies.

One such committee on which Farish served was the Gas Conservation Committee of the American Petroleum Institute. Following Farish's recommendation as retiring president of the Institute and a resolution of its board of directors, the new president in December, 1926, appointed a Committee of Seven to "devise and suggest" measures for petroleum, including gas, conservation. Marland was chairman, and the members included Farish and J. Edgar Pew.[21] A series of meetings attended by Farish in person or by Pratt as his representative, supplemented by the work of a technical subcommittee on which Suman, Humble's new petroleum engineer and director, represented Texas and Louisiana, eventually led to a report in favor of conservation supported by all but one member. This report recommended: that the API board call upon the industry "to adopt every reasonable and practical means to effect the conservation of natural gas" in the interest of economy, ultimate recovery, and conservation; that it "encourage the co-operative development of oil pools . . . and the passage of necessary legislation to permit" such development; and that it "impress upon its members . . . the need for state legislation . . . to prevent the waste of natural gas found in oil sands." The API board accepted the recommendation of state legislation for the conservation of gas but not that calling for co-operative development of oil pools.[22]

An account of the work of the Committee of Seven, especially of its technical subcommittee, was incorporated in H. C. Miller's *Function of Natural Gas in the Production of Oil*, published in 1929 under the joint sponsorship of the API and the Bureau of Mines. This publication was of great importance in the dissemination of the latest information about developments in reservoir science and technology.

Another important committee of which Farish was a member was the Committee of Nine, established in 1927 at the suggestion of Hubert Work, Secretary of the Interior and Chairman of the Federal Oil Conservation Board, to study the need for federal legislation. This committee consisted of three representatives each of the federal government, the American Bar Association, and the American Petroleum Institute. Farish, J. Edgar Pew, and Thomas O'Donnell, past presidents, were designated to represent the API.[23]

At a meeting of the Committee of Nine in December, 1927, Pew emphasized gas conservation, but Farish took a strong position in favor of unit operations. His testimony repeated the views that he had expressed so often during the year, emphasizing the necessity of unit operations for reducing the waste of gas and the overproduction of oil and pointing to obstacles in the way.

This committee in January, 1928, went far in recommending legislation. It recommended federal and state legislation that would recognize arrangements for the co-operative development and operation of single pools and, under proper safeguards, permit agreements among producers to curtail production in time of serious overproduction. It disapproved of compulsory unitization, however; it favored gas conservation laws but could not agree as to their "exact nature." [24]

In accordance with the committee's recommendations, Secretary Work in February, 1928, wrote the governors of twenty oil-producing states requesting co-operation with the federal government "to secure uniform state and federal legislation for the practical conservation of the country's national petroleum resources." He particularly requested study of the waste of natural gas in preparation for legislation that would "forbid such waste as fully as may be done without working injustices and unreasonable hardship." [25]

During 1928 the energies of Farish and other Humble executives concerned with conservation were directed chiefly toward improving the company's own operations and toward promoting co-operation among producers in the prorating of individual fields. Humble and other progressive companies were improving their knowledge of reservoirs, and the conviction was growing that such knowledge made possible some control of production in the interest of lower costs, long-time reserves, and better adjustment to market demand.

The increased understanding of reservoir conditions was well illustrated by the Texas Railroad Commission's hearings in Winkler County in 1928. The questions of Chairman Gilmore and the testimony of the engineers of Humble and of such other companies as Pan-American (Indiana Standard), Marland, and Roxanna (Shell) showed the great advances that were being made. A nucleus of support for production methods, based on new concepts concerning the nature and behavior of reservoirs, was obviously being developed.[26]

Yet, in 1929, despite growth in the knowledge of conservation principles, it was only after a hard fight that a new conservation act, prepared and sponsored by the Railroad Commission,[27] was, with some important deletions and amendments, put through the Texas legislature. The original bill, in addition to broadening and strengthening the powers of the Railroad Commission to prevent waste of oil and gas, authorized a majority of operators holding a majority of the acreage in an oil or gas pool, with the permission of the Railroad Commission, "to make and enforce orders . . . for the orderly development and operation of the separate holdings therein with a view to the prevention of waste."

Humble executives supported this bill with an energy that came from their conviction of both the possibility of production control and the urgent need for it in the interest of the reduction of waste and of a more orderly marketing of oil. The situation was then particularly critical because of pending injunction suits which, if successful, would in the words of Farish "leave the commission without any power of control over the waste of oil and gas."[28] Humble, of course, favored the provisions for gas conservation and for the strengthening of the Railroad Commission, but it was especially interested in the provisions for unit operations.

The company's support of this bill took a new form. Hitherto it had confined its "educational" efforts largely to the oil industry. Now for the first time it appealed directly to the general public, that is, to the voters and the legislature, through two pamphlets in support of the bill.

One pamphlet was entitled *Humble Oil & Refining Company's Position on House Bill 388*. It challenged the legislature "to determine the facts in this controversy and to take upon itself the final responsibility of saying whether or not Texas' natural resources are going to be produced in an orderly, intelligent manner, or whether we are going to have no restriction on volume or the manner in which they are produced." It protested strongly against the blame being heaped upon the oil industry for wasting the nation's resources when the industry was prevented by law from acting to curb wasteful practices, stating that "The public has no right, after putting shackles on a man, to complain at his failure to do something which requires a certain amount of freedom of action." The pamphlet called particular attention to the provisions that would permit agreements for unit operations.

"Because of its earnest conviction" that, without legislation to permit the industry to regulate itself or the Railroad Commission to control it, "there will be a perfect orgy of drilling, production, and waste of oil and gas," with great financial loss to the state, "this Company wishes now to restate its position which it originally took several years ago and has since maintained consistently, to wit:"[29]

First: The oil pool is the natural unit of competition;

Second: The most efficient recovery of the maximum amount of oil from a pool depends upon a conservative, orderly drilling and production program governed by the physical conditions in each particular pool together with the market demand for the oil;

Third: Overground storage of oil is wasteful and should not be tolerated where it can possibly be avoided;

Fourth: This Company favors any character of legislation which will permit the orderly production of oil and gas from a pool, either,

(a) by permitting the operators themselves to agree upon a production program, or,

(b) by authorizing the Railroad Commission to fix by order a program for such orderly production, and to enforce the carrying out of such order and the modification of it as circumstances may require;

Fifth: Unrestrained overproduction is wasteful, and therefore, bad for the industry and bad for the public. It will mean that oil will be produced and sold below the cost of production. This will result in Texas producing and selling its great natural resource to outside consumers at sacrifice prices.

The second pamphlet in support of the bill, entitled *The Problem of Oil and Gas Conservation and State Legislation As an Aid in Its Solution*, appeared over Farish's name and presented a general discussion of the conservation problem.[30] In twenty-two pages it reviewed the history of conservation in Texas since 1899, summarized clearly the arguments of scientist and engineer against waste, and reviewed at some length the findings of the various committees that had been studying conservation problems and possible solutions. It called attention to the fact that the state of Texas, particularly in connection with its university and school funds, had a direct landowner's interest in conservation.

Humble was the only large company actively supporting the original bill with the provision for legalizing agreements for unit operations. Gulf and Magnolia, in particular, were hostile to state legislation in general; and the majority of the independents, who feared undue control by the majors in pooling operations, were strongly opposed. Both majors and independents were also opposed to giving the Commission power to enforce proration in a flush field.[31] The opposition succeeded in weakening the measure, among other changes eliminating the section on unit agreements that Humble had particularly urged. The bill as amended was passed in March, 1929, by very large majorities in both houses.[32]

The act significantly provided that waste was to be construed to mean not *economic* but only *physical* waste, a provision that over a long period was to serve as an effective obstacle to real conservation. Although it was a much weaker measure than Humble had hoped for, it still broadened the authority of the Commission.

Humble executives apparently viewed with some satisfaction the support given the amended measure by The Texas Company and a number of independents, as well as the neutral position that Magnolia finally assumed. Farish considered Gulf directly responsible for the defeat of the unit-operations provision. "It would be very helpful to us," he wrote, "if Mr. Mellon (W. L.) would be good enough to indicate how we are to proceed in the Yates Pool, and in Texas generally, to do the things we both agree should be done. . . ." [33] Gulf was, of course, on principle opposed to any extension of government regulation of business; and its leading Texas representatives, F. C. Proctor and Underwood Nazro, were dyed-in-the-wool individualists of the old school. Texas, Magnolia, and Gulf, moreover, were in a far stronger position in oil production, relative to their crude oil requirements, than was Humble.

Despite partial defeat in the Texas legislature, Humble executives continued to advocate unit operations. Farish presented a particularly strong appeal at the October, 1929, meeting of the Petroleum Division of the American Institute of Mining and Metallurgical Engineers.[34] He urged unit operations as "the only method of reducing costs to a point where we can meet the competition of cheap foreign oil, itself a product of oil pools owned and operated as individual units." Costs had, to him, become a test of survival: "We must have low-cost production if we are to survive as producers." He urged further: "Unit operations will also solve our problem of overproduction which has plagued us so sorely for the last decade. . . ." He emphasized "the opportunity it affords of building up reserves in the ground—something we have never been able to do in the past in a competitive pool."

Brief excerpts from the remainder of the address indicate Farish's serious concern over the condition of the oil producer:

> We have seen our meagre profits dwindle, to be replaced by severe losses, periodically. We have debated remedies and argued as to facts. . . . We have been advised . . . to expand our markets for crude in order to relieve this condition of overproduction. . . . Some observers contend that this overproduction is temporary. . . . We have found as much oil in the last 5 years as we did in a generation preceding that period. . . . Must we produce all our reserves as fast as we find them. . . . ? We are staggering along with this [burden of] storage. . . . Storage of crude or products beyond bare working requirements is a millstone around the neck of the company carrying it, today. . . .

Unit operation by joint agreement after the discovery of oil was still without protection from the threat of prosecution under Texas antitrust law. Two years earlier Gulf's venerable legal counsel Proctor, "not writing . . . as a lawyer but as a business man," had declared that if he was an oil-company executive interested in bringing about "cooperation on joint operation" in fields where no substantial development had taken place, he would simply disregard legal uncertainties and risk prosecution.[35] In the autumn of 1929 Humble apparently decided to take the risk.

The first important joint-operations agreement in a proved field in which Humble participated was entered in the fall of 1929 and applied to 5,800 acres in the Van pool in East Texas. The Pure Oil Company, which brought in the discovery well in October, held more than four-fifths of the acreage; Humble, Sun, Texas, and Shell held the remainder. The agreement, which was drawn up by Hines H. Baker and Robert A. Shepherd, attorney for Pure Oil, went into effect after the discovery but before it was generally known, and the companies hoped—correctly, as it turned out—that their agreement would escape antitrust prosecution. The allocation of interests was determined according to the best current reservoir knowledge. For two years allocation was on an acreage basis in order to permit study of the production curves of wells. Eventually the formula adopted was "acre foot of producing formation times bottomhole pressure," an advanced formula for that time. Because of unitization Van escaped the vice, disorder, and lawlessness usually accompanying an oil-field boom, few dry holes were drilled, and a decade later the field still had an efficient reservoir pressure.[36] Here was co-operation at its best.

Humble also had a hand in negotiating a few other joint-operating agreements.[37] For some time, however, even prior to the defeat of unit operations in the Texas legislature, it had been obvious that voluntary unit operation was not in itself a solution to the problem of waste and overproduction. Even if voluntary unitization should be recognized as legal, a single operator in a field could disrupt the entire plan.

PURCHASING AND PRORATION

While Humble continued to practice and advocate gas conservation and unit operations, its executives had far greater success in promoting the prorating of production in individual fields. Proration means dividing a field's allowable production, determined either by voluntary agreement of the producers or by the state regulatory agency, among the various leaseholders with the objective of preventing waste and bringing about equitable withdrawal. Proration eventually proved to be the solution in Texas to the problem of waste, overproduction, and inequitable withdrawal, but only after a long and bitter struggle of which Humble bore the brunt. The early part of the proration effort, which extended over the years 1927–1930, furnished both experience and education to producers and regulatory agency in a conservation method that was eventually applied to the entire oil producing industry in Texas.

Humble took the initiative in bringing about a meeting early in September, 1927, that led to the first successful attempt in the United States to prorate the production of a large field. Efforts at Oklahoma's

Seminole field, to be sure, provided an example but not a perfect guide to success. The Yates field in West Texas, discovered late in 1926, was for a time the largest known oil pool in the world;[38] eventually it ranked in Texas second only to the great East Texas field. By September, 1927, the daily capacity of Yates was 192,000 barrels, but as yet the field had no pipeline outlet.

In August, Humble, which had the only pipeline in the vicinity, offered to extend its line to the pool and buy 30,000 barrels daily—the amount it estimated that it could market—if the producers would agree to ratable sharing of the outlet. Farish pointed out that the field's production, if not controlled in some way, would by December probably be nearly a third of a million barrels daily. He called attention to the resulting evils. Oil in such quantities could not possibly be tranported and sold, but tankage was expensive and, since the crude was high in sulphur content, corrosion of tanks would be rapid and ultimate salvage negligible. To build tankage for the storage of excess crude, when it could be "left in the ground and produced on an equitable basis fair to all," was in Farish's view "financial suicide." Producers without a market or storage would be forced to shut in their wells and allow their oil to be drained. Such uneven withdrawal would cause the water to bypass a large part of the oil, which would be trapped in the limestone and lost. Uncontrolled production would thus result both in waste of oil resources, with consequent loss to the public, and in financial disaster to the producers.[39]

It was, nevertheless, only grudgingly and tardily that the Yates operators finally assembled, agreed in principle on proration, and appointed a permanent committee. The attorney general of Texas, who was appealed to for an opinion on the plan's legality, refused to approve or disapprove, but he promised not to prosecute without notice. The proration agreement was accepted by nearly all the operators in the field with the conspicuous exception of Gulf, which declared that it intended to behave fairly but must be its own judge. Gulf had a valid argument against the Yates agreement: the agreement provided that each individual operator's runs to pipeline were to bear the same relation to the market outlet that his potential production bore to that of the entire field, but it did not limit the number of wells or the amount produced and stored. This proration formula was adopted because it was feared that to restrict production absolutely might run counter to antitrust law. But proration based on potential production, with no limitation on the number of wells, naturally encouraged a drilling competition to increase the wells on which potentials would be allowed. At the beginning of 1928 a new six-months' agreement, using acreage instead of well-potential as the basis for determining a well's share of the total field allowable, was accepted by Gulf. This plan, too, was not ideal, for it went to the other extreme of not allowing for differences in the productive capacity of wells.[40]

A committee was chosen to apportion the available outlet, and J. Elmer Thomas was hired as consulting geologist. W. A. Moncrief of the Marland Oil Company of Texas was elected chairman of the proration committee. The operators assigned men from their own staffs to study the reservoir under the direction of the committee; several of Humble's research and engineering staff participated. Data were collected for all the wells in the field. In order to control the rate of production, the oil was produced through tubing. By June, 1928, 150 wells on 14,000 acres, gauging a potential of 1,800,000 barrels a day, were held to a production of 52,500 barrels.

The Yates field was, however, merely the greatest of the West Texas fields, which early in 1928 were already producing about 300,000 barrels daily and were believed capable of five times this production. Of this amount, 80,000 barrels were then going to storage and the rest were being sold at a below-cost average price, sometimes at the distress price of 40 cents at the well. Winkler County's Hendricks field, in which Humble had large production, was producing over 164,000 barrels a day, 100,000 barrels more than the available market and transportation. One independent producer in desperation agreed to pay Magnolia one barrel out of two for six-months' storage of up to 3,000,000 barrels.[41]

Humble continued to work for an extension of co-operation in West Texas. Farish and Weiss wrote to company officers, urging proration or the shutting-in of wells. Farish urged upon the president of the West Texas Chamber of Commerce that "we can have a moderate measure of prosperity only through co-operative action within the industry and on the part of the state authorities with the industry, which . . . should center on the necessity of leaving the oil in the ground which cannot be produced without a sacrifice in price . . . , proration of output, no crude in tankage, producing only that quantity of oil that can be sold." [42]

Early in March, 1928, Farish addressed a meeting called by the Railroad Commission to discuss the situation in Winkler County. Geology and geophysics, he said, now made it possible to discover more oil than the market could currently absorb. During 1924 to 1927 Humble had invested $25,000,000 in pipeline facilities in West Texas and had purchased half the oil produced in the area, paying the highest posted prices. It could not continue to buy West Texas crude at a higher price than did competitors and put the oil into expensive steel storage, which would in four years add 75 cents per barrel to the cost. The company wished to share with other producers its ability to transport and market crude and hoped that West Texas oil could be equitably prorated so that each producer would have a fair percentage of the outlet. Prosperity could come only "through co-operation on the part of the industry and the government to balance production with consumption and create reserves of petroleum in the ground." Pointing to Yates and Oklahoma's Seminole, he declared that "proration is not an idle dream but an accomplished fact."

Farish's paper received considerable favorable comment, particularly from independent producers, as a contrast to the "dog eat dog" and "brute force" attitude ascribed to certain other major companies. His views, although strongly supported by W. B. Hamilton, chairman of the Oil and Gas Bureau of the West Texas Chamber of Commerce, were not unanimously accepted. One independent, C. D. Neff, declared that there was no domestic overproduction and blamed the situation on crude imports. The representative of the company which had agreed to store an independent's production for half a year in return for half its oil declared that proration "smacked of monopolism."[43]

A committee, including Farish, Hamilton, and Underwood Nazro, was appointed to make recommendations for a proration program. It reported that contracts and small acreage rendered "actual or complete proration by agreement . . . impossible." In the meantime reckless and unruly production methods continued to prevail, with consequent waste of gas and oil. Farish saw no chance for a solution unless the Railroad Commission did "something drastic."

The Commission in April held hearings on Winkler County production. Engineers of Pan-American (Indiana Standard), Marland, and Shell, as well as of Humble, gave testimony in support of control. Tom Cranfill, an independent, pleaded for freedom to produce.[44] On April 24 the Commission issued an order regulating production methods and limiting Winkler production to 150,000 barrels daily, prorated according to a formula giving equal weight to acreage and potential. Early in May the Commission issued new orders for prorated production in Winkler County applying to the Hendricks and Howard-Glasscock fields.[45] In June it assumed the administration of Yates and issued special rules under which that field continued to be operated. The new orders for Yates established 100 acres as the proration unit, allowables to be figured one-fourth on an acreage basis and three-fourths on the wells' potential.[46] The Yates rules, providing for wide spacing and recognizing the need for acreage in an allocation formula, constituted an important step forward.

Proration was thus established in 1928 in flush Texas fields under the authority of the Railroad Commission to conserve oil and gas. Voluntary agreement, despite Farish's best efforts, had failed to make much headway. Proration under the Railroad Commission's authority to prevent waste was to become the standard method in Texas, although several years were still to pass before that authority was firmly established by legislation and court decisions.

The development of the Yates field under proration, first by agreement of producers and later under the administration of the Railroad Commission, is a landmark in the history of conservation in the United States. One of the very earliest efforts at co-operative development of fields, Yates set an example for others to follow. From an engineering standpoint it was a great success, and for many years it was looked upon as an illustration of important new developments in production.[47] It demonstrated the feasibility of wide spacing and the value, from the standpoint of conserving a field's energy, of controlled production in accordance with engineering studies of the individual wells over a period of years.[48] The early bases for allocation of allowables were far from satisfactory, but progress was made toward that better understanding of reservoir conditions affecting the productivity of individual wells necessary for an equitable division of the field's allowable production among the various operators. As a business proposition, too, the Yates experiment was of wide interest, for it demonstrated the general advantage of regular production in an amount that the outlet to market would absorb, as compared with the old competitive production with its great waste and inequities. Farish, five years after proration at Yates had gone into effect, said that production there was "at a current cost . . . of less than 5¢ a barrel." Finally, by demonstrating the saving of the resource by controlled production and the feasibility, from an engineering point of view, of reasonably equitable allowables, Yates gave some basis for proration by the state regulatory agency. It was with justifiable pride that Farish could write in 1932: "The Yates pool is the best example of what has been accomplished by co-operative action on the part of producers and conservation authorities as compared to old line competitive development and is the nearest approach to one-ownership development or 'unit' development that the industry has to exhibit."[49]

Humble had taken the lead during 1927 and 1928 in establishing the precedent of proration in West Texas; in the following year it continued through example and precept to encourage all efforts in behalf of good production practices and the equating of supply and demand. The company opposed any increase in the allowables of the prorated fields and in some cases advocated still further decreases, co-operated in bringing about proration agreements in Gray County in the Panhandle and at Darst Creek in Southwest Texas,[50] suggested the advisability of statewide proration, and worked for a model conservation law in New Mexico. It is significant, however, that the company's representative in

North Texas was forbidden to agree to a program adopted by producers in Wilbarger County in December, 1929, not to drill wells and not to sell oil below the posted price. Humble could not for legal reasons, the representative was told, be a party to any agreement or discussion that might have in view limiting production or "fixing the price of oil."[51]

Successful as these proration efforts were in improving production practices, they were not enough to solve the growing problems of waste and overproduction. In the majority of the Texas fields, where the Railroad Commission was as yet attempting no control, drilling and production were highly competitive, and even in the prorated fields the Commission was subject to constant pressure to increase allowables. In California and the Mid-Continent similar efforts were made to unitize and prorate fields;[52] but, as in Texas, these were significant rather as steps in a process of education than as immediate solutions to the pressing problems of the industry.

While his company was promoting unit operations and the prorating of fields, Farish was also concerned with the national aspects of oil-production problems. As a member of a committee of the American Petroleum Institute that had been appointed to study and draw up a memorandum on oil supply, he had a statistical study made of the national supply situation. He was one of a large number of company executives appointed in February, 1929, to serve on regional subcommittees of the API's Committee on World Production and Consumption of Petroleum and Its Products, which was headed by President R. C. Holmes of The Texas Company. This committee outlined a program for holding production in the United States in 1929 to the level of 1928, which was unanimously adopted by the directors of the API and referred to the Federal Oil Conservation Board. The board, however, on the advice of the Attorney General of the United States, did not approve the recommendation.[53]

Out of this effort the idea of an interstate compact of oil states, which Humble executives enthusiastically supported, began to crystallize. E. E. Townes and Hines H. Baker prepared a form for an interstate oil and gas conservation compact which, under supervision of the proper public authorities, would remove the restraints of federal and state antitrust laws and thus permit agreements for co-operation in a single pool by approval of the state conservation agency; the compact would also allow interstate agreements in time of overproduction on approval of an interstate agency. Farish expressed very little expectation that such a compact would be adopted promptly, but he hoped the effort might prove educational.[54]

The Texas conservation act of March, 1929, however, was encouraging. By considerably extending and strengthening the Railroad Commission's authority to prevent waste of gas and oil, the act had presumably reinforced the validity of the Commission's proration orders. If enforced, proration could be as effective in individual fields as a general agreement for unit operations. If extended throughout the state, it could accomplish more than could be hoped for through voluntary agreement. Some advances were made in 1929, though not such spectacular ones as those made in 1928. Near the end of 1929 Farish was optimistic. "The spirit of conservation," he declared, "seems to have reached the industry." [55]

But, when the record for 1929 was finally in, it was far from encouraging. For the first time since 1923 Humble's crude oil in storage was higher at the end of the year than at the beginning, this time over a million barrels more. The *Oil & Gas Journal* in April, 1928, had pointed to Humble as "one of the few oil companies which did not store oil last year and is not doing it this year as a matter of deliberate policy." But in 1929, despite increased sales and refinery runs and efforts to curtail its own production and promote unitization and proration, the company found itself in a serious condition of oversupply.

What could be done? The extent to which Humble could shut down production even in its wholly owned fields was limited by its lease obligations; the Railroad Commission was subject to constant pressure for the increase of allowables in the prorated fields; and in the majority of Texas fields no control was attempted, and drilling and production were of necessity highly competitive. Overproduction, with its economic and physical waste and its threat to prices and to the stability of the oil industry, was a problem that neither Humble nor any other oil company, neither the state of Texas nor any other oil-producing state, no matter how enlightened and farseeing, could cope with individually. Oil companies and states, nevertheless, then saw no other alternative than to make the attempt.

In these circumstances Humble could only utilize its own influence as a large purchaser and transporter to improve its storage position. The company was forced to attempt limited production control through such time-honored but unpopular unilateral devices as drastic price cuts and purchase-storage arrangements. In doing so, it again came into conflict with independent producers, who chafed under their dependency on the large purchaser and often put the worst construction on Humble's actions without attempting to understand the conditions which had brought them about.

Early in 1930 the company took a step that aroused a storm of resentment even among those producers who had previously been most friendly. In January, six weeks after Farish had publicly declared that excess crude was not being produced (which at that particular time was actually true), Humble, simultaneously with Jersey's Mid-Continent affiliate Carter, instituted a drastic cut in the price of crude, stating that the reduction was made necessary by low gasoline prices resulting from excessive stocks. Those independent producers who had co-operated in the movement for proration, under what they had regarded as a tacit understanding that crude prices would be maintained, were bewildered, hurt, and in some cases bitter and vindictive.

Farish subsequently defended the price cut vigorously and at length. He showed a committee of the Texas division of the Mid-Continent Oil & Gas Association the company's books and convinced them that "competing units operating on the seaboard"—not Humble—were responsible for gasoline overproduction. The committee reported that Humble was drilling new wells only where it was obligated to do so under its leases and that at Moss Bluff it was paying royalty owners in advance in order to delay development.[56]

The general condemnation of the price cut was tempered in the minds of some producers by the knowledge that Humble, by taking the oil of West Texas producers even at the expense of shutting in some of its own production, had given more consideration to the producers than any other company.[57] Nevertheless, this abrupt cut left behind such a legacy of bitterness that for at least three or four years almost any rumor or charge—no matter how baseless—as to the selfish, unscrupulous, ruthless, and arbitrary character of Humble received credence from a considerable segment of the Texas oil industry.

The angry independents proceeded to retaliate for the price cut by attempts at legislation on both a national and a state level. Since Humble's principal stockholder, Standard Oil Company (New Jersey), was a large importer of crude, and the theory was abroad that overproduction was solely the result of imports, the Independent Petroleum Association had a bill introduced into the United States Congress calling for a tariff of one dollar per barrel on foreign crude; despite large-scale lobbying tactics, the bill was defeated, though by a narrow margin. The Texas legislature, however, on March 18, 1930, passed the so-called Common Purchaser Bill; this required any purchaser of oil in Texas affiliated in any way with a common-carrier pipeline to purchase oil ratably without discrimination between fields or producers, including the purchasing company's own production.[58]

Although this measure was widely looked upon as an effort to penalize Humble, the company's president had actually regarded the possibility of its passing with considerable satisfaction. He had, indeed, shortly after the January price cut, in a letter to the head of Standard of California expressed the hope "that the reaction that will follow this price cut. . . will be such as to give us some better machinery of control."[59] He found comfort in the fact that under this new legislation "the Railroad Commission would have the authority to prorate production over the entire state," since, if common purchasers were to be required to purchase ratably, the restriction of the state's production to the purchasing companies' needs would be essential. Moreover, Humble was purchasing more oil ratably than were a number of other companies; the executives believed that the new act would permit the shifting of some of its excess connections to other companies.

In the meantime the company adopted in its own operations a measure which it hoped would be followed by others. Some months earlier it had refused to participate in a movement for closing operations on Sundays as not going far enough, but on March 9, 1930, in response to a suggestion of the Federal Oil Conservation Board that refineries be shut down Sundays to prevent further overproduction of refined products, Humble shut down not only refining but also—wherever physically possible—drilling, producing, and transporting. This example was not followed generally in Texas, though in some fields Pure Oil, the Texas affiliate of California Standard, and Prairie Oil & Gas reduced production one-seventh. But on April 28 Humble announced the termination of its Sunday closing. The failure of its example to have a wide influence and its return to seven-day operations brought satisfaction to some independents, one of whom reminded "Father Farish" in a telegram that "God still rules the Universe." [60]

Early in June, shortly before the Common Purchaser Act was to go into effect, Humble took action that caused almost as great a shock as did its January price cut; it announced that, beginning July 1, it would discontinue purchasing in seven North Texas counties. Such a withdrawal, which the *Oil & Gas Journal* declared "an unprecedented move for a major oil company," involved a test of the Common Purchaser Act. Representatives of various oil and gas associations conferred with the Railroad Commission in regard to "a matching of the supply of crude with the current demand," that is, by a proration program of some sort under the Common Purchaser Act. Humble thereupon announced that it would continue purchasing in North Texas, pending the result of the proration efforts, even though this would involve buying oil that it did not need and would have to store.

Then came a significant step in proration. On August 14 the Railroad Commission, after extensive hearings and following an Oklahoma precedent, issued its first state-wide proration order, limiting Texas production to 750,000 barrels a day, an amount which was estimated to be sufficient to supply a reasonable market demand.[61] The Railroad Commission, however, soon discovered that it was one thing to issue a state-wide proration order and quite another to enforce it. A number of companies obtained injunctions that permitted them to produce without restriction, and The Prairie Oil & Gas Company withdrew as a purchaser in the Panhandle, as did Phillips. Proration broke down, and the Railroad Commission's prestige suffered everywhere. Again, Humble resorted to a price cut.

One of the concerns opposing the Commission's order was the Danciger Oil & Refining Company. This North Texas company, which had production, a pipeline, and a refinery, obtained a temporary injunction against the limiting order. It asserted that no law could prevent a company from producing as much oil as it had a market for and that the Commission's orders were concerned not with physical waste but with price fixing and economic waste, which were expressly excluded from consideration under the conservation act of March, 1929.

Here was a direct challenge to the Texas Railroad Commission's authority to prevent waste in general and to the principle of market demand in particular. Since Humble Pipe Line Company was the transporter of some Danciger oil, Humble became involved in the ensuing suit. This case, in which Hines H. Baker represented Humble, was to have great significance to conservation law and its administration (see Chapter 18), but at the end of 1930 it constituted a serious challenge to proration in Texas.

Early in 1930 a "Memorandum Concerning Conservation and Production Policy" was written by President Farish, with the aid of Hines H. Baker, for use within Humble. Excerpts from its final paragraph provide a succinct summary of the company's attitude toward petroleum engineering and conservation near the end of this, the middle period, in the Texas conservation movement:

> To sum up briefly: We are interested in conservation; we are interested in proration or other forms of cooperative development and production whether voluntary or compulsory; we are interested in unit operation; we are interested in producing our oil at the lowest cost under the best engineering practices; we are interested in getting the maximum amount of oil per acre from under our leases. . . . it is necessary that additional power to enforce sound and scientific production be given to our conservation authorities. The public interest and the correlative rights of all parties operating in a pool justify these measures. . . . Intelligent controlled production may influence prices to the extent that they be fair and reasonable, but as such controlled production . . . is going to be dependent upon . . . some political body in any State, it is reasonable to assume that fair prices will prevail and that the power to control can never be abused because public opinion will prevent. Whether the ideal can be realized or whether this type of production can be made more or less general may be subject to debate and doubt for some time to come. So far as our own company is concerned, we have made progress and are making progress along these lines. . . .

Three developments late in 1930 were prophetic of the future of the Texas oil industry. One was the evidence of the onset of the great depression in the form of the decline in crude oil sales (primarily responsible for increasing Humble's storage stocks by 4,000,000 barrels in 1930), refinery runs, and prices. The second was Danciger's challenging of the authority of the Railroad Commission. The third was the discovery of the East Texas field, the largest oil field ever discovered in the United States. These developments, combined with world-wide overproduction of crude oil and its products, threw the Texas oil industry into utter chaos. To perceptive observers it was a serious question whether the industry would continue its wasteful, erratic, and chaotic practices—perhaps ending in complete economic collapse or control by the federal government, or both—or achieve the orderly, less wasteful, controlled production that Humble executives and others throughout the years 1927–1930 had persistently championed. But before the important developments that were to answer this question are considered, our attention will be turned to other matters, particularly, in the next two chapters, to Humble's general administrative organization, policy, and practices and to its employment management and relations in the 1930s.

Chapter 14

CHANGING ADMINISTRATORS, POLICIES, AND PRACTICES IN A PERIOD OF TRANSITION, 1930–1941

As THE DECADE of the 1920s drew to a close, Humble's executives could look with satisfaction on what had been accomplished since 1918. The company's net worth had been increased from $11,000,000 to $171,-300,000 at the end of 1929. As a result of good earnings, principally from pipeline operations, and a conservative dividend policy, Humble had been able to expand largely from income and to become financially strong. It had also achieved organizational strength and made progress in applying science and engineering to refining and production. It had built a large and up-to-date refinery and a pipeline system that reached all the oil-producing regions of Texas, it had become a large producer and purchaser of crude oil, and it had acquired market outlets for its crude and products.

On the whole, the company's executives were optimistic. They envisaged a continued upward trend in the demand for oil products. They were anxious, however, about Humble's relatively low ratio of oil reserves to current production and needs, about the world-wide oversupply of oil and products accompanied by destructive competition, and about declining prices. But the policies and programs they had adopted in 1927 to strengthen their company's reserves and production bore much promise. They were encouraged by the fact that some awareness had developed within the oil industry and the state and federal governments of how the American system of competitive oil production could be strengthened and waste minimized by better production methods, voluntary restraint on the part of companies, and regulation by states.

But those men could hardly then foresee the developments of the 1930s that were to bring severe stress and strain to Humble and its industry. Two great crises that developed in 1930 and 1931 were to block progress: the great depression itself and the extravagant and wasteful production and the resulting market chaos that came with the development of the East Texas field and accentuated the disastrous effects of the general economic collapse. These crises, however, also were to bring unforeseen opportunities to companies that had the resources, flexibility, and foresight to seize them. Gradually, the depression would subside, the industry become more stable, and a growing demand for higher-quality products in large volume bring recovery and, on the eve of World War II, even stimulate expansion to unprecedented heights.

How Humble's policies, plans, and operations were developed in response to overproduction, depression, and recovery accompanied by a dynamic demand is the general interest of Chapters 14 through 21. The present chapter begins with the top policy-makers and planners, deals with the development of the headquarters organization in response to new needs, and sketches general policies.[1]

THE TOP POLICY-MAKERS AND PLANNERS

Humble entered the 1930s with a Board of Directors containing several members of high administrative and technological capacity, men who were keenly sensitive to the nature and possibilities of changes then in progress in the industry and who were able effectively to adjust their company's planning and operations to the changing conditions. This group included Farish, the general administrator and chief executive, and Wiess, Pratt, Suman, and Anderson, the men who had top responsibility for operations. Blaffer, whose special field was finance, and Townes, the general legal counsel, understood the implications of changing conditions and gave their support and advice to the directors in charge of operations. The three other directors confined themselves for the most part to departmental responsibilities.

This group guided the company through the early years of the depression, but in 1933 came major changes in the membership of the Board of Directors. The most important was the resignation of Farish on June 6, 1933, to accept the chairmanship of the Board of Directors of Standard Oil Company (New Jersey). Subsequent developments indicate that he was called to New York principally in order to prepare him for assuming within a few years the post of his old friend, President Teagle. Rumors that Farish would "go with Jersey" had been rife among the oil fraternity for over a decade. In 1927 he had been elected a Jersey director but had retained his Humble presidency. The Jersey board in 1933 was losing five directors by retirement and resignation and was in need of strong, new leadership; Farish was a logical choice. He left Humble with great reluctance and maintained his Houston residence. He spoke of his acceptance of these new responsibilities as necessitated by his duty as a "member of an industrial army," thus applying to himself his frequent insistence that employees behave as good soldiers.[2]

Before Farish severed his official connection with Humble, several other changes in the Humble board that had been impending for some time were made. John S. Bonner retired at the age of sixty under Humble's depression relaxation of its rule for later retirement.[3] Other directors who retired at this time were Frank P. Sterling and Walter W. Fondren.[4] Sterling, who was sixty-three years old, was eligible for retirement. Fondren, though only fifty-six, had been in the oil industry much longer than Sterling; he had been the first of all the Humble founders to enter the industry.

Fondren's career in retrospect illustrates how far the oil industry in Texas had progressed in a few decades. He had grown with the industry from nearly the beginning of production in the first oil field in the state and through the Spindletop boom to early prominence in the Texas oil industry. He had been a pioneer in rotary drilling and was in his day regarded as the outstanding driller on the Gulf Coast, with a greater practical knowledge of salt domes than any other man in Texas. As director of the company's Gulf Coast drilling he had made an indispensable contribution to Humble's early success. He was intelligent, open-minded, and progressive. But, without engineering education, Fondren, the orphan boy who had gone to work in a sawmill at the age of thirteen, had yielded place to Suman and young engineers and production executives until, while still in his prime, his duties had become those of only a director rather than an operator. Fondren, moreover, was not in the best of health, and his withdrawal from active business gave him more time for the religious and philanthropic interests which his great wealth enabled him to carry on and which had increasingly been occupying his attention. His retirement marked for Humble the end of an era; he was the last of the early Spindletop drillers and the last director of the original Humble Oil Company to occupy a seat on the board of Humble Oil & Refining Company.

These retirements in 1933 dramatically climaxed two significant tendencies toward change in the composition of the board. The old, practical, rule-of-thumb oilmen were nearly all gone, and only two of the original stockholders and founders remained. Of these two, Blaffer and Wiess, the latter had been educated as an engineer. The other four of the six board members were a lawyer, a geologist, and two engineers. Townes (the lawyer), Pratt (the geologist), and Suman (an engineer) were at this time advanced to vice-presidencies.[5] The sixth member, also an engineer, was James Anderson, whose major responsibilities as director and vice-president were for the Crude Oil Department and the subsidiary Humble Pipe Line Company.

The resignation of Farish left the highest executive position in Humble vacant and the succession uncertain. Farish may or may not have been "the greatest oilman who ever lived," to quote some of his loyal admirers, but his right at the time to the title of the greatest oilman of the American Southwest would seem, at any rate, to have stood on a secure foundation. His place would not be easy to fill. The two logical possibilities as his successor were Blaffer and Wiess, founders, vice-presidents, and large stockholders.[6] Pratt and Suman, although able and influential, were comparatively recent members of the board, directors rather than officers, and owners of relatively small stock interests.

Blaffer was ten years older than Wiess and had been in the oil business several years longer; he had for some time been recognized as the senior vice-president. He had always, however, been regarded as more interested in finance than in operations; and after the sale of stock to Jersey in 1919 and his own appointment as treasurer, he had become even more withdrawn from actual operations. Although Blaffer was officially head of the Crude Oil Department, Farish had been its chief policy-maker and James Anderson its manager. Blaffer's heart belonged to the treasurership.

Wiess, on the other hand, during the past fourteen years had been vested with the responsibility for building up from practically nothing Humble's refining and marketing organizations; he had fulfilled those difficult assignments with great conscientiousness and, particularly in refining, with notable success. Baytown was a technological triumph, and the Wiess interest in research and experimentation had extended to and benefited the entire company. Wiess, however, was the youngest member of the board with the exception of Suman.

Here was a difficult choice. Should the specialist in finance with comparatively little recent experience in the management of operations be given a position to which his ability in his special field, his loyalty to the company's interests, and his seniority would seem to entitle him? Or should the responsibility and the prestige go to a younger man, who had much the broader managerial experience and who was by training, experience, and, indeed, his very nature keyed to the new technology that had come to occupy a dominant place in Humble's thinking and operations?

The directors in 1933 temporarily solved the problem of executive succession by electing Blaffer to the presidency and Wiess to the newly created office of executive vice-president. Although the change in the bylaws creating the new office did not explicitly assign any special administrative authority and responsibility to the executive vice-president, perhaps it was hoped and believed that a division along the lines of each of the top officers' particular qualifications would work out in practice without any official statement; Humble's administration, after all, had never followed rigid organizational lines. The other vice-presidents, however, followed the letter of the bylaw and looked upon Wiess's executive vice-presidency merely as an officially recognized senior vice-presidency, such as Blaffer had previously held unofficially. Blaffer, having full confidence in the other vice-presidents and directors, gave them a free hand in operations. This demonstration of confidence was gratifying and had certain beneficial effects, but it also resulted in what some believed to be inadequate over-all administrative co-ordination. The problem was informally resolved in December, 1933, with the advice of Farish, by an understanding that Wiess should serve as the chief executive officer.

Wiess was actually to direct Humble's operations for fourteen years. In 1937 Blaffer, who was giving more and more attention to the increasing complications of company finance, suggested that he himself be made chairman of the board and Wiess elected president, which was then done.[7]

An understanding of Wiess's role beginning in 1933 is perhaps best approached through comparison with his predecessor, Farish. The two executives who, unofficially or officially, directed the operations of Humble Oil & Refining Company during its first thirty years were strikingly dissimilar in physique, personality, and administrative methods. Farish was tall and strongly built, an enthusiastic golfer and quail hunter, and an omnivorous reader; he was impatient of minute detail and rigid organizational schemes, willing to delegate authority, rapid in decision, his strong emotions masked by an imperturbable courtesy.[8] Wiess was of medium height and solid build, with impressively rugged features—in the graphic words of an associate, "a burly chunk of a man." He disclaimed literary interests and, although he manifested the Texas businessman's conventional interest in hunting and sports, he actually found his principal recreation in work—in the opinion of some, he never learned to play.[9]

The mainspring of Wiess's character as a business executive seems to have been an extreme conscientiousness and sense of personal responsibility. Again and again close associates have said of him, in essence: "I never knew anyone who tried harder to do right." He was anxious to come to exactly, and not merely approximately, the right decision. This required an indefatigable search for information, following the methods of the scholar rather than those of the man of action. His arriving at a decision, consequently, was frequently a slow process; sometimes he would draw up the pros and cons in two columns and then weigh and compare them in several closely typed pages with the alternatives carefully balanced. Although in his later years he was less insistent on following the reasoning and arguments of the experts to the last detail, he apparently always felt it his responsibility to examine a question at issue so carefully that the ultimate decision became his own.

Wiess's insistence on arriving at his own decisions naturally made it difficult for him to delegate responsibility. It was not that he did not trust those working with him; but, since as chief executive the ultimate responsibility was his, he felt that he must know and understand everything that was going on. A lesser man would soon have broken under the strain, but Wiess's indefatigable energy and strength of will enabled him not only to occupy the driver's seat but also to be aware of what was going on under the hood and in all other parts of the machine.

Wiess's own conscientiousness and his own tremendous drive were accompanied by high standards of performance for those who worked under him. He made heavy demands on them and tended to be impatient with those who did not measure up to his standards. He strove to be fair, however, and not unduly impatient with those who in his opinion were sincerely trying to do a good job even when their work did not always meet his requirements. Some men developed greatly through working with him, but he did not win the generally spontaneous loyalty and cooperation that several of Humble's other high executives were able to inspire.

Another side of Wiess's ultraconscientiousness was a spirit of *noblesse oblige*, an interest in the welfare of deserving or unfortunate Humble employees, which found quiet and undramatic expression and was consequently not generally known. His attitude toward labor unions was in part a reflection of his rigorous belief in personal responsibility. If he could not fully delegate authority to his own chosen and trusted subordinates, how could he commit any of the "prerogatives of management" to a self-appointed group of employees under outside influence? As to the alleged benefits of unionism and social legislation, his attitude was: "We'll take care of our own." That this attitude was sincere is confirmed by an abundance of unsought testimony. For example, when in a tragic accident in a Humble laboratory two well-known research chemists and an obscure welder were fatally injured, Wiess's first concern was for the welfare of the welder's widow, who, he feared, might be overlooked. A colored waiter in the Humble executives' dining room volunteered this comment: "Some thought Mr. Wiess was stiff and unfriendly, but he had a big heart. Any of us boys could go to him when we were in trouble."

An obviously logical part of Wiess's nature was his liking for order.

He wanted everything defined and down on paper. For example, the meticulously worked-out, and probably long overdue, Humble organization chart, which provided a place for every man and put every man in his place, was a product of the Wiess regime. So also was the formalization of certain procedures, as will be considered later in this chapter. During his presidency it came to be understood that even board members were expected to be in their offices during regular office hours.

Wiess's notable contributions as an executive derived from his scientific and analytical interests. Of all the Humble executives he was probably the most broadly informed on the oil industry. And, perhaps more than anyone else in a group that was predominantly inclined in the same direction, he was interested in research and in the application of science and engineering to the problems of his company. Moreover, he early emphasized the importance of economic analysis and of attention to cost considerations.

Humble was fortunate in possessing two such chief executives, each in his own time and place, as Farish and Wiess. Farish was the bold risk-taker, the imaginative builder for the distant future, the impressive and compelling leader. His rapid, seemingly intuitive, decisions were appropriate in leading the company in its early expansion and in the building-up of large crude reserves, and his broad grasp of the problems of the industry and his capacity for leadership made him an important figure in the conservation movement. Wiess's cautious temperament and his meticulous and disciplined methods were more especially adapted to the carefully plotted long-range forecasts, the decimal-point calculations, necessary in planning the development of a large-scale refinery or the expansion of a sales department, and they were indispensable in the management of the company in a period of depression and increasing competition. His interest in formalized procedures coincided with the needs of a company grown large. Wiess's energy and his conscientiousness and devotion to what he regarded as his obligations were at no time more effectively employed than in leading his company in its outstanding performance during World War II.

In conformity with a depression-inaugurated program of contraction, the vacant seats on the Humble board were not filled in 1933, but the remaining directors had no intention of permanently limiting their number to six. Pratt, Wiess, and Suman were youngsters in their forties, but Blaffer, Anderson, and Townes were in their middle or late fifties and were due to retire in a few years. Moreover, the burden on some of the board members was growing severe. Wiess, in addition to his duties as chief executive officer, continued to carry responsibility for manufacturing and sales; the extensive program of exploration and leasing weighed heavily on Pratt. The directors were, therefore, conscious of the need of strengthening their group by the addition of younger men.

The year 1937 brought the needed expansion. That year was marked by the appearance on the board of two representatives of a new and younger element, the first directors to be added since 1927. The new directors, L. T. Barrow and Hines H. Baker, were merely the vanguard of an influx that within the next decade would completely change Humble's Board of Directors. Unlike their predecessors, they had joined the company as young and inexperienced employees, at first indistinguishable from other beginners in their professions. They had worked their way up through long service until they were selected to swell the majority of technologists and lawyers in the company's governing body.

Baker was a native Texan and in his early forties. He had taught country school at the age of seventeen, served as a superintendent of schools at nineteen, roustabouted one summer in the Saratoga oil field, and received the B.A. degree at The University of Texas. He had worked his way through the same university's law school as a student assistant in economics, graduating with honors, had been in military service, and had practiced law in Beaumont for a short time before coming to Humble in 1919. Baker was at first engaged primarily in title work and legal problems in connection with lease acquisitions and the purchase of crude oil. He was soon called upon to consult with various departments and to write legal opinions on corporate and other problems as well as to participate in trial work. When the company became interested in conservation, he was put in charge of the important and grueling legal work associated therewith. At the same time he continued to deal with corporate legal problems and to handle the legal work of the Refining and the Sales Department. Townes relied heavily upon his advice, and Baker worked closely with Farish and other executives and directors as legal adviser.

As a director, Baker had a broad range of duties. He still had charge of matters relating to conservation and proration and consulted with E. E. Townes and Rex G. Baker on antitrust, natural-gas, and conservation matters in general. He also assisted President Wiess in the co-ordination of his executive work.[10]

Barrow, also a Texan in his early forties, had a pre-Humble record that included service in the air corps and an instructorship and a Master's degree in geology from The University of Texas. He had joined Humble as a geologist in 1924 and had been appointed chief geologist in 1929, in which office he had carried much responsibility for Humble's leasing and exploration, working closely with Pratt in the company's great campaign for acquiring reserves. He continued after his election to the board to serve as chief geologist accountable to Vice-President Pratt. However, when Pratt in June, 1937, resigned to become a director, vice-president, and member of the executive committee of Jersey Standard,

Barrow succeeded him as director for geology, geophysics, scouting, and leasing, and his responsibilities as chief geologist were given to L. P. Teas. Barrow was elected a vice-president in 1938.[11]

The resignation of Wallace E. Pratt was Humble's second great loss to Jersey Standard in a few years. Pratt was a slightly built and modest-spoken man, with more the appearance of a scholar than a man of action, who had early risen to a position of leadership in Humble's administration. Oilmen both inside and outside Humble who were acquainted with the company from its early years unanimously list him among the three or four men who contributed the most to its great success in its first decisive score of years.

Pratt's special contribution was his leadership of the company in building a strong leasing and exploration organization and acquiring enormous reserves, but his influence reached far beyond this important province. He was an executive of long-range vision. It was he who convinced Farish that Humble should go into petroleum engineering and urged the employment of John R. Suman. He early recognized the need for reservoir research and conservation and advocated their development within Humble and in the industry generally. He had a strong and constructive influence on the thinking of Farish and Wiess and in the making of many of Humble's policy decisions. Outside the company, recognition of his knowledge, integrity, and balanced judgment contributed to Humble's favorable reputation as a company.

A third new director was added in 1938. Wiess, who although officially president was still director in charge of manufacturing and sales, decided to shift his departmental responsibilities to the shoulders of a new director, Stuart A. Giraud, chairman of the manufacturing and marketing committees and for many years Wiess's "Man Friday." Giraud, who had been with Humble from its organization, had also worked his way up in the company through long service, in his case in accounting.[12] His election was evidence that new seats on the board were not exclusively reserved for men of university training but were open also to those who had entered the industry as very young men, had learned the business through practical experience, and had risen on the strength of their performance. Giraud's period of service as director was cut short by his death in 1940.

GROWTH AND CHANGE IN ADMINISTRATIVE ORGANIZATION AND PRACTICES

Between April, 1934, and October, 1935, was built a fifteen-story addition to Humble's overcrowded nine-story Houston office building.

The tower, with the United States flag at its mast, has ever since been a striking feature of the Houston skyline and a symbol to the general public of the company's importance. To those employed at headquarters in 1935 this addition to the Humble Building meant adequate space for the expanding personnel and work of the central administrative organization.

The 1930s brought not only more work but also work that was relatively new or of changing character. This necessitated expanding and also broadening the scope and influence of headquarters departments, developing new staff groups, and formalizing certain procedures. One new staff group that became influential throughout the company was the Industrial Relations Office. Other groups rose to importance within individual operating departments. Certain staff developments, however, were more exclusively than others of assistance to the top administration or in the company's outside relations.

The Legal Department felt strongly the increase in the company's business. Its growth and the change in its work at this time are illustrative of changes taking place generally throughout the organization.

The essential functions of the department continued as they had always been: to advise the directors and officers of the company in all legal matters and to see that the company's broad activities in its various relations were conducted in conformity with law, that its rights were safeguarded, and that it was properly represented in the trial of lawsuits to which it was a party. The department helped to shape company policy, and its members performed the dual function for the operating and administrative departments of handling their current legal work and advising them on the legal aspects of steps which they contemplated. The department also handled the company's trial work. Humble's policy was to keep litigation to a minimum by trying to settle difficulties out of court; but, where important legal principles or significant financial or operational issues were involved, the company did not hesitate to enter court action to defend itself, whatever the effect on public opinion or on its relations with a regulatory agency. Outside legal counsel were utilized for advice—for example, Robert E. Hardwicke on conservation matters —and for examining titles and assisting in the trial of cases in the courts.

The developments in the Legal Department that were particularly distinctive in the 1930s were the great increase in the amount and the range of its work and the consequent growth of specialized groups within the department. Few industries, if indeed any, surpass oil producing in the amount of legal work required; besides the wide range of legal issues and routines that any large business concern must attend to, the oil producing industry normally has an incredible amount of title and contractual work and of litigation resulting from the leasing of oil lands. Humble's tremendous program of purchasing and leasing oil lands in the 1930s increased this work to unprecedented proportions. Conservation and proration also brought much new work. As in other industries, new tax laws and regulations, social security, new employee regulations, and other new or changed forms of government relations multiplied the work of the lawyers in the 1930s. The stresses and strains of depression brought their usual problems.

The depression and falling oil prices were directly responsible for increased political attacks on the larger oil companies, but Humble was in an especially critical position because of its great importance as a purchaser of crude and as a pipeline carrier and also because of its affiliation with a large company that was a traditional whipping boy of press and politician. State and federal investigations of the oil industry and suits instituted by the state of Texas resulted in much work for company lawyers.

Though most of the investigations and suits in which Humble was involved in the 1930s were related to specific operations and will be considered in those particular relations, one suit had general corporate significance because of its threat to the company's charter. This was an antitrust suit filed in the Travis County District Court by the state of Texas in November, 1931, in the depths of depression and amid the chaos resulting from the excessively prolific development of the East Texas field.

The suit, *State of Texas* v. *Standard Oil Company of New Jersey, et al.*, was brought by Attorney General Allred against Humble, Standard Oil Company (New Jersey), and fifteen other defendants, including Socony-Vacuum, Shell, Standard of California, the American Petroleum Institute, and the Texas Petroleum Marketers Association. It was brought on the theory of alleged conspiracy by all the defendants under the Code of Fair Marketing Practices sponsored by the API and approved by the Federal Trade Commission. This code was intended to help eliminate some of the unfair and destructive competitive practices resulting from the overproduction that had begun to develop late in the 1920s. According to allegations in the state's 132-page petition, the code had been utilized by the defendants, in violation of Texas antitrust law, to monopolize the petroleum business in the state and to throttle the independent retailer. The petition, moreover, specifically alleged that Jersey Standard controlled and dominated Humble.

The penalties demanded included the annulment of the charters of concerns incorporated in Texas and the cancellation of permits of other companies to do business in the state. Writs of attachment and garnishment and fines totaling $17,000,000 were also demanded, principally against companies that were not incorporated in Texas or did not have permits to operate in the state but were allegedly doing business there through affiliates. This suit, accordingly, threatened Humble's charter and Jersey's Humble stock.

The case had a long career in the Texas courts. It was part of a general depression-born attack on business, but it met with a great deal of disfavor on the part of the public. Such organizations as the Houston and East Texas chambers of commerce warned Texans of the danger to the industry threatened by Allred's action, and editors reflected that a return to normal business was more important than the destruction of business and the frightening away of capital. While the original trial was in progress, the Petroleum Code under the National Industrial Recovery Act of 1933, modeled after the earlier code, was approved and put into effect. The attorneys for the defendants held that this new code made legal the acts complained of in the suit and also that the Texas antitrust laws were invalid under an earlier decision of the United States Supreme Court. The District Court held that the code did so apply and dismissed the case, but it was appealed. The Court of Civil Appeals at Austin affirmed the judgment of the lower court, but again the decision was followed by an appeal, this time to the Texas Supreme Court. Before the issue had been decided by the state's highest court, however, the Supreme Court of the United States declared the NRA unconstitutional, and in consequence the case was sent back to the trial court. On October 3, 1938, an agreed judgment was rendered in favor of all the defendants except the Texas Petroleum Marketers Association, which paid a fine. The issue of Jersey Standard's control of Humble was not tried, but the effect of the disposition of the case was to resolve the issue against the state's contention.[13]

Throughout this period E. E. Townes, the company's veteran general counsel, continued to head the Legal Department. Although his responsibilities as a member of the Board of Directors occupied much of his time, he continued to have general oversight of the department and helped to maintain a strong *esprit de corps*. The young men who had risen to responsible positions in the 1920s continued to serve as leaders within the department.

Trial work came to be directed mainly by R. E. Seagler, general attorney, assisted by the lawyers of the trial division, who, together with other trial lawyers, represented the company in the courts. The larger part of the litigation of major importance in the 1930s came from conflicts over titles and various damage suits, and under proration law and its administration. The most significant cases are considered in their proper relations elsewhere.

Hines H. Baker, until he became a member of the Board of Directors in 1937 as already noted, continued to carry the major responsibility for general corporate problems, antitrust matters, and conservation, besides handling the legal work of the Refining and the Sales Department. His responsibilities for refining and sales were in 1937 assigned to John Q. Weatherly, who also had charge of the increasingly complex field of tax law and of the legal aspects of employee relations. Most of Hines Baker's other work in the department was assigned to Rex G. Baker.

Rex G. Baker rose to leadership in the Legal Department in the 1930s. He was legal adviser to nearly all the operating and staff departments and handled the legal problems in connection with the large trades and acquisitions of oil properties made by the company during the period of great expansion prior to World War II. In 1937 he was given principal responsibility for antitrust matters, for general corporate problems, and also for conservation. In view of the scope and quality of his experience, he was the logical successor of Townes as general counsel on the latter's retirement in 1943.

By 1943 the department had attained essentially its structure as of today and its name was changed to Law Department.[14] Its work had become more distinctly compartmentalized. And with the exception of J. Q. Weatherly, who headed a small group of attorneys concerned principally with taxation and the legal work of the Sales and the Refining Department, younger men had risen to the headship of the various divisions of the work. Among them was H. P. Pressler, Jr., who had charge of the title and contract and other legal work of the Geologic, Lease and Scouting Department and also of the Production Department's legal work excepting conservation and proration; this was the largest group in the department. Nelson Jones had charge of conservation and proration matters and of the general legal work of the Crude Oil Department. The trial division, headed by R. E. Seagler, became next to the largest group within the department. Other special fields were handled by one or more men.

The Comptroller's Department and its subsidiary accounting offices, in contrast with certain other headquarters groups, entered the 1930s with an already highly developed organization. Comptroller L. H. Attwell, Jr., co-ordinated the company's accounting through the heads of the various accounting offices and a system of internal auditing. The department, with Gay Carroll as chief accountant, prepared the various reports and consolidated statements required by the corporation, compiled state and federal tax reports, and compiled financial and statistical information for the company's officers and Board of Directors. Each department—the Administrative Department and the operating departments—had its separate accounting office, which embraced all phases of accounting related to the investments and activities of the department; each of these offices prepared reports and statements for the Comptroller's

Department and provided the management of its own department with whatever information or assistance it required. This decentralization and specialization had developed early in the company's history.

New needs in the 1930s brought significant changes in Humble's accounting, and expansion in every aspect of the company's operations created more work for the Comptroller's Department. The great expansion in reserves and production, particularly, increased the load of the largest departmental accounting office, that of the Production Department headed by R. E. Sinclair. Every lease must have its separate set of complicated accounts, payments for bonuses, rentals, and royalties, and its own depletion records. New tax requirements and governmental regulation of the oil industry added to the accounting load throughout the organization. Particularly significant was the growing attention of management to costs, to problems of interdepartmental billing, and to the use in planning and budgeting of financial and statistical data provided by the Accounting Department. Throughout the whole accounting organization these new demands brought a need for enlarged personnel, but particularly for greater attention to order and system.

Certain developments suggest the trend of the changes. The Baytown refinery's problem of joint costs of products and transfer billing led its engineers to set up formulas for figuring costs, and both the Refining Department and the Production Department required increasingly detailed and specific cost data in their efforts to raise the efficiency of equipment and of operating practices in the 1930s. In 1934 Humble adopted a new accounting manual, which had grown out of an intensive study, with the help of Price, Waterhouse & Company, of its accounting organization and methods. This manual was designed, principally, to effect greater uniformity of accounting methods. Strengthening the influence of the comptroller and of the internal auditing group had the same objective. The adoption of a more formal system of company planning and budgeting in the later 1930s put heavier requirements on the accounting groups in the departmental offices, as well as on the comptroller and the Comptroller's Department. In 1938 the Sales Department's accounting office undertook a study of its own work. Three years later, under the direction of Gay Carroll, who had become comptroller in 1940, the Comptroller's Department instituted a study of the company's whole accounting organization. Its objective was to raise the department's general efficiency and to adapt its personnel, organization, and procedures to the expanding and changing needs of the corporation and its management.[15]

Significant innovations were also introduced in Humble's Administrative Department at this time by the addition of new staff men and functions to assist and inform the administration in specific areas. These additions were made in 1937, after Wiess had become president in name as well as in function and Hines H. Baker had been elected to the board. It was at Baker's suggestion that new staff men were appointed for engineering and for economics and statistics.

For technical assistance to management, Ralph J. Schilthuis, a graduate in petroleum engineering of the Colorado School of Mines with the unusual combination of several years of experience in refining and production, was transferred from production research. Engineers were, of course, familiar figures in Humble's departmental staff and operating organizations, but adding an engineer to the administrative staff was a new departure. Professionally trained economists and statisticians were even more unusual, not merely in Humble but in the oil industry in general. Dr. Richard J. Gonzalez, assistant professor in the economics department of The University of Texas, was chosen for the position of economist and statistician. Gonzalez had recently received his doctorate in economics from the same university, but had also completed sufficient work in mathematics and statistics to have taken his degree in that field as well. He came to Humble on July 1, 1937, on leave of absence from his teaching post, originally intending to stay for a year or two and then go back to teaching.

The introduction of these new functions was on a small scale. The engineer and the economist and statistician were added to the staff of W. N. Finnegan, Jr., the veteran assistant to the president who was in charge of both press relations and such statistical work as had been carried on in the Administrative Department. Schilthuis soon returned to the Production Department for work in the Gas division, which was then becoming an important part of the department's operations. Gonzalez' duties, however, developed into a permanent and important central staff function.

Dr. Gonzalez devoted himself to building up statistical techniques and a body of statistical information, useful in the quantitative representation and analysis of conditions in the oil industry and the general economy, which would serve as aids to management in the planning of expansion and operations. No longer did the top executives' own observations, aided by statistics compiled by untrained assistants, provide a sufficient basis for decisions that involved judgment about trends in the oil industry and the general economy. Gonzalez was put in complete charge of the economics and statistics staff early in 1941, when Finnegan decided to go into business for himself as a lease broker.

Another significant innovation in 1937 was the introduction of a formal system of budgeting. President Wiess in July issued a circular on budget procedures. Because of the rapid growth of the business, he stated, it was "advisable that a definite procedure be outlined, and that all those who propose expenditures should carefully consider them and present in a clear and full manner all pertinent facts and arguments in support of such proposed expenditures, in order that a sound program may be adopted." In the fall of each year, the circular continued, an estimate of operations should be prepared in detail for the following year. The first step was to be the preparation of a report by L. T. Barrow, as chairman of a committee charged with the responsibility of preparing and furnishing estimates for the next year, of production in the states in which Humble operated, of the amounts available for purchase, and of average prices. When approved by the board, such estimates should be made available for use in preparing departmental budgets. Those budgets, prepared by the individual departments with the aid of the director in charge, should include, among other data, estimates of the amount of the department's business and of its capital and operating expenditures. These departmental budgets, assembled by the Comptroller's Department, became the basis for board action.

Certain aspects of the procedures followed in the compilation of this budget are significant. It still originated at headquarters. That is, departmental budgets were planned by the top management of a department in consultation with the director in charge of the department and were compiled by the departmental accounting offices. From about 1939 the information on which this planning was based was broadened by Gonzalez' forecasts, based on statistical studies, of trends in the oil industry and the general economy that were significant to Humble's business. This budget was regarded as primarily a planning budget, control being a secondary objective. It was reviewed quarterly. Essentially it represented a necessary systematization in a company grown large of a task that had been done earlier in a less formal way. But it did not represent the broad concept of planning or of the use of the budget that Humble was later to adopt.

PUBLIC RELATIONS POLICIES AND PRACTICES

Humble's executives had always been conscious of their company's need for good public relations, but they had not visualized the advisability of strengthening those relations by special efforts to communicate with the general public. They had realized that in affiliating with Standard Oil Company (New Jersey) Humble had put itself in an exposed legal and public relations position, both because of that company's early clashes with Texas law and because association with a large out-of-state corporation was still a cause for suspicion with much of the Texas public. Humble's Board of Directors had operated on the policy that the company should strive to establish its character in the view of the public by careful observance of Texas law and the principle of fair dealing in all its operations. This called for vigilance on the part of the Legal Department and for good relations with the various interests with which the company's administrative and operating groups came into contact.[16]

The company worked hard to establish and maintain good relations with those groups, but it relied on deeds rather than words. Lease men were under instructions to take no advantage of farmers and ranchers or of Humble's own competitors. Crews for pipeline construction, drilling, and production were ordered to exercise the greatest care for the landowner's fences, crops, and livestock. Humble paid the posted price for oil and adopted the policy of buying proportionally as much from its connections' wells as from its own, or, when compelled to limit the amount purchased, of accepting the surplus for storage until a market was available. The Sales Department during the late 1920s and early 1930s inaugurated a policy of maintaining company-owned service stations, with dependable products, clean restrooms, and efficient and courteous service.[17] The improvement in Humble's standing with the Texas public over the years was probably in considerable measure the result of the good will created by the products and service of its retail marketing outlets.[18]

One method of giving public expression to its views of which Humble had taken full advantage was the public hearing or investigation, by Railroad Commission, legislature, or other public body. Humble was outstanding in its presentation of scientific and engineering information, particularly as related to production problems. Perhaps no achievement of the company won it more respect from those interested in the larger problems of the industry than its contributions in such hearings. Those contributions, however, reached only a small although an important group.

The old Humble slogan, "Our employees are our public relations department," expressed one way in which the company reached a more general public. Humble executives were aware of the importance of the company's employee-relations program not only as it affected its workers on the job but also from a public relations viewpoint. Employees had the opportunity to transfer their impressions of the company for which they worked to relatives, friends, neighbors, retail merchants, professional men, and persons casually encountered—a public more numerous and covering a much wider range of occupations and interests than could be reached by company representatives in any of its business relations except the retail sale of gasoline. There was no more effective missionary than the really enthusiastic employee next door or across the street.

Humble's practice of depending on deeds rather than words to maintain good public relations could not be relied upon exclusively. No large company could keep out of the newspapers entirely or depend wholly on individual departments for contact with the public. Farish, as president from 1922 to 1933, is credited with a greater consciousness than his associates of the public's importance, and with a greater interest in explaining the company's position. Because of his office and his personal attitude, complaints and criticisms were naturally channeled to him and always received prompt attention. Humble, indeed, boasts that no letter, even of the most trivial character, has ever been permitted to go unanswered—an examination of its files would seem to confirm this claim. W. N. Finnegan, Jr., who was one of Farish's assistants almost from the company's incorporation, helped the president in this area. Finnegan also gradually took over such a large proportion of public and press relations that much of his time came to be occupied by representatives of newspapers and trade journals, independent operators, and other representatives of the public who wished information about or explanations from Humble. It was, however, no part of his duties or of the company's policy to keep the public, and particularly the newspapers, regularly informed as to Humble's views or plans, or of its reasons for a particular course of action.

Humble executives were not particularly conscious of that great public with whom the company had little direct contact, but whose attitude was nevertheless of importance because of its votes for state legislators and members of the Railroad Commission and because of its influence in that pervasive climate of opinion in which legislators, commissioners, and judges operated. This general public, by and large, could be reached and to some extent influenced through newspapers and the radio, but Humble's policy was rather to avoid such publicity than to seek it. If attacked in reputable newspapers, the company would answer, briefly and with dignity, but for many years it never issued a preliminary or simultaneous explanation for any of its actions that might incur criticism—its reasons were given, if at all, only after the fact, and too often after public resentment had already crystallized. To the more extreme attacks of small sensational publications it would not reply.

In the 1930s circumstances forced Humble to examine its public relations policy. The company was not alone in this need, for American business was then generally being forced to consider its relations with the public, a large part of which blamed business for the unprecedentedly serious depression out of which the country was endeavoring to struggle. Humble, however, was not only subject to this generally critical attitude; it also became the object of a great deal of special criticism because of its price policy and its strong advocacy of the regulation of production, especially in East Texas, where at one time, in the picturesque language of a Texas editor, the company was about as popular as a skunk at a garden party.[19] Although by 1937 the conservation program that Humble had so vigorously supported was regarded with general favor, independent producers and royalty owners still maintained that crude prices were too low. "In our company," commented H. S. Warner of the Industrial Relations Department in 1939, "we have the paradox of a company with excellent employee relations but with regrettably poor public relations." [20]

The principal new development in Humble's public relations in the 1930s and early 1940s was a greater attention to winning the good will of its individual "publics." The method used was to explain the company's actions in the hope that the public would be persuaded of its fairness and effectively inoculated against attacks by politicians, hostile business interests, and labor union representatives. It took Humble some time, however, to learn to anticipate attacks through synchronizing explanatory press releases with actions, such as price cuts, that might call forth hostile reactions. The use of newspaper advertising to explain a price cut of August, 1939, manifested an awareness of the need of such explanation. Humble did not, however, at this time envisage any long-range and continuing program of winning the favorable regard of the public by keeping it informed of the company's policies and operations.

A first, though short, step toward making the management of public relations a specialized staff function came through changes in the president's office late in the 1930s that enabled W. N. Finnegan, Jr., to devote his attention primarily to his public relations duties. Finnegan's group was not elevated to the stature of a department with an administrative committee to give special attention to public relations, but it at least acquired staff status.

A special type of "public" to which Humble management began to give attention late in the 1930s was its stockholders. In common with most other large companies, Humble had assumed that the great majority of the stockholders took little interest in operations as long as they received regular dividends. From 1917 through 1937, consequently, the annual report never consisted of more than two pages, with balance sheet, income account, and earned surplus account; no explanation of the increase in the fixed assets or of the sources of the income was ever presented. Minority stockholders, avid for larger dividends, frequently questioned Humble's policy of "plowing under" most of the profits. Many of those stockholders were residents of Texas, and Humble's stock-purchase plans were making its own employees increasingly numerous among them—in his 1934 report President Blaffer stated that 1,100 employees already constituted 30 per cent of the total number of Humble stockholders and that the 1933 stock-purchase plan would shortly triple the number. The approval of the minority stockholders was consequently of double, even triple, importance from a public relations viewpoint. In 1939, two years after Wiess's accession to the presidency, the annual report became a neat booklet, which presented brief descriptions of the company's condition and its activities for the year as compared with the previous year, and gave the stockholder some insight into the use of the earnings that he was not receiving in the form of dividends.[21]

Although Humble attempted to strengthen its relations with its "publics" in these various ways, its administrators continued to regard the employees as the company's best representatives before the public. Despite their limitations as interpreters of the company, the employees were nevertheless indispensable in that capacity. The company expected them—from directors to rank-and-file employees—to become a part of their communities, to contribute to the Community Chest, and to participate in civic affairs. Humble endeavored to hire men who would worthily represent it in such capacities. Over the years, its employees gained a general reputation for personal uprightness and public spirit that reflected favorably upon the company and went far to make up for the lack of a highly organized public relations program.

Humble continued to believe that its standing with the public was dependent, fundamentally, on its character as a business concern. Obviously, words were important as an aid in developing a better understanding of the whys and wherefores of company action. In the long run, however, the quality of its products and the behavior of management and employees in their various relations were the acid tests of the company's standing before the public. This was a conservative position, but it was an honest one and proved in the long run to be sound.

GENERAL POLICIES AND PROGRAMS

One of the distinctive characteristics of Humble's administration has been its capacity to give attention to details of current operations while at the same time planning effectively for the future. Corporations characteristically envisage an indefinite existence, but to balance the present and the future successfully in planning and operations does not necessarily follow. While Humble executives have always had as a fixed objective the making of annual profits, they also have consciously endeavored so to manage their business as to make it strong for the long run and sufficiently flexible to take advantage of changing opportunities and to meet with success the inevitable vicissitudes of the future.

To understand Humble's operations, it is necessary to recognize this long time-horizon of its top executives. The long-term view affected the company's financial policies, its investments in capital assets, its emphasis on keeping well abreast of developments in science and engineering, its efforts to build a strong employee force, and its interest in conservation.

This long-term viewpoint found particular expression in the 1930s in the company's emphasis on its main interest, production, and on the acquisition of reserves. By 1931 pipeline and storage systems and a refinery had been built which, with minor additions and changes, were considered adequate for years to come. Humble's oil reserves were in no such satisfactory condition. The company's efforts to strengthen its reserve position in the early 1930s, however, were to go far beyond what other comparable concerns seemed at the time to consider necessary or desirable.

Humble's reserve policy was, first of all, to acquire immense reserves of oil in the ground. This meant an active program for obtaining new reserves, with emphasis on the extensive purchase of leases and on improved exploration and development techniques. A long-time reserve policy also made imperative the use of efficient oil-recovery methods. Since this was primarily a matter of science and engineering, Humble continued to extend its knowledge of reservoirs and to apply that knowledge to drilling and production. In order to do this effectively and with the least possible waste of oil and gas, it was necessary to gain the co-operation of other producers in given fields, and this Humble came to believe could be accomplished only through public regulation in the interest of conservation. Public regulation therefore became a principal objective motivating the executives in their strong support of the conservation movement.

An indication of Humble's emphasis on production in general and the acquisition of reserves in particular is provided by its capital expenditures in the years 1931–1941. The company's net investment in fixed assets more than doubled, while its investment in production facilities quadrupled. Of the total amount invested in fixed assets, about 75 per cent went into production, and of that amount about half was spent on acquiring reserves.

There was no significant change in Humble's operating policies in those years, but rather the adjustment of established policies to changing conditions—changes caused by depression, by a nearly chronic condition of overproduction, and by the eventual institution of a system of prorating in Texas. Throughout operations the emphasis was increasingly on efficiency—in the production and handling of oil, in equipment, and in men. A prime tool was science and engineering; a major concern, the reduction of costs.

As in the 1920s, Humble continued to dispose of unprofitable properties, salvaging as much of the investment as possible but in any event cutting losses. It reduced oil storage stocks in 1931 and 1932 at a considerable loss, but also thereby released $5,000,000 for other uses.[22] It cut losses and recovered some capital by selling or abandoning over 300 wells, including those in such once profitable fields as Powell, Mexia, and Orange, for which lifting costs were higher than believed to be warranted by prevailing prices.[23] A great salvage program undertaken to furnish equipment for drilling and production in East Texas was estimated to have saved over $7,000,000.[24]

The company, on the whole, succeeded in maintaining the policy of paying moderate but reasonably stable dividends. After an increase to $2.50 in 1930, dividends were cut back to $2.00 a share in 1931, which amount was paid in the next two years. At the end of 1933 the stock was split three for one, and in 1934 and 1935 a dividend of $1.00 a share was paid, the equivalent of $3.00 on the old shares. The rate was increased to $1.50 in 1936 and $2.00 in 1937, the level at which it remained through 1942. In the 1930s the proportion of the company's net income distributed was increased to about 50 per cent, which was a larger percentage than in the 1920s.

Expansion continued to be financed largely from internal sources, and long-term liabilities were kept low. About half of the net income was plowed back into the business, thus furnishing the major part of the funds for capital expenditures. Large amounts were also supplied by the recovery of capital through depreciation and depletion, and lesser amounts by the sale of crude storage stocks and wells, as noted above. The sale of capital stock brought a relatively small amount. In the years 1931 through 1933 the company paid up debenture bonds for $42,900,000, but in 1934 it borrowed $13,000,000 from banks to help pay for large lease purchases, a loan that was completely repaid by the end of 1935. In 1938, another year of heavy lease expenditures, Humble drew on Standard Oil Company (New Jersey) for $35,000,000 and borrowed $5,000,000 from banks. (See Appendix II, Tables I–VI.)

Such were the changes in Humble's leadership, its administrative organization and practices, and its general policies and programs during the years from 1930 through 1941. They all had one objective: to maintain and strengthen the company's business of producing, transporting, storing, refining, and selling oil and oil products. These various operations will be considered in subsequent chapters, with particular emphasis on adaptations and innovations to meet changing conditions and to take advantage of new opportunities. Humble's top administrators recognized, however, that operations depended to a large extent on the quality and morale of the rank-and-file employee. They consequently made a broad, organized effort to strengthen the company's employee group and to improve its employee relations.

Chapter 15

NEW DEVELOPMENTS IN EMPLOYEE RELATIONS, 1930–1941

IN THE PERIOD from 1930 to America's entry into World War II Humble adopted a positive philosophy of employee relations and developed an organization, techniques, and attitudes that made it effective in operations. This was no sudden development; it had its roots in the character and experience of Humble's founders and in the company's own experiences of the 1920s, as well as in the ideas and example of Jersey Standard. It grew in response to the new conditions and new needs of the 1930s. It was nourished by Texas individualism and by the labor movement of those years. It was guided by the Industrial Relations Office established in 1929.[1]

That organization provides a main thread by which to trace developments in Humble's employee relations in the 1930s. It occupied a special position as a staff group designed to study, to advise, and in general to help. It worked with the members of the Industrial Relations Committee of directors and executives to inform them of conditions and suggest means for improvement, the manager of the Industrial Relations Office serving as secretary of the committee. The office translated general company policy into terms that could be understood by the employees and into practices that could be employed by the managers of operations.

Humble's employee relations in this period can logically be treated as four principal and consecutive developments: setting up a new organization and program; solving employment problems rising out of the depression; meeting the developing need for collective bargaining; and expanding Humble's employee program after the depression.[2]

INAUGURATION OF AN EXPANDED PROGRAM

The industrial relations organization at the beginning of 1930 included the old annuities and benefits office under L. C. Ingram, which administered the company's annuities plan, sickness, accident, and death benefits, group insurance for employees, and employees' vacations, the related Medical Department under Dr. C. M. Aves, the recently added safety division, and the new personnel and training sections. Its head, Charles E. Shaw, had been trained under Jersey Standard's Hicks and Tiedemann and brought to Humble the philosophy and experience of the older company. According to Farish's notice to line employees on January 6, 1930, Shaw was to be "an intermediary between the employees and management."

After a study of Humble's employee activities late in 1929, Shaw had presented the main outlines of an expanded program. In addition to the well-established work of the old sections, he recommended extending safety and medical work, improving employment procedures by means of a centralized clearing house for employee records and ability rating of employees, undertaking an extensive training program including foreman training, and establishing a company-wide publication. Most of these recommendations were put into effect in 1930.

The general character of Humble's safety work was established under the direction of Chief Safety Engineer Roaper with the advice of a central safety committee, of which the head of the Petroleum Engineering Department was chairman. Roaper and his assistants made a detailed study of safety problems throughout all company operations, after which safety inspectors were placed in the different regions. These regional safety men advised managers and supervisors on safety matters, made regular inspections of machines and equipment, attended district safety meetings, held meetings with gangs in the fields, gave first-aid training courses with the assistance of instructors from the Bureau of Mines, helped to investigate the causes of accidents, and collected data to be used in compiling safe-practice pamphlets. The Houston office co-ordinated these activities, examined and distributed safety appliances, and collected and prepared information to promote safety. Roaper himself spent much time in the field, his special function being to win the co-operation of line managers, most of whom disliked this addition to their duties.

Safety was regarded as a line-management responsibility, and a comprehensive organization to promote it was set up within operations. In every district of company operations a safety committee of three men, each serving for three months, was appointed by the superintendent. The committees' main function was to make regular inspections of company properties and to report hazards to the Houston safety office. District safety meetings were held monthly. These meetings discussed safety problems and measures, the emphasis being on individual responsibility. Local safety groups were also organized to hold regular meetings. In 1930, moreover, the practice was initiated in the fields of taking five minutes at the beginning of each tour for the foreman to explain the work of the day and the safety precautions to be taken.

The rank-and-file employees, like the supervisors, were at first apathetic. In traditional Texas oil-field culture, accidents were a part of the day's work and concern for safety was a sign of weakness. Safety measures could not be forced upon the employee, but gross negligence was a cause for terminating employment. The problem was largely to gain interest and voluntary co-operation, and these were the chief objectives of local safety meetings. An early safety chairman in the old Goose Creek district related in later years that, after much discouragement, he began to open safety meetings with prayer and found that the result was a more serious participation in safety discussions. Opening safety meetings with prayer became common in Humble's producing fields, a practice as sincere as it was natural in the Texas way of life.

A report by Shaw in 1932 indicated progress in safety work and also showed that safety meetings were taking on a broad significance as a means both of communication between management and employees and of employee participation in decisions on operating matters. Shaw reported that the monthly "meetings have become similar to the old New England town meetings, and the modern Joint Conferences." Safety matters were discussed and safety rules suggested; these suggestions, together with others obtained from the supervisory force, Shaw reported, "have been accumulated and approved by the Central Safety Committee." By June, 1932, a pamphlet of safety rules for oil-field operations had been prepared, and similar ones were in preparation for pipeline and refinery employees.[3] Thus early was established the principle that rules should be made by the men who were to be most closely affected by them. It became a matter of pride with the men that they were writing their own rules—"Look at that rule," one would say, "*I* wrote that." Other questions affecting the mutual interest of the employees and management were also discussed at the meetings. Training work in the field actually started in these meetings.

The effect of those early safety efforts on accident frequency cannot be measured exactly. Construction, which was then generally attended by a high accident rate, was greatly curtailed after the unusual activity of 1929, particularly in the Baytown refinery and also on pipelines. On the other hand, production in East Texas was being developed, with all the dangers that accompanied the rapid drilling of an uncontrolled field; and reservoir conditions in certain Gulf Coast fields were especially conducive to dangerous blowouts.

The accident rate declined in the early 1930s. The number of disabling injuries per million man-hours of work for the whole Humble organization fell from 44.42 in 1929 to 23.21 in 1930 and 12.74 in 1932. Deaths from injuries decreased from 13 in 1929 to 5 in 1930; but they rose to 9 in 1932, owing principally to blowouts in the Raccoon Bend field. The number of men disabled permanently each year declined from 63 in 1929 to 51 in 1930 and 19 in 1932.

The accident rate in all departments was eventually to be reduced further, but the fundamental principles for achieving the reduction had been established in those few years: official backing, enthusiastic direction, inspection, improved equipment, individual responsibility, and education. It was a far cry from the old Texas slogan, "If you kill a mule you have to buy another, but if you kill a man you can hire another," to Farish's severe reprimand in a letter to Humble's production manager on June 4, 1932, in reference to a fatal accident to a roughneck: "Apparently we are paying too high a price for speed when this type of accident can take place. . . . I am under the impression that this man's life was sacrificed to speed and carelessness. We do not want any more of it."

The new personnel division under Howard S. Warner was expected to help stabilize employment and make hiring, firing, and promotion more intelligently selective. Humble had early adopted the policy of promoting from within—a logical result of the annuities and benefits program—but it had never set up any formal standards or system for promotions, and its hit-or-miss employment methods had not brought the best results so far as the quality of employees was concerned. These weaknesses Shaw and Warner attacked, but they had hardly got the work under way when they had to turn to the employment problems caused by the depression.

Two new practices were inaugurated at this time to help strengthen the interest of employees in making a career with Humble. Special recognition of long service was begun in 1930 by awarding a button at the end of every ten-year period of employment.[4] The same year a Coin-Your-Ideas Plan similar to Jersey Standard's was put into effect. This plan offered to Humble employees monetary awards for practical suggestions on how to increase operating efficiency. Local committees throughout operations submitted the suggestions of individual employees to a central committee consisting of the industrial relations manager as chairman, the manager of the three major operating departments, and the head of the training department.[5]

A special staff to guide and co-ordinate the development of an expanded training program was a logical outcome of both the general objective to improve the quality of the employees and the policy of promoting from within. Humble's typical skilled or semiskilled employee had generally learned his work on the job, usually by beginning in a labor gang presided over by a skilled craftsman or workman, watching his methods, showing intelligence and willingness, being promoted to helper, and so progressing upward. The need for specialized training had been recognized to some extent earlier and a few courses had been given, particularly at Baytown, but a more systematic and comprehensive program was needed.

Although training was considered a responsibility of management, Thomas W. Moore was given the task of developing a training program.[6] His function, as he saw it, was not to plan a comprehensive set of courses but rather to help to arrange for training whenever demand or need arose or opportunity presented itself. Believing that training could not succeed unless the operating staff was in accord with the program, he moved only when he felt that the co-operation of managers and employees was assured.

The training section was organized in the spring of 1930, and in that year and the next the work got well under way. The courses were given mostly outside working hours and without charge to the employees. Participation by employees was voluntary. The instructors were regular company employees, who were paid moderate fees for the extra work.

The first course was given for student engineers hired in 1929 and 1930, one section for refinery engineers and another for geologists, geophysicists, and petroleum engineers. The work consisted of a short period of formal study, followed by a series of jobs accompanied by the study of assigned materials and the writing of reports. A request from the geophysicists for instruction in structural geology led to a course with an enrollment of 266 men, of whom 75 per cent completed the work. Other special courses were also designed for technical personnel at Baytown and elsewhere. Courses were also given at Baytown for nontechnical employees, covering such a wide range of subjects as refinery processes, trade mathematics, pipe fitting, electricity, machine-shop practices, blueprint reading, and foremanship. Evening courses for Houston office employees and supervisors, started in October, 1930, included business English, public speaking, business arithmetic, bookkeeping, accounting, mathematics for engineers, refinery operations, and a general outline of the petroleum industry.

Sales training took several forms. District and local managers were given short, intensive training at Baytown in products and in company service-station policies. Training in the field consisted almost entirely of a series of district lectures. Classes in automobile lubrication were held in conjunction with the vocational department of the Houston Public Schools. A *Service Station Manual*, prepared jointly by the training section and the Sales Department, became available in 1931.

Courses were not offered in the producing fields because the employees were so widely scattered, but at the request of the Production Department a series of lectures was prepared for trial use in the Gulf Coast division. These lectures were on such topics as the geology of oil fields, the theory of oil emulsions, methods of lifting oil, principles of the orifice meter, and lubrication of equipment.

The depression ended many of the courses and generally impeded the expansion of the training program. In the summer of 1932 Industrial Relations Manager Shaw commented:[7]

> I personally believe that the advent of the five-day week gives Management an additional responsibility for providing its employees with an opportunity for personal development which should be mutually profitable to the Company and the employee. If, as expressed by Mr. Farish, the greatest asset of the company is its personnel and our training program can increase the effectiveness of our personnel one per cent, we have added considerably to the assets of the Company.

By then, however, the major interest of the industrial relations organization had shifted to employment problems brought by the depression. Most of the new activities were continued, although less actively, but the realization of the comprehensive program planned in 1929 and 1930 had to be postponed.

DEPRESSION AND THE DEVELOPMENT OF A PERSONNEL PROGRAM

The depression began to affect Humble seriously late in 1930. Although hope still persisted that the difficulty would be of short duration, the Humble board adopted a carefully formulated employment and layoff policy similar to that of Jersey Standard.[8] The primary objective of the intelligent and constructive program adopted late in 1930 was to deal with surplus labor in such a way as to minimize the loss to Humble and the hardship to employees.

The program aimed to minimize layoffs and to dismiss older and efficient employees as a last resort. It provided, first, for the elimination of overtime work and contract labor, the transfer of employees from slack to busy departments, and the undertaking of maintenance and repair work. Whatever surplus labor remained was to be laid off as follows: first, employees of less than a year's service, unless of conspicuous ability; next, substandard employees of more than one but less than ten years of service. If the dismissal of those two groups did not take care of the surplus, part-time work was the next possibility. If these measures proved inadequate, unusually capable employees of more than one year's service would be granted severance allowances and laid off or, if eligible for annuity, retired.

In April, 1931, however, on Shaw's recommendation, an ability-rating system, similar to Jersey Standard's, superseded the seniority provisions in the above employment program, its objective being to help evaluate men where transfers or layoffs were necessary. Supervisors were required to divide their subordinates semiannually into an outstanding 10 per cent, a loyal and efficient 65 per cent, and a questionable 25 per cent who would be the first to be laid off. The employees became bitterly hostile to this system, especially at Baytown, and some supervisors, particularly on the pipelines, disliked it, but Farish supported it strongly. Its obvious weakness, which its sponsor later recognized, was that it was so coldly mathematical and was applied to such small groups that one supervisor's lowest 25 per cent could easily overlap in efficiency another's middle 65 per cent, with the result that some of the employees laid off would be more desirable to retain than others who were kept.

Every effort was made, however, to hold dismissals to a minimum. Humble in its region spearheaded the national share-the-work movement. The eight-hour day, which it had put into effect on January 15, 1930, enabled the company to get through the year without a great reduction in personnel. During the depression years other cuts reduced the work week in various departments from forty-eight, to forty, to thirty-two hours, until for a couple of months early in 1933 the Mechanical Department at Baytown was down to twenty-four hours. The Petroleum Code, under the National Industrial Recovery Administration, effective January 1, 1933, stabilized the work week throughout the oil industry at an average of thirty-six hours in all departments except for clerical and technical employees, who were limited to forty hours. The hours of Humble office workers, including executives, had on July 1, 1932, been cut from forty-four to forty, with a corresponding salary reduction. These work weeks remained standard until 1941.[9]

Humble's early handling of this problem of surplus labor was, on the whole, successful. Employees were consulted as far as possible, particularly in the Baytown refinery's Joint Conference, which proved a useful medium for discussing depression problems with employee representatives. The employees generally approved of the share-the-work program —even though it was accompanied by a decrease in total earnings, though not in average hourly rates—as an alternative to even more extensive layoffs. Humble's program also favorably impressed the public as a contrast to the numerous reported instances of operators instituting layoffs while clinging tenaciously to a twelve-hour day and seven-day week.[10] In the summer of 1932, for example, the Atlantic and Humble were the only oil companies in Texas not reporting some employees working eighty-four hours a week. D. B. Harris believed that the share-the-work program did more to change the current hostility of East Texans toward Humble than anything else that could have been done.

The cut in weekly hours reduced take-home pay; the next question was whether or not to reduce salary and wage schedules. At the time when Humble began to consider reductions, smaller oil companies and operators, as well as such major companies as Sinclair and Texas, had cut their schedules; but Shell had reduced salaries only, and Sun, Gulf, and Magnolia had not changed their base rates. Farish and Suman were in agreement that the interests of morale forbade a cut in production wage rates. Suman maintained that "the working man in the field" had "borne the brunt of the depression."

Wiess's attitude was different. He believed that every tub should stand on its own bottom, and both refining and sales were taking a severe beating from the depression. Sales Department commissions and salaries were severely cut, as was the pay of certain salaried refining groups, particularly in the research division. Shaw was strongly opposed to cuts in the hourly wage rates, which were also seriously considered. No general reduction was put into effect, although the wage rates for a limited number of Baytown refinery men in certain classifications—including a cut in the wage rate of white unskilled laborers from 50 cents to 40 cents per hour—were reduced to bring Humble's rates more in line with the rates of other refineries. Unskilled labor and the technical group were presumably singled out for pay cuts because of the abundance of such employees for the amount of work then being done. These cuts, which were exceptional in a generally enlightened and generous program, had serious repercussions. The Baytown laboratory subsequently became a center of union agitation.

A by-product of the discussion of salary rates was the organization in 1932 of the Classification Committee, consisting of the comptrollers of the two Humble companies and the industrial relations manager. Suman had been influential in bringing about the establishment of uniform wage rates in 1927, but salaries had continued to depend largely on the department heads' generosity and Treasurer Blaffer's approval—under the general oversight of a salary committee of the Board of Directors instituted in 1924. The Classification Committee, working with department managers, analyzed every salaried position outside the special rolls, grouped them, compared the salaries with those of competitors, and recommended corrections of numerous inequities. The initiative for this move is said to have come from Farish, who was shocked by the disparities that he had discovered, but the need for a more systematic handling of salaries was also then being recognized by Jersey Standard and, indeed, by business in general.

The reduction in the average annual earnings of Humble employees, as a result of the share-the-work policy and the wage-rate cuts, amounted in some categories to only 17 per cent, from $1,903 in 1929 to about $1,580 in 1932 and 1933. Average earnings in the Refining Department declined about 20 per cent—from $1,680 to $1,348. In the Production Department, however, they declined from $2,216 in 1929 to $1,592 in 1933, a reduction of 28 per cent—the long hours which many production employees had worked in 1929 explained the greater reduction in production earnings. The reduction in take-home pay was, of course, accompanied by a decline in the cost of living, which between 1929 and 1933 amounted to approximately 25 per cent. On the average, therefore, it could be said that Humble employees received more purchasing power in the form of wages during this depression period—and for shorter hours per week—than during the prosperous 1920s. But the "average" employee is a fictitious character; common labor in the refinery, mostly because of shorter hours, had suffered cuts in take-home pay ranging from 40 to 60 per cent, which was a serious reduction in earnings that probably were barely at the subsistence level.[11]

Despite its share-the-work policy, Humble had to reduce the number of its employees. The total was reduced from 12,548 at the end of 1929 to 9,944 at the end of 1930; the lowest year-end point was in 1931, when the total stood at 8,988, but the decline continued into 1932. (See Appendix II, Table VII.) Some of this reduction, of course, was the result of normal and voluntary terminations without replacements, and departments varied widely in the degree to which they were affected. The number of sales employees was actually increased. The pipeline company in 1930 dismissed only about 15 per cent, largely temporary construction workers. The Production Department reduced its employees even less, its superintendents being ordered merely to "weed out lazy, indifferent, indolent, or disloyal men."[12] The Refining Department had the largest percentage of dismissals; the number of its employees was reduced from 6,087 at the end of 1929 to 3,854 at year's end in 1930, followed by a steady decline to a low of 2,744 at the end of 1933.

There were special reasons for the severe cuts in refinery employment. The decline in the demand for products reduced process work, and the abandonment of the hydrogenation project ended research in hydrogenation. In the research division the number of nontechnical helpers was reduced, their work being done largely by the technical men themselves. The greatest reduction, however, came from the dismissal of construction workers. The total number of refinery employees had risen from about 4,000 at the end of 1928 to about 6,000 at the end of 1929, mostly for construction work. The abandonment of the hydrogenation building project and the completion of other construction accounted for the larger part of the dismissals in 1930. Native white labor gangs and Negro and Mexican laborers, who had been doing the heavy and unskilled work of refinery construction, consequently suffered the most.

Humble at this time made a significant change in its handling of surplus labor. Previously, for example, when the company had had surplus employees in a field, it had simply laid them off, even though operations in other fields needed more men; transferring men from one department to another was nearly unheard of. But in 1931 and thereafter, the Personnel Department helped to transfer to East Texas not merely production men but even several hundred surplus refinery men. The uncontrolled East Texas field, which was such a problem for Humble management, in this respect proved an unmitigated blessing to the employees, though many grumbled over transfer. In 1932 the opening of new Gulf Coast fields further eased the situation.

Maintenance and repair work was also a part of Humble's depression program, as of Jersey Standard's, but the Humble Refining Department's application of this method of employing surplus labor proved unfortunate although well intentioned. In March and April, 1933, several hundred surplus Baytown employees were put to work at painting, cleaning, repairing, and pipeline-protection work—valuable activities but not immediately necessary—at 25 cents an hour for a forty-hour week. These relief workers continued to rate as regular employees and thus as eligible for benefits. The surplus men were glad at the time to get work at any wages rather than be laid off; but they also felt somewhat humiliated, and they subsequently remembered the "two-bit gang" with resentment.[13] They reasoned retrospectively that, if the relief work was worth doing at all, it should have been worth the normal wages, particularly in view of the fact that, although the Refining Department had suffered a loss in 1931, it had earned fair profits in 1932. Whatever the justification for this later attitude, both Charles E. Shaw, then industrial relations manager, and Robert C. Oliver, who became the leader of the union movement at Baytown, in recent conversation expressed the belief that an interest in unionism at Baytown began with the "two-bit gang."

Humble's executives learned several lessons from their experience with surplus employees at this time. They learned that the hiring of a large number of temporary workers for construction might bring serious problems; partly for this reason they thereafter followed the policy of having most of Humble's construction work done by contractors. Their unfortunate experience at Baytown also taught them that relief work at low pay might be very costly in morale. Finally, the transfer of employees and subsequent complaints about the poor quality of many of them demonstrated the need for higher employment standards.

The depression also brought a re-examination of Humble's benefit plans. In some cases the result was a liberalization, which was particularly welcome when decreased hours were cutting into family reserves. The maximum free death benefits were increased. Wage earners were given the privilege of accident benefits and, if they had three years of service, of sickness benefits also, beginning with the first day of disability—advantages that salaried employees had long enjoyed.[14]

The annuity program also was revised. One change provided that employees contribute part of the total cost formerly borne by the company. In 1930 the company had only one annuitant, but it was feared that, as a greater number reached retirement age, the payments would prove too severe a burden. Consequently, for service after January 1, 1932, the company provided only half as much annuity credit as formerly, but an employee could maintain the previous annuity rate by contributing the other half. In December, 1930, retirement at the age of seventy was made compulsory, and in May, 1933, special consideration in regard to annuities was granted to those willing to retire at sixty.[15]

In the summer of 1935 the federal Social Security Act brought to an end the old annuity plan and also the even older stock-purchase plan; a new annuity and thrift plan was substituted for them as of January 1, 1936. All employees who had one or more years of continuous active service with Humble were eligible to participate. The employee could contribute from 3 to 13 per cent of his compensation, to which the company added a regular contribution of dollar for dollar on the first 3 per cent and 50 cents on the dollar after 3 and up to 13 per cent. The company might also choose to make additional contributions to the fund and consistently did so.

Under this new system a specified minimum proportion of the total contributions went to the purchase of group annuities to supplement the Social Security pension. Since this was a thrift as well as an annuity plan, a part of the remainder could be used at the participant's option to purchase Humble stock or insurance, and a part could be withdrawn periodically. The new annuity plan lacked the uncertainty of the old one, which was based on compensation during the five years preceding retirement, and it was also less costly to the company. For the employees it had the added advantage that their annuity rights were no longer dependent upon their staying with the company until they retired.

The record of a low-salaried wage earner, who resigned when research on the history of Humble's Annuity and Thrift Fund was in progress in 1952, illustrates what the thrift feature of the plan could mean to an employee. This particular man, who had been employed by the company continuously from 1928, entered the new Annuity and Thrift Fund on January 1, 1936, and continued to participate at the highest rate allowed under that plan and its revision of 1946. He allocated all of his and the company's contribution, beyond the required payments to the pension fund, to the purchase of Humble stock. When he entered the Thrift Fund, he was a derrickman at an hourly rate of 90 cents; by transfers and promotions he rose to the position of pumper helper first class in the Baytown refinery with an hourly rate of $2.21, which were his classification and rate at the time he left the company. Converted to a monthly basis, his highest rate of pay from 1936 to 1952 never exceeded $383 per month. His total contribution to the Thrift Fund during those years amounted to $4,720; he withdrew during his participation $50 in cash and nine shares of stock which, because of two stock splits, would have represented thirty-six shares if left in the fund. At the termination of his employment, this employee's settlement consisted of $150 in cash and 421 shares of Humble stock having a current market value of approximately $31,700.

Humble's other depression-inspired employee welfare measures included reduction of rent on company houses at Baytown and deferment of payments on company-financed houses.[16] The company, moreover, furnished prepared land and seed for employee gardens and provided canning facilities at Baytown and in company camps.[17] Employees were also enabled to buy Humble products on credit and at a substantial discount.[18]

Humble's official actions to cushion the impact of the depression do not tell the whole story. Perhaps even better remembered are the private loans and benefactions of company officials to employees faced with the loss of their homes or the sacrifice of company stock. R. L. Blaffer proved in this emergency to be as generous with his own money as he was careful of the company's.[19] Wiess, in his more discriminating and reserved fashion, was equally, if not more, helpful, and other high executives—Farish in particular—likewise were generous in their assistance.[20]

Gradually the downtrend was reversed. An upswing in employment in 1933 came principally from an increase in the number of production employees to the highest point yet attained. But refinery employment continued to decline, and average annual earnings fell off. During 1934, however, improvements took place in all categories and in all respects. In May, 1934, when Harold L. Ickes, Petroleum Administrator under the National Industrial Recovery Act, ordered the adjustment of the skilled workers' compensation to the 1929 purchasing power, Humble readily complied; it also granted Baytown's mechanical workers forty hours' pay for thirty-six hours of work.[21] Production and mechanical employees later received a raise in take-home pay as a result of increased weekly hours, while pipeline and refinery process employees were given a bonus in order that their pay would remain the same despite reduced hours. A general 5 per cent cost-of-living allowance on June 1, 1935, brought the average Humble employee's real wage up to a little more than that of the predepression period—and for thirty-six hours a week instead of from forty-eight to seventy-two.[22] The average number of employees in 1935 was only two hundred less than in 1929, with a much smaller percentage of temporary employees. The Humble employees seem by 1935 to have been well over the hump of the depression.

Humble's young Industrial Relations Office should be given recognition for its part in cushioning the impact of the depression on the employees. Shaw, on principle, stood for as generous treatment of them as possible, and he had the support of most of the directors. The personnel section handled transfers and dismissals with a degree of order and an intelligence that contributed to minimizing the loss to both company and employee. This department also helped to prepare the company for the negotiations that later led to the establishment of collective bargaining between the company and its employees.

COLLECTIVE BARGAINING: JOINT CONFERENCE, EMPLOYEES FEDERATION, OR CIO?

While Humble was struggling with the employment problems of the depression, a national movement to organize workers that was itself a product of the depression and the resultant New Deal Administration was getting under way. During the middle 1930s, the company was intermittently involved in a struggle with an oil workers' union that strove to win recognition as the bargaining agency for Humble employees and in 1936 brought the company to the verge of a strike. Out of this struggle and other depression developments came genuine collective bargaining throughout Humble's operations. This was bound to come sooner or later, but the issue was what agency the employees would choose to represent them.

This development commands attention for several reasons. It brought a fundamental change in Humble's relations with employees. It meant to the Oil Workers International Union (CIO) not only failure to obtain recognition as the bargaining agency for the employees of one important company, but also the more significant failure to breach the traditional opposition of Jersey Standard and its affiliates to "outside" unions. And it provides a meaningful example of action and reaction on the part of one union and one company management in a movement of tremendous importance to American labor, business, and the public in general.

The issue originated in Baytown and was confined largely to that refinery. That such a controversy should have originated in the refinery may be explained by the general industrial situation and the special conditions prevailing within Humble. Unionism had in the past made little progress among drillers, production men, and pipeliners, who worked in scattered small groups or alone and who were generally highly individualistic. Craft unions of the American Federation of Labor, however, had had considerable success among the skilled workers in refineries. Refineries, furthermore, were more exposed to union influence because they were usually located in or near industrial centers and, perhaps most important, they had large, concentrated employee groups, as contrasted with the employees in the great open spaces where pipeliners, drillers, and production men worked.

Aside from this general situation, some of Baytown's employees had recently acquired enough of a sense of grievance to make them susceptible to the idea of unionism. For nearly a decade after the construction of the refinery, refining was generally profitable and the Baytown workers had little reason for complaint; if an individual was dissatisfied, he could find work in some other large refinery in the vicinity. The depression changed the situation. At first the Baytown employees accepted layoffs as inevitable and appreciated the share-the-work program. Their only serious grievance was the substantial de-emphasis on seniority as a factor in determining the sequence of layoffs and the substitution of an ability-rating system which, they argued, was unrealistic and gave undue authority to the individual foreman. An important factor, also, was the rise of a feeling that refinery employees were discriminated against as compared with those in other departments; since the company as a whole continued to make profits during the depression, the argument that the refinery had to reduce costs because it was financially in the red or making small profits did not appeal to them. The climax came in March, 1933, shortly after the Mechanical Department's work week had been reduced to twenty-four hours and several hundred surplus employees at Baytown were, as an alternative to dismissal, organized into a special labor gang at 25 cents per hour.

However glad still to have even a small weekly pay and to retain their privileges as employees, these men, many of whom were skilled, felt humiliated at their demotion and were a disturbing example to other employees.

Section 7(a) of the National Industrial Recovery Act of June, 1933, which provided that employees should "have the right to organize and bargain collectively through representatives of their own choosing," indicated how grievances could be translated into action. The NRA, with its industrial codes and its announcement that the federal government stood ready to protect workers who wished to organize for bargaining purposes, strongly suggested to discontented employees that they should look for relief to the government and to labor unions rather than to their employers.[23]

In the meantime, the emerging national labor movement lent force to Shaw's persistent urging upon Humble's directors and high executives, from the time he came to the company, that the system of employee representation should be extended and made a more vital part of the company's relations with its employees. Management had earlier considered the system neither useful nor practicable for small refineries or scattered pipeline and producing operations. Now, however, it decided to extend the system, and elections for employee representatives were immediately held in the Production Department, small refineries, and Humble Pipe Line Company. Nearly 90 per cent of the employees voted. The first Humble Joint Conference outside Baytown was held early in July, 1933.[24]

Improvement in the effectiveness of the old Baytown Joint Conference also became an obvious need. Powell, who for thirteen years had been its chairman ex officio, was an excellent superintendent of the old school, who ruled with an iron but impartial hand, administered discipline severely but impersonally, and, despite his harshness, was on the whole popular with the employees. However, the idea of free give-and-take between manager and employee, even across a joint conference table, was apparently entirely foreign to his temperament and training, as it probably was to most superintendents of his generation. He had treated the Joint Conference principally as a means by which he could dispense praise, censure, exhortation, warning, and information, and through which minor complaints and suggestions could be respectfully presented and decisively dealt with.[25] As such, the Joint Conference had undoubted value, but it did not mean "giving workers . . . a needed voice . . . in matters vitally affecting their interests," as Clarence J. Hicks had envisaged.[26]

The first threat of a challenge to the Baytown management's existing relations with employees came late in 1933 when an oil workers' union made its appearance. Superintendent Powell and Industrial Relations Manager Shaw took the position that the Joint Conference was more useful to the employees than representation by outsiders could be. Although neither in so many words opposed union membership, Powell warned that, if the employees joined the union, they would risk working for wages lower than their current scale, adding that the company might then also be "forced to withdraw the various benefits of the A & B Plan . . . such as vacations, sick pay, etc." [27]

Late in 1933 and throughout 1934 management put into effect a series of changes intended to strengthen the Baytown Joint Conference. In December, 1933, elections were taken out of the hands of departmental foremen and entrusted to representatives who were not running for re-election; voting by 81 per cent of the eligible voters resulted in the election of new men in all divisions. Management even suggested that the chairman be elected, but the conference voted down a change that they believed would widen the gap between themselves and management. In June, 1934, management's suggestion that an arbitration board be established was unanimously accepted. In December, conference minutes began to be signed jointly by an employee representative and a management representative instead of, as before, by Powell and a company representative.

The Joint Conference representatives reciprocated by a readiness to act independently. One new laboratory representative, Robert C. Oliver, began to show his independence early in 1934 at the first meeting he attended. Oliver, a member of the Baytown research division, was an enthusiastic and somewhat idealistic East Texan of twenty-five years of age who, after two years in the New Mexico Military Institute and two at The University of Texas, had gone to work in the Baytown Development Department in 1929.[28] This department soon suffered salary cuts, and many laboratory employees felt that they were in a blind alley. The "two-bit gang" and knowledge that the company as a whole was making profits later contributed to Oliver's dissatisfaction. He himself applied for work in the Sales Department, but that department was laying off men at the time. Oliver participated vigorously in the first Joint Conference he attended and left the meeting something of a hero.

The principal issue discussed was wages. The mechanical workers wanted a bonus. A management representative declared that Humble's large profits and the increased cost of living would justify revoking the 1932 cut. Wiess replied that the company's average rates were equal or superior to those of other companies and that Humble could not introduce the cost-of-living factor into its wage policy—compensation, he said, should depend on individual merit. He added, however, that the Board of

Directors would consider divisional adjustments. Oliver thereupon challenged the "prevailing wage" policy, defending the view that living costs and company profits should be considered. Powell replied that labor, like sugar, was worth just what you had to pay for it.[29]

Whether because of the growing strength of the Joint Conference or improvement in Baytown's profits as the depression subsided, or both, increases were soon made in refinery wages. Although salaries were left on an individual basis, Mechanical Department employees, including the unskilled laborers, were granted time and a half for overtime; those receiving less than a dollar an hour were given pay increases. Process employees were put on new hourly rates incorporating their temporary 11 per cent bonus.

The Baytown Joint Conference after this encouraging beginning became more active. In April, 1934, management acceded to Oliver's proposal that the elected representatives be permitted to caucus outside the conference. Both elected and company representatives bitterly denounced Shaw's ability-comparison sheets as too complicated and too much affected by personalities; six months later the ratings were suspended. Elected representatives assailed, though ineffectively, the use of low-paid contract labor. For the first time the Joint Conference voted to meet during the summer.

An important change was Powell's stepping down, officially because of ill health, from his chairmanship of the Joint Conference. He was succeeded on January 1, 1935, by the newly appointed Baytown superintendent, quietly forceful and diplomatic Gordon L. Farned, who during his seven years' superintendency at the Ingleside refinery had won a reputation for good relations with the working force—the "Little Boss," who, they said, got along well with the employees without trying.[30]

In the meantime important developments had been taking place on the union front. Early in 1934 Houston Local 227 organized an East Harris County branch covering the Baytown area. Bob Oliver, the youthfully impatient Joint Conference representative, became a member and was elected vice-president. An offer of the long-hoped-for better job in the Humble Sales Department came too late,[31] and in July, 1934, he left Humble to serve as full-time president of a separately chartered Local 333, International Association of Oil Field, Gas Well, and Refinery Workers (AFL), covering workers in the Baytown, Goose Creek, and Barbers Hill communities and claiming a membership of 1,600 refinery, production, and service-station workers.[32] In April, Local 316 had been chartered at the Ingleside refinery under the leadership of Henry W. Wier, a process-shift foreman in Humble's refinery; by June it had signed up about a hundred of 340 Humble employees.

Local 333 almost immediately requested recognition as a bargaining agency for the Baytown refinery. To the local's repeated and unsubstantiated claims that a majority of Baytown employees had chosen it as their collective bargaining agency and to its request that it should therefore be "recognized as the sole agency of collective bargaining in the Baytown Refinery" and that the Joint Conference should be discontinued, Humble management remained obdurate. It maintained that, even if a majority of the Baytown workers were members of the local, this fact would not entitle the union to represent employees who preferred another bargaining agency or wished to bargain individually.

The beginnings of organized and active unionism among Humble employees coincided with the appearance of a new industrial relations manager. Shaw, who had accepted a position as assistant industrial relations manager with Jersey, recommended as his successor David B. Harris, the original first choice for the post. Shaw's resignation and Harris' appointment were announced in June, 1934. That the man who had largely been responsible for the establishment of an effective industrial relations department, as well as for employee policies that had enabled Humble to solve its depression problems with comparatively little friction, should leave at the very time that the challenge of unionism began to appear might well have seemed untimely. Harris, however, proved to be a fortunate choice. Although he was without formal training in industrial relations, he had gained a varied experience in handling men as a captain in the United States Army in World War I and during many years in the producing fields as a division superintendent. In several producing divisions he had lived in bunkhouses with the men and had come to have a close acquaintance with them. He had a reputation for never asking a man to do anything he had not done himself or would not do, and the men had confidence in him and believed he had their interests genuinely at heart.[33]

For several years thereafter, the Baytown local strove to obtain a contract with Humble; the struggle went on with increasing tension and heat on both sides until an explosion occurred late in the summer of 1936. As so often in such controversies at that time, neither group had a sympathetic understanding of the other's position. Humble's directors and executives were not well acquainted with the labor movement, and unionism was new to the members of Local 333.

These Humble men then shared with American management generally a strong dislike for negotiating with employees except as individuals, or at the most through such organizations as a joint conference or an independent union of company employees. They took legitimate pride in Humble's progressive industrial relations in such matters as insurance, pensions, vacations, and wages. They wanted to be fair and even generous to all employees and believed that they had been, but regarded themselves as the only proper judges of what constituted fairness and generosity. They had firm views concerning the prerogatives of management, which included the right to decide who was to be paid how much and who was to be promoted, demoted, hired, or fired.

The attitude of management was intensified in President Blaffer and Executive Vice-President Wiess by the fact that they were among the organizers and founders of Humble; it was *their* company in a special sense. They felt that they had always tried to do right by their employees, and when their good intentions were questioned they were hurt and angered. Criticism from within the "Humble family" was bad enough, but for the company employees to call in outsiders seemed to them to involve deep disloyalty and gross ingratitude. Many Humble executives and supervisors who had risen from the ranks also felt an intense love and loyalty for the company that had given them their opportunities; they found it difficult to believe in the sincerity of employees whose attitude was different and they resented having to deal with them.

Many Baytown and Ingleside employees, on the other hand, had lost their earlier sense of security and satisfaction in their jobs. They shared a feeling of apprehension and resentment, which Local 333 embodied and encouraged, and they were aware of the improvements in hours and wages brought about by the Petroleum Code under the NRA. Hundreds of them, therefore—like thousands of industrial workers in Texas and countless others throughout the United States—began to look to the union and the federal government for help. Thus a historic change in American labor made itself felt in Humble.

That hundreds of Baytown and Ingleside employees were drawn to the oil workers' union may be less surprising than that more hundreds resisted its attraction. It is a testimony to the effectiveness of Humble's employee relations over nearly twenty years and to the recent accomplishments of the Joint Conference that, although other refineries on all sides were negotiating union contracts, the union local at Humble's Baytown refinery never became more than an aggressive minority. Had either of those factors been lacking, it can hardly be doubted that Baytown would eventually, like Shell's, Sinclair's, and other neighboring refineries, have accepted the Oil Workers International Union as its principal bargaining agency.

Humble management did not refuse to deal with the union and even affirmed a willingness to recognize it as a bargaining agency for its members. They asserted, however, that, since their company was not engaged in interstate commerce, the Wagner Act, which took the place of the labor code under the NRA, did not apply.[34] They tried to have as little to do with the union as possible. The management was desperately opposed to anything savoring of the "closed shop," both as an infringement on its prerogatives to hire and fire and as an impairment of the employees' freedom; any contract with a union was regarded as a step toward a closed shop. Accordingly, although plant superintendents were willing to discuss individual grievances, policy-making company representatives avoided discussion of such general matters as seniority rules and blanket pay increases. This was far from satisfying to the union, but, when late in 1935 Local 333 charged Humble with maintaining a company union and interfering with the right of its employees to bargain collectively, the regional chairman of the National Labor Relations Board found for the company.[35]

The struggle at Baytown and Ingleside was not solely between management and union locals; it was triangular, involving as it did the Joint Conference. Anxious to get as much as possible for those whom it represented and spurred on by the necessity of bidding against the union for employee support, the conference was frequently in agreement with what the union wanted to obtain from management and requested more in the way of higher wages, increased benefits, and longer vacations than the company was willing to concede. Management, however, usually granted at least a part of the conference's requests. The situation was complicated by the fact that some Joint Conference representatives were union members or sympathizers.

The Baytown Joint Conference continued to gain strength, both in opposition to Local 333 and in its emerging role as a collective-bargaining agency. The impatient young Local 333 weakened itself by ordering its members to boycott the conference, which brought the resignation from the union of several Joint Conference members. In April, 1935, the Baytown Joint Conference demanded a cost-of-living increase—which the Production Department had already requested and been refused. Wiess offered a limited and conditional 5 per cent bonus, an offer which the Humble board late in May extended to all Humble wage earners. Other Joint Conferences accepted the offer immediately, but the Baytown conference accepted it only on condition that the minimum monthly bonus be $5.00. This general bonus strengthened the Baytown Joint Conference's position and was a blow to union prestige.

The growth in the strength of the Baytown Joint Conference came at the very time when the federal government's support of unionism was weakening. The Schechter decision of the United States Supreme Court in May, 1935, invalidated the National Industrial Recovery Act and left the unions without government protection. The Wagner Act, which was intended to replace Section 7(a) of the NRA and became law in July, was immediately attacked as unconstitutional and did not become effective for nearly two years. The general situation of unionism, particularly the oil workers' union, showed no improvement during 1935 and 1936. Late in the summer of 1936 the oil workers' union was, nationally, on the decline; it was one of the unions supporting John L. Lewis in his projected drive for industrial unionization that were expelled from the craft-dominated AFL.[36]

Bob Oliver and Local 333, nevertheless, selected this time for a determined effort to obtain a contract with Humble.[37] The local situation, in contrast with the national, was, indeed, rather propitious. The cost of living was still on the upgrade. Subsequent to wage increases by Sinclair and Pure Oil, Humble had absorbed the previous year's 5 per cent bonus into the base pay, but, unfortunately, many employees were under the impression that the company had agreed to pay both the "prevailing wage" and the bonus.

Local 333 got its campaign off to a bad start with a piece of seeming discourtesy which reacted against it. Oliver, who later claimed that he had unavailingly tried to arrange a conference with Humble officials, addressed to John L. Finley, general superintendent of Humble refineries, a letter which appeared in the Houston *Chronicle* before it reached the company. In this letter he made demands for wage increases and recognition of seniority in promotions, demotions, transfers, and layoffs which evidenced a shrewd recognition of sensitive points at Baytown.

In his reply Finley asserted that the weighted average annual earnings of Humble refinery employees were more than $1,500, or approximately 80 cents an hour. No wage increases, he went on, could be granted, since the prevailing rates were already being paid. Seniority would govern only between men of equal capabilities. Finally, Humble would make no agreement that would require its employees to belong to a union or "pay tribute for the right to work." [38]

A conference between representatives of union and management was finally scheduled for September 4, 1936, after Oliver had requested a conciliator from the regional director of the National Labor Relations Board. The day before the conference, Wiess released to the Baytown employees a circular letter denouncing the movement to organize the oil industry as "a political move where a small group seeks to dominate and impose its will upon all of us." The letter further stated: "The success of efforts of this kind is dependent upon coercion. . . . This insidious force can best be combatted by the resistance of the employees themselves. . . . The company will stand behind you with all possible support."

Neither of the two highest refining executives, Wiess and Giraud, was present at the conference, and the discussion was conducted principally by Harris. The union claimed that, while Baytown was paying wages as good as or better than other refineries for similar work, the lower categories were not receiving a living wage and the company could afford higher wages and should share its substantial earnings with the employees. Management's views were that the company had done all that could be expected if the wages were as high as Shell's and Sinclair's, no matter how low the wages might be in terms of living costs, and that with higher wages it could not meet competition. Humble had met Sinclair's recently increased wages, but it refused to yield to the union demand that it take the lead in a new wage increase.

Convinced that further negotiations would be fruitless, Oliver suddenly called a strike vote at Baytown, which he claimed resulted in 787 votes for a strike to 57 against. He later admitted that the strike threat was a bluff intended to scare the company. The strike was set for September 19, to give opportunity for further negotiations, and Oliver requested mediation from the Department of Labor.

The Joint Conference's elected representatives immediately began to circulate an antistrike petition, which was given impetus by an episode on September 12. Among the unions that had offered support to Local 333 was the International Longshoremen's Association, in which Negroes were strongly represented. A few jitney loads of Negro longshoremen, with their cotton hooks—the tools of their trade—stuck into their back pockets, arrived at Baytown late that afternoon to attend a union mass meeting and proceeded to the Negro section of town. In a short time the impression was created that Negroes, brandishing cotton hooks, had paraded all through town in an attempt to terrorize white employees.

Oliver now waved a torch in front of an open powder magazine. He announced: "Our great fear is destruction of property. Some hothead outside the union who has a grudge against the company might fill a sewer full of casinghead gas, drop a match in it, and there would be no more refinery."[39] This provocative statement further alienated a local sentiment that up to the strike vote had on the whole not been unsympathetic with the union.

The businessmen of Baytown and neighboring Goose Creek and Pelly, alarmed by intimations that a strike might mean closing down the refinery, appealed to both company and union to settle their differences. A citizens' committee suggested an election under the supervision of Joseph Myers of the United States Conciliation Service to determine the wishes of the Baytown employees; the strike committee rejected it, ostensibly on the ground that it would involve nonunion participation in union business but primarily, no doubt, because it would have shown a large antistrike majority. Although the Joint Conference's claim that

2,436 out of 3,200 employees had signed the antistrike petition may have been exaggerated, the union had never claimed that more than one-fourth of the Baytown employees had voted for the strike.

Humble management, in the meantime, had taken action. The second wage increase within a fortnight, amounting to from 2½ to 8 cents per hour and affecting nearly all Baytown employees, was announced. Also, a representative of an Akron firm experienced in industrial disputes was called in for advice. Simultaneously with the wage increase, Humble built around the Baytown plant several miles of steel fence topped with barbed wire, installed large floodlights, hired fifty or sixty special officers, set up dormitory and mess-hall accommodations, and built a landing field. Antistrike employees organized to crash the expected picket lines.

The mediatorial work of Joseph Myers was in the meantime having its effect, as was the ground swell of public sentiment against the strike. Three days before the scheduled strike, Wiess at Myers' request promised that, if the strike was called off, he would "not . . . discharge any member of the union because of his membership in the union or because he voted for the strike." Another vote was conducted that was unanimous in favor of calling the strike off.[40]

Although Oliver claimed the settlement as a union victory, the strike threat resulted in defeat for Local 333. Harris, indeed, expressed some concern lest what he referred to as union accomplishments at Baytown might affect production and pipeline employees.[41] However, from the long-run viewpoint, the strike threat had resulted in a defeat from which Local 333 never recovered. The union had rushed impetuously into strike action without exhausting the possibilities of negotiation or adequately gauging its resources, flouted the wishes both of the majority of Baytown employees and of the Tri-Cities community in general, and rejected at the time of the wage increase the opportunity of withdrawing with unimpaired, perhaps even increased, prestige from what was becoming an impossible situation. Neither the community nor the majority of Baytown employees forgot or forgave that week of apprehension. And a substantial body of Baytown employees, thoroughly identifying their own interests with the company's, were now prepared to fight spontaneously and aggressively against any threat to existing management-employee relations.

After the cessation of the strike threat, management devoted itself to the improvement of communication with employees and, under Harris' leadership and the prodding of the Joint Conference, to the correction of certain inequities in the compensation of lower-paid employees. Local 333 utilized this time to recruit its forces for another attempt to gain effective bargaining rights. Realizing its mistake in having boycotted the Joint Conference, the union determined instead to capture it. An unusually heavy vote resulted in the election to the conference of nine union members or sympathizers out of seventeen employee representatives.

In February, 1937, the CIO inaugurated a national membership drive with the Baytown refinery as a principal objective. A group of Humble employees, mostly supervisors, under the leadership of W. A. Thomas, a Methodist minister working at the cracking coils, then organized the antiunion Security League. The Minute Men, as the leaguers called themselves, at first devoted themselves to propaganda, publishing two issues of a news sheet called *The Voice*, circulating an "anti-Lewis" petition, and distributing a pamphlet, by the notorious Joseph P. Kamp, entitled *Join the CIO and Help Build a Soviet America*.[42]

Circumstances soon gave the Security League the opportunity for more positive action. When on April 8 the United States Supreme Court found the Wagner Act constitutional, Humble's company-supported Joint Conferences became illegal and were promptly dissolved.[43] The permanent adjournment of the Baytown Joint Conference left a vacuum that Local 333 could not or did not fill; its strike threat of the previous autumn had greatly impaired its prestige with the main body of Baytown employees, and Bob Oliver had left Baytown—he was later to rise high in the CIO.[44]

Three days after the dissolution of the Joint Conferences, a meeting sponsored by the Security League drew up a constitution for an "Employees Federation," prepared a letter inviting Baytown employees to accept the federation as their bargaining agency, and scheduled an immediate four-day election to determine employee sentiment. Ballots attached to the letters provided for approval or disapproval of the federation and also served as membership blanks. Of 3,570 Baytown employees, 2,597 cast votes, and of these only 79 were opposed. Accusations of irregularities, some of which were subsequently supported by testimony, could not refute the fact that 2,038 voters—a substantial majority of the Baytown personnel—had signed applications for membership in the proposed Employees Federation. A few days later 330 out of 475 eligible voters at Ingleside chose a similar federation as their bargaining agency. Employees in other departments soon followed the example of Baytown and Ingleside.

The negotiation of contracts between Humble and the newly organized federations was a simple matter. The Baytown contract with the new federation, which set the pattern for the others, was similar to the old Joint Conference agreement. The Baytown federation recognized management's position that ability must take precedence over length of service as a basis for promotion and that the determination of ability and of the necessity for layoffs "must of necessity rest with management." The federation consequently accepted the restoration of ability ratings, which had been dropped three years earlier under pressure from the Joint Conference. In the meantime, however, much had been done to improve the rating system.[45]

The federations, particularly that at Baytown, soon manifested a spirit similar to that of the earlier Joint Conference. The Baytown group even used the same arguments for a wage increase that had been employed by representatives of Local 333—the cost of living and Humble's ability to pay—and requested that length of service be the governing factor in layoffs. The Production Department federation requested that wages be increased through increasing the working hours to forty per week, and it also attacked the use of low-paid contract labor. Humble denied all these requests for wage increases on the grounds that it was paying higher wages by 5 per cent than the prevailing rate of competitors and that living costs had increased but slightly. Nevertheless, it offered a still further liberalization of the vacation policy—two weeks after two years, three after fifteen years—and announced a contribution to the Annuity and Thrift Fund of $50.00 per employee, plus an additional contribution of $1,250,000 to be apportioned according to the amount credited to participants during the previous year.

Locals 333 (Baytown) and 316 (Ingleside), confronted with the *fait accompli* of Humble contracts with Employees Federations, turned to the NLRB. Late in August, 1937, they charged Humble with having restrained and coerced its employees and interfered in their right of self-organization, and with having sponsored, supported, and organized Employees Federations. For nearly three years the cases dragged on through the NLRB and the courts.[46] Humble claimed exemption from the Wagner Act on the ground that it was not engaged in interstate commerce. The NLRB examiner set this claim aside, as also the charge that Humble had dismissed employees for union activity. However, after six weeks of hearings beginning in March, 1938, the NLRB examiner found Humble guilty on the charges of forming, sponsoring, and dominating the Employees Federations and discouraging membership in the union through statements by company officials and the activities of supervisors. The decision was based on the similarity of the federations to the company-established Joint Conferences, on Wiess's attack on the CIO in his letter of September 3, 1936, and on the conspicuous part of supervisory employees in the organization of the Security League and the Employees Federations.

Humble appealed the case, but the NLRB confirmed the findings of its trial examiner and ordered the company to withdraw recognition from the Baytown and Ingleside federations and invalidate their contracts. The federations, however, refused to disband, and Humble petitioned the Fifth Circuit Court of Appeals at New Orleans to set aside the decision. The court did so when on June 26, 1940, it set aside the order that Humble should disestablish the Employees Federations and nullify its contracts with them—although it did order Humble to cease and desist from interfering with, restraining, or coercing its employees in the exercise of their rights under the Wagner Act and to post notices that it would do so. The CIO threatened to appeal to the United States Supreme Court, but no action was taken.

The decision was obviously a victory for Humble and the federations. Humble's persistent opposition to union organization had been entirely obvious, but the company was able to demonstrate to the satisfaction of the New Orleans Court that these efforts had terminated with the Supreme Court's recognition of the Wagner Act's constitutionality and that the company had not attempted subsequently either to discourage membership in or to set up and dominate any collective bargaining agency. The company's prompt action in disestablishing its Joint Conference system was valuable, perhaps decisive, evidence.

Baytown and Ingleside employees had chosen the Employees Federations, but not because they were coerced by Wiess's letter or by the evidence of management's hostility to "outside" unions. They were not inferior in stamina to other oil companies' employees who, in the face of more serious attempts at coercion, had organized and won bargaining rights for OWIU locals. One can only conclude from written records and a wide range of interviews that the majority of the Humble employees simply were not interested in an "outside" union. They had become convinced that their own federations were effective agencies for collective bargaining with management. Moreover, the experience of twenty years had created in them a basic confidence in and loyalty to their company that was currently being further strengthened by management's renewed efforts to implement its comprehensive employee program.

ADVANCING THE EMPLOYEE PROGRAM AFTER THE DEPRESSION

Humble's efforts to improve relations with its employees in the later 1930s were not motivated primarily, as some have maintained, by a desire to keep them from joining the oil workers' union, though such a desire was for a time an important factor. The principal motivation was the long-standing objective of the Humble directors to improve the company's employee group and to strengthen relations with employees, from a general interest in their well-being and as a means of increasing operational efficiency—a policy that long antedated effective unionism in the oil industry. Better general business conditions, prorated production, and Humble's own accumulating experience in employee relations made possible the company's more effective application of its employee program.

Perhaps the strongest motivation behind Humble's employee program after the depression was the executives' recognition of the increasing need for men able to handle progressively more difficult processes and complex equipment and to work effectively within an organization that was growing in size and complexity. The more volatile materials handled in the refineries, the greater problems met in drilling to deeper formations, the more highly mechanized equipment in nearly all operations, these all required skills, judgment, and dependability of a high order, while the growing need for co-ordinated effort made effective teamwork necessary. This was true of nearly all types and levels of work. A special need was for more engineers and men with advanced training in certain sciences, men who from the very nature of their training were not accustomed to working with others. What was increasingly required throughout the organization was a high degree of individual performance and responsibility coupled with the capacity to work as a group.

It was recognized that this combination required good morale as well as able employees but that in so large an organization neither came without special effort. What had been achieved quite naturally and informally in the early years of Humble Oil & Refining Company now required an organized and conscious effort. The strengthening of the structure and techniques of the employee relations organization continued in these later years of the 1930s, but probably the most distinctive development was a new element in relations with employees, one that served to give the employee a sense of belonging while at the same time challenging him to good performance.

In 1935 and 1936 the influence of the employee relations organization was broadened by its extension into operations. From February, 1935, to June, 1936, offices serving all operations were set up in each of Humble's four important operating regions, and the office earlier established at Baytown was expanded.

These offices were designed to serve operating management in a staff capacity and not as an integral part of the operating organization. Their managers, each of whom was to handle and co-ordinate all employee relations activities in his own region, were directly responsible to both the industrial relations manager in Houston and to the division superintendents in their areas. In the words of Harris: they were to be regarded as intermediaries between employees and management, "helpful to both but tied to neither"; they were to interpret company policy to employees and interpret employees to management; they were to be friendly with employees but "never assume a paternalistic attitude." They should, in brief, "furnish the human relationship desired by the company:—the missing link between the highest executives and the men in the ranks." [47]

These managers, Harris advised, should be of comparable quality and rank with division engineers, geologists, and assistant superintendents. They should be fair, honest, patient, friendly, and of good judgment. They should be recruited not from among men with special training in personnel work but from employees who were acquainted with operations and who understood the employee viewpoint, a recommendation that was adopted and that became a cardinal principle of Humble's employee relations.

The new managers—Leigh H. Cox, Thomas W. Moore, Ray H. Horton, LeRoy Wilkie, and William M. Holmes—had been formally educated in such fields as geology, chemical engineering, petroleum engineering, civil engineering, and social science. One was a graduate of the United States Naval Academy; another had been a personnel adjutant in World War I. One had begun his career with Humble in a minor job in refining; the others had begun low on the production ladder. The Humble experience of all included leadership or management positions as driller, safety engineer, leader of supervisory conferences, head of training department, elected representative in Joint Conference, and so on—sometimes in more than one such position. All had demonstrated the personal qualities considered necessary for the new posts. That they had risen in operations, and that some had represented their co-workers on Joint Conferences, made the company's claim that they were to look after the interests of employees as well as of management somewhat more realistic than if they had been brought in from outside as trained personnel workers unacquainted with operations.

Although the relationship of the industrial relations organization to management was carefully defined, it was not immediately clear in actual operations. In comparable companies, industrial relations men more commonly belonged and were wholly responsible to the operating organization. To get company policy understood and applied throughout management took time. Baytown and Ingleside refinery management, because of their old-school traditions and also because of a more difficult employee situation and consequently a greater preoccupation with labor problems than on pipelines and in production, was slow to co-operate. Production and pipelines, on the other hand, tended to shift the entire responsibility for their employees to the industrial relations organization and to request its enlargement.

To clarify any existing uncertainty about company policy and about the allocation of duties and responsibilities in employee relations matters, Suman, as chairman of the Industrial Relations Committee, which also included President Wiess, President Hanrahan of Humble Pipe Line Company, and Director Hines H. Baker, on January 19, 1938, sent a long explanatory statement to operating heads. This statement explained industrial relations policies and their origin in the company's highest echelon, the committee's responsibility for seeing that they were fairly administered, and the responsibilities of the industrial relations staff for co-ordinating industrial relations matters, acting as a service and advisory organization to operations and reporting to the committee. This function of keeping the committee informed was stressed: "If any industrial relations manager is worth his salt, he must report conditions to the management exactly as he finds them. He must be courageous enough on occasions to tell the management some things it doesn't want to hear. . . . Summed up: there is no need to try to fool ourselves. Either we want to know the facts or we don't. If we are sincerely trying to improve employee relations we must know the facts."

This explanation of the function of management in employee relations is such a precise and strong statement of Humble policy that it is worth quoting at length:

> Assuming that a company has fair policies, in my opinion, the responsibility for building and maintaining good industrial relations is distinctly the function of management. And, I might add, no function of management is of more importance than that of keeping the personnel in the proper state of enthusiasm and morale. Any industrial undertaking succeeds or fails to an appreciable degree on the efforts and efficiency of the men in the ranks. Only management is empowered to give orders, to enforce rules, to exact discipline, and to reward the most worthy employees in an industrial organization. Only the managerial force is in a position to evaluate the performance of individual employees on the job, to gain the intimate knowledge of the good and bad qualities of the men in the ranks. It is the responsibility of management to have this knowledge and to use it, fairly and impartially, in making promotions, demotions, and layoffs. Unless these are made fairly and impartially, it is nearly a foregone conclusion that, sooner or later, a poor state of industrial relations will follow. Nothing is more destructive to the morale and esprit de corps of a group of workers than failure on the part of management to recognize and reward those who are most deserving. Management, and management alone, is empowered to reward merit, and in time of layoffs or demotions to weed out the least deserving. In my opinion, the upper and intermediate management should, as far as it is practicable to do so, hold the foremen of gangs and units responsible for the proper administration of industrial relations in the units for which they are responsible in other matters. Foremen should be trained to assume this responsibility and to administer the Company's industrial relations policies

with painstaking fairness. They should be held responsible for efficiency and discipline in their units, and, by the same reasoning, should be permitted to make recommendations for the advancement of their subordinates in rank and pay when occasion justifies. If and when, but not before, a raise in pay or rank is actually made effective for any employee by proper approval of the upper management, the employee's immediate foreman should have the privilege of notifying him of his promotion and commending him for the qualities that justified the promotion, at the same time calling to his attention any improvement that might be made in the performance of his work. The upper and intermediate management must be alert to see that subordinate foremen do not abuse these responsibilities. It thus seems clear to me that management must accept the responsibility for building and maintaining good industrial relations.

The above statement expressed a broad concept of the responsibilities of the supervisory force that had for several years been developing in the Humble organization. The earlier attitude had been that the sole responsibility of supervisors was to get the work done—to give orders and to see that they were carried out—in other words, to be drivers. In recent years, however, Humble's top executives had come to expect more of supervisors; for example, they had delegated to foremen responsibility for safety and, increasingly, for the quality and morale of employees. They had come to look upon the foremen as leaders and as the embodiment of the company itself so far as the employees under them were concerned.

This changed concept of the supervisor's function made it necessary to have men capable of performing the broader function. Some men who at first had resisted the change eventually came to have great enthusiasm for it. Some who could not measure up to the new requirements left the company and were replaced by men who had proved capable of carrying the new responsibilities or who gave promise of so doing. Gordon L. Farned, for example, was brought to Baytown as superintendent because of his successful relations with employees at the smaller Ingleside refinery. Particular interest was displayed early in 1937 in replacing mediocre supervisors in the Process Department at Baytown with younger, better-trained, and more competent men. The operating management became increasingly conscious of the need to discover promising management material. Safety and other operational meetings gave management excellent opportunities for discovering promising men who were insufficiently aggressive to make an occasion to call the supervisors' attention to themselves but who in such meetings would participate freely and effectively. Performance rating records were surveyed for promising candidates for promotion to lower management positions.

By 1937 specialized training in supervision had come to be regarded as essential. Such earlier training of this nature as the foreman training initiated at Baytown in 1930,[48] together with the short series of evening discussion meetings instituted late in 1934 in some divisions under the leadership of Leigh Cox and Ray Horton, was said by Harris to have been worth while in leading "to better cooperation and coordination, better understanding and greater efficiency."[49] With increasing emphasis on foremanship, the extension of training to all foremen became desirable in order to cultivate qualities of leadership and to give supervisors a clear understanding of company industrial relations policies and methods. In view of the union organizers' insistence that the employees were not getting their fair share of Humble's "enormous earnings," Harris in 1937 suggested that company earnings should be discussed with foremen, with an explanation of how such earnings redounded to the workers' benefit. Some top executives believed that giving foremen broad understanding of company policies and operations would also have public relations value. Suman urged regular conferences on company time.

Conferences of supervisors soon got under way throughout operations. These meetings brought men together to discuss common problems and possible solutions and to pool experience under the guidance of leaders from management and the industrial relations organization. They helped to develop rules and standards for supervision, which were eventually incorporated in a *Supervisors' Manual*, and they also served to bring a closer co-operation between the industrial relations staff and the supervisors in operations.

Safety work, going beyond the training of employees in safety methods, also continued to be a form of supervisory training. Many new local safety groups were organized—in September, 1937, the Gulf Coast division alone boasted fifty-four local safety chairmen. Engineering had already accomplished much in making equipment safer, and most safety devices in use had been adopted earlier; a new contribution to oil-industry safety was the "hard hat," which Humble at this time adapted from the helmet used in mines.[50] The emphasis in safety training was becoming positive, being focused on "doing the job right" rather than on avoiding accidents. The slogan was: "If a thing is done correctly it is done safely." Accidents were investigated and discussed with a view to determining the cause. In May, 1936, a few mimeographed sheets—the forerunner of the later *Safety Information*—began to be issued monthly and were made available to all employees. By this time two general safety principles had become well recognized in operations: (1) safety is a responsibility of management; and (2) under no circumstances should safety be sacrificed to any other consideration.

Formal training of employees except in supervision and safety had made no particular progress up to this time—the directors and officers apparently had not been strongly interested. Courses were given at

Baytown and Houston as requested, with some increase as the depression waned. But by 1937 the building-up of a reserve of technically trained men at Baytown had again become desirable, and interest in the employing and training of refinery technicians was revived. The familiar problem of preventing dissatisfaction among highly trained technical men engaged in routine work reappeared. A voluntary training program was set up to acquaint such men with operations and to give them an opportunity to improve themselves.

An increase in the number of engineers and scientists, as the depression subsided and a larger number of such men was required, necessitated a more formal method of hiring. More attention was given to the selection of outstanding prospective graduates and postgraduate students in courses of study useful in the oil industry. Teams composed of men from the upper levels of Humble management and the employee relations organization visited engineering and other schools to interview students, individually and in groups. The men accepting employment with Humble nearly always entered low salaried starting positions, frequently to work at the lower levels of operations in accord with Humble's principle of acquainting its specialists with various levels and types of operations.

In the later 1930s systematic hiring, firing, and promotion were established throughout Humble's operations, for the first time under reasonably normal industrial conditions. An *Employment Manual*, compiled by the industrial relations group and operating management and approved at the top, was issued on July 1, 1936. Thereafter, the central or regional personnel offices interviewed and passed on all applicants for jobs. The quality of the applicants could thus be given more careful attention than would usually be possible from busy supervisors; and favoritism in the employment of relatives and friends was minimized, although such employment, which had become a considerable problem, was permitted if the candidate possessed adequate qualifications. Management still did the actual hiring, but the recommendations of the personnel office were generally followed.

The industrial relations offices also assisted management in promotions, demotions, transfers, discharges, and layoffs. All personnel records, including ability ratings, were co-ordinated through the central office in Houston. Demotions and discharges were relatively few, the highest number of the latter in any year of the decade 1932–1941 being 171 and the lowest 37. Transfers, on the other hand, were significant, in the same decade ranging from 6,500 in 1936 to 2,500 in 1938. The large number of transfers was caused partly by the practice of laying off less desirable men and transferring able surplus men, a method of upgrading the employee group, but largely by the shifting nature of oil-field work. The first year of employment with Humble was considered a probationary period, as it had been ever since the establishment of employee benefits.

The ability rating—performance rating as it was later called—which came to be considered a vital part of Humble's effort to eliminate the undesirable and to build an employee group of high quality, was necessarily improved. The controversial system of dividing each group into arbitrary percentage divisions was discontinued in 1935, and a new system of individual rating was adopted. Employees were rated twice a year, and each employee was allowed to see his rating and to discuss it with his supervisor. These ratings became a part of the employees' individual records in the personnel offices. Since it was recognized that, if ability ratings were to be used in determining promotions and layoffs, they must be dependable and fair, much attention was given to ways of rating. Desirable and undesirable qualities and how to gauge them were frequent subjects of lengthy discussion in foremen's conferences; and the industrial relations men instructed the foremen in methods of rating their men.

To make the ratings of employees as objective and realistic as possible was important for a company whose policy was to promote from within. That such promotion was extensive is illustrated by the situation at Baytown. Early in 1937, of 1,160 skilled jobs at the refinery, 1,046 were filled by men who had begun there as unskilled workers; most of the other 114 men, who had come there as skilled workers, had been with Humble since the early days and had helped to train the others.[51]

To stabilize employment further Humble in the 1930s adopted the definite policy of contracting temporary work as far as practicable—as several of its competitors were doing at the time. A primary reason was the bad effects on employee morale of the extensive dismissals and transfers and the unfortunate make-work episode at Baytown during the depression. Another was the new social security legislation, with its unemployment taxes, which made regular employment financially advisable. Contracting was resisted, however, by the Employees Federations; they claimed that it reduced employment and the possibilities for advancement. The company took the position that contracting made steady employment possible and that Humble employees were never laid off to make room for contractors' workers.

Circumstances beyond the company's control, however, in several years resulted in a surplus of employees and in heavy layoffs. For example, in 1938 new discoveries and unrestricted production in Illinois and other states greatly reduced the market for Texas oil and, consequently, reduced production in Texas; layoffs in the Production Department followed. The outbreak of war in Europe in 1939 had a similar effect.

Safeguards for the individual employees were built into the system of promotions, demotions, and transfers, but there is no specific measure of their effectiveness. Under the bargaining agreements with the federations, any employee could appeal from his immediate superior, even up to the Board of Directors, but such appeals were personal and did not become a matter of written record; their value to the employee cannot, therefore, be definitely assessed. But dismissals were reported to divisional and central personnel offices, where they are said to have been questioned at times with a resulting review of the case. A discharged employee could, and sometimes did, go to the industrial relations office to ask for an examination of his case; Harris himself might personally go to the employee's district to examine a dismissal in conference with those closely concerned. Promotions were recommended by an employee's immediate supervisor after consultation with the district superintendent and the industrial relations manager for the area. Some cases of dissatisfaction with promotions were brought to Harris as industrial relations manager, but by the end of the 1930s complaints of this nature had virtually disappeared.

Improvements in employment management were paralleled by a more systematic handling of salary and wage matters. Humble's salary and classification plan officially went into effect on January 1, 1934, following the Classification Committee's two-year study of the duties and responsibilities of all salaried positions and wage earners on one-rate jobs. This committee and the Salary Committee of high executives continued to be responsible for maintaining Humble's system of job and salary classification, which necessitated continuous study of old and new jobs and salaries and wages by a research division of the industrial relations office in close co-operation with operating department heads and payroll departments.

The "prevailing rate" policy of the company led to another innovation, a system of regular wage comparisons with a number of comparable companies. Such comparisons had previously been informal and occasional, with the result that the company's claims of paying prevailing rates were not always well founded. In 1934, therefore, Humble undertook to obtain the co-operation of comparable companies in comparing rates. By 1938 a satisfactory system of making rate comparisons had been established by the division of the industrial relations organization that had special charge of wage research.

Humble also began to take the initiative in wage adjustments in this period. The production and pipeline managers were the earliest to adopt the practice of suggesting adjustments as soon as it was discovered that their rates were out of line with those of comparable companies, a practice which Harris said, early in 1936, was at least partially responsible for the fine spirit prevailing among production and pipeline employees. Immediately after the elimination of the strike threat in 1936, Harris pointed out that about a thousand Humble employees were still being paid less than the National Industrial Conference Board's "reasonable wage" of $1,356 per year; he strongly advocated that Humble grant a 5 per cent increase before the employees asked for it. Management, however, delayed until it lost the initiative to the Baytown Joint Conference, which requested a cash bonus. Humble offered a general 5 per cent wage and salary increase and simultaneously announced a contribution to the individual employees' Annuity and Thrift Fund equivalent to two weeks' salary. In the future the company was to be more sensitive to the necessity for wage adjustments. In 1937 an examination of its wage rates revealed that, although the refinery process department's rate was higher than the national rate, Humble's "inordinately high number of laborers and mechanical helpers" rendered its general weighted average wage rate in refining lower than the national average.[52] In April, consequently, Humble not only raised its refinery wage rates an average of 6.49 cents per hour but also gave its other hourly wage workers a general 5 per cent increase and its salaried employees a minimum raise of $10.00 per month.

Authoritative figures on which to base a comparison of Humble's wages for specific jobs with those of comparable companies are not available for the 1930s, but some are available for 1940. In that year Humble reported to the United States Bureau of Labor Statistics the average hourly earnings in its production organization to be $1.158 and in refining $0.977; the general industry averages reported by the Bureau for that year were $0.887 in crude oil production, $0.974 in petroleum refining, $0.948 in the automobile industry, and $0.661 in all manufacturing. Humble's refinery rates were thus slightly, and its production rates substantially, above the industrial average. Benefits, which in Humble's case were highly important, were not included in these averages.

To the old-timers the most obvious change in the fields in those years was probably the improvement in living conditions. As proration slowed up the development of oil fields and gave them promise of a longer active life, the brawling boom town of flush production days disappeared. Humble, like other companies, then largely ceased to house and feed married employees in bunkhouses and mess halls; it continued to provide for unmarried men and also for married employees where it was impracticable to bring families, as, for example, later in offshore operations. After the middle 1930s, the company increased its building of attractive and comfortable camps. It not only supplied more houses for field supervisory personnel, at a monthly rental of $3.00 per room, but it also assumed a measure of responsibility for housing other employees and for providing more community facilities. In or near established communities, nonsupervisory employees usually found houses for themselves, but in the company-owned camps Humble assigned lots to employees who wished to build there and gave assistance in planning houses, obtaining materials, and so on. The company maintained in every camp an electric power plant and sewage system, provided water and gas, and planted trees, grass, and flowers. In each of the larger camps it also maintained a recreation hall and a first-aid center and quarters for the camp nurse, as well as providing schools in the rare places where public schools were not available or school buses where there were local schools.

The coming of families transformed social conditions in the camps. The vice, gambling, drinking, and fighting of the boom towns vanished, and in their place came family and community life, wholesome entertainment, gardening, and garden and book clubs. Supervisors and other employees, with their families, lived together more or less permanently in the same community.

Through Humble's employee relations records of the later 1930s runs like a refrain the statement that the basis for management-employee co-operation is understanding—understanding of the job, of safety, of principles of fair treatment, of responsibilities, of company policies, and so on. This concept of "understanding" apparently motivated much that Shaw and Harris did and said as managers of industrial relations; it was a fixed principle of some of Humble's highest executives.

Recognition of the need for making company policies and practices better known to employees was probably the principal motivation behind Humble's increased attention to company publications after the middle 1930s, a time when American business quite generally began to issue more house organs. The only company publication from 1930 to 1935 had been the *Humble Sales Lubricator*, which was primarily a sales-promotion organ. During the early years of the unionization drive, the *Lubricator* began to carry articles of a more general informational character, of which one, entitled "The Interests of Stockholders, Employee and Management Are Identical," was typical.[53] The *Lubricator* achieved a considerable circulation at Baytown, and in 1935 the old *Humble Bee* (discontinued in 1933) was revived as the biweekly *Humble Refinery Bee*, which was aimed primarily at Baytown personnel.

The *Bee* and the *Lubricator*, in addition to carrying news of Humble employees, increasingly called attention to the common interests of company and employees and to the benefits the latter enjoyed.[54] A series of articles on the company's benefits program, written in a clear and homely style by G. A. Mabry under the title, "You and Me and the Company," began to appear on the very day that Local 333 took its strike vote in September, 1936. These articles were later collected in a booklet; it was followed by another of a more general character, *Working with Humble*, which described Humble's ideals for "its relationships with its own people, with the petroleum industry, and with the public." Humble had learned that it was not enough to formulate and carry out policies intended to improve its various relations; it must also inform its "publics" of the existence of those policies and explain their purposes and achievements.

The form of communication, however, that was most distinctive in Humble, and that many executives prized the most, was the direct personal one. At the base was the foreman, who for five minutes at the beginning of each shift discussed with his gang the work before them. The industrial relations man was always ready to talk with the employees individually. There were the casual meetings of high executives with employees at various levels—which occurred more naturally and easily on the pipeline or in the oil field than in a refinery. Suman's gift for personal contact is a company legend, but he was not the only one who had that gift. Frame was another—employees, for example, like to tell of how "Dave" Frame, when production manager, would drop in for breakfast with one of the field workers in the kitchen of his oil-camp cottage.

The various meetings for training and other purposes gave regular opportunities for managers and employees to get together for discussion. Some directors and managers of operations occasionally attended safety meetings or supervisory conferences. Frame established the practice of regularly calling together production men and explaining to them plans for field development and opportunities for promotion in the subsequent six months or year.

Especially significant after the Wagner Act had gone into effect was the pattern established in collective bargaining in production and on pipelines. Frame believed that employees should be broadly informed about the company, and as a result the sessions with representatives of Production Employees Federations—he always attended the divisional as well as the central council meetings—became concerned largely with discussions of company policies, operations, and earnings, in fact whatever the representatives wanted to discuss. Motivating Frame's willingness to discuss such matters with the employee representatives was his firm belief that the employees' understanding of and confidence in the company and its operations were of greater significance to them than were wage contracts. Neath, who similarly attended meetings with representatives of pipeline employees, had the same attitude and followed the same practices. Neither Frame nor Neath seems ever to have forgotten what it was like to work in field operations, and both recognized the importance of the individual in operations.

Communication between managers and the rank and file of employees helped to build loyalty as well as understanding and confidence. It would, indeed, be inadequate to emphasize understanding as the only significant objective of such communication. Important also was a largely unspoken, even somewhat unconscious, recognition by managers and supervisors of the importance of feelings and attitudes, of a sincere interest in the employees and in their problems and good fortune, whatever they might be. Harris had a special talent for personal relations with employees. It is impossible to measure the influence that he came to have among the employees in the later 1930s and 1940s, but there is no question about the affection and confidence with which the rank-and-file employees regarded him. Managers in line operations similarly won their deep regard. When Frame told a man he had confidence in him, the employee believed that Frame meant what he said and would generally do everything possible to merit it. And of the pipeline president of those days it was said that if the CIO should manage to organize the Humble Pipe Line Company, the union members would probably then go to Ralph Hanrahan to ask him how to vote. The attitudes and behavior of these top men set the pattern as well for supervisors on lower levels.

The loyalty of Humble employees to the company was not feudalistic, however, nor was the attitude of employees toward management expressive of a master-servant relationship. They were not unmindful of the fact that many men in the higher echelons of management had started work with Humble in very minor positions. Their loyalty was in part based on the realization that Humble was a successful company, one that they were proud to work for. They respected the company's top management and believed that the executives knew their business, but they also rated themselves highly and believed they deserved a share of credit for the company's position. By the end of the 1930s—some time before America's entry into World War II—Humble employees, it is said, had begun to think of themselves as the "prima donnas" of the oil industry. The employees' loyalty to the company and its top management was thus not to some *thing* or to some *group* apart from or above themselves, but rather loyalty to a large group of which they themselves were members. Such loyalty, however, did not exclude disagreements, sometimes sharply phrased and stubbornly disputed. Humble's policy of stressing ability and performance had clearly helped to develop an independent as well as an able group of workers, as was emphatically demonstrated in collective-bargaining conferences between management and representatives of the employees.

The results of Humble's efforts to strengthen its employee group and to improve employee-management relations cannot be measured in terms of ability, productivity, or economy. The situation was too complex to isolate the contribution of any one factor, desirable though that might be. Some pertinent figures and general impressions, however, can be observed.

One tangible evidence is the decrease in accidents and consequently in the cost to the company of casualty insurance. The frequency rate of disabling injuries fell from 44.42 per million man-hours in 1929 to 12.74 in 1932 and to 5.97 in 1941; the number of permanently disabled fell from 63 in 1929 to 19 in 1932 and 13 in 1941; deaths were 13 in 1929, 9 in 1932, and 2 in 1941. A measure of the decrease in cost of accidents to the company is suggested by comparing Humble's credits or discounts against the casualty rates set by the Texas Insurance Commission: Humble Oil & Refining Company for 1929 received a credit on its premium of 30.7 per cent and in 1941 of 58.7 per cent; Humble Pipe Line Company, which in 1929 was penalized by an additional charge of 22.1 per cent, received in 1941 a credit of 49.4 per cent.

Certain statistics indicate that progress was also being made in stabilizing employment, and that working for Humble was becoming a lifetime career. At the end of 1941, of over 13,000 employees about 1,000 had been with Humble twenty or more years, 3,300 fifteen or more, 6,200 ten or more, 10,100 five or more, and 3,300 less than five years. A decade later those who had been with Humble ten or more years represented about two-thirds of the total number employed.

Scores of interviews with men inside and outside Humble give an impression of the quality and morale of the employees at the end of this period. The judgment is unanimous that they constituted a working force of high character. Many years of effort, based on a positive attitude toward employee relations—spurred on by such outside pressures as the threat of unionism and the demands of the employees themselves and nourished by the employees' pride in their company—had eliminated most vestiges of arbitrary dominance and paternalism and had substituted a large degree of voluntary co-operation between management and employees.

Humble men, both in the managerial group and among operating and staff employees, like to refer to Humble as a team. Certainly, an outstanding feature of Humble's operations, despite the trouble at Baytown in the 1930s, has been the teamwork within and between groups. This could have been achieved only by employing, training, and retaining employees of high quality. But even men of the highest intelligence and training and the widest experience are frequently unable to work harmoniously together. Perhaps the spirit of co-operation so characteristic of Humble can be traced to the principles of fair treatment and respect for the individual and his performance, which, despite occasional lapses, were basic in the company's employee relations from the days of the founders and which during the 1930s found a particularly intelligent and understanding organized expression.

Chapter 16

A GOLDEN AGE OF RESERVE ACCUMULATION, 1930–1941

IN ANY ANALYSIS of Humble's basic strength in later years, the importance of the tremendous reserves of oil and gas acquired in the 1930s can hardly be overemphasized. In those years Humble achieved what the distinguished geologist, E. L. DeGolyer, called its paramount position as a holder of domestic oil reserves. While adding to those reserves, the company also acquired large deposits of natural gas. The acquisition during the 1930s of reserves in several large oil-and-gas fields and gas-and-condensate fields made Humble the owner of the largest gas reserve on the Gulf Coast and in Southwest Texas. The company's subsequent record as a producer, particularly its great contribution to the petroleum requirements of World War II but also its continuing leadership after the war, could not have been achieved without a large backlog of reserves to draw upon.[1]

What accounts for Humble's brilliant success in increasing its reserves at this time? The company had always followed the policy of spending heavily to acquire reserves, but its success had varied, ranging from its notable accomplishments in the fault-line region in the early 1920s to disappointment in other places in the later years of the decade. In the early 1930s, however, Humble's reserve-acquisition campaign succeeded phenomenally, and it continued for several more years to add significantly to reserves. In general, in the decade preceding America's entry into World War II, the company's executives, notably Wallace E. Pratt, were strong reserve expansionists. They particularly sought to acquire large blocks, the development of which would be subject to a minimum of competitive drilling and production. "There is practically no limit," Farish declared in 1932, "to the amount of controlled reserves, unit operated, that we should own."[2] However, these men were not blind expansionists. They continuously gauged their company's strength and the cost of acquiring reserves against their forecast of future needs and prices. This meant considering many variables; as these changed from time to time, Humble's reserve-acquisition operations were also changed. The best explanation of Humble's success, therefore, is an examination in some detail of how its reserve-acquisition policy was tailored to particular circumstances.

ACQUIRING LARGE UNPROVED ACREAGE AND RESERVES IN GREAT FIELDS, 1930–1934

In 1930 Pratt was anxious about the future of Humble's oil finding. In the course of its history, he reported, the company had found approximately 400,000,000 barrels of oil, of which "100,000,000 were to be credited directly to geophysical exploration, which has been effective only over the last four years." But, he continued, "The success of geophysics appears to be already on the wane . . . and unless we can improve our technique so as to expand its application to new areas we seem likely soon again to begin to deplete rather than build up our oil reserves." Nearly all the shallow Gulf Coast domes had then been found, and the geophysical instruments being employed by Humble and others in Texas were, generally speaking, nearly useless for outlining the more deeply buried structures.[3]

Pratt's concern was well founded. As a result of its unfavorable reserve position from about 1925, Humble had greatly increased its expenditures for leasing and had expanded its exploration and wildcatting. Yet its new reserves had just barely equaled its production. The threat of an even greater drop in the ratio of Humble's own production to its commitments as a supplier of crude, particularly for its own and Jersey Standard's refineries, was becoming serious. Several of its competitors, moreover, had a far higher ratio of production to refinery requirements. Currently, it is true, there was an overabundance of oil on the market, but reserves were nevertheless the very lifeblood of a producing company.

Humble, which already had a strong geologic staff, had foreseen the need to strengthen its geophysical techniques and had in 1929 expanded its research. Late in 1930 the research efforts of the geophysics group were beginning to bear fruit. At that time two crews were equipped with reflection seismographs and sent into the field, and by the following mid-

January all Humble seismograph crews in the territory in which it was operating had been refitted with reflection equipment. This new type of instrument, which recorded sound waves from explosions on the surface as they were reflected from subsurface structures—that is, echoes of surface explosions—was to prove much more effective in mapping the more deeply buried structures than was the recording of refracted—or bent—sound waves by the earlier refraction seismograph. In May, 1931, O. H. Truman completed his work on the gravity meter on which he had been engaged for four years. This later became the first successful fieldworthy instrument of its kind; it was Humble's great geophysical contribution to the oil industry. In the same year Dr. Blau succeeded in devising a short-period torsion balance that showed definite promise. So far, however, all these new instruments were either not yet fieldworthy or had not been sufficiently tried in the field to have proved themselves definitely.

The first field trials took place in 1931 and 1932. The two reflection crews sent out near the end of 1930 worked in East Texas and the San Antonio district; at first it was believed that there was not enough difference in the character of the formations on the Gulf Coast to make possible the correlation of reflections, but this belief was soon found erroneous. One experimental gravity crew was put to work in Texas in 1931. In the following year four reflection crews were employed, mostly in Texas, six torsion-balance crews were scattered over wide areas that were believed to have promise, and crews using an improved Truman gravity meter began to survey the whole of Humble's operating territory. In 1932 Humble crews accounted for 42 per cent of the total geophysical crew-months worked by various companies in the whole territory in which Humble operated. During that and the two following years Humble also sent reflection crews on contract to Jersey affiliates in Oklahoma, Venezuela, Rumania, Argentina, Mexico, and Colombia.[4]

The new geophysical techniques at once proved their value. Experience in their use and continuing research brought about improvements in the instruments and greater assurance in the interpretation of data. These instruments revealed many areas of geologic interest that led to the leasing of acreage and the eventual discovery of new fields.

Humble continued to search aggressively for new oil even in the years of deep depression and amid the chaos caused by the prolific East Texas field (see Chapter 18). It maintained a full exploration staff and hired even more brokers than usual to buy leases. It increased lease purchases to the record high of $13,549,000 in 1934, a figure Humble was not to surpass until 1948 (see Table 7). It reduced its wildcatting, however, in 1931 and 1932; it had hoped to bring about such a reduction earlier but had been unsuccessful because of the highly competitive drive for new reserves in the late 1920s. Its drilling crews in 1931 and 1932 were occupied mostly in development work, particularly in the great and competitively developed East Texas and Conroe fields.

Humble's reserve program of the early 1930s differed sharply from that of much of the oil producing industry at the time. It is particularly significant that during the early depression years other majors greatly relaxed their leasing and exploration. Shell Petroleum, faced with heavy debt-service charges incurred in its recent great expansion and with operating deficits, adopted a policy of retrenchment. It gave up a tremendous lease acreage, in 1931 dropping leases that had cost $8,000,000, and it sold a potentially valuable property in East Texas and forfeited another.[5] It seems improbable, however, that, if Shell had believed this to be a propitious time to buy reserves, it could not have obtained the necessary funds. Gulf, which had severely strained its financial resources and was also losing on operations, lacked funds in the depth of the depression with which to buy proved or unproved acreage to any considerable extent and, under the terms of its earlier borrowing, was unable to seek further loans. Another major competitor, The Texas Company, had shifted its emphasis to refining and marketing several years earlier and was not developing production in Texas as aggressively as before.[6] Independent operators, such as Ed Bateman and George W. Strake, either were finding it difficult to get loans with which to develop their properties or thought the risks too high and were consequently ready to sell acreage as soon as they struck oil or gas.

The consequent decrease—though by no means absence—of competition for potential or proved oil lands provided a favorable situation for a company with the means, the will, and the courage to invest heavily. Even in the years of deepest depression, Humble Oil & Refining Company and Humble Pipe Line Company never failed to record net earnings; moreover, they had entered the depression with low fixed-interest obligations. Pratt and Farish were uncompromising reserve expansionists. One prominent producing company executive is quoted as saying even before the discovery of the great East Texas field, "We can't see anything but cheap oil. Why buy reserves?"[7] Pratt, on the contrary, even after the East Texas discovery had brought 10-cent oil, could look beyond the existing market chaos and see that, because of the current ratio of oil finding to production, reserves were being increased only slightly if at all to meet what he believed would be a greatly increased future demand. Pratt was ridiculed by some oilmen. But several of his associates on the Humble board, besides Farish, were likewise reserve-minded and others were convinced by his persuasiveness.

Table 7 shows what Humble was doing in the search for oil in the years 1930 through 1934. Indicative of the strong drive for reserves were

TABLE 7

SELECTED DATA ON EXPLORATION ACTIVITIES AND RESERVES, HUMBLE OIL & REFINING COMPANY, 1925–1941

	Geophysical Crew-Months Operated		Undeveloped Acreage under Lease[a]	Lease Purchases	Surrendered Leases	Total Exploration Costs (Excluding dry holes)	Wildcats Drilled		Expenditures for Dry Holes	Gross Crude Oil Reserves[b]	Humble's % of Crude Oil Reserves	
	Total Number	Humble's % of Area	(000 acres)	($000)	($000)	($000)	Total Number	Number Productive	($000)	(million barrels)	Of Area in Which Humble Operated	Of U.S.[c]
1925	17	...	2,250	7,776	1,327	8,282	30	2	1,810	61	...	0.7
1926	92	...	3,635	12,217	1,826	10,382	40	...	1,987	55	...	0.6
1927	146	...	3,820	5,595	3,167	8,625	41	3	2,300	82	...	0.8
1928	104	...	3,327	4,023	3,833	10,172	30	2	1,442	172	...	1.6
1929	120	...	3,896	5,147	2,781	14,659	41	1	2,156	223	...	1.7
1930	158	...	4,453	5,022	3,750	13,308	41	3	1,824	219	...	1.6
1931	144	...	3,438	5,540	5,616	8,663	14	3	745	591	...	4.5
1932	136	42.2	3,430	8,642	2,857	5,286	4	1	584	883	...	7.2
1933	162	28.8	4,748	9,043	2,068	4,841	28	2	949	947	17.1	7.9
1934	187	14.6	6,936	13,549	2,378	4,370	50	3	2,391	1,159	19.7	9.5
1935	195	14.2	7,146	6,945	3,505	6,281	41	1	3,025	1,438	20.7	11.6
1936	213	11.9	7,101	5,001	2,906	5,940	18	3	2,127	1,629	20.7	12.5
1937	225	10.7	7,543	7,976	2,911	6,380	34	5	2,810	1,905	20.9	12.3
1938	238	11.8	8,204	12,825	4,708	8,372	31	6	4,253	2,155	21.5	12.4
1939	223	12.3	7,418	3,061	5,251	8,379	35	2	3,445	2,433	18.9	13.2
1940	228	12.3	8,049	4,936	3,474	8,567	48	8	3,730	2,655	20.3	14.0
1941	223	10.9	10,710	3,624	2,381	8,187	28	5	3,010	2,726	20.0	13.9

[a] Unoperated acreage, not including royalty interest.
[b] Year-end estimate with revisions credited to current year and not to year of discovery.
[c] Figures for the U.S. used in calculating percentages are estimated year-end reserves prepared by the American Petroleum Institute; Humble estimates were used for the area in which Humble operated.

Source: Records of Humble Oil & Refining Company.

the increase in geophysical work, the high expenditures for leasing and exploration, the increase in undeveloped acreage, the expansion of wildcatting in 1933 and 1934 from the low point it had reached in 1931–1932, and, especially, the growth of the company's reserves, both in estimated barrels of oil and in percentage of total estimated industry reserves.

Particularly significant were two aspects of Humble's leasing and reserve-acquisition operations: the leasing of large blocks of acreage, and purchases in fields discovered by others. The former was a continuation of a well-established Humble policy that was being progressively strengthened by the growing knowledge of the behavior of reservoirs under production, by experience, and by the necessity for low-cost production. At this time Humble acquired unproved acreage on which it later developed several wholly owned or nearly wholly owned fields. Its most notable purchases in the early 1930s, however, were in major fields discovered by other operators.

The most important of these major fields was the East Texas field (see map), which has continued to hold the record not only as the greatest oil field ever discovered in the United States but also as containing Humble's greatest reserves in any one field.[8] This field was discovered on October 3, 1930, by the veteran drilling contractor and wildcatter, Columbus M. ("Dad") Joiner, who was waiting out the depression by "poor-boying" some wells in southern Rusk County. It was an ironical comment on the uncertainties of oil finding that, after many years of prospecting in Texas by means of geology and geophysics, such an oil field should have been discovered by virtually random drilling, the wildest of all wildcatting.[9] It is popularly believed in Texas that the major companies, particularly Humble, had condemned the area in which this field was discovered. Actually, several majors had long been interested in the region. Humble had earlier acquired considerable acreage in what became the East Texas field and had entered into an agreement for the drilling of a joint test well several months before the discovery well was brought in.

Humble had, indeed, been interested in East Texas ever since the development in the early 1920s of Mexia, Powell, and Wortham, fault-line fields with prolific production from the Woodbine sand, which also proved to be the producing sand in the East Texas field. After the discovery of oil in the Boggy Creek field in 1927, interest in East Texas increased. Humble started geophysical work in the area and transferred several geologists there for rapid reconnaissance. Rusk County was covered by L. T. Barrow and Gregg by E. A. Wendlandt, but the focus of the search was on salt domes and neither geologic study nor the refraction seismograph revealed any such formation in either county. Certain areas, however, were recommended for detailed coverage. L. W. McNaughton early in 1928 mapped a structure in the London area, as a

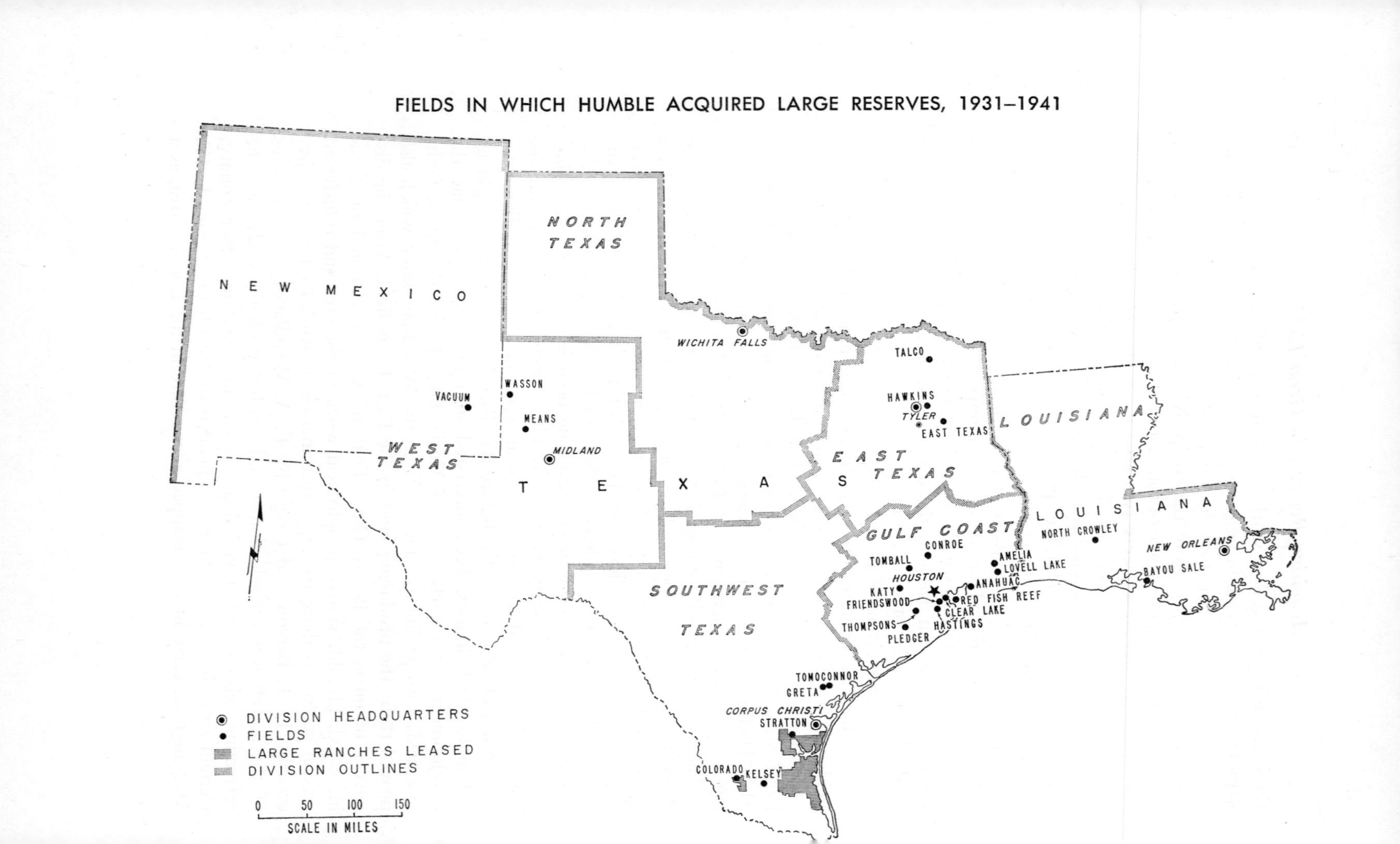
FIELDS IN WHICH HUMBLE ACQUIRED LARGE RESERVES, 1931–1941
NEW MEXICO
NORTH TEXAS
WEST TEXAS
TEXAS
EAST TEXAS
GULF COAST
SOUTHWEST TEXAS
LOUISIANA
LOUISIANA
VACUUM
WASSON
MEANS
MIDLAND
WICHITA FALLS
TALCO
HAWKINS
TYLER
EAST TEXAS
CONROE
TOMBALL
HOUSTON
KATY
FRIENDSWOOD
THOMPSONS
PLEDGER
HASTINGS
CLEAR LAKE
RED FISH REEF
ANAHUAC
LOVELL LAKE
AMELIA
NORTH CROWLEY
NEW ORLEANS
BAYOU SALE
TOMOCONNOR
GRETA
CORPUS CHRISTI
STRATTON
COLORADO
KELSEY
DIVISION HEADQUARTERS
FIELDS
LARGE RANCHES LEASED
DIVISION OUTLINES
0 50 100 150
SCALE IN MILES

result of which Humble leased 1,500 acres, one-third of which it sold to Gulf Production Company. Later work proved that no such structure was there, but the block was retained because it was in a likely area and its cost was low. This was the first acreage Humble acquired in what was to become the East Texas field.

The first written suggestion in the Humble records of a possible shoreline field in East Texas is found in a report by G. M. Knebel dated October 24, 1928. Knebel had mapped the surface geology of Gregg County. He mapped a structure with twenty feet of closure on the Cane River southwest of Longview and, referring to the earlier interest of Humble's geologists Cash, McLellan, and Wendlandt in the region, recommended leasing and drilling. Knebel became an enthusiastic advocate of leasing in the general area. Barrow recalls that, before leaving in 1929 to work with a Jersey Standard affiliate in Venezuela, Knebel spoke to him somewhat as follows: "Don't forget the possibility of a big oil field where the Woodbine pinches out on the west side of the Sabine Uplift. It may be that the oil will be on structures, even noses, but the oil might be trapped all along the pinchout."

As a result of the work of its geologists, Humble leased two blocks in addition to the London Block. Late in 1928, following Knebel's recommendation, it leased 8,000 acres southwest of Longview, of which it later sold one-third to Gulf. Humble purchased from Gulf a one-third interest in a block of over 5,000 acres in Gregg and Upshur counties—only a small portion of this acreage proved productive. Its interest in East Texas, like that of other companies, was heightened by Pure Oil's discovery of the Van field in the Woodbine in 1929.

In April, 1930, Humble, Gulf, and the Herbert Oil Company entered an agreement for a joint test well on acreage that proved to be in the heart of the East Texas field. The test was suggested by the Herbert Oil Company, which had leased several thousand acres around the Humble-Gulf London block. Humble was to be the operator if oil was found. Humble decided to accept the proposal, as also did Gulf. Had it not been for title and other difficulties, this would probably have been the discovery well.

Because of its lease interests and accumulated knowledge of the area, Humble was quick to recognize the probable importance of the first showing of oil in the Joiner well on September 6, 1930. Almost at once the company's East Texas geologist, H. J. McLellan, with authority from Pratt, bought Herbert's one-half interest in the 4,500-acre block and added another 2,000 acres to Humble's London holdings. Further additions were made in the London area on the basis of subsurface geology—all but the extreme southeastern part of the company's large London block proved productive. Between the first showing of oil in Joiner's well and the actual bringing-in of the well on October 3, Humble leased over 12,000 East Texas acres at a cost of about a quarter of a million dollars. It continued to acquire acreage. It considered an offer of an interest in a block of leases on which the fourth East Texas producing well was completed in January, 1931. This was a block in Gregg County totaling several thousands acres, a divided half of which Moncrief and Showers offered to Humble for $35.00 an acre. Humble men believed the acreage had some merit as a part of a possible large shoreline oil field but refused the offer, primarily because the sellers wanted to retain half of each lease; this would have been the worst kind of checkerboarding and, since the leases were typically small East Texas tracts, would have forced a competitive drilling campaign.

Humble's most important purchase in establishing its leading position in the East Texas field was made in January, 1931. On November 1, 1930, Ed Bateman and associates had started a well on the large Crim holdings southwest of Kilgore and ten miles north of the discovery well. On December 17, cores taken at from 3,638 to 3,651 feet showed that the bottom fourteen inches were saturated with oil. On December 28, casing was set and a drillstem test was made; in forty minutes the well flowed 600 barrels of 38° gravity oil. Crim No. 1 was immediately shut in, and Bateman went in search of funds with which to develop his holdings.

Unable to obtain loans, Bateman put his well and acreage on the market. He first sought buyers in Shreveport and Dallas; failing in both places, he went to Houston. He offered his well and 1,500 acres of leasehold to Humble for $1,500,000 cash and $600,000 to be paid out of the oil produced, which was considered a very high price. Although others had refused the offer, Pratt not only recommended but urged the purchase; the results of study of the area for several years by such able Humble geologists as Knebel, Wendlandt, and McLellan had convinced him of the great importance of this acreage. Also, Pratt himself, Farish, and practically all the directors, remembering Mexia and Powell, were interested in the Woodbine.

"Well do I remember," wrote Barrow in 1945 in his "Notes on the East Texas Field," "the conference in the old Board Room with Mr. Farish and Mr. Pratt probably having made up their minds to make the purchase, but thoroughly analyzing all facts and information, and convincing other Board members. . . ." Blaffer walked the floor "because 'Bill' wanted to make such a large expenditure." Chief Geologist Barrow wanted to make the trade, but subject to the well's satisfactory performance upon being tested. Bateman, however, since the fittings were so light that the well might get out of control, did not want to open it again. Farish, true to his belief in the play of men, finally asked Barrow: "What does Mac think of it?"—Mac being McLellan, Humble's geologist in East Texas, who was generally considered a conservative Scotsman. "He says," Barrow replied, "that if we take it we'll never need to look back." "Well, if Mac says that," Farish asked in a matter-of-fact voice, "what more do we want to know?" The Board of Directors was finally won over to Pratt's recommendation. Pratt, Barrow, and Rex G. Baker completed the negotiations on January 9, 1931, paying Bateman's asking price for what was to prove to be one of Humble's great lease acquisitions of the decade. In making this purchase Humble not only acquired a valuable property but also took a first step in its depression investment of large sums in proved oil lands.

Humble continued to lease in the neighborhood. As competition for leases increased, $50.00 per acre was first set as the limit, then $100, then $250, and then $1,000 and even higher. "At times," writes Barrow, "we stopped buying, thinking we had all we could handle," but "then Mr. Pratt and Mr. Farish would instruct us to start again." Among the larger trades were two made by Pratt with Byrd & Frost for a one-fourth interest in 2,800 acres, between Kilgore and Humble's Longview block, and for another block of 7,000 acres. Some of this acreage was traded to Gulf. Many other lease purchases were made in Houston, principally by Cooper, and even more in Tyler, largely by McLellan, the negotiations being directed by Barrow, who consulted frequently with Pratt.

The Humble men correctly concluded that the first three wells drilled in the general area defined a single, large field, instead of being the discovery wells of three new oil fields, ten or fifteen miles apart. (See Chapter 18 for a description and geologic drawing of this field.) On the basis of this conclusion and their geologic knowledge of the region, Humble purchased still more lease acreage, with the result that ultimately it was the largest owner in the East Texas field, with an estimated 16 per cent of the acreage of the entire field. It also purchased considerable oil and gas royalty interests.

The significance of Humble's acquisitions in the East Texas field is indicated by the fact that the company's gross (including royalty oil) ultimate production in the field, as estimated after the field was fully developed (1939), was over 600,000,000 barrels of oil. This was approximately three times as much as the company's total reserves in 1930.

Early in 1932, a time of deepening pessimism in the American oil industry and general economy, Humble also acquired large interests in two other major fields. These were Thompsons in Fort Bend County and Conroe in Montgomery, both on the Gulf Coast.[10]

The Thompsons acquisition,[11] like the Bateman in 1931, involved the purchase of proved property rather than discovery. Humble had bought some leases there several years earlier, when Scout Rostrom had reported the appearance of gas during the drilling of a water well. The

Gulf Production Company had leased 7,500 acres on the basis of surface indications and a torsion-balance survey and had traded a one-half undivided interest to H. R. Cullen and the West Production Company. In May, 1931, Cullen and West had brought in the discovery well, after which they had drilled on the property several producers in the Miocene. In November, Humble's Gulf Coast geologist, L. P. Teas, strongly recommended "the acquisition of all or any part of this property on anything like reasonable terms. . . ." [12] In March, 1932, Teas informed Pratt that the field could easily cover 3,000 acres and contain 127,000,000 barrels of oil. Pratt became convinced that this was a valuable property and urged its purchase, despite a price that made the Bateman trade seem small. Cullen and J. M. West, the president and principal owner of the West Production Company, approached Pratt with the idea of selling their leasehold. Pratt negotiated the trade by which Humble in March, 1932, bought the one-half interest of Cullen and West in eight leases at Thompsons for $3,000,000 in cash and $17,000,000 to be paid out of receipts from a portion of the oil produced, plus an overriding royalty of one-twenty-fourth on oil and gas and 33⅓ cents per long ton on sulphur.

That the strong major did not, as a matter of course, have its own way in such trades is illustrated by the negotiations for this interest. After preliminary discussions in which Pratt believed agreement had been substantially reached, he and Rex G. Baker of Humble joined Cullen and West and the latter's son, together with their legal counsel, in West's Houston office to complete the drawing-up of the contract. After many hours of discussion, West casually rose to leave with the explanation that he had to be off to a cattlemen's convention in El Paso. Unable to complete the contract with "the boys," as West had suggested, the Humble men had to await the return of West nearly a week later to complete a purchase for which they pledged their company to pay $20,000,000 plus overriding royalties.

Humble's acquisition of an interest in this valuable field was a result of its willingness to "shell out" for what it wanted and its ability to act quickly. Cullen and West had made almost the same proposition to the joint owner, but the Gulf's head office in Pittsburgh had turned down the offer. Humble's gross ultimate production in the Thompsons field was estimated, on the completion of the field's development in 1940, at about a hundred million barrels.

Humble's Conroe trade was for property not yet actually proved for oil.[13] This was a block of leases obtained in the name of the Strake Oil Corporation by George W. Strake, a young wildcatter, who "knew," on the basis of geophysical work by Pure Oil, that his leases covered a dome. He offered a portion of the block to Humble, which had done some refraction and torsion-balance work in the vicinity without finding any favorable indications, but Barrow on the basis of the data offered considered Strake's terms too high. Possibly Humble's own survey had not covered enough acreage—most Gulf Coast fields were then small, around a thousand acres, and before the development of the Conroe field companies generally looked for structures of that size or a little larger. Failing to find a buyer for his leases, Strake "poor-boyed" a well down to gas-condensate production in December, 1931. Most operators did not consider this discovery of importance because only gas condensate was found, and the producing sand, the Cockfield, was not known to be a producer. Humble, however, on the strength of Earle Short's effective scouting and because it had been interested in the area for years, was willing to make a trade.

Strake approached Humble in February, 1932, and in March Pratt closed a contract with the Strake Oil Corporation. This contract illustrates the kinds and amount of detail that might be included in such agreements. The provisions show that both parties were uncertain how much, if any, production could be obtained from the wells to be drilled. The contract assigned six of Strake's leases to Humble and provided for the payment of $100,000 by the latter. It provided for the drilling of four test wells, in addition to Strake's original well, to a depth of not over 5,500 feet and at a maximum obligatory cost of $50,000. Strake was to drill the first, Humble the second, and so on, each well to be commenced within a specified time—the first a certain number of days after the contract was effective and each of the others a specified time after the completion of the preceding well. Strake was to furnish Humble samples from the wells he drilled. Within thirty days after the completion of the four wells, Humble would have to decide whether it would keep the leases or reassign them to Strake. After providing for certain adjustments to cover costs out of any oil that might be produced by these wells, the contract further stipulated that, if Humble chose to retain the leases and the production of the wells on the property reached a certain amount per day, Humble would pay $350,000 in cash, alternative provisions being made in the event of smaller production. Finally, if Humble chose to pay the $350,000 and to develop the block of leases, it would pay Strake $3,500,000 out of one-fourth of seven-eighths (that is, the total production minus the original lessors' one-eighth) of the production of flowing wells and one-eighth of seven-eighths of pumping wells; and, after the completion of the payment, Humble would pay Strake a one-twenty-fourth overriding royalty on production. As was sometimes the case, what was considered a high-priced trade at the time proved to be cheap.

Strake commenced drilling as agreed, and Humble began to explore in the vicinity with a reflection seismograph under R. S. Duty. When on June 5, 1932, Strake brought in the first Conroe oil well at about 5,000 feet, Humble had a seismographic picture which, together with subsurface work by Teas, made it possible to proceed confidently with the purchase of additional leases. During that year and the next the company purchased leases on more than 3,000 acres in several blocks for $3,225,000 cash and $3,870,000 in oil payments, followed by the usual one-twenty-fourth overriding royalty. In nearly all the Conroe trades Pratt negotiated the principal terms, leaving the details to be worked out by Landman Cooper and Rex G. Baker of the Legal Department.

Humble succeeded in getting nearly half of the field's productive acreage. It would perhaps have obtained an even larger share had its first reflection work not been incorrectly interpreted to indicate that the south edge of the field had probably been reached—again, not a large enough area had been shot. (This incident led to Humble's adoption of the practice of covering a considerable area around each prospect.) Continued reflection work helped Humble to get as large a portion of the field as it did. According to estimates after the field had been fully developed (1934), Conroe added to Humble's oil reserves a gross of over 300,000,000 barrels, which then ranked as the company's second largest reserve in a single field. Although primarily an oil field, Conroe also added greatly to Humble's reserves of gas, constituting one of the company's largest gas reserves in a single field.

Many factors contributed to Humble's success in obtaining such large reserves at Conroe. Very few major companies bought heavily there, partly because of their curtailment of lease expenditures at that time, but probably also because they were slow to recognize Conroe's importance. Gulf, Shell, and Magnolia bought nothing; Sun, a few leases; Texas had earlier acquired two tracts, which it offered to sell to Humble after the discovery. Important competition, however, was furnished by newcomers like Tidewater, independent operators, drilling contractors, and lease brokers. Humble acquired this valuable property because of the scouting skill of Scout Earle Short, the judgment of its top men in geology and geophysics—Pratt, Barrow, Teas, Carlton, and LaRue—and the willingness of the Board of Directors to follow Pratt's recommendation to assume heavy obligations at what seemed to many oilmen an unpropitious time. The reflection seismograph enabled Humble to buy intelligently. No doubt the company's reputation for successful operations and fair play inclined Strake to negotiate with it and also helped Humble to get much acreage in the competitive lease play that followed the discovery of oil in June, 1932.

Conroe, however, proved to be a troublesome as well as a productive field for Humble. Some of the difficulties encountered will be considered in other connections, but two merit consideration here because of their possible effect on the amount of Humble's reserves in the field and because they illustrate certain hazards that accompanied investment in underground reserves.

One hazard to Humble's interest in Conroe, which it met with spectacular success, was a blowout on a neighboring lease of Harrison & Abercrombie, aggressive Houston wildcatters. This firm had a fifteen-acre tract in the middle of Humble's leases and brought in a well which, late in January, 1933, as a result of a blowout in a neighboring well itself blew out and began to crater. In June it began "boiling out" about 10,000 barrels daily, which the owners caught in a dammed-off creek and ran to a pipeline. Since the Conroe field was prorated by the Railroad Commission at about 100 barrels per well, the wild well was producing 100 times as much as any other well in the field—much of the oil was probably replaced by oil drawn from beneath neighboring leases. The crater, meanwhile, was spreading, gulping down trees and boulders.

Humble, as the largest leaseholder in the field, was particularly anxious that the well be brought under control, but the well's owners, finding this "act of God" highly profitable, refused to do anything about it. The Railroad Commission also would not interfere. Production Director Suman, after consultation with the petroleum engineering staff headed by W. W. Scott, was confident that the well could be killed by directional drilling, that is, by drilling a "relief well" deviated from the perpendicular in a controlled fashion until its bottom was near that of the well to be killed, when the wild well would be choked off by water pumped down the relief well. Humble offered to buy the lease so that it could attempt to shut off the well; Harrison & Abercrombie finally agreed to sell it for $300,000. They stipulated, however, that they should be entitled to all the oil the well produced until Humble succeeded in shutting it off, which many people doubted could be done, and that if the well should catch fire during Humble's efforts they would be paid for the oil consumed—independent operators were not backward in bargaining!

After taking every precaution against fire, Humble started drilling on November 13, 1933. Suman at about the same time flew to California where he obtained the services of John Eastman, who had been drilling deviated holes on town lots in Huntington Beach to tap oil from beneath tidewater. Under Eastman's direction the Humble crew began deviating at the depth of 3,000 feet by means of a whipstock—a wedge of steel inserted in the bottom of the hole at the point where deviation was desired. On January 7, 1934, when the bit was close to the bottom of the wild well, the crew began pumping 30,000 barrels of water per day down the relief well. Within twenty-four hours they succeeded in breaking through and killing the year-old wild well; this was probably the first time deviational drilling had been employed for such a purpose. Suman, true to his principle of selecting the best men for a job, giving them responsibility, and leaving them alone, is said never to have gone near the well during the operations. When the well was brought under control, he was out duck hunting. Nevertheless, he was justly proud of what he and his staff had accomplished. The success of this first effort to kill a wild well in this way did much to make directional drilling widely known.[14]

Conroe also presented a classic example of how confused land titles could be when oil was involved. The possibility existed in any field of "vacancies" being overlooked and of claims to limitation titles being made after a property had acquired value as an oil producer, but in the case of Conroe a rather special problem arose.

In 1838 the Republic of Texas had granted one-third of a league of land to an illiterate colonist named Wilson Strickland. In time it was discovered that all but approximately 495 acres of the grant conflicted with earlier grants; the net acreage of some 495 acres was within what became the Conroe field. In 1847 one Allen Vince sued Strickland for the land, and judgment was rendered in 1848 in favor of the plaintiff. Both Strickland and Vince either vanished or departed this life without making any use of the land. The leases which Humble purchased were under a title which went back for many years and was buttressed by much possession and use but did not, so far as was revealed by the public records, connect with either Wilson Strickland or Allen Vince. Humble further removed any doubt about its title by purchasing the claim of title of the descendants of Allen Vince. It did not recognize the claim of one John Vince that he was the successor to and holder of the claim of title of Allen Vince. Although Rex G. Baker had warned that the production of oil from this property would probably incite title litigation, it was believed that Humble was the owner and holder of the better and superior title and could successfully defend that title against any claim. Baker's prediction proved true, but it is doubtful that even he foresaw the scope and magnitude of the litigation that was to come.

Suit was filed by John Vince, who claimed to be the only successsor to Allen Vince, by the state of Texas, by persons seeking a lease from the state of Texas who contended that the original Wilson Strickland patent from the state was void, and by many other groups of persons acting independently of the others and each claiming to be the true heirs of the original patentee, Wilson Strickland.[15] The trial at Conroe, which lasted almost a year, was, in all probability, the lengthiest jury trial that ever took place in the state of Texas. There were other defendants in the case in addition to Humble. Humble was represented by John C. Townes, R. E. Seagler, Roy Pitts, and Edgar Townes, Jr. The final judgment entered in the trial court upheld Humble's title and denied recovery to the plaintiffs, a decision that was sustained by the appellate courts. Other phases of the litigation pertaining to the same land were tried separately, a part being heard by the same court at Conroe and another part by the federal court at Houston. Some ten years after Humble had first acquired the leases on this property and after the expenditure of large sums of money in preparing for and actually defending this title in the courts, the final appellate steps had been completed in all the Strickland cases. The trial court's judgments holding good the title of Humble and other defendants were affirmed.

The most spectacular example of Humble's leasing campaign was its purchase in 1933 of the largest oil or gas lease ever purchased in the United States, the million-acre King Ranch lease,[16] which seemed at the time one of the most speculative investments of any size into which Humble had ever ventured. Humble had had an exploration lease on the King Ranch in the early 1920s but had found little of interest; when the owners had asked for a large bonus for renewal, the company had let it go. Subsequent developments in Southwest Texas, however, had made the area appear more promising. Pratt felt that since any marine sedimentary beds were likely to hold oil, a million-acre ranch, scattered through eleven Texas counties with oil fields extending toward it from every side—even though there was only one major producing field in Southwest Texas at the time—should not be permitted to remain unleased. He was therefore interested when Robert J. Kleberg, Jr., manager of the King Ranch and grandson of its founder, suggested that Humble consider a lease.

The King Ranch, on which heavy estate taxes had been levied after the death of Mrs. Henrietta M. King in 1925, was then in debt more than $3,000,000, and the bottom had dropped out of the cattle market. The ranch owned some 40,000 steers, two years old and up, but it could not afford to put the steers on the market because the price of beef on-the-hoof was so low. Robert J. Kleberg, Jr., and the other trustees under the will of Mrs. King were anxious to make a deal by which they could sell an oil and gas lease on the ranch for enough money to pay off the ranch's indebtedness.

Pratt, accordingly, entered negotiations with Kleberg and the other trustees to acquire for Humble oil and gas leases on all of the King Ranch property, including the land owned by Kleberg and his mother, individually. After considerable negotiation, the terms of a trade were finally agreed upon, and contracts were drafted by Humble's Rex G. Baker and the legal representative of the King Ranch, Leroy G. Denman, Sr., of San Antonio.

In the meantime, Pratt had had to "sell" the proposition to the Humble Board of Directors. Farish was strongly opposed; disappointment over Kingsville and Piedras Pintas had left him with little interest in Southwest Texas. The board as a whole was dubious. Humble was in the middle of its reserve-accumulation campaign and had recently doubled its lease expenditures. Were not opportunities on the tried and true upper Gulf Coast sufficient without venturing into an area that was not generally considered promising oil country? A consulting geologist to whom Pratt turned for support did not consider the area very favorable, at least for large oil fields. Wiess, however, eventually became sympathetic, and the ebullient Johnny Bonner is said to have encouraged the doubting Thomases with the assurance that a ranch of over a million acres was bound to contain at least a few oil fields!

Pratt, as in connection with leasing at Mexia a dozen years earlier, finally persuaded Farish and the Board of Directors to take an interest in a lease on the ranch. Gulf, Shell, and Texas all, however, turned down the opportunity to participate—they were then not spending money even on much better prospects than an untested Southwest Texas cattle ranch.

Undaunted by failure to win the participation of those strong companies, Pratt finally won the Humble board's assent to leasing the entire King Ranch. Two leases totaling approximately 160,000 acres, covering areas having somewhat different title conditions and requirements, were acquired in addition to the main King Ranch lease. The latter, dated September 26, 1933, included nearly a million acres. The lease was for a term of twenty years and provided that at the end of that period Humble could select and retain all the acreage on the structures on which it had, at that time, obtained production. Humble was obligated to pay an annual rental of $127,824 during the twenty-year primary term and also a one-eighth royalty. Simultaneously with the execution of the leases, Humble loaned the trustees of the King Estate $3,500,000 at 5 per cent interest on the security of a deed of trust on the King Ranch; the annual rental could be applied by Humble on the interest; and, during the second ten-year period of the lease, royalties up to $150,000 each year could be applied as installment payments on the loan.

Humble followed the King Ranch lease with the purchase of leases on a number of other large Southwest Texas ranches. It consequently acquired an almost solid block of nearly 2,000,000 acres between Corpus Christi and the Rio Grande.

The leasing of what was said to be the largest ranch in the world owned by one family was the culmination of the policy of leasing large blocks toward which Humble had been working almost from its beginning and which it had adopted in 1927 as an official policy. Oil production was not to be developed on the King Ranch for several years, however, although a considerable exploration program was undertaken.

Almost at once litigation involving the King Estate lease arose, and a part of the leased property has been under nearly continuous litigation ever since—Felix A. Raymer, an attorney, who joined Humble in 1933 and who was still representing Humble at the time of his death in 1958, spent much of his career with the company on King Ranch litigation. The trouble over the King properties came from a branch of the family that had become separated, geographically if not otherwise, from the rest of the group. These were three unmarried grandchildren of the founder of the King Ranch; their mother had left home, married an army officer, and died before the death of her mother in 1925. At least two of these unmarried grandchildren, living in Chicago, were dissatisfied with either the terms of the will of their grandmother or the construction and interpretation being placed upon it by the trustees named in the will and various other persons entitled to share in the estate. They engaged a Chicago lawyer, Thomas Hart Fisher, to represent them, his fees to consist of specified percentages of their interest in the estate; Edwin Atwood testified in court in 1950 that he and his sister up to that time had conveyed 50 per cent of their interest in Mrs. King's estate to Fisher for his services.[17]

The Atwoods in 1933 and 1935 filed in federal court three suits in which Humble was a defendant because of its lease. These suits attacked the validity of the lease on the allegation that the trustees of the King estate had no right to encumber the property after the expiration of their trusteeship; they also called for an accounting of the funds of the King Estate, and asked for the setting aside of the partition made in 1935 in accordance with the provisions of Mrs. King's will by which the Atwoods received a southern portion of the main ranch. These suits finally, after many years of litigation, all ended in favor of Humble and, indeed, of all the defendants as to the principal issues. The validity of the lease was upheld by the United States District Court at Corpus Christi in 1940, which judgment was sustained by higher courts on appeal; this particular litigation ended in 1943 with the denial of an application for *certiorari* by the Supreme Court of the United States.[18]

The Atwoods have since pursued an unending series of lawsuits in an effort to set aside the lease so far as the acreage allotted to them in the division of the properties is concerned, to challenge Humble's royalty accounting and operations on the land, and to recover damages for a variety of asserted wrongs. All of this litigation which has terminated has ended unfavorably to the Atwoods; some of the litigation was still pending in 1958. On this particular portion of the ranch Humble developed considerable production in the Willamar field. The company has paid royalties of several million dollars on production from the lands allotted to the Atwoods.

As to the remainder of the King Ranch lease acreage, Humble and the Ranch have had no difficulty in interpreting and living under the provisions of the original instruments. The primary term of the leases has twice been extended, and Humble will have the opportunity to continue exploration and development under primary term conditions beyond the year 2000. Production has been developed in a number of fields upon this part of the King Ranch.

Although during 1933 Humble had comparatively little success in actually acquiring proved reserves, in May it participated in what was its most important discovery since Sugarland. Its reflection crews in 1932 had mapped a structure at Tomball in Harris County. The company had leased over 10,000 acres in the area and, owing largely to the work of Chief Landman Cooper, eventually obtained over 75 per cent of the field's acreage.[19] Magnolia drilled the discovery well on a block on which it had sold Humble a one-half interest for $1,000,000. Tomball, however, instead of being a second Conroe as had been expected, turned out to be of moderate size. Humble's share of its ultimate production was estimated, at the time the field was fully developed (1943), as a gross reserve of 42,200,000 barrels of oil.

The year 1933 also added greatly to Humble's gas reserves. The largest addition was in the Pledger field, on the Gulf Coast, a gas-condensate field in the trillion-cubic-foot category; holdings in this field constituted one of Humble's largest gas reserves. Next in rank among its gas reserves were the above Tomball field and the Greta, in Refugio County, both oil-and-gas fields discovered in 1933.

Humble's executives were justifiably pleased with the record to date, and their hopes for the future were correspondingly optimistic. The estimate of the company's crude reserves at about the middle of 1933 was almost a billion barrels, which proved to be not far from correct; its gas reserves were then estimated to be about 800,000,000,000 cubic feet. Humble's percentage of the crude oil reserves of the area in which it operated and of the whole United States was rising. Moreover, as dry holes had become proportionately few and larger reserves per field were acquired, Humble's oil-finding costs decreased; according to Pratt's estimate, the cost per barrel was very much less in 1932 than in 1925 and even 1930. But of the dozen fields which contained most of the lower-cost oil, only three or four, and those not the largest, were Humble discoveries, a record the company was soon to improve.

In the meantime Humble's geophysics was progressing. Its gravity work was beginning to be important; the gravity meter was even faster, and therefore less expensive to use, than the new short-period torsion balance. Gravity instruments made it possible to cover a great deal of territory rapidly and at comparatively little expense; gravity anomalies thus revealed could subsequently be more accurately checked by the reflection seismograph. By 1934, according to Pratt, geophysical instruments were effective in determining with considerable accuracy structures to depths as great as ten thousand feet.

Humble's success in acquiring reserves caused Pratt early in 1934 to urge the continuation of the aggressive reserves campaign. According to statistics, the oil industry in the United States was producing oil faster than it was finding new oil, whereas the earlier trend had been for subtractions and additions to be approximately equal. Pratt observed as a factor in this change the declining importance of the old wildcatter, drilling "on a shoestring, whose name was legion a few years ago" but whose number was greatly reduced by the expense of geophysical surveys—such a survey of a new location was currently, according to Pratt, costing as much as the well itself had cost ten years earlier. If the figures, he said, had "in reality the significance I attach to them, they show that our current finding rate in the American oil industry is desperately low." He had no doubt that intensified finding efforts, "such as we believe to be upon us," would discover new reserves and increase the national finding rate; but it seemed unlikely that the United States could again equal and maintain for a long period the rate attained from 1926 to 1930. Pratt was also alarmed by the increasing cost of finding oil, but he found special significance for Humble in the fact that its oil-finding costs, according to his information, were far below the national average. The currently adverse oil-finding trend might, he admitted, change: "If and when it does we may be justified in placing less emphasis on our oil-finding effort. But until it does so, we would appear to be justified in a vigorous effort to find new fields." [20]

Although the Board of Directors decided to continue the aggressive drive for reserves, a significant shift was made in the way in which reserves were acquired, a shift based on a growing confidence in the company's own exploration organization. The decision was made to spend 90 per cent of the lease-purchase budget on undeveloped properties. Lease expenditures were increased 50 per cent over 1933; 1934 was one of the outstanding lease-acquisition years in Humble's whole experience. Expenditures in geophysical and other oil-finding operations were also greatly increased, and more wildcats were drilled by Humble in 1934 than it had ever drilled in any preceding year.

In 1934, after two years in which it had done relatively little wildcatting and five years during which it had actually discovered only three fields, which yielded small or merely fair production, Humble again struck its stride with three discoveries. One was the largest clear-cut discovery since Sugarland, and it had special significance because of the region in which it was located. This was the Means field in Andrews County, West Texas, which was drilled principally as a result of subsurface work by J. Ben Carsey but partly on the basis of seismographic indications recorded in 1934 by the first Humble geophysical crew operating in the region. Means, as estimated after the field had been developed (1941), added a gross of 65,000,000 barrels to Humble's oil reserves. Deeper drilling to the Cockfield sand at Raccoon Bend in the same year added twice the amount of the estimated reserves of the field's original producing formation.

These reserves acquired by the discovery of new fields and a new sand in an old field were, however, only the beginning of a series of additions to Humble's reserves in 1934. O. H. Truman, who had resigned from Humble in 1931 but had continued to use the gravity meter he had developed while with the company, found for the Quintana Petroleum Corporation what he interpreted to be a prospect on the Tom O'Connor Ranch in Refugio County in Southwest Texas. H. R. Cullen of Quintana offered Humble a one-half interest in 4,000 acres for $50,000. Pratt, after consulting with various members of his staff as was his custom, accepted the offer; although there was little if any favorable geophysical or geologic information, there was general agreement among Humble's top exploration men that the purchase should be made. Humble also bought jointly with Cullen other leases in what became the Tomoconnor field.[21] This field eventually grossed crude reserves, as estimated when the field had been fully developed (1950), of nearly 150,000,000 barrels and also extensive gas reserves. Tomoconnor holds the record of being the largest oil field discovered in Southwest Texas. And it is generally regarded as Humble's greatest bargain, a result of the company's willingness to take a chance on not too clear evidence.

Humble also got about 20 per cent of the large Hastings pool in Brazoria County on the Gulf Coast, a field discovered by Stanolind in December, 1934. After the field had been developed (1940), Humble's share was estimated as a gross oil reserve of less than 100,000,000 barrels. Humble itself had been engaged in seismic work and leasing at Hastings before the discovery, but because of competition it had been unable to shoot and lease as large an area as it wanted to cover. That Humble obtained as much as it did of the field was the result of skillful seismographic exploration, which will be considered in connection with the discovery of the Friendswood field.

Humble entirely missed one Gulf Coast field discovered in 1934, the Old Ocean. This area was a well-known prospect, on which Humble had done refraction shooting in 1925 and 1928, torsion-balance work in 1929, and a small amount of reflection work in 1933. The earlier findings had not been encouraging, and the reflection work proved to be inadequate. Some time before the spring of 1934 (no written record can be found) DeGolyer offered Humble a one-half undivided interest in a lease, apparently on the Bernard River Development Company land, on the strength of reflection work. Pratt recalls that, although he considered the price very high, he had DeGolyer's geophysical map checked by reflection work and that Humble's "geophysics gave a negative answer." Harrison & Abercrombie accepted the offer of participation and discovered on the land one of the best fields on the Gulf Coast.

Humble added tremendously to its reserves in 1934. This increase was achieved not merely through its own discoveries and in such large fields as Tomoconnor and Hastings but also in approximately twenty fields scattered from New Mexico to Louisiana. Humble's success in southern Louisiana was the beginning of a change of fortune in that region, where the company had had small production since 1920.

In the autumn of 1934, when Humble's oil-seeking program for the next year was under discussion in connection with the preparation of the budget, the advisability of continuing so strong a drive to increase the company's reserves was considered. Humble's reserves were then estimated at well over a billion barrels, which was probably more than the combined reserves of the Gulf and The Texas Company. Humble also held a tremendous unproved lease acreage—nearly 7,000,000 acres at the end of the year—and its annual rental payments on undeveloped leases were approximately $1,400,000. The program for the future was discussed at length, but Pratt believed that world demand would grow faster than the discovery of new reserves.

GREAT RESERVE ACQUISITIONS THROUGH HUMBLE DISCOVERIES, 1935–1937

Early in 1935 Pratt, as was his custom, asked his associates to review Humble's reserve-acquisition program. He put the matter to them in the form of the question as to the possible effect on the value of oil reserves of a large excess of oil from new discoveries. Pratt was then in New York, where, according to later correspondence, he was discussing with his former associate in Humble, W. S. Farish, the situation as to oil reserves in the United States.

In replying to Pratt's query, Executive Vice-President Wiess and Chief Geologist Barrow were emphatic in their advocacy of continuing an aggressive reserve-acquisition program. "My real concern," wrote Barrow to Pratt, "is that we have budgeted too little money for drilling and the acquisition of undeveloped properties." He pointed out that in 1934 every district in Humble's operating territory except the Gulf Coast had produced more oil than had been added to reserves, and also that "our leading competitors have finally realized their unfavorable position and are increasing their activities." Wiess emphasized that the cost of producing oil was increasing, and he stated that he did not believe that the value of controlled reserves would be destroyed, "such as we have striven for years to find and as are exemplified by Sugarland, Thompsons, Anahuac, et cetera." Referring to the increasing cost of producing oil, he expressed the belief that the industry would realize enough to return the cost of the oil produced even to the high-cost producer.[22] The judgment as to production and reserves of Barrow and Wiess, and indeed of Farish, was confirmed by Pratt's tour of the California oil industry in the following September. His detailed report[23] of his findings with respect to production and reserves there—current and prospective—illustrates Pratt's indefatigable search for facts to guide in planning Humble's reserve-acquisition program.

These statements of Pratt, Wiess, and Barrow—rare in a company which continuously discussed issues but too seldom left a written record—indicate how the executives tried to plan on the basis of the best forecast they could make of many factors affecting the possible future value of reserves.

One significant factor in the situation developed in 1935: the increasing competition, which drove the cost of proved or prospective oil lands upward. Here several influences were at work. Certain companies had come to realize that they had been mistaken in decreasing their leasing so radically during the depression years; they realized, further, that under proration the holding of reserves would be less risky and that larger reserves would be required in order to maintain owned production in a desirable ratio to a company's requirements. Among the majors, The Texas Company, with the election of a new president, had begun an aggressive search for reserves; Shell was returning strongly to the oil-lands market; and Indiana Standard, through the Stanolind Oil & Gas Company, was becoming very active, as is illustrated by its purchase in 1935 of the Yount-Lee Oil Company in Texas.[24]

It was logical in this situation that Humble, instead of competing aggressively with its major rivals in the acquisition of leases, should curtail its leasing and shift its emphasis to testing and developing its many millions of acres of unproved lands. In 1935 Pratt recommended that Humble budget for lease purchases in 1936 an amount which was less than half the total expenditure for leases in 1934—unless, of course, changed conditions should make greater purchases advisable.

Statistics (Table 7) give a summary view of what was actually done from 1935 through 1937. Lease purchases in terms of dollars were greatly reduced, but the still considerable additions continued to increase, although at a reduced rate, the total undeveloped acreage. Total annual exploration expenditures, exclusive of dry holes, were larger than during 1932–1934 but averaged far less than expenditures in any year from 1925 through 1931. More wildcats were drilled on the average than in the years 1931–1934. The amount of Humble's geophysical work consistently increased, but it is significant that, whereas its geophysicists had in 1932 worked 42.2 per cent of the total geophysical crew-months worked by the industry in the area in which Humble operated, the percentage in 1935 was 14.2 and in 1937 only 10.7.

Humble's exploration in those years ventured into less familiar regions but was aided by increasingly effective geophysical instruments. A greatly improved gravity meter, largely the result of Dr. L. G. Howell's research, was put to work in 1935. This instrument proved especially useful for the rapid survey of an area. Reflection work was greatly expanded, in 1936 even entering upon the exploring of Louisiana's vast extent of swamp and bayou, for which work seismic crews were furnished with house boats and amphibious tractors known as marsh buggies. Several somewhat unsuccessful experiments were made with new devices, such as an instrument for measuring electrical transients in the earth as an indication of structures, and the research department studied the possible use of gamma rays and Geiger counters in well-logging. One new device, the Schlumberger method of electric well-logging, which Humble had begun to use experimentally in 1933, proved effective; by recording the differences in the resistance of different geologic strata to an electric current, this instrument indicated the character and thickness of successive formations penetrated in drilling. The Schlumberger was one of the important instruments that Europe contributed to the oil industry, earlier ones being the torsion balance and the seismograph.

Humble's outstanding addition to its reserves in 1935 was through the discovery of the Anahuac field, its largest discovery up to that time by its own drilling crews. Here also was an example of a prospect that, after earlier geophysical methods had failed to reveal favorable structures, eventually proved to be an oil field. In 1929 Humble had acquired a block of 40,000 acres in the same vicinity, but when the torsion balance indicated no anomaly the leases were allowed to expire. Late in 1932 a trade was made for 21,000 acres with some brokers who had unsuccessfully peddled the block around town before approaching Humble. For 35 cents an acre it obtained the right to explore the block, with the understanding that it could select any acreage for retention at $5.00 per acre. In 1933 Humble covered the block with a reflection seismograph, which found indications of a structure, a further illustration of the importance of the new instrument. Because the seismograph showed that the structure extended beyond the western limit of the Humble block, the company extended its seismic work and leasing but soon met considerable competition from Sun and other companies. Nevertheless, it acquired over three-quarters of the area that later proved productive. It completed the discovery well on March 15, 1935, in thirty-one feet of oil sand in the Frio formation beginning at 7,048 feet. Anahuac, as estimated when the field had been developed (1941), added gross reserves of over 200,000,000 barrels of high-gravity oil and also a large reserve of gas.

Other large additions were also made in 1935. Humble was the principal leaseholder in a unitized block in Waller County on the Gulf Coast on which was discovered the great Katy gas-condensate field, one of the largest of such fields in Texas. The company then owned more than a third of the field, which portion it increased as the field was extended. Katy became Humble's largest gas reserve. The company also added to its reserves in Southwest Texas, where the improved gravity meter proved effective.

Humble's discoveries in 1936 were moderate. The most important was Amelia, in Jefferson County on the Gulf Coast, discovered as a result of seismograph work; Humble owned nearly all of this field, which added a relatively small amount to its crude reserves. In this year the company obtained its greatest reserves in fields that it did not actually discover but to the discovery of which it in some way contributed. The principal field was Talco, in an area in East Texas in which Humble had been sporadically interested ever since Powell. It bought 400 acres of leases at $20.00 per acre from a wildcatting firm to enable that firm to drill on a tract near 9,000 acres which Humble already held. The well was successful and, by purchasing additional acreage, Humble came to own more than half of the field's reserves—a gross reserve of nearly 80,000,000 barrels of very low-gravity and high-viscosity oil, as estimated after the field had been developed (1940).

Pratt's review early in 1937 of Humble's oil-finding experience in the 1930s revealed a striking record. Instead of reducing its exploration work during the depression, Humble had kept its geologic and geophysical crews in the field. Pratt ascribed to geophysics the major credit for the discovery of more than 55 per cent of the oil fields found during the years 1932 to 1936 in the area in which the company operated; and, he wrote, Humble had come into possession of over a third of the total proved reserves on those geophysical prospects. The company had discovered so much oil, or got in so early and effectively in fields discovered by others, that its per-barrel cost of reserves was estimated as being much lower than the costs of the reserves of the two other domestic producing affiliates of Jersey. According to Pratt, Humble was the only one among Jersey's domestic affiliates whose reserve costs compared at all favorably with those of the South American affiliates.

Humble's greatest discovery by its own operated drilling came only a few months later, in the middle of 1937. This was the Friendswood (or Webster) field in Harris County on the Gulf Coast,[25] right in Humble's own backyard, where many companies had been searching for indications of oil for over a decade. Since there was no surface evidence of the deep-seated salt dome on which the field was discovered, there was nothing to suggest the presence of an oil reservoir prior to the development of adequate geophysical instruments. Humble had in 1926 shot the area with fan shots from two to five miles in length, using a mechanical refraction seismograph, but its shot-lines were too short to give indication of the deep oil-bearing structure that was later found. In 1929 it had leased a block from a group of independent operators on the strength of their torsion-balance data. After drilling two wells and making refraction tests without favorable indications, Humble had abandoned this Genoa block; neither the wells nor the refraction recordings reached the structure that later proved productive.

In the spring of 1933 two areas in the same general vicinity became of interest to Humble. A seismograph crew was sent to investigate a small area southeast of the Mykawa dome in Harris County. In order to complete a certain day in the field, some additional holes were shot in northern Brazoria and Galveston counties, near where they join Harris; but for the fact that the records obtained were not of usable quality, probably owing to faulting, Humble might then have obtained its first indication of the Friendswood structure. The second area that interested Humble was west of the town of Webster, where P. H. O'Bannon, a geologist, was working under L. P. Teas; the electric log of an abandoned well, of which a copy was obtained, yielded the very important information that the Discorbus zone there was several hundred feet higher than normal. Humble lease men were instructed to purchase leases that could be bought at reasonable prices in all directions from the abandoned well. Scattered acreage—some within the later Friendswood producing area—was obtained, and a reflection crew began work in April, 1934.

In attempting to get shooting permits, the Humble crew members ran across lease brokers and a seismograph crew of a competitor in the vicinity of Hastings, a circumstance that led the Humble men to suspect that a structure had been found there. Humble lease men were sent into the area. While waiting for shooting permits near Hastings, which were hard to obtain because of competition, the crew shot a number of points near Webster. When shooting permits were obtained at Hastings, the crew's shot-hole rig that had been used at Webster was left there, chiefly because a small bridge over Clear Creek was unsafe for the large drill, and another rig was used at Hastings.

With a shot-hole rig in each place and shooting permits difficult to get at Hastings, the crew shot in both areas. After shooting for three days they obtained sufficient data to indicate the presence of a dome at Friendswood, and by the fifth day to confirm the presence of the Hastings dome. The crew continued to work in both places in order to confuse their competitors. Fourteen days after the seismograph shooting had been started, information on which to begin leasing at Hastings had been obtained and the Friendswood dome had been outlined. Quick leasing enabled Humble to acquire much of what proved to be the Friendswood field.

The discovery well in the Friendswood field was spudded-in in June, 1937, and completed on July 10, after logging oil sand from the depth of 5,817 feet to 6,014. The thickness of the oil column was especially significant because it indicated that the reservoir probably extended beyond Humble's lease block. Humble bought additional leases as a result of this information.

Friendswood, a deep-seated salt dome, proved to be the Gulf Coast's third most productive field, exceeded only by Conroe and Hastings. Humble had been able to acquire less than half of Conroe and only about a fifth of Hastings; but in 1938, by the purchase of the West Ranch, it extended its holdings to 99 per cent of Friendswood—estimated on the full development of the field (1940) as a gross ultimate crude production of over 400,000,000 barrels, as well as a large gas reserve.

Friendswood's magnitude caused Humble's other two principal discoveries in 1937 to pale almost into insignificance. These were its seismograph discovery of the North Crowley field on the Louisiana Gulf Coast and its acquisition of a somewhat larger reserve in the Wasson field in Gaines County in West Texas.

The discovery of the Friendswood field marked for Humble the end of an era that had begun in 1931, the era of the acquisition of a succession of large reserves in a number of great fields. In subsequent years the company made far more numerous discoveries than ever before and also obtained productive acreage in many fields discovered by others, but only a few times during the next score of years did it acquire reserves of 100,000,000 barrels or more in a single field.

In the very year when its notable series of reserve acquisitions in great fields ended with Friendswood, Humble lost the man who more than anyone else is credited with its success in acquiring reserves. On June 30, 1937, Wallace E. Pratt resigned to become a director, vice-president, and member of the executive committee of Standard Oil

Company (New Jersey), of which his former associate, W. S. Farish, had been elected president.

Although his departure was a serious blow to the company, Pratt had been so successful in building up the Geologic, Lease and Scouting Department that the loss was less severe than it might otherwise have been. His personal qualities—his knowledge, integrity, and interest in and respect for the individual personality—and his methods contributed to his success in building a strong department. As an administrator, Pratt expected those working under him to exercise initiative and independence of judgment, and he had the ability—shared by so many Humble executives that it might be regarded as a company characteristic—of giving his men responsibility, watching them, deciding on their merits, and putting implicit confidence in those who met his standards. In the pursuit of the program of building up large reserves, Pratt's "play of men" was particularly important, but it was also a vital factor in the development of a staff of men who were strong both individually and as a group.[26]

Pratt's approach to a decision, whether in testing a man's ability or in buying a block of leases, involved an expert combination of double-checking and confidence, caution and daring. In principle Pratt believed in the most comprehensive and meticulous search for geologic information on which to base the selection of lands to test and develop, but he was willing in an emergency to act before all the desired information about acreage in question had been obtained. He knew that in a competitive lease play inaction might be more risky than action, but he never acted on what are popularly known as hunches. He had the quality, which is characteristic of both the creative scholar and the successful administrator, of finding in the known, even though incomplete, a basis for decision. Such a method at its best, as in Pratt's case, is founded on broad knowledge and a wealth of experience.

Pratt's courage—his willingness to think and act independently—merits special emphasis. At the very time when much of the American oil industry had greatly reduced or nearly ceased its search for oil, he led his company in an unprecedented campaign for building up its reserves. Similarly, in a number of instances he persuaded his associates on the Humble board to invest in oil lands in locations or in amounts not originally favored by them. He won support by the persuasiveness of his facts and arguments, which combined immediate practical considerations with a broad view of conditions and trends in the oil industry and the general economy.

Another of Pratt's salient characteristics, as indeed of the company with which he was associated, was the ability to change his mind, even abruptly, yet without embarrassment. He displayed this quality, for instance, in his decision to enter vigorously into geophysical research after having at first looked upon the seismograph and torsion balance with little confidence. This was, indeed, not so much a change of mind as a decision on the basis of new information. Pratt possessed the flexibility of decision that is a primary requisite to success in so fast-moving and competitive a business as the leasing of oil lands.

Pratt's high standing outside the company was an important factor in Humble's successful drive to increase its reserves. In his business and professional relations he worked for the advancement of petroleum geology, better production methods, and the conservation of resources, thus contributing to Humble's reputation as a progressive company. In the lease market he had a reputation for fair trading, which was undoubtedly one reason why so many opportunities to buy oil lands came to Humble. Pratt had the businessman's concern with costs and a keen sense of oil-land values, but he believed that a trade that was not mutually advantageous and satisfactory was not a good trade.

He was an outstanding geologist as well as an administrator. His counsel was sought by consultants and even geologists with competing companies. He did not make so many definite contributions to the science of geology as did some who devoted their careers to geologic study and research. But his professional stature was high, as is indicated by the fact that he was the first recipient of the Sidney Powers Medal of the American Association of Petroleum Geologists. In presenting this medal, Everette DeGolyer said of Pratt: ". . . he has raised the profession of petroleum geology to an eminence and a dignity which it would not otherwise have attained." [27]

Pratt was succeeded by L. T. Barrow as director responsible for leasing and exploration. A report of March 7, 1938, presented by Barrow to President Wiess on the expenditures and accomplishments of the department, was significant in its review of the past and its implications for the future. The past year (1937) had been one of the peak years in the history of the Geologic, Lease and Scouting Department. The total expenditure—$14,272,000—was larger than that of any previous year except 1926 and 1934 and was 40 per cent larger than that for 1936. Nearly $8,000,000 was spent for lease purchases. The 1937 geophysics expenditure of $1,745,000 exceeded the previous high mark of 1936, and the annual lease rental had risen to $2,845,500. However, these expenditures had "not increased in proportion to the increase in production and reserves."

Barrow nevertheless expressed concern over the expenditures that represented the bulk of the cost increase in 1937. He wrote: "We have been concerned at the increase in lease rentals, and have tried to decide what should be the criterion for the amount of rentals the Company is justified in paying. Each time we come to the conclusion that no set limit can be placed on this item, but that it must be determined by the amount of acreage with favorable geology on it that can be purchased." As to the geophysics expense: "In spite of the fact that we are spending more money in our geophysics effort, we are gradually dropping behind at least two of our competitors. This is not serious inasmuch as we had a jump on them in the early history of reflection work, and inasmuch as we have so much acreage under lease. . . . We do not anticipate that we will be able to reduce our [geophysics] expenditures for at least five years. . . ."

RESPONSE TO CHANGING CONDITIONS, 1938–1941

The men immediately responsible for exploration and leasing in the years 1938–1941 were L. T. Barrow and L. P. Teas. Shortly after his election to the Board of Directors in 1937, Barrow was succeeded as chief geologist by Teas, who as the geologist in Humble's most important producing division, the Gulf Coast, had played an important part in the building-up of the company's reserves. Morgan J. Davis followed Teas as Gulf Coast geologist. Barrow himself became a vice-president in 1938.

Both the general economy and the oil industry were in an uncertain condition for some time after 1937. Crude oil prices had recovered considerably, but the effect of the economic recession which began late in 1937 was increased in the crude market by the return of overproduction and an upsurge in drilling nearly everywhere. This condition was further aggravated after the outbreak of World War II by the loss of European markets.

At the same time, competition for new oil lands continued to increase, though at an uneven rate. Humble's competitors among the majors, some of whom had greatly reduced their leasing and exploration during the depression, had undertaken stronger reserve-acquisition programs. A relatively recent but an increasingly important element was the independent operator. He had formerly been a supplier of unproved or proved acreage, but in the later 1930s he developed more and more oil production himself. Proration removed much of the risk in oil production and made it easier for the small operator to obtain credit from a bank or a supply company to be used in developing his land. "Almost every drilling contractor," wrote Barrow in 1941, "has production of his own today."[28] As a result of greater competition on the one hand and decreased sales of proved lands by the small operator on the other, prices for proved or unproved acreage rose.

A factor influencing Humble's decisions on leasing and exploration was the mounting difficulty of finding new oil in its principal operating regions. Chief Geologist Teas, in his annual reviews of operations in 1938 and 1939, emphasized the trend, particularly on the Gulf Coast, toward deeper discoveries, thinner oil sands, a larger proportion of gas to oil, and smaller fields. The Gulf Coast continued to account for a major portion of the oil found in the general area, but the cost of finding and developing new fields was becoming serious. Moreover, large blocks of unproved lands in favorable areas were becoming scarcer and more difficult to acquire. For Humble, whose great strength lay along the coast, this was an ominous development.

Humble's top administrators evaluated these external factors in relation to their company's needs, resources, and obligations. They knew that they were far ahead of competitors in the volume of reserves actually held—the fear of an imminent shortage, which had plagued them in 1930, was gone. At the beginning of 1938 Humble had an estimated crude reserve of nearly two billion barrels, which at the company's current rate of production would be enough for about forty years. Although Humble's hunger for reserves was never satisfied, this was a sufficiently large supply to give some flexibility in planning leasing and exploration programs. One consideration in planning expenditures at this time was the fact that the company in 1937 and 1938 became indebted to Jersey Standard to the amount of $35,000,000 and borrowed $5,000,000 from banks; although the company's credit was as sound as ever, the officers and directors, who tended to be financially conservative, were not inclined to borrow for uncertain expansion. Humble, moreover, was carrying heavy lease rentals on undeveloped acreage and was committed by its leases to large expenditures for testing the leased acreage and developing production where oil was found. The weight of these considerations would, of course, depend on the course of crude prices and the prospects for profits, but the tendency in the later 1930s was to hold a firmer check on the expenditures of the Geologic, Lease and Scouting Department, particularly on its expenditures for leasing.

The ways in which Humble's reserve-acquisition operations were adjusted to changing conditions and the effect on the company's total reserves are indicated by annual statistics for the years from 1938 through 1941 in Table 7. In brief, Humble continued to add to its net reserves, but principally by greater attention to exploring, testing, and surrendering or developing the lands it already held than (except in 1941) by great net additions to its acreage. Actual operations and results, of course, varied from year to year.

Although in 1938 Humble did not discover large production in any one field, the year brought the company considerable cumulative discoveries and acquisitions. Humble by its own operated drilling found ten widely scattered fields, the most important of which was a seismographic discovery at Kelsey in Southwest Texas which added a substantial amount to its reserves. The company also contributed to and participated in discoveries by others. After thorough seismograph and torsion-balance surveys of an area near the old Spindletop field, it "farmed out" a forty-acre tract to an independent operator, the subsequently famous Glenn H. McCarthy, who brought in the discovery well of the Lovell Lake field; Humble's five-sixths share of the field's total amounted to a modest estimated ultimate oil production as well as a gas reserve.

One purchase in 1938 was reminiscent of the large trades of the earlier 1930s and involved the largest single cash expenditures in Humble's acquisition of oil lands up to that time. This was the purchase in fee of the 28,000-acre West Ranch. This land included the recently discovered Clear Lake field, but it was particularly interesting to Humble because the Friendswood field extended into the ranch by an estimated 800 acres containing an estimated ultimate production of about 60,000,000 barrels of oil. The seller—the same West who had been a principal in the Thompsons sale to Humble—set his initial price far above what he could possibly have hoped to get; Humble countered by an offer considerably below what it expected to pay. Months went by, during which Barrow would occasionally go to West's office with a slightly raised offer and West would sit for hours—with the traditional Texas hat on his head—silently pondering the matter, now and then interrupting his thoughts to discuss with Barrow the land's value or perhaps only the weather; Barrow would return to the Humble board with the latest offer. This procedure was repeated again and again, from August, 1938, throughout the remainder of the year. The contract, in the drawing-up of which H. P. Pressler, Jr., represented Humble, was signed on December 28, 1938. It provided for $8,500,000 in cash plus royalties ranging from three-sixteenths to three-eighths.

Humble acquired an estimated 200,000,000 additional barrels of oil reserves in 1938. In that year it increased, as compared with 1937, the percentage it held of the total reserves of the territory in which it operated. The company's reserves of about two billion barrels were believed to be larger than the combined reserves in the territory of its three nearest competitors—Gulf, Stanolind, and Texas. But the cost of acquiring reserves was rising.

The year 1938 was one of great activity in West Texas in which Humble shared, although not so successfully as to maintain its earlier relative position as a holder of reserves there. On the basis of seismic work it added a number of wildcat blocks in Mitchell and Scurry counties, on the east side of the Permian Basin. This acreage was based on the presumption that there was oil in the Ordovician. In his report for the year Teas commented—correctly, as later years were to prove—that the oil will be "difficult to locate on the sharp structures on which it may occur, and the finding and producing cost will therefore be high."

It was also in 1938 that Humble took the important step of moving its drilling out into the waters of the Gulf of Mexico. The location, named the McFadden-State No. 1 and selected on January 11, 1938, was on lease blocks offshore from Jefferson County purchased in 1935 from the state of Texas. The first well encountered cap rock and was abandoned at 2,655 feet in May, 1938. Two more wells were drilled in the same year, encountered cap rock, and were abandoned. Two were also drilled in the next year, to 6,576 and 7,603 feet, but were "lost" because of heaving shale. On the expiration of their primary term in 1940, these state leases were not renewed. This series of efforts in the Gulf, although close to shore, showed that Humble's search for oil was extending beyond its accustomed areas and helped the company to prepare for a later important development on this new frontier of American oil production.

The year 1939 brought retrenchment in leasing, less being spent by Humble on new acreage than in any other year since 1918. This was owing partly to the large West Ranch purchase of 1938, but other reasons were the decline in crude prices, the rise in lease acreage prices, and Humble's still extensive holdings encumbered by heavy lease rentals and obligations to explore and test and, if oil was found, to develop. Humble, accordingly, purchased only such acreage as its geologists judged to be unusually promising or relatively low in price, and placed its emphasis on the appraisal of acreage already held. It surrendered an unusually large amount—more, in terms of cost, than in any other year since 1931.

Humble's only discoveries in 1939 through its own operated drilling were two fields containing mostly gas and of no particular importance, but it held acreage in several fields discovered by others and got about one-eighth of the estimated production in the West Ranch–Vanderbilt field in Jackson County on the Gulf Coast. A large part of the acreage included in this field's producing area could have been leased before the discovery for $1.00 per acre plus an overriding royalty, but at the time this seemed exorbitant to Humble since it was buying similar large tracts for 50 cents. The purchase of the acreage by Magnolia—which drilled the discovery well—illustrates that companies were willing to pay higher prices for lease acreage. In this year Humble began to find oil on the million-acre King Ranch lease. The company had not yet done any wildcat drilling on the ranch and did not do so for a dozen years after the date of the lease (1933), but it drilled wells offsetting fields on adjoining land discovered by other operators. In 1939 it brought in its first King Ranch well, in the Colorado field; this was a modest reserve addition, although Humble obtained over half the field's total estimated ultimate production.

The year 1939 was in fact disappointing for Humble, its additional reserves coming mostly from upward revisions of the estimated reserves of old fields; the year was a disappointing one also for the oil industry of the region. Humble's chief geologist was discouraged at the time. "Today," reported Teas early in 1940, "in reviewing the events of the year 1939, we must implement our vocabulary of scarcity to say that the discovery of new oil has become extraordinarily difficult. . . ." The quality of the oil fields discovered in Texas, he wrote, continued to decline, the fields being in deeper sands and containing a larger percentage of gas. Southwest Texas appeared to be "drying up," except the area of large ranches, where development had lagged. In West Texas and New Mexico the search was active, but very little production was added. "We believe," wrote Teas, "that we are currently static to a large extent and will probably continue to be so for a number of years in the future."

Yet Humble was in an excellent position as a holder of natural gas reserves and, according to the estimates of the Geologic, Lease and Scouting Department, in its oil reserves was "more amply fortified than any three other companies in our areas, and any two other companies in the United States. . . ." Moreover, it still had 7,400,000 acres of undeveloped lands to explore. Here was ample work for Humble's geophysicists, geologists, and wildcat drillers for many years to come.

Despite its large undeveloped acreage and Teas's discouragement, Humble greatly increased its leasing in 1940. A principal reason was rising oil prices, which spurred the industry to a more aggressive effort to increase reserves. Humble in that year purchased 3,361,000 undeveloped acres at an average cost of about $1.40 an acre. The location of this acreage is significant in that it illustrates the trend toward leasing in regions that had not hitherto been very active. A total of 356,000 acres was bought in West Texas, and leases on 2,558,000 acres were purchased on the Gulf Coast of Louisiana, Mississippi, and Alabama, about four-fifths in the last two of these states.

The year 1940 was also Humble's best year since 1931 for the acquisition of new oil and gas reserves. The company then added markedly to its estimated percentage of oil reserves in the territory in which it operated and in the nation as a whole. Humble's increased wildcatting activity discovered eight fields, all relatively small, the most important being the seismograph discovery of Red Fish Reef in Galveston Bay, which added an estimated 14,000,000 barrels to its reserves. The greatest acquisition of reserves, however, was in a field where Humble did not drill the discovery well but held the majority of the acreage.

Humble had earlier leased a 15,000-acre block at Hawkins in East Texas, as a result principally of surface work by Wendlandt, geologist in the East Texas division, who more than anyone else was responsible for Humble's acquiring and holding so large a portion of this field. The company had delayed drilling a test well because of the oversupply of oil on the market at the time. As not uncommonly happened as a result of leasing by a company with a good exploration organization and oil-finding record, an independent operator, Bobby Manziel, drilled a wildcat on the edge of Humble's block; in December, 1940, he completed a well in the Woodbine. This discovery forced Humble to drill earlier than it had planned, but the full development of the field was delayed until after the war. When the field had been developed (1947), Humble held an estimated gross reserve of nearly 350,000,000 barrels of oil, one of the company's largest crude reserves in a single field, and a substantial gas reserve.[29]

Humble discovered few fields in 1941 but, according to its estimate, raised its percentage of total reserves both in the area in which it operated and in the whole country. One of its five discoveries was Bayou Sale, a seismograph discovery on the Louisiana Gulf Coast that yielded Humble a fair-sized reserve of oil and considerable gas; this was not only Humble's largest field in that area but also its own largest discovery since Friendswood, nearly four years earlier. In addition to this discovery, Humble participated in the discovery of another of the four fields found in southern Louisiana in 1941. In the same year it established the Louisiana Gulf Coast division of the Production Department. Humble also then completed on the King Ranch its first well in the moderate-sized Stratton field, in which it held over half the field's total oil reserves and also considerable gas.

Again in 1941 Humble reduced its expenditures on lease purchases, but the cost and the location of the 1,610,000 acres are worthy of note because they indicate two significant changes. The average cost, $2.15, was 75 cents more than the average in 1940; and less than half the total acreage acquired was in Texas. The largest acreage was obtained on the Gulf Coast eastward from Texas: 495,000 acres in Louisiana, 210,000 in Mississippi, 70,000 in Alabama, and 14,000 in Florida. Humble was expanding its leasing into undeveloped regions, particularly in the Gulf Coast type of terrain with which it had the greatest familiarity and had enjoyed the greatest success. Even with the purchase of this large acreage at a high average cost, Humble's net expenditure on lease purchases in 1941 was less than in any other year since 1924.

Several developments in 1941, however, pointed to the need for a reappraisal of the company's recent leasing and exploration and the adoption of a more aggressive program. The Geologic, Lease and Scouting Department urged such a reappraisal. It believed that Humble could invest five or six million dollars annually in buying undeveloped and developed acreage; under proration in Texas and with improved transportation small leases were believed to offer good prospects, and large areas in North Texas, Southwest Texas, and West Texas were still attractive for deeper drilling.[30] Crude prices were rising, and Humble's production profits promised in 1941 a considerable recovery from the low point of 1940, which was the lowest since 1935. The requirements for national defense, moreover, were already having an effect. Certain conditions were strongly favorable to the resumption of an aggressive oil-finding program, but the entry of the United States into World War II was for a time to turn the energy of the exploration group into other channels of greater immediate urgency.

The Geologic, Lease and Scouting Department faced conversion to war with a new chief geologist. L. P. Teas, whose work had meant so much to Humble, particularly on the Gulf Coast of Texas, after a year's leave of absence resigned in 1941 to go into business for himself. His successor was Morgan J. Davis, formerly Gulf Coast division geologist and acting chief geologist in Teas's absence. Davis had joined Humble in 1925 after graduation from The University of Texas, had left the company in 1929 to serve as resident geologist with a Jersey affiliate in the Dutch East Indies, and had returned to Humble in 1934. His work as a geologist had been outstanding. As early as 1929 he had contributed to the literature on the structure of the Permian Basin. He had demonstrated high general ability, good judgment, and capacity for management.[31]

Humble's long campaign to increase its reserves had proved outstandingly successful. At the end of 1941 the company had an estimated gross working interest of 2.7 billion barrels of oil reserves and 6.5 trillion cubic feet of gas. (See Appendix II, Table VIII.) Its oil reserves had been increased more than twelve times from 1930, and its gas holdings even more. No other domestic producing company had oil reserves of comparable size, and probably no major company held reserves in the United States that had cost less on the average than Humble's.

Those great reserves were to be the primary factor in the tremendous growth of Humble's production and, indeed, of all its operations in subsequent years. Their value, moreover, was being enhanced by other developments within the company that paralleled the growth of reserves. The cost of production; the efficient recovery of oil from a reservoir; economical transportation; the cost, quality, and amounts of products manufactured from the crude oil relative to refinery input; and realizations from the sale of crude and products—all affected the physical and economic productivity of those reserves. Attention is now turned to Humble's other operations in the 1930s, first of all to its scientific and engineering efforts to improve the efficiency and reduce the cost of producing oil.

Chapter 17

THE TECHNOLOGICAL REVOLUTION IN HUMBLE'S PRODUCTION, 1931–1941

DRAMATIC as were Humble's reserve acquisitions in the 1930s, of even greater long-term significance were the growth of the company's understanding of reservoirs and their behavior and its application of new techniques to oil recovery. These were part of an industry-wide movement, led by a number of progressive companies including Humble. Humble's strong position in the movement was based on the early commitment of President Farish and the Board of Directors to reservoir research and petroleum engineering and the consequent progressiveness of the company's Production Department. The resulting technological developments in the 1930s advanced the realization of policies adopted and changes initiated late in the previous decade. They enabled the company to produce oil more efficiently and to increase its reserves by making possible the ultimate recovery of a larger percentage of the oil in a reservoir.[1]

This story of Humble's reservoir research and petroleum engineering is more than a record of one company's accomplishment. To evaluate properly Humble's contribution to this technological revolution is impossible in the absence of any general descriptive exposition of the whole movement. But the one company's experience can be presented as an illuminating case study of problems encountered, the processes by which their solution was attempted, and results. What was accomplished by this one company, moreover, has a meaning far beyond its contribution to the company's success or the advancement of the oil industry. The resulting reduction of costs, tapping of deeply buried oil-bearing geologic structures, and increase in the ultimate recovery from reservoirs illustrate developments within the American oil industry that were of both immediate and long-term significance to the consumer of oil products and also contributed to the strength of the national economy.

THE PRODUCING ORGANIZATION

Humble had a strong producing organization to carry forward new developments. By 1931 its Production Department had been unified; the divided management resulting from the circumstances of the company's origin had disappeared and the department was under one general superintendent, David Frame. Operations were carried on in five regional divisions. Several staff groups, including accounting, employee relations, civil engineering, petroleum engineering, and production research, served the department. John R. Suman was the director for production and a member, together with other top management and staff personnel within the Production Department, of the departmental committee.

Organizational changes in the Production Department in the 1930s were in the direction of expansion, greater internal specialization, and closer integration of the various groups and activities. The department in 1931 took over the management of casinghead gas plants and in 1935 set up a subsidiary gas department under John O. Sue. In 1941 the Louisiana division was established to manage expanding development in the coastal region of that state. Departmental personnel increased from 2,200 in 1931 to 3,800 in 1941. The Petroleum Engineering Department* was nearly quadrupled; its technical personnel became more closely concerned with operations; many transferred to the line organization. W. W. Scott, chief petroleum engineer, became virtually assistant superintendent of production. The research group, which worked closely with the engineers and the line organization, in addition to carrying on research performed technical services for the producing organization—such as measuring reservoir pressures—until that work was in 1937 transferred to the Petroleum Engineering Department. A Proration division was organized in 1934 under William E. Hubbard, one of Humble's early geologists.

In the 1930s Humble's Production Department came to rank high in management, in the quality of its employees, and in the efficient functioning of the whole organization. The early opposition by some practi-

* In 1942 most of the separate groups within the Production Department were renamed divisions; for example, the Petroleum Engineering Department became the Petroleum Engineering Division.

cal men of all ranks to engineering and research gradually disappeared through a process of education or experience and the retirement of the few who could not adjust to the new ways. Suman, Frame, and Scott are given much credit for the excellent co-operation that developed between the old linemen and the engineers and for the generally exceptional morale of the whole department. The personnel of the department was strengthened by special attention to employment and training. In the later 1930s, particularly, much emphasis was placed on supervisory training. At all levels, from the department's top management to the gangs in the field, conference and consultation were widely employed.

STRENGTHENING DRILLING OPERATIONS

Greater economy and efficiency were primary considerations in Humble's drilling operations in the 1930s. Both became increasingly necessary as prices declined and as oil had to be drawn from deeper formations. The crude oil price decline and the need for reducing costs were then matters of concern for the whole industry; deeper drilling, however, was a problem of particular importance to operators on the Gulf Coast, where wells were on the average deeper than in other oil-producing regions in the country except California.

The Petroleum Engineering Department had chief responsibility for drawing up specifications for drilling tools and production equipment and for introducing improved drilling and production practices. The department had a central organization with several functional groups and a staff of field engineers in each producing division, who were responsible to their respective division superintendents as well as to the chief petroleum engineer. W. W. Scott continued to serve as chief petroleum engineer and in the early 1930s as a member of the departmental committee of the Production Department. He deserves much of the credit for organizing a competent petroleum engineering group, directing its work effectively, and winning acceptance of petroleum engineering by practical field men. Indeed, he promoted throughout the company an understanding of technological concepts of conservation practices. In 1936 C. E. Reistle, Jr., was employed by Humble as assistant chief engineer in charge of the Houston petroleum engineering staff. Reistle had been one of the early reservoir research men of the United States Bureau of Mines and field chairman of the East Texas Engineering Association since its organization. In 1940, after the death of Scott, he became head of the department.

As the work of the department grew, new groups were organized to carry on special functions. Among them were the drilling tools, proration, and production-practices sections and the economics bureau. The economics group, set up in 1931, illustrates the department's cost-consciousness and growing emphasis on economy; the group's stated function was "to analyze all production costs and to have such analysis available for comparison so that the most economical practice may be readily ascertained with the least delay and experimentation." [2] Its work came to include making regular and special cost reports and compiling the Production Department's annual and quarterly revised budget. Later in the 1930s the economics group was merged with the Production Department's accounting staff.

A major interest of the petroleum engineers was drilling and producing equipment. They continued the program of standardizing and improving equipment, which had been undertaken in the later 1920s and which became increasingly important as wells increased in depth. This was part of an industry-wide movement headed by committees of the American Petroleum Institute on which Suman, Scott, and other Humble engineers from time to time served. In 1931 Scott, as chairman of the API Committee on Production Practices, was instrumental in the formation of a subcommittee to study well-spacing; this committee came under the chairmanship of T. V. Moore in 1933. Humble's own production equipment committee, which had been established in 1929, approved the specifications included in a publication called *Equipment Standards.*

Systems and methods for controlling quality and inventory and for lengthening the life of equipment were also established. The petroleum engineering laboratory and central staff worked closely with the company's purchasing agent, both in drawing up specifications and in checking on the quality of purchases. They maintained a centralized system of inventory control and set up more efficient use of machine shops for repairs and salvage. They instituted service records for equipment. They studied lubrication, with the object of preparing lubrication charts for all kinds of equipment. They worked on corrosion problems. They were interested in anything having to do with improving equipment and prolonging its efficient life.

A significant achievement in the 1930s of Humble petroleum engineers in co-operation with the line organization was their contribution to the efficiency of drilling operations. At first much attention was given to the speed of dismantling, moving, and setting up rigs, a matter everywhere of importance as a factor in drilling costs but particularly so in such competitive fields as East Texas and Conroe. Formerly the various pieces of drilling equipment had been dismantled entirely by manhandling with the use of chain hoists, loaded on trucks in no particular order, moved to the new location, unloaded, and then reassembled, a process that often took two weeks. During the East Texas boom in 1931, J. U. Teague of the engineering staff prepared a blueprint showing the proper position of each part; a truck equipped with a crane picked up the parts and deposited them at the new location in their proper places.

Hu Harris, head of the new drill tools division, which was organized especially to provide centralized control of all drilling tools and equipment, introduced a radical improvement in 1932. The rotary-rig draw works had hitherto consisted of about seventy-five separately installed pieces; when moved, they all had to be taken apart. Harris permanently assembled several related rig parts on common steel bases or frames, so that the entire rig could be moved in several large units without need for dismantling and reassembling the many parts. In this way rigs could be moved and set up again with a saving of eight to ten hours in erection and dismantling time between rig moves. Further changes later made it possible to move any but the largest rigs "without the crews breaking tours, or, at the most, with only one crew doubling over." Harris' unitized rig was an important contribution to drilling operations and was the forerunner of the present-day draw works.

Improvements in equipment gave Humble, at best, only temporary advantages over its competitors; continuing competitive strength in drilling was largely the result of the sheer efficiency, skill, and teamwork of its crews. Each part of the drilling machinery was lubricated systematically and regularly; Humble rigs experienced comparatively few twist-offs, and Humble wells seldom deviated more than slightly from the vertical. Bringing in a well was commonly a scene of excitement, confusion, and anxiety; but when Suman appeared to watch the bringing-in of the first Tomball well in 1933 the old-time tool pusher in charge simply climbed into his car, apparently unconcerned about what was going on. "Aren't you going to be on the derrick floor when they bring the well in?" the director asked. "Hell, no!" the veteran replied, "I don't need to. Those boys know exactly what to do and when to do it." Suman realized then, he later reminisced, that engineering had really taken hold in production.[3]

At a time when low prices for crude were pressing hard on costs, the rapidity and efficiency of Humble crews in "making hole" was a matter of competitive importance. Humble rig No. 89, operating in the East Texas field in 1931 and 1932, achieved what was then declared to be a world record by completing twenty-four wells with an average depth of 3,750 feet in 366 days, an average for each well of slightly over 15 days and of about 250 feet a day. For shorter periods and in other fields Humble did even better: a casual inspection of a driller's log in the Anahuac field showed 2,400 feet drilled in twenty-four hours.[4] Humble's record in the East Texas field led in October, 1931, to the temporary discontinuance of contract drilling, which effected a saving in costs as well as assuring continued employment for company men.[5] In the year 1932 a monthly average of thirty-one company-owned rigs drilled an average of 318.4 feet per rig per day.

The Petroleum Engineering Department continued throughout the decade to direct its efforts toward improving drilling equipment and techniques and reducing costs. The increasing depth at which new oil fields were being discovered made it necessary to achieve lower drilling costs per foot if these fields were to compete with production from lesser depths. Similarly, the reduction in allowable production per well under proration in Texas made it desirable to reduce drilling costs to compensate for diminished earnings per well. A limiting factor at the time in deeper drilling and in the improvement of drilling and reduction of costs was the fact that steel equipment and pipe of greater strength and quality were not available. Humble engineers, according to a report of 1936, believed that drilling wells from 10,000 to 12,000 feet would require the use of steel alloys of greater strength and less weight; and that, with increased drilling speed, the cost of wells of 12,000 to 15,000 feet would depend largely on metallurgical developments. New techniques, however, increased the usefulness of materials then available, as, for example, the use of welded instead of threaded casing joints. The cost of drilling was also reduced by such other means as using casing that was only as large and strong as was absolutely necessary, adopting practices that extended the life of expensive equipment, reducing the cost of power, and improving drilling-mud control.

Special emphasis continued to be placed on increasing drilling speed. Improvements on the fishtail bit, on which Humble engineers worked with manufacturers in 1936, considerably increased the total footage drilled by a bit and the feet drilled per hour. Other changes helped to effect a saving of from five to seven days in average drilling time per well at Tomball and Anahuac. However, experiments with an automatic piston-type indicator to measure the weight of the drilling bit on a formation being penetrated proved unsatisfactory. So also did a new kind of bit for drilling soft formations, which made possible drilling at record speed but which, after about two years of use on scores of wells, was given up because of its tendency to deviate too greatly from vertical.

Humble's drilling organization on the Gulf Coast, like that of its competitors, ran into certain special problems that were in large part the result of drilling to deeper horizons. The chemical section of the Petroleum Engineering Department and the Production Research Department co-operated with the drilling organization in the search for solutions of such problems.

One problem was that of sloughing or heaving shales, which caused the abandonment of many wells on the Gulf Coast. Such shales on contact with drilling fluids swelled and disintegrated into a mass that squeezed into the hole and filled it up again as fast as the bit penetrated it. Principles of colloidal chemistry were employed in the efforts to solve this difficulty. Humble engineers experimented with various drilling fluids with but indifferent success until in 1939 they were encouraged by the results of the use of sodium-silicate mud; such mud was used successfully on the Bayou Sale discovery well in 1941. The problem of sloughing shales, however, was to continue to plague the driller for several more years.

Another problem was blowouts, which were both dangerous and costly. Blowouts, always a hazard, became more frequent in Humble's operations in the early 1930s and challenged both engineer and driller. The first problem was to discover the cause. The engineers observed that most blowouts occurred as the drill pipe was being removed from the hole. By mid-decade, through use of the recording bottom-hole pressure gauge, they had learned that both normal and abnormally high pressures were being encountered, and by 1937 they knew that in most reservoirs a direct relationship could be traced between pressure and depth below sea level.

Research men, engineers, and drillers co-operated in solving the problem. One way was to remove the drill pipe less frequently, because the swabbing action induced by pulling the pipe—under normal as well as abnormal pressures—was especially hazardous where the pressure was high. The frequency of the "round trips" of the drill pipe was reduced by improvements on the fishtail drilling bit, and a method was devised for obtaining cores without pulling the pipe. Abnormally high pressures encountered were brought under better control by using heavily weighted and treated muds. And mechanical blowout preventers were improved. In the meantime the field personnel were acquiring a better understanding of how to drill where pressures were abnormally high. Progress was thus made, but the problem was not entirely solved.

When in spite of all precautions a blowout did occur, not only the individual well was endangered but also the field, which might be seriously injured by the rapid depletion of its energy. An important new technique for getting a wild well under control was dramatically introduced by Suman at Conroe in 1933 (Chapter 16), that is, drilling a well slantwise toward the bottom of the wild well and forcing water down around the hole to choke off the gas and oil. In 1941 this technique was used at East Flour Bluff to kill a burning blowout that was producing 50,000,000 cubic feet of gas and 100,000 barrels of water a day. Stopping that blowout took months of time. The cost of stopping the blowout and of the original drilling totaled $560,000. When the well was finally brought under control, it was merely a useless crater, but the further waste of gas was prevented.

Cementing, that is, surrounding the lower part of the outside of the casing with cement in order to seal out gas or liquids from formations other than the one being produced, had always been a problem; but as the depth of wells increased it became even more difficult. The portland cement in use would "set" before it could be pumped to the bottom of the deeper wells, a difficulty accentuated by the higher temperature of deep wells, which hastened the process of setting. The problem was to find retarders that would prevent the cement from setting too soon and yet not delay the process so long as to waste the crew's time. Humble engineers devoted themselves primarily to testing various retarders offered by manufacturers rather than to devising new ones. By 1938 high-temperature, slow-setting cements of adequate strength had been developed.

The search for new fields under water in the Texas and Louisiana coastal region also brought problems and innovations for solving them. Drilling in water was nothing new for Humble; it had drilled from platforms supported by pilings on the shallow water of Black Duck Bay at Goose Creek as early as 1917,[6] and entry into southern Louisiana in the 1920s had forced it to adapt operations to a variety of watery circumstances. In 1930 Humble designed and installed, in conjunction with the General Electric Company, the first Diesel electric equipment on a floating barge for use with a rig drilling from a piling foundation. Two years later it installed a small gasoline-powered drilling rig on a floating drilling barge built by the Freeport Sulphur Company. Floating barges, however, were not stable enough for deep drilling and were also affected by changes of the tide. The solution was the use of the submersible barge, which The Texas Company had introduced in 1933. This barge was floated out to a drilling location and sunk to provide a firm platform for the rig; when it was no longer needed in one location, it was refloated and moved to another. Humble built its first submersible barge rig, a steam rig, in 1937. In the two following years it also experimented with offshore drilling, a few thousand feet out in the Gulf of Mexico, from platforms built on piling; even though production was not established, the experiment in drilling on the Gulf was successful.

All these general improvements and devices, many of which were developed by the Production Department's line-and-staff men, together with countless refinements of detail, made possible not only a significant reduction in costs but also drilling to ever greater depths. In 1941 a wildcat at Bayou Sale in Louisiana was drilled to about 12,500 feet. These developments, however, were along more or less familiar lines. The really revolutionary changes in the 1930s were in production practices based on a growing understanding of reservoirs and their behavior.

STUDYING RESERVOIRS AND THEIR BEHAVIOR

Humble's reservoir research group in the 1930s was small but brilliant in its accomplishment. H. D. Wilde, Jr., was its head until his transfer to Baytown in 1933 to succeed Stewart P. Coleman as head of the Baytown Research and Technical Service Department; his successor was T. V. Moore. Both Wilde and Moore were graduates in chemical engineering of the Massachusetts Institute of Technology. Among the other top Humble production research men were Ralph J. Schilthuis, a graduate in petroleum engineering of the Colorado School of Mines, William Hurst, a chemical engineering graduate of Massachusetts Institute of Technology, and Stuart E. Buckley, who had a Master's degree in chemical engineering from The University of Texas. These engineers were all to contribute significantly to advancing the knowledge of reservoirs. Dr. Lewis of MIT continued to serve as consultant to this research staff, which until its transfer in 1936 to the Production Department was a division of the Research and Technical Service Department of the Refinery Department.

The Humble men exchanged ideas and findings, under a research contract, with Jersey Standard and its affiliates. H. H. Hill, formerly of the United States Bureau of Mines, was co-ordinator of production research among Jersey affiliates. Throughout the decade, Humble was the leader among Jersey affiliates in production research.

Humble's reservoir research staff sought to answer several questions of paramount importance in production: What were the most efficient methods and producing rates for fields and wells from the viewpoint of ultimate recovery? What spacing of wells would best accomplish the two objectives of efficient long-time recovery and economy of operations? How could reasonable equity be attained in the allocation of allowables in a field?

Answering these questions required information that could be divided into four categories. The first involved the shape or geometry of the producing reservoir. The location of the wells with respect to reservoir boundaries and the angle of dip of the formation could be included in this category. The second was the nature of the formation rock itself, that is, its porosity and permeability and degree of stratification. Another concerned the physical characteristics and the relative volumes of the reservoir fluids, which could range from gas that migrated readily through the sands to oil so thick that it resembled asphalt and was for practical purposes immobile. The fourth category was related to the natural source of energy available to drive the oil to the producing wells and thence to the surface. The first of these, the geometry of the reservoir, including its nature and uniformity, was, of course, a primary concern of the geologists, while study of the remaining reservoir phenomena and their effect on production was left primarily to the production research staff.

It is important to note that there was wide co-operation within the American oil industry in reservoir research. It was generally recognized that it was necessary to improve knowledge and techniques and to make them known broadly within the industry as a basis for establishing the most efficient industry-wide production practices designed to obtain the maximum practicable oil recovery and thus minimize the loss or waste of the resource. Humble research men, therefore, not only contributed to Jersey and its affiliated companies and profited from their research; they also participated in the work of committees of the American Petroleum Institute, the American Institute of Mining and Metallurgical Engineers, and the American Association of Petroleum Geologists, and they co-operated with scientists in universities and technical schools. Along with academic scientists and the research men of other oil companies they presented their findings before scientific and engineering groups and in published papers. Humble's reservoir research was, therefore, part of a broad advance, to which the company contributed and from which it benefited.

It is probably fair to say, however, that no American oil company in the 1930s surpassed Humble's contribution to the study of oil reservoirs and its application to production. Among the companies operating in the same region as Humble, Gulf was the only other company that in those years developed significant reservoir research; its contributions were particularly outstanding in the study of theoretical aspects of reservoir behavior. Several other large companies were also active in production research, but their interest was principally in the broader field of petroleum engineering rather than in reservoir engineering. Important factors in the progress of Humble's production research effort were the full support of the company's Board of Directors and the complete co-operation of the petroleum engineers and the producing organization at all levels. So close was the integration of Humble's research, engineering, and production that the reservoir research men as well as the petroleum engineers served as a technical service group for production. From time to time, however, as the results of research were increasingly applied in the field, certain functions were transferred from production research. Pipeline technical problems were transferred to Humble Pipe Line Company in 1931; design and operations evaluation of gas plants, to the Gas Department in about 1935; and subsurface pressure measurements and treatment of drilling muds, to the Petroleum Engineering Department in 1937 and 1938, respectively.

Humble's research emphasized the study of actual reservoirs in order to obtain information that would confirm laboratory and theoretical data and that could be used in the study of processes actually taking place many thousands of feet below the surface. In the laboratory, research engineers studied the flow of oil, gas, and water through various types of rocks, the solubility of gas in oil, and the behavior of oil under changes in reservoir pressure. Considerable time was also spent in analyzing samples of the reservoir rock itself and in developing methods to measure its physical properties accurately. In the field, emphasis was placed on the measurement of bottom-hole pressures and the effect of production rates on reservoir pressure behavior. As early as 1929, company engineers recognized "that the effect of dissolved gas in oil, permeability, porosity, gas-oil ratios, and bottom-hole pressure could be resolved into predictions of reservoir condition and recovery of oil," and although their early work was elementary in the light of today's knowledge of reservoir behavior, it was a start in the science of reservoirs.

A limitation on research that had to be overcome if progress was to be made was the difficulty of getting adequate measurements and samples. For example, in 1929 Humble's Coleman, Wilde, and T. W. Moore had worked out an equation expressing the relationship between reservoir pressure, the quantities of gas and oil produced, and the gas and oil content of the reservoir.[7] With the use of this equation, it was theoretically possible to estimate the effect on reservoir pressure of controlling production to reduce gas withdrawals or of injecting gas to increase recovery. Valuable as this formula was as a hypothesis, and important as it proved to be as a tool in reservoir analysis, exemplifying the kind of imaginative thinking that was basic to progress in production research, one essential element was lacking—that is, precise reservoir data, such as pressures, the character and physical properties of the oil and gas in place, and reliable production data on oil, gas, and water.

A major concern, therefore, of the production research group was to design and build instruments for obtaining exact reservoir information, especially, and to devise the most effective methods for their utilization. In April, 1931, Humble put to work in the East Texas field its first subsurface pressure gauge.[8] Although this instrument, which was lowered by a wire line, was too large to be used in the smallest tubing and although it recorded only the maximum pressure encountered, it did make possible the measurement of pressures at the bottom of a well and was thus of enormous importance. The gauge was subsequently improved in various ways, particularly by the development of a chart section for continuous recording. In 1939 a gauge with an outside measurement of only seven-eighths of one inch was built for use in wells with small tubing. In 1932 an instrument was built and put to use that made possible the obtaining, for laboratory analysis, of samples of oil as it actually existed in the reservoir. In 1933 a practical expansion gas porosimeter was developed to help in studying the porosity of reservoir rocks. In 1937 a subsurface temperature gauge was made and put to use in determining reservoir temperatures. Finally, as a result of the development of nonaqueous drilling muds, it became possible to get cores of reservoir formations uncontaminated by water from the drilling mud.

An early and a continuing interest of Humble's research men and engineers, as indeed of those in many companies, was reservoir pressures. With its new and improving pressure gauge, Humble's research staff kept continuous records of the bottom-hole pressure of wells and fields and made special studies to determine correlations between such pressures and rates of production. They regarded the behavior of the pressure, relative to the rate of production, as a primary indication of whether or not efficient use was being made of the active or potential forces capable of moving or displacing oil in a reservoir.

But what were those forces? Pressure alone, although a guide to reservoir behavior, could not explain *why* a reservoir behaved as it did. The sources of a field's natural energy had for some time been a subject of investigation by research men of the United States Bureau of Mines and several companies besides Humble. Until 1930, however, interest had been centered in the role of gas dissolved in oil and the extent to which it could expand and displace oil from the reservoir rocks when pressure in a particular area was lowered. This concept of reservoir energy led to attempts to keep the ratio of gas to oil in production as low as possible and to return to the formation the gas separated from the oil, as Humble did at Sugarland.

In the early 1930s the interest of Humble's reservoir men in their search for the source of a pool's energy, as also that of researchers of other companies and agencies, shifted from a nearly exclusive emphasis on gas in solution in oil to the study of the function of water in the displacement of oil. Wilde of Humble and Lahee of Sun, in research sponsored by the API, worked on glass-windowed, sand-packed laboratory models of reservoirs to investigate the effect of the production rate on the pattern of water encroachment and the efficiency of oil recovery. These models demonstrated the importance of controlled production in effecting a regular displacement of oil by water.[9] Also during the early 1930s significant theoretical work on the movement of water in oil sands was being done by M. Muskat and R. D. Wyckoff of the Gulf Research and Development Corporation.[10]

Humble made its most important contribution to the understanding of water as an energy factor in production by its work on the effect of the compressibility of water in the reservoir. Here the new East Texas field played a stellar role—in one of the greatest oil-field mystery dramas of all time. Humble's research men and petroleum engineers, using their new bottom-hole pressure gauge, observed that different rates of production were accompanied by apparently significant changes in pressure. Since their problem was to explain those variations, obviously they had to identify the source of the field's energy. Their first thought was that the East Texas field derived its energy from gas in solution; but, although as yet they had no adequate way of sampling the oil in the reservoir so as to ascertain the exact relationship of oil and gas, they soon concluded that at existing pressures dissolved gas was of little if any importance.

The surface outcropping of the Woodbine producing sand some 150 miles west of the field suggested the possibility of a water drive from the entry of surface water (see Chapter 18 for drawing). But it was then still believed that, in order to displace the oil produced from a reservoir, water would have to flow through the entire producing sand. The research men, therefore, examined cores from the East Texas reservoir for permeability to water and, applying the fundamental equation for the flow of water through porous rocks, calculated the rate at which water would flow to the reservoir. The findings indicated that water could not trickle through the Woodbine from the surface outcrop fast enough to displace the current production of the field. The research men concluded, therefore, that the water drive was of little significance and recommended that the gas produced with the oil be returned to the reservoir in order to help maintain the reservoir pressure.

A year later Humble scientists and engineers had come to believe that both dissolved gas and water drive provided the natural energy of the East Texas field and that the latter was the more important of the two. They had learned from laboratory research the importance of an even encroachment of water to avoid the trapping of oil in the formation; they also recognized the importance of keeping the production of oil throughout a field at proper rates in order to prevent the liberation and production of dissolved gas, which would result from a too rapid and uneven lowering of pressure. These observations indicate how their concept of the fluid mechanics of the reservoir was developing, but the source of the East Texas field's water-drive energy was still a mystery.[11]

In 1933 Ben E. Lindsly of the United States Bureau of Mines supplied a missing link in the chain of evidence that was to solve the mystery. From subsurface oil taken with the recently developed sampler, Lindsly was able to calculate the actual gas content of the oil and hence its relative displacement power. The data provided by study of numerous bottom-hole samples were decisive. Lindsly demonstrated that the crude from the East Texas field was undersaturated with gas and that, therefore, dissolved gas could not be the effective source of its energy.[12] What, then, was the source of the field's natural energy?

The solution was finally supplied by Humble's research men. T. V. Moore, Wilde, and Schilthuis, who had been studying the flow of fluids by means of laboratory models and field studies, had become interested in the compressibility of water, apparently on the suggestion of Dr. Lewis.[13] Scientists were well aware that water was compressible, but its possible compression was so infinitesimal as to have escaped serious consideration in connection with reservoir energy. Schilthuis and Hurst began to work on the hypothesis that the natural energy in the East Texas field came from the expansion of water. They collected data from which Hurst made brilliant mathematical computations.[14] Their significant conclusion was stated simply in 1934 in a paper presented before a section of the American Institute of Mining and Metallurgical Engineers: [15]

> The data on the East Texas field indicate clearly that water drive or water encroachment is by far the most important agency in maintaining the reservoir pressure or in producing the oil. From the analyses described herein, it appears that the water moves into the field by virtue of its own expansion upon reduction of pressure, and not, as in many cases, by flowing through the entire formation from its surface outcrop to the field.

Schilthuis and Hurst at the same time presented a method, tested in the East Texas field, for predicting the reservoir behavior and the flowing life of water-drive fields at various producing rates. Thus, characteristically, Humble research men translated a new concept into a formula for practical use in field operations.

This concept of the expansibility of water as a source of reservoir energy led to a revision of current views concerning the geologic conditions under which a water drive could be effective.[16] Further studies by Humble and others made it apparent that water was a more common source of reservoir energy than had earlier been thought, indeed that most fields in which Humble operated, especially in the Gulf Coast area, were largely or wholly water-drive fields. This type of drive was generally the most efficient and the easiest to handle. Water, the heaviest of the fluids in a producing formation, would rise evenly below the oil zone if the rate of production in a field was not so rapid or so uneven as to cause water-coning, or water-fingering. To accomplish an even encroachment of water, however, it was necessary to exercise sound production controls, taking into account the geologic configuration of the reservoir and the strength of the water drive. Buckley of Humble, using the equation developed by Hurst and Schilthuis, showed from mathematical calculations for the East Texas field the effect of the rate of oil production and the volume of water produced on pressure behavior, pointing out expressly the need to restrict water production to prevent excessive pressure decline.[17]

Increased understanding of the water drive, particularly of the expansibility of water, was the greatest contribution of the 1930s to the understanding of reservoir energy. Dissolved gas and free gas—a gas cap above the oil in the producing formation—were also studied, as sources of energy, in laboratory and field for a more precise understanding of their behavior and effects. In no two fields were the energy factors found to be exactly the same. The reservoir energy in the East Texas field was furnished chiefly by the expansion of water. Sugarland derived its energy from both dissolved gas and water drive. Hilbig proved a perfect example of a dissolved gas field. The strength of these drives, moreover, varied from field to field, and where they existed in combination their relative contribution to the field's energy varied. Their effective utilization necessitated careful study of each field from the beginning of its development.[18]

The object of such study was, particularly, to determine the rate of withdrawal or other production controls that would utilize these different kinds of drives most efficiently. By 1932 Humble men had concluded from laboratory experiments that, in order to use a water drive most effectively, all the wells in a field should be produced at rates that would cause the water to rise uniformly throughout the entire field as it displaced the oil; theoretical work by Gulf research men confirmed this finding.[19] Humble men also studied various aspects of gas energy, such as the solubility of gas in oil, the conditions affecting efficient displacement of oil by gas-cap gas, and the formation of secondary gas caps by the liberation of dissolved gas. In a gas-cap field, too high a rate of production could cause the gas to move from the gas cap to the well bore, bypassing and trapping oil and thus wasting gas energy and adversely affecting ultimate oil recovery. Thus it was necessary to determine the rate of production, for reservoirs and even individual wells, beyond which the most effective energy and oil-displacement relationships between the various fluids in a reservoir could not be realized.[20]

Reservoir research was aimed at determining the most effective use of the original natural energy of a pool and the methods of restoring energy already dissipated and of supplementing energy when the natural drive forces were insufficient. Pressure maintenance by returning gas to the producing formation had been practiced in the 1920s, but it was then done almost blindly, without much knowledge of the character of the reservoirs or of their natural energy. Humble research men and engineers in the 1930s continued the experiment, started in 1927, of restoring the energy earlier dissipated in the production of oil from the Desdemona field. They also continued for several years an experimental gas repressuring project begun in 1929 at Olney, which threw much light on the benefits to be derived from gas injection in flushing oil out of a reservoir and obtaining additional recovery. However, their attempt to maintain the pressure at Raccoon Bend was ineffective, because of the high degree of natural obstructions to the flow of the gas and oil in the formation, and was discontinued. They learned from experience how to maintain the reservoir pressure at Sugarland. Outstandingly successful was their experiment at Hilbig. A better understanding of reservoirs made possible a more effective use of pressure maintenance as a method of increasing oil production. Maintenance of the water drive by water injection, however, gained little attention in Texas until late in the 1930s. Buckley's study of water production in the East Texas field pointed to the necessity of limiting water production or returning water to the reservoir to help maintain pressure and thus increase ultimate recovery.[21]

Humble's reservoir research group in the 1930s also studied other reservoir conditions affecting oil production. They worked on the flow characteristics of oil, particularly the effect of viscosity; if not the first oil company to study viscosity, Humble seems for many years to have been the most active in both theoretical research and the analysis of samples from reservoirs. Its research group also studied the permeability of sands, using laboratory models and reservoir samples.[22] They studied the concept of relative permeability that Gulf research men had developed through their research on the flow of fluids.[23] Humble men thus learned much about how to employ exact reservoir data to calculate the rate of flow under specific pressure conditions of a given oil in a sand of known permeability.

Reservoir studies also contributed to an understanding of areal drainage, which was necessary for economical and efficient spacing of wells. Spacing was then a highly controversial subject; in the 1920s W. W. Cutler, Jr., and S. C. Herold had contributed to the popular notion that the greater the density of wells, the greater the oil recovery from a reservoir.[24] In 1932, however, Humble research men took the radically opposite position that oil recovery was independent of well-spacing and that spacing should be based on actual reservoir data; their research and observations in fields had indicated that drainage in a reservoir was practically without limits within a continuous and permeable oil-bearing formation, a conclusion which Gulf research subsequently supported.[25] In 1934 Suman went so far as to suggest, on the basis of Humble's research and field experience, that wider spacing, by making possible more effective control of a reservoir's energy, might yield a greater ultimate recovery.[26]

Humble men thus employed the results of research as a bridge on which to pass from the earlier emphasis on the well to an emphasis on the reservoir as a whole and the efficient use of its natural energy. Subsequent research by Humble and other companies corroborated the importance of studying reservoirs and added refinements required by special conditions.

Humble's production research staff also worked on devising formulas for determining allowables of individual wells in prorated fields. Their primary emphasis was on efficient recovery of oil from a reservoir; however, since nearly all fields were divided among many owners, equity was another essential consideration. Humble men had early opposed the traditional open-flow test for determining a well's potential capacity to produce; they held it to be not only inaccurate but also harmful to the reservoir. In 1931 T. V. Moore and Wilde proposed a formula for prorated fields under which 25 per cent of the field quota would be allotted among the various tracts in proportion to their productive acreage and 75 per cent on the basis of capacity as measured by bottom-hole pressure drawdown.[27] Progress in reservoir studies was reflected in a formula that Wilde developed in 1933 for the Allocation Committee of the API. This formula considered the surface area represented by a well, the thickness and porosity of the underlying producing formation, and the ability of the well to produce as determined by its bottom-hole pressure and productivity.[28] This was an effort to base allowables on the recoverable oil actually in place under the surface as allocated to a well. Another proposal for the determination of allowables was the principle of volumetric withdrawal; according to this principle, gas and water as well as oil should be considered in computing the allowable volume produced by a well.[29] The purpose of this method was to encourage conservation of reservoir energy and protect a progressive operator from wasteful practices on offset leases.

Humble's research group also contributed toward a better understanding of connate waters. The earlier assumption in estimating the oil content of a reservoir and in planning pressure maintenance and secondary recovery had been that oil and gas completely occupied the pores of the producing zone; water, it had been believed, was always by force of gravity beneath the oil zone, although with some contamination at the interface. The possibility that water might also be present in the pores of the oil zone was recognized by Humble men and others for many years; some evidence of its existence had been found by a number of investigators. To prove whether or not water in substantial amount actually was present in the oil zone and, if it was, to determine its relationship to oil, was, however, impossible so long as cores free from contamination with water from drilling fluid were unobtainable. When, after the mid-thirties, the use of nonaqueous drilling mud made it possible to obtain uncontaminated cores, Humble's Schilthuis, by analyzing samples of reservoir rocks from three different formations in three fields—East Texas, Anahuac, and Tomball—demonstrated not only that water was present in substantial quantity in the oil zone of those sands but also that there was an inverse correlation between water saturation and permeability. In 1937 he presented his findings to the Petroleum Division of the American Institute of Mining and Metallurgical Engineers with practical suggestions on how to determine the proportion of water to oil in an oil sand,[30] thus making possible greater accuracy in estimating the reserves in a field.

As their instrumentation and techniques improved and their knowledge grew, the Humble reservoir research men undertook refinements of their earlier work. One subject that very much needed such study, particularly as fields were discovered at greater depths, was the physical behavior of the hydrocarbon systems occurring in reservoirs; not enough was known concerning these hydrocarbons to make it possible to calculate their behavior in reservoirs under high pressure or to determine how best to separate them on the surface. In the later 1930s the Humble men carried on extensive research on this subject. They studied gas-condensate reservoirs, on which Lacey and Sage of the California Institute of Technology did early theoretical and experimental work.[31] Similarly, the Humble group undertook studies of some of the more difficult aspects of reservoir mechanics, such as the capillary properties and two- and three-phase flow in oil sands.

Less dramatic than the study of oil reservoirs and their behavior was research by Humble engineers on lifting methods and on dealing with oil after it had been produced. Methods of treating crude oil to break emulsions and to separate from it water and other foreign matters were studied throughout the decade with increasing urgency as more salt water was produced from aging and deeper wells. The more efficient separation of condensate was another continuing challenge; in 1935 a project was initiated to experiment with low-temperature separation equipment and techniques. In 1940 a new flow treater was designed, which reduced not only installation and operating costs but also losses from evaporation.

To discover new uses for liquefied gas was the object of experimentation as well. As the natural energy of many of Humble's older wells diminished, artificial lifting methods called for increasing study.

The objectives of Humble's production research were in the 1930s, as later, accomplished by working along two routes. One was to develop general concepts, or principles, and formulas which would describe or govern the production process; the other was to develop methods of obtaining pertinent basic data about specific fields and wells to assist in determining how they could best be operated.

The early emphasis in gathering field data was on measuring reservoir pressures. Such data were the first for the collection of which adequate instrumentation was devised and thus the earliest evidence of a field's behavior during production that could be systematically observed. The research men supplied pressure measurements and interpretation of them until 1937, when this service was taken over by the new production practices division of the Petroleum Engineering Department. Thereafter, the engineers made systematic pressure surveys of fields—of 25 in 1937 and 115 in 1939; the increase in the number of fields surveyed illustrates the emphasis placed on maintaining good records of reservoir behavior.

At the same time, research men and petroleum engineers were also making comprehensive studies in individual fields of the various phenomena affecting recovery. The 1929, 1931, and 1933 engineering reports on the Sugarland field comprise an early study of a reservoir. In 1939 was completed a study of the Talco field. On the basis of this study the amount of oil in the reservoir was estimated and various plans were proposed for developing the field, with forecasts of the probable effect of each plan on the reservoir.

A result of a decade of work by Humble's reservoir research staff and petroleum engineers was the completion in 1940 of *The Principles of Reservoir Behavior*. This text, prepared for the use of Humble's field engineers, was designed to state systematically those principles of reservoir engineering that had been derived from reservoir research and field experimentation.[32] As described by Suman, it "outlined the fundamental equations describing the performance of the dissolved-gas drive, water drive, and gas-cap drive of reservoirs, as well as other principles."

As the decade of the 1930s passed, the growing understanding of the nature and behavior of petroleum reservoirs and the developing production techniques resulting from widespread research progressively changed the producing operations of Humble and of the industry to which it belonged. In that process a dramatic and significant role was played by one new field, the East Texas field, which challenged the scientist to greater effort and the engineer to new skills, while it also demonstrated that some means had to be found for curbing the old competitive practices of the American oil industry. The result was a transformation in oil industry-government relations that was as revolutionary as was the change in the technology of oil production.

Chapter 18

THE EAST TEXAS ORDEAL AND THE ESTABLISHMENT OF PRORATION, 1931–1935

With the inexorability of fate in an ancient Greek tragedy many forces combined in the early 1930s to drive the conservation movement in Texas to a climax. Action centered in a region known as East Texas, but its ramifications were state-wide and even nationwide. Although Humble Oil & Refining Company was only one of several principal actors in the drama, this phase in the development of the conservation movement must here be recounted at some length, both because of the importance of Humble's participation and because of the significance of the outcome to its operations.[1]

The backdrop against which the action took place was familiar but now appeared in sharpened lines and colors. The overproduction of recent years was being intensified by the cumulative success of the scientific and engineering revolution in oil finding and by the great depression. Such a combination of circumstances would in itself have created difficulties; in addition came a flood of oil from the newly discovered East Texas field, which could for a short time have supplied, although with great waste, all the country's oil needs. In East Texas, indeed, was re-enacted on a grand scale the familiar history of flush production, at this time under conditions of greater competition and a less dynamic demand than in earlier decades.

Texas oil operators would have been helpless before this new flood of oil had they not recently learned something of the science and practice of conservation through the development of production research and engineering and through efforts to cope with overproduction in West

Texas and the Panhandle.[2] Without the discovery of East Texas, however, the conservation movement in Texas and, indeed, in the whole country would undoubtedly in the 1930s have gone forward more slowly —if it had progressed at all. The East Texas crisis precipitated action that eventually led to the establishment of effective state-wide conservation in Texas and in other important oil-producing states.

CHAOS AND THE FAILURE OF PRORATION IN EAST TEXAS IN 1931

On October 3, 1930, a veteran wildcatter, Columbus M. Joiner of Ardmore, Oklahoma, completed the East Texas discovery well about six miles south of Overton, near a place later called Joinerville. This was about a month after the first state-wide proration order had been announced in Texas and less than a week after the Danciger Oil & Refining Company had obtained a temporary injunction against that order.[3]

A description of the geology of the East Texas field is now possible because of information accumulated since its discovery by geologists, reservoir research men, and engineers. On the surface this field is rolling piney-woods country; underneath lies the greatest oil pool ever discovered in the United States.

The field is located in the East Texas Geosyncline, a large regional trough which, in its present structural form, is affected by the Sabine Uplift on the east and the Bend Arch on the west (see drawing in Chapter 1). These positive features helped to shape and contain the basin into which the prolific oil-producing Cretaceous sediments were deposited. The city of Tyler is located near the axis on the deepest part of the basin. Extending away from this axis, successively older beds outcrop at the surface. All the formations that are penetrated by wells in the middle of the basin outcrop at the surface, with the exception of the Jurassic sediments. For instance, the Woodbine formation, which outcrops in a belt near Fort Worth approximately 150 miles west of Tyler, lies at a depth of about 5,400 feet in the north central portion of the trough. To the east of the trough, the Woodbine rises on the west flank of the Sabine Uplift; and in that eastward rise it is penetrated in the East Texas field at a depth of about 3,600 feet.

The Woodbine sand pinches out between impervious strata on the west flank of the Sabine Uplift. This pinchout, plus the later upward movement of the Sabine Uplift, formed the great East Texas oil trap. (See accompanying drawing.) The producing sand is an old shoreline deposit composed of differing combinations of sand, shale, gravel, and altered volcanic material. This same Woodbine sand is also the producing formation at Mexia, Powell, Boggy Creek, Van, Hawkins, and Neches. Although the character of the sand in the East Texas reservoir varies, it is generally highly porous and permeable. The sand pinch-out occurs at a depth of 3,100 feet below sea level. When production was first established, the oil column was about 200 feet high. Salt water underlies much of the oil column and is the chief displacing agent that tends to maintain reservoir pressure and causes the oil to flow to the well bores. The source of the oil has not been definitely determined, but most geologists believe the source beds are either the Eagle Ford shales or the Woodbine formation itself, or both.

"Dad" Joiner's discovery, although only a small producer, set in motion a frenzy of activity, but it was not realized that the field would

GEOLOGIC CROSS SECTION OF THE EAST TEXAS FIELD

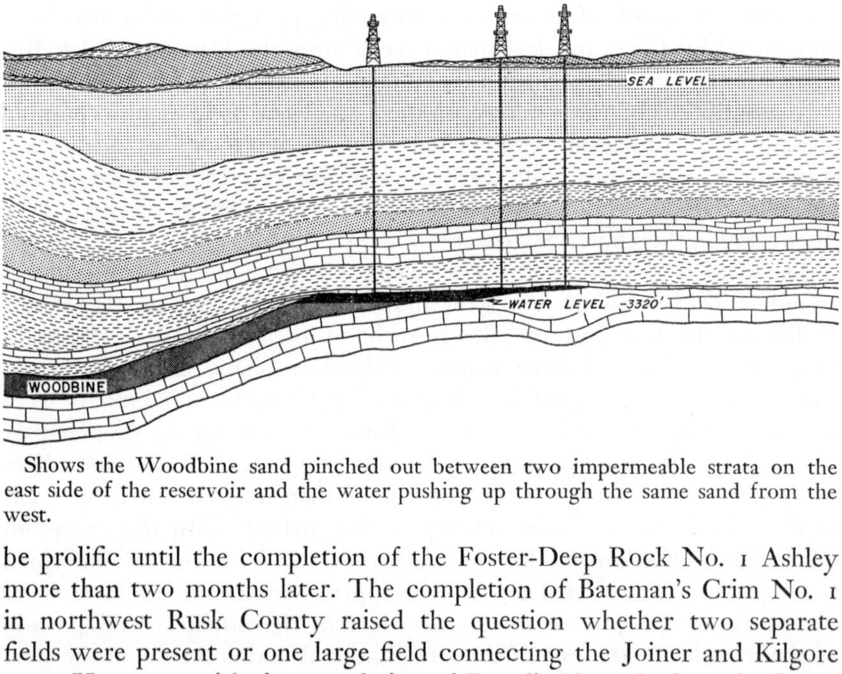

Shows the Woodbine sand pinched out between two impermeable strata on the east side of the reservoir and the water pushing up through the same sand from the west.

be prolific until the completion of the Foster-Deep Rock No. 1 Ashley more than two months later. The completion of Bateman's Crim No. 1 in northwest Rusk County raised the question whether two separate fields were present or one large field connecting the Joiner and Kilgore areas. However, with the completion of Farrel's No. 1 Lathrop in Gregg County, it was generally concluded that all three producing areas were parts of one enormous field, although how enormous nobody knew. By the latter part of May, 1931, the field was estimated to be thirty-seven miles long, north and south, and seven miles wide, and to contain 100,000 productive acres. Well after well was brought in near Overton, Kilgore, and Gladewater. Production increased very rapidly—reaching 340,000 barrels on April 29, 1931—owing to the extremely large potential of the wells, some of which exceeded 15,000 barrels per day.[4]

Humble entered the East Texas field early and in strength. Because it had been interested in the region since 1928 and had made arrangements for a test in the area that might have been the discovery well except for Joiner's earlier success, Humble on the first showing of oil in Joiner's well on September 5, 1930, was ready to move fast to increase its holdings (Chapter 16). Within a few months it held nearly 16,000 proved acres, or 13 per cent of the proved acreage of the field, which was by far the largest holding of any one company.

In developing production on its leases Humble followed the practices recommended by its technologists. Like other large integrated companies and some large independents, it practiced relatively wide spacing of wells. Unlike most producers, however, it early began to study the nature and behavior of the reservoir. The new bottom-hole pressure gauge devised by the research group was employed to measure pressures at the bottom of wells at the face of the producing formation; the use of the gauge in East Texas began in April, 1931, with the recording of pressures for twenty-five wells. By continuing to record such data Humble engineers built up a fund of information about the correlation of pressures and rates of production for different parts of the field, which gave significant indications of the behavior of the reservoir under varying conditions of production from time to time and varying rates in different parts of the field at a given time.[5] They early began to study the source of the reservoir's energy, but, as has already been observed, that mystery was unraveled only after several years of research. Yet, without understanding the fluid mechanics of the reservoir, they found, even so early, a close relationship between bottom-hole pressures and rates of production.

Humble offered on January 15, 1931, to enter the East Texas field as a purchaser of oil. It proposed to extend to this field its line from the Van field to the Louisiana boundary and to share its market ratably—that is, to purchase proportionately as much oil from others' leases with which its pipeline would be connected as the amount run from its own leases—on the condition that orderly, ratable production be established. Humble was unwilling to enter the field so long as production was unrestrained.

Farish and Suman were active in the subsequent effort to promote agreement among East Texas interests to prorate the field, but the effort failed.[6] Proration was already vigorously opposed, many producers holding that this field, like earlier ones, was entitled to a period of flush production. Therefore, on February 27, 1931, Humble announced that it was building its own private facilities for taking care of the production of its properties in the East Texas field and that it would not enter the field as a purchaser.

This announcement contained an explanation of Humble's position. The reasons for the company's interest in the regulation of production were stated thus: "On account of its large producing interests it has been and is now vitally interested in securing the largest ultimate recovery from its oil properties; it is interested in securing this at the lowest possible cost of production; and it is interested in securing for its oil the highest price obtainable." The announcement set forth the advantages of controlled production:

> Orderly production secures these results by preventing physical underground and aboveground waste, by eliminating unnecessary and costly expenditures incident to rush operations, and by preventing the dumping of distress oil on a crowded market and thus breaking the price structure locally with a final resulting break of the price structure generally. . . . If East Texas produces oil in distress quantities without reference to market demand therefor, not only will there be actual waste of oil indicated above and increased cost of production, but the price of all oil in Texas inevitably will fall to the price basis established for the distress oil of East Texas.

After voluntary proration had proved unattainable, the only agency that could help was the Railroad Commission, but for six months after the completion of the East Texas discovery well the Commission did not attempt to regulate production in that field. Some delay was understandable. The Commission might, for example, wish to accumulate more extensive information before setting a tentative field allowable and prorating it among the wells, although it could have limited individual wells concerning which information was available. Moreover, the authority of the Commission to prorate production had not yet been clearly defined by either legislature or courts and had been strongly challenged by the Danciger suit, which was then in process of litigation.

The Danciger case was a crucial one, the first important case involving the exercise of the police power of the state of Texas in state-wide prorating. The Danciger Oil & Refining Company had obtained a temporary injunction against the Railroad Commission's proration orders in the fall of 1930, on the allegation that those orders deprived the company of property without due process of law and in violation of Article 19 of the Texas Constitution. Three companies were involved, including Humble Pipe Line Company as a carrier of Danciger Oil.

Hines H. Baker of Humble, as well as Robert E. Hardwicke of Dallas and John E. Kilgore of Wichita Falls, counsel for a producers' proration committee, worked with the state's attorney general and his assistants in preparing the argument for the defense. Baker advised, especially, on the controversial issue of market demand as a basis for the proration allowable. Danciger's principal reliance was on the claim that it was not permitting actual waste of oil. The defendants held, however, that it was not necessary to show actual physical waste on Danciger's part, but that the reasonableness of the order could be supported on the ground that Danciger's action in producing its wells to capacity, when followed by protective measures by offsetting producers, necessarily resulted in waste in two respects: large aboveground storage would be required, which would result in the evaporation of the more volatile fractions; and the waste of gas and the encroachment of water in the reservoir resulting from flush or uneven production would cause underground waste of oil. The defendants' attorneys held that even under the principle of ownership of oil in place there was a common interest in the pressure of water and the expansive pressure of gas in a pool.

The prorationists won the first round in the Danciger case on February 13, 1931, when the District Court of Travis County delivered an opinion in favor of the Railroad Commission and the other defendants. The decision held that the order was a reasonable one for the prevention of waste and within the power and authority of the Commission.[7] Danciger, however, appealed the decision, which meant that the issue would not be settled until later.

While the litigation cast doubt on the authority of the Railroad Commission to prorate production and perhaps partially justified its hesitancy in attempting to do so, there can be no doubt as to the Commission's right to enforce Rule 37. Under this old rule—which specified the minimum distance between wells and from wells to property lines, with a provision for an exception—the Railroad Commission granted exceptions so freely that 65 per cent of the wells in the East Texas field were said to have been drilled as exceptions to the rule. The Commission actually permitted twelve wells to be drilled on a lot 60 by 150 feet in Kilgore—after a bank building occupying that corner had been torn down for the purpose! Exceptions of this nature could hardly be supported on the basis of equity or the prevention of waste.[8]

Explanations of the Commission's failure to take a firm stand on Rule 37 in East Texas are easier to suggest than to evaluate. The Commission was under political and other pressures that militated against strict enforcement even of well-established conservation rules. There was the usual lure of quick profits from a rich field. Moreover, East Texas was an area of small holdings, which brought innumerable requests for spacing exceptions. The depression and resultant poverty influenced the small landholders to demand as large an immediate income as possible. Clarence Gilmore's death had recently removed from the chairmanship of the Commission a staunch supporter of the new engineering approach to production problems and had brought to it a man unfamiliar with the issues and the new reservoir engineering. Firm administration in accordance with law, equity, and good engineering practice was to come only with a better understanding of the issues and the ways of meeting them on the part of legislators, commissioners, judges, operators, landowners, and the public in general. The East Texas field had, perhaps, been discovered too early for the normal processes of democracy to have prepared the ethical codes and institutional methods capable of dealing with so large and important a field.

Counterpressures on the Railroad Commission, however, brought some action, but only after the field had been developed for a number of months almost without restraint. The Oil States Advisory Commission, at a meeting which Governor W. H. Murray of Oklahoma had called to consider oil industry problems and in which Governor Ross S. Sterling of Texas and representatives of the governors of Kansas and New Mexico participated, in March, 1931, issued a report that recommended proration based on market demand and the application of that principle to the East Texas field. Humble's refusal to purchase oil in East Texas until after the establishment of proration exerted local pressure. Other oil companies urged action. The Commission issued an order on April 4 which, amended twice, became effective May 1 for the proration of the East Texas field. A principal East Texas antiproration organization agreed to a sixty-day "truce" to give the effort a chance to prove itself.[9]

Humble, which had been active in the discussions leading up to the order, then extended its pipeline to the field. It made connections with as many leases as it could serve on the basis of the allowable production and posted the Mid-Continent price.

The Railroad Commission's proration order divided the East Texas producing area into units of twenty acres or fractions thereof and set the initial total daily allowable of the field at 70,000 barrels, which amount was to be increased gradually; the allowable of each unit was to be determined by the relation that its potential production bore to that of the entire area, except that every unit or fractional unit was to be permitted to produce a minimum of 100 barrels per day.[10] Unfortunately, this order encouraged the drilling of additional wells, since each well increased a unit's total production, although not proportionately.

The truce proved entirely ineffective. Many operators simply ignored the Commission's orders, and others brought injunction suits. Sometimes the courts issued restraining orders, which permitted the plaintiffs to produce to capacity; only one major company is said to have utilized this device. In other cases the operator simply filed suit and then, in the belief that the mere filing of a suit would give immunity if the order was later declared valid, proceeded to violate the proration order. Operators who might have preferred to obey the order were forced to produce proportionately with their offsetting neighbors or suffer drainage of their oil.[11] Humble suffered excessive offset or adjacent production by certain independent and major companies for several weeks before finally calling on the Commission to enforce its orders, vacate them, or permit Humble to produce sufficiently in excess of its allowables to protect itself.[12]

Production soon increased to twice the Commission's allowable, and posted prices for East Texas crude ceased to have any relationship to the actual market price. Since about half the production was moving at 35 cents or less per barrel, on May 26, 1931, four major companies, including Humble, cut their posted price from 65 cents to the actual going price of 35 cents. A week later, after the price structure had been almost destroyed, Humble cut all its crude prices and ceased to post a price for East Texas crude; but it continued to take oil ratably from its own properties and those with which its pipelines were connected, promising to pay the "going price" at the regular time of settlement. Humble decided that that price was 15 cents per barrel, although at the time some crude was sold at as little as 6 cents and "spot sales" were reported at as low as 2 cents. When the daily production of East Texas had reached 250,000 barrels, Humble was buying 18,000 of less than 40,000 barrels of crude being taken ratably from properties operated by independents.[13]

By June, 1931, the first attempt to prorate East Texas production had collapsed, and a movement was under way to promote legislation for proration according to market demand. Governor Sterling, however, took no action, despite an avalanche of telegrams urging him to call a special session of the legislature at once in order to prevent the complete destruction of the Texas oil industry. Tom Cranfill, who had led the opposition to proration in West Texas in 1928, now promoted the "East Texas plan," which proposed an initial total field allowable in excess of 200,000 barrels daily, to be increased to a maxium of 500,000 as the market permitted. The distinctive feature of the Cranfill plan was the provision that the owners of tracts larger than the proration unit of twenty acres might produce the allowable for as much as 100 acres through a single well. The allowables of the numerous wells on tracts of less than twenty acres would be determined by an arbitration committee.[14]

Farish expressed Humble's willingness to co-operate in any equitable program that would bring about ratable taking and relieve the situation, but he warned that success was dependent primarily upon the approval of all producers. Cranfill's plan, unfortunately, had in it nothing to attract the men with wells on five-acre, one-half acre, or town-lot tracts, who could hardly expect to get from an arbitration committee a larger allowable than the minimum of 100 barrels per well permitted under the existing order.

On July 2, nevertheless, the Commission issued an order embodying the Cranfill plan's principles in modified form. This order provided that the field allowable be increased to 250,000 barrels per day and that prorating be by acreage unit instead of well-potential, but it permitted the assignment of the allowables of only two twenty-acre units to a single well.

Despite this order, production continued to mount with a consequent drop in prices. East Texas sales pulled down prices in other fields. On July 8 Humble reduced its postings on all West Texas–New Mexico crudes to 10 cents and on certain low-gravity crudes in North Texas and central East Texas to the same amount.[15] Opponents of proration denounced price cuts as intended to bring pressure for "monopolistic legislation," meaning a proration bill. A meeting of East Texas landowners who had earlier opposed proration, however, sent a telegram of congratulations to Governor Sterling on learning that he had called a special session of the legislature to adopt a conservation measure that would remove any doubt of the legality of production control by the Railroad Commission.[16]

Although proration was gaining friends in the summer of 1931, antiproration forces in East Texas were at their strongest. Small producers, often inexperienced and operating on borrowed capital, preferred, for example, to produce 10,000 barrels daily over a few months even at 25 cents a barrel rather than 300 daily at $1.00 over several years. Similarly, many operators who had swarmed into East Texas to make a "fast killing" wanted no restraint on production. Small refineries, hastily built with makeshift equipment, were dependent on cheap oil to enable them to meet the competition of larger and better-equipped plants. Some companies operating larger refineries were willing to avail themselves of an opportunity to stock up on cheap oil. Some majors—especially Gulf—feared anything savoring of government regulation. Many East Texas landowners, who for generations had been barely eking out a living growing sweet potatoes and goobers (peanuts) on their sandy soil and were now suffering from the double impact of a protracted drought and depression, were easily induced to believe that oil production on their lands was being restricted and they themselves were being despoiled as a result of a conspiracy of the big interests.

Proration in East Texas at the same time enjoyed a wide range of support. The most influential supporters were those independents who were not compelled by immediate financial stringency to produce as much as they could and who were farseeing enough to recognize the advantages of keeping the remarkable East Texas field flowing indefinitely, in the hope of selling the oil at a reasonable price instead of "letting it blow its head off" at a few cents a barrel. Proration had a special appeal to companies with a long-term view, with pipelines to keep full, refineries to supply, and customers to satisfy. They held that proration by restricting production and conserving gas pressure—the water drive was not yet understood—would enable the producer to obtain oil from one field for perhaps forty years at a tempo that would keep pipelines, stills, and customers supplied, but not swamped, and at prices above the cost of production. Proration also derived support from those East Texas land and royalty owners who saw that they would make more from their properties if the field could be controlled and pressure and income maintained over a long period of time. Businessmen of the region, moreover, recognized that continuing prosperity could not be based on feast today and famine tomorrow. Some members of the general public also understood that cheap gasoline would be dearly bought at the cost of the rapid depletion of the East Texas field and the sale of its oil at ruinous prices.

East Texas production was not merely a local issue. Ten-cent oil there threatened to force the abandonment of thousands of wells in older and higher-cost fields, especially in North Texas and West Texas, with the loss of the reserves remaining to be recovered from those wells. The state of Texas itself, which was largely dependent on its revenues from oil, was directly concerned. East Texas was also having a depressing effect on the national oil market. It was soon to become the largest problem field in the whole history of the American oil industry.

The calling of a special session of the Texas legislature made proration a state-wide political issue and thus the concern of others than oilmen and public officials. Winning support for proration, therefore, was no longer a matter of dealing with more or less informed oilmen and the friendly Railroad Commission, but of convincing legislators and the general public, who represented all ranges of information, attitude, and opinion. This broad public, and indeed the legislators and judges, had not gone through the process of education that Humble and other companies had experienced. That they should have little knowledge of the problem of waste was understandable, but this lack of familiarity with the industry and its problems was a serious obstacle to what Farish called a rational solution of industry problems.

In these circumstances it was easy to arouse suspicion of the motives and objectives of the conservationists where such suspicion did not already exist. A traditional fear of monopoly and big business was still strong in Texas and was a ready instrument for antiprorationists to play upon. Farmers outside oil regions were especially suspicious of anything that might raise the price of gasoline when wheat was selling at 25 cents a bushel and cotton at 8 cents a pound.

Fundamental political and economic questions were also concerned. A quarter-century later we may have forgotten that in 1931 state or federal control of oil production was looked upon as revolutionary in the extreme. Most Americans—at least most of those engaged in business—still firmly believed that every man had the right to do as he pleased with his own property; and many accepted the view that government should keep its hands off economic matters except to prevent restraint of trade by monopolistic practices, to regulate working and health conditions, and perhaps to aid agriculture. In their consideration of current problems of the oil industry, voters, legislators, public administrators, and judges were influenced by a philosophy of governmental noninterference in economic activities that was deeply ingrained in American—particularly Texan—tradition and could not easily be adjusted to sanction the invocation of the state's police power to meet the problems at hand.

Such was the state of interest and attitude when the special session of the Texas legislature convened in the summer of 1931 to consider conservation issues. A bill was introduced, following an Oklahoma statute, that specifically authorized the limitation of production to reasonable market demand. Its proponents—prominently including Humble—contended that such limitation was absolutely necessary in order to prevent physical waste. The spokesmen for the opposition claimed that it was a price-fixing and monopolistic scheme of the big interests. The opposition succeeded in delaying action and bringing about an investigation of the oil industry which frequently became an informal trial of Humble.

This investigation was conducted by the lower house of the Texas legislature as a committee of the whole.[17] Individuals from the oil industry were called for questioning. Humble was represented by Farish—"Now the little boy of the Standard Oil Company of New Jersey," one legislator commented as Farish rose to be questioned. Farish's answers were direct and factual, and they demonstrated his comprehensive knowledge of the oil industry and of general economic conditions. His answers were forthright, even when a question called for a reply that would put his company in a bad light. He was courteous, patient until worn down by hours of questioning, and poised except when a question cast doubt on his own integrity. But he did not play to the galleries, and near the conclusion of his testimony he gave the impression that he was "talking down" to the legislators.[18]

The hearing was charged with emotion and prejudice. One legislator by direct questions and innuendo endeavored to turn the investigation into a case of Monopoly versus The People. A leading witness of the antiprorationists, Joseph Danciger, not only put himself on the side of "the people" but held that engineers were nothing but theorists and fourflushers and that production should be left to the working of the law of supply and demand, even though he admitted that this might waste the resource and bankrupt the small operator.[19]

The antiprorationists in and outside the hearings accused Humble of advocating restriction of output while itself drilling unnecessary wells, and of having reduced crude prices as a part of a "scheme to take that East Texas field at theft prices" by squeezing out the small operators. Humble, they declared, had "already made a profit on those equivalent thefts of not less than $300,000,000," although the truth was that during the period of price cuts the company had actually invested not much over $100,000 in East Texas leases and had paid bonuses of from $750 to $1,000 an acre. Defenders of Humble, on the other hand, testified that it had connected with leases of independents when no other company would do so and that it had kept its production within its allowables. Farish admitted that Humble was drilling wells that were "not necessary . . . to keep the leases, or to offset wells on adjacent leases," but he justified such drilling on the ground that Humble could not leave its lessors' properties undeveloped. His company, he said, had leases on 16 per cent of the proved acreage in the East Texas field but had produced less than 10 per cent of the oil; it was entitled, he asserted, to bring its production into line with its acreage.[20]

Humble could legitimately have been presented as a true friend of the small independent—the man with neither storage nor refining facilities—who, in the absence of production control and stable prices, might be forced to sell his oil at the well at a below-cost distress price. Indeed, E. J. Sadler, Jersey Standard's vice-president for production, opposed proration on the very ground that it made large producing units pay "an abnormally high price for crude to smaller competing units." [21] But even had Humble been inclined to rise to its own defense, its Jersey connections, which enabled opponents to weaken any measure it supported by dubbing it a "Standard Oil proposition," would have made Humble's open championing of the smaller operator particularly difficult. Moreover, many of Humble's co-workers for proration among the independents—men like Charles F. Roeser, Robert R. Penn, J. D. Collett, and W. B. Hamilton—were susceptible to the charge that they were owners of West Texas and North Texas wells that were higher-cost producers and hence suffered from the competition of the East Texas field.

Some observers have stressed the political ineptness at this time of the prorationists, including Farish, but it is questionable whether, under the conditions then existing, any leadership could in so short a time have brought legislative action favorable to proration in Texas.[22] Such revolutions in public policy normally come only after a period of preparation—by means of experience and education—of legislators, judges, public administrators, and the general public.

A decisive blow to the market-demand bill in this session was dealt by a three-judge federal District Court in an East Texas case similar to the Danciger case. While the legislative investigation was still going on, the court decided in *Alfred MacMillan et al.* v. *Railroad Commission of Texas et al.*[23] that the East Texas proration orders of April, 1931, were invalid because they were designed to prevent "economic waste" contrary to the specific prohibition of the 1929 statute and because they deprived the plaintiffs of property without due process of law, impaired obligations under contracts, and interfered with interstate commerce. The court, in an opinion written by Judge Hutcheson, discounted as largely theory and speculation the testimony of geologists, petroleum engineers, and operators that dissipation of reservoir energy and irregular water intrusion at high rates of flow resulted in physical waste; it held that proration was merely a device to solve the problem of glut.[24] The case was appealed with the support of Sun, Texas, Shell, and Humble, with Robert E. Hardwicke as counsel.

Governor Sterling then declared that he would veto any bill that authorized the limitation of production to market demand.[25] The legislature, which had been called on the specific assumption that it would enact market-demand legislation, on August 12 passed a statute which, although prohibiting every type of physical waste, specifically forbade any attempt to limit the production of oil to existing market demand.[26]

Farish was at a loss as to what attitude to take toward the new "conservation law." He was convinced that the measure did not give "any direct authorization . . . to effectively prorate any individual field and the bill expressly prohibits proration of the state as a whole." But, since the "general reaction throughout the state is that a conservation bill with merit has been passed," he was reluctant to throw cold water on the hopes and efforts of those concerned.[27]

The new conservation statute was generally interpreted as annulling all previous proration orders. This, together with its provision for ten days' notice and a hearing before new orders could be issued, had the effect of releasing East Texas from all restraint. During the week of August 16 its production reached a daily average of over a million barrels.

An article in the September, 1931, issue of *World Petroleum* commented that the East Texas field would go down in history as the world's most recklessly developed oil field. It described the field as follows: The current production was over a million barrels a day, which was believed to be the record for a single field. On August 15 the field had 1,600 wells on 93,000 proved acres, 19 refineries, and what were probably the most extensive railroad loading racks for oil ever built, plus extensive pipelines. The direct costs for developing production alone were said to have been $236,000,000. A total of 56,000,000 barrels had by that time been produced, a flood of oil which had plunged crude prices in Texas from $1.07 to as low as 2½ cents, had shattered prices in other states, and had even made it possible to undersell the Russians in foreign markets.[28]

In the field itself, chaos reigned: a widespread disregard of Railroad Commission orders, the production of illegal oil in large amounts, a disordered market which nearly destroyed values, tremendous amounts in storage, decline in reservoir pressures, wells going to water, and even outright theft of oil. East Texas had amply realized the fears of Humble executives and others who had urged proration in the interest of a stable oil industry and efficient production.

GROWING REALIZATION OF INDUSTRIAL PROBLEMS, 1931–1933

The effect of releasing East Texas from all restraint was immediately apparent. The reservoir energy of the field dropped seriously; some wells had to be "put on the pump" and some began to "go to water." A gas cap was forming on the east side of the field, which meant that gas in solution in the oil was escaping from the oil because of too rapid production and the consequent lowering of pressure. Many operators, realizing that the Railroad Commission was unable to control the situation and fearing that the field would be ruined, called upon Governor Sterling to close the field under martial law. Precedent for such action already existed in Governor Murray's closing of the Oklahoma fields early in the same month.

On August 17, when East Texas crude was selling for 13 cents, the governor ordered all the field's wells shut in and put the Texas National Guard in charge.[29] Farish declared the action justified; the Texas and Vacuum companies also expressed approval; independents were divided on the question.

The shutdown brought immediate improvement. The Railroad Commission, following hearings, on September 2 issued new proration orders for the state. These orders were voluntarily obeyed nearly everywhere outside East Texas, where they were enforced by the presence of the Texas National Guard. The East Texas field was reopened with a daily allowable of 400,000 barrels, which the testimony in hearings had generally agreed was the maximum if waste was to be prevented. Unfortunately, however, the field was prorated at 225 barrels per well without regard for equity or efficient recovery of oil. The temporary shutdown and restricted production, nevertheless, strengthened the reservoir's pressure. Five days after the shutdown Humble had posted new crude prices slightly higher for all grades than those in effect before the debacle of the summer; on August 27 it announced a price of 68 cents a barrel, which it continued to pay for over two months.[30]

Military control, of course, could be only a temporary measure. Farish declared, "There is no chance for the Texas situation to be in shape . . . without the type of legislation which Sterling killed." He expressed the belief that they might "have to go through the terrific pressure of low prices again in order to get the necessary legislation." [31]

Control of the East Texas field by martial law lasted until a three-judge federal court in February, 1932, found that the governor had no right to assume the Railroad Commission's functions and prorate oil production by force of arms, a finding later confirmed by the United States Supreme Court.[32] The court, however, ordered the operators not to open up their wells until the Commission could resume control, which it did on February 25 with an order setting the field's daily allowable at the reasonable amount of 325,000 barrels. Again, however, this total amount was allocated on the basis of a flat per-well allowable, this time of seventy-five barrels, which encouraged further drilling on smaller tracts. Humble immediately announced, nevertheless, that it would take the allowable from the leases to which its pipeline was connected.

This promising beginning did not last long. For the Texas oil industry the year 1932 was a time of uncertainty and recurrent confusion. Many producers and refiners, taking advantage of a continuing struggle between the Railroad Commission and the federal courts, resisted or violated proration orders on a wholesale scale. During the year, nineteen different orders were issued and vigorously attacked. The courts refused to recognize the judgment of petroleum engineers concerning the East Texas field's proper maximum production. To reinforce their original view that a market-demand limitation had no reasonable relation to physical waste the courts now had the statute of 1931, which specifically prohibited both physical waste and the limitation of oil production to market demand. They consequently tended to regard any attempt whatever to control the field allowable as actually a market-demand limitation, which was held to be but thinly disguised price fixing.[33]

The Railroad Commission, in its turn, persistently weakened its own case by disregarding not only the efficient producing capacity, or potential, of wells but also the acreage represented by individual wells, and by insisting on a flat per-well allowable, which exposed its orders to challenge on the ground of inequity. A judicial intimation in July and a definite decision in December that field allowables were too small, the distribution of allowables unjust, and the Commission's orders tantamount to price fixing, were go-ahead signals for the disregard of proration orders and widespread overproduction. Control of production, whether for maintenance of reservoir energy, prevention of undue water intrusion, or stabilization of prices, seemed impossible without a statute specifically authorizing limitation of production to market demand.

As the largest purchaser of crude oil in Texas, Humble, by following realistic price and purchase policies, probably contributed to the growth of support in that state for some control of production. It refused, except in a few instances, to pay more for crude than seemed justified by the general demand for crude and products, but it strictly adhered to its policy of not buying distress oil at prices below its posted offers. Humble also consistently took all the oil produced by leases connected with its pipelines; although it sometimes refused to purchase all the allowables of those connections, it was always willing to store what it did not purchase.

Humble made both friends and enemies by its purchasing policy and tried occasionally to meet the attacks of the latter by explaining the reasons for its price decisions. Such an explanation was made in a statement of April, 1932, when, after a lapse of ten days, Humble followed a general price increase by Magnolia which brought East Texas crude to 98 cents. Humble then explained that the delay in meeting the new prices resulted from a conviction that current economic conditions did not warrant an increase, but that it had decided to raise prices "in part due to numerous urgent appeals from individuals, oil producers, trade organizations, newspapers and state officials and in part to the desire not to penalize the producers who sell to it and who probably could find no other market." The statement asserted that, although Humble "desired higher prices for crude oil just as much as any producer does," over the five months since the last advance it had been "unable to secure for products from its refineries and from the operation of its transportation system to its refineries any profit on the crude bought, transported, and refined." The company was at the time buying more oil than it wanted, and had been trying for weeks to reduce its takings but had been unable to do so without working a hardship on the producers whom it served.[34]

This reluctance to raise prices was based on some harsh realities. During 1931 Humble had sold over 5,000,000 barrels of storage oil at a heavy loss; in 1932, under the pressure of increasing depression and a payment of about $20,000,000 on a bond issue due on July 15, it was trying to decrease its inventory still further. Even before the price increase, moreover, it was on the average paying from 15 to 20 cents per barrel more than it thought the crude worth. An increase of 10 cents a barrel would cost its crude account $15,000 a day, plus storage, loss from evaporation, and other costs, without considering loss from a possible further decline in price. An oil company buying crude in a volume more nearly matched to its current needs, or buying a part of its oil by spot purchases at less than posted prices, would not incur or risk so heavy a loss.

Mounting production in the East Texas field continued to press on Humble as a purchaser. Early in September, after allowables per well had been increased, Humble Oil & Refining Company announced that, effective September 12, it would restrict its purchases in East Texas, the Panhandle, and a number of specified counties to 50 per cent of the production allowables of the leases with which its pipelines were connected. Humble Pipe Line Company simultaneously announced that "at the request of owners" it would run the other half of allowable production to storage, subject to gathering and transportation charges and two cents a barrel per month for storage.

Attorney General Allred interpreted these announcements to mean that Humble, contrary to the Common Purchaser Act, intended to run its own entire production while halving its purchases; he filed suit against the company on September 11, 1932, and obtained an injunction requiring it to purchase oil ratably and to maintain existing connections. Humble made known that it had never intended to run to pipelines a larger proportion of its own production than it purchased from others, a position that is recorded in a plea to the state court of September 15 and supported by company practice from at least as early as the Yates proration agreement of 1927. On September 17 Humble obtained from the Supreme Court of Texas an order temporarily restraining the judge of the Travis County Court from enforcing the original injunction; a few days later it raised its purchase order to 60 per cent, again offering to store the remainder. It then turned to the United States District Court at Austin, alleging that the Common Purchaser Act was unconstitutional and asking for a restraining order against the Texas attorney general and the Railroad Commission. Three days before the federal court's hearing on this petition, the attorney general took the novel action of asking for a state court order restraining himself from enforcing the Common Purchaser Act against common purchasers of oil, pending final determination of the suit in the state court, and further ordering that no common purchaser should be subjected to any penalties for any violation of the act occurring before such determination. The federal court on November 5 granted Humble's plea for an injunction against the attorney general pending the decision in the state court. No further action was taken by the attorney general in the suit he had instituted in the state court, and in 1936 the case was dismissed.[35]

Conditions in East Texas continued to worsen in 1932, and support for production control to grow. Overproduction, under protection of injunctions and through clandestine bypasses, finally alarmed even some of the most vocal opponents of production control, including Editor Carl Estes, who, with a radical shift of position, declared that opposition to proration was now being employed as an "umbrella" by people who wanted cheap oil.[36] Out-and-out theft of oil, with which existing laws and enforcement agencies seemed incapable of coping, also increased alarmingly and, along with the bootlegging of untaxed gasoline, endangered product prices far and wide and further threatened the already weak crude price structure.[37] Humble, in fear of theft and sabotage, began to have its pipelines patrolled by armed and mounted guards.[38] The East Texas reservoir showed the effects of uneven and rapid development and high production; many of its wells ceased to flow or began to produce salt water, and bottom-hole pressures fell. Many royalty owners, producers, and businessmen in East Texas came to see that, instead of merely profiting from a period of flush production, they were actually suffering loss because of injury to the field, low prices, and a general decline of values owing to the chaotic conditions in the field. Mrs. Miriam Ferguson, who had been nominated for the governorship of Texas in the decisive Democratic primaries, called for a law to permit the Railroad Commission to consider economic waste and market demand.[39]

A strong factor in the change of opinion in Texas, especially in East Texas, was the growing influence of the engineers. Humble engineers continued the investigations they had begun early in 1931; they gathered data on their own company's and others' wells, seeking to draw as nearly complete a picture as possible of the nature of the whole reservoir and its behavior under different conditions of production. These studies were intended to make it possible to define proper spacing in terms of costs and efficient rates of production; the close relationship between reservoir pressures and volume of production thus discovered was of particular significance. The engineers of other companies and of the United States Bureau of Mines were carrying on similar investigations.

A system of voluntary exchange of information among engineers of oil companies and of the Bureau of Mines was initiated under the leadership of W. W. Scott of Humble and M. Albertson of Shell.[40] This early co-operation resulted in the assembling of a considerable body of engineering data that was useful in operations, as evidence before the Railroad Commission and courts, and in the education of the public.

This informal co-operation led to the establishment in 1933, again under the leadership of Scott and Albertson, of a formal organization, the East Texas Engineering Association. The broad acceptance of reservoir engineering at that time is indicated by the association's membership, which besides Humble and Shell included the Arkansas Fuel Company, Atlantic Refining, Sun, Texas, Amerada, Barnsdall, Gulf, Ohio Oil, and Tide Water. Albertson of Shell was the first chairman, and Carl E.

Reistle, Jr., of the Bureau of Mines was employed to head the association's activities, which were described as the collection, analysis, and dissemination among its members of engineering data pertaining to the East Texas field. Beginning in August, 1933, this association issued regular monthly and special reports, which included new findings and conclusions concerning the field, pressure data and information about water intrusion and pumping wells, and estimates of "hot" oil production.

Here and there organizations sprang up to support or to oppose conservation, especially proration. By far the strongest organization promoting the proration movement in Texas in 1932 was the Texas Oil & Gas Conservation Association. This organization, which became active at the beginning of the year, was a combination of five, largely regional, groups: a group of Southwest Texas operators; the North Texas Oil & Gas Association; The East Texas Home & Landowners Association; The East Texas Steering Committee; and the Texas Oil Emergency Committee.[41] Gulf Coast independents were conspicuously absent, probably largely because of their favorable location near tidewater.

The Texas Oil & Gas Conservation Association was by design composed principally of independent oilmen. Humble supported it with engineering information, advice, and financial aid, as did other majors interested in the organization's objectives and cognizant of the greater influence of the independent oilman with both Texas industry and the public. The president of the association was Charles F. Roeser of Fort Worth, a veteran and indefatigable proponent of the conservation movement. Among the twenty-four original vice-presidents were such well-known conservationists as J. D. Collett and E. A. Landreth of Fort Worth and Frank P. Zock of San Antonio, and such prominent independents operating in East Texas as J. K. Hughes of Mexia, H. L. Hunt of Kilgore, and Jake Hamon of Gladewater (later Dallas). Also among the vice-presidents was Ernest O. Thompson, an attorney of Amarillo, who in 1932 was to begin a long and distinguished career as a member of the Texas Railroad Commission. The association had a manager and a small engineering staff. Its membership reached 5,000 in June, 1932.

The stated purpose of this organization was to carry on an active and vigorous campaign in support of a platform which had as its first and principal plank the "stabilization of the oil industry and conservation of petroleum resources through regulation of production to balance supply with current demand and through ratable taking from all producers."[42]

The association's activities were broad. From January, 1932, to July, 1933, it published *The Conservationist*, a bimonthly which contained articles and addresses by prominent oilmen, engineering information about oil fields, statistics comparing production and prices and, for the

East Texas field, production and pressures, information about illegal production of oil in East Texas, and so on. It urged limiting the production of a field in accordance with good engineering practice and market demand. The association also submitted information to the Railroad Commission, provided engineering data and hired outstanding legal talent to advise in crucial court cases, sent representatives to hearings, promoted petitions in support of certain allowables for East Texas, provided speakers for various occasions, and carried on lobbying activities.

The association during its short life undoubtedly had a strong influence. By June, 1932, according to that month's issue, *The Conservationist* was being sent to 10,000 persons, 700 daily and weekly newspapers in Texas, 600 chambers of commerce, and 100 public libraries. Oil-field communities were appealed to in the interest of law and order; royalty owners, operators, and businessmen indirectly concerned with income from oil were constantly told that control meant better prices for oil and longer life for fields; taxpayers received the assurance that a stable industry meant more taxes from oil and better income from the state's oil lands. The publication also presented a broad view of industry conditions and instructive information on engineering matters and legal issues. But the association broke up in 1933, apparently because of differences within its membership as to whether authority to regulate production should be lodged in the state or in the federal government.

Humble in 1932 did not publicly advocate the proration movement in Texas. Its support of the market-demand bill in 1931 had proved an element of weakness, inasmuch as it enabled opponents to identify the bill with Standard Oil and monopoly. As Farish testified in 1934, speaking as Chairman of the Board of Standard Oil Company (New Jersey), "We have learned from experience . . . that one of the easiest ways to defeat a thing is for us to ask for it." [43] There were special reasons, however, why Humble in 1932 should refrain from publicly advocating a legislative program. In November, 1931, Attorney General Allred had filed against Humble and certain other major oil companies an antitrust suit which, though eventually decided in favor of the defendants, temporarily contributed to their ill favor. In 1932, also, the prominence of Humble employees in the campaign against the attorney general's renomination caused the company to be accused of instigating and assisting their activities, and probably contributed to Allred's renomination and a further decline in Humble's popularity.[44] Moreover, in 1932 Humble's price policy reduced the company's popularity with independent producers to its lowest point. In addition to all these special reasons was the general consideration that Humble's interest was too much keyed to engineering and economic considerations for the company to be effective in influencing general opinion.

Although Humble did not enter the political lists or participate in efforts to "educate" the public, it continued throughout the East Texas struggle to present scientific data and economic arguments to official, professional, and commercial bodies. Its geologists and petroleum engineers gave expert testimony on reservoir and production matters before legislators, members of the Railroad Commission, and judges, presenting evidence to demonstrate that uncontrolled production actually led to decline in underground pressure and premature exhaustion of a field. Supported by engineering data, Humble's lawyers strove to get effective conservation bills drawn up, to induce the Railroad Commission to issue effective orders, and to convince the courts that such orders were legal. Farish and other Humble spokesmen simultaneously presented the proration argument before official, commercial, industrial, and technical organizations.

Until he joined Jersey Standard as Chairman of the Board of Directors in 1933, Farish was Humble's leading spokesman for conservation and by 1932 had also become the American oil industry's most strenuous advocate of conservation, in succession to Henry L. Doherty. Farish contributed to the development of the conviction among leaders in industry and government that something must be done about the problems of the oil industry of which such uncontrolled production as that in East Texas was basically the cause. In 1932 he addressed the United States Chamber of Commerce in San Francisco in May, the Petroleum Division of the American Institute of Mining and Metallurgical Engineers at Ponca City, Oklahoma, in September, and three Texas association meetings in Dallas in October.

Farish's San Francisco address, entitled "What the Oil Industry Needs," was an exposition of his company's convictions and principles that had evolved over the preceding six years.[45] The speaker presented as the industry's primary need controlled production, with ratable withdrawals from the various properties in a pool and the limitation of its total output to reasonable market demand. Such controlled production would conserve the resource, would eliminate unnecessary storage aboveground and the waste attending such storage, and, "more important, it would minimize the underground waste that results from uncontrolled production practices." It would greatly increase recovery and decrease costs: "Intelligent control of production in a pool may easily mean the recovery of twice as much oil as uncontrolled production methods would yield, with only one-third as much expense for drilling wells and less than one-half the cost per barrel for lifting the oil. In other words, yield can be doubled and unit costs divided by four through intelligent controlled production."

Farish on this occasion especially addressed himself to the broad effects of uncontrolled production and the need for regulation of production as a means of stabilizing the industry. In the absence of control, he said, the volume fluctuates, "with short periods of flush flow . . . during which prices fall to ridiculously low levels followed by longer periods of failing supply . . . with prices rising to absurd heights." A result of extreme price fluctuations was an unstable producing industry:

> The advent of high prices stimulates great activity, bringing additional capital and workers into the producing industry. Recurring low prices destroy the value of this investment as well as old investment in production, throwing thousands of workers out of employment and bringing distress and confusion into industry.

The effects of uncontrolled production spread throughout the whole oil industry:

> But the greatest burden which the petroleum industry has brought upon itself through its inability to control its production of crude oil is, undoubtedly, the economic waste that has arisen through the overexpansion of manufacturing and distributing facilities. Small inefficient refineries; over-built large refineries; duplication of sales equipment; thousands of unnecessary retail outlets. . . . The costs of marketing have pyramided and multiplied until they have become fantastic.

Seeing the American industry in relation to the world oil industry, Farish stressed the need in this country of both low costs and low prices:

> Low-cost production, with correspondingly low prices of products and a stabilized producing enterprise, is essential to the welfare of American industry and of the American people. Other nations, and oil producers in other nations, already enjoy the advantages that grow out of this control, since foreign oil fields are generally held in large ownerships which make possible their operations as units under single management, and since producers in foreign countries generally are free to enter into agreements to control production.

In two articles appearing in the *Oil & Gas Journal* in June and October, 1932, Farish more especially discussed programs for preventing the waste of oil and gas and for stabilizing the industry.[46] The June article, entitled "Problem of Preventing Waste of Oil and Gas and Stabilizing the Petroleum Industry," proposed a program for attaining the three objectives that Humble men constantly emphasized: preventing waste, assuring equitable participation of interests in a pool, and stabilizing the petroleum industry. The importance of conserving the energy of pools was stressed, as was the regulation of imports. The article discussed the differences between oil and other types of mineral deposits that necessitated special regulations for and practices in the oil industry, the inadequacy of voluntary co-operation among operators, and the hindrance to efficient unit operations presented by antitrust laws. The need was pointed out for a program of curtailment by voluntary agreement among operators or by administrative agencies under a state's police power, for the formation of conservation agencies, for relief from antitrust laws, and for definite proration policies.

The October article was the address on "A Rational Program for the Oil Industry," which Farish had delivered before the AIMME. On this occasion he was concerned especially with broad policy issues. Although cognizant of "a spirit of intense individualism" then prevailing in America, he nevertheless believed it necessary to formulate a program for the sake of the industry and the public interest. The existing overproduction and waste in the producing industry must, he said, be remedied by a program that was reasonable to all branches of the industry, to both large and small operators, and to the public. A fundamental characteristic of a rational program was to regulate production in accordance with demand, but such regulation would require an intelligent understanding of world markets. No program was rational, however, that sought to raise prices. Proration, said Farish, was not properly a device to secure higher prices, as so many producers appeared to believe, and the curtailment of supply was justifiable only to the extent that it was necessary to prevent waste of oil or of equipment or of effort. A rational program should not require abandoning stripper wells. It did demand the application of sound engineering practices—wide spacing, unit operation, and rational allocation formulas—and also the protection of correlative rights. Such a program would work toward steady employment, which Farish considered a public obligation. The accomplishment of such a program, he said, would require education, adequate conservation laws, and the modification of antitrust laws. Enforcement he held to be almost entirely a function of the police power of states, and a rational program almost identical with a conservation program.

These addresses and articles have been presented here at some length because of their meaning in the history of Humble. They not only demonstrated the strong position Farish had attained in the American industry and his own views on how to attack industry problems, but, as he said again and again, they presented the experience and the convictions of his company as evolved through the years. His statements were, indeed, the essence of the experience of the whole organization, the knowledge of its engineers and scientists, the thinking of its lawyers, and the policies of the company, as written with the assistance, especially, of Hines H. Baker and Wallace E. Pratt. Farish himself added to these his own broad knowledge of the oil industry and the strength of his reputation.

One national development of the time that helped to clarify conservation issues was the tariff on crude oil imports that went into effect in 1932. The antiprorationists had been asserting that the unrestrained import of foreign crudes was solely responsible for overproduction in the United States, an especially telling argument in attacking Humble because of its affiliation with Jersey Standard, a large importer. When Humble and Carter had cut crude prices early in 1930, the Independent Petroleum Association inaugurated a determined campaign for a tariff. When overproduction had become very serious in Texas in 1931, Farish was ready to support a movement for voluntary agreement to restrict imports, and, when the board of directors of the American Petroleum Institute had endorsed a petroleum tariff in principle, both Farish and Pratt of Humble voted affirmatively. The tariff measure of 1932 buried the issue for the time being.[47]

Although the year 1932 was distinguished by overproduction, low prices, and instability in the oil industry generally and in East Texas particularly, it was also a period during which conservation issues began to be clarified and opinion to crystallize. Support for greater regulation increased, in Texas especially for that form of regulation called proration.

Under the American system of government the development of effective state or federal regulation is a slow process, even where opinion is favorable, for it necessitates gaining the support of all three branches of government—legislative, judicial, and administrative—and deciding in the process whether regulation in a particular matter is properly a function of the state or of the federal government. In 1931 proration in Texas had failed to gain or hold the support of any of the three branches of the state government; it was to attain that support only through a long struggle, which was complicated by the controversy over whether the chief authority and responsibility should rest with the states under their police power or in the federal government under its constitutional authority to regulate interstate commerce.

VICTORY OF PRORATION IN LEGISLATURE AND COURTS, 1932–1933

Proration according to market demand won a victory (although a Pyrrhic one) in Texas in the spring of 1932, when the Court of Civil Appeals at Austin reaffirmed the decision of early 1931 dissolving the temporary injunction of the Danciger Oil & Refining Company against the Texas Railroad Commission and three companies, including Humble

Pipe Line Company.[48] The crucial issue, as observed earlier, was the legality of proration according to market demand. The court upheld the argument of the defense. The opinion read: " . . . any order of the commission bearing a reasonable relationship to the general duty imposed upon the commission, which is not unreasonable or unjust, and which is reasonably calculated to prevent waste, comes, if not within the express powers granted to the commission, clearly within those necessarily implied. . . ." The validity of a general order, the opinion stated, was not dependent on whether or not waste was taking place at an individual well or lease, since such a criterion would render impossible the enforcement of any general conservation measure. One producer might extract oil without physical waste to a particular well and yet cause coning and dissipation of reservoir energy in the pool. The individual wells, hence, would have to be considered in relation to all with a view to conserving the whole. The opinion specifically held that production in excess of reasonable market demand caused or resulted in physical waste. Although the decision in this case was of little practical importance, since it was contrary to the judgment of the federal court in the MacMillan case and to the Texas anti-market-demand act of 1931, it was significant as an expression of an important Texas court on one of the most controversial conservation issues.

Only a few weeks later, however, the Supreme Court of the United States handed down a decision, upholding Oklahoma's conservation statute and orders, that was in line with the Texas court's decision in the Danciger case. In *Champlin Refining Company* v. *Oklahoma Corporation Commission*[49] the court sustained a denial of an application for a temporary injunction against the orders of the state's Corporation Commission, on the allegation that those orders were repugnant to due process under the Fourteenth Amendment and violated the commerce clause of the United States Constitution. The orders had been issued under Oklahoma's conservation statutes, which prohibited the production of petroleum in such ways as to cause underground waste or waste incident to production in excess of marketing facilities or reasonable market demand. The court found that there was serious overproduction in the United States and in flush pools in Oklahoma; that full potential production in the case at issue exceeded transportation and marketing facilities and demand and, therefore, caused waste; and that no one, even with ways of disposing of his oil, had the right to produce so as to cause waste to others. Significantly, it took the position that "the effect, if any, upon price" of limiting production to reasonable market demand "was merely incidental." Robert E. Hardwicke had earlier written concerning the Champlin case: "If the Supreme Court of the United States affirms the judgment in the Champlin case, I take it that the next legislature in Texas will be asked to re-write the conservation statutes. The bug-a-boo of market demand will be overthrown." [50]

The time was obviously ripe in the autumn of 1932 for a Texas market-demand bill, and J. Edgar Pew of the Sun Oil Company, Farish's early gas conservation ally, took charge of guiding such a bill to success. Pew inaugurated his campaign on October 15 with an increase in Sun's crude prices, advancing East Texas crude to $1.10, an action that was intended to win the favor of the politically potent independent producers.

Several other companies followed Sun's example, but Humble repeated its statement of April, 1932, that product prices did not justify an increase in crude prices. The storm of resentment and criticism which then burst about Humble's head almost equaled in fury the one stirred up by its January, 1930, price cut. Editor Estes of Tyler, Texas, formerly the principal antiproration leader in East Texas, now accused Humble of "wanting to break down proration in order to buy . . . cheap oil." Humble refused to budge, maintaining that if production was limited to consumptive demand prices would take care of themselves. Humble did not remind its critics that during the year the company had curtailed its own production in order to connect with shutdown wells and had taken over connections from other companies that were withdrawing as purchasers.[51]

A spur to legislative action soon came as a result of still another court decision. On October 24, 1932, the federal court in the People's case upheld an injunction against the Railroad Commission's latest proration order on the grounds that it was actually an attempt to limit production to market demand contrary to the Texas statute of 1931, that its flat per-well basis was discriminatory, and that the allowable of 400,000 barrels a day was not reasonably necessary to prevent waste.[52] This decision, which made the Railroad Commission practically powerless, left the East Texas field again without control. The logic of events finally convinced even some of the archfoes of proration that regulation of production was necessary and that a law specifically declaring the production of petroleum in excess of transportation facilities or reasonable market demand to be waste was a requisite to acceptance of proration in Texas by the courts.

On November 12, 1932, a special session of the Texas legislature, after a bitter controversy and by a close vote, finally passed the controversial market-demand bill. [53] The statute specifically included in its definition of waste "the production of crude petroleum oil in excess of transportation or market facilities or reasonable market demand," and it did not prohibit the consideration of economic waste in the regulation of production.

The Railroad Commission's initial East Texas proration order under the new law fixed a total daily field allowable of 290,000 barrels. Considering reservoir pressures and the attitude of the courts, this was lower than was necessary and wise, but illegal production made the actual output of East Texas much larger. The prorating of the allowable among the wells of the field was continued on the objectionable per-well basis, which the major operators strongly opposed and which the federal court had given as one of the reasons for invalidating earlier orders.

J. Edgar Pew, who was anxious to strengthen proration and to advance a movement for including acreage as a factor in determining allowables, again urged the bolstering of crude prices as a means to win the independent producers' support. For help in maintaining prices, Pew now turned to Humble as the largest purchaser in Texas. When prices subsequently fell, Humble had to bear the brunt of criticism. The Fort Worth *Star-Telegram*, expressing the views of the more moderate independent producers, took the position that, since Humble had obtained from the state, the independents, and the small producers all that it had asked, it should pay the mid-October price of $1.10 for East Texas crude.[54] Humble's president again refused to raise prices, explaining that his company already had more oil than it wanted and was losing money on every barrel purchased. Farish wrote to Pew: "The only influence that we have . . . to limit production to market demand is to refuse to take more than we want and, through educational efforts . . . reach the Commission to the end that they will reduce the allowables to the actual consumption demand. . . . My opinion is that we shall come nearer to getting production limited to market demand if everybody realizes that it is necessary to do this in order to have any stable price." [55]

The recurrence of this price issue in the history of both East Texas and Humble calls for some explanation. Basically, it points to a divergence of opinion concerning the relationship of price and proration. Many producers believed that the chief end of proration was higher prices. The Texas Oil & Gas Association's *Conservationist* sometimes carried graphs or tables showing the relation between the volume of production and price. Advocates of conservation used the price appeal—about the only appeal that had weight with many producers—to win support for proration. Farish himself, early in 1931, in an effort to stem the tide running against the regulation of production, had emphasized the effect on prices. Proration, he said, as quoted in the *National Petroleum News*,[56] had secured for the producer an average price far in excess of what he would otherwise have received. However, the fear that a flood of oil might be released, he held, had had a depressing effect on crude and product prices, the wholesale values of refined products then being less than the cost of raw materials and manufacture. He maintained that proration was not "price freezing," but that effective proration would assure a "fair market price." Such statements, of course, could be and were interpreted in various ways.

What was Humble's position on the price question? Farish and his Humble associates in those controversial years took pains to dissociate proration from "price fixing," but they frankly stated that proration would *influence* price through its effect on supply. Hines H. Baker expressed this position in 1933: "Production in excess of the reasonable market demand . . . inevitably leads, through the operation of the law of supply and demand, to inordinately low prices of oil. Proration, properly understood, therefore, does prevent the collapse of price due to inordinate over-supply, but it does not lead to an artificial price by the limitation of price below the reasonable demand for oil." [57] In other words, Farish and Baker held that conservation in general and proration in particular would enable the producers to withhold oil from the market when to sell would mean selling at a loss, and would also help to eliminate the extreme fluctuations resulting from uncontrolled flush production. Their object was a more stable price structure and a price that would enable producers to sell their oil at a profit. Regulation did not, they emphasized, mean fixing or raising prices; rather it would enable petroleum producers to follow the normal practice of other suppliers of goods for the market, which, the Humble executives maintained, still left the determination of price to the interaction of other supply and demand factors in the market.[58]

Such was Humble's theory, but what determined its pricing practice? The most important factor in causing Humble near the end of 1932 to adopt the policy of posting a lower price than Sun and its followers was that Humble itself, although only one of several large buyers, was the largest crude purchaser in Texas; it was buying on an average over 150,000 barrels daily, most of which had to be put into expensive steel storage. It was also the largest Texas producer. Companies with a smaller production or with fewer lease connections, whose incoming oil was better matched to their immediate needs, could afford from a short-run viewpoint to pay more for their oil than could a company whose production and purchases were so out of balance with its needs that a large part was going into storage. When Humble, therefore, was paying a price that after careful consideration it believed to be as high as was economically justifiable, a smaller company or an independent refinery could often be found that for the time being was posting or paying a higher price, with the result that Humble would be accused of forcing the price down in order to ruin the independent operators and force them to sell their properties.[59]

Humble was really in a dilemma so far as crude prices were concerned. As a producer of crude it was interested in high prices, and as a heavy purchaser it was cognizant of the importance of the price factor in holding the good will of suppliers. In the 1920s it had been able to maintain leadership in increasing crude prices in Texas, but, for reasons that will be considered in Chapter 20, in the 1930s it was no longer able to do so. It is doubtful, however, that Humble would have paid higher prices for reasons of good will even if it could have afforded to take the losses; the executives believed that to pay more than was justified by the demand merely gave an artificial stimulus to wildcatting and production, thereby aggravating the malaise of the producing industry. Farish's position, expressed again and again in correspondence, was that low prices alone would bring many producers to accept regulation, and he believed that this influence should be permitted to run its natural course. This attitude on the part of Humble, realistic though it was, for the short run at least made enemies.

In refusing late in 1932 to raise prices, Humble executives realized that their company's connections were getting 12 cents a barrel less than they would have received had their leases been connected with the pipelines of buyers paying the higher price. They felt, however, that this temporary disadvantage was balanced by the security Humble gave its connections, since, although it sometimes stored a portion of their oil in lieu of immediate purchase, it never in East Texas cast them adrift, however serious the overproduction. Humble maintained that, once a normal supply-demand situation was established, a competitive market would prevail and producers would be free to sell to anyone who offered the best price.

The Railroad Commission, which was usually responsive to the wishes of the majority of oil operators, on December 10, 1932, issued an order providing an allocation formula based only two-thirds on the well and the remaining third on acreage and bottom-hole pressure. Humble engineers had for some time been advocating recognition of bottom-hole pressure as a true measure of a well's capacity to produce.[60] East Texas, however, in November was producing 100,000 barrels a day above the field's allowable, and crude was being bootlegged for as low as 50 cents a barrel.[61] Because of this situation both Humble and Carter, Jersey's Mid-Continent affiliate, on December 15 met a general crude cut initiated in the Mid-Continent by The Texas Company. Humble lowered the price of East Texas oil from 98 to 75 cents. The Texas Company and Shell promptly followed Humble's reduction in Texas, the latter even cutting East Texas crude to 65 cents. Again Humble was blamed, especially for lowering the price just before Christmas, which was implied to be tantamount to robbing Santa Claus.[62]

The Railroad Commission, now confronted with overproduction and lower prices and already staggered by a storm of protest from the operators on small tracts against the inclusion of bottom-hole pressures as a factor in determining allowables, on December 18 shut in the East Texas field in order to obtain a breathing spell for determining a future course.[63] During the shutdown a proration association attempted to find pipeline connections for all East Texas wells, but Humble refused to accept additional connections; it already had surplus connections with about 300 wells and also had to take some oil from the new Conroe field.[64]

The year 1933 did not begin promisingly for the proration movement. The Railroad Commission returned to the old flat per-well allowable and overproduction increased. Stanolind promptly cut its East Texas price to 50 cents, and production continued to mount until in February the average was again 100,000 barrels above the legal daily allowable.

The East Texas situation appeared even more desperate in the spring of 1933 than when, in 1931, Governor Sterling had put the field under martial law. East Texas landowners and operators in 1933 began to organize to fight "hot oil"—oil produced in excess of the legal allowable—and several pipelines were mysteriously dynamited. On March 16, 1933, Humble halved its East Texas price to 25 cents; on the next day the federal court in a second Peoples case declared invalid the Commission's order allocating the allowable on a per-well basis and setting the East Texas top allowable at 290,000 barrels.[65] The Fort Worth *Star-Telegram*, spokesman of the moderate independents, now denounced the Railroad Commission as a "total failure" and a "standing joke" and held that it had deliberately written invalid proration orders.[66] The Commission and the attorney general, after having been cited for contempt of court for issuing orders that represented "no real variation" from the flat per-well basis that the federal court had condemned, apparently determined to write an order that could not possibly be found invalid and could be enforced. On April 22 the Commission established the field allowable at 750,000 barrels, more than twice the amount that T. V. Moore, a Humble engineer, had recommended in the hearings as the maximum; and, to avoid the inequity charged against the per-well basis, it allocated the allowable of about 10,000 wells according to well-potential but without considering acreage.[67]

Farish was discouraged. Early in April, 1933, when the character of the Railroad Commission's proposed order doubling the East Texas allowable was already known, he summed up in a letter to Teagle his opinion of the past and future of proration. Humble's early abstention from drilling its East Texas properties up to the limit, he said, had resulted in the loss of several million barrels of oil, and at the new Conroe field the company had received no co-operation in its attempts to obtain orderly development. Humble consequently intended to protect itself by developing its leases at the same rate as the surrounding properties. Adequate control in Texas, Farish said, involved "two indispensable and major accomplishments: . . . a new Commission . . . beyond political control, or the control of any independent or major company," which "would deal with proration orders on their merits"; and "a low price for crude over a sufficient . . . time thoroughly to discourage uncontrolled development . . . to make the industry conscious . . . that in order to produce at a profit it must have the benefit of the low-cost production that follows control and unit operation." [68]

Six years of struggle for conservation and proration in Texas had apparently accomplished little or nothing. Of two conservation laws, one had actually served as a barrier to effective regulation and under the second the Railroad Commission had proved incapable of writing or unwilling to write a valid order for the protection of the East Texas field. An order was about to go into effect that would legalize what was, according to engineering data, more than twice the proper maximum production. Farish was beginning to feel that perhaps only the law of tooth and claw, the dominance of which he had so long opposed, could bring about some order.

The initial results of the Texas Railroad Commission's order of April 22, 1933, were what the more farseeing had expected. The larger companies objected that the field allowable was far too large, from the viewpoint of both efficient recovery and the market-demand principle, and that a distribution of well allowables according to potential production without considering acreage was almost as discriminatory as the flat per-well basis. The usual suits were filed, the usual overproduction ensued, and the inevitable price cuts followed. The Texas Company cut its East Texas price to 10 cents, its lowest posted price to date; this reduction was followed by Humble and all other major companies except Magnolia. Gulf withdrew its East Texas posted price entirely, followed on May 2 by Humble, which then cut its price in North Texas and related fields to 25 cents. East Texas was completely out of control, producing over a million barrels daily, which was about half the total United States requirement and double the current market demand.

The situation had reached a breaking point. Some independent producers pathetically called for another attempt at voluntary proration; others preferred to blame the major companies—particularly Humble—for the overproduction, accusing them of running more hot oil than all the independents combined. Some called for federal regulation and were supported by Governor Ferguson, who declared that the states could no longer cope with the situation. Hines H. Baker agreed with those who advocated federal prohibition of transporting in interstate commerce oil or products produced in excess of market demand or contrary to state laws.[69]

The shock of 10-cent oil, however, had an immediate effect. Production fell off, though it was still far out of line with the market demand. Humble promptly, on May 13, established a posted price of 25 cents and a 100 per cent purchase program.[70]

The company then faced the problem of disposing of the oil that its pipeline subsidiary had in storage. For eight months Humble Pipe Line Company had been storing large percentages of its connections' allowables, subject to a gathering fee of 10 cents a barrel and storage charges of 2 cents a barrel per month; although from time to time the Crude Oil Department had purchased part of this storage oil, at the beginning of 1933 Humble Pipe Line held 1,500,000 barrels belonging to its connections. When Humble Oil & Refining Company finally offered to buy this East Texas storage crude at its posted price of 25 cents, it volunteered to absorb the gathering charge and half the storage charges after the first month. This meant that a producer would receive 16 cents a barrel for crude that had been in storage eight months, instead of owing Humble one cent.

From Humble's viewpoint this was a generous offer, but the producer was more likely to remember that, when Humble had stored that oil instead of purchasing it, the company's posted price had been 98 cents a barrel instead of 25 cents—and the posted price of the Sun and certain other companies had been $1.10. The producer retrospectively saw an 80- or 90-cent loss instead of a 17-cent gain. Some producers accepted Humble's offer, preferring to dispose of their oil in storage and start afresh; others, who were financially and psychologically able to gamble on higher future prices, refused. In September, with nearly 500,000 barrels of the oil of its pipeline connections still on hand, Humble repeated its May offer; by then, however, the posted price had risen to $1.00, and by the end of the year the process of liquidation was virtually completed.[71]

The inescapable economic and psychological conflict between crude oil producer and purchaser in a period of overabundance is clearly demonstrated by this episode. The helplessness of the producer and the economic necessities of the purchaser combined to create a situation in which the latter's most generous action, within the bounds of economic possibilities, seemed hopelessly niggardly to the former. The only solution to this impasse, in the judgment of Humble executives, was the balance between supply and market demand for which Humble had been striving for six years.

The shifting of the courts to the side of production control in 1933 and 1934 removed a serious obstacle to the enforcement of the Texas

Market Demand Act and to proration in general. In May, 1933, a federal court refused injunctions against the April orders of the Railroad Commission; in June, in a second Danciger case, it held the Commission's order restricting production in the Panhandle to market demand under the statute of 1932 as reasonable and necessary to prevent waste.[72] The decision by a federal court in February, 1934, in an East Texas case, *Amazon Petroleum Corporation* v. *Railroad Commission*,[73] ended any remaining uncertainty about the constitutionality of the Texas market-demand statute and about the authority of the Railroad Commission. The court's opinion, written by the same Judge Hutcheson who in the MacMillan decision in 1931 had referred to the evidence of the engineers as mere theory and speculation, now took a favorable position with respect to such evidence: "... we are bound to say that all this vast amount of evidence, submitted in favor of the Commission's findings, is too ponderable to be brushed aside as no evidence at all. We find ourselves wholly unable to see that the conclusion the Commission reached is not one which reasonable minds could entertain." Since the Supreme Court of the United States had earlier upheld the market-demand statute of Oklahoma, these decisions virtually settled the question of the constitutionality of the Commission's orders under the statute of 1932.

Thus the principle of proration according to market demand, in the promotion of which Humble had been the original leader in Texas, was established as a valid part of that state's law. Science and engineering, with the aid of astute lawyers, had won in the courts over the contention that the state was powerless to prevent production in excess of market demand—a triumph over chaos. They had yet, however, to triumph in the administration of conservation law and in oil-field practice.

COMPLETING THE LEGAL AND ADMINISTRATIVE STRUCTURE, 1933–1935

By late spring of 1933 the problems of the oil industry centering in East Texas had become merged with those of a nationwide depression. The oil industry was merely one element, though an important one, in a depression-born movement, under the leadership of an aggressive federal administration, for the national regulation of the American economy in the interest of general industrial recovery. Consequently, for nearly two years thereafter the petroleum conservation movement was promoted along two lines, state and federal. This parallel development was finally joined in a workable system of regulation.

In this later development Humble did not directly provide leadership as a spokesman, although Farish, then with Jersey Standard, still maintained the position in the conservation movement that he had attained as president of Humble. Humble's contributions in this later phase were chiefly toward the growth of understanding of reservoirs and their behavior and toward translating that understanding into legal thinking on correlative rights in a reservoir and into sound production practices. Here our interest is primarily in the completion of the regulatory structure itself and secondarily in Humble's part in the process.

The chaos in the Texas oil industry that resulted from the Railroad Commission's high allowable for the East Texas field in April, 1933, helped to cause a break in the ranks of Texas conservationists over the question of state versus federal regulation. The directors of the North Texas Oil & Gas Association petitioned President Franklin D. Roosevelt for federal supervision of the oil industry for the duration of the emergency, asserting that the Texas oil industry was in a state of complete collapse and that failure to enforce conservation statutes was rendering inevitable the bankruptcy of hundreds of independent operators. J. S. Bridwell, a veteran conservationist, together with other Texas oil industry leaders, attended a conference in Washington that urged federal regulation of the oil industry, even the fixing of prices for oil and its products. Although much opposition to a federal "oil dictator" manifested itself in the Texas legislature, Governor Miriam Ferguson urged President Roosevelt and Secretary of the Interior Harold Ickes to take prompt action.[74]

The National Industrial Recovery Act of the following month provided for federal regulation of the oil industry. Shortly after that act had gone into effect the federal government issued an order banning the shipment, interstate or abroad, of oil produced contrary to state laws; in September it promulgated the Code of Fair Competition for the Petroleum Industry, which had been drawn up with the help of industry representatives; and soon thereafter it established the Petroleum Administrative Board to set up and administer regulations.[75] The industry generally, notably the board of directors of the American Petroleum Institute, accepted the regulation of industry activities according to the code and with the support of the federal government.[76] Farish and Teagle had recommended the adoption of a code as a method of self-regulation of the industry early in 1925, but they had not then envisaged participation by the federal government.

Side by side with the movement for federal regulation came a stiffening of conservation law and its administration in Texas. The court decisions of May and June, 1933, strengthened the Railroad Commission, and a law enacted in May made unlawful the production of crude beyond the Commission's allowables, thus by specific statute putting the state's enforcement agencies behind the Commission's orders.[77]

Conditions in Texas improved for a time. In September, 1933, Humble took the lead in an increase in posted prices, which brought East Texas crude up to $1.00, an increase made possible, the company explained, by the rise in products prices that followed President Roosevelt's signing of the Petroleum Code in August. In the autumn the Railroad Commission began to use the United States Bureau of Mines estimates, under the Petroleum Code, of the consumptive demand for oil in setting its proration totals for the state. Engineering evidence of water intrusion and of the decline in reservoir pressure in the East Texas field influenced the Commission in December to reduce its allowable to 400,000 barrels.[78]

R. L. Blaffer, president of Humble, made this optimistic statement early in 1934: "The past year has marked a turning point in the oil industry. . . . We have emerged from a condition of chaos and threatened collapse of all conservation efforts . . . to a fair degree toward orderly production and termination of the wasteful and ruinous practices of the past."[79] For this favorable condition the emergency measures of the federal government were given some credit, although the administrative machinery was still far from complete; an important contributing factor was the oil industry's growing conviction that it had to exercise restraint in production.

Humble's executives, like the oil industry generally, fully accepted regulation under the NIRA. Farish's statement in the autumn of 1934, as Chairman of the Board of Standard Oil Company (New Jersey), was also true of his former associates: ". . . we have given whole-hearted support to the Oil Administration in its efforts under the act and code to bring about crude production control and thereby effect a stabilization of the oil industry as part of the administration's national program of recovery."[80] Not only was the National Industrial Recovery Act the law of the land; Humble executives, in common with oil executives generally, had become convinced that the emergency situation could not be solved by individual state action. Virtually all past efforts to establish voluntary co-operation of the oil states under the Federal Oil Conservation Board and the Oil States Advisory Committee had failed to have a lasting effect. Humble men from 1929, at the latest, had favored the establishment of a system for estimating the national consumptive demand and recommending to each oil state the proportion it should produce; and they had urged the formation of a formal organization for bringing about interstate co-operation in setting up uniform systems of regulation. The Petroleum Code went much further, and in February, 1934, Hines H. Baker saw in the existing chaos a hopeful prospect for the federal enforcement of quotas. But the Humble executives also saw difficulties, constitutional and administrative, in such a system. "The accomplishment of the desired program is a problem in practical politics," commented Pratt, adding that "at the moment the legal and political hurdles bar further progress."[81]

Humble executives, however, at that time firmly opposed more than limited participation by the federal government. They favored an authoritative determination of consumptive demand and its allocation among states—for which they regarded the United States Bureau of Mines as the best-equipped agency—and some form of federal administration and enforcement of production quotas in states without adequate, or well-enforced, conservation laws.[82] They believed, however, that regulation of production was as far as the federal government should in any event go, and they opposed the proposed regulation of refining through a system of quotas as without foundation "in principle or logic or experience" (in the words of Hines H. Baker) and as leading "to consideration of the whole field of price control and price-fixing with all its complications and with the necessary creation of machinery for carrying it out." [83]

This position was an expression of the company's general philosophy concerning regulation, which Baker then explained as follows:

> The spirit of the American system of government is that there should be as little interference with the private control of business as possible. This is not a statement that such effective measures as are necessary should not be adopted to protect the industry and the public from the effects of over-supply. It is intended to say, however, that in approaching this problem, as in the approach to the solution of all social problems, it is best to proceed as far as may be along recognized methods of procedure and to apply as far as may be remedies that have proved their worth in the light of practical experience. In all experimentation in the solution of social problems it is important to give each method a thorough test before another method is applied, so that results may be carefully observed and confusion as to what remedy secures results may be avoided.

Developments in Texas in the spring and summer of 1934 again weakened confidence in the state's administration of its oil regulations. The enactment in March of a bill requiring all refineries in the state to report the source of the oil they processed—a measure that was fought bitterly by scores of small refineries—was, however, a gain.[84] When the small refineries complained that the majors were preventing them from obtaining crude, Humble took the lead in offering to share its crude supply with such independent refineries as were operating in accordance with Commission regulations, were financially responsible, and would pay the posted price. Some refineries accepted the offer of the majors to allocate 5 per cent of their East Texas output to the independents, and some closed down; but it was generally believed that most East Texas refineries could still obtain bootleg crude at 40 to 50 cents below the posted price.[85]

The stability which East Texas had seemed about to attain again proved highly precarious. Dollar oil itself, as well as the opportunity to bootleg hot oil, stimulated overproduction; bottom-hole pressures declined. The state authorities again seemed helpless to cope with the situation. A serious rift, moreover, was said to have come between the Commission and its East Texas representatives; and the Commission's new policy of granting permits, when requested, for direct and equidistant offsets in East Texas would, according to the calculations of Humble engineers, add many thousands of new wells.[86]

Humble opposed this new policy, which struck at the very roots of the conservation program for which it had been working those many years. Humble engineers estimated that, if the East Texas field was drilled to the density that was being made possible by these permits, the drilling cost alone would approximate $200,000,000, which would bankrupt many small producers. If all the 30,000 wells possible under the new ruling were granted the statutory minimum of twenty barrels daily allowed marginal wells, the total daily field allowable would rise to 600,000 barrels; this volume of production, experience had proved, would cause pressures to drop so rapidly that within a few months all the wells in the field would have to be pumped. To provide pumping equipment, it was estimated, would cost an additional $135,000,000. The increases in drilling and production costs would, it was believed, bring about a demand for producing beyond the allowable and render enforcement more difficult. Such intensification of drilling and production by destroying the natural reservoir pressures would not only increase costs but would also, Humble engineers confidently asserted, reduce by hundreds of millions of barrels the amount of oil ultimately recoverable.

A report in Humble's intracompany *Weekly Digest* of May 15, 1934, however, indicates a strengthening support of better administration of oil law in East Texas: "Those of us who were in East Texas found that it was the opinion of the majority of the independent operators, who had just got out of debt in the operation of their properties, that they did not want to start a new drilling campaign. The only operators who did want new locations were those who had small tracts and hoped to drill to a greater density than they now have and then sell their properties to major oil companies on the basis of $40,000 per well."

Humble executives, despite their concern, were reluctant to oppose this new policy directly. To protect their own leases in East Texas, they decided to drill more wells. They also increased their efforts to strengthen the engineering argument for wider spacing. And they continued with a suit they had instituted in 1933 against a permit to drill a well which, they alleged, was in violation of Rule 37. This suit, which in June, 1935, was decided in their favor by the Supreme Court of Texas, was important as a test of the Railroad Commission's power to grant exceptions to the rule (see Chapter 19).[87]

In the year 1934 the conservation movement reached something of a climax, both inside and outside Texas. Much interest and conflict centered in the efforts of the Petroleum Administrative Board to stabilize the oil industry and in the question of federal regulation after the expiration of the two-year emergency regulation under the NIRA. A subcommittee of the Committee on Interstate and Foreign Commerce of the federal House of Representatives, headed by William P. Cole, Jr., of Maryland, conducted an investigation of the industry at the time when bills providing for clearer statutory authority for continued federal regulation were before Congress.

The early impressions of the Cole Committee formed by President Wiess of Humble during the committee's visit to Houston in July indicate a sympathetic attitude: "They are intelligent, are taking their work seriously, and give every indication of having the determination to get the facts, and having done so, to deal with them to the best of their ability." [88] The thoroughness and impartiality of that committee's work were to have a strong influence on the resolution of the conservation issue.

The Cole Committee's hearings revealed within the industry itself a broad support of conservation but also deep and continuing rifts concerning how it should be attained, particularly as to the federal government's proper role. A large majority strongly supported conservation; Farish, Pew, and Marland, strong advocates of state regulation from the early days of the conservation movement, were now members of a large company of conservationists representing both the majors and the independents. Farish and his early conservation allies were all still firmly committed to regulation under the police power of the states.

At the time of the committee hearings in the autumn the program favored by Humble's executives combined several elements: proration by the states based on a federal agency's estimates of consumptive demand, federal prohibition of interstate shipment of oil produced in violation of state regulations, and an interstate oil compact.[89] Humble's lawyers had always maintained that the constitutional authority for regulating the oil producing industry resided in the police power of the states, but during the NIRA emergency they had reserved judgment concerning the powers of the federal government under its constitutional authority to regulate interstate commerce. They were, at the same time, cognizant of the risks involved in entrusting to representatives of all the states the regulation of an industry operating in only a minority of states. Their opposition to federal regulation was based not only on the constitutional issue, but particularly on the belief that national regulation of the oil industry was impracticable.

So far, indeed, even in so restricted an area of regulation as federal efforts to control interstate shipments from East Texas, the federal agency had not been a success. According to Humble's *Weekly Digest* in the summer and fall of 1934, conditions in East Texas continued bad despite the efforts of the Railroad Commission and the federal government. In early June production was around 75,000 barrels above allowable, only twenty-three of sixty-nine refineries were reporting to the Commission, and "the consensus of opinion is that East Texas is probably at its worst since the Petroleum Code was inaugurated." The *Weekly Digest* of September 25 reported that federal efforts to regulate shipments had been ineffective, and that East Texas refineries were then running approximately 82,500 barrels of hot oil per day.

The climax, according to the *Weekly Digest*, came early in October. A daily average of 110,000 barrels of products was then reportedly being shipped by tank cars from East Texas refineries, and estimates of the production of "hot" crude varied from the 102,000 per day reported by Humble scouts to the 145,000 reported by Gulf's. The OES-6 forms which shippers, in tendering oil for interstate shipments had to furnish as evidence of legality, were characterized as a joke. "Some of the affidavits," noted the *Weekly Digest*, "have been signed by fictitious names, such as Ed Wynn, Mrs. Franklin D. Roosevelt, Will Rogers, Julius Caesar, and others." Government agents, it was said, caught a man "who had 172 of these affidavits signed by these various names and he confessed . . . he was receiving $4.00 apiece for these affidavits." One cause of this state of affairs was disagreement between the Department of the Interior, under which the Petroleum Administrative Board operated, and the Department of Justice.

This early October report in the *Weekly Digest* apparently marked the nadir of recent efforts to regulate production in East Texas; new administrative developments were soon to bring improvement. Late in October another deputy administrator of the Petroleum Administrative Board came to head a new Federal Tender Board in East Texas. Tenders approved by the Railroad Commission were, thereafter, required for interstate shipments from the field—Humble representatives had been in contact with the industry's Coordination and Planning Committee and with the Petroleum Administrative Board itself to promote such a program. Commissioner Thompson of the Railroad Commission indicated at a proration hearing that the Commission would hold the state's allowable within the volume of demand for Texas oil as determined by the federal government; he reported full co-operation between the state and federal administrative agencies, each of which, he said, was acting in its own sphere in enforcement efforts in East Texas. In December the Texas Railroad Commission instituted a state-wide tender system to regulate the movement of crude oil and products. The strengthening of control was indicated by arrests for evasion of federal taxes on production and refining in the East Texas field.

Better enforcement soon showed results. Early in November Humble scouts reported that illegal production in East Texas was down to about 33,000 barrels. On December 18 the *Weekly Digest* reported that the Federal Tender Board was functioning satisfactorily, their work having been "of value not only in controlling interstate movement, but in revealing the facts so clearly they have contributed a great deal to the effectiveness of control of intrastate operations."

In the fall of 1934, nevertheless, opposition to broad federal regulation gathered strength. Under the code, national production had consistently exceeded allowables. The Cole Committee hearings had already revealed much opposition to federal regulation, except for the prohibition of the interstate shipment of hot oil; and the opposition was strengthened by the attempts of Secretary of the Interior Ickes to set up a comprehensive program of federal regulation, particularly by his suggestion in November that the oil industry be declared a public utility. The board of directors of the American Petroleum Institute then came out against the extension of federal control. The movement against federal regulation was given direction by Governor Marland of Oklahoma, supported by Governor Allred of Texas. Marland took the initiative in starting a series of meetings to consider the old suggestion of a compact among oil-producing states.[90]

The movement away from federal regulation was strengthened by two developments. The Cole Committee Report of January 2, 1935, influenced by the interest in an agreement among oil states, recommended no federal legislation but urged upon the states the adoption of an interstate oil compact.[91] Also, early in January the Supreme Court of the United States, in the Amazon and Panama cases which had originated in East Texas, invalidated the subsection of the National Industrial Recovery Act on which federal hot-oil regulation had been based; in May the invalidation of the act itself by the Supreme Court removed the statutory basis for the remaining federal regulation under that act.[92]

Yet out of this controversial experiment with national regulation of the oil industry one important instrument was salvaged. The states were saved from losing what had proved to be strategic federal assistance in enforcing conservation legislation by a bill introduced in Congress by Senator Tom Connally of Texas—shortly after the invalidation of the hot-oil regulation in January—which was promptly passed and was signed by President Roosevelt on February 16, 1935.[93] This measure prohibited the shipment in interstate and foreign commerce of crude oil and products produced contrary to state law, and a new Federal Tender Board was immediately established in East Texas to perform the same function as the previous one under the NIRA. This form of federal intervention was generally recognized as a decisive factor in making possible the curbing of illegal overproduction in the petroleum industry.

The movement for co-operation among oil-producing states also achieved some success after several earlier efforts. Representatives of oil states met in Dallas in February, 1935, and, after sessions marked by strong differences over conservation principles—Governor Allred taking a successful stand for the principle of regulation to prevent waste, long one of Humble's cardinal principles, as opposed to price control—a compact was agreed upon for proposal to the Congress of the United States and to the individual states. The agreement was in due course acted upon favorably by the Congress and President of the United States, by the state of Texas, and by a number of other states.[94] The Interstate Oil Compact, for a period of time, provided for a permanent but voluntary association of oil states to consider and advise on conservation matters. Although without legislative or enforcement powers, it was potentially an influential agency for education in conservation and for the furtherance of interstate co-operation in its support.[95]

In the winter and spring of 1935 Texas improved its own regulation of oil production. A new law extended and strengthened the market-demand law of 1932, a favorable vote in the state senate of twenty-three out of twenty-six indicating the general acceptance which the market-demand principle had by that time won. Other acts provided for better regulation of intrastate oil movement, with provision for the confiscation of hot crude oil and products, for more care in granting injunctions against Railroad Commission orders, and for more effective collection of oil taxes.[96]

These regulations, together with federal control of shipments out of the state, were soon applied to all of Texas. On June 18, 1935, the Railroad Commission issued a new state-wide tender order putting into effect regulations for the entire state relating to the transporting, storing, and handling of crude oil and products and to the reports required of all branches of the industry. This order was adopted only after long hours of conference and study, and it proved highly effective in reducing the

Rex G. Baker

Morgan J. Davis

David Frame

Harry W. Ferguson

Stuart A. Giraud

DIRECTORS ELECTED TO BOARD 1938–1948

D. B. Harris

J. A. Neath

Carl E. Reistle, Jr.

Largest crude oil tank farm, with pump station in foreground, at Webster, between Houston and Galveston. Storage capacity, 2,675,000 barrels.

Interior of compressor plant at Lovell Lake. Here gas was compressed and returned to the oil reservoir to maintain pressure and increase oil recovery.

London natural gasoline plant, one of three operated in the East Texas area. Note orderly spacing of wells and tank batteries in woods.

Katy gas cycling plant from the air. Shows how the 500-million-cubic-feet-per-day plant fits into the surrounding rice-growing area.

Equipment development shows contrast. At left, derrickman racks pipe manually from thribble board; at right he sits and operates mechanical racker developed by Humble in experimental rig at Sugar Valley.

On field trip in the 1940s to Sitting Bull Falls in the Guadalupe Mountains of New Mexico was this group of geologists, all of whom spent long years in exploration work with Humble. Left to right: Wallace E. Pratt (Humble's first geologist, then on the Executive Committee of Standard Oil Company (New Jersey), William B. Hoover, Sol Bunnell (in rear), John W. Skinner, Morgan J. Davis (later Humble president), Richard D. Holt, and L. T. Barrow (Humble director and later chairman of the Board).

Typical Humble rig in West Texas. Big derrick and Diesel-powered equipment were designed for deep drilling in hard West Texas formations.

Polk Street view, looking north, of Humble Building shows post-World War II addition in central well foreground. Houston skyline in back.

Employees file out of Humble Building's Dallas Street (north) entrance at the close of day.

This huge Diesel-powered barge rig was designed for deep well drilling in shallow bays and other inland water up to 15 feet in depth.

"Billion Gallon Day," to celebrate Humble's manufacture of one billion gallons of 100-octane aviation gasoline, was observed at Baytown on December 14, 1944. Thousands of employees heard their wartime efforts lauded by officials of the company, government, and armed services.

Aerial view of Baytown refinery.

Wartime view of the heart of the Baytown refinery. Light-ends fractionating towers in the foreground; toluene facilities in the background. (Facing page)

Kilgore, Texas, in the heart of the East Texas field, illustrates the close spacing allowed under townsite drilling before development of conservation rules and practices.

Contrasted with the above picture is this aerial view of the Conroe field showing orderly 20-acre spacing.

Typical of the attractive employee communities built near major oil fields is this street scene in the Friendswood camp, near Houston.

In the vast Permian Basin area of West Texas a pumping well in the prolific Yates field seems to stand guard over a Humble Pipe Line Company pump station and employee housing community.

Agriculture and cattle raising continue in the midst of a major oil operation, as is shown by this peaceful scene in the Raccoon Bend field.

Typical Humble station of today, a type which has been in use since the middle 1940s.

Among the various post-World War II benefits introduced by Humble was this mobile Driver Education Unit.

Earliest drilling ventures in the deep waters of the Gulf of Mexico were undertaken with units like this: a platform to carry the derrick and drilling machinery, accompanied by a converted LST tender to house power plant, mud-mixing facilities, storage, and living quarters for the crews.

amount of hot oil produced and in eliminating impractical provisions of previous orders.

This story of the forging of regulations and administrative agencies to prevent waste and to help stabilize the oil industry is unusual in certain respects, but in many others it is a common one. The establishment of government regulation in any field of activity is usually a slow process; it involves trial and error, the development and dissemination of pertinent information, and long experience before apparently conflicting interests can be sufficiently reconciled to establish the necessary basis of agreement and before adequate policies and administrative mechanisms can be devised, organized, and put into effect to accomplish the desired objectives.

In any such movement leadership is essential. A large number of persons, companies, and associations participated in the oil conservation movement. Farish and Humble provided particularly significant leadership in the early years, and Farish continued to do so on a national scale in the 1930s. The company's role became less conspicuous as the movement broadened and won increasing support, but it remained important, particularly in reservoir research and engineering and in conservation law. The chairman of the Petroleum Division of the Institute of Mining and Metallurgical Engineers commented in a letter of August, 1935, to a Humble executive: "I think there is no doubt your company has contributed more constructive thought to sound conservation practice than any other American company." [97]

The legal and administrative structure for the regulation of the oil industry in the regions in which Humble had its principal operations had thus been established by the summer of 1935, but giving it specific formulation and application in actual practice still remained to be accomplished. The progress of that aspect of conservation, particularly as it applied to proration, is illustrated in the next chapter in connection with Humble's producing operations in the 1930s.

Chapter 19

OIL AND GAS PRODUCTION UNDER THE NEW TECHNOLOGY, 1931–1941

The dramatic development of the East Texas field after 1930 and the simultaneous struggle over public regulation of production tended to overshadow other important changes in the production of oil and gas. Humble's producing activities continued to progress along the lines laid out by its research and engineering, and in a few years the process of transition from rule-of-thumb operations to production according to scientific engineering principles was completed. Although other companies were progressing in the same direction, the interest in this chapter is again focused on Humble.

Change within a company always creates internal problems, but in the 1930s Humble's production also had to adjust to a number of pressing external complications, including those attending the development of the East Texas field. Deep depression was followed by an irregular and uncertain recovery that continued until World War II brought a great expansion. Moreover, state regulation of oil production in Texas was developing unevenly; even after new laws had provided for an adequate system of regulation and such regulation was found constitutional, effective and equitable administration developed only gradually.

APPLYING NEW RESERVOIR CONCEPTS TO OIL PRODUCTION

Humble's policy was to apply new concepts of the nature and behavior of reservoirs to production as soon as appropriate methods could be devised for putting them into practice, a policy which had become established in operations in the late 1920s but was to be applied more broadly in the next decade. The transition to scientifically guided production, however, was made both difficult and uneven by the conflict of interest and differences in viewpoints that complicated the development of conservation law and its administration.[1]

Throughout this period Humble consistently advocated and attempted to practice the following production principles: (1) to consider the reservoir as a unit for production, inasmuch as each well affected the others in a field; (2) to produce from a reservoir in such a way as to obtain the largest ultimate recovery that was economically feasible; (3) to space wells as widely as possible within the limits of efficient drainage; and (4) to allocate production allowables so that the owner of each lease would be afforded the opportunity to recover his proper share of the oil-pool allowable.

Since most of its producing operations were in Texas, conditions in that state were of the greatest significance to Humble. The principle was well established that reservoirs should be produced with the least possible waste. And the 1932 law, as already observed, included under waste any production in excess of reasonable market demand, and specifically authorized the Railroad Commission to restrict production to that demand. But how to administer the law so as to prevent waste and how to allocate the state's allowable production among the various pools and each pool's allowable among its producers were matters of controversy for a number of years.

Humble's research men and production engineers in the early years of the decade concluded that in most fields proper drainage was not so much a matter of spacing as of the efficient use of reservoir energy, and that both greater economy and less waste of the resource could be attained with wider spacing than was then customary. Many operators and royalty owners, on the contrary, held to the popular theory that greater well density meant greater oil recovery and consequently advocated close spacing. Humble's engineers pointed out that the statistics used in support of this theory concerned pools where wide-open production existed and that they did not prove that the ultimate recovery from an entire pool, as distinguished from recovery from specific portions over a limited period of time, would be increased by greater well density. During the early 1930s, when the rush for close spacing threatened to bankrupt even large companies, W. W. Scott was extremely active in advocating wide spacing at meetings of the API and the AIMME and as a Humble representative before the Railroad Commission.

Humble's production research staff and petroleum engineers, on the basis of observed reservoir data, could estimate with reasonable accuracy the total oil in a reservoir and the amount in place under a given area. Moreover, they devised formulas for allocating the total allowable within a given pool that would give each producer the opportunity to recover approximately his proper share of the pool allowable. Some operators argued, however, that, regardless of well density or the size of tracts, allocation should be on a per-well basis or on the relative potentials of wells without regard for other factors that indicated the relative amount of oil in place under the tract represented by a well.

The advocates of controlled production were in a difficult situation. Under the earlier unregulated production, wells were produced to their maximum capacity. Neighboring leases could in most instances be protected from drainage by the drilling of offset wells, with the result that the several wells competing for oil in a pool represented about the same size of surface area. But when the production of a pool and the location of the wells therein were restricted, the formula used for allocating production among wells or leases took on paramount importance. Assume, for example, that the spacing rules for a pool prescribed one well for each forty acres and that exceptions were granted so that some wells were drilled on tracts of less than forty acres. Allocation of production on a per-well basis, or even on the basis of 50 per cent on acreage and 50 per cent on wells, made it possible for the owners of the wells on the smaller tracts to drain large quantities of oil from under the larger forty-acre units. As a result, a well on a town lot twenty-five feet square might produce during its lifetime a hundred times the amount of oil originally in place beneath the lot. This situation epitomizes the economic basis of conflicts involving spacing and allowables.

The simplest way to afford an opportunity for a reservoir to be produced according to good production practice, Humble executives believed, was to have complete control of its leases by means of some form of unitized or co-operative plan. In the later 1920s Humble had obtained complete operating control of three producing fields—Boggy Creek, Sugarland, and Raccoon Bend—and, for experimental purposes, of Olney. The operation of these fields demonstrated the efficiency that was possible with an adequate plan of operation for an entire pool. It had proved impossible, however, to accomplish much in the way of unitization by voluntary co-operation of producers. But by the early 1930s Humble executives had come to believe that, with intelligent spacing of wells and proper field rules and allocation formulas, efficient operations could be attained without unitization.

Humble continued to lease large areas in the hope that one or more pools would be found within an area and thus afford the company the opportunity to treat each pool as a unit. Its additions to reserves in this period were recorded in the annual reports of the Production Department, together with the estimated percentage of the productive acreage owned by Humble in each field. According to these records, all or nearly all the productive acreage of a few fields was acquired, including the small Hilbig and the Clear Lake field and the great Friendswood field in Texas and North Crowley in Louisiana. Humble acquired estimated percentages ranging from about 50 to over 90 per cent of the productive acreage of many other fields, including such important ones as Conroe, Thompsons, the Katy gas field, Means, Tomoconnor, Anahuac, and Hawkins. It also obtained substantial participations in a large number of other fields, including Hastings, Talco, Kelsey, and Avoca in Texas, Vacuum in New Mexico, and Lake Washington, Potash, and Roanoke in Louisiana. These participation factors changed in later years as the development of the fields progressed. But, whether they were increased or decreased, the fact remains that Humble in the 1930s succeeded notably in its policy of leasing large parts or even all of individual fields.[2]

The advantages in holding all or large portions of a field lay partly in the greater economy of operations but particularly in the measure of control afforded over the location of wells and production practices. When Humble held all or large blocks of a field, it could obtain reservoir data from a correspondingly large portion of the area; and such data could be used both to determine the best production practices for the reservoir and to present as evidence in Railroad Commission hearings. Moreover, the danger of drainage from neighboring leases was not so great in the interior of large blocks as in small holdings.

In its wholly leased fields, Humble followed the production practices for obtaining maximum ultimate recovery indicated by reservoir data and applicable engineering principles. Hilbig, which the company began to develop in 1933, is a clear illustration. In the development of this field, reservoir engineers studied the reservoir factors that had a bearing on production. Structurally, the Hilbig reservoir is the porous upper portion of an igneous plug, intruded from greater depths through sedimentary bedded rocks, some of which were presumably oil-bearing. Oil from the ruptured edges of these source beds moved into the upper part of the plug and there accumulated. The formation gave no evidence of an effective water drive or of a gas cap and was found to derive its energy from gas in solution. Its oil zone varied in thickness up to 300 feet and lay about 2,500 feet below the surface. On the basis of data concerning the character of the reservoir rock and its fluid contents, Humble drilled twelve producing wells and one gas injection well on the field's 260 acres. Production was carefully regulated to make the best use of the energy-potential of the dissolved gas. The gas produced with the oil, excepting a small amount which was unavoidably lost, was returned to the oil zone. Thus, by the continuous injection of produced gas, maximum use was made of the reservoir's only energy source, gas in solution. About twenty-five years after its discovery, Hilbig was still producing oil with energy derived from gas. It was then estimated that the oil already recovered exceeded by about 20 per cent what the ultimate total would have been without the return of gas to the reservoir, and that with gas return Hilbig would continue to produce at a declining rate for about another score of years.

Humble, however, had most of its operations in fields with divided ownership, and in such fields it co-operated with other producers in support of production practices in keeping with the new reservoir knowledge. It favored agreement among the operators in a given Texas field as to the practices to recommend to the Railroad Commission for that field. Such co-operation was most easily effected in fields where operators were relatively few and holdings large, because most of the larger producers favored spacing orders and allocation formulas that gave some consideration to the oil in place under the area represented by individual leases. Accordingly, in the early 1930s some fields were developed on twenty-acre spacing, though ten-acre spacing was still the prevailing pattern in Texas from 1931 through 1935. A forty-acre spacing order of the Texas Railroad Commission was issued in 1932 for Howard-Glasscock and in 1935 for the Greta field (deep); in the latter Humble held an estimated fifth of the productive acreage.[3] In 1934 Humble owned 43 per cent of the wells in pools for which the spacing pattern was twenty acres or more per well, although it was then operating only 6 per cent of the total number of wells in Texas. In some fields, well-allocation formulas included such factors as oil-sand thickness, acreage, and bottom-hole pressure. Greta in 1933 was prorated entirely on acreage; Van, Conroe, Thompsons, Tomball, and other newer fields were being developed with allocation formulas that Humble executives considered reasonable. During 1936–1940 the over-all spacing trend in Texas was toward the twenty-acre pattern. In fields in which all or nearly all the operators had recommended specific spacing patterns and allocation formulas, the Commission in those later years of the decade tended to accept such recommendations, although it sometimes showed a disposition even in closely held fields to order ten-acre or approximately ten-acre spacing.[4]

Humble's greatest problem with spacing and allowables was in fields with many and scattered small holdings, particularly in the East Texas field. That field was especially important to the company, since in the first half of the 1930s it had more reserves in that field than in any other and drew therefrom nearly a third of its production.

Humble recognized that in the case of small holdings the cost of drilling seemed to give some justification for granting to the small tract more than its share of production under the field order, but it did not agree with such practices in principle. It advocated as an alternative, in many instances successfully, the pooling of tracts that were not large enough under a field's spacing rule to permit a well to be drilled in compliance with the pattern fixed by the rule. But when well allowables were based wholly or largely on well or potential, holders of small tracts could recover more oil by obtaining an exception to Rule 37 than they could by pooling.[5] Some states remedied this situation by providing for compulsory pooling of small tracts to form units in conformity with the prescribed spacing pattern. Humble voiced no objection to compulsory pooling of tracts to drill a well, but it consistently opposed compulsory field-wide unitization.[6]

Like the larger operators generally, Humble as a practical matter was not seriously concerned over exceptions to Rule 37 so long as such exceptions were relatively few per field. But the situation in the East Texas field was serious. In 1933 and 1934 Humble drilled many more wells than it considered necessary for properly draining its leases—in 1934 it spent $5,500,000 on wells that were unnecessary except to maintain its percentage of the allowable; like other large producers, it made a special effort to protect those leases that were exposed to serious drainage by wells on neighboring small tracts. At the same time, like certain other companies, it consistently presented evidence in Railroad Commission hearings in support of wide spacing and of allowables that would give some recognition to the amount of recoverable oil originally in place under a lease. But the Commission continued to grant permits for exceptions to the spacing rule and, generally, to allocate allowables according to well-potential or on substantially a per-well basis. When the Commission refused such permits, the District Court of Travis County often intervened and granted injunctions against the enforcement of the spacing rule.

Humble and a number of other companies sought recourse in the courts against the exceptions to Rule 37. Its most important East Texas case in the earlier years of the decade was one of several such cases involving permits for spacing exceptions. Humble's suit involved 1½ acres of a 3-acre portion of a 102-acre tract of which it held the other 99 acres under lease. After the Commission had set the spacing pattern for the field, the owner of the 3-acre tract obtained a permit to drill a well on 1½ acres as an exception to Rule 37, and he later obtained a permit for a well on the other half of the tract. Humble applied to the Travis County District Court to set aside the second permit. The issue was whether owners of small tracts could, by voluntary subdivisions made after a spacing rule for a field had been established, acquire the right to drill wells on such subdivided tracts closer to property lines or to other wells than the rule stipulated and thus recover more than the tract's proper share of oil. The District Court refused Humble's plea to set aside the second permit, whereupon Humble appealed to the Court of Civil Appeals at Austin and won a favorable decision. The owner of the lease then appealed to the Supreme Court of Texas. In June, 1935, this court in *Brown* v. *Humble Oil & Refining Company* affirmed the decision of the Court of Civil Appeals.[7]

This decision established the important principle that "Where Rule 37 is in force in a certain territory, a voluntary subdivision of a tract of land subject to development for oil and gas as a whole would not entitle the owner of said divided tract, or tracts, as a matter of right, to an exception to Rule 37 on the ground of vested right, because such act would destroy the rule and render the conservation law a nullity. . . ." However, when a subsequent suit brought by the lease owner for the whole three-acre tract as a unit was remanded to the trial court, the permit for the second well was upheld on the basis of "substantial evidence" to the effect that two wells were necessary for the recovery of the oil to which the tract was entitled.[8] Although this later decision allowed the second well, it did so on the ground that the two wells were necessary for the recovery of the oil under the three-acre tract. Wrong as this position was from the viewpoint of Humble's engineering evidence, it nevertheless was important as a recognition of the principle that a landowner is entitled to the opportunity to produce or obtain the recoverable oil under his tract.

Humble executives eventually became convinced that little could be done to improve the East Texas situation because, once bad spacing had been permitted on a large scale in a field, it was practically impossible to change the pattern. They had at one time been hopeful that a formula for determining allowables might sometime be adopted that would be more nearly equitable and less injurious to the field than the well-potential formula. By 1935, however, they saw little chance of achieving such a formula without special legislation. Court action against a spacing order that was in flagrant disregard of Rule 37 was possible, but to get action against well-potential as the sole basis for the allocation of the East Texas field's production was probably impossible at the time. "I am afraid," one Humble executive wrote in April, 1935, "that East Texas will be forever a mess and that we should seek to protect our investments elsewhere by undertaking to secure proper holdings under a more favorable fact set-up." [9]

It may have seemed that by the end of 1935 a large measure of equity, order, and stability should have been established in the oil fields of Texas. By then many questions regarding the validity of statutes and practices, including restriction to market demand, had been settled there; and the Interstate Oil Compact gave some promise of influencing other oil states to carry out effective conservation programs. However, Texas law, like the law of other states, necessarily left much discretion to the state administrative agency. Although great progress had been made toward providing a scientific and engineering basis for regulation, the members of the Texas Railroad Commission were elected by popular vote and hence were highly sensitive to the pressures of public opinion and the condition of the oil market. The circumstances were ideal for conflict. Under a ceiling on total production, the individual producer fought for what he claimed to be his fair share of the allowable; but "fairness" seemed to have no clear definition or generally recognized basis, although the courts had recognized the right of each operator to have a reasonable opportunity to produce the recoverable oil and gas in place under his land or lease.

In 1936 Humble's executives became disturbed over a situation that for the next five years was to create serious problems and threaten the value of their company's reserves. They observed a tendency for the number of wells to increase faster than market demand, a usual response to higher prices which was now aggravated by the restraint on the volume produced by the individual well. In some new fields the Railroad Commission delayed issuing spacing orders until a relatively narrow spacing pattern had been established by drilling, particularly in certain salt-dome fields, which the Commission claimed were by law exempt from the usual spacing regulations under Rule 37. In 1936 the Humble men were especially anxious over the failure to set rules for the Amelia field, in which the company held by far the larger portion of the proved acreage. The Railroad Commission continued to grant exceptions to Rule 37 in the East Texas field, thus permitting extensive additional drilling.

Humble was also concerned over the high allowables being ordered for some new fields, which encouraged excessive drilling that could lead to production rates adversely affecting ultimate oil recovery. It preferred the policy of wide spacing in new fields, whether or not they were competitively held, so as to avoid the excessive and wasteful production rates that were prompted by too close drilling and overinvestment in any given field.[10]

In 1936 and 1937 Humble continued in Railroad Commission hearings to press for wider spacing patterns and for allocation formulas that would give reasonable recognition to the quantity of recoverable oil under the various tracts in a field. The executives believed that a better understanding of reservoirs, as well as cost considerations, would eventually bring the Railroad Commission to order spacing patterns and allowables more in keeping with equity as indicated by the new reservoir knowledge; it seemed to them, however, that to attempt at the time to correct specific inconsistencies and uncertainties in the Commission's interpretation of the law and in some of its orders might bring greater difficulties than already existed. But in 1937 the amount of oil in storage in the United States increased, largely from new and unregulated production in Illinois, and depressed the market. This increase stimulated the drilling of more wells by those who, from choice or necessity, wanted to balance lower prices with a larger volume of production.

The situation was bad in Texas and other states, and Humble participated in an industry-wide movement to formulate and propose remedies. The Independent Petroleum Association of America—in which the Texas independent producer, Charles F. Roeser, was very influential—and the American Petroleum Institute sponsored extensive studies by committees of members. Hines H. Baker and John R. Suman were on the API committee on well-spacing; Baker was also a member of its legal subcommittee, and T. V. Moore and C. E. Reistle, Jr., were members of its technical study committee. The study committee of the IPA in 1938 pointed especially to overdrilling in the East Texas field, where the committee estimated that unnecessary wells had cost $200,000,000.[11] President Wiess of Humble at the time took a strong stand against excessive rates of drilling and too rapid depletion of reserves. But, despite studies, reports, and public statements, the situation with respect to spacing and allowables continued to deteriorate.

By 1939 Humble executives considered two problems particularly serious. The more rapid increase in the number of wells than in the state's allowable and production brought especially severe cuts in average well allowables for non-marginal—that is, the more productive—wells, which included a large percentage of Humble's own wells. The other problem was the decrease in the allowables of many fields in which the company held all or a large part of the acreage. Humble's proration division had calculated early in 1938 that, whereas the East Texas field at its current production rate would be depleted in fifteen years, certain other fields in which the company had large interests would be depleted in from forty to eighty-nine years, the latter period being the estimate for Humble's unit-operated Sugarland. Thompsons was held to a low field allowable despite a shortage of the kind of crude it produced, which was in demand for lubricants; Humble was said to have had for several years insufficient storage stock of low-cold-test types of crude to assure Baytown of an adequate supply.

The periodic shutdown, or the restricting of the producing days of fields in order to hold total production within the state's allowable, gave opportunity for further discrimination. For example, when overproduction in September, 1939, caused a state-wide shutdown of nine days a month, 145 fields in Texas with a scheduled allowable of 450,000 barrels were exempted. It seemed to many that the Commission, for reasons which it no doubt considered sufficient, tended to favor the small tracts in a field or the fields with a large number of small owners.

Field allowables were Humble's greatest problem in the later 1930s. Although Texas conservation law contemplated a state-wide allowable production that would not exceed market demand and the distribution of that allowable among the pools without discrimination, it made no specific provision for allocation among fields. From 1931 on, such allocations had been based largely on demands by purchasers for crude from individual fields. Requests for field allowables, together with pertinent field data, were generally presented by companies or individuals at regular or special Railroad Commission hearings; and the various conflicting interests strove competitively for a larger share of the total state allowable. During a period of decline in the demand for crude, for example, West Texas producers, fearing that Humble would reduce its considerable purchases in West Texas in favor of its own Gulf Coast production, seem to have brought pressure to bear for decreasing the allowables of certain Gulf Coast fields.[12]

The Humble executives who were closest to this problem advocated, according to memoranda written in 1938 and 1939, that, within the capacity of the individual pools to produce without waste, the total state allowable should be divided among pools according to a general formula. Such a formula should consider the field's reserves and other appropriate factors; the estimated reserves should be given heavy weight in determining a field's allowable, not less than 50 per cent and preferably more. It was recognized that adjustments would have to be made to conform with statutory provisions for marginal wells, to allow for actual differences in the demand for specific crudes, and to keep a field's allowable within its marketing facilities.

Overdrilling continued to be the most serious threat to Humble's large interest in the East Texas field, where the Railroad Commission persistently granted exceptions to Rule 37 and set well allowables virtually on a per-well basis without serious regard for the size of a tract and the relative quantity of oil under the various tracts. The result was a very small differential between marginal wells and closely spaced flowing wells, on the one hand, and widely spaced flowing wells, on the other.

In 1939 Humble joined with several other companies in an effort to test in the courts the orders of the Railroad Commission for well allowables in the East Texas field. The first case was that of the Rowan & Nichols Oil Company, an independent producing firm, which applied for an injunction against the enforcement of the Railroad Commission's allocation order. The company alleged that the order would permit the owner of five wells on a single acre in one of the less productive parts of the field to produce as much as Rowan & Nichols' five wells on a twenty-five-acre tract in the most productive part, thus discriminating against the company and in effect giving its property to another or others. Alleging that the order was confiscatory and arbitrary, in violation of its rights under the Fourteenth Amendment of the Constitution of the United States, Rowan & Nichols brought suit in the federal District Court at Austin, Texas. Both the trial court and the Circuit Court of Appeals of the Fifth Circuit held that the order was invalid.[13]

As a result of this decision, the Railroad Commission in June, 1939, issued a new allocation order. Humble claimed that, although it owned approximately 14 per cent of the total recoverable reserves of the East Texas field, under the new order it was permitted to produce only a fraction over 9 per cent of the field's total allowable. It requested the Commission to issue an order that would permit the company to produce its fair share of the recoverable oil. When the Commission failed to grant this request, Humble filed suit in a three-judge federal court at Austin, basing its action on the equal-protection and due-process clauses of the Fourteenth Amendment. Rowan & Nichols similarly instituted action in a second suit. The two companies filed in the federal rather than the state courts, primarily to save time because of the thousands of barrels of oil per day involved.[14] Presumably the cases would thus reach the Supreme Court of the United States for decision on the constitutional question sooner than if they first went through the state courts and then to the United States Supreme Court.

A three-judge federal court on August 11, 1939, granted Humble's plea for a temporary injunction, later made permanent, which permitted the company to produce 5,000 additional barrels per day in the East Texas field. This court found no serious dispute as to the facts in the Humble and Rowan & Nichols cases and held that the Commission's orders were unreasonable, discriminatory, arbitrary, and confiscatory.[15] The Railroad Commission appealed the cases to the Supreme Court of the United States.

The Railroad Commission had already appealed to the Supreme Court the first Rowan & Nichols case, which had been decided in favor of the company by the United States Court of Appeals. The majority decision of the Supreme Court on this case, delivered in June, 1940, upheld the order of the Commission, principally on the ground that it was not a proper function of the federal courts to interfere with a state administrative agency so long as some evidence supported the agency's action and the issues could be tried in the state courts.[16] "This opinion," according to a memorandum of June 12, 1940, written by Humble's Hines H. Baker, "appears to make valid any order by an administrative body if supported by any evidence, however slight, even though the proof shows conclusively in the trial of the case that the order is highly confiscatory and discriminatory."

This decision set the pattern for the high court's disposal of the Humble suit and the second Rowan & Nichols suit.[17] It virtually closed the federal courts, at least the lower courts, to those who sought to invalidate a commission's order as being violative of constitutional rights.

The decision of the Supreme Court of the United States in these cases was not, therefore, based on the merits of the contention that under the Commission's orders the companies were being deprived of property without due process of law through arbitrary and discriminatory allocation orders. The arguments presented by Humble's Rex G. Baker before the United States Supreme Court in *Railroad Commission et al.* v. *Humble Oil & Refining Company*, in support of the allegation that the orders were discriminatory, remained largely unanswered.

Humble, and other companies similarly situated, had been caught and buffeted by changing rules. These cases were disposed of by a court, the majority of whose members had been recently appointed and who seemed to be inclined to support the authority of administrative agencies, which were then growing in importance. The dissenting opinion in the Rowan & Nichols case, written by Chief Justice Hughes and concurred in by Justice McReynolds and Justice Roberts, held that the court had reversed its established position in regard to due process under the Fourteenth Amendment and had decided contrary to the recent opinion of Justice Brandeis, written for a unanimous court, in *Thompson* v. *Consolidated Gas Utilities Corporation*, a case which dealt with a proration order affecting gas.[18] Many students of constitutional law agreed that this Rowan & Nichols decision went contrary to a long-established rule of law, based on statute, that a federal court had jurisdiction to decide, and should decide, the validity of an order of a state agency if a substantial federal question was involved. Discussion of the validity of the court's decision in the Humble and Rowan & Nichols cases was merged with the current controversy over the growth of administrative agencies and their authority.

As so often happens, however, even as the decision of the Supreme Court of the United States seemed to block Humble's attainment of a more equitable position under the Railroad Commission's orders, counterbalancing forces were at work. Better administration of conservation law was developing in Texas, particularly in newer fields, as it was in neighboring states in which Humble operated. Companies were increasingly employing engineers and advocating sound practices based on reservoir data. Moreover, much better information on reserves was available. The Railroad Commission itself was beginning to acquire an engineering staff and to have greater confidence in the engineering approach to production problems, as was illustrated by an article of Ernest O. Thompson of the Texas Railroad Commission in the February, 1939, issue of the *Oil & Gas Journal.* Necessity also played a part in curbing reckless drilling; the high cost of drilling, the low allowables per well (averaging 14.2 barrels per day in Texas in 1942), and the low prices of crude, all tended to deter drilling. The number of wells drilled in Texas was considerably less in relation to existing wells in 1939–1941 than it had been in 1935–1938.

The administration of Texas conservation law in 1940 and 1941, consequently, underwent important changes. In February, 1940, the Railroad Commission issued its first state-wide twenty-acre spacing order, a signal gain despite the exceptions that continued to be granted. Forty-six of the special field orders issued in 1940 included allocation formulas, and of these only one failed to give 50 per cent or more weight to acreage; these orders applied to 99 per cent of the total reserves in the fields concerned. The greatest advance was in allocation among pools. In an order of December, 1940, the Commission for the first time applied a general formula based on acreage, wells, depth of oil sand, and type of crude produced. At the same time the Commission nearly ceased granting to individual pools exemption from shutdowns. The formula for allocations among pools was strengthened early in 1941 by making more explicit and practicable the basis for the classification of individual fields. The year 1941 brought even greater progress, as was reported by Humble's Proration Department at the end of the year:[19]

> Texas crude demand changed from one of civilian needs at the first of 1941, to national defense needs in midyear, and to total war needs at the end of the year. During this time, as compared with previous years, proration matters in Texas were administered on a sounder basis. The Commission completely abandoned the policy of granting special allowables, and announced the following guiding principles: (1) crude demand will be considered as individual state demand rather than individual field demand in setting allowables; (2) there will be strict adherence to the formula for allocation between pools; (3) state production is to be kept within the recommendation of the Bureau of Mines.

Production in Texas in 1941 was held to the estimates of the Bureau of Mines, and the trend toward wider spacing was accelerated.

Texas was not the only state in which Humble operated that was strengthening its conservation law and administration, although it was by far the most important to Humble because of the company's large operations there and relatively small interests in other states. During the 1930s Humble also had production in Louisiana and New Mexico. In New Mexico good practices had prevailed from the time of the development of the Hobbs field in 1929. In both states effective conservation laws were developed somewhat later than in Texas, and both profited from their neighbor's long and controversial experience. New Mexico adopted a conservation measure in 1929 and enacted a basic conservation law in 1935; a ratable purchasing amendment was adopted in 1940. In the view of Humble executives—some of whom advised on the writing of that state's law—New Mexico's conservation law proved notably successful in promoting good conservation practices and in protecting correlative rights in the production of oil. In 1940 Louisiana adopted a comprehensive conservation statute, which on the whole followed the example of Texas and New Mexico but added compulsory pooling and the authority to compel gas cycling. In both states the administration of these laws was reasonably effective from the very first.[20]

By 1941 Humble could look with satisfaction on its own production practices and on the progress of conservation law and administration in the states in which it operated. The struggle for such law, and for nondiscriminatory allocation orders and other practices protective of property rights, had been long and often discouraging. But in the territory in which Humble operated the fact that regulations had become legally established and widely accepted made it possible for oilmen to employ practices that reservoir research and engineering had indicated to be sound. The twin development of science and engineering, on the one hand, and state regulation, on the other, had brought revolutionary changes in Humble's producing operations and in the practices of the oil industry in the region in which it operated.

HUMBLE BECOMES A LARGE PRODUCER OF NATURAL GAS

While improving and expanding its oil production in the 1930s, Humble was developing even more rapidly its production of natural gas.[21] Factors having a strong effect on this operation were the new technology, a greatly increased market demand, and the discovery of great gas reserves.

In expanding natural gas production in the 1930s, Humble reversed its policy of the 1920s, when it had deliberately sought to avoid the production of gas. The main reason for the earlier policy was an insufficient demand for natural gas to make its production on a large scale profitable; the local market was then definitely limited and relatively inelastic, and transmission to distant markets was still impracticable. Humble had, therefore, assigned the gas rights in the gas fields it discovered to a local gas company or to oil companies which had entered the gas business; for example, in 1925 it sold its gas reserves in the Ibex field to the Phillips Petroleum Company.[22] In some fields it built plants to extract the gasoline from the "wet," or casinghead, gas produced with the oil, which it used principally for upgrading refinery gasoline; in other fields it endeavored to sell its casinghead gas to local gas companies or carbon-black plants.

As the function of gas in oil production came to be recognized, Humble began to utilize gas to increase oil recovery. It first used gas as a lifting agent for oil. As noted earlier, in 1930 it built a plant at Sugarland for returning gas to the oil formation in order to help maintain the pressure essential to oil recovery. This was the first large pressure maintenance operation in the United States, and the Sugarland plant was the first of several such plants built by Humble within a few years.

The transfer of the old Casinghead Gasoline Department to the Production Department as of January 1, 1931, was a result of the growing recognition of the importance of gas in production. The increasing realization of the function of gas in efficient oil recovery made imperative a close co-ordination of gas operations and oil production. Moreover, a developing demand for light hydrocarbons necessitated the use in their production of the new techniques being developed within the Production Department.

The value of the union of the Casinghead Gasoline Department and the Production Department was soon demonstrated in Humble's operations in the East Texas field. Its large oil production there raised the problem of how to dispose of the casinghead gas. The solution adopted was to build casinghead gasoline plants to strip the casinghead gas of its natural gasoline. The residue gas could be returned to the lease for lease use or sold if a market was available. In 1932 two such plants, with auxiliary gas pipelines for gathering systems, were built at Kilgore and London. These plants were designed for a daily production of 75,000 gallons of debutanized casinghead gasoline. It was then estimated that a margin of one-fourth of a cent per gallon between the cost and the selling price of the gasoline would represent a good profit.[23] A similar plant was completed at Conroe in 1934.[24]

By then, however, it had become obvious that Humble's gas reserves were so large that other outlets had to be found. From 1931 to 1933 the Conroe, Pledger, Tomball, and Greta fields had been discovered, and in all of these Humble had large interests. Although all but Pledger were principally oil fields, all were also large gas producers. Humble by 1933 was believed to have larger gas reserves than any other company in southern and Southwest Texas, larger even than the United Gas Corporation and the Houston Pipe Line Company, which then dominated the gas business in the area.

Humble employed the Hope Engineering Company to advise on how to market its Conroe and Tomball gas. This firm recommended that the company should either operate as an industrial-gas marketing company, serving major industries outside Houston, or, since 80 per cent of its gas reserves were within forty miles of Houston, enter the Houston market by acquiring control of the Houston Natural Gas Corporation, an affiliate of the Houston Pipe Line Company. Failing to obtain control of Houston Natural Gas and wishing to avoid the duplication of distributing facilities, Humble attempted, without success, to sell a large part of its gas reserves to United Gas and Houston Pipe.

In the meantime, the discovery of the great Tomoconnor, Anahuac, and Katy fields, in which it acquired large reserves, increased Humble's gas problem. The company by then felt that it had no alternative but to enter industrial-gas marketing. As Wiess put it, "We feel that we are forced into the business by the discovery of enormous gas reserves under our properties, which are in close proximity to a large consuming market." [25] The first question was whether Humble should market gas directly or set up a new corporation. The decision awaited the outcome of agitation in Texas for the regulation of gas production and distribution, particularly for the divorcement of gas and oil properties. A report of the United States Bureau of Mines issued early in 1935 spotlighted the Texas Panhandle area where about 60 per cent of the current natural gas production was being wasted, a condition that threatened to deplete the recoverable reserves in ten to twenty-five years. Governor Allred of Texas recommended legislation to provide for effective gas conservation and ratable taking, for the divorcement of gas pipelines from oil interests, and for the prohibition of interlocking ownership of the several branches of the industry by means of holding companies.[26]

In the spring of 1935 the Texas legislature passed the Gas Waste Act.[27] This measure required the regulation of the production of gas from gas wells to prevent waste and to accord with market demand, authorized the Railroad Commission to consider both well-potential and acreage in allocating production, authorized agreements for the co-operative development and operation of gas fields under the attorney general's approval, and provided for ratable taking. Humble had long urged some of these provisions and believed that this measure was a definite improvement over earlier ones, but Wiess doubted that to prorate gas according to market demand was practicable, holding that it was neither sound economics nor sound engineering.[28]

When the Texas legislature took no action on proposals for the divorcement of gas and oil properties, Humble decided to operate its gas business through a division of the Production Department, as The Texas Company and the Magnolia Petroleum Company were already doing. Accordingly, in 1935 it established the Gas Department, which included the old Casinghead Gasoline Department, with John O. Sue as superintendent. Henceforth this group had the responsibility for operating gas wells, for handling the gas produced with oil, and in general for supplying staff service on gas matters to the Production Department.

In 1936 an obstacle to Humble's entry into the large-scale commercial sale of gas was eliminated. That obstacle was the contention of the Texas Railroad Commission that Humble's contract of June 7, 1928, to sell gas from the Raccoon Bend field to the M. and M. Pipe Line Company, a gas utility, made Humble itself a gas utility subject to regulation by the Commission under the state's public utility statutes. Humble, denying the Commission's jurisdiction, had applied to the Travis County Court for an injunction against the enforcement of the order setting a substantially lower rate for the sale of the gas than that agreed upon in the contract in question. The Travis County Court granted Humble's application for the injunction in January, 1936, a decision which was affirmed by the Court of Civil Appeals at Austin in 1939. Thus it was established that, under the laws of Texas, the sale of gas at the point of origin to a utility did not make a producing company a public utility.[29]

The development of commercial gas production on a large scale hinged, of course, on finding a profitable market for the gas. Entering a market that already has established suppliers is never easy, but in this instance the company was favored by a growing industrial demand for gas in its area. Humble's first substantial contract for the sale of gas was negotiated by Pratt with the Texas Gulf Sulphur Company, which was said to be the largest consumer of gas in the state. Under this contract, effective January 1, 1936, Humble agreed to sell to the sulphur company the gas requirements for its Gulf, New Gulf, and Long Point plants for ten years at a delivered price of 9 cents per thousand cubic feet, with a clause entitling the buyer to any lower price that Humble might grant during the term of the agreement. The Houston *Press* on June 11, 1935, acclaimed the contract as "the forerunner of a new industrial era for the Houston Ship Channel and its vicinity."

Humble arranged to supply the Texas Gulf's requirements from the Pledger gas field, which was only eight miles from the sulphur company's main point of consumption at Boling. The Danciger Oil & Refining Company, which owned approximately as much of the Pledger field as did Humble, had a gasoline plant there and was blowing large quantities of residue gas into the air. Humble agreed with Danciger to supply as much as 80 per cent of the requirements for this contract from Pledger, to treat Danciger's interests as equal to its own, to have its gas processed through the Danciger plant at cost plus 5 per cent, and to buy Danciger's residue at 5 cents per thousand cubic feet, with a provision to adjust the price proportionately to any change in the price under the contract with the Texas Gulf Sulphur Company. Humble also purchased two-thirds of Danciger's pipeline to New Gulf and constructed a seventeen-mile line to Long Point and a thirty-mile line to the Texas Gulf plant.

Humble's contract with the Texas Gulf Sulphur Company inspired an acrimonious dispute with the president of the Houston Oil Company that illustrates one of the problems encountered in breaking into industrial-gas marketing. The Houston Oil Company had previously had the contract to supply the sulphur company at 14 cents per thousand cubic feet. The sulphur company had offered it the opportunity to meet Humble's rate of 9 cents per thousand cubic feet, but Houston Oil had replied that a sale at less than 14 cents would mean its ruin. Houston Oil's president held that it was unethical for a wealthy oil company like Humble, which was already making large profits, to enter into the gas-distribution business in competition with his comparatively small company; Humble, instead of taking advantage of its large gas reserves and proximity to a market to sell directly to industrial establishments, should permit his company to enjoy the middleman's role and profit. This view, though understandable, hardly fitted into the pattern of competitive enterprise avowedly favored by the executives of both Houston Oil and its new rival.

Other large gas consumers then began to approach Humble, and the company itself explored every possibility for contracts with industrial concerns and for sale of gas at the well. In the fall of 1936 it entered into two five-year contracts with The Texas Company, effective April 1, 1937, for the sale of its Tomball gas. In one contract Humble agreed to sell and deliver natural gas to The Texas Company's refineries at Port Arthur, Port Neches, and Houston at 9 cents per thousand cubic feet; in the other it agreed to purchase from The Texas Company some of its Tomball gas production for processing, in addition to Humble's own gas, in amounts and at prices to vary in accordance with certain variable factors.

In order to provide this gas, Humble built a gasoline plant at Tomball with a system of gas transmission lines. It built a ten-inch main pipeline to Houston, with a capacity of 60,000,000 cubic feet daily, to be supplied from Tomball and other Humble gas reserves. It purchased from the Pan-American Petroleum & Transport Company a ten-inch line running from Houston to Baytown, and it built lines from Baytown to Port Arthur and Port Neches. The company began to deliver gas on schedule to The Texas Company in March, 1937.

Although they invited orders from industrial consumers, Humble's executives let it be known that they intended neither to sell gas for domestic use nor to enter into the general purchase and sale of industrial gas. They had entered gas distribution primarily to provide a market for Humble's own gas production after extracting the natural gasoline, and they did not intend to lay lines to fields in which the company was not interested or to purchase gas generally. They were purposely trying to avoid getting into a position that might necessitate their purchase of gas.

Humble's gas reserves continued to grow through the discovery of Lirette, Friendswood, Heyser, Lovell Lake, Navarro Crossing, Hugoton (Texas Panhandle), Hawkins, Erath, and other fields; and the company continued to seek outlets for gas. After September 15, 1937, it began to supply from Tomball the gas-fuel requirements of the Houston Lighting & Power Company and the Eastern States refinery. In 1939, it arranged for United Gas to take gas from the Lirette field in Louisiana, and established the Montegut gas pipeline system. From 1936 when it began to sell and distribute natural gas for industrial purposes through 1941, Humble's gas sales increased about two-thirds. The expiration of its own old gas-purchase contracts provided another outlet by enabling Humble to supply its own gas-fuel requirements at Baytown in 1940 and at Ingleside in 1941.[30]

After the middle thirties a virtually new demand swelled Humble's gas recovery, the demand for butane, propane, and other light hydrocarbons which resulted from the growth of gas technology and the increasing use of high-octane gasoline. The utilization of those light hydrocarbons in manufacturing refinery products was an important subject of research by the Research and Technical Service Department at Baytown, and valuable new uses were devised. (See Chapter 21.) At the same time, Buckley and other research men of the Production Department also studied various aspects of the recovery and utilization of light hydrocarbons.

In recognition of the increase in the variety of gas products and in their demand, Humble continued to expand its gas operations. Its gross investment in plants doubled from the end of 1935 to the end of 1941, the net amount of gas processed nearly quadrupled, and liquid-gas products more than tripled. In 1937 and 1938 the Kilgore and London plants were expanded to extract light ends—East Texas crude was especially rich in butane and propane—and an eight-inch pipeline from East Texas was adapted, with a new extension to Conroe, to transport natural gasoline, butane, and propane from those two fields to Baytown. In 1937 additional equipment was installed at the London and Kilgore plants for recovering butane and propane from 700 outside wells in addition to Humble's own wells already connected. A plant was purchased in East Texas, and in 1937 and 1938 plants were constructed at Tomball, Dickinson, Heyser, and Flour Bluff. Humble's gasoline plants produced various proportions of casinghead gasoline, butane, and propane.

Thus Humble made great progress in utilizing the casinghead gas produced with crude oil, but the efficient utilization of the gas from its gas fields continued to pose serious problems for both the company and its industry. Humble executives in the later 1930s were disappointed in their hope that the Fischer-Tropsch process for the synthesis of motor fuel from natural gas might be improved so that the company could utilize that process for increasing the value of its gas reserves. New to the industry but more promising for profitable gas-field operations was cycling, that is, the extraction of condensate (natural gasoline) and other useful gases from the gas produced from gas reservoirs and the return of the residue to the producing formations. In 1937 the Tide Water Associated Oil Company and others planned the first major cycling operation in Texas.[31]

Although Humble's executives recognized the potential importance of cycling, they were aware of the current tendency of the supply of light ends to outrun the demand. Moreover, an oversupply of condensate meant a cutback in crude oil production. Condensate production was by 1940 expanding rapidly, particularly in Southwest and east central Texas; and Humble had reserves in thirty-nine of ninety-six fields in Texas in which condensate was being produced.

In 1941, however, when the greatly increased demand for gasoline promised to make the operation profitable, Humble entered an agreement for unitized operations and the building of a cycling plant in the Katy field. It agreed to manage the construction and operation of the plant and to build pipelines to carry the products to its Baytown refinery.[32] But the Katy plant, which was to become Humble's most important gas operation, was at the end of 1941 still in the planning stage.

SUMMARY OF EXPLORATION AND PRODUCTION

The primary accomplishments of Humble's exploration and producing operations in the 1930s were the strengthening of the company's reserves and the expansion of its producing facilities. Humble's crude oil reserves in those years increased about thirteenfold, a growth that compares strikingly with an estimated increase of about 50 per cent in reserves in the territory in which Humble operated and in the United States. (See Appendix II, Table VIII.) By the time of America's entry into World War II, Humble had also acquired large gas reserves. The number of Humble's oil and gas wells had more than quadrupled in the years 1931–1941; this was a large increase but, because of wider spacing, was proportionately less than the increase in reserves. The gross value of the Production Department's fixed assets (including crude oil storage) had risen from $85,600,000 at the end of 1930 to $318,400,000 at the end of 1941.

The production of oil and gas came to be by far the most important of Humble's operations. The position of leadership which the Production Department attained within the company is illustrated by comparing the investments in the various operating departments. The Production Department's investment constituted 34 per cent of Humble's fixed assets at the end of 1930 and 61 per cent at the end of 1941. Production had, indeed, always represented the company's largest investment, but in the later 1920s the investment in both refineries and pipelines had nearly doubled, whereas production had remained fairly constant and at the end of 1930 it was nearly equaled by the pipeline company's assets. The trend in the relative growth of Humble's production established in the 1930s has been maintained ever since.

TABLE 8

DAILY AVERAGE NET CRUDE OIL AND CONDENSATE PRODUCTION, HUMBLE OIL & REFINING COMPANY, 1931–1941
(In barrels)

Year	Louisiana	New Mexico	Texas: East	Texas: Gulf Coast	Texas: North	Texas: Southwest	Texas: West	Total
1931	49	3,777	32,265	20,193	3,331	11,576	7,557	78,748
1932	144	2,864	30,710	19,863	2,658	9,221	5,364	70,824
1933	208	3,208	48,189	29,464	2,669	7,549	4,555	95,842
1934	700	3,027	45,374	30,695	2,822	8,533	4,445	95,596
1935	3,140	2,853	44,604	32,591	2,241	9,928	5,380	100,737
1936	4,937	3,755	42,502	38,715	1,919	12,856	6,654	111,338
1937	5,357	5,051	49,168	46,587	2,032	20,367	10,097	138,660
1938	6,192	4,066	45,314	42,206	2,293	16,940	10,014	127,025
1939	6,886	3,945	47,412	42,776	2,491	16,386	10,529	130,425
1940	8,258	3,900	46,082	45,066	2,335	17,579	10,862	134,082
1941	10,386	3,775	44,235	58,005	2,572	18,233	12,766	149,972

Source: Records of Humble Oil & Refining Company.

Humble also realized its aim of achieving a more nearly stable oil production. The increase in the volume of crude oil produced was not commensurate with the increase in reserves and producing facilities; oil production in 1941 was less than double what it had been in 1931. (See Appendix II, Table IX.) This slower increase was owing principally to conservation and proration in accordance with market demand. Even when production in East Texas was nearly unregulated, the increase in Humble's total production was fairly steady, except in 1937, which was characterized by a resurgence of drilling in Texas reminiscent of oil-field booms of earlier days. South Louisiana also contributed substantially to

Humble's rate of growth, its daily average production in that region rising from 49 barrels in 1931 to over 10,000 in 1941. The faithful old Gulf Coast division in 1931 lost its leadership to East Texas with its great East Texas field, as it had to Powell for a short time in the 1920s, but in 1941 it regained its primacy.

Humble's gas processing experienced a growth that established it as an important part of the company's producing operations. In 1934 the company processed a net of 6.8 billion cubic feet of gas in all its plants; in 1941 it processed 33 billion. In the same years liquid products derived from the gas processed increased from 427,000 to 1,792,000 barrels.

PER CENT GEOGRAPHIC DISTRIBUTION OF HUMBLE'S NET PRODUCTION

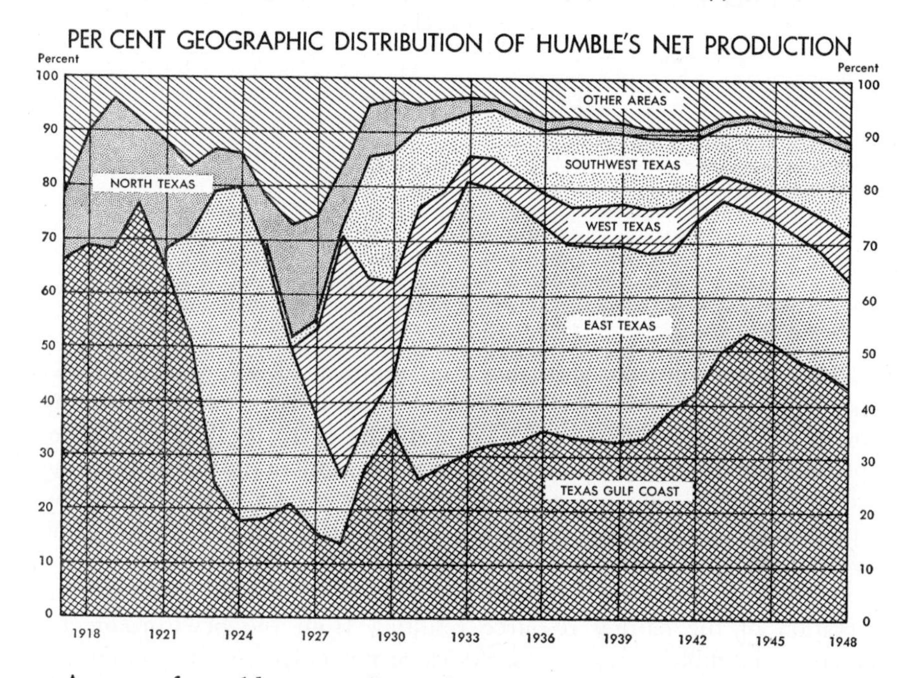

A more favorable cost-price relationship for the producer was also attained than that of the 1920s, when the total cost of producing crude oil was not infrequently higher than the returns. Although the average price Humble obtained for its crude in the 1930s was very much lower than in the preceding decade, the trend after 1931 was upward, as compared with a downward trend after 1920. Taxes and expenditures for social security and employee welfare, of course, increased considerably. Lease and well expenses, however, declined in the early 1930s, though they rose later in the decade. The greater effectiveness of Humble's search for oil reduced exploration expenses; expenditures for dry holes were lower. The more stable and efficient production that resulted from engineered and regulated operations contributed to a decline in costs.

Improvements in drilling, which helped to counter the higher cost of deeper drilling, contributed importantly to this decline. During the 1930s the average depth of Humble wells increased greatly. (See Table 9.) Because the per-foot cost normally increases considerably with depth, Humble's average per-foot cost might have been expected to increase. But so successful was the company in reducing drilling costs that, despite the increase in the depth of its wells, the average cost per foot remained fairly stable.

TABLE 9

AVERAGE DEPTH OF WELLS OF HUMBLE OIL & REFINING COMPANY
1933–1941
(In feet)

	Wells in Proved Areas	*Wildcat Wells*	*Total Wells*
1933	4,138	5,934	4,167
1934	3,964	5,228	4,008
1935	4,322	5,027	4,350
1936	4,325	5,484	4,349
1937	4,799	4,971	4,803
1938	5,017	6,760	5,074
1939	5,422	7,115	5,506
1940	5,437	7,480	5,594
1941	5,439	7,208	5,523

Source: Records of Humble Oil & Refining Company.

Other important savings cannot be represented by figures. Wider spacing of wells obviously resulted in a very large saving; utilizing the oil reservoirs' natural energy to bring the oil to the surface was responsible for another. Important also was the reduction of costs resulting from the stabilization of certain expenditures over a longer period by lengthening the effective producing life of fields and eliminating the cycle of flush production and rapid decline.

Of greatest basic and long-run importance, of course, was the conservation of the natural resource resulting from the new production practices. Humble's greater reserves came not only from the discovery of new fields and producing horizons but also from practices that assured a greater ultimate recovery of the fluids in reservoirs.

Rising prices after the low of 1931, which was about half the lowest average for any earlier year since Humble Oil & Refining Company's organization in 1917, contributed to a substantial increase in the gross income of the Production Department from 1931 through 1941. The average annual posted prices per barrel for Humble's net production, which had been $1.0590 in 1930, were as follows:

Year	Price	Year	Price
1931	$0.5698	1937	$1.1876
1932	0.8298	1938	1.1549
1933	0.5990	1939	1.0273
1934	0.9854	1940	1.0448
1935	0.9819	1941	1.1573
1936	1.0962		

Despite depression, the period 1931 through 1941 was profitable for the Production Department. In 1931 it suffered a loss, but thereafter it always earned a profit, not infrequently a considerable one. In 1934 production for the first time surpassed pipelines as the chief breadwinner of the Humble family, which record was maintained and strengthened in subsequent years. The record of the 1930s was in striking contrast to that of the 1920s, when for four years, despite far higher prices than in the later decade, the Production Department operated in the red and in only two years made a satisfactory profit.

The Production Department in the 1930s, consequently, financed a large portion of its expansion with its own profits. More than 50 per cent of production profits were plowed back to provide nearly half of the gross addition to the department's investment in fixed assets. Production in the 1930s, like the pipelines earlier, thus supplied large funds for financing growth.

On America's entry into World War II Humble was prepared to contribute heavily to the wartime needs for crude oil. It had tremendous reserves, efficient plants and equipment, and a producing organization that in technology, skill, and morale was equal to the best in the American oil industry. The history of Humble's Production Department in the 1930s, indeed, epitomizes a revolution that had taken place throughout the American oil industry and that had strengthened it for the war. That decade was a period of transition between two eras: the old era of rule of thumb, erratic and wasteful; and the era of highly technical, regulated, and efficient operations, in which efficiency manifested itself not only in immediate economies and effective production but also in terms of the ultimate recovery of a valuable and irreplaceable natural resource.

Chapter 20

PURCHASING, TRANSPORTING, AND MARKETING CRUDE OIL IN A PERIOD OF OVERABUNDANCE, 1931–1941

ALTHOUGH HUMBLE in the 1930s greatly strengthened its reserve position and increased its production, it still continued to be a heavy purchaser of crude oil. However, the problem was no longer how to obtain an adequate supply, as it had been during much of the 1920s under the general fear of shortage, but rather how to deal with a superfluity of oil.

The experience of Humble as a purchaser at this time illustrates the pressures upon a large purchaser and supplier and the adjustments that must be made when considerable change occurs in the crude oil market. Many things must always be taken into account in making decisions about crude purchasing, but in the 1930s an unusual combination of unfavorable circumstances had to be considered. In the early years of the decade especially, prices were low and unstable, demand was uncertain and depressed, and an unprecedented flood of oil strained the market. Still, Humble had to utilize its refineries and pipelines nearly to capacity in order to make profits, always had to have oil available to supply its own and its customers' refineries in amounts and qualities required, and at all times, if possible, had to maintain good relations with suppliers. It was within the limits of such circumstances that Humble's executives had to manage their crude oil business in the decade before America's entry into World War II.[1]

ADJUSTMENT TO A CHANGING MARKET, 1931–1934

In the early years of the decade any hopes that Farish and other Humble executives may have entertained of a more stable market were shattered by the continued oversupply of oil, particularly by the large production of the East Texas field. Two other developments simultaneously assailed the American oil industry: the depression and rising oil production outside the United States.

The growth of production abroad was especially threatening to Humble because of the large additions to the lower-cost foreign production of Humble's largest customer, Jersey Standard. In the preceding five years, 1926–1930, Jersey and its affiliates had taken a yearly average of about 66 per cent of Humble's crude oil and 85 per cent of its refinery products, and as a result Humble had not been seeking to develop its own market aggressively. In the later 1920s, however, the holding company's foreign affiliates had acquired so much production in Peru, Colombia, and, especially, Venezuela that in 1931 the group's foreign production exceeded its domestic. In 1932 that production was doubled by Jersey Standard's purchase of the foreign properties of Standard Oil Company (Indiana), which included rich concessions in the Maracaibo Basin in Venezuela with production that was reported to cost considerably less than the domestic oil. With this purchase Jersey Standard also acquired a large, modern refinery on the island of Aruba, off the coast of Venezuela.[2] These acquisitions gave Jersey more oil at a time when prices had fallen and competition for markets was severe everywhere. For economic and political reasons it had to find a market for its foreign oil. To do so without curtailing its purchases from Humble was a problem.

Humble's own loss of the foreign markets which it had supplied through Jersey Standard was in part made up for by temporary gains at home, which helped it to weather the period when home consumption was most severely affected by depression. The tariff act of 1932, which was a precipitating factor in Indiana Standard's sale of the foreign producing and refining properties from which it had been supplying a large part of its domestic requirements, forced the Indiana company to look for crude at home. Indiana Standard, which had become a stockholder of Standard Oil Company (New Jersey) in consequence of the sale of its foreign properties to that company, favored purchasing crude oil from Jersey affiliates until it could acquire adequate domestic production of its own. Humble arranged to dispose of considerable quantities of oil to Indiana's Stanolind Oil Purchasing Company and to turn over to another Indiana affiliate, the Pan American Petroleum & Transport

Company, connections from which Humble itself was purchasing about 9,000 barrels daily in the East Texas field. Humble also provided pipeline transport and storage facilities for these companies.[3] Humble was thus able to compensate in part for the loss sustained from the shift in the supply pattern of Jersey Standard resulting from the latter's large purchase of producing properties in Venezuela.

Almost two years before the Jersey-Indiana trade was consummated, however, Humble had become anxious over its future supply relations with Jersey Standard and Standard Oil Company of New Jersey (the Delaware Company), which had been incorporated in Delaware in 1927 to own and operate Jersey's East Coast refineries and marketing facilities. In the spring of 1930 the Delaware Company had requested that its daily purchases of Ranger crudes from Humble be reduced from 4,000 to 1,000 barrels a day, on the grounds that its European bright-stock business had fallen off and that a higher profit could be derived from running crudes from the Burbank field in Oklahoma. This was a blow to Humble; since 1919 it had treated Jersey, and more recently Delaware, as a dependable customer for the scarce and valuable Ranger crudes. If it acceded to Delaware's request, it would have to look for a new customer, in the meantime storing the crude on a falling market. Humble denied the request, particularly since adequate notice had not been given.

The Delaware Company was also taking progressively less of the Reagan County oil which Humble, principally in order to supply its large customer, had in 1924 contracted to purchase to the amount of 20,000 barrels daily for fifteen years. In 1930 Delaware was buying only 8,000 barrels daily and wished to cut its takings still further, although Humble was then running 9,000 barrels of Reagan oil to its own refineries at what was said to be an annual loss of over $2,000,000. On Humble's insistence, however, Delaware continued to take 8,000 barrels daily. The Reagan contract was not Humble's only long-term purchase commitment; in 1932 about half of its purchases were on a similar basis.

This Reagan contract was about to cause Humble serious trouble in another way. In 1931 the State of Texas—representing The University of Texas as owner of the land from which the oil came—sued the Reagan County Purchasing Company and Humble, alleging that the latter during the period September 1, 1928, to November 30, 1931, had underpaid for Reagan oil by $4,600,000. The state had reportedly realized in royalties under this contract $800,000 more, and the producers $6,300,000 more, than if the oil had been sold in West Texas on the open market. But bad as this contract was proving to be for Humble, the case remained in litigation until 1945, when the Supreme Court of Texas decided it in Humble's favor.[4]

Fortunately for Jersey's Texas affiliate, the Delaware Company continued for a time after 1930 to buy heavily. Because of its own increasing efficiency and aggressiveness in domestic retail and wholesale marketing, Delaware was able to continue to buy from Humble. It took a daily average in 1931–1934 of 119,400 barrels, as compared with an average of 77,400 for the same refineries and markets in the preceding five years; its purchases increased not only absolutely but also relatively to Humble's own production plus its purchases.

In order to hold their business, Humble had made one significant concession to Delaware and other customers—the reduction of marketing charges. Those charges, which before April, 1921, had been 15 cents per barrel on crude sold to Jersey Standard and affiliates and 20 cents to non-Jersey companies, had been reduced from time to time until in June, 1931, Humble was charging 3½ cents to the Delaware Company and 5 cents to others.

On the whole, Humble's crude oil sales held up remarkably well in the years of deep depression. While they did not increase at so rapid a rate as in the later 1920s—except for a notable increase in 1931, which was partly the result of the sale of storage stock at a loss—the average daily sale of crude in the years 1931–1934 was 153,000 barrels as compared with an average in the four preceding years of 121,100.

How far and by what means did Humble succeed in balancing its crude purchases and sales in those years? This question requires consideration of pipeline policies and operations as well as of purchasing.

Humble's degree of success in balancing supply and sales may be illustrated by its inventory at year's end. In the late 1920s, after losing heavily on storage stocks, the company had adopted the policy of attempting to hold crude oil stocks down to the amount believed necessary to meet current demands; that is, not to store in anticipation of a possible drop in production and consequent shortage of supply. Despite this policy, Humble's inventory had risen by more than 4,000,000 barrels in 1930—to more than 19,600,000 at the year's end. In 1931 Humble sold about 5,000,000 barrels of this oil at a heavy loss. By the next year's end, it had brought its inventory down to about 12,000,000 barrels, which was estimated as a proper amount to meet current demand. Through 1934 the company kept its year-end crude inventory at about that figure. (See Appendix II, Table IX.)

Fortunately, in the early 1930s there was some stabilization of production outside the East Texas field, with the result that the pressure on Humble as a purchaser was not so heavy as might otherwise have been the case. The slowing-up of development in new fields resulting from lower prices and a reduced search for new oil by many companies, together with proration under the Texas Railroad Commission, helped to limit production outside the East Texas field and to some extent within that field even in the earlier years of the decade. The East Texas field confronted Humble with its most urgent problems as a purchaser in the early 1930s; the chaotic conditions there and the results to Humble as a purchaser have already been observed.

More serious than the volume of crude offered for purchase were the drop in prices and price instability. The annual average price in Texas per barrel of crude, which had been as high as $1.85 in 1926 and 99 cents in 1930, was 51 cents in 1931, 83 in 1932, 56 in 1933, and 95 in 1934. Even these figures do not express the extreme gyrations at particular times and places, especially in the East Texas field; moreover, the prices were considerably lower than the general level of crude prices in the 1920s. To adjust to lower and rapidly changing prices was a problem for the whole industry in all its operations. As the largest purchaser in Texas, Humble bore the principal onus of transmitting the price decline to the producer, with consequent repercussions on its public relations.

In the years of deep general depression and of chaos in East Texas, Humble used various means in attempting to balance sales and purchases. One method was not to enter a field to buy oil until some regulation of production had been instituted; for example, it refused to purchase in the East Texas field until the Railroad Commission had issued orders for the limitation of production. In many fields, as was earlier observed, no serious problem existed because, on the unanimous recommendation of the individual field's producers, regulation of production was established by the Commission at the beginning of development. As in the 1920s, Humble followed the policy of not buying at less than its posted prices. Contrary to its practice in the earlier decade, however, it now strove to pay only such prices as a realistic appraisal of the current market seemed to warrant; to carry more than a working stock to meet current demand seemed unnecessary, partly because of the company's own expanding reserves and partly because of the probability of a continued plentiful supply. However, instead of refusing to buy the oil of its connected leases in the East Texas field when there was a large surplus, as some purchasers did, Humble qualified as a public storer under a new state regulation and offered, as in the previous decade, to store at a charge the oil which it did not purchase. It entered upon public storage in the belief that state regulation would soon become effective in East Texas and would then eliminate the surplus of oil there.[5] It continued to purchase ratably, that is, to run to pipelines proportionately as much of its connections' oil as of its own.

Both Humble's prices and its storage policy aroused much criticism —one of the intangible costs of depression and oversupply. When the company reduced prices or failed to follow the increases of others, or when storage charges piled up on a falling market, Humble reaped a harvest of ill will from the owners of the oil, the public, and government officials. Although it eventually absorbed some of the accumulated East Texas storage charges, the better course from a public-relations viewpoint might have been to purchase all the oil from the beginning and take the full loss rather than to arouse so much animosity; but other short-term and long-term considerations had to be weighed against any gain in good will. When the stored oil had finally all been disposed of, Humble withdrew as a public storer.

Humble's heaviest purchases, however, were not made in the East Texas field. In that field it bought 4,600,000 barrels in 1931 and a million more in 1932 but thereafter reduced purchases, after 1935 to a relatively insignificant amount. Throughout the decade most of its purchases were made from fields with more stable production, about a third to nearly a half coming from West Texas and New Mexico and large amounts from west central Texas, Southwest Texas, the Panhandle, and even the coastal area.

A number of considerations apparently guided the Humble executives in deciding where to purchase. Of basic importance was the necessity of being able to supply a great variety of crudes, some types in larger amounts than others, in order to fill the refiners' varied requirements. This necessitated purchasing in certain areas—notably West Texas and New Mexico and the Panhandle—where Humble was not customarily a large producer. A further very important consideration was the economic advisability of keeping the pipelines operating as near to capacity as possible. Humble's crude oil purchasing had to be managed with reference to the company's total operations.

Until 1934 the sale of crude and products held up fairly well, but in that year came a considerable decline. Humble had to reduce purchasing because of that reduction and its own expanding production. It consequently disposed of many pipeline connections, particularly in 1934 but also in 1935, by turning over a substantial portion of the purchasing in East Texas to Indiana Standard's Pan American and even selling some of its own production in the East Texas field. In West Texas it gave up to other purchasers connections yielding over 10,000 barrels daily, and it withdrew entirely from purchasing in the Wichita Falls district and disposed of the pipeline serving the area. Humble maintained that the oil produced in that district, being largely of a stripper nature, was of too small volume to move profitably the long distance to the Gulf and that it should be gathered into the nearer Mid-Continent pipelines. As a matter of fact, the damming of the outlets to foreign markets by the increasing production of foreign oil and the growth of demand in the north central states made it economically advisable thus to reverse the flow of oil from northern Texas. But this withdrawal by Humble, however defensible economically, aroused the wrath of North Texas producers, who considered it a violation of the spirit of ratable taking and felt that their support of the conservation movement at a time when most independents were hostile entitled them to especially favorable consideration.[6]

Humble was able to keep purchases within the limits of its current market outlets. Its daily average supply of crude for the years 1931–1934 was within 3,000 barrels of the average for the four preceding years, which indicated that expansion of the supply beyond requirements had been arrested. A larger proportion of Humble's supply was furnished from its own production; purchases fell from a daily average of 188,600 barrels in 1927–1930 to 154,700 in 1931–1934. Nevertheless, Humble still continued to obtain the major part of its oil supply by purchasing.

ADJUSTMENT OF HUMBLE PIPE LINE COMPANY TO NEW PRESSURES, 1931–1941

Nowhere is the mutual dependence of two divisions of an oil company's operations better illustrated than by the relationship at this time between Humble's crude oil purchasing and its pipelines. Purchasing operations depended on pipelines for an economical outlet for oil, and the pipelines depended on purchasing to help supply a sufficient volume of throughput to make their operations profitable.[7]

At the end of 1930 Humble's 4,000 miles of trunk lines reached all the producing regions of Texas and New Mexico and had outlets to two points on the Gulf of Mexico, to northern Louisiana, and to Humble's own refinery at Baytown, as well as connections with a number of refineries of other companies in Texas. No other system in Texas then reached so many oil regions and had so many outlets. The most important of Humble's trunk-line extensions were those tying the Talco and East Texas fields into the original main-line system. In the years 1931–1941 the company's total trunk-line mileage was increased by about a thousand miles and gathering lines by only a few hundred, some mileage in both categories, of course, being abandoned. (See Appendix II, Table XI.)

Humble's large pipeline system was both advantageous and disadvantageous in the early thirties. On the one hand, this system enabled the company to deliver on short notice at various points many types and grades of oil from the extensive region served; this high flexibility in supplying the market was important at a time when purchasing for refining was becoming more selective as to the quality of crudes and when competition in the sale of products was becoming increasingly severe. On the other hand, in a time of depression it was a considerable problem to keep fully occupied a system that had been built to serve an anticipated expansion of production. Pipelines operate at diminishing costs up to a capacity determined largely by their diameter and power; to move both Humble's own production and its purchases at the lowest costs necessitated keeping the lines occupied up to their optimum volume.[8]

Since few producers other than Humble Oil & Refining Company at this time tendered oil to Humble Pipe Line Company for transportation, throughput was determined largely by Humble's own production and purchasing; but, inasmuch as the capacity of the lines was far beyond Humble's own production, purchasing made the difference between profit and loss, and sometimes a large difference. In order to take advantage of the economies of large-scale transportation, therefore, Humble, because of the large additions to its lines in 1927–1930, had to expand its purchasing even in times of depression. And, if all lines could not be fully occupied, to favor the long lines was preferable. When, therefore, Humble's executives in 1934 decided that some of their company's pipeline connections must be given up in order to balance purchases with decreased sales, they were guided by the interests of the pipelines. Their policy was to try to keep their longer lines occupied in preference to the short ones because, everything else being equal, long lines not only bring in more revenue than short lines but also are more profitable mile for mile. Humble, accordingly, gave up some short-haul crudes, selling some of its own Gulf Coast and East Texas oil in the field, and supplied customers with purchased long-haul oil; thus it retained the advantage of added revenue from the long lines, some parts of which had become wholly or partly idle, to West Texas and the Panhandle. It was not by chance that in the 1930s Humble's purchases in West Texas and New Mexico ranged from about a third to nearly half of the total purchases nor that from a fourth to nearly half of the total volume carried by the trunk lines of Humble Pipe Line Company came from the same region.

On the whole, Humble succeeded remarkably well, considering the circumstances, in keeping its pipeline system occupied. The volume handled by the gathering lines decreased from a high of 73,471,000 barrels in 1929 to 44,929,000 in 1934, but thereafter rose more or less every year to 114,354,000 barrels in 1941. The more important trunk-line volume dropped very little in 1930 and 1931 from its 1929 high of 91,869,735, but it thereafter rose to 148,541,000 in 1937 and averaged about 140,000,000 barrels in the next four years.

So far as revenue was concerned, however, this rise in volume was more than canceled out by reductions in charges. To be sure, Humble owned most of the oil it carried at this time, doing relatively little public carrying; but the percentage of its pipelines transport that was for companies other than Humble Oil & Refining Company increased progressively in the later years of the decade, partly as a result of proration, which encouraged production by independent producers. Humble was also in a somewhat special situation as compared with some other large pipeline operators in that it was selling most of the oil carried to other companies—that is, to Jersey Standard's affiliates and increasing amounts to outsiders—and that oil had to bear the cost of pipeline transport. Humble's pipeline income, therefore, was not merely a matter of internal bookkeeping but directly affected total profits.

The pipeline company's return on investment in gross fixed assets, which during its first ten years had ranged from 21 to 29 per cent, had been criticized for some time, particularly by Humble's principal customer and largest stockholder. Humble had seen no reason earlier to relinquish any part of the profits, which could be put to such good use in financing expansion, particularly since the charges were not out of line with the charges of other pipeline companies. But in 1931 the company made the first general pipeline tariff cut in its history as a result of the discovery of the tremendously prolific East Texas field, the consequent dilemma of producers with interests in more remote areas, and pressure from Jersey for lower rates. Independent producers, who usually sold their oil in the field, had not hitherto cared greatly how much pipeline tariffs increased the price of oil to the refiner;[9] but, with greatly reduced prices, pipeline tariffs became of greater competitive importance as among both regions and companies.

Pipeline rates became notably important to West Texas producers when prices fell steeply in 1932. As long as prices were high enough, oil could stand gathering and trunk-line charges to the Gulf that totaled 52½ cents a barrel, as compared with a range of from 15½ cents to 27½ cents on oil from Gulf Coast fields, even though, because of a high sulphur content, the West Texas oil commanded lower prices. The tremendous volume of West Texas production enabled the oil from that distant region to compete at shipside with oil from other regions, despite high pipeline tariffs and posted prices from 26 to 65 cents lower than the average prices in Gulf Coast fields.

The development of the vast East Texas field, with its uncontrolled flood of oil, changed this situation. Six weeks after Humble had established a posted price for East Texas crude, the price was 15 cents. Delivered to tankers, the oil cost a total of 50 cents, which was slightly less than merely the gathering and trunk-line charges on West Texas crude; this was an obviously impossible situation if oil from West Texas was to find a market. Humble, particularly apprehensive for the more remote areas in which it had substantial interests, proposed a reduction in its pipeline tariffs and was able to introduce on June 6, 1931, "a general reduction in rates approximating 20 per cent . . . in order to increase the demand and stimulate the movement from fields more distantly located than the new East Texas field." Humble also cut its posted prices outside East Texas. Even then, the transportation charges applied to West Texas crude for movement from the well to the Gulf exceeded the total shipside cost of the superior oil from East Texas.[10]

Despite this pipeline tariff reduction, Humble Pipe Line Company was handling such a tremendous amount of oil from West and East Texas—more than in any previous year except 1929—that in 1931 its returns on gross investment after taxes amounted to approximately 25 per cent. Such profits, for a year when the average price of Texas crude had sunk lower than ever before in Humble's history, brought agitation in Texas for pipeline divorcement—that is, the complete separation of the pipeline companies from the producing and refining companies, which, under The Texas Company Act of 1917, were entitled to own 100 per cent of pipeline-company stock. Farish was apparently not seriously disturbed; he even expressed the belief that in some respects divorcement might be a good thing.[11] Humble nevertheless took action in 1932 to reduce pipeline profits by transferring to the Crude Oil Department the gathering of Humble's own production in a number of fields, thus taking from the pipeline company an annual income of 7½ cents a barrel on approximately 30,000,000 barrels. The gathering operations in those fields, except Anahuac, were returned to the pipeline company in 1940, and the Anahuac operation in 1942.[12]

Although the price of East Texas crude recovered somewhat in 1932 as a result of martial law in the East Texas field and various attempts at proration, it was still so subject to downward fluctuations that the Texas Railroad Commission and legislature were under constant pressure from independent producers with interests in regions remote from the coast to reduce pipeline rates, particularly for long hauls, so that they would be able to sell in competition with the oil from East Texas wells. By 1934 attacks on pipelines had developed into a national movement; the independent producers were joined by independent refiners and marketers, who complained that they could not compete with the major companies, which, supported by pipeline profits, could manufacture and sell gasoline at a loss.[13] The divorcement issue figured in the Congressional investigation of the oil industry in 1934, but no action resulted. However, pressure from the Railroad Commission and the Interstate Commerce Commission, orders of the Railroad Commission, and increasing competition with other pipeline companies, particularly those of Texas, Atlantic, and Shell, forced Humble during the decade after 1931 to make several general tariff reductions and also to cut rates on specific lines. Several cuts reduced gathering charges from a range of 20 to 7½ cents to a range of 10 to 5 cents; and trunk-line charges ranging from 50 to 15 cents were reduced to a range of 22½ to 5 cents. These reductions brought a severe decline in pipeline earnings.[14]

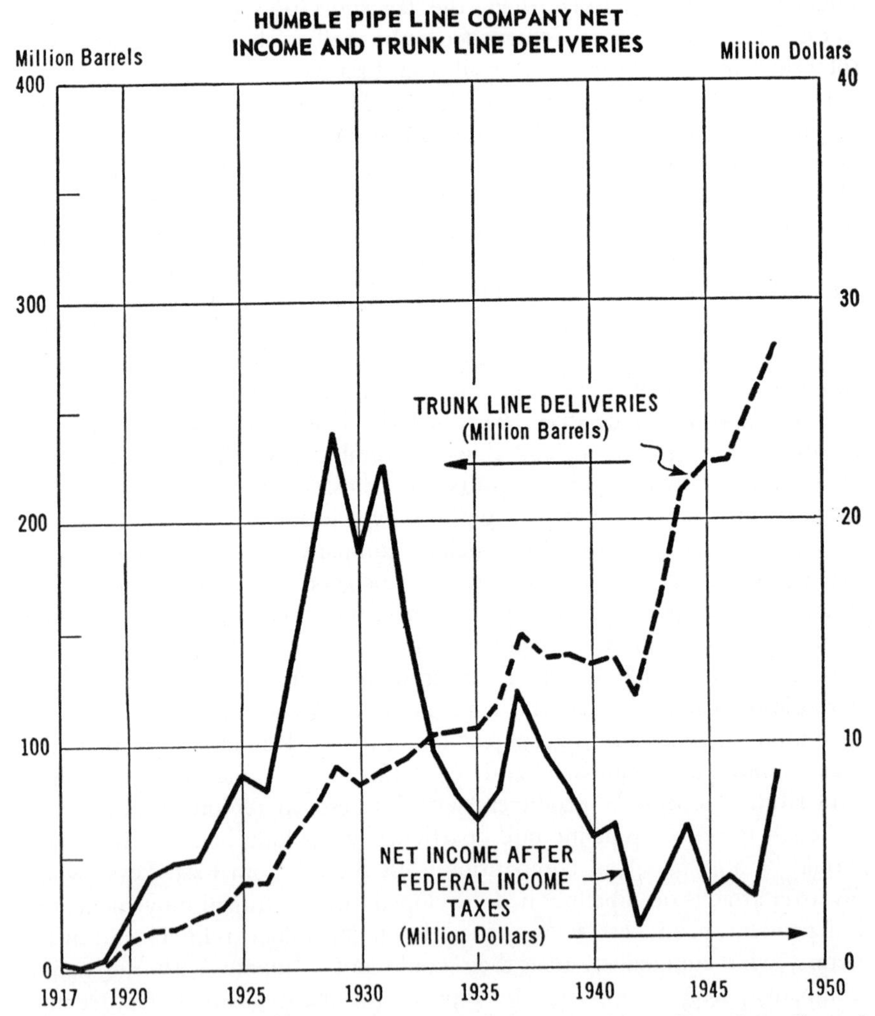

Tariff reductions were not the only factor that adversely affected pipeline profits. The independent producers also objected to deductions for "wastage." By long-standing practice, pipelines charged producers 2 per cent for loss supposedly incurred in gathering the oil; of each 100 barrels the pipeline company took at a lease, the producer was paid for only 98. The pipeline company also charged the owner of the oil—the company to which it was being shipped—a 1 per cent allowance for evaporation, leakage, and other losses, between the "rail head"—the beginning of the trunk line—and the point of delivery; that is, out of every 100 barrels the pipeline company ran to the trunk line, it was required to deliver only 99 barrels. These allowances had probably been reasonable to begin with, since a good deal of oil was lost in the lines; but, as the pipelines and tanks were improved and less and less was lost, the deduction percentage remained the same.

In the early 1930s the producers became particularly anxious, because of conservation and drastic limitations on production, to get paid for every drop of oil that they believed they were entitled to. They also objected to paying a gross production tax on oil for which they did not receive payment, particularly when in 1933 the price of crude was low and the tax became a flat per-barrel charge instead of a percentage. The Railroad Commission finally ordered the pipeline companies to show cause why the deduction should not be reduced or eliminated altogether. The records of the pipeline companies could not justify such an allowance; Humble usually derived annual profits of between one and two million dollars from the sale of "surplus" oil. On December 1, 1933, the gathering allowance was consequently reduced to 1 per cent; on October 1, 1937, after a struggle in the courts, it was abolished entirely. The trunk-line deduction of 1 per cent remained. Humble's actual loss in both gathering and trunk-line systems on oil handled during 1940 was estimated at somewhat less than 1 per cent.[15] Justified though it was, the abolition of the gathering deductions obviously still further reduced pipeline profits.

Losses in revenue were in part canceled out by reductions in costs. These came largely from research that helped to cut losses from corrosion, from better engineering and cost control, and from generally increased efficiency. Conservation and proration and improved techniques for oil finding also reduced costs by helping to stabilize the pipeline system; before these became effective, laying pipes to new fields, where production was uncertain and which might prove to have only a short period of flush production, had resulted in much waste. Less building and tearing-up of lines and slower development of fields also made it possible to stabilize the pipeline organization and to run the systems more efficiently.

Corrosion was an important factor in pipeline costs, and considerable progress was made in the 1930s in understanding its causes and in devising ways of attacking them.[16] Humble's own research group continued its corrosion studies. An industry study centering in the Bureau of Standards in Washington made great progress, as is indicated by reports published in the *Proceedings* of the Production Division of the American Petroleum Institute for 1931, 1932, and 1934. One of the important conclusions from this co-operative research was that the principal forces tending to destroy pipe coatings are physical—such as soil stress—and not chemical. From this research came better knowledge of preventive measures, particularly of what constituted an effective coating for protection against moisture and other destructive elements in the soil and for shielding the pipe from soil stress. Asbestos felt, together with a bituminous material in a molten state, was found to be a good wrapping in that it distributed soil pressures and was long-lasting. Better methods were also devised for cleaning and preparing pipe for the application of protective materials. Standardization of materials made it possible for manufacturers to design machines for performing these various processes. These materials, which lengthened the life of pipes, and the mechanization of their application helped materially to reduce costs.

The major new development in corrosion control in the 1930s was the use of cathodic protection against electrolytic action in soil and water. This method had originated with gas utility companies whose gas pipes were injured by electricity escaping from trolleys or other electric lines. By 1935 the value of cathodic protection for pipes and tanks was well recognized in the oil industry.

Internal corrosion was a different problem. For pipeline companies it was more serious on gathering than on trunk lines; in the former the slower movement allowed the salt water and other destructive elements, such as hydrogen sulphide, to separate from the oil, but in the latter separation was largely prevented by the turbulent motion of the oil. The problem was partly met by better separation equipment in the producing fields, but experiments were begun on using noncorrosive materials for lining pipes. Tanks had a special internal problem in that the vapor from sour crudes condensed on the roofs and induced corrosion.

Humble Pipe Line made considerable progress in the 1930s, adopting new preventive measures as they were developed. It carried on an extensive pipe-reconditioning program, using the new coatings and wrappings and also the new mechanical equipment. In reconditioning old pipe by welding the screwed joints, it made them stronger and sealed them better than with screwing. After about 1932 it began to use electric-arc welding exclusively, and in 1935 to install cathodic units to reduce electrolytic action. Humble Pipe Line's first generators were wind-driven, but wind power proved to be inadequate and too variable. Other sources of electric current were used as they became available through widespread extension of power lines to rural areas. Public utilities were found the most economical source. In 1941 cathodic protection was installed on the big Webster tank farm south of Houston. In the 1930s an attempt was made to cope with corrosion inside tanks by building nearly flat roofs. The theory was that oil-wetting the under sides of roofs by completely filling the tanks would prevent corrosion. This theory proved incorrect, since condensed moisture and corrosive materials stick more firmly to nearly horizontal surfaces than to slanting or vertical ones and are not effectively removed by the oil. Floating roofs, which reduced the vapor space and thus reduced both corrosion and evaporation, were found to be the best answers where the expense was justified. In 1940 Humble installed its first concrete bottoms in oil-storage tanks; such bottoms proved to be of practically unlimited life as compared with steel bottoms, which in similar service lasted approximately ten years.

All these measures, expensive though most of them initially were, contributed to cost reduction. They were utilized on new construction, especially. Only a beginning was made in applying them to old equipment, since the war reduced construction, reconditioning, and maintenance in general to what was immediately necessary.

Much of the saving from cost reduction in the 1930s, however, was absorbed by increased taxation. The total tax bill of Humble Pipe Line Company from 1931 through 1941 ranged from the decade's low of $504,000 in the former year to the high of $5,320,000 in the latter. An intangible assets tax, levied on actual value as indicated by earning capacity, went into effect in 1934. The largest tax item, however, was the federal corporation-income tax, which ranged from no tax in 1931 and 1932 to $3,335,000 in 1941.

In 1940–1941 the agitation against pipelines, which had smoldered throughout most of the preceding decade and had burst into flames again in recent years, brought a change in the status of pipeline companies and placed a legal limitation on their profits. In 1940 the United States Attorney General filed suit against nearly 400 oil companies throughout the country including Humble, alleging violation of various federal statutes and asserting in particular that the payment of dividends by pipeline companies to their producing and purchasing owners constituted the granting of rebates in violation of the Elkins Act. Rather than fight the case in the courts, the oil companies agreed in the following year to settle this phase of the suit by a consent decree, which provided that dividends to shipper-owner stockholders in pipeline corporations should be restricted to 7 per cent on the valuation.[17]

This consent decree, however, did not affect the dividends paid by Humble Pipe Line Company to its shipper-owner, Humble Oil & Refining Company.[18] Reduced tariffs, abolition of the deduction for waste in gathering oil, and increased taxes had already reduced the pipeline company's profits, despite greatly increased oil movements, to less than the prescribed minimum. Daily average trunk-line deliveries of 254,400 barrels in 1932 were slightly higher than the previous record of 1929, but the pipeline company's net income after taxes was $23,941,000 in 1929 and $15,739,000 in 1932; in 1937 daily trunk-line deliveries of 407,000 barrels yielded a net income after taxes of $11,713,000; daily deliveries of 380,400 barrels in 1941 yielded $6,518,000 after taxes.

Despite the reduction in income, the pipeline system remained an effective and integral part of Humble Oil & Refining Company's total oil operations. Efficient co-ordination of all the company's functional activities could still continue as long as that "perfect petroleum unit," which was envisaged in 1920 and developed in the following decade, remained intact. Nowhere was the importance of the pipelines greater than in providing flexibility and speed in the movement of oil in the 1930s and, indeed, during World War II.

GREATER INDEPENDENCE FROM JERSEY IN CRUDE OIL OPERATIONS, 1935–1937

The year 1935 brought a reappraisal of Humble's crude oil supply policies. There was still a superfluity of oil relative to demand. Moreover, it appeared that Humble could no longer depend on the affiliates of Jersey Standard to take their accustomed large portion of Humble's increasing oil supply. Humble, consequently, faced the alternatives of becoming a more aggressive marketer or of reducing its crude oil operations.

A further reduction of pipeline connections was considered. But the extent of this reduction was limited both by Humble's policy of ratable purchasing, which since 1932 had been reinforced by state law, and by the economic inadvisability of either turning its pipelines over to rival companies or of permitting them to lie empty and idle. Humble, in the words of an executive, "could not alter receipts of crude without involving serious embarrassment and incurring ill will—subjecting the company to serious criticism and probably adverse or discriminatory action on the part of the State Commission." The situation would become more serious with every new field that Humble discovered or in which it became a large participant. "The territory served by our lines will grow and our receipts will increase more than the mere increase in Humble's own production" was Wiess's judgment. Conservation was prolonging the life of flowing wells and slowing up the natural decline of other wells connected to Humble pipelines. However, the company hesitated to get rid of pipeline connections, even when possible, because those that could most easily be disposed of were usually the most desirable.[19]

Hines H. Baker recommended that, before shrinking the pipelines to achieve a balance between supply and demand, Humble should undertake "a broadly aggressive crude marketing program." The pipeline investment gave the company a ready access to all parts of Texas and southeastern New Mexico and enabled it to deliver on shipboard all grades of crude in almost any quantities. Baker wrote: "If we are to market our own supply to advantage, we must have larger markets. The greater the volume moved through the pipe lines the lower the final cost of moving our own oil. We should be so aggressive at the business of contacting people for the sale of crude that they will always think of us when they need crude."[20] W. R. Trelford, assistant manager of the Crude Oil Department, pointed out that Humble's production would increase as a result of its accumulated reserves, whereas the probable decline in the production of other companies was likely to put them in the position of prospective customers.[21]

By the spring of 1936 Humble executives had definitely decided that, for personal, political, and business reasons, their company should maintain the "splendid position" that resulted from its pipeline connections. Trelford held:[22]

> [Humble should] avoid the unfavorable reaction which would follow withdrawal from areas, or the refusal to purchase crude in areas reached by us. Self-enforced proration, price cuts, and other such remedies on our part to control supply must be avoided if possible. . . . It is probable that in the reasonably near future a more secure balance of supply with demand may be brought about. Whenever this occurs, the crude oil marketer who has available established supplies of crude will be enabled to reap the benefit of his position.

Humble's executives believed that the pipeline position of their company would enable it to gather and transport crudes more cheaply than competitors could do. They did not intend to take advantage of this position by "adopting an aggressive position as a purchaser," but they did intend to continue to purchase ratably and expected to increase their company's purchases each year by perhaps 5,000 barrels daily.[23]

Although during 1935 Humble's own production increased approximately 1,750,000 barrels and its outside purchases 1,500,000, and although sales to Jersey were cut nearly 3,000,000 barrels, Humble succeeded not only in balancing outgoing and incoming crude but also in taking more than 1,000,000 barrels out of storage. This was accomplished principally by increasing sales through processing contracts with the Pan American Refining Corporation, the Hartol Oil Corporation,

Sun, Shell, Tide Water, and others (Chapter 21). These contracts, some of which had been made in 1931 and continued to run through 1939, were particularly important from 1934 to 1937. The company also made contracts for the sale of crude. For several years from 1936 to 1942 it was selling on contract to the Pan American Refining Corporation from 4,000 to 8,000 barrels daily of Anahuac crude, and during 1937 and 1938 it sold 5,000 to 6,000 barrels daily of East Texas and Van crude to Pure Oil. It also sold up to 15,000 of southern Louisiana crude to Standard of Louisiana.

One aspect of Humble's aggressive sales campaign was the attempt to sell crude for export, although opportunities for such sales were narrowly limited. The Italo-Ethiopian situation had enabled Humble in September, 1935, to sell through brokers over 500,000 barrels of Mirando crude for the use of the Italian Navy, but the Neutrality Act of August 31, 1935, was embarrassing to further shipment. Attempts to sell crude for export through Jersey's D. L. Harper were hampered at first by Humble's unfamiliarity with the business; several sales were lost before Humble realized that it must "price the crudes at one cent per barrel under the relative price quoted our friends in the East," as Anderson put it, in order to allow for the broker's commission.[24]

During this period Humble executives felt that their company was not being allowed to furnish its proper proportion of the Jersey affiliates' crude requirements and, moreover, was not being given sufficient notice of changes in Delaware's commitments.[25] Delaware, on its part, had long felt that Humble's pipeline tariffs and other charges were excessive. Humble's aggressive campaign for crude oil markets was a motivating factor in the revision of those charges. In May, 1935, the company reduced the marketing charge to Jersey companies from 3½ to 3 cents a barrel, absorbed the 1 per cent pipeline deduction, and even agreed to sell to Delaware a cargo of Mirando-Refugio crude from storage without a marketing charge. Other purchasers seem also to have been granted unspecified concessions. The Robinson-Patman Act of June 19, 1936, which forbade price discrimination that might impair competition or tend to create a monopoly, ultimately put an end to Humble's commission differential in favor of the Jersey interests.[26]

During 1936 and much of 1937 the crude oil situation continued to improve as a result of the upward trend in business and the general acceptance of the Texas proration program. For nearly two years, according to Humble's *Weekly Digest*, "a very satisfactory situation" prevailed, "when the problem was to find enough crude."[27] During 1937 Humble's refinery runs and sales and its production and crude purchases were all at a peak. A general increase in the price of Texas crudes—the first since late in 1933—took place at the beginning of

1936; an increase in gasoline consumption, which reached a new high during the year, helped to bring about another general price increase early in 1937. The condition of the market is illustrated by the fact that in June, with East Texas crude at $1.35, the East Texas Refining Company was trying through a 7½ cent premium to take connections away from major companies.

OVERSUPPLY AGAIN AND A LESSON IN PUBLIC RELATIONS, 1937–1941

Stimulated by the return of favorable marketing conditions to increase production, the oil industry again began to build up its crude and products stocks to burdensome levels. By the summer of 1937 a recession had set in which, quoting Farish, changed "that very satisfactory situation" of the "past year and a half to two years, when the problem was to find enough crude to meet the demand of the buyer, into the more normal condition where the problem of the supplier is to find a market for his crude." [28] In the spring Humble had intended to build up its crude stocks to 12,000,000 barrels to ensure flexibility; by autumn it was apparent that 3,000,000 barrels instead of the intended 2,000,000 would have to be added to storage.

New discoveries in 1937 and 1938 again brought a flood of crude on the market. Production in Illinois, where a search for oil had been going on for some time but where there was no effective regulation of production, was the most disturbing factor. Discoveries were also made in other states. Particularly important to Humble was The Carter Oil Company's success in developing production in Arkansas and Mississippi. This Mid-Continent affiliate of Jersey's Delaware Company, which developed large production in Illinois, also took over the producing interests of Louisiana Standard. It started a strong campaign to develop new production in Arkansas and in Louisiana and Mississippi north of the Gulf Coast region. Carter's success made it a competitor with Humble as a crude oil supplier of Louisiana Standard's Baton Rouge refinery and Delaware's refineries in New Jersey. Humble's sales to Jersey affiliates held up fairly well, but they did not increase in proportion to the increase in the company's supply of oil.

In the winter of 1938, when sales to Jersey affiliates were falling from the record high of the previous year, Humble decided to inaugurate another campaign for the sale of crude outside the Jersey group. In April it issued a crude oil catalogue describing its principal grades, the territory served by its pipeline system, and its methods of selling, holding out the probability of being "from time to time . . . in position to offer crude for spot sale," and giving a schedule of tariffs and prices.[29]

Together with a downturn of prices again arose the issue of marketing commissions and other charges. Contrary to its unwillingness in 1936 to make any of the reductions requested by Jersey—or even to give Jersey information about its costs, which might put the business on a cost-plus rather than a competitive basis—Humble agreed early in 1938 to reduce its oil-loading charge to Jersey from 2½ to 1½ cents per barrel. According to the director in charge of Humble's Crude Oil Department, competitive conditions were then such that there were "no fair or just grounds" on which Humble could offer any further objections. When Jersey in 1939 requested the elimination of Humble's 3-cent marketing charge, Humble proposed a marketing charge of 1 cent plus a pipeline deduction equal to 1 per cent of the field price of crude. Jersey's Delaware Company, Humble's large crude-oil customer, maintained that a commission on crude oil sales was appropriate only in a sellers' market, not in a situation in which large volumes of crude were moving below posted prices and refineries were operating at a loss. When it was pointed out to Humble that a marketing fee was not charged by the crude oil supplier of the refineries of certain of Delaware's competitors, Humble's president reminded its large purchaser that under the original agreement with Jersey Standard, as well as according to Texas law under which Humble operated, "the business between Jersey and Humble could not be conducted as in the case of parent and wholly owned subsidiaries." Moreover, "as a matter of equity, Humble should not be asked to perform service for the Jersey Company on a basis which would not provide a fair return above actual cost." All these arguments notwithstanding, the economics of the situation finally forced Humble to make a concession; but by reducing the charge, instead of eliminating it altogether, it maintained both a charge and a principle.[30]

The great increase in production in Illinois and new production in Arkansas in the meantime had caused price cuts in adjacent states and a substantial movement of crude at substandard prices. Humble, consequently, inaugurated a general price reduction, which was followed by other major purchasers.[31] Although this price cut inspired the usual attacks on large companies, which were particularly vulnerable because of their leadership in price reductions and their own crude imports, the cut was not criticized so severely as might have been expected, perhaps because it left the average price of Texas crude at over a dollar, a price that was generally regarded as fair.[32]

Large quantities of crude continued, however, to move in Texas below posted prices. Dr. Gonzalez, Humble's newly appointed economist, tended to doubt the advisibility of a further price cut; crude prices were already so low that they were barely returning a profit.[33] On

August 10, 1939, however, Sinclair-Prairie cut its crude prices 20 cents, on the ground that "product prices do not return the cost of raw materials." [34] This was the first important downward adjustment of crude prices since the hectic East Texas days. The next day Humble cut its own crude prices by from 5 to 32 cents.[35]

Although Humble was becoming increasingly conscious of the political aspects of price changes, this price cut could hardly have come at a more unfortunate time for its public relations. It occurred simultaneously with a court decision that was interpreted as a victory for the major companies over the small East Texas producers. This was the decision of the United States District Court at Austin that granted Humble a preliminary injunction against the Texas Railroad Commission's enforcement of a recent proration order. The decision, unless it was reversed by a higher court, meant that Humble would be permitted under the existing order to produce approximately 5,000 additional barrels of East Texas oil per day.[36] For Humble to cut its prices on the very day of this decision seemed to many to be saying, in effect, that it could afford to cut prices because it was going to be allowed to produce more oil in the East Texas fields.[37]

Again Humble was severely attacked. Public animosity was focused on it rather than on companies that for months had been purchasing at less than Humble's posted price. As the largest purchaser in Texas, Humble was always subject to attack when prices fell, but to the decline was now added the coincidence of the price cut with the East Texas decision and the failure of other large producers, because of the furious resentment aroused, to follow Humble's reduction.[38]

Jerry Sadler of the Railroad Commission warned Farish of Jersey Standard that, unless Humble either cut the retail price of gasoline at least 5 cents per gallon or restored the crude price cut, the "Standard Oil Company" would stand convicted of having determined, through its "Texas puppet company," to rule or ruin the oil industry, to drive every independent out of business, to deprive the state of Texas of funds for the care of its blind and aged, to deplete the state's oil reserves for the benefit of "the money barons of Wall Street," or to turn control of the oil business over to the federal government. Farish and Wiess replied that Standard Oil Company (New Jersey) did not control Humble's actions and that Humble had been losing business because of the 500,000 to 600,000 barrels of crude daily moving at below its posted price. David G. Gray of the North Texas Oil & Gas Association, however, claimed that this crude did not represent overproduction but was rather "distress crude" from fields to which the major producing companies refused to furnish a market outlet. On August 14 Commissioner Thompson in a radio address denied that there was overproduction and accused Humble of wanting to fill its storage tanks with cheap oil.[39]

On the same day, the Texas Railroad Commission ordered a fifteen-day shutdown of all Texas fields effective the morning of August 15. The Commission stated that this shutdown was required to enable it to investigate whether or not waste was occurring or imminent, but the immediate objective was presumably to decrease the available supply of crude. Texas was joined by Louisiana, Oklahoma, Arkansas, New Mexico, and Kansas, with the result that two-thirds of the national output was plugged. The Texas attorney general also began a probe to see if Humble was violating antitrust laws.[40]

Humble obviously needed to defend its general price cut, but the way in which it responded to the situation may have been influenced by an earlier suggestion of Wallace E. Pratt to President Wiess. Pratt, then with Jersey Standard, had suggested to Wiess in 1937 that Humble might apply to its long-standing "policy of issuing explanatory statements in connection with crude price adjustments" the advice of Robert T. Haslam, co-ordinator of retail sales of the Delaware Company.[41] Commenting on Delaware's decision to "accompany any announcements of an important adjustment in the price of leading products with a statement of the reasons that have made it necessary," Haslam had remarked that "the person who is . . . responsible for co-ordinating this activity" should "have at all times in mind the public's reaction to price changes rather than making an effort to explain it from the company's viewpoint." Humble's earlier announcements of price cuts and other measures irritating to its crude oil suppliers had probably been written primarily from the very viewpoint that Haslam was criticizing—to express the company's views rather than to convince the public—and, since the company was not in any doubt as to the wisdom and justice of its policy, these explanations had tended to be rather perfunctory and not very persuasive.

On August 17, 1939, Humble took its case to the general public by inserting in the daily papers of the state a paid explanatory statement. This statement showed how much crude oil was moving below the going market price at the time of the recent price cut, emphasized that Humble's prices were in no case lower than Sinclair-Prairie's, and pointed out that Humble was a large producer whose own crude was adversely affected by the price cut. It placed the blame for the below-price movement which had been responsible for the cut on "the flood of oil from Illinois and Louisiana," most of which, it said, was "being produced wastefully, in violation of conservation principles."

This was by far the fullest, clearest, best-expressed, and most convincing public statement that Humble had ever made in such circumstances, and it represented a distinct advance in the company's relations with both its crude oil suppliers and the general public. The publication of the statement several days after the cut, however, had permitted public feeling to get out of control, and Wiess's excellent statement was consequently less effective than it would probably otherwise have been.

Criticism continued to mount. Charles F. Roeser, an independent producer who had been one of Humble's staunchest friends in the conservation struggle but who stood to lose from the price change, now attacked the company bitterly and even resigned from the executive committee of the API in order to demonstrate his feeling that this organization was irrevocably committed to the viewpoint of the majors and was incapable of understanding that of the independents.[42] Other independents and their allies were even more severe in their attacks. One independent circularized newspaper editors with postal cards, suggesting a chain-letter campaign in behalf of the proposition that anyone who bought Humble products was a "traitor to Texas." [43] Another sent Humble a photostated page from his Bible to illustrate his comparison of Humble's crude price cut with Herod's slaughter of the children of Bethlehem. A number of holders of Humble credit cards turned them in. On the other hand, a number of independents wrote in support of Humble because of its assistance with wildcat wells and its readiness to furnish a market outlet.

The shutdown soon had its effect. On August 28 Wiess testified before the Railroad Commission that Humble's working stock of crude was far below its minimum level of 11,000,000 to 12,000,000 barrels.[44] The Railroad Commission then ordered the extension of the shutdown for two more days, Humble promptly rescinded its price cut retroactively, and the Commission immediately terminated the shutdown.[45] Commissioner Thompson then proclaimed that Texas had showed the "Standard Oil Company" that its "fair-haired child" could not trample the rights of Texas producers under its "golden boot heels." [46]

Humble had helped to bring about a decrease in production, but at a serious and perhaps not entirely necessary cost to its public relations. The loss was not without compensation, however, for the episode seems to have shocked the company into a greater realization of the deficiences of its public relations program, particularly when changes in the crude oil situation were involved, and thus to have marked a turning point in that program. Humble began to realize the advisability of anticipating criticism and answering it before it could be uttered, for example, in the case of a crude oil price adjustment explaining to the less well-informed sellers of crude oil and the general public the economic conditions determining the action.[47]

The two-week August shutdown reduced Humble's storage stocks to less than 9,000,000 barrels. Since Delaware sometimes abruptly and unexpectedly called on Humble for deliveries of from 500,000 to 700,000 barrels, Humble then regarded approximately 13,000,000 barrels of storage crude as a reasonable working stock.[48] In view of this 4,000,000-barrel deficiency and an anticipated wartime demand, Humble was forced to scramble frantically for crude; it bought storage oil from the Magnolia, Stanolind, and Sun companies, entered into six-month purchase contracts, and acquired new connections. In at least one case it paid a 5- or 6-cent premium for high-gravity crude. Early in October the company raised its prices for Gulf Coast, Southwest Texas, and Talco crudes. By the end of the year its working stock was up to 12,000,000 barrels.

Humble's executives realized, however, that this shortage had been artificial and temporary. The territory in which the company operated contained more than half the nation's known oil reserves, and Humble's own leaseholds constituted the largest single operating ownership in it. Humble's extensive pipeline system in that productive area meant that, as new fields were brought into production, Humble would be regarded as a potential outlet and its increasing supply of crude would continue to be out of proportion to the needs of its own and its affiliated companies' refineries. The enlargement of crude sales through other outlets was, therefore, imperative.

The anticipated wartime demand did not materialize during 1940. In fact, the invasion of the Low Countries and France and the occupation of Denmark and Norway caused an almost complete loss of Delaware's export market. Humble's principal customer was then drawing a large portion of its domestic crude from Carter Oil's production in Arkansas, Louisiana, and the new oil-producing state, Mississippi. Humble's increased refinery runs and a reduction in outside purchases did not compensate for the decrease in its sales to Jersey affiliates, which fell to their lowest point since 1932.

Although scattered price cuts by other purchasers in various fields suggested to Humble a downward adjustment in the prices of certain crudes, Suman successfully argued against such a step on the ground of public relations, which Humble was more and more recognizing as a factor that could not properly be excluded from any consideration of crude price changes. As a consequence Humble's crude price schedule did not change throughout 1940.

Relief, however, soon came to the crude market. During 1941 the preparation of the United States for participation in the world-wide conflict caused Humble's crude operations to attain a new peak in all respects, in production, purchases, refinery runs, and total sales. In March Humble recognized the increasing demand for crude by inaugurating a general price increase, which was promptly met by the majority of crude oil purchasers. Price adjustments during 1941 brought the average price of Texas crude for the year to $1.12 per barrel. The long period of overabundance of oil with its consequent problems for the crude oil purchaser was over.

Confronted by the threat of a contraction in the amount of crude that it could sell, Humble might have attempted to reduce its purchases. For a time it did so, particularly by dropping stripper, short-haul, and other unprofitable connections; but it coupled this contraction with an aggressive and successful campaign for outside markets for its crude oil and products.

Humble met two tests of success in its crude oil and pipeline operations in the years 1931–1941, tests of profits and growth. The profits on crude oil purchases and sales and pipeline transportation were good, particularly in view of the depression and an overabundance of oil and lower prices during a large part of the period. The growth in the volume of transactions was considerable: crude oil purchases increased in those years by almost two-thirds and trunk-line deliveries slightly more. Humble was thus able to maintain its position as a large purchaser and transporter of crude oil while also greatly increasing its production.

Many factors contributed to this success. Proration, the market-demand law, and the Connally Hot Oil Act all helped to stabilize oil operations, and hence to eliminate some of the earlier risks and pressures in purchasing and to reduce the costs of operations. The confidence of Humble's executives in the future of the oil industry led them to seek new markets aggressively when Jersey Standard affiliates were taking relatively less of crude and products. Important also were the superb pipeline and refinery facilities that Humble had built in the preceding decade. The former enabled it to supply economically an unusually large variety of crudes to companies that did not have sufficient production to supply their own stills; and the latter, to manufacture products for companies whose marketing facilities exceeded their crude supplies or refining equipment.

Chapter 21

RESPONSE BY THE REFINING AND SALES ORGANIZATIONS TO MOUNTING COMPETITION, 1930–1940

As in the production, transportation, and purchasing of crude oil, Humble's policy-makers and planners in the 1930s had to adjust their company's manufacturing and marketing to a combination of deep-seated problems and rapid changes. In these operations they shared with all business executives the necessity of adjusting to depression and recovery. Like others throughout the oil industry, they had to meet problems resulting from a serious oversupply of manufacturing and marketing facilities, which were particularly intensified in Texas by the development of the East Texas field. They also had to recognize the increasing importance of the quality of products as a factor in competition. And, as in other Jersey affiliates in the United States, they had to adjust to shifts in the Jersey group's products supply pattern that largely eliminated domestic products from foreign markets.

How did Humble's Board of Directors respond to this stream of difficulty and change in planning refining and sales in the 1930s? In exploration and production, as has been seen, their response was to expand vigorously, particularly in the acquisition of reserves and in applying research and engineering to the improvement of operations. In pipeline transportation their principal policy was to make every effort to fill the lines to capacity in order, so far as possible, to maintain earnings despite declining rates and charges. The response in manufacturing and marketing was different than in these other operations.[1]

CHALLENGE AND RESPONSE IN THE MARKETING OF PRODUCTS, 1930–1934

The years from 1930 through 1934 were especially difficult in both branches of Humble's sale of refined products, that is, in refinery marketing and in the operations of the Sales Department in Texas. Table 10 shows that the general trend of the company's total sales was downward through 1934, the lowest point for the decade, as was also the trend of the prices of the most important product, gasoline. Humble's sales, moreover, fell at a greater rate than did the total national demand. The company's sales total inside and outside Texas was in 1934 only a little over half what it had been in 1929, while the national demand fell by about 9 per cent from 1929 to the low point in 1932 and rose in 1934 to only about 1 per cent below the figure for 1929.

TABLE 10

SELECTED STATISTICS ON SALE OF PRODUCTS, HUMBLE OIL & REFINING COMPANY 1929–1940

	Total U. S. Demand for Products (Thousands of barrels)	Annual Sales of Humble			Annual Average Price of Regular Grade Gasoline	
		Total	To Jersey Affiliates	In Texas	Houston Tank Wagon[a]	Gulf Cargo
		(Thousands of barrels)			(Cents per gallon)	
1929	940,083	48,339	40,967	2,042	11.9	8.48
1930	926,450	46,132	39,125	2,219	10.8	7.62
1931	903,206	35,736	31,608	1,740	9.0	4.68
1932	835,482	32,151	29,644	1,323	9.6	5.30
1933	868,488	34,103	30,032	1,433	8.8	4.74
1934	920,164	27,465	19,461	1,561	8.4	5.38
1935	983,686	28,573	24,657	1,671	8.4	5.42
1936	1,092,754	30,411	24,279	1,871	9.1	6.08
1937	1,169,682	42,386	34,570	2,076	9.4	6.27
1938	1,137,123	51,882	45,158	2,304	9.5	5.49
1939	1,231,076	55,856	48,675	2,582	8.7	5.54
1940	1,326,620	60,239	52,128	2,904	7.7	4.84

[a] Houston tank-wagon price is exclusive of tax. The state tax throughout the period was 4 cents per gallon; the federal tax averaged 1.3 in 1932; it was 1 cent in 1933–1939, and 1.3 in 1940.

Sources: Records of Humble Oil & Refining Company except the first and last columns, which are from *Petroleum Facts and Figures*, 1950, pp. lf., and the *NPN Handbook*, respectively.

Because of its heavy dependence on the Jersey group for outlets for its products, Baytown was strongly affected by the reduction in the purchases of the Delaware Company. In 1931 and 1932 Humble was informed again and again that sales to the Jersey affiliate must be reduced because of the decline in the domestic and export gasoline business.[2] But of greater long-term significance were developments in the Jersey group's sources of supply. Colombian crude oil, for example, was being used by Delaware's New Jersey refineries and consequently was displacing Baytown lubricants in Delaware's Atlantic seacoast business, including shipments abroad.[3] Most disturbing to Baytown, however, was the purchase of the great Aruba refinery in the Caribbean. In July, 1932, Jersey notified Humble: "With the acquisition of the Aruba Plant practically all our export markets will be served from refineries outside of the U. S., leaving for the refineries in this country little more than the domestic business." [4] It was the purchase of this refinery that largely accounts for the great reduction in Baytown's sales to Delaware after 1932 and for the great decline in Humble's products sales at a time when demand in the United States was beginning to rise.

Humble reacted to this deteriorating situation in two ways. It protested against what it considered too low volume and prices and employed whatever pressures it could to get both raised, and it undertook negotiations with the Delaware Company for a long-term arrangement to cover Baytown's manufacturing for Jersey markets, as will be considered in a later section. In objecting to the competition of Colombian oils, Humble resorted to its old argument, that its investment in a lubricating plant was solely for the purpose of supplying Jersey's foreign markets. Jersey responded by urging the salespeople abroad to "make every conceivable effort to push the sale of Humble Coastal Lubricating Oils" and not to offer lubes made from Colombian crude unless necessary to meet Russian competition.[5] Humble also protested that Delaware's prices were too low. Its manager of refinery marketing became convinced that Delaware's sales managers were so obsessed with the idea of "holding business regardless of price" that they were selling Humble products "without proper regard for cost." [6] Lube prices, as before, were an especially controversial point. When Wiess in 1932 insisted on a new price basis for heavy distillates, on the ground that the old would not return full costs, Delaware replied that in that case it would make "other arrangements." [7] Delaware, of course, was in the front line of the fight for markets, and it had to adjust to a continuing decline in prices and intense competition. In such a situation costs are not the major consideration.

Humble's Sales Department, which operated in Texas only, in the early 1930s faced the same problems of declining demand and, especially, of rising competition and falling prices that troubled Baytown's largest customer and all large and many small American distributors of oil products. More serious than the decline in consumption, which for a time was moderate, was the country's overexpansion of refining capacity and marketing outlets, which became particularly serious as prices declined. Hundreds of unemployed during the depression invested their scant savings or borrowings in filling stations; and, beginning in 1931, the East Texas boom—with its flood of cheap, "hot," often stolen oil—led to the mushrooming of small refineries and market outlets, particularly within trucking distance from the field. The situation raised major questions of policy for both refining and marketing.

Like other companies, Humble at first met the difficulties in marketing with increased efforts to sell products. It continued to expand its sales facilities, and the directors even decided to allow the Sales Department to adopt some of the prevailing competitive practices which they had not sanctioned in earlier years. The Humble stations issued "courtesy" cards, entitling customers to the so-called commercial discount, so indiscriminately that almost anyone holding a competitor's card could buy at a discount at Humble stations. Recognizing that most retail gasoline business was at the so-called commercial discount of 2 cents a gallon, Humble also established a general 4-cent differential between its tank-wagon price to retail dealers and the retail gasoline price posted in the company's own stations. Most significantly, Humble adopted the lease-and-license system. It entered contracts with over 600 dealers—known as Authorized Dealer Agency (ADA) contracts—whereby the company leased a dealer's station (usually at one cent per gallon of sales) with a guaranteed minimum rental and then subleased the station back to the dealer with the understanding that Humble furnish him products on consignment and that he handle Humble products exclusively.[8]

Despite increased sales, these liberal practices and declining prices brought a loss on sales operations in Texas in 1930. By the early autumn of the year the Board of Directors had to face the fact that the Sales Department was in a bad way. They then adopted a program aimed at increasing sales through existing facilities. Robert Bruce White, a dynamic supersalesman who had been sales manager of the Valvoline Oil Company, was employed as sales manager.[9] Arrangements were made with the Delaware Company to permit Humble to use the Esso brand name for its premium motor fuel and, in order to provide a motor oil of competitive quality, with the Vacuum Oil Company for Humble to sell Mobiloil. (This oil, however, was soon displaced by an improved motor oil, "997," resulting from research at Baytown.[10]) Humble also, like large distributors generally at the time, broadened the range of the so-called specialty products sold; it sold its own products and also Stanco products provided by a Jersey affiliate.[11] The Board of Directors considered following the example of certain other companies by selling tires at service stations; but Humble's attorneys advised that, since, according to the precedent established by cases adjudicated up to that time, tires were not petroleum products, their marketing probably lay outside the company's charter powers. This situation illustrates how, because of the limited powers under its Texas charter, Humble was operating under a handicap compared with rival companies incorporated in states with more favorable corporation statutes.

Sales Manager White initiated an aggressive program of advertising and sales promotion. Outdoor and direct sales media were emphasized. The Reddington agency was engaged to handle poster advertising and McCann-Erickson for newspaper advertising. The *Humble Lubricator*, a departmental monthly established in December, 1930, and committed to the direction of T. W. Moore and G. A. Mabry of the Industrial Relations Department's new training section, was expanded and renamed the *Humble Sales Lubricator*. This sales-promotion organ was distinguished for attention-catching headlines, inspirational stories (frequently from the sales manager's own typewriter), practical sales suggestions, and profuse illustrations. High-pressure sales meetings, attended by nearly 1,500 men, were used to acquaint the sales organization with 997. A similar campaign inaugurated Esso. "Know Your Products" booklets were distributed, a new sales manual was prepared, and in August Humble's first protracted sales-training school was held at Baytown.[12]

This campaign was carried out in the very year when Texas was flooded with oil from small refineries using cheap East Texas oil and when numerous retail outlets sprang up to sell their products. In attempting to meet competition from "bootleg" gasoline, Humble was forced to lower its posted retail gasoline prices and reluctantly followed other major distributors in introducing a third-grade gasoline, bearing the Jersey brand name Acto.[13] Marketing became especially unstable in the territory close to the East Texas field. Indeed, chaos reigned nearly everywhere in the American retail gasoline market; to the normally increased competition from an oversupply was now added the tax evader, the seller of hot-oil products, and the dumper.

To Humble's marketing difficulties in the fall of 1931 was added an attack on the company by the attorney general of Texas. A suit was brought against Humble and sixteen other concerns, most of which were large companies marketing in Texas. The attorney general alleged that the defendants had conspired to monopolize the petroleum business under the National Code Practices for Marketing Refined Petroleum Products promulgated by the Federal Trade Commission. This collusion allegedly enabled the defendants to seize control of retail marketing and thereby to throttle independent retailers. The penalties demanded included the annulment of the charters of companies incorporated in Texas and heavy fines. The suit met considerable disfavor on the part of the general public, but it nevertheless acted as a threat to the companies involved until it was finally settled in the defendants' favor in 1938. (See Chapter 14.)

In spite of some gains from the department's ambitious plans and whirlwind campaigns, the results for the year 1931 were not good. On the positive side were the increasing of gasoline sales by service stations and holding Humble's share of tax-paid gasoline sales in Texas at 7 per cent. But decreased bulk-station sales canceled gains by the service stations, and a decline in direct sales to other companies greatly reduced the department's total gasoline sales. The Sales Department's year-end statement registered a loss, principally because of declining prices and rising unit costs. In the summer of 1931 Director Wiess had reported that Humble's average marketing cost per gallon of gasoline had risen since 1929 to a cost which he described as the highest in the state and nearly twice that of cut-price stations.

Foreseeing the direction in which the Sales Department was moving, the Humble directors in September, 1931, decided to set the department on still another course. They decided to cut losses, even to the point of sacrificing volume and reducing the number of outlets. This was contrary to the policy at the time of such large marketers as Jersey's Delaware Company and Shell.[14] The decision to retrench, rather than to expand with a prospect of losses for a number of years, was no doubt influenced by the Board of Directors' conviction that investment in oil reserves then promised the best long-term returns. Humble had always been primarily a producing company, and at this time the strongest expansionists among its directors were producing men. Sales, on the contrary, had been without forceful representation on the board. Even Director Wiess, who was in charge of refining and sales, was primarily interested in refining, and he firmly believed that every department should strive to make profits at all times.

The Board of Directors' new program was not long left to Sales Manager White to carry out. His strength was in sales promotion and he had built up a high order of service; but, according to Wiess, his plans had been too ambitious and extravagant.[15] They were not suitable for a program of retrenchment. In March, 1932, after several months during which the department had a temporary manager, the appointment of Stuart Giraud was announced.[16] Giraud at first drove with a tight rein; but, after he began to assume heavy responsibility for the Refining Department in 1933, the new Marketing Committee—consisting of the general manager and the men in charge of the department's various divisions—became virtual manager of sales in Texas.

The main strategy in reducing costs was to abandon unprofitable operations. Several of Humble's small refineries were closed; the reduction in their sales and hence in their crude runs, mostly because of competition from new small refineries that could fill the demand for the lower grades of products, had made them uneconomical to operate.

Over a third of the bulk stations were also eliminated, particularly those formerly served by the closed refineries but also some in other areas that had a record of small volume or unprofitable operations or that could be served more economically from other stations. A few new stations were opened, including five to sell lubricants in parts of Texas from which Humble withdrew as a gasoline marketer.

Many unprofitable retail outlets were also disposed of. Some company-operated service stations were eliminated, mostly in territory formerly supplied by the closed refineries or exposed to intense competition from East Texas gasoline. Many of the ADA stations, which averaged sales of only 2,200 gallons of gasoline in December, 1931, were also eliminated. By September, 1933, Humble had disposed of nearly 400 out of 1,100 retail outlets.

A change in the ADA stations was by then already well under way, primarily because of the NIRA Petroleum Code adopted in August, 1933. Since the code provided for the cancellation of contracts that tended to eliminate independent dealers, it raised the question of what to do about this consignment type of station. Giraud, who was convinced of the public relations value of efficiently operated service stations, suggested an imaginative plan, including profit-sharing, for integrating the commission agents and their employees into the company organization.[17] Instead, following the example of other large marketers, Humble leased the stations to new contract dealers to whom it agreed to sell gasoline at a stated amount from 3 to 4 cents below the posted retail price in its own stations.[18] By the end of 1934 Humble had about 700 stations; slightly more than half were company-operated and the remainder were contract-dealer stations.

In its efforts to increase the volume of sales per station, Humble broadened the line of products sold in Texas. In September, 1933, the specialty manufacturing division, which had been started very modestly in 1930, went into full-time operation as a unit of the Sales Department. It manufactured industrial paints, slushing compounds, cutting oils, a household lubricant, lighter fluid, liquid soap, type cleaner, furniture polish, Breaxit, and Rust-Ban. In 1934 the Sales Department added to its stock in trade Jersey's Uniflo Winter Oil, Jersey-bonded marine oils, and Bayou City motor oil (a low-price competitor). It also began to sell motor oils in sealed cans. And it increased its marine lubricating business. Unlike other majors, Humble still did not undertake the sale of TBA products.

While working to reduce unit costs by increasing the volume of business per outlet, efforts were also made to reduce expenses throughout the organization. No comprehensive study of costs was made, but they were reduced wherever feasible. Overhead and general operating costs were pared. The number of employees was cut, although this reduction was reversed late in 1933 after the NIRA Petroleum Code set forty-eight hours as the weekly maximum. In 1931 the Sales Department for reasons of economy abandoned some of the competitive practices it had earlier adopted. It tightened up on credit sales by canceling about 100,000 courtesy cards; the writing-off of nearly $400,000 in uncollectible accounts showed that volume sold on credit was of dubious value. Thereafter, credit (courtesy) cards were issued only to customers approved by the department's credit division. And it established a flat 2-cent spread between tank-wagon and its own posted retail prices.

Humble fully subscribed to the National Code Practices for Marketing Refined Petroleum Products—which, however, became ineffective early in the depression—and to the NIRA Petroleum Code of 1933. It frowned on easy credit and indiscriminate granting of commercial discounts, which the larger distributors had generally abandoned; but it granted discounts to large consumers and large contract customers, as was then generally done by distributors. Like other large companies it tried to promote sales by selling coupon books through employees, inaugurating a touring service, stressing clean restrooms in service stations, and sponsoring broadcasts.[19] Humble's broadcasting of Southwest Conference football games, initiated in 1934, proved so popular that it has been continued ever since. Unlike some companies, however, Humble held advertising to a relatively low figure,[20] although with an increase after 1932. Obviously, its small-volume stations scattered over an immense area did not justify advertising extensive enough to have much effect on volume.

Humble's price policy was on the whole conservative.[21] In gasoline pricing the company generally followed "major competition, up or down, as it may occur," and it tried to keep the differential between the three grades from becoming more than 2 cents. For a time its price competition centered in the third grade, which was intended to compete with the cheap and unbranded gasolines from East Texas. It endeavored to price that grade without covering overhead, but this often resulted in such a large differential between the regular and third grades that the sale of the former suffered. Early in 1933 Giraud took the position that it was not necessary to meet the competition of the cut-rate stations on a price basis, for the bootlegger operating on "hot" East Texas oil, the tax evader, and the dumper would always be able to supply gasoline at a retail price 1 or 2 cents below the major companies' prices. The public, the sales manager believed, would respond to the appeal of quality products, attractive stations, and courteous service. However, if competition with the majors necessitated cutting third-grade prices, then the whole price structure should be reduced in order to maintain the 2-cent differential.[22]

In 1933 Humble refused to meet a reduction in the price of the third grade resulting from a price war but countered the reduction with an advertising campaign. Advertisements emphasized the quality of Humble Motor Fuel and stated that U. S. Motor Gasoline met all government specifications, was tax-paid, and complied with all NIRA regulations. Radio broadcasts and a pamphlet entitled *What Price Gasoline?* proclaimed the impossibility of paying the standard price of a dollar a barrel for East Texas crude and selling gasoline manufactured therefrom at less than 15 cents a gallon. After refusing for several months to reduce the third grade, however, in May, 1934, Humble finally decided to meet competitors' prices.[23]

At the end of 1934 the Sales Department was still far from being profitable and from occupying the position that it aimed to reach in the Texas market. The volume of its sales was less in 1934 than in 1931, although slightly more than in 1933. The department's percentage of total tax-paid gasoline sales in Texas had declined from 7.05 per cent in 1930 and 7 per cent in 1931 to 5.72 in 1934. Although the department's net investment was considerably reduced, operations in 1932 barely covered costs and in 1933 and 1934 resulted in substantial losses.

Might more aggressive policies and practices have made Humble's sales efforts in Texas at this time more effective? Information is not available for comparing the company's experience with that of other concerns marketing exclusively in Texas, in a large part of which developments flowing from the East Texas field created an especially difficult marketing situation. It is pertinent to note, however, that Shell, which on the whole was an aggressive marketer in this period, also had loss operations in Texas; it later reported that, outside a small area adjacent to Houston, its marketing operations in that state "had never been on a profitable footing . . . ."[24]

CONTRACTION AND ECONOMY IN REFINING OPERATIONS, 1930–1934

The early response of Humble's refining operations to the decline in prices and in the volume of products sold was to curtail operations and reduce cost. In so doing the company was paralleling the action of such other large refiners as Jersey's Delaware Company, Indiana Standard, and Shell.[25]

Contraction at Baytown came about in several ways. The completion in

1930 of parts of an extensive program of expansion brought the dismissal of many temporary construction employees. Baytown's first pipe still—so called because the oil was heated while passing through pipes instead of in a tank—which was a part of a program for the greater utilization of sour West Texas crudes and which had been put into operation in April, 1930, was closed down in September. The construction of a hydrogenation plant, started in the fall of 1930, was permanently suspended the next spring, after an expenditure of $3,000,000. This project, designed to increase the percentage of gasoline obtained from a barrel of oil, was abandoned because of the sudden availability in tremendous quantities and at low prices of high-gasoline-content and low-sulphur-content crude from East Texas; the expensive hydrogenation process was believed to be appropriate only to a situation of crude scarcity, in which it was necessary to get the maximum of desirable products out of each barrel of crude. The abortive hydrogenation plant was the last unit of major construction at Baytown until 1935.

The capacity of Baytown was also reduced very considerably during the depression, as was generally true in large refineries at the time. In 1932 the percentage of its rated capacity utilized declined to 68. The next year the rated capacity was reduced from 125,000 barrels daily to 80,000 by the withdrawal from service of cracking and topping equipment.

As has already been noted, contraction also brought the closing of small plants in 1931 and 1932. The topping plants at Breckenridge and Chilton and the refinery at McCamey, which were operating at less than half their rated capacities, were closed. Only the small San Antonio and Neches refineries, besides those at Baytown and Ingleside, were retained. In the interest of economy all but six of the sixteen gasoline plants in the fields were also shut down, and for reasons of efficiency the remaining six were, as of January 1, 1931, returned to the supervision of the Production Department.

Cost reduction became an urgent necessity as prices declined and the margin between what a refinery paid for crude and what it received for its products became narrower. The payroll was reduced by cutting weekly hours and by laying off surplus workers, transferring them to other operations, or putting them on relief work. (See Chapter 15.) Substantial savings were made by careful planning and use of plant and equipment and the more effective cost control brought about by the technical service division of the Technical Service and Development Department.

The technical service work became particularly important to refining in the depression years. The engineers studied both physical and economic aspects of refining plant and operations. They planned alternate ways of accomplishing given results, devised methods of using equipment most economically from the viewpoint of the whole refinery, and were concerned with better planning for the refining of crudes of different qualities in order to use the ones that would yield the largest amount of given products and quality at the lowest cost.

Pressure from declining product prices also in the early 1930s necessitated more attention to billing or transfer prices. By studying economic and engineering aspects of refinery costs, the economic analysis group, under Stewart Coleman's direction, developed the principle of replacement costs for figuring the cost of specific refinery products. According to this principle, the major product of a refinery was motor gasoline, with fuel oil as the most important by-product. Other products, such as kerosene and lubes, were made from fractions that could either be cracked into gasoline or used as fuel oil. Their replacement costs could therefore be determined in terms of the gasoline and fuel oil that might have been made instead of these other products—in other words, an opportunity cost. The principle of replacement costs made possible the more specific determination of what products actually cost and, as a result, more realistic billing from the refinery's viewpoint. It was principally because of his work in directing Humble's application of economic and engineering analysis to problems of cost that Coleman was invited in 1933 to join the Coordination Committee of Standard Oil Company (New Jersey).

The research work of the Baytown Technical Service and Development Department was curtailed during the depression. The hydrogenation laboratory at Baytown was discontinued and experimental cracking was dropped. Early in 1931 Coleman wrote concerning the department's expenses that "most of the estimated reduction of expenditures has been on allowance for research, which means that our effort will be concentrated on plant problems and technical service work." A year later he reported that they were then conducting no research work of a broader nature, that is, investigating general principles or developing new ideas. But they were doing "laboratory experimental work primarily for the purpose of improvement of plant operation" that was "forward-looking" and not concerned with "routine testing or service matters."[26]

Some research already under way was continued, however, particularly on motor oils, in the manufacture of which a great deal of trouble had been encountered. Lubricants made from Texas crudes with the conventional processing methods could not compete in quality with those manufactured from Pennsylvania oils. Humble engineers recognized that Panhandle crude represented a potential source of high-quality lubricants, but it had the undesirable qualities of high asphalt and wax contents.

In addition to other problems in the manufacture of motor oils, therefore, the research group was concerned with the removal of asphalt and wax. The eventual result of the research on lubes was the new motor oil manufactured at Baytown that went on the market in 1931. It was called "997" because laboratory tests indicated that at a temperature of 997 degrees Fahrenheit, only 50 per cent of the oil would be distilled, because it was supposed to be 99.7 per cent carbon-free—and, some claimed, because it was only on the 997th attempt that the difficulties in its manufacture were finally solved.[27]

The Baytown research men were maintained. But their earnings were reduced and the work of many of the men was changed, even lowered to the grade of work previously done by transferred or dismissed non-technical employees. The effect on morale was bad. The slackening of research meant that the department's organization faced a problem when expansion later became imperative.

Even with strong efforts to economize, the total costs of the Refining Department in the period 1930 through 1934 exceeded gross income by millions of dollars. Operating losses were particularly heavy in 1931 and 1932. As a result of a large cut in expenses and a small increase in the products sold, plus the income from processing for other companies, the department made a profit in 1933, but even then the situation was precarious and the outlook far from promising.

The year 1934 brought something of a crisis but also a turn for the better. The total amount of Humble's sale of refined products fell to 27,400,000 barrels (see Appendix II, Table X). The Delaware Company reduced by about a third the volume it purchased; this meant a percentage reduction from 88.1 of Humble's total products sales in 1933 to 70.9 in 1934. The Refining Department earned a nominal profit in 1934 but, excepting losses in 1931 and 1932, the smallest profit since 1923. In 1934, however, the department was put on a more stable basis by a processing contract with an affiliate of Standard Oil Company (Indiana) and a new arrangement for the sale of products to the Delaware Company.

A SALES AGREEMENT AND PROCESSING CONTRACTS

The agreement with Delaware arose out of Humble's long-standing arrangements to provide Jersey Standard and its affiliates with refined products. In 1930 Humble had contributed over 20,000,000 barrels of products to Jersey's foreign trade, which was 55 per cent of the total trade; in 1933 it supplied only 8,000,000 barrels, or 47 per cent of a greatly reduced total. The decline in the sale of gasoline for export was particularly severe—from over 10,000,000 barrels, or 61 per cent of Jersey's exports, to less than 2,000,000 barrels, or 37 per cent. Humble was left to depend largely on the sale of lubes and gas oil for export, which declined less steeply, and on sales to Delaware for its domestic market.

The Humble executives knew that in depression the company could not expect the refining profits of the golden late twenties, but they held that Jersey Standard had some responsibility for helping their company to find other outlets in place of the European markets, which Jersey was supplying with products manufactured at Aruba from Colombian and Venezuelan crudes. Humble had spared no expense in building up its own oil reserves and refining capacity, with Jersey's encouragement; and it had made no strong effort to develop markets, except in Texas, because its refined products were primarily committed to Jersey (from 1927, to Delaware). Its executives consequently held that Jersey Standard should not treat Humble as a marginal supplier; and that, if Jersey was going to purchase products from Humble, and thus place on the latter company the burden of making the necessary investments, Jersey should furnish a dependable market.

Jersey Standard was in a difficult situation. Its top executives were concerned about Humble's situation, but Jersey could obtain refined products at lower cost by processing Latin American crudes at the Aruba refinery than by buying from the affiliate in Texas. To expand sales enough to dispose of all the products of both was made difficult, if not impossible, by the fact that Jersey's marketing affiliates were encountering serious refining and marketing competition both at home and abroad.[28]

Temporary relief came to Humble from the very purchase that had displaced so much of its oil in foreign markets. The tariff act of 1932, which was largely responsible for the sale of Indiana Standard's foreign properties to Jersey,[29] made the seller look for domestic supplies at home. Indiana especially needed gasoline for the American Oil Company, which it had earlier supplied from its foreign properties. The Indiana group accordingly planned that the Pan American Petroleum & Transport Company should acquire domestic producing properties and build a refinery to supply Amoco's needs.[30] Complications within the Indiana Standard group, together with the general overcapacity of the American refining industry, led to the decision that for the time being Pan American would supply Amoco with the help of Humble.[31] It was arranged that Humble should turn over to a new purchasing affiliate of Indiana Standard the oil from wells with which Humble Pipe Line Company's gathering lines were connected in the East Texas field but that Humble Pipe Line would gather the oil and carry it to Mexia. From Mexia the Stanolind Pipe Line Company would carry the crude in its own trunk line to a spur to be built by Pan American to Baytown. Baytown would process for Pan American the East Texas crude and also Conroe oil to a combined total of from 20,000 to 28,000 barrels daily from January, 1934, to December, 1936, and possibly longer, at 22½ cents a barrel, subject to increase if the cost of labor or materials should rise. According to the recently published history of Indiana Standard, the processing charge of 22½ cents a barrel "was lower than the cost in any refinery of Standard of Indiana."[32]

Humble was already processing under contract for various other companies. It had begun with a total of 601,000 barrels in 1931, which was increased to 2,154,000 in 1933; but the Pan American contract swelled the amount of oil processed for other companies far beyond the earlier volume. In the years 1934 through 1939 the Baytown refinery processed under such contracts 65,857,000 barrels of crude; over half of this was for Pan American and the remainder principally for the Sun Oil Company and the Hartol Corporation. Such obviously temporary processing, however, could promise no long-term substitute for sale to Jersey's affiliates.

In the meantime Humble and Jersey executives were discussing the position of Humble as a supplier of the Delaware Company. As early as October, 1931, Wiess had suggested that Baytown and Ingleside be put on a cost-plus arrangement. Jersey considered several other solutions, but its Houston legal counsel saw grave difficulties for them under Texas antitrust law. One suggestion—that Jersey purchase the refineries—seemed to Humble executives "too radical a move"; it is doubtful that Humble's principal minority stockholders seriously considered at the time the proposal that they exchange their company's stock for Jersey's.[33] As late as August, 1934, Director Sadler of Jersey Standard was thinking of a ten-year lease of the refineries, renewable for the same period, with an option to purchase should it ever become politically safe for Jersey to own property and do business in Texas.[34]

The long discussion was finally brought to a conclusion in October, 1934, when a sales contract was signed, which was retroactive to July 1, 1934, and was to run for fifteen years. Under this contract Delaware should purchase from Humble substantial volumes of refined products at prices that would cover costs plus a fair return on Humble's investment. Certain formulas were agreed upon that took into account changes in construction costs, so that in times of inflation the investment on which a return was calculated could exceed the depreciated book cost considerably. The principal issue was the percentage return. Over the ten years since Baytown had become a going concern, the Refining Department had averaged between 5 and 6 per cent on net investment. They agreed on 5.75 per cent.

The Delaware sales contract brought something of a change in

Humble-Jersey relations. Because Humble had been accustomed to selling about 80 per cent of its refined products to Jersey or its Delaware subsidiary, the Refining Department had always had closer relations with Jersey than had any other department; indeed, to ascertain whether the resulting product would find an adequate outlet in the Jersey group, Humble had customarily consulted Jersey or Delaware before installing new equipment at Baytown. The new arrangement unquestionably tightened this connection and strengthened Jersey's influence on Humble's refining.[35] Proposed capital expenditures by Humble's Refining Department were subject to review by Delaware, which could veto the inclusion of the expenditure in the investment on which Humble's return under the contract was based.[36] Humble was as free under this arrangement as earlier to proceed independently of Jersey in expanding refining and in seeking new markets, but as a practical matter there was no advantage in an aggressive marketing campaign outside the area in which it had chosen to operate.

The processing contracts and the Delaware Company agreement were chiefly responsible for a substantial increase in the output of Humble's refineries from 1934 to 1941. Contract processing was most important in 1934–1937, when it constituted about a third of the refinery crude runs. The daily average crude runs to stills at Baytown, including oil processed on contract, rose from 86,300 barrels in 1934 to 134,200 barrels in 1940.

Table 10 shows that Humble's total annual sale of products from 1934 through 1940, contrary to the years 1929 through 1934, increased at a far more rapid rate than the total rise in demand in the United States. The company's sales approximately doubled. The percentage sold to the Delaware Company under the new sales contracts increased from the period's low of 70.9 per cent in 1934 to 86.5 in 1940.

The considerable increase in both the volume and the percentage sold to Delaware was the result not only of recovery from depression. Another important factor was the greatly improved quality of Baytown products, as will be indicated later in this chapter. Important also were the expansion of the sales territory of the Delaware Company and the notable improvement in the effectiveness of the marketing operations of that company and of other Jersey affiliates.

MARKETING PRODUCTS IN TEXAS, 1935–1940

Some significant changes in the later 1930s came in the kinds and quality of products sold by the Sales Department in Texas. An important policy change was Humble's decision to begin in 1935 to sell tires, batteries, and accessories; the Legal Department had decided that, in view of the general practice of marketers, Humble could legitimately enter the TBA business. The Sales Department sold chiefly the Atlas brand. The Atlas Supply Company, which was owned by a group of companies, customarily sold only to its stockholders and at cost.[37] But Humble, wise in its generation and with a three-year-old antitrust suit still hanging over its head, refused to purchase Atlas stock and arranged to buy on a cost-plus basis.[38] Liquefied gas (butane and propane) was added to the products line in 1937 and asphalt in 1939. Of greatest immediate importance, however, was the improvement in the quality of Baytown products, particularly of gasoline.

Despite some recovery in the Texas market for oil products, Humble made no effort to re-establish sales operations in the parts of Texas from which it had withdrawn in the earlier 1930s. Business continued to be unattractive in the more sparsely settled parts of the state and was promising only in a few centers in the southeastern part of the state.[39] At the end of 1940 Humble still had sales operations in only about 60 per cent of the state (containing 80 per cent of the population). To serve this territory—an area larger than all of New England, New York, and the Middle Atlantic states—Humble-operated or dealer retail stations had been increased from about 700 to 1,000 in number.

The Texas chain-store-tax act of 1935 challenged Humble's policy of maintaining a large number of company-operated service stations. This act provided that mercantile establishments, not including "any place of business engaged exclusively in storing, selling, or distributing petroleum products and servicing motor vehicles," should pay annual license fees ranging from $1.00 for one store to $750 per store for each establishment in excess of fifty. Although Humble's lawyers were of the opinion that the sale of tires, batteries,and accessories was included under the servicing of motor vehicles, they were not so sure of this interpretation that they felt it wise for Humble, with nearly 300 company-operated stations, to run the risk of investing in more stations. In 1939 the Texas attorney general ruled that Humble's sale of tires and accessories made the company liable to the tax and, when Humble declined payment, filed suit. In 1941 Humble lost the suit and had to pay nearly a million dollars in full satisfaction for the tax and interest. Two months earlier, however, the law had been amended to allow 25 per cent of proceeds from service-station sales to be from the sale of the controversial tires, batteries, and accessories.[40]

The Social Security Act of 1936 had a stronger effect on the salient feature of Humble's retail distribution plan, which was company operation of a large part of the stations handling Humble products. In order to escape the provisions of the act, most other companies carried out to the limit the program of leasing their stations to contract dealers, which they had inaugurated when the NIRA Petroleum Code went into effect in 1933. Early in 1937, when Humble still had 297 company-operated stations, none of its major competitors had more than five. Humble executives, however, felt that putting the stations on a dealer basis would be more disadvantageous than having to pay Social Security taxes on the earnings of station employees. If Humble abandoned its company-operated stations, it would not only be deprived of the profits from the sale of non-petroleum products but it would also lose effective control over its retail outlets, with a consequent impairment of the opportunity to improve public relations through the good services offered by the stations.

Nevertheless, the necessity of cutting costs finally influenced Humble to reduce the number of its company-operated retail stations.[41] Commission agents operated an increasing percentage of its bulk stations, but the greatest change came in retail stations. At the end of 1934 over half of about 700 stations selling Humble products had been operated by the company; by the end of 1940 Humble had only 228 company-operated stations and 780 contract dealers. Although it had reduced the number of its operated stations, it did not follow the general movement among large distributors to respond to the Social Security Act and widespread chain-store legislation by converting nearly all company-operated to contract-dealer stations.

There was no significant change in Humble's competitive practices. The Sales Department adopted a well-co-ordinated but modest advertising program.[42] When necessary to meet competition, it granted quantity discounts on regular-grade gasoline to large consumers, particularly to road contractors. In 1938 it abandoned a sliding-scale basis for determining tank-wagon prices and put into effect a flat 4-cent margin below posted retail prices in its own commission stations. It continued to emphasize the performance of its premium motor gasoline, which late in 1939 was renamed Esso Extra. For a time it focused on Thriftane its efforts to increase sales volume; this new leaded third-grade gasoline introduced in 1939 was intended by its price appeal to check the downward trend in service-station volume. At first the only leaded third-grade gasoline in Texas, Thriftane brought an increase in service-station sales; but competitors were soon selling a leaded third grade and meeting Humble's price. Humble did not participate in the "giveaway" competition which reappeared in the late 1930s. It continued to stress the quality of its products and the service and clean restrooms of its service stations.[43]

The total products sold by the department in Texas doubled between 1934 and 1940; gasoline sales increased somewhat more than sales as a whole. The major gasoline increase came from bulk-station sales to new dealers and to road-building contractors and from the sale of aviation gasoline, in the manufacture of which Baytown made great strides at the time. In 1938 Humble supplied the United States Air Corps in Texas with about 70 per cent of its requirements. And, in spite of strong competition, it also had the larger part of the commercial aviation business.[44] Moreover, it supplied a considerably larger percentage of the state's consumption of motor oils than of gasoline, and its portion of industrial lubricants sales continued to be high. Humble was at this time becoming especially well equipped to meet quality competition in these products, and it maintained its earlier strong position in the sale of motor oil and other lubricants. It sold Esso Motor Oil purchased from Delaware and during 1937 and 1938 improved the quality of its own oils.[45]

In every year from 1936 through 1940 the Sales Department was profitable. The percentage return on gross investment rose fairly steadily from a relatively heavy loss in 1935 to a substantial profit in 1940. This profit would have been even higher if the Sales Department had been billed by the Refinery Department "at the market" rather than on the basis of the Delaware Sales Agreement. But in 1940 the department sold only 5.74 per cent of the total tax-paid gasoline sold in Texas.

BAYTOWN'S LIGHT HYDROCARBONS PROGRAM AND MOTOR OIL TREATING, 1935–1940

Humble's policy-makers—the Board of Directors, with Wiess having special responsibility for refining until 1938 and Giraud as his successor thereafter—were well aware that strength in competition in the oil-products market was becoming more and more dependent on the up-grading of old products and the manufacture of new ones. Small refineries employing simple equipment and old processes could still serve a large demand that was more interested in price than in quality; "teakettle" refineries had practically captured the market for third-grade gasoline. But, as always, the race in the long run obviously would go to the innovators, that is, to the concerns that could supply the rising demand for higher-quality products at competitive costs. The significant new demand in the late 1930s was for improved lubricants and for fuels for high-compression engines, particularly for airplanes. Another potential source of profit was the manufacture from petroleum hydrocarbons of synthetic products that could compete, costwise, with such old products as alcohol, glycerine, ammonia, and solvents. Whatever the quality or type of product, the competitive race would be won by the refineries that could obtain the greatest value out of a barrel of crude oil.

In the postdepression years of the 1930s advances in refining constituted a technological revolution in that industry. The revolution, indeed, had been well under way in the 1920s, when a number of companies, including Humble and Jersey Standard, carried on research in petroleum chemistry and began to apply chemical engineering to refining. Several groups had then made great strides in such processes as thermal cracking and vacuum distillation. But many of those research efforts were relaxed, although not altogether discontinued, during the depression years. Humble, as observed earlier, maintained its research personnel; but, with the exception principally of work on motor oils, it was concerned mainly with reducing costs in order to adjust to declining prices. The early postdepression years brought a resurgence of emphasis on research and the adoption of new processes and improved equipment; the research chemist and chemical engineer rose to unquestioned leadership within progressive refining operations.[46]

Humble's Refining Technical and Research Department became a vital center of Baytown's operations. Dr. Wilde, Coleman's successor as the department's head, had had a long and varied experience in research in refining and production and in recent years had been in charge of production research. One important organizational change, which came late in 1936, was designed to bring about an even closer integration of engineering and refinery operations than had earlier prevailed. Following the example of the Delaware Company's Baltimore refinery, a process-control group was set up in 1937 within the Baytown operating organization to carry on the more or less routine work in operations that had earlier been performed by the technical service staff.[47] Although this change appeared sound in principle, it did not work well in practice; the men preferred to be a part of the Technical and Research Department, where they had more opportunity to keep informed of new developments. In 1941 they were returned to the technical service division.

The technical service division, headed in the later 1930s by Smith D. Turner, had been maintained fairly well throughout the depression. An increase in its personnel began in 1936, and even with the loss of men to the new operating process-control group the division contained fifty-five technical men in 1940. Technical service was concerned with plant equipment and design and with all economic aspects of current and proposed refinery operations. It was the standards-setting division, as contrasted with the process-control group, which was responsible for seeing that standards were applied. The economic analysis section was especially concerned with cost studies, but the focus of the whole division was on operating efficiency and costs.

In accordance with a program of expansion undertaken in 1935, the research division was enlarged until it included 314 employees in 1940. Sherman S. Shaffer was in charge, with Herbert H. Meier as assistant director. Both men had been associated with Baytown research for approximately a decade. The work of the division was carried on in several specialized sections, which, in addition to the testing laboratories, included the light hydrocarbons laboratory, a crude oil assay laboratory, a plant experimental laboratory, and one for chemical analysis. To raise the octane rating of gasoline and improve lubricants were the central objectives.

In refinery research Humble worked closely with Standard Oil Development Company and the research groups of other Jersey affiliates. Unlike Humble's reservoir research division, which was for many years far in advance of any other such research group among Jersey affiliates, its refinery research division co-operated on an equal basis with the others. Humble's formal relations with them were governed by the Mutualization Contract of 1928 with Standard Oil Development Company and revisions of that contract made in 1938. Under this agreement the research of the participating affiliates was shared on a cost basis and patents were held by Standard Oil Development Company. Humble thus was spared the litigation and other difficulties arising out of patent conflicts, and it benefited from the research of Imperial Oil, Limited, Jersey's Canadian affiliate, and of the research groups of Standard Oil Development and Louisiana Standard. A method of sharing knowledge and research experience, which was becoming of particular importance at this time, was the periodic conference of research men from Jersey affiliates. Humble's refinery research men thus were able to communicate personally with others working on the frontiers of new refinery processes and products.

It is important to recognize that the research and engineering efforts of Humble and of other Jersey affiliates were part of a broad movement within the oil industry to apply chemical research and engineering to the production of new products and the improvement of refining processes and equipment. Many companies, particularly among the majors, by this time had specialized groups doing fundamental and applied research. While the emphasis was on improving the traditional products and their manufacture, particularly lubricants and fuels for high-compression engines, some research was also done on the manufacture of products formerly not made to any important extent from petroleum, such as alcohol, ammonia, and new solvents.[48] Humble's research in the later 1930s was concerned primarily with the improvement of fuels and lubricants. But so broad was the work done by the industry on those products, and so numerous the patent difficulties and cross-licensing agreements entered into by groups of companies at the time, that it is nearly impossible to say what was the contribution of any given company.

While research was increasing in importance at Baytown, chemical engineers rose to the top in the management of refining operations. Three chemical engineers replaced old-school managers in various managerial posts. Dr. E. F. Voss, who already was chief engineer, in 1935 became a member of the manufacturing committee.[49] In the same year Gordon L. Farned, superintendent at Ingleside, was appointed Baytown superintendent, and Harry W. Ferguson, earlier head of technical service, was in 1937 appointed assistant general manager of refining.[50] The three veterans whom these engineers replaced had served well in earlier years, but their retirement left room for men better equipped to manage refinery operations undergoing great technological changes.

The efforts to provide a management equipped to meet new conditions of refining was also carried down to the lower supervisory levels and to the nonsupervisory process and maintenance employees. The better selection and training of foremen, instituted after the depression, had the specific objectives of developing the new understanding necessary for supervising both the progressively more complex process and maintenance work and the practices in employee management designed to strengthen the refinery working force. Workers were required who had skills, judgment, and the capacity for concentration on the job far beyond what had been necessary in earlier operations using smaller and simpler equipment and dealing with less volatile materials. The current upgrading of refinery personnel, through more selective hiring and firing, training, and the improvement of morale, was an important aspect of the technological change taking place in Humble's refining in the 1930s.

Without Baytown's engineering staff and management and its generally high-grade organization, the changes in equipment and processes from 1935 on would obviously have been impossible. Baytown's rated capacity was raised to 140,000 barrels daily in 1940, which according to figures of the United States Bureau of Mines was then the highest rated capacity among refineries in the United States. This, together with the abandonment of old units, meant large investments, year by year, in new equipment—in 1937 nearly $9,000,000. This expansion was not primarily in new cracking equipment, as in the earlier decade, although in 1937 a flash coil was converted to a visbreaker in order to process the heavier residue into lighter products. What particularly distinguished Baytown in this period was the addition of new and advanced equipment for raising the octane rating of gasoline and for improving the quality of motor oils.

The most significant phase of Baytown's development in the years between the depression and World War II was its light-hydrocarbons utilization program.[51] This program had its embryonic beginnings in Humble's gasoline plants, which recovered from the "wet" gases, produced with crude oil, highly volatile gasoline fractions that were used to improve the gravity of refined gasoline. In the early 1930s, also, several combination natural-gasoline and repressuring plants were operated by the Production Department.[52] These plants produced great quantities of propane, butane, and other light hydrocarbons. The hydrocarbons, for which there had been little commercial demand, became tremendously important in the 1930s in improving the quality of gasoline, as did certain waste gases from refinery cracking operations. Their utilization, moreover, meant the conversion of a nearly valueless product into a valuable one. It was, of course, important from the viewpoint of conservation.

The principal quality problem in the 1930s was to manufacture gasolines of low "knocking," or detonation, quality for high-compression engines. In the 1920s the conventional tests for gasolines included gravity, distillation behavior, boiling point, odor, sulphur content, and other qualities. As the compression ratio of engines began to be raised late in the 1920s, however, a new quality of gasoline rose to importance; because the high-compression engines "knocked" more readily, they required gasolines that burned, or exploded, more slowly than the older gasolines. So important did this quality of gasoline become that the setting of standards for rating it became necessary. In 1930 the United States Army Air Corps adopted the octane scale for this purpose.[53] On this scale a particular iso-octane molecule with a low "knocking" quality is rated as 100, and normal heptane, which has a high one, is rated as zero; the scale is determined by the percentage of iso-octane in a liquid made up of a mixture of the two. For example, a gasoline with an octane rating of 70 would have the same "knocking" characteristic as a mixture of 70 per cent iso-octane and 30 per cent heptane.

As detonation became increasingly important because of the use of engines with higher compression ratios, various means were used for retarding the explosion rate of gasolines. One way was to use crude oils in the manufacture of gasoline that contained gasoline fractions which burned, or exploded, more slowly. Another was to add something to retard the burning, the most important additive being tetraethyl lead, which came into use late in the 1920s.

By 1935 Humble was having serious difficulty in meeting the heavy demands of the Delaware Company for high-octane aviation gasoline. It had been manufacturing aviation gasoline since 1927, when it produced a total of about 45,000 barrels. During 1931, after the installation of a special aviation gasoline unit for redistilling naphthas from selected coastal crudes, it produced over 400,000 barrels, and in subsequent years it increased the amount. Its first octane-number aviation gasoline was reported on April 3, 1931, the rating being 72. Humble could not, however, for some time produce straight-run gasoline of higher than about 70 to 74 octane number; and cracked gasoline, since it overheated the engine, could not be used alone as an aviation fuel. In order to meet competition, it was necessary to raise the octane rating to 77, at least, and to increase greatly the production of aviation gasoline. In 1929 Jersey Standard and the Ethyl Corporation had produced iso-octane in small quantity for use in laboratories as the basis for the iso-octane scale, but the first iso-octane (hydrogenated di-isobutylene) produced in commercial quantity was a thousand gallons delivered by the Shell Oil Company to the Army Air Corps in 1934. This was blended with gasoline produced from selected crudes and with tetraethyl lead to raise the blend back to 100 octane.[54]

The problem was attacked by the Baytown research organization, which found a solution temporarily acceptable. The research group knew that gasoline made from crudes from Conroe, Tomball, and Raccoon Bend (deep), for example, were of unusually high octane content, and they reached the conclusion that this was caused by the presence of aromatics in those crudes. Attention was consequently directed to isolating the light aromatics. It was found that at relatively low temperatures (about minus 60° F.) sulphur dioxide is a very selective solvent for aromatics; this discovery led to the development of a process for their segregation. In 1935 a conventional Edeleanu plant at Baytown for extracting aromatics from kerosene was converted into a low-temperature naphtha extraction unit. Low temperature SO_2 extraction yielded a high-quality blending agent, called Avomatics, which raised straight-run gasoline to the desired 77-octane rating. This blending agent was produced in sufficient quantity to meet the Delaware Company's needs at the time, but gasoline of higher octane was soon required.

More important than Avomatics to Humble's high-octane aviation gasoline program and a great stimulus to the use of gases in gasoline production was the industrial application at Baytown of the principle of polymerization, on which many oil companies were working at that time.[55] Polymerization is a process by which the small, simple molecules of fixed or "dry" gases, which are incapable of being liquefied by pressure, are induced to combine into larger molecules and then condensed into liquids. Polymerization can be achieved either by great heat at high pressure or, less expensively but also less effectively, by the use of a catalyst, usually sulphuric acid, at much lower temperatures.

Since polymer gasoline was capable of greatly increasing the octane number of ordinary gasoline with which it was blended, Humble decided to polymerize isobutylene gases resulting from thermal cracking to di-isobutylene (dimer, for short), using a cold sulphuric-acid catalyst; the process had first been experimented with by Standard Oil Development in 1928 and was put into plant operation at Bayway in June, 1935.[56] The Humble dimer plant went into operation in August, and Humble's aviation gasoline production in 1935 rose to nearly 1,500,000 barrels. But a serious limiting factor in the use of this process was the amount of isobutylene available.

Since the cold-acid dimer plant had proved so effective in producing high-octane aviation gasoline, Humble decided to construct a large thermal polymerization plant for the production of motor fuel to utilize the large quantities of propane and butane available from the gasoline plants in the East Texas field. In order to obtain a sufficient supply, the company late in 1935 entered a five-year contract to purchase 3,000 barrels per day of a butane-propane mixture from Hanlon-Buchanan, Inc., which owned gasoline plants connected with 5,100 wells in the East Texas field. It expanded its own plants and rebuilt a crude pipeline to transport a butane-propane mixture from East Texas and Conroe to Baytown. In the next few years it also built new plants in several fields (Chapter 19).[57]

At Baytown in the meantime a stabilization plant consisting of six light-ends fractionating columns, designed to separate the mixture of light hydrocarbons into its individual components, was completed in February, 1937, at a cost of over a million dollars. The thermal polymerization plant itself, constructed under licenses obtained by Standard Oil Development Company from the Phillips Petroleum Company after whose Borger plant it was modeled, was operating satisfactorily by November of 1937. This plant, constructed at a cost of $2,700,000, converted propane and butanes, normally gases, to a valuable gasoline fraction by high-temperature (1,025° F.) and high-pressure (1,700 pounds per square inch) thermal cracking.

Immediately after the completion of the thermal polymerization plant, Humble placed an order for the construction of a hot-acid catalytic polymerization plant to replace the cold-acid dimer plant. The dimer plant utilized isobutylenes exclusively, whereas the new codimer plant, or co-polymer plant as it was sometimes called, employed a hot (150° F.) sulphuric-acid catalytic process developed by the Shell Oil Company to unite an isobutylene molecule with a normal butylene molecule, thus increasing the copolymer yield.[58] The codimer plant was completed in February, 1938.

A few months later Humble put into operation its third catalytic polymerization plant, which was also the world's first commercial alkylation plant. Alkylation is a process of passing isobutane (separated from uncracked field gases), together with butylene or with amylene or pentylene (extracted from cracked refinery gases), at low pressure and temperature through a bath of strong sulphuric acid, which acts as a catalyst in promoting a chemical reaction between the two and results in a molecule of each combining to form a heavier molecule of alkylate. Alkylate, being a mixture of high-octane hydrocarbons, was particularly useful as a blending agent to produce 100-octane aviation gasoline.[59]

The theoretical basis for the process of combining isobutane and butylene had been developed by the research department of the Anglo-Iranian Oil Company, but that company had not yet been able to put the theory to practical use. An article describing the process, which appeared in *Petroleum Technology* in June, 1938, caught the attention of Humble's Meier. After a preliminary experiment to verify the results, Dr. Wilde on July 14 recommended bench experiments and the investigation of the patent and royalty situation. Arrangements were made by Jersey Standard with Anglo-Iranian, and fifty-eight days after the first bench-scale experiment at Baytown the first barrel of plant product was manufactured in the old cold-acid dimer plant converted to alkylation.

While a satisfactory plant operation on butylenes was being developed, experimental studies were also made of the use of amylenes as a means of avoiding the feed-stock limitation in relying solely on butylenes. The use of amylenes, if satisfactory, would make possible the recovery of large quantities of isopentane. After pilot unit tests had demonstrated a practicable operation, plant-scale alkylation of amylenes was initiated late in 1939.

The report of the Baytown research division for 1938 referred to its work on alkylation as "unquestionably the most interesting and far-reaching accomplishment" of the year. This process was to be of tremendous importance in increasing the yield for blending purposes of co-polymer from field and refinery gases without expensive hydrogenation.

The manufacture of alkylate by this process soon got under way at various places. Additions to Humble's alkylation plant in 1939, together with other facilities, made Baytown the world's largest manufacturer of aviation gasoline for the war effort. A second major expansion of Baytown's facilities for the production of aviation gasoline, by producing an alkylate from pentylenes, was to be made in 1941. In the meantime alkylation plants were also built at the Anglo-Iranian refinery at Abadan in the Persian Gulf, by Jersey Standard affiliates at Baton Rouge, Palembang in Sumatra, and Aruba in the Caribbean, and by Shell in the United States and abroad.[60]

Aviation gasoline with a 100-octane rating was an indispensable element in the success of the Allies in the war; Geoffrey Lloyd of the United Kingdom's Oil Control Board expressed the belief that "without 100-octane we should not have won the Battle of Britain." [61] Some of the 100-octane gasoline that gave the Spitfires an advantage over the *Luftwaffe* in the air struggle over Britain was provided by the alkylation process, from plants in the United States and the Caribbean.

Through the alertness and ability of its research group and the readiness of management to be guided by their findings and suggestions, Humble had stepped up near the head of the procession in the important development of polymerization, as it had a decade earlier in tube-and-tank cracking and vacuum distillation. This was, however, not only a technological triumph of tremendous importance in the war; it also meant the utilization in vast quantities of gases that had earlier been wasted, and it augmented income from refining and increased the economic value of a barrel of oil and a cubic foot of gas.

Simultaneously with Humble's development or adoption of processes for manufacturing high-octane gasoline from hydrocarbon gases came the company's application of improved processes for treating lubricants. Panhandle crude had early been recognized at Baytown as a potential source of high-quality lubricants, but its high asphalt and wax contents precluded processing by conventional methods. Accordingly, Baytown gave attention to the newer processing techniques of propane deasphalting, acid-treating, and dewaxing, at a time when these techniques were being worked on by several companies but were still mostly in the test-tube stage. So many companies, indeed, were working on these problems that the results led to much confusion as to patent rights. Jersey, because of its affiliates' early work in propane dewaxing and deasphalting and phenol extraction and fractionation and consequent patent rights, had in 1933 entered into an agreement with Indiana Standard, the Union Oil Company, and the M. W. Kellogg Company to cross-license their various processes and thus to avoid litigation over patent rights. Not all the processes, however, had been put into commercial operation.[62]

After nearly a year of experimentation with a pilot plant, Humble contracted with the M. W. Kellogg Company to design and construct a propane plant for the deasphalting, dewaxing, and acid-treating of lube distillates and residua, primarily from waxy Panhandle and Ranger crudes. The plant, which was completed in November, 1937, at a cost of $2,300,000, consisted of three units: in the first, liquid propane was used to dissolve the undesirable naphthenic, asphaltic, and resinous constituents of the feed-stocks which, being heavier than the desirable paraffinic element, then settled out of the solution; in the second, evaporation of a portion of the propane lowered the temperature sufficiently to solidify the wax; and, in the third, treatment with sulphuric acid eliminated most of the remaining impurities.

This method of treating, in comparison with the older method of naphtha centrifuge dewaxing and acid treatment in batch agitators, resulted in higher yields and a better quality of finished oils as well as a material reduction in manufacturing costs. Distillates from crudes of naturally poor lubricating qualities could be effectively treated, smaller quantities of sulphuric acid were required, desirable fractions were less affected chemically by the acid, and the final finishing operation necessitated less expensive clay-contact filtering. The high capacity rates realized at the propane plant made it possible in July, 1939, to shut down the naphtha centrifuge plant previously used for dewaxing. In order to supply lube distillates to the propane plant, an old battery of ten atmospheric shell stills was torn down, and in its place was erected the second Baytown pipe still, which began to charge Panhandle crude in February, 1938. Thus another old refinery unit—one that "was the tops in her day," according to a stillman who had watched over Battery H since "she" was "put on the line" in 1922—gave way to the new.[63]

Although propane lube treatment was somewhat more economical than the orthodox acid treatment and resulted in a lubricant of lower carbon residue and less affected by high or low temperature, it did not materially improve the viscosity index. In April, 1939, however, another lube plant constructed by the M. W. Kellogg Company, at a cost of over a million dollars, went into operation; it used phenol as a solvent and was intended primarily to improve the viscosity index of nonwaxy coastal lube distillates and residuum distillates. This phenol process had been discovered by Jersey's Canadian affiliate, Imperial Oil. The construction of the phenol plant for treating Gulf Coast distillates was followed by the installation of a third pipe still for processing Gulf Coast crudes. This still, which was put into operation in March, 1941, eliminated the necessity of rerunning coastal lube stocks.

With the introduction of phenol treating on a plant scale at Baytown in 1939, an improved line of 997 motor oil was placed on the market. This oil, according to the report of the Baytown research division for 1939, was equal to any motor oil currently sold with respect to varnish and sludge formation and other performance characteristics, but it was not as good as Esso Extra in extremely low temperatures. A year later, however, it was reported that premium motor oil of Esso quality could be made from extracted neutrals from Panhandle, Salt Flat, and mixed Reagan crudes.

Humble's research division was in the later 1930s co-operating with other companies in a search for new processes and products that were

TYPICAL FLOW DIAGRAM OF BAYTOWN REFINERY IN 1939

(Simplified)

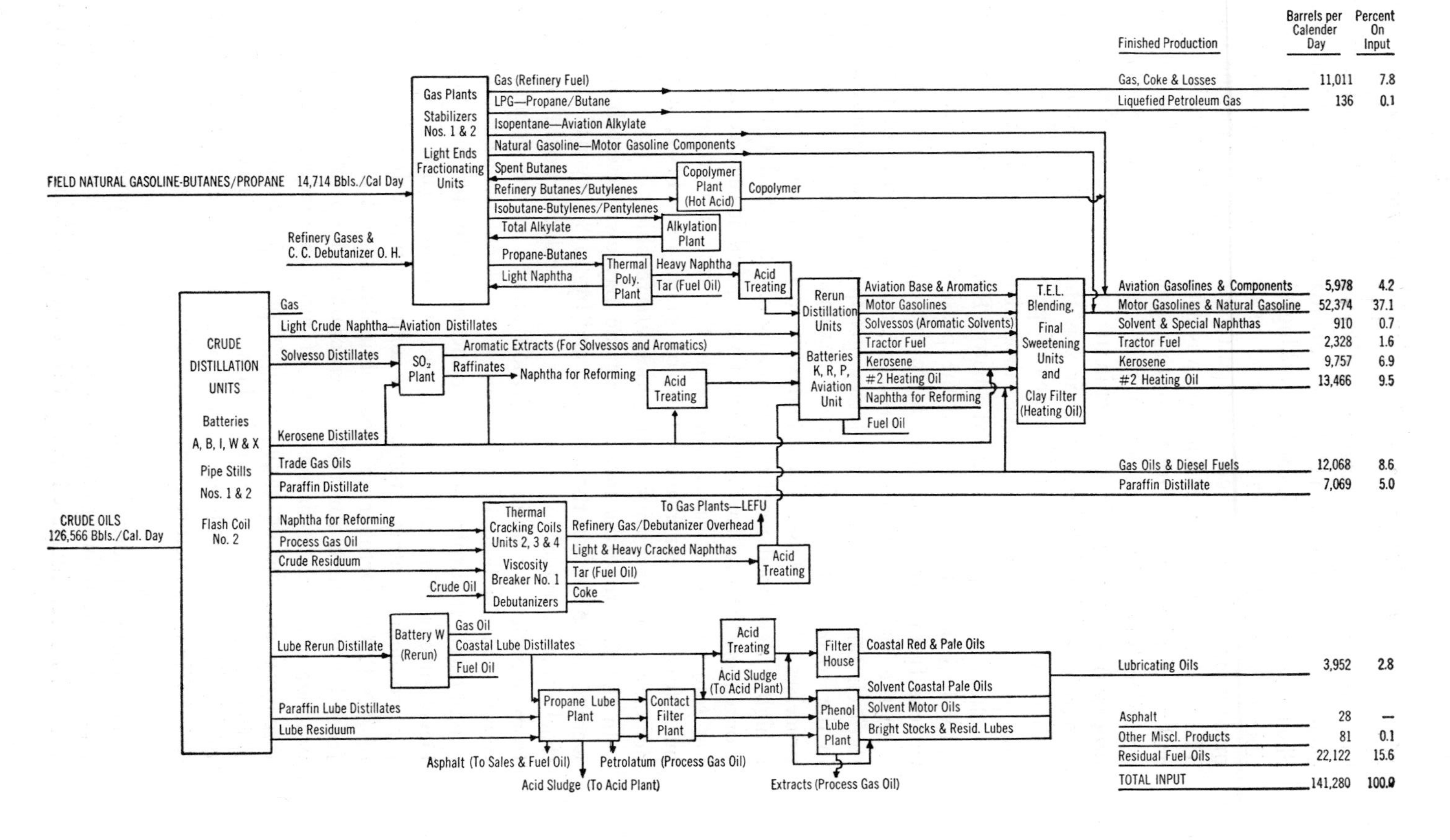

Finished Production	Barrels per Calender Day	Percent On Input
Gas, Coke & Losses	11,011	7.8
Liquefied Petroleum Gas	136	0.1
Aviation Gasolines & Components	5,978	4.2
Motor Gasolines & Natural Gasoline	52,374	37.1
Solvent & Special Naphthas	910	0.7
Tractor Fuel	2,328	1.6
Kerosene	9,757	6.9
#2 Heating Oil	13,466	9.5
Gas Oils & Diesel Fuels	12,068	8.6
Paraffin Distillate	7,069	5.0
Lubricating Oils	3,952	2.8
Asphalt	28	—
Other Miscl. Products	81	0.1
Residual Fuel Oils	22,122	15.6
TOTAL INPUT	141,280	100.0

later to become of importance to the war effort. One of these was catalytic cracking, on which Jersey Standard, Indiana Standard, Texas, Shell, and other companies were working. Another was research on possible processes for making synthetic rubber from petroleum. Humble made its most important contribution to the process for making toluene. The process, as finally developed, was a method of producing a cheap and plentiful source of pure toluol to augment the limited supply of the explosive TNT (trinitrotoluene) that could be made by the known process from toluene, a by-product in the manufacture of coke.

Petroleum chemists knew that it was theoretically possible to obtain natural toluene from certain types of petroleum, but also that it was not practicable to supply any substantial amount in that way. Researchers at Louisiana Standard's Baton Rouge refinery in 1933 apparently had been the first to see the possibility of producing synthetic toluene from petroleum. They made this discovery while experimenting with the hydrogenation of petroleum; this was a part of the extensive research undertaken by the Jersey group following Jersey's purchase in the 1920s of the hydrogenation patents and the right to use other processes of the I. G. Farbenindustrie, a German concern which had a highly developed research organization.[64] Standard Oil Development worked on the problem for several years, and it succeeded in producing toluene synthetically. Although the results were not sufficiently pure for the direct manufacture of grade one TNT, a pilot plant demonstrated that quantity production was feasible.

In the meantime the members of the Baytown research organization were also working on the problem, and by 1938 they had demonstrated that nitration-grade (99+ per cent pure) toluene could be produced from naphthas by utilizing a method known as the double extraction system. On the basis of this discovery, which involved a process too complicated to explain in this connection, Humble and Standard Oil Development eventually worked out a commercially feasible method for producing synthetic toluene of sufficient purity for the manufacture of TNT. On October 12, 1940, Humble signed a contract with the federal government for the construction and operation of a plant to produce about 2,000 barrels daily of nitration-grade toluene. That the discovery and the development of a practicable process of manufacture had come none too soon is shown by the fact that the first tank car of nitration-grade toluene was shipped from the Baytown Ordnance Works six weeks before Pearl Harbor.[65]

Humble had undertaken its chemical research program and efforts to strengthen the refining organization, processes, and equipment in 1935 in order to meet increased competition by providing products of competitive quality at competitive costs. This it succeeded in doing, with the result that both its refining and its sales in Texas made moderate profits. Although the company had not undertaken its light-hydrocarbons utilization program, lube-treating experiments, and other research in preparation for war, nevertheless, on the eve of World War II, the Baytown refinery was remarkably well prepared for the production in large quantities of high-octane aviation gasoline, high-viscosity-index lubricants, and toluene, products that were to prove decisive weapons in the shattering of the Axis powers.

Chapter 22

PRODUCING, PURCHASING, AND TRANSPORTING CRUDE OIL AND GAS FOR WAR, 1941–1945

THE ENTRY of the United States into World War II in December, 1941, at once changed Humble, as it did all American oil companies, from a private enterprise competing in the market to a segment of a vast industry welded into a bond of co-operative effort in defense of national security.[1] Viscount Curzon is often quoted as having said that in World War I the Allies floated to victory on a sea of oil; in World War II petroleum, refined and transformed into aviation gasoline, high explosives, motor oil, Diesel naval fuel, and synthetic rubber, was the very lifeblood of victory.

Humble is an excellent example of what the American oil industry in partnership with the government contributed toward the achievement of victory. The Army-Navy Petroleum Board at the end of the war gave that industry high praise: [2]

> . . . without question . . . one of the great industrial accomplishments in the history of warfare. Because of the resourcefulness, untiring and unceasing efforts, and outstanding accomplishments of the Petroleum Administration for War and the petroleum industry, not a single operation was delayed or impeded because of a lack of petroleum products. . . .

Not a single operation delayed or impeded! Quite apart from the logistical difficulties involved in making that record was the problem of producing the necessary quantities and kinds of oil products. Each B-29 required 10,000 gallons of 100-octane gasoline for a long-range round trip. The Allied forces, not including Russia, used 22,000,000,000 gallons of petroleum products in conquering Germany. The floating base supplying fighting ships for the invasion of Okinawa pumped enough fuel oil into the ships to fill a train of tank cars 238 miles long. About two-thirds of the increased production required for the anti-Axis powers, not including Russia, was provided by the United States alone. This meant an increase in the last year of the war as compared with 1942 of about a million barrels of crude oil and refinery runs per day, approximately a 25 per cent increase in this country.

In the volume of feed-stocks supplied to the stills and cracking coils of its own and other United States refineries in the war years Humble surpassed all other companies, many with notable records, and in the manufacture of oil products it was among the leaders. The company bent its energies to whatever activities would aid the war effort, thus demonstrating that "spirited devotion to the great cause, entailing the sacrifice of company advantage and an uncommon disregard of the normal considerations of 'good business' " which the official history of the United States Petroleum Administration for War described as characteristic of the American oil industry in wartime.[3]

COMPANY MEN AND ORGANIZATION IN WARTIME

When the United States became involved in the war, Humble had reached a new peak of strength. Its oil and gas reserves were very large, the former at the end of 1941 being estimated at over 2,700,000,000 barrels, or nearly 14 per cent of the total national reserves, and the latter at 6.6 trillion cubic feet. Humble Pipe Line Company had over 5,000 miles of trunk lines and about half as many miles of gathering lines connected with 18,500 wells. Humble had refineries at Baytown, San Antonio, and Ingleside, and until May, 1942, a topping plant at Neches. The Baytown refinery was one of the largest and most advanced in the country, and in its equipment for manufacturing high-quality products for war ranked above such large refineries abroad as that of the Anglo-Iranian Oil Company at Abadan in the Persian Gulf and the refinery of an affiliate of Jersey Standard on the island of Aruba in the Caribbean. Humble also had many plants in the fields, with associated systems of gathering lines, for producing liquid hydrocarbons.

As a result of the loss of some men and the promotion of others, the membership of the top administrative and operating management experienced the usual changes in the early 1940s. The promotions to high positions were all made from among men with long service in the company, who had been tempered by the difficult years of the 1930s.

Several changes in the membership of the board came on the very eve of America's entry into the war. The death of Giraud in 1940 had left one vacancy, and the retirement of Blaffer in 1941 was impending when the 1941 election of new directors took place. Two new directors, consequently, were elected early in 1941. David Frame, general production superintendent, was the obvious choice when the increasing importance of production caused the board to add another producing man besides Suman, vice-president for production. Frame was consequently designated as director in charge of production. No general superintendent of production was appointed at that time, but the position was filled in 1945 by the appointment of Carl E. Reistle, Jr. A directorship for industrial relations was new, but David B. Harris' achievement as head of Humble's Industrial Relations Department made his elevation to the board in 1941 a logical step.[4]

The careers of the "two Daves," as they were frequently called, had been closely parallel. Both were native Texans, Harris born in 1888 and Frame two years later; both had left banking to serve in the United States Army; and both had been mustered out with the rank of captain, Harris in the infantry and Frame in the artillery. They had gone to work for Humble in 1919, Harris as a roustabout and clerk in the Production Department and Frame as a scout. Both had speedily risen to the rank of division superintendent in production, from which they had been promoted to head the work of their respective departments.

Simultaneously with the election of Frame and Harris to the Board of Directors, Hines H. Baker, who four years earlier had become a director and recently had succeeded Stuart A. Giraud as director for refining and sales, was elected to a vice-presidency.[5] Because the refining operations had grown so large as to require a manager who was not also a director with other responsibilities, Harry W. Ferguson was made manager of that branch of operations. He had been with Humble since 1924, had worked in research, had been head of technical service at Baytown, and had become assistant manager of refining in 1937.[6]

In August, 1941, R. L. Blaffer reached retirement age. The last of the Humble directors whose actual experience in oil industry operations extended back to early boom days at Spindletop, he was also the first to reach in office the usual compulsory retirement age. He was the last but one of the original directors to leave the company's service. The role Blaffer for nearly a quarter of a century had played in the Humble organization is difficult to assess because of its intangibility.[7] One aspect of his contribution may be indicated by the comment made after his retirement—when Blaffer left, the company "lost its heart." This, of course, was not correct; certain other directors, even the organizing, planning Wiess, were equally interested in the employees and their welfare; but the comment illustrates the affectionate regard for Blaffer among the employees and suggests the role of his personality in building employee morale. Blaffer's definable contribution to Humble's functioning was principally in finance. His death took place slightly over a year after his retirement, and it preceded by only a month that of his old friend and associate, Farish.

Two other directors at the outbreak of war were approaching retirement, James Anderson and E. E. Townes. The former had managed the early construction and operation of Humble's pipeline system, and since 1921 had been a director of Humble Oil & Refining Company with special responsibility for pipelines and the particularly difficult and sensitive operation of crude oil purchasing. Since Blaffer's retirement he had been treasurer of the company. Anderson reached retirement age in April, 1942, and was succeeded as treasurer by Director Harris.[8] Townes, who had served as Humble's general counsel from its organization and as director from 1918, retired in September, 1943. In addition to his broad responsibilities as general counsel, his particular contribution had been to lead Humble through the intricate mazes of antitrust law. He had led the company successfully through two important antitrust cases and within the company had exercised a restraining influence, particularly on the Sales Department, whose volume-conscious salesmen were impatient with such abstractions as legal questions bearing on competitive practices. As a member of the Board of Directors he had had a broad influence in policy matters. In general he was conservative and had an unusual sensitivity to the multiplicity of factors bearing upon a particular problem.

J. A. Neath succeeded Anderson as director for pipelines and crude purchasing.[9] An outstandingly successful field superintendent, Neath had been promoted in the 1920s to the position of general superintendent of pipeline operations, to the pipeline company's board, and to a vice-presidency. As the chief operating executive under Hanrahan as president, he had been in charge of pipeline operations in the company's greatest period of growth.[10] He had proved particularly successful in his relations with men inside and outside the company. Perhaps a key to that success was his willingness to discuss with individuals fully and fairly their problems or grievances, as for example with small producers who felt that the company's price for crude was too low. O. Q. Lomax, Neath's successor as general superintendent who had entered the company's employment in 1918 and had by 1937 risen to the position of assistant general superintendent, was in 1942 elected to the board and a vice-presidency of Humble Pipe Line Company.[11]

Rex G. Baker, because of the quality and range of his work and his broad experience in the Legal Department, was Townes's obvious successor as director and general counsel. Baker had been a member of the Legal Department since 1920. Before coming to Humble he had been principal of the Batson public schools, earned the A.B. and the LL.B. degree at The University of Texas, and served in the Army, from which he had been discharged in 1919. In the 1920s he had been in charge of Humble's title and contract work and all the legal work for exploration and production excepting conservation matters, which had become the special province of Hines H. Baker. In the 1930s he had been given broader responsibilities, particularly in heading Humble's work in conservation law after Hines H. Baker became director.

No further changes were to come in Humble's board and top management until near the end of the war. These directors and managers and others who already occupied high managerial positions—including in operations Trelford as head of crude oil purchasing, Davis as chief geologist, and Reistle as chief petroleum engineer—were to be responsible for Humble's policies, plans, and operations until near the war's end in 1945.

They managed an operating organization made up of able and loyal employees exceptionally well integrated as a working unit. But Humble, like American business generally, had to release a large number of its employees to war service and to civilian work for war. One of the company's greatest wartime problems was to maintain adequate manpower, which was a particularly serious matter in the oil industry because of the skills required in most of its operations. More than 4,000 Humble employees—about 29 per cent of those employed August 31, 1939—entered military service. Nearly 1,300 were engaged as civilians in governmental and industrial activities outside the normal operations of the Humble companies. Besides, many executives and other employees contributed voluntary part-time services with various governmental and industrial groups.

Many of those on leave for nonmilitary purposes participated with men from other companies in civilian war activities requiring special administrative or technical knowledge and skills. Sixteen men left Humble for service with the Petroleum Administration for War, twelve with the Civil Aeronautics Administration, forty-five with other government agencies, forty-three to work on the Southwest Emergency Pipe Line, a group to design and supervise the construction of the Portland-Montreal pipeline, and so on.

A large percentage of Humble's technical and research staffs served on government war-research projects. Humble's exploration executives followed an especially liberal policy in granting leaves for men who felt they could make a greater contribution to the war effort by accepting offers from military laboratories. The executives knew that the Office of Scientific Research and Development was having great difficulty in staffing laboratories doing urgent war work, and they believed that because of Humble's large reserves these men could be spared. Men with a knowledge of electronics being in especially short supply, nearly all the senior members of the geophysics research staff were early granted leaves of absence for such special work, as were also many from the reservoir research and petroleum engineering staffs. These men were assigned to service with numerous scientific groups, including the research groups of the United States Army and Navy, the Radio Research Laboratory at Harvard University, the Applied Physics Laboratory at Johns Hopkins University, the Department of Terrestrial Magnetism of the Carnegie Institution of Washington, the Underwater Sound Laboratory at Columbia University, the Radiation Laboratory at Massachusetts Institute of Technology, and the Naval Ordnance Laboratory at The University of Texas. In these laboratories many Humble men worked on devices for use in antisubmarine and mine warfare and on special ballistic devices. Others did research on the atomic bomb, flame thrower, and proximity fuse. Still others were engaged in reservoir studies under the Petroleum Administration for War for determining the maximum efficient rates of production of individual fields.[12]

In a letter to Humble's L. T. Barrow, Dr. Vannevar Bush, director of the Office of Scientific Research and Development, wrote with reference to the contribution of Humble men to government research projects: [13] ". . . I know of few, if any, organizations which have contributed so liberally of their staffs to the manning of these vital central laboratories whose entire efforts have been devoted to developing the new and improved weapons which have played so important a role in our military operations."

Humble also contributed directly of its own scientific equipment and knowledge. Its geophysics shop and research laboratories did much work. Under contracts with the Navy and subcontracts through several universities, they designed and built radar-test and harbor detection equipment, developed various devices, made specialized measurements, and did other highly classified work. The company also turned over to the government certain special methods that its research staffs had developed for protecting electronic equipment in humid and tropical climates; and it loaned equipment urgently required by various governmental research groups, which its laboratories and shops had developed but which was not obtainable from commercial sources.

The company's executives also assisted in the administration of war agencies, which drew widely on the oil industry for staff and top administrators. As already noted, many employees were on leave for work with the Petroleum Administration for War. Fifteen Humble men—President Wiess, directors, and operating executives—added to their regular duties with Humble by serving on important governmental and industry boards and committees having to do with industrial manpower and, especially, with the petroleum industry. President Wiess was a member of the Petroleum Industry War Council, and he and others served on various national committees under the Petroleum Administration for War (PAW) and other agencies.

Because of its greatly increased wartime work, one administrative staff group, the Law (Legal, until 1943) Department, was particularly affected by the loss of men to the armed forces. This department had to keep itself and all departments of the company informed in regard to the manifold governmental orders, rules, and regulations that affected almost every activity in which the company was engaged. In addition, it handled the many legal problems involved in Humble's building and operating for the government the Baytown Ordnance Works, the Butyl Rubber Plant, and the Butadiene Plant, as well as the legal work associated with Humble's other contractual relations with the government. During the war period Nelson Jones was given responsibility for seeing that the company complied with government orders, rules, and regulations; Carl Illig represented the Refining Department in drafting contracts with the government and ascertaining that all legal requirements under those contracts were met in operations.

Humble's loss of a large portion of its personnel at a time when work was increasing was compensated for in several ways. The total number of employees was increased from about 13,400 at the end of 1941 to 16,000 at the end of the war, including 1,100 working in government plants. This was a small increase in view of the greatly increased amount of work done during the war. The difference was made up largely by increasing the production per well, running refineries to capacity, and keeping pipelines fully occupied. Increased automation also helped to save manpower. Also, the work week was lengthened, and many men worked not only longer hours but harder.

With the necessity for replacing over 5,000 employees on leave for all or part of the war and with its total employment increased by about 2,500, Humble had to meet a stupendous training problem. The addition of such a large new labor force was complicated by the strain of long hours and of working under pressure and by the highly volatile materials that went into the manufacture of war products. Nearly all workers were trained on the job. This need for extensive training added to the responsibilities of an already overburdened supervisory force. Absorbing so large a number of additional workers also brought its own problems of morale, although with local exceptions Humble's employee relations during the war were generally as amicable as in the preceding years. The company's wartime operations unquestionably benefited greatly from the good relations that had been nurtured over the years.

In accordance with Humble's prevailing-wage principle, and to some extent as a result of union pressure, the employees were given wage increases at least commensurate with those generally granted in the oil industry at the time. Humble had given two increases in 1941, one in the autumn.[14] In July, 1942, following the precedent set by the National War Labor Board's decision in the "Little Steel" case that wages might be raised to meet a 15 per cent increase in the cost of living since January, 1941, Humble declared a general increase of 5½ cents an hour for wage workers and $10.00 a month for salaried employees. In May, 1943, because of wartime exigencies the work week had to be increased from forty to forty-eight hours; with time and a half paid for all hours over forty, this meant a 30 per cent increase in the rate of pay.[15]

Humble made special provisions for the welfare of its employees in the war services. An employee who had been in the service of the company for one or more years at the time of enlisting or of being drafted was granted a leave of absence and, on induction, received full pay for two months. Dependents of an employee in military service received an allowance designed to keep his income at not less than half his normal income from the company and, in addition, the company contributed toward the annuity funds of employees on military leave.[16]

The pressure of war work was heavy in all departments and divisions of Humble's operations. It was particularly burdensome for top administrators, managers, lawyers, and technologists, who had to work long days in order to carry the increased loads. Despite its strength at the beginning of the war, Humble was heavily strained to supply the mounting wartime requirements. Not only did volume have to be greatly increased; also, the ever-growing demand for new products and for raising the quality of old ones challenged the ingenuity and energy of technologists and managers and of employees on all levels. The sense of urgency that drove those men and the strain they were under during the war years, in Humble as in much of American industry, cannot be adequately described.

LEADERSHIP IN DOMESTIC PRODUCTION

Humble's petroleum production in the war years was an outstanding achievement.[17] From September 1, 1939, to September 1, 1945, the company produced 525,000,000 barrels of crude oil. The production of 56,000,000 barrels in 1942, its record at that time, was followed by over 86,000,000 in 1943 and 113,000,000 in 1944. Its daily average at the end of the war was well over 300,000 barrels. Humble more than doubled its production between 1941 and 1945 and supplied more than one-fifth of the nation's production increase after 1941. From 1942 it was the largest crude oil producer in the United States. Its percentage of the total United

States production rose from 3.7 per cent in 1939 to 6.7 in 1944. In 1945 Humble produced nearly one out of every twenty barrels of petroleum produced throughout the world. A comparison of the amount and rate of increase of the company's crude oil production with that of selected geographic areas is afforded by Table 11. (For total annual production, see Appendix II, Table IX.)

TABLE 11

CRUDE OIL PRODUCTION BY HUMBLE AND IN SELECTED GEOGRAPHIC AREAS 1939–1945

(Thousands of barrels per day)

			Western Hemisphere						
	Humble[a]	*Texas*	*U. S.*	*Canada*	*Vene-zuela*	*Other Coun-tries*	*Total*	*Eastern Hemi-sphere*	*World*
1939	154	1,325	3,466	21	566	331	4,384	1,332	5,716
1940	157	1,348	3,697	23	507	349	4,576	1,298	5,874
1941	175	1,385	3,842	28	626	336	4,832	1,252	6,084
1942	178	1,324	3,799	28	405	295	4,527	1,208	5,735
1943	274	1,628	4,125	28	487	314	4,954	1,229	6,183
1944	354	2,040	4,585	28	702	340	5,655	1,428	7,083
1945	348	2,068	4,695	23	885	349	5,952	1,157	7,109

[a] Total from Humble-operated properties.

Source: Records of Humble Oil & Refining Company; U.S. Bureau of Mines (U.S. figures); and *World Oil*.

Humble's output of light liquid hydrocarbons, some of which were exceedingly important in the manufacture of 100-octane aviation gasoline, was also greatly increased. The company operated nine plants, six of which it owned entirely. It had partial ownership of three plants operated by others; it owned 50 per cent of the most important one of these three, a plant in the Hawkins field which began operations in 1944. Humble's production of such hydrocarbons increased from nearly 2,000,000 barrels in 1941 to 5,000,000 in 1945; during 1942–1945 it totaled 12,688,000 barrels.

The increase came largely from the Katy cycling plant for extracting liquid hydrocarbons from gas and returning the residue to the producing sands. This plant, which went into operation on January 1, 1943, was built and operated by Humble for a group of companies that unitized their interests in the field. So important was the Katy plant to the war effort, and in general to the utilization of petroleum resources, that it merits special attention.

Cycling—a method of obtaining maximum recovery of liquid products from a gas field while avoiding the flaring and waste of the residue gas for which there was at the time little or no available market—had taken hold in Texas since 1938, but it was not widely employed until the war required light hydrocarbons in tremendously increased quantities. The Katy field had been discovered by a well drilled by Stanolind under a pooling agreement in which Humble was a large participant.[18] Such was the effect of the war demand that, because of its tremendous reserves and its fortunate location only about thirty-five miles from the large refineries in the vicinity of Houston, Katy became the most important gas-condensate field in the nation. In July, 1943, Katy gas reserves, in terms of British Thermal Units, were equivalent to one billion barrels of oil. Based on reserve estimates at that time, this gas reserve was exceeded only by those of the Panhandle fields.

As early as 1940 Humble and other operators had been studying the engineering and economic aspects of building a cycling plant at the Katy field; the demand for light liquid hydrocarbons, particularly for aviation gasoline stocks, helped to crystallize the project, which received a high-priority government rating. By November, 1941, field unitization and plant-operating agreements had been executed; and Humble, the plant operator, had awarded the construction contract for a $3,000,000 cycling plant to process from 250,000,000 to 275,000,000 cubic feet of produced gas daily, extract from it 5,000 to 6,000 barrels of products, and return about 200,000,000 cubic feet of residue gas daily to the reservoir. An important saving from unitized operations was achieved by producing this large field from only fourteen wells, with four more wells for returning the unused residue gas to the producing formation. Humble, one of the ten Katy operators financing the plant and one of the thirteen companies pooling a block of 11,272 acres, owned a 46.5 per cent interest in the plant and 44.7 per cent of the unitized acreage, though the latter was operated by Stanolind until Humble took over field operations in 1944. Additional drilling proved the field to be much larger than originally believed, and in 1944 over 17,500 acres surrounding the original unit were unitized as Katy Gas Field Unit II and the plant was enlarged to handle 500,000,000 cubic feet per day. Humble Pipe Line Company constructed and operated two four-inch pipelines from the field for the transportation of the products to Baytown.[19]

The Katy cycling plant's war production was important and impressive. The plant was designed to extract a maximum of isobutane for making alkylate, which was valuable in the manufacture of aviation gasoline, and also isohexane and isoheptane, which were premium-quality aviation base stocks. But the demand for Katy products was so heavy that the original plan was expanded even before the plant went into operation, and expansion continued until in January, 1945, when the plant reached a wartime peak of 13,000 barrels a day, of which nearly half was 91-octane gasoline. From January, 1943, through August, 1945, about 34 per cent of the plant's 7,500,000-barrel production of liquid products was 91-octane gasoline.[20]

Despite the great growth in the demand for light hydrocarbons, Humble was able to make little use of the increased gas production that accompanied the increase in its production of crude oil. The expansion of its crude oil production to meet war needs had the first claim on its manpower and construction materials and left little of either for the construction or expansion of plants for processing the gas produced with the oil or, indeed, for other conservation or utilization efforts. Although Humble completed a gas conservation project at the Tomball field in 1944, in the following year it was releasing to the atmosphere about 52 per cent of the gas produced with its oil—one of the unavoidable wastes involved in waging the war.[21]

Most of the increase in Humble's oil production came from no such dramatic achievement as the building of the Katy plant. In the early war years, in fact, the increase came with relatively little additional effort, the result of long-time planning and activity in acquiring reserves, developing fields, and selecting and training a superb operating organization that gave full and unbroken support to the company's war effort. The extent of the production employees' loyalty, even before the United States entered the war, is indicated by the Production Employees Federation's nonstrike pledge of support to "free enterprise" and "to the Government of the United States and . . . the Humble Companies," which even went so far as to commend a severe Texas antistrike law.[22]

Although doubling its production in 1942–1944, Humble drilled fewer wells than it had in the immediately preceding years and operated with a considerably reduced production personnel. It averaged only 318 wells in these later years as compared with an average of 640 wells (oil and gas, dry and producing) annually during 1939–1941. The resultant savings in manpower and steel were, of course, important in an industry affected by shortages in both.

Humble was able to double its production while halving its drilling because in the preceding decade it had increased its proved reserves tenfold and had developed and produced those reserves in accordance with the best-known production principles. Maintaining reserves, instead of exhausting them in competitive drilling and production, had been possible largely because of Texas conservation law. At the outbreak of the war the Texas oil industry was producing crude at a rate determined by market demand; since the allowable production of many fields was lower than the amount that could be produced effectively without reducing ultimate recovery, such fields had reserve capacity to meet the increased wartime demand.

With the knowledge gained from extensive reservoir studies, Humble, without difficulty or danger to ultimate recovery, was able to increase its production greatly in many fields. For example, the production from the Friendswood field was raised from a daily average of about 8,000 barrels in 1941 to over 60,000 barrels in March, 1945. Its production in Hawkins was raised from a daily average of approximately 2,000 to over 28,000 barrels, but this field was largely developed during the war. The approximate daily production averages of even such comparatively old fields as Raccoon Bend and Sugarland, both operated entirely by Humble, were increased from 3,600 to over 10,000 and from 1,700 to 7,760, respectively. Humble had drilled and produced those fields with particular care; had they originally been developed and produced competitively and unrestrictedly, with close spacing and open flow after the manner of Spindletop and Powell, they would have been exhausted within a few years or reduced to stripper proportions. In March, 1945, half of Humble's production came from five fields: East Texas, Hawkins, Conroe, Anahuac, and Friendswood. With the exception of the East Texas field, in which Humble had a large reserve but a minor fraction of the acreage, the company's holdings in those fields ranged from nearly half of Conroe to all but four wells of Friendswood.

The wartime production of the East Texas field, great though it was, contrasts significantly with that of Friendswood. Because of the way in which East Texas had been developed and produced, it had little reserve capacity beyond what was required to maintain its prewar production. In fact, Humble's production from East Texas in the years from 1940 through 1945 never attained the daily average of 1939. In other words, the increase in Humble's crude production came from fields that had not been overdrilled and produced at capacity but rather from fields developed in accordance with good conservation principles and held to less than their maximum efficient rates by the existing proration formulas.

The war years brought an even wider application of conservation practices in Texas. The changes included wider spacing as well as recovery more nearly in accordance with the rule of ownership in place. Humble had begun in the early 1930s to advocate 100 per cent acreage as the most reasonable and practicable method of allocation of allowables among oil wells and had consistently requested it in Railroad Commission hearings. In the years 1941–1945 the Texas Railroad Commission ordered the spacing of most wells according to a forty-acre pattern, with twenty acres as a second pattern, until the PAW in 1942 ordered forty-acre spacing for new oil wells. The Railroad Commission also allocated production by acreage and well, applying formulas by which allocations were based 50 per cent on acreage plus 50 per cent on wells, or 75 per cent on acreage and 25 per cent on wells.

These developments were significant. The wider spacing of wartime was important as a means of saving critical materials and manpower; it also reduced costs for producers, although less for Humble and such other companies as had earlier practiced wide spacing. The heavier weighting of acreage in the allocation of allowables, moreover, removed or at least reduced the inequities resulting from earlier allocation formulas that had completely or largely disregarded acreage.

Even with improving practices, wartime production drew heavily on reserves. Neither the industry nor Humble could simply go on increasing without limit the amount of oil drawn from producing wells and developed fields. By 1943 the wartime demand was so great that allowables of fields in the territory in which Humble operated were approaching their maximum efficient rate (MER), so that further increases could have an adverse effect on ultimate recovery. Under the initiative of the federal government, an industry committee (the Ivy Committee), in which Humble took an active part, set maximum efficient rates of production for all pools in District 3, in which Texas was included. In order to ensure adequate capacity Humble, along with the industry generally, had to increase its search for new reserves, drill new wells, and seek new production, although on the reduced scale necessitated by wartime shortages of manpower and equipment.

In this area of its operations Humble had early begun to feel the effect of losing many men to war research, the military services, and other government needs. The geophysics division lost over half of its technical personnel. The geologic, lease, title, and scouting staffs were also hard hit, almost 30 per cent being in military service. By the autumn of 1942 Humble had fallen to sixth rank in the number of seismograph crews operated by companies in the area—some of its competitors had added to their crews immediately after the declaration of war; the company's percentage of the geophysical crew-months worked in its area fell from 12.3 in 1940 to 8.7 in 1942. Since Humble had to find new oil in order to continue to increase its production so as to keep up with war requirements, the loss was serious. It succeeded in adding to the exploration staff slightly.[23]

Humble carried on a greatly enlarged leasing program after 1941. Its total net dollar expenditures for lease acreage rose from about $3,500,000 in 1941 to nearly $10,000,000 in 1944. In the three years after 1941 the company's undeveloped acreage under lease rose to nearly 16,000,000 acres, a 50 per cent increase; this did not, however, mean a comparable increase in current leasing but resulted in part from the fact that, since the exploration staff was not able to survey as much territory as the larger prewar staff, less leased acreage was being surrendered. The balance of Humble's leased acreage tipped to the east of the Mississippi. Within the state of Texas the company was most active in West Texas, although it was highly selective in purchasing because of its large untested holdings and the high cost of lease acreage. According to a report of the Geologic, Lease and Scouting Department, the average price of lease acreage in the whole territory in which Humble operated rose in the first ten months of 1944 by about 75 per cent and rentals by 10 per cent. Wildcat acreage east of the Mississippi was much lower than in West Texas, but even there the price of strictly wildcat acreage had increased to two, three, and even four times the prewar price. If reserves were to be maintained, Humble's lease budgets obviously had to be raised.[24] Obviously, also, more selective buying was important, particularly in the high-price areas. With increased rental costs, it was necessary to survey and test leased lands early and drop leases that did not look promising. This need became especially pressing because in the more competitive regions the primary term of leases was being reduced.

It was impossible, however, during the war to carry on geologic and geophysical work commensurate with Humble's lease holdings and leasing program. Much gravity surveying was done; considerable territory was covered by this greatly improved and rapid exploration method, particularly on Humble's large holdings east of the Mississippi. Surface work by the geologists was, however, greatly reduced. The seismograph crews were used where the need was most urgent and their effectiveness the greatest. In some regions the seismograph was not yet effective; this was particularly true in the Edwards Plateau of Texas, in southern Mississippi, and in southern Florida, limestone regions where the lime "absorbed" the shock waves. In such places the only way to study formations was from outcrops on the surface, cores and cuttings from wells, and electric logs. The geologists mainly worked on wells being drilled.

Drilling similarly had to be done where the immediate promise of oil was greatest. One reason was the shortage of materials and equipment. "At present," according to a report in the autumn of 1944, "large drilling engines, drawworks, and pumps require approximately one year for delivery. Drill pipe with tool joints require nine months to a year. . . ."[25] As always, most of the drilling was in proved areas; after 1943 Humble's development drilling took a sharp upward turn, for its proved but undrilled locations were increasing. A significant shift came in the location of such drilling: in 1945 for the first time in its history Humble included in its drilling program more wells in Southwest Texas than on the Texas Gulf Coast; and the percentage increase in Louisiana and North Texas was considerable.

In 1943 Humble entered upon the greatest wildcatting program that it had ever undertaken.[26] Its exploration and leasing staffs had located and leased a great deal of promising acreage which had not yet been tested, and the company's own interest, together with government pressure for locating more oil, led to the drilling of the most attractive locations. In 1943 Humble drilled fifty-five wildcats, of which nine were producers; in 1944, ninety-six, of which eighteen were producers; and in 1945, eighty, of which eighteen were productive. This was not only a large number of wildcats but a high percentage of discovery wells. Humble, of course, also participated with other companies in drilling test wells.

Notable features of the wartime discoveries were their wider geographic distribution and their greater depth. The increasing activity in Southwest Texas, the focus of wildcatting interest on West Texas and New Mexico, the discovery of oil in Florida and in other parts of Humble's newly created Eastern division, and the discoveries in southern Louisiana were proof of the widening search for oil by Humble and the industry. Perhaps even more significant was the great increase in the depth at which new reservoirs were found. Humble's 1944 discovery well in New Mexico was almost 12,000 feet deep, and in that year the company also drilled in southern Florida its deepest well up to that date, a depth of 13,512 feet. The average of all wells drilled with Humble tools increased from 5,764 feet in 1942 to 6,909 in 1943 and 7,445 in 1944. The percentage of Humble wells that exceeded 10,000 feet in depth increased from 1.5 in 1940 to 18.1 in the first six months of 1944, according to a report for the first half of the latter year.[27] Drilling to such depths inevitably increased costs greatly, quite apart from the general rise in costs during the war years.

Humble's most publicized oil-find in the war years was its discovery in 1943 of the Sunniland field, near the southern tip of Florida, by a well drilled to a depth of over 11,500 feet. As a participant in a strong leasing campaign in Florida beginning late in the 1930s, the company had leased a large acreage in the southern part of the peninsula on the basis of gravity-meter survey and core drilling and had started drilling operations in 1939. Several companies, especially majors, had similarly been investing heavily in the search for oil in the state, but Humble's discovery was the first to prove that there really was oil in Florida. The discovery well was drilled on land leased in 1942, and on a location selected by geologist LaRue on the basis of gravity data and core drilling. Humble drilled several more wells in the vicinity of the discovery well, but all were dry. Sunniland turned out to be a small field, and, since no other field has been discovered in Florida (except one discovered by Gulf, which was soon abandoned), Humble's expensive pioneering in the Everglades has proved more productive of prestige than of petroleum. But the search in Florida has been continued.

During the war the company acquired production in still another state, Mississippi. It had obtained a permit to do business there in 1930, but it was not the discoverer of the state's first commercial oil well, that honor having been won in 1939 by the Union Producing Company. Humble had followed up this initial discovery by a very active lease play and had thus obtained a large acreage at a reasonable cost compared with later costs. The war years brought great activity in Mississippi, particularly in what is known as the Salt Dome Basin. Humble's best wartime acquisition of reserves in the state was the gas reserve it acquired in the Gwinville field in 1944. The following year it discovered two small oil fields, one of which, the Hub drilled on the basis of seismic data, was also a good-sized gas field.

By its discoveries and acquisitions in Florida and Mississippi, Humble gained a strong foothold in production east of the Mississippi, but its success was even greater in Louisiana, where it had been searching for oil for many years. The company's most promising discovery in 1942 was the salt dome on Avery Island, on land leased on the basis of surface evidence and subsurface geology. Avery Island, actually a part of the Louisiana coastal mainland, is in the old French-Acadian country; Humble's operations there a few years later provided the theme for Robert Flaherty's documentary film, *Louisiana Story*, which with rare beauty portrays the impact of the oil industry on people of an old culture and old ways of life. In 1942 Humble also, on the basis of seismic data, discovered in Louisiana the Deer Island gas field and acquired fair oil and gas interests from leases acquired earlier in the new Paradis field. In 1943, by a well drilled with a barge rig, it discovered another Louisiana gas field, Pecan Island on the Gulf Coast. And in 1944 the company discovered a rather small oil field and two gas fields, besides acquiring a fair gas reserve through the discovery by Gulf of the Krotz Springs field.

Eastern Texas and the Gulf Coast continued to add to Humble's reserves, but the discoveries were few compared with those of earlier years. In 1943 Humble discovered Halls Bayou, a gas-condensate field on the Texas Gulf Coast. Its largest gas reserve acquisition, however, was the extension of the Katy field. In 1944 it discovered a relatively small oil field on the Gulf Coast. East Texas and the Gulf Coast continued to be regarded within Humble as good hunting grounds for oil and gas, but the company's greatest wildcatting in Texas in the war years was in the newer oil regions.

Southwest Texas during these years became a very rewarding region in Humble's search for oil and gas. In 1944 the company discovered three relatively small fields, and early in 1945 extended the Tijerina-Canales field, discovered a year earlier by The Texas Company, into its great King Ranch property, thereby adding substantially to its reserves of oil and gas. Near the end of the year, on the basis of subsurface geology and seismic investigation, it brought in Borregas, its first King Ranch discovery, with even larger estimated reserves of oil and gas than at Tijerina-Canales —indeed the greatest addition to its gas reserves since the acquisition of the Katy reserves. Humble also in 1945 made discoveries by seismograph of two wholly owned Southwest Texas gas fields of moderate size.

West Texas, together with a neighboring portion of New Mexico, during the war years took on the aspects of one of the world's major oil provinces, and Humble participated strongly in the aggressive drive to find new oil in that region. Oil had been produced there for about two decades, and certain fields discovered in the Permian were prolific producers. But in studying the varied geology of the region, particularly in the pre-Permian horizons of the Permian Basin on which interest came to be focused, difficulties had been encountered which had nearly stopped the oil seekers' progress. During the war, however, an exciting advance was made. The influx of companies into the region which had begun in the late 1930s continued, and increased exploration and wildcatting brought some spectacular discoveries, which further increased activity. "By far the most active area in Humble's territory in 1944, as well as in 1943," reads a report of Humble's Geologic, Lease and Scouting Department late in 1944, "has been the West Texas–New Mexico area, where there were 456 active drilling operations on November 1, 1944." Most promising were several discoveries of high-gravity, sweet crude in the Ellenburger formation of the Ordovician; these discoveries focused the search in the region on the pre-Permian, particularly on the Ellenburger. Previous geological conceptions concerning the pre-Permian were found incorrect, and much of the earlier geophysical work was found to be unusable. The report of Humble's exploration department explained at the end of 1945: "The complicated nature of the pre-Permian structure was suspected, but only recently have sufficient data been available to positively reveal overturning and faulting together with steep normal fields and large normal faults."

Humble made some important advances in West Texas in the war years, although it was still far from being a leader in production there. It discovered seven fields there in 1944–1945.[28] Heading the list of its oil discoveries in the region in 1944 was the finding of high-gravity oil at 11,816 feet in the Ellenburger lime by its Federal-Leonard well in Lea County, New Mexico. Humble also discovered the Midland field in Texas, which then gave indication of only small production but had special geologic significance because of being in the Pennsylvanian Strawn formation. Humble's percentage of the estimated reserves of the region rose. Although the company ranked eighth in the amount of oil produced in the later war years in the West Texas division, its small geophysics and geologic staff operating in the area had made substantial progress in adding reserves in the region.

Humble's discovery of new fields and its reserves in fields discovered by others, together with the extension of older fields, resulted in a strong addition of new oil and gas in the war years. Despite the tremendous increase in production, the company was able to maintain approximately its prewar reserves. It also maintained about the same percentage of the reserves of the area in which it operated and of the United States as a whole. Nevertheless, its ratio of reserves to annual production fell.

In all parts of Humble's exploration and production, research was severely reduced during the war years. The nearly complete absence of formal research, however, does not mean that nothing was accomplished. No advance was made in the search for new prospecting methods, but the use of known methods and techniques was improved. For example, even during the war years substantial progress was made in obtaining usable reflection data in parts of the Permian Basin where ten years earlier seismograph results had been so poor that some companies had discontinued geophysical work there altogether.

Humble's reservoir research and production engineering were similarly curtailed during the war because of a general loss of personnel to war service and the need to use available employees principally for increasing production. The reservoir research staff was reduced from 41 men at the end of 1941 to 25 at the end of 1943, and the production engineering group from 181 to 149. Beginning in 1944 these groups were increased, but chiefly by the addition of nontechnical employees.

During the war Humble's production research and petroleum engineering were concerned mainly with the effective application of principles and techniques that had been learned and developed earlier rather than with additions to knowledge and practice from new investigations. A number of articles written by Humble men or produced jointly with outsiders—on such subjects as the mechanism of fluid displacement in sands, control of filtration characteristics of salt-water muds, and dimensional model studies of oil-reservoir behavior—were published in 1942 and 1943, but they represented prewar research.[29] Humble's S. E. Buckley and R. C. Craze wrote "The Development and Control of Oil Reservoirs" and "A Factual Analysis of the Effect of Well Spacing on Oil Recovery," which summarized the work of special study committees of the American Petroleum Institute. These appeared in 1943 and 1945 in *Drilling and Production Practice* issued by the API.

Humble's production research staff during the war devoted much of their time, as was generally true among oil companies, to studies of reservoirs in order to obtain the necessary basis for efficient production—among others, the Colorado, Amelia, Halls Bayou, and Gregory reservoirs. Nevertheless, many patents issued in the names of the staff members in the later war years testify to considerable innovation. Among some thirty patents obtained from 1942 through 1945 were those on a subsurface fluid sampler still used in substantially its original form; a method of measuring viscosity, which has come into standard use throughout the industry; and a capillary equilibrium method for measuring the connate water in core samples, which has become a standard by which other methods are judged.

The petroleum engineers in the meantime were concerned chiefly with obtaining necessary materials and equipment, especially by salvaging old equipment and adapting it to new uses. The expanding drilling activity of the later years stimulated efforts to increase efficiency by the use of new and improved methods and equipment. The year 1945 brought increased emphasis on gas conservation and on the determination of MER.

The shortage of research and engineering personnel during the war brought an innovation in training that was to become an important and permanent part of Humble's engineering training program. This was the Reservoir Engineering School, under T. A. Huber, which was established to help overcome the shortage of technical personnel trained in reservoir engineering.

Although a ceiling was put on the Production Department's realization per barrel of crude by the federal government's freezing of prices [30] as of October, 1941, moderate profits were made per unit of volume produced. This was largely a result of the fact that Humble was able to increase very greatly the amount produced by drawing on its tremendous, low-cost reserves acquired and developed during the 1930s. It is pertinent to observe, however, that the reserves depleted during the war were replaced at far higher costs.

CRUDE OIL PURCHASING, MARKETING, AND TRANSPORTATION, 1941–1945

During the war, as earlier, purchased crude oil made up the difference between Humble's own production and the requirements of its refineries and customers. Transportation between the original sources of supply and Texas refineries or the loading points for shipping out of the state was supplied principally by Humble Pipe Line Company.[31] Both these branches of Humble's operations were put under unusual strain during the war as they strove with reduced personnel and materials to supply greatly increased volumes of oil. The problems of both were magnified greatly by the disruption of normal tanker traffic from Texas shipping points.

Neath as director and Trelford as manager were in charge of crude purchasing. Throughout the entire period they and the Humble board were spared one generally persistent headache: they no longer had to decide whether, or when, they should initiate, or follow, increases or cuts in crude prices. The Office of Price Administration (OPA), after permitting slight increases in 1941, held the average price of Texas crude at $1.21 throughout the war and into 1946, despite persistent efforts by the Independent Petroleum Association, the Patman Small Business Committee, and even the PAW to obtain price increases averaging 35 cents per barrel. Stripper wells pumping less than ten barrels daily were, however, granted government subsidies.

Full participation by the United States in World War II, with a consequent increase in the demand for petroleum and petroleum products, should, it would seem, have ended for the duration Humble's long-standing problem of how to dispose of the crude which it purchased. But the intense U-boat activity that followed the declaration of war on Germany reduced oil movement by tanker from the Gulf Coast to a small fraction of the prewar proportions and temporarily cut down the outlet for Texas crude.[32] Because of the shortage of transport facilities, Jersey and its affiliates in 1942 reduced their purchases from Humble by about 40 per cent—a reduction that was not nearly compensated for by increased sales to outsiders. Runs to Humble's own refineries also fell off more than 10 per cent in 1942. Humble, consequently, cut its purchases by over 11,000,000 barrels in that year but still increased its storage stocks by more than 5,000,000 barrels above the 12,000,000 norm.

In this emergency the available refining capacity and transportation to distant markets had to be reserved for the crudes and products most needed for military purposes. On several occasions early in the war, therefore, Humble was forced to prorate its purchases of crude from West Texas, Southwest Texas, and New Mexico because of the high sulphur content of West Texas crude and the insufficiency of the transportation facilities to the Atlantic Coast refineries. Fortunately for Humble, the Gulf Coast and East Texas, with their particularly desirable crudes, normally furnished about two-thirds of the company's own production.

Humble explained to the Texas Railroad Commission the necessity for proration in the surplus areas in a carefully worded analysis of the situation, which was also distributed in a circular letter, "To Those From Whom We Purchase Oil in West Texas-New Mexico and Southwest Texas." The company expressed its willingness to "turn over connections permanently to other companies, to lease or rent its gathering systems on a reasonable basis to those having a market for the crude, or to gather and sell to others crude from fields where it is forced to prorate purchases." It released connections to other companies and also stored crude for which there was no immediate use until, before the end of 1942, the storage tanks were filled to capacity. Although a bill was introduced into the Texas legislature penalizing purchasing companies for failure to buy 100 per cent of the allowable from wells with which their pipelines were connected and specifically banning the defense that refinery equipment or techniques prevented taking the full allowable of a particular crude, the general public reaction to Humble's action was not severe. This was doubtless the result of the public's concentration on the war effort and of Humble's explanation of the situation to those most immediately affected, as well as its obvious willingness to do everything possible to relieve the situation.

In May, 1942, Humble instituted a program of constructing facilities for loading tank cars with crude, which were completed early in 1943. During the war period Humble Pipe Line Company loaded over 30,000,000 barrels of crude on tank cars for delivery to Midwest and Atlantic Coast refineries. This expensive form of oil transport, the extra cost of which was borne by the federal government, had to be used when other means were unavailable.

By the middle of 1943 the transportation situation had improved to the extent that Humble was again usually able to purchase full or nearly full allowables, except in certain fields where the pipeline capacity was inadequate. The decline in tanker movements had by then been partially compensated for by a great increase in the movement of oil by tank cars and pipelines.

The principal and permanent relief to the transportation problem of the Gulf Coast and of Southwest Texas came from the twenty-four-inch War Emergency Pipe Line built from Longview in East Texas to the New York refining area, a line popularly known as The Big Inch. Several of Humble Pipe Line's key men worked on the construction and operation of this line. The first segment—to Norris City, Illinois—was completed by the end of 1942; the first crude moved into the line on New Year's Eve and arrived at Norris City in February, 1943. The line began to deliver crude to eastern refineries in July and September.[33]

Humble Pipe Line Company helped to provide the system of feeder lines, made up of existing private lines, required to supply The Big Inch. Humble reversed its East Texas line so that crude could be moved north to Longview instead of south to the Gulf. The company's most important part in providing crude for The Big Inch was to act as agent for the government in converting, reconditioning, and extending 150 miles of an old, badly corroded, fourteen-inch and sixteen-inch gas line between Refugio and Pierce Junction to form the Southwest Emergency Pipe Line and to move crude from Southwest Texas to the Houston area and thence to East Texas for delivery to The Big Inch. In its work on this emergency line Humble Pipe Line Company acted, without compensation beyond costs, for the Defense Plant Corporation, which had purchased the lines from a gas company. It operated the line as agent of the Reconstruction Finance Corporation. Starting in October, 1943, about 80,000 barrels of crude were moved through this line daily from Southwest Texas to Houston.[34]

Humble pipeline deliveries to The Big Inch in 1943 averaged nearly 70,000 barrels daily, and during the fourth quarter reached a daily average of 117,000; in 1944 they averaged over 107,000 barrels a day. Tank-car loadings of crude were in consequence reduced about 5 per cent, thus freeing cars for other service. About one-third of the total crude transported through The Big Inch from Texas to the East Coast was supplied by Humble.

Humble men also assisted in building other emergency lines. J. A. Neath directed twenty-six men, including H. M. Stevenson as chief engineer, who had full authority for constructing a line from Portland, Maine, to Montreal for the Portland Pipe Line Company. The company also co-operated with Shell, Texas, Pan-American, Pure Oil, and Crown Central in building the Bayou Pipe Line, entirely from secondhand pipe, from the Houston refining area to Baton Rouge, Louisiana. This was a feeder line for the Plantation Pipe Line completed in 1942 for piping petroleum products —chiefly gasoline—from Baton Rouge to Greensboro, North Carolina, and eventually to Richmond, Virginia. Humble owned the largest interest, but the Shell Pipe Line Corporation served as agent of the group for the construction and operation of the Bayou Pipe Line, which was completed by mid-February, 1943.

Humble Pipe Line did not do much construction of its own in the war years. It built only about 150 miles of trunk line, in order to reach new fields or step up capacity, and it even reduced its gathering mileage. Yet, by driving its system to capacity, it was able to increase substantially the amount of oil handled. Its gathering was increased from a total of 114,000,000 barrels in 1941 to 201,000,000 in the peak war year of 1944; and the crude transported by trunk line rose from nearly 139,000,000 barrels in 1941 to over 225,000,000 in 1945. During 1942–1945 Humble Pipe Line gathered a total of about 636,000,000 barrels and transported about 727,000,000 barrels of crude oil.

Crude oil transportation from Texas by tank car, and even more importantly by the War Emergency Pipe Line, enabled Humble to satisfy its customers' greatly increased wartime demands for petroleum. Sales to Jersey affiliates, after dropping off abruptly in 1942, gradually increased until in 1945 they amounted to 48,000,000 barrels—2,000,000 barrels more than in 1941—but sales to outsiders more than quadrupled, from nearly 32,000,000 in 1941 to 129,000,000 in 1945. During 1942–1945 Humble sold a total of 158,000,000 barrels to Jersey affiliates and 380,000,000 to others, of which 96,000,000 were to the Defense Supplies Corporation for movement through The Big Inch.

In order to supply the increased demand, Humble in 1942–1945 doubled its own production and increased its outside purchases to the largest they had then ever been. Increased demand and expanded transportation also made possible the reduction of excess crude storage stocks.

The marketing and transportation of crude oil brought Humble no high wartime profits. Despite the large volume of crude handled, drastically reduced marketing charges—which the company had been forced to adopt during the buyers' market of the late 1930s—kept the profits from the purchase and sale of crude oil down to the lowest they had been for any length of time since the early 1920s. Pipeline earnings, though higher than those of the Crude Oil Department, were also low, the result of a decade of steady tariff reduction. In 1942, with Humble's oil movements, particularly from the company's more remote operating areas, considerably reduced because of the submarine menace, the pipeline net earnings dropped to their lowest point—less than $2,000,000 after taxes, or a little less than 2 per cent on the gross investment. Humble Pipe Line Company's highest net income was earned in 1944—over $6,000,000 after taxes, or slightly more than 6 per cent on gross investment. Crude oil buying and selling and pipeline operations had become practically service functions. Humble profits had consequently come more and more to depend on its own crude oil production.

The tabulation below summarizes, in terms of daily average number of barrels by years, Humble's work in supplying crude oil during the war years: [35]

	1942	*1943*	*1944*	*1945*
Supply of Crude Oil				
Net production	154,200	236,500	308,600	305,000
Purchases	218,000	281,300	386,600	399,200
Total	372,200	517,800	695,200	704,200
Disposal of Crude Supply				
Used by Humble	169,400	195,200	229,700	219,500
Sold at leases	44,100	55,900	67,900	75,200
Other sales	144,000	277,500	398,400	410,500
Total	357,500	528,600	696,000	705,200
Stock change	+14,700	−10,800	−800	−1,000
Crude Transport by Humble Pipe Line Company				
Oil gathered	279,000	378,000	550,000	537,000
Trunk-line deliveries	325,000	454,000	584,000	617,000

Chapter 23

GASOLINE, RUBBER, AND TOLUENE AGAINST THE AXIS, 1941–1945

AVIATION GASOLINE, toluene, and synthetic rubber: in the manufacture of these strategic materials for war Humble made an outstanding record. Humble also produced for military use tremendous quantities of other gasolines, fuel oils, lubricants, asphalt for airplane runways, fuel for flame throwers and smoke screens, and scores of other products. And in addition to its manufacture for direct use by the armed forces, it provided great quantities of products for war industry and for countless civilian needs.

Of the several hundred American refineries that supplied by far the major part of the oil products used by the United States and its allies—not including Russia—in the war, three belonged to Humble; its Baytown refinery was one of the four or five largest in the world and probably equal to any in the range of its equipment, processes, and products. Humble's refineries handled about 5 per cent of the total crude processed in the United States during the war years, manufactured almost 10 per cent of the 100-octane gasoline, and provided about 50 per cent of the toluene used in making the explosive known as TNT(trinitrotoluene). Baytown produced large quantities of synthetic rubber and more 100-octane aviation gasoline than any other refinery in the world, besides providing some other refineries with its surplus of certain components of that gasoline.

Humble was able to manufacture this great variety and quantity of products because of its strength in refining at the beginning of the war. The strong technical and operating organization and the advanced equipment and processes developed at Baytown in the later 1930s had put that refinery among the foremost in the country's manufacture of petroleum products. They also had given it the flexibility of organization and plant required for quick conversion to the manufacture of special war products in large quantities.

Despite shortages of manpower and materials and other wartime difficulties the new plants, new processes, and new skills demanded by the war were provided in record time. Baytown was an organizational model and an example of effective teamwork throughout its organization. The only flaw in the generally good relations in the Humble refineries was at Ingleside; a struggle there with the CIO highlights by contrast the excellent employee relations in the company's other refineries.[1]

Most of Humble's refinery products in wartime, as before, were sold wholesale—to the government by contract, to affiliates of Jersey Standard, and to other large buyers. The Sales Department, although continuing to serve the civilian needs of Texans, supplied an even larger volume of products to industrial plants and military establishments within the state than for retail distribution.

REFINING IN WARTIME

When World War II broke out, petroleum refining throughout the oil industry was nearing the summit of an evolution that had been in progress for some time. An industry formerly managed by "practical" men and carrying out relatively elementary processes with simple equipment was now run by scientists and engineers, who developed and directed chemically and mechanically complex and exacting processes and equipment. A large refinery had become a vast array of pipes, pumps, furnaces, and tanks and towers operating under incredibly high temperatures and pressures and automatically regulated from large central control boards.

No short account can convey an adequate appreciation of the scientific and engineering knowledge and the high skills, or of the minute attention to details, constant alertness, and trained judgment, necessary to operate a refinery as large as that at Baytown. In such a refinery, weakness in a metal or a slight human error can change what is normally a roaring but controlled plant into a veritable inferno. Accidents can, of course, happen in peacetime, but in World War II the danger was increased by the building of new types of installations, the use of more volatile materials, and the employment of new workers.

A description in *The Humble Way* of one of the new wartime installations at Baytown, of a type installed in a number of large refineries, conveys a sense of the size and operation of such a unit and of the infinite care necessary to maintain it in proper condition. The installation described was what is known as a "cat cracker": [2]

> Build a roller-coaster as high as a 20-story office building. . . . Use more steel than is in the cruiser *Houston*, and spread it over a city block. Then construct a vertical chute to the bottom, bend it, and bring it back to the top. Now send a series of ten-ton trucks down this vertical track with velocity enough to complete the round trip in one minute. Keep these trucks in operation 24 hours a day.
>
> Incredible, isn't it? Yes, for a roller-coaster, but not for a catalytic cracking unit. The No. 1 Fluid Catalytic Cracking Unit at Humble's Baytown refinery is 260 feet high, contains 8,500 tons of steel, and circulates catalyst and oil at the rate of ten tons per minute. Originally designed for a capacity of 13,800 barrels per day, the unit has been operating on a stepped-up schedule of 24,000 to 26,000 barrels per day. . . . In a single day, it produces enough components for the aviation gasoline used in a thousand B–25 medium bombers.

Such a unit, operating under terrific strain, not only must always be watched carefully while in operation but also must be periodically inspected, cleaned, and repaired. The description of the cleaning and repairing of this cat cracker after five months of continuous operation—work known in refinery language as a turnaround—gives an idea of how sensitive such equipment is and of the meticulous care that must be used in keeping it in good condition. Under the guidance of metal inspectors and engineers and the direction of the supervisory personnel, men of many crafts went to work—brickmasons, tube cleaners, boilermakers, pipe fitters, welders, machinists, carpenters, and laborers with their wheelbarrows:

> This particular turnaround presented some special problems in stress relief. When certain alloys containing chromium, nickel, molybdenum and other elements are welded or bonded together, stresses and strains in the metal are set up as the weld cools. By carefully controlled heat treatment of the weld and surrounding metal surfaces, the molecules and crystalline structure of the metal are rearranged in such manner that these stresses and weaknesses are relieved. Under changing temperatures of operation, lines and other equipment should expand and contract as evenly and smoothly as possible.
>
> Ordinarily, stress relieving is done at the welding shop's furnace. This time, however, a giant 72-inch line . . . needed a new flange connection. It was impracticable, of course, to remove the line, so a furnace was built around it. A circular system of gas and air lines was piped around the welding area, and fires were lighted. Keeping careful check with an instrument recording temperature, instrument men brought the preheat temperature of the area up to 500 degrees fahrenheit and held it there for 137 consecutive hours. Meanwhile, welders working in shifts inside the big line applied the weld. When the welding job was completed, the actual stress relieving was begun. At the rate of 300

degrees per hour, temperature was brought up to 1250 degrees and held there for three hours. Then the temperature was lowered to 600 degrees at the rate of 200 degrees per hour and the metal allowed to cool from that point to atmospheric temperature. Thus, 145 hours—more than five days—were spent in stress relieving this one line. Thirteen similar jobs were done on lines from 60 inches to four inches in diameter.

This effort to prevent the development of dangerous weaknesses in the metal illustrates the care with which this behemoth had to be handled. Three separate shifts of men working around the clock for a month were required to perform this tremendous cleaning and repair job. After a successful test run following the turnaround, "the cat cracker was brought back on stream."

One of the great sources of danger in refinery operations at this time was the necessity of working with unprecedentedly volatile hydrocarbons. This may have been the main cause of a rising trend in the frequency rate of accidents at Baytown and in the refining industry generally from about 1942, a trend that continued until 1949. Nine fatalities resulted from three explosions at Baytown in the war years—in the butadiene plant, in the Butyl laboratory, and at a cracking coil. Contributing factors may have been the large number of new employees without previous refining experience and also the pressure to get work done.

The pressure to complete tasks on or ahead of schedule necessitated much improvisation and tremendous effort on the part of the Baytown organization during the war. Not only technologists and managers were profoundly affected by the urgency of the need for products, old and new, but also the supervisors, who simultaneously had to train many inexperienced workers and instruct the entire operating force in the carrying-on of new manufacturing processes. In addition, Baytown had to provide the necessary supervisors to direct five new government plants operated by the Baytown organization. An extended work week plus increased automation made it possible to operate with fewer employees in proportion to the work done by the refinery.

The normal necessity of keeping all aspects of refinery operations in balance—maintaining the various crude oil and base stocks, chemicals, power, steam, water, and other materials and equipment in the proper ratios for producing the essential products in required quantities—became more difficult under wartime pressures and shortages. The addition of one particular manufacturing unit might throw the relationship of several out of balance and necessitate considerable changes in old equipment or the building of new at the very time when shortages of both manpower and materials were particularly acute. The necessity of producing on tight schedules specific quantities of particular war products increased the usual problems of supply and disposal. Not infrequently, certain crudes that were particularly desirable for the manufacture of important products could not be obtained, and it became necessary to determine in a short time which available crude was next best and how most effectively to utilize it. Moreover, in order to manufacture the desired amount of toluene, for example, it was sometimes necessary to produce as a by-product a much larger amount of gasoline than, because of transportation shortages, could be disposed of. In 1943 gasoline was in such oversupply at Baytown and storage so limited that to burn the gasoline as waste—as in the early days of the kerosene-oriented oil industry—was at one time considered the only solution.

Baytown's staffs for research, technical service, and economic analysis played strategic roles in the planning and co-ordination of refinery operations. The Baytown staff men, applying principles that were already known, worked on processes and products—on providing adequate base stocks from available crudes, developing maximum production of essential war materials as quickly as possible, making the most economical use of available equipment and manpower—and, in general, on co-ordinating the planning and building of new equipment and the operations of the diverse units of the refinery so as to get the greatest possible production in the shortest time.

Humble, like other technologically progressive refiners, also contributed to the efforts of the Petroleum Administration for War to bring about the fullest possible utilization throughout the industry of the most advanced refining knowledge and techniques. Under the PAW, knowledge, techniques, and patents were pooled for the whole industry, the emphasis being on the collection and distribution of available information that would increase the critical war materials rather than on research.

The Refining Department, as observed above, made three especially important contributions to requirements for war. These were largely the results of research and development by Humble and the Jersey Standard group in the years immediately preceding the outbreak of war. Their research drew heavily on knowledge obtained by Jersey from I. G. Farbenindustrie, a German concern from which it had purchased certain patents and processes in the 1920s.

Humble's production of high-octane aviation gasoline was a particularly outstanding wartime accomplishment. This was the fuel that carried fighters and bombers over the Southwest Pacific, North Africa, and Europe—"the superfuel that meant more speed, more power, quicker take-off, longer range, greater maneuverability—all the things that meant the victory margin in combat"—and this fuel, according to *A History of the Petroleum Administration for War*, was always "perilously close" to a supply shortage.[3]

Humble's share in the contribution of such gasoline was a result in the main of its own and Standard Oil Development's research, with some borrowing from other companies, and of its own plant development at Baytown just before the war. During the years 1935 through 1938 Humble had built several polymerization plants for the production of blending agents to increase the octane number of gasoline. In 1938 it had constructed the world's first commercial alkylation unit, and in 1939 and 1941 had added three more such plants. These alkylation units had necessitated the construction during 1939–1941 of additional light-ends fractionating units for separating the gases to be subjected to alkylation. (See Chapter 21.)

By the end of the 1930s thermal cracking for improving the octane rating of gasoline had gone as far as it could because of the high temperature required. The industry had consequently undertaken research to discover some other way of cracking oil molecules. Several companies had adopted a catalytic cracking process invented by Eugene J. Houdry. Jersey Standard considered contracting for the right of its affiliates to use the Houdry process but found the cost too high. It therefore decided late in 1937 to undertake research on catalytic cracking, and in the next year, together with I. G. Farbenindustrie, Standard Oil of Indiana, and other companies, formed the Catalytic Cracking Associates, a group which was joined later by several other large companies. Each member began to do research and reported to the others. The laboratories of a Jersey affiliate, Standard Oil Development Company, discovered the fluid catalytic process. By this process gas oil was subjected to lower temperature and pressure than in thermal cracking but under rapid movement in the presence of a catalyst (a fine sandlike material) which helped to split the oil molecules.[4] Quoting the PAW history, catalytic cracking, by the fluid and Houdry processes, was "one saving grace for the 100-octane program."[5] It produced larger quantities of high-octane gasoline than did thermal cracking from the same amount of charge stock, resulted in smaller and more valuable residues, and was not so hard on equipment. In the autumn of 1940 Humble authorized the construction of a fluid catalytic-cracking unit at Baytown, the unit already described. Although work was begun immediately, the first cat cracker was not completed until November, 1942.

These polymerization, alkylation, and catalytic-cracking projects, which had been undertaken before there was any immediate threat of this country's involvement in war or even of war itself, enabled Humble in the period immediately after Pearl Harbor to produce 20 per cent of all the 100-octane gasoline being manufactured in the United States. It was logical, therefore, that shortly after America's entry into the war a contract should be signed between Humble and the Defense Supplies Corporation providing for the sale of such quantities of 100-octane gasoline as might be required for delivery in the state of Texas.

Humble at once set about expanding its capacity for manufacturing

100-octane aviation gasoline. Its plans called for Baytown to turn out by mid-1943 approximately 20,000 barrels per day, and a year later 30,000 barrels. Pre-Pearl Harbor production had been 13,000 barrels daily by Humble and other Jersey affiliates and 44,000 by the entire United States refining industry.

Several new manufacturing units were, accordingly, built at the Baytown refinery. In 1942 and 1943 an isomerization and a naphtha fractionating unit, each with a capacity of about a thousand barrels daily, were constructed. The isomerization unit produced, from normal butane, isobutane to supply the alkylation plant; the naphtha plant produced aviation base stock of improved quality. In 1942 a fourth alkylation plant was added; the resultant alkylate was the type of blending agent used in producing most of the 100-octane gasoline manufactured in the United States. Naphtha fractionating units—for removing low-octane constituents from aviation gasoline base stocks and providing additional isopentane, in order to increase the production of 100-octane aviation gasoline—were completed in November, 1942, and in the following May had a total capacity of about 20,000 barrels daily. A second fluid catalytic-cracking unit, authorized late in 1942, was completed early in 1944. By charging maximum fresh feed to its catalytic units, Humble was able to produce not only maximum yields of high-quality gasoline fractions but also isopentane for aviation gasoline and isobutane and olefinic charge-stocks for the production of aviation alkylate; catalytic cracking also produced isobutylene and normal butylenes to be used in the manufacture of synthetic rubber.

Baytown's aviation gasoline program was completed in August, 1944, by the installation, at the cost of $4,600,000, of a government-sponsored hydrogenation unit. This unit increased the production of high-quality aviation gasoline base stocks by hydrogenating the light gasoline fractions from the catalytic crackers through the use of hydrogen-bearing gas produced at the Baytown Ordnance Works and the butadiene plant.[6]

Thus, as a result of its early attention to the production of high-octane gasoline, Humble took the leading role in supplying aviation gasoline for World War II. The Baytown refinery, as already noted, produced and delivered more 100-octane aviation gasoline than any other refinery in the world and also manufactured a surplus of blending agents above those needed for finishing its own high-octane gasoline. On December 14, 1944, the refinery celebrated the production of its billionth gallon of 100-octane gasoline; it was the first refinery in the world to make this record and one of three to do so during the war. The San Antonio refinery manufactured over half a million barrels of 100-octane, but its production of aviation gasoline was confined principally to 91-octane quality; and all the Ingleside refinery's aviation gasoline was of 91-octane number. From the outbreak of the war in Europe until V-J Day Humble refineries manufactured—nearly all at Baytown—a total of 30,000,000 barrels of 100-octane aviation gasoline. This was almost 10 per cent of the total United States production of 100-octane gasoline and more than 7 per cent of the total production of the United States and its allies exclusive of Russia.[7]

Humble's second vital contribution to the war effort was the manufacture of toluene, the main ingredient of TNT, the chief explosive used in modern warfare. Humble, after working for some time with Standard Oil Development Company in search of a way to produce synthetic toluene from petroleum, had in 1938 discovered a method for extracting nitration-grade toluene from naphtha (see Chapter 21). In response to the Army's urging, and through the co-operative efforts of Standard Oil Development Company, Humble, and other Jersey affiliates, the process was developed for quantity production. In the manufacture of the first 20,000 gallons of nitration-grade (99+ per cent pure) toluene—which were turned over to the Ordnance Department in August, 1940—the various fractions had to be shipped from Baytown to Bayway (New Jersey), then back to Baytown, and finally to Baton Rouge (Louisiana), for successive stages of processing; at no one refinery was all the necessary equipment available. For commercial production it was obviously important to have the various processes concentrated in a single plant, and the most advantageous location for such a plant was near Baytown, where large quantities of naphtha were available.[8]

Humble, therefore, in co-operation with Standard Oil Development Company and with the assistance of the M. W. Kellogg Company, E. B. Badger & Sons Company, and C. F. Braun & Company, leading refinery construction concerns, began to work on plans for a plant as early as May, 1940. On August 15 it submitted a proposal for the construction of the Baytown Ordnance Works, the first commercial synthetic toluene plant in the world. The proposed plant was to be owned by the government but built and operated by Humble on a cost-plus-fixed-fee arrangement, was to have a daily capacity of 82,000 gallons, or about 30,000,000 gallons per year, and was to be completed within twelve months from the beginning of construction. So anxious was Humble to get this vital defense material into production that its subcontractors were ordered to start work early in October, 1940, before all details had been settled and the contract finally signed. The unit was "put on the line" early in September, 1941, six weeks ahead of schedule; the first consignment of toluene was shipped forty-five days before Pearl Harbor; and within three months the plant was producing at the prescribed rate. This plant was the model followed in building several other plants for manufacturing toluene from petroleum.

Humble's technicians worked from the beginning of operations to improve the plant's performance. In the spring of 1942 it was found that additional equipment at the sulphur dioxide plant would increase toluene production. The installation of such equipment, expected to be completed by September, was actually accomplished in July, essential equipment being borrowed from the Baytown refinery pending the arrival of that specially purchased for the Ordnance Works. The toluene plant's production eventually exceeded 200 per cent of the capacity for which it was designed.

In connection with this plant Humble took a step in keeping with its policy of avoiding large profits on government business during wartime, thus forestalling action by the government agency regulating war profits. It had agreed to supply prime-cut naphthas to the toluene plant at 12 cents per gallon, subject to adjustment according to increases or decreases in the weighted average of the posted field prices of certain grades of crude oil received at the Baytown and Ingleside refineries. The annual fee for operating the plant was fixed at $300,000. On August 26, 1942, however, the company decided that the naphtha prices and operating fee were too high and voluntarily reduced the base price from 12 cents a gallon to 8 cents, retroactive to the beginning of operations; it simultaneously reduced the fee to $175,000.

The contribution of toluene to the war effort by the Humble-operated Baytown Ordnance Works was without equal. During 1942 the plant produced 50,000,000 gallons; until early in 1943, when other similar plants went into operation, it was, in fact, producing two-thirds of the nation's entire output. During the course of the war the Baytown Ordnance Works produced a total of over 5,500,000 barrels of toluene, nearly half of the whole supply of this ingredient of an essential explosive.

Japan's capture early in 1942 of the Far East's rubber supplies, which forced the United States to undertake a synthetic rubber program,[9] led to still another important contribution by Humble to the war effort. Steps in the direction of manufacturing synthetic rubber had been taken several years earlier. Standard Oil Development Company, through an agreement made in 1929 with the German concern, I. G. Farbenindustrie, had acquired a number of patents, including one for buna rubber, which the Germans had used for tires; one of the principal ingredients was butadiene, which could be manufactured either from alcohol or from butane or butylene, which are petroleum products. Standard Oil Development Company, in the course of working with other I. G. Farben patents, had also developed a type of synthetic rubber known as Butyl, which proved to be particularly suitable for inner tubes, barrage balloons, and certain other rubber products. The Baton Rouge refinery already had a small butadiene plant early in 1942.

On March 23, 1942, Humble entered into a contract with the Defense

Plant Corporation to build and operate a plant at Baytown for the manufacture of butadiene by the dehydrogenation of butylenes. The plant was to have an annual capacity of 30,000 short tons of butadiene and to cost nearly $19,000,000. Upon its completion—after the usual difficulties with wartime shortages and restrictions had been surmounted—the plant was leased to Humble at a nominal rental and went into operation in September, 1943. The operation of this butadiene plant also required the construction of the second fluid catalytic-cracking plant, which was built at Humble's own expense and completed early in 1944 at a cost of about $9,500,000.

By the terms of a contract of December 17, 1942, a "quickie" butadiene plant was established at the Ingleside refinery, the crude capacity of which had been increased the previous year from 22,000 barrels daily to 30,000. Three tube-and-tank thermal cracking coils were converted, at a cost of $4,285,000, into a plant for the production of 12,500 short tons of butadiene annually by means of a high-temperature, low-pressure steam cracking process. Although scheduled for completion in June, 1943, this government plant did not begin operations until October, 1943, when it also was leased to Humble.[10]

On May 18, 1942, Humble contracted with the Defense Plant Corporation to build and operate a Butyl rubber plant at Baytown. (Two other Butyl plants were built by Jersey affiliates, one at Baton Rouge, Louisiana, and the other at Sarnia in Canada.) Humble's plant was to have an annual capacity of 20,000 (later 30,000) long tons and to cost a little over $26,000,000. Upon completion, following the precedent of the butadiene plants, it was leased to Humble. Changes in the plans, low priorities, and other circumstances postponed Baytown's first satisfactory production of Butyl until September, 1944, but during the next twelve months the plant produced nearly 24,000 long tons of Butyl rubber, approximately half the total amount produced in the United States under the government's program.[11]

Humble was compensated for its work in the construction and operation of these synthetic rubber plants by the sale of their entire output of butadiene and Butyl to the Rubber Reserve Company at a price consisting of an agreed-upon charge for feed-stocks, plus direct operating expenses and a graduated fee based upon the volume of output.

In addition to manufacturing high-octane aviation gasoline, blending agents for bringing aviation gasoline up to the 100-octane number, toluene for high explosives, and two types of synthetic rubber, Humble also contributed to the war effort large quantities of Navy fuel oil and superior aviation lubes. Its propane and phenol plants had put it in the forefront of the manufacture of lubricants, just as its polymerization, alkylation, and catalytic-cracking plants had given it a leading position in the manufacture of 100-octane aviation gasoline.[12]

The following quantities of the principal war products manufactured from petroleum were produced by Humble refineries during the war period, that is from September 1, 1939, to September 1, 1945:

100-octane aviation gasoline	29,944,900 barrels
91-octane aviation gasoline	5,632,800 "
Other aviation gasolines and components	13,980,000 "
Xylenes	1,395,600 "
Toluene	5,590,700 "
Navy Diesel fuel	7,944,200 "
Navy fuel oil	20,697,300 "
Aviation and heavy-duty lube oils and components	5,031,100 "
Butadiene	81,700 short tons
Butyl rubber	23,600 long tons

Because of the critical need for strategic war materials, it was important that Humble should even exceed the requirements of its contracts with the government. Both 100-octane aviation gasoline and toluene were delivered several months ahead of schedule; because of shortages and low priorities, the delivery of butadiene was late. All three were supplied in far greater quantities than contracts called for.

In order to produce the enormous quantities of products intended for special wartime needs it was necessary, as already noted, to enlarge tremendously Humble's refinery capacity and crude runs. At the Baytown Ordnance Works, for example, since only about 9 per cent of the original naphtha could be converted into toluene, Humble arranged to purchase naphtha from other refineries in an amount equivalent to about half of the crude charged. In addition, the company had to increase its total rated refining capacity from 169,000 barrels daily in 1939, of which 137,000 were at Baytown, to nearly 224,000 in 1945, of which 190,000 were at Baytown. The total crude runs were increased from over 152,000 to 215,000 barrels daily.[13] In 1944, when the utilization of its rated capacity was over 100 per cent, Humble's refinery runs amounted to nearly 17 per cent of the total runs in Texas and 5 per cent of the United States total.

This great increase was difficult to achieve under wartime conditions. Steel for new equipment was generally in short supply, a situation Humble met by restoring obsolete equipment to service, using old equipment in the construction of such new plants as an isomerization unit and the Ingleside butadiene plant, and "robbing Peter to pay Paul" by borrowing equipment from one important plant in order to put one of even greater importance on the line, as in the case of the Baytown Ordnance Works.[14] The loss of men to war service and the sharp 1942 decline in refinery operations, because of the enemy submarine campaign which reduced shipments by tankers, had resulted in a cut in Humble's refining personnel. In 1943, confronted with a shortage not merely of steel but also of manpower and temporarily depleting its group of skilled refinery men by furnishing skeleton workers for operating the war plants, Humble increased its work week from forty hours to forty-eight, as was commonly done in the industry, extended automation in its plants, trained additional refining personnel, and put more oil than before through its stills per man-hour.[15]

For these accomplishments in wartime, credit must go to the refinery organization—to Hines H. Baker, Ferguson, Farned, Meier, and others who had chief responsibility for refinery operations, to lower echelons of management, and to the many technologists who with imagination, skill, and energy contributed to construction and operation. Recognition must also be given to those many other employees who, particularly at Baytown, had been welded into a strong team by a process of selection, training, and morale-building in the later 1930s. In refining, especially, vital new construction and operations were driven by an urgency stemming from the realization that victory or defeat might be determined by the quality and quantity of the products. Men knew that refining operations were important in wartime, particularly the manufacture of the gasolines and lubes for fighter planes and bombers, toluene for their explosives, and rubber for the many vital military and civilian uses.

UNIONISM AT INGLESIDE, 1942–1945

An important factor, indeed, in making possible Humble's contribution to the war effort was the generally excellent condition of management-employee relations that characterized the company organization during the war. In the Baytown refinery, at the sales stations, on the pipelines, and in the producing fields, morale was high and close co-operation was characteristic. Employee relations in those operations, because of their smoothness and lack of complexity, require no detailed consideration. There was, however, one exception in the war years. It was centered in the protracted effort of the Oil Workers International Union of the CIO to organize the employees in Humble's Ingleside refinery.[16]

The struggle was a minor episode in Humble's wartime operations and had little influence on the company's total war effort, but it has a significance beyond its immediate effect. In the history of Humble it stands as the first strike of any importance in which the company was involved, far outweighing the unimportant boilermakers' strike at Baytown in 1920 and Humble's involvement in the unsuccessful general strike of oil-field workers that affected the entire Gulf Coast oil industry during World War I.[17] This unionization drive probably accelerated certain changes in Humble's relations with its employees. And it reveals the attitude of the company's management and of the majority of its employees to "outside" unions, together with some of the reasons for that attitude. Beyond the company itself, the protracted struggle at Ingleside affords one example of the process by which the organization of labor was advanced at the time, particularly showing the strength and the methods of the CIO.

On July 6, 1942, despite two recent 5 per cent general wage increases and only a few days before a third, OWIU Local 316 at Ingleside successfully petitioned the National Labor Relations Board for an election to determine the plant bargaining agency at the Humble refinery. The result was that, out of 284 valid votes cast, 212 were for the OWIU Local and only 69 for the Employees Federation.[18] Never before had Humble employees cast such a vote for an "outside" union.

What had changed the attitude at Ingleside? A common explanation was that Ingleside had been staffed largely by employees who had been transferred in the early 1930s from abruptly closed inland refineries, such as McCamey, and who felt that they were being pushed around—but in 1937 Ingleside had voted overwhelmingly against the CIO. Unionism was sweeping the Gulf Coast refineries, and the CIO had won bargaining rights in the Texas refineries of Shell, Texas, and Pan American; yet the union drive did not win the Baytown employees, who were paid the same wages as at Ingleside and enjoyed the same benefits. One important factor apparently was the fear that the Ingleside refinery might be closed down. The CIO used the argument: "Join the union or you'll never get another job in a refinery." Since the CIO was organizing the employees of refineries all around, this was convincing. Considerable influence must also be credited to a refinery employee who apparently was in closer communication than refinery management with the employees. Henry W. ("Slick") Wier was a long-service employee and a supervisor who was an active organization man, whether in his church, the Boy Scouts, or his several fraternal organizations. He was known in the community for his strong advocacy of social reform. From the time of the first effort of the CIO to unionize Ingleside in the 1930s, he had been Local 316's principal leader; he had continued to be in close communication with the CIO ever since. When the unionization drive was resumed in the Ingleside refinery in 1942, Wier was the logical leader. In this small refinery where —partly because of him—a strong independent union had not developed, he exerted an influence that in the long pull was apparently a powerful and perhaps the decisive factor.

Negotiations between Local 316 and Humble management got under way early in 1943 and went on for nearly three months. Disagreement centered in racial discrimination, minimum wages, seniority, and maintenance of union membership.

On racial discrimination the union presented the standard CIO provision, that "The Company shall not discriminate against any employee because of race, creed, color, or sex." Management pointed out the implications of such a provision and declared that, if the company accepted it, they would expect to live up to it. The union thereupon accepted the innocuous substitute: "All employees shall receive equal pay for equal work regardless of race, creed, or sex." The union negotiators, however, held out so stubbornly for a standard labor rate of 89½ cents, instead of two classifications with the lower on a 76½ cent rate, that the controversy went to a United States conciliator. He ruled for the company.[19]

The recognition of seniority, which the union demanded and the company had to accept, weakened one of Humble's most treasured prerogatives of management. The 1943 contract of the Baytown Employees Federation still provided that, in layoffs or promotions, seniority should govern only when other factors, such as "demonstrated ability" and leadership, were "relatively equal." The new Ingleside contract, however, stipulated that layoffs should take place in the inverse order of seniority; it further provided that employees should have the right to bid on vacancies and new positions, the senior employee to be awarded the job if he had "relatively the fitness and ability to perform the work." If the company rejected a senior bidder, the employee or the workmen's committee might file a grievance with the superintendent; and, if his decision was not satisfactory, they might submit the matter to arbitration.

One union demand that Humble refused to grant was for a maintenance-of-membership provision. When Humble had refused to agree to a union shop, the local had substituted a request for a clause providing that all employees who were members of the union should, as a condition of employment, maintain their membership in good standing for the period of the contract. Humble based its objection on its unwillingness to abrogate its traditional principle of "no discrimination by the Company . . . against any employee on account of membership or nonmembership in any church, society, fraternity, or union."

By April 30, 1943, union and management had agreed that the contract should be signed, subject to the right of the union to present the maintenance-of-membership provision to the War Labor Board and the right of the company to oppose and contest a directive covering such a provision. On May 14, 1943, the contract with the CIO union was signed.[20]

In the meantime, OWIU Local 333 at Baytown, asserting that it represented a majority of the Baytown employees, had petitioned the WLB for an election. Humble and the Baytown Employees Federation opposed the petition on the ground of an existing contract, but the WLB finally ordered an election to be held in November, 1943. The CIO union on its part asserted that the promotions were "made . . . without regard to seniority," and that the refinery was not, as claimed, paying the highest wages in the region, because a disproportionately large number of employees were helpers. Humble's own figures, indeed, had indicated that in 1941 Baytown was using more helpers in proportion to craftsmen than any other Jersey-affiliated refinery, a situation that was of some concern to Humble management. The union also declared that Humble sickness benefits could be "withheld at will by the Company without notice"; although this was technically true, it is doubtful that anyone believed it was likely to happen. The federation, on its side, brought up the race issue with the assertion: "A vote for the CIO is a vote for absolute equality between the white and colored races on every job in Baytown from labor gang to department head"—an argument which the CIO denounced as "Hitlerat propaganda." [21] The Baytown Employees Federation in November, 1943, by a vote of almost two to one, again, as in 1937, won the right to bargain for the process and maintenance employees. The AFL machinists' and electrical workers' unions and the Brotherhood of Railroad Trainmen's union, who claimed the right to represent employees in those trades, were, however, victorious in their particular small groups.[22]

The Baytown Employees Federation subsequently asked for and obtained more emphasis on seniority in promotions. Its contract of May 10, 1944, included a provision somewhat similar to the corresponding one in the Ingleside agreement, with the important exceptions that seniority was to apply neither to technical and engineering employees nor to employees of special or unusual fitness and ability. During the spring of 1944 electricians, trainmen, and machinists also won contracts. Humble agreed that, if compelled to accept maintenance of membership in the Ingleside contract, it would not resist efforts of the AFL unions to obtain a similar provision.[23]

In the meantime the Ingleside maintenance-of-membership dispute was grinding along from stage to stage. In April, 1944, the War Labor Board reversed a decision of the regional board and ordered Humble to accept such a clause; [24] Humble refused on the ground that maintenance of membership was wrong in principle.[25] When on September 6, 1944, it appeared that the Petroleum Administration for War might take over the Ingleside refinery, Humble obtained from the federal District Court in Dallas an injunction against such action on the ground that acceptance of the order would endanger the peaceful relations with its 14,000 employees by violating the company's long-standing policy of noninterference with their right to join or not join labor organizations.[26]

At this point the union took a significant step. The Smith-Connally Act provided that an interruption of work must actually have taken place, or at least be seriously threatened, before the PAW could enforce an order of the WLB by taking over a plant. The Ingleside union, therefore, petitioned the WLB for the right to hold a strike vote. But strikes and lockouts were banned by the existing contract between Humble and the Ingleside union. The union is said not to have intended to strike; it regarded a vote for a strike as merely a vote for maintenance of membership. Whatever the union's intention, it seemed to be threatening to violate its contract with Humble in order that the government might take a step that would be illegal except under the assumption that such a violation was actually intended. On November 16 the Ingleside union voted 187 to 110 for a strike. But no further action was taken at the time.

Although Humble was nearing the end of its judicial resources, several months elapsed before these were entirely exhausted. On December 21, 1944, the United States Circuit Court of Appeals dissolved the District Court's injunction. On June 5 the President ordered the PAW to take over the Ingleside plant; on June 18 the United States Supreme Court sustained the Circuit Court's dismissal of the District Court's injunction. And on June 20 a District Court judge, from whom Humble had obtained a temporary restraining order and to whom it had applied for an injunction against the seizure of the plant on the grounds that no actual interruption of work had taken place and that the attempted seizure was merely a method of applying illegal sanctions in support of an unenforceable order of the WLB, declined to grant such an injunction. Humble management in the meantime had suggested to the Ingleside union that it might consent to observe written authorizations for payroll deductions, but the workmen's committee unanimously refused anything short of maintenance of membership. On June 22 the PAW "seized" the Ingleside plant.[27]

The seizure was merely a token one, since the company continued to operate the refinery for its own account under the superintendency of Frank Goss.[28] Under the Smith-Connally Act the refinery was to be returned to the company within sixty days after the restoration of normal operations. Although operations had never actually been interrupted, it was not returned until September 10 and then still without a maintenance-of-membership provision in the contract. The War Labor Board's order to observe maintenance of membership had proved unenforceable.

Humble's victory had wide application. The controversy was regarded by many as more than a struggle between a powerful oil company and a 300-member refinery local; it was a test of strength between "Standard Oil," the bulwark of opposition to "outside" unionism, and the powerful Congress of Industrial Organizations, which had picked the Jersey Standard affiliates as among its principal targets. Local 316—the little union, which, according to a history of the OWIU, by its victory in a WLB-sponsored election had "humbled high and mighty Humble" [29]—was a symbol of industrial unionism in the oil industry, just as Humble was regarded as a symbol of the companies affiliated with Jersey Standard. If Local 316 could enforce a maintenance-of-membership provision, it would be another leak in the dike that Humble and Jersey Standard had for over a quarter of a century built up against national-union infiltration. Humble's victory in connection with the maintenance-of-membership provision did much to plug the hole.

Troubles at Ingleside, however, were not yet over. The new issue was the CIO's demand, after the war had ended, that a reduction of weekly hours from forty-eight to forty should be accompanied by an increase of 30 per cent in the wage scale in order that take-home pay should not be reduced. The oil companies generally offered a 15 per cent increase. OWIU-organized refineries began to strike in the middle of September, 1945, first in North and East Texas, then on the Gulf Coast. By the end of that month all refineries in the Beaumont–Port Arthur area were closed; in the Houston–Texas City area, only Humble's refinery at Baytown and the Eastern States refinery were still in operation. On October 3 the Ingleside local, despite its nonstrike contract, closed down the plant. Even the Baytown Employees Federation, which had demanded the same 30 per cent increase as the CIO unions, began to talk darkly about a strike. President Truman, however, on October 4 ordered the Secretary of the Navy to occupy the struck plants, and work was resumed at Ingleside under the hours and wages in effect at the time of the stoppage.[30]

Humble offered its employees' bargaining agencies a 15 per cent wage and salary increase, a reduction in weekly hours to forty, probably beginning a month later, and a continuance of negotiations in regard to the 30 per cent increase. The Employees Federations accepted the offer; Ingleside rejected it.[31]

Sinclair, the first company to sign a contract with the OWIU in 1934, was also the first to come to an agreement with the union in the early postwar period. Sinclair offered, and the union finally accepted, an increase of 18 per cent when it went on a forty-hour week, plus a differential of 4 and 6 cents per hour for the evening and midnight shifts. Other companies and refineries followed. On February 1, 1946, Humble, in conformity with its prevailing-wage policy, accepted the new standard. A month earlier it had voluntarily granted a two-weeks' vacation after a single year's service.

Ingleside unionists did not benefit from the strike, because by mid-November, 1945, the long anticipated shutdown had finally taken place. Some persons were inclined to believe that the refinery was closed in order to get rid of the only contract Humble had ever had with a CIO union. Humble management was obviously annoyed with a group that had broken through the wall of its resistance to outside unionism, forced it to engage during wartime in two years of litigation over the maintenance-of-membership issue, twice violated the no-strike clause in its contract, and twice brought about the seizure of the plant by the government. The strike may well have been the proverbial last straw.

Circumstances indicate, however, that closing would probably have come at about the same time even if there had been no CIO union at the refinery. As early as January, 1945, Humble was considering what to do with Ingleside after the expiration of its government butadiene contract, which it had been informed would come approximately two years after the war with Japan had ended. Since the Ingleside refinery was obsolete compared with Baytown, its eventual fate was foreshadowed. By early August Humble, having learned that the postwar requirements of the Delaware Company were not sufficient to justify operating the Ingleside refinery, was considering shutting down the refinery "as soon as arrangements could be made to supply the feed stock . . . for the Government's butadiene operations at Baytown from other refineries in the Texas Gulf Coast." [32] Late in October the government contract for the manufacture of butadiene at Ingleside was canceled.

A few days later Humble announced its decision to close the Ingleside refinery. It explained that, because the cracking facilities at Ingleside had been converted to butadiene work, the refinery was merely a topping plant and no longer economical to operate.[33] To modernize this refinery would require an investment not considered justifiable at the time when the market was in a slump.

In closing Ingleside Humble, as it had earlier done in similiar emergencies, assisted its employees in making the necessary adjustments. It gave them the choice between transfer to such jobs with Humble as were available and severance pay. Some employees accepted transfers, but most, including all the union leaders, took severance pay. Termination allowances alone cost Humble nearly $200,000. The Humble Employee Relations Department helped those who chose not to stay with Humble to look for jobs in the Corpus Christi–Ingleside area and elsewhere in Texas. Many were placed with industrial plants in Ingleside. The smoothness with which the operation was carried out created general good will for the company.

The struggle with unions at Ingleside was far more than temporary and local in its importance. It aroused considerable bitterness in management over the methods employed by the union and by government agencies, and it failed to win favor for the union with many Humble employees. At the same time, it permanently weakened the company's stand against seniority as the determining factor in promotions and layoffs and management's freedom to select what it considered the best men and good men for retention and promotion. To the OWIU it meant failure to complete its organization of the most important companies in the American oil industry.

OPERATIONAL DIFFICULTIES AND FINANCIAL TRIUMPH OF THE SALES DEPARTMENT, 1941–1945

The Humble Sales Department, although beset during the war years with many operational difficulties, emerged from the struggle with flying colors. The large sales to aviation training camps and war plants contributed strongly to its unprecedented earnings.[34] Its difficulties originated from shortages of strategic materials and manpower.

Even before Pearl Harbor, the construction and repair of service stations were under strict governmental supervision, although work in progress might be completed if completion was possible before March 31, 1942. The Sales Department had long hesitated because of the Chain Store Tax Act to undertake construction and was thus not prepared to take full advantage of an amendment of that law on May 1, 1941. The company was able to complete three new stations before the deadline, but thereafter it found difficulty even in keeping the existing retail outlets in good repair.

A week after Pearl Harbor the sale of tires was frozen, and the next month new tires and tubes were put under strict rationing and price control. Their withdrawal from general sale deprived Humble and its commission dealers of important retail sales. Between the time of freezing and of outright rationing, Humble prepared its service-station personnel for the future in a series of rationing schools; in order to help offset its agents' loss on commissions by encouraging retreading of tires, prompt repairs, and so on, it presented an engineering program entitled "Twenty Ways to Get Longer Life from Your Car." [35]

When in April, 1942, the government, in order to save tank cars for the shipment of crude oil to the East, forbade the use of cars for the transportation of products within a radius of 200 miles from refining points, Humble had to convert, without warning, to tank truckage for the distribution of refined products. The company was able to obtain considerable gasoline for particular outlets through purchase-and-sale arrangements with other companies, but some of its dealer stations could not be supplied in this way. Tank trucks were already scarce. Humble was able eventually to obtain four 3,500-gallon trucks, but these were entirely inadequate for its needs. A Texas law passed in the spring of 1945, which increased the gross load limit for trucks from the 7,000 pounds of a 1932 law to 48,000 pounds, came too late to improve materially the wartime transportation situation. To obtain tires and parts for trucks was also difficult, because equipment for the distribution of petroleum products to civilians had a low priority. Humble, consequently, had to depend primarily on common-carrier trucks.

Gasoline rationing on the East Coast began in May, 1942, and, over the protests of Texas and Louisiana spokesmen for the oil industry, became nationwide on December 1, 1942.[36] In order to cushion the shock to its commission agents, Humble instituted a temporary plan for extra compensation. The volume of paper work imposed on Humble sales personnel by gasoline rationing was enormous; it was estimated that a million manhours were spent merely in handling ration coupons.

The lowering of the quality of motor gasoline also affected Humble's sales. In order to save blending agents and lead for use in improving the octane number of aviation gasoline, Humble's premium grade, Esso Extra, was cut from 78 octane to 76, and Humble Motor Fuel from 74 to 72 and in 1944 to 70; the use of lead in Thriftane, its third-grade gasoline, had been discontinued earlier. In September, 1944, the civilian consumption of premium gasoline was cut 50 per cent. Since sales of Esso Extra had accounted for 60 per cent of Humble's gasoline sales through company-operated stations, these restrictions, particularly, affected Humble more than companies with a smaller proportion of premium-grade sales.

The sale of certain lubricants was also regulated. On January 1, 1941, Humble had replaced a Standard of California product with Humble Esso-lube H. D., a superior or heavy-duty automotive and Diesel lubricant. But because of the great demand in essential defense industries for this heavy-duty, detergent oil, its sale to civilians was at once put under severe restrictions.

Gasoline rationing and transportation difficulties that rendered some small stations uneconomical, as well as enlistments, the draft, and opportunities for better-paying jobs in war plants, caused the number of Humble's contract-dealer stations to decline by about a third, approximately the same percentage reduction as throughout the country.[37] Since the company was determined not to lose the public relations and other values of its company-operated stations, it maintained approximately the same number of company-operated stations throughout the war. To do so, however, necessitated a replacement of personnel amounting to nearly 100 per cent annually in 1942–1944.

Wartime regulations were not all adverse. The PAW's ban on credit, or courtesy, cards early in 1943 reduced operating expenses. Humble also withdrew its coupon books. A temporary PAW ban on keeping other than twenty-four-hour stations open more than seventy-two hours in a week helped Humble's manpower shortage by making it possible for a single agent to operate a station without relief. When the order was withdrawn, Humble instructed the field force to institute such hours as each station called for.

Wartime rationing of gasoline and tires caused a shift in Humble's advertising. It was changed from aggressive sales promotion to an institutional program; motorists were advised as to conserving tires and cars and Humble's name was kept before the public as a leader in the production and transportation of petroleum and in the manufacture of petroleum products, particularly for defense purposes.[38] The *Humble Sales Lubricator* was devoted more to the maintenance of employee morale than previously and was renamed the *Humble Lubricator* in May, 1943.

Rationing cut Humble's gasoline sales for civilian use. Sales through company-operated service stations declined from 29,000,000 gallons in 1941 to 23,000,000 in 1943; they rose to nearly 27,000,000 gallons in 1944 and maintained the same average through the war months of 1945. Bulk-station gasoline sales to commercial and individual users and dealers followed the same general pattern, although the decline was proportionately greater and the recovery relatively slight.

The decline in sales in Texas for ordinary civilian purposes was, however, far more than offset by sales to the government—largely for use in the numerous air force training fields throughout Texas—and by commercial sales to large Texas war plants. From 1942 through 1945 the Sales Department's refinery sales to the United States government (not including sales in cargo lots by the Refining Department) represented over 30 per cent of total sales; a total of 304,000,000 gallons was made up of 100-octane aviation gasoline, lower-octane aviation gasoline, motor gasoline, and lubricants. Commercial sales of over 429,000,000 gallons of petroleum products during the same period accounted for 44 per cent of the total volume of the Sales Department.

These sales in large quantities, since they cost considerably less per barrel than the service-station and bulk-station sales, were chiefly responsible for the Sales Department's higher net earnings in the war years. Intense competition and abnormally low retail gasoline prices resulted in service-station and bulk-station losses in 1941, but aviation and other direct sales prevented the Sales Department from showing a loss. Service-station sales showed a loss in 1942 as well.[39] During the years 1943 through 1945, retail sales shared moderately in the prosperity of the department. Sales to airfields and war-industry plants contributed two-thirds of the earnings, however, because of large volume and consequently lowered unit costs.

FINANCIAL RESULTS OF HUMBLE'S WARTIME OPERATIONS

Obtaining capital for expansion during wartime was no problem. The construction of the government-owned war plants operated by Humble was financed by the government. Humble's own additional investments in fixed assets were financed by the recovery of capital, chiefly from depreciation, and by current income, of which 59 per cent was plowed back into the business in the years 1942–1945. Net investments in fixed assets increased from $313,100,000 at the end of 1940 to $384,200,000 at the end of 1945.[40] (See Appendix II, Table IV.)

Costs, of course, tended steeply upward. One cost that Humble was able to reduce was the interest on its indebtedness, through refinancing its debts at lower interest rates. In 1945 it paid off $40,000,000 of debentures carrying interest rates of from 2.50 to 2.85 per cent, maturing from 1953 to 1960, by borrowing the same amount from banks on notes bearing 1.75 per cent, to be repaid in 1952–1955, an operation which reduced the annual interest load by about $370,000.[41] Labor costs rose steeply; the average annual employee earnings increased from $2,382 in 1941 to $3,460 in 1945, and benefits, particularly contributions to the thrift fund, increased at an even greater rate.

One of the most important costs, that of finding new oil, climbed sharply for a number of reasons. Not only did the drilling of new wells have to bear the generally increased wartime costs; the necessity to drill to greater average depths than earlier added significantly to the expense. The average cost of dry holes drilled rose from $62,000 in 1943 to $105,000 in 1944; the average cost of new producing wells increased at the same time from $47,000 to $66,500.[42]

Income was determined largely by government controls. Humble's earnings from operating government-owned plants were fixed by contract, subject to renegotiation. The gross-income ceiling on Humble's other operations was set by price controls through the Office of Price Administration. Prices, therefore, did not rise to a point where Humble derived much benefit from the saving in unit costs resulting from increased volume, as would presumably have been the case under normal operations of the market. And its tremendously increased production, by far the larger source of earnings, depleted low-cost reserves which were replaced at far higher costs.

Humble Oil & Refining Company's net earnings were relatively low in 1942, when the submarine menace interfered with shipment by tanker. The earnings increased in 1943 and 1944 but fell again in 1945. For the four war years Humble had total net earnings, before federal income taxes, of $289,000,000; the average net earnings on net worth (after taxes) were 13 per cent.

Of these earnings in the war years, Humble plowed back more than half, an average of 53.5 per cent in 1941–1945 as compared with 51.2 in 1936–1940 and 57.7 in 1931–1935. In 1942 stockholders received $2.00 per share, as they had every year from 1937; in 1943 shares were split two to one, and on the doubled number the owners received $1.25 a share in 1943 and $1.50 in 1944 and 1945. (See Appendix II, Tables I and II.)

Humble's earnings during the war years, 1942–1945, came largely from the Production Department. Of the company's consolidated net income before federal income taxes, about three-quarters was derived from the production of crude oil—the result of a tremendous volume and the comparatively small production expense in the early war period resulting from the earlier high development of its enormous reserves. Less than 10 per cent of the total was earned by pipeline operations; reduced tariffs, despite capacity operations, produced a considerably lower income than the 7 per cent ceiling provided for by the consent decree of 1942. Refining owed its earnings of approximately 10 per cent of the total to capacity operations at the Baytown refinery and to cost-plus operations of government war plants. The Sales Department's earnings of about 4 per cent of the total were derived principally from sales to airfields and war-industry plants. Crude oil purchasing and sales, in spite of large volume, brought up the rear with a contribution of approximately 1.5 per cent of Humble's total net earnings.

In the years of America's participation in World War II Humble produced crude oil measured in hundreds of millions of barrels and furnished pipeline transportation for its own crude and even a larger volume purchased from others. It manufactured such products vital to the war effort as aviation gasolines and fuel oils in tens of millions of barrels, toluene in millions of barrels, and over a hundred thousand tons of butadiene and Butyl for making rubber products. These were some of the company's tangible contributions to the war effort. There is no way of measuring the savings to the nation, strained by war shortages, resulting from Humble's reserve capacity in nearly all its operations at the start of the war. Nor is it possible to evaluate the work of its administrative and technological specialists who served in government agencies and war-research laboratories and in other ways outside the company's own operations. Such were the contributions of this company to "one of the great industrial accomplishments in the history of warfare," as the official history of the Petroleum Administration for War characterizes the record of the American oil industry in World War II.

Chapter 24

POSTWAR MANAGEMENT, MANUFACTURING, AND MARKETING 1945–1948

While Humble was still supplying oil for war, its Board of Directors and top managers began to plan for conversion to peace. They knew that, after several years in which military needs had had to be met, regardless of costs and operations, and prices had been under close government controls, the company would have to be ready to make comprehensive changes throughout all operations in converting to a peacetime economy.[1]

The question was how abrupt those changes would be. A 1944 analysis of Humble's probable postwar problems was predicated on the assumption that the country's global responsibilities would permit only gradual demobilization and that conversion to the civilian market would accordingly be gradual, so that the decreasing demands of the armed forces would be offset by increasing civilian requirements. As the end of the war approached, however, the expectation of gradual conversion gave way before the prospect of rapid demobilization. In the summer of 1945, on the advice of distinguished economists and in agreement with the views of nearly all oil industry leaders, the Humble Board of Directors decided to prepare for a severe and protracted slump in the oil market after the conclusion of hostilities.[2]

They planned a broad program of conversion. Expecting a decline in demand for some time after the war, they planned for a reduction in most operations, but they decided upon an aggressive campaign to increase sales in Texas. Anticipating a great increase in demand over the long run, they placed the greatest emphasis on the search for new oil. Obvious immediate needs were to recondition plant and equipment, strengthen research, convert the operating force to peacetime operations, and assimilate into the Humble organization the employees returning from military or other war services.

THE POSTWAR ORGANIZATION

Effective as the Humble organization had proved to be during the war, certain groups would obviously have to be strengthened, and thousands of men returning from war would have to be placed in positions suitable to their skills and rank. The restiveness late in the war of American labor in general, and of a portion of Humble's own refinery employees in particular, foreshadowed a more difficult time in employee relations. However, the first steps in organizational changes came at the very top, where the growth of the administrative function necessitated the addition of new executives or managers and where normal vacancies brought promotions.

The responsibilities of the company's chief executive had in recent years grown to be exceedingly heavy, and President Wiess was ready to transfer some of his burden to other shoulders. Early in 1945 Hines H. Baker, director and vice-president, was elected executive vice-president, not to act as chief executive but to share some of Wiess's work. Baker's experience since he joined Humble in 1919 had been broad, and for many years he had worked closely with Wiess.

Early in 1945 Humble lost one of its strongest executives with the resignation of Vice-President John R. Suman to become a director and vice-president of Standard Oil Company (New Jersey).[3] Suman's influence in Humble had been both broad and deep. More than any other man, he was responsible for the technological revolution in Humble's production methods. He had also taken a lead in the reorganization and strengthening of the producing organization; he had promoted both its unification and the decentralization of authority and responsibility, thus setting an example for the whole Humble organization; and he had been influential in the training and selection of strong men for the Production Department's top operating management. He had also helped to initiate and had contributed to the development of Humble's employee relations organization and program. His influence had, moreover, reached far beyond the bounds of the company. He had been one of the leaders in the Texas oil industry in promoting the improvement of production methods. And, by attending meetings of professional and oil industry associations, serving on industry committees, and appearing at hearings before government agencies, he had been influential in helping to spread throughout the entire industry interest and confidence in more efficient and less wasteful methods of oil recovery.

Suman's resignation and Baker's new responsibilities necessitated several moves up the executive ladder. Frame, director for production, was promoted to a vice-presidency. Carl E. Reistle, Jr., who since 1940 had been chief petroleum engineer, was appointed general superintendent of production and the next year was made manager of the Production Department. Harry W. Ferguson, who since 1941 had been manager of refining operations, was elected director and was given Baker's responsibility for refining and, two years later, for sales.

Other appointments and promotions helped to make the years 1945–1948 an outstanding period in Humble's organizational history. Early in 1945 Frank A. Watts was made sales manager, and Dr. H. D. Wilde was put in charge of all the research groups—geophysics, production, and refining—with the title of research manager. In 1946 Chief Geologist Morgan J. Davis was appointed manager of the Exploration Department (the new name of the Geologic, Lease and Scouting Department). Ray H. Horton, since 1944 head of the Production Department's employee relations, was appointed general manager of employee relations under Director Harris. And Donald F. Haynes, who had joined the company in 1918 as secretary to Vice-President Fondren and had been assistant manager of the Crude Oil Department since 1940, was appointed to the managership under Director Neath. Two years later Harris and Neath were elevated to vice-presidencies, and Nelson Jones was promoted to general attorney and head of the trial division of the Law Department.

These appointments and promotions illustrate Humble's increasing tendency to set up departmental managerships below the board level. During the years of expansion and increasing specialization in operations, division of responsibility on the higher administrative levels had become imperative. The Board of Directors had become almost wholly a policy-making body; departmental managerships were intended to free the directors from immediate supervision of operations as well as to prepare the managers for possible board membership. Ferguson, the one new director elected during the early postwar years, had been advanced from a departmental managership. And two of the six managers appointed in the same period, Reistle and Davis, were within another three years to be elected to the board.

In these years, also, efforts were resumed to strengthen the administrative staff organization and administrative tools and practices.[4] Progress had been made in this area of administration before the war, but during the man-poor war years all energies were directed toward meeting more urgent needs. The rapid growth of the company's operations, together with the lack of time and personnel for making changes that were desirable but not immediately necessary, left many problems to be met after the end of hostilities.

One illustration of this situation is the Comptroller's Department. A broad postwar program, plans for which had been begun in 1944, was initiated as soon as the war was over. This meant changes in policies and objectives as well as in routine procedures. Significantly, it was recognized that, as the corporation grew and responsibility was necessarily more and more delegated to lower levels, the top administrators and managers would have to rely increasingly on accounting and operating reports. In order to produce useful data, it was necessary for the accountants to learn to understand operations better and record information that would be more useful in planning and control. Moreover, the work had grown to such proportions that more efficient methods of handling it had to be devised. For example, in 1946—a year in which the volume of routine accounting and clerical work reached an amount unequaled in Humble history—20,000,000 entries were made in accounting ledgers, nearly 3,000,000 customers' invoices were rendered, about 400,000 suppliers' invoices paid, and 500,000 payments made for oil purchases. Also, over 13,000 reports and tax returns were made to federal and state governments. In the next year entries in accounting ledgers increased 20 per cent and customers' invoices rendered rose by 67 per cent.

An obvious necessity was the simplification and standardization of accounting procedures. A first step was the preparation by the Comptroller's Department of a new accounting manual. This project, which was started before the war ended, required the analysis of the accounting policies and practices of the general and departmental accounting offices. Many changes and improvements were made and, so far as possible, were applied uniformly throughout the whole organization. The resulting manual was completed in 1946. A small staff was provided to assist the various accounting offices in using the manual, and plans were made for continued revision and improvement. Steps were also taken to establish control over the hundreds of statements and reports prepared by the Comptroller's Department and to simplify and standardize their contents.

Many organizational changes were made and projects initiated in the years 1945–1948 to strengthen the Comptroller's Department. A planning and research division was established; it was headed by O. L. Luper, who later became Controller (the present name of the position). A project was undertaken for analyzing and classifying jobs. A development program for accounting employees, emphasizing on-the-job training in company-wide operations and related accounting functions, was designed to provide better-trained personnel. Primary responsibility for the administrative aspects of all the company's taxes, except ad valorem, was centered in the tax division. Study and reorganization of the work within certain accounting offices provided a more effective allocation of functions and better administrative guidance. A more extensive installation of electric "punched-card" accounting machines was begun; crude-oil-purchase accounting was mechanized in 1948. These machines made possible the handling of expanding volumes of work at reduced cost, provided data more promptly, and made their use more flexible.

The aim was not merely to increase routine efficiency but particularly to improve the department's general effectiveness as a part of the administrative mechanism. For example, a realization had grown up over the years that the internal auditing staff should develop a better understanding of operations and work more constructively toward strengthening accounting as a management tool. Accordingly, in 1946 the auditors began to spend much time in the field, talking with the men, observing operations, and studying ways to improve the accounting with a view to using it more effectively for control purposes.

Studies were also undertaken of budget procedures and objectives. A first step toward using the budget for planning and control purposes was taken by closely comparing the field cost records of wells with budget estimates, a practice that was later expanded in co-operation with the management of the Production Department to include all capital expenditures. This procedure was designed to assist in the better estimating and control of field operating expense. In order to do this effectively, arrangements were made to provide cost data in a shorter time.

These first steps, and others that followed, contributed toward using the budget more effectively for planning and control. Under the system of budgeting formally adopted in the 1930s, departmental operating and capital budgets had been prepared by the departments' managers, largely on the basis of past operations, the forecasts of the Economics and Statistics Department, look-aheads on production and the drilling program by the Exploration Department, and the general goals and allocation of funds determined by the Board of Directors. Gradually here and there, but apparently first on a broad scale in the Production Department, the practice developed of having the preparation of departmental budgets begin at the lower operating units. The Production Department had a tradition of decentralization, but the immediate reasons for this new practice were a great increase in operations and the prospects of rapidly increasing costs, particularly for the expensive new offshore operations. From consultation with supervisors in the fields, district managers drew up proposed plans and budgets, guided by the general objectives and limits set by the board in Houston. These were then co-ordinated at divisional headquarters, and then, in turn, by departmental offices and by the Comptroller's Department in Houston. Final decision, of course, rested with the Board of Directors.

These developments in budgeting, together with the closer relations between the auditors and accountants and the field operating personnel, exemplify a general change long under way in the management of the company: the broadening of the functions and responsibilities of lower management and the increasing communication between the various levels of management from the top administrative officers to regional or local units. While the Board of Directors still set the general goals, decided what funds would be available, and had final authority over the budget, the originating of plans and budgets for operations had become broadly dispersed. This dispersal forced the front-line supervisors to examine their operations critically with a view to possibilities and costs; and it required them to make plans, in consultation with their supervisor, for work over which they would have primary responsibility. Once a budget had been authorized, the division superintendent could proceed with more authority than formerly, without consulting the departmental manager but merely informing the latter of project expenditures under a regular reporting procedure. Periodic budget reviews, with revisions where necessary, gave sufficient flexibility to correct errors or meet changed conditions.

The impact of the expansion of Humble's operations was similarly felt after the war in other staff departments. For example, considerable reorganization took place in the Law Department. The earlier general functional groups were maintained, but the company's expanding operations necessitated a somewhat more detailed distribution of work in the nontrial division. The patent division was enlarged because the expansion of the company's research was greatly increasing the legal aspects of that work. At this time, also, branches of the Law Department began to be set up in the company's operating divisions, particularly in those outside Texas. Expansion also necessitated the employment of many new men, who were annually selected from among the best students in the graduating classes of law schools. The practice was adopted at this time of rotating the young lawyers, as opportunity offered, within the department in order to broaden their experience in handling various legal problems and thus counteract the narrowing effect of specialization.

These efforts to expand and strengthen the company's administration and administrative procedures were paralleled by the rebuilding and expansion of the employee force. A large percentage of employees on military leave returned after separation from the services; although a wartime army poll had revealed that 50 per cent of the men in the United States Army preferred not to go back to their old jobs, 83.5 per cent of Humble's employees on military leave had returned by the end of 1946. Seventy-nine Humble men were reported to have died in service. Out of 18,000 employees at the end of 1947, nearly half had been with the company ten years or more; the average length of service was ten years and the average age was thirty-six.[5]

A large number of new employees had to be added after the war. The total increase in the first year or two was hardly more than the number of returned veterans, but the many retirements and voluntary separations after the war made necessary hiring on a large scale. By the end of 1946 over 3,000 veterans who had never worked for Humble had been hired. By the end of 1948 the total number of the company's employees had increased to nearly 19,000 from less than 16,000 at the end of 1944. The turnover rate, however, had fallen.

In these disturbed and inflationary postwar years Humble liberalized the application of its old employee policies.[6] External pressures, notably the rise of living costs, were forcing wages upward all over the country. The Oil Workers International Union was exerting pressure upon the whole oil industry, and Humble's Employees Federations were demanding and stiff bargainers. Like the oil industry generally, in which labor costs are relatively lower than in some other large industries, Humble was able to follow comparatively generous practices. As President Wiess said, Humble "was privileged" to be able to pay its employees well.[7] The result was a stable operating organization of high ability and outstanding morale.

As of January 1, 1946, changes were made in the Annuity & Thrift Plan. The principal new annuity feature was the guarantee to the retired employee of a life annuity of $2.00 annually for each $3.00 he had contributed, with provision for payments for five years to qualified beneficiaries in case of earlier death. Humble also continued to make special annual contributions to the Thrift Fund—$2,550,000 in 1946 and $5,650,000 in the banner year 1948. And late in 1948 it recognized inflation by voluntarily providing additional retirement income of not less than $25.00 to annuitants whose income, including Social Security, was less than $250 per month; however, the total payment, including the special payment, could not exceed $250 per month. The Annuity & Thrift Plan was so popular that on January 1, 1948, 97.7 per cent of all eligible employees were participants; the vast majority were contributing the maximum amount.[8]

Revisions in the Benefits Plan included the elimination in 1946 of the seven-day waiting period during which a sick employee with less than three years' service was ineligible for benefits. A new plan, which went into effect in the autumn of 1947, generally liberalized survivor benefits, increased the amount of benefits to a totally disabled employee, and permitted retired employees under certain circumstances to continue a part of their group insurance.[9] In 1947, also, Humble installed a group hospitalization and surgical benefit plan on a company-wide basis for which it paid a part of the premium. Humble employees had for some time had hospitalization and surgical plans, but earlier these had been administered by various insurance carriers through contracts with the bargaining agencies and the Houston Humble Club.[10]

The Humble vacation program, which had always been progressive compared with general industrial practice, was further liberalized on January 1, 1946. All employees were then granted two weeks' vacation after a single year's service; two years later, following Magnolia's example, twenty-five-year men were granted four weeks of vacation.

Safety continued to receive careful attention with good results. In 1947, when over forty-nine accidents per million man-hours occurred in drilling, Chief Safety Engineer Roaper emphatically described this record as "probably the worst in the industry." This record apparently resulted from the large number of recently hired and inexperienced men as well as from deeper and more difficult drilling. The refinery accident rate still continued its upward trend, a trend in the entire industry which may have been due to a combination of circumstances, including additions of inexperienced personnel, increased construction activity, and the handling of increasingly volatile materials. The terrible Texas City disaster of 1946, resulting from an explosion in the harbor on a ship in no way connected with Humble, cost the company heavily in tanks of oil awaiting shipment but demonstrated the sincerity of the company's interest in its employees' welfare. President Hanrahan of Humble Pipe Line Company is quoted as having given instructions that, if the attempt to save company facilitites should involve the risk of injury or death to employees, the property must go. Though two Humble employees were hospitalized as a result of the explosion and fire, not a single one was killed. This attitude contributed to public as well as employee good will. In 1948 the accident frequency rate for the whole company was low, and in the next year it reached the lowest point in the company's history.[11]

The average Humble employee apparently regarded annuities, benefits, insurance, paid vacations, and a safety program as less important than the money in his pay envelope. The inflation which set in with the dropping of price controls on June 30, 1946, inspired the Humble Employee Federations to request pay increases or bonuses. Robert Oliver, formerly president of the Baytown OWIU local and now state CIO director, in mid-October announced a drive to organize Humble's pipeline and refinery employees. In October the OWIU's national wage-policy committee demanded a wage increase of 30 cents per hour.[12] Humble, however, granted a general $25.00 per month cost-of-living allowance, thus postponing an increase in the basic rate of pay which, experience indicated, if once granted could not be retrieved. Sinclair was the first to respond to the demand of the CIO; on November 15 it granted an increase of 18 cents an hour ($31.20 a month), with an escalator clause. The Texas Company granted an increase of $30.00 per month.

Humble's action in 1946 set its pattern for the next two years. During 1947 it inaugurated a series of pay raises in the form of both increased cost-of-living allowances and wage and salary increases which were well ahead of the OWIU's 1948 campaign for a "third round" of wage increases. In May, 1948, when the Baytown Employees Federation was asking for an increase of 21½ cents per hour base pay, Humble offered, and the bargaining agency accepted, a wage increase of 12 cents per hour, a salary increase of 5 per cent with a minimum increase of $21.00 per month, and a continuance of the current cost-of-living allowance. During this period the OWIU was trying to supersede the Employees Federation as the bargaining agency for the Baytown refinery employees, but, in the election of June 2–3, 1948, conducted by the National Labor Relations Board, it polled only 29 per cent of the votes cast as compared with 35 per cent in 1943.[13]

In the postwar period the Baytown Employees Federation was especially demanding. In January, 1947, for example, certain employees, acting individually and as officers of the federation, sued Humble for $6,000,000 in back wages for "walking and make-ready time," in keeping with the currently popular portal-to-portal claims, plus an equal amount as a penalty. This suit was shortly dismissed by the court.

Certain old areas of contention, such as seniority and alleged improper classification of employees, and, especially, the contracting of work to outsiders, persisted. Complaints about contract labor were a recurrent theme on the pipelines, in production, and at the refinery. The production employees complained that, when so much work was done by outside contractors, their own opportunities for advancement to gang pusher or driller were reduced. Employees further objected to the "scab wages" allegedly paid by some contractors, particularly by those who employed principally Negroes and Mexicans. The company answered that such work as the building of derricks and tanks had always been done principally by contract, that other companies contracted all their pipeline construction and even drilling—Humble did more of its own drilling than most of the other major companies in the area in which it operated—and that contracting stabilized Humble's employment.

The argument that contracting contributed to the stability of the working force and helped to prevent layoffs was certainly to a large extent justified by past experience, but there were also other justifications for its use. A decrease in the proportionate amount of drilling by company rigs, with a consequent reduction in opportunities for promotion, was a price that, in a competitive economy and industry, the employees of Humble and comparable companies had to pay for their other advantages. The "Gimmes," as the Humble benefits are sometimes called, plus overtime and travel time, were so expensive that the company found it advantageous to use contractors to drill many of its wells and to handle major construction projects.

One cost eliminated by contracting was portal-to-portal pay. For example, field employees in production and on the pipelines in the 1920s and 1930s had gone to work on their own time and returned on the company's time, but in 1941 Humble had agreed to pay for all the time over one hour spent in going to and from company headquarters to the place of work. The significant portal-to-portal decision of the United States Supreme Court had subsequently required Humble to pay for all the time spent in going to and from work. Consequently, a Humble crew that drove two hours each way to repair a pipeline would work four hours and be paid for eight. To arrange with a nearby contractor to keep the line in good working order would reduce expenses—and also the amount of pipeline work available to Humble employees. The rule of law established by the court was, however, altered by the Portal-to-Portal Act of 1947.

Transfer and travel-expense allowances to the Humble employees transferred on the company's initiative also increased labor costs, particularly in the Production Department. Travel allowances had originated when the company adopted the policy of transferring men from a surplus in one place to a shortage in another. After the mid-1930s Humble also paid "transfer allowances," which were intended to compensate the employee for the expenses of moving a household. During World War II these transfer allowances were put on a flat basis, varying with the employee's family status and other considerations.

Apparently the employees' discontent over certain matters did not outweigh their realization that Humble's wage rates were among the highest and its employee benefits were not equaled by any other oil company in the territory in which it operated. Baytown employees felt that in many respects the CIO members employed by other companies were merely catching up with the material benefits that Humble employees had long enjoyed.

Despite the hiring of a large number of new employees and the general postwar restiveness of American labor, Humble soon after the end of the war restored its total working force to the degree of skill and morale that had characterized the prewar organization. To maintain such a level of quality among employees, however, promised to become increasingly difficult. This was an important consideration in the decision of the company's top administrators to undertake a vigorous program of selection and training for executive positions.

Humble began immediately after the war to give greater attention to the appraisal of junior executives and supervisors and to programs for the development of men for middle and high managerial posts. T. W. Moore was assigned the work of organizing a new management development program. For two years he studied training problems and possibilities and examined the executive training programs of various schools and of other companies. He especially consulted with the director of Jersey Standard's program of executive development, which had been undertaken during the war in order to assure an adequate supply after the war of potential executives with the breadth and experience required for effective management.

Humble adopted two programs for executive development. It sent to the Advanced Management Program at the Graduate School of Business Administration, Harvard University, such key executives as the company's comptroller, the managers of the exploration, production, and sales departments, the assistant to the director for refining, and the vice-president of Humble Pipe Line Company. And it adopted a program of formal training within the company. Humble's own course, launched experimentally in 1948 in West Texas, was designed particularly for middle management. The course, which occupied five eight-hour days, was conducted by the training division of the Employee Relations Department, but the instructors were from operating management and from the Board of Directors. The subjects included the history and philosophy of the company, basic information in regard to its operations, and concepts of management, particularly human relations in such matters as handling grievances. The case system was used, and discussions were carried on by the conference method.

The establishment of a formal management development program constituted further recognition of the fact that relations within the company could not be left to chance, and that executive development could not safely be entrusted solely to the individual manager. The size of the company and the complexity of its operations, the growing independence of the employees, the large number of new technical employees without experience in refining or field work, and the increasing difficulty of maintaining informal communication—all these underscored the need for special attention to training for management. At the same time, new concepts of group leadership pointed to the possibility of training managers and supervisors to a competence in managing men similar to the engineers' or the skilled workmen's ability to deal with materials and machines. The professionalization of management was thus reaching down into the ranks.

CONVERSION OF REFINING TO PEACETIME OPERATIONS

Of all Humble's operations, refining was the first to be strongly affected by the ending of hostilities, and it was also the most easily converted from war to peace. Baytown's total number of employees remained about the same as before, although some turnover was experienced and the research and technical-service staffs were enlarged. The refinery's principal new problems were to plan manufacture for the civilian market and to adjust old equipment to new uses. Faced with neither manpower, equipment, nor crude oil shortages, Baytown's research, engineering, and operating organizations not only converted smoothly to manufacture for a civilian market but also improved products and expanded output in the early years after the war.

Most of the war work of the Refining Department, as had been anticipated, was discontinued abruptly.[14] With V-J Day in sight, the government canceled its contract for toluene, and on August 20, 1945, accordingly, the Baytown Ordnance Works was closed down.[15] The Defense Supplies Corporation also canceled its contracts for 100-octane aviation gasoline, and the production of that gasoline at Baytown was discontinued, as were operations at the fractionation units and at nine thermal cracking coils. Humble's Ingleside refinery was closed when the government butadiene contracts with the higher-cost plants were canceled shortly after the end of the war. This left the San Antonio refinery as the last of Humble's smaller refineries. The Butadiene Plant at Baytown continued to operate, however, as did the Butyl Rubber Plant. The latter continued to run well above its rated annual capacity of 30,000 tons, and, in fact, at the end of 1945 was producing enough synthetic rubber to supply nearly half the inner-tube requirements of the whole country.[16]

Humble quickly adjusted its refining operations to supplying civilian needs; within a week after the end of the war, Baytown was manufacturing new high-quality products for civilian use. The adjustment of price ceilings on different products at different times caused some difficulty in balancing refinery yields with the demand, so that for a few months after the war there was a surplus of gasoline and a shortage of fuel oil.[17] But the imbalance was soon corrected. Light crude naphthas, which in wartime had gone to the toluene plant, and co-polymer and alkylate, which had gone into 100-octane gasoline, were now available for the improvement of motor gasoline. These made possible Humble's sensational high-octane Esso Extra.

Only a few days after the government's closing of the Baytown Ordnance Works, Humble reopened it under lease from the government. Early in 1946 the company purchased the plant for $7,000,000, a price "based on the cost of the usable equipment purchased, less 10 per cent annually for depreciation and obsolescence." [18] No longer manufacturing a constituent of TNT, this plant instead produced aromatic solvents, such as Solvesso Toluene and Solvesso Xylene, for use in paints, varnishes, and insect sprays, and for the improvement of the quality of gasolines.[19] It was an important factor in Humble's early and firm entry into the postwar market for solvents, aviation gasoline, and high-octane motor gasoline.

The Baytown research and technical-service staffs were expanded and were assigned to work on the manufacture of civilian products. While the latter group concerned itself largely with questions of planning and costs, the research men worked principally on finding ways to improve the quality of products and on raising the proportionate yields of the more valuable products from a given quantity of crude oil. The new higher-compression automobile engines, especially, required a better-quality gasoline.[20] Little time then remained for fundamental research.

An unexpectedly large postwar demand for petroleum products, particularly for gasoline, soon caused the Baytown refining organization to restore its equipment to full use. There was a brief slackening of demand in 1946, but thereafter, contrary to earlier expectations, it became necessary to utilize well over 100 per cent of the Baytown refinery's rated capacity. In the spring and summer of 1947 the thermal cracking coils were restored to service, the naphtha fractionating units were reactivated, the co-polymer unit was put back on stream, and the output of Catalytic Cracking Unit No. 2 was increased by 7,000 barrels daily. In September, 1947, Baytown broke all its records with a throughput of 257,000 barrels in a single day, although its daily rated capacity was still only 190,000 barrels. On May 8, 1947,[21] the Baytown refinery celebrated the processing of its billionth *barrel* of crude oil; this was even more impressive, though greeted with less fanfare, than its wartime production of its billionth gallon of 100-octane gasoline.[22]

Important additions soon had to be made at Baytown. The demand for motor gasoline stimulated the demand for motor oil and brought about the building of Humble's MEK (methyl-ethyl-ketone) plant, for the solvent extraction of wax from coastal, light West Texas, and Panhandle lube stocks; the plant went into operation early in 1948.[23] And work was started on pipe still No. 4, which, with a daily capacity of 45,000 barrels, was intended to replace outmoded shell stills and achieve sharper fractionation of lube crudes. Its completion in 1949 was to bring Baytown's capacity to 260,000 barrels daily and to make that refinery for a time the largest* in the United States.[24]

Other important additions at Baytown were also made or started at this time. In 1948 a new tanker loading dock was constructed.[25] A very large central shop building, completed the next year, was designed to bring most of the mechanical crafts under one roof so that repairs could be made more efficiently and economically.[26] The building of a new research center at the Baytown refinery was begun.

Developments at Baytown in these postwar years may be summarized by a few selected statistics. Capital expenditures totaled $33,000,000. Crude runs were about 25 per cent higher in 1948 than in 1945. But net earnings dropped severely in 1946 and, despite expansion in refinery

* In 1948 refineries of Gulf and Humble in Texas and of Esso Standard in Louisiana, according to Bureau of Mines figures, had capacities close to 200,000 barrels daily, Gulf's with 206,000 being the largest.

investments and runs, in 1948 were about the same as in the last year of the war. (See, also, Appendix II, Table X.)

Although the dynamic demand of the postwar market was favorable to the refining industry, Baytown's growth was also based on the improvement of the quality of its products, notably gasoline. This was one reason for the tremendous volume of sales to Esso Standard—an average of 85.2 per cent of a greatly increased Baytown output in the years from 1946 through 1948. It was also an important factor in the strengthening of Humble's position in the Texas market immediately after the war.

INCREASING SALES AND PRESTIGE IN TEXAS

One of the most interesting developments late in the war and in the early postwar years was the change in Humble's policy with respect to marketing in Texas and the consequent strengthening of the Sales Department. The directors and executives had long hoped to make the company's sales operations commensurate with its other activities in the state, but they had never strongly committed Humble's resources to the realization of that hope. In 1945 they made such a commitment. The Board of Directors had by then come to believe that the growing Texas market would provide a potentially profitable outlet for Baytown's high-quality products.[27] Competition would obviously be strong, but many of the conditions that had made the market so chaotic in the 1930s had largely disappeared.

Nearly a year before the end of the war the Humble board decided upon an aggressive postwar campaign to increase sales in Texas. Plans were accordingly made for the reorganization of the department, the improvement of products for the postwar civilian market, the expansion and strengthening of sales outlets, the development of more economical distribution facilities, and a vigorous sales-promotion program.

The reorganization of the department was begun in January, 1945. Frank A. Watts was then given full charge of the department, a responsibility that had for many years in effect been borne by the Marketing Committee. An engineer by training, Watts had come from California in 1919 to join Humble during the Ranger boom and had in 1928 been appointed sales engineer in charge of construction. Since 1938 he had been head of the company's central Purchasing Department, except during fifteen months when he served as director of the Materials Division of the Petroleum Administration for War.[28]

A systematic reorganization of the department, with a clear-cut distribution of responsibility and authority, was put into effect as soon as the war was over. The department's head office in Houston included staff and operational groups directly concerned with sales. Specialized salesmen handled large contract sales to airlines, railroads, industrial plants, and road-building and maintenance concerns. Engineers were used extensively to service large customers, for example, to advise railroads and industrial plants on lubricants and anticorrosion products. One salesman specialized in conducting meetings to promote sales to farmers. A division for specialty products, besides having charge of sales, worked on the development of such products in a special plant run by the Sales Department. The marketing of tires, batteries, and accessories was under a manager who served as the liaison between the Atlas Supply Company and the retailers.

Responsibility for sales territories was also clearly defined. The marketing territory for sales other than large direct contract sales was divided into four divisions, each of which consisted of four districts. The division managers were assisted by staffs similar to those at headquarters in Houston, were responsible only to the general manager at headquarters, and had considerable authority over operations. The district managers had charge of district salesmen and of bulk-station and retail-station personnel, and referred only the more important matters to the division manager. The district office had chief responsibility for sales promotion within its area, but it could call on divisional staffs and specialists from the head office for assistance.

The first postwar move to strengthen sales was the introduction of greatly improved motor gasolines without raising prices.[29] Two weeks after gasoline rationing was terminated in August, 1945, automobiles, powered by wartime gasoline of 70 or 76 motor octane rating, drove into Humble stations with their engines knocking and departed humming, fueled by Humble's premium gasoline, Esso Extra, with a research octane number of 95, or by the regular grade, Humble Motor Fuel, with a research octane number of 85. Because of the quick shift of the Baytown refinery to manufacturing high-octane motor gasoline, Humble was the first company in Texas to supply such gasoline to the civilian market after the war. Although its competitors eventually improved their gasolines for the retail market, Humble kept a comfortable lead. The Texas motoring public, as a result, came to identify high octane and high performance with Humble gasoline. The marked superiority of its gasolines was probably the greatest asset in the quest for new business. Whereas total Texas gasoline sales increased by 9 per cent in the first three postwar months, the company registered a 39 per cent increase.

The rise in gasoline quality, together with the great postwar increase in the demand for products, spurred the expansion of Humble's marketing facilities. The Board of Directors stood ready to provide generous funds. The Sales Department's budget and planning staff, headed by Sales Manager Watts and Assistant Sales Manager R. M. Stephens, drew up programs. They were assisted by a newly organized market-research group and an enlarged and strengthened cost-accounting organization, which advised on the most profitable ways of increasing sales. These two groups maintained a continuous study of markets and of factors affecting costs and ultimate profits.

The most rapid and flexible method of increasing retail outlets, since building restrictions and materials shortages did not end with the war, was to sign up a large number of contract dealers. In the postwar months of 1945 the number of such dealers was increased by about a third. Humble had a substantial core of company-owned commission stations for which it set high standards, but these were not greatly increased in number.

Late in 1945, by returning to large-scale operations in the relatively thickly populated marketing territory of northeast Texas, Humble began to reclaim the territory from which it had withdrawn in the early 1930s. The first move was to purchase the properties in the Dallas–Fort Worth area of the Texas Pacific Coal & Oil Company, which had decided to withdraw from retail marketing. These properties, consisting of bulk stations, owned and leased service stations, and the delivery equipment of several agencies, had an average monthly sales volume of over a million gallons of gasoline. Nearly all Texas Pacific's 139 independent dealers joined Humble.[30]

Although Humble concentrated on expanding its sales effort in heavily populated northeastern Texas, it also regained some lost ground in West Texas. The Sales Department did not attempt at this time to re-enter the trans-Pecos area in West Texas, nor to enter the Panhandle. It did, however, expand its West Texas operations by adding bulk stations and retail outlets.

This campaign to expand the outlets for Humble products resulted in a considerable increase in the company's total number of bulk and retail stations. In the three years after 1945 the contract dealer stations more than doubled; they numbered about 1,700 at the end of 1948. The company-owned commission retail stations increased to only about 250. Because of the larger area served by each station, proportionately fewer bulk than retail stations were added.

The whole distribution pattern was affected by changes in the quality of products and in the plants required for their manufacture. High-octane gasoline could be produced only at plants equipped for catalytic cracking, and the refineries without such cracking equipment could no longer compete in the quality-gasoline market. Humble's Baytown refinery, like other plants equipped for catalytic cracking by the fluid or the Houdry process, consequently had a great competitive advantage over the small interior refineries which, because of their location near fields and markets, had earlier been strong competitors in the marketing of gasoline in Texas.

The geographic expansion of Humble's markets, together with the pressure of competition, made the reduction of transportation costs an especially vital element in successful competition. Some costs were rising steeply after the war, such as wages and the costs of materials and equipment. Yet in long-distance transportation as well as in local distribution the Sales Department reduced costs greatly, compared with what they would have been if old methods had been used. The significance of what might seem to be a small reduction per unit may be illustrated by the fact that an average saving of a small fraction of a cent per gallon on the transportation of gasoline from Baytown to retail outlets might in a year add up to a million dollars or more.

The most important development in Humble's long-distance transportation of products was the building of a products pipeline from Baytown to the Dallas–Fort Worth area. Although this line was built nearly twenty years after the first products line had been put into operation in the United States, that of the Jersey Standard group in Pennsylvania, it was the first important products line in Texas. In September, 1946, despite postwar shortages of pipe, Humble Pipe Line Company completed the construction of the line from Baytown to the Dallas–Fort Worth area, with terminals at Baytown and Irving and with three intermediate distributing points. The total cost was over $6,000,000. The line's worth was demonstrated at once; by September, 1947, it was delivering approximately half the gasoline sold by the Sales Department. By July, 1948, it was moving 400,000 gallons per day at a considerable saving as compared with tank-car and transport-truck charges.[31]

The closing of the Ingleside refinery near Corpus Christi in the autumn of 1945 and the earlier introduction of improved Esso Extra, which could be manufactured only at Baytown, also confronted the Sales Department with the problem of economically supplying gasoline to lower Southwest Texas. The problem was solved by leasing a tank terminal at Corpus Christi and transporting petroleum products from Baytown by barge via the Intercoastal Canal; this saved nearly nine-tenths of a cent per gallon in transportation costs.[32]

Still another course was adopted for supplying West Texas, which was too far from Baytown to be supplied from there without too high transportation costs. At first the regular grade was purchased from a refinery at Sweetwater and Esso Extra was brought the long distance from Baytown. Plans were made to overcome this transportation disadvantage by arranging with the Cosden Petroleum Corporation to supply both premium and regular grades according to Humble specifications from its Big Springs refinery. Cosden agreed to build a catalytic cracking unit in order to manufacture the Esso Extra grade.

Substantial savings were also made in the local distribution of products, changes that had come earlier in other progressive companies—for example, the Delaware Company—doing a large-volume business and not held to low maximum truckloads by state regulations as in Texas. The raising of the maximum truckload to a gross weight of 48,000 pounds, under the pressure of the wartime need for transportation and the shortage of tank cars, enabled Humble, by using large transport trucks carrying 5,000 gallons of gasoline per load, to make direct deliveries to retail outlets within a radius of eighty miles from its products pipeline and barge terminals and refineries and to supply stations at greater distances by contract carriers. Many of these trucks were obtained on contract at rates 20 per cent lower than tank-car rates.[33] This method of direct delivery of gasoline from terminals to retail outlets proved a real boon to cost reduction.

Simultaneous with the adoption of the use of these large transport trucks was the inauguration of a "big dump" program. Storage tanks of sufficient size to receive motor fuel in full transport loads were installed at service stations managed by commission agents; and dealers with sufficient volume to justify the installation of large underground tanks, if it appeared that they would continue to do business with the company, were given credit where they were not able to pay for the full load. This direct delivery program enabled Humble to effect sizable economies through bypassing bulk plants; adjustments were made to compensate bulk-station commission agents for the loss of business.

Substantial progress was also made in reducing the cost of distributing packaged products and specialties from Baytown and the Houston specialty manufacturing plant. The use of truck vans with half the capacity of a boxcar reduced the warehouse space required, speeded up deliveries, and reduced transportation costs substantially.[34]

Cost was also a paramount consideration in the great construction and modernization program which the new sales policy made necessary. When the Sales Department's planning staff had determined what should be done and had allocated available funds, the engineering staff had primary responsibility for planning and constructing stations, terminals, and bulk plants and for equipping them for efficient operations. The engineering group was also responsible for the rehabilitation of many properties that had necessarily been neglected in the war years. This modernization and expansion program in the years 1945–1948 added approximately $11,000,000 to the department's gross investment.

The expansion and improvement of distribution facilities was paralleled by the enlargement and upgrading of the personnel of the sales organization. No outsiders were brought into management. But the number of employees was approximately doubled in the years from 1946 through 1948, and the postwar availability of new manpower made possible more careful selection and consequent improvement of the quality of the sales personnel.

An extensive training and sales-promotion program was instituted to raise the standards and effectiveness of the sales effort. The program was initiated early in 1945 by a meeting of district managers in Houston for briefing on products, distribution, and sales training. In 1946 annual sales and cost meetings were started which were attended by members of the various levels of the management organization, ranging from sales districts to the head office in Houston. These gatherings gave to men who otherwise had no way of meeting one another an opportunity to discuss problems of mutual interest, and they helped to build morale and enthusiasm for the company's sales program. Annual division and quarterly district meetings were also started, and training units were installed in districts. An important feature of the retail training program was the operation on a salaried basis of five retail stations to serve as models for service stations selling Humble products and as training schools for station personnel. Special training in product information, sales techniques, operations management, and safety was also given to salesmen and bulk agents who called on dealers, consumers, and commercial and industrial users.

District sales-promotion units were responsible for continuous new business solicitation.[35] They introduced the advertising and other promotional campaigns developed in co-operation with the Houston staff. For publicizing the opening of new Humble stations the sales-promotion group utilized captive balloons, banners, and Hawaiian orchids in a spectacular fashion. Loyal Humble employees on such occasions turned out by the hundreds to swell the blocks-long bumper-to-bumper procession of automobiles waiting to be filled. No one in the neighborhood could help knowing that a new Humble station had been opened.[36] The usual result was the prompt establishment of an adequate basis in customer and community good will for the subsequent development of a satisfactory business.

Humble employed newspaper advertising in these early postwar years far beyond its earlier practice. It accompanied the introduction of the new Esso Extra gasoline with advertising in virtually every newspaper in Texas. It continued to broadcast the Southwest Conference football games, which had proved a particularly effective advertising device. In the spring of 1945 it established *The Humble Way*, which was the company's first general house organ since the demise in 1922 of the *Humble Magazine*.

The establishment of a general house organ was suggested to the Board of Directors by Hines H. Baker, then executive vice-president for refining, sales, and public relations. Although aimed principally at the enlightenment of stockholders and employees, *The Humble Way* was widely distributed by mail and through schools and public libraries. It was edited by G. A. Mabry in such a fashion as to appeal to all members of the reading public who were interested in oil—which in Texas meant almost every adult. It specialized in simple, well-written, nontechnical articles, effectively illustrated with photographs and easily understandable graphs and charts. It was distinguished by its colored reproductions of paintings of oil-field and other Texas scenes by such artists as Kenneth Harris, Jackson Lee Nesbitt, Avery Johnson, Jerry Bywaters, and particularly E. M. Schiwetz. Humble's encouragement of regional art pleasantly affected a discriminating section of the public that was less susceptible to direct publicity measures.

Humble's products price policy continued to be to follow major competition rather than to lead in making price changes. Its prices, grade by grade, were not higher than other companies' even though it consistently held the octane rating of its gasoline higher than its competitors'. The record of changes in the price of regular gasoline shows that in no instance did Humble lead in the six advances and one reduction made after the end of war controls, although it did not lag far behind in adjusting prices to changed conditions. It maintained a fixed spread between the tank-wagon prices and the retail prices posted in its commission agents' stations; the margin was raised from 4 cents per gallon to 4½ in March, 1947, and to 5 cents in September of the next year.

By the end of 1948 Humble had nearly achieved its objective of increasing its sales to a position commensurate with its leadership in other phases of the oil industry in Texas. In that year it was responsible for over 14 per cent of the total tax-paid gasoline sales in Texas. Although still second to The Texas Company in Texas sales of tax-paid gasoline, Humble was first in the territory in which both operated; and the Sales Department was confident that, by continuing along the lines already laid down, it would before long stand first in the entire state of Texas. Gratifying as the Sales Department's new position was to Humble's pride, it was also significant that increased gasoline sales had accompanied and contributed to a steady rise in Humble's reputation as a "really good company." More and more Texas motorists were becoming familiar with its Esso Extra gasoline, clean restrooms, and courteous and efficient service-station attendants.

From the viewpoint of both volume and net revenue, gasoline was by far the most important product sold. During the years from 1946 through 1948 the total consumption of tax-paid gasoline in Texas increased 50 per cent but Humble's sales increased 187 per cent, while its net sales revenue from gasoline increased over 300 per cent. An important factor in this rise was of course the quality of Humble gasoline. Esso Extra in 1948 was still more than five octane numbers ahead of the premium grades of competitors and even three points above Esso Standard's rating. By July 1, 1948, Humble had virtually discontinued the service-station sale of its third-grade gasoline, Thriftane. Sales of aviation gasoline fell off sharply after the war; but, by the aggressive solicitation of airline accounts, aviation sales were raised greatly in the second half of 1946. By October, although its aviation lubricating-oil sales were confined to a single airline, Humble was selling gasoline to six out of eight of the leading airlines operating in Texas and supplying 65 per cent of the state's airline consumption. Its aviation gasoline sales doubled during 1947 and nearly doubled again in 1948.

Although the sale of motor oil also increased, it lagged far behind gasoline sales, primarily because of the smaller amount of oil consumed by the new automobiles. Humble never relaxed its efforts to increase motor-oil sales by such devices as its 1946 "Quarts That Count" contest for service stations and dealers. The company's sales of industrial lubricating oil fell off by nearly 30 per cent from 1945 to 1948. While the cessation of wartime demand was the principal reason for this decline, other important factors were improvements in lubricating engineering and the gradual disappearance of the old group of industrialists who had been accustomed to purchasing from Humble because of personal friendship with "Johnny" Bonner, who had retired as a director in 1933.

A highly specialized group responsible for Houston office sales and for technical service to buyers of products aided materially in registering substantial increases in sales from 1945 to 1948. In January, 1947, Humble began to supply the TBA line to its contract dealers as well as its commission agents; the net revenue from these products nearly quadrupled. The Sales Department's net revenue from specialty products more than doubled; the sales force emphasized Humble's own products, including a recently developed full line of high-quality protective coatings and a DDT emulsible concentrate for the farm and ranch trade. Fuel oil showed the greatest percentage increase, but the amount sold was relatively small. Although the sale of all these products increased, in total sales they were individually of relatively little importance.

While achieving the objective of raising Humble's share of sales in Texas, the Sales Department also raised its profits. The rate of return on gross investment, which had been negative or small in the 1930s and substantial in the war years, declined severely in 1946 but rose slightly in 1947 and considerably in 1948. Higher prices, larger volume, and greater efficiency contributed to this record despite a substantial rise in wages and costs of materials and equipment.

The program of expansion, sales promotion, training, and cost reduction instituted in 1945 had thus in the early postwar years already brought excellent results. The faith of Humble's directors and officers in their company's veteran salespeople was justified when, with high-quality products, new and capable help, adequate financing, and unqualified support from the top, the sales management established records in both volume of sales and efficiency of operations. Field personnel, secure in the knowledge that their efforts were being recognized and confident of management's full support, joined in bringing about a notable accomplishment. The Sales Department's operations were still small compared with Humble's other operations. But the department was no longer insignificant, operationally or financially. It was important in making Humble favorably known in Texas.[37]

Chapter 25

THE NEVER-ENDING QUEST FOR OIL AND GAS

THE GREATEST CHALLENGE to Humble's planners and operations managers at the end of the war was to assure the company of adequate crude for the years ahead. Although Humble still had the largest oil reserves in the United States and possibly as large gas reserves as any other company, its ratio of oil reserves to current production had fallen—as had the industry's—during the war. The executives held that Humble must find at least enough oil each year to replace the amount produced and thus maintain or increase reserves each year.[1]

As the end of the war approached, Humble's administrators made plans to manage producing operations as far as possible in accordance with current demand, to drill on proved properties the wells required to protect leases, and generally to restore the company's production and transportation of oil to their accustomed efficiency and to build up surplus capacity. However, they planned to place the strongest emphasis on the acquisition of new reserves.[2]

But the rapid recovery of the civilian market upset all plans. So great was the early postwar demand that by the end of 1945 the national oil inventory had been reduced to 13,500,000 barrels below that at the end of the crucial war year 1944. The rise in prices after the removal of government controls in 1946 gave a tremendous spur to the industry. All operations were soon driven to their limits. In Texas, oil wells were allowed to produce 291 days in 1946, 324 days in 1947, and every day in 1948—even in the crucial war year, 1944, they had been allowed only 281 days.

The situation was reminiscent of that which had developed after World

War I, but with important differences. There was the same upsurge in demand, prices, and costs, the same plentiful supply of capital, and the same drive to get control of proved or prospective oil lands. However, there was not the same fear of the actual exhaustion of the natural resource, although oilmen knew that to find new oil and to produce it were becoming more difficult in our country. And some feared that oil finding and production might in the not-very-distant future reach costs so high that the domestically produced crude could not compete with lower-cost production abroad or with alternate sources of energy.

PRODUCING OIL FOR A BOOMING MARKET

Instead of being forced to reduce its 1946 production to the expected 1941, pre-Pearl Harbor level of 55,000,000 barrels, the Production Department—under Frame as director for production, Reistle as production manager, and R. C. Barbour as general superintendent—actually raised the crude produced to approximately 113,000,000 (a daily average of 309,473 barrels), which was slightly more than the production in the peak wartime year, 1944. Demand continued to rise. In 1947 production was increased to over 125,000,000 barrels (343,219, daily average) and in 1948 to approximately 135,000,000 (368,322, daily average)—almost three times as much as had been produced ten years earlier.

The increase was largely provided by development drilling. In 1946 war restrictions having been lifted, 600 wells were drilled on proved acreage, a large number in the Hawkins field in order to make up for the company's earlier inability on account of wartime restrictions to drill the number that would permit it to compete under the Railroad Commission's allocation formula. For similar reasons, many wells were also drilled in West Texas and on the King Ranch. The number drilled in proved areas fell off somewhat in 1947, after the completion of the Hawkins program, but in 1948 it rose even above the 1946 figure.

The accomplishment was greater than the number of wells would seem to indicate. Shortages in skilled manpower and materials continued for some time to be serious. Contract drillers were relatively scarce. And—most significant for the long run—it was necessary to drill deeper and deeper wells. In 1946 the average depth of all Humble's new wells was 7,000 feet as compared with 4,300 ten years earlier, and in 1948 Humble set a record by completing in Chambers County on the Gulf Coast, at a little over 12,000 feet, the deepest producing well in Texas.[3] Table 12, which gives the depth of the deepest well drilled by Humble year by year over a period of time, illustrates one of the most significant developments in American oil production.

Drilling costs rose steeply. One reason, of course, was the general rise in wages and the cost of materials; from 1941 through 1948 the cost of labor rose 69 per cent and of materials 55 per cent. An important factor was the greater depth of wells; in 1946 the average cost per foot of Humble wells in proved areas drilled to a depth of from 9,000 to 9,999 feet was about 40 per cent higher than the average cost per foot of wells ranging from 5,000 to 5,999 feet deep. The increased proportion of multisand wells and of wells drilled in hard-formation areas also raised costs. In 1948 Humble drilled at a cost of $75,000,000 only about a third of the number of wells it had drilled for $67,000,000 in the years 1939–1942.[4]

TABLE 12

DEEPEST WELLS DRILLED ANNUALLY BY HUMBLE OIL & REFINING COMPANY 1933-1948

Year	*Depth in Feet*	*Well and Field Location*	*Geographic Location*
1933	8,115	Pierce Estates 2, Pledger Field[a]	Texas Gulf Coast
1934	9,811	White & Baker 1, Pecos County[a]	West Texas
1935	11,144	W. L. Pollock, Upton County[a]	West Texas
1936	10,254	Continental Land & Fur Co., North Castell[a]	South Louisiana
1937	12,168	Ellender 1, Lirette Field	South Louisiana
1938	11,767	R. Verret 1, Lirette Field	South Louisiana
1939	11,920	Milliken & Farwell Inc. 1, Labadieville	South Louisiana
1940	12,600	Caldwell Sugars 1, E. Labadieville	South Louisiana
1941	12,487	E. F. Marin 1, Bayou Sale Field	South Louisiana
1942	11,857	Galveston Bay State A–32, Red Fish Reef Field	Texas Gulf Coast
1943	13,253	Houston Farms Dev. Co. B–1, Halls Bayou Field	Texas Gulf Coast
1944	13,512	Gulf Coast Realties Corp. 2, Sunniland Field	Florida
1945	14,093	G. S. Means 88X, Means Field[a]	West Texas
1946	15,452	E. F. Milo 10, Tomball Field[a]	
1947	15,140	Humble Cote Blanche 2, Cote Blanche Isle[a]	
1948	16,347	R. P. McWatters No. 1, Freestone County[a]	East Texas

[a] Wildcat well.

Source: Records of Humble Oil & Refining Company.

In the early postwar years, one of the principal objectives of the Petroleum Engineering Division, under Bowman Thomas, was to raise the efficiency of drilling operations in order to brake the rate of cost increase and to develop tools and equipment designed to reduce the strain on men from deeper and more difficult drilling.[5] Equipment research on drilling rigs was intensified. A research project was undertaken in 1946 to make a detailed investigation of all the factors affecting the drilling rate of different types of rigs, including a manpower study. A five-man crew was found to be adequate for the operation of land-based steam rigs. The outstanding achievement of the engineers was the designing of a high-fluid-velocity bit, known as the jet bit, which was introduced into operations in 1948 and which so increased drilling speed that two company rigs set what was believed to be a new record by drilling 2,488 and 2,575 feet, respectively, in eight-hour tours.[6] Two years later, in 1950, the year's use of jet bits was estimated to have saved Humble a million dollars. The engineers in 1948 also experimented with an automatic control device to maintain uniform pressure on the drilling bit. At the same time the Petroleum Engineering Division was active in the development of various types of automatic equipment for rigs to reduce the work of the drilling crew in such operations as racking, coupling, and uncoupling pipe.

In 1948 a rig that was described in the *Oil & Gas Journal* as "probably the world's most automatic drilling rig" was working for Humble in the Sugar Valley field on the Texas Gulf Coast.[7] This Humble rig number 30, a heavy-duty steam rig, was in fact a field laboratory for drilling equipment. It represented the Petroleum Engineering Division's many efforts to reduce both the costs of deeper drilling and the accidents that had come with the use of heavier machinery. Among the results that added up to more efficient drilling at lower costs in manpower and money were the lessening of crew fatigue, a more rapid and constant rate of drilling, straighter holes, and less frequent blowouts. It was found impracticable to adopt all the new features of this rig, which was a prototype with many possibilities for future improvements in drilling.

The engineers, with help from the research men, continued in these postwar years to work on certain specific problems in the drilling and completion of wells. They practically completed their conquest of heaving shales. They helped to develop improved mud, in which pipe, if necessary, could remain suspended for a long period of time without sticking. They also contributed to improvements in cementing, introducing a lightweight cement containing a high percentage of bentonite. They did much work on casing perforators; they developed a jet perforator which they introduced into operations in 1948. They devised a permanent type of well completion that eliminated the earlier necessity of pulling the tubing for remedial purposes, which had become increasingly costly as Humble's wells became older and many needed reworking. Permanent completion became especially valuable in offshore operations. The engineers also gave attention to problems of offshore drilling.

A significant trend in production was the increasing number and seriousness of problems that developed because of the increased depth and age of wells and fields. One problem was the greater corrosion of subsurface equipment. A beginning was made in its solution by installing cathodic protection against electrolytic action; studies were also made of the application of alloys and plastic coatings. The disposal of produced salt water became an increasingly persistent problem. Even before the war the producers in the East Texas field had formed a nonprofit corporation to build a water-injection system. After the war Humble had to increase, substantially, the facilities for taking care of the salt water produced with oil, especially disposal wells, in order to prevent the contamination of streams and tillable lands. Workover jobs on wells also increased in number; in 1946, for example, 304 workovers on 281 wells—of which 71 per cent were considered successful—cost nearly $3,000,000. Also, a large number of wells needed lifting equipment.

As technical personnel returned from the service, it became possible to place greater emphasis on reservoir studies. A new instrument was at this time put into use that made possible calculations relating to water-drive reservoirs, which, because of the time required, had not been practicable earlier. This was an automatic calculator developed by The Carter Oil Company. To ensure maximum recovery from each reservoir, studies were made of its maximum efficient rate of production, and special attention was given to the possibility of gas conservation in individual fields and also to secondary recovery. Comprehensive studies were made of the Hawkins field, in particular, in order to provide evidence in support of Humble's claim that permits to others to drill wells as exceptions to the field's spacing rule resulted in draining oil originally in place under the company's leases.

Humble took important steps to provide better-trained engineers for this work and to apply the best principles of reservoir engineering. Its special advanced course for reservoir engineers, first offered in 1944 but subsequently discontinued, was resumed. A *Reservoir Engineering Manual* was also prepared; the first edition of 1,100 copies became available in 1949.

The engineers continued to give much attention to the handling of the oil and gas produced. They worked on the treating of emulsions, which presented increasing problems. They resumed work, discontinued during the war, on the development of low-temperature separation equipment for obtaining maximum liquid recovery from natural gas.

The Production Department's research group worked on problems that were of importance to reservoir engineering and to drilling and production. Among their activities were studies of heaving shales and drilling muds, referred to above, and of the characteristics of fluids in limestone fields, of sand permeability, the viscosity of oil, and the angle of dip of a formation. They initiated a comprehensive study of the mechanics of oil recovery by gas-cap drive. They continued to work on the hydrodynamics of water and gas production in oil wells. They placed particular emphasis on phase behavior of hydrocarbons under reservoir conditions. And, in general, they carried forward fundamental studies of the behavior of fluids in reservoirs with a view to increasing ultimate recovery.

In the period of postwar readjustment a stabilizing factor was the restriction of production to market demand. By this time all the states in which Humble carried on producing operations, except California, had comprehensive systems of state regulation. Consequently, the uncertainty, unnecessary costs, and waste of the resource that had formerly characterized the American industry had been reduced, although not eliminated. Conservation and proration were no longer serious political issues in most oil states, although there was a growing movement, largely outside the oil industry but supported by some operators, against restriction of production to market demand. Its promoters held that such restriction raised prices unduly.

Humble's executives maintained that not only the oil industry but also the consumers of oil products and the general public gained from proration. They held that reserves in the ground were available for increasing production and that restriction to market demand actually increased reserves by encouraging the search for new oil, particularly by the smaller operators who under this system were assured a share of the market. Moreover, the more efficient utilization of a limited natural resource and of manpower and materials reduced costs, which reduction was reflected in prices. Most important was the indication from experience that a far larger percentage of the oil in a reservoir ultimately would be recovered where production was so regulated as to make full use of sound reservoir engineering principles. And, by leaving the oil in nature's own storehouses, conservation and proration eliminated the physical and economic waste that resulted from the extensive storage earlier required to take care of flush production and to assure adequate supplies when production declined.

Of immediate importance to Humble's postwar efforts to keep costs from rising unduly was the regulation of well-spacing. In most states in which the company operated, spacing was so regulated that the number of wells allowed per field was gradually being reduced to a little nearer the number actually necessary for efficient drainage. In all fields in Texas small-tract owners were granted permits to drill as exceptions to the fields' spacing patterns, which resulted in the sinking of much capital in wells unnecessary for efficient drainage. In the postwar years, however, the trend was definitely toward wider spacing. The savings from draining a given area through fewer wells were of great importance in the reduction of producing costs. This reduction helped to keep prices to consumers from rising as much as the general price level, and also strengthened the American oil industry in its competition with oil produced abroad, which had the cost advantage of wide spacing on large concessions.

The greater degree of equity achieved in the allocation of production to wells and leases, in conjunction with the well-spacing pattern for individual fields, in most instances did not yet approximate the actual ownership of oil in a reservoir. The Texas Railroad Commission in these postwar years used three formulas in allocating to leases their share of production from new pools. One formula gave equal weight to acreage and wells on a lease; another gave acreage a weight of 75 and wells 25, this formula being applied to nearly three times as much acreage as the 50-50 formula; a third considered acreage only, but it was applied to a relatively small percentage of the total under production.

Although some progress had been made in the allocation of the allowable in individual Texas fields, controversy had not been eliminated. A persistent source of conflict was the tract that was smaller than the spacing pattern set by the Railroad Commission for a field. Exceptions to the famous Rule 37 continued to be granted in the East Texas field. In one field developed in the 1940s—Hawkins in East Texas—Humble considered the small-tract allowables to be seriously discriminatory against its own and its lessors' interests.

Under the Railroad Commission's Hawkins field order of 1944, which was a revision of the original order, the field's spacing pattern was twenty acres and the per-well allowable formula gave equal weight to acreage and wells. The order stipulated, however, that a forty-acre well, Humble's common spacing because of PAW restrictions during the war,[8] should have not more than twice the allowable of a twenty-acre well; and that the twenty-acre unit should have not more than twice the allowable of tracts less than an acre, that is, the Hawkins townsite lots.

Humble, with its lessors, brought suit against the Railroad Commission's Hawkins order, alleging that it was confiscatory as between Humble's own wells, which were largely one well on forty acres, and those on small tracts. Humble alleged that it was allowed to produce only 71.4 per cent of the field's allowable, although its engineers estimated that it owned 76.5 per cent of the recoverable oil in the pool; the company maintained that, under the existing order, the loss from its leases by drainage would during the life of the field amount to 30,000,000 barrels. Outside the townsite, Hawkins on February 1, 1945, had 314 wells on 9,363 productive acres; the townsite had 87 wells on 73.7 acres.[9]

This Hawkins litigation was instituted in the Travis County District Court in 1945 and ended in the Supreme Court of the United States in 1947. Humble won in the first court, but it lost on the Railroad Commission's appeal to the Court of Civil Appeals. It tried every possible additional judicial recourse, finally applying to the United States Supreme Court for a hearing. The application was denied.[10]

The case was concerned wholly with the question of equity, and the issue was whether or not the order was confiscatory. The decisive reasoning and opinion were those of the Court of Civil Appeals. The court held that "there was no conflict regarding the existence of substantial uncompensated excess drainage." In support of its opinion the court said, among other things, that reserves did not constitute the only factor to be considered in determining the validity of a proration order, that the rule of capture, as well as the rule of ownership in place, was a part of the

Texas law of ownership of oil in a pool, that it would seem that the right to drill on a small tract implied the right to a reasonable profit, and that, in the absence of agreement between the reservoir experts of the two sides, "the Commission's discretionary powers should not be subject to judicial review, and the substantial evidence rule should apply." In further support of its opinion, the court pointed to compensations for the disparity in allowables which accrued to Humble from the very fact of regulation, saying that more widely spaced wells benefited from the restriction of production to market demand, that wider spacing meant less costly production, and that the amount of drainage was less than under unregulated production.[11]

The real basis of the court's decision seems to have been an unwillingness to interfere with the Railroad Commission's exercise of its judgment. This decision in effect left the determination of allowables for small tracts to the discretion of the Commission. In the judgment of Humble's counsel, the system worked to the advantage of small tracts. The determination of allowables continued to depend on the Commission's judgment as to equity in individual cases and fields. Hawkins and other fields notwithstanding, however, great progress had been made in Texas in reducing waste and in protecting correlative rights in a reservoir.

During the immediate postwar period, progress was also made in Texas in achieving a higher degree of equity in the allocation of the state's total production among the individual fields through the MER system. The Railroad Commission continued after the war to use the MER concept—the maximum efficient rate of production without the loss of recoverable oil, that is, without physical waste—in allocating the state's total production among the fields in Texas. Humble then, as during the war, was a firm supporter of this system. In many cases, however, especially in new fields, the Commission reverted to the use of a yardstick formula similar to that adopted in 1940 (Chapter 19).

Having once found oil, a company could have some assurance that production would be reasonably efficient and that the market would be supplied in a more orderly fashion than in the days of the familiar cycles of oversupply and shortage. In other words, in producing oil from a reservoir speculation had in a measure given way to competition on the basis of efficient operations. But the search for oil was still costly and risky. Indeed, it was becoming increasingly so, as will be seen later in this chapter.

CRUDE OIL PURCHASING FOR A DYNAMIC MARKET

The postwar demand restored the condition of certain years in the 1920s when the problem had been to get enough oil to supply eager customers rather than, as in the 1930s, to find customers for crude that had to be purchased in order to maintain connections with wells and thus to retain the good will of the independent producers. It also restored the sellers' market, with the result that the pressure for price increases was strong.

The Crude Oil Department, under Donald F. Haynes as manager, had the responsibility for purchasing the tremendous amount of oil required to supplement Humble's own production, the total purchases each year actually exceeding the company's net production. (See Appendix II, Table IX.) Even in 1946, when the demand dropped slightly, Humble purchased a daily average of 134,400 barrels of oil from 10,000 wells and hundreds of producers, and in 1947 it had to make substantial spot purchases from other large companies. Inventories rose in 1946 and 1947 because of insufficient transportation out of West Texas and from the Hawkins field, but in 1948, with a steeply rising demand and the movement of large volumes of West Texas and Hawkins oil by tank car, storage stocks were again reduced. Throughout all those years, Humble's crude oil inventory remained fairly low in proportion to its total requirements.[12]

Crude prices began to rise as soon as federal wartime price controls were lifted in 1946. Humble immediately announced a general price increase of 25 cents per barrel. When in the summer of 1947 the average price of Texas crude approached $2.00 per barrel, Eugene Holman, president of Standard Oil Company (New Jersey), declared that crude prices were adequate. A representative of the Independent Petroleum Association promptly attacked President Holman's statement, maintaining that prices must be increased by at least 35 cents per barrel in order to cover replacement costs and a normal profit margin. Humble again was under strong pressure from producers to raise prices. It did not subsequently initiate price increases, but late in the year it followed the substantial increases of such other purchasers as the Phillips Petroleum Company, Stanolind Oil Purchasing Company, and the Sun Oil Company. By the end of the year crude prices in Texas averaged $2.64 per barrel—the highest since 1920. They remained approximately at that average level through 1948.[13]

When Phillips in September, 1948, increased its price 35 cents per barrel, Humble refused to follow, on the grounds of an improved petroleum supply, a slackening in the rate of increased demand, and large additions to industry stocks. The action of the market later corroborated the company's stand. Excepting the Southern Minerals Corporation and Sinclair, the other large purchasers did not raise their prices. Humble lost lease connections to Phillips amounting to approximately 15,000 barrels daily, but it was not criticized as much as might have been expected. Before the end of the year, Phillips, Southern Minerals, and Sinclair had reduced their postings to competitive levels.[14]

The magnitude of Humble's crude oil operations during the years 1946 through 1948 and the increase in prices were not reflected in the Crude Oil Department's profits. By this time the department was operating almost as a service organization. Actually, the conditions under which it operated had changed radically, so that much of the earlier risk from having to carry large inventories as a hedge against possible scarcity had been removed by proration. The principal source of income was a marketing charge of one cent per barrel, but this charge was barely adequate to cover expenses. In 1946 and 1947 the department had small losses, in the latter year primarily because of the destruction of crude inventory by explosion and fire at the shipping terminal in Texas City. In 1948 crude oil operations were back in the black, but the profit was small.

THE PIPELINES' PROBLEMS AND PROGRESS

Humble Pipe Line Company's early postwar plans were based on the obvious need to repair the wear and tear of wartime and to meet new conditions and objectives. Among these were the anticipated decline in demand, the Sales Department's program of sales expansion, which made imperative the relatively low-cost carrying of products to the Dallas–Fort Worth area and hence necessitated building a products line, the expectation of continued shortages in manpower and steel, and the need to keep costs as low as possible. The execution of this program by O. Q. Lomax, general superintendent, A. E. Pecore, chief engineer, and the pipeline organization in general was a large undertaking.

Humble's pipeline system in the three postwar years, 1946–1948, experienced its greatest expansion and largest annual investment since late in the 1920s. The pipeline company invested nearly $36,000,000 to meet the unpredicted increase in the demand for crude and products. A twenty-inch, forty-mile crude line was built from the Satsuma pipeline station to Baytown. This followed the complete destruction of the facilities at Texas City, which resulted in the decision to shift Humble's tanker loading terminal from that place to the Baytown docks. The additional facilities for crude transport, however, principally took the form of gathering lines. The only increase in crude trunk lines was the further looping of the line from West Texas to the Corpus Christi area.[15] The most important pipeline construction by far was the 276-mile, eight-inch products line from Baytown to the Dallas–Fort Worth area. Natural gasoline lines were also constructed from the Clear Lake and Anahuac fields to Baytown.

A frontal attack was made on costs. An annual average of $2,000,000 per year above normal maintenance was spent in the years 1945 through 1947 to recondition the pipeline system, and various other steps were taken to raise the efficiency of the lines and reduce expenses. Vigorous efforts were made to reduce operating costs. For example, the substitution of aerial inspection of pipelines for the traditional walking or riding of lines saved Humble Pipe Line Company about $400,000 per year. The resumption on a large scale of the prewar program of corrosion prevention resulted in substantial savings.

HUMBLE PIPE LINE COMPANY SYSTEM, 1948

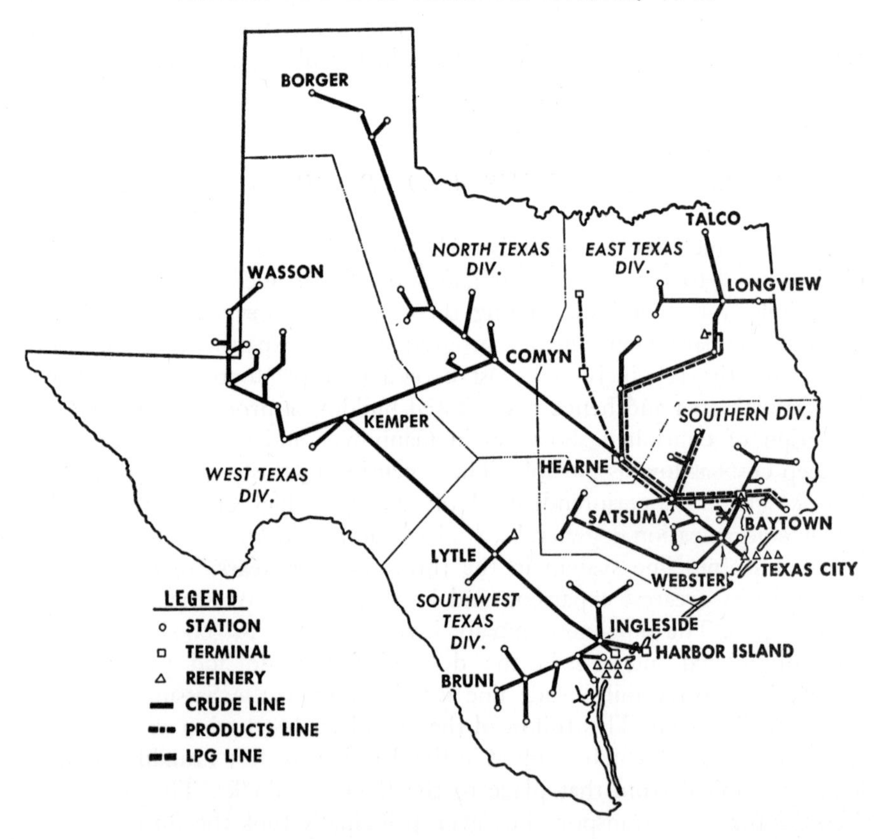

The corrosion problem became more acute because of the increasing age of the entire system and the greater amount of sour crude moved from the West Texas area, while the losses from oil leaks caused by internal and external corrosion became higher and hence less tolerable. At the same time, however, better means became available for coping with the problem. The cathodic-protection program initiated before the war was resumed on a large scale; but not until 1948, when modern equipment was more readily available and electric power became more extensively distributed in rural areas, did this program become really comprehensive and widely effective. The use of galvanic anodes, which had been improved by a chemical company during the war, proved to be a convenient and economical alternate source of electric power for cathodic protection. New processes for applying coatings to the inside of pipes were also developed, including a process for the in-place coating of existing pipelines. The substitution of floating for fixed tank roofs was also resumed in order to reduce both evaporation and corrosion by eliminating the vapor space. The greater use of concrete bottoms to replace corroded steel bottoms further reduced tank corrosion and maintenance costs.

These and other measures brought a substantial reduction in the costly repairs necessitated by corrosion and in the loss of oil from leaks and evaporation. The effectiveness of cathodic protection is illustrated by Table 13, which shows the sharp reduction in pipe corrosion at one tank farm after cathodic protection was started. Such accomplishments may seem routine and inconsequential in the total operations of an oil company. Actually, corrosion and evaporation, although more serious in some oil industry operations than in others, are far from inconsequential in any of them and can have a significant effect on maintenance costs and on oil losses.

TABLE 13
CORROSION FAILURES ON TANK-FARM PIPELINES AT WEBSTER STATION
1938–1950

Year	*Number of Failures*	*Year*	*Number of Failures*
1938	78	1944	4
1939	73	1945	4
1940	71	1946	4
1941	53	1947	7
Cathodic protection started on May 13, 1941		1948	3
		1949	2
1942	15	1950	0
1943	12		

Source: Records of Humble Pipe Line Company.

Humble Pipe Line Company performed a herculean transportation job in those years. Trunk-line deliveries in 1946 did not increase much over those in 1945, but the next year they rose to record heights and in 1948 reached a daily average of 758,000 barrels (see Appendix II, Table XI). By 1947 Humble's pipeline capacity out of certain areas became seriously inadequate, the situation being especially critical in West Texas. The company in that year had to move nearly 10,000,000 barrels of crude from West Texas by tank car at a cost estimated to have been nearly $4,000,000 more than comparable costs by pipeline.[16]

Realizing that the West Texas lines had no spare capacity, Humble Pipe

Line increased the capacity of the line to the Corpus Christi area by looping, as noted above. The old system to the Houston area, a dogleg instead of a direct line, would require a relatively large amount of power and extensive looping, thus making it unwise to expand that line. Building a new line, nevertheless, was not undertaken immediately after the war for a number of reasons. The trend of production in West Texas was believed to be too uncertain to warrant investment in a new line. The anticipated severe slump in demand for crude oil, moreover, seemed in any event to make a new line unnecessary. Standard Oil Company of New Jersey, Humble's largest customer, had warned that after the war it would require a relatively small volume of oil from West Texas.

The critical situation that developed in 1947, however, in 1948 brought the decision to build a new line. The next year, when pipe was again available, construction was begun on the projected eighteen-inch, 372-mile line from Kemper to Satsuma, which was designed to carry 136,000 barrels daily and to cost an estimated $14,500,000.[17] This line followed a more direct route, which was fifty miles shorter than the old one and downgrade most of the way. Being of large diameter, it required less power and operating personnel to move the same quantity of oil.

The contrast between the projected new line and the old lines pointed up a serious problem confronting Humble Pipe Line Company after the war. Its pipeline system was less efficient than newer large-diameter lines, a fate that has befallen most pioneers in industrial development involving high plant investment. To be sure, other major companies also had such pipeline systems, but none in Humble territory had comparable systems that came so near to being obsolete throughout. Most of the Humble lines were made up of multiple, small-diameter pipe and had been looped from time to time in order to increase capacity; their pump stations were powered by obsolete equipment, and their routes were largely determined by the location of the oil fields of the 1920s and early thirties. These obsolete Humble lines consequently had higher operating costs than the newer large-diameter competing lines leading more directly from important new fields to refineries or tanker terminals.

The big question facing Humble Pipe Line Company was what it should do about its old lines. Should it scrap them and build new lines? Should it electrify its old stations but continue to use the old lines? Would the saving in operating costs justify abandoning the largely depreciated old systems and incurring the heavy, long-term capital costs of building new ones? Would the future pipeline business, moreover, justify those heavy fixed costs?

In this situation Humble faced the result of its consistent policy of not participating in lines built jointly with other companies—the only exception was the wartime Bayou line. Such co-operation had not been necessary in the 1920s, when the company was building small-diameter lines and the volume of business was increasing. Some of its competitors, on the contrary, had built jointly, which made possible the construction of large-diameter lines with a greater assurance of sufficient volume at a lower cost per barrel of throughput.

Although Humble Pipe Line Company did not have the volume advantage of jointly owned lines, it had a substantial amount of business from nonaffiliated companies. The larger portion of its business, to be sure, continued to be for Humble Oil & Refining Company, but the deliveries to outside companies had increased considerably in recent years.

The decision was reached to have comprehensive studies made of the company's pipeline situation in order to determine how to meet the problems of obsolescence and inefficiencies in the old systems. Preparations were made to start these studies in 1949 by a new planning and economics division under H. M. Stevenson.

The trend of Humble Pipe Line Company's net earnings was downward. There was no general increase or reduction in tariff rates; for the most part only minor changes were made to meet competition. There were some tariff reductions on long-haul, large-volume business, principally from West Texas and the Panhandle, but the average tariff per barrel remained about constant. Costs, however, rose steeply. Although increased volumes and unremitting efforts to reduce expenses tended to counteract increased wage rates and costs of materials, earnings during these postwar years were substantially below the 7 per cent on the valuation of carrier facilities permitted under the consent decree of 1941.[18]

NATURAL GAS: PRODUCTION AND MARKETING PROBLEMS

The pressure to meet increasing demands for crude oil created problems as to the conservation and disposition of natural gas. This was of special concern to Humble because its gas reserves doubled during the war and postwar years and made the company one of the largest potential producers of natural gas in the country. The problem was increased by the fact that the company could not altogether control the output of the gas.[19]

Humble had quadrupled its gas production from 1941 to 1945. This increase came from expanded crude production, and from the production of natural gas by the Katy cycling plant and of smaller amounts from Humble's 9 per cent interest in a cycling plant operated by The Texas Company at the Erath field in Louisiana and its 50 per cent interest in a plant at the Hawkins field put into operation in 1944. The rapid expansion of crude production to meet the needs of the war effort had made it impossible for the company to obtain either the manpower or the materials for constructing or expanding casinghead gasoline plants or otherwise utilizing the gas produced. Even with its increased utilization of the gas produced with the crude oil, Humble was in 1945 flaring 42 per cent of the casinghead gas, an estimated 143.1 million cubic feet of gas per day.

This large amount of unused casinghead gas was increased after the war by the growing demand for oil products and the continued shortage of materials, which for some time made it impossible to provide adequate plant facilities for utilizing the natural gas. The chief road block, however, was the lack of an immediate market for natural gas. Humble's gas sales from its natural gas systems increased from approximately 21 billion cubic feet in 1945 to nearly 34 in 1948; and total gas sales to outsiders, that is, from both oil wells and gas wells, increased at the same time from 75 billion to 127. This was but a fraction of what might have been produced for sale had a market been available.

Most of the gas was sold for use in Humble's own producing region. The company was itself a large consumer of gas; its refineries, with expanded wartime and postwar operations, were great consumers of gas. Baytown and Ingleside had increased their consumption nearly fourfold from 1941 to 1945; in 1948 Baytown alone used over 54 billion cubic feet. Baytown was furnished gas from the Tomball System, but gas for Ingleside was purchased from an outsider. The largest outside buyers of Humble gas were the United Gas Pipe Line Company, The Texas Company, the Texas Gulf Sulphur Company, and the Interstate Natural Gas Company. Sales to the first three of these dated from the later 1930s (Chapter 19), but during the 1940s other gas, chemical, and carbon-black companies became purchasers of gas from various Humble fields in Texas, Louisiana, and Mississippi.

One of the company's most important contracts for the sale of gas was executed in 1945 with the Jersey-affiliated Interstate Natural Gas Company; deliveries were started in 1946. This contract provided for the sale of gas from the North Tepetate and Pecan Island fields in Louisiana at 5 cents per MCF (thousand cubic feet). Humble agreed to build a seventy-five-mile gas line from Pecan Island to Interstate's facilities, which line was to be leased to Interstate for five years; Interstate agreed to build the other necessary facilities and to deliver the gas to the Baton Rouge refinery of Standard Oil Company of Louisiana, one-half of whose daily gas requirement of 80,000,000 cubic feet was to be supplied with gas purchased by Interstate from Humble. In 1946 Interstate also contracted to take Humble's gas at North Crowley, and it started taking gas from Humble at Carthage Point, Mississippi, for movement northward in interstate commerce. In the same year United Gas, in addition to its Katy purchase, began to buy at Paradis, Roanoke, and other fields in Louisiana.

In 1947 Humble began to supply the Dow Chemical Company from its new Angleton natural gas system, and the following year it contracted all its Gwinville (Mississippi) production to the Southern Natural Gas Company, which marketed gas in Alabama and Georgia. In Texas Humble's Tomball natural gas system supplied a large part of the sales to major purchasers and supplied Baytown's natural gas requirements.

Humble was not satisfied with the prices received for its gas, although its average realization was apparently higher than the average in the state of Texas. Its average rose from 5.2 cents per MCF in 1943 to 5.9 cents in 1948, but the latter price was still considerably lower than the 9 cents per MCF at which its first important contract for the sale of gas had been negotiated in 1935.[20]

Although Humble had potential gas production far larger than the possible market in the states in which it produced gas, it showed little interest in selling gas to the interstate gas transmission companies that were engaged in large-scale construction of pipelines for conveying gas from Texas to the industrial North and East. Among its natural gas purchasers in Texas at the end of 1948 was only one such company, the Tennessee Gas Transmission Company, which during 1946 and 1947 purchased small amounts of Humble's residue Katy and Tomoconnor gas.

Two principal considerations made Humble hesitate to sell to interstate carriers: low prices and the threat of federal price regulation. The company considered gas prices far too low in terms of the fuel value of gas. Inasmuch as 6 MCF of gas equal the fuel value of one barrel of oil, equivalent fuel values of gas and oil at the well in 1948 were 30 cents and $2.65, respectively. Gas was obviously at a supply-demand disadvantage compared with oil because of the large available supply of gas, the impossibility of storage aboveground in substantial amounts, and the cost of transportation to distant markets. However, Humble executives believed that, with improving transportation and expanding markets, gas prices should eventually come nearer to their proper levels in terms of comparative fuel values if they were not restrained by federal price control. They were fearful of the possibility that the production of gas, in the event of sale in interstate commerce, might come to be treated as if it were a public utility subject to the control of the Federal Power Commission.

The question as to what should be done with the increasing production of casinghead gas and the rapidly expanding gas reserves in Texas had become a crucial problem for the state of Texas and its whole oil industry. Three separate but related issues had come under consideration: gas conservation, prices, and state versus federal control of the gas industry. Texas sentiment, of course, was favorable to gas conservation and higher prices and opposed to federal control. And increased prices were generally recognized as an important and perhaps an essential stimulus to conservation.

The Texas Railroad Commission had been empowered by a law of 1929 to prevent the waste of gas produced with oil. In December, 1945, its engineering committee reported that 57 per cent of a total daily Texas production of nearly 2.5 billion cubic feet of casinghead gas was being flared, and recommended that this inordinate amount be reduced by such measures as gas injection for pressure maintenance. The oil companies were reluctant, however, to incur the expense of conserving a product of so little market value, and shortages rendered it difficult if not impossible to observe the conservation recommendations. A bill, backed by the Railroad Commission and about twenty oil companies, including Humble, which would have called for compulsory cycling and repressuring where such measures would increase the ultimate recovery of gas and oil and which aimed to reduce the expense of gas conservation by authorizing voluntary pooling agreements, failed of passage because of the usual argument that such agreements were in violation of the anti-trust law. Although Humble favored the conservation of gas as far as was economically feasible, it saw difficulties in over-all compulsory cycling and repressuring; but it was willing to accept such regulation as an alternative to federal control. To prevent the extension of federal control of the gas business within the state consequently became a common objective of Humble, other Texas oil companies, and the Railroad Commission.

Early in 1946 hearings of the Federal Power Commission in Texas explored the issues. Humble was represented at these hearings by Rex G. Baker, who served on a committee appointed by Governor Coke Stevenson to present the case for Texas and its natural gas industry. The testimony favored higher prices of gas at the well and state regulation of gas production, processing, and gathering. On the controversial point of gas wastage Humble's witnesses, the technologist Stuart E. Buckley and the economist Richard J. Gonzalez, emphasized the fact that the price of gas was so low that, although more than half of Texas's casinghead gas production was vented, the cost of saving it would be almost prohibitive. Conservation of casinghead gas, they declared, particularly in small fields, depended on prices that would render the gathering and compressing of gas financially feasible. The natural gas industry took the position that, in view of the large known reserves of natural gas, the replaceability of oil and gas by synthesis from coal, and the prospects for atomic energy, there was no further need for the Federal Power Commission to extend its control in the interest of conservation.

In the summer of 1946 the natural gas producing industry was disturbed by an opinion written by Judge Joseph C. Hutcheson, Jr., of the Fifth United States Circuit Court of Appeals in New Orleans which upheld the

FPC's authority, under the federal Natural Gas Act of 1938, to force the Interstate Natural Gas Company to reduce prices on natural gas sold within the state of Louisiana to companies that delivered the gas in interstate commerce. This decision was confirmed by the United States Supreme Court the following year.[21] President Wiess of Humble declared that the decision would retard conservation, since the threat of control over the price of a commodity that was already priced too low would cause the gas producer to "resist in every way making connections to interstate pipelines." [22]

The Federal Power Commission's administrative order of August, 1947, however, assured the independent natural gas producers and gatherers that they could sell and deliver such gas "at arm's length" to interstate pipelines without danger of coming under the commission's jurisdiction. But this was not sufficiently reassuring to Humble's executives. They still feared that, by selling gas to interstate transmission companies, their company might be classed as a natural gas company and its interstate gas operations regulated as a quasi-public utility business. Humble declared that, to prevent this interpretation of the Natural Gas Act, the adoption of the amendment advocated by the National Oil & Gas Committee was necessary. This amendment would limit the jurisdiction of the Federal Power Commission to trunk-line interstate transportation of natural gas and to its sale by the interstate pipelines for resale, and would prohibit the commission from controlling the production, gathering, and field price of gas. Humble also advocated, as it had nearly a score of years earlier, a Texas law permitting the unitized development and operation of oil reservoirs. Such a law would enable the operators, without danger of antitrust proceedings, jointly to provide facilities to recover or return to the reservoir the gas produced with crude.[23]

Humble was at the same time carrying forward a program aimed at the complete utilization of its casinghead gas.[24] At the end of World War II it owned or had an interest in thirteen gas-conservation projects, but it was then venting 52 per cent of its total casinghead production—a lower percentage than that of the whole industry in Texas. It had planned additional conservation projects in twenty-two fields, but shortages of material and labor had held up construction. By 1947, fourteen of the new projects had been completed and were conserving 62,000,000 cubic feet of gas per day and increasing Humble's casinghead gas utilization to 76 per cent. During the years 1945 through 1948, the company's net investment in gas conservation projects increased from nearly $9,000,000 to over $22,000,000.

The principal incentive to such an extensive and expensive program of building casinghead plants was Humble's recognition of the economic importance of conserving and selling casinghead gas wherever possible, of repressuring oil reservoirs depleted during the war, and of utilizing the rich hydrocarbons that were increasingly demanded for the production of higher-quality gasoline, synthetic rubber, and plastics. The substantial profits in 1944 from investments in natural gasoline and cycling plants dropped slightly in 1945 and greatly in 1946, but thereafter came a sharp upward turn which continued through 1948.[25]

The Texas Railroad Commission felt impelled to use its influence in those years to increase gas conservation regardless of the market, even to the extent of shutting down oil fields. In March, 1947, the Commission issued an order against gas waste in the Seeligson field, but the order was held up in the courts until the autumn of 1948. The Commission then ordered operators in seventeen fields to show cause why production should not be shut in so as to prevent the flaring of casinghead gas. Humble, as an operator in twelve of the seventeen fields, was producing 60,000,000 cubic feet of casinghead gas daily and flaring 65 per cent, but it testified that it had projects under construction to eliminate the waste of 27,500,000 cubic feet daily, had authorized other projects at a total cost of over $19,000,000 to conserve an additional 40,000,000 cubic feet, and was negotiating for the sale to the Tennessee Gas Transmission Company of residue gas at Heyser.

The Commission, however, on December 1, 1948, ordered Heyser, where Humble was one of a number of major operators, to be shut down until the 21,000,000 cubic feet of residue gas from the gasoline plant could be utilized for one or more of the purposes provided by the law; a few days later it ordered the shutdown of the other sixteen fields. Shortly thereafter it called for show-cause hearings in regard to twenty-six additional fields. Humble and other operators applied for and obtained injunctions against the Commission's orders. Humble's position was that the orders were poorly timed and failed to consider what the company, despite wartime and postwar shortages and the program currently under way, had already accomplished. Early in 1949 the Texas Supreme Court upheld the Heyser order.

Hines H. Baker, president of Humble, writing in the January-February, 1949, issue of *The Humble Way*, explained that the only real difference between the Commission and the industry had been one of timing. On the whole it appeared that the industry, including Humble, had done all that could reasonably have been expected, considering the complicated nature of the problem, the available time, and the continued shortage of materials. Since 1945 Humble had made capital expenditures of nearly $20,000,000 for casinghead gas plants and conservation equipment and had processed nearly 715,000,000 cubic feet of gas daily in Humble-operated plants. It had thereby greatly reduced the relative amount of gas flared on Humble-operated leases. And it had publicly committed itself to a full gas-conservation program, maintaining the same position with regard to gas as a natural resource that it had so long held in the production of oil.

Humble's natural-gas problems were far from being solved at the end of 1948. The possibilities of casinghead-gas conservation were to be greatly advanced in 1949 by an act of the Texas legislature permitting the co-operative development of gas fields. New postwar uses and markets for gas had somewhat improved the price, thus rendering casinghead-gas conservation more feasible economically. However, the gas producer's specter of federal regulation, with the possibility of resulting price regulation, still haunted Humble and the Texas gas industry generally and still made the company cautious about selling gas for shipment in interstate commerce.

THE QUEST FOR OIL AND GAS

Although great progress had been made in exploration, the old saying that "oil is where you find it" still applied. Great progress, indeed, had been made in the past quarter-century in locating geologic structures favorable to the formation or entry of oil and to its trapping. But the gains therefrom had been narrowed continuously by the necessity of seeking oil at greater depths in the earth's crust, in regions still largely unknown geologically, or in less and less accessible places on the surface of the earth. However far or fast the oil-seeker progressed, the demand for oil was rarely far behind.[26]

Humble's administrators were not pessimistic about the prospects of discovering new oil after the war was over. But they knew that the cost of oil finding was rising and that oil was becoming harder to discover in the older producing regions. They believed, moreover, that the long-term trend of demand was upward, while the competition for proved or prospective oil lands was increasing.

Humble operated in an entirely different market for oil lands during the later war and the early postwar years than when it had made its great reserve acquisitions in the early 1930s. Since late in the 1930s, large integrated companies and independents had been increasingly active in exploration and in the purchase of unproved or proved lands. Some companies were in serious need of strengthening the ratio of their reserves to current production. Moreover, producing companies generally had come to value reserves in the ground more highly than during the years of overproduction. And many former wildcatters, assured of an equitable share of the market under proration, chose to operate as producers and hence did not offer to sell the leases on which they had discovered oil. Small concerns that had earlier been handicapped by the lack of a research staff and specialists in exploration could now for a fee hire consulting geologists and geophysical exploration crews. Also, the generally stabilized earnings of the industry and the recovery of a considerable portion of invested capital through normal depreciation and depletion provisions supplied much capital for investment in reserves. Companies, large or small, that chose to borrow for such investment found credit plentiful and interest rates comparatively low. Consequently, leasing was becoming increasingly competitive, bonuses and rentals unprecedentedly high, and proved lands, in the judgment of some oilmen, prohibitively costly.

The plans of the Humble Board of Directors were designed, as before, to find as great new reserves of both oil and gas as the company's earning power would permit. The directors knew, however, that, unlike many companies, Humble was not under the immediate necessity of increasing its reserves. Confident of the comparative strength of their exploration and drilling organizations and unwilling to pay the high prices asked for the scarce proved lands offered for sale, they chose to depend almost entirely on the company's own efforts to find new reserves rather than to purchase leases on which oil had been discovered. This was Humble's old policy, which had in the past been departed from in particular instances only when the need for new reserves was urgent or the opportunity to purchase was especially attractive. In the early postwar years, there seemed to be neither the necessity nor the attractive opportunity to depart from that policy.

To search for lands to lease and to select lands for testing by drilling on the scale contemplated after the war required a large exploration organization. Most of the men on leave from the various exploration groups returned as soon as the war was over. New men could be added only as they became available and could be hired in an intensely competitive market for geologists and geophysicists. For a time, also, the outfitting of new geophysical crews was retarded by a shortage of instruments. Yet, the number of crew-months worked by Humble's geophysicists in 1948 was larger by 50 per cent than in 1945. The increase in the number of geologists and geophysicists, however, did not at once bring a commensurate increase in effectiveness; a first-class exploration man, even one with excellent academic preparation, can be developed only with special training and experience.

It is significant that, although the number of Humble's geophysical crews increased in the years from 1946 through 1948, Humble did not then enjoy the comparative technological advantage in exploration of earlier years. In these postwar years, Humble crews carried on an average of only approximately 7 per cent of the total geophysical operations in the territory in which the company operated, whereas in 1932 they had done 42 per cent. This comparison illustrates the general rise in the level of oil industry technology and the narrowing of the margin of advantage enjoyed by the early innovators.

Technology, however, is never static, particularly in so dynamic a situation as then prevailed in the American oil industry. After the war, Humble gave added attention to the training of field men, and it expanded exploration research. The research groups worked on certain geochemical techniques, but these did not prove promising at the time. They continued to improve their interpretation of geologic and geophysical data and the effectiveness of geophysical instruments. They were particularly successful in improving the reflection seismograph.

The exploration group continued to meet old and new challenges. The geophysics research staff succeeded in adapting the reflection technique to the search for salt domes beneath the waters of the Gulf. Operating from an exploration fleet built around six retired submarine chasers, reflection crews in 1946 and 1947 discovered a number of areas of interest on the continental shelf.[27] In some places on land the seismograph proved entirely ineffective, particularly in southern Florida and on the Edwards Plateau in Texas, regions where limestone "absorbed" the shock waves so that there were no satisfactory echoes to record. Geologic study in such regions was consequently left to surface exploration and the analysis of cores and electric logs from wells being drilled. Even in the older producing regions, difficulties increased. A common reason was the need to search for reservoirs at greater depths, which challenged both the geophysicist and his instrument and the driller and his rig. Exploration in West Texas was especially difficult.

Postwar interest in that region was focused on the pre-Permian formations of what was known as the Permian Basin. Much exploring had been done in the area since the middle 1920s, and many relatively shallow fields had been found there in the Permian period of geologic time, for example, the prolific discoveries of the later 1920s. But interest had developed over the years in earlier geologic periods, which proved much more difficult to study than the Permian. Not only was the pre-Permian generally found at greater depths, but its geology was also extremely complex and distorted—with an unusual degree of folding and faulting. To explore it by either geologic or geophysical methods and to interpret the data collected were very difficult. Humble found that the geophysical data recorded on the pre-Permian earlier were not dependable. However, the geophysicists gradually improved their instruments for more effective use in these older formations.

Humble continued to increase its leased acreage after the war. At the end of the war it had the largest total unoperated leased acreage that it had ever held—16,500,000 acres, which was more than twice its holdings at the time of the attack on Pearl Harbor. This meant that it was paying heavy rentals and had a tremendous obligation under its leases to explore and drill test wells, but also that it was not under extreme pressure to acquire new lands. In the three postwar years it dropped a very large

NORTH–SOUTH CROSS SECTION OF GEOLOGIC FORMATIONS IN THE BIG LAKE FIELD, WEST TEXAS

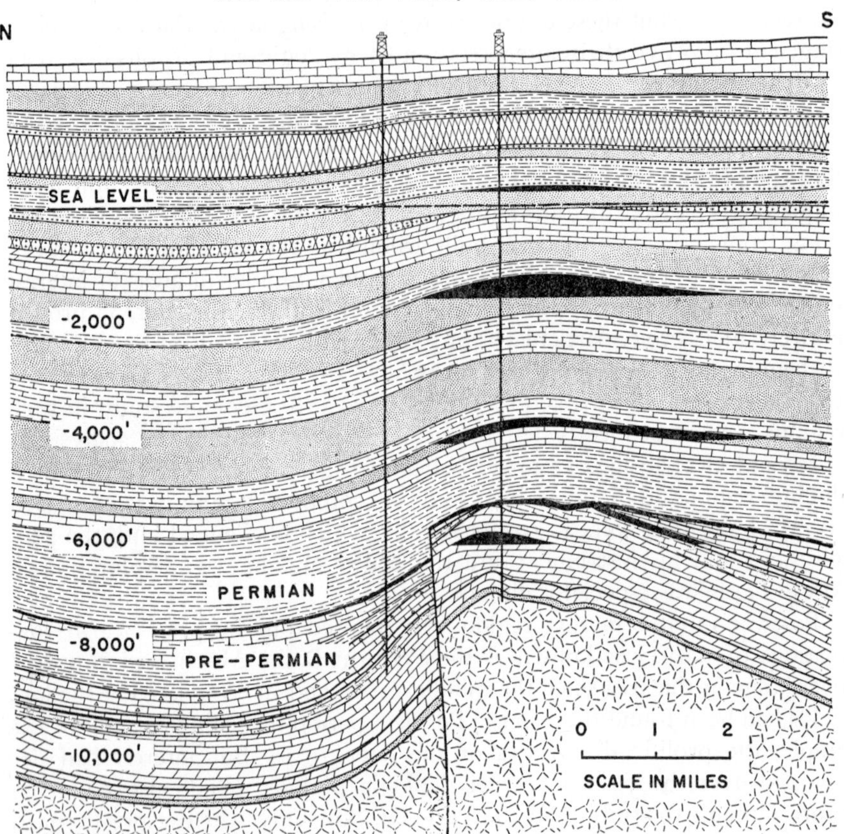

This drawing illustrates the folding and faulting of the pre-Permian strata in the Permian Basin. It shows one well penetrating several reservoirs and another missing them all.

total acreage on which the prospect of finding oil proved to be insufficiently promising to warrant the renewal of leases. But it more than replaced the acreage dropped, with the result that at the end of 1948 it held under lease approximately 17,500,000 acres of unoperated lands. In the years 1946 through 1948 it spent a net of $35,000,000 on lease bonuses and paid $21,000,000 in rentals on unoperated leases. This made a total of $56,000,000 spent on acreage from which no oil or gas was being obtained and from much of which neither might ever be obtained.

In the older and particularly in the more competitive areas—where bonuses and rentals rose steeply, royalty percentages were increased, and the primary terms of leases not infrequently were shortened—Humble was especially selective in its leasing. It already had tremendous acreage in West Texas and New Mexico and in Southwest Texas. In 1947 and 1948 it went heavily into the Anadarko Basin in the Panhandle. But it bought leases very modestly in North Texas, where fields were typically small. It continued to lease extensively but selectively on the Gulf Coast and in East Texas. One unusual lease purchase was the 113,500 acres on the continental shelf purchased from the state of Texas at a bonus of $1,500,000.

High costs and generally increasing difficulties in finding oil in the older oil regions, as well as confidence in the company's own exploration organization, made Humble look increasingly for oil lands outside Texas. In 1947 its Exploration Department began reconnaissance work in northeastern Arizona. In 1948 the company reached across nearly half the continent to enter California, Texas' great petroleum rival, in which no Jersey-affiliated company had operated since 1911. Although Humble in 1948 joined with other companies in a survey of the California continental shelf, it was primarily interested in finding oil on land, both in producing areas and in several of the relatively untested basins of California and the Northwest.

More immediately important in its operations and on a large scale were Humble's exploration and leasing on the Gulf Coast eastward from Texas. The cost of leases there was rising, but it was still generally modest compared with the older oil-producing regions. The company added to its already large leased acreage in the Louisiana division, that is, in southern Louisiana and Mississippi. In 1946 and 1947 it participated in a strong lease play by nearly a score of companies on the continental shelf off the Louisiana coast; it leased ten offshore blocks from the state, paying an average bonus of $21.73 per acre.

The Louisiana offshore operations were interrupted for some time because of the decision of the United States Supreme Court of June, 1947, in *United States* v. *California*, that the United States had "paramount rights" over "the lands, minerals and other things of value, lying seaward of the low water mark on the coast of California." [28] This decision had obvious potential applicability to Louisiana and other littoral states,[29] and it was not long before the federal government filed suits against Texas and Louisiana in which it claimed paramount rights to the offshore area beyond the low-water mark of the coasts of those states. Although oil companies would in any case have to pay royalties to whichever government established its claim, Humble's executives shared the belief of most oilmen that the resources of the continental shelf would be more satisfactorily developed under state than under federal ownership and regulation.

In its newly established Eastern division—which operated in southern Alabama, southwestern Georgia, and Florida, with headquarters at Tallahassee—Humble continued to explore, to drop acreage found not to be promising, and to lease new acreage. It probably had a larger total leased acreage there than any other company, although many majors and some independents were carrying on extensive exploration operations in those states.

Humble's testing of its leased lands by wildcatting was expanded nearly everywhere, even beyond the wildcatting of the record year of 1944. More than two-thirds of its exploratory wells were "rank" wildcats—that is, in entirely unproved territory—rather than "field" wildcats drilled to explore deeper zones or extensions outside what was considered proved acreage in a field. The percentage of successful wildcats was high; in the three years, 1946–1948, 38 out of 248 rank wildcats discovered oil, and 41 out of 105 field wildcats were productive. And yet, despite this relatively good record, dry holes totaled a cost of $64,000,000.

In its search for new pools Humble drilled to far deeper horizons and at higher costs than ever before. The average depth of the company's wildcat wells in 1946 for the first time exceeded 9,000 feet; ten years earlier it had been 5,500 feet. The deepest well was an East Texas wildcat drilled in 1948 to a depth of 16,347 feet. The most expensive well Humble had ever drilled on land was a gas well completed in 1946 at over 12,000 feet and at a cost of $767,248. More costly still were wells drilled on the Louisiana continental shelf, an operation that more than any other demonstrates to what lengths companies were going in searching for oil.

Several oil companies, in searching for oil before the war, had gone out from land, emerging from swamp and bayou, lake and bay, into the open waters of the Gulf of Mexico. Their efforts had been costly and not productive of oil, for example, Humble's drilling off the coast of Jefferson County in Texas. After the war they renewed that search. In November, 1947, after its exploration crews had found areas of interest and many blocks had been leased, Humble, in spite of the uncertainty as to whether the state of Louisiana or the federal government owned the offshore area, began to construct in the open sea, nearly seven miles southeast of Grand Isle in forty-eight feet of water, a double-decked marine platform from which to drill.

This platform measured 206 by 110 feet and weighed 2,000 tons. It was supported by a hundred steel piles driven from 147 to 197 feet into the bottom of the Gulf and was built to withstand the probable maximum wind, waves, and tides expected to attend a major hurricane at this location in the Gulf. This one platform cost over $1,200,000. It was completely equipped for drilling purposes and was also fitted out as permanent living quarters for a crew of fifty-four men. According to the plans, seven directional wells would be drilled from this single platform. Five smaller platforms were also built during 1948, with space only for the drilling equipment; their crews and materials were quartered in converted United States Navy LSTs (Landing Ship Tanks).[30] A complete new camp, with headquarters for the new district organized to operate on the Gulf, was built on Grand Isle, which was little more than a sand bar off the mainland about fifty miles south of New Orleans.

Humble's first continental shelf well was dry, but the next hole drilled from the large platform was completed as an oil well on August 15, 1948. A second producing well, at Caminada Pass and approximately seven miles offshore from Grand Isle, was completed late in November. These were neither the first producing wells drilled in the open waters of the Gulf nor the farthest out. In November, 1947, Kerr-McGee Oil Industries, Inc., in a joint operation with Phillips and Stanolind, had completed a well approximately eleven miles from land but in only seventeen feet of water.[31] Humble's drilling of its first successful well was based on seismic and surface data and the second on seismic only. These wells, which were later found to be on two different salt domes, were believed at the time to have considerable promise. But their cost was the highest in Humble's experience—$785,700 and $848,400, respectively.

These high costs raised the question of whether it would be profitable to drill and maintain wells on the continental shelf. A completed well in the Gulf, it was estimated, would cost from three to five times as much as a well of the same depth on land. A single tropical hurricane in September, 1948, cost Humble nearly half a million dollars in damages to two of its drilling platforms. The depth of the water obviously left numerous known structures out of bounds for drilling at that time. Altogether, the continental shelf hardly seemed as yet the answer to the reserve problems of either the industry or Humble. Nevertheless, expensive as the Gulf operations were, they provided something of a hedge against possible future scarcity.

In contrast with success on the continental shelf was a serious stroke of bad luck in West Texas in 1947 in Humble's failure to find oil in Davis No. 1 drilled on a large block in Scurry County.[32] This well was drilled to 8,027 feet in the Ellenburger, a pre-Permian dolomite formation. After only water was found in that formation the well was abandoned as a dry hole. The geologists completely overlooked the presence of a reef containing oil approximately 2,000 feet further up the hole. In consequence of finding no oil in this and in still another well drilled nearby, Humble dropped a considerable acreage in Scurry County which it had held for about ten years, a more or less routine procedure after an area has proved insufficiently promising for renewing leases. Late in 1948, however—after Humble and Sun Oil in the jointly drilled Schattel No. 1 had discovered oil in the Canyon reef in Scurry County—Standard Oil Company of Texas, a subsidiary of California Standard, found oil in a wildcat drilled a few miles east of Humble's Davis No. 1. This was the discovery well of the North Snyder field. The producing formation was the Canyon reef in the pre-Permian Pennsylvanian. After the first show of oil in Standard's Brown No. 1, Humble at once renewed all its renewable leases in the neighborhood and immediately drilled on the leases that could not be renewed. Standard of Texas later found oil in Humble's abandoned Davis No. 1—in the same Canyon reef—and a considerable portion of the acreage Humble dropped in 1947 was proved to contain oil. By not finding oil in this well, Humble failed to discover the largest oil field found in over a decade of Texas exploration.

This experience demonstrates how uncertain the search for oil can be. Both inordinately bad luck and error contributed to the failure to find oil in Davis No. 1. There was a long record of a fruitless search for oil in Scurry County after the discovery of the Sharon Ridge field at a depth of 1,700 feet in 1923. Despite a diligent search by several companies, no more oil was discovered in Scurry for nearly a quarter of a century. In the years from 1937 through 1941 Humble leased half a dozen blocks totaling 73,000 acres. However, until Humble in 1943 drilled its Newman No. 1, no company drilled deeply enough to test the pre-Permian formations that were later found to contain oil. This well, abandoned at 8,336 feet in the Ellenburger, was only 7,500 feet beyond the western edge of the North Snyder field discovered in 1948—an example of how short the distance between success and failure could be. Humble continued to do exploratory work in and around Scurry. In 1946 it discovered the Polar field in the Ellenburger in Kent County, just across the Scurry boundary and, again, only a short distance from the North Snyder field later discovered. Because of this Polar discovery in the Ellenburger and other discoveries in the same formation in that region Humble had decided to drill its Davis No. 1 on a seismograph prospect, hoping to find oil in the Ellenburger. The seismograph had failed to find any indication of the Canyon reef. But a sufficiently large area had not been covered by the seismic survey, and Humble's test well was later found to be at the very edge of the reef. Geologists had not up to that time recognized the real possibilities of the Canyon reef, and it was only after the Humble-Sun discovery of Schattel No. 1, followed by the Standard of Texas discovery in 1948, that attention was focused on this reef. The next year was to yield nine more new fields in Scurry County, two of which were found by Humble.

The irregularity of the pre-Permian underneath Scurry is well illustrated by the fact that, of those nine fields, three were discovered in the Canyon, three in the Strawn, two in the Ellenburger, and one in the Mississippian.

The overcoming of heavy odds on the continental shelf and the failure of a wildcat in West Texas were dramatic developments in what proved to be a successful three years' search for oil and gas. Even in West Texas, where nature's obduracy was extreme, Humble added considerably to its reserves. It found several new fields of importance, including the major Martin-Ellenburger and Yarborough-Allen fields, and it discovered, in a joint test drilled with Pure Oil, the Dollarhide field (in both the Devonian and the Silurian period of the Paleozoic era of geologic time). Humble's search in Southwest Texas, where the company maintained its earlier leadership, was rewarded by a considerable addition to reserves. It extended its holdings in old fields outward and downward and found several new fields, none of which, however, was large. On the Gulf Coast, in spite of much geologic and geophysical work and drilling of wildcats, Humble, like its competitors, made no really important discoveries. The new fields and the new producing horizons in old fields that were discovered were modest. The company's continuing faith and diligent search in East Texas, however, were to be rewarded several years later by its discovery of the major Neches field. In its Louisiana division, particularly in Louisiana but also in Mississippi, Humble added significantly to its reserves. In Mississippi it discovered the large Sandy Hook gas field, which was chiefly owned by Humble, and in Louisiana the two discoveries, already mentioned, on the continental shelf. In Florida, and, indeed, the whole Eastern division, Humble's quest was not at the time very rewarding—as, indeed, was no company's search there. The company succeeded in adding five more flowing wells to its Sunniland field near the southern tip of Florida, but even with those additions that field's total production in 1948 was only 274,694 barrels from eight wells. The Exploration Department, nevertheless, continued to believe that significant amounts of oil would eventually be found in Florida.

The total estimated volume of new oil reserves, from new fields and the extension of old ones, was large. In the years 1946, 1947, and 1948 Humble added to its gross estimated reserves more than 100,000,000 barrels above the amount withdrawn for the enormous production of 373,039,000 barrels (see Appendix II, Table VIII). But, in the words of one Humble director, 10-cent oil had been replaced by $2.00 oil. Costs had, indeed, been high; and higher royalties on recently leased lands would make the cost even higher as the oil found on the new leases was produced. Because of the greatly increased production, the ratio of Humble's reserves to current production had fallen slightly, a decline that was experienced by the entire American oil industry. There was as yet no clear trend, however, and changes in either demand or discoveries could raise the ratio of reserves to production.

The trend of Humble's gas reserves was clear. Table 14 shows a notable increase in the company's reserves in the 1940s. At the end of 1948 Humble held an estimated 12.3 per cent of the gas reserves in the territory in which it operated.

TABLE 14
YEAR-END GAS RESERVES, HUMBLE OIL & REFINING COMPANY
1940–1948
(Million cubic feet)

Year	*Gross*	*Net*
1940	5,303,730	4,587,726
1941	6,596,453	5,705,932
1942	9,141,164	7,907,107
1943	10,356,460	8,958,338
1944	9,846,786	8,517,470
1945	10,505,458	9,087,221
1946	12,124,984	10,488,111
1947	13,103,811	11,334,797
1948	12,958,195	11,208,839

Note: The figures prior to 1944 are not entirely comparable with those for the later years.

Source: Records of Humble Oil & Refining Company.

The full measure of accomplishment in those early postwar years, however, was not the new reserves found. There was good reason to believe that, because of the strengthening of its exploration organization and techniques, Humble was in a far stronger position at the end of the three postwar years than at their beginning. Moreover, the Exploration Department had learned much about the geology of the greatly expanded territory in which it was operating. Would its strengthened organization, improved techniques, and increased knowledge enable the company to continue to discover new oil reserves at least as fast as the old ones were produced? That was one of the most important questions facing Humble, and indeed the entire American oil industry, at the end of 1948.

THE END OF AN ERA

On May 10, 1948, the date of the Humble stockholders' annual meeting, President Wiess was approaching sixty-one years of age; July 30, 1952, as he and his associates were well aware, was the day of his retirement under the company's rules. Probably, however, few of the approximately eighty stockholders assembled for the 1948 meeting were prepared for the announcement that he was retiring from the presidency to become chairman of the board. Wiess informed the stockholders that the directors would elect as president Hines H. Baker, executive vice-president.

The identity of Wiess's successor in the presidency came as no surprise to those who knew of the role that Baker had long played in the company. The main question posed by the change in the titles of the two executives was the division of authority between them. The energetic, conscientious, hard-working chief executive of the company could hardly be visualized in the traditional role of a chairman presiding at directors' meetings and performing the duties of the president during his absence, as provided in the bylaws. However, this problem had been considered and discussed in advance, and a modification of the bylaws had been worked out which provided that the chairman should be the principal officer of the company and the president the chief administrative officer, responsible for the execution of the plans and policies authorized by the Board of Directors. This division of authority was designed to permit Wiess to yield gradually and watchfully his close supervision over the great company in which most of his substantial fortune and his own business career were invested, but it was also a step in the right direction for a large corporation in which the responsibilities and work of the chief executive had become so heavy as to call for sharing by a team. So ill-defined a division of authority, however, could be effective only between two men who, like Wiess and Baker, enjoyed mutual confidence and were accustomed to working together.

At the same meeting the importance of exploration and production was further recognized by the election to the Board of Directors of two additional members from those branches of the company's operations. They were Morgan J. Davis, since 1946 manager of the Exploration Department under Vice-President Barrow, and Carl E. Reistle, Jr., since 1946 manager of the Production Department under Vice-President Frame.[33] Exploration and production were thus doubly represented on the board, each by two directors, one of whom in each instance was a vice-president, whereas both crude oil purchasing and pipelines were under Neath, director and vice-president, and refining and sales under Director Ferguson.

To add to the historical significance of the 1948 stockholders' meeting, Humble's capitalization, which in 1946 had been increased from $175,000,000 to $300,000,000, was further increased to $475,000,000, by transfer from surplus to capital, in order to bring the company's capitalization more nearly in line with its net worth. Humble continued to follow its traditional policy of retaining a large portion of earnings in order to finance expansion by distributing in dividends to stockholders 38.6 per cent of net earnings, or $4.00 per share out of a net income of $10.35 per share.[34]

The division of executive authority between chairman of the board and president provided for in May did not long continue. Wiess had not been in good health for a year or more, although his decision to retire as president was apparently motivated by the approach of compulsory retirement rather than by considerations of health. A few weeks after the annual meeting he underwent an operation, which at first seemed to be successful. A second operation soon became necessary, and six weeks later, on August 26, 1948, the last Humble founder still active in the company succumbed at his home in Houston.

Harry C. Wiess was commonly spoken of by men acquainted with Humble Oil & Refining Company from its early years as one of three or four men who had contributed the most to the company's success. Perhaps his career can best be summarized by pointing out that he represented three streams of thought and action in the business of his company and industry: one old, one new, and one a timeless component of private enterprise. He was of the old in his belief in centralized authority and direct personal responsibility. He was of the new in his early and continuing support of the application of science and engineering in his company's operations and in his advocacy of economic analysis and cost accounting as instruments of planning and control. And, in a time when other considerations were increasingly receiving organized emphasis inside and outside business, Wiess stood firmly for the timeless principles that the good of all interests requires the efficient utilization of capital, labor, and natural resources, and that the strength of a company primarily rests on how well and how efficiently it performs its function of providing goods or services for the market.

The death of Wiess left the newly elected president as sole chief executive. Conscious of the scope and weight of the company's top administrative responsibilities and cognizant of the strategic importance of exploration and production, Hines H. Baker looked to L. T. Barrow to share the administrative burden. The latter reluctantly consented to accept the chairmanship of the board under bylaws then revised for the second time in 1948. The revision provided that the president should be the chief executive officer, with general supervision and control over the company's affairs and with responsibility for executing the plans and policies authorized by the board. It also provided that the chairman, in addition to presiding at meetings of the stockholders and the Board of Directors, should be responsible to the board and to the officers of the company for leadership in the formulation of long-range plans and broad corporate policies, should consult and advise with the president on executive problems of all kinds, and should assist in the discharge of executive responsibility.

Barrow's election to the chairmanship brought other changes. Morgan

J. Davis was elected to succeed Barrow as director in charge of exploration, and his increased responsibilities necessitated changes in the Exploration Department. Consequently, W. A. Maley was appointed manager of the department and J. Ben Carsey was made chief geologist.[35]

The death of Wiess, the last member of the Humble board who owed his original position to his contribution of large properties to the consolidation which became Humble Oil & Refining Company, marked the end of an era and the culmination of an administrative change that had long been in progress. Humble's Board of Directors was now entirely made up of men who had joined the company as young lawyer, geologist, or engineer or in such nontechnical positions as scout and roustabout, and who had worked their way up through the ranks. The board consisted of six professionally trained men—two lawyers, two geologists, and two engineers—and three without formal professional training who had risen to vice-presidencies as heads of important departments.

By the end of 1948 Humble Oil & Refining Company had returned to what could be called normal peacetime operations. The return to serving the civilian market, contrary to expectations, had meant a great increase in the scope and scale of operations. During 1948 Humble produced, transported, bought, sold, and refined more crude, marketed more refined products, and made higher dollar profits than in any other year in its history. It also increased its capitalization to $475,000,000.

During the three postwar years Humble had not merely expanded its operations to unprecedented proportions; it had also accomplished much toward putting those operations on a sounder basis for future development. The administrative organization and practices had been changed to meet changing needs. The employee force had been restored and strengthened, and employee-management relations were probably in a healthier state than ever before. Baytown had been reconverted to serve peacetime needs, and construction that would again greatly increase its capacity was nearing completion. The Sales Department had made a sensational advance. The pipeline system had been extended by the addition of a long products line, and the older lines had been reconditioned. Production and exploration had been strengthened by improvements resulting from research and engineering, and the two departments had added greatly to the company's gas reserves and had provided a greatly increased quantity of oil for the booming market while finding enough new oil to add moderately to reserves.

This history of Humble Oil & Refining Company ends with the year 1948. In the complex continuum of a successful corporation's operations, few points in time can be designated as marking broadly important beginnings or endings: the new generally comes gradually and the old disappears in the same way. Even the full commitment of the future of Humble Oil & Refining Company to professional managers brought no break in the continuity of policy or practice. Yet, in a broad sense, the year 1948 can be looked upon as the end of an era that had begun approximately at the time of the incorporation of Humble Oil & Refining Company, an era of great growth and of fundamental transformations within Humble itself and the entire American oil industry.

Chapter 26

THREE DECADES OF ENTERPRISE

"It is enterprise which builds and improves the world's possessions," wrote J. M. Keynes, the noted British economist.[1] This history of Humble Oil & Refining Company shows what one group of enterprising men did in the way of such building and improving over some thirty years. The account is more, however, than a record of one company's work; it is in effect a case study of such matters of broad importance as the growth of a vital industry, the process of economic growth and development, and the nature, function, and operation of our business system.

Humble's performance of its function of providing crude and products for the market can be measured statistically. Over the whole span of its operations from 1917 through 1948, the company produced crude oil and condensate to the amount of 1.4 billion barrels (of 42 gallons), provided a market for other producers' oil totaling 2.4 billion barrels, ran to its own refineries 1.3 billion, and delivered from its trunk pipelines 3.2 billion.

Certain aspects of Humble's operations in producing these products and services are more meaningful than even such enormous totals. Through the decades the company's manufacturing operations supplied the market with products of increasing diversity and utility and of rising quality; this was dramatically demonstrated in Humble's response to the needs of the Allies in World War II. But it was in production, Humble's most important operation, that the company made its most significant contribution. As a member of an industry serving an increasing demand for petroleum products, it more than kept pace with that demand. Located in the most rapidly growing oil region in the United States, Humble produced a proportion of the crude oil production in the heartland of that region, the state of Texas, which rose from about 9 per cent for the year 1918 to 13 per cent for 1948. This growth came not from absorbing other producing companies or even to a major extent from the purchase of proved oil-producing properties, but largely from expansion by means of the company's own exploration and producing operations.

Humble early acquired a reserve capacity in its various operations that enabled it to supply its customers despite changes from time to time in the ratio of oil finding and production to consumption. In the 1920s its large storage capacity enabled it in times or areas of flush production to build up inventory with which to supply demand when production declined. Later, when oil under proration could be kept in nature's own storehouses, the company acquired reserves that made possible a notable increase in its production to meet critical war needs and a rising postwar demand. At the end of 1948, despite tremendous wartime and postwar drafts on reserves, Humble still had estimated reserves adequate to provide throughout a period of nearly twenty years an annual amount of crude oil equivalent to its production in that year. This was a substantial hedge against future scarcity and an important service to a country vitally dependent on petroleum products.

Humble's "improving" took various forms. The company was one of the early and continuing leaders in the American oil industry in bringing about fundamental changes in practices which radically changed the industry. As a large company, it could finance research that a small company could not support. It was progressive in applying science and engineering in all principal operations, and it was among the research-minded and engineering-oriented companies that contributed significantly toward reducing the waste of the natural resource and increasing the operating efficiency of the industry. The scientific and engineering advances made by Humble, as by other progressive companies, also helped to provide the necessary basis for the development of new government policies and more effective regulation of oil and gas production, notably at first in Texas but also in other oil states.

Humble was an early leader in promoting regulation under the police powers of states to enable producers to develop production in accordance with the new reservoir knowledge and engineering practices and to produce oil in accordance with consumptive demand. It supported the Texas Railroad Commission in the development of what became a noted system of administration of oil and gas law. Proration, particularly, made possible a reduction in the waste of the resource and in the cost of producing and handling oil; and it also reduced the inequities inherent in the earlier system of competitive field development. At the same time, proration allowed unrestricted exploration and wildcatting, thus enabling individual companies and hence the industry to build up reserves on which to draw to meet market demand. This form of regulation did not work perfectly; there were still unsolved problems in 1948. However, it is probable that, without such regulation, American oil reservoirs would have been exhausted more rapidly, costs and prices would have risen more than they did rise, and the United States and its allies would have suffered from shortages of petroleum products in World War II.

The broad economic and social significance of a company of Humble's size and influence obviously extends far beyond the products and services it supplies. Over the decades the company furnished employment to tens of thousands of employees and paid in wages and benefits at least as much as, and probably more than, comparable companies in the area—which for most employees meant a comfortable living and security. It also offered rank-and-file employees training in new skills and afforded the able and ambitious opportunities to develop their potential capacities and to advance to responsible positions—such possibilities for the realization of an individual's potential are essential objectives of a democratic system and constitute an important contribution to general social advance. Humble, in addition, provided work in lesser or greater amounts for countless large and small suppliers of materials, equipment, and services, and for thousands of service-station dealers. Moreover, it earned royalty income for landowners who could not themselves test their lands for oil or develop production if oil was discovered. And it offered a market for the crude oil of thousands of specialized producers and storage and transportation for those who did not own such facilities. In brief, Humble's experience illustrates the extensive ramifications of one company's operations and shows how broadly a large company serves to provide opportunity in great variety to employees and to facilitate and co-ordinate the efforts of a wide range of specialists outside its own corporate fold.

Humble's per-unit realizations from these contributions and services from 1917 through 1948 were clearly modest. It is impossible to calculate for this whole span of years the exact average net earnings on a specific amount of work done, such as carrying a gallon of oil a given distance by pipeline. But it is possible to calculate averages that have some significance. In the case of transportation, the net income of $258,326,000 realized by Humble Pipe Line Company represented an average profit of 7.88 cents per barrel delivered by trunk pipelines, or about a fifth of a cent per gallon. This relatively small profit per unit bespeaks a large operation conducted efficiently at low cost. To figure net earnings per unit of product for other operations is impossible. It is meaningful to observe, however, that Humble's realization from the crude oil it produced averaged $1.396 per barrel, or 3.32 cents per gallon. In view of all the exploration, drilling, and production activities involved in providing crude, the gross realization for this valuable raw material cannot be regarded as anything but reasonable. This figure—which covers all costs as well as profits—epitomizes the effectiveness of progressive, mass-production operations.

It is significant that the prices of petroleum and its products during the three decades did not rise as much as the general wholesale commodities price level or labor rates in the United States. The trend of oil prices is illustrated by the accompanying chart showing the course of the price of Humble regular gasoline in Houston. Sales taxes on gasoline, which

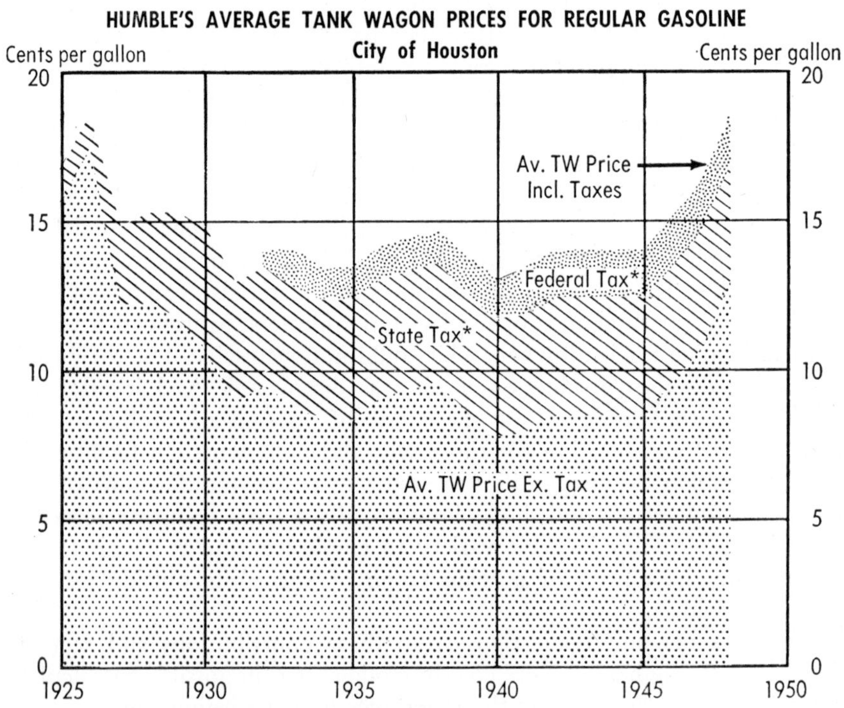

had their beginning in the period and gradually came to constitute a substantial share of the cost of gasoline to the consumer, are also shown on this chart.

Despite the modest per-unit profit from transportation and per-unit realization from the sale of Humble's crude oil production, the total profit earned for the company's owners was substantial. Humble's net earnings for the years 1917–1948 were $258,326,000 from Humble Pipe Line Company, its wholly owned subsidiary, and $765,588,000 from all other operations. Throughout its history Humble Oil & Refining Company—which received the pipeline subsidiary's earnings as dividends—followed the policy of paying its stockholders moderate but steady dividends and plowing back a large percentage of earnings. (See Appendix II, Table II.)

Humble actually generated most of the capital for its growth. At first it borrowed heavily to finance expansion—mostly from its largest stockholder, Standard Oil Company (New Jersey). But over the whole span of the decades covered by this history Humble's earnings supplied all but a small fraction of the funds for increasing its net worth from $8,400,000 at the end of 1917 to $673,500,000 at the end of 1948. Even if allowance is made for the depreciation of the dollar, this increase represents a substantial rate of growth.

No one set of circumstances accounts for Humble's record of service, influence, and growth. Certain environmental factors, obviously, were indispensable to the company's success, particularly the rich petroleum resources of its home territory. Important also was the time of its organization and growth, a period when the demand for oil products was rising sharply and advanced science and engineering were available for use in the oil industry. But not all external factors were favorable. In its earlier years, particularly, Humble had to adjust to the widespread suspicion in Texas of large corporations; this was of special importance to Humble because it was the only large company with by far the larger part of its operations in that state. An especially serious difficulty with which the company long had to cope, in common with the entire American oil industry, was the extreme and destructive form of competition that characterized the production of oil in this country until in the 1930s. Under the unregulated operation of the rule of capture, it was nearly impossible for a company to acquire an adequate backlog of reserves, or to hold production costs at levels that would be competitive with the more efficient unit production that was being developed on large concessions in other countries. Moreover, the same factors that stimulated Humble's growth also brought a tremendous expansion of the whole oil industry, at home and abroad, and an intense competition for markets. The result was a high degree of uncertainty and instability.

In such a dynamic and often unstable situation—which, of course, presents opportunities as well as difficulties—success is determined principally by a company's own administration. Administration is the function of men—men who determine objectives and set standards, who must choose between various alternatives in making decisions and plans, and who direct, co-ordinate, and control operations. Success, within the limits of circumstance, in the long run depends on the appropriateness and timeliness of decisions and on the competence with which they are carried out.

One of Humble's original directors, who resigned a few months after the company was organized but who was always an astute observer of its progress, attributed the company's success to owner-management. This is an old explanation of success in business, one set forth by no less an authority in matters economic than Adam Smith himself. Undoubtedly, owner-management was an important factor, particularly in plotting the course which the company was to follow. It was significant that the men who organized the company had full authority as owners, and that they were men of experience in the oil industry who committed their fortunes and their careers to the company. Two original owners early provided outstanding leadership and continued to do so as long as they were associated with Humble: Farish, who set new objectives for the company, who was the over-all planner and strategist, and who more than anyone else was responsible for adding certain strong men to management early in the company's existence; and Wiess, who was especially important in promoting research and engineering and careful economic and cost analysis.

But Humble could not have progressed as it did without the addition of men with trained and experienced competence in special fields. Within ten years of its founding, four professionally trained men had been added to its governing board: Townes, the lawyer, who knew petroleum and antitrust law and had a sensitive perception of that public opinion which is the ultimate lawmaker; Anderson, an engineer, who brought to Humble broad experience in pipeline management and crude oil operations; Pratt, a geologist, who combined the best qualities of the scholar and the businessman, and who proved to be a farseeing and courageous planner; and Suman, a petroleum engineer, who raised the efficiency and effectiveness of drilling and producing equipment, methods, and men, and who had a strong influence on the company's employee policies and practices and on its recognition of broad responsibilities as a large company. These men set the pattern for the addition of younger men to the management groups and ultimately to the top administration and the Board of Directors. In this way Humble early acquired an administrative group which had the capacity to provide responsible and progressive leadership in a dynamic industry.

Humble's administrators followed no one grand strategy; and no single decision or policy accounts for the company's strength. Their primary objective was to make profits in carrying on an oil business; but, although they sought to make profits year by year, they did not lose sight of the long-run implications of their policies and planning. They were firm negotiators and strong competitors. They had certain principles of action that conformed with their image of Humble as a progressive company and one that strove to be fair in all its relations. But they were pragmatists, who based their decisions on their company's changing needs and potential and on conditions and prospects as they saw them.

There is no single explanation of Humble's success except the general one that the company's administrators made a preponderance of right decisions and saw that these were effectively implemented. Certain decisions were more important than others, but actually few were independent of others. The degree of success with which a given decision was carried out was dependent on earlier ones—even the great reserve campaign of the 1930s would not have been so successful if it had not been preceded by certain strategic decisions and developments. There was a vertical and horizontal interdependence which determined the company's particular pattern of development.

The decision to organize Humble Oil & Refining Company was the first of a series that led to the expansion of the company and its operations to a size which made possible an emphasis on research and engineering, the lowering of unit costs through large-scale operations, and the effective use of capital in large amounts. The decision to form the new company was especially timely, for it came on the threshold of one of the oil industry's periods of greatest expansion. It was accompanied by the adoption of a policy followed consistently thereafter, that of paying moderate dividends and using a large percentage of net earnings for expansion, a policy which provided funds for growth and kept the company from acquiring heavy fixed capital costs.

Less than two years after Humble's incorporation came one of the most important decisions in its history—to sell stock to Standard Oil Company (New Jersey). The consequent association with the large company at once provided funds for expansion and a large market for oil. This association, moreover, without weakening the authority of its own Board of Directors, gave Humble the opportunity to draw upon the experience of Jersey Standard and its affiliates. In the 1920s Humble was able to expand its production, build an up-to-date refinery and a large pipeline and storage system, and enter upon extensive purchasing of crude oil. Its pipeline system, which provided an outlet from fields in all the producing regions of Texas, was especially profitable. Within a decade Humble had grown greatly in size and had become financially successful and strong.

Another series of early decisions provided the beginnings of the transition from old empirical methods to the rational, technological operations which played a fundamental role in Humble's success. The first was the decision in 1918 to hire a geologist; the second, in 1919, to employ an engineer with long pipeline experience to have charge of the construction and operation of a pipeline system; and the third to introduce chemical research and engineering in the company's refining.

The outstanding developments in the progress of Humble's transition to science-oriented operations in the first decade occurred in the search for oil. The employment of Pratt as geologist very soon brought important changes in the company's exploration and leasing. Pratt began at once to build what became a strong geologic staff. This group adopted advanced techniques, including micropaleontology and geophysics, and early became strong in geologic and geophysical research and exploration. A very important development was Pratt's being given charge in 1924 of scouting and leasing, which position was strengthened by his election to the Board of Directors in 1925. Humble thus, in contrast with many companies, adopted the significant policy of placing a geologist at the head of what is the most strategic branch of a producing company's operations.

Humble's early interest in science and engineering proved of particular importance when the company ran into trouble soon after the middle 1920s. With heavy investments, responsibilities as a supplier of crude and products to Jersey Standard and others, and obligations to purchase the oil of many crude oil producers, Humble found itself in an uncertain position. It had to have an adequate supply of oil at all times at almost any cost. But under the prevailing system of competitive production it could have no assurance of adequate reserves to meet future needs, and because of falling prices for crude oil and products it faced increased risks on inventory and also high producing costs relatively to prices.

In order to meet successfully the problems posed by this complex set of circumstances, Humble's Board of Directors in 1926 and 1927 made several decisions that rank among the most important in the company's history. These had their origin in the conviction of at least three men—Farish, Pratt, and Wiess—that the producing industry's waste of the natural resource and high costs could be reduced substantially only by the application of science and engineering to production. Accordingly, action was taken in two directions. In order to provide knowledge of the nature of reservoirs and their behavior under production, reservoir research was started in a small way in 1926 by refinery research men and was formally organized under a specialized reservoir research group in 1929. Also, late in 1926 John R. Suman was invited to join the company in order to introduce and develop petroleum engineering. The Board of Directors then formally adopted the policy of leasing prospective oil lands in large blocks in the hope of obtaining control of all or nearly all of a field or fields that might be developed on a block so as to apply desirable production practices. Moreover, they had come to believe that, in order to curb the worst excesses of competitive field development, it was necessary to modify oil and gas law and its administration.

These decisions were important both in themselves and in their timing. They enabled Humble to benefit from the relatively early improvement of its own operations and also to help raise industry standards and to contribute to the development of proration and other conservation regulations under the police powers of Texas and other states. To Humble, as to the industry, the results of the new technology and the new state regulation were more efficient and lower-cost production, the ultimate recovery of a larger percentage of the oil or gas in a reservoir, and the possibility of controlling the rate of production more nearly in accordance with market demand.

One of the outstanding contributions to Humble's strength in the 1930s was the company's program to acquire extensive reserves. Several policies and circumstances contributed to the success of this effort. One was the fact that Humble, as a result of its profitability and its policy of plowing back earnings, had funds with which to acquire proved or unproved acreage. Another was the company's policy of purchasing leases on a tremendous acreage during the years of depression in the oil industry when the market for oil lands was especially favorable. Important also was the 1927 decision to lease large blocks, which enabled Humble to exercise greater control of production in a number of large fields found on such blocks because of its ownership of all or nearly all the productive acreage of the fields. A basic factor in the success of Humble's reserve campaign was the strong exploration organization that had been built up in the earlier decade. To these must be added the developing system of state regulation which made possible the holding of reserves in the ground until needed, instead of producing from them competitively and hence wastefully, as had been done earlier.

Refining, like exploration and production, was strengthened by the early adoption of research and engineering for improving processes and products. Costs were reduced and efficiency raised by an increasing emphasis from about 1930 on economic studies and the analysis of costs, especially comparative costs for different crudes, processes, and equipment. In the period of recovery from the deep depression of the early 1930s, research was greatly expanded, and management was strengthened by promoting engineers to top managerial positions and by providing better training for the supervisory force. These developments reduced costs and made possible the manufacture of products of greater utility as well as of greater economic value. They enabled Humble to supply the higher-quality products demanded by the market in the 1930s and to provide aviation gasoline, synthetic toluene, and rubber to meet the crucial needs of the United States and its allies in the war.

At the same time that Humble was working to make more efficient use of its natural resources and operating facilities, it also improved and made more effective its human organization. An aspect of this development was the continuing effort to build a stable and high-quality employee force. This had its formal beginning in the decision made in 1920 to establish a system of annuities and benefits; it was furthered by the decision to set up an employee relations organization in 1929. The first of these led to the adoption of employee practices which contributed to stabilizing employment and improving morale. The second looked particularly toward improving the quality of the Humble organization. It brought improved methods of hiring and promotion, better training, more effective supervision, and generally strengthened performance. Gradually, also, was brought about a better co-ordination of the total administrative function, the allocation of greater responsibility and authority to the lower managerial levels, and more effective vertical and horizontal communication throughout the company.

By the time of World War II Humble had achieved great strength. It was strong financially. It had an outstandingly able and effective organization. With its extensive plant and facilities, advanced methods, and high-capacity operations, despite heavy expenditures for research and employee benefits, it generally had the advantage of relatively low unit costs. Its early application of chemical engineering to refining enabled it to manufacture old products of high quality and new ones of vital importance to the war effort. Finally, its success in carrying out its reserves-acquisition program gave it a position of comparatively great strength in production.

To assess the results to Humble of its outstanding contribution of products and services to the war effort is difficult. This contribution brought profits resulting largely from a substantial increase in production from extensive but low-cost reserves, which were depleted at frozen prices for crude and products. Humble's war record strengthened the company's standing in its home territory and in the national oil industry. Moreover, the company's top administrators and managers derived from their experiences a broadened view of the public responsibilities of their company and industry. The demonstration Humble had given of the importance of such an oil company to national security, however, was probably not known to the general public outside its home territory.

After the war was over, Humble continued to progress along the same general course that it had been following in the 1930s. Again, the company entered upon an extensive program to increase its reserves. It now threw more of its energy into the search for oil and the development of production in geographic regions hitherto little explored for oil and gas. It also moved in the direction of a more nearly balanced integration by a significant strengthening of its marketing in Texas, particularly increasing the distribution of its products through service stations. At the same time it took further steps to improve its management. These included a broadened and more effective utilization of economics and statistics and of accounting and budgeting as instruments of planning and control. Perhaps most significant as an indication of Humble's recognition of the growing pressures on a large oil company's management was the establishment of a formal program for selecting and developing men for higher managerial positions within the company.

The recognition of the need for specialized attention to providing men for the higher echelons of management symbolizes a change that had for some time been developing within Humble, and indeed Jersey Standard and its affiliates generally, as well as in other sectors of American business. It was clear to Humble's Board of Directors after the war that the company then faced a complexity of circumstances and challenges, internally and externally, beyond their earlier peacetime experience.

Several developments had for some time been narrowing the margin of advantage which Humble, like other progressive companies, had enjoyed because of its leadership in innovation in important aspects of operations. One was the generally high level of technology that had come to prevail in the oil industry. The pioneers in its development had borne the heavy costs of research and development, but as a result they had also for a time enjoyed the advantage of greater strength in competition with less progressive companies. As the utilization of research and engineering had broadened, however, the margin of advantage of the early innovators had gradually narrowed. No one doubted in 1948 that there was still room for further technological progress, but competition in that area had obviously become stronger. To maintain a comparatively advanced technological position would require Humble to place increasing emphasis on research and engineering.

Other developments had similarly narrowed the competitive advantages of the early leaders. For example, Humble no longer occupied the same advantageous position in the employment market that it had held earlier because of its reputation as an outstandingly progressive and dynamic company offering employees great opportunities for advancement, comparatively high total compensation, unusual stability of employment, and exceptional employee relations. It was still a leader, but the general improvement in the opportunities for and conditions of employment in the oil industry had raised general industry standards and practices, while pressure from organized labor had similarly tended to raise and equalize wage rates throughout the industry. In order to maintain a comparatively strong and productive employee force Humble would obviously have to give increasing attention to its employee policies and training, particularly to provide managers and supervisors especially competent in maintaining a stable and productive operating organization.

Most difficult to meet were certain developments that were external to the company and the oil industry. As in business generally after the war, both Humble and the oil industry felt the impact of an increasing drive for a higher standard of living that took such forms as higher wages, increased taxation, and price regulation in the interest of the consumer. The continuing pressure for higher wages and salaries posed the question of whether added compensation was accompanied by a proportionate increase in productivity, to which there was no easy answer. Political attacks on the depletion allowance on income from oil and gas production raised some serious issues. The threat of setting the price of gas at the wellhead by the Federal Power Commission in the interest of the out-of-state consumer foreshadowed the possibility of a ceiling on income that might become particularly serious for a company like Humble with large gas reserves. Significant also was evidence of a resurgence of attacks on big business by certain politicians and the courts.

These developments had not yet progressed far by 1948, and the problems they posed were potential rather than real. Certainly, the American oil industry had no cause for complaint under the condition of rising prices in the early postwar years. But rising costs and any threat of a ceiling on earnings were particularly important to the oil industry because of the increasing difficulty of finding new oil and the growing competition of oil from unit-operated production abroad. American oilmen did not doubt that they would find new reservoirs, but they were concerned over costs. Even if prices were allowed to rise, increasing costs might force them up to a point where other products would be substituted for certain oil products or foreign oil might supplant the American in the domestic market sufficiently to weaken the national industry.

Under normal conditions and in less strategic industries, such issues could be left to decision in the market place. However, because of the widespread use of petroleum products in the United States and particularly because of the importance of those products to national security, the problems of the oil industry were closely tied to issues of national well-being and security. The United States had gone far on the road to federal interference with the processes of the market, and there was no certainty, in the crosscurrents of political pressures from sectional and economic interest groups, that the good of the industry or even the general good would prevail where oil-industry issues were concerned. Moreover, there was no simple answer to the question as to how far the United States should go in protecting the domestic oil industry from foreign competition.

A basic difficulty was the fact that, for reasons too complex to examine here, there existed no adequate fund of knowledge or informed opinion about the industry on which to base national oil policy. The situation was reminiscent of the state of knowledge and opinion, even in the oil-producing states and on the part of the industry itself, when the conservation movement had first got under way. Many years of research and education had been required to provide the understanding of reservoirs on which to base industry practices and government policies that would bring about a less wasteful and more nearly equitable recovery of petroleum resources. A similar process of research and education was obviously needed at this later time to contribute toward some understanding of how, within the framework of the American system and with fairness to the diversity of interests involved, the American oil industry could best continue to play its vital role.

The men responsible for Humble's administration in 1948 faced far different challenges than those faced by their predecessors three decades earlier, challenges which bespoke great changes in the company itself, in the oil industry, and in the large national and international community of which Humble was a corporate member. At this later time, the company's administrators were responsible for managing operations representing tremendous fixed capital investments, for meeting enormous obligations to supply the current and future markets, and for maintaining and directing a large employee force, which on the lowest levels required a large measure of skill and dependability and in the highest ranks called for great scientific and engineering capabilities. At the same time these administrators had to meet vigorous competition. Because of the generally high technological and administrative competence of its competitors, Humble had to continue to progress beyond its own high levels, which were already straining the best efforts of its scientists, engineers, and administrators. Significant also were the developing public attitudes and policies which foreshadowed increasing restrictions on the oil industry, on the interplay of free competitive forces, and on large corporate enterprise.

There was every prospect at the end of 1948, however, that, within the limits of circumstance, the men responsible for Humble's policies, planning, and management would keep their company strong. They were broadening and deepening the base of their planning and working with sharpened tools of cost analysis and an improving technology to reduce costs. They were continuing to expand the company's research. They were also giving increasing attention to employee training—particularly for specialists in advanced technology in various fields—and to executive development. They were striving to maintain a workable balance among the many interests concerned in or affected by their company's operations. And they were pressing with increasing vigor Humble's quest for gas and oil.

Appendix 1

DIRECTORS AND OFFICERS ELECTED IN THE YEARS 1917–1948 WITH TERMINAL DATES THROUGH 1958

A. Humble Oil & Refining Company

Directors

R. L. Blaffer	June 21, 1917—September 4, 1941
L. A. Carlton	June 21, 1917—July 22, 1925
W. S. Farish	June 21, 1917—June 6, 1933
W. W. Fondren	June 21, 1917—June 12, 1933
C. B. Goddard	June 21, 1917—October 7, 1929
Jesse H. Jones	June 21, 1917—February 11, 1918
F. P. Sterling	June 21, 1917—June 12, 1933
R. S. Sterling	June 21, 1917—February 16, 1925
H. C. Wiess	June 21, 1917—August 26, 1948
E. E. Townes	February 11, 1918—September 9, 1943
W. S. Smullin	February 9, 1920—February 14, 1921
James A. Anderson	February 14, 1921—April 27, 1942
J. S. Bonner	February 20, 1922—June 12, 1933
Wallace E. Pratt	February 16, 1925—May 31, 1937
John R. Suman	January 17, 1927—January 31, 1945
Hines H. Baker	February 8, 1937—April 29, 1957
L. T. Barrow	February 8, 1937—May 9, 1955
S. A. Giraud	February 14, 1938—December 22, 1940
David Frame	February 10, 1941—May 9, 1955
D. B. Harris	February 10, 1941—August 8, 1953

J. A. Neath . . . . April 27, 1942—November 16, 1957
Rex G. Baker . . . . September 10, 1943—August 29, 1956
H. W. Ferguson . . . . . February 12, 1945—
Morgan J. Davis . . . . . May 10, 1948—
C. E. Reistle, Jr. . . . . . May 10, 1948—

Chairmen of the Board

R. S. Sterling . . . . October 23, 1922—February 16, 1925
R. L. Blaffer . . . . February 8, 1937—August 4, 1941
H. C. Wiess . . . . May 10, 1948—August 26, 1948
L. T. Barrow . . . . October 28, 1948—May 9, 1955

Presidents

R. S. Sterling . . . . June 21, 1917—October 23, 1922
W. S. Farish . . . . October 23, 1922—June 6, 1933
R. L. Blaffer . . . . June 7, 1933—February 8, 1937
H. C. Wiess . . . . February 8, 1937—May 10, 1948
Hines H. Baker . . . . . . May 10, 1948—April 29, 1957

Executive Vice-Presidents

H. C. Wiess . . . . June 7, 1933—February 8, 1937
Hines H. Baker . . . . . . February 12, 1945—May 10, 1948

Vice-Presidents

R. L. Blaffer . . . . June 21, 1917—June 7, 1933
W. S. Farish . . . . June 21, 1917—October 23, 1922
F. P. Sterling . . . . June 21, 1917—June 12, 1933
H. C. Wiess . . . . June 21, 1917—June 7, 1933
W. S. Smullin . . . . March 20, 1920—February 14, 1921
James A. Anderson . . . February 15, 1921—April 27, 1942
J. S. Bonner . . . . February 20, 1922—June 12, 1933
Wallace E. Pratt . . . . June 12, 1933—May 31, 1937
John R. Suman . . . . . . June 12, 1933—January 31, 1945
E. E. Townes . . . . June 12, 1933—September 9, 1943
L. T. Barrow . . . . February 14, 1938—October 28, 1948
Hines H. Baker . . . . . February 10, 1941—May 10, 1948
David Frame . . . . February 12, 1945—May 9, 1955
D. B. Harris . . . . May 12, 1947—August 8, 1953
J. A. Neath . . . . May 12, 1947—May 9, 1955

General Counsel

E. E. Townes . . . . February 13, 1922—September 9, 1943
Rex G. Baker . . . . September 10, 1943—August 29, 1956

Treasurers

Florence M. Sterling .. June 21, 1917—April 8, 1919
R. L. Blaffer .... April 8, 1919—August 4, 1941
James A. Anderson ... August 4, 1941—April 27, 1942
D. B. Harris .... April 27, 1942—June 30, 1953

Comptrollers

L. H. Attwell, Jr. .... September 15, 1919—September 19, 1940
Gay Carroll .... September 20, 1940—October 31, 1953

Secretaries

Florence M. Sterling .. June 21, 1917—February 16, 1925
F. O. Freese .... February 16, 1925—February 14, 1938
J. S. Crate .... February 14, 1938—December 14, 1940
H. K. Arnold .... February 10, 1941—August 22, 1958

B. Humble Pipe Line Company

Presidents

R. S. Sterling .... March 3, 1919—March 2, 1920
James A. Anderson ... March 2, 1920—February 12, 1921
W. M. Cleaves .... February 21, 1921—February 2, 1925
Ralph V. Hanrahan ... February 2, 1925—October 9, 1950

Appendix II

STATISTICAL TABLES

TABLE I

CAPITAL STOCK AND OWNERSHIP, HUMBLE OIL & REFINING COMPANY, 1917–1948

Year	Changes in Authorized Shares of Stock				As of December 31		
	Date	Par Value	Shares	Amount	Outstanding Shares	No. of Share-holders	Shares Owned by SONJ
1917	June 21[a]	$100	40,000	$ 4,000,000	40,000	131	....
1918	Oct. 1	100	40,900	4,090,000	40,900	144	....
1919	Feb. 10	100	82,000	8,200,000	....	....	....
	Oct. 26	100	250,000	25,000,000	250,000	288	140,000
1920	....	....	....	....	250,000	554	140,931
1921	....	....	....	....	250,000	624	140,931
1922	Dec. 31	25	1,750,000	43,750,000	1,750,000	694	1,063,524
1923	....	....	....	....	1,750,000	1,267	1,063,524
1924	....	....	....	....	1,750,000	1,260	1,063,524
1925	....	....	....	....	1,750,000	1,524	1,103,524
1926	Mar. 1	25	3,000,000	75,000,000	2,924,703	2,301	1,839,207
1927	....	....	....	....	2,947,428	2,773	1,839,207
1928	....	....	....	....	2,964,132	2,899	1,839,207
1929	....	....	....	....	2,967,545	3,648	1,839,207
1930	....	....	....	....	2,966,338	5,681	1,918,507
1931	....	....	....	....	2,964,138	5,446	2,048,870
1932	....	....	....	....	2,964,138	5,092	2,144,832
1933	Dec. 19	NPV	9,000,000	....	8,954,145	5,133	6,441,096
1934	Dec. 17	NPV	....	175,000,000[b]	8,968,479	5,445	6,441,096
1935	....	....	....	....	8,985,662	7,114	6,441,096
1936	....	....	....	....	8,987,840	8,197	6,441,096
1937	....	....	....	....	8,987,840	7,657	6,441,096
1938	....	....	....	....	8,987,840	9,712	6,441,096
1939	....	....	....	....	8,987,840	9,332	6,441,096
1940	....	....	....	....	8,987,840	9,139	6,441,096
1941	....	....	....	....	8,987,840	8,941	6,441,096
1942	....	....	....	....	8,987,840	9,033	6,441,096
1943	Nov. 22	NPV	18,000,000	....	17,975,680	8,970	12,922,192
1944	....	....	....	....	17,975,680	9,945	12,926,192
1945	....	....	....	....	17,975,680	10,601	12,967,192
1946	May 13	NPV	....	300,000,000[b]	17,975,680	11,399	12,967,192
1947	....	....	....	....	17,975,680	11,472	12,967,192
1948	May 10	NPV	....	475,000,000[b]	17,975,680	11,532	13,017,192

[a] The date of incorporation.
[b] Stated capital was increased by transfer of surplus without changing the number of shares.

Source: Records of Humble Oil & Refining Company.

TABLE II

NET INCOME, DIVIDENDS, NET INCOME INVESTED IN THE BUSINESS AND SHAREHOLDERS' INVESTMENT

HUMBLE OIL & REFINING COMPANY AND SUBSIDIARY COMPANY, 1917–1948

(Million dollars)

Year	*Net Income*	*Dividends*[a] *Total*	*Dividends*[a] *As Per Cent of Earnings*	*Net Income Invested in Business*	*Shareholders' Investment*[b] *(Net Worth)*
1917	0.9	...	...	0.9	8.4
1918	3.1	0.7	21.0	2.4	11.0
1919	−1.3	0.8	...	−2.1	51.9
1920	6.5	2.0	30.0	4.5	56.5
1921	−1.1	2.0	...	−3.1	53.6
1922	−1.2	2.0	...	−3.2	51.2
1923	5.1	2.1	41.5	3.0	54.2
1924	9.8	2.1	21.4	7.7	61.9
1925	22.6	2.1	9.3	20.5	82.4
1926	19.4	4.9	25.3	14.5	126.5
1927	7.1	5.9	82.6	1.2	129.1
1928	19.3	5.9	30.7	13.4	143.6
1929	32.5	5.9	18.2	26.6	171.3
1930	18.1	7.4	41.1	10.7	180.2
1931	2.8	5.9	214.3	−3.1	183.2
1932	14.9	5.9	39.8	9.0	191.2
1933	20.8	5.9	28.6	14.9	206.6
1934	22.0	9.0	40.8	13.0	212.4
1935	24.0	9.0	37.5	15.0	228.2
1936	34.2	13.5	39.4	20.7	249.6
1937	46.9	18.0	38.3	28.9	277.9
1938	35.8	18.0	50.2	17.8	295.4
1939	30.0	18.0	60.0	12.0	307.1
1940	28.1	18.0	64.0	10.1	313.1
1941	35.4	18.0	50.8	17.4	328.8
1942	29.2	18.0	61.5	11.2	339.7
1943	45.7	22.5	49.2	23.2	363.0
1944	60.5	26.9	44.5	33.6	396.5
1945	70.9	27.0	38.0	43.9	444.6
1946	71.8	29.2	40.7	42.6	489.2
1947	124.1	53.9	43.5	70.2	559.4
1948	186.1	71.9	38.6	114.2	673.5

[a] See Table I for changes in number of shares and amount of capital.
[b] As of December 31.

Source: Records of Humble Oil & Refining Company.

TABLE III

CONSOLIDATED BALANCE SHEET: ASSETS
HUMBLE OIL & REFINING COMPANY AND SUBSIDIARY COMPANY, 1917–1948

(Million dollars)

	Current Assets								
	Cash	*U. S. Gov't. Secur.*	*Receivables*	*Inventories*	*Total*	*Invest-ments & Advances*	*Net Fixed Assets*	*Net Deferred Charges & Credits*	*Total Assets*
1917	0.1	0.1	1.0	0.9	2.1	....	8.0	....	10.1
1918	.6	.5	1.5	1.5	4.1	0.1	9.9	0.4	14.5
1919	.5	.6	19.4	12.6	33.1	.1	34.1	.2	67.5
1920	1.1	.6	7.9	35.8	45.4	.1	51.0	.8	97.3
1921	1.0	.6	7.4	39.5	48.5	.1	57.9	1.1	107.6
1922	1.8	....	6.5	43.7	52.0	.1	59.0	.7	111.8
1923	1.1	....	4.9	48.7	54.7	.2	65.6	1.1	121.6
1924	4.6	....	6.5	51.3	62.4	.2	69.0	.9	132.4
1925	4.4	....	7.9	55.2	67.5	.2	88.6	–.3	156.1
1926	3.8	....	13.5	53.6	70.9	.6	107.9	–.3	179.1
1927	2.2	....	16.5	41.1	59.8	1.1	128.3	.7	189.9
1928	3.2	....	29.2	39.7	72.1	2.1	130.8	.2	205.2
1929	5.5	....	36.9	48.9	91.3	3.9	143.6	.5	239.3
1930	6.5	.6	37.5	48.4	93.0	5.4	145.7	.2	244.3
1931	8.5	....	32.4	32.3	73.2	5.5	162.5	.1	241.3
1932	4.2	....	23.9	26.3	54.4	6.2	167.6	.1	228.3
1933	4.4	.1	25.5	25.0	55.0	13.0	179.0	.5	247.5
1934	6.2	....	13.7	25.7	45.6	6.5	193.1	–1.3	243.9
1935	5.6	....	11.7	24.1	41.4	7.0	204.1	–.2	252.3
1936	7.0	....	10.6	24.7	42.3	7.0	226.3	.8	276.4
1937	6.9	....	8.8	34.1	49.8	7.6	269.9	1.3	328.6
1938	10.4	....	17.4	30.1	57.9	7.8	295.4	1.7	362.8
1939	16.8	....	13.8	30.1	60.7	7.8	304.3	1.8	374.6
1940	20.6	....	11.7	32.7	65.0	6.3	313.1	1.2	385.6
1941	21.8	5.0	13.1	36.4	76.3	4.3	325.1	1.1	406.8
1942	12.4	5.0	21.3	45.1	83.8	3.8	336.6	.9	425.1
1943	35.4	25.0	33.0	38.3	131.7	3.1	341.5	1.2	477.5
1944	36.7	48.2	39.8	39.0	163.7	1.9	353.6	1.4	520.6
1945	49.2	48.3	32.1	42.9	172.5	1.4	384.2	.8	558.9
1946	56.2	10.2	33.2	51.5	151.1	1.4	437.5	.9	590.9
1947	60.0	45.0	59.2	54.2	218.4	2.6	481.7	1.0	703.7
1948	55.0	53.0	121.1	68.2	297.3	2.3	560.7	1.0	861.3

TABLE III (Continued)

CONSOLIDATED BALANCE SHEET: LIABILITIES AND SHAREHOLDERS' INVESTMENT
HUMBLE OIL & REFINING COMPANY AND SUBSIDIARY COMPANY, 1917–1948

(Million dollars)

	Current Liabilities				*Long-Term Liabilities*					
	Accts. Pay. & Accr. Liabs.	*Notes Pay. Banks*	*Est. Liab. For Fed. Inc. Tax*	*Total*	*Notes Pay. Banks*	*Deben. Bonds*	*Purch. Oblig. & Other Long-Term Liabs.*	*Total*	*Share-holders' Invest-ment*	*Total Liabs. and Shareholders' Investment*
1917	0.5	0.6	0.3	1.4	0.3	....	....	0.3	8.4	10.1
1918	1.2	1.7	.6	3.5	....	....	....	....	11.0	14.5
1919	15.0	.2	.2	15.4	.2	....	....	.2	51.9	67.5
1920	39.3	.1	1.2	40.6	.2	....	....	.2	56.5	97.3
1921	27.2	.1	.7	28.0	26.0	....	....	26.0	53.6	107.6
1922	33.8	.2	.8	34.8	.7	25.0	....	25.7	51.2	111.8
1923	41.2	....	.8	42.0	.5	25.0	....	25.5	54.2	121.6
1924	43.5	....	1.8	45.3	.2	25.0	....	25.2	61.9	132.4
1925	45.5	....	3.1	48.6	....	25.0	....	25.0	82.4	156.1
1926	18.6	6.0	3.0	27.6	....	25.0	....	25.0	126.5	179.1
1927	10.1	....	1.5	11.6	....	49.2	....	49.2	129.1	189.9
1928	11.4	....	3.0	14.4	....	47.2	....	47.2	143.6	205.2
1929	19.1	....	4.3	23.4	....	44.6	....	44.6	171.3	239.3
1930	15.2	....	2.1	17.3	.1	43.8	2.9	46.8	180.2	244.3
1931	11.2	....	.3	11.5	.1	42.9	3.5	46.5	183.2	241.3
1932	10.2	....	.3	10.5	.1	18.9	7.6	26.6	191.2	228.3
1933	13.1	....	1.3	14.4	....	18.9	7.7	26.6	206.6	247.5
1934	12.5	6.5	1.4	20.4	6.5	....	4.7	11.2	212.4	243.9
1935	10.6	6.5	2.2	19.3	....	....	4.8	4.8	228.2	252.3
1936	18.5	....	3.8	22.3	....	....	4.6	4.6	249.6	276.4
1937	41.3	....	3.5	44.8	....	....	6.0	6.0	277.9	328.6
1938	17.4	....	3.0	20.4	5.0	....	42.0	47.0	295.4	362.8
1939	17.3	....	3.1	20.4	5.0	....	42.1	47.1	307.1	374.6
1940	19.7	....	4.1	23.8	5.0	....	43.6	48.6	313.1	385.6
1941	21.9	....	8.5	30.4	5.0	....	42.6	47.6	328.8	406.8
1942	21.0	....	6.8	27.8	....	50.0	7.6	57.6	339.7	425.1
1943	29.4	....	31.6	61.0	....	50.0	3.5	53.5	363.0	477.5
1944	35.5	....	45.9	81.4	....	40.0	2.7	42.7	396.5	520.6
1945	41.1	....	29.6	70.7	40.0	....	3.6	43.6	444.6	558.9
1946	41.4	....	17.6	59.0	40.0	....	2.7	42.7	489.2	590.9
1947	70.6	....	31.3	101.9	40.0	....	2.4	42.4	559.4	703.7
1948	81.2	....	57.0	138.2	40.0	....	9.5	49.5	673.5	861.3

Source: Records of Humble Oil & Refining Company.

TABLE IV

INVESTMENT IN FIXED ASSETS AT DECEMBER 31
HUMBLE OIL & REFINING COMPANY AND SUBSIDIARY COMPANY, 1917–1948

(Million dollars)

	Gross					Net				
	Oil & Gas Prod.[a]	*Mfg. and Mktg.*	*Pipe Line*	*All Other*	*Total*	*Oil & Gas Prod.*	*Mfg. and Mktg.*	*Pipe Line*	*All Other*	*Total*
1917	8.5	0.3	0.1	0.2	9.1	7.5	0.3	0.1	0.1	8.0
1918	12.0	.9	.1	.1	13.1	9.0	.7	.1	.1	9.9
1919	25.3	5.0	9.0	.7	40.0	19.9	4.9	8.8	.5	34.1
1920	34.7	11.7	14.3	2.1	62.8	24.9	11.2	13.1	1.8	51.0
1921	41.5	16.1	16.6	3.8	78.0	26.2	14.3	14.1	3.3	57.9
1922	44.9	18.4	17.6	4.5	85.4	26.3	15.5	13.5	3.7	59.0
1923	53.3	21.3	20.4	4.8	99.8	30.1	17.0	14.8	3.7	65.6
1924	55.9	24.1	26.3	3.8	110.1	29.2	18.3	18.7	2.8	69.0
1925	67.7	32.8	33.6	4.7	138.8	37.0	24.9	23.3	3.4	88.6
1926	82.1	38.4	43.8	5.1	169.4	45.8	27.9	30.5	3.7	107.9
1927	86.1	43.5	68.9	4.3	202.8	45.3	29.5	50.8	2.7	128.3
1928	85.5	51.5	76.2	4.4	217.6	41.1	34.1	52.9	2.7	130.8
1929	81.4	66.1	81.1	4.6	233.2	43.4	44.5	52.8	2.9	143.6
1930	85.6	74.3	83.2	4.6	247.7	44.3	48.2	49.8	3.4	145.7
1931	98.1	74.4	86.7	5.0	264.2	54.1	48.3	56.5	3.6	162.5
1932	104.1	74.5	87.0	5.0	270.6	65.1	45.5	53.6	3.4	167.6
1933	124.0	74.4	86.1	4.7	289.2	83.3	42.6	49.9	3.2	179.0
1934	149.0	66.3	86.0	5.3	306.6	108.3	34.1	46.9	3.8	193.1
1935	168.0	66.6	84.8	6.2	325.6	123.7	32.0	44.0	4.4	204.1
1936	193.2	69.8	87.4	6.6	357.0	144.0	32.9	44.9	4.5	226.3
1937	234.4	77.5	93.6	7.1	412.6	177.4	39.2	48.3	5.0	269.9
1938	268.5	81.7	94.9	6.8	451.9	203.0	41.1	47.1	4.2	295.4
1939	284.2	84.8	95.4	7.6	472.0	212.1	41.6	45.6	5.0	304.3
1940	299.0	89.5	97.3	7.9	493.7	220.2	43.8	44.0	5.1	313.1
1941	318.4	95.9	97.4	9.2	520.9	229.9	47.2	41.7	6.3	325.1
1942	332.9	108.9	98.2	8.1	548.1	233.7	57.4	40.8	4.7	336.6
1943	349.9	114.5	99.1	8.2	571.7	239.1	59.0	38.7	4.7	341.5
1944	383.6	115.4	101.4	8.3	608.7	256.4	54.6	37.8	4.8	353.6
1945	441.1	110.2	104.4	8.6	664.3	295.7	47.2	36.6	4.7	384.2
1946	499.5	121.2	113.5	8.6	742.8	334.0	56.1	42.6	4.8	437.5
1947	548.6	133.2	123.3	9.1	814.2	361.4	64.1	51.0	5.2	481.7
1948	639.0	146.4	129.1	9.8	924.3	424.6	74.4	56.0	5.7	560.7

... plants for all years except 1921-1930, when gas plants are included in Manufacturing Department.

SELECTED DATA ON SOURCE AND DISTRIBUTION OF CAPITAL FUNDS AND WORKING CAPITAL
HUMBLE OIL & REFINING COMPANY AND SUBSIDIARY COMPANY, 1917–1948

(Million dollars)

	Source of Funds						Capital Expenditures					
			Money from Outside Sources									
	Recovery of Previous Capital Expend.[a]	*Retained Earn.*	*Borrowed*	*Sale or Pur. of Stock*	*Other*	*Total Avail. for Capital Expend.*	*Total*	*Oil & Gas Prod.*[b]	*Mfg. and Mktg.*	*Pipe Line*	*All Other*	*Working Capital*
1917	2.0	0.9	0.3	7.5	0.1	10.8	10.1	9.5	0.3	0.1	0.2	0.7
1918	3.6	2.4	–.3	.2	–.5	5.4	5.5	4.3	.7	. . .	.5	.6
1919	8.4	–2.1	.2	43.1	–.2	49.4	32.3	18.4	4.7	8.8	.4	17.7
1920	16.5	4.5	. . .	. . .	–.7	20.3	33.3	19.7	6.5	5.3	1.8	4.7
1921	14.4	–3.1	25.9	.2	–.1	37.3	21.6	13.7	3.9	2.6	1.4	20.4
1922	14.6	–3.2	–.3	. . .	1.4	12.5	15.7	11.6	2.7	1.3	.1	17.2
1923	16.6	3.0	–.2	. . .	–.6	18.8	23.2	16.4	2.9	3.9	. . .	12.8
1924	14.7	7.7	–.3	. . .	4.7	26.8	22.5	9.8	4.2	8.4	.1	17.1
1925	19.8	20.5	–.2	. . .	1.4	41.5	39.7	21.4	9.3	9.0	. . .	18.9
1926	22.3	14.5	. . .	29.6	1.5	67.9	43.4	24.7	6.8	11.8	.1	43.4
1927	22.9	1.2	24.2	1.4	–2.4	47.3	42.5	10.2	5.7	26.6	. . .	48.2
1928	25.7	13.4	–2.0	1.2	.6	38.9	29.3	10.0	10.1	9.1	.1	57.8
1929	29.8	26.6	–2.6	.5	. . .	54.3	44.2	20.9	16.8	6.2	.3	67.9
1930	26.5	10.7	–.7	. . .	1.5	38.0	30.1	14.5	11.9	3.6	.1	75.8
1931	17.9	–3.2	–.9	.1	3.6	17.5	31.6	17.5	6.9	7.1	.1	61.7
1932	18.8	9.0	–20.2	. . .	–2.9	4.7	22.5	19.5	1.3	1.7	. . .	43.9
1933	14.8	14.9	–.1	.8	–2.6	27.8	31.1	27.5	1.2	2.2	.2	40.6
1934	17.2	13.0	–11.9	.3	6.1	24.7	40.1	36.0	1.4	2.1	.6	25.2
1935	18.8	15.0	–6.5	.9	. . .	28.2	31.3	26.3	1.6	2.1	1.3	22.1
1936	18.6	20.7	2.5	.1	–1.0	40.9	43.0	32.1	4.5	6.2	.2	20.0
1937	20.1	28.9	22.7	. . .	4.8	76.5	66.2	47.8	10.0	7.5	.9	30.3
1938	21.9	17.8	14.8	. . .	2.3	56.8	49.7	41.0	6.1	2.9	–.3	37.4
1939	22.1	12.0	. . .	. . .	2.7	36.8	33.9	24.9	5.1	3.0	.9	40.3
1940	21.0	10.1	1.9	. . .	–.2	32.8	32.0	23.7	6.8	1.4	.1	41.1
1941	21.9	17.4	–.6	. . .	3.2	41.9	37.2	25.1	8.1	2.5	1.5	45.8
1942	23.8	11.3	10.3	. . .	3.3	48.7	38.5	19.4	15.1	3.9	.1	56.0
1943	26.9	23.2	–3.7	. . .	4.0	50.4	35.7	24.5	8.2	3.0	. . .	70.7
1944	33.9	33.6	–10.6	. . .	3.3	60.2	48.6	42.0	2.8	3.9	–.1	82.3
1945	40.1	43.9	–.6	. . .	10.2	93.6	74.1	65.1	3.9	4.8	.3	101.8
1946	37.0	42.6	–.5	. . .	4.5	83.6	93.3	67.7	14.8	10.4	.4	92.1
1947	47.0	70.2	–0.4	. . .	3.7	120.5	96.1	67.5	14.0	14.2	.4	116.5
1948	54.5	114.2	. . .	. . .	12.2	180.9	138.3	110.2	16.2	11.3	0.6	159.1

[a] Includes intangible development costs for years 1917 through 1930; these costs were expensed through those years but were capitalized in 1931 and subsequent years. Also recovery by depletion, depreciation, sale of properties, etc., is included.
[b] Includes Crude Oil Department, gas plants, and gas systems for all years except 1921-1930, when gas plants are included in Manufacturing Department.
Source: Records of Humble Oil & Refining Company.

TABLE VI

STATEMENT OF INCOME
HUMBLE OIL & REFINING COMPANY AND SUBSIDIARY COMPANY, 1917–1948

(Thousand dollars)

	Revenue								
	Operating Revenue								
	Sales of Crude Oil	*Sales of Products*	*Sales of Natural Gas*	*Other Sales and Services*	*Total Operating Revenue*	*Non-operating Revenue*	*Total Revenue*	*Costs, Expenses, and Taxes*	*Net Income*
1917	2,890	668	14	131	3,703	21	3,724	2,846	878
1918	6,383	3,645	159	13	10,200	29	10,229	7,176	3,053
1919	6,585	4,476	150	19	11,231	257	11,488	12,762	−1,274
1920	55,020	10,144	335	210	65,709	165	65,874	59,401	6,473
1921	42,411	11,192	442	240	54,285	225	54,510	55,653	−1,143
1922	40,922	12,431	422	467	54,242	246	54,488	55,644	−1,156
1923	42,459	21,179	434	211	64,282	135	64,417	59,359	5,058
1924	53,230	36,450	277	374	90,331	131	90,462	80,627	9,835
1925	75,397	56,434	359	179	132,369	321	132,690	110,066	22,624
1926	76,298	77,085	336	204	153,923	216	154,139	134,753	19,386
1927	71,029	83,868	263	450	155,611	381	155,992	148,880	7,112
1928	63,377	103,722	393	416	167,910	1,119	169,029	149,752	19,277
1929	77,881	116,158	483	524	195,046	4,716	199,762	167,227	32,535
1930	57,268	102,639	478	722	161,107	1,372	162,479	144,396	18,083
1931	44,346	55,309	361	2,443	102,459	840	103,299	100,534	2,765
1932	55,035	53,936	242	4,260	113,472	816	114,288	99,391	14,897
1933	48,200	52,057	253	4,620	105,130	363	105,493	84,645	20,848
1934	72,155	52,145	85	5,136	129,522	859	130,381	108,391	21,990
1935	72,366	53,162	133	6,931	132,592	369	132,961	108,995	23,966
1936	90,034	56,265	695	9,037	156,031	437	156,468	122,284	34,184
1937	118,289	86,005	921	8,524	213,738	572	214,310	167,386	46,924
1938	94,014	105,116	866	5,738	205,733	446	206,179	170,379	35,800
1939	89,349	105,315	810	4,311	199,786	507	200,293	170,343	29,950
1940	82,144	111,994	1,149	3,792	199,079	352	199,431	171,323	28,108
1941	94,936	133,321	1,038	3,311	232,606	363	232,969	197,612	35,357
1942	82,762	136,894	2,109	4,394	226,159	353	226,512	197,269	29,243
1943	148,507	170,585	3,280	8,094	330,465	362	330,827	285,115	45,712
1944	209,179	202,407	4,214	12,553	428,353	471	428,824	368,298	60,526
1945	220,630	207,714	3,724	11,909	443,977	667	444,644	373,749	70,895
1946	249,695	197,071	3,429	6,993	457,188	592	457,780	385,948	71,832
1947	430,827	281,294	4,654	8,583	725,358	523	725,881	601,774	124,107
1948	649,264	384,327	7,524	11,118	1,052,233	1,619	1,053,852	867,783	186,069

(Thousand dollars)

	Costs & Operating & Gen'l. Expenses	Dry Hole Costs	Expenses Not Requiring Funds: Surrendered Leases	Expenses Not Requiring Funds: Deprn., Depln., Amortz., and Retiremts.[a]	Interest Charges	Total Taxes	Memo: Gasoline and Lubricating Oil Taxes Collected for State and Fed. Gov't.
1917	373	251	257	1,740	36	189	N.A.[b]
1918	2,953	....	9	3,563	50	601	"
1919	3,839	244	363	8,048	18	250	"
1920	37,328	2,892	1,875	14,581	927	1,798	"
1921	34,930	2,308	2,737	11,662	3,140	876	"
1922	33,621	2,286	1,280	13,320	4,238	899	"
1923	37,021	1,089	1,504	15,123	3,353	1,269	"
1924	58,314	1,238	1,475	13,210	3,782	2,608	"
1925	80,785	1,810	1,327	18,519	3,643	3,982	"
1926	104,412	1,987	1,826	20,492	2,265	3,771	"
1927	118,996	2,300	3,167	19,742	2,660	2,015	934
1928	116,200	1,442	3,832	21,908	2,734	3,636	1,040
1929	127,252	2,156	2,781	27,009	2,584	5,445	1,570
1930	109,043	1,824	3,750	22,775	2,640	4,364	2,452
1931	77,289	745	5,616	12,295	2,443	2,146	2,341
1932	75,333	584	2,857	15,895	1,846	2,876	2,483
1933	63,207	949	2,068	12,722	1,107	4,592	3,759
1934	82,238	2,391	2,378	14,825	976	5,583	3,171
1935	79,934	3,025	3,505	15,317	479	6,735	3,440
1936	92,718	2,127	2,906	15,662	520	8,351	3,789
1937	132,727	2,810	2,911	17,193	505	11,240	4,207
1938	132,099	4,253	4,708	17,241	910	11,168	4,391
1939	132,704	3,445	5,251	16,823	1,197	10,923	4,574
1940	133,011	3,730	3,474	17,490	1,416	12,202	4,848
1941	154,088	3,010	2,381	19,484	1,420	17,229	5,989
1942	151,912	3,230	3,586	20,256	1,965	16,320	6,034
1943	208,352	5,279	2,445	24,421	1,696	42,922	7,574
1944	271,644	11,714	2,992	30,931	1,709	49,308	7,675
1945	292,507	15,064	3,606	36,458	1,981	24,133	8,566
1946	304,253	20,474	3,872	32,452	1,895	23,002	11,124
1947	486,850	16,772	6,815	39,134	1,656	50,547	14,518
1948	704,847	26,498	4,661	48,924	730	82,123	18,487

[a] Does not include depreciation treated as a part of dry-hole costs. Depreciation, depletion, amortization, and retirements includes intangible development costs for years 1917 through 1930 which were expensed in those years and capitalized in 1931 and subsequent years. [b] Not available prior to 1927.

Source: Records of Humble Oil & Refining Company.

TABLE VII

EMPLOYEES: SELECTED DATA
HUMBLE OIL & REFINING COMPANY AND SUBSIDIARY COMPANY, 1917–1948

	Total Number of Employees December 31	Thousand Dollars		
		Total Payroll	Total Benefits	Total Employee Compensation
1917	541	524	N.A.	N.A.
1918	1,078	1,198	"	"
1919	7,285	5,055	"	"
1920	5,935	8,801	"	"
1921	6,100	8,317	"	"
1922	4,073	8,640	"	"
1923	5,748	9,277	"	"
1924	8,169	10,889	"	"
1925	8,579	14,694	"	"
1926	12,256	16,626	"	"
1927	12,266	19,556	"	"
1928	10,442	18,757	"	"
1929	12,548	21,874	"	"
1930	9,944	19,782	"	"
1931	8,988	17,844	"	"
1932	9,207	14,433	"	"
1933	10,352	15,451	"	"
1934	11,420	18,658	"	"
1935	11,185	20,033	"	"
1936	12,949	23,009	2,363	25,372
1937	13,732	27,978	3,760	31,738
1938	13,235	28,695	3,752	32,447
1939	12,943	28,352	2,977	31,329
1940	12,610	27,928	6,209	34,137
1941	13,194	30,794	3,339	34,133
1942	12,557	34,587	3,126	37,713
1943	13,409	41,989	3,816	45,805
1944	14,359	49,126	4,404	53,530
1945	16,056	53,259	7,667	60,926
1946	17,375	58,831	9,380	68,211
1947	18,023	70,082	16,501	86,583
1948	18,954	82,310	23,118	105,428

Source: Records of Humble Oil & Refining Company.

TABLE VIII

CRUDE OIL RESERVES, HUMBLE OIL & REFINING COMPANY, 1917–1948[a]

(Million barrels)

	A.P.I. Estimates United States	Humble Estimates	
		Area in Which Humble Operated	Humble (Gross Working Interest)
1917	N.A.	....	31
1918	6,200	....	32
1919	6,700	....	48
1920	7,200	....	55
1921	7,800	....	58
1922	7,600	....	58
1923	7,600	....	75
1924	7,500	....	71
1925	8,500	....	61
1926	8,800	....	55
1927	10,500	....	82
1928	11,000	....	172
1929	13,200	....	223
1930	13,600	....	219
1931	13,000	....	591
1932	12,300	....	883
1933	12,000	5,538	947
1934	12,177	5,886	1,159
1935	12,400	6,939	1,438
1936	13,063	7,871	1,629
1937	15,507	9,132	1,905
1938	17,348	10,020	2,155
1939	18,483	12,863	2,433
1940	19,025	13,061	2,655
1941	19,589	13,643	2,726
1942	20,083	13,839	2,649
1943	20,064	13,589	2,591
1944	20,453	14,075	2,540
1945	20,827	14,039	2,525
1946	20,874	14,201	2,641
1947	21,488	14,745	2,662
1948	23,280	15,034	2,668

[a] Year-end estimates with revisions credited to current year and not to the year of discovery.

Source: Records of Humble Oil & Refining Company.

TABLE IX

CRUDE OIL PRODUCTION, PURCHASES, AND YEAR-END STOCKS
HUMBLE OIL & REFINING COMPANY AND SUBSIDIARY COMPANY, 1917–1948

(Thousand barrels)

	Net Crude and Condensate Production	*Crude Purchases*	*Crude Oil Stocks Exclusive of Lease Stocks (December 31)*
1917	3,200	837	242
1918	4,292	642	133
1919	6,040	2,719	4,876
1920	7,826	12,410	8,160
1921	12,291	16,301	13,152
1922	11,199	17,853	15,743
1923	17,027	18,957	20,626
1924	15,852	24,967	20,515
1925	18,029	31,483	18,084
1926	13,707	36,589	15,434
1927	13,250	60,575	14,699
1928	15,503	71,171	14,076
1929	23,451	78,952	15,405
1930	26,214	64,868	19,632
1931	28,743	58,131	14,675
1932	25,921	60,293	12,156
1933	34,982	56,603	12,116
1934	34,893	49,173	11,574
1935	36,769	51,162	10,354
1936	40,750	61,102	10,031
1937	50,611	82,495	13,071
1938	46,364	80,766	12,760
1939	47,605	88,236	12,109
1940	49,074	86,172	13,427
1941	54,740	91,757	12,342
1942	56,266	79,563	17,618
1943	86,328	102,611	13,493
1944	112,930	141,460	12,998
1945	111,338	145,743	12,677
1946	112,958	135,476	15,457
1947	125,275	170,115[a]	16,395
1948	134,806	195,112[a]	15,198

[a] Because of having to carry crude proffered for shipment by means other than common-carrier pipelines from West Texas and the Hawkins field in 1947 and 1948, Humble had to purchase the oil to be shipped at the receiving point and sell it back to the shipper at the delivery point. Such purchases have been included in the above figures for 1947 and 1948 and account for a substantial part of the increases reflected in these years; actual purchases for sales to Humble's own customers were somewhat lower.

Source: Records of Humble Oil & Refining Company.

REFINERY OPERATIONS AND REFINERY PRODUCT SALES
HUMBLE OIL & REFINING COMPANY, 1917–1948

	Crude Runs to Stills			Baytown Input[b]	Per Cent Yield on Raw Material at Baytown				Total Refy. Sales[c] (Thousand Barrels)
	Baytown[a]								
	Thou. Bbls. Daily	Mil. Bbls.	Mil. Bbls. Total[a]	Thou. Bbls. Daily	Gaso.	Kero.	Dist.	Resid.	
1917	....	....	0.2	....	....	....	....	....	174
1918	....	....	0.4	....	....	....	....	....	578
1919	....	....	0.6	....	....	....	....	....	530
1920	3.4	0.8	1.5	2.2	6.3	1.8	30.3	28.2	1,133
1921	5.8	2.1	2.5	5.8	9.3	−0.6	15.9	43.6	1,998
1922	11.5	4.2	4.7	11.5	12.0	1.4	22.9	15.2	3,363
1923	21.7	7.9	8.9	21.7	11.3	0.7	17.6	27.0	8,002
1924	35.2	12.9	16.0	35.2	14.1	5.0	17.0	40.8	15,159
1925	42.1	15.4	18.3	42.1	21.5	5.4	17.0	31.6	16,245
1926	57.0	20.8	21.5	57.0	31.6	8.7	14.2	26.9	20,867
1927	77.6	28.3	32.0	77.6	32.9	5.3	16.9	29.9	32,308
1928	99.6	36.5	43.5	101.0	33.9	5.0	22.1	27.6	43,804
1929	111.8	40.8	49.0	112.5	35.8	5.6	24.4	25.2	48,339
1930	99.8	36.4	43.8	100.3	36.8	6.7	23.5	23.9	46,132
1931	90.8	33.2	38.5	91.1	40.2	7.9	17.6	26.2	35,736
1932	85.6	31.3	35.4	85.6	39.7	8.2	19.8	22.2	32,151
1933	86.8	31.7	37.0	86.8	38.0	8.4	20.8	23.3	34,103
1934	86.3	31.5	35.7	86.4	34.2	9.8	27.8	18.7	27,465
1935	101.3	37.0	40.7	103.5	38.0	7.6	19.4	22.8	28,573
1936	115.1	42.1	46.9	117.8	38.2	6.4	21.4	24.1	30,411
1937	124.7	45.5	53.4	142.6	38.4	7.9	21.6	20.7	42,386
1938	131.2	47.9	56.6	146.8	41.1	6.6	23.3	17.0	51,882
1939	126.6	46.2	55.6	141.3	41.3	6.9	24.7	15.6	55,856
1940	134.2	49.1	59.0	146.8	35.7	7.7	28.3	18.8	60,239
1941	153.2	55.9	68.3	165.3	39.6	5.5	25.5	19.3	67,927
1942	137.3	50.1	60.6	156.9	36.0	3.1	23.7	18.8	61,037
1943	159.2	58.1	70.1	179.2	32.1	5.4	23.6	20.9	75,089
1944	187.9	68.8	82.7	212.7	33.7	4.6	22.3	20.5	82,375
1945	184.6	67.4	78.6	213.4	39.1	5.5	22.4	17.1	78,887
1946	196.8	71.8	73.9	212.3	33.3	9.9	27.1	15.1	71,376
1947	220.6	80.5	83.0	235.2	34.4	9.1	26.4	14.4	83,588
1948	242.4	88.7	91.3	257.3	31.7	8.6	28.5	14.4	90,868

[a] Crude runs include crude processed for others, all at Baytown, in the years 1931-1939.
[b] Crude oil and other net raw materials, such as natural gasoline, butane-propane mixtures. Includes crude processed for others.
[c] Does not include greases, asphalts, black oil, etc.

Source: Records of Humble Oil & Refining Company.

TABLE XI

SELECTED DATA
HUMBLE PIPE LINE COMPANY, 1917–1948

	Miles of Line December 31		*Thousand Barrels Daily*			*Net Income in Thou. Dollars*
				Trunk Line Deliveries		
	Trunk	*Gathering*	*Oil Gathered*	*Total*	*Products*	
1917	....	....	....	....	....	308
1918	....	8	....	....	....	105
1919	60	85	7.6	3.9	....	465
1920	443	245	33.8	35.0	....	2,442
1921	331	629	48.5	48.0	....	4,227
1922	654	643	53.6	51.7	....	4,639
1923	734	846	86.0	62.0	....	4,998
1924	846	1,108	94.7	78.9	....	6,446
1925	1,447	1,351	98.8	98.7	....	8,513
1926	1,781	1,793	87.1	106.6	....	7,951
1927	2,957	2,220	135.6	153.7	....	13,126
1928	3,182	2,542	161.8	201.3	....	19,343
1929	3,728	2,445	201.3	248.0	....	23,941
1930	3,918	2,357	169.5	223.8	....	18,584
1931	4,220	2,303	181.6	243.6	....	22,150
1932	4,252	2,281	164.9	254.4	....	15,739
1933	4,276	2,108	124.1	284.6	....	10,152
1934	4,314	2,019	123.1	287.6	....	7,676
1935	4,227	1,968	132.4	291.5	....	6,746
1936	4,476	2,025	166.7	321.2	....	7,957
1937	4,728	2,341	233.3	407.0	....	11,713
1938	4,973	2,228	234.6	378.1	....	9,283
1939	5,053	2,269	239.9	382.2	....	7,582
1940	5,099	2,623	257.5	369.9	....	5,892
1941	5,293	2,590	313.3	380.4	....	6,518
1942	5,321	2,457	279.2	334.5	....	1,920
1943	5,454	2,408	377.7	454.0	11.1	4,131
1944	5,411	2,512	549.5	584.3	15.0	6,367
1945	5,447	2,492	537.0	617.2	11.9	3,260
1946	5,769	2,666	507.9	619.0	10.5	4,167
1947	5,794	2,908	559.3	694.0	16.6	3,164
1948	5,757	3,068	608.5	758.6	21.7	8,821

Source: Records of Humble Pipe Line Company.

Notes

The term "Records" appearing throughout these notes refers to the various types of business records of companies. The company is indicated by an abbreviated form of its name: Humble for Humble Oil & Refining Company; SONJ for Standard Oil Company (New Jersey). Because of the great volume of company records used, references are given only for quotations or to some letter, memorandum, etc., of particular significance. Specific references are given where information was obtained from company publications, which are available in many libraries, and from other published materials.

CHAPTER 2

1. Information on the early Texas oil industry and on the forerunners of Humble Oil & Refining Co. was obtained from such early oilmen as G. Clint Wood, C. B. Goddard, H. C. Wiess, R. S. Sterling, Ed Prather, and Bert Broday, and also Edgar E. Townes, an attorney early specializing in petroleum law.

2. For general information on early oil developments at Corsicana, the following were consulted: Carl Coke Rister, *Oil! Titan of the Southwest* (Norman, Okla., 1949), 43–48; "The Petroleum Industry, 1859–1934," *Oil & Gas Journal-Oil City Derrick* (Diamond Jubilee Publication, 1934), 97; Ralph W. Hidy and Muriel E. Hidy, *History of Standard Oil Company (New Jersey), Pioneering in Big Business, 1882–1911* (N. Y., 1955), 276 and 393.

3. George E. Cannon and Thomas Pennington, "History of Rotary Drag Type Drilling Bits," a chapter in a history of petroleum engineering, in preparation for publication by the American Petroleum Institute.

4. For general accounts of early Gulf Coast developments, particularly at Spindletop, see Rister, *op. cit.*, 50–65, and C. A. Warner, *Texas Oil and Gas since 1543* (Houston, 1939), 20, 34–47, 50. Oil-production figures are from *Petroleum Facts and Figures* (American Petroleum Institute, various editions), unless other sources are specified. Firsthand impressions have been furnished by Patillo Higgins and C. G. Hamill, as well as by several named in note 1.

5. Interview with Patillo Higgins, July 17, 1948; Boyce House, "He Started It All," *The Lamp*—house organ of Standard Oil Co. (N.J.)—Aug., 1939.

6. For the actual drilling of the first successful Spindletop well, the following are firsthand accounts: Al Hamill's story in *Spindletop, A Texas Titan* (American Petroleum Institute, Jan., 1945) and, in an abbreviated form, in Robert Ingram, "Spindletop . . . Its Roar Echoed Around the World," *Oil & Gas Journal* (hereafter cited as *O. & G. Jour.*), Apr. 17, 1941; C. G. Hamill's story in Houston *Chronicle*, Mar. 28, 1939; Captain Lucas' account in Reid Sayers McBeth, *Pioneering the Gulf Coast: A Story of the Life and Accomplishments of Capt. Anthony F. Lucas* (n.p., about 1918, in the Columbia University Library), which is also used in Edwin C. Bell, "History of the Southwestern Fields," *O. & G. Jour.*, May 30, 1919. Anthony F. Lucas, "The Great Oil-Well near Beaumont, Texas," *Transactions of the American Institute of Min-*

ing Engineers (Feb., 1901), is mostly about control of the well, quality of oil, etc., and devotes only a page and a half of the total thirteen to drilling of the well. A contemporary account appeared in the Houston *Post*, Jan. 11, 1901.

7. For the Spindletop boom, see Rister and Warner, above, and *O. & G. Jour.*, Oct. 9, 1941, p. 15.

8. Houston *Post*, Jan. 13, 15, and 16, 1901.

9. Warner, *op. cit.*, 373, 375, 383; *Oil Investors' Journal* (hereafter cited as *Oil Inv. Jour.*), Nov. 1, 1902, pp. 1f., Aug. 16, 1903, p. 8, Apr. 1, 1904, p. 7, and Jan. 3, 1906, p. 3.

10. Constitution, State of Texas, 1917, Art. 16, sec. 59a.

11. *O. & G. Jour.*, Dec. 27, 1918, p. 35.

12. Rister, *op. cit.*, 47f., 63–65, and 78f.

13. *Oil Inv. Jour.*, Sept. 1, 1904, p. 3.

14. Hidy and Hidy, *op. cit.*, 276, 284, 393f., and 400; Warner, *op. cit.*, 45–56; *O. & G. Jour.-Oil City Derrick* (Diamond Jubilee Publication), 110, 112, 172, 174; *Magnolia News*, Apr., 1931, p. 16; Burt E. Hull, "Founding of The Texas Company" (mimeographed address, Mar. 31, 1941), p. 22.

15. *Journal of the House of Representatives*, 29th Legislature, State of Texas, pp. 226f., 735; *Oil Inv. Jour.*, 1905: Feb. 3, pp. 2–5, Feb. 8, pp. 2–7, Feb. 18, p. 8, Mar. 3, pp. 9, 12f., 16, Mar. 18, p. 10, Apr. 3, p. 12.

16. *General Laws of the State of Texas:* 1897: ch. 130, sec. 1 (3a); 1899: p. 202, sec. 1; 1907: p. 312, sec. 5. Also, John G. Tod, *Principal Corporation Laws of the State of Texas* (Austin, 1902), 3; F. C. Weinert, *Principal Corporation Laws of the State of Texas to Date* (Austin, 1914), 37f.; John G. McKay, *Principal Corporation Laws of the State of Texas* (Austin, 1916), 4, 38–40; *Oil Inv. Jour.*, Apr. 1, 1904, p. 7, Mar. 3, 1905, pp. 10, 23, Apr. 3, 1905, p. 12; Jewel P. Lightfoot, *Anti-Trust Laws of the State of Texas* (Austin, 1907), 6–12, 15–22, 26f., 32, 34, 54; *Complete Texas Statutes* (K. C., Mo., 1920), 1341–1343.

17. Hidy and Hidy, *op. cit.*, ch. 12.

18. *Oil Inv. Jour.*, June 7, 1902, p. 12, Mar. 3, 1905, pp. 10f., Feb. 6, 1909, pp. 68–71; *O. & G. Jour.*, Jan. 21, 1915, p. 15, Jan. 28, 1915, p. 18, June 28, 1917, p. 32; various interviews.

19. The principal informant on Fondren's parentage and youth was his nephew, Frank Sparkman, son of Fondren's older sister. Other informants on his early life were J. S. Bozeman, his foster brother; G. Clint Wood, a former partner; C. G. Hamill and C. L. Brown, early oil-field acquaintances; C. E. Richards and D. F. Haynes, former secretaries; and such other associates in the Humble organization as the informants in note 1, as well as M. Manning and C. E. Stanley. Additional testimony to his ability, moral character, and popularity was furnished by F. L. Carpenter, A. H. Smith, C. W. DeLancey, F. M. McGehee, and J. W. Fincher.

The printed authorities consulted were Ellis A. Davis and Edwin H. Grobe, *The New Encyclopedia of Texas* (Dallas, 1926), I, p. 538, II, pp. 1586, 1589; Houston *Chronicle*, Jan. 6, 1939, pp. 1, 3; *Humble Refinery Bee* (hereafter cited as *H. Ref. Bee*), Jan. 12, 1939, pp. 8f.; *Humble Sales Lubricator* (hereafter cited as *H. Sales Lub.*), Jan. 10, 1939, pp. 17f.

Fondren's oil-field activities up to 1905 are known only from his reminiscences to later associates, but his operations during 1905–1917 are frequently referred to in the *Oil Inv. Jour.* and *O. & G. Jour.*

20. *Oil Inv. Jour.*, Mar. 3, 1905, p. 9, and Jan. 5, 1908, p. 4.

21. The printed accounts of W. S. Farish's early life are confused and contradictory. The accounts in Davis and Grobe, *op. cit.*, I, 310, and II, 1900, are generally inaccurate and uncritical. The sketches in *Who's Who in America*, various vols., also contain inaccuracies. These and other inaccuracies have often been repeated elsewhere. Family, associates, and acquaintances have, however, been helpful in supplying fuller and more accurate information. The principal authority was Hazelwood P. Farish, a first cousin who accompanied Farish to Beaumont in 1901. S. P. Farish, a younger brother, was also helpful.

R. L. Blaffer's early life is also rather obscure. Information appears in Alva Blaffer's manuscript, "Brief Notes on Robert Lee Blaffer," about 1933, which is principally, however, on ancestry and family; Davis and Grobe, *op. cit.*, I, 326; *Who's Who in America, 1938–1939;*

H. Sales Lub., June 15, 1933, pp. 4f., Aug. 14, 1941, p. 4, and Nov., 1942, p. 4.

Information concerning the oil-field activities of R. L. Blaffer and W. S. Farish, 1902–1917, was derived principally from the frequent references in the files of the *Oil Inv. Jour.* and *O. & G. Jour.*, but interviews with C. C. Clifton, an early clerk, and Maxey Ward, a veteran oil worker, have been of unique value.

Information regarding the business and personal relations and respective temperaments of Blaffer and Farish was also obtained from the informants in note 1 and from Mrs. Libbie Rice Farish, Mrs. Sarah Campbell Blaffer, J. A. Neath, W. E. Pratt, H. K. Arnold, J. W. Fincher, D. B. Harris, and Farish's former secretaries, B. D. Haltom and W. N. Finnegan, Jr.

22. *Oil Inv. Jour.*, July 15, 1903, p. 6.

23. Davis and Grobe, *op. cit.*, II, 1899; interview.

24. John Henry Brown, *Indian Wars and Pioneers of Texas* (Austin, n.d.), 473–476; Davis and Grobe, *op. cit.*, I, 984; Warner, *op. cit.*, 42; Florence Stratton, *The Story of Beaumont* (n.p., 1925), 171; *Beaumont* (Houston, n.d.), 50, 55; *Oil Inv. Jour.*, Apr. 18, 1906, p. 10; *O. & G. Jour.*, June 18, 1914, p. 8.

25. Information about the Paraffine Oil Co., 1903–1912, has been drawn principally from the company's minutes in the possession of Humble Oil & Refining Co. and from *Oil Inv. Jour.*, which has been useful for the general background as well. Interviews have also added local and personal color.

26. Warner, *op. cit.*, 189.

27. On the Reliance Oil Co. the principal source is the company's minutes, in the possession of Humble Oil & Refining Co.

28. *Oil Inv. Jour.*, Feb. 1, 1904, p. 7, and Mar. 3, 1905, p. 7.

29. Information on R. S. Sterling and his business activities, particularly Humble Oil Co., was drawn from Frank W. Johnson, Eugene C. Barker, and Ernest William Winkler, *A History of Texas and Texans* (Chicago, 1914), IV, pp. 1764–1766; Davis and Grobe, *op. cit.*, I, 210–212, 322, 713, 964; Houston *Chronicle*, June 22, 1905; Houston *Post*, Jan. 22, 1917; Sterling letters and Humble Oil Co. records in possession of Humble Oil & Refining Co.; and interviews with and statements from informants in note 1, as well as N. K. Robb, George W. Armstrong, J. W. Fincher, and F. L. Carpenter.

30. *Oil Inv. Jour.*, Nov. 6, 1909, p. 28.

31. Information from P. H. Walber.

32. *O. & G. Jour.*, Apr. 24, 1913, p. 3; Rister, *op. cit.*, 228; Jimmie Clark, "Old Justice of Peace Gave Humble Company Its Name Indirectly," Houston *Press*, Nov. (?), 1937 (clipping); information from Mrs. Ella Humble, Hull, Texas.

33. The history of Ardmore Oil Co. was drawn principally from the company's records, in the possession of Humble Oil & Refining Co., supplemented by information from *O. & G. Jour.* (1913: Dec. 25, p. 6; 1914: Mar. 26, pp. 10, 12, Oct. 8, p. 4; 1915: Mar. 4, p. 31; 1917: Feb. 15, p. 14), but interviews have also been helpful. Information in regard to some of Ardmore's original officers was drawn from *Oil Inv. Jour.*, Mar. 3, 1905, and Davis and Grobe, *op. cit.*, I, 1938.

34. The story of Humble's success in Oklahoma was drawn principally from company records and the *O. & G. Jour.*, Nov. 20, 1913, p. 14, Feb. 12, 1914, p. 14.

35. *Oil Inv. Jour.*, Nov. 28, 1908, p. 18; *O. & G. Jour.*, Sept. 12, 1912, p. 26, Jan. 1, 1914, p. 14, Sept. 3, 1914, p. 29, Sept. 17, 1914, p. 18, Jan. 7, 1915, p. 13, Nov. 4, 1915, p. 14, Jan. 13, 1916, p. 67; Wallace E. Pratt and L. G. Weeks, "History of Oil Exploration . . . ," in *Finding and Producing Oil* (Dallas, 1939), 7–18.

36. *O. & G. Jour.*, Aug. 26, 1915, p. 16; Rister, *op. cit.*, 108–118.

37. *Ibid.*, 145f., 158–161, 164f. Information was obtained from Wallace E. Pratt on discoveries in north central Texas.

38. The story of Schulz Oil Co. and the partnership which preceded it was drawn primarily from the records of the company in the possession of Humble Oil & Refining Co., but this source was supplemented by interviews. For an outside viewpoint, see *O. & G. Jour.*, Apr. 2, 1914, p. 16, May 13, 1915, p. 14, May 20, 1915, p. 12.

39. Information from A. H. Smith.

40. *O. & G. Jour.*, Nov. 4, 1915, p. 14.

41. Humble's success on the Gulf Coast, 1916–1917, is revealed not only in company records but also in the *O. & G.*

Jour., 1916: Sept. 7, p. 14, Dec. 14, p. 14, Dec. 21, p. 12, Dec. 28, p. 14; 1917: Jan. 4, pp. 14, 16, Feb. 1, pp. 14, 16, Feb. 22, p. 16.

42. Davis and Grobe, *op. cit.*, I, 322.

CHAPTER 3

1. For the organization of Humble Oil & Refining Company, the events leading up to it, and the general industrial background, interviews with men experienced in the industry and involved in the organization were indispensable. The principal informants were the late H. C. Wiess and the late R. S. Sterling, the last survivors of the company's most prominent founders, and E. E. Townes, who was familiar with the legal aspects of the industry and of the company's organization.

2. *Oil Inv. Jour.*, 1905: Jan. 15, pp. 7f., and Mar. 3, p. 12; 1908: Jan. 5, p. 4, May 10, p. 14, June 15, p. 24, July 6, p. 16, Dec. 20, p. 11; and 1909: Mar. 20, pp. 28f., and Apr. 20, pp. 23f.

3. House Bill 324 (1905).

4. For example, see Hidy and Hidy, *Pioneering in Big Business*, 180f., 380f.

5. George S. Gibb and Evelyn H. Knowlton, *History of Standard Oil Company (New Jersey), The Resurgent Years, 1911–1927* (N. Y., 1956), 50.

6. Industrial Conference Board, *The Petroleum Almanac* (hereafter cited as ICB, *Pet. Almanac*) (N. Y., 1946), 281.

7. *O. & G. Jour.*, Jan. 21–Mar. 11, 1915, *passim; Gen. Laws of Texas*, 1915, ch. 152, sec. 1, and ch. 41, sec. 1; *Senate Journal*, 35th leg., reg. sess., pp. 449–454.

8. ICB, *Pet. Almanac*, 281.

9. 61st Judicial District Court, Houston, Harris Co., Texas, District Clerk's Office, Case 79030, *Blaffer & Farish et al.* v. *Gulf Pipe Line Co.* On Jan. 24, 1920, the Court of Civil Appeals upheld the judgment of the District Court in favor of Gulf Pipe Line Co.

10. Records of Imperial Oil, Ltd., A. C. Bedford to W. C. Teagle, May 13, 1915.

11. For the general background of the struggle between independents and majors over the use of the latter's pipelines at this time, see Gibb and Knowlton, *op. cit.*, 166–178.

12. *O. & G. Jour.*, Dec. 9, 1915, p. 16.

13. A complete text of Farish's speech has not been located. The most significant portions were published in the Tulsa *Daily World*, July 11, 1931; Farish publicly acknowledged authorship before the Texas legislature (*House Journal*, 42d leg., 1st called sess., Austin, Texas, July 30, 1931, pp. 483–488).

14. *Ibid.*; Houston *Post*, Dec. 16, 1915, p. 8; *O. & G. Jour.*, Dec. 23, 1915, p. 22.

15. *O. & G. Jour.*, Jan. 27, 1916, pp. 23f.

16. *O. & G. Jour.*, 1916: Dec. 14, p. 22, Dec. 21, p. 12; 1917: Jan. 18, p. 36, Feb. 8, p. 36. E. E. Townes, "How the Company was Organized," *H. Ref. Bee*, Jan. 13, 1938, pp. 4–6; *Humble Sales Lub.*, Jan. 20, 1938, pp. 6–8.

17. Information on gasoline production and marketing by Humble predecessor companies has been drawn principally from the records of the Globe Refining Co. and the Schulz Oil Co. and from the Blaffer & Farish correspondence, all in possession of Humble Oil & Refining Co. On the Globe, interviews with S. P. Farish, C. H. McNair, J. L. Dunman, Maxey Ward, J. A. Neath, J. R. Mulvey, and Gay Carroll were also valuable; and on the Schulz, information from W. B. Calhoun. For Southern Pipe Line Co. and the background of its purchase the principal source is the company's records, in possession of Humble.

18. Rister, *Oil! Titan of the Southwest*, 70, 74, 78f.

19. *Ibid.*, 182. For an example of the rising importance of gasoline, see Gibb and Knowlton, *op. cit.*, 681.

20. For the Globe and its predecessor, see also *O. & G. Jour.*, 1916: Mar. 16, pp. 12–14, Mar. 23, p. 12, Aug. 17, p. 12; Feb. 15, 1917, pp. 12, 32; May 30, 1919 (supplement), pp. 131f. Also, *Humble Magazine* (hereafter cited as *H. Magazine*), Nov., 1921, p. 5.

21. For Southern Pipe Line Co. and the background of its purchase, see also *O. & G. Jour.*, Aug. 13, 1916–May 10, 1917, especially 1917: Feb. 1, p. 14, Mar. 22, p. 14, Apr. 12, p. 12, and May 10; Warner, *Texas Oil and Gas*, 370; Houston *Post*, Jan. 26, 1917, p. 1.

22. 80th Judicial District Court, Houston, Harris Co., Texas, case 72158, *Southern Pipe Line Co.* v. *J. M. West et al.*

23. The discussions leading up to the decision to organize Humble Oil & Refining Co. are not a matter of record; the authors have relied principally on the recollections of the principal participants and of Bert Broday and Ed Prather.

24. Common Carrier Act: Texas, 35th leg., reg. sess., *Journal of the Senate*, Feb. 13, 1917, pp. 449–454; *Revised Civil Statutes of Texas*, secs. 6038–6049a.

The Texas Company Act: Texas, 35th leg., reg. sess., *Journal of the Senate*, Feb. 12, 1917, pp. 29, 34, 92f., 216, 248, 273, 413f., 423, 449–454; *Revised Civil Statutes of Texas*, art. 1307, ch. 24, title 25.

See also *O. & G. Jour.*, 1917: Jan. 18, p. 36, and Feb. 15, p. 35.

25. The discussions in regard to the final stages of the organization of Humble Oil & Refining Co., particularly those dealing with such matters as the date of the actual merger and the valuation of the properties turned over to the joint enterprise, were also not recorded. The recollections of H. C. Wiess were helpful to the authors as were those of a member of the new company's Legal Dept. and a member of its Accounting Dept. For the final organization of Humble Oil & Refining Co. the manuscript sources are the company records and the records of such predecessor companies as Humble Oil Co. and Paraffine Oil Co., in possession of Humble Oil & Refining Co., and the new company's charter, together with an affidavit listing properties and their values that is in the office of the Texas Secretary of State.

No contemporary record exists fixing either the date when joint operations were to begin or the basis of the valuation for all the properties turned over to Humble Oil & Refining Co. Both these omissions eventually led to trouble for the new company; the Bureau of Internal Revenue used them as the basis for a tax suit, which was, however, after many years, settled in the company's favor (*U. S.* v. *Humble Oil & Refining Co.*, 69 Fed. 2d 214). In this suit, Humble's legal counsel maintained that a quasi-corporation existed from March 1, 1917.

26. Humble Oil & Refining Co. records (hereafter cited as Humble Recs.), Minutes of Meeting of Board of Directors, Sept. 10, 1917.

27. *O. & G. Jour.*, 1915: Apr. 22, p. 1, May 6, p. 25. Gibb and Knowlton, *op. cit.*, 583.

28. Quoted in interview with Gay Carroll.

CHAPTER 4

1. Beginning with this chapter, the principal source of information was the records of Humble Oil & Refining Co., chiefly the executive correspondence and directors' minutes but also reports on various operations. Specific references to this material will be made only when the matters involved are unusually controversial or important and the exact source is of peculiar significance, or when direct quotations are used. Another type of company material that has proved of particular value is typewritten or mimeographed departmental and company histories prepared, usually under the supervision of a departmental head or manager, for use in training programs or for circulation among administrators; they are normally based on company or departmental records, but usually include reminiscences as well. Particularly useful for the period and subjects dealt with in this chapter were "Company Organization, 1934," which includes accounts, up to that date, of the various departments by important departmental executives; L. T. Barrow, "Notes on the History of the Geologic, Lease and Scouting Department of Humble Oil & Refining Co."; Gay Carroll, "Financial Summary of the Transactions of Humble Co., the Issuance of New Capital Stock and Borrowing Money"; "Organization of Humble Oil & Refining Co."; and "These Thirty Years." The reader may assume that the above items have been consulted on the subjects to which they are pertinent. Interviews with Bert Broday, H. C. Wiess, E. E. Townes, and R. S. Sterling were also helpful on the subjects treated in this chapter.

2. Information concerning general administrative organization in this period was derived from the directors' minutes and from interviews with former directors and with H. K. Arnold and Gay Carroll. On the organization of production activities, information from M. Manning, S. P. Farish, and R. D. Farish supplemented the manuscript material.

3. Humble Recs.; information from Bert Broday; J. S. Bonner, "Selling Oils," *H. Magazine,* Mar., 1922, pp. 18f.

4. Information as to Humble's development of refining and the marketing of refined products during its first two years has been derived principally from the records of Humble, the Globe refinery, and Dixie Oil & Refining Co., and from Eugene Reese, W. B. Calhoun, Ray Sinclair, J. R. Mulvey, C. B. Goddard, Joyce Adams, Gus Borgstrom, D. T. Monroe, J. E. Niland, R. H. Brinton, C. H. McNair, and W. C. Teagle.

5. Humble Recs. Also, *O. & G. Jour.*, 1918: Nov. 8, p. 49; 1919: Apr. 11, p. 58, May 30 (Supplement), pp. 131–135, June 13, p. 30, June 16, pp. 30–38.

6. Various interviews and personal letters; see also *H. Sales Lub.*, Aug. 1, 1944, p. 408.

7. Dixie and Humble Recs.; interviews; *H. Magazine,* Nov., 1921, p. 5; *O. & G. Jour.*, 1917: Aug. 9, p. 16, Aug. 16, pp. 6, 14; and 1919: Apr. 4, p. 4.

8. Humble Recs.; interviews; *O. &. G. Jour.*, 1917: Aug. 30, p. 28, Nov. 8, p. 12, and 1918: June 6, p. 18.

9. See *H. Magazine,* Aug. 1, 1921, p. 4 (photograph of first Humble-built filling station).

10. Humble Recs.; C. H. McNair, "Oil by Rail," *H. Sales Lub.*, May 12, 1938, pp. 14f.; *H. Ref. Bee,* May 19, 1934, pp. 8f.

11. *O. & G. Jour.*, 1918: May 2, pp. 18, 20, June 21, pp. 22, 24.

12. *Ibid.*, 1918: June 7, pp. 20, 22, June 14, pp. 18, 20, June 28, pp. 18, 20, July 19, pp. 18, 20, Aug. 16, pp. 16, 18; Humble Recs.; interviews.

13. General information as to production and prices in this period was derived primarily from company records and from interviews with C. W. DeLancey, M. Manning, Hines H. Baker, Charles King, and J. A. Neath.

14. Information regarding Humble's entrance into the North Texas boom fields was drawn from *O. & G. Jour.*, Oct. 4, 1934, p. 39; Warner, *Texas Oil and Gas,* 59, 233; and numerous interviews.

15. For information on Wallace E. Pratt and the introduction of geological methods into Humble's oil-finding program, see E. L. DeGolyer, "Wallace Everette Pratt: An Appreciation," *Bulletin of the American Association of Petroleum Geologists* (hereafter cited as *Bull. of AAPG*), XXIX (May, 1945), 476–490. Information from W. E. Pratt, L. T. Barrow, and Alva Ellisor was also indispensable.

16. *O. & G. Jour.*, 1918: Feb. 14, p. 10, Feb. 28, p. 36, Mar. 14, pp. 18, 20, Mar. 28, p. 12. Humble Recs., W. S. Farish to Daniel E. Garrett, Aug. 29, 1917; Farish to J. F. Lucey, Sept. 17, 1917, and to M. L. Requa, Feb. 20, 1918; Thomas A. O'Donnell to M. L. Requa, June 13, 1918.

17. Texas Legislature, *House Journal,* 42d leg., 1st called sess. (July 30, 1931), p. 485; *O. & G. Jour.*, Mar. 28, 1918; information from Robert E. Hardwicke.

18. *O. &. G. Jour.*, 1917: Sept. 13, p. 33, Oct. 25, p. 43, Dec. 27, p. 14; 1918: May 16, p. 4, July 5, p. 47, July 12, p. 41, Aug. 23, p. 16, Nov. 8, p. 20.

19. Union activity among oil workers on the Gulf Coast and in California is described with a strong prounion bias and many inaccuracies as to facts by Harvey O'Connor, *History of Oil Workers International Union–CIO* (Denver, 1950), 4–17. The *O. & G. Jour.* presents the employer's viewpoint; its issues of Nov., 1917–Feb., 1918, *passim,* so regularly contain information on the Gulf Coast strike that only particularly important items will be given specific reference. A short general treatment of the strike, including its background and immediate effects, is given in Ruth Allen, *Chapters in the History of Organized Labor in Texas* (The University of Texas Publications, 4143, Austin, Nov. 15, 1941), 221–228.

Interviews with the following men who were in the oil fields at the time, including supervisors and field workers, strikers and nonstrikers, have been helpful: C. L. Brown, F. L. Carpenter, Maxey Ward, E. J. Parks, Frank Bass, P. H. Walber, A. H. Smith, C. C. Clifton, H. J. Derrick, S. P. Farish, N. K. Robb, J. L. Burton, J. L. Dunman, and J. D. Hunnicut. Information as to the wage scales of Humble and its predecessor companies during the period immediately preceding the strike was derived from a variety of time books and pay cards, 1915–1917.

20. Information from Bert Broday.

21. *O. & G. Jour.*, 1917: Jan. 18, p. 36, Feb. 15, p. 27; Humble Recs.
22. *O. & G. Jour.*, 1917: Oct. 25, p. 43, Nov. 1, p. 18.
23. O'Connor, *op. cit.*, 15.
24. *O. & G. Jour.*, 1917: Nov. 8, p. 14, Nov. 15, p. 14, Nov. 22, p. 30.
25. *Ibid.*, 1917: Nov. 15, p. 16, Nov. 22, p. 6, Nov. 29, p. 41.
26. For example, the Bisbee, Arizona, affair, described in Robert Glass Cleland, *A History of Phelps Dodge, 1834–1950* (N. Y., 1952), 171–192.
27. *O. & G. Jour.*, Dec. 20, 1917, pp. 14–16.
28. The Mediation Board's findings, the operators' reply, and the results of their protest are presented in two pamphlets published by the Texas Gulf Coast and Louisiana Oil and Gas Producers' Association: *Proceedings of Oil and Gas Producers of Texas Gulf Coast and Louisiana . . . Houston, Texas, Jan. 2, 1918;* and *Report of the Executive Committee of Texas Gulf Coast and Louisiana Oil and Gas Association and Agreement with the President's Mediation Commission* (Feb. 12, 1918).
29. *O. & G. Jour.*, 1918: Jan. 31, p. 32, and Feb. 7, p. 2; *Report of the Executive Committee of Texas Gulf Coast and Louisiana Oil and Gas Association. . . .*
30. *O. & G. Jour.*, 1918: Jan. 10, p. 3, Feb. 28, p. 50, Mar. 14, pp. 3, 47, July 12, p. 50, July 19, p. 3, Aug. 30, p. 47, Sept. 13, pp. 3, 51, Sept. 20, p. 6, Sept. 27, p. 51, Oct. 25, p. 3, Nov. 22, p. 18, Dec. 6, p. 3, Dec. 20, pp. 51, 58.
31. Humble Recs.; *O. & G. Jour.*, Mar. 28, 1918, p. 53.
32. Humble Recs.; *O. & G. Jour.*, Sept. 20, 1918, p. 26; information from J. A. Neath.
33. Mrs. A. D. Murphee, "Living Conditions . . . are Improving . . . ," *H. Magazine*, Aug., 1921, p. 18; *O. & G. Jour.*, 1918: Aug. 23, p. 16, Dec. 20, p. 14.
34. Humble's financial problems from incorporation up to the end of 1918 have been discussed in interviews with directors of the day and with Gay Carroll, R. E. Sinclair, and Bert Broday.
35. Testimony of W. S. Farish, Dec. 12, 1923, in *State of Texas* v. *Humble Oil & Refining Co.*, printed in *O. & G. Jour.*, June 5, 1924, pp. 132f.
36. Humble's unsuccessful attempts to negotiate a large long-term loan are dealt with in Humble Recs.; *State of Texas* v. *Humble Oil & Refining Co.* (263 S. W., 319–325); *O. & G. Jour.*, June 5, 1924, pp. 132f.; New York *American*, Nov. 27, 1923; *Daily Times Herald* (Dallas), Sept. 9, 1923.
37. In the records of Standard Oil Co. (N.J.) is the first written record found of Farish's discussions with Teagle: "Memorandum of Information Relative to Humble Oil and Refining Company, given by Mr. Farish at a conference today in Mr. Teagle's office, September 24th, 1918." Inside views of the agreement between Jersey and Humble have been given by Sterling, Wiess, Townes, and W. C. Teagle. Farish's testimony in regard to the negotiations was published in the *O. & G. Jour.*, June 5, 1924, pp. 132f.
38. For information on Jersey's position in production about 1918 see Gibb and Knowlton, *The Resurgent Years*, chs. 3 and 4.
39. Standard Oil Company (New Jersey) records, hereafter referred to as SONJ Recs.
40. The Jersey Standard side of the negotiations for the purchase of an interest in Humble, particularly the legal aspects of the transactions, has been drawn from the SONJ Recs.
41. Humble Recs., Gay Carroll, "Financial Summary." "Bills Payable" (photostat).

CHAPTER 5

1. The principal sources used for this chapter were the company records, particularly executive correspondence and directors' minutes, and interviews, especially with men of executive rank and so situated as to have been able to observe the policy-making process.
2. SONJ Recs., Guy Wellman to James K. Jones, June 13, 1919.
3. Gibb and Knowlton, *The Resurgent Years*, 33–36.
4. *State* v. *Humble Oil & Refining Co.*, in *Southwestern Reporter*, 263, pp. 319–325 (1924). Interview with Rex G. Baker.
5. W. S. Farish testimony, *House Journal*, 42d leg., 1st called sess., 1931, p. 487.
6. Information from Robert E. Hardwicke and L. T. Barrow.
7. For the personalities, roles, and contributions of members of the Humble

board during this period one must draw to a large extent on the recollections and opinions of their associates and acquaintances, inside and outside the company. The comments of E. E. Townes, James Anderson, and W. E. Pratt, Humble directors of this period, have been broadly useful.

Some Humble directors of central importance during the company's first decade have become legendary figures, the objects of admiration, affection, and, rarely, of some degree of antagonism; these men are the ones most often the subjects of character analysis and anecdotes. Others, of equal or sometimes greater importance, were less colorful personalities; their achievements and character therefore belong primarily to the written record and are less subjects of common fame. Still others attained their greatest importance during the 1930s and later and are but slightly touched upon below.

On Sterling, in addition to Sterling himself and some of the informants in Chap. 2, n. 29, the principal commentators were M. Manning, D. F. Haynes, R. H. Brinton, T. H. Hamilton, W. A. Eberle, and Joe A. Collerain.

On Blaffer, in addition to commentators in Chap. 2, n. 21: Gay Carroll, B. H. Brown, R. E. Sinclair, R. V. Hanrahan, W. B. Calhoun, Joe A. Collerain, Alva Ellisor, J. L. Burton, H. S. Warner, A. A. Nance, G. B. Corless, Frank Cullinan, Sigmond Rothschild, and T. H. A. Tiedemann.

On Farish, in addition to informants referred to in Chap. 2, n. 21: Hines H. Baker, L. T. Barrow, Gay Carroll, D. F. Haynes, T. H. Hamilton, H. H. Hill, Heinrich Riedemann, J. S. Bridwell, G. S. Mabry, R. C. Barbour, C. E. Shaw, Clint Murchison, George W. LeVan, Jesse H. Jones, Frank Cullinan.

On Anderson: J. A. Neath, W. R. Trelford, N. K. Robb, G. W. LeVan.

On Bonner: J. R. Mulvey, D. T. Monroe, A. L. Dingle.

8. *H. Sales Lub.*, Oct., 1943, pp. 9f.; interview with Robert E. Hardwicke.

9. *O. & G. Jour.*, Nov. 2, 1922, p. 52; interviews.

10. A. R. Hinton, "Standard Back in Texas . . . ," Los Angeles *Times*, dated from Ranger, July 2, 1919 (clipping); *O. & G. Jour.*, Apr. 11, p. 16 and May 2, p. 20, 1919, and Sept. 3, 1920, p. 34; information from W. C. Teagle; Humble Recs.

11. Humble Recs., Directors' Minutes; *H. Ref. Bee*, May, 1942, p. 4; *H. Sales Lub.*, May, 1942, p. 7; interviews; *O. & G. Jour.*, Mar. 5, 1920, p. 4.

12. Davis and Grobe, *New Encyc. of Texas*, I, 558; *H. Ref. Bee*, June 1, 1939, p. 9; *H. Sales Lub.*, June 8, 1939, p. 8; interviews.

13. Information concerning Sterling's affiliations and activities and in relation to his retirement was derived from Humble Recs. and SONJ Recs.; Houston *Chronicle*, Jan. 12, 14, 17, 19, and 22, 1923, and Oct. 30, 1924; Houston *Press*, Oct. 15 and 30, 1924; Fort Worth *Record*, Nov. 1, 1924; and numerous interviews.

14. Numerous anecdotes illustrate Farish's consideration for others. R. V. Hanrahan told of his refusal to have his office air-conditioned unless the whole building was air-conditioned, and W. E. Pratt of his declining to take a short cut to a golf course because the shorter way was "a shell street and our car will throw dust all over those little houses."

15. Conversations with Hines H. Baker and H. K. Arnold.

16. Conversation with R. S. Dewey.

17. For information about pipeline practices at this time, see Gibb and Knowlton, *op. cit.*, 460–463.

18. *Ibid.*, 465–468.

19. An organization plan, which internal evidence indicates was prepared about Aug. 1, 1919, presents a much more highly developed organization than the actual workings of the company at the time would seem to have justified.

20. Further details on the organization of these various production departments and subdepartments are given in subsequent chapters on production operations.

21. On the general character of Humble's employee relations, both before and after the formal adoption of an employee program, testimony has been available from within the company and from outsiders, from high company executives and from field workers. Witnesses include C. B. Goddard, D. B. Harris, A. H. Smith, A. H. Rowan, Joyce Adams, and W. H. Wheatley.

On the general development and

early history of Humble's formal employee relations program, information was furnished by D. B. Harris, Hines H. Baker, John R. Suman, C. E. Shaw, Henry Wilson, and T. H. A. Tiedemann.

Humble's high accident rate and long struggle to improve it are revealed in the monthly accident reports. General information on this problem has also been obtained from R. B. Roaper and T. W. Moore; W. H. Wheatley, Frank Bass, P. H. Walber, and F. L. Carpenter discussed accidents and safety programs from the viewpoint of the production man in the field; R. V. Hanrahan, A. E. Pecore, and H. M. Stevenson from the viewpoint of the pipeline executive.

Our understanding of the "weekly hour" problem, and particularly the controversy over the six-day week, has benefited from interviews with Suman, Harris, K. R. Dailey, Harold Ward, and Howard Warner of Humble, Tiedemann (then of Jersey), and R. L. Clifton and J. J. Conry of Carter.

22. For the employee policies and activities of Standard Oil Co. (N.J.), see Gibb and Knowlton, *op. cit.*, ch. 18.

23. *Humble Annuities & Benefits*, booklets issued 1920, 1922, 1924; *Humble Bee* (hereafter cited as *H. Bee*), Nov. 19, 1923, p. 3.

24. Humble Recs.; *H. Bee*, Apr. 15, 1922, p. 2, Apr. 21, 1923, p. 2, May 26, 1923, p. 2.

25. Humble Recs.; *H. Bee*, 1921: Mar. 24, p. 1, and Apr. 14, pp. 1f.; *H. Sales Lub.*, May, 1944, p. 9.

26. Humble Recs.; *H. Bee*, Apr. 14, 1921, p. 1, and Mar. 17, 1922, p. 1; *H. Magazine*, Mar., 1922, p. 23.

27. On the Jersey system: Gibb and Knowlton, *op. cit.*, 583f.; *O. & G. Jour.*, Aug. 22, 1919, p. 2, Aug. 29, 1919, p. 6, Nov. 26, 1920, p. 58, and Jan. 27, 1922, p. 6. On Humble's: Humble Recs.; *H. Bee*, Apr. 1, 1927, pp. 2f.; *H. Ref. Bee*, Mar. 26, 1936, pp. 10f.

28. Gibb and Knowlton, *op. cit.*, 150, 579; *O. & G. Jour.*, July 23, 1925, p. 23; Humble Recs.; interviews.

29. The most significant information on the controversy preceding Humble's adoption of the six-day week was drawn from Humble Recs., particularly W. C. Teagle to D. R. Weller (Standard Oil Co. of La.), Oct. 25, 1927; Hicks to W. S. Farish, Oct. 17, 1927; D. B. Harris to John R. Suman, Jan. 19, 1928; Suman to Farish, Jan. 24, 1928; Teagle to Farish, Feb. 14, 1928.

30. *Humble Club Bulletin*, Oct., 1928, pp. 38f.

31. Humble Recs.; *H. Bee*, July 1, 1929, p. 3; *O. & G. Jour.*, Aug. 14, 1930, p. 106.

32. Humble Recs., Wiess to Farish, Jan. 30, 1929.

33. Humble Recs.; *H. Sales Lub.*, June 24, 1934, pp. 4f.

34. All financial figures in this section are from the records of the Comptroller's Department of Humble Oil & Refining Co.

35. Gibb and Knowlton, *op. cit.*, 40–42.

36. *O. & G. Jour.*, 1919: Oct. 24, p. 54, Oct. 31, p. 64, and Nov. 7, p. 32; Humble Recs.

37. Gibb and Knowlton, *op. cit.*, 602.

38. Interview with J. A. Neath.

39. Humble Recs., Farish to Roy Heermans, Dec. 17, 1929.

40. Gibb and Knowlton, *op. cit.*, 672f.

41. Correspondence between Teagle and Farish in August, 1919, reveals early consideration of building; by Dec. 1, 1920, a total of $667,048.48 had been spent for the building and some of its furnishings.

42. *H. Magazine*, May, 1921, pp. 7f.

CHAPTER 6

1. Although some information on production methods is found in the Humble records, interviews with and personal letters from veteran Humble production men have been more useful; the contemporary company records have been much more important as to specific fields, although interviews have also supplied information concerning Humble activities.

The Humble records of greatest importance for information regarding production activities and methods during this period were the executive correspondence, particularly of W. S. Farish, W. S. Smullin, and W. E. Pratt of Humble, and W. C. Teagle, president of Standard Oil Co. (N.J.). Minutes of directors' meetings were also useful.

Several manuscript histories, papers, speeches, and reports have also been frequently drawn on for this chapter: L. T. Barrow, "Notes on the History of the Geologic, Lease and Scouting

Department"; Wallace E. Pratt, "High Lights in the Development of Petroleum in Texas," dated Mar. 4, 1924 (particularly useful for Humble's employment of petroleum geology); D. P. Carlton, "The History of the Geophysics Department"; "The Scout of Yesterday" (recounting the experiences of a scout on the Gulf Coast), intended as background for a speech on "The Role of Scout or Landman in the Well Spacing Problem," about 1939; "History of Changes in Humble's Work Week," dated Apr. 27, 1948; Joe H. Russell, "Improved Drilling and Production Methods in the Gulf Coast Fields"; Harry L. Edwards, "Improved Drilling and Production Methods" (prepared for a meeting of the American Institute of Mining and Metallurgical Engineers, Tulsa, Okla., Oct. 11, 1926); report of J. R. Suman to W. S. Farish on inspection trip, Northern division, dated Mar. 9, 1927; "Summary of Humble's Net Crude Oil Production by Divisions."

Interviews and, in some cases, letters written in reply to requests for specific information have been particularly valuable. Information of a general and varied nature was furnished by Wallace E. Pratt, L. T. Barrow, D. P. Carlton, Hines H. Baker, and Charles E. Richards. Scouting and leasing were dealt with by R. B. Cooper, N. E. Tanner, Joe C. Rostrom, John F. Bricker, Bonneau Peters (of Standard Oil Co. of La.), Mrs. Howard S. Tullis, R. D. Farish, Henry K. Arnold, R. S. Sterling, E. E. Townes, H. C. Wiess, and Rex G. Baker. Geological scouting was emphasized by J. E. LaRue, Alva C. Ellisor, Morgan J. Davis, H. J. McLellan, E. A. Wendlandt, W. A. Maley, and Olin G. Bell. D. P. Carlton, J. E. LaRue, and Alva Ellisor contributed information on the development of geophysics. Valuable information on drilling and production, largely from the viewpoint of the practical man in the field, was supplied by D. B. Harris, S. P. Farish, Bert Broday, F. L. Carpenter, P. H. Walber, Frank Bass, M. Manning, R. L. Sloan, F. M. McGehee, C. B. Goddard, C. E. Stanley, T. J. Lamb, Joyce Adams, Donald C. Glass, A. H. Smith, R. E. Stearns, M. F. Lester, H. S. Warner, Harold Ward, A. H. Mitchell, R. E. Sinclair, and W. N. Finnegan, Jr. Early developments in and controversies over petroleum engineering were described by many of the drilling and production men above, and with particular emphasis by C. W. DeLancey, S. C. Moor, Frank Watts, R. G. Hamaker, J. R. Suman, G. B. Corless, R. E. Bridges, R. V. Hanrahan, and G. A. Mabry. Nearly all those mentioned above furnished information on particular regions and fields: special emphasis on North Texas in this period came from J. A. Neath, W. C. Teagle, W. B. Calhoun, R. C. Barbour, and C. C. Moore; on the Gulf Coast from J. L. Burton, W. H. Wheatley, A. A. Klein, D. F. Haynes, Mercer H. Parks, and Sigmond Rothschild; and on the Panhandle from David Frame.

2. For information on scouting and leasing in general, see E. L. DeGolyer, editor, *Elements of the Petroleum Industry* (N. Y., 1940), 101f., and Max W. Ball, *This Fascinating Oil Business* (Indianapolis, 1940), 29f. Additional information on Humble scouting and leasing was drawn from Humble Recs. and interviews. See also *Humble Way* (hereafter cited as *H. Way*), "The Search for Oil," Jan.–Feb., 1947, p. 23, and "Drill Here," Nov.–Dec., 1948, p. 23.

3. Humble Recs., D. E. Woods to E. L. Owens and All Employees in Scouting Dept., Sept. 3, 1919.

4. Information about the use of geology in oil finding in this period, and particularly the work of the Humble geologists under Wallace E. Pratt, has come from Humble Recs. and interviews. Also from Alva C. Ellisor, *Rockhounds of Houston, an Informal History of the Houston Geological Society* (Houston, 1947); Carey Croenis, "Micropaleontology—Past and Future," *Bull. of the AAPG*, July, 1941, pp. 1208–1255; J. Elmer Thomas, "The Origin and Growth of the American Association of Petroleum Geologists," *O. & G. Jour.*, Apr. 11, 1940, pp. 30–34, 37, 40; Alexander Deussen, "Two Decades of Progress in the Art of Oil Finding," *Bull. of the AAPG*, July, 1934, pp. 942–944; Pratt and Weeks, "History of Oil Exploration" in *Finding and Producing Oil; Report of the Temporary National Economic Committee* (hereafter cited as TNEC Report), VI, 388

(testimony of E. L. DeGolyer, Sept. 30, 1939); DeGolyer, "Wallace Everette Pratt"; *H. Sales Lub.*, Mar. 3, 1938; *H. Way*, Sept.–Oct., 1946.

5. *H. Way*, Sept.–Oct., 1945, pp. 10–12. None of the old Humble drilling and production employees interviewed ever mentioned rig building as one of his occupations.

6. Ball, *op. cit.*, 30–33, gives a brief and admirably clear description of the various categories of drilling and production men. *H. Way*, Sept.–Oct., 1948, pp. 24–27, describes cable-tool drilling, while the rotary crew and the functions of its members are dealt with in *H. Way*, Mar.–Apr., 1948, pp. 2–5, July–Aug., 1948, pp. 22–27, and Mar.–Apr., 1953, pp. 11, 14. Numerous interviews with veteran drilling and production employees were highly useful.

7. Humble Recs.; *H. Magazine*, Aug., 1921, p. 6; *O. & G. Jour.*, June 10, 1921, p. 28.

8. The extent to which pumping is an older man's job is brought out by the latest jobs of 150 Humble production employees, retiring 1945–1953, according to *H. Way*, *passim.* No fewer than 55—well over a third—were pumpers.

9. The opportunities for advancement available to Humble drilling and production employees are illustrated by the fact that of the 150 retiring, 1945–1953, well over a fourth were of ranks equal or superior to those of driller and gang pusher. They included 6 drillers, 10 tool pushers, 9 roustabout gang pushers, 3 farm bosses, and no fewer than 11 district superintendents.

10. Humble Recs. and interviews; *O. & G. Jour.*, Sept. 22, 1927, pp. 136 A–K, Mar. 27, 1930, p. 151, Sept. 28, 1933, p. 76.

11. *O. & G. Jour.*, Mar. 17, 1922, p. 20.

12. *Report of Electric Motor-Driven Rotary Drilling Operation on Humble Oil & Refining Company Well No. 12, L. P. Douglas Lease, Electra, Wichita County, Texas, April 19, 1923* (issued by Wichita Falls Electric Co.); *O. & G. Jour.*, Mar. 25, 1921, p. 86; Humble interviews and Recs.

13. *O. & G. Jour.*, Mar. 25, 1921, p. 86; Humble Recs.

14. *H. Magazine*, Mar., p. 10, and June, 1922, pp. 13, 15; *O. & G. Jour.*, 1921: Apr. 1, p. 52, May 13, p. 54.

15. *Financial American*, Apr. 9, 1919; *O. & G. Jour.*, Dec. 5, 1919, p. 38, Mar. 25, 1921, p. 86; *H. Magazine*, June, 1922, pp. 10, 12; *H. Bee*, Mar. 31, 1921, p. 1.

16. Harry L. Edwards, "Better Equipment and Improved Oil Field Appliances," *National Petroleum News*, Nov. 17, 1926; *H. Magazine*, Aug., 1921, pp. 17, 24, June, 1922, p. 36; Humble Recs. and interviews.

17. A. R. Hinton, "Standard Back in Texas . . . ," Los Angeles *Daily Times*, dated from Ranger, July 2, 1919 (clipping); *O. & G. Jour.*, Apr. 11, 1919, p. 16, May 2, 1919, p. 20; Humble Recs.; interview with W. C. Teagle. Smullin was a controversial figure, evidently capable of inspiring strong likes and dislikes. Opinions about him, ranging from the most adversely critical to the most favorable, were expressed in interviews with approximately a dozen Humble employees and executives of the period. Those who were most closely associated with him, however, generally seemed the most friendly in their judgment.

18. Humble Recs. and interviews; *O. & G. Jour.*, Aug. 29, 1919, p. 52. Surviving Humbletown menus indicate that the quality of the meals has been little exaggerated, if at all. The traditions of the lavishly stocked commissary are also apparently well founded; when it was closed in 1922 the stock on hand included 7 barrels and 230 cases of olives, 85 cases of catsup, large amounts of Jiffy Jell, a goodly store of silver polish, and no fewer than 625 pairs of shoes. Probably, indeed, the commissary was then overstocked, but this was not necessarily Smullin's responsibility, since he had left Texas in the summer of 1920.

19. Humble Recs., W. S. Smullin to W. S. Farish, Oct. 22, 1919, to R. S. Sterling, Feb. 23, 1920, and to R. D. Farish, May 13, 1920.

20. Humble Recs. and interviews; *H. Magazine*, Aug., 1921, pp. 5, 14; *O. & G. Jour.*, Aug. 15, 1919, p. 16; Boyce House, *Were You in Ranger?* (Dallas, 1935), 110.

21. Humble Recs. and interviews; SONJ Recs.; *O. & G. Jour.*, Sept. 3, 1920,

p. 34; Gibb and Knowlton, *The Resurgent Years,* 372.
22. Humble Recs.; *H. Magazine,* Aug., 1921, pp. 21, 31.
23. Interviews; *O. & G. Jour.,* May 23, 1919, p. 52.
24. *H. Magazine,* June, 1922, p. 38.
25. Humble Recs.; *H. Magazine,* May, 1921, p. 23; *O. & G. Jour.,* June 20, 1919, pp. 30–34.
26. *H. Magazine,* 1921: May, p. 23, Aug., p. 31, Nov., p. 39; Humble Recs.
27. *H. Magazine,* Aug., 1921, pp. 5f.; Humble Recs.; *O. & G. Jour.,* June 10, 1921, p. 28.
28. See note 4 above, esp. Pratt and Weeks, *op. cit.,* 10.
29. Deussen's mention of a fault appeared in "Geology and Underground Waters of the Southeastern Part of the Texas Coastal Plain," *Water Supply Paper* No. 335, U. S. Geol. Survey. Information on the early months of the Mexia boom has been derived from *O. & G. Jour.,* 1921: July 29, p. 44, Aug. 12, pp. 70f., 76, Sept. 9, pp. 1, 14, Sept. 23, pp. 1, 33, 52; DeGolyer, "Wallace Everette Pratt," 482; Humble Recs. and interviews.
30. General information on the Powell field was drawn from Warner, *Texas Oil & Gas,* 64, 166–168, and from Humble Recs. and interviews.
31. Humble Recs. and interviews; also *H. Magazine,* Aug., 1921, pp. 15–17, Mar., 1922, p. 38, Sept., 1922, p. 24.
32. Humble Recs. and interviews. Also, W. Henry Rector, "Legal History of Conservation of Oil and Gas in Arkansas," *Legal History of Conservation of Oil and Gas* (Section of Mineral Law of the American Bar Association, 1938), 19f.
33. Something of the general background of Humble's Southwest Texas operations, 1922–1925, is found in Warner, *op. cit.,* 284–286, 288, 305f., 422–432. Information on Humble's own part in the quest for oil in this region was drawn principally from company records and interviews.
34. Humble Recs.; *O. & G. Jour.,* July 9, 1925, p. 36, Dec. 10, 1925, p. 39, Oct. 7, 1926, p. 54, May 5, 1927, p. 51.
35. Rister, *Oil! Titan of Southwest,* 174f.; Humble Recs.
36. *O. & G. Jour.,* 1926: Jan. 7, p. 18, Jan. 14, p. 52, Feb. 4, p. 33; Humble Recs.
37. Humble Recs. and interviews; W. E. Pratt, "Oil and Gas in the Texas Panhandle," *Bull. of the AAPG,* May–June, 1923, pp. 237–249; Rister, *op. cit.,* 275f.; Warner, *op. cit.,* 258–261.
38. *O. & G. Jour.,* May 13–June 24, 1926, *passim,* esp. June 3, p. 158; Warner, *op. cit.,* 261; Humble Recs.
39. Warner, *op. cit.,* 318–323, 443–459; Rister, *op. cit.,* 287–292, 296; interviews with Humble men.
40. Warner, *op. cit.,* 242.
41. Committee on Stock List, *New York Stock Exchange, Humble Oil & Refining Company . . . September 19, 1925; O. & G. Jour.,* Oct. 4, 1934, p. 39; *H. Magazine,* Aug., 1921, p. 31, Mar., 1922, pp. 9, 11; Humble Recs.
42. Humble Recs.; Warner, *op. cit.,* 169.
43. Rister, *op. cit.,* 229, quoting *Oil Weekly,* Mar. 12, 1926, p. 79.
44. Information as to early developments in geophysical prospecting on the Gulf Coast was found in E. L. DeGolyer, "Notes on the Early History of Applied Geophysics in the Petroleum Industry," *Journal of the Society of Petroleum Geophysicists,* July, 1935, 245–254; E. L. DeGolyer, "Geophysical Methods in Economic Geology," *Economic Geology,* May, 1926, p. 297; E. A. Eckhardt, "A Brief History of the Gravity Method of Prospecting for Oil," in *Geophysical Case Histories,* L. L. Nettleton, editor (Society of Exploration Geophysicists, 1948), I, 24; Donald C. Barton, "Gravity Anomalies of Nash and Damon Mounds, Fort Bend and Brazoria Counties, Texas," *ibid.,* I, 35; Donald C. Barton, *Gulf Coast Oil Fields* (Tulsa, 1936), x-xi; Thomas, article cited in note 4; P. Wagner, "Seismographic System for Exploration of Underground Formations," *National Petroleum News,* Apr., 1923, p. 87; P. Wagner, "Location of Subsurface Fault Planes with 'Seismos' Tried in Texas," *ibid.,* Dec. 12, 1923, p. 51; Charles E. Kern, "Seismograph Search of Rock Formations," *O. & G. Jour.,* Mar. 6, 1924, p. 21; David Donoghue, "Oil Development of the Gulf Coast during 1924," *Production of Petroleum in 1924* (*Transactions,* Amer. Inst. of Mining and Metallurgical Engi-

neers, 1925), 127f.; *O. & G. Jour.*, June 12, 1924, p. 44.

45. *Ibid.*, 1924: Aug. 7, p. 52, Sept. 18, p. 46, Sept. 25, p. 42, Oct. 16, p. 42, Nov. 13, p. 38, Nov. 27, p. 52, Dec. 4, p. 115.

46. *Ibid.*, June 17, 1926, p. 58; Warner, *op. cit.*, 229; Humble Recs.

47. L. E. Smith, "Restoration of Pressure to Oil Sand Increasing in Oil Fields," *National Petroleum News*, May 7, 1924, p. 71; Humble Recs.

48. *H. Magazine,* Nov., 1921, p. 30, Sept., 1922, p. 6; Humble Recs.

CHAPTER 7

1. For the history of Humble's pipeline construction and operation, and particularly for an understanding of the development of company policies, the Humble executives' correspondence is sometimes supplemented by similar material from the Standard Oil Co. (N.J.) records. A useful single document is "Brief History of the Pipeline Company, 1919 through 1949," which contains information on pipeline construction, investment, profits, lengths and capacities of trunk and gathering lines, amount of crude transported, etc.

The Humble pipeline organization has been a closely knit group in which the personal touch has been particularly important, especially in construction. Personal information through interviews, conversations, and an occasional letter or memorandum, principally from members of the pipeline organization but also from other Humble executives and employees and a few outsiders, has thus been of great importance. Our principal informants were R. V. Hanrahan, H. M. Stevenson, J. A. Neath, O. Q. Lomax, and James Anderson, but valuable information on special subjects has also been supplied by C. C. Moore, A. D. Wilbur, S. G. Loy, W. R. Trelford, C. H. McNair, F. D. McMahon, Ray Horton, George Lee, C. B. Stults, A. A. Nance, H. M. Lingle, R. G. Hamaker, C. B. Goddard, Wallace E. Pratt, E. F. Voss, R. A. Brannon, and Frank Cullinan.

Humble's pipeline construction through 1924 is described in James Anderson, "Fast Spreading Pipe Lines in Texas," *The Lamp,* Apr., 1925, pp. 21–26. An illustrated article, "From Three Miles to 6,000," *H. Sales Lub.*, May 3, 1934, pp. 4–8, describes Humble's pipeline system at time of publication and tells something of its history. A brief account also appears in *H. Ref. Bee,* Feb. 24, 1938, p. 7.

2. Humble Recs.; *H. Ref. Bee,* May, 1942, p. 4; *H. Sales Lub.*, May, 1942, p. 7; *O. & G. Jour.*, Mar. 5, 1920, p. 4.

3. Interview; *O. & G. Jour.*, Aug. 1929, p. 24.

4. "The Petroleum Industry, 1859–1934," *O. & G. Jour.-Oil City Derrick* (1934), 123, 193; Humble Recs.; *O. & G. Jour.*, Apr. 4, 1919, p. 22.

5. See Rister, *Oil! Titan of the Southwest*, 152f.

6. *O. & G. Jour.*, 1919: July 18, p. 16, Sept. 5, p. 32, July 25, p. 50; 1920: Jan. 23, p. 46, Feb. 6, p. 6.

7. *Ibid.*, May 28, 1920, p. 26; 1921: Sept. 9, p. 1, Sept. 30, p. 18.

8. *Ibid.*, Mar. 17, 1922, p. 40.

9. *Ibid.*, Sept. 5, 1919.

10. Humble Recs.; R. V. Hanrahan, "Humble Pipe Line Activities in North Central Texas," *H. Magazine,* June, 1922, pp. 11f.

11. John Joseph Mathews, *Life and Death of an Oilman: The Career of E. W. Marland* (Norman, Okla., 1951), 173f.; *O. & G. Jour.*, 1925: Jan. 1, p. 30, Apr. 9, p. 145, Apr. 23, p. 24, May 7, p. 124, June 25, p. 142, July 23, p. 73; 1926: Mar. 25, p. 56. Also, Rister, *op. cit.*, 289; interview.

12. Warner, *Texas Oil and Gas,* pp. 98, 325f.; Rister, *op. cit.*, 297f.; *Wall Street News*, July 5, 1927.

13. Humble Recs.; *O. & G. Jour.*, 1926: Jan. 7, p. 18, Jan. 14, p. 52, Feb. 4, p. 33, May 20, p. 58, June 3, pp. 50, 158, July 22, p. 135, Aug. 19, p. 37, Dec. 16, p. 51; 1929: Jan. 3, p. 134; 1930: Mar. 13, p. 86, Apr. 24, p. 78, June 5, pp. 52f., 56f., Sept. 11, p. 71.

14. *Ibid.*, 1927: July 14, p. 94, July 28, p. 120, Aug. 11, p. 34; 1928: Mar. 15, p. 176, Mar. 24, p. 187, Apr. 12, p. 155, Aug. 2, p. 164, Aug. 9, p. 112, Aug. 30, p. 71; Corpus Christi *Caller*, Feb. 8, 1928; the Dallas *Morning News*, Mar. 11, 1928; Humble interviews.

15. Humble Recs. and interviews; *O. & G. Jour.*, Sept. 1, 1927, p. 124.

16. Mathews, *op. cit.*, 184.

17. Humble Recs.; *O. & G. Jour.*, May 5, 1927, p. 40.
18. "Desert Nuisance," *H. Way*, Jan.–Feb., 1946, pp. 21–23.
19. "Looping the Line," *H. Way*, May–June, 1947, pp. 9–11; *O. & G. Jour.*, Aug. 11, 1927, p. 34.
20. *O. & G. Jour.*, May, 1951, pp. 419, 421f.
21. Interviews; *O. & G. Jour.*, Aug. 11, 1927, p. 34.
22. *O. & G. Jour.*, Apr. 19, 1928, p. 153.
23. *Ibid.*, Aug. 29, 1929, p. 74.
24. George S. Wolbert, *American Pipelines, Their Industrial Structure, Economic Status, and Legal Implications* (Norman, Okla., 1952), 22–25.
25. "From Three Miles to 6,000," *H. Sales Lub.*, May 3, 1934, pp. 5f.; "Refinery Stillman Sees Pipe Line Operations," *H. Way*, Mar.–Apr., 1949, pp. 24–27; *O. & G. Jour.*, July 28, 1927, p. 120.
26. *Ibid.*, Jan. 10, 1924, p. 60.
27. "Delivered on Schedule," *H. Way*, Sept.–Oct., 1928, pp. 8–11.
28. Ball, *This Fascinating Oil Business*, 211f.; *O. & G. Jour.*, June 3, 1926, p. 50.
29. "Refinery Stillman Sees Pipe Line Operations," *H. Way*, Mar.–Apr., 1949, pp. 24–27; "Delivered on Schedule," *H. Way*, Sept.–Oct., 1948, pp. 8–11.
30. C. O. Wilson, "Southwest Is Hub of the Pipe-Line Industry," *O. & G. Jour.*, May, 1951, pp. 400–426, esp. 414f.
31. Humble Recs., Farish to Teagle, July 19, 1919.
32. Wolbert, *op. cit.*, 9.
33. Humble Recs., Teagle to Sterling, Aug. 24, 1920; Sterling to Teagle, Aug. 7 and 27, 1920; Teagle to Farish, Sept. 9, 1920; Farish to Teagle, Aug. 31, 1920; E. E. Townes to Farish, Aug. 31, 1920.
34. Humble Recs., Teagle to Farish, Feb. 10 and Mar. 1, 1922; Farish to Teagle, Feb. 21 and Mar. 8, 1922.
35. Humble Recs.; Gibb and Knowlton, *The Resurgent Years*, 465–472.
36. SONJ Recs., Teagle to Farish (personal and confidential), Sept. 12, 1928, and Nov. 2, 14, 1928; Farish to Teagle, Nov. 8, 1928.

CHAPTER 8

1. In addition to Humble executive correspondence and directors' minutes, contracts for the purchase and sale of crude, notices to producers from whom Humble bought crude, memoranda in regard to pipeline rates, oil in storage, etc., were significant sources for this chapter. Standard Oil Company (N.J.) records also provided valuable information.

Correspondence usually emphasized matters of general policy; for the details of actual operations, interviews with the men in the office and field were indispensable. J. A. Neath's long service with Humble Pipe Line Co. and, subsequently, on the board of the parent company enabled him to give information on almost every point; he was particularly informative in regard to purchase and sales contracts and the development of ratable taking, as was also Hines H. Baker. James Anderson, who was for many years director in charge of crude oil operations, and W. R. Trelford, his assistant, were also generally informative. H. C. Wiess furnished indispensable information in regard to early negotiations with Jersey. N. K. Robb and George W. LeVan contributed to our understanding of the organization of the Crude Oil Dept. and Committee. Gay Carroll gave key information on crude oil accounting. The important role of the pipelines was discussed by such pipeline executives as R. V. Hanrahan, O. Q. Lomax, A. E. Pecore, H. M. Stevenson, and H. M. Lingle, and in a conference with pipeline superintendents. The crucial problem of storage was discussed by the above-mentioned pipeliners, by such representatives of other groups as C. B. Goddard, Bert Broday, Clyde Vardaman, C. W. DeLancey, R. L. Clifton, R. E. Sinclair, and M. F. Moffett, and in a conference with Crude Oil Dept. executives. Bert Broday and David Frame gave information on the background of Humble's entrance into the Panhandle as a purchaser. C. L. Brown gave a favorable estimate of Humble's crude purchasing policy from the viewpoint of the small independent producer.
2. Humble Recs., Farish to J. C. Wilson, Mar. 31, 1919.
3. Information from Robert E. Hardwicke.
4. SONJ Recs.
5. Humble Recs. See also *Wall Street*

Journal, Apr. 28, 1919; *O. & G. Jour.*, Dec. 12, 1919.
6. Humble Recs.; interviews; also R. V. Hanrahan, "Humble Pipe Line Activities in North Central Texas," *H. Magazine*, June, 1922, pp. 11f.
7. Humble Recs. Also *O. & G. Jour.*, Dec. 26, 1919, pp. 3, 42.
8. On storage: interviews; Humble Recs.; *H. Magazine*, Nov., 1921, p. 30.
9. Humble Recs.; *O. & G. Jour.*, Nov. 26, 1920, p. 50, May 13, 1921, pp. 18, 20ff.
10. Humble's purchasing policy during the first few months of this period of overproduction is revealed in Humble Recs.; SONJ Recs.; Wichita Falls *Record-News*, Feb. 14, 1921. Also, *O. & G. Jour.*, 1920: Oct. 15, p. 37, Dec. 24, p. 72; 1921: Jan. 7, pp. 50, 82, Jan. 14, p. 24, Jan. 28, pp. 6, 26, Feb. 28, p. 56.
11. Humble Recs.; Wichita Falls *Record-News*, Apr. 5, 1921; *Oklahoman*, Aug. 3, 1921; *O. & G. Jour.*, 1921: Apr. 8, p. 44, Apr. 15, p. 66, Aug. 12, p. 20.
12. Gibb and Knowlton, *The Resurgent Years*, 436.
13. Interviews; Gibb and Knowlton, *op. cit.*, 439.
14. Humble Recs.; *O. & G. Jour.*, Sept. 6, 1923, p. 49, Apr. 3, 1924, p. 57; *H. Magazine*, Mar., 1922, p. 7, quoting *The Lamp*.
15. Humble Recs., Farish to Teagle, Nov. 7, 1921.
16. On the problem of storage during the "years of abundance": Humble Recs.; interviews; *H. Magazine*, Nov., 1921, p. 30, and Sept., 1922, p. 6; *O. & G. Jour.*, Feb. 15, 1923, p. 20; *The Lamp*, Apr., 1925, pp. 21–26.
17. *O. & G. Jour.*, 1923: Jan. 25, pp. 54, 86, 104, Feb. 15, p. 32, Feb. 22, pp. 32, 34, Mar. 22, p. 36, Mar. 29, p. 22; Wichita Falls *Record-News*, Feb. 10, 1923.
18. American Petroleum Institute, *Petroleum Facts and Figures* (hereafter referred to as *Petr. Facts and Figures*), 1950, p. 3.
19. *O. & G. Jour.*, 1923: May 3, p. 46, June 28, p. 17.
20. The report is undated, but internal evidence indicates that it was written in the summer of 1923.
21. *O. & G. Jour.*, 1923: May 17, p. 57, May 24, pp. 15, 118–120, May 31, p. 28, June 28, p. 45, July 19, pp. 82f., July 26, p. 61, Aug. 2, p. 39; Humble Recs.
22. Humble Recs.; *O. & G. Jour.*, 1923: July 5, p. 74, Aug. 2, p. 66, Aug. 23, p. 28. Prairie Oil & Gas Co. and Sinclair had announced in June that they would prorate their purchases to market demand in the Mid-Continent fields (*O. & G. Jour.*, June 28, 1923, p. 44).
23. Humble Recs., Farish to Hanrahan, July 30, 1923.
24. Humble Recs.; *O. & G. Jour.*, 1923: Sept. 27, p. 27, Oct. 11, p. 31, Oct. 18, p. 49, Oct. 25, pp. 31, 41, 43, Nov. 1, pp. 31, 55.
25. *O. & G. Jour.*, 1923: Sept. 6, p. 42, Sept. 20, p. 50, Oct. 18, p. 43, Oct. 25, pp. 31, 41, 43, Nov. 22, p. 93; New York *American*, Nov. 27, 1923; Humble Recs.
26. Edwin C. Clapp, in New York *American*, Nov. 28, 1923.
27. *O. & G. Jour.*, 1923: Nov. 22, p. 17, Nov. 29, pp. 25, 54, Dec. 6, p. 46.
28. Hidy and Hidy, *Pioneering in Big Business*, 671–684.
29. *State* v. *Humble*, 1924, 263 S. W., 319–325; SONJ Recs.
30. *Petr. Facts and Figures*, 1950, p. 170.
31. *O. & G. Jour.*, 1923: Nov. 22, p. 17, Nov. 29, pp. 25, 54, Dec. 6, p. 46.
32. New York *American*, Nov. 27, 1923; *O. & G. Jour.*, Dec. 27, 1923, p. 26.
33. Humble Recs.; *O. & G. Jour.*, 1924: May 22, p. 19, June 5, p. 50, June 12, pp. 27, 36, July 3, p. 27, July 10, pp. 19, 23, 80, July 17, pp. 19, 27, 36, 130, July 24, pp. 27, 54, July 31, pp. 19, 27.
34. Humble Recs., Farish to Teagle, Mar. 29, 1924.
35. Humble Recs., Teagle to Farish, Nov. 18, 1924; Farish to Teagle, Nov. 22, 1924.
36. Humble Recs., Farish to Teagle, Nov. 25, 1924.
37. *O. & G. Jour.*, Sept. 6, 1923, p. 49, Apr. 3, 1924, p. 57.
38. Interview with Russell Barbour.
39. *H. Sales Lub.*, Feb. 27, 1941, pp. 16–18.
40. Humble Recs.; *O. & G. Jour.*, 1923: Nov. 1, p. 31, Nov. 15, p. 31; 1924: June 5, p. 50, June 12, pp. 27, 36, July 3, p. 27.
41. Humble Recs.; *O. & G. Jour.*, Jan. 1, 1925, p. 30.
42. *O. & G. Jour.*, 1926: May 20, p. 58, June 3, pp. 50, 158, July 22, p. 135, Aug. 19, p. 37, Dec. 16, p. 51.
43. Humble Recs.; *O. & G. Jour.*, Aug. 19, 1926, p. 37, Apr. 7, 1927, p. 39.

44. SONJ Recs.; Humble Recs.
45. *O. & G. Jour.*, 1926: July 8, p. 127, Sept. 30, p. 123, Oct. 28, pp. 39, 143, Nov. 4, p. 145.
46. Humble Recs., Teagle to S. B. Hunt, Oct. 15, 1926; Houston *Press*, about July 19–20, 1927, quoting *Wall Street Journal;* Amarillo *Daily News*, Oct. 4, 1927.
47. Humble Recs., Farish's statement at Railroad Commission hearing, Austin, Mar. 10, 1928.
48. SONJ Recs., memo., "Pipe Line Rates, Gathering Charges and Selling Commissions," Jan. 28, 1927.
49. *Petr. Facts and Figures*, 1950, p. 170.

CHAPTER 9

1. Humble records include a number of typewritten or mimeographed histories of refinery developments and operations, based on official sources: Edwin A. Bynum, Jr., "Notes on Colony Creek Refinery and Burkburnett Refinery, Nov. 5, 1948"; "Baytown and Ingleside Refineries, July 27, 1934"; "Dates of Initial Operation of and Major Changes to Major Baytown Equipment, July 19, 1944"; "Baytown Refinery Expansion from 1921 to 1948, Feb. 18, 1949"; "Highlights on Organization and Development of Refining Operations, 1944."

For employee relations, the Minutes of the Baytown Joint Conference were indispensable.

Interviews were of particular value because of the technical nature of refining. H. C. Wiess, who died in 1948, was helpful in the early stages of research. On the difficulties of early construction and operations, interviews with D. F. Haynes (Wiess's secretary), R. H. Brinton and T. H. Hamilton (early engineers), W. A. Eberle (superintendent), Bob Roberts and Joe Reilly (foremen), and W. G. Lopas, D. T. Monroe, F. T. Fendley, C. E. Rodecape, Maxey Ward, and J. L. Dunman were useful. L. W. Schrader, a Jersey engineer, gave insight into "the other side" of the early difficulties at Baytown. Information as to technical improvements was furnished by S. P. Coleman, W. K. Lewis, H. D. Wilde, James Harrop, H. W. Ferguson, R. N. Dyer, and Karl E. Martin. Information on employee relations was contributed by T. W. Moore, David Hunt, James Beasley, Knox Thomas, R. B. Roaper, Jake Hodges, Joseph Boudelouche, and W. H. Wheatley.
2. On the small refineries and casinghead plants: Humble Recs.; interviews; *H. Magazine*, Nov., 1920, p. 8, Aug., 1921, pp. 12f., 18, Nov., 1921, pp. 5, 8; *H. Bee*, 1921: Mar. 24, p. 1, Apr. 7, p. 1.
3. *O. & G. Jour.*, July 6, 1919, pp. 30-38, June 13, 1919, p. 30; interview.
4. Humble Recs., Wiess to Farish, June 16 and Oct. 5, 1925.
5. H. C. Wiess, "The Humble Oil & Refining Company as a Refiner of Petroleum Products," *H. Magazine*, Nov., 1921, p. 5; A. T. E. Newkirk, "Baytown as an Industrial Community," *ibid.*, Nov., 1921, pp. 15f.; Howard E. Humphrey, "Pleasant Memories of Seventeen Years," *H. Ref. Bee*, Apr. 22, 1937, pp. 4–6, May 6, 1937, pp. 13–15; other reminiscences in *H. Ref. Bee*, 1939: Mar. 23, pp. 4–6, May 18, pp. 4–6, Aug. 24, pp. 6–10.
6. Interview with R. H. Brinton.
7. *O. & G. Jour.*, Aug. 23, 1918, p. 51, Jan. 24, 1919, p. 26.
8. *H. Bee*, May 26, 1921, p. 1; *H. Ref. Bee*, Oct. 19, 1939, pp. 4–6.
9. Humble Recs; interviews; *H. Bee*, June 23, 1921, p. 1; *H. Magazine*, Aug., 1921, p. 21; *H. Ref. Bee*, July 28, 1938, pp. 7f., Nov., 1942, pp. 5f., Nov., 1945, p. 8, Apr., 1946, pp. 5f.
10. *H. Ref. Bee*, June 17, 1937, pp. 10f., Nov. 16, 1939, pp. 8–10, Nov. 14, 1940, pp. 21f., Apr., 1946, pp. 5f.
11. *H. Ref. Bee*, July 13, 1939, pp. 5f.; *O. & G. Jour.*, Dec. 5, 1919, p. 38.
12. *H. Ref. Bee*, July 18, 1936, p. 23; Dec. 16, 1937, pp. 10f.; 1939: Oct. 5, pp. 4f., Nov. 16, pp. 8–10, Nov. 30, pp. 6–8; Oct., 1943, pp. 8f.; Aug., 1946, p. 12.
13. Interviews; Humble Recs.; *H. Magazine*, Aug., 1921, p. 26; Allen, *Organized Labor in Texas*, p. 228.
14. Humble Recs., Wiess to Teagle, Feb. 20 and Apr. 20, 1920; also *H. Ref. Bee*, Dec. 28, 1939, pp. 7f., May, 1942, pp. 10f.
15. Humble Recs.; *H. Ref. Bee*, Dec. 31, 1936, p. 11.

16. *H. Bee,* Mar. 17–Apr. 21, 1921, *passim; H. Magazine,* 1921: May, p. 10, Aug., p. 26, Nov., pp. 7, 11f., 15f., and Sept., 1922, p. 8.
17. Humble Recs.; interviews; *H. Bee,* Apr. 21, 1921, p. 1; *La Prensa* (San Antonio), Apr. 1, 1921; Houston *Post,* Mar. 23, 1921, p. 5.
18. *H. Magazine,* Aug., 1921, p. 15; Humble Recs.
19. *H. Magazine,* Mar., 1922, p. 7; *H. Bee,* Mar. 17, 1922, p. 2; *H. Ref. Bee,* Aug. 12, 1937, p. 7; Humble Recs.; Houston *Post,* Jan. 18, 1946.
20. Interview with R. H. Brinton.
21. Gibb and Knowlton, *The Resurgent Years,* 525; Paul H. Giddens, *Standard Oil Company (Indiana), Oil Pioneer of the Middle West* (N. Y., 1955), 252.
22. Humble Recs.; *H. Ref. Bee,* Mar. 25, 1937, pp. 6f., July 29, 1937, p. 7, Nov. 2, 1939, pp. 5f.
23. Gibb and Knowlton, *op. cit.,* 537f.: "In 1921 Jersey's consultant, W. K. Lewis, set up the first of his so-called bubble towers at Bayway," but these towers were experimental. The official Baytown refinery history holds that the two batteries at Baytown were equipped with the first commercial bubble towers in the United States, as well as the first large heat exchangers.
24. *Ibid.,* 115–122, 532–538, 547–554; Giddens, *op. cit.,* 152f., 255–266.
25. Humble Recs.; interviews; Eugene H. Leslie, *Motor Fuels: Their Production and Technology* (N. Y., 1923), 357–366, 368, 373, 378–381; Frank A. Howard, "The Ancient Art of 'Cracking,'" *O. & G. Jour.,* Nov. 23, 1922, reprinted from *The Lamp.*
26. Humble Recs.; especially Wiess to Clark, Mar. 12, 1926, including extract from R. Steinschneider's Dec. 17, 1925, report of trip to the U. S., Oct.–Nov., 1925.
27. Information about the beginnings of Humble's Development Dept. was obtained from voluminous correspondence in the Humble records, interviews with S. P. Coleman, Oct. 1, 1948, and with W. K. Lewis, July 14, 1950.
28. Gibb and Knowlton, *op. cit.,* 573f.; Stuart Chase, "A Generation of Industrial Peace," *The Lamp,* Oct., 1946, pp. 2–6; Clarence J. Hicks, *My Life in Industrial Relations* (N. Y., 1941), 54, 87; Houston *Chronicle,* Feb. 13, 1948, pp. 1, 22–B; *O. & G. Jour.,* 1919: Apr. 4, p. 36, Apr. 11, p. 3, Apr. 18, p. 28, May 2, p. 47, May 9, p. 36, May 30, p. 42, June 14, p. 70.
29. Minutes, First General Joint Conference, Baytown Refinery, Dec. 10, 1920.
30. *Ibid.,* Sept. 12, 1922.
31. *H. Bee,* 1921: Mar. 17, p. 1, Apr. 28, pp. 1f., May 12, pp. 1f.; 1922: Mar. 1, p. 1, Sept. 23, p. 2, Oct. 21, p. 2, Nov. 18, p. 1; Mar. 26, 1923, p. 2.
32. Humble Recs.; interviews; *H. Bee,* Apr. 14, 1921, p. 1, Mar. 17, 1922, p. 1; *H. Magazine,* Mar., 1922, p. 23.
33. *H. Bee,* 1926: Dec. 1, p. 2, Dec. 15, p. 2; 1927: Mar. 15, p. 4, Apr. 15, p. 2; 1928: June 15, p. 2, July 7, p. 2; July 1, 1929, p. 3.
34. *H. Bee,* May 26, 1921, p. 1; *H. Ref. Bee,* Feb. 28, 1935, pp. 12f., June 18, 1936, p. 23, Oct. 8, 1936, pp. 9f., June 30, 1938, pp. 8f., Apr. 6, 1939, pp. 10–12, Nov., 1945, p. 8, Apr., 1946, pp. 5f.; Humble Recs.
35. Humble Recs.; *H. Ref. Bee,* Nov., 1945, p. 8, Apr., 1946, pp. 5f.
36. *H. Bee,* 1923: Feb. 12, p. 2, Apr. 21, p. 2; 1925: Jan. 31, pp. 2f., Aug. 3, pp. 2–4, Nov. 1, p. 4; Sept. 1, 1926, p. 4; Mar. 21, 1929, p. 1; *H. Ref. Bee,* Aug. 1, 1935, pp. 4–6, Dec. 31, 1936, p. 11; Humble Recs.; interviews.
37. Interview with Joseph Boudelouche.
38. Humble Recs., Teagle to Farish, Aug. 11, 13, 23, 1926; Farish to Teagle, Aug. 17, 1926.
39. Humble Recs. Also, *O. & G. Jour.,* Feb. 13, 1930.
40. *O. & G. Jour.,* Feb. 13, 1930; H. D. Wilde, Jr., Brian Mead, and S. P. Coleman, "Methods . . . to Decrease Losses," *O. & G. Jour.,* Oct. 3, 1929, pp. 222, 226, 229. Interviews.
41. Humble Recs.; *O. & G. Jour.,* Oct. 29, 1925, pp. 131, 140.
42. Humble Recs., Humble-Standard Oil Development Co. correspondence, Jan.–Feb., 1926, and "Mutualization Agreement between Standard Oil Development Co. and Humble," May 14, 1928.
43. Humble Recs., Wiess to Harden, Oct. 24, 1929, and to Finley, Coleman, Brown, Powell, and Giraud, Oct. 23, 1929.

44. Humble Recs., especially Wiess to E. J. Sadler, Apr. 26, 1927; interviews.

CHAPTER 10

1. In addition to the executive correspondence, various Humble statistical records, memoranda, contracts, and accounts proved useful. The Standard Oil Co. (N.J.) records used consisted almost entirely of the correspondence of top executives.

The voluminous correspondence on the subject of marketing reduces the comparative importance of interviews. Interviews with H. C. Wiess and B. H. Brown, however, helped to clarify various aspects of the Humble side of marketing; interviews with Hines H. Baker and R. H. Brinton were also helpful. Interviews with Frank B. Balling, P. C. Miller, and G. M. Davison were of especial value for the Jersey side of the story.

The sale of refined products within Humble's own operating area naturally received a good deal of attention in the press, but our knowledge of Humble's sales policies and activities within this region and period is, nevertheless, dependent primarily on Humble records, particularly correspondence of Humble's Farish, Wiess, Bonner, M. J. Monroe, and Brown, and of Jersey's Teagle.

Particularly important written accounts are E. A. Share, "A History of Humble Oil & Refining Company's Marketing Operations in Texas"; and, briefer but useful, J. R. Mulvey, "Sales Department, 'Company Organization,' Nov. 28, 1934." Bynum's "Notes on Colony Creek Refinery and Burkburnett Refinery" is useful for what it suggests concerning sales and marketing for those and Humble's other small refineries.

The development of a sales program usually involves personalities and field activities that are unlikely to receive adequate attention on the top-executive level and particularly in correspondence. Hence, the interviews with Roy M. Stephens, Dan T. Monroe, J. R. Mulvey, E. E. Townes, B. H. Brown, J. L. Dingle, G. A. Mabry, and H. W. Ferguson were of particular value.

2. Inside views of the agreement between the two companies were obtained from interviews with Sterling, Wiess, and Townes. *O. & G. Jour.*, June 5, 1924, pp. 132f., contains information given by Farish.

3. Humble Recs., Frank Andrews to Swain, July 26, 1921.

4. Humble Recs., H. C. Wiess to E. M. Clark, Dec. 30, 1922.

5. Humble Recs., Farish to Teagle, June 30, 1923.

6. Gibb and Knowlton, *The Resurgent Years*, 488–494.

7. Humble Recs., Farish to Teagle, Sept. 4 and Nov. 9, 1923; Teagle to Farish, Sept. 7, 1923; financial records. On industry experience: *O. & G. Jour.*, 1923, *passim*, esp. Aug. 23, p. 48.

8. Humble Recs., Farish to Teagle, May 15, 1924.

9. Humble Recs., Farish to Teagle, 1924: June 5 and 14, Aug. 17, Oct. 31; Teagle to Farish, 1924: July 17, Aug. 7, 16, and 28.

10. Humble Recs., Teagle to Farish, Oct. 25, 1924; Farish to Teagle, Oct. 27, 1924.

11. Humble Recs., Farish to Teagle, May 13, Oct. 4, 1924.

12. Humble Recs., Teagle to Farish, Oct. 9, 1924; Farish to Teagle, Oct. 13, 1924.

13. Humble Recs., F. H. Bedford to Farish, Oct. 9 and 20, 1924; Farish to Bedford, Oct. 14, 1924.

14. *Ibid.*, Teagle to Farish, Oct. 30 and Nov. 19, 1924; Farish to Teagle, Nov. 6 and 22, Dec. 15, 1924; *O. & G. Jour.*, 1925, *passim*, refinery and tank-wagon prices.

15. Humble Recs., Wiess to Farish, Sept. 3, 4, 5, 1925.

16. SONJ Recs.; interviews; J. S. Bonner, "Selling Oils," *H. Magazine*, Mar., 1922, pp. 18f.; *H. Ref. Bee*, June 1, 1939, p. 9; *H. Sales Lub.*, June 8, 1938, p. 8; Davis and Grobe, *New Encyclopedia of Texas*, I, 558.

17. Humble Recs.; TNEC Report, I, 418 (testimony of John E. Shatford).

18. Humble Recs., Brown to Wiess, June, 1922; Wiess to Farish, June 20, 1922; M. J. Monroe to Farish, Dec. 27, 1922; *H. Bee*, Apr. 28, 1921, p. 3; *O. & G. Jour.*, Oct. 1, 1920, p. 88, Oct. 7, 1921, p. 44; Houston *Press*, Apr. 12, 1922.

19. Humble Recs., memo., Farish, Aug. 11, 1923.

20. Humble Recs., Brown to Farish, May 17, 1923; Wiess to Farish, May 31, 1923. Also, TNEC Report, VI, 418.
21. Humble Recs.; *O. & G. Jour.*, Sept. 13, 1923, p. 50.
22. Humble Recs.; TNEC Report, VI, 418.
23. Gibb and Knowlton, *op. cit.*, 488f.
24. Humble Recs.; *O. & G. Jour.*, Sept. 13, 1923, p. 80.
25. Gibb and Knowlton, *op. cit.*, 488.
26. *Ibid.*, 489.
27. *H. Magazine*, May, 1921, and Sept., 1922, back covers.
28. Humble Recs., *Products of Known Quality* (pamphlet with specimen ads).
29. Humble Recs., memo. by Wiess on Sales Dept. matters, Dec. 17, 1925.
30. Humble Recs.; *O. & G. Jour.*, July 24, 1924, p. 82.
31. Humble Recs., Wiess to Farish, May 13, 1926.
32. *H. Bee*, Sept. 15, 1926, p. 3, and Oct., 1926.
33. Humble Recs.; Gibb and Knowlton, *op. cit.*, 541–544.
34. Humble Recs., Wiess to Bonner, Apr. 6, 1927.
35. Humble Recs., Bonner to Wiess, Nov. 5, 1926; Wiess to Bonner, Nov. 6, 1926.
36. Humble Recs., Wiess to Farish, July 13, 1927, Apr. 11, 1928.
37. Humble Recs., M. J. Monroe to Wiess, Dec. 18, 1928; Wiess to Monroe, Jan. 3, 20, 1929.
38. Humble Recs. and interviews; *H. Sales Lub.*, Oct., 1931, p. 3 (picture).
39. Humble Recs.; *API Bulletin*, July 30, 1929.
40. For the background of this difficulty, see Gibb and Knowlton, *op. cit.*, 335–338. Information on the Anglo purchase was obtained from SONJ Recs.; *New York Times*, Oct. 29, 1929; and *The Petroleum Times*, Oct. 2, 1937.
41. This effort to stabilize the foreign market will be considered at some length in a forthcoming volume on the history of Standard Oil Co. (N.J.)
42. Humble Recs. See Hidy and Hidy, *Pioneering in Big Business*, 141.
43. Humble Recs., Wiess to Clark, Oct. 27, 1926, and to C. E. Graff, Dec. 13, 1926.
44. Humble Recs., Wiess to D. L. Harper, Dec. 23, 1929, and to Farish, Dec. 28, 1929.
45. Humble Recs., Farish to S. B. Hunt, Aug. 3, 1928.
46. SONJ Recs., memo., Orville Harden (?), Nov. 30, 1927.
47. Humble Recs., Wiess to Brown, Jan. 15, 1929; Townes to Farish, Jan. 25, 1929; Wiess to Harden, Jan. 30, 1929.

CHAPTER 11

1. Information about the attitude of Humble executives toward conservation during 1919–1926 was derived principally from the executive correspondence of W. S. Farish. Interviews with Hines H. Baker, Wallace E. Pratt, and Carl E. Reistle, Jr., were also very helpful.
2. *O. & G. Jour.*, May 25, 1916, p. 31.
3. Warner, *Texas Oil and Gas*, 33f., 42–44, 49, 57, 59–61; Robert E. Hardwicke, "Legal History of Proration of Oil Production in Texas," *Texas Law Review*, Oct., 1937, pp. 99-128; and "Texas" in *Legal History of Conservation of Oil and Gas* (Amer. Bar. Assn., 1938).
4. Humble Recs., W. S. Farish to W. C. Teagle, July 19, 1919.
5. Humble Recs.; *O. & G. Jour.*, July 25, 1919, p. 69; Warner, *op. cit.*, 61f.
6. Humble Recs.; interviews; Philadelphia *Public Ledger*, Nov. 28, 1919; Warner, *op. cit.*, 61.
7. Humble Recs., Farish to C. K. Clarke (Standard Oil of La.), Oct. 27, 1931; interview with Clint Murchison.
8. Humble Recs., especially Bert Broday to W. S. Farish, Apr. 15, 1920; Texas R. R. Commission, *Revised Conservation Rules and Regulations*, Mar. 1, 1923.
9. Humble Recs., W. E. Pratt to W. T. Cushing, May 24, 1920.
10. Charles Richard Van Hise, *The Conservation of Natural Resources* (N. Y., 1917).
11. A. W. Ambrose, "Only 20 Per Cent. of Oil is Recovered," *O. & G. Jour.*, Oct. 10, 1919, pp. 62, 66.
12. J. O. Lewis, *Methods for Increasing the Recovery from Oil Sands*, U. S. Department of Interior, Bureau of Mines, Bulletin 148, Petroleum Technology 37 (Washington, 1917).
13. Ambrose, *loc. cit.*
14. R. Van Mills, "The Relations of Texture and Bedding to the Movements of Oil and Water through Sands," *Economic Geology*, Mar., 1921, p. 24.
15. "Relation of Drilling Campaign to

Income from Oil Properties," in *Reports of Investigations*, Bureau of Mines, Aug., 1921.

16. Humble Recs., W. S. Farish to R. L. Welch, May 24, 1921; W. S. Farish, "Oil Production in the Southwest," *O. & G. Jour.*, Dec. 14, 1922, pp. 94, 96, 98 (address before meeting of the API, St. Louis).

17. *Petr. Facts and Figures*, 1950, p. 3.

18. Report to the directors of the API dated Sept. 22, 1923; API Directors' Minutes, Sept. 24, 1923. See Leonard Marion Logan, *Stabilization of the Petroleum Industry* (Norman, Okla., 1930), 144f.

19. *Mining and Metallurgy*, July, 1924, pp. 336f.

20. Doherty's addresses and writings and other materials dealing with his reform efforts constitute a considerable literature. *O. & G. Jour.*, 1923: Sept. 17, pp. 58, 106f., 110f., 114f., Dec. 13, pp. 23, 107; 1924: Nov. 20, p. 23, Dec. 11, pp. 98, 101f., 104; 1925: Feb. 19, pp. 26, 117, Feb. 26, pp. 26, 211. Also, H. L. Doherty, "Suggestions for Conservation of Petroleum by Control of Production," in *Production of Petroleum in 1924* (N. Y., 1925); Logan, *op. cit.;* and Robert E. Hardwicke, *Antitrust Laws . . . vs. Unit Operations of Gas and Gas Pools* (N. Y., 1948).

21. For example, an article in the *O & G. Jour.*, Jan. 10, 1924, p. 28, expressing California Standard's opposition to the theory that wide spacing is preferable and citing both experience and authorities (Cutler and Clute) in support of the belief that close spacing results in greater production (note 15, above).

22. Logan, *op. cit.*, 144f.; *O. & G. Jour.*, Nov. 20, 1924, p. 23.

23. *O. & G. Jour.*, Oct. 11, 1923, pp. 68, 86, 104; 1924: Nov. 27, p. 103, and Dec. 11, pp. 98, 101f., 104.

24. President Coolidge's letter of Dec. 18, 1924, was widely reproduced and commented upon.

25. Humble Recs., W. S. Farish and W. C. Teagle to A. C. Bedford, Jan. 5, 1925 (copy), enclosed in letter from Teagle to Farish, June 10, 1927.

26. API, *Bulletin*, Jan. 24, 1925, is devoted to the subject of the Federal Oil Conservation Board. It reproduces the Coolidge letter, the resolution of the API board, and the questionnaire which the federal board sent to oil executives and specialists. Also Logan, *op. cit.*, 144f.; and Hardwicke, *Antitrust Laws*, 179–190.

27. The report on supply, which is a major section in the report of the Committee of Eleven to the API board, was published as *American Petroleum, Supply and Demand* (N. Y., 1925). Also Hardwicke, *Antitrust Laws*, 23–26; Logan, *op. cit.*, 145f.

28. *American Petroleum, Supply and Demand*, 3–5.

29. Humble Recs., W. S. Farish to Hubert Work, Mar. 31, 1925.

30. Humble Recs., W. S. Farish to R. L. Welch, May 24, 1921, and to Teagle, Mar. 29, 1924; *O. & G. Jour.*, Dec. 14, 1922, pp. 94, 96, 98.

31. Humble Recs., W. E. Pratt to Isaac Marcosson, Nov. 3, 1927.

32. Humble Recs., H. C. Wiess to F. H. Farwell, July 9, 1930.

33. Hardwicke, *Antitrust Laws*, 8–13.

34. Humble Recs., W. S. Farish to H. L. Doherty, Nov. 3, 1928.

35. Hardwicke, *Antitrust Laws*, 17f.

36. See the *Hearings* of the Federal Oil Conservation Board (hereafter cited as FOCB), 1926.

37. C. E. Beecher and I. P. Parkhurst, "Effect of Dissolved Gas on the Viscosity and Surface Tension of Crude Oil," *Transactions*, AIMME, 1927.

38. Hardwicke, *Antitrust Laws*, pp. 29f., note 26, and bibliography, pp. 277–293; Logan, *op. cit.*, pp. 149f.; Leonard M. Fanning, *The Rise of American Oil* (N. Y., 1936), 143; information from C. E. Reistle, Jr., who was with the Bureau of Mines at the time.

39. Hardwicke, *Antitrust Laws*, 4–8, lists, with brief notes, important early publications.

40. FOCB, *Complete Record of Public Hearings*, Feb. 10–11, 1926, pp. 8f.

41. W. S. Farish, address to West Texas Chamber of Commerce, Amarillo, June 23, 1926; address before the third public conference on education and industry held under the auspices of the University of Chicago and the Institute of American Meat Packers, Oct. 27, 1926; annual address of the president, API, Tulsa, Dec., 1926. The texts of these addresses are in the Farish Papers in the Humble records.

42. *Report of the Federal Oil Conservation Board* (Washington, 1926).
43. An excellent survey of the price situation in the 1920s is in Joseph E. Pogue's "The Trend of the Petroleum Situation," in the 1927 AIMME, Pet. Div., *Transactions*.
44. See Gibb and Knowlton, *The Resurgent Years*, 335–358.

CHAPTER 12

1. Since this chapter is concerned very largely with the acquisition of prospective oil lands and technological developments in production, petroleum engineering, and production research, the executive correspondence, although important, is not so basic as for chapters dealing primarily with business policy.

Basic to our knowledge of Humble's quest for and discovery of oil were L. T. Barrow, "Notes on the History of the Geologic, Lease and Scouting Department," and D. P. Carlton, "History of the Geophysics Department," revised in 1949, both supplemented by special reports of the Geologic, Lease and Scouting Department and by notes by Barrow on specific fields. Invaluable also were the files of the Legal Department on individual lease trades.

For petroleum engineering and production research: Monthly Petroleum Engineering Reports, beginning with 1929, and the Monthly Progress Reports of the Production Research Division, beginning Mar. 1, 1929.

The results of the quest for oil are shown in tables of production by fields compiled by the company.

For a chapter involving so many legal and technical problems, interviews and personal information are particularly valuable. L. T. Barrow and W. E. Pratt have been generally informative on the quest for oil. D. P. Carlton, J. E. LaRue, and Alva C. Ellisor contributed specific information on the use of geophysics. Barrow, Pratt, Eugene Holman, and Rex G. Baker were very helpful on the acquisition of large lease blocks. John R. Suman was generally informative on all aspects of production. D. B. Harris, G. B. Corless, and R. L. Clifton (of The Carter Oil Co.) discussed production methods as affected by new petroleum engineering developments. H. D. Wilde, T. W. Moore, and T. V. Moore gave indispensable information on production research. Various items of information on production organization and methods were furnished by Rex G. Baker, Hines H. Baker, David Frame, Bert Broday, C. B. Goddard, and J. Ben Carsey.
2. *Petr. Facts and Figures*, 1950, pp. 2f.
3. Figures from reports of the Bureau of Mines.
4. Information concerning this acquisition and field was obtained principally from Humble Recs., contract files; letters from Harry Pennington, Wallace E. Pratt, and L. T. Barrow; interviews with Barrow and Rex G. Baker; and L. P. Teas and C. R. Miller, "Raccoon Bend Oil Field," *Bull. of AAPG*, vol. XVII, p. 1459.
5. Humble Recs., contract files.
6. On the acquisition of the Sugarland acreage: Humble Recs., especially contract files; notes by L. T. Barrow and Rex G. Baker; letter from Wallace E. Pratt; and interviews with Barrow, Rex G. Baker, and Eugene Holman. Also on Sugarland, W. B. Carter and P. H. O'Bannon, "Sugarland Oil Field," *Bull. of AAPG*, vol. XVII, p. 1362.
7. Humble Recs., including a letter of Edward J. Hamner to Farish, May 3, 1929, and a copy of a letter of Hamner to his children, May 1, 1929.
8. Humble Recs., Geologic, Lease and Scouting Department, "A Résumé of Petroleum Development in the Gulf Coast of Texas and Louisiana in 1930," dated Feb. 7, 1931.
9. Humble Recs. and interviews, especially with L. T. Barrow and Rex G. Baker; Warner, *op. cit.*, 284–286, 288, 290–292, 305f.; Rister, *Oil! Titan of the Southwest*, 180, 222f.
10. L. T. Barrow, letters and interviews.
11. Interview with John R. Suman.
12. Humble Recs., report of John R. Suman to W. S. Farish, Mar. 9, 1927, on his inspection trip to the Northern division.
13. API, *Bulletin*, 1927.
14. Humble Recs., Pratt to Wiess, Aug. 1, 1927.
15. Humble Recs. and interviews; *O. & G. Jour.*, May 31, 1928, p. 139.
16. Scott's testimony in the hearings of the Texas Railroad Commission on Conroe, 1932.

17. AIMME, Petroleum Division, *Transactions,* 1927, pp. 51–70.
18. A good view of the thinking and research in the production field may be gained from the 1927 *Transactions* of the Petroleum Division of the AIMME, particularly the review by G. B. Umpleby, chairman of the Production Engineering Division, on pp. 11–18. The findings of the Gas Conservation Committee were used in the preparation of H. C. Miller, *Function of Natural Gas in the Production of Oil, A Report of the U. S. Bureau of Mines in Cooperation with the Division of Development and Production Engineering of the American Petroleum Institute* (1929). For names of chairmen and members of committees, see pp. 1f. and 7f.
19. T. V. Moore, "Saving the Oil," *Technology Review,* 1942, p. 4.
20. H. D. Wilde, Jr., "Producing Oil with Minimum Pressure Decline at the Sugarland Field," API, Production Division, *Proceedings,* 1930, pp. 18–20; Mercer Parks, "Conservation and Utilization of Gas, Sugarland Oil Field, Texas," *ibid.*, pp. 21f.
21. John R. Suman, "The Well Spacing Problem—Low Density Increases Ultimate Recovery," *ibid.*, 1934, p. 158; H. D. Wilde, "A Repressuring Experiment Project to Measure the Effect of Early Gas Injection," *ibid.*, 1930.
22. T. V. Moore, "Determination of Potential Production of Wells without Open-Flow Test," *ibid.*, 1930, pp. 27–29.
23. W. W. Scott, "Improvements in Production Practice," *ibid.*, 1930, pp. 30f.
24. Humble Recs.; H. D. Wilde, "Cementing Problems on the Gulf Coast," AIMME, Pet. Div., *Transactions,* 1930, pp. 371ff.
25. Published in AIMME, Pet. Div., *Transactions,* 1929.
26. See Note 24, above.
27. Wilde, "A Repressuring Experiment," and "Producing Oil with Minimum Pressure Decline"; Parks, "Conservation and Utilization of Gas, Sugarland"; Moore, "Determination of Potential Production"; Scott, "Improvements in Production Practice."
28. Humble Recs. and interviews; Rister, *op. cit.*, pp. 302f.
29. Humble Recs., F. H. Pierson (conservation agent, Texas Railroad Commission), Daily Report, Corsicana, Texas, July 22, 1929; Pierson to Humble Oil & Refining Co., July 30, 1929.
30. AIMME, Pet. Div., *Transactions,* 1930, p. 102.
31. Humble Recs., Ira Rinehart's *Oil Report,* Special Supplement to Report 23, Jan. 28, 1930, and Mar. 14, 1930.

CHAPTER 13

1. For Humble's participation in the movement for oil and gas conservation in this period, the company's executive correspondence was particularly valuable. Important on the legal aspects of conservation were many long expositions and memoranda, written mostly by Hines H. Baker. The Humble records were drawn upon for numerous documents, such as Railroad Commission orders, which are also available in public repositories.

Among those interviewed, W. B. Hamilton gave information from the special viewpoint of an independent producer.
2. Hardwicke, *Antitrust Laws,* 35.
3. For valuable perspective on this matter: Walter L. Summers, "The Modern Theory and Practical Application of Statutes for the Conservation of Oil and Gas," *Legal History of Conservation of Oil and Gas, a Symposium* (Section of Mineral Law of the American Bar Association, 1938).
4. James A. Veasey, "Legislative Control of the Business of Producing Oil and Gas," *Report of the Fifteenth Annual Meeting of the American Bar Association* (1927), 576–630.
5. API, *Bulletin,* Jan. 31, 1927, p. 3.
6. Interviews with Hines H. Baker, Rex G. Baker, and E. E. Townes.
7. Humble Recs., esp. E. E. Townes, memos., Apr. and July 6, 1927; Townes to H. E. Bell, Apr. 26, 1927.
8. Humble Recs., bound collection of important conservation papers.
9. Humble Recs., Farish to Bell, Dec. 24, 1926.
10. Humble Recs., W. E. Pratt to E. E. Townes, Jan. 20, 1927.
11. Humble Recs., Farish to W. N. Davis, Feb. 17, 1927.
12. Humble Recs., Teagle to Farish, June 10, 1927.
13. Humble Recs., F. C. Proctor to

Farish, Mar. 29, 1927; Hardwicke, *Antitrust Laws*, 39.
14. Humble Recs., E. W. Clark, presidential address to API, Dec. 6, 1927.
15. Humble Recs., notes on interview of W. C. Teagle and C. C. Swain with Charles Evans Hughes, June 22, 1927.
16. Humble Recs., Farish to Teagle, June 21, 1927.
17. Humble Recs., Farish to Teagle, June 20, 1927.
18. Humble Recs., statement of W. S. Farish and W. C. Teagle to Hubert Work, May 2, 1927; *The Bache Review*, May 21, 1927; "The Meaning of Unit Operations," *The Lamp*, June, 1927, pp. 6f.
19. Humble Recs., E. E. Townes, memo., July 6, 1927.
20. Fort Worth *Telegram*, May 20, 1928; *O. & G. Jour.*, 1928: Apr. 19, p. 168, May 10, p. 47, and May 24, p. 10; Humble Recs.
21. API, *Bulletin*, Dec. 9 and 15, 1926; Hardwicke, *Antitrust Laws*, 29.
22. API, *Bulletin*, Jan. 12, Oct. 31, Dec. 2, Dec. 9, 1927, and Jan. 6, 1928, *Summarized Report of Meeting Held by the Technical Sub-Committee of the API Gas Conservation Committee . . .*, Oct. 17–19, 1927; *The Conservation of Gas: Report of the Technical Sub-Committee of the American Petroleum Institute . . .*, Dec. 2, 1927; Hardwicke, *Antitrust Laws*, 41; Humble Recs.
23. Hardwicke, *Antitrust Laws*, 42–44.
24. *Report of Federal Oil Conservation Board of February 25, 1929*, App. I; Hardwicke, *Antitrust Laws*, 43–46, 202–205.
25. API, *Bulletin*, Mar. 7, 1928; Humble Recs.
26. Railroad Commission Docket, Oil and Gas, No. 101 (1928).
27. *O. & G. Jour.*, Feb. 14, 1929, p. 102.
28. Statement of W. S. Farish, *O. & G. Jour.*, Feb. 14, 1929, p. 102.
29. This undated and unsigned four-page pamphlet was reprinted in the *O. & G. Jour.*, Feb. 14, 1929, p. 102.
30. This pamphlet, although undated, was referred to in Farish's statement in the *O. & G. Jour.*, Feb. 14, 1929, p. 102.
31. *O. & G. Jour.*, Jan. 21, 1929, p. 34; Northcutt Ely, compiler, *The Oil and Gas Conservation Statutes* (Washington, 1933), 332; Robert E. Hardwicke, "Legal History of Conservation of Oil in Texas," *Legal History of Conservation of Oil and Gas: A Symposium* (America Bar Association, 1938), 220; Humble Recs.
32. *General and Special Laws of the State of Texas Passed by the Forty-First Legislature at the Regular Session* (1929), chap. 313, pp. 694–696; Hardwicke, "Legal History of Conservation of Oil in Texas," 219f.
33. Humble Recs., Farish to Teagle, May 14, 1929.
34. AIMME, Petroleum Division, *Transactions*, 1930, pp. 101–104.
35. Humble Recs., F. C. Proctor to Farish, Aug. 11, 1927.
36. Warner, *Texas Oil and Gas since 1543*, 71, 171f.; DeGolyer, "Wallace Everette Pratt," 483; Humble Recs.
37. *House Journal*, 42d leg., 1st called sess., July 24, 1931, pp. 193–197; Humble Recs.
38. Moore, "Saving the Oil," 3.
39. Humble Recs., esp. Farish to Yates pool operators, Aug. 11 and Aug. 25, 1927; *O. & G. Jour.*, Aug. 25, 1927, p. 41.
40. Humble Recs.; J. Elmer Thomas, "Production Curtailment in Texas," API, Section III, *Proceedings*, 1930, pp. 5–11; *O. & G. Jour.*, Sept. 8, 1927, pp. 29, 88; interviews.
41. Railroad Commission's Hearings, Mar. 10, 1928; Ira Rinehart's *Oil Report*, Mar. 10, 1928.
42. Humble Recs., Farish to W. B. Hamilton, Mar. 6, 1928.
43. Ira Rinehart's *Oil Report*, Mar. 12, 1928.
44. Railroad Commission, Oil and Gas Docket, No. 101.
45. Humble Recs., esp. Railroad Commission Order, May 2, 1928.
46. *Ibid.*, June 20, 1928, establishing special field rules governing the Yates field; Hardwicke, "Legal History of Conservation in Texas," 220; Rister, *Oil! Titan of the Southwest*, 299. Interviews.
47. Yates was frequently mentioned in discussions at meetings of professional associations, particularly the petroleum divisions of the API and AIMME. A valuable paper was H. C. Hardison, "Proration of the Yates Pool, Pecos County, Texas," in the *Transactions* of the AIMME, 1931. Moore's "Determination of Potential Production of Wells

without Open-Flow Test" is devoted partly to Yates. *The Petroleum Engineer*, Jan., 1930, contains a proposal of the Yates committee for proration based on rock pressure.

48. Hardison, *op. cit.*

49. Humble Recs., W. S. Farish to Clarence Wharton, July 9, 1932.

50. Humble Recs.; *O. & G. Jour.*, June 26, 1930, pp. 31, 115; Warner, *op. cit.*, 264f., 292–294.

51. Humble Recs., John R. Suman to Bert Broday, Dec. 30, 1929.

52. See, for example, API, *Bulletin*, Sec. III, Jan., 1929, for reports of efforts to control production in Texas, the Mid-Continent, and California.

53. Hardwicke, *Antitrust Laws*, 54, 123n.

54. Humble Recs., Farish to James P. Maher, Nov. 28, 1929.

55. Humble Recs., *ibid.*

56. Ira Rinehart's *Oil Report*, Jan. 28, 1930.

57. *Ibid.*, Mar. 14, 1930.

58. *General Laws of the State of Texas Passed by the Forty-first Legislature . . .* (1930), chap. 36, pp. 171–175; Ely, *op. cit.*, 351f.; Hardwicke, "Legal History of Conservation of Oil in Texas," 221.

59. Humble Recs., Farish to K. R. Kingsbury, Jan. 18, 1930.

60. Humble Recs., G. A. Henshaw, Jr., to Board of Directors of Humble, Apr. 30, 1930.

61. Hardwicke, "Legal History of Conservation of Oil in Texas," 222f.

CHAPTER 14

1. Although administrative and policy changes are described in a company's minutes and other records and sometimes in its publications and, in the case of such an important company as Humble Oil & Refining Co., frequently in both trade and general journals, the reasons behind such changes are rarely discussed. We must consequently, in this chapter, depend to an unusual extent upon interviews. James Anderson and E. E. Townes, who were directors throughout this entire period, were, of course, so situated as to be able to furnish particularly pertinent information. Hines H. Baker, W. N. Finnegan, Jr., Dr. R. J. Gonzalez, and Gay Carroll, comptroller, have also furnished so much general information that they, as well as Anderson and Townes, will not hereafter be specifically referred to except when conveying information for which their individual knowledge is indispensable.

2. *O. & G. Jour.*, 1933: June 8, p. 31, and Aug. 3, p. 9; *New York Times*, July 30, 1933, p. 23, Jan. 12, 1934, p. 35; William J. Kemnitzer, *Rebirth of Monopoly: A Critical Analysis of Economic Conduct in the Petroleum Industry of the United States* (N. Y., 1938), 135f.; Alex McCurdy, "Standard Oil's Making Big Merger Plans," *Oil Trade Journal*, Oct., 1922, pp. 13f.; Humble Recs., "First Address Made by Mr. Farish to Jersey Company Sales Department Meeting, Oct., 1933."

3. *H. Sales Lub.*, June 8, 1939, p. 8; interviews.

4. Humble Recs.; *H. Ref. Bee*, Jan. 12, 1939, pp. 8f., quoting from the Houston *Press*, Jan. 6, 1939; *O. & G. Jour.*, Sept. 1, 1932, p. 70, and Sept. 28, 1933, p. 76.

5. Humble Recs.; *H. Sales Lub.*, June 15, 1933, pp. 4f., and June 29, 1933, pp. 4f., 8.

6. The directors' choice of a president, the factors involved, the subsequent uncertainties, and the way in which the matter was temporarily settled were discussed with the persons mentioned in note 1 and with Bert Broday and C. B. Goddard.

7. *H. Ref. Bee*, Feb. 25, 1937, p. 6; Humble Recs., including *Weekly Digest*, Feb. 8, 1937; interview with Jesse H. Jones.

8. Various interviews. See Chap. 5 for a more detailed discussion of Farish's appearance and personality.

9. Informants on Wiess's personality, attitudes, and methods are in remarkable agreement, complementing one another. They include those listed in note 1 and L. T. Barrow, B. H. Brown, D. T. Monroe, G. A. Mabry, Charles E. Shaw, Robert E. Hardwicke, W. K. Lewis, D. B. Harris, John R. Suman, T. H. A. Tiedemann, A. A. Nance, W. B. Calhoun, and Jesse H. Jones.

10. *H. Sales Lub.*, Mar. 4, 1937, pp. 7f.; Humble Recs.; interviews with H. H. Baker and Miss Kessler, a former secretary.

11. *H. Sales Lub.*, Mar. 18, 1937, pp. 6f., June 10, 1937, p. 4, Feb. 17, 1938, p. 4; Humble Recs.

12. Humble Recs.; *H. Sales Lub.*, Feb. 17, 1938, pp. 4, 22.
13. Humble Recs.; interview with Hines H. Baker, Oct. 10, 1945; Texas *House Journal*, 1st called sess., July 28, 1931, pp. 438, 517; Houston *Chronicle*, Nov. 12 and Dec. 14, 1931; Houston *Labor Journal*, Nov. 20, 1931; Fort Worth *Star-Telegram*, Oct. 6, 1933; Tulsa *World*, Oct. 18, 1933; 103 Tex. 313; 107 S. W., 2d, 550.
14. The first extant organization chart of the Law Department is dated 1943.
15. Humble Recs., particularly "Accounting Organization and Functions," Sept., 1941; also information supplied by J. R. Mulvey, assistant comptroller.
16. The general character of Humble's public relations has been described in interviews with W. N. Finnegan, Jr., and Dr. R. J. Gonzalez.
17. *H. Ref. Bee*, Apr. 9, 1936, p. 8.
18. For details, see the sections on Texas sales for 1930–1941 and 1945–1948 in Chapters 21 and 23.
19. Interviews with Carl Estes, W. B. Calhoun, and A. A. Klein.
20. Humble Recs., H. S. Warner to Hines H. Baker, Dec. 6, 1939.
21. Humble Recs.; Joe B. Frantz, "The Annual Report as a Public Relations Tool in Three Industries," *Bulletin of the Business Historical Society*, Mar., 1950, pp. 28f. Dr. Frantz, who does not, however, include the oil industry in his study, places the addition of "expository material" in the 1920s and the appearance of the "slick paper . . . highly decorated annual report . . . in the late 1930's."
22. Humble Recs.; interview with M. F. Moffett.
23. Humble Recs.; *O. & G. Jour.*, Mar. 24, 1932, p. 91; interview with C. L. Brown.
24. Humble Recs., *Weekly Digest*, Apr. 2, 1931; interviews with J. L. Burton, R. E. Stearns, and D. B. Harris; *O. & G. Jour.*, Aug. 13, 1931, pp. 26f.

CHAPTER 15

1. See section on employees in Chapter 5. The names of the industrial relations office and its various divisions were changed from time to time, and the official names were not always used. The Industrial Relations Office was generally called the Industrial Relations Department—although it was not officially so named until 1941—and its divisions as well were commonly called departments, although officially they were sections.
2. The Humble manuscript material used in this chapter was largely letters or memoranda passing between the Industrial Relations managers and members of the Humble top management; and also reports, statements, chronologies, histories, etc., on such subjects as employee statistics, disabling injuries, changes in the workday and week and in the rates of pay, annuities and benefits, collective bargaining, etc., which the Industrial Relations Office (or Department), always statistically and historically minded, prepared either for the information of management or for the special purpose of this history.

For the employees' side of the story, the minutes of the various Joint Conferences and Employees Federations, and particularly the minutes of the Joint Conference at the Baytown refinery, have been indispensable. On the subject of collective bargaining, the minutes of discussions and negotiations between management and its representatives on the one hand and representatives of Joint Conferences, Local 333, and Employees Federations on the other, and the contracts and agreements between management and such conferences and federations have been basic.

Interviews with Industrial Relations managers C. E. Shaw and D. B. Harris, and with T. W. Moore, who at various times in this period was head of the training section and also industrial relations manager at Baytown, have been useful on almost every point of this general subject. Robert C. Oliver, as an elected representative on the Baytown Joint Conference and subsequently president of the Baytown local of the oil workers' union, presented a special employee's viewpoint.

On important special subjects interviews with the following have also been useful: safety, R. B. Roaper; the depression period, H. S. Warner, Henry Wilson, G. A. Mabry, K. R. Dailey; annuities and benefits, Jack H. Gudger and

Wayne H. Haines; collective bargaining, H. S. Warner, Hines H. Baker, T. H. A. Tiedemann, A. A. Nance, J. D. Hunnicut; the employee program after the depression, Ray Horton, K. R. Dailey, Leigh Cox, LeRoy Wilkie, Harold Hunt, James Beasley, A. A. Nance, S. C. Moor, and Russell Barbour.

3. Humble Recs., Charles E. Shaw to H. M. Ford, June 17, 1932.

4. *Humble Club Bulletin*, Aug. 31, 1930.

5. Humble Recs.; *H. Bee,* Apr. 1, 1922, p. 1, June 27, 1931, pp. 1f.; *H. Sales Lub.*, July, 1931, p. 7, June 16, 1932, p. 13; *The Lamp,* Sept., 1918, p. 3.

6. See Chapter 5.

7. Humble Recs., Shaw to Wiess, Aug. 31, 1932.

8. Humble Recs.; *O. & G. Jour.*, Dec. 25, 1930, p. 133.

9. Humble Recs.; *H. Bee,* July 12, 1932, pp. 1f.; *H. Sales Lub.*, 1932: July 5, pp. 13f., July 14, pp. 17f.

10. Humble Recs.; Robert E. Gregg, Secretary, Bureau of Labor Statistics, State of Texas, Austin, Jan. 1, 1932, to the Officers and Members of the Governor's and Legislative Committee for Unemployment Relief; Robert E. Gregg to Oil Companies, Nov. 21, 1931.

11. Humble Recs.; *Historical Statistics of the United States,* 1789–1945 (Washington, D. C., 1949), 236.

12. Humble Recs., D. B. Harris to A. D. Behling and others, Dec. 10, 1931; Report of Isador Lubin to Cole Committee in its *Report,* pt. 1, p. 523.

13. Humble Recs. and interviews; Baytown refinery, minutes of Joint Conference; *H. Ref. Bee,* Mar. 11, 1937, pp. 12f.

14. Humble Recs.; *H. Bee,* July 25, 1930, p. 1, Aug. 12, 1930, pp. 1, 3, and Apr. 11, 1932, p. 1.

15. Humble Recs.; G. A. Mabry, *You and Me and the Company* (Houston, 1937), 58–61.

16. Baytown refinery, minutes of Joint Conf.; *H. Ref. Bee,* Mar. 11, 1937, pp. 12f.

17. Baytown refinery, minutes of Joint Conf.; *H. Ref. Bee,* Aug. 13, 1936, pp. 11f.

18. *H. Bee,* 1931: Feb. 26, pp. 1, 4, Dec. 23, p. 2, and Jan. 11, 1932, p. 1; Humble Recs.; Baytown refinery, minutes of Joint Conf.

19. For further information about Blaffer, see Chapters 2 and 5.

20. Interviews with Hines H. Baker, Gay Carroll, W. E. Pratt, J. R. Suman, and James Anderson; circular letter, W. S. Farish, R. L. Blaffer, and H. C. Wiess, To All Employees . . . , Nov. 14, 1929.

21. Harold L. Ickes, Wage Differential Order, May 21, 1934; Humble Recs.; Baytown refinery, minutes of Joint Conf.; interviews.

22. *H. Sales Lub.*, Dec. 27, 1934, pp. 4f., May 30, 1935, pp. 15f.; *H. Ref. Bee,* 1935: June 6, pp. 4–6, Oct. 24, p. 7; Baytown refinery, minutes of Joint Conf.

23. For Humble management's relations with refinery labor from 1933 to Apr. 23, 1937, one of the most useful sources is the above-mentioned Baytown refinery, minutes of Joint Conf. The *Weekly Digest,* intended for the use of company executives, represents an attempt to present the actual situation as a guide for action. Interviews with members of the industrial relations group have been a source of otherwise unrecorded information. Robert C. Oliver, who, during 1933–1936, was first an elected representative on the Baytown Joint Conference and subsequently president of the Baytown local of the oil workers' union, was thus in a position to give a very special insight into one side of the controversy; he was retrospectively frank in his criticism of union tactics. O'Connor, *History of Oil Workers International Union (CIO),* 114–117, 229–231, treats Humble's labor relations at the Baytown and Ingleside refineries with no pretense of impartiality.

24. Humble Recs. and interview; O'Connor, *op. cit.*, 96f., 209f., 222.

25. Persons interviewed in regard to Superintendent Powell and the Baytown Joint Conference represented a variety of relationships to the refinery and the Joint Conference; they were, in general, personally friendly toward Powell but critical of the Joint Conference under his chairmanship. They included employees without positions on the Joint Conference, Norman d'Olive, J. L. Dunman, W. G. Lopas, Sr., and Karl E. Martin; elected representatives on the conference, B. D. Alleman and R. C. Oliver; elected representatives, who were later appointed company representatives, R. N. Dyer and G. A. Mabry; an industrial relations manager and representative ex officio, T. W. Moore; and company representatives, R. H. Brinton and Joe Reilly.

26. Hicks, *My Life in Industrial Relations,* 87.

27. Humble Recs.; Baytown ref., minutes of Joint Conf., Oct. 10, Nov. 15, 1933.

28. Houston *Chronicle,* Aug. 9, 1936.

29. Interview with Joe Reilly; Baytown refinery, minutes of Joint Conf.

30. *H. Sales Lub.,* Sept. 19, 1940, pp. 7f.

31. Interviews with G. A. Mabry and R. C. Oliver.

32. *The Democrat* (Goose Creek), Apr. 20, 1934; *The Daily Sun* (Goose Creek), June 11, July 9, 12, 1934.

33. On D. B. Harris, interviews with T. H. A. Tiedemann, W. B. Calhoun, and Clyde Vardaman, among others, have been informative.

34. Houston *Chronicle,* June 14, 1935; *International Oil Worker,* June 28, 1935.

35. Houston *Press,* Dec. 2, 3, 4, 1935; Houston *Chronicle,* Dec. 3, 4, 1935; Houston *Post,* Dec. 4, 5, 1935.

36. Humble Recs. Houston *Chronicle,* Aug. 8, 12, 1936; Houston *Post,* Aug. 20, 22, 1936; *Daily Oil Digest,* Aug. 18, 1936.

37. Humble management's side of Local 333's Aug.–Sept., 1936, campaign for a contract is presented in considerable detail in a letter from D. B. Harris to F. W. Pierce, Sept. 18, 1936, written at white heat just after the conclusion of the struggle (Humble Recs.). Interviews with representatives of the viewpoints both of management and of the union have given a sense of the spirit of the controversy. The *Press, Chronicle,* and *Post* (Houston) and the *Daily Sun* (Goose Creek) have something on the negotiations and the threatened strike almost every day from Aug. 27 to Sept. 19, 1936.

38. Humble Recs., J. L. Finley to R. C. Oliver, Aug. 28, 1936.

39. Houston *Press,* Sept. 11, 1936.

40. Humble Recs.; *O. & G. Jour.,* Sept. 24, 1936, p. 53.

41. *Ibid.;* Humble Recs., Harris to Blaffer, Nov. 20, 1936.

42. NLRB, 16th Region, Humble Oil & Refining Co., and Oil Workers International Union, Locals 333 and 316, Cases, Nos. C–590 and C–591, Brief for Respondent, Humble Oil & Refining Co., pp. 22f.; *Daily Sun* (Goose Creek), Mar. 9, 11, 1937.

On Kamp: Stetson Kennedy, *Southern Exposure* (Garden City, N. Y., 1946), 235–237, 245; John Roy Carlson (Arthur Derounian), *Under Cover: My Four Years in the Nazi Underworld of America* (N. Y., 1943), 132f., 455, 467f., 470.

43. *H. Ref. Bee,* May 6, 1937, pp. 12f.; *O. & G. Jour.,* Apr. 29, 1937, p. 26.

44. Oliver eventually returned to Texas as State Director of the CIO, in 1951 was sent to Europe as labor adviser to the Economic Cooperation Administration, in 1952 was appointed executive assistant to Walter Reuther, the president of the CIO, and in 1953 was also designated co-ordinator of CIO legislative affairs (*New York Times,* Dec. 13, 1951, 21: 3; June 6, 1953, 20: 2). In 1957 he organized Robert Oliver Associates, consulting firm in Washington.

45. Humble Recs., Agreement between Humble Oil & Refining Company and the Baytown Employees Federation, Aug. 14, 1937.

46. Humble Recs.; NLRB Order, Oct. 18, 1939, in Humble Oil & Refining Co., Cases C–590 and C–591; In the United States Circuit Court of Appeals, No. 9323, *Humble Oil & Refining Co., Petitioner,* v. *NLRB,* June 24, 1940, before Sibley, Hutcheson, and McCord, Circuit Judges; Houston *Press,* Mar. 7, 1938; Houston *Chronicle,* Apr. 3, 1938; *O. & G. Jour.,* 1938: Mar. 17, p. 28, May 12, p. 100.

47. Humble Recs., Harris to Wiess, Suman, and Hanrahan, Jan. 15, 1935.

48. See the first section of this chapter.

49. Humble Recs., Harris to J. A. Neath and David Frame, May 19, 1937.

50. The first announcement of the safety hat in the *H. Ref. Bee* was in the issue of Apr. 9, 1936; however, a man in a picture in the issue of May 9, 1935, was wearing such a hat.

51. *H. Ref. Bee,* Jan. 28, 1937, pp. 4–6.

52. Humble Recs., Harris to Wiess, Suman, and Hanrahan, Jan. 29, 1937.

53. *H. Sales Lub.,* June 28, 1934, pp. 4–8.

54. See, for example, *H. Ref. Bee,* June 20, 1935, pp. 1–6.

CHAPTER 16

1. On the general subject of Humble reserves and their acquisition L. T. Barrow's "Notes on the History of the Geologic, Lease and Scouting Department of the Humble Oil & Refining Company," Sept. 16, 1949, was of great and continuous help. J. V. Boyce's "Report of Major Fields," June 1, 1933, was useful on reserves acquired previous to that date. On the special problem of the quest for oil, D. P. Carlton's "History of the Geophysics Department," Feb. 1, 1949, was indispensable; and his article, "The Search for Oil," *H. Way*, Nov.–Dec., 1946, pp. 10–16, gives much in smaller compass. Reports and memoranda on the activities of the Geologic, Lease and Scouting Department and the Production Department, both annual and special, have been used frequently. Invaluable was the information obtained in conversations, interviews, and correspondence with L. T. Barrow, W. E. Pratt, Hines H. Baker, Rex G. Baker, H. C. Wiess, D. P. Carlton, G. B. Corless, and many others. For the operational chapters, of which this is the first in the period 1930–1941, the *Weekly Digest*, a mimeographed company publication which summed up for the benefit of the Humble executives the principal developments in the week within the company and affecting the industry as a whole, has been constantly useful (beginning in 1933) and will therefore not generally be specifically mentioned.

2. Humble Recs., Farish to E. J. Sadler, Oct. 4, 1932.

3. Humble Recs., Pratt to Farish, July 28, 1930.

4. For this brief résumé and for the geophysical work of the later 1930s the authors have relied on sources mentioned in note 1, on "Progress in Geophysical Exploration in Humble Territory, Seaview Conference, May 9, 1938," and on an interview with Dr. Ludwig Blau.

5. Kendall Beaton, *Enterprise in Oil: A History of Shell in the United States* (N. Y., 1957), 364–367.

6. John G. McLean and Robert William Haigh, *The Growth of Integrated Oil Companies* (Boston, 1954), 385f.

7. Information from Hines H. Baker.

8. The main source on Humble's interest and acquisition of acreage in the East Texas field was L. T. Barrow's "Some Notes on the History of Humble's Acquisition of Leases in the East Texas Field." Other information was found in Humble correspondence and reports or was obtained in interviews with Eugene Holman, H. J. McLellan, and G. M. Knebel. The viewpoint of East Texas landowners and lessors was presented by Malcolm Crim and "Shack" Laird. Standard Oil Company (N.J.) records were also of value on this subject.

9. Rister, *Oil! Titan of the Southwest*, 307–310.

10. Concise information on Gulf Coast fields in general can be found in *World Oil*, June, 1950, pp. 60–120, and *Oil Weekly*, July 25, 1938, pp. 137–228.

11. L. T. Barrow, "Some Notes on the History of Thompsons." The story of the final negotiations was related by Rex G. Baker.

12. Humble Recs., L. P. Teas to L. T. Barrow, Nov. 6, 1931.

13. Information on Humble's holdings in Conroe was obtained principally from L. T. Barrow, "Some Notes on the History of Conroe"; also from conversations and correspondence. See *O. & G. Jour.*, 1932: June 16, p. 72, July 14, p. 55, Oct. 20, pp. 33 and 35; and May 18, 1933, pp. 15, 48.

14. The story of this "wild well" was drawn from Humble Recs., Petroleum Engineering Dept., "Drilling of the Humble Oil & Refining Company's Alexander H-7 Directed Injection Well and the Subsequent Controlling of Harrison-Abercrombie's Alexander No. 1 Crater Well by Water Injection, Conroe Field, Montgomery County, Texas, Humble Oil & Refining Co., Mar. 9, 1934"; interviews with J. R. Suman and W. N. Finnegan, Jr.; executive correspondence; *H. Sales Lub.*, Jan. 11, 1934, pp. 9–12 (illustrated); *O. & G. Jour.*, Oct. 4, 1934, p. 39; R. Mills, "Killing the Conroe Crater," *Oil Weekly*, Jan. 15, 1934, pp. 8f.; Fort Worth *Star-Telegram*, Jan. 11, 1934; Ball, *This Fascinating Oil Business*, 133–135; J. R. Suman, "Drilling, Testing and Completion," *Elements of the Petroleum Industry*, 171–178.

15. A colorful description of the claims

involved in the Wilson Strickland case appeared in *Time,* Aug. 11, 1941, p. 64.

16. Information on Humble's King Ranch lease was drawn from Humble Recs.; Tom Lea, *The King Ranch* (Boston, 1957), 343, 526, 600, 611f., 633–635, 790; DeGolyer, "Wallace Everette Pratt," 485; *O. & G. Jour.*, 1933: Oct. 19, p. 32, Nov. 23, p. 20; interviews with M. Manning and Jack Shephard.

17. Lea, *op. cit.*, 343, 526, 600, 633, 635; Testimony of Edwin K. Atwood in *Edwin K. Atwood et al.* v. *Robert J. Kleberg, Jr., et al.* and *Edwin K. Atwood et al.* v. *Richard King, Jr., et al.* in the U. S. District Court, Southern District of Texas, Corpus Christi Division, Apr. 20, 1950.

18. 133 F. 2d 69; 135 F. 2d 452; 320 U. S. 744. The case was *Atwood et al.* v. *Kleberg et al.* An interview with Felix A. Raymer was helpful in gaining an understanding of the nature and significance of this litigation.

19. Humble Recs.; *O. & G. Jour.*, May 18, 1933, pp. 14, 86; Fort Worth *Star-Telegram,* May 13, Dec. 31, 1933; Warner, *Texas Oil and Gas since 1543,* p. 214.

20. Humble Recs., Pratt to E. J. Sadler, Mar. 5, 1934.

21. Humble Recs.; DeGolyer, "Wallace Everette Pratt," 484f.; Warner, *op. cit.*, 299; interviews with J. E. LaRue, John Sue, and Douglas Ragland.

22. Humble Recs., telegram, Barrow to Pratt, Feb. 24, 1935; telegram, Wiess to Pratt, Feb. 24, 1935.

23. Humble Recs., Pratt to Wiess, Sept. 16, 1935.

24. Beaton, *op. cit.*, 466f.; McLean and Haigh, *op. cit.*, 263, 386.

25. H. G. Patrick, "Case History of the Friendswood (Webster) Oil Field, Harris County, Texas," *Geophysical Case Histories* (The Society of Exploration Geophysicists, 1948), 74–84.

26. Observations in regard to Pratt's characteristics and contributions were drawn principally from interviews with his associates, especially those mentioned in note 1. The authors also had several conversations with Pratt from which they gained impressions that reinforced the views of their other informants. His correspondence was, of course, revealing.

27. DeGolyer, "Wallace Everette Pratt," 484f.

28. Humble Recs., memo. in budget files, Oct. 8, 1941.

29. Humble Recs.; and interviews, particularly with R. L. Sloan.

30. Humble Recs., memo. in the budget files, Oct. 8, 1941.

31. *H. Way,* May–June, 1948, p. 1; Morgan J. Davis and Grant Blanchard, Jr., "Permian Stratigraphy and Structure of Parts of Southeastern New Mexico and Southwestern Texas," *Am. Assoc. of Petroleum Geologists Bull.*, Aug., 1929, pp. 957–995.

CHAPTER 17

1. Humble management had long since committed itself as a matter of policy and practice to the extensive use of research and scientific development. Consequently, the Humble executive correspondence, with its emphasis on policy determination, is of little or no pertinence to this chapter. The material in it is, however, largely drawn from company sources, principally the reports of the Petroleum Engineering Dept., 1931–1941; the monthly reports of the Production Research Dept., 1930 and on through the decade; the reports of the Production Dept., 1936–1941; John R. Suman's manuscript, "History of Humble Petroleum Technology"; memo. for David Frame (undated). On so complicated a subject, interviews with such technologists and field men—or both—as John R. Suman, Carl E. Reistle, Jr., G. B. Corless, S. E. Buckley, and S. C. Moor have been particularly helpful.

Since the "technological revolution" was an industry-wide matter, printed sources have been of unusual value, but these will be referred to in their proper places.

2. Humble Recs., Report of Petroleum Engineering Department, 1931, pp. 1f.

3. *The Lamp,* Aug., 1932, pp. 25–28; interviews.

4. Interview with John R. Suman; *The Lamp,* Aug., 1932, pp. 25–28; *O. & G. Jour.*, Sept. 1, 1932, p. 73.

5. *The Lamp,* Aug., 1932, pp. 25–28.

6. *O. & G. Jour.*, 1917: Mar. 22, pp. 12–14, Apr. 5, p. 18, Apr. 12, p. 14, Apr. 26, p. 14, May 17, pp. 12–15, May 31, p. 14, June 21, pp. 12–16, *et passim.*

7. Coleman, Wilde, and Moore, "Quantitative Effect of Gas-Oil Ratios on Decline of Average Rock Pressure," AIMME, *Transactions, Pet. Dev. and Tech.*, 1930, pp. 174–184.
8. Other companies were also developing gauges. See D. G. Hawthorn, "Review of Sub-Surface Pressure Instruments," in API, Prod. Div., *Proceedings*, May, 1935, pp. 11–22.
9. H. D. Wilde, "The Value of Gas Conservation and Efficient Use of Natural Water-Drive as Demonstrated by Laboratory Models," API, *Prod. Bull.*, No. 210 (Nov., 1932), pp. 4–10; Wilde and F. H. Lahee, "Some Principles of Efficient Oil-Field Development," *Bull. of the AAPG*, Aug., 1933.
10. For example, M. Muskat and R. D. Wyckoff, "An Approximate Theory of Water-Coning in Oil Production," AIMME, *Transactions, Pet. Dev. and Tech.*, 1935, pp. 144–163; also Muskat in *Physics*, 1934, p. 71.
11. Humble Recs., statement of W. E. Pratt, June, 1932. Also, Wilde, article in note 9 above, pp. 4–10.
12. Ben Lindsly, "A Study of Bottom-hole Samples of East Texas Crude Oil," U. S. Bureau of Mines, R. I., 3212, 1933 (abstract in API, Sec. IV, *Proceedings*, May, 1933, pp. 40–52).
13. T. V. Moore, R. J. Schilthuis, and W. Hurst, "The Determination of Permeability from Field Data," *Oil Weekly*, May, 1933, p. 69.
14. William Hurst, "Unsteady Flow of Fluids in Oil Reservoirs," *Physics*, 1934, pp. 20ff.
15. Ralph J. Schilthuis and William Hurst, "Variations in Reservoir Pressure in the East Texas Field," AIMME, *Transactions, Pet. Dev. and Tech.*, 1935, pp. 164–176. Gulf research men had come close to a similar conclusion at about the same time.
16. T. V. Moore, "Saving Oil," *The Technology Review*, Jan., 1942, p. 5.
17. S. E. Buckley, "The Pressure Production Relationship in the East Texas Field," API, *Drilling and Production Practice*, 1938, pp. 140–145.
18. The various drives in reservoirs are clearly explained in an article by a Humble engineer, Norman J. Clark, "A Review of Reservoir Engineering," *World Oil*, May, 1951.
19. Muskat and Wyckoff, *op. cit.*
20. R. J. Schilthuis, "Active Oil and Reservoir Energy," AIMME, *Transactions, Pet. Dev. and Tech.*, 1936, pp. 31–50.
21. Buckley, article cited in note 17, pp. 140–145.
22. T. V. Moore, R. J. Schilthuis, and W. Hurst, "The Determination of Permeability from Field Data," API, Prod. Div. Proc., *Bulletin*, 1933, p. 211. Also *Oil Weekly*, May, 1933, cited above.
23. R. D. Wyckoff and H. G. Botset, "The Flow of Gas-Liquid Mixtures through Unconsolidated Sands," *Physics*, 1936, pp. 325ff.
24. W. W. Cutler, Jr., "Estimation of Underground Oil Reserves by Oil-Well Production Curves," U. S. Bur. of Mines, *Bulletin 228*, 88f.; S. C. Herold, "Jamin Action—What It Is, and How It Affects Production of Oil and Gas," *Bull. of the AAPG*, 1928, p. 659.
25. Moore, Schilthuis, and Hurst, *op. cit.*; Hurst, *op. cit.*; M. Muskat and M. W. Meres, "The Flow of Heterogeneous Fluids through Porous Media," *Physics*, 1936, pp. 346f.
26. John R. Suman, "Well Spacing Problem—Low Well Density Increases Ultimate Recovery," API, *Drilling and Production Practice*, 1934, pp. 158–166.
27. H. D. Wilde, Jr., and T. V. Moore, "A Method of Determining Production Allowances in Prorated Fields," API, Prod. Div., *Proceedings*, 1931, pp. 71–77.
28. H. D. Wilde, Jr., "An Allocation Formula," API, *Drilling and Production Practice*, 1934, pp. 30–33.
29. T. V. Moore, "Application of Principle of Volumetric Withdrawal to Allocation of Production," API, *Drilling and Production Practice*, 1934, pp. 23–27.
30. Ralph J. Schilthuis, "Connate Water in Oil Sands," AIMME, *Transactions, Pet. Dev. and Tech.*, 1938, pp. 199–212; Humble Recs., F. A. H. to Baker, June 14, 1937.
31. The first recognition and characterization of a condensate reservoir is Lacey and Sage's report of their study of the Kettleman Hills (California) field which was presented at the November, 1936, meeting of the American Petroleum Institute (*Proceedings*, Section IV).
32. T. V. Moore in May, 1940, gave a

paper before the American Petroleum Institute entitled "A Review of the Principles of Oil-Reservoir Performance" (*Proceedings*, Section IV), which is a useful summary of what had been learned.

CHAPTER 18

1. Since the struggle for proration in East Texas and elsewhere was carried on very largely in Railroad Commission hearings, in the state legislature, and in the courts, and was a matter of public notice and record, the authors were not so dependent on Humble records and interviews in writing this chapter as they were for most chapters. Nevertheless, for Humble's own views and activities, and particularly for the processes by which its executives arrived at the policies that they publicly advocated, the company's records are indispensable. Particularly useful are the executive correspondence, the Law Department files, the Production Research Department reports, and announcements to the public in regard to posted prices, storage, etc.

Interviews sometimes give a vividness and an immediacy to a situation that do not appear even in newspaper accounts and also, of course, frequently include information that, for obvious reasons, has not previously been recorded in either manuscript or printed form. Hines H. Baker was particularly informative on legal problems and has been helpful also on such matters as the legislative hearing of 1931 and Humble's crude oil price policy; on the latter J. A. Neath was particularly helpful. Robert E. Hardwicke, the principal authority on the legal history of conservation in Texas, gave a noncompany view of these and other problems, including the role of the independent oil operators. L. T. Barrow, W. E. Pratt, Carl E. Reistle, Jr., Ben Carsey, and W. N. Finnegan, Jr., and "Shack" Laird were all informative—the last from the landowner's view—on early leasing and drilling activities in East Texas. Finnegan, Hardwicke, Clint Murchison, W. B. Hamilton, and J. S. Bridwell described the legislative hearing of 1931 from various viewpoints—Finnegan as secretary to Humble President Farish, Hardwicke as a legal representative of the proration viewpoint, Murchison as an independent opposing proration, and Hamilton and Bridwell as independents favoring it. Hardwicke, Murchison, Hamilton, and Bridwell dealt with the various attitudes of the independent producers in the proration controversy, as also did Carl Estes, an East Texas newspaper editor who was at first a strong opponent of proration and then came to favor it, and the late David Gray, then a spokesman for independent producers, subsequently a Humble legislative representative. General conditions in East Texas, particularly lawlessness, hot oil, etc., were described by Laird, Estes, R. E. Stearns, and W. B. Calhoun. James V. Allred explained his reasons for proceeding against Humble under the Common Purchaser Act. H. L. Stone, Calhoun, Stearns, and M. L. Latham described the "Humble employees' campaign" against Attorney General Allred in the 1932 primary, as also did Estes from a different viewpoint.

A valuable record of geologic and engineering aspects of the history of the East Texas field is the mimeographed 1944 and 1953 reports of the East Texas Engineering Association, entitled "East Texas Oil Field, 1930–1940" and "East Texas Oil Field, 1930–1950." These reports were distributed to the association's members.

2. Hardwicke, "Legal History of Conservation of Oil in Texas," 228f.; statement by H. C. Wiess, stockholders' meeting, May 10, 1948.

3. Brief general accounts of the East Texas field and the attempts to control it are Rister, *Oil! Titan of the Southwest*, 307–326; Gerald Forbes, *Flush Production* (Norman, Okla., 1942), 65–67, 87–95, 112f., 188–192, 195f.; and Warner, *Texas Oil and Gas since 1543*, pp. 72–76, 127–130, 172–176, 356. The more picturesque aspects of the East Texas boom are treated in a popular fashion in Ruel McDaniel, *Some Ran Hot* (Dallas, 1939), esp. 81–85, 98f., 122f., 146–148. For legal and judicial aspects the indispensable source is Hardwicke in *Legal History* (article cited in note 2), pp. 214–268 and esp. 226–256. A valuable source for conflicting viewpoints is the published report of the special session of the Texas

legislature held in the summer of 1931.

4. Humble Recs. and interviews; East Texas Engineering Association, "East Texas Oil Field, 1930–1940," p. 19; Hardwicke in *Legal History*, 229; Hardwicke, *Antitrust Laws*, 87, n. 92; Rister, *op. cit.*, 306f.; Warner, *op. cit.*, 172f.; *O. & G. Jour.*, May–June, 1932, *passim*, and Oct. 6, 1932, p. 65.

5. DeGolyer, "Wallace Everette Pratt," 484; *O. & G. Jour.*, 1931: Oct. 1, p. 25, and Oct. 15, p. 25; Humble Recs. and interviews.

6. Tyler *Daily Courier-Times*, Feb. 9, 1931.

7. Copy of unpublished decision in Humble Recs.

8. Forbes, *op. cit*, 66f., 188f.; Tyler *Daily Courier–Times*, Feb. 3, 1931; Railroad Commission, statewide order, Oil & Gas Docket 112, Apr. 4, 1931; Humble interviews.

9. Humble Recs.; Tyler *Daily Courier–Times*, Feb. 3, 9, 1931; Tulsa *Daily World*, May 10, July 29, and Aug. 6, 1931; *O. &. G. Jour.*, 1931: Feb. 12, pp. 29, 132f., Feb. 26, p. 49, Mar. 5, pp. 39, 69, Mar. 19, pp. 22, 93, Apr. 2, pp. 21, 122–125, Apr. 9, p. 109, Apr. 16, p. 21, Apr. 23, pp. 19f., 32, 49, and May 7, p. 65; *House Jour.*, 42d leg., 1st called sess., July 24, 1931, pp. 224f., 438; "East Texas and Proration," *The Lamp*, June, 1931, pp. 15–22.

10. Hardwicke in *Legal History*, 229; Rister, *op. cit.*, 317; Railroad Commission of Texas, Oil and Gas Division, Cancellation of Order of Apr. 22, 1931, and Amendment of General Order of Apr. 4, 1931, Apr. 29, 1931.

11. Dallas *Morning News*, May 16, 1931; Fort Worth *Star–Telegram*, May 12 and 24, 1931; Rister, *op. cit.*, 317.

12. Hardwicke in *Legal History*, 229f.; Marshall *Evening Messenger*, May 29, 1931; *House Jour.*, 42d leg., 1st called sess., July 20, 1931, p. 68, July 22, 1931, p. 116, and July 28, 1931, p. 354; Humble Recs.

13. Fort Worth *Star–Telegram*, May 26, 1931; *O. & G. Jour.*, May 28, 1931, pp. 11, 24; Houston *Post–Dispatch*, May 27, 1931; *House Jour.*, 42d leg., 1st called sess., July 28, 1931, pp. 348–367; *The Lamp*, June, 1931, p. 20. Humble Recs.

14. Fort Worth *Star–Telegram*, 1931: May 26 and June 7, 19, and 21; *O. & G. Jour.*, May 28, 1931, pp. 11, 24; Marshall *Evening Messenger*, May 29, 1931; Houston *Post–Dispatch*, May 27, 1931; Houston *Chronicle*, June 11, 1931; *Daily Oklahoman*, June 24, 1931; *O. & G. Jour.*, 1931: June 18, p. 13, and June 15, pp. 13 and 126f.

15. Humble Recs.; *H. Sales Lub.*, 1931: June, pp. 1, 4, and July, pp. 1f., 6; Fort Worth *Star–Telegram*, July 8, 1931; *O. & G. Jour.*, July 2, 1931, p. 13.

16. Tulsa *Daily World*, Aug. 6, 1931; Waco *News Tribune*, July 10, 1931.

17. *House Jour.*, 42d leg., 1st called sess., 452–508.

18. *Loc. cit.*

19. *Ibid.*, 396–412.

20. *Ibid.*, 135, 144f., 209f., 348–367, 455f., 470–472, 484, 586, 608f., 632, 659; *Daily Oklahoman*, July 5, 1931; Tulsa *Daily World*, Aug. 6, 1931; Tyler *Daily Courier–Times*, Sept. 24, 1931; *O. & G. Jour.*, 1931: July 2, p. 118, and July 30, p. 33; Humble Recs.; interviews.

21. Humble Recs., E. J. Sadler to members of the [SONJ] Board, Jan. 12, 1933.

22. For example, *Moore's Oil Field Agency News Letter*, Sept. 10, 1931.

23. 51 F. (2d) 400.

24. *Ibid.*, 400–405.

25. Governor's Message to 42d Legislature, Aug. 3, 1931; Hardwicke in *Legal History*, 231f.

26. *Texas Acts*, 42d leg., 1st called sess., 1931, ch. 26, p. 46.

27. Humble Recs., telegram of Farish to E. E. Townes, Aug. 13, 1931.

28. *World Petroleum*, Sept., 1931, pp. 534–536, quoted in the East Texas Engineering Association's "The East Texas Oil Field, 1930–1950."

29. Rister, *op. cit.*, 320.

30. Hardwicke in *Legal History*, 232–234; Forbes, *op. cit.*, 88f., 190f.; Warner, *op. cit.*, 173f.; Houston *Press*, Aug. 17, 1931; Fort Worth *Star–Telegram*, Sept. 6, 1931; Tyler *Daily Courier-Times*, Sept. 14, 1931; Supplemental Order, Railroad Commission of Texas, Sept. 18, 1931; Humble Recs.

31. Humble Recs., Farish to W. C. Teagle, Dec. 11, 1931.

32. 75 F. (2d) 227; 287 U. S. 378; 53 S. Ct. 190.

33. *People's Petroleum Producers, Inc.* v. *Sterling*, 60 F. (2d) 1041.

34. Humble Recs., circular letter of W. S. Farish, Apr. 11, 1932; Tulsa *Daily World*, 1932: Mar. 27 and Apr. 3, 9, 12; *Daily Oklahoman*, 1932: Apr. 6, 9, 12.
35. *O. & G. Jour.*, 1932: Sept. 8, p. 40, Sept. 15, p. 8, Sept. 22, p. 11, and Sept. 29, p. 18; Fort Worth *Star-Telegram*, Sept. 12, 1932; interviews; also, Law Dept. records on: *State of Texas* v. *Humble Oil & Refining Co.*; *Humble Oil & Refining Co.* v. *Jas. V. Allred et al.*; *Humble Oil & Refg. Co. et al.* v. *W. F. Robertson* (Judge of the Dist. Ct. of Travis Co., Texas).
36. *Daily Oklahoman*, Oct. 6, 1932; Tulsa *Daily World*, Oct. 20, 1932; Houston *Press*, Nov. 10, 1932.
37. *O. & G. Jour.*, 1932: May 5, p. 14, and July and August, *passim.*
38. Tyler *Daily Courier-Times*, Aug. 17, 1932; Humble Recs.; interviews.
39. Tulsa *Daily World*, Oct. 2, 1932; *The Ferguson Forum*, May 26, 1932.
40. East Texas Engineering Assn., "The East Texas Oil Field, 1930–1950," 603.
41. Information about this organization was obtained from its publication, *The Conservationist*, which was issued from Jan., 1932, to July, 1933.
42. *Ibid.*, vol. I, no. 1, Jan. 23, 1932.
43. U. S. House of Representatives, 73rd Congress, *Hearings before a Subcommittee of the Committee on Interstate and Foreign Commerce* (Washington, 1934), Part I, 748.
44. Fort Worth *Star-Telegram*, Feb. 28, 1932; Houston *Post*, July 22, 1932; Houston *Chronicle*, July 21, 1932; "1000 Denials to One Charge," clipping from an unidentified Houston newspaper, undated but obviously July, 1932. Interviews.
45. A copy is in the collection of conservation materials in Humble's Law Dept.
46. *O. & G. Jour.*, June 30 and Oct. 6, 1932.
47. Clippings in Farish files from New York and Chicago financial journals, Jan.–Mar., 1930, on the crude price cut and proposed tariff; Hobbs *Daily News*, Jan. 4, 1931; *U. S. Daily*, July 18 and Sept. 26, 1931; *Daily Oklahoman*, June 24, 1931; Tulsa *Daily World*, Feb. 15 and May 10, 1931; *Dallas Morning News*, June 27, 1931; report in Farish files of meeting of Board of Directors, API, Chicago, Nov. 11, 1931; *O. & G. Jour.*, Jan. 7, 1932, p. 88; *Investigation of Concentration of Economic Power, Hearings before the Temporary National Economic Committee, Congress of the United States*, Part 14–A, p. 7783. The tariff bill was signed by President Hoover June, 1932 (*O. & G. Jour.*, 1932: Apr. 21, p. 22, and June 9, pp. 19, 34f., 47).
48. 49 S. W., 2d, 837ff.
49. 52 S. Ct. 559.
50. Humble Recs., R. E. Hardwicke to Fred Upchurch, Hines H. Baker, Marion S. Church, and John Kilgore, Mar. 28, 1932.
51. Humble Recs.; *O. & G. Jour.*, 1932: Aug. 11, p. 42, Oct. 20, p. 9, Oct. 27, pp. 9, 31f., and Nov. 3, p. 32; Tulsa *Daily World*, Oct. 20, 23, 27, 30, and Nov. 3, 1932; *Daily Oklahoman*, Oct. 22 and Nov. 6, 1932; Houston *Post*, Oct. 24, 1932.
52. 1 F. Supp. 361.
53. *Texas Acts*, 42d leg., 4th called sess., ch. 2, p. 3; Houston *Press*, Nov. 10, 1932; *O. & G. Jour.*, 1932: Nov. 3, pp. 10f., and Nov. 10, pp. 8, 31f.
54. Fort Worth *Star-Telegram*, Dec. 10, 1932.
55. Humble Recs., Farish to Pew, Dec. 13, 1932.
56. Jan. 7, 1931, p. 37.
57. Humble Recs., "Definition of Production," a memo. of Feb. 24, 1933.
58. Reference to the peculiar nature of oil production, which under the old rule of capture made it impossible for producers to control the amount they produced and put on the market, appears almost as a refrain in statements on proration by Humble representatives.
59. Interviews; *House Jour.*, 42d leg., 1st called sess., pp. 144f.
60. For example, H. D. Wilde, Jr., and T. V. Moore, "Substitute for Potential Production," in *O. & G. Jour.*, June 4, 1931, pp. 20, 280f.; also *O. & G. Jour.*, 1932: Dec. 1, p. 9, and Dec. 8, pp. 8f., 12f.
61. Houston *Press*, Nov. 10, 1932; *O. & G. Jour.*, 1932: Nov. 3, pp. 10f., 32, and Nov. 10, pp. 8, 31f.
62. Humble Recs.; *Chicago Jour. of Com.*, Dec. 16, 1932.
63. *O. & G. Jour.*, Dec. 22, 1932, pp. 15, 25.
64. Humble Recs.; Fort Worth *Star-*

Telegram, Dec. 29, 1932; *Chicago Jour. of Com.*, Dec. 30, 1932.

65. *People's Petroleum Producers, Inc.* v. *Smith et al.*, no. 479 in Equity, Eastern District of Texas, Tyler Div. (an unreported decision referred to in *Legal History of Conservation of Oil and Gas*, 241). Also, *O. & G. Jour.*, 1933: Jan. 5, pp. 8, 38, Jan. 12, pp. 12, 37f., Jan. 26, pp. 15, 33, 102, Feb. 9, p. 36, Mar. 2, p. 7, Mar. 16, pp. 7, 9, Mar. 23, pp. 8, 28, and Apr. 27, p. 42; Fort Worth *Star-Telegram*, Jan. 6, 1933; interviews.

66. Jan. 26 and Mar. 30, 1933.

67. *O. & G. Jour.*, 1933: Mar. 23, p. 32, Mar. 30, p. 92, and Apr. 27, p. 11; Humble Recs.

68. Humble Recs., Farish to Teagle, Apr. 3, 1933.

69. Fort Worth *Star-Telegram*, 1933: Apr. 25, 26, 29, and May 3, 6, 30; Kilgore *Daily News*, Apr. 28, 1933; *Chicago Jour. of Com.*, May 3, 8, 1933; *O. & G. Jour.*, 1933: Mar. 30, p. 92, Apr. 6, p. 44, Apr. 20, p. 43, Apr. 27, pp. 13, 26, 42, and May 4, pp. 7, 9f., 14, 16; statement of Miriam A. Ferguson, Governor of Texas, May 1, 1933, to 43d Legislature.

70. Fort Worth *Star-Telegram*, May 16 and 21, 1933; *O. & G. Jour.*, 1933: May 11, pp. 32 and 37, and May 18, p. 43.

71. *O. & G. Jour.*, Apr. 27, 1933, p. 42; Fort Worth *Star-Telegram*, Apr. 29 and May 16, 1933; Humble Recs.

72. References for *Danciger Oil & Refining Co.* v. *Smith et al.*: 4 F. Supp. 236; 290 U. S. 599; 54 S. Ct. 209; 78 L. Ed. 256. Humble's Wilde presented engineering evidence in this litigation.

73. 5 F. Supp. 633.

74. Fort Worth *Star-Telegram*, May 6 and 30, 1933; Hardwicke in *Legal History*, 247.

75. Blakely M. Murphy, editor, *Conservation of Oil and Gas, a Legal History* (Section of Mineral Law, American Bar Association, 1948), p. 644; Hardwicke in *Legal History*, 247f.

76. *Ibid.*, 251.

77. *Laws of Texas*, 43rd leg., reg. sess., ch. 165.

78. Fort Worth *Star-Telegram*, Aug. 25 and 26, 1933.

79. *Daily Oklahoman*, Feb. 14, 1934.

80. U. S. House of Reprs., 73rd Congress, *Hearings before a Subcommittee of the Committee on Interstate and Foreign Commerce*, Part 1, 673.

81. Humble Recs., especially Pratt to Farish, Feb. 19, 1934.

82. See Hardwicke in *Legal History*, 251, for discussion of the problems.

83. Humble Recs., Hines H. Baker, "Measures of Control in the Stabilization of the Oil Industry," a paper submitted to the Petroleum Administrative Board.

84. *Laws of Texas*, 43rd leg., 2d called sess., ch. 45.

85. Fort Worth *Star-Telegram*, Mar. 15 and 20, 1934.

86. Humble's *Weekly Digest*, May 15, 1934.

87. 83 S. W., 2d, 935.

88. Humble Recs., Wiess to Farish, July 21, 1934.

89. *Hearings before a Subcommittee of the Committee on Interstate and Foreign Commerce*, pp. 671–719, 737–750, and 2159–2191.

90. Blakely M. Murphy, ed., *op. cit.*, 558–560; Hardwicke in *Legal History*, 250f.

91. 74th Congress, 1st sess. (1935), *House Report*, no. 2.

92. Murphy, *op. cit.*, 564; *Amazon Petroleum Corporation* v. *Ryan*, 55 S. Ct. 241; *Panama Refining Co.* v. *Ryan*, 55 S. Ct. 241; *A. L. A. Schechter Poultry Co.* v. *United States*, 55 S. Ct., 837.

93. 49 U. S. Stat., 33 c. 18.

94. Hardwicke, in *Legal History*, 252f.; Murphy, *op. cit.*, 560, 570; *Laws of Texas*, 44th leg., reg. sess., ch. 81; *O. & G. Jour.*, May 3, 1934–Feb. 21, 1935, *passim*; *Weekly Digest*, Feb. 27, 1934–Mar. 26, 1935, *passim*, and May 7, June 25, July 2, 9, and 30, and Oct. 26, 1935.

95. Hardwicke, *Antitrust Laws*, 97f.

96. *Laws of Texas*, 44th leg., reg. sess., ch. 76 and ch. 246.

97. Humble Recs., Earl Oliver to Wallace Pratt, Aug. 15, 1935.

CHAPTER 19

1. The history of Humble's struggle for the application of new reservoir concepts to oil production is drawn principally from the records and reports of the Production Department, especially its Proration division; from the files of the Law Department; and from the executive correspondence. Inasmuch as the subject is highly technical, from the viewpoints of both engineering and law, we have leaned heavily on memoranda drawn up by W. E. Hubbard, proration engineer, and Hines H. Baker, director in charge of the legal aspects of proration.

2. Humble Recs., data on fields from the Annual Reports of the Production Department, 1937–1941. See also Chapter 16.

3. Humble Recs., Orders of Texas Railroad Commission, May 7, 1932, and Jan. 7, 1935.

4. Humble Recs.; Hardwicke, "Texas," in *Legal History of Conservation of Oil and Gas*, 258.

5. See Robert E. Hardwicke, "Oil-Well Spacing Regulations and Protection of Property in Texas," *Texas Law Review*, XXXI, 99–127.

6. Interview with Rex G. Baker and Herman P. Pressler.

7. 68 S. W. (2d) 622–624; 83 S. W. (2d) 935; 126 Texas 296.

8. 122 S. W. (2d) 222.

9. Humble Recs., Hines H. Baker to H. C. Wiess, Apr. 8, 1935.

10. William E. Hubbard, "Economics and Well Spacing in Texas," AIMME, *Transactions, Pet. Dev. and Tech.*, 1936–37, pp. 341–349; *Oil Weekly*, Oct. 26, 1936, p. 36.

11. "Progress Report of the American Petroleum Institute Committee on Well Spacing," API *Proceedings*, May, 1938; *Independent Monthly*, Jan., 1937, p. 19, and Dec. 4, 1937, p. 26; *O. & G. Jour.*, Dec. 28, 1936, p. 28; Hardwicke, "Texas," 256; H. C. Wiess, "Some Current Problems in Oil Conservation," *O. & G. Jour.*, Feb. 24, 1939.

12. *Texas State House Reporter*, Oct. 22, 1940.

13. *Rowan & Nichols Co.* v. *Railroad Com.*, 28 F. Supp. 131; 107 F. 2d 70.

14. Discussion with Hines H. Baker and Rex G. Baker.

15. 35 F. Supp. 573.

16. 310 U. S. 573 (1940).

17. 311 U. S. 578 (1941); 311 U. S. 579 (1941).

18. 300 U. S. 55.

19. Humble Recs., Report of Production Dept., 1941, p. 57.

20. Murphy, editor, *Conservation of Oil & Gas . . . 1948*, 198–220, 237f., 312–327, 333.

21. For the history of the development of Humble as a large producer and distributor of natural gas, we have depended principally on reports and memoranda emanating from the Production Dept., in the authorship of which W. W. Scott, J. O. Sue, and Stuart E. Buckley were conspicuous, on correspondence of top executives and on the *Weekly Digest*. Interviews with J. O. Sue and Ralph Schilthuis were especially helpful.

22. Humble Recs.; *O. & G. Jour.*, Jan. 29, 1925, p. 256.

23. Humble Recs; *O. & G. Jour.*, 1931: Aug. 13, p. 122, Aug. 27, p. 16, Nov. 12, p. 122; Warner, *Texas Oil & Gas*, 181.

24. Humble Recs; *O. & G. Jour.*, Nov. 16, 1933, p. 26.

25. Humble Recs., H. C. Wiess to George A. Hill, Jr. (Houston Oil Co.), June 17, 1935.

26. Warner, *op. cit.*, 271–273; statement of G. R. Hopkins (U. S. Bureau of Mines), Feb. 6, 1935, regarding gas waste in the Texas Panhandle, 1933–1934; Humble Recs.

27. *Texas Acts*, 1935, ch. 120. See Maurice Cheek, "Legal History of Conservation of Gas in Texas," in *Legal History of Conservation of Oil and Gas*.

28. Humble Recs.; Ira Rinehart's *Oil Report*, Apr. 27, 1935.

29. 128 S. W. 2d 9.

30. Humble Recs., Humble Oil & Refining Co., *Annual Report*, 1940, p. 7.

31. Warner, *op. cit.*, 100, 182.

32. Humble Recs., H. C. Wiess, "Natural Gas, Buried Treasure of the Gulf Coast," *H. Way*, Nov.–Dec., 1945, pp. 12–16; "Annual Report to the Stockholders," *H. Lub.*, Feb. 12, 1942, p. 5.

CHAPTER 20

1. The purchase and sale of crude oil and its transportation by pipeline involved high-level policy considerations both by Humble and by its principal purchaser, Jersey Standard. Our knowledge of these developments, therefore, is based primarily on the Humble executive correspondence. The *Weekly*

Digest has been useful. Statistics have been drawn from company sources.

2. This purchase is discussed in Giddens, *Standard Oil Company (Indiana), Oil Pioneer of the Middle West*, ch. xvii.

3. Humble Recs. See also Chapter 21 of this volume.

4. *Reagan County Purchasing Company et al.* v. *State et al.*, 65 S. W. 2d 353. A statement of the case was also prepared by R. F. Higgins of the Humble Law Dept.

5. Interview with J. A. Neath.

6. Humble Recs. The viewpoint of the independent producers was expressed in interviews with Clint Murchison and J. S. Bridwell, and Humble's viewpoint by J. A. Neath and Hines H. Baker.

7. Although our knowledge of this period of Humble Pipe Line Company's history was derived primarily from company records, our understanding was greatly enlarged through conversations with R. V. Hanrahan, O. Q. Lomax, James Anderson, A. D. Wilbur, S. G. Loy, Hines H. Baker, M. F. Moffett, H. M. Stevenson, and A. E. Pecore.

8. On the economics of pipeline operations, see Leslie Cookenboo, Jr., *Crude Oil Pipe Lines and Competition in the Oil Industry* (Cambridge, Mass., 1955).

9. Testimony of Ernest O. Thompson, Oct. 3, 1939, TNEC *Hearings*, VI, 479; testimony of R. D. Parker, Texas Legislature, *House Journal*, 42d leg., 1st called sess., July 21, 1931, p. 105.

10. SONJ Recs., W. C. Teagle to W. S. Farish, Apr. 30, 1931; Guy Wellman to W. C. Teagle, May 1, 1931.

11. Humble Recs., Farish to Guy Wellman, Feb. 8, 1932.

12. Information from S. G. Loy.

13. For a historical summary of attacks on pipelines see Wolbert, *American Pipe Lines*, 3–108.

14. Humble Recs. Also, Texas Legislature, *House Jour.*, 42d leg., 1st called sess., July 30, 1931, pp. 520f.; TNEC *Hearings*, VI, 488 (Humble rates) and 479 (testimony of Ernest O. Thompson).

15. *Independent Petroleum Association Opposed to Monopoly, Tax Overage Oil* (leaflet); Humble Recs.

16. Information on corrosion and corrosion control was obtained from Russell A. Brannon, corrosion engineer, Humble Pipe Line Co.

17. Wolbert, *op. cit.*, 142–160.

18. For a statement of its general ineffectiveness, see Wolbert, *op. cit.*, 159f.

19. Humble Recs., Wiess to H. L. Shoemaker, Nov. 8, 1934; S. A. Giraud, memo. of phone conversation with F. H. Abrams, Apr. 3, 1935; Wiess to Farish, Aug. 3, 1935; Sadler to J. E. Lindroth, Aug. 30, 1935.

20. Humble Recs., Hines H. Baker to Wiess, Aug. 16, 1935.

21. Humble Recs., W. R. Trelford to Wiess, Sept. 20, 1935.

22. Humble Recs., W. R. Trelford, memo. on "Outside Sales of Crude by Humble as Crude and through Processing or Products Sales Contracts, Seaview Conference, Apr., 1936."

23. Humble Recs., Wiess to F. W. Abrams, Apr. 27, 1936.

24. Humble Recs., Anderson to Wiess, July 15, 1938, May 31, 1939.

25. Humble Recs.; interview with W. R. Trelford.

26. Humble Recs.; interview with Carl Illig.

27. *Weekly Digest*, Sept. 28, 1937.

28. Humble Recs., H. C. Wiess, "Notes on W. S. Farish's Remarks at API Directors' Meeting, Chicago, Mar. 15–16, 1938."

29. Humble Recs., "A Catalogue of Texas Crude Oil, Humble Oil & Refining Company, Houston, Texas, Apr. 29, 1938."

30. Humble Recs., F. W. Abrams, memo. of June 23, 1939, in regard to "Commission being Paid by Delaware Company on Domestic Crude Oil"; Wiess to Abrams, July 13, Nov. 8, 1939; Abrams to Wiess, July 21, 1939.

31. Humble Recs.; *O. & G. Jour.*, 1938: Oct. 6, p. 19, Oct. 13, pp. 25, 42.

32. Houston *Post*, Oct. 11, 1938; Humble Recs.

33. Humble Recs., R. J. Gonzalez to Wiess, May 2, 1938; Gonzalez to Hines H. Baker, May 25, 1939, commenting on "Oil Price Change Seen by Industry," *New York Times*, May 21, 1939.

34. Houston *Post*, Aug. 10, 1939.

35. Humble Recs.; Houston *Press*, Aug. 12, 1939.

36. Humble Recs.; *H. Sales Lub.*, Aug.

17, 1939, pp. 4–6; *H. Ref. Bee*, Aug. 10, 1939, pp. 4–6; interview with Clint Murchison; *O. & G. Jour.*, 1939: June 15–Aug. 17, *passim.*

37. Interview with Robert E. Hardwicke.

38. Fort Worth *Star-Telegram*, Aug. 14, 1939; Humble Recs.

39. Humble Recs., telegrams, Farish to Wiess, Aug. 15, 1939, with copy of telegram from Jerry Sadler (Aug. 13, 1939) to Farish (also in *Texas State Reporter*, XXX, Aug. 14, 1939); Farish to Wiess, Aug. 15, 1939, with copy of telegram from Farish (Aug. 15, 1939) to D. G. Gray; statement of H. C. Wiess, Aug. 14, 1939, to Associated Press. Also, Houston *Post*, Aug. 16, 1939; Houston *Chronicle*, Aug. 16, 1939; *O. & G. Jour.*, Aug. 24, 1939, p. 27.

40. *Texas State House Reporter*, III, Aug. 14, 1939, containing a complete copy of the order of Aug. 14, 1939, with various comments; Houston *Post*, Aug. 17, 1939; *O. & G. Jour.*, 1939: Aug. 17, p. 23, Aug. 24, pp. 26f.; Houston *Chronicle*, Aug. 16, 1939; *Texas State House Reporter*, Aug. 15, 1939.

41. *The Lamp*, Aug., 1937, pp. 1f.; Humble Recs., R. T. Haslam to R. W. Gallagher, Aug. 20, 1937; W. E. Pratt to Wiess, Aug. 30, 1937.

42. Fort Worth *Star-Telegram*, Aug. 19, 1939.

43. Humble Recs., postal card, M. Z. Dibble to newspaper editors, Aug. 13, 1939.

44. Houston *Chronicle*, Aug. 28, 1939.

45. *Ibid.*, Aug. 29, 1930; *O. & G. Jour.*, Sept. 7, 1939, p. 34.

46. Humble Recs., address, Ernest O. Thompson, over TQN, Aug. 31, 1939.

47. Interviews with W. N. Finnegan, Jr., and R. J. Gonzalez.

48. Humble Recs.; interview with W. R. Trelford.

CHAPTER 21

1. Information on Humble's refining and refinery marketing in this period was drawn principally from the following company records: correspondence between Humble's top management and the operational managers and the technological staff at Baytown; annual reports of the Technical Service and Research Department; Humble's mimeographed *Weekly Digest*, beginning in 1933; and documents of a historical, chronological, statistical and scientific nature, which summarized a great deal of information upon particular aspects of Humble manufacturing, such as expansion of and changes in refining equipment, refinery throughput, quantity of refined products, products specifications, developments in light-hydrocarbons utilization, etc. Minutes of directors' meetings were also useful. The Standard Oil Co. (N.J.) records were particularly useful for contracts between such Jersey Standard affiliates as Delaware and Humble and for minutes of the discussions leading up to such agreements; the Humble records also include some such material, especially contracts with companies outside the Jersey group.

For the partial understanding, at least, of a subject so highly technical in many of its aspects, conversations with top-level refinery managers, technologists, and practical operators have been indispensable. In descending order of the number of times such informants have been consulted, they are: H. W. Ferguson, H. D. Wilde, H. H. Meier, E. N. Lewis, J. M. Mettenheimer, H. C. Wiess, S. P. Coleman, Brian Mead, S. S. Shaffer, G. L. Farned, W. J. Edmonds, T. W. Moore, Joe Reilly, Norman d'Olive, Knox Thomas, D. F. Haynes, and Roy M. Stephens. L. W. Schrader was particularly informative on the "Jersey side" of Humble's refining activities.

On sales operations in Texas, in addition to executive correspondence, many documents of a statistical, historical, and legal nature in the Humble records yielded much information. Of special assistance was Share's "A History of Humble Oil & Refining Company's Marketing Operations in Texas." Mulvey's "Sales Department, Company Organization, Nov. 28, 1934" was also of general use for the period it covered. The *Weekly Digest*, from 1933, was of use at almost every point. Minutes of directors' meetings and of the Baytown Joint Conference were also useful. The Sales Department gave special assistance on product grades and brands and on agents' commissions.

Information on the operations of the Sales Department was also obtained from R. M. Stephens, G. A. Mabry, G. M. Borgstrom, Sr., D. T. Monroe, F. A. Watts, H. H. Meier, A. B. Penny, and J. E. Niland; and, on legal aspects, from Rex G. Baker.

2. Humble Recs., H. L. Shoemaker to Wiess, Feb. 16 and May 6, 1931, Feb. 23, Mar. 8, and Apr. 13, 1932.

3. Humble Recs., memo., B. H. Brown to Farish, with pencil notations by Wiess, Oct. 27, 1931.

4. Humble Recs., Harden to Wiess, July 11 and 15, 1932; telegram, Shoemaker to Wiess, June 7, 1932.

5. Humble Recs., Shoemaker to D. L. Harper, Oct. 27, 1931; Harper to W. D. Crampton, Oct. 26, 1931.

6. Humble Recs., telegrams, Wiess to Farish, Nov. 1 and 3, 1931; and to Shoemaker, Nov. 1, 1931.

7. Humble Recs., H. L. Shoemaker to Wiess, June 6, 1932; B. H. Brown to Wiess, June 9, 1932.

8. Humble Recs. *Texas House Journal*, 42d leg., 1st called sess., July 30, 1931, pp. 3–17.

9. Humble Recs.; *H. Dealer*, Mar., 1931, p. 1; *O. & G. Jour.*, Mar. 5, 1931, p. 199.

10. Humble Recs.; *H. Dealer*, Mar., 1931, p. 1; *H. Sales Lub.*, May, 1931, p. 6.

11. Humble Recs.; *H. Sales Lub.*, 1931: Sept., pp. 5f., Oct., pp. 1, 4f., Nov., pp. 1, 3f. See Giddens, *Standard Oil Company (Indiana), Oil Pioneer of the Middle West*, 449f.; and Beaton, *Enterprise in Oil, a History of Shell*, 408.

12. Humble Recs.; *H. Sales Lub.*, 1931, *passim*, esp. May, p. 2, Aug., p. 6, and Sept., pp. 1f., 5, 8.

13. Humble Recs.; *H. Sales Lub.*, Oct., 1931, p. 1; Giddens, *op. cit.*, 474f.

14. Beaton, *op. cit.*, 420–422; chap. 6 of the forthcoming third volume of *History of Standard Oil Company (New Jersey)*.

15. Humble Recs., Wiess to J. H. Senior, Jan. 16 and 29, 1932; to J. A. Moffett, Jan. 16, 1932; "To All Concerned," Jan. 29, 1932; interviews.

16. On Giraud: Davis and Grobe, *New Encyc. of Texas*, I, 498; *H. Sales Lub.*, Apr., 1932, p. 1; interviews.

17. Humble Recs.; *H. Sales Lub.*, Aug. 24, 1933, p. 10.

18. Humble Recs., Wiess to E. J. Sadler, Sept. 2, 1933; Marketing Agreement, Dec. 7, 1933.

19. Humble Recs., especially the *Weekly Digest; H. Dealer*, 1931: Mar., p. 2, and Apr., p. 1; *H. Sales Lub.*, 1932: May 19, p. 15, June 2, p. 18, July 5, pp. 11f., July 28, pp. 11f., and May 26, 1938, p. 4; *H. Ref. Bee*, Aug. 29, 1935, pp. 4–6. Also, Giddens, *op. cit.*, 481, 509; Beaton, *op. cit.*, 396, 416f.

20. Giddens, *op. cit.*, 451, 472, 479, 509f., 518; Beaton, *op. cit.*, 415–417.

21. For comparison with price competition met and policies of other companies, see Edmund P. Learned, "Pricing of Gasoline: A Case Study," *Harvard Business Review*, Nov., 1948, pp. 723–766; Giddens, *op. cit.*, 462–464, 471f., 474–477, 480f., 511–524; Beaton, *op. cit.*, 391–394.

22. Humble Recs., Giraud to Wiess, Jan. 3 and Dec. 18, 1933, and Feb. 21, 1934; answers to a questionnaire distributed by the Planning and Coordination Committee for the Petroleum Code, Nov., 1933.

23. Humble Recs.; *H. Sales Lub.*, 1934: Mar. 8, pp. 4f., Mar. 22, pp. 9f., May 31, p. 3.

24. Beaton, *op. cit.*, 451.

25. See *ibid.*, 364, and Giddens, *op. cit.*, 468. Delaware's experience is described in chap. 4 of the forthcoming third volume of *History of Standard Oil Company (New Jersey)*.

26. Humble Recs., Coleman to Wiess, Feb. 25, 1931, Mar. 22, 1932.

27. *H. Sales Lub.*, May 1931; interviews.

28. Chap. 6 of the third volume of *History of Standard Oil Company (New Jersey)*, now in preparation, will discuss the developments in the marketing of the Jersey Standard group from 1927.

29. *Ibid.;* Paul H. Giddens, *op. cit.*, 489–493.

30. *Ibid.*, 494f.

31. *Ibid.*, 497.

32. *Ibid.*, 497–501; TNEC Report, I, 558f., 576–580; Houston *Chronicle*, Apr. 3, 1938; Humble Recs. and interviews.

33. Humble Recs., Frank Andrews to E. J. Sadler, Aug. 25, 1933; Wiess to Pratt, July 3, 1934.

34. Humble Recs., memo., Wiess, about July, 1934, probably recording a telephone conversation with a Jersey official; SONJ Recs., "Discussions of Proposed Products Sales Agreement between the Humble and Delaware Companies, July–Aug., 1934," and memo. of E. J. Sadler's conversation with Christy Payne, Aug. 7, 1934; Humble Recs., memo., Hines H. Baker, Sept. 18, 1934, on conference at Greenbrier Hotel, Sept. 17, 1934.

35. Interview with Wallace E. Pratt.

36. SONJ Recs., memo., "Relations of Humble with Jersey, Delaware and Other Companies of the Jersey Group," Oct. 6, 1938.

37. Chap. 6 of the forthcoming third volume of *History of Standard Oil Company (New Jersey);* Giddens, *op. cit.*, 448–450.

38. Humble Recs.; *H. Sales Lub.*, Feb. 21, 1935, pp. 2–4, July 2, 1936, p. 15, Jan. 21, 1937, pp. 4f., and Mar. 4, 1937, inside cover; interview with J. Q. Weatherly of the Law Dept.

39. For Shell's view of the situation, see Beaton, *op. cit.*, 451.

40. On the Chain Store Act, the rulings of the judge, and related matters: *Vernon's Penal Code of the State of Texas Annotated* (Kansas City, Mo., 1948), Titles 12–14, Arts. 695–1268, ch. 11a, Stores & Mercantile Establishments, pp. 629–638; *H. Sales Lub.*, Jan. 4, 1940, p. 5; Humble Recs., including the *Weekly Digest* and the legal files.

41. Humble Recs.; *H. Sales Lub.*, Feb. 29, 1940, p. 6.

42. Humble Recs., including directors' minutes; *H. Ref. Bee*, 1936: Apr. 9, p. 13, and Sept. 24, pp. 9–11; *H. Sales Lub.*, June 27, 1935, p. 16; 1937: Mar. 18, pp. 4f., Apr. 29, pp. 4f., and May 13, pp. 9–12, and 1940: Sept. 2, pp. 8f., Aug. 1, pp. 4f., Nov. 21, pp. 14f.

43. *H. Sales Lub.*, May 26, 1938, p. 4, May 11, 1939, p. 2, and 1940: Apr. 11, pp. 8f., and Dec. 5, p. 6.

44. Beaton, *op. cit.*, 406.

45. SONJ Recs.; Humble Recs.; *H. Sales Lub.*, July 18, 1940, p. 4.

46. For information on research in petroleum chemistry in the 1930s, see Charles Sterling Popple, *Standard Oil Company (New Jersey) in World War II* (N. Y., 1952); the forthcoming third volume of *History of Standard Oil Company (New Jersey);* Beaton, *op. cit.;* Giddens, *op. cit.;* and S. D. Heron, *Development of Aviation Fuels* (Boston, 1950).

47. Humble Recs.; *H. Ref. Bee,* May 20, 1937, pp. 4–6.

48. For example, on Shell see Beaton, *op. cit.*, 519–534.

49. Humble Recs.; *H. Sales Lub.*, Sept. 19, 1940, pp. 7f.

50. *H. Ref. Bee,* May 20, 1937, pp. 4–6.

51. General information on the utilization of light hydrocarbons has been drawn from Ball, *This Fascinating Oil Business*, 155f., 197, 207, and from Walter Miller, "Petroleum Refining," *Elements of the Petroleum Industry*, 352–358. Information on Humble operations in this field has been derived from a variety of company documents.

52. Humble Recs. Also, *O. & G. Jour.*, 1931: Aug. 13, p. 122, Aug. 27, p. 16, Sept. 24, p. 112, Oct. 15, p. 90, Nov. 12, p. 122; 1933: Nov. 16, p. 26; 1934: Oct. 11, pp. 10f.; and Warner, *Texas Oil & Gas since 1543*, 181f.

53. Popple, *op. cit.*, 21.

54. *Ibid.*, 21f.; Beaton, *op. cit.*, 535, 560, 587.

55. Giddens, *op. cit.*, 563–565.

56. Popple, *op. cit.*, 24.

57. Humble Recs.; *O. & G. Jour.*, Nov. 19, 1936, p. 19, Nov. 18, 1937, p. 43, Jan. 20, 1938, p. 33.

58. Beaton, *op. cit.*, 565f.

59. Winona Patton, *United States Petroleum Refining, War and Post War* (Washington, 1947), 4; S. F. Birch, A. E. Dunstan, F. A. Fidler, F. B. Pim, and T. Tait, "Condensation of Olefines with Iso-Paraffins in Sulphuric Acid," *O. & G. Jour.*, June 23, 1938, pp. 49, 52–55, 58; Humble Recs.

60. Popple, *op. cit.*, 28f.; Beaton, *op. cit.*, 568f.

61. Quoted in *A History of the Petroleum Administration for War* (Washington, 1946), 3.

62. General information on motor-oil treating has been drawn from Miller, *op. cit.*, 363–369, 372; also Giddens, *op. cit.*, 483–485. Information on Humble's own operations is from company records.

63. Humble Recs.; *H. Ref. Bee,* Mar. 25, 1937, pp. 6f.

64. Popple, *op. cit.*, 7–12.

65. *Ibid.*, 97–107.

CHAPTER 22

1. Humble had a number of histories written of its various wartime activities in addition to the more general departmental histories. The wartime and general histories (mimeographed or typed) written under company auspices and pertinent to the theme of this chapter include: "Humble's Search for Oil during World War II"; "Oil for Victory: The War-Time Record of Humble's Production and Drilling"; "Wartime Crude Oil Marketing"; "Transporting Oil for War: Review of Humble Pipe Line Company Operations, Sept. 1, 1939–Sept. 1, 1945"; D. P. Carlton, "The History of the Geophysics Department, Sept. 28, 1949"; L. T. Barrow, "Some Notes on the History of the Geologic, Lease and Scouting Department, Sept. 16, 1949"; "Brief History of the Humble Pipe Line Company, 1919 through 1949."

The annual departmental reports were very useful; those of the Geologic, Lease and Scouting Department became more comprehensive in the later war years. The *Weekly Digest* was used frequently. Statistics were drawn from the above special histories, from company and industrial reports, and from departmental records. The published *Annual Report* of Humble Oil & Refining Company contains much information about operations in the war years.

The abundance of synopsized material reduced our dependence on the executive correspondence, except when policy matters were involved.

Since Humble is one of the Jersey Standard's principal domestic affiliates, Popple's *Standard Oil Company (New Jersey) in World War II* is generally useful; it should be noted, however, that figures in the Popple volume sometimes differ from those in the Humble records.

2. John W. Frey and H. Chandler Ide, editors, *A History of the Petroleum Administration for War, 1941–1945* (Washington, 1946, 7)—hereafter referred to as *History of PAW*.

3. *Ibid.*, 69.

4. *H. Ref. Bee*, Feb. 20, 1941, pp. 7f.; *H. Sales Lub.*, Feb. 13, 1941, pp. 9f.; Humble Recs., E. J. Sadler to W. C. Teagle, Jan. 27, 1932; *O. & G. Jour.*, Feb. 20, 1941, p. 121.

5. *H. Ref. Bee*, Jan. 23, 1941, p. 23.

6. *Ibid.*, Mar., 1945, p. 7; *H. Lub.*, Mar., 1945, pp. 4f.

7. For a few of the numerous acquaintances, both from inside and outside the company, who have commented on Blaffer's lovable disposition and his intangible, difficult-to-assess contributions to Humble, see Chap. 5, note 7.

8. *H. Sales Lub.*, May, 1942, p. 6.

9. *H. Ref. Bee*, May, 1942, p. 5.

10. *H. Lub.*, Oct., 1943, pp. 9f.

11. *H. Way*, Sept.–Oct., 1957, p. 8.

12. See James Phinney Baxter, 3rd, *Scientists against Time* (Boston, 1946); projects on which Humble men worked are those mentioned in the following chapters and pages: chap. VI, pp. 83, 87, 90, 92, 94f.; chap. IX, pp. 145, 148; chap. X, pp. 164f.; chap. XI, pp. 174–176, 178, 182–184; chap. XII, p. 195; chap. XIV, pp. 214, 217; chap. XV, pp. 225, 227f., 230, 232, 234, 237, 239. Also, Popple, *op. cit.*, 216; Humble Recs., "Humble Employees in World War II."

13. Humble Recs., "Humble Employees in World War II."

14. Humble Recs.; O'Connor, *Oil Workers International Union-CIO*, 295.

15. Humble Recs.; Houston *Chronicle*, Feb. 11, 1941; Popple, *op. cit.*, 220.

16. Humble Oil & Refining Company, *Annual Report*, 1943, pp. 9f.; Humble Recs.; interview with G. Howard Kelley.

17. Humble Recs. See also Popple, *op. cit.*, 162–164, 166, 168f., 216, 309, 313, 613.

18. Humble Recs.; *World Oil*, June, 1950, p. 89.

19. H. C. Wiess, "Natural Gas, Buried Treasure of the Gulf Coast," *H. Way*, Nov.–Dec., 1945, pp. 12–16; "Annual Report to Stockholders," *H. Sales Lub.*, Feb. 12, 1943, pp. 4–7; Humble Recs.

20. Humble Recs.; company's *Annual Report*, 1944, p. 9.

21. Humble Recs.; "Farewell to Flares," *H. Way*, Mar.–Apr., 1947, pp. 7–12.

22. *H. Sales Lub.*, Jan 2, 1941, pp. 12–14; "Report Employee Federation, Production and Crude Oil, Central Council, Apr. 11, 1941." For the so-called O'Daniel Act, see *New York Times*, 1941: Mar. 28, p. 17, Apr. 4, p. 15, Apr. 5, p. 8. The AFL and CIO opposed the bill on the ground that it would permit a strikebreaker to attack a peaceful picketer without being guilty of more than a misdemeanor, whereas a picketer who struck back might be found guilty of a felony.

23. Popple, *op. cit.*, 216; Humble Recs., L. T. Barrow to H. C. Wiess, Oct. 14, 1942; Carlton, *op. cit.*, pp. 23–25.

24. Humble Recs.

25. Humble Recs., Report of the Geologic, Lease and Scouting Dept., 1944.

26. *Loc. cit.*

27. *Loc. cit.*

28. *Ibid.*, 1944 and 1945.

29. S. E. Buckley and Dr. M. C. Leverett, "Mechanism of Fluid Displacement in Sands"; T. S. Chapman, J. L. Foster, and Dr. G. R. Gray, "Control of Filtration Characteristics of Salt-Water Muds"; Dr. M. C. Leverett, Dr. W. B. Lewis, and M. E. True, "Dimensional-Model Studies of Oil-Field Behavior"; W. Hurst, "Water Influx into a Reservoir and Its Application to the Equation of Volumetric Balance." These articles appeared in AIMME, *Transactions, Pet. Dev. & Tech.*, 1942 and 1943.

30. *History of PAW*, 185f.

31. For Humble's crude oil purchasing, marketing, and transportation, in addition to the company and departmental histories: "Let Freedom Flow," *H. Lub.*, Aug., 1943, pp. 4–7, 13, and Popple, *op. cit.*, 144f., 148f., 156, 167f., 192.

32. This problem and how it was met for the whole country is considered in *History of PAW*, chap. VII, with statistics on pp. 449 and 454.

33. *Ibid.*, 107; Rister, *Oil! Titan of the Southwest*, 355–361.

34. Interviews with R. V. Hanrahan, H. M. Stevenson, Dr. R. J. Gonzalez, and others; Humble Recs.; *H. Ref. Bee*, Nov., 1943, pp. 4–8.

35. Humble Oil & Refining Co., *Annual Report*, 1945, p. 8; Humble Recs., "Transporting Oil for War . . . ," referred to in note 1 above.

CHAPTER 23

1. For refining during wartime the following Humble compilations have been particularly important: "Wartime Leadership of Humble Refineries in Aviation Gasoline and Toluene"; "Production of War Products at Humble Oil & Refining Company's Baytown Refinery, Feb. 25, 1943"; "Baytown Refinery Expansion from 1921 to 1948"; "Dates of Initial Operation of and Major Changes to Major Baytown Equipment, July 19, 1944." The *Weekly Digest* has also been useful, as have company and departmental statistics and reports.

Helpful on the general background were *A History of the Petroleum Administration for War, 1941–1945* and Popple's *Standard Oil Company (N. J.) in World War II.*

2. *H. Way*, Nov.–Dec., 1945.

3. *History of PAW*, 193.

4. Popple, *op. cit.*, 12–15.

5. *History of PAW*, 200.

6. *H. Lub.*, Sept., 1944, pp. 12f.

7. Humble Recs.; Popple, *op. cit.*, 45–48; *History of PAW*, 455f., gives U. S. and United Nations' production.

8. For the contributions of Jersey Standard and the Standard Oil Development Co. to the toluene program, see Popple, *op. cit.*, chap. 6, "Toluene."

9. Rubber Reserve Co., *Report on the Rubber Program, 1940–1945* (Feb. 24, 1945), esp. pp. 21, 23, 29, 38, 43; W. S. Farish, *Synthetic Rubber, International Relations Patents* (Washington, D. C., Mar. 31, Apr. 1–2), 19–42; Popple, *op. cit.*, 64–68, 108, 116, 242f., 246.

10. Interview with Dr. H. D. Wilde; *H. Ref. Bee*, Dec., 1943, pp. 4f.; Popple, *op. cit.*, chap. 4, "Butadiene and Synthetic Rubber."

11. *H. Ref. Bee*, Sept., 1944, pp. 4–8; *H. Lub.*, Oct., 1944, pp. 12–16; Popple, *op. cit.*, 67, 70, 76.

12. *Ibid.*, 116.

13. *Ibid.*, 88, 93.

14. See *History of PAW*, chap. X.

15. Popple, *op. cit.*, 82, 84f., 89, 93, 213, 218f.

16. The union's side of the general drive of the OWIU to organize the oil industry during this period is told in O'Connor, *History of Oil Workers International Union–CIO*, 47–56, 229–231, 293–296, 309–311, 360f. Interviews with the following members of Humble's Employee Relations Department gave various aspects of management's viewpoint: D. B. Harris, K. R. Dailey, H. D. Ward, J. N. Beasley, and A. A. Nance.

Unionism and contracts with unions and other employee organizations were matters profoundly affecting company policy, and they consequently received a great deal of attention in correspondence among Humble's top management, particularly those executives in charge of refining, local refinery managers, the employee relations group, and union representatives.

Contracts between Humble on the one side and Local 316 at Ingleside and the Baytown Employees Federation on the other, and the minutes of the negotiations between Humble and the union representatives at Ingleside, are documents of particular importance.

17. Humble management, during its difficulties with the Ingleside union, more than once asserted that Humble had "never had a strike" (petition of *Humble* v. *WLB,* Fed. Dist. Court, Northern Div. of Texas, Dallas, Sept. 7, 1944; Hines H. Baker, Statement before WLB, July 6, 1944; Houston *Post,* Oct. 4, 1945). It is understandable that the unimportant Baytown boilermakers' strike of 1920 should have been forgotten or neglected, but the Gulf Coast strike of 1917–1918, which affected Humble in three fields, was a different matter. However, it occurred so early in Humble's history that few of the top administrators or managers of 1944 were with the company at the time. That it was a general Gulf Coast strike, and not directed specifically against Humble, may have been the main reason for the failure of a latter-day Humble management to remember it as a Humble strike.

18. *CIO News,* June 22, 1942; Humble Recs., Edwin A. Elliott, NLRB, to Humble, July 7, 1942, and to H. H. Baker, Oct. 16, 1942; Corpus Christi *Caller-Times,* Aug. 25, 1942.

19. Humble Recs., Memos. on Negotiations for Agreement at Ingleside Refinery, Mar. 30, Apr. 19, 1943; D. B. Harris to C. E. Shaw, May 5, 1943.

20. Humble Recs., esp. Articles of Agreement between Humble Oil & Refining Company and the Oil Workers International Union, Local Union No. 316 . . . Ingleside, Texas . . . May 17, 1943.

21. *Questions and Answers* (Goose Creek), Jan., 1943; interview with Robert C. Oliver; Humble Recs., K. R. Dailey to H. H. Baker, Oct., 1937; Baytown Employees Federation, Bulletin No. 63, Apr. 27, 1943.

22. Humble Recs., esp. E. A. Elliott, WLB, to Humble, OWIU, BRT, IAM, IBEW, and Baytown Federation, Nov. 17, 1943.

23. Humble Recs., esp. Contract between Humble and Baytown Employees Federation, May 10, 1944.

24. Humble Recs., War Labor Board Directive Order, Apr. 1, 1944, Case No. 111–1819–D.

25. Humble Recs., correspondence between Humble officials and representatives of the WLB and the OWIU, May 16–June 7, 1944.

26. Humble Recs.; *O. & G. Jour.,* Oct. 7, 1944, p. 109.

27. Humble Recs.; *O. & G. Jour.,* June 30, 1945, p. 134.

28. Humble Recs.; Corpus Christi *Caller-Times,* June 24, 1945.

29. O'Connor, *op. cit.,* 229.

30. Humble Recs.; Houston *Post,* Oct. 5, 1945.

31. Humble Recs.; Houston *Chronicle,* Oct. 18, 1945.

32. Humble Recs., memo. on phone conversation of M. J. Rathbone and H. H. Baker, Jan. 17, 1945, and of M. J. Rathbone with H. H. Baker and H. W. Ferguson, Aug. 10, 1945.

33. Humble Recs.; *O. & G. Jour.,* Nov. 3, 1945, pp. 130f. According to the *History of PAW,* p. 225, after V-J Day "the more economical of the petroleum butadiene plants were designated as the sole peacetime source for butadiene for Government's synthetic rubber manufacturers."

34. Of general importance for the Humble Sales Department during the war years are: "Distribution of Petroleum Products in World War II," by the Sales Department; E. A. Share, "A History of Humble Oil & Refining Company's Marketing Operations in Texas"; and the annual reports and statistical records of the company and department. Also, *History of PAW,* 116–145, and helpful information from W. H. Willis, R. M. Stephens, and G. M. Borgstrom.

35. Humble Recs.; *H. Sales Lub.,* Dec. 18, 1941, pp. 4–6.

36. *History of PAW,* 118–125.

37. *Ibid.,* 144.

38. Humble Recs.; *H. Sales Lub.*, Mar., 1943, pp. 8f.
39. Humble Recs.; *H. Sales Lub.*, Feb. 12, 1942, p. 6.
40. The financial data for this section were drawn principally from the following Humble compilations: Comptroller's Black Book; "Financial Results of Humble's Wartime Operations"; "Organization of Humble Oil & Refining Company"; Gay Carroll's "Financial Summary of the Transactions of Humble Co., The Issuance of New Capital Stock and Borrowing of Money"; "Statistical Record, 1917–1954."
41. Humble Oil & Refining Co., *Annual Report*, 1945, p. 19.
42. *Ibid.*, 1944, p. 6.

CHAPTER 24

1. The Humble records most useful for this chapter were the mimeographed *Weekly Digest* and a variety of minutes, memoranda, reports, and statistical and historical documents. Interviews were helpful on every subject.
2. *H. Way*, July–Aug., 1945, pp. 1–4.
3. *The Lamp*, Apr., 1945, p. 22; *H. Ref. Bee*, Feb. 8, 1945, p. 8.
4. Information on administrative changes in general and certain special developments was obtained from many interviews. In the Controller's Department J. R. Mulvey was very helpful, as were Rex G. Baker and John Q. Weatherly of the Law Department. Many others from the Administrative Department and operating departments similarly gave assistance when asked.
5. Humble Oil & Refining Co., *Annual Report*, 1946, p. 11, and 1947, p. 12.
6. Information in regard to Humble employee relations during the postwar period, especially those directly or indirectly influenced by the rise of collective bargaining, has been drawn principally from the minutes of various Employees Federations and of meetings between members of management and employee representatives. "Chronological Report of Pertinent Dates and Records in Collective Bargaining in the Humble Conference" is a typewritten document of general interest. Interviews with Ray Horton have been broadly useful; also, on safety, Karl Martin; collective bargaining, H. D. Ward, J. N. Beasley, C. C. Moore, and H. W. Ferguson; on wages, Paul V. Lucas; and on training, T. W. Moore.
7. Quoted by Dr. R. J. Gonzalez.
8. Humble Recs.; *H. Way*, 1947: Jan.–Feb., p. 1, July–Aug., pp. 8–10; *Plan for Supplementing Humble Annuity & Thrift Plan Annuities . . . Effective October 1, 1948;* Houston *Post*, Oct. 24, 1948.
9. *H. Way*, Sept.–Oct., 1947, pp. 24–27.
10. Humble Recs.; *H. Bee*, 1930: July 11, p. 1, Nov. 28, p. 1; also *H. Ref. Bee*, 1935: Nov. 7, pp. 5f.; 1936: May 7, p. 11, July 30, p. 11; 1944: Feb., p. 10, Mar., pp. 10f.
11. Humble Oil & Refining Co., *Annual Report*, 1948, p. 11, and 1949, p. 10.
12. O'Connor, *Oil Workers International Union*, 60.
13. Houston *Post*, Apr. 14, 29, June 2, 4, 1948; Humble records and interviews.
14. For refinery expansion in the immediate postwar period, interviews with H. W. Ferguson, Dr. H. D. Wilde, E. N. Lewis, and Joe Reilly were especially helpful in supplementing the company records.
15. Humble Recs.; *H. Way*, Sept.–Oct., 1947, pp. 17f.
16. *H. Way*, Mar.-Apr., 1949; *Annual Report*, 1945, pp. 11f., and 1946, p. 9.
17. *Ibid.*, 1945, pp. 10, 15.
18. *Annual Report*, 1945, p. 11; *Weekly Digest.*
19. Humble Recs. and interviews; *H. Way*, Nov.–Dec., 1947, pp. 22–24.
20. *Annual Report*, 1948, p. 11.
21. *H. Way*, Sept.-Oct., 1947, pp. 17f.
22. Humble Recs.; *H. Way*, May-June, 1947, p. 1.
23. *Ibid.*, May–June, 1948, pp. 15–17; interviews; Walter Miller, "Petroleum Refining," *Elements of the Petroleum Industry*, 372.
24. *H. Way*, July-Aug., 1951, pp. 8–10.
25. Humble Recs.; *H. Way*, July-Aug., 1948, pp. 20f.
26. *H. Way*, Jan.–Feb., 1949, pp. 10f.
27. Of the documents, other than purely statistical compilations, on which our knowledge of the postwar activities of Humble's Sales Department is based, of particular value were Share's "History of Humble Oil & Refining Company's

Marketing Operations in Texas," and J. E. Niland, Training Lecture, 1945. A discussion of Sales Department problems with a group of its key men was of the greatest value. Individual interviews with R. M. Stephens, J. R. Mulvey, G. A. Mabry, and Choyce Allison were also very helpful.

28. *H. Lub.*, May, 1944, p. 15, Feb., 1945, pp. 3, 7, 10, Mar., 1945, p. 10; *H. Way*, May–June, 1947, p. 19; interviews.

29. Information on Humble's high-octane gasoline has been drawn from the following sources: *H. Way*, Nov.–Dec., 1946, pp. 17–19; July–Aug., 1949, pp. 10–14; *Annual Reports*, 1945, 1946; Humble Recs.; SONJ Recs.

30. Humble Recs.; *H. Way*, Nov.–Dec., 1946, pp. 17–19.

31. *Ibid.*, 1946: May–June, pp. 18f., and Nov.–Dec., pp. 17–19; July–Aug., 1948, pp. 16–19; 1949: July–Aug., pp. 10–14; Jan.–Feb., 1951, pp. 4–7.

32. *Annual Report*, 1949; *H. Way*, Jan.–Feb., 1951, pp. 4–7; interview.

33. *H. Way*, July–Aug., 1948, pp. 16–19; Humble Recs.

34. *H. Way*, Jan.–Feb., 1951, pp. 4–7.

35. Humble Recs.; *H. Way*, Nov.–Dec., 1946, pp. 17–19, and July–Aug., 1949, pp. 10–14.

36. *H. Way*, July–Aug., 1949, pp. 10–14.

37. In a public opinion poll of the attitude toward several large oil companies in Texas after the war, Humble received its highest rating in the areas where it had marketing operations.

CHAPTER 25

1. *H. Way*, July–Aug., 1945, pp. 7f.

2. This chapter is based principally on annual company and departmental reports and statistical compilations, particularly for the Production and the Exploration Department. The intra-company *Weekly Digest* was also useful. Information on specific subjects, such as pipeline corrosion, depth of wells, and certain petroleum engineering problems, was provided by company specialists concerned with the particular operations involved. Among the engineers who were especially helpful in furnishing such compilations or in discusssing specific problems were Douglas Ragland and Thomas Pennington in petroleum engineering and Russell A. Brannon and F. O. Stivers of Humble Pipe Line Co. O. Q. Lomax, president of Humble Pipe Line Company, contributed a broad perspective on some of Humble's pipeline problems. Director E. J. Hamner and Director C. E. Reistle, Jr., similarly helped to clarify certain significant issues and developments in exploration and production.

3. *O. & G. Jour.*, Feb. 26, 1948, p. 88.

4. Humble Oil & Refining Co., *Annual Report*, 1948, pp. 5 and 12.

5. On petroleum engineering and reservoir research, of special importance was a chapter (mimeographed) on the history of petroleum engineering by John R. Suman, which is to be included in a forthcoming volume on the subject to be published by the API.

6. *H. Way*, May–June, 1949, p. 3, May–June, 1950, pp. 19–23, 29, and July–Aug., 1950, p. 23; Humble Oil & Refining Co., *Annual Report*, 1948, p. 11, and 1950, p. 7.

7. *O. & G. Jour.*, Aug. 8, 1948, pp. 54, 58–62; *H. Way*, July–Aug., 1948, pp. 22–27, and July–Aug., 1949, pp. 15–17.

8. *History of the PAW*, 179; page 2 of Brief for Appellee, Humble Oil & Refining Co., in *Railroad Commission of Texas, et al.* v. *Humble Oil & Refining Co.*

9. Pages 4, 5, and 14 of Appendix of Petition for Appeal, Assignment of Errors, and Prayers for Reversal, of Humble Oil & Refining Co. to U. S. Supreme Court, October term, 1946, in *Humble Oil & Refining Co.* v. *Railroad Com. of Texas, et al.*

10. 331 U. S. 791.

11. 193 S. W. 2d 824.

12. Humble Oil & Refining Co., *Annual Report*, 1946, p. 7, 1947, p. 8, and 1948, p. 7.

13. Humble Recs. This question of crude prices was widely discussed in the oil industry periodicals at the time.

14. Humble Recs.; SONJ Recs.

15. Humble Oil & Refining Co., *Annual Report*, 1946, 1947, and 1948.

16. *Ibid.*, 1947, p. 7.

17. *Ibid.*, 1949, p. 8.

18. *Ibid.*, 1948, p. 8.

19. Information on how Humble coped with natural gas problems during the years immediately after World War II has been drawn principally from various statistical compilations, the *Weekly Digest*, and executive correspondence of Humble.

20. *H. Way*, Mar–Apr., 1947, pp. 9–12; Jan.–Feb., 1949, pp. 1–4; *Annual Report*, 1948, p. 7; Humble Recs.

21. 156 F. 2d 949.

22. Humble Recs., especially H. C. Wiess to W. R. Boyd, Jr., of the API, Oct. 4, 1946; *Annual Report*, 1946, pp. 6f.

23. Humble Recs., *H. Way*, Jan.-Feb., 1949, pp. 1–4.

24. Humble Recs., *H. Way*, Mar.–Apr., 1947, pp. 9–12, Jan.–Feb., 1949, pp. 1–4, Mar.–Apr., 1949, p. 11; July–Aug., 1950, pp. 6–8; *Annual Report*, 1944, p. 9.

25. Humble Recs.; *H. Way*, Mar.–Apr., 1949, p. 17.

26. This section is based principally on the annual reports of the Exploration Department, 1946–1948. Interviews with L. T. Barrow and E. J. Hamner were invaluable.

27. *The Lamp*, June, 1947.

28. 332 U. S. 19; Ernest R. Bartley, *The Tidelands Oil Controversy* (Austin, Texas, 1953), 162–181.

29. *H. Way*, Sept.–Oct., 1947, pp. 1–5.

30. Mercer H. Parks and James C. Postgate, in *O. & G. Jour.*, Nov. 11, 1948, pp. 230, 360–368, 371, 373f., 376; *H. Way*, 1948: Jan.–Feb., pp. 24–27, July–Aug., pp. 6–9, and May–June, 1949, pp. 14–20; the Grand Isle *Gazette*, May 15, 1948; *O. & G. Jour.*, 1948: Sept. 16, p. 72, and Nov. 25, pp. 82–84, 123f.

31. J. Ben Carsey, "Basic Geology of the Gulf Coastal Area and the Continental Shelf," *O. & G. Jour.*, June 4, 1948, pp. 251f., Giddens, *Standard Oil Company (Ind.)*, 650.

32. This statement on Davis No. 1 and the brief sketch of the search for oil in Scurry County is based principally on the following material from Humble Recs.: L. T. Barrow, "Notes on History of Oil Development in Scurry County"; copy of letter of L. T. Barrow to Max W. Ball, Mar. 11, 1952.

33. *H. Way*, May–June, 1948, pp. 1f.

34. Humble Oil & Refining Co., *Annual Report*, 1948, p. 12.

35. *H. Way*, Nov.-Dec., 1948, p. 4.

CHAPTER 26

1. We are indebted to Charles Wilson's *The History of Unilever* (London, 1954), vol. II, p. 397, for this quotation from Keynes' *Treatise on Money* (London, 1938).

Index